מקראות גדולות

Mikraoth Gedoloth

ירמיהו
חלק א׳

JEREMIAH
VOLUME ONE

מקראות גדולות

ירמיהו
חלק א׳

תורגם מחדש לאנגלית

מתורגם ומבואר עם כל דבורי
רש״י ולקט המפרשים על ידי

הרב אברהם י. ראזענבערג

הוצאת יודאיקא פרעסס

Mikraoth Gedoloth

JEREMIAH

VOLUME ONE

A NEW ENGLISH TRANSLATION

TRANSLATION OF TEXT, RASHI
AND OTHER COMMENTARIES BY

RABBI A. J. ROSENBERG

THE JUDAICA PRESS, INC.

Jeremiah, Vol. One — A new English translation

Part of the *Judaica Books of the Prophets* series

Fifth printing — 2018

ISBN: 978-0-910818-59-9

THE JUDAICA PRESS, INC.
123 Ditmas Avenue / Brooklyn, NY 11218
718-972-6200 / 800-972-6201
info@judaicapress.com
www.judaicapress.com

Manufactured in the United States of America

CONTENTS

RABBI MOSES FEINSTEIN
455 F. D. R. DRIVE
New York 2, N. Y.

ORegon 7-1222

משה פיינשטיין
ר"מ תפארת ירושלים
בנוא יארק

בע"ה

הנה ידוע ומפורסם טובא בשער בת רבים ספרי הוצאת יודאיקא פרעסס על תנ"ך שכבר יצא לאור על ספרי יהושע ושמואל ועכשיו בחסדי השי"ת סדרו לדפוס ג"כ על ספר שופטים והוא כולל הפירושים המקובלים בתנ"ך הנקוב בשם מקראות גדולות ועל זה הוסיפו תרגום אנגלית שהוא השפה המדוברת במדינה זו על פסוקי תנ"ך וגם תרגום לפרש"י מלה במלה עם הוספות פירושים באנגלית הנצרכים להבנת פשוטו של קרא והכל נערך ע"י תלמידי היקר הרב הגאון ר' אברהם יוסף ראזענבערג שליט"א שהוא אומן גדול במלאכת התרגום, והרבה עמל השקיע בכל פרט ופרט בדקדוק גדול, וסידר את הכל בקצור כדי להקל על הלומדים שיוכלו לעיין בנקל ואפריון נמטיה למנהל יודאיקא פרעסס מהור"ר יעקב דוד גאלדמאן שליט"א שזוכה ומזכה את הרבים בלימוד התנ"ך שמעורר לומדיה לאהבה וליראה את שמו הגדול ולהאמין בו ובעבדיו הנביאים שהוא יסוד ושורש בעבודתו יתברך ואמינא לפעלא טבא יישר ויתברכו כל העוסקים בכל ברכות התורה וחכמינו ז"ל בברוך אשר יקים את דברי התורה הזאת.

וע"ז באתי עה"ח ביום ה' שבט תשל"ט

משה פיינשטיין

FOREWORD

This book, volume one of Jeremiah, is the ninth of the Judaica series of the Prophets, the third of the Latter Prophets. For convenience, we have divided the Book of Jeremiah into two volumes, since it would be very awkward in one. As in the preceding volumes, we have translated the text into a modern language, except in instances in which accuracy would suffer. In such cases, we have rendered the text literally. As in our previous volumes, our translation is based mainly on Rashi's commentary, which is of primary interest. As the reader will notice, the difference between Rashi and other commentaries is much more pronounced in the Latter Prophets than in the Early Prophets. This is because the works of the Early Prophets are predominantly historical and consequently, prosaic. The Latter Prophets, however, are mostly prophetic and consequently, poetic, leaving much leeway for various interpretations. Although we have sometimes encountered difficulty in rendering the text according to Rashi's interpretation, we have seldom deviated from this pattern. In addition to basing our translation on Rashi, we have presented Rashi verbatim, drawing attention to variant readings from Rashi mss. presented in the Jerusalem edition of the Latter Prophets, published by *Etz Chaim,* 1974. We have also consulted *Shem Ephraim* by Rabbi Ephraim Zalman Margalioth for emendations of the Rashi text. Unfortunately, these two sources shed little light on Rashi's commentary on Jeremiah.

After Rashi, we drew from Redak, Rabbi Joseph Kara, and Mezudoth, whose commentaries all appear in Nach Lublin. Among other early commentaries, we have consulted Rabbi Isaiah da Trani, Abarbanel, and Rabbi Joseph Ibn Nachmiash, an unusual gem, found only on Jeremiah, Proverbs, and Esther. Since a large part of this commentary is based on Redak, we have compared our edition of Redak to that quoted by Ibn Nachmiash to determine the correct reading.

Although Mezudath David is usually based on Abarbanel, we have quoted many explanations in the name of Mezudath David since it is printed in Nach Lublin and is readily accessible to the reader. In addition to the explanations based on Abarbanel, many original ones are found in Mezudath David, making it indispensable to the student of Nach. It is known that Rabbi Elijah of Vilna encouraged the study of Nach with Rashi and Mezudoth.

Of the modern commentaries, we have quoted often from Malbim and Alschich, which bring unusual clarity to the text. We have not neglected

contemporary authors and have quoted from Daath Soferim by Rabbi Chaim D. Rabinowitz, a famed Bible scholar and educator. We have also used Daath Mikra, composed and published by Mosad HaRav Kook, where we find many recent discoveries that shed light on the meaning of the text.

Last, but of major importance, we have quoted frequently from Talmudic and Midrashic literature. We have attempted to trace each passage to its original source, not being satisfied with secondary sources, such as Rashi, Redak, and Yalkut Shimoni. In some instances, however, the original midrashim are no longer extant, except for fragments quoted by medieval authors who were in possession of these prized gems.

A.J.R.

ACKNOWLEDGEMENTS

We wish to thank our friend, Dr. Paul Forchheimer, who, as in earlier volumes, has enlightened us regarding Old French expressions found in Rashi's commentary.

PREFACE

I. Authorship

The Talmud (Baba Bathra 15a) ascribes the recording of Jeremiah's prophecies to the prophet himself. Rashi (ad loc.) explains that the prophets did not write their prophecies until shortly before their death. This, perhaps, accounts for the more detailed information of Zedekiah's fate in Jeremiah than appears in II Kings, which was probably written earlier, and, as the Talmud states, by the same author.

Although the moderns understand Chapter 36:2 to mean that Jeremiah instructed Baruch to write his prophecies, the Rabbis explain this verse as a reference to the Book of Lamentations. The Book of Jeremiah, however, was composed by the prophet himself. Abarbanel (ad loc.) explains that Jeremiah was written through the spirit of prophecy, which assisted the prophet to commit his words to writing. Lamentations, however, was written through *ruach hakkodesh,* Divine inspiration, a step lower than prophecy. This required much seclusion and exertion, preventing him from committing his own words to writing.

In the transmission of the Oral Law Jeremiah followed Zephaniah and his tribunal (Introduction to Mishneh Torah), making him the twentieth recipient from Sinai and the sixteenth of the prophets. According to Abarbanel, he received from Joel and his tribunal, making him the twenty-fifth recipient from Sinai and the eleventh of the prophets (Seder Hadoroth). Although a disciple of Zephaniah, he prophesied during the same period, as the Rabbis state (*Pesikta Rabbathi* ch. 26): Three prophets prophesied in that generation: Jeremiah, Zephaniah, and Huldah. Jeremiah prophesied in the streets, Zephaniah in the synagogues, and Huldah to the women. As the second verse states, Jeremiah prophesied from the thirteenth year of Josiah until the exile of Jerusalem at the end of the eleventh year of Zedekiah's reign, a total of forty years.

II. Position

According to the Talmud (Baba Bathra 14b), the order of the Latter Prophets is as follows: Jeremiah, Ezekiel, Isaiah, and the Twelve. Although

chronologically Isaiah preceded Jeremiah and Ezekiel, the Book of Jeremiah is the first of the Latter Prophets, following Kings, since Kings ends with destruction and Jeremiah deals completely (i.e. mainly) with destruction. Ezekiel begins with destruction and ends with consolation, and Isaiah deals entirely (i.e. mainly) with consolations, we juxtapose destruction to destruction and consolation to consolation. Concerning the Twelve, i.e. the Minor Prophets, although Hosea was the first of that perioid, preceding Isaiah, since his prophecy is brief, it was incorporated into one Book, ending with Haggai, Zechariah, and Malachi, who were the last prophets. Upon close scrutiny of the numbers of the *remazim* of *Yalkut Shimoni,* it becomes apparent that he, too, followed the Talmudic order.

The popular order, however, places Isaiah as the first Book of the Latter Prophets, followed by Jeremiah, Ezekiel, and the Twelve. Redak testifies that 'in all the good books that we have seen, that were written in Spain since many years, they are arranged according to their period, Isaiah before Jeremiah, as his period preceded his, and similarly, Jeremiah before Ezekiel. And in the Twelve, which follows, they followed the order of the Rabbis o.b.m. although some of them preceded Jeremiah and Ezekiel. Since their prophecies were short, they did not write each one in a separate book lest they be lost, as our Rabbis said. . .'

III. Piety of the People

Superficial reading of the Book of Jeremiah, as well as other prophetic Books, may give the impression that the Jews who lived in Jeremiah's time were a nation of evildoers, oppressors of the poor, even murderers, a nation akin to Sodom and Gemorrah. If we delve deeper into the Scriptures, however, we find that this is indeed far from the truth. We must remember that Jeremiah commenced his prophetic career in the thirteenth year of Josiah's reign. In the eighteenth year, Hilkiah the priest found Moses' Sepher Torah in the Temple. After this, there was a general revival, as the Bible tells us in II Kings. 22, 23. Josiah relied on this revival among the people to defy Pharaoh-neco, when he attempted to cross his land to attack Assyria. He was unaware that many of the people still worshipped idols clandestinely, even hiding these idols from the inspectors sent to eradicate idolatry from the land. They had inherited this practice from the time of Manasseh and Amon, and they could not emancipate themselves from it.

The Talmud states that during the reign of Jehoiakim, although the king was wicked, the people were righteous, whereas, during the reign of Zedekiah, the righteous king, the people were wicked. The Rabbis go so far

as to state (*Sanhedrin* 103a): The Holy One, blessed be He, wished to return the entire world to its original void because of Jehoiakim. He looked at his generation and was satisfied. The Holy One, blessed be He, wished to return the entire world to its original void because of the generation of Zedekiah. He looked at Zedekiah and was satisfied. Although Scripture of Zedekiah: 'And he did what was evil in the eyes of the Lord' (II Kings 24:19), since he had the power to protest and did not do so, it is regarded as though he had committed all these sins. Cf. Commentary Digest on II Kings.

It is apparent from Chapter 26, that in Jehoiakim's time, Jeremiah had many supporters and protectors, whereas in Zedekiah's time, he was imprisoned and cast into a pit where he would have died, were it not for the intervention of Zedekiah and Ebed-melech Hakushi, who rescued him (37, 38). Also, we find that in the time of Jehoiakim, a fast was declared in the fifth year of his reign, probably because of the threat of Babylon. Obviously, one who does not believe in God does not fast and pray to Him for salvation.

It appears that the people were confident that the presence of the Temple would save them from attack and destruction. Moreover, the false prophets, perhaps people misled by dreams, wished to bolster the morale of the people by assuring them that there would be peace. Jeremiah castigates them very severely for misleading the people in this manner. He demands that people recognize the difference between a dream and a prophecy. No doubt, it was very perplexing to the people to discern between the prophets predicting peace, and Jeremiah, predicting war and destruction. Later on, when he preached surrender to Babylon, he doubtlessly appeared as a traitor to his country, for which reason he was relentlessly pursued by the officers of the king. Even King Zedekiah had not the courage to surrender to Nebuchadnezzar, but attempted to escape.

IV. Historic Background

As mentioned above, Jeremiah's prophetic career commenced during the thirteenth year of Josiah's reign. During this period, many prophets prophesied the capture of Jerusalem, as is mentioned in many places in this book, as well as the prophecy of Huldah, mentioned in II Kings 22:15–20. To avert this calamity, Josiah conducted a campaign to uproot idolatry from the land. Unfortunately, he was uanble to do so because of the provocations of Manasseh (II Kings 23:26f.). As mentioned above, many of the people still followed the practices of Manasseh, who, although having repented his own sins, had left an impression on the people. At this time,

Jeremiah commenced to prophesy and to preach to the people to cease their sinful activities. Even the righteous were blamed for not protesting the acts of the wicked. Seeking to prevent Pharaoh-Neco from entering his land to attack Assyria, he was slain in battle. After his death, his son Jehoahaz was crowned king. He reigned only three months, when he was removed by Pharaoh-Neco and imprisoned, first in Riblah and later in Egypt, where he died.

After his death, Jehoiakim his brother was crowned by Pharaoh-Neco. At this time, Nebuchadnezzar commenced his conquests. Judah was attacked by troops of Chaldeans, Arameans, Moabites, and Ammonites. Jehoiakim was a wicked king as in II Kings 24 and in II Chronicles 36:8. Many of Jeremiah's prophecies are directed against him. He is warned that he will be buried 'the burial of a donkey,' that he would be 'dragged and thrown past the gates of Jerusalem.' This was fulfilled when the Chaldeans dragged him with copper chains to take him to Babylon and he died. He was never buried, just as the prophet had predicted. In addition to the sins he committed, as expounded on in Commentary Digest, II Kings 24:5, Jeremiah takes him to task for exploiting the people by making them work for him to build his elaborate palaces and houses (22:13f.).

During Jehoiakim's reign, Jeremiah suffered considerably. See 26:7–24, 36:26.

After Jehoiakim's death, his son Jehoiachin, or Jeconiah, reigned. His reign was very brief, only three months. In his days, the second exile took place. At this time, most of the important people, including the *harash* and *masger,* the great Torah sages, were exiled. They preserved Judaism among the exiles. As the prophet expresses himself in Chapter 24, the exile of Jeconiah is compared to good figs, whereas the exile of Zedekiah is referred to as bad figs. At this time, many of the vessels of the Temple were taken to Babylonia.

Nebuchadnezzar crowned Zedekiah as king instead of Jeconiah, who was exiled to Babylon. Although Jeconiah is labeled an evil king, he repented in Babylon and was taken out of prison to be honored by Evil-Merodach, Nebuchadnezzar's successor. See the end of the Book for details, also the end of II Kings. Zedekiah, as mentioned above, was a righteous king. He was a weak king, however. He did not have the courage to castigate his generation for their evil deeds, nor did he have the courage to surrender to the Chaldeans, as the prophet had commanded him. In his reign, too, Jeremiah suffered considerably. For his unfavorable prophecies and for his orders to surrender to Babylon, he was branded a traitor to his people. He was branded a false prophet by Hananiah son of Azzur, who predicted the

return of the holy vessels, as well as the return of the exiles from Babylon. He was imprisoned by Zedekiah when the Chaldeans besieged Jerusalem (32:3, 33:1). When the Chaldeans withdrew from the city because of the approaching Egyptians, Jeremiah attempted to go to Anathoth in the land of Benjamin, his home town. He was apprehended by officers of the king, who accused him of defecting to the Chaldeans. He was imprisoned in a dungeon where he almost died of starvation. The king removed him from the dungeon to the prison yard where he was given a daily allotment of a loaf of bread. He was later cast into a pit, where he sank into the mire, to be rescued by Ebed-melech Hakushi (Chapter 38).

Jeremiah remained in the land when Nebuchadnezzar exiled the Jews remaining from the exile of Jeconiah. Only the poorest of the people were left, and Jeremiah remained with them, after originally having planned to accompany his brethren to Babylon in chains. He was released from the chains by Nebuzaradan, chief of the guard, and permitted to choose for himself whether or not to go into exile. By Divine instruction, he remained in Mizpah with Gedaliah son of Ahikam, the governor appointed by Nebuchadnezzar. When Gedaliah was assassinated, he gave over God's message to the people that they were to remain in their place and no evil would befall them. Instead, they fled to Egypt. He accompanied them to Egypt where he died. Scripture is silent concerning his death. We find, however, in *Shalsheleth Hakabbalah* that when the Jews went to Egypt against his will, he castigated them and they stoned him, subsequently burying him in Egypt. Since the Egyptians had been plagued by locusts and had beseeched Jeremiah to pray for them, thereby saving them from the locusts, they defied him after his death and offered up sacrifices to him. According to Seder Hadoroth, quoting Seder Olam, Nebuchadnezzar took him and Baruch to Babylon, where they died.

In addition to Jeremiah's suffering at the hands of the kings and their officers, he suffered at the hands of his townsmen, the men of Anathoth. These threatened him with death should he prophesy in the name of God (11:22). A worse death was predicted for them than for the rest of Israel that would be attacked by Babylon. They were denied a remnant. However, some of them repented and were exiled to Babylon whence they returned.

V. Chronology

Josiah — ruled thirty-one years (3285–3316) — killed by Pharaoh-Neco in war. Jeremiah commenced to prophesy (3298).

Jehoahaz his son — reigned three months (3316) — deposed by Pharaoh-Neco, who replaced him with his brother Eliakim, whose name he changed to Jehoiakim.

Jehoiakim son of Josiah — reigned eleven years (3317–3327) — bound by king of Babylonia to take to Babylon — died on the way.

Nebuchadnezzar (Nebuchadrezzar) — ascended throne of Babylon (3319) — conquered Jehoiakim (3320).

Jehoiachin his son — reigned three months (3327) — exiled to Babylon with princes of Judah — succeeded by his uncle Mataniah, whose name was changed to Zedekiah.

Zedekiah, son of Josiah — ruled eleven years (3327–3338) — chained and blinded by Babylonian king — taken to Babylon — Nebuzaradan, officer of king of Babylon burned Temple, palace, and all houses in Jerusalem, demolished walls of Jerusalem, exiled the entire populace with all the Temple vessels, left Jerusalem desolate until the first year of Cyrus king of Persia.

Gedaliah son of Ahikam — appointed governor over Judea (3338) — assassinated (3339).

Nebuchadnezzar conquered Egypt (3346).

OUTLINE OF JEREMIAH

I. 1–10. Jeremiah's call to prophesy.
11. The vision of the almond rod.
13–19.The vision of the bubbling pot.
II. Reproach for idolatry, bloodshed, and for going to Egypt for aid.
III. 1–13. Reproach for idolatry, comparing it to adultery.
14–18. Prophecy of Messianic era and ingathering of exiles.
19–25. Appeal to repent.
IV. Prophecy of Babylonian invasion and destruction.
V. Reproof for adultery, idolatry, and deceit, prediction of invasion.
VI. Warning to Benjamites to flee Jerusalem to fortify their cities, reproof for sins lest the enemy attack.
VII. Prophecy to proclaim in the Temple gate.
VIII. Prediction that the invaders will exhume the graves and lamentation of the prophet for his people.
IX. Prophet's desire to leave his people because of their falseness and prophecy of exile.
X. Ridicule of idolatry and exhortation against idolatry while in Babylonian exile.
XI. 1–17. Command to exhort Israel to observe the covenant.
18–23. Jeremiah's prayer to God to punish the people of Anathoth for their attempt to poison him.
XII. 1–6. Jeremiah's question concerning the success of the men of Anathoth, God's answer and His exhortation to beware of the princes of Judah.
7–17. Promise to restore Israel to its land after the exile.

XIII. 1–11. The parable of the girdle.
11–14. The parable of the wine jug.
15–27. Appeal for humility because of the impending exile of Jehoiachin.
XIV. 1–10. Prophecy of the droughts and Jeremiah's prayer.
11–22. God's command to Jeremiah not to pray for the people and the blame on the false prophets.
XV. 1–14. Prophecy of the siege and the exile.
15–21. Jeremiah's plaint of his persecution due to his prophecy and God's answer.

XVI. 1–13. Condemnation of the men of Anathoth.
14–21. Promise of ultimate redemption.
XVII. 1–3. Reproof for idolatry.
4–11. Reproof for not observing the Sabbatical year.
12–18. Jeremiah's prayer to put to shame those who forsake God.
19–27. Reproof for profanation of the Sabbath to be proclaimed in the gates of Jerusalem.
XVIII. 1–12. Parable of the potter.
13–17. Prophecy of desolation of land.
18–23. Plot of men of Anathoth against Jeremiah and his prayer against them.
XIX. Parable of the earthen jug and prophecy of the Valley of Ben Hinnom.
XX. 1–6. Jeremiah's humiliation and imprisonment by Pashhur and his prohecy of Passhur's exile and burial in Babylon.
7–18. Jeremiah's declaration of how he is forced to prophesy and his curse of the day he was born.
XXI. 1–2. Zedekiah's supplication to Jeremiah to pray that Nebuchadrezzar withdraw.
3–7. Jeremiah's reply that the city is doomed.
8–10. Jeremiah's appeal to the people to surrender to Babylon in order to be saved.
11–14. Appeal to the house of David to improve their ways and to execute justice.
XXII. The dire prophecy concerning Jehoiakim.
XXIII. 1–8. Reproof of kings of Judah and prophecy of Messiah.
9–32. Reproof of false prophets.
33–40. Reproof of the people for lack of respect to God's prophecy.
XXIV. The vision of the two baskets of figs.
XXV. Prophecy of subordination of all nations to Babylon for seventy years.
XXVI. Jeremiah's prophecy in the Temple court and his attack by the princes.
20–23. Account of Uriah who was slain by Jehoiakim.
XXVII. Parable of the yoke and exhortation to surrender to Babylon.
XXVIII. Episode of Hananiah son of Azzur.
XXIX. Message to the exile of Jeconiah that the exile would be long and dire prophecies concerning the false prophets who assure the people that it would soon terminate.
XXX. Prophecy of Messianic era.
XXXI. Prophecy of Ingathering of Exiles and Messianic era.

XXXII. 1–5. Jeremiah's prophecy of Zedekiah's fate (during his imprisonment).

6–15. Jeremiah's purchase of Hananel's field.

16–25. Jeremiah's question of God as to the use of the purchase.

26–44. God's reply.

XXXIII. Promise of redemption and of preservation of the priesthood and kingship.

XXXIV. 1–6. Promise to Zedekiah that he would die in peace and be lamented.

7–22. Covenant to free slaves and subsequent abrogation thereof.

XXXV. Moral learned from the Rechabites.

XXXVI. Episode of the scrolls.

XXXVII. 1–11. Prophecy that the Egyptians would withdraw and the Chaldeans would return.

12–16. Jeremiah's imprisonment in dungeon.

17–21. His prophecy to Zedekiah and his transfer to the prison yard.

XXXVIII. 1–6. Jeremiah cast into pit.

7–13. Jeremiah's rescue.

14–28. Jeremiah's command to Zedekiah to surrender and be spared.

XXXIX. 1–14. Breach of the walls, Zedekiah's capture and exile.

15–18. Promise to spare Ebed-melech Hakushi.

XL. 1–6. Jeremiah freed from chains, given choice to go to Babylon or stay in the land of Israel, chooses to stay with Gedaliah in Mizpah.

7–12. Gedaliah joined by all Jews left in Judea and in neighboring countries.

13–17. Warned of plot against his life, does not heed warning.

XLI. Assassination of Gedaliah by Ishmael son of Nethaniah.

XLII. The people warned by God not to go to Egypt.

XLIII. 1–7. Prophecy ignored, migrate to Egypt.

8–13. Prophecy of Nebuchadnezzar's conquest of Egypt.

XLIV. 1–14. Warning to the Jews in Egypt against idolatry.

15–20. Refusal of Jews to heed warning.

21–30. Jeremiah's prophecy of the doom of the Jewish community in Egypt.

XLV. Jeremiah's prophecy to Baruch.

XLVI. 1–12. Prophecy of Nebuchadnezzar's defeat of Pharaoh-Neco.

13–25. Prophecy of second attack on Egypt by Nebuchadnezzar.

XLVII. Prophecy of fate of Philistines.

XLVIII. Prophecy of fate of Moab.

XLIX. 1–6. Prophecy of fate of Ammon.

7–22. Prophecy of fate of Edom.
23–27. Prophecy of fate of Damascus.
28–32. Prophecy of fate of Kedar, Hazor, and sons of Kedem.
34–39. Prophecy of fate of Elam.

L. Prophecy of fate of Babylon.

LI. 1–58. Continuation of previous prophecy.
59–64. Jeremiah's order to Seraiah to read prophecy in Babylon and to cast the scroll into the Euphrates.

LII. 1–3. Account of Zedekiah's reign.
4–6. Chaldean siege.
7. Breach of walls.
8–11. Zedekiah's capture, torture, and imprisonment.
12–30. Destruction of city, Temple and the exile of remaining Jews.
31. Jehoiachin's release from Babylonian prison and his esteemed position.

ספר ירמיה

חלק א

•

מקראות גדולות

JEREMIAH

VOLUME ONE

א א דִּבְרֵי יִרְמְיָהוּ בֶּן־חִלְקִיָּהוּ מִן־
הַכֹּהֲנִים אֲשֶׁר בַּעֲנָתוֹת
בְּאֶרֶץ בִּנְיָמִן׃ ב אֲשֶׁר הָיָה דְבַר־יְהוָה
אֵלָיו בִּימֵי יֹאשִׁיָּהוּ בֶן־אָמוֹן מֶלֶךְ יְהוּדָה
בִּשְׁלֹשׁ־עֶשְׂרֵה שָׁנָה לְמָלְכוֹ׃ ג וַיְהִי
בִּימֵי יְהוֹיָקִים בֶּן־יֹאשִׁיָּהוּ מֶלֶךְ יְהוּדָה
עַד־תֹּם עַשְׁתֵּי־עֶשְׂרֵה שָׁנָה לְצִדְקִיָּהוּ
בֶן־יֹאשִׁיָּהוּ מֶלֶךְ יְהוּדָה עַד־גְּלוֹת

ת"א דברי ירמיה. סנהדרין לה: בימי יהויקים. מגלה י:

ירושלם

תרגום

א פתגמי נבואת ירמיהו בר חלקיהו מן רישי מטרת כהניא מן אמרכליא דהוו בירושלם גברא דקביל אחסנתיה בענתות בארע שבטא בנימן: ב דהוה פתגם נבואה מן קדם יי עמיה ביומי יאשיה בר אמון מלך שבטא דבית יהודה בתלת עסרי שנין למלכיה: ג והוה ביומי יהויקים בר יאשיה מלך שבטא דבית יהודה עד דשלימא חדא עשרי שנין לצדקיה אחוהי בר יאשיה מלך שבטא דבית יהודה עד דאתא נבוכדנצר מלכא דבבל וצר על ירושלם תלת

רש"י

א (א) **דברי ירמיהו בן חלקיהו וגו'.** ליתי בר קלקלתא דתקנן עובדוהי ירמי' בא מרחב הזונה ולוכה בר מתקנתא דמקלקלן עובדוהי אלו ישראל שקלקלו מעשיהן שבאו מזרע כשר: (ב) **אשר היה דבר ה' אליו וגו'.** אשר התחילה שכינה לשרות עליו בהותו הזמן: (ג) **ויהי בימי יהויקים.** ויהי נביא כל ימי יאשיהו הנותרים וימי יהויקים בנו וימי צדקיהו בנו עד תום עשתי עשרה שנה היא השנה עד גלות ירושלים בחדש החמישי:

מהר"י קרא

א (א) **דברי** ירמיהו בן חלקיהו מן הכהנים אשר בענתות בארץ בנימין: (ב) אשר היה דבר ה' אליו בשלש עשרה שנה למלכו. התחיל להתנבאות: (ג) ויהי בימי יהויקים בן יאשיהו. פת' ונמשכה נבואתו כל ימי יהויקים. עד תום

רד"ק

(א) **דברי** ירמיהו בן חלקיהו. כתב א"א ז"ל כי חלקיהו זהו חלקיהו בן שפן הכהן שמצא ספר התורה בבית ה' בימי יאשיהו וירמיהו בנו נבא בימי יאשיהו ותחלת נבואתו היתה בשנת שלש עשרה למלכו ועדין לא שבו יאשיהו ויהודה מרעתם עד שמנה עשרה שנה למלכו שמצא ספר תורה: מן הכהנים. ת"י מן רישי משרת כהניא מן אמרכליא דהוו בירושלם גברא דקביל אחסנתיה בענתות: בענתות. היא עיר מערי הכהנים כמ"ש בספר יהושע ומה שהחל בדברי לפי שכולל בספר הזה כל דברי נביאות שנבא על ישראל ועל העכו"ם וכן דברי עצמו מה שקר' לו בנבואתו עם ישראל. ובדרש ג' נביאים על ידי שהיתה נבואתם דברי קנתורין לפיכך נתלה נבואתן בעצמן ואלו הן דברי קהלת דברי עמוס דברי ירמיהו ר"ל בעצמן שדברו בדברי עצמן כמו שלמה שאמר אני קהלת הייתי מלך וכל הענין שספר בעצמו וכן עמוס ספר בדברי עצמו קשר עליך עמוס וכל הענין כמ"ש וכן ירמיהו ספר בתחלת ספרו דברי עצמו בטרם אצרך בבטן ידעתיך וכל הענין וכן בתוך ספרו מה שספר מן הרעות שעשו לו: (ג) ויהי בימי. דבר ה' שהיה אליו היה גם כן בימי יהויקים בן יאשיהו וכן בימי צדקיהו עד תום מלכותו שמלך י"א שנה בשנת אחת עשרה נפל ביד מלך בבל וגלות ירושלם בחדש החמישי כמ"ש בספר מלכים:

מנחת שי

א (א) **דברי** ירמיהו. טעם המלה מירכא:

מצודת דוד

א (א) **דברי** ירמיהו. אלה הם דברי ירמיהו וגו' אשר בענתות אשר ישב בענתות שהיא בנחלת בנימין: (ב) אשר היה וגו'. בימי יאשיהו. התחלת דבר ה' בו היה בימי יאשיהו וגו': (ג) ויהי בימי יהויקים. היה מתנבא גם בימי יהויקים בנו והתמיד' נבואתו עד כלות עשתי עשרה שנה לצדקיהו וגו' ולתוספת ביאור אמר עד גלות ירושלים שהיה' בחדש החמישי הוא חדש אב:

מצודת ציון

א (ג) **תום.** ענין השלמה כמו כי אם תם הכסף (בראשית מ"ז):

2. **To whom the word of the Lord came**—*Upon whom the shechinah commenced to rest at that time.*—[*Rashi*]

3. **And he was in the days of Jehoiakim**—*And he was a prophet all the remaining days of Josiah, the days of his son Jehoiakim, and the days of his son Zedekiah, until the end of the eleventh year—that is the year—until the exile of Jerusalem in the fifth month.*—[*Rashi*]

Others render: And it was. . ., referring to *the word of the Lord*; i.e., the word of the Lord came to him also in the days of Jehoiakim son of Josiah and likewise in the days of Zedekiah until the end of his kingdom, for eleven years. In the eleventh year, he fell into the hands of the king of Babylon, and the exile

1

1. The words of Jeremiah son of Hilkiah, of the priests who were in Anathoth in the land of Benjamin. 2. To whom the word of the Lord came in the days of Josiah son of Amon, king of Judah, in the thirteenth year of his reign. 3. And he was in the days of Jehoiakim son of Josiah, king of Judah, until the end of eleven years of Zedekiah son of Josiah, king of Judah, until the exile of

1. **The words of Jeremiah**—*Jonathan* renders: The words of the prophecy of Jeremiah. The Rabbis ask: Did Jeremiah prophesy only these words? Did he not write two books [viz. Kings and Lamentations]? . . . Why then does it say: The words of Jeremiah? This teaches us that they were words of reproof. . . . (*Yalkut Shimoni* from *Sifre*, Deut. 1:1). *Redak* explains this expression to mean: the affairs of Jeremiah, including his prophecy concerning Israel and the nations and his personal history, what happened to him because of his prophecy. *Abarbanel* adds that the Book is written frequently in the first person, indicating that Jeremiah is relating the happenings of his life.

Redak continues to expound on this matter, quoting a midrash that three prophets spoke harshly, and their prophecy was attributed to them. They were Koheleth, Amos, and Jeremiah. All of them spoke harshly to Israel, and their prophecies begin with "the words of . . ." *Redak* explains this to mean that since they spoke harshly to Israel, in their prophetic books were included incidents of misfortunes that befell them.

Alshich explains: These are the words fit for Jeremiah; he was indeed deservant of reproving Israel, for not everyone has the right to reprove Israel. Jeremiah, however, was a righteous man with whom no fault could be found. Moreover, he was the son of Hilkiah, also a prophet and a righteous man, as will be discussed further.

The words of Jeremiah son of Hilkiah—*Let the son of the corrupt woman, whose deeds are proper—Jeremiah was descended from Rahab the harlot—and let him reprove the son of the righteous woman, whose deeds are corrupt—these are Israel, who corrupted their deeds, who are descended from legitimate seed* (*Rashi* from unknown midrashic source). This is based on the Talmudic maxim that Joshua married Rahab after her conversion, and was the progenitor of eight prophets, all of them priests (*Meg.* 14b).

of the priests who were in Anathoth—Jonathan paraphrases: Of the heads of the priestly watches, of the trustees who were in Jerusalem, a man who received his heritage in Anathoth. Anathoth was one of the priestly cities enumerated in Joshua (21:18) [*Redak*].

יְרוּשָׁלַ͏ִם בַּחֹדֶשׁ הַחֲמִישִׁי׃ ד וַיְהִי דְבַר־
יְהוָה אֵלַי לֵאמֹר׃ ה בְּטֶרֶם אֶצּוֹרְךָ
בַבֶּטֶן יְדַעְתִּיךָ וּבְטֶרֶם תֵּצֵא מֵרֶחֶם
הִקְדַּשְׁתִּיךָ נָבִיא לַגּוֹיִם נְתַתִּיךָ׃
ו וָאֹמַר אֲהָהּ אֲדֹנָי יְהוִה הִנֵּה לֹא־

ת"א אצרך בבטן. יומא פב עקדה שער לט זוהר ברא׳ אחרי ולהדרת נשא: יתיר ואו

תרגום

שְׁנִין וְאִתְגְּלִי עַמָּא דְבֵית
בְּיַרְחָא חֲמִישָׁאָה׃
ד וַהֲוָה פִּתְגָם נְבוּאָה מִן
קֳדָם יְיָ עִמִּי לְמֵימָר׃
ה עַד לָא בְרֵיתָךְ בִּמְעַיִן
אִתְקְנָתָךְ וְעַד לָא
אֲתֵיתָא לְעָלְמָא נְסֵיתָךְ
נְבִי מַשְׁקֵי כַס דִּלְוָט
לְעַמְמַיָּא מַנֵּיתָךְ׃
ו וַאֲמָרֵית קַבֵּיל בָּעוּתִי
יְיָ אֱלֹהִים הָא לֵית אֲנָא

מהר"י קרא

עשתי עשרה שנה לצדקיהו בן יאשיהו מלך יהודה. שמלך אחרי יהויקים: (ה) בטרם אצרך בבטן ידעתיך. בטרם יצרתיך צורה ידעתיך בימי משה בשעה שאמרתי לו נביא אקים להם מקרב אחיהם כמוך:

רש"י

(ה) בטרם אצרך בבטן וגו׳. מימי אדם הראשון הראהו הקב"ה לאדם דור ודור ונביאיו: אצרך. לשון צורה: ידעתיך. (קנייוסטו"י בלע"ז) כמו לא נודעתי להם (שמות ו׳): הקדשתיך. זמנתיך לכך: נביא לגוים. לישראל שהם נוהגים עצמם כגוים כך נדרש בספרי נביא מקרבך וגו׳ (דברים י"ה) יקים לך ולא למכחישי תורה הא מה אני מקיים נביא לגוי׳ נתתיך בבנ"י שנוהגים מנהגי גוים. ועוד יש לפתור נביא לגוים כמו על הגוים להשקותם כוס התרעלה להנבא עליהם פורענות כמו שנאמר קח את כוס היין החימה הזאת מידי והשקיתה אותו את כל הגוים (לקמן כ"ה) ד"א בטרם תצא מרחם הקדשתיך עליך אמרתי למשה נביא אקים להם כמוך (דברים י"ח) זה הוכיחם וזה הוכיחם זה נתנבא ארבעים שנה וזה נתנבא ארבעי׳ שנה: (ו) אהה. לשון יילל (קונפלייני"ש בלע"ז): כי נער אנכי. איני כדאי להוכיחן משה הוכיחן סמוך למיתתו כבר נחשב בעיניהם בכמה נסים שעשה להם הוציאם ממצרים וקרע להם את הים הוריד את המן הגיז את השליו נתן להם את התורה העלה את הבאר אני בתחלת נביאותי אני כא

מנחת שי

(ה) אצורך בבטן. כן כתיב בוא"ו וקרי הצד"י בקמץ חטוף והוא חד מן פליו יתירין וא"ו וחסרין קמצין על פי המסורת: (ו) ואמר אהה. ה"א פנייה במפיק בספרים כ"י ודפוסים ישנים וכן כל א ה ה שבמקרא.

רד"ק

(ה) בטרם אצורך. כן כתיב בוי"ו וקרי הצד"י בקמץ חטף כמשפטו עם הכנוים ואין עמו וי"ו והכנין אחד וענין בטרם אצרך כתב א"א כאשר בא היסודות הד׳ ידעו בכח הטבע ואחר כך הוציאו לפעל וכן אמר ישעיהו מעת היותה שם אני בכח היסודות הייתי מזמן שהייתה עת בעולם ועתה הוציאני מכח לפעל ושלחני ברוחו או פי׳ ידעתיך כמו ידעתיך בשם שאמר למשה ימורה עליו. ובטרם תצא מרחם הקדשתיך. מל׳ קדושה. וידעתיך ל׳ גדולה ולפי׳ הראשון יש לשאול והלא כל הנביאים והצדיקים וכן הרשעים בטרם הבראם ידעם והכירם אך יורה זה שאביו ואמו נזהרו בקדושה וטהרה בעת ההריון שיהיה הנביא מקודש והחכם הגדול ר׳ משה בר מיימון ז"ל כתב כי זה ענין כל נביא אי אפשר לו מבלתי הכנה טבעית בעיקר יצירתו שיהיה נכון לנבואה עם ההתלמדות ויש לדעתו לישאל למה לא אמר זה הענין לנביא אחר אלא לירמיהו ונוכל לומר לפי שידע האל ית׳ שירמיהו יסרב בשליחות האל הודיעו כי הוא מוכן לנבואה מן הבטן כדי שיחזק לבו ללכת בשליחות האל ואם תאמר והלא משה רבינו ע"ה היה מסרב ג"כ בשליחות האל ולא אמר לו כן הנה הראה לו אות גדול לחזק את לבו והוא אות הסנה והאותות האחרים שנתן בו יכולת לעשותן לפני פרעה וגם נוכל לומר כי משה רבינו כבר ידע זה מעצמו כי חכם גדול היה וידע כי בעיקר יצירת האדם יש הכנה טבעית לנבואה למי שהוא עתיד להתנבא ולא זה בלבד אלא כל חכמה וכל טבע שיש באדם שהוא גובר בו יש לו קצת הכנה בו בעיקר היצירה יגבר בה עם ההתלמדות וי"ת הפסוק כן עד לא בריתך וגו׳ כבעמוד: (ו) ואומר אהה. ל׳ קריאה על הצער ועל הדאגה ומה שאמר לא ידעתי דבר ר"ל דברי תוכחה כי אני נער ואיך אוכיח עם אחד ואין תימה אם באה לו נבואה והוא נער כי הנה ג"כ שמואל היה נער בתחלת נבואתו כמ"ש ורוח הנבואה החכימה אותם אף על פי שהיו נערים ואפשר כי נער ר"ל משרת ואף על פי שהוא גדול בשנים יקרא נער כמ"ש ומשרתו יהושע בן נון נער והיה משרת נביא אחד שהיה בימיו או חכם ר"ל ביד גדול ממני ראוי לשלוח זה השליחות לא בידי כמו שאמר משה רבינו שלח נא ביד תשלח והמפרשים פירשו כי נער היה בשנים בהנבאו וכן שמואל חכריהו בן עדוא וי"ת

מצודת ציון

(ה) אצרך. מלשון יצירה: ידעתיך. ענין הכרה כמו ושמואל טרם ידע את ה׳ (ש"א ג׳): הקדשתיך. מל׳ קדוש׳: נתתיך. ענין מנוי ופקידות כמו נתתיך אלהים לפרעה (שמות ז׳): (ו) אהה.

מצודת דוד

(ד) ויהי דבר ה׳. וזהו דברי ירמיה שאמר לישראל: (ה) בטרם. עד לא ילדתיך בבטן אמך הכרתי בך שתהי׳ הגון ומוכן לנבוא׳: הקדשתיך. קדשתי אותך והזמנתיך ופי׳ לו׳ כזה קדשתיך כאשר נתתיך להיו׳ נביא להתנבאו׳ על הפכו"ם כולם: (ו) ואומר וגו׳. אמרתי אהה ה׳ אוי לי על המגיע׳ והמכשול הנמצא כי אשר לא ידעתי לסדר דברי הנבוא׳ כאמות הלשון כי עדיין אני רך בשנים

ets, only regarding Jeremiah. We can possibly answer that, since the Almighty knew that Jeremiah would hesitate to accept his mission as a prophet, He informed him that from his mother's womb he was already prepared for prophecy, in order to encourage him to accept God's mission.

Redak proceeds to question this principle, since Moses too refused to accept God's mission when He sent him to Egypt to redeem Israel, yet he was not informed of his prenatal preparation for prophecy. He replies that the great wonders shown Moses, such as the sign of the burning bush and the signs he was to

Jerusalem in the fifth month. 4. And the word of the Lord
came to me, saying: 5. When I had not yet formed you in the
womb, I knew you, and when you had not yet emerged from
the womb, I had appointed you; a prophet to the nations I
made you. 6. And I said, "Alas, O Lord God! Behold,

of Jerusalem was in the fifth month, as in the Book of Kings [II:25:2].—[*Redak, Kara, Mezudath David*]

in the fifth month—This is the month of Ab.—[*Mezudath David*]

4. **And the word of the Lord**—These are Jeremiah's words to Israel.—[*Mezudath David*]

5. **When I had not yet formed you in the womb etc.**—*Since the days of the first man. The Holy One, blessed be He, showed Adam each generation and its prophets.*—[*Rashi* from *Seder Olam*, ch. 31]

I . . . formed you—Heb. אֶצָּרְךָ, *an expression of* צוּרָה, *a form.*—[*Rashi*]

I knew you—*connois toi in O.F. Comp.* (Exodus 6:3), *"I was not known* (נוֹדַעְתִּי) *to them".*—[*Rashi*]

I appointed you—*I appointed you for this.*—[*Rashi*, based on *Jonathan*] According to *Redak*: I sanctified you. See below.

a prophet to the nations—*To Israel, who behave like the nations. In this manner it is expounded in Sifre on the verse: "A prophet from your midst etc.* (Deut. 18:15)," *will set up for you and not for those who deny the Torah.* (Venice edition reads: *For you and not for the nations.* Jerusalem edition 1974 reads: *For you and not for the pagans.*) *How then do I fulfill "A prophet to the nations I made you"? To the children of Israel who deport themselves with the customs of the nations. It can further be interpreted: "A prophet for the nations," like "About the nations," to give them to drink the cup of poison, to prophesy retribution upon them, as it is said: "Take this cup of the wine of wrath from My hand, you shall give all the nations to drink of it* (infra 25:15)." *Another explanation of "When you had not yet emerged from the womb I appointed you" is:—Concerning you I said to Moses: "I will set up a prophet . . . like you* (Deut. 18:18)." *This one reproved them, and this one reproved them. This one prophesied for forty years and this one prophesied for forty years.*—[*Rashi* from *Pesikta d'Rav Kahana*, p. 112]

Redak, in addition to the usual rendering, suggests: "When I had not yet formed you in the womb, I made you great, and when you had not yet emerged from the womb, I sanctified you." He questions the ordinary rendering, since God knew all the righteous as well as the wicked before they came into being. If so, what is exceptional about Jeremiah? He replies that the intention is that the prophet's parents behaved with purity and sanctity at the time of his conception so that he would be holy, and *Rambam* writes that no one can become a prophet without the proper preparation in his very formation, in addition to his own training. According to this theory, we can ask why this is not mentioned regarding other proph-

ידעתי דבר כי נער אנכי: ז ויאמר
יהוה אלי אל תאמר נער אנכי כי על
כל אשר אשלחך תלך ואת כל אשר
אצוך תדבר: ח אל תירא מפניהם
כי אתך אני להצלך נאם יהוה:
ט וישלח יהוה את ידו ויגע על פי
ויאמר יהוה אלי הנה נתתי דברי
בפיך: י ראה הפקדתיך היום הזה
על הגוים ועל הממלכות לנתוש
ולנתוץ ולהאביד ולהרוס לבנות

ולנטוע

תרגום

ידעא לאתנבאה ארי רבי אנא ומשירותי עקא ונלו אנא מתנבי על עמא הדין: ז ואמר יי לי לא תמר רבי אנא ארי לכל אתר דאשלחינך תהך וית כל דאפקדינך תתנבי: ח לא תדחל מן קדמיהון ארי בסעדך מימרי לשיזבותך אמר יי: ט ושלח יי ית פתגמי נבואתיה וסדר בפומי נאמר יי לי הא שויתי פתגמי נבואתי בפומך: י חזי דמניתך יומא הדין על עממיא ועל מלכותא למעקר ולתרעא ולאבדא ולפגרא ועל בית ישראל ולמבני ולקימא:

ת"א ויאמר ה'. גיטין ו' בתרא כה. הגרי"ב. לקמן ל"א כ':

רש"י

להוכיח': (ז) על כל אשר אשלחך. אל העכו"ם: את כל אשר אצוך. לישראל תדבר: (ט) וישלח ה' את ידו. כל שליחות שהוא אצל יד לשון הושטה ל"א כתרגומו ושלח ה' ית פתגמי נביאותיה: (י) הפקדתיך. מניתך על העכו"ם: לנתוש ולנתוץ. (דיספלי"ר בלע"ז) ועל ישראל

מהר"י קרא

(ט) הנה נתתי דברי בפיך. וכן נאמר לו למשה ונתתי דברי בפיו וגו': (י) לנתוש ולנתוץ ולהאביד ולהרוס. את החוטאים: לבנות ולנטוע. את השבים מפשעם וכן הוא אומר רגע אדבר

רד"ק

כן ואמרית קביל בעותי וגו' כבעמוד: (ז) כי על כל אשר אשלחך. על במקום אל וכן וילך אלקנה הרמתה על ביתו כמו אל ביתו ומה שאמר אשלחך תלך כי בענתות באה לו הנבואה בתחילה ורצה האל לשלחו לירושלם מקום המלוכה להוכיח את המלך ואת עמו והבטיחו שיחזק לבו ללכת למקום שלא היה רגיל שם ויתקן דבריו בפיו שידע לדבר דברי תוכחות בלא מורא: (ח) להצילך. בא בפתחא בסגול חלמ"ד לפי שיש לו העמדה ופעמים יש לו משפט ההפסק לא הבטיחו שלא יגעו בו אלא יגעו בו ויכוהו ויצילהו מידם שלא ימיתוהו אע"פ שהיה ברצונם להמיתו כמ"ש וכשבאו להמיתו ואת ברוך אמר ויסתיר' ה': (ט) וישלח ה' את ידו. הוא המלאך הנראה אליו ודבר אליו בשם השם ונקרא בשמו ונראה במראה הנבואה שהושיט ידו אליו והגיע הדברים על פיו ונראה לו כאילו שם בפיו דבר שיש בו ממש לתקן אף על פי שאין הגעת הדבר אלא על האוזן לא על הפה במראה הנבואה נראה לו כאילו שם בפיו דבר שיש בו מכש לתקן בו בפיו לדבר בחתוך ל' בלא מורא וכן אמר בישעיהו ויגע על פי שהגיע הרצפה על פיו כי שניהם ויגע בפתח היו"ד מבנין הפעיל וי"ת הפסוק דרך משל ושלח ה' ית פתגמי נבואתיה וגו' כבעמוד: (י) ראה הפקדתיך. שמתיך פקיד וממונה עליהם לטוב ולרע כי כאשר תתנבא עליהם כן יבא עליהם וכפל הלשונות הנתיצה וההריסה לפי שהרבה לדבר רע על ישראל ועל האומות והטוב היה מעט באומות כמו

מנחת שי

(י) לנתוש ולנתוץ. התוי"ן רפויות:

מצודת דוד

ולא סורגלתי כזה: (ז) אל תאמר. ר"ל אל תמאן בדבר בעבור סנערות: כי על כל. אלא על כל הדברים אשר אשלחך תלך ותדבר את כל אשר אצוך: (ח) אל תירא. אל תפחד מפני מי אשר אשלחך אליה' פן תכשל בלשונך ויקפלו עליך כי אני עמך להצילך מיד סבאי' להרע עמך: (ט) וישלח. בנבוא' נראה לו כאלו המקו' הושיט ידו ונגע על פיו כאלו נותן הנבוא' אל פיו: הנה נתתי. בזה שנגעתי ידי בפיך נתתי דברי הנבוא' בפיך: (י) הפקדתיך היו'. בזה מניתי אותך על כל עכו"ם לנבאות עליהם חורבן והשקט

מצודת ציון

ענין לשון יללה הוא כמו ואומר אהה ה' (יחזקאל ד'): (ט) וישלח. ענין הושטה וכן שלח ידך ואחוז (שמות ד'): (י) הפקדתיך. מל' פקידות ומינוי כמו ופקדו שרי צבאות (דברים כ'): לנתוש. ענין עקירה כמו ונטעתי אותם ולא אתוש (לק' מ"ב): ולנתוץ. ענין הריסה ושבירה כמו תנור וכירים יותץ (ויקרא י"א): ולהרוס.

indeed touch him and smite him. God promised him only that they would not kill him although they attempted to do so, as we read (infra 36:26) that when the king ordered his servants to seize Jeremiah and Baruch, his disciple, God concealed them.—[*Redak*]

9. **And the Lord stretched forth His hand**—Lit. sent forth. *Every sending mentioned concerning a hand is an expression of stretching forth. Another explanation is like the Targum: And the Lord sent the words of His prophecy.*—[*Rashi*] *Redak* explains the verse as referring to the

I know not to speak for I am a youth. 7. And the Lord said to
me: Say not, "I am a youth," for wherever I send you, you shall
go, and whatever I command you, you shall speak. 8. Fear
them not, for I am with you to save you, says the Lord. 9. And
the Lord stretched out His hand and reached my mouth, and
the Lord said to me: Behold, I have placed My words in your
mouth. 10. Behold, I have appointed you over the nations and
over the kingdoms, to uproot and to crush, and to destroy and
to demolish, to build and to plant.

perform before Pharaoh, encouraged him to accept his mission, and made it unnecessary to inform him of his preparation for prophecy. Another answer is that Moses was very wise and understood by himself that everyone destined to prophesy was endowed with that property before his birth.

6. **"Alas**—This is *an expression of wailing (konpljjnt in O.F.).—[Rashi]* *Redak* and *Mezudath Zion* explain in the same manner. *Jonathan* renders: Accept my supplication.

for I am a youth—*I am not worthy to reprove them. Moses reproved them shortly before his death, when he was already esteemed in their eyes through the many miracles that he had performed for them. He had taken them out of Egypt, split the Red Sea for them, brought down the manna, caused the quails to fly, given them the Torah, brought up the well. I come to reprove them at the beginning of my mission.—[Rashi]*

His youth would not serve as an impediment to his prophecy, for we find that Samuel prophesied when he was young. It can only mean that he hesitated to reprove the people. It is also possible that נַעַר is used in the sense of *servant*. Perhaps Jeremiah was the servant of a prophet or a sage of his time, whom he deemed worthier of God's mission than he himself. The exegetes explain, however, that Jeremiah was indeed young when he commenced to prophesy, as were Samuel and Zechariah son of Iddo. *Jonathan* renders: Accept my supplication, O Lord God; I know not how to prophesy for I am young, and from my inception, I am to prophesy troubles and exile upon this people. —[*Redak*]

7. **wherever I send you**—*to the heathens.—[Rashi]*

and whatever I command you—*to Israel you shall speak.—[Rashi]*

Redak explains that God wished to send Jeremiah from Anathoth to Jerusalem to castigate the king and his people, and He promised to give him courage to go to an unfamiliar place and to arrange the words in his mouth so that he would be able to reprove them without fear.

8. **to save you**—God did not promise him that the people would not touch him, for they would

וְלִנְטוֹעַ׃ יא וַיְהִי דְבַר־יְהוָה אֵלַי לֵאמֹר
מָה־אַתָּה רֹאֶה יִרְמְיָהוּ וָאֹמַר מַקֵּל
שָׁקֵד אֲנִי רֹאֶה׃ יב וַיֹּאמֶר יְהוָה אֵלַי
הֵיטַבְתָּ לִרְאוֹת כִּי־שֹׁקֵד אֲנִי עַל־
דְּבָרִי לַעֲשֹׂתוֹ׃ יג וַיְהִי דְבַר־יְהוָה ׀ אֵלַי
שֵׁנִית לֵאמֹר מָה אַתָּה רֹאֶה וָאֹמַר
סִיר נָפוּחַ אֲנִי רֹאֶה וּפָנָיו מִפְּנֵי צָפוֹנָה׃

יא וַהֲוָה פִּתְגָם נְבוּאָה
מִן קֳדָם יְיָ עִמִּי לְמֵימַר
מָה אַתְּ חָזֵי יִרְמְיָה
וַאֲמָרִית מַלְךְ דְמוֹחֵי
לְאַבְאָשָׁא אֲנָא חָזֵי׃
יב וַאֲמַר יְיָ לִי יָאוּת
חֲזֵיתָא אֲרֵי מוֹחֵי אֲנָא
עַל פִּתְגָמֵי לְמֶעְבְּדֵיהּ׃
יג וַהֲוָה פִּתְגָם נְבוּאָה מִן
קֳדָם יְיָ עִמִּי תִּנְיָנוּת
לְמֵימַר מָה אַתְּ חָזֵי
וַאֲמָרִית מַלְךְ דְרָתַח
כְּדוּד אֲנָא חָזֵי וּמַקּוֹם
מִשֵּׁירְיָתֵיהּ דְמִדְבְּרָן

מהר"י קרא

על גוי ועל ממלכתו לנתוש ולנתוץ ושב הגוי ההוא מרעתו תחמתי על הרעה אשר דברתי לעשות לו: (יא) מקל שקד אני רואה. של פירות שקדים ולכך נקרא שמם שקדים שמקדימין פירותיהן לכל הפירות: (יב) כי שקד אני. כי ממהר אני על דברי לעשותו: (יג) סיר נפוח. סיר רותח: ופניו מפני צפונה.

רש"י

לבנות ולנטוע אם ישמעו כך תרג' יונתן: (יא) מקל שקד. (מנדולי"ר בלע"ז). ויונתן תרגם מקל שקד מלך דמוחי לאבאשא: (יב) היטבת לראות. השקד הזה הוא ממהר להוציא פרח קודם לכל האילנות אף אני ממהר לעשות דברי. ומדרש אגדה השקד הזה הוא משעת חניטתו עד גמר בישולו עשרים ואחד יום כמנין ימים שבין שבעה עשר בתמוז שבו הובקעה העיר לתשעה באב שבו נשרף הבית: (יג) סיר נפוח. רותח (בוייל"ק בלע"ז): ופניו. רתיחותיו

רד"ק

שאמר בבני עמון ואח"כ אשיב את שבות בני עמון ואמר בעילם יהיה באחרית הימים אשיב את שבות עילם ואמר לבנות כנגד לנתוש ולנטוע כנגד לנתוץ ויונתן חלק הפ' הרע לאומות והטוב לישראל שתרגם חזי דמניתך יומא הדין על עממיא ועל מלכותא למעקר תרעא ולאבדא ולפגרא ועל בית ישראל למבני ולקיימא: (יא) ויהי דבר ה'. זה ו"ה במראה הראשונה כי בתחלה אמר לו שילך באשר ישלחהו ואחר כן באותה המראה עצמה הראה לו במראת הנבואה מקל שקד כאמרו מקל שקד אני רואה נראה כי ראה המקל בלא עלים ובלא פרחים והתבונן אליו במראת הנבואה והכיר בו שהוא מעץ שקד לפיכך אמר לו הטבת לראות שאילו ראה אותו בעלים ובפרחים מה היתה הטבת הראיה נקל הוא להכיר זה הראה לו האל מקל שקד להיות משל על הפורענות העתידה לבא על ישראל שתבא להם במהרה כמו שעץ השקד ממהר לפרוח יותר משאר העצים לפיכך נקרא שקד כי השקידה ענין המהירות וההשתדלות וכן אמר כי שקד אני על דברי לעשותו ואמר לשקוד על דלתותי יום יום וי"ת מקל שקד מלך דמוחי לאבאשא אנא חזי: (יג) ויהי דבר ה' אלי שנית. מה שאמר שנית לפי ששתי המראות היו בענין אחד ואף על פי שהדברים נראים לו נשתנו אמר כי בענין זה נראה לו פעם שנית ששאלו גם כן מה הוא רואה ופי' לו גם כן המשל תוך המראה לא שבא לספר הפעמים שנראה לו כי לא ספר אלא זאת וכן ויהי דבר ה' אל יונה שנית לפי שדבר עמו בענין ניניה ב' פעמים לפיכך אמר שנית לא כדברי בעל הדרש שאמר שנית דבר עמו שלישית לא דבר עמו: סיר נפוח. נפוח תאר ופירושו רותח והסיר כשהוא רותח מעלה הבל כמו הנופח באש שמוציא הבל מפיו בעת הנפיחה: ופניו מפני צפונה. הצד מן הסיר שיצקו ממנו יקרא פנים: מפני צפונה. היה לו לומר אל פני צפונה אלא באמרו במ"ם באר בו שני ענינים כי פני צפונה מורה כי פני הסיר היו פונים פני צפונה ואמר אותו במ"ם להורות כי המרתיחים אותה היו מארץ צפון והיא בבל שהיא מזרחית צפונית לארץ ישראל. וא"א ז"ל פירש ופניו פני השפתים או הכירה ששופתין עליה הקדרה אמר כי פני

מצודת ציון

מל' הריסה והריסה: לבנות. מל' בנין: (יא) מקל. מטה: שקד. שם פרי שקדים כמו ויגמול שקדים (במדבר י"ז): (יב) שוקד. ענין מהירו' כמו וישקוד ה' (דניאל ט'): (יג) סיר. קדרה וכן על סיר הבשר (שמות ט"ז): נפוח. ר"ל מעלה רתיחה ע"ש בגרלה

מצודת דוד

כפי מה שאלוה לך: (יא) מה אתה רואה. במראה הנבוא': מקל שקד. מטה מאילן בגדילים בו שקדים: (יב) היטבת לראות. ר"ל ראית דבר ראוי לפי הזמן כי שוקד אני על דברי לעשותו וא"כ ראית דבר המרמז רמז על מה שעתיד להיו' כי מקל שקד ראית ואני שוקד על דברי והמה אחד בל': (יג) שנית. ר"ל שאלני פעם שנית: מה

אתה רואה. במראית הנבוא': סיר נפוח. קדירה מעלה רתיחה: ופניו. פני הרתיחה מקו' שמעל' רתיח' מדוכה הוא מעבר הצפון:

משלי חכמים פירוש ע"ט

Nachmiash] This symbolizes the army attacking with wrath.—[*Isaiah da Trani*]

whose foam—Lit. and its face, *its seething* (*et ses ondes in O.F.*) and its waves.— [*Rashi*]

Others explain this as the side into which the liquid is poured. The intention is that those who cause the pot to seeth are from the north. Rabbi Joseph Kimchi explains it as the side upon which the pot is placed over the fire. The intention is the same, that the side from which the fire is placed under the pot is on the north. The pot symbolizes Jerusalem, as in Ezekiel's prophecy (26:1–14). Those pouring in the liquid or placing the fire under the pot symbolize the Chaldeans who

11. And the word of the Lord came to me, saying: What do you see, Jeremiah? And I said, "I see a rod of an almond tree." 12. And the Lord said to me: You have seen well, for I hasten My word to accomplish it. 13. And the word of the Lord came to me a second time, saying: What do you see? And I said, "I see a bubbling pot, whose foam is toward the north."

angel who appeared to the prophet and spoke to him in the name of God, therefore called by His name. He appeared in the prophetic vision as stretching forth his hand and causing the words of the prophecy to reach his mouth, and it seemed to him that the angel was placing something tangible into his mouth to enable him to speak fearlessly. We find the identical word in Isaiah 6:7 in reference to the beginning of his prophetic career.—[*Redak*]

10. **I have appointed you**—*I have appointed you over the heathens.*—[*Rashi*] *

11. **And the word of the Lord came**—This was part of Jeremiah's first prophecy. First God told him that he would go wherever He would send him, and in this same vision He showed him a rod of an almond tree.—[*Redak*]

a rod of an almond tree—(*amendlèèr in O.F.*) *Jonathan, however, renders: A King who hastens to do evil.*—[*Rashi*]

Redak explains that Jeremiah saw a bare branch of an almond tree with neither leaf nor blossom, which he recognized through prophecy as a branch of an almond tree. Otherwise, if he had seen a rod with leaves and blossoms, why would God say, "You have seen well"? It is not difficult to recognize an almond branch from its leaves and blossoms.

12. **You have seen well**—*This almond tree hastens to blossom before all other trees. I, too, hasten to perform My word. And the Midrash Aggadah* (Ecc. Rabbah 12:8) explains: *An almond tree takes twenty-one days from its blossoming until it is completely ripe, as the number of days between the seventeenth of Tammuz, when the city was broken into, until the ninth of Ab, when the Temple was burnt.*—[*Rashi*]

Indeed, the almond is called שָׁקֵד because of its quick ripening period. The word שְׁקִידָה denotes hastening and endeavoring.—[*Redak*]

13. **And the word of the Lord came to me a second time**—I.e. a second time in this manner. Just as in the first vision, God questioned the prophet concerning what he saw and interpreted the parable within the vision, so did He do in the second vision. Scripture does not mean to count the visions, since no other visions are numbered but these two. We find the same in the Book of Jonah, where the word of the Lord came to him a second time, i.e. a second time concerning the doom of Nineveh.—[*Redak*]

a bubbling pot—Lit. Blown up, *seething* (*boillant in French*).—[*Rashi*]

I.e. a pot from which steam ascends, as one who blows, emitting vapor from his mouth.—[*Redak, Ibn*

* For Rashi's commentary turn to page 211.

וְאָתְיָן מֵאַפֵּי צִפּוּנָא׃
יד וַאֲמַר יְיָ לִי מִצִּיפּוּנָא
תִּשְׁרֵי בִּישְׁתָּא לְמֵיתֵי
עַל כָּל יָתְבֵי אַרְעָא׃
טו אֲרֵי הָא אֲנָא מְכַלֵּי
לְכָל זַרְעִית מַלְכְוָת
צִפּוּנָא אֲמַר יְיָ וְיֵיתוּן
וְיִרְמוֹן גְּבַר כּוּרְסוֹהִי
לָקֳבֵל תַּרְעֵי יְרוּשְׁלֵם
וְעַל כָּל שׁוּרָהָא סְחוֹר
סְחוֹר וְעַל כָּל קִרְוַיָּא
דְבֵית יְהוּדָה׃ טז וַאֲמַלֵּיל
פּוּרְעָנוּת דִּינֵי מִנְּהוֹן עַל
כָּל בִּשְׁתְּהוֹן דִּשְׁבָקוּ
פּוּלְחָנִי וְאַסִּיקוּ בוּסְמִין
לְטָעֲוַת פַּלְחֵי כוֹכְבַיָּא
וְאִשְׁתַּעְבַּדוּ לְעוֹבָדֵי
יְדֵיהוֹן׃ יז וְאַתְּ תִּתְקַף

יד וַיֹּאמֶר יְהוָה אֵלָי מִצָּפוֹן תִּפָּתַח
הָרָעָה עַל כָּל־יֹשְׁבֵי הָאָרֶץ׃ טו כִּי הִנְנִי
קֹרֵא לְכָל־מִשְׁפְּחוֹת מַמְלְכוֹת צָפוֹנָה
נְאֻם־יְהוָה וּבָאוּ וְנָתְנוּ אִישׁ כִּסְאוֹ
פֶּתַח ׀ שַׁעֲרֵי יְרוּשָׁלִַם וְעַל כָּל־חוֹמֹתֶיהָ
סָבִיב וְעַל כָּל־עָרֵי יְהוּדָה׃ טז וְדִבַּרְתִּי
מִשְׁפָּטַי אוֹתָם עַל כָּל־רָעָתָם אֲשֶׁר
עֲזָבוּנִי וַיְקַטְּרוּ לֵאלֹהִים אֲחֵרִים
וַיִּשְׁתַּחֲווּ לְמַעֲשֵׂי יְדֵיהֶם׃ יז וְאַתָּה

תאזר

ת״א כי הנני. פקדה שבע פט:

רש״י

(אביזאינדי״ש בלע״ז): (יד) מצפון תפתח הרעה. בבל לצפונה של ארץ ישראל היא: (טז) ודברתי משפטי

רד״ק

השפתים שמכניסים משם האש תחת הסיר היו לצד צפון מורח שהמבעיר האש תחת הסיר יבא מצפון והסיר היא ירושלם כמו שהמשיל אותםג״כ בנבואת יחזקאל לסיר ואמר שפות הסיר שפות וכל הענין ושם מבואר הענין וי״ת סיר נפוח מלך דרתח כדוד אנא חזי וטקום משריתיה דמדברן ואתיין מאפי צפונא: (יד) תפתח. ענין התרה כמו ויפתח את הגמלים כאילו היתה קשורה עד הנה ועתה תהיה מותרת לבא על ישראל ועל הדרך הזה ת״י תשרי בישתא כמו שת״א ויפתח את הגמלים ואשרי ית גמליא ואפשר ג״כ ענין פתיחה כי שני הענינים קרובים: (טו) כי הנני קורא. כאילו אני קורא להם שיבאו כלו׳ אשים בלבם שיבאו: משפחות ממלכות צפונה. המשפחות אמר על העם וממלכות אמר על המלכים ראשי הממלכות ועל שכם נקראים ממלכות ואומר זה על מלכי ארץ בבל והמלך הגדול היה נבוכדנצר ועל המלכות אמר ובאו ונתנו איש כסאו ר״ל כשיצורו על ירושלם והם נרגל שראצר רב מג וכל רבי מלך בבל שוכר למטה כאשר נלכדה ירושלם: (טז) ודברתי. דבור האל עמהם הוא הביא המלכים עליהם וכן אמר אליהוא כי באחת ידבר אל וגו׳ ואמר ובמסרם יחתום והוא הדבור שידבר עמהם שיביא יסורים עליהם להוכיחם: למעשי ידיהם. ביו״ד ויש ספרים שכ׳ בהם למעשה בה״א מטות הוא וע״פ המסורת הנה ידענו זה: (יז) ואתה האזור מהניך. ללכת בזריזות כמ״ש

מנחת שי

(טו) לכל משפחות. בס״ס הכ״ף במארך ועיין מ״ש בפרשת ראה על כל הבכור: ונתנו. בס״ס הוא״ו בגעיא: (טז) למעשי ידיהם. חד מן י״ח דכתיבין יו״ד וסימנם במסרה רבתא ורד״ק כתב יש ספרים שכתוב בהם למעשי בה״א וטעות הוא וע״פ המסורת ידענו זה: (יז) ואתה תאזר. בספרי הדפוס הה״א בחטף

מצודת דוד

(יד) מצפון תפתח הרע׳. זה ירמז אשר מבבל העומדת מצפון תפתח הרעה כי עד הנה כאלו היתה הרעה קשור׳ לבל תבוא ועתה הותר הקשר ותבוא הרעה על יושבי א״י והמשיל׳ לסיר כמו הסיר מאספים הנתחי׳ אליה ואח״ז מרתיחין אות׳ כן כולם יכנסו במצור העיר והאויב ילחם בם וכן נאמ׳ שפות הסיר שפות וגו׳ אסוף נתחיה אליה וכו׳ רתח רתחיה (יחזקאל כ״ד): (טו) הנני קורא. ר״ל אעיר לבוא כל משפחות של ממלכו׳ לפוני והם בבל וכל הרלו׳ ממשלת בבל לבוא על ירושלים: ונתנו איש כסאו. כל אחד יתן כסאו מול פתחי השערים ועל החומות לצור עליה מסביב: (טז) ודברתי. אז אדבר

מצודת ציון

נפוחים ואבטבוטות וכן כדוד נפוח ואגמון (איוב מ״א): (יד) תפתח. ענין התרת הקשר כמו יתפלי פתח (שם ל׳):

that in the very spot where the Sanhedrin convened to decide points of *halachah*, there the princes of Babylon would make their court.—[*Ibn Nachmiash*]

This may also refer to the kingdoms subservient to Babylon, who will accompany Nebuchadnezzar and his hosts in their attack on Jerusalem.—[*Mezudath David*]

16. **And I will utter My judgments against them**—*I will debate with them, with Judah and Jerusalem.*—[*Rashi*]

Others explain that the attack by the kings of Babylon and the de-

14. And the Lord said to me: From the north the misfortune
will break forth upon all the inhabitants of the land. 15. For,
behold I am summoning all the families of the kingdoms of the
north, says the Lord, and they will come and place, each one his
throne at the entrance of the gates of Jerusalem and against all
its walls around and against all the cities of Judah. 16. And I
will utter My judgments against them concerning all their evil,
that they left Me and offered up burnt-offerings to other gods
and they prostrated themselves to the work of their hands.

will come from the northeast to destroy Jerusalem.—[*Redak, Ibn Nachmiash*] Similarly, Rabbi Isaiah da Trani explains it as the side where the wood is placed under the pot. *Jonathan* renders: I see a king seething like a pot, and the battle array of his camps that are coming from the north.

Abarbanel explains it as a pot under which the embers have been fanned with a bellows, and the front of it, the side from which the people would fan the flames was on the north, denoting that from the north the Chaldeans would bring misfortune upon Jerusalem.

14. **From the north the misfortune will break forth**—*Babylon is on the north of Eretz Israel.*—[*Rashi*]

will break forth—Or, will be unleashed, an expression of untying. It is as though the misfortune were tied up and now it would be released to come upon Israel. It may also be rendered: will open.—[*Redak*]

Jonathan renders: will begin. *Abarbanel* explains that God alluded to the two destructions, the first by Babylon, and the second by Rome. The destruction will begin from the north, i.e., the first destruction will be perpetrated by the Chaldeans who live in the north of Eretz Israel.

upon all the inhabitants of the land—This may refer to all the cities of Judea, as is mentioned further, or to the other nations conquered by Nebuchadnezzar.—[*Abarbanel*]

15. **For behold I am summoning**—It will be as though I am summoning them to come; i.e., I will inspire them to come and attack Jerusalem.—[*Redak*]

families of the kingdoms of the north—The families are the people; the kingdoms are the kings, the heads of the kingdoms. This refers to all the potentates of Babylon, including Nebuchadnezzar, the king over all the kings.—[*Redak*]

and they will come and place each one his throne—I.e., when they besiege Jerusalem. These are Nergal-sarezer, Samgar-nebo, Sarsechim Rab-saris, Rab-mag, as is related below (36:3), who came and sat in the middle gate with all the other princes of the king of Babylon when Jerusalem was taken.—[*Redak*]

The Rabbis (*San.* 103a) tell us

תאזר מתניך וקמת ודברת אליהם
את כל־אשר אנכי אצוך אל־תחת
מפניהם פן־אחתך לפניהם: יח ואני
הנה נתתיך היום לעיר מבצר ולעמוד
ברזל ולחמות נחשת על־כל־הארץ
למלכי יהודה לשריה לכהניה ולעם
הארץ: יט ונלחמו אליך ולא־יוכלו לך
כי־אתך אני נאם־יהוה להצילך:
ב א ויהי דבר־יהוה אלי לאמר: ב הלך

ת"א סלוך וקראת: סנהדרין קי: וקראת

תרגום

חרצך ותקום ותתנבי להון ית כל דאנא מפקיד לך לא תתמנע מלאוכחותהון דלמא אתבריניך קדמיהון:
יח ואנא הא יהבתך יומא דין תקיף כקריה כריכא וכעמודא דברזל וכשור דנחש לאשקאה כס דלוט לכל יתבי ארעא למלכא דבית יהודה לרברבהא לכהנהא ולעמא דארעא:
יט ויהון דיינין ומגיחין לקבלך למסתר ית פתגמי נבואתך ולא יכלין לך ארי בסעדך מימרי אמר יי לשיזבותך:
א והוה פתגם נבואה מן קדם יי עמי למימר: ב אזיל ותתנבי קדם עמא די בירושלם למימר כדנן

רש"י

אותם. מתווכח עמם עם יהודה וירושלים: (יז) תאזור מתניך. לשון זירוז כאיש חיל: (יח) למלכי יהודה. כנגד מלכי יהודה: (יט) ונלחמו אליך. ויהון דיינין ומגיחין לקבלך למסתר ית פתגמי נבואתך:

מהר"י קרא

רתיחתו של סיר נופח כלפי צפון: (יז) אל תירא מפניהם פן אחיתך. אל תירא שאני אחיתך לפניהם שלא אתנך בידם: (יח) ואני הנה נתתיך היום לעיר מבצר. שהיא בצורת וחזקה והכל נלחמים בה ולא יוכלו לרדותה כך לא יוכלו לך וכל כך למה: (יט) כי אתך אני. להצילך:

רד"ק

באליהו וישנס מתניו וירץ לפני אחאב: פן אחתך. אם לא תירא מהם ותבטח בי אצילך מידם ואם תירא מהם אחתך ואפילך לפניהם: (יח) על כל הארץ. ואחר כך פירש למלכי יהודה אמר תהיה כנגדם כעיר מבצר שלא יוכלו לך כמו שלא יוכל אדם לכבוש עיר מבצר כל שכן אם יהיו לה חומות נחשת ומה שאמר לעמוד ברזל שלא יוכל אדם להפותו ולשברו וי"ת על כל הארץ לאשקאה כס דלווט על כל יתבי ארעא: (יט) ונלחמו אליך. כמו שת"י ויהון דינין ומגיחין לקבלך למסתר ית פתגמי נבואתך: להצילך. שלא ימיתוך: (ב) הלך. מקור או צווי וכן

מנחת שי

מגול ומלא וא"ו ובספרים כ"י מדוייקים האל"ף בשוא לבדו וחסר וגם רב ספלים כתב שהאל"ף בשוא נח ע"כ. וכן נ ח ו ר בגבורה סילים פ"ס האל"ף בשוא לבדו: (יח) ולחמות. במקצת ספרים מלא וא"ו קדמאה בתר חי"ת וחסר וא"ו תניינא בתר מ"ס ובספרי ספרד נכתב ומסורת מסייעא להו דוק ותשכח. ויונתן תרגם וכשור דנחש אולי היה קורא ולחמת בלשון יחיד דומיא דעיר מבצר ועמוד ברזל. וגם במקרא ישנה דפוס ויניציאה יש הגהה מזה אבל לא מצאתי כן בשום ספר: ב (ב) הלך. כרוב אלנו מהמסורת שהוא חסר וא"ו וכן הוא

מצודת ציון

(יז) תאזור. מל' אזור וחגורה: תחת. אחתך. מנין פחד ושבר כמו אל תערוץ ואל תחת (יהושע א'): (יט) יוכלו. מל' יכולת והתגברות:

מצודת דוד

ממהם משפט ר"ל אביא עליהם משפט הגמול בעבור רעתם: (יז) תאזור מתניך. הוא ענין זרוז כי המגור במתניו הוא מזורז: אל תחת מפניהם. אל תפחד מפניהם מלומר להם את כל דברי פן אחתך. כי כשתפחד אעזוב אותך לפניהם ויוכלו לך להזיקך לכן אל תפחד ובטח עלי ואז לא יוכלו לך: (יח) נתתיך היום. נתתי כח בידך להיות חזק כעיר מבצר בו להתגבר על כל הארץ וחוזר ומפרש על מלכי יהודה ועל שרי יהודה ועל כהנים ועל כל עם הארץ מיתר העם: (יט) ונלחמו אליך. כולם ילחמו עמך ולא יוכלו לך כי אני עמך להצילך מידם:

thereof, to fight against them according to their strength, against the kings, who are the strongest, against the princes, who are after the kings, against the priests, who are after the princes, against the people of the land, who are the lowest and the most humble.

19. **And they shall fight against you**—*They shall quarrel and fight against you to refute the words of your prophecy.*—[*Rashi, Redak* from *Jonathan*]

They will all fight against you, yet they will not prevail against you, since I will be with you to save you because you trust in Me.—[*Abarbanel, Mezudath David*]

to save you—so that they should not kill you.—[*Redak*]

17. And you shall gird your loins and arise and speak to them all that I command you; be not dismayed by them, lest I break you before them. 18. And I, behold I have made you today into a fortified city and into an iron pillar, and into copper walls against the entire land, against the kings of Judah, against its princes, against its priests, and against the people of the land. 19. And they shall fight against you but they shall not prevail against you, for I am with you, says the Lord, to save you.

2

1. And the word of the Lord came to me, saying:

struction of the Temple is God's way of talking to Israel to castigate them.—[*Redak, Abarbanel*]

17. **And you shall gird your loins**—This is *an expression of quickening like a man of valor.*—[*Rashi*]

We find that Elijah girded his loins in order to run swiftly before Ahab's chariot, in I Kings 18:46.—[*Redak*]

be not dismayed by them—Lit. do not break down from before them. I.e., do not fear to tell them everything that I command you, for if you do fear them, I will indeed break you before them, and they will be able to hurt you. Therefore, do not fear them, and hope for My protection. Then, I will save you.—[*Redak, Mezudath David*]

Since you are aware of the impending doom, gird your loins despite your youth and commence quickly to deliver My message to the people. Fear them not lest I break you and cast you down before them.—[*Abarbanel*]

If you strengthen yourself, I will add to your strength, and if you break down before them, I will add to your being broken. How, then, can you not strengthen yourself?—[*Ibn Nachmiash*]

18. **against the entire land**—Then He elaborates: against the kings of Judah, against its princes, etc. God says that Jeremiah will be like a fortified city, invincible to attack. He says: They will not be able to prevail against you as no one can prevail against a fortified city, surely if it is surrounded by copper walls. He promises to make him like an iron pillar, which no one can bend or break. *Jonathan* renders: to give all the dwellers of the land to drink the cup of the curse.—[*Redak*]

against the Kings of Judah—*lit. to the Kings of Judah.*—[*Rashi*]

Abarbanel explains: If you believe My words, I will make you today, while you are still a youth, into a fortified city etc. against the entire land, against the various members

אמר יי דכירנא לכון טבות יומי קדם רחמת אבהתכון דהימנו במימרי ואזלו בתר תרין שליחי בתר משה ואהרן במדברא ארבעין שנין בלא זודין בארעא דלא מזדרעא: ג קודשא אינון בית ישראל קדם יי ועל בזויהון כדמעה ארמות עללא דמן דאכל מניה חיב למימת וכשירו חצד עומר ארמותא דעד לא מקרבין מניה כהניא בני אהרן קורבניא על מדבחא מן דאכיל מניה מתחיב אף כן כל בזויהון דבית ישראל יחובון בישתא תיתי עליהון אמר יי: ד קבילו פתגמא דיי בית יעקב וכל זרעית בית ישראל:

וְקָרָאתָ בְאָזְנֵי יְרוּשָׁלַם לֵאמֹר כֹּה אָמַר
יְהוָֹה זָכַרְתִּי לָךְ חֶסֶד נְעוּרַיִךְ אַהֲבַת
כְּלוּלֹתָיִךְ לֶכְתֵּךְ אַחֲרַי בַּמִּדְבָּר בְּאֶרֶץ
לֹא זְרוּעָה: ג קֹדֶשׁ יִשְׂרָאֵל לַיהוָֹה
רֵאשִׁית תְּבוּאָתֹה כָּל־אֹכְלָיו יֶאְשָׁמוּ
רָעָה תָּבֹא אֲלֵיהֶם נְאֻם־יְהוָֹה: ד שִׁמְעוּ
דְבַר־יְהוָֹה בֵּית יַעֲקֹב וְכָל־מִשְׁפְּחוֹת

ת"א קודש ישראל. קדושין כג: תבואתו קרי קמץ בז"ק בית

רש"י

ב (ב) זכרתי לך. אם הייתם שבים אלי תאותי לרחם עליכם כי זכרתי חסד נעוריך ואהבת כלילות חופתך שהכללתיך לחופה ולשון הכנסה הוא. כלולותיך (נוליד"ש בלע"ז). ומה הוא חסד נעוריך לכתך אחרי שלוחי משה ואהרן מארץ נושבת יצאתם למדבר ואין לדה לדרך כי האמנתם בי: (ג) קודש ישראל. כתרומה: ראשית תבואתה. כראשית קציר לפני העומר שאסור באכילה

מהר"י קרא

ב (ב) זכרתי לך חסד נעוריך. את שבהת חסד שעשיתי לך מנעוריך שגאלתי אתכם מתחת סבלות מצרים והולכתי אתכם במדבר וספקתי צורכיכם במדבר ארבעים שנה והריני מזכיר לך חסד שעשיתי לך מנעוריך כשהלכת אחרי במדבר בארץ לא זרועה. וקראתיך קודש כמו שנאמר ואתם תהיו לי ממלכת כהנים וגוי קדוש. וזהו הוא: (ג) קודש ישראל לה'. כלומר באותו פרק ובאותו העונה כיניתי לכם השם הזה ושמא תאמר מה הנאה יש בו מה טיבו של שם זה לקרות אתכם קודש דבר גדול הוא לכם אלו לא חללתם את שמכם בעבירות שהרי מה קודש כל הנהנה ממנו חייב אשם אף ישראל כל אוכליו יאשמו: תבואתה. ה' כתיב כנגד בכורים ושלשה תרומות ומעשר ראשון שנקראו כולם ראשית ואית דמפיק מעשר ועייל ראשית הגז: רעה תבא עליהם נאום ה'. באותו הפרק בדור המדבר אמר כך. ועכשיו שעזבתם אותו ותקפרו

רד"ק

זכור את יום השבת תמוך אשורי: באזני ירושלים. ר"ל עם ירושלם ומדבר כנגד העיר כאלו מדבר כנגד העם: זכרתי לך חסד נעוריך. אף על פי שאני מביא עליך רעה בעבור מעשיך הרעים לא אעשה אותך כלה וגם אעניש המריעים לך כי זכרתי לך חסד נעוריך וענין חסד נעוריך אהבת כלולותיך כמו שת"י דכיר אנא לכון טבות יומי קדם רחמת אהבתכון דהימנו במימרי וגו' כבעמוד. ואפשר שהיה דעתו באמרו ימי קדם על האבות אברהם יצחק ויעקב שהיו אנשי חסד או אהבת כלולותיך פירוש חסד נעוריך והכל ענין אחד על דור המדבר וקורא הימים הקדמונים ימי נעורים בדרך השאלה כמו שהנערים קודמין לבחורים ולזקנים ופי' כלולותיך שם מן כלה כי כנסת ישראל נדמת לכלה ביום מתן תורה והקב"ה נדמה לחתן: (ג) קדש ישראל. נחשב כמו קדש שלא יאכלנו זר ומה שאמר ראשית תבואתה הוא כפל ענין במ"ש כי התרומות שהיא ראשית התבואה הוא קדש וכל זרים אוכליו יש עליהם אשם כן ישראל אף על פי שהקב"ה מביא עליהם האויב הוא נענש עליהם כי זוכר להם חסד נעורים שהוא חסד האבות כמו שראינו בסנחריב וכן בנבוכדנצר ולעונש ישראל נחרבה בבל כמ"ש: תבואתה. כתיב בה"א במקום וי"ו כמו אהלה והדומים

מנחת שי

בספרים מדוייקים ומלאים כי מדרשנה בסוף וילא: וקראת. בספרים כ"י מדוייקים הוא"ו בגעיא. (ג) ראשית תבואתה. כתוב בה"א והתי"ו בחולם וכן תברו שבסמוך יחזקאל וכיתה שבואתה ללחם ע' זהר פרשת משפטים דף קכ"א ופרשת האזינו דף ר"ז ותיקונים תיקון ט"ו: יאשמו. האל"ף בשוא לבדו רד"ק: (ד) וכל משפחות. בס"ס כב"פ במאריך כמו שכתבתי לעיל סימן ה':

מצודת דוד

ב (ב) באזני ירושלים. באזני יושבי ירושלים: זכרתי לך. זוכר אני לך את החסד אשר עשיתי עמך בימי נעוריך. בעת בחרתי אותך לי לעם כי מצאת חן בעיני: אהבת כלולותיך. האהבה שהי' לי עליך בעת היית ככלה בזמן חופה' וזהו במעמד הר סיני לקבל התורה: לכתך. ר"ל זכור לפני האמנ' שהאמנת בי שהלכת אחרי במדבר בארץ שאין בה זרע זרוע ואין מה לאכול: (ג) קודש ישראל. ולזה הוא קודש לה': ראשית. הוא המיטב שבכל תבואתו ר"ל המובחר שבכל העכו"ם: כל אוכליו. כל הגוזלים ומכלים את ישראל יהיו אשמים והרעה תבא עליהם ר"ל אף שישראל יהיו נמסרים ביד העכו"ם בעבור חטאם עכ"ז על כי המה קדש לה'

מצודת ציון

ב (ב) כלולותיך. מל' כלה ונקראת כן שהיא ענין כלול היופי כמו כלילת יופי (איכה ב') והכלה בימי חופתה היא כלולה בכל מיני יופי וקישוט: (ג) ראשית. ענין מיטב כמו ראשית גבורתם (לק'

you shall be to Me a kingdom of priests and a holy nation."

3. **Israel is holy**—*like terumah.*—[*Rashi*]

the first of His grain—*Like the first of the harvest before the Omer, which it is forbidden to eat, and whoever eats it is liable, so will all those who eat him be guilty. So did Jonathan render it.*—[*Rashi*]

At that time I called you this name. Should you ask, "What benefit do I gain from it? What is the essence of this name?" I will answer

2. Go and call out in the ears of Jerusalem, saying: So said the
Lord: I remember to you the lovingkindness of your youth, the
love of your nuptials, your following Me in the desert, in a land
not sown. 3. Israel is holy to the Lord, the first of His grain; all
who eat him shall be guilty, evil shall befall them, says the Lord.
4. Hearken to the word of the Lord, O house of Jacob, and all
the families of the house of Israel.

2. **Go and call out**—*Jonathan* paraphrases: Go and prophesy before the people who are in Jerusalem.

Our sages (*Mechilta, Beshallach* 7) tell us that this is the beginning of Jeremiah's prophecy, not the prophecy of the exile in Chapter 1.

in the ears of Jerusalem—I.e. in the ears of the people of Jerusalem. He is speaking of the city as though speaking of its people.—[*Redak, Mezudath David*]

I remember to you—*Were you to return to Me, I would desire to have mercy on you for I remember the lovingkindness of your youth and the love of the nuptials of your wedding canopy, when I brought you into the wedding canopy, and this* (כְּלוּלֹתָיִךְ) *is an expression of bringing in. Your nuptials* (*Noçes in O.F.*). *Now what was the lovingkindness of your youth? Your following My messengers, Moses and Aaron, from an inhabited land to the desert without provisions for the way since you believed in Me.*—[*Rashi*]

Redak explains in a similar manner: Although I am bringing misfortune upon you because of your evil deeds, I will not destroy you completely. I will even punish those who harm you since I remember to you the lovingkindness of your youth. This is paraphrased by *Jonathan*, who renders: I remember to you the goodness of the days of old, the love of your forefathers who believed in My word and followed My two messengers, Moses and Aaron, in the desert forty years without provisions, in a land not sown. His mention of *the days of old* may be an allusion to the patriarchs, Abraham, Isaac, and Jacob, who were men of lovingkindness, or perhaps the expression, *the love of your nuptials* is an explanation of *the lovingkindness of your youth,* both referring to the generation of the desert . . . *The love of* your nuptials refers to the giving of the Torah, when Israel was compared to a bride and the Holy One, blessed be He, was compared to a bridegroom.

Kara explains the verse in an opposite manner: You forgot the lovingkindness I performed for you from your youth, that I redeemed you from the bondage of Egypt and led you in the desert and supplied your necessaries in the desert for forty years, and behold I remind you of the lovingkindness I performed for you when you followed Me in the desert, in a land not sown, and I called you 'holy' as it is said: "And

בֵּית יִשְׂרָאֵל: ה כֹּה ׀ אָמַר יְהוָה מַה־
מָּצְאוּ אֲבוֹתֵיכֶם בִּי עָוֶל כִּי רָחֲקוּ
מֵעָלָי וַיֵּלְכוּ אַחֲרֵי הַהֶבֶל וַיֶּהְבָּלוּ:
ו וְלֹא אָמְרוּ אַיֵּה יְהוָה הַמַּעֲלֶה אֹתָנוּ
מֵאֶרֶץ מִצְרָיִם הַמּוֹלִיךְ אֹתָנוּ בַּמִּדְבָּר
בְּאֶרֶץ עֲרָבָה וְשׁוּחָה בְּאֶרֶץ צִיָּה
וְצַלְמָוֶת בְּאֶרֶץ לֹא־עָבַר בָּהּ אִישׁ וְלֹא־
יָשַׁב אָדָם שָׁם: ז וָאָבִיא אֶתְכֶם אֶל־
אֶרֶץ הַכַּרְמֶל לֶאֱכֹל פִּרְיָהּ וְטוּבָהּ

תרגום

ה כִּדְנָן אֲמַר יְיָ מַה
אַשְׁכָּחוּ אֲבָהַתְכוֹן
בְּמֵימְרִי שְׁקַר אֲרֵי
אִתְרְחָקוּ מִדַּחַלְתִּי וּטְעוּ
בָּתַר טַעֲוָתָא נַהֲווֹ
לְלָמָא: ו וְלָא אֲמַרוּ
נִדְחַל מִן קֳדָם יְיָ דְּאַסִּיק
יָתָנָא מֵאַרְעָא דְמִצְרָיִם
דְּדַבַּר יָתָנָא בְּמַדְבְּרָא
בְּאֲרַע מֵישַׁר וְחָרוּב
בְּאֲרַע צַדְיָא וְטוּלֵימוּתָא
בְּאֲרַע דְּלָא עֲדָא בַּהּ
אֱנָשׁ וְלָא אִתּוֹתַב אֱנָשָׁא
תַּמָּן: ז וְאָעֵלִית יַתְכוֹן
לַאֲרַע דְּיִשְׂרָאֵל דַּהֲוַת
מְנַצְבָא כְּכַרְמְלָא לְמֵיכַל
אִבַּהּ וְטוּבַהּ וְעַלְתּוּן
וסאיבתון

ת"א מה מלאו חגיגה ט. באר נא עבר, ברכות לא סוטה מו: ואביא אתכם. עקידה שער פו: ותטמאו את ספר הזוהר פ' אחרי מות הכהנים וגו' ספר הזוהר פ' לו:

מהר"י קרא

לאלהים אחרים קורא לכל משפחות ממלכות שיבאו ויתנו איש כסאו פתח שערי ירושלים: (ה) מה מצאו אבותיכם בי עול. שנעשו כפויי טובה שלא זכרו החסד שעשיתי עמהם מנעוריהם והוא החסד המפורש למעלה ומפרש עוד והולך כענין שאמר אחריו: (ו) ולא אמרו איה ה' המעלה אותנו ממצרים. ושמא תאמר אם שאר העם נעשו כפויי טובה הכהנים ותופשי התורה מחזיקין הן בתורת ה' וזכורין הן הטובות שעשיתי עמהן לשעבר

רש"י

והאוכלו מתחייב כך כל אוכליו יאשמו כן תרגם יונתן: (ו) ולא אמרו איה ה'. כי נלך אחרי אלהים אחרים: ערבה. (פלנטור"א בלע"ז): ושוחה. (נסוי"ה אינפוסיא"ה בלע"ז): ציה. (דיסגאט"ה בלע"ז): וצלמות. לשון חושך הוא: (ז) אל ארץ הכרמל. לארעא דישראל

מנחת שי

(ז) ואביא אתכם אל ארץ הכרמל. מלא יו"ד ואל"ף כמ"ש בספר זה סימן ל"ה:

רד"ק

לו וי"ת קדש ההרומה וראשית תבואתה העומר שתרגם כן קודשיא אינון בית ישראל קדם ה' ועל בזיזיהון וגו' כבעמוד: יאשמו. האל"ף בשו"א בלבד: (ה) כה אמר. מה מצאו אבותיכם. הדורות הראשונים משנכנסו לארץ שעבדו עכו"ם: (ו) איה ה'. לא נתנו על דעתם לאמר איך נעבד אלהים אחרים ואיה ה' המעלה אותנו כלומר איך השלכנו אותו אחרי גוינו ולא פנינו אליו: ערבה ושוחה. כתרגומו מישר וחרוב: ולא ישב אדם שם. שמא תאמר כבר בימים ההם נתישבו המקומות ההם ואחר כך חרבו ושבו מדבר זה לא היה כי אין המקומות ההם ראוים לישוב כי אינם מקום זרע ומה שדרשו רז"ל בזה ידוע, ופי' אדם. אדם הראשון ואמר מאחר שלא עבר מהיכן ישב אלא כל ארץ שגזר עליה אדם הראשון לישב נתישבה ושלא גזר עליהם אדה"ר לישוב לא נתישבה: (ז) אל ארץ הכרמל. מה שסמך אותה אל הכרמל לפי שהארץ הנעבדת בשדות ובכרמים ואילנות טובים נקרא כרמל ולפי שארץ ישראל היתה כן כמ"ש עליה ארץ חטה ושעורה וגפן ותאנה ורמון וגו' קראת ארץ הכרמל וי"ת לארעא דישראל דהות מנצבא ככרמלה: לתועבה. כתרגו' לפולחן טעותא שהם תועבת ה'. ומה שאמר ארצי נחלתי ר"ל הארץ הראויה לי לשרות שכינתי בה כי היא נבחר' מכל הארצות לטעם ידוע אצל

מצודת ציון

מ"ט): יאשמו. מל' אשם: (ו) ערבה. הוא כמו מדבר: ושוחה. מקום גומות וכורות כמו בשחת עשו (תהלים ט'): ציה. ענין שממון: וצלמות. נלו צל מות ר"ל חשכת הקבר: (ז) הכרמל. ענין מקום שדות וכרמים וכן ונופל כשן וכרמל (ישעיה ל"ג):

מצודת דוד

אהיה נפרע כבוף מן העכו"ם על שהרעו להם: נאום ה'. וזהו מאמר ה': (ה) מה מצאו וגו'. מה דבר עולה מצאו כי אשר בעבורם רחקו מעלי: ההבל. זהו העכו"ם שהוא הבל ואין בו ממש: ויהבלו. ובעבור זה נעשו גם המה הבל מבלי ממש כי כמש: ממשלת' עדי ארץ: (ו) ולא אמרו. לא חזרו מדרכ' לומר איה ה' ר"ל נשוב לעבוד את ה' אשר העל' אותנו מארץ מצרים: המוליך וגו'. ר"ל ולא תעינו בדרך ולא חסרנו דבר: בארץ וגו'. כפל הדבר כמ"ש פעמים רבו' להפלג' הענין ובדרך המליצה: לא עבר. בדרך העבר': ולא ישב. בקביעות מקום: (ז) ואביא. הנה הבאתי אתכם משם אל ארץ הכרמל. ר"ל מקום שדו' וכרמים: ותטמאו. במה שעבדתם בה לעכו"ם: ונחלתי. א"י שהיא נחלתי

you think that in earlier times these places were inhabited but were since abandoned, Scripture states that no man had ever dwelt there, that these places were not fit for settlement since they are not places where seeds can be sown. Our Sages (*Ber.* 31a) ask: If no man passed there, why must Scripture state that no man dwelt there. They, therefore, expound it to mean that any land that Adam decreed that it be inhabited was inhabited, and any land that he decreed that it should not be inhabited was not inhabited. [Hence, we render: *and where Adam had not decreed that it be inhabited*]. —[*Redak*]

7. **to a forest land**—*To the land of Israel which is planted like* כַּרְמֶל,

5. So says the Lord: What wrong did your forefathers find in
Me, that they distanced themselves from Me, and they went
after futility and themselves became futile? 6. And they did not
say, "Where is the Lord, Who brought us up from the land of
Egypt, who led us in the desert, in a land of plains and pits, in a
land of waste and darkness, in a land where no man had passed
and where no man had dwelt. 7. And I brought you to a forest
land to eat of its produce and its goodness,

you that there is great benefit to you, had you not profaned your name with sins, for just as hallowed things, whoever derives benefit from them is liable to a guilt-offering, so it is with Israel, all who eat him shall be guilty.—[*Kara*]

5. **What wrong did your forefathers find**—I.e. your forefathers who entered the Holy Land and worshipped idols.—[*Redak*]

What wrong did they find in Me that they became ungrateful, forgetting all the kindness that I bestowed upon them in their youth? That is the lovingkindness mentioned above. Then he proceeds to elaborate on all the kindness God bestowed upon Israel for which they showed no appreciation.—[*Kara*]

and they went after futility—An allusion to the idols.—[*Jonathan, Ibn Nachmiash, Mezudath David*]

6. **And they did not say, "Where is the Lord**—*that we should follow other gods?*—[*Rashi*] They did not call to mind, saying, "How can we worship other gods? Now where is God Who brought us up from the land of Egypt? How did we cast Him behind our backs and not turn to Him?"—[*Redak*]

plains—Heb. עֲרָבָה, (*planure* in O.F.), related to *pianoro* in Old Italian, meaning 'a plateau.'—[*Rashi*]

and pits—Heb. וְשׁוּחָה, (*enfossés in O.F.*), pitted.—[*Rashi*] This interpretation is followed by *Ibn Nachmiash* and *Mezudath Zion*. *Redak* follows *Targum Jonathan,* who renders: waste.

waste—Heb. צִיָּה (*dégât in French*).—[*Rashi*]

and darkness—Heb. וְצַלְמָוֶת, *an expression of darkness.*—[*Rashi* from *Menachem* p. 150 and *Dunash* p. 89] Some explain it as a combination of two words: צֵל מָוֶת, *the shadow of death.*—[*Redak, Shorashim; Saadia Gaon*] This appears to be *Jonathan's* translation. According to *Ibn Nachmiash,* however, *Jonathan* renders: שְׁלְהוּתָא, *darkness,* agreeing with *Rashi, Menachem* and *Dunash*. *Mezudath Zion* appears to combine both derivations, defining it as the darkness of the grave.

Ibn Ganah (*Sepher Haschoraschim,* p. 431) explains that darkness, because of its desolation and man's fear of it, is depicted as the shadow of death, as though death were a person with a shadow. Darkness is depicted as that shadow.

and where no man had dwelt—Lest

וַתָּבֹאוּ וַתְּטַמְּאוּ אֶת־אַרְצִי וְנַחֲלָתִי
שַׂמְתֶּם לְתוֹעֵבָה: ח הַכֹּהֲנִים לֹא אָמְרוּ
אַיֵּה יְהוָֹה וְתֹפְשֵׂי הַתּוֹרָה לֹא יְדָעוּנִי
וְהָרֹעִים פָּשְׁעוּ בִי וְהַנְּבִיאִים נִבְּאוּ
בַבַּעַל וְאַחֲרֵי לֹא־יוֹעִלוּ הָלָכוּ: ט לָכֵן
עֹד אָרִיב אִתְּכֶם נְאֻם־יְהוָֹה וְאֶת־בְּנֵי
בְנֵיכֶם אָרִיב: י כִּי עִבְרוּ אִיֵּי כִתִּיִּים
וראו

ת"א כי עברו. הכניה א ח:

וְסָאֵיבְתּוּן יַת אֲרַע בֵּית שְׁכִינְתִּי וְאַחְסַנְתִּי שַׁוֵּיתוּן לְפוּלְחַן טַעֲוָתָא: ח כַּהֲנַיָא לָא אֲמַרוּ נִדְחַל מִן קֳדָם יְיָ וּמַלְפֵי אוֹרַיְתָא לָא אֲלִיפוּ לְמִידַע דַּחֲלְתִּי וּמַלְכַיָא מְרָדוּ בְּמֵימְרִי וּנְבִיאֵי שִׁקְרָא מִתְנַבַּן בְּשׁוּם טַעֲוָתָא וּבָתַר דְּלָא יְהֲנוּן לְהוֹן אֲזָלוּ: ט בְּכֵן אֲנָא עָתִיד לְאִתְפְּרָעָא מִנְּכוֹן אֲמַר יְיָ וּמִן בְּנֵי בְנֵיכוֹן דְּאִם יַעְבְּדוּן כְּעוֹבָדֵיכוֹן אֲנָא עָתִיד לְאִתְפְּרָעָא: י אֲרֵי עֲבַרוּ לִנְגָוַת כִּתָּאֵי וַחֲזוֹ וְלִמְדִינַת עַרְבָאֵי שְׁלַחוּ וְאִסְתַּכַּלוּ לַחֲדָא וַחֲזוֹ עַמְמַיָא דְּגַלָּן מִכְּבַךְ

רש"י

דהות מגלגה ככרמלה פירוש נטועה כיער: (ח) ותופשי התורה. סנהדרין: והרועים. המלכי': נבאו בבעל. בשם הבעל: (ט) עוד אריב. טרם אביא עליכם רעה אתווכח עמכם עוד ע"י נביאי אע"פ שרבתי עמכם כבר ימים רבים: (י) איי כתיים. לאיי כתיים. איי. (איסל"ש

מהר"י קרא

לכך נאמר: (ח) הכהנים לא אמרו איה ה'. כלומר איה ה' המעלה אותם מארץ מצרים: ותופשי התורה לא ידעוני. אף הם שכחו הטובות שעשיתי להם. לא ידעוני. פת' לא הכירו הטובות כמו שנאמר והיא לא ידעה כי אנכי נתתי לה את הדגן ואת התירוש ואת היצהר וכן ויקם דור אחר אחריהם אשר לא ידעו את ה' (ואת כל הטובה אשר עשה ה' לישראל): והרועים פשעו בי. אלו מלכי ישראל ואחז ומנשה ויהויקים מלכי יהודה שהדיחו את ישראל מעל ה' והחטיאום חטאה גדולה: (ט) לכן עוד אריב אתכם נאום ה'. כלומר לבד ממוסר זה שהוכחתי אתכם שהייתם כדיי לזכור הטובות שעשיתי עמכם לשעבר ועוד אריב אתכם שהיה לכם לקחת מוסר מן האומות שאין לך עם שיחליף גוי אלהיו אע"פ שאין העובדו נהנה ממנו כל ימיו כמו שמפרש והולך: (י) כי עברו איי כתיים וראו וקדר שלחו והתבוננו מאוד. שב' אומות הללו יושבי אוהל ומקנה הם ואינן קבועים במקום אחד אלא נדין ממקום למקום לתור אחרי מרעה הטוב תושאין וסובלין את עץ פסלם על כתיפם בכל מקום הליכתן ואע"פ שאינו מכירין בו שיוכל להרע או להיטיב להם אינן

רד"ק

המשכילים: (ח) הכהנים. איה ה'. פירשנוהו והכהנים שהם לפני ה' כל היום ומקריבים קרבנות לפניו היה להם לומר לעם העובדים לבעל איה ה' שתעבדו לזולתו: ותופשי התורה. הם החכמים לומדי התורה לא ידעוני שלא למדו התורה לשמה לקיים מה שכתוב בה אלא לומדים בפה ולא בלב וזהו לא ידעוני כי המחשבה הטובה והמעשים הטובים הוא דעתה לא הלמוד לבד וי"ת ומלפי אורייתא לא אליפו למדע דחלתי: והרועים. הם המלכים שהם רועי העם כמו שהרועים רועי הצאן וכת"י ומלכיא מרדו במימרי: והנביאים. הם נביאי השקר: (ט) לכן עוד אריב אתכם. אדבר אתכם עוד דברי ריב ותוכחה ואמר עוד כי הקדים בדברי תוכחה באמרו מה מצאו אבותיכם ואמר כמו שאמרתי על אבותיכם כן אני צריך לומר לכם כי גם אתם רעים כמותם וכן אהיה צריך להריב עם בני בניכם כי גם הם ירעו ככם וזה הדרך שאמר משה רבינו כי ידעתי אחרי מותי כי השחת תשחיתון וסרתם מן הדרך ודברי תוכחה אלה האחרונים כי עברו איי כתים וראו וכל הענין וי"ת בכן אנא עתיד לאתפרעא מנכון אמר ה' ומן בני בניכון אם יעבדון כעובדיכון אנא עתיד לאתפרעא: (י) כי עברו איי כתיים. מלא בשתי יודי"ן פירשו רז"ל כי לפיכך זכר אלו האומות כי הקדרים עובדים לאש והכתים עובדים למים ואע"פ שיודעים עובדי האש כי המים מכבים האש אף על פי כן אינם ממירים אלהותם וי"ת כן ארי עברו לנגוות כתאי וחזו ולמדינת

מצודת דוד

שמתם להיות מתועב לפני: (ח) הכהנים אשר עליהם. להורות דרכי ה' כמ"ש כי שפתי כהן ישמרו דעת ותורה יבקשו מפיהו (מלאכי ב') : לא אמרו איה ה'. לא הזהירו לעם לומר איה ה' למה עזבו אותו: ותופשי התורה. הם הסנהדרין אשר עליהם משפטי התור': לא ידעוני. לא רצו לדעת ולהכיר גודל רוממותי: והרועים. המלכים מרדו בי: והנביאים. נביאי השקר מתנבאים בשם הבעל: ואחרי לא יועילו הלכו. הולכים אחר דברים שאין בהם תועלת והם הפסילים שאין בהם ממש: (ט) לכן עוד אריב אתכם. מלבד מה שהוכחתי את אבותיכם על רשעם הנה עוד אריב אתכם וידעתי שגם את בני בניכם אריב כי החכמה הזאת תלך מהאבו' לבנים דור אחר דור וכולם ראוים לתוכח' ומריב': (י) איי כתיים. גאי' כתיים והם אגלות המערב כי כתיים הם רומיים כי וצים מיד כתים (במדבר כ"ד) ת"א וסיען ילטרכן מרומאי:

מצודת ציון

(ח) ותופשי. ענין אחיזה כמו כי יתפוש איש באחיו (ישעיה ג'): בבעל. שם עכו"ם: יועילו. מל' תועלת: (י) אי. כמו הן

and those who hold onto the Torah—*The Sanhedrin.*—[*Rashi*]

I.e., the Sages who learn the Torah did not know Me, for they did not learn the Torah for its sake to fulfill what is written therein, but they learned with their mouths and not with their hearts. This is the meaning of *did not know Me,* for good thoughts and good deeds constitute knowledge of the Torah, not mere lip service by studying it.

*10. **the isles of the Kittites**—*To the isles of the Kittites.* אִיֵּי *is* (*isles* in French).—[*Rashi*]

The Kittites were descended from

* For Rashi's commentary turn to page 212.

and you came and contaminated My land, and made My heritage an abomination. 8. The priests did not say, "Where is the Lord?" And those who hold onto the Torah did not know Me and the rulers rebelled against Me, and the prophets prophesied by Baal and followed what does not avail. 9. Therefore, I will still contend with you, says the Lord, and with your children's children will I contend. 10. For pass over [to] the isles of the Kittites

meaning: planted like a forest.—[*Rashi* from *Jonathan*] *Rashi*, obviously, understands כַּרְמֶל as a forest. *Redak*, however, explains it as a fertile land composed of fields, vineyards, and fruit trees. Eretz Israel is called *karmel* since it is 'a land of wheat and barley, vines and fig trees and pomegranates, a land of oil-producing olives and honey' (Deut. 8:8).

and made My heritage an abomination—Eretz Israel, which is My heritage, you have made abominable to Me.—[*Mezudath David*] *Jonathan* renders: And made My inheritance for idol worship.

The land of Canaan was designated to be under God's direct supervision, without the heavenly princes as intermediaries. Since the Canaanites were corrupt in their deeds, they were expelled from that land, which was then purified for the reception of the Shechinah. Then Israel entered with the Holy Ark and the holy Torah into a purified land, ready for God's direct providence. Hence, when they commenced to worship idols, they contaminated a pure land.—[*Abarbanel*]

8. **The priests**—I.e., the priests who stand daily before the Lord and offer up sacrifices before Him should have said to the people, "Where is the Lord, that you worship other deities?"—[*Redak*]

Alternatively, the priests, whose mission is to instruct the people, as in Malachi 2:7: "For the priest's lips shall guard knowledge, and they shall seek instruction from his mouth," should have reproved the people by saying, "Where is the Lord? Why have you forsaken His worship?"—[*Mezudath David*]

The priests, who noticed the miracles of the Temple, and also noticed the cessation of those miracles, should have asked the people, "Where is the Lord?"—[*Abarbanel*]

This may also allude to the casting of lots on Yom Kippur to designate which of the goats was to be the sin-offering to God and which was to be sent to Azazel. In early times, the lot bearing God's name would invariably come into the High Priest's right hand. Forty years before the destruction of the Temple, it started to come into his left hand. Nevertheless, the priests did not ask "where is the Lord?" Why is His name not in its proper place?—[*Azulai*]

וראו וקדר שלחו והתבוננו מאד
וראו הן היתה כזאת: יא ההימיר גוי
אלהים והמה לא אלהים ועמי המיר
כבודו בלוא יועיל: יב שמו שמים על־
זאת ושערו חרבו מאד נאם־יהוה:
יג כי־שתים רעות עשה עמי אתי

ת״א ההמיר גוי. שם עקידה שער ס: כי שתים. כפר הזהר פ׳ואתחנן: כבודו ת״ע החת כבודי

לכבך וסמדינה למדינת נטלין ית טעותהון ומובלין להון עמהון ובאתר דאינון שרן פרסין ית משכניהון ומקימין ית טעותהון וסגדין להון אידא היא אומה ולישן בעבדת כנתכון בית ישראל: יא הא עממיא לא שבקו פולחן טעותא ואינון טען דלית בהון צרוך ועמי שבקו פולחני די בדיליה אנא מיתי עליהון יקרא ואזלו בתר דלא יהנון להון: יב אתאבלו שמיא על כדין על ארעא דישראל דעתידא למחרב ועל בית מקדשא דעתיד לאצטדאה ועל דעובדין בישין עבדו עמי להדא אמר יי: יג ארי תרתין בישן עבדו עמי פולחני שבקו די בדיליה אנא

רש״י

בלע״ז): וקדר שלחו. ולקדר שלחו לראות מנהגם: והתבוננו מאוד. ושימו לב להסתכל בדבר יפה: הן. כמו אם. אם המיר גוי מהם את אלהיו ואע״פ שהמה לא אלהים ועמי המיר את כבודו אשר בו היה נכבד וכתיים וקדרים יושבי אהלים ורועי מקנה ונוסעים והולכים ומטלטלין ממרעה למרעה וממדבר למדבר ונושאים את אלהיה׳ עמהם למקו׳ שחונים שם ואני נשאתי אתכם עד אשר קבעתי אתכם והנחתם אותי כך תרגם יונתן ורבותינו אמרו כתיים עובדים למים וקדריי׳ עובדים לאש ואע״פ שיודעי׳ שהמים מכבין את האש לא הניחו את אלהיהם: (יא) בלא יועיל. בעכו״ם שאין בה תועלת: (יב) שומו שמים. לשון תמהון כמו השתוממו והוא לשון צווי כמו אם כה יאמרו אלינו דומו (שמואל א׳ י״ד): ושערו. לשון סער: חרבו מאד. כאילו אתם נחרבי׳ על ביהמ״ק שעתיד ליחרב: (יג) שתים

מהר״י קרא

סמירין בו לבהיר אלהים חדשים ועמי שמכירין בי שאוכל להרע ולהיטיב להם שהוא דבר המועיל ואעפ״כ המירו בי ותפשו בדבר שלא יועיל: (יג) כי שתים רעות עשה עמי. אילו עזבוני ולא הלכו להם אחרי אלהים אחרים עדיין הייתי כדיי

רד״ק

ערבאי וגו׳ כבעבור והאריך הוא על זה הפסוק: הן היתה כזאת. בדרך שאלה לא שיהיה הן בדרך אם כמ״ש רבינו יונה אבל הן כמשמעו לקיים הדבר בחבריו ויבא ענין השאלה בלא ה״א השאלה ובלא אם כמו אתה זה בני והדומה לו: (יא) ההימיר. כן כתוב ביו״ד בין הה״א והמ״ם תכתב כן להביא במלה ב׳ ענינים ענין ההחלפה כמו ואם המר ימיר מנחי העי״ן והענין השני מן ובכבודם תתימרו מנחי הפ״א והוא הענין גדולה ר״ל אם החליף גוי אלהיו ואם הגדיל אלוה גוי אחר ואף על פי שהמה לא אלהים לא זה ולא זה כל אחד דבוק בשלו: (יב) שומו. כלומר ראוי העולם שיהיה חרב על זאת הרעה שומו ענין שממה: שערו. ענין סער׳: חרבו. ענין חרבן והחי״ת נקראה בקמץ חטף והוא צווי מן הקל והמסורת עליו לית חטף וכתב רבי יונה כי יש אנשים שהיו קוראים אותו חרבו כמו חרבו פני האדמה והיו מפרשין אותו גם כן צווי אבל מן הדגוש כמו פרקו נזמי הזהב והשיב הוא עליהם מן המסרה ועוד המסרת על חרבו פני האדמה שנים ובפסוק כן ות״י הפסוק כן אתאבלו שמיא על כדין על ארעא דישראל דעתידה למחרב כבעמוד: (יג) כי שתים. המשיל הטוב המשפיע לישראל בעודם מחזיקים בתורתו למקור מים

מנחת שי

(י) והתבוננו. בספרים מדוייקים כ״י המאריך בה״א לא בבי״ת ומכאן ראיה שאין מאריך כזה מניע השוא הבא אחריו דאל״כ לא היתה הבי״ת דגושה ודומה לו אחר התגלתו דפרשת נשא התכנדי מארכה דסוף ניחוח ורבים כיוצא בהם בל׳ התפעל שהם דגושים אחר החי״ו וככר דברתי מזה במאמר המאריך ואין להאריך כאן: (יא) ההימיר. במקצת ספרים כ״י חסר יו״ד ראשונה ורד״ק כתב כתוב ביו״ד בין הה״א וכמ״ס: ועמי המיר כבודו בלוא יועיל. זהו אחד מן י״ח תיקון סופרים שבמקרא והיל״ל כבודי אלא שכינה הכתוב מדרש ילמדנו ומכילתא פ׳ בשלח ומסורת ופי׳ ת״ס אבאר בהרבה בזכריה ב׳: (יב) ושערו. בס״ן שמאלית כמו בסמ״ך ענין סערה: חרבו. החי״ת נקראת בקמץ חטוף והוא צווי מן הקל

מצודת ציון

ותחסר ס״א התימא וכן תרקיע עמו לשחקים (איוב ל״ז) ומשפט התרקיע בה״א התימא: (יא) ההמיר. מל׳ תמורה וחלוף וכן ואם המר ימירנו (ויקרא כ״ז): כבודו. זה תקון סופרים והכאוי כבודי: (יב) שומו. מל׳ שממון: ושערו. כמו סערו בסמ״ך ור״ל רוח סערה: חרבו. מל׳ חורבן: מאד. ר״ל גדול וחזק: (יג) מקור.

מצודת דוד

וראו. משפט מנהגם: וקדר שלחו. שלחו מלאכים לקדר הם בני ערב אשר הם בפאת המזרח: והתבוננו מאד. הקרו מאד בתכונ׳ יתירה: וראו הן היתה כזאת. לאו מעשה העכו״ם ההם וכי באמת היה׳ ביניהם כתועבה הזאת: (יא) ההימיר. וכי גוי מהם החליף אלהיו באחר: והמה. ואף כי גם אלהיהם לא אלהים המה עכ״ז כיון שהחזיקו בהם לא החליפום: ועמי. אבל עמי החליף כבוד המקום בעכו״ם שהוא דבר שאין בו תועלה: (יב) שומו שמים. ר״ל ראוי שיהיה בעולם שממון וסער׳ והורבן גדול בעבור התועבה הזאת: (יג) שתים רעות. ר״ל רעה כפול׳ ותחשב לשתים: מקור מים חיים. שאני כמעיין הנובע מים חיים ר״ל

points *as*: "(I Sam. 14:9) *If they say thus to us, 'Wait* (דֹּמּוּ)! . . .'"—[*Rashi*] Others render it as an expression of desolation, meaning that the world should become desolate because of Israel's evil doing.—[*Redak, Mezudath David*]

13. **two evils**—I.e. a twofold evil, counted as two.—[*Mezudath David*] *Had they exchanged their Deity*

and see, and send to Kedar and consider diligently, and see whether there was any such thing, 11. Whether a nation exchanged a god although they are not gods. Yet My nation exchanged their glory for what does not avail. 12. Oh heavens, be astonished about this, and storm, become very desolate, says the Lord. 13. For My people have committed two evils;

Javan, as in Gen. 10:4. They dwelt on the isle of Cyprus.—[*Abarbanel* ad loc.]

and send to Kedar—*And send to Kedar to see their custom.*—[*Rashi*]

The Kedarites are descendants of Ishmael, as in Gen. 25:13, here representing Arabia, as Jonathan renders.

and consider diligently—*And put your heart to it to consider the matter diligently.*—[*Rashi*]

whether—Heb. הֵן, *like* אִם, *if. Whether either of those nations exchanged its god although they are no gods, yet My nation exchanged their glory, with which they were honored. The Kittites and the Kedarites were tent dwellers and cattle herders, who would travel, go, and wander from pasture to pasture and from desert to desert, and they carry their gods with them to the place where they encamp. But I carried you until I established you, yet you forsook Me. This is how Jonathan paraphrased it. Our Sages said however: The Kittites worshipped water and the Kedarites worshipped fire. And although they know that water quenches fire, they did not forsake their god.*—[*Rashi* from *Taanith* 5b]

Redak, following *Ibn Ganah*, prefers to render this as a question: Was there any such thing? Did any nation exchange its god. . . ? The peculiar spelling of the word הֵהֵימִיר leads *Redak* to believe that it is a combination of the root ימר, *to aggrandize*, and מיר to *exchange*, thus explaining: Did any nation exchange its god for a god of another nation and aggrandize that god? They would not do so although neither one is a god.

11. **although they are not gods**—*Jon.* renders: They are idols that have no power.

for what does not avail—For an idol that does not avail.—[*Rashi*]

Abarbanel explains that Scripture chooses these two nations since the Kittites were the forerunners of the Romans, thus representing the western nations, and the Kedarites were the Arabs, representing the eastern nations. The intention is that one can go from east to west and not find any nation exchanging its god for another although it is of no avail.

their glory—My worship for which I bring glory upon them.—[*Jon.*]

The Rabbis explain this as a euphemism, for *My glory.*—[*Minchath Shai* from *Mechilta, Beshallach* 15:6: *Tanchuma, Beshallach* 16]

*12. **O heavens, be astonished**—Heb. שֹׁמּוּ, *an expression of astonishment, like* הִשְׁתּוֹמְמוּ. *It is the imperative form,* with the same vowel

* For Rashi's commentary turn to page 212.

עזבו מקור מים חיים לחצב להם
בארות בארת נשברים אשר לא
יכלו המים: יד העבד ישראל אם יליד
בית הוא מדוע היה לבז: טו עליו
ישאגו כפרים נתנו קולם וישיתו ארצו

סיתי אליהון יקרא
כסבוע דסיין דלא
פסיק ושעו בתר
טעותא דאינון להון
כגובין תבירין דלא
יכלין לקיימא מיא:
יד הכעבדא הוה ישראל
אם יליד ביתא הוא
סבין אתמסר לבזוזין:
טו עלוהי יכלין מלכיא
ידימון קלהון ושוו

ת"א העבד ישראל. פקידה שפר טו: עליו ישאגו. פס: פתח בס"פ לשמה

רש"י

רעות. אם המירו ירא תס בכיולא בו יש כאן רעה אחת ועכשיו שאותי עזבו שאני מקור מים חיים ללכת אחרי עכו"ם שהם כבורות של מים מכונסין ונשברין ונסדקין ומימיהם נבלעים בסדקיהם הרי שתים רעות: לחצוב. לחפור: אשר לא יכילו. (טינדרוני"ש בלע"ז) את מימיהם שהמים מטפטפין את שפתם וכותליה' והם נופלין:

(יד) יליד בית. בן האמה: (טו) ישאגו. שואגים לשון הווה: כפירים. מלכים: נצתו. נלתו כאש:

מהר"י קרא

שאקצוף עליהן על שקבלו אלהותי עליהן ועזבוני כל שכן שאותי עזבו והלכו להם אחרי אלהי נכר שאין בו ממש למה דבר זה דומה לאדם שיש לו מקור מים חיים ומניחן ומבקש מים מכונסין שהן מצויין בבורות נשברים אשר לא יכילו המים. והיה להם להשים על לב מה נשתנו ישראל להיות לבז ולמשיסה בעולם מכל האומות. וכי: (יד) העבד. מקנת כסף ישראל: אם. עבד יליד בית הוא. שהאומות מושלין בו: מדוע היה לבז. שאנו

רד"ק

חיים שנובע מים בלא הפסק כן הייתי להם אני ועזבותי לעבוד אלוהות שהם להם כמו בארות נשברים: בארות. הם חריצים עשוים בבנין לאסוף לתוכם מי המטר ואם הם נשברין יצאו המים מהם כמו שיכנסו בהם והנה תוחלת הבוטחים בהם נכזבה והנה טוב האל למיחלין לו הוא נמשל למקור מים חיים לשני פנים לטובה אחת שלא יבאו לו המים ממקום אחר אלא ממקומו הם נובעין ועוד שאין להם הפסק כן טוב האל למיחלים לו כי הטובה יצא להם כאתו יהוא לא יקבלנו מאחר וטובו גם כן אין לו הפסק וכן המשיל הטוב שביחלין ישראל כהאלוהות ומהאומות העובדים אותם והיו בוטחים במלך אשור ובמלך מצרים שהיו בוטחים בו שיעזרום מהאויבים הצרים אותם כמו הבארות הנשברים כי אפי' יהיו שלמים יש להם הפסק כשיכלו המים המכונסים כי ממקום אחר יבאו להם המים המכונסים לא מעצכם כן הכח שהיה לעוזריהם היה בא להם מאחר כי המלך לא יעשה דבר אלא בעזר צבאותיו גם כן אם לא בעזר אלהים כמו שנאמר אין המלך נושע ברב חיל ואם הם בוטחים שאלהיהם יעזרום הנה הם ככו בארות נשברים שלא יכילו המים כי אפי' ישים אדם בהם מים יצאו בעד השברים ולא ימצא בהם מים כן הם שבוטחים באלהים אחרים אפי' יהיו עם רב אפי' יהיו להם כלי זיין הרי הם כאילו אינם וינצחום אויביהם ואפי' יהיו מדוקרים וכן דגנם ותרושם יהיו למארה כמו שאמר פנה אל הרבה והנה מעט ואמר והבאתם הבית ונפחתי בו: יכילו. יחזיקו כמו אלפים בת יכיל: (יד) העבד. הה"א פתוחה כי היא להמות כלומר אם עבד הוא או יליד בית ואם הוא יליד בית שנולד מן השפחה שיש לו לאדם בביתו והלא נקרא בני בכורי בנים אתם לה' אלהיכם ומנהג האב לרחם על הבן ואיך נטשו האל שיבוזו אותו אויביו וכי עבד הוא שאין משגיח האדון כל כך עליו כמו שמשגיח האב על הבן. ומדוע: (טו) עליו ישאגו כפירים. ונתנו קולם עליו הבהילוהו בקולם ובזזוהו בידם ומדוע היה זה והכפירים הם מלכי העכו"ם נדמו לכפירי אריות והשאלה הזאת כאילו ישראל שואלים מדוע היה להם זה והנביא משיבם הלא זאת תעשה לך עזבך את ה' אלהיך: נצתה. חרבו ושממו וכת"י צדיין ושרשו נצת וכתיב בה"א וקרי בוי"ו כמו ידינו לא שפכה והדומים לו או יהיה נצתו ענין הדלקה והבערה כמו ותצת בסבכי היער והוא על דרך עריכם

מנחת שי

כמו שמו ושערו והמסורת עליו לית חסף וכתב ר' יונה בספר הרקמה כי יש אנשים שהיו קוראים אותו כמו תרכו פני האדמה והיו מפרשים אותו ג"כ לווי אבל מן הדנוש כמו פרקו נזמי הזהב והשיב הוא עליהם מפני המסרה הנ"ל ועוד המסרה על חרבו המים אומרת שהם שנים ובפסוק רד"ק בפי' ושרשים ומכלול דף י"ט: (יג) בארות בארת. כן ראיתי בספרים מדוייקים וגם במקצת דפוסים קדמאה מלא וא"ו תניין חסר ובמקרא גדולה כתוב בספרים

מצודת דוד

כשפיע להם טובות בכל עת: לחצוב. למען לחצוב לעצמם באורו' רבום נשברו' כותליהם אשר לא יחזיקו את המים אשר נתנו בהם ר"ל עובדים למזלו' השמים המקבלים ההשפעה מאת המקום ואף אין בידם להחזיק את ההשפע' הבאה בכל עת וכאו' הנה המחליף דבר בדבר הטוב לו הנה לרע יחשב אף כי המחליף דבר בדבר הגרוע ממנו: (יד) העבד ישראל. וכי ישראל הוא כעבד מקנת כסף או יליד בית בן השפחה כי אלו מפני פחיתותם לא ישגיח האדון עליהם בהשגחה פרטיו' ולכן המה נעזבים אל המקרים ואמר וכי ישראל הוא כמותם להיות נעזב אל המקרים ומדוע א"כ היה לבז: (טו) עליו. על ישראל ישאגו ככפירים לאיים עליו והם מלכי העכו"ם: נתנו קולם. עליו נתנו קול' וכפל הדבר כמ"ש: וישיתו.

מצודת ציון

מעין: לחצוב. זה הל' נופל על החפירה כמקו' האבני' וכן ובורות חצובים (דברים ו'): יכילו. ענין המחזקה כמו קטן מהכיל את העולם (מ"א ח'): (יד) לבז. מלשון בזה ושלל: (טו) ישאגו. ענין זעקת קול: כפירים. אריות: וישיתו. ענין שימה כמו שתו בשמים פיהם

Mezudath David] Is Israel like a slave purchased for money or one born of a maidservant that they should be completely neglected by their Master? On the contrary, Israel is called the firstborn son of God, and it is natural for a father to show kindness to his own child and to protect him.—[*Redak*]

why has he become a prey?—Why then has he become a prey?—[*Mezudath David*]

15. **roar**—Although grammatically this is the future form, the meaning is that they *roar, a present tense*.—[*Rashi*]

young lions—Symbolic of *kings*.—[*Rashi* from *Jonathan*]

they have forsaken Me, the spring of living waters, to dig for themselves cisterns, broken cisterns that do not hold water.
14. Is Israel a slave? Is he a home-born slave? Why has he become a prey?
15. Young lions roar over him; they have raised their voice, and they have made his land

[*lit.* *their fear*] *for one His equal, it would be one evil, and now that they have forsaken Me, that I am a spring of living waters, to follow idols, which are like cisterns of stored-up water, and they are broken and cracked, and their water is absorbed in their cracks, these are two evils.*—[*Rashi*]

Scripture compares God, Who lavishes good upon Israel when they hold onto His Torah, to a spring of living waters, which flow endlessly. So was I to them, yet they forsook Me to worship pagan deities, which are like broken cisterns.—[*Redak*]

to dig—Heb. לַחְצֹב, lit. to hew.—[*Rashi*]

cisterns—Heb. בֹּארוֹת. These are trenches built up for the purpose of gathering rain water. If they are broken, the water will leak out of them just as it comes into them, and those who rely on them are disappointed. Now the goodness bestowed by God upon those who trust in Him is compared to a spring of living waters in two respects: one, that the water does not come from another source, but originates from its place, and secondly, the water does not cease to flow. So is the goodness bestowed by God upon those who rely on Him; the goodness originates from Him; He does not receive it from anyone else, and it is endless. In contrast, He compares the favors Israel hoped to receive from pagan deities and from the nations that worship them, e.g. the king of Assyria and the king of Egypt, upon whom they relied to save them from attacking nations, to broken cisterns. Even a perfect cistern is not always full of water since the water comes from another source; it does not spring up from the earth. So is the aid they receive from heathen nations; it does not come from the king. He must rely on his hosts, if not on the help of God, as the Psalmist words it: "*A king is not saved with a great army*" (Psalms 33:16). If they depend upon their deities, it is as though they are depending on broken cisterns, which do not hold water. Even if one fills them with water, it will seep out through the cracks, and no water will remain. So it is with those who rely on other gods; even if they are a mighty multitude, equipped with adequate armaments, they are as nought, and their enemies will defeat them although they will be wounded by the sword. Also, their corn and their wine will be destroyed by a curse.—[*Redak*]

that do not hold—(*Tendront in O.F.*) *their water, for the water will make their edge and their walls muddy, and they cave in.*—[*Rashi*]

14. **Is Israel a slave?**—I.e. is Israel a slave bought by his master for money?—[*Kara*]

Is he a home-born slave?—*The son of a maidservant.*—[*Rashi, Redak,*

לְשַׁמָּה עָרָיו נִצְּתָה מִבְּלִי יֹשֵׁב: טז גַּם־
בְּנֵי־נֹף וְתַחְפַּנְחֵס* יִרְעוּךְ קָדְקֹד: יז הֲלוֹא־
זֹאת תַּעֲשֶׂה־לָּךְ עָזְבֵךְ אֶת־יְהוָה
אֱלֹהַיִךְ בְּעֵת מוֹלִכֵךְ בַּדָּרֶךְ: יח וְעַתָּה
מַה־לָּךְ לְדֶרֶךְ מִצְרַיִם לִשְׁתּוֹת מֵי
שִׁחוֹר וּמַה־לָּךְ לְדֶרֶךְ אַשּׁוּר לִשְׁתּוֹת
מֵי

נצתו קרי ותחפנחס קרי

תרגום

אַרְעֵיהּ לְצַדּוּ קִרְוֵהי צַדְיָן מִבְּלִי יָתִיב: טז אַף בְּנֵי מְפִּיס וְתַחְפַּנְחֵס יְקַטְלוּן גִּבָּרָךְ וְיִבְזוֹן נִכְסָךְ: יז הֲלָא דָא פּוּרְעָנוּתָא תִּתְעֲבִיד מִנִּיךְ עַל דִּשְׁבַקְתְּ יָת פּוּלְחָנָא דַּייָ אֱלָהָךְ דְּאַחְזְיָךְ אוֹרְחָא תַקְנָא וְלָא הֲלֵיכְתָּא בַהּ: יח וּכְעַן מָה לְכוֹן לְאִתְחַבְּרָא לְפַרְעֹה מַלְכָּא דְמִצְרַיִם לְמִרְמֵי דְּכוּרֵיכוֹן בְּנַהְרָא וּמָה לְכוֹן לְמִגְזַר קְיָם עִם אַתּוּרָאָה לְאַגְלָאָה יָתְכוֹן לְהָלְאָה מֵעֵבֶר פְּרָת:

רש"י

(טז) גם בני נוף והתפנחס. הם מצרים שאתם בוטחים עליהם לעזרה. ירעוך קדקד. ירצצו גולגלתכם. ירעוך לשון רצילה כדמתרגמינן ורצוץ ורעוע: (יז) הלא זאת תעשה לך. הלא את הרעה ואת הפירענות הזאת תגרום לך האשמה והעון אשר עוזבת את ה' אלהיך: בעת מוליכך בדרך. שהיה מלמד אותך דרך הטובה והישרה: (יח) מה לך לדרך מצרים. למה תעזבי אותי ותבטחי על מצרים: לשתות מי שיחור. שטבעו זכוריכם בנילוס שיחור הוא נילוס כמה שנאמר מן השיחור אשר על פני מצרים בספר (יהושע י"ג): ומה לך. למרוד כי למען תגלי לדרך אשור

מהר"י קרא

רואין בכל יום שעלינו שואגין האומות המושלין ככפירים ונותנין קולם וישיתו ארצינו לשמה וערינו נתצו מבלי יושב: (טז) גם בני נוף ותחפנחס. שהיא שפלה מן הממלכות: ירעוך. הראש שבכם זה יאשיהו שהרגו פרעה נכה בלכתו להציב ידו בנהר פרת: ירעוך. לשון שבירה: (יז) הלא זאת תעשה לך. תשובה לדבר היא זו כלומר אל תתמה על החפץ שהאומות שולטין בכם שאת גרמת לך ביום עזבך ה' אלהיך. בעת מוליכך בדרך. ולא זכרת העת שהוליכך במדבר ושם סיפק לך כל צורכך: (יח) ועתה מה לך לדרך. לרדת מצרים לעזרה לעם שנעשה אכזרי עליכם בהיותכם גרים בינותם שגזרו עליכם להשליך זכוריכם ביאור. בשיחור ומה לך לדרך אשור. שתשלחו אליו שיבא ויושיעכם כשם שמצינו באחז ששלח למלך אשור לאמר עבדך ובנך אני עלה והושיעני מכף מלך ארם וגו' וסופו להגלותכם

רד"ק

שרפות אש וא"א ז"ל פירש נצתו צבחו כי המקום החרב יעלה צמחים: (טז) גם בני נף. אמר הנביא והשיב להם כתופש דבריהם כן הוא כמו שאתם אומרים ועוד כי אפי' בני נף ותחפנחס שאת בוטחת בהם והולכת למצרים לבקש עזר ממצרים גם הם ירעוך קדקד ומה יעשה לך כל זה עזבך את ה': ירעוך. ישברוך כמו רעה התרועעה ורעו את ארץ אשור ומה שאמר קדקד כי מכת הקדקד מכה רבה מוהצת הראש באמצע כי הוא חוצה הראש וטרף זרוע אף קדקד ות"י ירעוך קדקד יקטלון גוברך ויבזו נכסך. ותחפנס כתיב וקרי ותחפנחס והיא עיר בארץ מצרים הקרא כזה וכזה כי קרובים הם: (יז) הלא זאת תעשה לך. אמר תעשה בל' נקבה על עזבך שהוא מקור לפי שהמקור הוא כדמות השם ויבא ל' זכר ול' נקבה ואמר בל' זכר כי רע ומר עזבך את ה' אלהיך וכשאבר הלא זאת תעשה לך עזבך כאילו אמר עזיבתך כי היא דמות השם וכן בא בל' נקבה כמו הנקלה בעיניכם התחתן במלך: בעת מוליכך בדרך. הוא היה מוליך אותך בדרך ישרה ואת נטית מעליה ועזבת את ה' ללכת אחרי אלהים אחרים ואמר בדרך בידיעה כלומר הדרך הידועה שהלכו בה אבותיך הראשונים: (יח) ועתה מה לך. למה תלכי לבקש עזר ממצרים ומאשור ועזרך בםקומך אם תרצי ללכת דרך ישרה לא היתה צריכה לטרוח דרכים רחוקים כאילו התאוית לשתות מי

מנחת שי

אחרים בניכם חסרים וי"ש מחלוקת בדבר: (טו) נצתה. נצתו קרי: (טז) ותחפנס. ותחפנחס קרי: (יז) הלוא. מלא וא"ו ע"פ המסורת: עזבך. העי"ן בקמץ

מצודת דוד

ישימו ארצם לשממה ועריו נתצו שממה מבלי איש יושב בהם ואל מלכות אפרים ילמד שגלו ככר מארצם: (טז) גם בני נוף ותחפנחס. שהם מארץ מצרים אשר אתה בוטח בהם ותשאל מהם עזר גם המה ישברו אותך וחוזר ומפרש את הקדקוד ישברו וכאומר וכי זהו בטחו' שנעזבו אל המקרים וכי מהראוי שיהיו נעזבים אל המקרים וכי המה כעבד או כיליד בית: (יז) הלא זאת תעשה לך. ר"ל לא זהו בעבור בנעזבים אל המקרי' אלא זאת היא הדבר הגורם את הרע' והיא עזיבתך אשר עזבת את ה' ולא הלכת אחריו בעת שהי' מוליך אותך בדרך הישר' ובעונש כל מה שבא ולא במקר': (יח) ועתה. הואיל והכל בהשגחה למה לך ללכת לדרך מצרים ואשור לרוח

מצודת ציון

(תהלים ע"ג): נצתה. ענין שממון כמו נלתה כמדבר (לקמן פ'): (טז) ירעוך. ענין שבירה כמו ורעו דליותיו (לקמן י"א): קדקד. היא אמצעית הראש יהולקבם השער אילך ואילך: (יח) שיחור.

He would lead you on the straight way, but you turned away from it and forsook the Lord to follow other gods. The definite article denotes the well known way on which our ancestors trod.—[*Redak*]

Others explain this as a reference to the time God led them on the way from Egypt. You did not remember the time that the Lord led you through the desert and supplied you with all your necessaries.—[*Kara*]

18. **what have you to do in the way of Egypt**—*Why do you leave Me and trust in Egypt?*—[*Rashi*]

to drink the water of the Shihor—

a desolation; his cities were burnt without an inhabitant.
16. Also the children of Noph and Tahpanhes will break your
crown. 17. Is not this caused to you by your forsaking the Lord
your God at the time He leads you by the way? 18. And now,
what have you to do in the way of Egypt to drink the water of
the Shihor and what have you to do in the way of Assyria to
drink

were burnt—Heb. נִצְּתוּ, *were burnt with fire.*— [*Rashi, Redak*] Rabbi Joseph Kimchi renders: were overgrown. A desolate place, where no one treads, soon becomes overgrown with grass and weeds. Most exegetes render: became desolate.—[*Jonathan, Redak, Mezudath Zion*]

16. **Also the children of Noph and Tahpanhes**—*They are the Egyptians upon whom you trust for aid.*—[*Rashi*] You even go down to Egypt to appeal to them for aid.—[*Redak*]

Noph—Identified by *Jonathan* as Memphis. This was a city in lower Egypt.—[Biberfeld, *Universal Jewish History*, vol. 1, p. 175]

Tahpanhes—Identified as Daphnae Pelusii. This was on the eastern bank of the Nile, on the road to Eretz Israel.—[*Rabinowitz*]

will break your crown—Heb. יִרְעוּךְ. *They will break your skull.* יִרְעוּךְ *is an expression of breaking* (רְצִיצָה), *as we translate* וְרָצוּץ, *and crushed* (Deut. 28:33) וּרְעִיעַ.—[*Rashi*]

The prophet seizes their words, saying, "It is indeed true as you say; even the children of Noph and Tahpanhes, upon whom you rely for aid, will break your crown." I.e., they will slay your mighty men and plunder your belongings, as *Jonathan* renders it.—[*Redak*]

Others render: will feed on your crown.—[*Ibn Kaspi*] This is followed by most English translations. However, most Jewish commentators follow *Rashi*.—[*Redak, Mezudath Zion, Isaiah da Trani, Ibn Nachmiash*]

Others explain that even the humble kingdom of Egypt, whose capitals were in Noph and in Tahpanhes, will break your crown; they will slay your most exalted person, King Josiah, who was slain by Pharaoh-Neco when he opposed him on his way to attack the king of Assyria (II Kings 23:29).—[*Kara*]

17. **Is not this caused to you**—*Is not this misfortune and this retribution caused to you by the guilt and the iniquity that you have forsaken the Lord your God?*—[*Rashi*]

This is the reply to your question. Do not be astonished at the fact that the nations rule over you, for you have caused it since the day you forsook the Lord your God.—[*Kara*]

Your troubles are not the result of God's leaving you to chance. It is due to your having forsaken Him.—[*Mezudath David*]

at the time He leads you by the way—*For He would teach you the good and the straight way.*—[*Rashi*]

מִי נָהָר׃ יט תְּיַסְּרֵךְ רָעָתֵךְ וּמְשֻׁבוֹתַיִךְ
תּוֹכִחֻךְ וּדְעִי וּרְאִי כִּי־רַע וָמָר עָזְבֵךְ
אֶת־יְהוָה אֱלֹהָיִךְ וְלֹא פַחְדָּתִי אֵלַיִךְ
נְאֻם־אֲדֹנָי יֱהוִה צְבָאוֹת׃ כ כִּי מֵעוֹלָם
שָׁבַרְתִּי עֻלֵּךְ נִתַּקְתִּי מוֹסְרוֹתַיִךְ
וַתֹּאמְרִי לֹא אעבוד* כִּי עַל־כָּל־גִּבְעָה

יט אַיְתֵיתִי עֲלָךְ יִסּוּרִין וְלָא מְנַעְתָּא מִבִּישְׁתִיךְ וְעַל דְּלָא תַבְתָּא לְאוֹרַיְתָא פּוּרְעָנוּתָא תִּתְעֲבִיד מִנִּיךְ וּדְעִי וַחֲזִי אֲרֵי בִישְׁתָא וּמְרִידָא אַיְתִי עֲלָךְ יְרוּשְׁלֵם עַל דִּשְׁבַקְתְּ יָת פּוּלְחָנָא דַיְיָ אֱלָהִךְ וְלָא שַׁוִּיתָא דְחַלְתִּי לְקָבֵל עֵינָךְ אֲמַר יְיָ אֱלֹהִים צְבָאוֹת׃ כ אֲרֵי מֵעַלְמָא הַעֲבָרִית נִיר עַמְמַיָּא מִצַּוְּרֵיכוֹן פְּסָקִית הַנִּיקֵיכוֹן וַאֲמַרְתּוּן לָא נוֹסִיף עוֹד לְמֶעְבַּר עַל מֵימְרָךְ אֲרֵי עַל רָמָא

ת"א תיסרך וגו'. שם כו פקרים מ"ג כו: כי מעולם עקידה שער כו   קמץ בז"ק אעבור קרי

רש"י

למעבר נהר פרת: (יט) תיסרך רעתך. סוף שרעתך תביא עליך יסורין: ומשובותיך. לשון בנים שובבים (לקמן ג'): תוכיחוך. לשון מוסר: ולא פחדתי. פחד שלי לא היה בלבך ליראה אותי: (כ) שברתי עולך. העול של עץ נופל בו לשון שבירה והמוסרו' שהן של עור נופל בהן לשון נתיקה: מוסרותיך. הם רצועות שקושרין בהם העול: ותאמרי לא אעבור. על דבריך: כי על כל גבעה. אך אתה לא שמרת הבטחתך ועל כל גבעה

מהר"י קרא

כעבר לנהר פרת וזהו לשתות מי נהר: (יט) תיסרך רעתך. יש לך אדם שמקבל מוסר עד שלא ילקה וזה הוא חכם אבל הכסיל אינו מקבל מוסר עד שילקה גם את כשתבוא עליך רעה אז תוסרי: ומשובותיך. מרד שמרדת בי תוכיחוך אז תרעי ותראי כי רע ומר עזבך את ה' אלהיך: ולא פחדתי אליך. מעולם לא שמת פחד יראתי על לבך: (כ) כי מעולם שברתי. עול האומות מעליכם ונתקתי מוסרותיכם: ותאמרי. לא אוסיף עוד לעבור על פיך ועל כל

רד"ק

שיחור או מי נהר מלך אשור וי"ת וכען מה לכון לאתחברא לפרעה מלכא דמצרים וגו' כבעמוד: (יט) תיסרך. אחר שנסית כמה פעמים כי בעשותך רעה יבא לך רע ובעבור משובותיך שאת מורדת בי ימשלו בך האויבים הם בעצמם רעתך ומשובותיך יהיו לך מוסר ותוכחה ליסרך שלא תשובי עוד בדרך הרעה שהרי נסית כי יבא לך רעה בעבורה וזהו ודעי וראי כי רע ומר עזבך את ה' אלהיך: פחדתי. שם בשקל פחדת אהבה אחוה אמר יראתי ופחדתי לא היתה אליך ולא פחדת שאביא עליך רע בעונש מעשיך הרעים: (כ) מעולם. מזמן קדמון שברתי עול מצרים מעליכם וכן בכל דור ודור נתקתי מוסרות הגוים מעליך וכשהייתי מציל אותך היית אומרת לא אעבור עוד על מצותיך והכתוב אעבוד לא אעבוד עוד עכו"ם

מנחת שי

(כ) אעבוד. אעבור קרי ברי"ש וכתיב בדל"ת והם שרש לבד וזהו מסוף:

מצודת דוד

למאוך כמי אלכם ר"ל נבקש מכם עזר' להיות נושע על ידיהם הלא הכל בהבנת' ומה יועילו לך: (יט) תיסרך רעתך. הרעות שאתה עושה המה ייסרו אותך במוסר יסורי ר"ל בעבורם תייסר ביסורין: ומשובותיך. מה שהלכת בדרכי לבך תוכיחוך כמאמר וכפל הדבר במ"ש: ודעי וראי. תן לב לדעת ועינים לראות אשר רע ומר דבר העזיב' אשר עזבת את ה' ולא היה פחד ה' אליך כאומר אין מכריחי לעזוב את מפאת העזר הבאה ממנו את מפאת יראת העונש: (כ) כי מעולם. הלא מימות עולם הייתי לך לעזר' ושברתי העול אשר הכבידו עליך העכו"ם: נתקתי. העתקתי מעל צוארך קשרי רצועות העול: ותאמרי. והא אמרת לא אעבור עוד על דבר ה': כי על כל גבעה. כאו' והנה לא קיימת כי על כל וכו':

מצודת ציון

זהו הנילוס: נהר. ר"ל נהר פרת: (יט) תיסרך. מל' יסורין: ומשובותיך. ענין מרד והליכה כדרכי הלב כמו וילך שובב (ישעיה נ"ז): תוכיחוך. ענין משפט הגמול כמו והוכח במכאוב (איוב ל"ג): ומר. מל' מרירות: (כ) עולך. מל' עול הכושם על צואר הבהמה והוא משל על הכבדת העבודה: נתקתי. ענין העתק והסרה: מוסרותיך. הם קשרי רצועות העול: גבעה. ענינו כמו

Egyptians off you, and in every generation I tore the yoke-bands of the nations off you.—[*Redak*]

I broke your yoke—*To the wooden yoke an expression of breaking applies, and to the yoke-bands which are of leather an expression of tearing open applies.*—[*Rashi*]

and you said, "I will not transgress."—*your words.*—[*Rashi*] I.e., whenever I saved you from the nations, you would say, "I will no longer transgress Your commandments." The *kethib* is: *I will not worship,* meaning that you promised no longer to worship idols.—[*Redak*]

but on every lofty hill—*But you did not keep your promise, for on every lofty hill you recline* (צֹעָה). *This is an*

the water of the river? 19. Your evil will chastise you, and your backslidings will reprove you, and you shall know and see that your forsaking the Lord your God is evil and bitter, and fear of Me was not upon you, says the Lord God of Hosts. 20. For of old I broke your yoke, I tore open your yoke-bands, and you said, "I will not transgress," but on every lofty hill

For they drowned your male children in the Nile. Shihor is the Nile, as it is said: "From the Shihor which is before Egypt," in the Book of Joshua (13:3).—[*Rashi*] According to *Kaftor Vaferach*, ch. 11, this refers to Wadi-el-arish.

and what have you to do—*to rebel against Me so that you should be exiled to the way of Assyria, to the other side of the Euphrates River?*—[*Rashi*]

Why should you go to Egypt and to Assyria to seek aid when your aid is here in your place? If you follow the straight path, you will not have to travel to distant places as if you wished to drink the waters of the Shihor or the waters of the river of the king of Assyria. *Jonathan* renders: And now, why should you befriend Pharaoh the king of Egypt to cast your male children into the river, and why should you enter into a treaty with the Assyrians to exile you to places past the Euphrates?—[*Redak*]

Kara explains: Why should you go down to Egypt for aid, to the country where you suffered during your sojournings there, and why should you go to Assyria for aid, as Ahaz entered into a treaty with Assyria so that they assist him against Aram in II Kings 17:7.

19. **Your evil will chastise you**—*Eventually, your evil will bring suffering upon you.*—[*Rashi*]

Some people accept reproof before they are punished. They are the wise. The fool, however, does not learn his lesson until he is chastisted. You, too, do not learn your lesson until evil befalls you.—[*Kara*]

and your backslidings—Heb. וּמְשֻׁבוֹתַיִךְ, *an expression related to "backsliding children* (שׁוֹבָבִים)" (infra 3:22).—[*Rashi*]

will reprove you—Heb. תּוֹכִחֻךְ, *an expression of reproof.*—[*Rashi*]

and you shall know and see etc.—After you have experienced many times that whenever you sin, evil befalls you, and whenever you rebel, the nations rule over you, your evildoings and your backslidings will serve as reproof to you, and you will know therefrom that it is evil and bitter to forsake the Lord.—[*Redak*]

and the fear of Me was not—*My fear was not in your heart that you should fear Me.*—[*Rashi*] I.e., you did not fear Me that I would bring retribution upon you because of your evil deeds.—[*Redak*] The Rabbis interpret this verse as referring to retribution in the hereafter. Your evil will chastise you in the hereafter . . . because you did not fear Me in this world (*Mid. Psalms* 14:5).

20. **For of old**—From time immemorial I broke the yoke of the

גְּבֹהָ֗ה וְתַ֙חַת֙ כָּל־עֵ֣ץ רַֽעֲנָ֔ן אַ֖תְּ צֹעָ֥ה
זֹנָֽה׃ כא וְאָֽנֹכִי֙ נְטַעְתִּ֣יךְ שֹׂרֵ֔ק כֻּלֹּ֖ה זֶ֣רַע
אֱמֶ֑ת וְאֵ֨יךְ נֶהְפַּ֥כְתְּ לִ֛י ס֖וּרֵי הַגֶּ֥פֶן
נָכְרִיָּֽה׃ כב כִּ֤י אִם־תְּכַבְּסִי֙ בַּנֶּ֔תֶר וְתַרְבִּי־

ה"א ואנכי נטעתיך. ס' הזוהר פ' וירא: כי אם תכבסי ר"פ ח' חגיג' ב פו יבמות קה:

תרגום

מִנַטְלָא וּתְחוֹת כָּל אִילָן עֲבוּף אַתְּ פָּלְחָא לְטַעֲוָתָא: כא וַאֲנָא קַיְמִתְכוֹן קֳדָמַי כְּמִנְצַב גּוּפְנָא בְּחִירָא כּוּלְכוֹן עָבְדֵי קְשׁוֹט וְאֵיכְדֵין אִשְׁתַּנִּיתוּן קֳדָמַי בְּעוֹבָדֵיכוֹן מְקַלְקְלַיָּא סְטֵיתוּן מִבָּתַר פּוּלְחָנִי הֲוֵיתוּן כְּגוּפַן דְּלֵית בֵּיהּ הֲנָאָה: כב אֲרֵי אִם תְּדַמִּין לְאִתְנַקָּאָה מֵחוֹבַיִךְ כְּמָא דְמִנַקַּן

מהר"י קרא

זאת לא עזבת מעבוד ע"ז על כל גבעה: את צועה זונה. נשכבת זונה צועה לשון מצע: (כא) ואנכי נטעתיך שורק. אשר כולה זרע אמת. בני יעקב שהיו כולן מיטה שלימה: ואיך נהפכת. לי לסור כאחרי: הגפן נכרית. שאינה מוציאה פירות: גפן נכריה. קורין אותו גפן שמוציאין ענבים שקורין בל' אשכנז תרמילנ"ק: (כב) כי אם תכבסי בנתר. אפילו אם היית רוצה לנקותך מעון כאדם

רש"י

את לועה ל' משכב ומלע כי מששם ל' אלה: (כא) נטעתיך שורק. שורק הוא זמורות גפן טוב כלומר בני אבות כשרים ולדיקים ומדרשו נטעתיך שורק הוספתי לך על שבע מלות של בני נח שש מאו' ושש כמנין שורק: סורי. (דישטוולסויר"ש בלע"ז): הגפן נכריה. הלוממות ביערים: (כב) בנתר. מין אדמה שחפין ושפין בה את הבגדים: בורית. נקיון כמו ובר לבב (תהלים כ"ד) ויש לועזים בורית (שאבו"ן

מנחת שי

במסורת וחברו בעזרת ח' כמ"ש שם: (כא) כלה זרע אמת. כתוב בה"א וכן ראוי פ"ע המסורת שנמסר בשמואל ב' סי' ב' דכל ספר ירמיה כתוב כ ל ה בה"א בר מן תרין כחד פסוקא כי מקטנם ועד גדלם וגו' בסימן ו' ואף דכתיב כתם במסורה וסי' כי מקטנם ועד גדולם דירמיה סימן ו' ז"ל ב' בפסוק אבל אותה שבפסוק כי מקטן ועד גדול בירמיה סי' ח' שניהם בה"א ועיין מ"ש בסוף מלאכי בס"ד ומדקדקי פ' בראשית כלה זרע אמת כלה כתיב רמז לכלה הכלולה מן הכל

רד"ק

ולא עשית כן אלא בנות לך עברת על מצותי ושבת לעבוד עכו"ם כמו שאתה עושה עתה כי על כל גבעה גבוהה וגו': צועה זונה. דמה אות' בעבודתם אלהים אחרים כמו הזונה שתדבק מעט זמן בזונה אחד ואחר כך תחשוק זונה אחר ותלך אחריו ובזה המשל הם רוב דברי יחזקאל כן את עבדת עכו"ם פלו' זמן אחד ואח"כ עכו"ם פלו' ואת הולכת מגבעה אל גבעה ומעץ רענן אל עץ רענן לעבוד עכו"ם: צועה. הולכת ונוסעת ממקום למקום וכן מהר צועה להפתח וכן צועה ברב כחו אך הוא פועל יוצא: (כא) ואנכי. שורק. הוא הגפן המשובח שבמיני הגפן ואומר כי בענביו לא ימצא תרצן ואמר זה על אברהם אמר איך היה זה ואיך יצאת כמו גפן נכריה כי מטעתך היה גפן נבחר וזרע אמת והיה ראוי שיצא ממנו גם כן פרי טוב והענבים שיטעו ממנו יהיו טובים ואיך נהפכת לי סורי הגפן הרע והיא נכרי למטע שהיה שורק ונטע אמת הוא לי כמו נכרי זר כאילו לא יצא ממנו וסורי הגפן הם הבדים הרעים שמסירין אותם מן הגפן שאין בהם צורך אמר נהפכת לי כמו סורי הגפן או כמו גפן נכריה שפירותיה באושים לא ענבים והגפן תמצא בל' זכר ובל' נקבה בל' זכר גפן ביקק וימצא גפן וילקט ממנו ובל' נקבה והיא כפורחת לגפן אחת והגפן האדרת והגפן נכריה: (כב) כי אם תכבסי. כמו שמכבסין הבגד בנתר ובבורית להעביר ממנו הכתם כן אם תכבסי עצמך ותנקי עצמך כלומר שתשובי בתשוב' אף על פי כן אענישך על עונך כל כך הוא רב ועצום והנה כתוב כבסי מרעה לבך ירושלם למען תושעי התשובה לזאת השאלה כי על כל פנים אם עשו ישראל שבאותו הדור תשובה היו נושעים מהאויב ולא היה מגלה אותם אבל היו מקבלים עונש עונם. חרב בארצם כי יש עון שאינו מכופר בתשובה לבדה אלא עם היסורין שממרקין העון אחר התשובה ורז"ל הקשו אלו הפסוקים ותרצו כי זה חה אחר גזר דין אלא כאן בגזר דין שאין עמו שבועה כאן בגזור דין שיש עמו שבועה כי גזר דין שיש עמו שבועה אינו נקרע כמו שנאמר לכן נשבעתי לבית עלי אם יתכפר עון בית עלי בזבח ובמנחה עד עולם: בנתר. יש מפרשים הוא שקורין לו

מצודת ציון

סר: רענן. ענין לחות ורטיבות כמו בשמן רענן (תהלים צ"ב): צועה. ענין טלטול ונוע ממקום למקום וכן ושלחתי לו צועים ולעהו (לקמן מ"ח): (כא) שורק. זמורות משובחים וכן ויטעהו שורק (ישעיה ה'): סורי. מל' הסרה והפלה: נכריה. זרה: (כב) תכבסי. מלשון כבוס ורחילה: בנתר. מין אדמה רכה

מצודת דוד

את צועה זונה. הולכת ונוסע' ממקו' למקו' ר"ל כמו הזונ' אין דרכ' לשב' במקום אחד וכמ"ש בה בביתה לא ישכנו רגליה (משלי ז') כן הלכת אתה מבית עכו"ם זו לבית עכו"ם זו: (כא) ואנכי נטעתיך שורק. מתחילה נטעתיך מענפי גפן משובח והוז' ומפ' הכל מזרע אמת הם אברהם יצחק ויעקב וא"כ ראוי היית להיות כמוהם ואיך נהפכת למולי להיות כדים רעים המוסרים מן הגפן אשר כל אחת נכרי' וזרה מן הנטיע' ולא תבוא אליה: (כב) ותרבי לך בורית. תרבי לעצמך בורי' להלאת עלמך ע"י ר"ל אף אם תרא' לפני הבריו' לדקות ומעש"ע הכר' לא תועיל בזה כי עונך שאתה עוש' בסת' נראה לפני ככתם כי לא העבירם הנתר והבורית כלומר הלדק' שאתם

and under every leafy tree, you recline as a harlot.
21. Yet I planted you a noble vine stock, throughout of right seed; now how have you turned yourself into a degenerate wild vine to Me?
22. For if you wash with natron and use much

expression of a bed and a sheet (מַצָּע). כִּי *serves as an expression of 'but'.*—[*Rashi*]

you recline—Heb. צֹעָה. As explained above, this is *Rashi*'s explanation of the word. *Kara* and *Isaiah da Trani* concur. *Redak* and *Mezudath Zion*, however, explain it to mean, you wander as a harlot. Just as a harlot goes from place to place seeking lovers, living first with one and then with another, so did you worship first one idol and then another one.

21. **I planted you a noble vine stock**—שׂוֹרֵק *is the branches of a good vine; that is to say the children of pious and righteous fathers. Its midrashic interpretation is: I planted you* שׂוֹרֵק. *I added for you to the seven commandments of the children of Noah, six hundred and six, as is the numerical value of* שׂוֹרֵק.—[*Rashi* from obscure midrashic source]

300 = ש
6 = ו
200 = ר
100 = ק

606

The seven Noachide commandments are enumerated in *Sanhedrin* 56a: (1) Laws, (2) prohibition of blasphemy, (3) prohibition of idolatry, (4) prohibition of incest and adultery, (5) prohibition of murder, (6) prohibition of robbery, (7) prohibition of eating a limb taken from a live animal. Israel was given six hundred and six more commandments, totalling six hundred and thirteen.

Redak interprets this as the choicest of the species of vines, which produce seedless grapes. This symbolizes Abraham. God wonders how that is possible. I planted you from the best vines of true seed, from which the best grapes should grow and the best branches to plant other vines. Now how have you turned yourself into the bad branches of a strange vine? A vine that is strange to its planting since it was planted from the best branches. סוּרֵי means bad branches that must be pruned. Another explanation is: the bad branches of a wild vine, which produces wild berries (בְּאֻשִׁים).—[*Redak*] See *Commentary Digest*, Isaiah 5:2.

degenerate—Heb. סוּרֵי (*Destoultours in O.F.*).—[*Rashi*]

wild vine—*that grows in the forests.*—[*Rashi*] See above *Redak*'s interpretation.

22. **with natron**—*A type of earth with which garments are cleansed and*

לך בורית נכתם עונך לפני נאם אדני
יהוה: כג איך תאמרי לא נטמאתי
אחרי הבעלים לא הלכתי ראי דרכך
בגיא דעי מה עשית בכרה קלה
משרכת דרכיה: כד פרה ׀ למד מדבר

ת"א נכתם עונך. ר"ס א' ית:

באות

בנתרא וסמתורין
בבוריתא הא כרושם
כתמא דלא דכי כן
סגיאו חוביך קדמי
אמר יי אלהים:
כג איכדין תימרין לא
אסתאבית ובתר טעות
עממיא לא הליכית
זקופי עיניך על
אורחתיך כד הוית
יתבא בחילתא לקביל
בית פעור דעי מא עבדת הוית דמיא לינקא קלילא דמקלקלא אורחתהא: כד כערודא דמדוכה

רש"י

בלע"ז): נכתם עונך. הא כרושם כתמא דלא דכי כן סגיאו חוביך קדמי. כתם. (סתק"א בלע"ז): עונך. על עון העגל נאמר שהוא קיים לעולם כמו שנאמר וביום פקדי ופקדתי עליהם (שמות ל"ב) כל פקידות הבאות על ישראל יהיה מקצת עון העגל בהם: (כג) ראי דרכך בגיא. מה עשית מול בית פעור ועד עתה את מחזקת באותו הדרך כבכרה קלה המשרכת דרכיה: בכרה. גמלה נקבה בחורה שהיא אוהבת לגוע בכרי מדין (ישעיה ס') מתורגם הוגני מדין והם גמלים בחורים כמו שמצינו בסנהדרין נפישי גמלי סבי דטעיני משכי דהוגני: משרכה. מחזקת בדרכי נעוריה ל' מסריך סריך ויש לחברו עם שרוך הנעל (בראשית י"ד) קושרת דרכי נערותי' בלבה: (כד) פרה. (שלוואטיק"ו

מהר"י קרא

שמכבס בגדיו בנתר ובאהל ובבורית לא יועילך כי עונך נכתם ביותר שאם תאמר לא נטמאתי: (כג) ראי דרכך בגיא. בעון פעור שגרם שנפלו מישראל כ"ד אלף. בכרה קלה. את דומה לבהמה קלה שלועזין פולייד"ר שמעקלת דרכיה ואינה הולכת ישר כשבורחת מבני אדם: בכרה. כמו בכרי מדין ועיפה: (כד) פרה למוד במדבר. כנסת ישראל דומה לפ"א לימוד מדבר שאינה מקבלת מרות כעניין שנאמר באיוב מי שלח פרא

רד"ק

בלע"ז אלומ"י וי"מ שהוא העפר שרוחצין בו הראש ובו מנקין כל דבר: בורית. י"מ שהוא שקורים לו בלע"ז סבו"ן ויש מפרשים שהוא עשב שמכבסין בו: (כג) איך תאמרי. ר"ל כל כך עונך בגולה שאם רצית להכחישו לאמר לא נטמאתי ואחרי הבעלים לא הלכתי לא תוכלי לכחש: ראי דרכך בגיא. הלא על הגבעות היתה עבודתה איך אמר בגיא אלא ר"ל ראי דרכך שהוא דרך בגיא לעלות אל הגבעה וזכר הגיא בעבור כי הגבעה כמו ההר היא אבן ולא יכיר בה אדם הדרך כמו בגיא לפיכך תוכלי לראות הדרך שיש לך בגיא שלא היה לך דרך בה אלא לעלות על הגבעה לעלות עולות ואת תמידה ללכת שם עד שהדרך נעשה מסלה נכרת לכל שדורכין בה בני אדם ואין באותו הגיא דרך כי אם לגבעה הסמוכה לו דעי מה עשית מעבודת הבעל בגבעה ולמה שפירש בו יונתן הוא פי' נכון. שתרגם כן ראי דרכך זקפי עיניך וגו' כבעמוד ולפי דרך יונתן נפרש הפ' כן איך תוכלי לומר אחרי הבעלים לא הלכתי ראי דרכך שהוא כמו שהיה בגיא מול בית פעור שהלכת אחרי בעל פעור כן את הולכת עתה אחרי הבעלים ואיך תוכלי לכחש: דעי מה עשית. בגיא מול בית פעור והנה גם כן בארצך הנה את כבכרה קלה שמשרכת דרכיה פעם תרוץ הנה ופעם תרוץ הנה כן את פעם את עובדת עכו"ם פלונית ופעם עכו"ם פלונית ות"י הוית דמיא כינקתא קלילא המקלקל' ארחהא ובכרה היא גמלה הקטנה עולת ימים והיא רצה יותר מהזכר. משרכת. מענין שרוך הנעל שקושרין אותו סביב הנעל כמה פעמים: (כד) פרה. בה"א כמו באל"ף פרא אדם הן פראים במדבר והוא

מנחת שי

שהיא זרע אחת כד"א אמן אמת ליעקב וגו': (כג) אחרי הבעלים. כן כתוב אחרי בלא וא"ו בראשית השטה וראיתי מי שנסתפק בזה וגם בס"א כ"י וכנביאים עם פירוש הרי"א כתוב ואחרי וכן נראה מהתרגום ובספרים אחרים אינו כן:

מצודת דוד

עוש' לפני ההביו' לא כפרו על העון בהסת': (כג) איך תאמרי. איך תכחשי לו' לא נטמאתי עתה בעכו"ם ומעולם לא הלכתי אחרי הבעלים: ראי דרכך בגיא. כלו' איך תוכל לומר כן הלא ראי דרכך בגיא מול בית פעור ששם עבדת הבעל ודעי מה שעשית היום הזה ותדע ותשכיל שאותו העון אשר התחלת שם הוא עמך עד היום הזה: בכרה קלה. והרי אתה כגמל' נקב' בחור' שקלה לרוץ יומ' מהזכר אשר נתקש' עמה דרכה ומנהג' עד שכל ימי' תתמיד במנהג ההיא לרדוף ולרוץ בכל עת וכן אתה כאשר התחלת בעבודת בעל פעור נדבקת בעבודת הבעלים עד היום הזה ולא תעזבם: (כד) פרה. הרי את כפרא הזה הלמוד והרגיל במדבר אשר באות

מצודת ציון

ומכבסין בו וכן חומץ על נתר (משלי כ"ה): בורית. שם עשב המנקה וכן וכבורית מכבסים (מלאכי ג'): נכתם. מל' כתם ורושם: (כג) בגיא. הוא מול בית פעור כמ"ש ונשב בגיא מול בית פעור (דברים ג'): בכרה. גמלה בחורה כמו בכרי מדין (ישעיה ס'): משרכת. ענין קשירה והוא מלשון שרוך נעל (בראשי' י"ד) שהוא הרצועה שקושרין בו הנעל: דרכיה. ענין מנהג וסדר: (כד) פרה. כמו פרא באל"ף והוא חמור הבר: למוד. ענין

Holy One, blessed be He, and says, "I am from So-and-so who committed me," and the Holy One, blessed be He, appoints it and it stands there to watch to destroy him when it has an opportunity to rule over him. Concerning this, it is written: Your sin is stained *before Me*.—[*Zohar, Noach* 73b]

* 23. **How do you say**—Your sin is so blatant that if you wish to deny, you are unable to do so and to say that you have not been defiled and have not followed the Baalim.—[*Redak*]

* 24. **A wild donkey**—(*salvatico in O.F.*), *wild, and some interpret it as poulain in O.F., a foal.*—[*Rashi*]

* For Rashi's commentary turn to page 213.

soap, your iniquity is stained before Me, says the Lord God.
23. How do you say, "I have not been defiled; I have not gone
after the Baalim"? See your way in the valley, know what you
have done, [like] a swift young she-camel, clinging to her ways.
24. A wild donkey accustomed to the desert,

rubbed.—[*Rashi*] *Redak* identifies it as alum, used for bleaching wool. See also *Sefer Hashorashim*.

soap—Heb. בֹּרִית, *cleanliness. Comp. "And pure* (וּבַר) *of heart"* (Ps. 24:4). *Some explain* בֹּרִית *as savon in French, soap.*—[*Rashi*]

your iniquity is stained—*Jon.* renders: *Like the mark of a stain that is unclean, so have your sins increased before Me.* כֶּתֶם *is tka in O.F.* tache in modern French, a stain.—[*Rashi*]

your iniquity—*This is said concerning the iniquity of the 'calf,' which remains in existence forever, as it is stated: "And on the day of My visitation, I will visit upon them their sin"* (Exodus 32:34). *All visitations that come upon Israel have part of the iniquity of the 'calf' in them.*—[*Rashi*]

God says to Israel: Although you repent and cleanse yourself of your sin, I will still punish you for it, it is so grave. This verse appears to contradict the prophet's statement (below 4:14): "Cleanse your heart of evil, O Jerusalem, in order that you be saved." The solution is that if Israel in that generation had repented, they would have been saved from the enemy, and they would not have been exiled. They would, however, have been punished in their land for their grave sins, for there are sins that are not expiated with repentance alone, but which require suffering after the repentance to complete the atonement. [Those sins punishable by *kareth,* spiritual excision, and death by the court require suffering to complete the atonement (*Yoma* 81a).] The Rabbis, too, considered this difficulty and solved it by qualifying this prophecy to a sin for which the verdict was already issued with an oath. For such a sin, repentance is not effective. If no oath accompanies the verdict, however, repentance is effective. A verdict accompanied by an oath cannot be nullified, as Scripture states: "And therefore, I have sworn to the house of Eli that the iniquity of the house of Eli shall not be purged by sacrifice or by offering forever" (I Sam. 3:14).—[*Redak* from *Rosh Hashanah* 18a]

The *Zohar* explains as follows: Come and see! If a person sins once before the Holy One, blessed be He, it makes a mark, and when he sins a second time, that mark becomes intensified. When he sins a third time, that stain spreads from one side to the other. In such a case, Scripture states: Your sin is stained before Me.—[*Zohar Chadash,* Gen. 11a] [I.e., the sin becomes like a stain that has penetrated the fabric from one side to the other and cannot be completely removed.]

Elsewhere, the *Zohar* states: If one transgresses the words of the Torah, that sin ascends before the

בְּאַוַּת נַפְשׁוֹ שָׁאֲפָה רוּחַ תַּאֲנָתָהּ מִי
יְשִׁיבֶנָּה כָּל־מְבַקְשֶׁיהָ לֹא יִיעָפוּ
בְּחָדְשָׁהּ יִמְצָאוּנְהָ׃ כה מִנְעִי רַגְלֵךְ

ת"א מנעי רגלך. יומא ח טו: נפשה קרי מיחף

בְּמַדְבְּרָא בִּרְעוּת נַפְשַׁהּ שָׁתְיָא רוּחָא כְּיָרוּדָא כֵּן כְּנִשְׁתָּא דְיִשְׂרָאֵל מָרְדַת וּטְעָת מִן אוֹרַיְתָא וְלָא צְבִיָא לְמֵיתַב נְבִיָא אָמַר לַהּ כָּל בְּעָהָא דְאוֹרַיְתִי לָא יִשְׁתַּלְהוֹן בְּזִמְנָא יִשְׁכְּחוּנַהּ׃ כה מְנַעִי רַגְלַיִךְ מִלְּאִתְחַבְּרָא לְעַמְמַיָא וּפוּמִיךְ מִלְּמִפְלַח לְטַעֲוַת פַּלְחֵי

מהר"י קרא

חפשי. פרה כתיב כי הפרה נעשה פרא: שאפה רוח. מצפה לרוח כמו כעבד ישאף צל: תאנתה מי ישיבנה. אי זה אדם יכול לכופה שתשדד עמקים אחריו לחרוש חרישו ולדוש דישו ולטעון משאו: תאנתה. לשון אנאו ורמיית: כל מבקשית. להשיבה ממה שהיא למודה ולמושכה אחר תרבות שורך ותמורך הגדלין על אביסך: לא ייעפו. אין צריכין להתייגע אחריה כי לא יועיל אבל חדש אחד יש הוא חדש תמוז יכולין לה לפי שיושבה במקום אחד שביעה ושמינה והיא נהפשת וזה הוא. בחדשה ימצאונה. כן ישראל למודין במעשיהן הרעים שמימי אבותיהם סרו מן הדרך ולא שמעו אלי וכשם שפרא הזה מצפה לרוח כך הם מצפין לעזרת האומות שלא יועילו להם לעזרת מצרים ואשור וכן הושע אמר אפרים רועה רוח ורודף קדים כל היום כזב ושד ירבה וברית עם אשור יכרותו ושמן למצרים יובל וכשם שאין אדם יכול להשיב הפרא הזה מתאנתו ומעניינו הרע כך שלחתי אליכם עבדי הנביאים להשיבכם אלי ולא יוכלו. ומה הפרא הזה נמצא בחדשו אף ישראל יבא חדש אחד והוא אב ויפרע מהם: (כה) מנעי רגלך. מלכת אחר ע"ז שגורמת לעובדיה שיהו הולכין יחיפין בגלות וגורמת לכל הקרואין אליה להיות בגרון

רש"י

בלע"ז) ויש לועזין (פוליי"ן בלע"ז): למוד מדבר. הלמוד להיות במדברות כן אוהבת לנוע: שאפה רוח. פותחת את פיה ושואפת רוח ולעולם הוא הוזר למקומו: תאנתה מי ישיבנה. אותה מדת תניניס שיש בה כי גם התנין שואף רוח כמה שנאמר שאפה רוח כתנים (ירמיה י"ד) מי ישיבנה מאותה מדה כן אתם מי יוכל להשיבכם מדרככם הרעה: כל מבקשיה לא ייעפו. כי על הגס ייעפו שלא יוכלו להשיגה ומה סופה בחדשה ימצאונה חדש אחד יש בשנה שהיא ישנה כל ההדר' ואז היא נלכדת אף אתם חדש אחד (הוא אב) הוכן לכם כבר מימות המרגלים שקבעו אבותיכ' בכיית חנם בו תלכדו. תאנתה. ש"ן (דגרונמינ"ס בלע"ז) וכן תרגם יונתן כערודא. ד"א לשון יללה כמו תאניה ואניה (איכה ב') ל"א (שאקונטריא"ה בלע"ז) כמו תאנת שילה (יהושע ט"ו): (כה) מנעי רגלך מיחף. זו

מנחת שי

(כד) נפשו. נפשה קרי: בחדשה. אין בחי"ס מאריך: (כה) וגורנך. וגרונך קרי:

רד"ק

חמור הבר אמר והנה את כמו הפרא שהוא למוד מדבר שהוא רגיל במדבר והיא ארץ מישור לרוץ בו מאד חמר הפרא בפסוק זכר נקבה כי פרא הוא ל' כלל לזכר ולנקבה כמו חמור ושור ויהי לי שור וחמור ואפשר שהנקבה רצה יותר לפיכך זכר ל' נקבה ואמר באות נפש' אבל אחר שהוא כתוב נפשו ל' זכר נאמר המשל הזה על זה והקרי נפשה כמו שהוא רוב הפסוק בל' נקבה ואמר באות נפשה שאפה רוח כי היא רצה למקום שתאוה לא יכול אדם להשיבה ממקום תאותה וענין שאפה רוח כמו שאפו רוח כתנים והיא ההרחה ומשיכת האויר אל האף והשאיפה היא במרוצה כמו שכתב החכם הגדול ר' שלמה בן גבירול כי רכוז חוש הריח באמרו כי לא לקלים המרוץ מפני שהמרוץ יהיה בשאיפת האויר מחוץ לרתף או לנושף על החמימות הטבעי אשר בתוך גוף האדם והשאיפה תהיה בחוש האף ולולי האף לא היתה הנשיכה שהיא מביאה לידי התנועה ויונתן תרגם שאפה רוח שתיא רוח כירודא הוסיף בו כתנים כמו שנא' שאפו רוח כתנים: תאנתה. מן אנה לידו שהוא גרם הדבר וסבובו כלומר כאשר מאנת עצמה ללכת למקום תאותה מי יוכל להשיבה: כל מבקשיה לא יעפו. כי בחנם ירוצו אחריה כי לא יוכלו להשיגה: בחדש' ימצאונה. יש מפרשים החדש שתשלם הריונה אז היא מלאה וכבדה ואז יוכלו להשיגה ולמצאה כן כנסת ישראל והמבקשים אותה הם הנביאים המוכיחים אותה לשוב אל ה' ולא יועילו אמר כי בחדש שיכבד עליה פשעה ונפלה והוא חדש אב שנפל הבית והוחרב אז ימצאוה ותודה על פשעה כי לא שמעה אל הנביאים (רק) כשתראה בחורבנה ויש מפרשים בחדש' בחדושה כלומר בכל עת ימצאוה כאלו עתה תחל לרוץ והיא חדש' במרוצה ויונתן תרגם בזמנה ישכחונה: (כה) מנעי. כשהנביאים אומרים

מצודת ציון

הרגל וכן כעגל לא לומד (לקמן ל"א): באות. מלשון תאוה וחשק: שאפה. ענין משיכה אל בית הבליעה וכן שאפה רוח כתנים (לקמן י"ד): רוח. כן נקרא האויר: תאנתה. ענין לער ואבלות כמו תאניה ואניה (איכה ב'): ייעפו. ענין יגיעה: (כה) מנעי.

מצודת דוד

נפש' שאפה רוח ר"ל אין מי מכרימ' לרוץ ולרדוף אבל כיא בהפלי תרון ותרדוף בכל עת ומושכת את האויר אל בית הבליע' כדרך הרלים מהרה: תאנתה מי ישיבנה. ר"ל בכל פעם הרון ותחזור במרולה למקומה כאלו היה לה לער ואבלות ואנס מי ישיבנה למקומה ולזה תרון מהרה והיא ענין מלילה: כל מבקשיה. כל המבקשים אותה לתפשה ביד אינם לריכי' להתייגעות לרדוף אחריה כי בחדשה בהתמלא הריונה ימלאו' אות' בקלות כי אז היא כבדה ואינה יכולת לרוץ וכן ישראל כמה כפרא הזה כי ע"י מעשיהם אשר לא טובים בא עליהם האויב והמה מסוטסים למלא עזר ממלכי העכו"ם למען יוכלו עמוד במרל' א"כ כל המדור הזה בא באות נפשם וכן סופם יהיה כסוף הפרא כי האויב הבא עליהם לכבשם לא יהיה לו יגיע' רבה כי בקל יכבשם בחדש המוכן לפורעניות והוא אב שהוקבע בכיה לדורות בזמן המרגלים כמ"ש רז"ל: (כה) מנעי

also be interpreted in a derogatory manner. Israel was like a wild donkey, snuffing the wind, i.e. wild, free to pursue her desires. She was, therefore, enticed to follow the idols, who are, in fact, nothing but wind and futility, without any tangibility. Therefore, their wailing will not be hindered, as explained above.

25. **Withhold your foot from going barefoot**—*This your habit, like the wild donkey that loves to wander. My prophets say to you, "Withhold your foot from idolatry lest you go barefoot into exile and withhold your throat from dying of thirst.*—[*Rashi*]

Those driven into exile go barefoot and very often they go thirsty since their captors give them no water. The prophet exhorts them to

that snuffs up the wind in her desire, her tendency like the sea creatures, who can hinder her? All who seek her will not weary; in her month they will find her. 25. Withhold your foot

her tendency like a sea creature—Heb. תַּאֲנָתָהּ, *son dagronemant in O.F.*, dragon nature. *Jonathan rendered it in this manner,* כַּעֲרוֹדָא. *Another explanation: It is an expression of wailing, comp. 'moaning and* wailing' (תַּאֲנִיָּה וַאֲנִיָּה) (Lam. 2:5). *Another explanation:* (*sa contrée in French,*) her country, *comp. Taanath-Shiloh* (Josh. 16:6).—[*Rashi*] *Rashi* apparently renders *Taanath-Shiloh* as 'the country of Shiloh.'

Others render: Her cause. She cannot be returned when she causes herself to go to the place of her desire.—[*Redak, Ibn Nachmiash*]

All who seek her will not weary—They will not weary to pursue her because they will be unable to overtake her.—[*Redak*]

in her mouth they will find her—In her final month of pregnancy, when she is heavy with child, they will be able to overtake her and find her. So it is with the people of Israel. The prophets who pursue her to reprove her for her sins will be unable to overtake her for they will not heed them. Their reproof will not avail them until the month of Ab, when they will be heavy with sin and they will fall, then they will confess their sins, as they actually did when the Temple was destroyed. Others explain: In her renewal, they will find her. I.e., whenever they find her, she is in a state of renewing her sins. It is as though they are now commencing to run and cannot be overtaken.—[*Redak*] Since they find them ready to renew their sins at all times, they refrain from reproving them, since it is better that they be inadvertent sinners than intentional sinners.—[*Ibn Nachmiash*]

Abarbanel explains this verse in a very unique manner. The prophet compares Israel to the wild donkey accustomed to the desert. Israel, after being freed from Egyptian bondage, were led through the wilderness, where they 'snuffed the wind', they strove for the prophetic spirit that they attained at Mount Sinai, but later—her wailing, who can hinder it? Who can prevent the destruction and the wailing? Those who seek her do not weary. They will easily find her in her month. I.e. the month of Ab, designated for misfortunes to Israel. In that month, it was decreed upon our forefathers that they would die in the desert and not enter the Holy Land. It was on the ninth of Ab. On that day, both temples were destroyed. On that day, the Jewish community of Alexandria was destroyed. On that day, the Jews were expelled from England. On that very day, the Jews were expelled from France in the year 5055. When the king of Spain decreed expulsion upon all the Jews in his kingdom and gave them three months to leave, that period terminated with the ninth of Ab. Although he knew nothing of that date, he was directed from heaven to the time designated by the prophet. It may

מִיָּחֵף וּגְרוֹנֵךְ מִצִּמְאָה וַתֹּאמְרִי נוֹאָשׁ
לוֹא כִּי־אָהַבְתִּי זָרִים וְאַחֲרֵיהֶם אֵלֵךְ׃
כו כְּבֹשֶׁת גַּנָּב כִּי יִמָּצֵא כֵּן הֹבִישׁוּ בֵּית
יִשְׂרָאֵל הֵמָּה מַלְכֵיהֶם שָׂרֵיהֶם
וְכֹהֲנֵיהֶם וּנְבִיאֵיהֶם׃ כז אֹמְרִים לָעֵץ
אָבִי אַתָּה וְלָאֶבֶן אַתְּ יְלִדְתָּנִי כִּי־פָנוּ

ת"א אומרים לעץ. יבמות דף מט : כי פנו. חולין ח׳. מקידש שפר קל : וגרונך קרי ילדתנו קרי

כוכביא ואמרת הבית
מבתר פולחנך לא ארי
רחימית לאתחברא
לעממיא ובתר פולחן
טעותהון אהך׃
כו כבהתת גבר
דמתחשיב מהימן
ומשתכח גניב כן
בהיתו בית ישראל
אינון מלכיהון רברבהון
וכהניהון ונביהון
דשקרא׃ כז אמרין לצלם
אעא אבונא את ולמה
דמתעביד מן אבנא אמרין ליה את בריתנא ארי אחזרו בפולחני קדל ולא שויאו דחלתי

רש"י

היא מדהך כפרא האוהבת לנוע. נביאי אומרים ליך מנעי עצמך מעכו"ם שלא תלכו יחף בגולה ומנעי גרונך מלמות בצמא: ותאמרי. על דברי הנביאים: נואש. אין מיחוש נואשתי בדבריכם. נואש (נוקליי"ר בלע"ז): (כו) כי ימצא. בתחלה כשהוא נמצא גנב והוא היה מוחזק נאמן כך תירגם יונתן: (כז) ובעת רעתם יאמרו. אלי קומה והושיענו

מהר"י קרא

צמאה ובחוסר כל אף את: מנעי רגלך. מלעובדה כדי שלא תלכי בגלות ברגל יחף *): וגרונך. כלומר גם מבצורות גרונך מקרא אליה כדי שלא יבא גרונך לידי צמאה: ותאמרי נואש. כאדם שמתיאש מעבירה שבידו ואינו נותן לב לחזור ולתקן עצמו: (כו) כבושת גנב כי ימצא. ת"י כבהתת גבר דמתחשב מהימן ומשתכח גנב כן בהיותו בני ישראל אונין מלכיהון רברבנוהון כהניהון ונביאהון דשקרא עכשיו הם פונין אלי עורף ולא פנים: (כז) ובעת רעתם יאמרו. עתידים הן לפנות

*) נ"ב והר׳ ישעיה פי׳ פיתף שם המקור הוא כמו מדבר עם יעקב. העתק מהנדפס

רד"ק

לך מנעי רגלך מיחף שלא תלך יחף וגרונך מנעי גם כן מצמאה כלומר שלא תלכי בדרכים רחוקים להעזר מן האומות ובדרכים יקרה לאדם צמא והלך יחף כי יבלו בנעליו בדרכים וכן לא ימצא בכל מקום מים ואם תרצי לא תצטרכי לזה כי במקימך יהיה לך עזר מהאל אם תלכי אחריו ואת אמרת להם נואש כלומר נואש לבי מלכת אחרי ה׳ לא אלך עוד אחריו אלא אחרי זרים שאני רואה שהם מצליחים ואהבתי אותם ואחריהם אלך ויונתן תרגם מנעי רגלך מלאתחברא לעממיא ופומך מלמפלח לטעות עממיא וגו׳ כבעמוד: יחף. שם כי אילו היה תואר היה אומר יחפה כי רגל היא בלשון נקבה או יהיה זכר ונקבה כמו יד והנה יד שלוחה אלי והנה בו מגלת ספר: צמאה. שם בשקל שמלה: וגרונך. וגורנך כתיב והענין אחד אולי הם שני משקלים: (כו) כבשת גנב. פירוש הנכון כתרגומו כבהתת גבר דכתחשב נאמן ואשתכח גנב כי הגנב המפורסם אין לו בשת: כן הובישו. פירוש היה להם להוביש כי הם לא היה להם בשת כי אילו היה להם בשת היו שבים מדרכיהם הרעים אלא היה להם להוביש ממעשים הרעים כי הם היו עם אשר בחר ה׳ בהם ובאבותיהם והם תעו אחרי אלהים אחרים הנה הם במשל כאדם שהיה מוחזק בנאמן ונמצא בגנבה שיתבייש כהמעשה אשר קרהו באמת כן ישראל היו מוחזקים בעם ה׳ עושים מצותיו ודבקים בו ושבו לעבוד אלהים אחרים היה להם להוביש כי יצאו מחזקתם: שריהם. בלא וי"ו כמו בוי"ו כמו שמש ירח ראובן שמעון והדומים להם: וכהניהם. כהני הבעל: נביאיהם. נביאי השקר: (כז) אומרים לעץ ולאבן. לצלמי העץ והאבן: אבי אתה. גדולי ואדוני: ילדתני. כמו יצרתנו וכן בטרם הרים יולדו: כי פנו אלי עורף. רוצה לומר כל עבודתם אינה אלא לעכו"ם אינם פונים לעבודתי כלל ופנותם אלי אינו

מנחת שי

(כז) ילדתני. ילדתנו קרי:

מצודת דוד

רגליך מיחף. ר"ל לא נתקן מעביך ולא תלכי בגול׳ יחף ולמאה גמים: ותאמרי נואש. אמרת אני מתייאש מעבודת המקום ולא אשוב אליו כי אוהב אני את הזרים הם עבודה הבעלים: ואחריהם אלך. לעבוד אותם: (כו) כבושת גנב כי ימצא. כמרבית בושת הגנב אשר היא בעת ימצא שהוא גנב אחר שהיה מוחזק לנאמן כן יהיה בושת בית ישראל בעיני העכו"ם על כי היו מוחזקים לעובדי ה׳ ונמצאו עכו"ם ככל העמים: המה. המון העם: וכהניהם. כהני הבעל: ונביאיהם. נביאי הבעל: (כז) אומרים. על אשר אומרים לפסל העשוי מעץ אתה אבי ולצלם מאבן יאמרו אתה ילדתנו כאלו הפסילים ברא העולם ומלוא׳: כי פנו אלי עורף. ר"ל אינם שומעים לדברי כאדם המהפך עורף מול רעהו ולא יאבה לשמוע

מצודת ציון

חדלי: מיחף. כן נקרא ההולך מבלי מנעלים וכן ערום ויחף (ישעיה כ׳): וגרונך. מל׳ גרון ולוא: נואש. מל׳ יאוש ועזיבת הדבר וכן ואמרו נואש (לקמן י"ח): זרים. מל׳ זר ונכרי: (כו) הבישו. מל׳ בושה: (כז) אבי. ענין אדון וגדול וכן אבי דבר גדול הנביא

stone —I.e. to images of wood and stone.—[*Targum Jonathan, Redak*]

"You are my father"—You are my great one and my master.—[*Redak*]

"You bore us"—I.e., you formed us.—[*Redak*]

In that generation, they did not worship idols as intermediaries to bring down God's bounty upon themselves, but they believed the idols to be their creators.—[*Malbim*]

for they turned to Me their nape—That means that all their worship was directed to the idols. They did not turn to My worship at all. Their turning to Me was only with their nape, i.e. to deny Me.—[*Redak*]

from going barefoot and your throat from thirst; but you said, "I despair. No, for I love strangers, and I will follow them."
26. As the shame of a thief when he is found out, so have the house of Israel been ashamed; they, their kings, their princes, their priests, and their prophets. 27. They say to the wood, "You are my father," and to the stone, "You bore us," for they turned

repent of their sins. Then they will be spared the ordeal of going barefoot and thirsty into exile.—[*Abarbanel*]

Redak explains: Withhold your foot from going barefoot, that you shall not go barefoot on long journeys to secure aid from the nations. On long journeys, travelers' shoes frequently wear out, and very often they do not find water. If you wish, you will not need this, for your aid will be given you in your place if you follow God. *Jonathan* renders: Withhold your foot from joining with the nations and your mouth from worshipping idols.—[*Redak*]

but you said—*concerning the words of the prophets.*—[*Rashi*]

I despair—*It is of no concern. I despair of your words.* נוֹאָשׁ *is* (*nonkalajjr in O.F.*) nonchalair in modern French.—[*Rashi*]

I.e., my heart has despaired of following the Lord. I will no longer follow Him but I will follow the strangers since I see them prospering. Therefore, I will love them, and I will follow them.—[*Redak*]

It is like a person who despairs of his sins and does not think of attempting to rectify them.—[*Kara*]

26. **when he is found out**—*At the beginning, when he is found to be a thief, and he was presumed to be faithful. In this manner, Jonathan rendered it.*—[*Rashi*]

Should an unfaithful person be found to be a thief, he is not ashamed of being found out, for a known thief has no shame.—[*Redak*]

so have the house of Israel been ashamed—I.e., so should the house of Israel have been ashamed, but they were not ashamed, for, if they were, they would have repented of their sins. They should have been ashamed of their evil deeds, since they were the nation whom God had chosen, both they and their forefathers, yet they strayed after pagan deities. This is the analogy to the honest person who is found to be a thief, who will, undoubtedly, be ashamed. So it is with Israel, who were presumed to be the people of God, observant of His commandments and cleaving to Him. Yet they turned to idolatry. For this deviation from their presumed status, they should be ashamed.—[*Redak*]

their priests—The priests of Baal.—[*Redak, Mezudath David*]

and their prophets—The false prophets.—[*Jonathan*] The prophets of Baal.—[*Redak, Mezudath David*]

27. **to the wood ... and to the**

אלי ערף ולא פנים ובעת רעתם
יאמרו קומה והושיענו׃ כח ואיה
אלהיך אשר עשית לך יקומו אם־
יושיעוך בעת רעתך כי מספר עריך
היו אלהיך יהודה׃ כט למה תריבו אלי
כלכם פשעתם בי נאם־יהוה׃ ל לשוא
הכיתי את־בניכם מוסר לא לקחו
אכלה חרבכם נביאיכם כאריה

ת"א למה תריבו . בבא קמא צב : לשוא הכיתי . שבת לג כתובות ח

משחית

תרגום

לקביל אפיהון ובעדן
דבישתא אתיא עליהון
כפרין בטעותהון ומודן
קדמי ואמרין רחים
עלנא ופרוקנא׃ כח ואן
דחלתכון דעבדתון לכון
יקומון אם יכלין
למפרקכון בעדן
בישתכון ארי מנין
קרויכון הואה דחלתכון
דבית יהודה׃ כט למא
אתון מתמלמלין לקבל
פתגמי כולכון מרדתון
במימרי אמר יי׃ ל למגן
אלקיתי ית בניכון
אולפן לא קבילו קטלת
חרבכון נבייכון כאריא

מהר"י קרא

אלי ולומר קומה והושיענו. ואני משיבם איה אלהיך. שעשית לך: (כח) יקומו אם יושיעוך בעת רעתך. שהרי רבים הם כמספר עריך ויכולין להושיעך וזה הוא: כי מספר עריך היו אלהיך יהודה. וגם זו כן התשובה שאני משיבם בעת קוראם אלי בעת רעתם כשיצעקו אלי לומר למה פניך תסתיר. אני משיבם. למה תריבו אלי וגו': (ל) לשוא הכיתי אתכם. שאע"פ שהכיתי

רש"י

וכן ת"י ובעידן דבישתא אתיא עליהון כפרין בטעותהון ומודן קדמי ואמרין רחם עלנא ופרוקנא: (כח) מספר עריך היו אלהיך. בכל עיר ועיר אלוה אחר: (כט) למה תריבו. איך תבואו להתווכח כריב ולומר לא חטאנו: כולכם פשעתם בי. אף הצדיקים כמשמע היינו דאמרי אינשי בהדי הוצא לקיא כרבא: (ל) לשוא הכיתי. על חנם כי לא הועיל שיקחו מוסר: אכלה חרבכם. את

רד"ק

אלא בעורף והיא כפירה בי וכן נזכר הפנה בעורף הפנה עורף מואב כוש: ובעת רעתם. כשתבא עליהם הרעה ויראו כי אין אלהיהם מושיע אותם יאמרו אלי קומה והושיענו כמו שאמר צדקיהו דרוש נא בעדינו את ה' כי נבוכדנצר מלך בבל נלחם עלינו: (כח) ואיה. כי מספר עריך. ואם תאמר אין לי אלהים אחרים כמספר עריך היו אלהיך כי בכל עיר יש לך אלוה: (כט) למה תריבו. ענין מריבה ותלונה אמר כשיבא האויב עליכם אתם מריבים אלי ואומרים למה עזבנו ה' ויתננו ביד אויבינו ולמה זה אתם מריבים אלי והלא כלכם פשעתם בי ופי' כלכם גדוליכם וקטניכם וי"ת ענין דין למה אתון מדכן למידן לקביל פתגמי: (ל) לשוא. אמר בניכם לפי שאמר כלכם אמר למה אתם מריבים אלי ואם תאמר למה אני מכה אתכם ביד האויבים אתם פשעתם בי ואם תאמרו למה אני מכה בניכם לפי שהם למדים מקטנותם לדבר שוא ואם מיסרים אותם נביאי ה' מוסר לא לקחו אם כן למה תריבו אלי ויונתן תרגם לשוא למגן כלומר בחנם הכיתי אותם כי מוסר לא לקחו ורז"ל פי' לשוא על עסקי שוא שאמרו בעון נדרים בנים מתים שנאמר לשוא הכיתי את בניכם מוסר לא לקחו: אכלה חרבכם נביאיכם. יש מפרשים כי אמר זה על זכריה ועל אוריה הנביאים שהרגום ואין זה הפי' נכון כי לא היה אומר נביאיכם כי לא היו נביאיהם אלא נביאי השקר כמו שאמר כהניהם ונביאיהם אלא הנכון כמו שפירש אדוני אבי ז"ל אמר נביאיכם שהם נביאי השקר אתם הרגתם אותם כשמעכם דבר ה' ונבואתם גרמה לכם אבוד הנפשות לפיכך אמר כאריה משחית שמשחית הבשר וקורעו

מצודת ציון

דיבר אליך (מ"ב ה') : ילדתנו. הוא כמו ילדתנו וכן בפרס כרים ילדו (תהלים ל') פנו מלשון הפנה וכיבוש : עורף. הוא אחורי פנים והצואר : (כט) תריבו. ענין תרעומות והתלונה : (ל) לשוא.

מצודת דוד

אמריו : ובעת רעתם. בעת בא עליהם הרעה יתפללו אלי ויאמרו קומה והושיענו מן הרעה : (כח) ואיה. ר"ל והנה אשיב לך איה אלהיך אשר עשית לך כפועל ידיך יבואו הם ויקומו אם יוכלו להושיע לך בעת בא עליך הרעה : כי כמספר עריך. לפי חשבון מספר עריך היו אלהיך יהודה א"כ רבים המה ואף אחד לא ימלא מהם שיוכל להושיעך : (כט) למה תריבו אלי. למה תתרעמו למולי על שאין אני מציל אתכם מן הרעה הבאה הלא כולכם פשעתם בי איש לא נעדר ומהו הזכות הנמצא לכם : (ל) לשוא. על חנם הכיתי את בניכם כיון שעכ"ז לא לקחו מהמכות מוסר ועדיין עומדים במרדם וכל עצם כונת המכות הבאות היא למען יוסרו המכות : אכלה. כי

loc. adds that even the prophet is included. The neighbors of the wicked suffer together with him, much as the cabbage suffers when it is uprooted together with the thorns growing close by. *Daath Sofrim* explains that the righteous were lacking in the piety expected of them. Had their piety been up to par, they would have affected the multitude, so that they would not have sunk to the level to which they did sink.

30. **In vain have I smitten**—Heb. לַשָּׁוְא *For no purpose, for it did not avail that they should receive correction.—[Rashi]*

Others explain לַשָּׁוְא as *for falsehoods.* For falsehoods I smote your children. From their childhood, they

to Me their nape and not their face, and at the time of their misfortune they say, "Arise and save us." 28. Now where are your gods that you have made for yourself; let them get up if they will save you at the time of your misfortune, for as many as your cities were your gods, O Judea. 29. Why should you strive with Me? All of you have rebelled against Me, says the Lord. 30. In vain have I smitten your children, they received no correction. Your sword devoured your prophets like a destroying lion.

and at the time of their misfortune they say—I.e. they say *to Me, "Arise and save us." Jonathan, too, translates in this manner: And at the time that misfortune befalls them, they deny their idols and confess before Me, and say, "Have mercy upon us and save us."*—[*Rashi*]

I.e., when misfortune befalls them, and they see that their gods do not save them, they say to Me, "Arise and save us," as Zedekiah said, "I beg you, pray for us to the Lord, for Nebuchadnezzar, king of Babylon, is warring against us" (infra 21:2).—[*Redak*]

28. **Now where are your gods**—I reply to them, "Now where are your gods etc."—[*Kara*]

let them get up—Let the gods you have made with your own hands attempt to save you if they can save you when misfortune befalls you.—[*Mezudath David*]

as many as your cities were your gods—*In every city was another god.*—[*Rashi*]

Should you deny that you have other gods, I tell you that as many as your cities were your gods.—[*Redak*]

The *Midrash* (*Proem* 22, *Lam. Rabbah*) depicts the origin of these idols representing each city. At first they placed images in the fields. When no one protested, they put them at the beginning of the roads. When this was allowed to remain, they put idols in the cities. *Daath Sofrim* explains that this was not originally meant as idolatry, but it was a vestige of the Canaanite culture which the Jews had adopted, believing that these images would bring them luck. Since they were allowed to remain, they were gradually placed in more and more prominent places, only to be eventually regarded as deities.

29. **Why do you contend**—*How do you come to contend with the quarrel and say, "We do not sin"?*—[*Rashi*]

When the enemy comes, you will contend with Me and say, "Why did the Lord forsake us and deliver us into the hands of our enemies?"—[*Redak*]

All of you have rebelled against Me—*Even the righteous are meant. This is what people say, "With the thorn the cabbage suffers."*—[*Rashi* from *Baba Kamma* 92a] *Rashi* ad

דִּמְחַבֵּל: לא עַם דָּרָא אַתּוּן קַבִּילוּ פִּתְגָמָא דַּיְיָ הָא כְּמַדְבַּר צְדֵי דְּלֵית בֵּיהּ הֲנָאָה וַהֲוָה מֵימְרִי לְיִשְׂרָאֵל אִם כַּאֲרַע חוּרְבָא מַה דֵּין אֲמַרוּ עַמִּי אִטַּלְטֵילְנָא לָא נְתוּב עוֹד לְפוּלְחָנָךְ: לב הַאֶפְשַׁר דְּתִתְנְשֵׁי בְּתוּלְתָּא תִּקּוּנַהּ כַּלְּתָא קִשּׁוּטַהָא וְעַמִּי שְׁבָקוּ פוּלְחָנִי יוֹמִין דְּלָא מִנְיָן: לג מָה אַתְּ מִשְׁתַּפְּרָא

מַשְׁחִית: לא הַדּוֹר אַתֶּם רְאוּ דְבַר־
יְהֹוָה הֲמִדְבָּר הָיִיתִי לְיִשְׂרָאֵל אִם־
אֶרֶץ מַאְפֵּלְיָה מַדּוּעַ אָמְרוּ עַמִּי רַדְנוּ
לוֹא־נָבוֹא עוֹד אֵלֶיךָ: לב הֲתִשְׁכַּח
בְּתוּלָה עֶדְיָהּ כַּלָּה קִשֻּׁרֶיהָ וְעַמִּי
שְׁכֵחוּנִי יָמִים אֵין מִסְפָּר: לג מַה־תֵּיטִבִי
דרכך

ב׳ טעמים

רש״י

נביאכם הרגתם את זכריה וישעיה: (לא) ראו דבר ה׳. הוצי׳ להם צנצנת המן אמר להם ראו כאן מה דבר ה׳ מועיל: המדבר הייתי לישראל. לשון תימה הוא לכך נקודה מ״ם רפי וה״א בחטף פתח כלום נדמה לאבותיכם שהוא מדבר כשהלכו בו שהורדתי להם לחם זה דבר יום ביומו: מאפליה. לשון הפך: מדוע אמרו עמי רדנו. נבדלנו ממך כמו הרודה פת מן התנור כך מדרש ר׳ תנחומא ומנחם פירש רדנו לשון ירידה ・ ועוד פנים אחרים: (לג) תיטבי.

מהר״י קרא

אותם מוסר לא לקחו: אכלה חרבכם נביאכם. הנבאים לשקר היא אכלה אתכם: (לא) המדבר. שהוא חרב ואין בו הנאה היה דברי לישראל והלא אין לך מצוה בתורה שלא כתוב כתן שכרה בצידה זה הוא פשוטו ותרגומו וגם המדרש נוטה אחר פשוטו אמר להם ירמיה לישראל למה אין אתם עוסקין בתורה אמרו לו ואם אנו עוסקין בתורה במה נתפרנס הוציא להם צנצנת המן שהיה מונח למשמרת אמר להם אבותיכם שעסקו בתורה ראו במה נתפרנסו שהיה יורד להם המן בכל יום: המדבר הייתי לישראל. הכהולכים במדבר הייתי לישראל כשהולכתים במדבר הלא כל צורכן סיפקתי להם: אם ארץ מאפלית. הלא לפניהם הייתי מאיר בעמוד אש: מדוע אמרו עמי רדנו. נפרדנו ממך כמו וירדהו על כפיו שפתרונו ויפרדהו מגוית האריה אל כפיו ובת״י ונסחיה לידית דרך ארץ כשאין האב מספיק לו לבן את צורכו שהבן פורש ממנו ואינו שומע לו אבל ראית מימך שהאב מספיק לו את צרכיו והבן פורש ממנו ומסרב לדבריו ואני כמה טובות עשיתי להם והם אמרו לא נבוא עוד אליך: (לג) מה תיטיבו דרכך. פת׳ מה תרבי דרכיך

רד״ק

כרעים בטרפו כן אתם השחתם אותם בנפשותם ובגופותם: (לא) הדור. הה״א ה״א הקריאה כה״א הקהל חקה אחת לכם: ראו דבר ה׳. הבינו מה שהוא אומר לכם כי יש ראיה בלב כמו ולבי ראה הרבה ראה דבריך טובים והדומים להם. ובדרש כי צנצנת המן הראה להם לפיכך אמר להם ראו ולא אמר שמעו: המדבר הייתי. אם הייתי להם כמו המדבר או ארץ מאפלית שלא ימצא בהם האדם צרכו אלא כל צרכם וספוקם מצאו בי בל זמן שהלכו אחרי אך כן מדוע אמרו עמי רדנו כלומר יש לנו ממשלת מלכים ושרים לא נבא עוד אליך. רדנו מענין רד עם אל שהוא ענין ממשלה. מאפליה מלה אחת בשוא הלמ״ד ונקידתה מחלוקת בין הספרים יש ספרים שנקוד׳ מאפליה המ״ם בפתח והאל״ף בשוא ויש ספרים שנקוד בהם מאפליה המ״ם בשוא והאל״ף בפתח והפ״א דגושה ופירוש ארץ אפל ולהגדיל האפל סמך אותו למלת י״ה וכן שלהבת י״ה כהררי אל עיר גדולה לאלהים ותהי לחרדת אלהים וי״ת מאפלית חרובה כי היא כמו ארץ אופל שלא ימצא בה דבר והרגם רדנו אטלטלנא וכן תרגם עניים מרודים מטלטלין: (לב) התשכח בתולה עדיה. בתולה כלה. וכפל הענין במלות שונות כי אין כלה בעדי׳ וקשוריה כ״א בתולה וכן אין בתולה בעדי׳ ובקשורי׳ כ״א כלה וישראל נמשלו לכלה ביום מעמד הר סיני ואיך שכחו אותי היום והלכו אחרי אלהים אחרים זה כמה ימים ושנים ובאמרו אין מספר הוא להפלגה: (לג) מה היטבי. התקני׳ דרכך לבקש אהבה כלומר אהבת האומות כמו שאמר מה לך לדרך מצרים

מנחת שי

(לא) מאפליה. במקצת ספרים כ״י מדוייקים המ״ם בפתח והאל״ף נחה בלי ניקוד ומקצתן האל״ף בשוא וכולן המ״ם בלא מאריך והפ״א בלירי ודגש קל והיא מלה אחת בספל מַאְפֵּלְיָה כמ״ש רד״ק בשרש אפל ואת שלהב ובעל לוית חן בפ׳ י״א : מהטעם השמיני ובחרי טעמי א״מ המסורת והה״א רפויה וכן נמסר במ״ג סוף פרשת בשלח וגם רד״ק כתב בפירוש ובשרשים שהמ״ם בפתח והאל״ף בשוא. עוד כתב שיש ספרים שנקוד בהם מַאֲפֵלְיָה המ״ם בשוא והאל״ף בפתח והפ״א בדגש חזק עכ״ל. עוד מצאתי במקצת ספרים האל״ף בחטף פתח ובדפוס אחר שתי מלות ואלו ואין נוגע להם: (לג) למדתי. למדת קרי:

מצודת דוד

הרבכם הרגה את נביאיכם כי הרגו את ישעיה ואת זכרי׳: כאריה משחית. כארי׳ המשחי׳ בני אדם: (לא) הדור אתם. אתם בני הדור ראו בהבנת הלב את מלות ה׳ אשר יש תשלום גמול עליהם: המדבר. וכי עד הנה הייתי לישראל כמדב׳ ואר׳ מאפלי׳ אשר לא ימלא במה די צורך האדם כ״ל וכי לא היה ספוק בידי לשלם גמול טוב על המלות בעשו: רדנו. ככר נבדלנו ממך ולא נבוא עוד אליך: (לב) התשכח. וכי הדרך הוא בתבכח הבתול׳ להשים עדיה עליה להתקשט בו וכי תשכח הכלה את קשוריה הם חוטי המשי שקושר׳ בהם להתקשט וכאו׳ הלא אין דרך האדם לשכוח דבר הנלרך ביות׳: ועמי. הבל עמי שכחו אותי ימים הרבה ואין מספ׳ להם עם שזהו עיק׳ הייסם על האדמה: (לג) מה היטבי דרכך. מה התקני מנהגך בעבוד׳ הבעל לעשו׳ בדמיון גמו׳ אל מעש׳ הטכו״ם

מצודת ציון

לחכם: (לא) ראו. יאמר גם על הבנת הלב וכן ולבי ראה הרבה הכמה (קהלת א׳): מאפליה. מל׳ אופל וחושך וכשבא להגדיל הדבר סומכו למלת יה וכן שלהבת יה (ש״ה ח׳) והוא כמו מדב׳ וכפל הדבר כמ״ש: רדנו. ענין הבדלה ממקום הדבוק כמו רדה הדבש (שופטים י״ד): (לב) עדיה. מל׳ עדיו וחכשיט: (לג) תיטבי. ענין

jewelry, a bride her ribbons?—The two are synonymous since a bride bedecked with jewelry is invariably a virgin, and a virgin bedecked with jewelry is a bride.—[*Redak*]

Yet My nation have forgotten

31. O generation, you see the word of the Lord. Was I a desert to Israel or a land of thick darkness? Why have My people said, "We have been separated; we will no longer come to You"?
32. Will a virgin forget her jewelry, a bride her ribbons? Yet My people have forgotten Me for countless days. 33. How you adorn

learn to speak falsehoods, and even when the prophets reprove them, they do not accept correction. Therefore, I delivered them into the hands of the enemy, who smote them.—[*Redak, Ibn Nachmiash*]

Our Sages (*Shabbath* 32b) explain that the falsehood refers to that of the parents, not that of the children. If the fathers are guilty of false vows, vows that they did not keep, the children die.—[*Redak*]

*31. **See the word of the Lord**—*He took out to them the jar of manna. He said to them, "See here how helpful the word of the Lord is."*—[*Rashi* from *Mechilta, Beshallach* 5:33] The complete *Mechilta* reads: "And place there an omer-full of manna and place it there before the Lord to be kept for your generations" (Exodus 16:33) . . . Rabbi Eliezer says: For the days of the Messiah and for the days of Jeremiah the prophet, for when Jeremiah said to Israel, "Why do you not engage in Torah study?" they said to him, "How will we earn a livelihood?" He produced for them the jar of manna and said to them, "O generation, you see the word of the Lord. Your forefathers, who engaged in Torah study—see how they were maintained. You too—if you engage in Torah, the Holy One, blessed be He, will maintain you from this."—[*Kara*]

Redak cites this as a *derash*, maintaining that the simple meaning is: *Understand the word of the Lord.* We find the expression of seeing in the sense of understanding in Ecc. 1:16, "And my heart saw much wisdom and knowledge."

Targum Jonathan renders: Hearken to the word of the Lord.

was I a desert to Israel—Heb. הֲמִדְבָּר. *This is the interrogative form. Therefore, the 'mem' is punctuated 'weak'*—i.e. without a *dagesh—and the 'hey' with a hataph pattah. Did it seem to your forefathers that it was a desert when they traversed it? For I brought down for them this bread, the necessity of each day in its day.*—[*Rashi*]

thick darkness—Heb. מַאְפֵּלְיָה, *an expression of darkness.*—[*Rashi*]

The addition of יָ־ה, the name of God, serves to intensify the sense of the word, making it 'thick darkness.' Did I take you through a land of thick darkness where you could not obtain your necessities?—[*Redak*] Did I not illuminate the way with the pillar of fire?—[*Kara*]

we will no longer come to You—*Jon.* paraphrases: We will no longer return to Your worship.

32. **Will a virgin forget her**

* For Rashi's commentary turn to page 214.

דרכך לבקש אהבה לכן גם את־
הרעות למדתי את־דרכיך: יד גם
בכנפיך נמצאו דם נפשות אביונים
נקיים לא־במחתרת מצאתים כי על־
כל־אלה: לה ותאמרי כי נקיתי אך
שב אפו ממני הנני נשפט אותך על־
אמרך

תרגום

באורחתיך למעבד רחמי לאתחברא בעממיא בכן אף ית בישן אליפת מן אורחתיך: יד אף בסתרא אשתכחת דאשדת דם זכאי דם נפשת דמסכנין זכאין לא כמא דמשכחין במחתרתא אלהין על כל אלין עבדת: לה ואמרת ארי זכיתי ברם תב רוגזיה מני הא

ת"א גם בכנפיך. שבת סט: למדת קרי

סהר"י קרא

כמו כי ייטיב אבי את הרעה עליך דיהונתן שפתרונו כי ירבה וכן הטיבו מצבות פי' הרבו מצבות: לכן גם את הרעות. שעושין האומות: לבדת את דרכיך. כשאת הולכת אליהם לבקש אהבה מהן: (לד) גם בכנפיך. לשון קרן זוית: לא במחתרת מצאתים. פת' מצאת אותם כמו את זמתך ואת תזנותיך את נשאתים שפתרונו את נשאת אותם לא נמצאו במחתרת שתוכלו לומר חייבין הן אם במחתרת ימצא הגנב: כי על כל אלה. על כל תועבות הנזכרות למעלה שעשית הוספת לעשות גם את זאת: (לה) ותאמרי כי נקיתי אך שב אפו ממני. כלומר אחרי עשותך את כל אלה את אומרת נקיתי מעון וראוי אני להשיב אפו ממני כלומר אין הדבר תלוי בי שהוא כועס עלי שהרי נקיה אני מחטא אך דין הוא שישוב אפו ממני וזו קשה שבכולן שאחרי שהרבית לחטוא את אומרת נקיתי ועל זאת אני שופט אותך על אמרך לא חטאתי: נשפט. שופט כמו כי באש ה'

רש"י

תקשטי עצמך לקראת נואפיך כמו (מלכים ב' ט') ותיטב ראשה דאיזבל בפרשת יהוא: גם את הרעות למדה. חזרת על כל רוע דרך ללמוד את המקולקלת שבכולם. גם ל' אפילו: לכן. לשון שבועת אמת אך את הדרך הרעה שבכל הדרכים למדת לעצמך: למדת. הנהגת: (לד) לא במחתרת מצאתים. לא מצאת אותם במחתרת כשהרגת אותם: מצאתים. כה יאמר לנקבה לשון פעלת והרבה זה בספר (יחזקאל ט"ז) את נשאתים: כי על כל אלה. שהיו מוכיחים אותך בדברים האלה: (לה) ותאמרי. בלבך: כי נקיתי. אשר זכאה אני נפשי: נשפט אותך. אבא עמך במשפט:

רד"ק

יפה לך לדרך אשור ונמצא לשון הטבה ברעת כי רוצה לומר תקון הדבר או חוזקו כמו התיטב חרה לך כי יטיב את אבי הרעה עליך על הרע כפים להטיב: גם את הרעות. כלומר האומות הרעות למדת את דרכיך כלומר שהרעות מהם והם למדו מרעותיך וכתיב לבדתי והוא כאמר האל רוצה לומר למדתי אותך בדרכיך שהן רעות ויבא לך בעבורן רע כאילו למדתי אותן מדרכיך שיוסרו עליך והקרי למדת כמו שפירשנו: (לד) גם בכנפיך. בכנפי בגדך על דרך ויז נצחם על בגדי וכל מלבושי אגאלתי ויונתן תרגם אף בסתרא אשתכחת דאשדיתא דם זכאי תרגם בכנפיך סתרא כמו ולא יגלה כנף אביו שמפרשין אותו סתר אביו והיא אשתו וכת שאמר נמצאו ואמר דם כאילו אמר דמים שהרי אמר נפשות: לא במחתרת. שנאמר אם במחתרת ימצא הגנב והכה ומת אין לו דמים ואת לא מצאת אותם במחתרת למה הרגת אותם והם נקיים: מצאתים. מצאת אותם כי כן תחבר הנקבה הנמצאת עם הכנוי בחירק התי"ו: כי על כל אלה. טעמו דבק עם הפסוק הבא אחריו: (לה) ותאמרי. אמר כי על כל אלה אני מוכיחך על שאת הולכת אחרי העמים ועובדת אלהיהן ושופכת גם כן דם נקי ואת אומרת כי נקית ממעשים רעים ושב אף האל ממני ולא ירע לי עוד ובזה עונך כפול כמה שאמר החכם כפירת העון

מצודת ציון

תיקון כמו ותיטב את ראשה (מ"ב ט'): דרכך. מנהגך: (לד) בכנפיך. שולי הבגד: במחתרת. ר"ל במקום נסתר והוא מל' מחיר' וחפירה כמו אם במחתרת ימצא הגנב (שמות כ"ב): (לה) נשפט. ענין ויכוח וכן כי באש ה' נשפט (ישעיה ס"ו):

מצודת דוד

לבקש מהם אהבה בעשותך כמעשיהם: לכן. באמת גם את העכו"ם הרעו' למדת אתה מנהגיך ר"ל אתה הרעו' לעשו' יות' מכולן ואף להרעות שבהן למד' להרשיע יות' כמוך: (לד) גם בכנפיך. גם בכנפי בגדיך נמצאו דמי נפשו' אביונים נקיים מעון מיתה ועל חנם הרגתם: לא במחתרת מצאתים. דמי הנפשות האלה לא מצאתים במחתר' ובמקום נסתר כ"א בגלוי על כל אלה הכנפים המוכרים למעל' ר"ל לא עשית הדבר בהסת' כי אם בפרסום רב מבלי בושה: (לה) ותאמרי. ר"ל אם אמנם כל אלה עשית בפרסום איך תאמרי לא כן הוא כי נקי אני מעביר' ואין האמת עם הנביאים שאומרים שחר' כי אף ה' אך שב אפו ממני הואיל ואני מנוקה מעון: הנני נשפט אותך. לכן הנני מתווכח עמך גם על מה שתכחש לומר לא חטאתי ר"ל מלבד גמול החטא אוסיף עוד עונש על מה שתכחש חטאיך וטעותך כזה תחשב לויכוח כי כזה יודיע שפשעו בדבר הזה:

all these. I.e. in addition to the sins of idolatry, you are guilty of murder as well.—[*Kara*]

Others render: For concerning all these. I.e., concerning all these crimes I castigate you.—[*Abarbanel*]

Redak connects this to the following verse: For concerning all these, I reprove you, and you said, "But I am innocent . . ."

*35. **And you said**—I.e. you said *in your heart*.—[*Rashi*]

I reproved you for all these sins, for following the heathens, worshipping their idols, and shedding innocent blood, but you say, "No, but I am innocent of evil deeds, and His wrath has gone away from me.—[*Redak*]

But I am innocent—*That I have*

* For Rashi's commentary turn to page 215.

your way to seek love! Verily, even to the most evil you accustomed your ways. 34. Also in your skirts is found the blood of the souls of the innocent poor; you did not find them breaking in, but for all these. 35. And you said, "But I am innocent, surely His wrath has gone away from me." Behold, I contend with you concerning

Me—Israel was compared to a bride when they stood at Mount Sinai to receive the Torah. Now, how is it that they have forgotten Me for countless days? The term countless is an exaggeration.—[*Redak*]

*33. **even to the most evil you accustomed**—*You searched throughout all the evil ways to learn the most corrupt of them all.* גַּם *is an expression of 'even.'*—[*Rashi*]

verily—Heb. לָכֵן, *an expression of a true oath. Verily, to the most evil way of all the ways you accustomed yourself.*—[*Rashi*]

you accustomed—Heb. לִמַּדְתְּ, lit. you taught.—[*Rashi*]

Verily, even the worst you have taught your ways—I.e., even the worst of the heathens you have taught your ways. You have dealt more corruptly than they, and you have taught them your ways. The *kethib* is: I taught your ways. I.e., I taught you of your ways that they are evil and that you would be punished for following them.—[*Redak*]

34. **Also in your skirts**—I.e. in the skirts of your garments. Comp. Isaiah 63:3: "And their lifeblood sprinkled on My garments, and all My clothing I soiled." *Jonathan* renders: Also in secret you were found that you shed innocent blood. He compares כְּנָפַיִךְ to: "And he shall not uncover his father's secret (כְּנַף)" (Deut. 23:1).—[*Redak*]

you did not find them breaking in—*You did not find them breaking in when you slew them.*—[*Rashi*]

you did not find them—Heb. מְצָאתִים. *So does Scripture say for a feminine second person singular, and there are many such examples in the Book of Ezekiel* (16:58) "*You bore them*" (נְשָׂאתִים).—[*Rashi*] *Rashi* explains that, despite the 'yod', the verb is in the second person rather than the first.

The Torah ordains: "If while breaking in, the thief be found and he be smitten and die, he has no blood guilt" (Exodus 22:1). These dead were not found as thieves breaking into the house. Why then did you slay them when they were innocent?—[*Redak*]

Others explain: You did not slay them in secret, while they were breaking into a house, but in the open, where every one could see. This corresponds with the blood mentioned above that it was found on the skirts, meaning that their crimes were visible.—[*Mezudath David, Abarbanel*] *Ibn Nachmiash* questions how this coincides with *Jonathan*'s translation of the beginning of the verse, where he states that the killings were in secret.

but for all these—I.e. *because they were reproving you for all these things.*—[*Rashi*]

Others render: for in addition to

* For Rashi's commentary turn to page 215.

אָמַרְתְּ לֹא חָטָאתִי׃ לו מַה־תֵּזְלִי מְאֹד
לְשַׁנּוֹת אֶת־דַּרְכֵּךְ גַּם מִמִּצְרַיִם תֵּבֹשִׁי
כַּאֲשֶׁר בֹּשְׁתְּ מֵאַשּׁוּר׃ לז גַּם מֵאֵת זֶה
תֵּצְאִי וְיָדַיִךְ עַל־רֹאשֵׁךְ כִּי־מָאַס
יְהוָה בְּמִבְטַחַיִךְ וְלֹא תַצְלִיחִי לָהֶם׃
ג א לֵאמֹר הֵן יְשַׁלַּח אִישׁ אֶת־אִשְׁתּוֹ
וְהָלְכָה מֵאִתּוֹ וְהָיְתָה לְאִישׁ־אַחֵר

ת״א לאמר. יומא ח סו סנהדרין ז ט: — הישוב

תרגום

אֲנָא עֲבִיד עִמִּיךְ פּוּרְעָנוּת דִּין עַל דַּאֲמַרְתְּ לָא חֲטֵיתִי: לו מָה אַתְּ מִסְתַּכְּלָא לַחֲדָא לְקַלְקָלָא יַת אוֹרְחָתַיִךְ אַף מִמִּצְרַיִם תִּבְהֲתִין כְּמָא דִבְהֵתְתְּ מֵאַתּוּרָאֵה: לז אַף מִלְוַת דֵּין תִּפְּקִין וּבְהָתַת חוֹבִיךְ עַל רֵישִׁיךְ אֲרֵי רְחִיק יְיָ רוּחְצָנַיִךְ וְלָא וְלָא תַצְלְחִין לְהוֹן: א לְמֵימַר הָא יִפְטַר גְּבַר יַת אִתְּתֵיהּ וּתְהַךְ מִלְוָתֵיהּ וּתְהֵי לִגְבַר

רש״י

(לו) תזלי. ל׳ זלזול: לשנות את דרכך. לעזוב אותי ולסמוך על מצרים לעזרה בימי יהויקים ולדקיהו (לקמן ל״ז): לשנות. ל׳ שינוי: כאשר בושת מאשור. שסמך אחז עליו ויצר לו ולא חזקו כמה שנאמר (בדברי הימים כ״ח):

ג (א) לאמר הן ישלח וגו׳. יש לי לומר שאין עוד את

מהר״י קרא

נשפט והוא מגזרת נשבע: (לו) מה תזלי מאד. מה את מזילת ומבזה עצמך לשנות דרכייך מדרכי אבותיך הטובים: גם ממצרים. שאת יורדת לשם לעזרה: תבושי כאשר בשת מאשור. כששלח אחז למלך אשור עלה והושיעני מכף מלך ארם וכתיב בדברי הימים ויצר לו ולא חזקו כי חילק אחז את בית ה׳: (לז) גם מאת זה תצאי וידיך על ראשך. פת׳ סוף הבטחון הזה לתקלה ולקלון כאדם שאוחז בשערות ראשו ותולשן מרוב צער: תצאי. לשון סוף ואחרית הוא ולשון בני אדם הוא כשאדם רוצה לומר לחבירו סוף דבר זה יבא לחרפה אומר מדבר זה תצא לבסוף לחרפה: כי מאס ה׳ במבטחיך. הם מלכי מצרים ומלך אשור שאתם בוטחים בהן:

ג (א) לאמר. כה ציוני ה׳ לאמר: הן ישלח איש. הישוב אליה. שאם ישוב אליה חנוף תחנף הארץ דכתיב לא יוכל בעלה הראשון

רד״ק

שתי עונות ובזה אני נשפט איתך ומעני שך בזה על אמרך לא חטאתי: (לו) מה תזלי. שרשו אזל והוא ענין הלוך כתרגומו אמר מה תלכי הנה והנה לבקש עזר ותשנה את דרכך פעם לאשור פעם למצרים ומה שאמר מאד כמו שאמר מה תיטיבו דרכך כמו שפירשנו: כאשר בושת מאשור. ששלח לו אחז שחד ואומר בדברי הימים ויצר לו ולא חזקו וכן בימי חזקיהו תפש כל ערי יהודה הבצורות ואמר גם כן תבושי ממצרים שנתן יהואחז שחד לפרעה נכה והעריך את הארץ לתת השחד ויעזור לו במלך בבל ולא הועיל כי יצאו גדודי כשדים ולא הוסיף עוד מלך מצרים לצאת כי לקח מלך בבל מנחל מצרים והנה בושה יהודה מעזרת וכשל עוזר ונפל עזור לפיכך אמר אחר זה הפסוק: (לז) גם מאת זה תצאי. רוצה לומר מן המקום הזה שלא יועיל לך מבטחיך שהיית בוטחת בהם: ולא תצליחי להם. רוצה לומר בעבורם וכה שאמר וידיך על ראשך כי כן דרך האשה הצועקת על אידה הולכת וידיה על ראשה כמו שאמר בתמר ותשם ידה על ראשה ותלך הלוך וזעקה וי״ת ובהתת חוביך על רישיך: (א) לאמר. ענינו עם כי מאס ה׳ הוא ריאס בך בעבור מבטחיך ואומר לך הן ישלח איש את אשתו: חנוף תחנף הארץ ההיא. שיעשה בה זה המעשה כמו שאמרה תורה כי תועבה היא לפני ה׳ ולא תחטיא את הארץ

מצודת דוד

(לו) מה תזלו מאד. למה תרבי ללכת לבקש עזר מן העכו״ם: לשנות את דרכך. פעם לאשור פעם למצרים: גם ממצרים תבושי. על אשר לא תמלא עזר על ידו: כאשר בושת מאשור. כי אחז מלך יהודה שלח מלאכים למלך אשור לעזור לו והיצר לו עוד כמ״ש ויבוא וכו׳ מלך אש׳ ויצר לו ולא חזקהו (דה״ב כ״ח): (לז) גם מאת זה. כמו שיצאת בדאגה ויללה מאת מלך אשור כן תצאי מִמלך מצרים בדאגה וידיך יהיו מונחים על ראשך כדרך המקונן: כי מאס ה׳ במבטחיך. דבר בגאוי ונמאס בעיני ה׳ מה שאתה בוטח בעזרת העכו״ם ולכן לא תהיה לך הצלחה להם למצוא חן בעיניהם להיות לך לעזר מול הקמים עליך:

ג (א) לאמר. ר״ל מהראוי לאמר לישראל את זאת הנה אם יגרש איש את אשתו והלכה מאתו והיתה לאיש אחר ואף אם לא בא עליה הישוב. וכי יוכל בעלה הראשון לשוב עוד אליה לקחתה אחר שמת השני או גרשה הלא בעבור עון כזה התחייב הארץ הסיס

מצודת ציון

(לו) תזלי. ענין הלוך כמו אזלו מים מני ים (איוב י״ד): מאד. הוא כמו הרבה: לשנות. מל׳ השתנות:

ג (א) ישלח. ענין סלוק וגרושין וכמו׳ מכיתו (דברים כ״ד):

the one to be helped fell. This verse refers to that incident.—[*Redak*] [It was actually Jehoiakim who sent the tribute to Pharaoh-neco, not Jehoahaz, who was deposed by Pharaoh-neco. The tribute was levied on the land when he deposed Jehoahaz, but it was collected after Jehoiakim was placed on the throne.]

37. **Also from this one**—I.e., just as you left the king of Assyria with worry and wailing, so shall you leave the king of Egypt with worry and wailing and with your hands on your head as people do when lamenting over their sorrow.—[*Abarbanel, Mezudath David*]

1. **to say**—*I have to say that you*

because you say, "I have not sinned." 36. How you degrade
yourself exceedingly to change your way! You shall also be
ashamed through Egypt as you were ashamed through Assyria.
37. Also from this one shall you go out with your hands on
your head, for the Lord has despised those whom you trust,
and you shall not prosper through them.

3

1. [I have] to say: If a man sends away his wife, and she goes
away from him, and marries another man,

purified my soul.—[*Rashi*] This appears to be *Rashi*'s intention, although it is not clear.

because you say, "I have not sinned."—You say, "I am innocent; surely His wrath has gone away from me, and He will no longer bring misfortune upon me." For this, your sin is twofold, as the sage says: Denial of sin constitutes two sins. I, therefore, will bring you to judgment and punish you for saying, "I have not sinned."—[*Redak*]

36. **degrade yourself**—Heb. תֵּזְלִי, *an expression of degradation.*—[*Rashi*]

Others derive it from the Aramaic root, אזל, *to go.* How you go here and there to seek aid!—[*Redak*]

to change your way—*To leave Me and to rely on Egypt for aid in the days of Jehoiakim and Zedekiah* (infra 37).—[*Rashi*]

to change—Heb. לְשַׁנּוֹת, *an expression of change.*—[*Rashi*] Others explain: to change your way by first going to Assyria and later going to Egypt.—[*Redak, Mezudath David*] Since the kings of Judah were sending emissaries to Egypt for aid against Babylon, the prophet castigates them for changing their way, going first to Assyria and then to Egypt.—[*Abarbanel*]

as you were ashamed through Assyria—*Upon whom Ahaz relied and 'he oppressed him and did not strengthen him'* (II Chron. 28:20).—[*Rashi*]

Although Ahaz sent a bribe to Tiglath-Pileser, he did not aid him but, on the contrary, he oppressed him. Also, during Hezekiah's reign, he seized all the fortified cities of Judea. The prophet admonishes Judea, telling them that they will be ashamed through Egypt in the same manner. Indeed, Jehoahaz gave a bribe to Pharaoh-neco and he levied a tax on the population to pay the bribe so that Pharaoh-neco would save him from the king of Babylon, but it did not avail him, for troops of Chaldeans emerged, and the king of Egypt did not continue to go out to war, for the king of Babylon took from the river of Egypt to the Euphrates river (II Kings 24:7). Thus, Judah was ashamed because of its helper, and the helper stumbled and

הֲיָשׁוּב אֵלֶיהָ עוֹד הֲלוֹא חָנוֹף תֶּחֱנַף
הָאָרֶץ הַהִיא וְאַתְּ זָנִית רֵעִים רַבִּים
וְשׁוֹב אֵלַי נְאֻם־יְהוָֹה: ב שְׂאִי־עֵינַיִךְ
עַל־שְׁפָיִם וּרְאִי אֵיפֹה לֹא שֻׁגַּלְתְּ עַל־
דְּרָכִים יָשַׁבְתְּ לָהֶם כַּעֲרָבִי בַּמִּדְבָּר
וַתַּחֲנִיפִי אֶרֶץ בִּזְנוּתַיִךְ וּבְרָעָתֵךְ:
ג וַיִּמָּנְעוּ רְבִבִים וּמַלְקוֹשׁ לוֹא הָיָה

שכבת קרי ומצח

ת"א ויִמנעו וגו'. תענית כ"ו יבמות ח' מ:

תרגום

אוֹהֲדָן הַאֶפְשַׁר דִיתוּב לְוָתַהּ עוֹד הֲלָא מֵחָב תְּחוּב אַרְעָא הַהִיא וְאַתְּ טְעֵיתָא וְאִתְחַבַּרְתְּ לְעַמְמִין סַגִּיאִין וְתוּבִי מִכְּעַן לְפוּלְחָנִי אֲמַר יְיָ: ב זְקוֹפִי עֵינַיִךְ עַל נַגְדִין וַחֲזָא הֵיכָא לָא אִתְחַבַּרְתְּ לִיךְ לְמִפְלַח לְטַעֲוָתָא עַל אוֹרְחַת בֵּית מִישְׁרֵיהוֹן אוֹרְכַת לְהוֹן כְּעַרְבָאֵי דְשָׁרַן בְּשְׁכוּנִין בְּמַדְבְּרָא וְחַיֵּבְתְּ אַרְעָא בְּטַעֲוָתִיךְ וּבְבִישָׁתִיךְ: ג וְאִתְמְנַעוּ

רש"י

רחויה לי כי כן דרך המגלה את אשתו והלכה לה וגו': ואת זנית רעים רבים. עם אוהבים רבים ואעפ"כ שובו אלי: ושוב אלי. כמו עשות ולשוב אלי אני חושק כך: (ב) שפים. יגלי מים: לא שוגלה. לשון פלגש: ישבת להם. להיות נכונה לקראתם: כערבי. יושב אוהלים שהוא תמיד מצוי בחוץ במדברות ועל שם כך הוא קרוי ערבי ששוכן בערבה: (ג) ומלקוש. המטר היורד בניסן על המלילות ועל הקשין ומלקוש (טרדיי"א בלע"ז):

מהר"י קרא

וגו': ושוב אלי. שובי אלי ותמצאי כופר: (ב) על דרכים ישבת. לכנאפים: כערבי. השוכן באהלים לפי שהם

מנחת שי

ג (ב) שגלת. שכבת קרי:

רד"ק

כן אמר הנה חנוף תחנף הארץ כלומר תחטא: ואת זנית רעים רבים ושוב אלי. במקומות רבים המשיל הכתוב כנסת ישראל לאשה והקב"ה בעלה כלומר שלקחם לו לעם נחלת והיא לו כאשה והוא לה כבעל וכמו האשה שזונה תחת בעלה שהיא חייבת כן ישראל שהלכו אחרי עמים רבים ודבקו בטעותם קרא הכתוב זה זנות וזה הענין נמצא בנביאים שדברו בזה המשל וקראו ענין זה ענין זנות ושמשו בו בכל לשון של זנות וזה הרבה בספר יחזקאל אמר ואחר שהלכת לבעלים איך תשובי אלי עוד ואפי' תשובי בתשובה לא תוכלי לשוב אלי עד שתגלי מארצך ותשבי שם ימים רבים עד תשכחי עונך הראשון ולא יעלה על לבך עוד עבודת אלילים ואחר כן תשוב אלי ואשוב אליך: (ב) שאי. שפים. מקומות גבוהים כמו ההרים הרמים והגבעות הנשאות כי כן היה דרך עובדי עכו"ם בזמן ההוא כמו שכתוב: שגלת. כתיב שכבת קרי כמו ישגלנה ישכבנה לשון נקיה וכבר פירשנו כי לשון הזנות והשכיבה הוא ענין העכו"ם: על דרכים ישבת להם. פי' לעובדי עכו"ם כלומר ישבת מיחלת עוברי דרכים שהם מכסת מקומות רוצה לומר עם ועם עובד אלהיו ואת התאוית לכלם לעבדם כמ"ש כי מספר עריך היו אלהיך יהודה: כערבי במדבר. כי כן דרך הערביים השכנים במדבר יושבי' להם על הדרכים מיחלי השיירות העוברות לככור להם ולקנות מהם וי"ת שפים נגרין כמו נגרי ברייתא בתלמוד ותרגום לא שכבת לא אתחברת ליך למפלח וגו' כבעמוד: בזנותיך. בסיטן רבוי אחד לבד והרומים לו כתבנו בספר מכלל בחלק הדקדוק כבנו: (ג) וימנעו רביבים. הוא המטר והוא היורד במרחשון והוא הנקרא יורה ומורה וכן בדברי רז"ל יורה במרחשון ומלקוש בניסן כי אלה שני הזמנים הם זמני המטר לצורך התבואה וברוב הזמנים רוב המטר יורד במרחשון לפיכך נקרא ירח בול מענין מבול ונקרא המטר

מצודת ציון

חנוף תחנף. ענין חיוב ואשמה כמו ולא תחניפו את הארץ (במדבר ל"ה): (ב) שפים. כן נקראו המקומות הגבוהים כמו אפתח על שפים נהרות (ישעיה מ"א): איפה. איה פה וכן איפה הם רועים (בראשית ל"ז): שגלת. ענין משכב המשגל וכן ואיש אחר ישגלנה (דברים כ"ח): להם. לגרל': כערבי. שם אומה: (ג) רביבים. הוא המטר החזק וכן וכרביבים עלי עשב (שם ל"ב): ומלקוש. כן נקרא המטר המאוחר היורד על הקשין ועל המלילות

מצודת דוד

הנמשה בה כזאת ותקבל גמולה מבעלה: ואת. הכל אתה ישראל עם כי בעודך תחתי זנית באיסור עם אוהבים רבים ר"ל עם כי עבדת עכו"ם הליקות עכ"ז ש"ב הני ואקבלך בתשובה: (ב) שאי עיניך. הרימי עיניך להביט אל ההרים הגבוהים וראי איה המקום אשר לא נשכבת שמה עם נואפים ר"ל אשר לא עבדת שמה עכו"ם: על דרכים וגו'. לפי בהמשילה לזונה אמר ל' הנופל בזונה היושבת על הדרכים להיו' מזומנ' אל הנואפים ור"ל היית מצליח עצמך לכל מין עכו"ם: כערבי במדבר. כערבי הזה הרגיל לשבת במדבר במקומו' במקום שאין אנשים כן הסתרת עצמך על הדרכים להסתחר שם עם הנואפים ור"ל מאד היית נרדף אחרי עבודת הפסילים: ותחניפי ארץ וגו'. עם זנותך לעכו"ם ועם יפל רשעך חייבת את הארץ להיות הרבה ושוממה: (ג) וימנעו. הנה בעונך נמנעו הרביבים ולא

idolaters who came from various places, each one with his particular deity, and you longed for all of them, as the prophet states above (2:28): 'For, as many as your cities were your gods, O Judea.'—[*Redak*]

like an Arab—*A tent dweller, who is always found outside in the deserts, and because of this, he is called* עֲרָבִי, *since he dwells in the* עֲרָבָה, *the plain.—*[*Rashi*]

It is customary for the Arabs who live in the desert to sit by the roads awaiting the caravans, to buy from them and to sell to them.—[*Redak*]

3. **the rains**—Heb. רְבִבִים. This refers to the rain that falls in the month of Marcheshvan, usually

may he return to her again? Will not the land become defiled? But you have played the harlot [with] many lovers, yet return to Me, says the Lord. 2. Lift up your eyes upon the rivulets and see, where have you not been lain with? By the roads you sat for them like an Arab in the desert, and you defiled the land with your harlotries and with your evil. 3. And the rains were withheld, and there has been no latter rain,

are no longer fit for me, for so is the way of one who sends away his wife and she goes away etc.[*Rashi*]

Mezudath David explains the verse similarly: It is proper to say to Israel etc.

Kara paraphrases: So did the Lord command me to say: If a man . . .

Redak connects it to the preceding verse: For the Lord has despised those whom you trust . . . saying: If . . .

Will not that land become defiled?—The prophet alludes here to the Pentateuch prohibition of remarrying one's divorced wife after she has been married to another man. In this case, the Torah (Deut. 24:4) states: 'Her first husband who sent her away shall not be able to take her again to be his wife after she became defiled for that is an abomination before the Lord, and you shall not cause the land to sin." This is represented by the prophet's words, 'Will not the land become defiled?'

But you have played the harlot [with] many lovers—*With many lovers. Rashi* supplements the word 'with,' missing in the text. He also explains that רֵעִים is synonymous with אוֹהֲבִים, *lovers. Nevertheless, return to Me.*—[*Rashi*]

yet return to me—Heb. וְשׁוֹב, lit. *and to return to me, like* עֲשׂוֹת, *to do, and to return to Me, I long for you.*—[*Rashi*] This is not the imperative, but the infinitive. Rabbi Joseph Kara explains it as the imperative although the form is very irregular. It should be וְשׁוּבִי. *Jonathan*, however, appears to explain it in this manner. The complete Targum will be presented below.

2. **rivulets**—Heb. שְׁפָיִם, *rivulets of water.*—[*Rashi*] This appears to be *Jonathan*'s translation as well. See *Lexicon Chaldaicum* נְגַד.

Others render this as 'high hills.'—[*Redak, Mezudoth, Ibn Nachmiash*] These were the usual locations of the pagan shrines in those days.—[*Redak*]

and see—from this vantage point.—[*Ibn Nachmiash*]

where were you not lain with—See the entire surrounding area and tell Me where you did not play the harlot. I.e., tell Me where you did not worship idols.—[*Redak*]

you were not lain with—This follows the *keri*, the traditional reading, שֻׁכַּבְתְּ. The *kethib*, the written text, is שֻׁגַּלְתְּ, *an expression of a* פִּילֶגֶשׁ, *a concubine.*—[*Rashi, Redak*]

you sat for them—*to be prepared to greet them.*—[*Rashi*] I.e. to greet the idolaters. You sat, awaiting the

וּמֵ֨צַח אִשָּׁ֤ה זוֹנָה֙ הָ֣יָה לָ֔ךְ מֵאַ֖נְתְּ
הִכָּלֵֽם׃ ד הֲל֣וֹא מֵעַ֔תָּה קָרָ֥את לִ֖י אָבִ֑י
אַלּ֥וּף נְעֻרַ֖י אָֽתָּה׃ ה הֲיִנְטֹ֣ר לְעוֹלָ֔ם
אִם־יִשְׁמֹ֖ר לָנֶ֑צַח הִנֵּ֧ה דִבַּ֛רְתְּ וַֽתַּעֲשִׂ֥י
הָרָע֖וֹת וַתּוּכָֽל׃ ו וַיֹּ֨אמֶר יְהוָ֜ה אֵלַ֗י

ת"א ומלא אנס. ברכין ג טו: אלוף נעורי. חגיגה ג טו: יתיר י' יתיר י'

דְסִיסְיָא וּמַלְקוֹשָׁא לָא
הֲוָה וְחוּצְפָּא כְאִתְּתָא
נָפְקַת בָּרָא הֲוָה לִיךְ
מְסָרְבַת לְאִתְכְּנָעָא׃
ד הֲלָא מִכְּעַן הַצְלָן
קֳדָמַי רִבּוֹנִי אַתְּ פָּרְקִי
דְמִן עַלְמָא׃ ה הַאֶפְשַׁר
דְתִתְנַטְרוּן לִיךְ חוֹבִיךְ
לְעָלַם אִם תִּתְקַף עֲלָךְ
מָחָא לְאַפְרֵישׁ הָא
מַלֵּילְתְּ וַעֲבַדְתְּ בִּישִׁין
וְאַסְגֵיתְ׃ ו וַאֲמַר יְיָ לִי בְּיוֹמֵי יֹאשִׁיָה מַלְכָּא הַחֲזֵיתָא מָה דַעֲבַדוּ דְמִתְחַסְנִין לְמֵיתַב לְפוּלְחָנִי דְבֵית יִשְׂרָאֵל

רש"י

(ד) הלוא מעתה. הלואי שבת מרעתך וקראת לי אבי אם תעשי כך היינטור לך אדוניך לעולם את אשר חטאת לו אם ישמור לנצח לא ישמור: (ה) הנה דברתי. בפיך לא נבוא עוד אליך ואותה הרעה תעשי ולא תתני לב לשוב: ותוכל. ונלאת למרוד: (ו) משובה. נלאת ומוכחת בימי יאשיה

מהר"י קרא

אנשי מקנה: (ד) הלא מעתה. מיכן ואילך קראת לי אבי ואלוף נעורי: (ה) הינטור. הקב"ה לעולם לפשעי אדם אבל את: דברת ותעשי הרעות ותוכל. ותצליחי בהן:

רד"ק

ההוא רביבים במקום שקראו במקום אחר יורה וענין הפסוק אומר כי נמנעו הגשמים מפני מעשיהם הרעים כמו שאמר בתורה וסרתם ועבדתם אלהים אחרים וגו' וחרה אף ה' בכם ועצר את השמים ולא יהיה מטר ועם כל זה שמנעתי חרביבים בעונך ומלקוש לא היה לא נכלמת ממעשיך והיה לך מצח כאשה זונה שאינה בושה בנאפופיה ומדיכה מצח ומעיזה פניה אף על פי שהנביאים מוכיחים אותך ואומרים לך בושי ממעשיך ראי העונש שמשיגך בעבורה עם כל זה מאנת הכלם וזהו שאמר מאנת כלומר שהיית ממאנת בתוכחת הנביאים ולא בושה מפניהם ורז"ל דרשו הפסוק ואמרו אין הגשמים נעצרים אלא בשביל עזי פנים שנאמר ויכנעו רביבים וגו' ות"י וחוצפא כאתתא נפקת ברא הוה לך ועז פנים יקרא חצוף בלשון רז"ל: (ד) הלא מעתה קראתי. כתיב ביו"ד כאילו הוא מדבר בעדו וקרי בלא יו"ד כמו לנמצא ופי' הכתוב אמר הלא מעתה כלומר היה לך מעתה לקרוא לי אבי כיון שקראתי לך ע"י נביאי בני היה לך לענות ולומר לי אבי אלוף נעורי אתה ולא עשית כן ופי' הקרי אמר הלא מעתה כיון שראית שעצרתי הגשמים היה לך לשוב אלי ולקרוא לי אבי אלוף נעורי אלופי וגדולי כימי הנעורים והוא זמן יציאת מצרים כי אז נכנסו ישראל תחת כנפי השכינה ונתחנכו במצותיו ובידיעת אלהותו כמו הנער הנכנס ללמוד ומחנכין אותו בידיעת תורה וחכמה ותרגם יונתן אלוף נעורי פרקי דמן עלמא: (ה) הינטור. אמר הנביא אם עשית זה הינטור האל לך לעולם עונך אם ישמור חטאתך לנצח לא יעשה זה אלא בשובך אליו ישוב אליך ויטיב לך ואת לא עשית כן אלא דברת ותעשי הרעות ותוכל. דברתי כתיב ביו"ד אמר הנביא הנה דברתי לך לשוב ולא עשית אלא הרעות לעשות ותעשי הרעות וקרי דברת בשוא התי"ו כנוי הנמצאת אמר הנביא הנה דברת לעשות רעות ועשית כמו שדברת: ותוכל. תרגם יונתן ואסגית כלומר הרבית לעשות רעות בכל יכלתך וזה הפירוש הוא נכון אמר עשית הרעות כמו שיכולת עשות או פירושו כאשר יכולת לעשות ויש וי"ו במקום כאשר כמו אם לא ישבעו וילינו ושפתי רננות יהלל פי ובאמרו ותעשי לשון נקבה ותוכל לשון זכר כן הוא מנהג המקרא במקומות רבים כשדובר כנגד כנסת ישראל ידבר בלשון נקבה כנגד הכנסה ולשון זכר כנגד העם והכל אחד. ואדוני אבי ז"ל פירש שני אלו הפסוקים כן הלא מעתה קראת לי אבי מעתה מקרוב כשחזר יאשיה המלך בתשובה ושבו אנשי יהודה עמו מוכרחים היו כמו שהוא מפורש שאמר בכל זאת לא שבה אלי בגודה אחותה יהודה בכל לבה כי אם בשקר הינטור לעולם כך היו אומרים הם והנביא אמר להם הנה דברת ועשית הרעות ותוכל: (ו) ויאמר. בימי יאשיהו המלך. למה אמר זה והלא ידוע כי בימי יאשיהו נתנבא אלא לפי שנתנבא אף בימי יהויקים ובימי

מנחת שי

(ד) קראתי. קראת קרי: (ה) הנה דברת. במקצת דפוסים ישנים כתוב דברתי בי' וקרי בלא י' וכן מצאתי במקצת ספרים כ"י וגם רד"ק כתב כן אמנם בספרים אחרים מדוייקים כת' בלא י' גם לא נמנה במסורת בריש ספר מלכים עם מלין דכתיבין יו"ד בסוף תיבותא ולא קריא והאיתי גם כן מסרה אחת כ"י ממלות אלו

מצודת דוד

היה המלקוש ואע"כ היה לך להיות בוש במעשיך: ומצח. אבל יש לך מצח מגולה כדרך אשה זונה שאינה מכסה מצחה בעבו' בושה מה לא כדרך הצנועות המכסות מצחן אם יקרה להן דבר בושה: מאנת הכלם. אתה מאנת להיות נכלם ובוש ממעשיך: (ד) הלא מעתה. הלא בעת מנעתי הגש' בעונך קראת לי בפה אבי ואמרת עלי אלוף וגו' ר"ל אתה האדון שלי מעת נעורי מיום שבחרת בי: (ה) הינטור. ואמרת בחשב' וכי המקום ישמור השנאה לעולם וכי ישמור האיבה לנצח והיא כפל ענין במ"ש: הנה דברת. הנה הדברים האלה דברת בפיך בלבד אבל במעשה עשית הרעות וכל מה שיכולת לעשות מן הרעות עשית ומוסב למעלה לומ' איך לא תכלמי אם אין לבך שלם עמי איך תדבר בתפלה כדברים האלה:

מצודת ציון

וכן יורה ומלקוש (שם י"א): ומצח. הוא הפדחת: מאנת. מל' מיאון: הכלם. מל' כלימה: (ד) אלוף. שר והאדון וכן אל תבטחו באלוף (מיכה ז'): (ה) הינטור. ענין שמירה כמו נוטרה את הכרמים (ש"ה א'): לנצח. כמו לעולם: ותוכל. מל' יכולת:

you return to Him, He will return to you and do good to you. This is the meaning according to the *'keri,'* the traditional reading, קָרָאת. According to the *'kethib,'* the written text, קָרָאתִי, it is to be interpreted: Is it not from now, that I called you My children through My prophets, that you should say to Me, "My Father, You are the Master of my youth."—[*Redak*]

Behold, you have spoken—*with your mouth, "We will no longer come to You," and that evil you will do, and you will not give any thought of returning.*—[*Rashi*]

and you had a harlot's forehead; you refused to be ashamed.
4. Will you not from this time call me, "My Father, You the
Master of my youth." 5. Will He bear a grudge forever? Will
He keep it to eternity? Behold, you have spoken, and you have
committed evil things, and you were able. 6. And the Lord said
to me

October or November. It is the early rain, referred to in Scripture as יוֹרֶה or מוֹרֶה. We find also in the Talmud (*Ta'anith* 5a): The early rain (יוֹרֶה) falls in Marcheshvan and the latter rain (מַלְקוֹשׁ) in Nissan, for in these two seasons the rains necessary for grain usually fall. Since most of the rain falls in Marcheshvan, this month is called Bul, akin to *mabbul*, a flood. Here, the early rain is called רְבִיבִים, *the great rains,* instead of יוֹרֶה. The intention of the verse is that the rains were withheld because of Israel's straying after pagan deities. A parallel is found in the Pentateuch (Deut. 11:17): 'And the Lord's anger will be kindled against you, and He will shut up the heaven, and there will be no rain, and the earth will not give forth its produce . . .'—[*Redak*]

Rashi (Deut. 32:2) defines רְבִיבִים as the drops of rain shot down from the heavens like arrows. [Accordingly, יוֹרֶה and רְבִיבִים are very close in meaning, the former also denoting the rain that shoots.]

and you had a harlot's forehead; you refused to be ashamed—You had a forehead like a harlot, who is not ashamed of her harlotries and lifts up her forehead brazenly. You were brazen despite the prophets' constant reproof and warning of impending doom. You refused the prophet's reproof, and you were not ashamed before them. Our Sages inferred from this verse that rains are withheld because of brazen people (*Ta'anith* 7b). *Jonathan* renders: And you had the audacity of a harlot.—[*Redak*]

4. *Will you not from now—If only you repent of your evil and call me "My Father." If you do so, will your Lord bear a grudge forever* for *what you have sinned? Will He keep it to eternity? He will not keep it.*—[*Rashi*]

I.e., since you see that I have withheld the rains because of your sins, you should have returned to Me and called Me, "My Father, You are the Master of my youth." You have been my Master from my youth, from the time of the Exodus, for then Israel entered under the wings of the Shechinah and were trained in the observance of His commandments and in the knowledge of His Godly powers, just like a youth who enters school to learn Torah and wisdom. *Jonathan* renders: My Redeemer from days of yore.—[*Redak*]

*5. **Will He bear a grudge forever?**—The prophet announces to the people: Had you done so, would God bear a grudge for your iniquity forever? Will He keep your sin to eternity? He will not do so, but if

* For Rashi's commentary turn to page 216.

בימי יאשיהו המלך הראית אשר
עשתה משבה ישראל הלכה היא
על־כל־הר גבה ואל־תחת כל־עץ
רענן ותזני־שם: ז ואמר אחרי עשתה
את־כל־אלה אלי תשוב ולא־שבה
ותראה בגודה אחותה יהודה:
ח וארא כי על־כל־אדות אשר נאפה

ותרא קרי

תרגום

אזלין אינון על כל רמא מנטלא ולתחות כל אילן עבוף ופלחין אנון לטעותא : ז ואמרית כתר בעברו ית כל אלין לפולחני יתובון ולא תבו נחוו משקרא אחיהון דבית יהודה : ח וגלי קדמי ארי על כל עיסק דטעו דמתחסנין למיתב לפולחני דבית ישראל

ת"א חשר נחפה. עקידה שער ס"ח

רש"י

המלך כשלוני להחזיר עשרת השבטים הרחית חשר עשתה משובה ישרחל השובבה (חגכוזייח"ה בלע"ז) : ישראל. עשרת השבטים: הולכה היא. כעודה על חדמתה קודם שגלתה בימי חזקיהו עם הושע בן חלה. הולכה. היתה הולכת על כל הר גבוה: ותזני שם. לעכו"ס. ותזני כמו ותזן יו"ד יתירה: (ז) ואומר. ע"י נביחי עמוס והושע בן בחרי ושחר נביחים חלי תשוב: ותרא בגודה אחותה יהודה. כל זה׳ בגודה קשה ממשובה ישרחל שהם רחשונים לקילקול ולח רחו פורענות ללמוד ממנו ולשוב קרויין משובה יהודה שרחו שגלו חלו ולח לקחו מוסר קרויין בגודה: (ח) וארא כי על כל אודות וגו׳. נקודות טעמי מקרח זה מלמדין על פירושו ישרחל נקוד זקף מוכדל משלחתיה שלחתיה נקוד זקף גדול לעצמו וזה פירושו וחרח נסתכלתי בה ליפרע ממנה ולמה כי על כל חודות חשר נחפה משוב׳ ישרחל ומה היתה נקמתי שלחתיה מעל פני ולח ירחה בגודה יהודה שרחתה כפורענות של שומרון לתת לבה לשוב :

מנחת שי

חלין זה מכלכם : (ז) ותרחה . ותרח קרי :

רד"ק

צדקיהו אמר כי נבואתו היתה בימי יאשיהו קודם שעשת השובה יאשיהו ויהודה שהרי יאשיהו בער עכו"ם מן הארץ וכאן הוא אומר ותנאף את האבן ואת העץ אם כן הנבואה נאמרה קודם התשובה ומה שאמר בכל זאת לא שבה אלי כי אם בשקר שדומה שעשו תשובה אלא שעשו אותה בשקר אפשר כי בתוכחות הנביא ירמיה שהתנבא עליהם אפשר ששבו מקצתה בנראה ובגלוי לא בסתר זהו שאמר בשקר וגם יש לפרש שנבואה זו נאמרה אחר התשובה ואף על פי שאומר ביאשיהו אשר שב אל ה׳ בכל לבבו ובכל נפשו יאשיהו הוא ששב בכל לבבו אבל אנשי דורו שבו מוכרחים מאימת המלך וזהו שאמר לא שבה אלי כי אם בשקר: הראית אשר עשתה. זה לא היה בימי יאשיהו שכבר גלו ישראל בשנת שש לחזקיהו ואיך ראה ירמיהו מה שעשו ישראל קודם גלותם והלא בתחלת נבואת ירמיהו היה לגלות ישראל כ"ג שנה והוא אמר לא ידעתי דבר כי נער אנכי ואם כן נפרש הראית שמעת או הידעת כמו וירא יעקב כי יש שבר במצרים והדומים לו או נפרש אשר עשתה על השארית הנמצא מישראל מפוזרין בארץ מצרים וממנשה ומשמעון ומנפתלי שהיו שם בימי יאשיהו שאמר בדברי הימים ובערי מנשה ואפרים ושמעון ועד נפתלי ואמר אשר אספו הלוים שומרי הסף מיד מנשה ואפרים ומכל שארית ישראל: משובה. שם תאר וענינו מורדת מן שובו בנים שובבים: הלכה היא. לפירוש הראשון פירש שהיתה הולכת היא ולפי׳ השני כי עתה הלכה היא ולא לקחה מוסר כאשר גלו: ותזני שם. היו"ד במקום ה"א למ"ד הפעל והוא כמו ותזנה וכן צור ילדך תשי וחטאתם מלפניך אל תמחי: (ז) ואומר. אמרתי כיון שעשתה כל הרעות האלה ומצאוך צרות רבות ורעות עליה תתחרט על מעשים הרעים ותשוב אלי והנה לא שבה עם כל זה: ותרא בגודה אחותה יהודה. כלומר ראתה שעשתה כל זה משובה ישראל ולא שתה אל לבה והכתוב חסר הענין אבל מן הכתוב נבין כה שאינו כתוב וכן פסוקים רבים במקרא כמו נגיד חסר תבונות חולתו כמו שכתבנו בספר מכלל בחלק הדקדוק ממנו: ותרא. ותראה כתיב ואחד הוא. בגודה. שם תאר בא בקמץ חבי"ת על דרך היחיד: (ח) וארא. ואני ג"כ ראיתי כי היא ראתה ולא שבה ומה ראתה כי על כל אודות אשר נאפה משיבה שלחתיה עם כל זה לא יראה בגודה אחותה יהודה שאשלח אותה ג"כ ולא שבה אלי ומה שאמר וארא טעמו נקשר בסוף הענין כי אם בשקר לפיכך אמר וארא כי בני אדם לא ראו זה אבל אני ראיתי כי תשובתם בשקר ולא בכל לבה ואני בוחן לב ראיתי

מצודת ציון

(ו) הראית. הה"א השאלה: משובה. ענין מרד והליכה בדרכי הלב כמו וילך שובב (ישעיה נ"ז): רענן. לח ורטוב: (ז) בגודה. ענין מרד כמו כל רעיה בגדו בה (איכה א׳): אחותה. רעותה ומכלתה: (ח) אודות. ענינו כמו עסק וכן על אודותי (יהושע י"ד):

מצודת דוד

(ו) הראית. אם נתת לב לראות אשר עשתה עדת ישראל המורדים הם בני עשרת השבטים: ותזני שם. עבדת שם לפסילי׳: (ז) ואמר. אמרתי לה על ידי נביאים. שוב אלי בתשובה: ולא שבה. ולא רצתה לשוב: ותרא. ר"ל ועוד סכלה שאחותה בגודה יהודה ראתה מעשיה ונמדה ממנה: (ח) וארא. ר"ל ואני רואה וגלוי לפני כי עם היות שעל כל אודות אשר נאפה משובה ישראל בעכו"ם שלחתיה וגו׳ רואה אני שלא סראה ממנה בגודה אחות׳ יהוד׳ ותלך והזן

7. **And I said**—*through My prophets, Amos and Hosea son of Beeri and the other prophets, 'You shall return to Me.''*—[*Rashi*]

Rashi obviously explains this as a command, as does *Mezudath David. Redak,* however, explains it as a future form: And I said: Since she has committed all these evils and all these misfortunes have befallen her, she will regret her deeds and return to Me. But she did not return.

8. **And I saw, because of all that backsliding Israel had committed**

* For Rashi's commentary turn to page 216.

in the days of King Josiah: Have you seen what the backsliding Israel has done? She goes on every lofty mountain and under every leafy tree, and she played the harlot there.
7. And I said after she had done all these things: She shall return to Me. But she did not return. And her treacherous sister Judah saw [it].
8. And I saw, because of all that backsliding Israel had committed adultery,

6. **And the Lord said to me in the days of Josiah**—Since Jeremiah prophesied also during the reigns of Jehoiakim and Zedekiah, he specifies that this prophecy came to him during the reign of Josiah. This was before Josiah's return to God, for at that time, he purged the land of idolatry, yet here the prophet states that they 'committed adultery with stones and with wood.' Although Scripture states that they did not return with all their heart, indicating that they did, in fact, repent, perhaps some of the people repented upon hearing the prophet's reproof, but this was only an outward manifestation of repentance, not a sincere repentance with all their heart. It is also possible that this prophecy came to Jeremiah after Josiah's repentance. Although Josiah repented with all his heart, with all his soul, and with all his possessions, as in II Kings (23:25), and he abolished paganism from the land, many of his subjects still worshipped pagan deities in secret, concealing their practice from him out of fear. [See verse 10.] Therefore, the prophet states (verse 10): 'And yet, for all this, her treacherous sister Judah has not returned to Me with all her heart, but falsely, says the Lord.'—[*Redak*]

In the days of King Josiah—*when He commanded me to bring back the Ten Tribes, "Have you seen what the backsliding Israel has done?* מְשֻׁבָה *is the same as* שׁוֹבֵבָה, *(envejjsede in O.F.)*.—[*Rashi* as emended by *Shem Ephraim*]

Israel—*The Ten Tribes.*—[*Rashi*]

This was not in the days of Josiah, for Israel was driven into exile in the sixth year of Hezekiah's reign. How then could Jeremiah see what they had done before their exile? He commenced to prophesy in the ninety-third year of the exile, when he hesitated to accept God's mission because of his youthfulness. We must, therefore, interpret 'have you seen' as 'have you heard.' Alternatively, this refers to the remnants of the Kingdom of Israel who were scattered in the land, from Ephraim and Manasseh, Simeon, and Naphtali, as is stated in II Chron. 34:6, 9.—[*Redak*]

she goes—*I.e., when she was still on her land before she was exiled in the days of Hezekiah with Hoshea son of Elah.* הֹלְכָה *means, she would go on every lofty mountain.*—[*Rashi*]

According to the other interpretation, that the prophet refers to the remnant of Israel, it can be understood literally, that she still goes on every lofty mountain.—[*Redak*]

מְשֻׁבָה יִשְׂרָאֵל שִׁלַּחְתִּיהָ וָאֶתֵּן אֶת־
סֵפֶר כְּרִיתֻתֶיהָ אֵלֶיהָ וְלֹא יָרְאָה
בֹּגֵדָה יְהוּדָה אֲחוֹתָהּ וַתֵּלֶךְ וַתִּזֶן גַּם־
הִיא׃ ט וְהָיָה מִקֹּל זְנוּתָהּ וַתֶּחֱנַף אֶת־
הָאָרֶץ וַתִּנְאַף אֶת־הָאֶבֶן וְאֶת־הָעֵץ׃
י וְגַם־בְּכָל־זֹאת לֹא־שָׁבָה אֵלַי בָּגוֹדָה
אֲחוֹתָהּ יְהוּדָה בְּכָל־לִבָּהּ כִּי אִם־
בְּשֶׁקֶר נְאֻם־יְהוָה׃ יא וַיֹּאמֶר יְהוָה אֵלַי

יִשְׂרָאֵל אַגְלֵיתִינוּן כְּמָה
דְיָהֲבִין אִגֶּרֶת גֵּט
פִּטּוּרִין וּמְשַׁלְּחִין וְלָא
דְחִילוּ מְשַׁקְרַיָא דְבֵית
יְהוּדָה אֲחֵיהוֹן וַאֲזַלוּ
וּטְעוֹ אַף אִינוּן: ט וַהֲוָה
כַּד קַלִּילָא בְּעֵינָהָא
טְעוּתָהָא וְחַיֵּבַת יָת
אַרְעָא וּטְעַת עִם פַּלְחֵי
אַבְנַיָא וְאָעַיָא: י וְאַף
בְּכָל דָּא לָא תָבוּ
לְפוּלְחָנִי מְשַׁקְרַיָא
אֲחֵיהוֹן דְבֵית יְהוּדָה
בְּכָל לִבְּהוֹן אֱלָהֵין
בְּשִׁקְרָא אֲמַר יְיָ:
יא וַאֲמַר יְיָ לִי נְבִיאוּ

רש"י

(ט) ותנאף את האבן. וטעת עם פלחי אבניא ואעיא. ויונתן תרגם מקל זנותה לשון קלות מדקלילא בעינהא טעוותהא: (י) וגם בכל זאת. שראו בקלקלת פורענות חבריהם: כי אם בשקר. דורו של יאשיה מראין עצמם שהם צדיקים והם רשעים היו וגרים צורות של עכו"ם על דלתותיהם מכפנים חציה על זו וחציה על זו וכשהיו מבערי

קמץ בטרחא

מהר"י קרא

(ט) והיה מקל זנותה. [מקול שיצא על זנותה. ד"א מקול זנותה]מקלות זנותה מקל חסר ו' לפי שאינו בגזרת קול אלא מלשון קלות וכן ת"י והוה מדקליא בעינהא טעוותא: ותנאף את האבן ואת העץ. זנו מאחרי בשביל צלמים של אבן ושל עץ:

רד"ק

כל זה ואתן את ספר כריתותיה אליה והנה אמר ישעיהו איזהו ספר כריתות אמכם אשר שלחתיה וירמיהו אמר ואתן את ספר כריתותיה אליה פי' המפרש כי ירמיה דבר כנגד עשרת השבטים שנתן להם ספר כריתות שלא יהיה עוד מהם מלך כי בקבוץ גליות אמר ודוד עבדי נשיא להם לעולם ואמר ולא יחצו עוד לשתי ממלכות אבל ליהודה לא נתן ספר כריתות אלא כבעל שמוציא אשתו מביתו שקצף עליה אבל לא נתן לה ספר כריתות מפני שעתיד להחזירה אליו וכן יהודה עתיד להחזיר המלכות אליו ונוכל לפרש ג"כ לפי שעשרת השבטים לא שבו בשוב הגלות מבבל ועוד משגלו לא יצאו ממקום גלותם וארך להם הגלות מאד הרי הם כאילו נתן להם ספר כריתות ואע"פ שעתידים לחזור אבל שבט יהודה הרי הם כאילו לא נתן להם ספר כריתות שהרי שבו לארצם אחר שבעים שנה וישבו בארצם ת"כ שנה ואע"פ ששבט יהודה לא גלו עדיין הנביא דבר על העתיד ונחמת שמנחם ישראל שהם בזה הגלות שישובו כי לא נמכרו כי אם בעונותיהם ובשובם אל האל ישיב שבותם ואמר כנגד יהודה אי זה ספר כריתות כלומר כי קרובים אתם לשוב אלי כמו ששבתם פעם אחרת כי אין ביני וביניכם כריתות ובשובם ישובו ג"כ שאר השבטים כי דוד ימלוך על כל השבטים וכ"א יחזקאל הנה אני לוקח את עץ יוסף אשר ביד אפרים ושבטי ישראל חבריו ונתתי אותם עליו את עץ יהודה ועשיתים לעץ אחד ואפילו שנתן להם ספר כריתות כבר היה הכריתות גדול וארך גלותם מאד והנה ישיב שבותם עם שבט יהודה: בגדה. בא בצרי עין הפעל על דרך היחיד וכן נוטרה את הכרמים והדומים להם: (ט) והיה מקל זנותה. ענין קלות ואמר המסרת עליו לית חסר בקלילותא ופירושו כתרגומו והות מדקלילא בעינהא טעוותהא וחייבת ית ארעא וטעת עם פלחי אבניא ואעיא וכבר פירשנו כי לשון זנות ונאוף הנזכר בזה הענין הוא ענין הדבקות בעכו"ם: (י) וגם בכל זאת. בכל זאת שראתה ששלחתי אחותה לא שבה אלי בכל לבה וזה קודם תשובת יאשיהו או אחר תשובתו כמו שפי' למעלה בפסוק ויאמר ה' אלי: בגודה. שם תאר היה משפטו בשוא פ"א הפעל כמי קרובה רחוקה ונשאר עם הקמץ כמו שהוא לזכר: (יא) ויאמר ה' אלי צדקה נפשה. אע"פ שחטאה משובה ישראל תחלה הנה אחותה יהודה הוסיפה לחטא עד שנחשבת אחותה ישראל צדקת כנגדה והוספת החטא ביהודה הוא לבזותה בית האל להכנים שם פסיליהם ואליליהם ולבטל שם עבודת האל ולעבוד עכו"ם בבית עצמו כמו שנאמר באחז

מנחת שי

(ט) ותחנף. החי"ם בחטף סגול:

מצודת דוד

גם היא בעכו"ם כאחותה ישראל: (ט) והיה מקל זנותה. בעבור הקלות שיש עמה בדבר הזנות לעכו"ם חייבה את הארץ להיות חרבה ושוממה: ותנאף וגו'. עשתה עכו"ם מעץ ואבן: (י) וגם בכל זאת. עם כל הרעה שראתה שבאה על ישראל עכ"ז לא שבה

מצודת ציון

נאפה. מל' ניאוף וזנות: שלחתיה. ענין טירוד וגרושין: ספר כריתותיה. כן נקרא גט האשה וכן וכתב לה ספר כריתות (דברים כ"ד) ע"ש שכורת ומפריד בינו לבינה: ותזן. מלשון זנות: (ט) מקל. מלשון קלות: את האבן. עם האבן:

I.e., although they saw that I sent away their sister kingdom, they did not repent sincerely. This was before Josiah repented, or perhaps even afterwards, as explained above, v. 6.—[*Redak*]

but falsely—*Josiah's generation would show themselves as righteous although they were wicked. They would make forms of pagan deities on the inside of their doors, half on this door and half on this one, and when the destroyers of idols would inspect, the door would be open, and they would not notice it.*—[*Rashi* from *Lam. Rabbah* 1:53.] See Pseudo-Rashi II Chron. 35:20, where he quotes Kinoth of Rabbi Eleazar

I sent her away, and I gave her her bill of divorcement, yet treacherous Judah, her sister, did not fear, and she too went and played the harlot. 9. And it was through the lightness of her harlotry, that she polluted the land, and she committed adultery with the stones and the wood. 10. And yet for all this, her treacherous sister Judah did not return to Me with all her heart, but falsely, says the Lord. 11. And the Lord said to me:

adultery—*The signs of the intonation of this verse teach us its explanation.* יִשְׂרָאֵל *is punctuated with a zakef katan, separated from* שִׁלַּחְתִּיהָ, *I sent her away.* שִׁלַּחְתִּיהָ, *I sent her away, is punctuated with a zakef gadol by itself. And this is its explanation: I saw*; i.e., *I contemplated her to exact punishment upon her. And why? Because of all that backsliding Israel had committed adultery. And what was My vengeance? I sent her away from before Me. And treacherous Judah did not fear when she saw the retribution of Samaria, to set her heart to repent.*—[*Rashi*]

Redak explains: And I, too, saw that she saw and did not repent. Now what did she see? That because of all that backsliding Israel had committed adultery, I sent her away. Despite all this, treacherous Judah did not fear that I would send her away as well. The words 'and I saw' are connected to the end of verse 10, with the word 'falsely.' Although human beings did not discern the falseness of their repentance, I, Who search the heart, saw it, and I, therefore, gave her her bill of divorcement. This verse seems to contradict Isaiah's prophecy, in which he states (50:1): "Where is your mother's bill of divorce that I sent her away?" The exegetes reply that Jeremiah was addressing the Ten Tribes, to whom God did indeed give a bill of divorcement, for they lost their sovereignty completely, never to place a king on the throne of Israel. In Messianic times, all Israel will be under the dominion of the house of David, as the prophet Ezekiel states: "(37:24) And My servant David shall be king over them." In the same chapter he states: "(v. 22) . . . and one king shall be for all of them as a king, and they shall no longer become two nations, and they shall no longer be divided into two kingdoms." To Judah, however, He did not give a bill of divorcement. This is analogous to a man who becomes angry with his wife and sends her away. He does not give her a bill of divorcement, because he intends to take her back. So it is with Judah, whom God intends to reinstate in its position of sovereign over Israel.

*9. **through the lightness of her harlotry**—I.e., because she considered her harlotry of little consequence.—[*Targum Jonathan, Redak, Kara*]

10. **And yet for all this**—*that they saw the misfortune of the retribution of their companions.*—[*Rashi*]

* For Rashi's commentary turn to page 217.

צדקה נפשה משבה ישראל מבגדה
יהודה: יב הלך וקראת את־הדברים
האלה צפונה ואמרת שובה משבה
ישראל נאם־יהוה לוא־אפיל פני בכם
כי־חסיד אני נאם־יהוה לא אטור
לעולם: יג אך דעי עונך כי ביהוה
אלהיך פשעת ותפזרי את־דרכיך
לזרים

ה"א הלוך וקראת. סנהדרין נא קי:

תרגום

נפשיהון דמתחסנין
למיסב לפולחני דבית
ישראל מסשקריא דבית
יהודה: יב איזיל ותתנבי
ית פתגמיא האלין
בארע צפונא ותימר
תובו דמתחסנין למיסב
לפולחני דבית ישראל
אמר יי כד תתיבון לא
אשלח רוגזי בכון ארי
סגי למעבד טבון אנא
אמר יי ולא יתנטרון ליך
חוביך לעלם: יג ברם
דעי חוביך ארי בסיקרא
דיי אלהך מרידת

מהר"י קרא

(יא) צדקה נפשה משובה ישראל. הם י' שבטים לא היה דור לפניהם שגלו בעונם ולא היה להם ממי ללמוד שיקחו מוסר אבל שבט יהודה שראו שגלו י' השבטים לפניהם בימי הושע בן אלה ובכל זאת לא יראו ולא שבו אל ה' נמצאו י' שבטים צדיקים מהן: (יב) ואמרת שובה משובה ישראל. מיכן יש ללמוד שירמיה הלך להחזיר י' השבטים ויאשיה מלך עליהן שהרי למעלה בענין הוא אומר ויאמר ה' אלי בימי יאשיהו המלך הראית את אשר עשתה משובה ישראל: (יג) אך דעי עונך. אך אם תעשו תשובה והתוודו חטאתיכם בווידוייכם וכך האמרו על כן באה אלינו הצרה הזאת כי בה' אלהינו

רש"י

עכו"ם בודקים היה הדלת פתוח ולא היו מכירין בה: (יא) צדקה נפשה משובה ישראל. נקת' ופטרה עצמה מן הדין שלא היה לה ממי ללמוד: (יב) הלוך וקראת וגו'. הלוך כתרגומו אזיל לשון צווי כאן ליווהו לילך ולחזור עשרת השבטים בימי יאשיהו כמו שאמר למעלה שבימי יאשיהו נאמרה לו נבואה זו וחזרו מקצת מהן כשמונה עשרה ליאשיהו: צפונה. אל המקומות שגלו שם לאשור: פני. רוגזי. כן תרגם יונתן: (יג) פשעת. מרדת: ותפזרי

מנחת שי

(יג) הלוך וקראת. בספרי ספרד היא בגעיא: לצונה. מלא וא"ו ועיין פ"ב בסימן כ"ג:

רד"ק

שצוה לעשות מזבח בב"ה דמות המזבח אשר בדמשק ובטל עבודת מזבח ה' וגו' ויסגר את דלתות בית ה' ונאמר ויכבו את הנרות וקטרת לא הקטירו ונאמר עליו וגם את בניו העביר באש כתיעבות הגוים וכן במנשה נאמר וישתחו לכל צבא השמים ונאמר והעביר את בנו באש ועונן ונחש וכשף ועשה אוב וידעוני הרבה לעשות הרע בעיני ה' ונאמר עליו הרע מכל אשר עשו האמרי אשר לפניו והחטיא גם את יהודה בגלוליו ונאמר וגם דם נקי שפך מנשה הרבה מאד עד אשר מלא ירושלם פה לפה חללים: (יב) הלוך וקראת. אינו אומר לנביא שילך צפונה במקום שגלו עשרת השבטים כי הגלה אותם מלך אשור בחלח וחבור ועדי כדי והם צפון העולם כלפי מזרח אלא פירושו הלוך ענין זרוז כמו לכה נא אנסכה בשמחה לבו ונפילה גורלות והדומים להם ומה שאמר וקראת ר"ל שיקרא הדברים האלה בירושלם לפני זקני יהודה ויקרא הדברים כנגד ישראל שגלו כאילו מדבר עמהם פנים בפנים ואמר להם שובה בשובה ישראל רמז להם שעתידים לשוב באחרית הימים וזהו שאמר לא אטור לעולם כלומר שלא ישמור עינם לעולם אלא ישיבם אליו אחר זמן ארוך ויקבצם עם גלות יהודה וכה שאמר לא אפיל פני בכם ר"ל לעולם וטעם העולם לשנים ללא אפיל פני וללא אטור כי כבר הפיל פניו בהם בגלותו אותם ופני פירוש כעסי כמו ונתתי אני את פני באיש ההוא פני ה' חלקם והדומים להם ומה שאמר כי חסיד אני ר"ל כי אע"פ שחטאתם והייתם חייבים כליה אני חסיד כמו שאמר במדות האל ורב חסד והחסד הוא יתרון הטובה יותר על הראוי: (יג) אך דעי. אך קודם שאשיבך אלי צריך שתדעי עונך ותכירי בעצמך על מה הגליתיך כי בה' אלהיך פשעת וכיון שתכירי זה תשובי אלי ואשובה אליך: ותפזרי. כי לא עבדת עכו"ם אחת לבדה אלא פזרת את דרכך לזרים לזה ולזה כמו שאמר כי מספר עריך היו אלהיך יהודה: ובקולי לא

מצודת ציון

(יב) הלוך. הוא ענין לשון זרוז: אפיל. ענין הניה והשכנה כמו ע"ס כי אהיו נפל (בראשית כ"ה): פני. ענין החמה וכעס כמו פני ה' חלקם (איכה ד') ע"ש שהכעס יוכר בפני האדם: אטור. ענין שמירה: (יג) ותפזרי. מל' פזור ופרוד: דרכיך. רגליך ע"ש שדורכי'

מצודת דוד

אלי וגו' ככל לבה כ"א בשקר מהספה ולהין: (יא) צדקה נפשה וגו'. ר"ל עם כי ישראל חטא להבינה הנה יהודה הבגידה כ"כ בפשעם עד שלמולה נחשבת ישראל לצדקת: (יב) צפונה. אל מול לפון לאשור מקום שגלה ישראל: לא אפיל. לא אשכין חמתי בכם: כי חסיד אני. ר"ל לא כמלך ב"ו שאינו מוחל למורדים בו אף אם עשו התשובה: לא אטור. לא אשמור האיבה לעולם כי מיד כשתשובו אלך לה האיבה: (יג) אך דעי עונך. אתי מכרת בעצמך שהרבית עון כי פשעת בה': ותפזרי. פזרת רגליך זה מזה לנאוף עם הזרים ור"ל עבדת עכו"ם הרבה: ובקולי לא שמעתם. ר"ל לא עבדתם

[*Rashi*] This is based on *Targum Jonathan* and the Talmud (*Yoma* 36b) where פְּשָׁעִים are classified as rebellious sins.

and you have scattered your ways—*This is an expression of harlotry, spreading the legs to the woman's private parts.*—[*Rashi*] The implication is that they were ready and willing to accept many gods.—[*Mezudath David*]

Redak explains: You scattered your ways by running here and there to worship many gods, similar to 'for as many as your cities were your gods, O Judea.'—[*Redak*]

Backsliding Israel has proven herself more righteous than treacherous Judah. 12. Go and proclaim these words to the north, and say: Return, O backsliding Israel, says the Lord. I will not let My anger rest upon you, for I am pious, says the Lord; I will not bear a grudge forever. 13. Only acknowledge your iniquity, for you have rebelled against the Lord your God, and you have scattered your ways

Hakalir; Kinot for the Ninth of Av, pp. 102f. See also Isaiah 57:8, Commentary Digest; II Kings 23:29, Commentary Digest.

11. **has proved herself more righteous**—*She has been cleared and she has freed herself from an unfavorable verdict, for she had no one to learn from.*—[*Rashi*]

Although Israel sinned first, her sister Judah continued to sin and increased her sins until her sister Israel appears righteous as compared to her. Judah's sins were more severe in that they disgraced the Temple by bringing their idols there and by curtailing their Temple service, even worshipping idols in the very sanctuary, as is written concerning Ahaz, who ordered an altar built in the Temple, modeled after the altar in Damascus, he curtailed the service and closed the doors of the house of the Lord (II Chron. 28:24). He also extinguished the lights of the menorah, and they did not burn the holy incense (29:7). It is also written of him that 'he passed his son through fire in the abominable manner of the nations' (II Kings 16:3).

Concerning Manasseh, too, it is stated: 'And he caused his sons to pass through fire in the valley of Ben Hinnom, and he practiced soothsaying, divination, and sorcery, and he practiced necromancy and divination with the jidoa bone; he did much evil in the eyes of the Lord, to provoke Him' (II Chron. 33:6). It is also stated concerning him, 'he has done more wickedly than all the Amorites who were before him, did, and he caused Judah to sin with his idols' (II Kings 21:11). 'Moreover, Manasseh shed very much innocent blood, until he filled Jerusalem from one end to the other' (II Kings 21:16).—[*Redak*]

*12. **Go and proclaim etc.**—*Go, as the Targum renders, אֱזִיל, the imperative form. Here he commanded him to go and bring back the Ten Tribes during the days of Josiah, as he states above that during the days of Josiah this prophecy was said to him and some of them returned in the eighteenth year of Josiah.*—[*Rashi* based on *Megillah* 14b]

13. **Only acknowledge your iniquity**—Before I return you to Me, you must acknowledge your iniquity and recognize the reason for your exile, that you rebelled against the Lord your God. When you recognize this, you will return to Me, and I will return to you.—[*Redak*]

you have rebelled—Heb. פָּשַׁעַתְּ.—

* For Rashi's commentary turn to page 217.

לַזָּרִים תַּחַת כָּל־עֵץ רַעֲנָן וּבְקוֹלִי לֹא־
שְׁמַעְתֶּם נְאֻם־יְהוָה׃ יד שׁוּבוּ בָנִים
שׁוֹבָבִים נְאֻם־יְהוָה כִּי אָנֹכִי בָּעַלְתִּי
בָכֶם וְלָקַחְתִּי אֶתְכֶם אֶחָד מֵעִיר וּשְׁנַיִם
מִמִּשְׁפָּחָה וְהֵבֵאתִי אֶתְכֶם צִיּוֹן׃
טו וְנָתַתִּי לָכֶם רֹעִים כְּלִבִּי וְרָעוּ אֶתְכֶם
דֵּעָה וְהַשְׂכֵּיל׃ טז וְהָיָה כִּי תִרְבּוּ
וּפְרִיתֶם בָּאָרֶץ בַּיָּמִים הָהֵמָּה נְאֻם־
יְהוָה לֹא־יֹאמְרוּ עוֹד אֲרוֹן בְּרִית־יְהוָה

וּקְלָקִילְתְּ יַת אוֹרְחָתִךְ
אִתְחַבַּרְתְּ לְעַמְמַיָא
פְּלָחֵי כוֹכְבַיָא תְּחוֹת כָּל
אִילָן עֲבוּף וּלְמֵימְרִי לָא
קַבֵּילְתּוּן אֲמַר יְיָ :
יד תּוּבוּ בְנַיָא דְמִתְהַפְּכִין
לְמֵיתַב אֲמַר יְיָ אֲרֵי אֲנָא
אִתְרְעֵיתִי בְכוֹן וַאֲקָרֵיב
יַתְכוֹן כְּאִלוּ אַתּוּן
מִשְׁתַּאֲרִין חַד מִקַּרְתָּא
וּתְרֵין מִזַּרְעִיתָא וְאַעֵיל
יַתְכוֹן לְצִיוֹן : טו וְאֵמַנֵי
עֲלֵיכוֹן פַּרְנָסִין עָבְדֵי
רְעוּתִי וִיפַרְנְסוּן יַתְכוֹן
בְּמַדַּע וּבְחוּכְמָא: טז וִיהֵי
אֲרֵי תִסְגוּן וְתִפְשׁוּן
בְּאַרְעָא בְּיוֹמַיָא הָאִינוּן
אֲמַר יְיָ לָא יֵימְרוּן עוֹד
אֲרוֹן קְיָמָא דַיְיָ וְלָא יִסַּק

ת״א אנכי. יומא פו סנהדרין לו קיא חגיגה ט ע״א ז׳ בכורות לה : והיה כי. פקדה ב״ב לה :

רש״י

את דרכיך. לשון זנות פיסוק רגלים למעברי אשה : (יד) שובבים. (אנוויישי״ר בלע״ז) ששובבתם דרככם מרוב כל שהייתם בשלוה ועונג כמו שהוא אומר הפורעים על פי הנבל (עמוס ו׳) השותים במזרקי יין (שם) : כי אנכי בעלתי בכם. ונקראתם בשמי שאני אדון לכם ואין כבודי להניח אתכם ביד אויבי : (טז) לא יאמרו עוד ארון.

מהר״י קרא

פשענו. ועל שפיזרנו דרכינו לע״ז אם תעשו כך לא אשמור לעולם אבל אסלח לכם : (יד) ולקחתי אתכם אחד מעיר ושנים ממשפחה והבאתי אתכם ציון. אילו הייתי ממתין שיהיו כל בני הדור צדיקים לא מדת הדין נותנת שתהיו נגאלין עולמית אלא בזכות צדיק אחד שימצא בעיר ובזכות שני צדיקים מן המשפחה והבאתי אתכם ציון זה הוא מדרשו. ופשוטו אני עתיד ללקט אתכם אחד בעיר ושנים ממשפחה שאתם פזורין בכל המקומות ונשארתם מתי מספר והבאתי אתכם ציון ושם תפרו והענין יורה על פתרונו שכתב אחריו והיה כי תרבו ופריתם בארץ : (טו) ונתתי לכם רועים כלבי. לפי שנאמר למעלה והרועים פשעו בי חזר ואמר כאן ונתתי לכם רועים כלבי ורעו אתכם דעה והשכל. לדעת את ה׳ : (טז) לא יאמרו עוד ארון ברית ה׳. שלא תהיו צריכין לומר עוד נקחה ארון ברית ה׳ ויבא

רד״ק

שמעתם. כי הייתי מתרה בכם תמיד על ידי הנביאים ולא שמעתם : (יד) שובו בנים שובבים. מורדים כמו משובה שפירשנו : כי אנכי בעלתי בכם. כלומר אבעל בכם אחר שגרשתי אתכם ות״י אתרעיתי בכון ואאז״ל פירש בעלתי קצתי לפי שהוא קשור בבי״ת וכן אנכי בעלתי בה נאם ה׳ ודמה אותו כן בזה הענין בלשון ערבי : אחד מעיר. אפי׳ יהודי אחד יהיה לבדו בעיר מערי הגוים משם אקחנו וכן אם יהיו אפי׳ שנים לבדם באומה אחת משם אקחם ואומה נקראת משפחה כמו ואם משפחת מצרים לא תעלה וכן לכל משפחות ממלכות צפונה ורז״ל פירשו אחד מעיר מזכה את כל העיר שנים ממשפחה מזכים את כל המשפחה ובזכותן יצאו כלם מהגלות : (טו) ונתתי. כלבי. שירעו אותם כלבי וחפצי לא כרועים הראשונים והם מלכי ישראל ויהודה שהיו מדריכים אותם בדרך רעה ולעבוד עכו״ם אבל אותם הרועים שאתן להם בזמן הישועה ירעו אותם דעה והשכל והרועים הם פרנסי ישראל שיהיו עם מלך המשיח כמו שנאמר בנבואת מיכה והקמונו עליו שבעה רועים ושמונה נסיכי אדם : (טז) והיה כי תרבו. לא יאמרו עוד ארון ברית ה׳ ולא יעלה על לב כלומר אע״פ

מצודת דוד

אותי אף בשתוף : (יד) שובו. אתם בנים מורדי׳ שובו אלי כי אנכי האדון והמושל בכם לכן מהראוי שתשובו אלי : ולקחתי אתכם. ואז אקח אתכ׳ מסגולם : אחד מעיר. ר״ל אף אם מעט ישובו אלי אקח אותם ולא ישקעו שם עם העומדים במרדם : (טו) רעים כלבי. מלכים צדיקי׳ וכפי רצון לבי לא כמו לבעל׳ שהמליכו מדעתם מלכים רשעים וכם הכיהו אות׳ לעכו״ם כי לעתיד המשיח ימלוך עליהם : ורעו. ידעו אתכ׳ בדרך דעה והשכל : (טז) לא יאמרו עוד ארון ברית ה׳. ר״ל לא יאמרו עוד זה נלך לפני הארון להתפלל שמה כי לפני מרכיב השם לא יוכלו כלם לבא שמה

מצודת ציון

ופוסעים בו וכמו שמלת פעם מבוקף על ענין ההולך ועל הרגל כמ״ש פעמי מרכבותיו (שופטים ה׳) ונאמ׳ פעמי דלים (ישעיה כ״ו) : (יד) בעלתי. ענין סר ואדון כמו אם בעליו עמו (שמות כ״ב) : (טו) ופריתם. מל׳ פרי ר״ל תלדו בנים מרובי׳ : יפקדו.

and they will feed you with knowledge and understanding—This may also be translated: And they will lead you with knowledge and understanding.—[*Mezudath David, Ibn Nachmiash*]

16. **when you will multiply**—Since God will gather but one from a city and two from a family, the number will be small. Then they will multiply and be fruitful in the land.—[*Malbim*]

they will no longer say, "The ark of the Lord's covenant"—*For your*

to strangers under every leafy tree, and you did not hearken to
My voice, says the Lord.
14. Return, backsliding children, says
the Lord, for I possessed you, and I will take you, one from a
city and two from a family, and I will bring you to Zion.
15. And I will give you shepherds according to My heart, and
they will feed you with knowledge and understanding.
16. And
it shall be, when you multiply and are fruitful in the land in
those days, says the Lord, they will no longer say, "The ark of
the Lord's covenant,"

So shall you say in your confessions: This trouble has befallen us because we have rebelled against the Lord our God, and we have scattered our ways to strangers. If you confess this, I will not bear a grudge forever, but I will forgive you.—[*Kara*]

and you did not hearken to My voice—I.e., you did not worship Me even in conjunction with pagan deities.—[*Mezudath David*]

Redak explains: For I constantly warned you through My prophets.

14. **backsliding children**—(*Envasec in O.F.*) *That you perverted your way because of much good, that you enjoyed tranquility and pleasure, as Scripture states: They hum snatches of song to the tune of the lute* (Amos 6:5), *those who drink from bowls of wine* (v. 6).—[*Rashi*]

backsliding—Heb. שׁוֹבָבִים, rebellious, like מְשֻׁבָה, as explained above.—[*Redak*]

for I possessed you—*and you are called by My name, that I am your Master, and it is not honorable for Me to leave you in the hands of My enemies.*—[*Rashi*]

Redak explains: for I *will* possess you. After I have driven you away, I will again take possession of you. He may also mean: After I have divorced you, I will become your husband. R. Joseph Kimchi renders: For I despised you.

one from a city—If there will be but one Jew in a city of the gentiles, I will take him out of there.—[*Rashi*]

and two from a family—A whole nation is called a family, as above (:15). If there will be two Jews amidst an entire gentile nation, I will take them out.—[*Redak*]

15. **according to My heart**—I.e., leaders who will lead you according to My will, not like the earlier leaders, the kings of Judah and Israel, who misled the people on evil ways, to worship idols, but these leaders whom I will appoint at the time of the redemption, will lead you with knowledge and understanding. These are the leaders of Israel who will be with the Messiah, as is mentioned in Micah's prophecy, 'And we will set up over him seven shepherds and eight princes of the sons of men' (Micah 4:5).—[*Redak*]

וְלֹא יַעֲלֶה עַל־לֵב וְלֹא יִזְכְּרוּ־בוֹ וְלֹא
יִפְקֹדוּ וְלֹא יֵעָשֶׂה עוֹד: יז בָּעֵת הַהִיא
יִקְרְאוּ לִירוּשָׁלַםִ כִּסֵּא יְהוָה וְנִקְווּ אֵלֶיהָ
כָל־הַגּוֹיִם לְשֵׁם יְהוָה לִירוּשָׁלָםִ וְלֹא־
יֵלְכוּ עוֹד אַחֲרֵי שְׁרִרוּת לִבָּם הָרָע:
יח בַּיָּמִים הָהֵמָּה יֵלְכוּ בֵית־יְהוּדָה עַל־
בֵּית יִשְׂרָאֵל וְיָבֹאוּ יַחְדָּו מֵאֶרֶץ צָפוֹן
עַל־הָאָרֶץ אֲשֶׁר הִנְחַלְתִּי אֶת־

עַל לִבָּא וְלָא יִדְּכְּרוּן עוֹד
בֵּיהּ וְלָא יְזוּעוּן וְלָא
יְגִיחוּן בַּהּ עוֹד קְרָב :
יז בְּעִדָּנָא הַהִיא יִקְרוּן
לִירוּשְׁלֵם אֲתַר בֵּית
שְׁכִנְתָּא דַייָ וְיִתְכַּנְשׁוּן
לְמִפְלַח בַּהּ כָּל עַמְמַיָא
לִשְׁמָא דַייָ לִירוּשְׁלֵם
וְלָא יְהָכוּן עוֹד בָּתַר
הִרְהוּר לִבְּהוֹן בִּישָׁא :
יח בְּיוֹמַיָא הָאִינוּן
יִתְחַבְּרוּן דְבֵית יְהוּדָה
עִם בֵּית יִשְׂרָאֵל וְיֵתוּן
כַּחֲדָא מֵאֲרַע צִפּוּנָא
לְאַרְעָא דְאַחְסֵינִית יָת
אֲבָהָתְכוֹן

מהר"י קרא

בקרבינו ויושיענו מכף אויבינו כי שלום יהיה: (יח) ילכו בית יהודה על בית ישראל. לפי שדיבר למעלה בגלות י' השבטים דכתיב וארא כי על כל אדות אשר נואפה משובת ישראל שלחתיה וגם בגלות יהודה כתיב כי הנני קורא לכל משפחות ממלכות צפונה נאם ה' ובאו ונתנו איש כסאו פתח שערי ירושלים וגו' חזר וריפא. כאן בימים ההם ילכו בית יהודה על בית ישראל פת' עם בית ישראל כמו והקרבתם על הלחם שפת' עם הלחם וכן והחתנים עליו שפת' והחותנים עמו: ויבאו יחדיו מארץ צפון וגו'. לפי שאמר למעלה הנני קורא לכל משפחות צפונה חזר ואמר כאן ויבאו יחדיו מארץ צפון על הארץ וגו':

רש"י

כי כל כניסתכם תהא קדושה ואשכון בה כאלו הוא ארון: יפקדו. כמו יזכרו: ולא יעשה עוד. מה שנעשה בו כבר בשילה שהביאוהו במלחמה עם פלשתים בימי עלי (שמואל א' ד'): (יז) ונקוו. ונקבצו לשון מקוה מים: שרירות. ל' ראיה כמו אשורנו (במדבר כ"ד): (יח) ילכו בית יהודה על בית ישראל. עמם יתחברו ויתוספו

רד"ק

שתרבו ופריתם בארץ לא יקנאו בכם הגוים שיבאו להלחם בכם והצטרכו לצאת למלחמה וארון האלהים עמכם כמו שהיה מנהגם שהיו מוציאים הארון במלחמה ובימים ההם לא יצטרכו לזה כי לא יהיה להם מלחמה עוד ולזה אמר לא יאמרו ולא יעלה על לב ולא יזכרו בו ולא יפקדו ולא יעשה עוד כלומר לזה הדבר להוציאו למלחמה ותרגום ולא יעשה עוד ולא יגיחון ביה עוד קרב: (יז) בעת ההיא. אין צריך לומר שלא יבאו הגוים על ירושלים להלחם אלא יקראו אותה כסא השם ונקוו אליה כל הגוים לשם ה'. ולעבדו לא להלחם ומה שאמר לירושלם אחר שאמר אליה רוצה לומר שיאמר אחד לחברו נלך לירושלם ולא ילכו עוד אחרי שרירות לבם הרע לא ישראל ולא הגוים: שרירות לבם. חוזק לבם כדברי רז"ל שריר וקים: (יח) בימים ההמה. בקבוץ גליות: על בית ישראל. עם בית ישראל וכן ויבאו האנשים על הנשים: מארץ צפון. כמו שכתבנו כי

מצודת ציון

ענין זכרון: (יז) ונקוו. ענין אסיפה וקבוץ כמו יקוו המי' (בראשית א'): שרירות. ענין ראיה והבטה כמו אשר שורני אנשי' (איוב ל"ו): (יח) על בית ישראל. עם בית ישראל כמו ויבואו האנשים על הנשים (שמות ל"ה):

מצודת דוד

כי המקום לא יכילם: ולא יעלה על לב. לא יעלה מי בלבו ללכת שמה יחידי כי מאד יקשה לבא שמה מדוחק המון העם: ולא יזכרו בו. לא יזכור מי בלבו ללכת שמה וכפל הדבר במ"ש ולא יפקדו: ולא יעשה עוד. לא יהיה נעשה עוד ארונות לגזרות ולמען ילכו כלם לבא לפני אחד מהם ולשכר שמה למען שהשכינה בשכינה יהיה בכל ירושלים ושמה תקובל תפלת המתפללים: (יז) כסא ה'. ר"ל גם במה שהיה שהשכינה בשכינה: ונקוו אליה. כל האומות יתקבצו אליה בעבור שם ה' השורה בה ומזה אל ירושלים יתקבצו כי שמה שהיה שהשכינה בשכינה: שרירות לבם הרע. אלהות לבם שמראה להם את הרעה ושמים אותם לנשוקת: (יח) ילכו. ממקום שגלו: בית יהודה. אלו שגלו מפני יסודי ע"י סנחריב מלך אשור ולא חזרו בבית שני: על בית ישראל. עם בני עשרת השבטים: יחדו. יהודה וישראל: מארץ צפון.

nical formula שָׁרִיר וְקַיָּם, *strong and permanent*, rendering: stubbornness.—[*Redak*]

18. **In those days**—I.e. in the days of the ingathering of the exiles.—[*Redak*]

the house of Judah will go with the house of Israel—*They will join them and they will be added to them to be one kingdom.*—[*Rashi* from *Jonathan*]

will go—from the place of their exile.—[*Mezudath David*]

and they will come together from the north land—As mentioned above, the Ten Tribes were exiled to lands northeast of Babylon, whence they will return.—[*Redak*]

The apparent explanation of this verse is that the kingdom of Judah, known as the house of Judah, will join the Ten Tribes, known as the

neither shall it come to mind, neither shall they mention it, nor shall they remember it, nor shall it be done anymore. 17. At that time, they will call Jerusalem The Throne of the Lord, and all nations shall gather to it in the name of the Lord, to Jerusalem, and they shall no longer follow the idea of their evil heart. 18. In those days, the house of Judah will go with the house of Israel, and they will come togeather from the north land to the land that I caused your forefathers to inherit.

entire assembly will be holy, and I will dwell therein as though it were an ark..—[*Rashi*] Isaiah da Trani takes this as a reference to the city of Jerusalem, which will be the seat of the Shechinah, as in verse 17.

nor shall they remember it—Heb. יִפְקְדוּ, *like* יִזְכְּרוּ, *remember or mention.*—[*Rashi*]

nor shall it be done anymore—I.e. it shall not be done *what was done with it already in Shiloh, that they brought it into the battle with the Philistines in the days of Eli.*—[*Rashi*]

Redak explains the entire verse in this context. When you will multiply and be fruitful in the land, the nations will not envy you, that they should wage war against you, and you should find it necessary to go forth to war and take the Holy Ark to war with you, as it was their custom to take the Holy Ark out with them to battle. At that time, however, they will not need it since there will be no more wars. Therefore, they will neither mention it nor remember it, and this thing, i.e. to take the ark out to battle will no longer be done.—[*Redak*]

Jonathan renders: And they will no longer mention it, neither will they fear, nor will they wage war with it anymore. He, apparently, interprets יִפְקְדוּ like יִפְחֲדוּ, *they will not fear.*

Others render: Nor will it be made anymore. Since the Shechinah will rest throughout the entire city of Jerusalem, there will be no need to make other arks so that the people will be able to pray before them. Wherever they will pray in the Holy City, their prayers will be accepted. —[*Isaiah da Trani, Mezudath David*]

17. **In those days**—Not only will the nations not march on Jerusalem to wage war, but they will call it The Throne of the Lord and all nations shall assemble to it in the name of the Lord to serve Him, not to wage war.—[*Redak*]

shall gather—Heb. וְנִקְווּ, *an expression of* מִקְוֵה מַיִם, *a gathering of water.*—[*Rashi*]

to Jerusalem—The repetition of 'to Jerusalem' after 'to it' may mean that one will say to his companion, "Let us go to Jerusalem," and they will no longer follow the stubbornness of their heart.—[*Redak*]

the idea of—Heb. שְׁרִרוּת, *an expression of seeing. Comp.* אֲשׁוּרֶנּוּ, *I see him* (Num. 24:17).—[*Rashi*]

Others derive it from the Rabbi-

אֲבוֹתֵיכֶם׃ יט וְאָנֹכִי אָמַרְתִּי אֵיךְ
אֲשִׁיתֵךְ בַּבָּנִים וְאֶתֶּן־לָךְ אֶרֶץ חֶמְדָּה
נַחֲלַת צְבִי צִבְאוֹת גּוֹיִם וָאֹמַר אָבִי
תִּקְרְאוּ־לִי וּמֵאַחֲרַי לֹא תָשׁוּבוּ׃
כ אָכֵן בָּגְדָה אִשָּׁה מֵרֵעָהּ כֵּן בְּגַדְתֶּם
בִּי בֵּית יִשְׂרָאֵל נְאֻם־יְהוָה׃ כא קוֹל־עַל־

תרגום

אבהתכון: יט ואנא אמרית איכדין אצלחינך בבניא ואתן ליך ארע חמדתא אחסנת חדות תושבחת עממיא ואמרית רבוני תצלון קדמי ומבתר פולחני לא תתובון: כ בכן כמה דמשקרא אתתא בבעלה כן שקרתון במימרי בית ישראל אמר יי: כא קלא על נגדין

ת"א ואתן לך. כתובות קיב: בגדתם בי. סנהדרין ס פט:

תקראי קרי תשובי קרי

רש"י

עליהם להיות ממלכה אחת: (יט) ואנכי אמרתי. בלבי ולכן הנחלתים לאבותיכם: איך אשיתך בבנים. את עדתי ואומתי בתוך שאר בנים מעורבת בין העובדי כוכבים לפיכך בררתי מנה יפה ואתן לך ארץ חמדה: צבי צבאות גוים. נוי של כל צבאות גוים: (כ) אכן. אבל אתם לא עשיתם מהשבתי כי אם כמו אשה שבוגדת מרעה על שאינו יכול להספיק מזונותיה כן בגדתם בי המספיק לכם כל טוב כך מדרש אגדה: (כא) על שפיים נשמע. קרוב

מהר"י קרא

(יט) ואנכי אמרתי כשהנחלתיה לאבותיכם: איך אשיתך בבנים. איך אתן לך נחלה בין האומות: ואתן לך ארץ חמדה. כאדם שמפריש מנה יפה לבנו כך הפרשתי הלקכם: נחלת צבי צבאות גוים. ארץ שהיא צבי לכל הארצות ואומר בעצמי מאחר שנתתיה לכם מעתה אבי תקראי לי ומאחרי לא תשובו: (כ) אכן בגדה אשה מרעה. כאשר בגדה אשה רעה בבעלה המספיק לה כל טוב כן אתם בגדתם בי שהייתי מספיק לכם כל צרכיכם ובעון זה סופכם. שקולכם: (כא) על שפיים [נשמע. בבכי ובתחנונים על שפיים] בגליות וכל זאת לפי שהעוו את דרכם שכחו את ה׳ לכן אני אומר לכם עד שלא יבואו ימי

מנחת שי

(יט) תקראו. תקראי ק׳: תשובו. תשובי קרי:

רד"ק

השבטים בארץ צפון כלפי מזרח כהלאה לבבל: (יט) ואנכי אמרתי. זה שנאמר עד הנה אני עתיד לקיים כלם באחרית הימים אע"פ שהיו בגלות ימים רבים אבל אם תרצו לא תגלו כי אנכי אמרתי איך אשיתך בבנים כלומר במאמר שתקראו לי בנים כמו שאמר בנים אתם לה׳ אלהיכם: ואתן לך. כלומר אשאירך בהם כמו שנתתיה לך הארץ שנקראת ארץ חמדה שחומדין אותה כל הגוים: נחלת צבי. כפל הענין במ"ש כי צבי פי׳ חפץ והוא כמו חמדה שזכר שהחפצים בה צבאות הגוים וי"ת צבי צבאות גוים חדות תושבחת עממיא ואיך יהיה זה ובאי זה ענין שאתננה לך ואמר בזה הענין יהיה שאשיתך בבנים ואתן לך ארץ חמדה שתקראי לי אבי ומאחרי לא תשובי תקראו כתיב וקרי תקראי כנגד הכנסת והכתוב כנגד העם ואחד הוא אם תקראו לי אב אקרא לכם בנים כמו שאמר אשיתך בבנים תשובו כתיב לשון רבים וקרי תשובי לשון נקבה כמו שפי׳ במלת תקראו: (כ) אכן בגדה. כמו שבגדה אשה מרעה הוא בעלה כן בגדתם בי ומה שקשר זה הלשון עם ב"ם שלא כמנהג ר"ל כי בבגדה בבעלה הולכת מאתו לאיש אחר: (כא) קול על שפיים נשמע. נפעל בינוני כי הוא קמץ ופי׳

מצודת דוד

ממקום בגלי במה: על הארץ. אל הארץ: (יט) ואנכי אמרתי. מתחלה כשלקחתיך לי לעם אמרתי בלבי באיזה ענין אשימך בין הבנים ודומה להסר"ל להיות דומים למלאכי מעלה הנקראים בני אלהי׳ כמ"ש ויבואו בני האלהים (איוב א׳): ואתן לך. ולזה נתתי לך ארץ חמדה נחלה מפואר׳ לכל צבאות הגוים כי כלם מתאוקקים ומתאוי׳ לה ומפארים אותה על כיהוא מקו׳ הפראת השכינ׳ והוא מבוא גדול לירא את ה׳ להיות כמלאכי מעלה: ואמר. אמרתי בענין אם תקראו לי אבי ולא תשובו מאחרי עד עולם: (כ) אכן. באמת לא כן הוא כמו שבגד׳ אשה מאת ריעה היא בעלה והולכת מאתו כן אתם בית ישראל בגדתם בי: (כא) קול על שפיים נשמע. ר"ל ראוי היה להיו׳ נשמע קול על המקומות הגבוהים להשמיע למרחוק

מצודת ציון

(יט) אשיתך. ענין שימה: צבי. ענין הדר ופאר וכן לצבי ממלכות (ישעיה י"ג): (כ) בגדה. מרדה: מרעה. מלשון ריע וחבר:

Others explain: [19] **And I said: How shall I place you among the sons?**—When Israel was in Egyptian bondage, God said: How can I elevate you from your present state of slavery to be placed in a status of 'sons,' as the Torah says: 'You are sons to the Lord your God' (Deut. 14:1), as though you are the sons of the living God on a level with the angels? How can I give you a land desired by all the nations? I said: Only if you call Me 'my Father,' and do not turn away from following Me. I.e., only if you humble yourselves before Me and always call Me Father.

[20] **Truly, as a woman betrays her beloved**—But you did not do so; you betrayed Me as a woman betrays her beloved and goes to another man.—[*Abarbanel*]

Mezudath David explains that 'But I will give you a desirable land . . .' is the beginning of God's answer. I will give you a desirable land, a land where the Shechinah rests. In this manner, I will be able

19. And I said: How shall I place you among the sons? But I will give you a desirable land, an inheritance of the beauty of hosts of nations, and I said: Call Me 'my Father,' and do not turn away from following Me. 20. Truly, as a woman betrays her beloved, so have you betrayed Me, O house of Israel, says the Lord. 21. A voice on

house of Israel, and they will come together from the north land. This is difficult since the house of Israel, hidden away in unknown regions, will more likely join the house of Judah on their way to the land of Israel. Moreover, the house of Judah is not exiled in the north land, but all over the world. How will they come together from the north land? Abarbanel, therefore, prefers to explain that 'the house of Judah' refers to those Judeans exiled by Sennacherib from the cities of Judah prior to the exile of Judah by Nebuchadnezzar. These Judeans were exiled to Assyria and sent to the north land and did not return to Eretz Israel during the time of the Second Temple. He bases this supposition on a letter brought to him by spice merchants who traveled from Portugal to India. They reported to him that they had seen many Jews in India, and they brought him a letter from one of their sages, stating that they were the descendants of the Judahites and the Benjamites exiled by Sennacherib from the cities of Judah prior to the destruction of Jerusalem by Nebuchadnezzar, as is mentioned in *Seder Olam*. They were settled beyond the mountains of darkness and did not return with the rest of Judah during the time of the Second Temple. Abarbanel concludes that, since they were exiled to a place near the Ten Tribes, it is very likely that Jeremiah prophesies that, when the Lord will return those exiled from Zion, the Judeans in the north land will join the Ten Tribes, and both groups will return together from the north land to the land of Israel. This explanation is followed by *Mezudath David*.

19. **And I said**—*to Myself, etc. and therefore, I caused your forefathers to inherit them.*—[*Rashi*] The correct reading is probably 'to inherit it,' as in Kara's commentary.

How shall I place you among the sons?—I.e. how shall I place *you, my congregation and My nation, among the other sons, mingled with the heathens. I, therefore, selected a handsome portion, and I gave you a desirable land.*—[*Rashi*]

the beauty of hosts of nations—*The beauty of all the hosts of nations.*—[*Rashi*]

20. **Truly**—*But you did not live up to My expectations* (lit. do My thought), *but like a woman who betrays her beloved because he cannot provide her sustenance, so did you betray Me, Who provides you with all good. So is the Midrash Aggadah* (*Tanhuma Mishpatim* 17).—[*Rashi*]

שְׁפָיִים נִשְׁמָע בְּכִי תַחֲנוּנֵי בְּנֵי יִשְׂרָאֵל
כִּי הֶעֱווּ אֶת־דַּרְכָּם שָׁכְחוּ אֶת־יְהוָה
אֱלֹהֵיהֶם׃ כב שׁוּבוּ בָּנִים שׁוֹבָבִים
אֶרְפָּה מְשׁוּבֹתֵיכֶם הִנְנוּ אָתָנוּ לָךְ
כִּי אַתָּה יְהוָה אֱלֹהֵינוּ׃ כג אָכֵן לַשֶּׁקֶר
מִגְּבָעוֹת הָמוֹן הָרִים אָכֵן בַּיהוָה

תרגום

נגדין אשתמע דבכן ומתאנחין בני ישראל ארי קלקילו ית אורחתהון אתנשיאו ית פולחנא דיי אלההון׃ כב תובו בניא דמתחסנין למיתב אשבוק לכון כד תתובון הא בכל עדן אתון אמרין הבנא לפולחנך פרוקנא ארי את יי אלהנא׃ כג בכן לשקרא פלחנא על רמתא ולא להנאה

ת"א שובו בנים שובבים. יומא ח פב חגיגה ב טו סנהדרין לו עכו"ם א ז בכורות דף לא עקידה שער א כל הפרשה עד ולא תנוד: ארפה וגו׳. יומא ח פו:

מהר"י קרא

תרעה: (כב) שובו בנים שובבים. פי׳ ששבון מרדכי הקב"ה הולכין אחרי דרכי לבם שובו מדרכיכם ולכו בדרכי וארפא משוביתיכם ואברו אלי הנני אתאנו לך כי אתה ה׳ אלהינו ועיד זאת תאברו: (כג) אכן לשקר. עשינו כהכון גבעות והרים והמון הרים שעבדנו עכו"ם בם: אכן. באמת:

רש"י קמץ בז"ק כצ"ל

הוא להשמע: (כב) הננו אתנו לך. הנביא מלמדם להתוודות ולומר כן הננו אתאנו לך אכן לשקר וגו׳ והכשת אכלה וגו׳ נשכבה בבשתנו כל זה ל׳ תפלה שהנביא מלמדם לומר: אתנו. באנו: (כג) אכן לשקר. במרנו מגבעות

מנחת שי

(כב) ארפה. לית דכתיב ה"א: הננו. בקלות בני ה נו"ן ובבות הראשונה ע"פ המסורת כמ"ש ביהושע סי"ט: (כג) המון. בספרים רבים הה"א בחטף פתח ורד"ק כתב בספרים בהוא קמוץ וכן ס"א מטולטולא נכתב בלדו יפה בספר

רד"ק

שפים המקומות הגבוהים ואמר על שפים כדי שישמע קולם למרחוק בהתודותם ופי׳ הפסוק אמר היה ראוי להם שישמע קולם למרחק על שפים ויבכו ויתחננו לאל בני ישראל ויתודו לו כי הם העוו את דרכם ושכחו את ה׳ אלהיהם כי אם היו עושים זה אני הייתי מקבל אותם בתשובה ואומר להם שובו בנים שובבים ארפא משובותיכם והם יאמרו הננו אתנו לך כי אתה ה׳ אלהינו: (כב) שובו. ארפה. כתיב בה"א והוא כמו באל"ף ענין רפואה ואמר ענין רפואה על הסליחה דרך השאלה וכן רפאה נפשי כי חטאתי לך כי כמו שמכת הגוף נרפאת ברפואה שעושין לה כן מכת הנפש והוא העון רפואתה הסליחה עם התשובה: הננו. קל ובשוא הנו"ן: אתנו. נקרא בקמץ כבעלי האל"ף והיא כבעלי הה"א מן ואתא מרבבות קודש: (כג) אכן לשקר. יתודו ויאמרו לשקר עבדנו עבודת כו"ם כי לא הועילה לנו כי העכו"ם היו עובדים על ההרים ועל הגבעות לפיכך אמר מגבעות המון הרים ופי׳ מגבעות התשועה שהיינו מקוים מעבודת הגבעות לשקר היא כי אין תשועת ישראל כי אם בה׳ אלהינו והמון קמץ הה"א ואיננו סמוך להרים שאם היה סמוך היה אומר המון בשוא ובפתח הה"א כמו אב המון גוים ופירושו התשועה שהיינו מקוים מהגבעות בעבודת שהיינו עובדים עליהם לשקר היא וכן ההמון שהיינו מתקבצים בהרים לעבוד שם עכו"ם לשקר היא וההרים הם בית השמוש כמו הנמצא בית ה׳ לזונות בית אביה וזולתו והדומים להם שכתבנו בספר מכלל בחלק הדקדוק ממנו ועל הדרך הזה פירש יונתן הפסוק בכן לשקרא פלחנא על רמתא ולא להנאה אתרגישנא על טוריא ויש לפרש הפסוק בענין אחר: אכן לשקר מגבעות. אנחנו שהיינו מצפין מהגבעות עזר מהאומות וכן מההרים היינו מצפין שיבא ההמון מן הגוים לעזרתנו לשקר היה כמו שאומר בצפיתנו צפינו אל גוי לא יושיע וכן פי׳ אאז"ל ובאמרו תשועת ישראל לפי שעינו עליהם לטובה כשילכו

מצודת ציון

(כא) שפיים. מקומות גבוהים: העוו. מל׳ עוות ועקום׳: (כב) ארפה. מלשון רפואה ועם כי היא בה"א ועל הסליחה יאמר כדרך משלה וכן רפאה נפשי כי חטאתי לך (תהלים מ"א): אתנו. ענין ביאה כמו אתא בוקר (ישעי׳ כ"א): (כג) המון. ענין

מצודת דוד

והקול יהיה מבכי תחנוני בית ישראל לבכות על מעלם ולבקש עליהם סליחה כי הרבה רעות עשו העקימו את דרכם מה שבין אדם לחבירו ושכחו את ה׳ ולא עבדוהו: (כב) שובו בנים שובבים. אתם בנים מורדים שובו אלי למען ארפא ואסלח על המרידה במרדתם כי ואמרו הננו באנו אליך בתשובה כי אתה מעולם ה׳ אלהינו: (כג) אכן לשקר מגבעות. באמת לשקר קוינו עזר מהעכו"ם העומדים על הגבעות ומהמון הפסילים שעל ההרים: בה׳

ings." Then he hears another voice, replying, "Here we are; we have come to You, for You are the Lord our God." It is also possible that this is all one voice, the voice of the people, saying to God, "Have You not promised us that if we return to You that You will cure our backslidings? Therefore, here we are; we have come to You.

[23] **Truly, in vain**—Truly, we know that our multitude went up to the hills and the mountains in vain, for the idol worship on these hills and mountains is to no avail, for only in the Lord is Israel's salvation.

the rivulets is heard, the weeping of the supplications of the children of Israel, for they perverted their way, they forgot the Lord their God. 22. Return, backsliding children, I will cure your backslidings. "Here we are; we have come to You, for You are the Lord our God. 23. Truly, in vain [we awaited help] from the hills, the multitude of mountains, but in the Lord

to elevate you to the status of 'sons.' Additionally, I said: Call Me 'my Father.

21. **A voice on the rivulets is heard**—*It is likely to be heard.*—[*Rashi*]

Rashi, as *Jonathan,* renders שְׁפָיִים as rivulets. See above v. 2. *Redak,* as above, renders: high places. It is proper that a voice be heard on the high places, where it can be heard in the distance, that the children of Israel are weeping in supplication to God and confessing their sin, that they perverted their way and forgot the Lord their God. Were they to do so, I would accept their repentance and say to them, "Return, backsliding children, I will cure your backslidings. And they would say, "Here we are, we have come to You, for You are the Lord our God."

22. **I will cure**—Just as a physical wound is cured with the proper medications, so is a spiritual ailment, namely sin, cured by forgiveness with repentance.—[*Redak*]

Here we are, we have come to You—*The prophet teaches them to confess and to say as follows, "Here we are, we have come to You . . . Truly, in vain . . . But the shameful thing has consumed etc., Let us lie in our shame. All this is the language of the prayer that the prophet teaches them to say.*—[*Rashi*]

We have come—Heb. אָתָנוּ.—[*Rashi*]

This is the poetic form, derived from the Aramaic, found only in poetry and in the prophetic books.

23. **Truly, in vain**—*we awaited from the hills and the multitude of mountains where we worshipped idols.*—[*Rashi*]

Redak explains: The salvation we expected from the hills, i.e. from worshipping pagan deities on the hills was vain, as was the multitude that gathered on the mountains. Alternatively, the hills and the mountains represent the nations whose help they had expected.

[21] **A voice is heard upon the high hills**—I.e. the voice of the Israelites exiled in the north land.

for they perverted their way—I.e. they were delinquent in their dealings with their fellowmen.

they forgot the Lord their God—They were delinquent in their observance of the commandments between man and God.

[22] **Return, backsliding children**—It is as though he hears a second voice, that of the Almighty, replying to them. This represents Divine inspiration arousing them to repent and saying to them, "Despair not of mercy. Return, rebellious children; there is still a cure for your backsliding, and I will cure your backslid-

אֱלֹהֵינוּ תְּשׁוּעַת יִשְׂרָאֵל: כד וְהַבֹּשֶׁת
אָכְלָה אֶת־יְגִיעַ אֲבוֹתֵינוּ מִנְּעוּרֵינוּ אֶת־
צֹאנָם וְאֶת־בְּקָרָם אֶת־בְּנֵיהֶם וְאֶת־
בְּנוֹתֵיהֶם: כה נִשְׁכְּבָה בְּבָשְׁתֵּנוּ
וּתְכַסֵּנוּ כְּלִמָּתֵנוּ כִּי לַיהוָה אֱלֹהֵינוּ
חָטָאנוּ אֲנַחְנוּ וַאֲבוֹתֵינוּ מִנְּעוּרֵינוּ וְעַד־
הַיּוֹם הַזֶּה וְלֹא שָׁמַעְנוּ בְּקוֹל יְהוָה
אֱלֹהֵינוּ: ד א אִם־תָּשׁוּב יִשְׂרָאֵל | נְאֻם־

תרגום

אִתְרְגֵישְׁנָא עַל טוּרַיָא
בְּרַם בְּמֵימְרָא דַיְיָ
אֱלָהָנָא פּוּרְקַן יִשְׂרָאֵל:
כד וּבְהֲתַת חוֹבִין אֲכִיפַת
יַת לֵיאוּת אֲבָהָתָנָא
מִזְּעוּרָנָא יַת עָנְהוֹן וְיַת
תּוֹרֵיהוֹן וְיַת בְּנֵיהוֹן וְיַת
בְּנָתֵיהוֹן: כה נִשְׁכּוּב
בִּבְהֲתַת חוֹבָנָא
יְתַחֲפִינָנָא אִתְכְּנָעוּתָנָא
אֲרֵי קֳדָם יְיָ אֱלָהָנָא
חַבְנָא אֲנַחְנָא וַאֲבָהָתָנָא
מִזְּעוּרָנָא וְעַד יוֹמָא הָדֵין
וְלָא קַבֵּילְנָא לְמֵימְרָא
דַיְיָ אֱלָהָנָא: א אִם תְּתוּב
יִשְׂרָאֵל לְפוּלְחָנִי אֲמַר

רש"י

(כד) והבושת. עכו"ם שעסקו בה כד"א ויגזרו לבשת (הושע ט'): אכלה את יגיע אבותינו. בעון עבודתה היה יגיעם לבז:

ד (א) אם תשוב ישראל. בתשובה זו אלי תשוב לכבודך וגדולתך הראשונ': ואם תסיר שקוציך מפני.

מהר"י קרא

שעבדנו לבעלים שם ועל חנם בטחנו אלא בה' אלהינו שהוא תשועת ישראל: (כד) והבשת אכלה את יגיע אבותינו. כל הדברים הללו קחו עמכם להתוודות בהן: והבשת. היא ע"ז כאמור וינזרו לבושת: (כה) נשכבה בבשתינו. פת' באותו רשע שבו עמדנו מנעורינו בו אנו עומדין היום כמו שמפרש והולך: כי לה' אלהינו חטאנו אנחנו וגו'. וגם המקרא זה מן תוידוי והקב"ה עתיד להשיבן כשיתוודו על עוונם ועל עון אבותם:

ד (א) אם תשוב וגו'. אלו שבתם אלי בעוד שהייתם בשלוה בארצכם כשם שאתם שבין אלי עכשיו והייתם מעבירים שיקוצים מפני

רד"ק

בדרכיו ישמרם תמיד ולא כן שאר האומות: (כד) והבשת. ויתודו ג"כ ויאמרו כי הבשת והיא העכו"ם אכלה את יגיע אבותינו מנעורינו הבעל שהיו עובדים נקרא בשת כמו וינזרו לבשת שהוא כמו לבעל וכן נקרא ירובשת ירובעל כי הבעל בשת וכלמה למי שיתעסק בו והיגיע היא תבואת השדה כי בעונש זה העון היה בתבואתן השדפון או ירקון או ארבה או אויב וכן אכלה את צאנם ואת בקרם ואת בניהם ואת בנותיהם שהיו מתים בדבר בעונש עון עכו"ם הנה שאנחנו יודעים כי הבשת והיא עכו"ם אכלה הכל וי"ת ובהתת חובין אסיפת ית לאות אבהתנא ובאמרו אבותינו ואמר מנעורינו ר"ל כי אנחנו ראינו מנעורינו כי יגיע אבותינו נאכל בעונינו: (כה) נשכבה בבשתינו. אנחנו ג"כ כמו אבותינו שהיו כלים בבשתם כן אנחנו אחריהם אחזנו דרכיהם ונשכבה בבשתינו ובאמרו נשכבה לפי שהאדם שהוא בצרה גדולה לא ידע מה לעשות יפיל עצמו בשינה ושוכב וכן על הדרך הזה אם תשכבון בין שפתים והיית כשוכב בלב ים וכשוכב בראש חבל וכ"א ותכסנו כלימתינו על דרך ובשת פני כסתני: מנעורינו. פי' מנעורינו עשינו הרע כמו שראינו לאבותינו: (א) אם תשוב. אם תתודו בדברים הנאמרים ותשובו אלי אני אקבל אתכם בתשובה ותנוחו ולא תגלו מארצכם תשב השני ענין מנוחה כמו בשובה ונחת תושעון וכפל הענין במלות שונות ואמר אם תסיר שקוציך מפני ולא תנוד כלומר לא תנודו מארצכם וי"ו ולא כוי"ו וישא

מנחת שי

מוגה בקמץ: (כה) ותכסנו. בס"ס סוא"ו נמארין וכ"כ כלמתי:

מצודת דוד

בעזר ה' כא תשועת ישראל: (כד) והבשת. העכו"ם שהיא לבושת ולכלימה לעובדיה עון עבודתה כלה והפסיד את אשר אספו אבותינו ביגיעה ועמל: מנעורינו. ר"ל הכליון והפסד שהיה מעת נעורינו היה בעון הזה: את צאנם. עכשיו מפ' לנו את זה הפסדנו מה שאספו הם את לאל וגו': (כה) נשכבה. ר"ל הנה הבוש' מסבבת אותנו, מסביב כאלו נשכב על מלבוש הבושת וכאלו הכלימ' מכסה אותנו ממעל והוא ענין מליצה: כי לה' וגו'. ואין בושת גדול מזה: מנעורינו. ר"ל מעת שלקח אותנו לעם: ולא שמענו וגו'. כפל הדבר במ"ש:

ד (א) אם תשוב. מוסב למעלה נו' אם אתה ישראל תשוב בוידוי ופיוסים כאלה אז תחזור והשוב אלי להיות לפני כמאז סגולה

מצודת ציון

רכוי: (כד) אכלה. מל' כליון:

voice of the supplications of the children of Israel. He depicts Israel as a lost sheep, and God as a Shepherd standing on the lofty mountains, calling to the sheep in the valley, that she recognize his voice and return to him. The sheep cries because she does not recognize the shepherd's voice and she is lost. The prophet accounts for the presence of these two voices. He first accounts for the voice of Israel, the sheep.

1. **If you return, O Israel**—*with this repentance, to Me, you will return to your original glory and greatness.*—[*Rashi*]

Redak renders: you shall be granted tranquility. He explains the entire passage as follows: If you confess in accordance with the confession stat-

our God is Israel's salvation. 24. But the shameful thing has
consumed the toil of our fathers since our youth, their flocks
and their cattle, their sons and their daughters. 25. We lie in
our shame, and our disgrace covers us, for we have sinned
against the Lord our God—we and our fathers—since our
youth until this day, but we did not hearken to the voice of the
Lord our God."

4

1. If you return, O Israel, says

Israel's salvation—Israel's salvation is only from the Lord our God, Who looks upon them favorably when they go in His ways, and He will watch them constantly, not so the other nations.—[*Redak*]

Abarbanel pictures the prophet hearing two voices, the voice of Israel crying to God from the northland and the voice of God replying to them.

24. **But the shameful thing**—*The idolatry with which we occupied ourselves, as Scripture states: 'And they turned aside to the shameful thing'* (Hosea 9:10).—[*Rashi*]

This expression is a pejorative for 'Baal,' for Baal worship is indeed a shameful thing for those who engage in it. In several other places also, 'bosheth' is substituted for 'Baal.'—[*Redak*]

consumed the toil of our fathers—*Because of the iniquity of its worship, our toil was pillaged.*—[*Rashi*]

They will confess that because they worshipped Baal, God punished them that their toil was in vain. The produce of the fields was destroyed by blast, yellowing, locusts, or attacks by the enemy. Their flocks and their cattle, their sons and their daughters, died from pestilence, all because they worshipped Baal. They will confess that they acknowledge that all this befell them as a punishment for worshipping Baal. They confess that since their youth they witnessed their fathers' possessions being destroyed because of their sins.—[*Redak*]

25. **We lie in our shame**—Just as our fathers were destroyed because of their worship of the shameful thing, so do we follow their ways after them. He uses the expression, 'we lie in our shame' as an illustration of a person plagued by a catastrophe from which he cannot extricate himself, and as an escape, he lies down in bed and falls asleep.—[*Redak*]

since our youth—In our youth we worshipped Baal as we saw our fathers do.—[*Redak*]

Malbim paints a pathetic picture of Israel in exile. He pictures the prophet hearing two voices, one voice on the high places, resounding through the mountains, and one

יְהֹוָה אֵלַי תָּשׁוּב וְאִם־תָּסִיר שִׁקּוּצֶיךָ
מִפָּנַי וְלֹא תָנוּד: ב וְנִשְׁבַּעְתָּ חַי־יְהֹוָה
בֶּאֱמֶת בְּמִשְׁפָּט וּבִצְדָקָה וְהִתְבָּרְכוּ
בוֹ גּוֹיִם וּבוֹ יִתְהַלָּלוּ: ג כִּי־כֹה | אָמַר
יְהֹוָה לְאִישׁ יְהוּדָה וְלִירוּשָׁלִַם נִירוּ
לכם

תרגום

יי תתקבל תיובתך עד
לא תתחתם גזירתך
ואם תעדי שקוצך מן
קדמי לא תטלטל:
ב אם תקים בשמי קים
הוא יי בקושטא בדינא
ובזכותא ויתברכון
עממיא בישראל וביה
ישתבחון: ג ארי כדנן
אמר יי לאנש יהודה
וליתבי

ת"א נירו לכם ניר. פסחים י קי: הגרי"ב סנהדרין נח:

מהר"י קרא

לא הייתם צריכים לניד ממקומכם וכן אם הייתם נשבעין חי ה' באמת ובמשפט ובצדקה אז היו מתברכין בו גוים ובו יתהללו: (ג) נירו לכם ניר ואל תזרעו אל קוצים. חרשו חרישת השדה קודם שתזרעוהו ואל תזרעוהו אם לא חרשתם קודם לכן שכל הזורע שדהו קודם שנתרש לשוא מצפיהו לקוצרו שאינו זורע כי אם אל קוצים שהקוצים רבים על זריעת התבואה ומאבדין את הזריעה אבל אם אתה מבקש שתבא זריעתך לידי קמה הוי חורש שדך עד שלא תזריעינו כדי לכלות קוצים ודרדרין שצמחו בו ואחר כך זורע ואז תעלה זריעתך שתתן ארצך את יבולה כך אל תתפלל כל זמן שאתה מלוכלך בעבירות שכל המרבה בתפילה עד שלא ישוב כדרכו הרעה תחילה למה תפילתו דומה לזורע אל קוצים שכשם שזה מאבד את זריעתו כך זה שתופס מעשים רעים ומאריך בתפילתו לשוא הוא מתפלל אלא אם רצונכם שתהיו תפילתכם נשמעת המולו לה' והסירו ערלת

רש"י

אז לא תנוד ללאת בגולה: (ב) ונשבעת חי ה' באמת. כשתשבע בשמי תשבע באמת ולא כאשר עתה שכתוב בכם (לקמן ה) אם חי ה' יאמרו אכן לשקר ישבעו: והתברכו בו גוים. אם תעשי כן אז יתברכו בישראל הגוים כל גוי יאמר לבנו תהא כפלוני ישראל: יתהללו. יגידו שבחכם ד"א יתהללו מי שיוכל להדבק בישראל יתפאר בדבר (פורוונטי"ר בלע"ז): (ג) כי כה אמר ה' וגו' נירו לכם ניר. הוו למידין מעובדי אדמה שנרים אותו בימי הקיץ להמית שרשי העשבים שלא תהא

רד"ק

אברהם את עיניו באמרו מפני רוצה לומר בכל מקום שהם בארצכם השקוצים והגלולים כי בכ"מ שהם הם לפני ויותר בארצכם שהוא מקום קבול רוח עליוני ויותר בית המקדש ששמו שם השקוצים וי"ת תשוב תשני קבול התשובה אמר אם התוב ישראל לפולחני אמר ה' תתקבל תיובתך עד דלא תתחתם גזרתך: (ב) ונשבעת. לא כמו שאתם נשבעים עתה שאתם נשבעים בשם ה' לשקר כמו שאמר ואם חי ה' יאמרו אכן לשקר ישבעו ומה שאמר באמת במשפט ובצדקה פי' אאז"ל באמת כשתדע שהוא באמת במשפט כשתתחייב מן הדין בשבועה ובצדקה שאם תכיר שהמשפט אינו בצדקה לא תקבל השבועה וי"ת ונשבעת ואם נשבעת ואם תקיים בשמי קים הוא ה' בקושטא ובדינא ובזכותא רוצה לומר אם תצטרך להשבע השבע באמת ויתכן פי' ונשבעת כמו ובשמו תשבע כי השבועה בשם ה' הוא כבוד והדר למי שיראנו ויעבדנו בלב שלם השבועה בדבר שיזדמן לו להשבע הוא מצוה הרי הוא כמו שמהללו ומגדלו כשנשבע בשמו כמו שדרך העולם להשבע במה שיאהב יותר כמו נפשו וראשו וכן הנביאים היו נשבעים תמיד בדבריהם ולא כל אדם ראוי להשבע אפי' באמת אלא יראי השם ואוהביו לפיכך אמר באמת במשפט ובצדקה וכן אמר בתורה את ה' אלהיך תירא ואותו תעבוד ובו תדבק ובשמו תשבע ופירשו רבותינו זכרם לברכה כשיהיו בך כל המדות האלה ראוי לך להשבע בשמו ואם לאו אי אתה רשאי להשבע בשמו: והתברכו בו גוים ובו יתהללו. כי עוד יבא זמן שאפילו שאר הגוים יתברכו בו ויתהללו בו ולא באלילים ויתכן לפרש כנוי בו שם לישראל כלומר אם תעשה כל זה יתברכו הגוים בך כמו שכתוב והתברכו בזרעך כל גויי הארץ וכה שאמר ונשבעת לנכח ואמר בו שלא לנכח כן דרך המקרא במקומות רבים: (ג) כי כה אמר ה' נירו לכם ניר. נירו כמו הנירו כמו שימו השימו כי ה"א הבנין נופלת להקל והניר הוא חרישת השדה קודם הזריעה ובחרישה ההיא יעקרו הקוצים והעשבים הרעים מן השדה ויהיה ראוי לזריעה אחר כן והמשל הוא שישיבו את לבם להבין דברי השם ולקבלם בלב נכון והיא כחורש האדמה לקבל הזרע לא שיאמרו בפה נשמע את דבר השם ולבם לא נכון עמו כמו שאמר למעלה לא שבה אלי בכל

מצודת ציון

ד (א) שקוציך. ענין תעוב כמו שקץ תשקצנו (דברי' ז'): ולא. הוי"ו היא במקו' אז וכן אם בחקותי תלכו ונתתי גשמיכ' בעתם (ויקרא כ"ו): תנוד. מל' נדוד ונעה: (ב) יתהללו. מל' הלול ושבח: (ג) נירו. ענין חריש' כמו רב אוכל ניר ראשים

מצודת דוד

מכל העמים: ואם תסיר. אם תעבי' הפסילים מארצי ומירושלים סירי אז לא תנוד ללכת בגולה: (ב) ונשבעת וגו'. ואם תשבע חי ה' באמת לא כמו שאתם נשבעים עתה לשקר כמ"ש ואם חי ה' יאמרו לכן לשקר ישבעו (לקמן ה'): במשפט ובצדקה. הענין כפול במ"ש: והתברכו. אז יתגדל מאד עד שעכו"ם יתברכו בו לאמר בברכתם ישימך אלהים כישראל: ובו יתהללו. המהלל עצמו יאמר הנה אני מהוללת כישראל: (ג) לאיש יהודה. כמו לאנשי יסודם: נירו לכם ניר. מתחלה חרשו השדה לחתוך שרשי הקוצים ואח"ז זרעו על שדה נקיה ולא תזרעו על הקוצים בעודם מחוברים

boast—Heb. יִתְהַלָּלוּ, *they will recite your praise. Another explanation of* יִתְהַלָּלוּ *is: Whoever is able to cleave to Israel will boast about the matter* (*porvanter in French*).—[*Rashi*]

3. **For so said the Lord etc. Plow for yourself a furrow**—*Learn from the tillers of the soil, who plow it in the summer to kill the roots of the grasses, that it should not grow thorns*

wise, you may not swear in My name.—[*Redak*] The Midrash cites Abraham, Joseph, and Job as examples.

nations will bless themselves with him—*If you do so, then nations will bless themselves with Israel. Every non-Jew will say to his son, "You shall be like So-and-so the Jew."*—[*Rashi.*]

the Lord, to Me, you shall return, and if you remove your detestable things from My Presence, you shall not wander.
2. And you will swear, "As the Lord lives," in truth and in justice and in righteousness, nations will bless themselves with him and boast about him.
3. For so said the Lord to the people of Judah and to Jerusalem: Plow

ed above, and you return to Me, I will accept your repentance and you will be granted rest and traquility.

and if you remove your detestable things from My Presence—*Then you shall not wander to go out in exile.*—[*Rashi*]

detestable things—Your idols, things fit to be detested, as in Deut. 7:26.—[*Mezudoth*]

from My Presence—I.e., from wherever they are in your land, for, wherever they are in the world, they are in My Presence, especially in the Holy Land, the land that receives the Divine Spirit [of prophecy], and still more, in the Temple, where they placed the idols.—[*Redak*]

Jonathan renders: If you return, O Israel, to My worship, says the Lord, your repentance will be accepted before your verdict is sealed . . . He apparently renders the second תָּשׁוּב: your repentance will be accepted.—[*Redak*]

2. **And you will swear, "As the Lord lives," in truth**—*When you swear by My name, you will swear in truth, not as now, that it is written concerning you, "And if they say, 'As the Lord lives,' surely they swear falsely"* (5:2).—[*Rashi*] *Redak* and *Mezudath David* also point out this contrast.

in truth—I.e., when you know that the matter is true.

in justice—When you are called upon to swear by the court.

in righteousness—If you know that justice is being perverted, refrain from swearing.—[*Redak* quoting his father]

Jonathan renders: If you swear by My name, meaning: If you find it necessary to swear, you shall swear in truth. It is also possible that we should render: "And you shall swear by My name." This is similar to "And you shall swear by His name" (Deut. 10:20), which means that it is honor and glory to the Lord if one who fears Him and serves Him wholeheartedly swears in His name when the occasion arises to swear. In that case, it is a positive commandment to swear in God's name. It is as though he praises Him and exalts Him when he swears in His name, just as the masses swear by something they love deeply, such as the soul or the head. The prophets, too, were wont to swear by God's name as we find in their Books. Not everyone should adopt this practice, however, only those who fear God and love Him, as the Torah states: "(ibid.) You shall fear the Lord, you shall serve Him, and you shall cleave to Him and swear in His name." The Rabbis comment (*Tanhuma, Mattoth* 1): If you possess all these traits, you shall swear in My name. Other-

לכם ניר ואל־תזרעו אל־קצים׃
ד המלו ליהוה והסרו ערלות לבבכם
איש יהודה וישבי ירושלם פן־תצא
כאש חמתי ובערה ואין מכבה מפני
רע מעלליכם׃ ה הגידו ביהודה
ובירושלם השמיעו ואמרו ותקעו
שופר בארץ קראו מלאו ואמרו
האספו ונבואה אל־ערי המבצר׃
ו שאו נס ציונה העיזו אל־תעמדו כי

ולְיָתְבֵי יְרוּשְׁלֵם עֲבִידוּ
לְכוֹן עוֹבְדִין טָבִין וְלָא
תִבְעוֹן פּוּרְקַן בְּחוֹבִין׃
ד תּוּבוּ לְפוּלְחָנָא דַיְיָ
וְאַעְדוּ רְשַׁע לִבְּכוֹן אֱנָשׁ
יְהוּדָה וְיָתְבֵי יְרוּשְׁלֵם
דִלְמָא יִדְלַק כְּאֶשָּׁתָא
רוּגְזִי וִישֵׁיצֵי וְלָא יְהֵי
חַיִּם מִן קֳדָם בִּישׁוּת
עוֹבָדֵיכוֹן׃ ה חַוּוֹ
בִּיהוּדָה וּבִירוּשְׁלֵם
בַּסְּרוּ וְאִמְרוּ תְּקַעוּ
שׁוֹפְרָא בְּאַרְעָא אַכְלִיזוּ
אִסְנוּ וְאִמְרוּ אִתְכַּנְּשׁוּ
וְנֵיעוֹל לְקִרְוִין כְּרִיכָן׃
ו זְקוּפוּ אָתָא עַל צִיּוֹן
גְּלוֹ לָא תִתְעַכְּבוּן אֲרֵי

הגרי"ב ובערה וגו'. לקמן כא יב:

תקעו קרי חמ' בפתח

רש"י

מעלה קוצים בעת הזרע בחורף אף אתם היטיבו מעשיכם בטרם תבא עליכם הרעה שלא תהא תפלתכם נמאסת כשתצעקו: ואל תזרעו אל קוצים. ואל תהי צעקתכם לפני מתוך הרשע כי אם מתוך תשובה שלא תהיו דומים לזורע בלא ניר והיא נהפכת לקוצים (קרדו"ש בלע"ז): (ד) המולו לה'. בטרם תצא חמתי כאש זהו כניר לפני הזרע: (ה) ואמרו תקעו שופר. הזהירו את יושבי הארץ שיתקעו בשופר לברוח: מלאו. ל' אסיפה והרבה יש במקרא אשר יקרא עליו. מלא רועים (ישעיה ל"א) יקראו אחריך מלא (לקמן י"ב) יחד עלי יתמלאון (איוב ט"ז): (ו) שאו נס. לברוח לציון: העיזו. האספו כמו שלח

מהר"י קרא

לבבכם: (ה) והגידו ביהודה ובירושלים. אתם נביאי ישראל פורענות העתידה לבוא עליהם: קראו מלאו. קראו בפה מלא: (ו) שאו נס ציונה. אתם נביאי ישראל הניפו יד כזה שכניף

רד"ק

לבת כי אם בשקר זהו כזורע אל הקוצים שלא יצמח וי"ת עבידו לכון עובדין טבין ולא תבעון פורקן בחובין: אל קוצים. כמו על קוצים. כמו ויך הפלשתי אל מצחו כמו על מצחו והדומים לו: (ד) המלו לה'. זאת היא מילת הלב ופירושו לפניו והסירו ערלת לבבכם: (ה) הגידו. אומר לשומעים נבואתו שיגידו איש לחברו שמלך בבל עתיד לבא עליהם מפני רוע מעלליהם השמיעו ע"י כרוז ולהשמיע יותר יתקעו בשופר: קראו מלאו. צווי מהדגוש והיה ראוי להדגש ופירושו אספו כמו מלא רעים קראו אחריך מלא שפירושו ענין אסיפה וכל זה כדי שיאספו אל ערי המבצר ועוד ישאו נס במגדל ציון כדי שיראוהו מרחוק וינוסו ויאספו אל ערי המבצר או לירושלם ואע"פ שכלם עתידים להכבש ערי המבצר וירושלם אמר להם זה להצלת זמן מועט או אמר להם זה לפי מחשבתם שינצלו: (ו) שאו נס ציונה. אל ציון כלומר במגדל ציון כי הוא מקום גבוה ויראו' למרחוק: העיזו. כמו שלח העז את מקנך

מנחת שי

ד (ה) ותקעו. תקעו קרי: מלאו. צווי מהדגוש והוא קל הלמ"ד והיה ראוי להדגש. רד"ק בפירוש ובשרשים ורבי יונה בספר הרקמה ועיין מ"ש

מצודת דוד

באמת כי לא תלאה הזריע' ור"ל מתחילה הסירו הפסילים ואח"ז יקובל תפלתכם לפני ולא כשעדיין לא עזבתם הפסילים: (ד) המולו לה'. ולתוספות ביאור אמר הסירו אוטם לבבכם לשם ה' להתבונן בדרכיו ולדבקה בו: איש יהודה. אתם אנשי יהודה ויושבי ירושלים: פן תצא וגו'. פן תצא חמתי כאש הדולק ובערה בכם ואין מי יכבה אותה ר"ל לא ימלא מי ממעכב' החימה מפני רוע מעלליכם אשר גברו ואין במי זכות להעביר החימה: (ה) הגידו. כאלו לשרי העם יאמר הגידו ביהוד' וגו': תקעו שופר. להשמיע ולזרז: קראו מלאו. קראו את העם ואספו אותם ואמרו להם האספו וגו' להכנס שם מפני האויב: (ו) שאו נס. הרימו נס לרמז להתאסף לציון להכנס בה: מביא. על הארץ הזה: מצפון. זהו בבל:

מצודת ציון

(משלי י"ג): אל קוצים. על קוצים: (ד) המלו. ענין חתוך וכריתה וכן ומל ה' אלהיך (דברי' ל'): ערלות. ענין אוטם וכן ערלי לב (יחז' מ'): מעלליכם. מעשיכם: (ה) מלאו. ענין אסיפ' כמו קראו אחריך מלא (לקמן י"ב): (ו) נס. כלונס ארוך וכראשו דגל

looking at the light. He likens this to a cover that envelops their heart, making it insensitive and not allowing it to respond to any inspiration to do good. He, therefore, exhorts them to circumcise themselves and to remove the foreskins of their heart until the heart becomes sensitive and will respond to God's word and His commandments.

*5. **Tell in Judah**—He says to those who hear his prophecy that each one tell His friend that the king of Babylon is destined to attack them because of the evil of their deeds.—[*Redak*]

6. **Raise a standard**—*to flee to Zion.*—[*Rashi*]

Others explain: Raise up a standard in the tower of Zion where it

* For Rashi's commentary turn to page 219.

for yourself a furrow, and do not sow upon thorns. 4. Circum-
cise yourselves to the Lord and remove the foreskins of your
heart, O people of Judah and dwellers of Jerusalem, lest My
anger go forth and burn with none to quench it because of the
evil of your deeds. 5. Tell in Judah and in Jerusalem; let it be
heard and say, "Sound a shofar in the land"; cry out, assem-
ble, and say, "Gather, and let us come into the fortified cities."
6. Raise a standard to Zion, assemble, do not stand, for

at the time of sowing in the winter. You, too, improve your deeds before the evil befalls you, so that your prayer should not be rejected when you cry out.—[*Rashi*]

Redak explains: Improve your heart to understand the word of God and to accept them with a proper heart. In this way, you will be like one plowing the ground to accept the seed. They should not say with their mouth that they will hearken to God's word when in their heart they are insincere, as the prophet states above (3:10): "Your treacherous sister Judah did not return to Me with all her heart, but with falsity." This is like sowing upon the thorns, which will not grow.—[*Redak*]

and do not sow upon thorns—*And let not your cry before Me be from amidst wickedness, but from amidst repentance, that you shall not resemble one sowing without plowing, and that turns into thorns* (*kardons in O.F.*, chardons in modern French).—[*Rashi*]

Jonathan renders: Do good deeds for yourselves and you will not beg for redemption with sins.—[*Redak*]

4. **Circumcise yourselves to the Lord**—*Before My anger comes forth like fire. This is like plowing before the sowing.*—[*Rashi*]

This is the circumcising of the heart, as he explains further: and remove the foreskins of the heart.—[*Redak*]

The intention is to remove the clogging of the heart for the sake of God, to think of His ways and to cleave to Him.—[*Mezudath David*]

Malbim explains these two verses as God's reply to the people who claim that they do not recognize God's voice, whether it is the message of those prophesying in God's name or the message of those prophesying in the name of Baal. To this, He replies that they must plow deeply in their heart to uproot all evil traits and all the impressions and imaginations with which they were inculcated. Then they will recognize God's word. If they do not uproot their former impressions, the 'thorns' will again spring up amidst the 'grain' and choke it.

Secondly, He wishes to reply to their excuse that they have become so attached to Baal that they no longer have any hope of repenting. This was caused by the foolishness that is like a cloud covering the light of their souls until they despair of

רָעָה אָנֹכִי מֵבִיא מִצָּפוֹן וְשֶׁבֶר גָּדוֹל:
ז עָלָה אַרְיֵה מִסֻּבְּכוֹ וּמַשְׁחִית גּוֹיִם נָסַע
יָצָא מִמְּקֹמוֹ לָשׂוּם אַרְצֵךְ לְשַׁמָּה עָרַיִךְ
תִּצֶּינָה מֵאֵין יוֹשֵׁב: ח עַל־זֹאת חִגְרוּ
שַׂקִּים סִפְדוּ וְהֵילִילוּ כִּי לֹא־שָׁב חֲרוֹן
אַף־יְהוָה מִמֶּנּוּ: ט וְהָיָה בַיּוֹם־הַהוּא
נְאֻם־יְהוָה יֹאבַד לֵב־הַמֶּלֶךְ וְלֵב

ת״א עלה אריה. ברכות ס נו מגילה א יא סנהדרין לב:

תרגום

בִישְׁתָא אֲנָא מַיְתֵי מִצִפּוּנָא וְתַבְרָא רַבָּא: ז גְלָא מַלְכָּא מִקַּרְבֵיהּ וּמְחַבַּל עַמְמַיָא נְטַל מִמַשְׁרְיָתֵהּ נְפַק מֵאַתְרֵיהּ לְשַׁוָאָה אַרְעִיךְ לְצָדוּ קִרְוַיִךְ יִצְדְיָן מִבְּלִי יָתֵיב: ח עַל דָא יִיסְרוּן סַקִּין יִסְפְּדוּן וִיַילְלוּן אֲרֵי לָא תָב תְּקוֹף רוּגְזָא דַיְיָ מִנָנָא: ט וִיהֵי בְּעִידָנָא הַהִיא אֲמַר יְיָ יִתְּבַר לִבָּא דְמַלְכָּא וְלִבָּא דְרַבְרְבַיָא וְיִצְדוּן כַּהֲנַיָא

רש״י

העו (שמות ט׳): (ז) עלה אריה. נבוכדנצר: מסבכו. דרך אריה לישב במארב סבכי היער (אשפיי״ש בלע״ז): תצינה. לשון ליה: (ח) על זאת. מה הוא זאת כי לא שב וגו׳ ואע״פ שדבר למעלה בנבוכדנצר על החורבן כאן חזר לדבר במיתת יאשיהו: כי לא שב חרון אף וגו׳. ואע״פ ששב יאשיהו בכל לבו נאמר בו (מלכים ב׳ כג) לא שב ה׳ מחרון אפו על כל הכעסים אשר הכעיסו מנשה: (ט) והיה ביום ההוא. ביומו של יאשיהו יתמהו למה עלתה בו כל כך והם אין יודעין שאין דורו חוזר יפה כשבא

מהר״י קרא

ידו בכלונס וכרמז לבני אדם שיבואו כך אתם הניפו יד והרימו קול לכל משפחות ממלכות צפונה שיבא ציתח ואמרו לכל יושבי ערי פרזות שבארץ יהודה: העיזו ואל תעמודו. כלומר הקבצו אל ערי המבצר מפני חיל הכשדים: העיזו. לשון קיבוץ כמו שלח העז: עלה אריה מסובכו. אריה זה נבוכדנצר שמלך על כל העולם כאריה זה שמולך על כל החיות: מסובכו. כסבכי היער שלו: (ח) על זאת חגרו שקים. כי לא שב חרון אף ה׳ ממנו. שמא תאמר אם עלה אריה מסובכו מה בכך ה׳ יצילנו כמו שהציל חזקיה מיד סנחריב שבא לירושלים ובא הנביא ואמר וגנותי על העיר הזאת שם פחדו פחד לא היה פחד כי אלהים בדור צדיק אבל על זאת חגרו שקים וספדו והילילו כי לא שב חרון אף ה׳ ממנו וכן הוא אומר אך לא שב ה׳ מחרון אפו הגדול אשר חרה אפו ביהודה וגו׳: (ט) והיה ביום ההוא. יאבד לב המלך והשרים. הה״ד ותבקע העיר וכל אנשי המלחמה הדרך שער בין החומותים אשר על גן המלך וכשדים על העיר סביב

רד״ק

ענין המנוסה והאסיפה אל העיר: מצפון. מבבל שהוא צפון לארץ ישראל: (ז) עלה אריה מסבכו. זהו מלך בבל והמשילהו לאריה שאין עומד לפניו כן נבוכדנצר כבש כל הארצות ולא עמד איש בפניו ופי׳ המשל לפניו ומשחית גוים. מסבכו. היא סכתו שהוא שוכב בה תמיד ולפי שנעשית מסבכי עצים נקראת כן: תצינה. תחרבנה כמו גלים נצים וכן ת״י קרוין צדין ואאו״ל פי׳ תצמחנה מענין הנצו הרמונים ויהיה לפי זה הפתרון שנים שרשים וענין אחד והערים התרבות יצמיחו דשאים ועשבים: (ח) על זאת. כי לא שב חרון אף ה׳ ממנו. כי לא שבנו אליו וחרון אפו לא שב ממנו אלא עתיד לבא עלינו: (ט) והיה ביום ההוא וגו׳ יאבד לב המלך ולב השרים. כי דרך המלך והשרים לחזק לב העם בבא עליהם אויב והם יאבד לבם ויהיו נבהלים בבא עליהם השבר הגדול והמלך הוא צדקיהו. הכהנים הם כהני הבמות ואז יהיו נשמים כי בטלה עבודתם והנביאים נביאי השקר יתמהו כי שקר נבאו לעם שהיו אומרים להם שלום יהיה לכם וכת״י יתמהו ישתעממון

מנחת שי

ביחזקאל ט׳: (ז) מסבכו. הבי״ת דגושה וכתב המכלול במשקל פעל שהנפרד ממנו סבך והיה לו לומר סֻבְּכוֹ הבי״ת בחטף קמץ אלא שהכפיק לו בוי״ו לבדו להקל כמו שאמרו מכתנות וישאום בכתנותם. ת״י בשוא לבדו ועיין עוד שם וכספרים כתוב מסבכו הבי״ת בשוא ופתח וי״ס בשוא לבדו ודנש הבי״ת לספרים פ״כ. וכספרי הדפוס וגם במקצת ספרים כ״י הבי״ת בשוא לבדו וי״ס כ״י שהבי״ת בחטף קמץ כמשפטו: (ט) והכהנים יתמהו. בס״ס חסר יו״ד קדמאה גם במסורת דכפרה סימן כ״ו לא נמנה עם המלאים:

מצודת דוד

מעומדת מצפון נא״י: ושבר גדול. הרעה תהיה שבר גדול: (ז) עלה אריה מסבכו. דרך האריה לשכב בתוך סבכי האילנות ועל כ״כ יאמר: ומשחית גוים. זה כ״כ שהשחית כל האומות וכפל הדבר במ״ש: עריך תצינה. הערים שלך תהיינה שממה מאין מי יושב בהן: (ח) על זאת. על השמועה הזאת: ממנו. מישראל: (ט) יאבד לב המלך. ר״ל יבוא בו מורך לב: ונשמו. ר״ל נא

מצודת ציון

לרעו להתאסף: העיזו. ענין אסיפה כמו שלח העז (שמות ט׳): (ז) מסבכו. ענינו ענפים אחוזים אלה באלה כמו עד סירים סבוכים (נחום א): תצינה. ענ׳ ליה ושממון: (ח) חגרו. ענ׳ הגור

eous, but this generation should gird themselves with sackcloth and lament and wail 'for the fierce anger of the Lord has not turned back from us.'—[*Kara*]

9. **And it shall be on that day**—*On the day of Josiah they will wonder why so much befell him, for they do not know that his generation did not repent properly. When he came to abolish idolatry, what did the scorners of the generation do? They would engrave an image of a pagan deity on their doors, half of it on this door and half of it on this door. When he would open it, it was not discernible, and when he went away from there, he would close it, and it would*

I am bringing evil from the north, and a great destruction. 7. A lion has come up from his thicket, and a destroyer of nations has traveled, has come forth from his place, to make your land into a waste, your cities will be desolate without an inhabitant. 8. Because of this, gird yourselves with sackcloth, lament and wail, for the fierce anger of the Lord has not turned back from us. 9. And it shall be on that day, says the Lord, the heart of the king and the heart of the princes shall fail,

will be visible from afar.—[*Redak, Ibn Nachmiash*]

assemble—Heb. הָעִיזוּ. *Comp.* "*Send, gather* (הָעֵז)" (Exodus 9:19).—[*Rashi*]

This denotes the fleeing and the gathering into the city.—[*Redak*]

from the north—From Babylon, which is north of Eretz Israel.—[*Redak, Mezudath David*]

and a great destruction—That evil will be a great destruction.—[*Mezudath David*]

7. **A lion has come up**—That is *Nebuchadnezzar.*—[*Rashi* from *Meg.* 11a]

Just as no one resists a lion, so did Nebuchadnezzar conquer many lands, encountering no resistance. The interpretation of the allegory is given immediately after it, 'and a destroyer of nations.'—[*Redak*]

Others explain that Nebuchadnezzar was the ruler of the world, just as the lion is the king of the beasts.—[*Kara*]

from his thicket—*It is customary for a lion to lie in wait in the thickets of the forest* (*espaises in O.F.*).—[*Rashi*]

Redak explains that this is his den, made of the thickets of the forest.

will be desolate—Heb. תִּצֶּינָה, *an expression of desolation.*—[*Rashi*]

Rabbi Joseph Kimchi renders: Your cities will become overgrown because of no inhabitant.—[*Redak*] Since no one will walk there, the grasses and weeds will grow unhampered.

8. **Because of this**—*What is 'this?' For the fierce anger etc.' Although he spoke above concerning Nebuchadnezzar in regards to the destruction, here he returns to speak of the death of Josiah.*—[*Rashi*]

for the fierce anger of the Lord etc.—*Although Josiah repented wholeheartedly, it is stated concerning him:* "(II Kings 23:26) . . . *the Lord did not turn back from his great wrath . . . because of all the provocations that Manasseh had provoked Him.*"—[*Rashi*]

For we did not return to Him, and His fierce anger did not turn back from us, but is destined to come upon us.—[*Redak*]

Although Sennacherib had marched on Judah and was repulsed just before he attacked Jerusalem, this is no indication that the same will happen to Nebuchadnezzar, for Hezekiah's generation was right-

השרים ונשמו הכהנים והנביאים
יתמהו: י ויאמר אהה ׀ אדני יהוה אכן
השא השאת לעם הזה ולירושלם
לאמר שלום יהיה לכם ונגעה חרב
עד־הנפש: יא בעת ההיא יאמר לעם־
הזה ולירושלם רוח צח שפים במדבר
דרך בת־עמי לוא לזרות ולוא להבר:

תרגום

כהניא ונביי שקרא
ישתעממון: י נאמרית
קביל בעותי יי אלהים
בכן הא נביי שקרא
מטען לעמא הדין
וליתבי ירושלם למימר
שלמא יהי לכון וכען הא
חרבא מקטלא בעמא:
יא בעדנא ההיא יתאמר
לעמא הדין וליתבי
ירושלם כרוח טיהרין
על רישי נגרין דמיין
במדברא כן אורח
כנשתא דעמי לא

פתח בס״פ

רש״י

לבער את עכו״ם מה היו לולני הדור עושין חוקקין לורת עכו״ם על דלתותיהן חליה בדלת זה וחליה בדלת זה כשהיה פותחו לא היתה ניכרת וכשהלך משם סוגרה והיא מתחברת: (י) השא השאת. (אטינטא״ר בלע״ז) לשון הנחש השיאני (בראשית ג׳) שנביאי השקר נבאו׳ להם שלום יהיה לכם: (יא) לעם הזה. על העם הזה כשיגלו כולם: צח שפים. מכבד ומטאטא אף את שדות יבלי המים לשיתם מדבר. ל״א לא לשון למא דמתרגמינן לחותא: דרך בת עמי. אותו רוח בא וגם לא לזרות מוץ מגורן

מהר״י קרא

וירדפו חיל כשדים אחרי המלך וישיגו אותו וגו׳: (י) השא. אטימ״ז בלע״ז: השאת. את נביאי השקר על העם לאמור שלום יהיה לכם ואני רואה שנגעת חרב עד הנפש: (יא) רוח צח שפיים. רוח הבא בזוהר חזק וארוך הוא מאותו רוח הבא במעונו הוא אותו רוח שיוצא חוץ על שפת ים דרך מקום שאין שם הרים להגן בחן הרוח שאותו רוח אינו ראוי לא לזרות ולא להבר: לזרות. את הקש מן התבואה ונו״ר בלע״ז: להבר. לברור את התבואה מן התמוץ כך היה דרך בת עמי להם שלא תפשו דרך הטוב שיהא להם

רד״ק

כמו שתרגם אונקלוס ובתמהון לבב ובשעמימות לבא והוא אבדת הלב וההבנה: (י) ואמר. אכן השא השאת. כיון שאתה מאריך אף לנביאי השקר המטעים אותם ומשיאין אותם שלום שלום הרי הוא כאילו אתה משיא אותם ויחשבו רוב העם כי ה׳ דבר אתם והם על שני הסעיפים אם ישמעו לי ואם ישמעו להם והנם נוטים אחריהם לפי שהם רבים או פי׳ כמו אני ה׳ פתיתי את הנביא ההוא שענינו הערת חפץ כדי לגלות שקריהם ודעתם שעושין בסתר ועוד נפרש זה הענין בספר יחזקאל בפסוק והנביא כי יפותה וי״ת בכן הא נביאי שקרא מטען לעמא הדין וליתבי ירושלם ובאמרו לעם הזה ולירושלם פירוש ולעם הזה לעם שזכר וזכר בפרט ירושלם לפי שהיא העקר ורבינו סעדיה פירש השאת רוצה לומר גלות נביאי השקר המשיאים אותם וכן אני ה׳ פתיתי את הנביא בארתי עליו שהוא מפותה ומליצה זו כמו והצדיקו את הצדיק והרשיעו את הרשע: ונגעה חרב עד הנפש. והנה חרב האויב נגעה עד הנפש כלומר שהחלו להרוג בעם לא שבי ולא בזה לבד אלא אף הורגים ואיך יאמרו שלום יהיה לכם וי״ת הא חרבא מקטלא בעמא: (יא) בעת ההיא. בעת יבא האויב אמר להם הנה האויב בא עליהם כמו רוח צח העובר על שפיים שהם מקומות הגבוהים כמו הרים והגבעות או כמו רוח העבר במדבר שבאלה המקומות יעבור הרוח מאין מונע כי בישוב כשתעבור הרוח תמצא מונעים הרבה שלא תעבור הבתים והכותלים והגדרות אבל בשפיים ובמדבר לא תמצא מונע כן האויב בא ואין מונע אותו ואיזה דרך בא דרך בת עמי וזה

מנחת שי

(יא) יאמר לעם הזה. בספרים מדוייקים כ״י הלמ״ד במאריך והמקף בין שתי

מצודת דוד

ידמו מה לעשות: (י) ואומר. הנה מאמ׳ הנביא שאמ׳ אהה ה׳ באמת כאלו אתה השאת את העם הזה לאמ׳ להם שלום יהיה לכם אל מילאי כי כן נבאו להם נביאי השקר ועל כי לא עשית בהם משפט חשבו העם שהאמת אתם וכאלו אתה פתית אותם: ונגעה. ר״ל בעבור זה לא שבו לה׳ והנה נגע׳ החרב עד הנפש כי הפורעניו׳ קרובה לבוא: (יא) בעת ההיא. בעת בוא הפורעניו׳ יאמ׳ לעם וגו׳ הנה רוח יבא סוער במקומו׳ גבוהות אשר במדב׳ שמטאטא ומכבד הכל הולך ואין שם דבר לעמוד בפני הרוח ולעבור והרוח הזה יבוא דרך בת עמי לטאטא את כלם ללכת גולה: לא לזרות. לא יבוא

מצודת ציון

ואזו׳: ספדי. מל׳ הספד: והילילי. מל׳ יללה: (ט) תשמו. ענין תמהון כמו על יומו נשמו (איוב י״ח): (י) אהה. הוא ענין לשון יללה: השא השאת. ענין הפתאה ופתוי כמו הנחש השיאני (בראשית ג׳): (יא) צח. ענין יובש כמו לחם צמא (ישעיה ה׳): שפים. מקומות גבוהי׳: בת עמי. עדת עמי וכן בת בבל (תהלים קל״ז): לזרות. ענין פיזור וזריקה וכן ואזרם כמזרה (לקמן ט״ו):

[since they wonder] that the sword has reached the soul."

*11. **At that time**—I.e. at the time of the enemy invasion.—[*Redak*]

of this people—Heb. לָעָם הַזֶּה, usually 'to this people.' *Concerning this people when they are all exiled.* —[*Rashi*]

has swept the rivulets—Heb. צַח. *It sweeps even the fields with rivulets of water to make them into a desert. Another explanation:* צַח *is an expression of thirst, which is translated:* צְחוּתָא.—[*Rashi*] [Accordingly, we render: A dry wind on the fields with rivulets of water, making them like a desert.]

[on] the way of the daughter of My people—*That wind will come, and also, not to winnow the chaff from the*

* For Rashi's commentary turn to page 220.

and the priests shall be astonished and the prophets shall wonder. 10. And I said, "Ah, O Lord God! You have surely misled this people and Jerusalem, saying, 'You will have peace,' yet the sword has reached the soul." 11. At that time it shall be said of this people: A wind has swept the rivulets in the desert [on] the way of the daughter of My people, not to winnow and not to cleanse.

join together.—[*Rashi* from *Lam. Rabbah* 1:53. See Buber's edition.] See also *Kinot for the Ninth of Av*, pp. 102f. See above 3:10.

R. Joseph Kara interprets this verse as referring to the day the wall of Jerusalem was breached and King Zedekiah fled as did the soldiers. See below 52:7–9, II Kings 25:4–7.

the priests—These are the priests of the high places who will be astounded at the curtailment of their worship.—[*Redak*]

and the prophets—The false prophets who constantly prophesied peace, will become confused.—[*Redak* from *Jonathan*]

10. **Surely You have misled**—Heb. הַשֵּׁא הִשֵּׁאתָ (*(à)tenter in O.F.*), *tempting, an expression like* "(Gen. 3:13) *The serpent misled me* (הִשִּׁיאַנִי), *for the false prophets prophesy for them, "You will have peace."*—[*Rashi*]

The fact that God was patient with the false prophets who were misleading the people by promising them peace was as though God Himself was misleading the people since they would think that God had inspired these prophets. Most of the people were wavering between believing the false prophets and believing Jeremiah. Since the false prophets were more numerous, the majority of the people followed them. *Redak* suggests further that we render: You caused to mislead. You inspired them to prophesy falsely in order to reveal their falsity and their evil deeds that they commit secretly. *Abarbanel* rejects this interpretation, for, if they were inspired by God, they would not be blamed for their false prophecy, neither could their followers be blamed for following them.

Saadiah Gaon renders: Surely You have revealed the false prophets who mislead the people.—[*Redak*]

yet the sword has reached the soul—The sword of the enemy has commenced to kill the people, not only to capture them and rob them. How, then, can they say, "You will have peace"? Jonathan renders: Behold, the sword is slaying among the people.—[*Redak*]

Abarbanel explains that Jeremiah complains or asks the Lord, that since the false prophets will wonder about the calamity, this will indicate that God indeed conveyed this message to them, for if they had fabricated the prophecy, they would not be surprised that it was not fulfilled. Therefore, they will say, "Surely you have misled this people and Jerusalem, saying, 'You will have peace,'

יב רוּחַ מָלֵא מֵאֵלֶּה יָבוֹא לִי עַתָּה גַּם־
אֲנִי אֲדַבֵּר מִשְׁפָּטִים אוֹתָם: יג הִנֵּה ׀
כַּעֲנָנִים יַעֲלֶה וְכַסּוּפָה מַרְכְּבוֹתָיו קַלּוּ
מִנְּשָׁרִים סוּסָיו אוֹי לָנוּ כִּי שֻׁדָּדְנוּ:
יד כַּבְּסִי מֵרָעָה לִבֵּךְ יְרוּשָׁלִַם לְמַעַן
תִּוָּשֵׁעִי עַד־מָתַי תָּלִין בְּקִרְבֵּךְ

מחשבות

ח"א כבסי מרעה. ר"ס א יס:

תרגום

לְסוּדְרֵי וְלָא לְכַדְרָא: יב עַל דְטָעוּ בָּתַר נְבִיֵּי שִׁקְרָא דְמִתְנַבְּן לְהוֹן כְּרוּחַ דְשִׁקַּר כְּכֵן מַשְׁרְיַת עַמְמַיָּא סָאלִין קַלִּילִין כְּרוּחָא יֵיתוֹן עֲלֵיהוֹן כְּעַן אַף כְּסִיטְרֵי אֲיְתִינוּן נָאמַלֵּיל פּוּרְעֲנוּת דִינֵי סִנְהוֹן: יג הָא מַלְכָּא בְּמַשְׁרְיָתֵיהּ יִסַּק עֲלֵיהוֹן כַּעֲנָנָא דְסָלֵיק וְחָפֵי יַת אַרְעָא וּכְעַלְעוֹלִין רְתִיכוֹהִי קַלִּילִין מִנִּשְׁרַיָּא סוּסְוָתֵיהּ וַי לָנָא אֲרֵי אָתֵי לְמִבְזְזָנָא: יד אִתְחַוַּרִי מִלְּמֶעְבַּד בִּישָׁא לִבִּךְ יְרוּשְׁלֵם בְּדִיל דְתִתְפַּרְקִין עַד אֵימָתַי יוֹרְכוּן וְיִתְקַיְמוּן עֻבְדֵי אוֹנָס דִי בְגַוִיךְ:

מהר"י קרא

כתרים בפני הפורענות: (יב) רוח מלא מאלה יבא לי. פת׳ לפי שכך נגל׳ה לי מעם אלה שדרכן דומה לרוח מלא כלומר לרוח הזק שאינו ראוי לא לזרות ולא להבר עתה גם אני אדבר משפטים עמו: (יג) הנה כעננים יעלה וכסופה מרכבותיו. הנני מביא עליהם גוי שדומה לרוח חזק כפרק הרים כן הגוי הזה: וכסופה מרכבותיו קלו מנשרים סוסיו. ור׳ מנחם בר חלבו פירש לשון ויכוח: (יג) וכסופה.

רש"י

(אבהבוגיי"ר בלע"ז) כמו ויזרס במזרה (לקמן ט"ו): ולא להבר. ולנקות תבואה הוא בא כלומר לא לטובה כי אם לרעה להגלות אתכם (וכסים) סף וכהמה: (יב) רוח מלא. מאלה הפורעניות יבא לי: רוח מלא. רוח שלם שלא אחזור בי ולא אנחם. רוח (סלנ"ש בלע"ז): משפטים. (איקומפארוכילו"ן בלע"ז):

מנחת שי

ספלום: (יג) יבוא לי. בספרים מדוייקים כ״י ודפוס ישן בגלגל בי״ד:

רד"ק

הרוח לא ימצאו בו שום נחת רוח כמו רוח שזורים בו התבואה ומבררים אותה מן המוץ ע״י הרוח הנה הרוח כשלא תהיה חזקה יותר מדאי אע״פ שהזיק לדברים תועיל לדברים אבל הרוח הזה שנמשל בו האויב לא יבא לישראל אלא להרע להם ולא ימצאו בו שום דבר טוב והו שאומר אחר כן רוח מלא כאלה זהו הרוח יותר חזק מאלה כלומר כרוח שהוא לזרות ושהוא להבר ופירושו רוח צח זך ובהיר כמו דודי צח ואדום צחו כחלב ורצה לומר שהאויב הוא ככל רצונו בעם רב בסוסים ופרשים לבושי מכלול כולם או פי׳ רוח צח רוח יבש מן והשביע בצחצחות נפשך כלומר שיבש הארץ ויחריבנה וי״ת ברוח מיתרין על רישי וגו׳ כבעמוד: (יב) רוח מלא. חזק כלומר יבא הרוח מלא בכל כחו וכן על הדרך הזה מלא ידו בקשת: יבא לי. מאמר הנביא בבקום ישראל עתה קודם בואו: גם אני אדבר משפטים אותם. פי׳ על ישראל ובאמרו גם אני לרבות על משפט הנבואה והתוכחותיה אדבר גם אני מעצמי משפט תוכחה עמם ואולי ישובו בהרבותי תוכחתי עליהם וי״ת על דטעו בתר נביאי שיקרא וגו׳ כבעמוד: (יג) הנה כעננים. כמו שהעננים עולים מן הארץ כמו שנא׳ ואד יעלה מן הארץ ועולים קל מהרה כן יעלה האויב על ארץ ישראל ואומר יעלה כי ארץ ישראל גבוהה מכל הארצות: וכסופה. היא הרוח החזקה שהולכת במרוצה ובחוזקה כן ילכו מרכבותיו: קלו מנשרים. כי הנשר קל לעוף משאר עופות ועף בגובה האויר יותר מכלם וכן אמר כאשר ידאה הנשר: כי שודדנו. כי לשדוד אותנו יבא: (יד) כבסי. לא תהיה תשובתך בנראה לבד אלא אף בנסתר וזהו שאמר לבך כמו שאמר למעלה ולא שבה אלי בכל לבה כי אם בשקר וכן אמר הנה ג״כ תלין בקרבך מחשבות אונך זהו כי תשובתה לא היתה מלב ומה שאמר תלין לשון זכר והוא מדבר כנגד נקבה שהיא ירושלם כבר פירשנו למעלה כי כשמדבר הנביא כנגד כנסת ישראל ידבר פעם לשון זכר פעם לשון נקבה כי הנקבה כנגד הכנסת והזכר כנגד העם וכן כשמדבר כנגד ירושלם. והנה אמר הנה כבסי למען תושעי ולמעלה אמר כי אם תכבסי בנתר ותרבי לך בורית

מצודת ציון

לחבר. מל׳ ברור ונקי: (יב) רוח מלא. רוח שלם וכן ומלוא סהכל (שמואל ב׳ ח׳): משפטים. מנין ויכוח: (יג) כעננים. כעבים: וכסופה. רוח חזק: קלו. מל׳ קלות: שדדנו. מנין מושק ונזל: (יד) תלין. מנין המעמד כמו לדק ילין בה (ישעיה א׳): אונך.

מצודת דוד

הרוח לזרות המין מן הגורן ולא לנקות את התבואה מן העפר ר״ל לא יבוא לטובה כ״א לרעה: (יב) רוח מלא. רוח שלם תמלא הרוחו׳ הנושבו׳ במקומות הגבוהו׳ שבמדבר הנה יבא לצרכי להפרע מהם: עתה. ר״ל בזמן קרוב אתוכח עמהם גם אני כי עד הנה היה הנביא מתוכח עמהם להגיד להם משפט ועתה אתוכח גם אני כי בהביאי עליהם הפורעניות כאלו אגיד להם בזה משפט אשר נגרו למעלה: (יג) כעננים יעלה. האויב יעלה עליהם חיש מהר כעננים העולים ברום השמים: וכסופה. כרוח סופה כן ימהרו מרכבותיו: כי שדדנו. קרובים אנו להיות נשדדים ביד האויב: (יד) כבסי. לכן עשי תשובה וכבסי לבך מן הרעה למען יבא לך תשועה: תלין בקרבך. תתמיד להיות בקרבך מחשבת עמל ואון שאתה רגילה בהם:

Just like the strong and swift whirlwind, so will the enemy's chariots approach.—[*Redak*]

swifter than eagles—Since the eagle is swifter than other birds and flies higher than they, Scripture compares the enemy's steeds to eagles.—[*Redak*]

for we have been plundered—I.e., he will come to plunder us.—[*Redak, Ibn Nachmiash*]

14. **Cleanse your heart of evil**—Your repentance shall not be superficial, manifested only by fasting and confessing, but it should be from the heart, sincere repentance, not as

12. A full spirit of these shall come to me; now, I too will debate with them. 13. Behold, like clouds he will ascend, and like the whirlwind his chariots; his steeds are swifter than eagles; woe is to us for we have been plundered. 14. Cleanse your heart of evil, O Jerusalem, in order that you be saved; how long will you lodge in your midst

threshing floor (*[à]vanner in O.F.*). *Comp.* "(infra 15:7) *And I winnowed them with a sieve* (וָאֶזְרֵם בְּמִזְרֶה)".—[*Rashi*]

12. **A full spirit**—*of these retributions shall come to me.*—[*Rashi*]

A full spirit—*A full spirit, that I will not retract and not repent.*

spirit—(*talant in O.F.*)—[*Rashi*]

debate—Heb. מִשְׁפָּטִים *an expression of debating.*—[*Rashi*]

Redak renders: A wind stronger than these will come to me. I.e. a wind stronger than those winds used for winnowing and cleansing the grain, will come to me, Israel. Lit. a full wind, a wind with its full strength.

I too will bring charges against them—In addition to the reproof of the prophecy, I too will add my own words of reproof—.[*Redak*]

Abarbanel, as a continuation of his commentary on verse 10, explains that God replies to the prophet's question that the false prophets' wonder at the destruction appears to prove that God conveyed a prophetic message to them that there would be peace. God replies:

[11] **At that time, it shall be said to this people and to Jerusalem, "A clear spirit of breaking in the desert is the way of My people, not to winnow and not to cleanse."** The intention is that a clear prophetic message was conveyed to the true prophets, a message that the people will be broken (שְׁפָיִם) in their exile into the desert, which will be the way of My people, not to winnow and not to cleanse. I.e., it is not a spirit that can be interpreted as good or bad, like a wind that can be used for useful purposes, e.g. for winnowing or cleansing. Here is a play on words, רוּחַ is used as 'spirit' and as 'wind'.

[12] The prophet confirms God's statement by saying, **"A spirit full of these comes to me; now too I will speak of judgments with them."**—I.e., I too received a message from God full of these descriptions of breaking and destruction. Now too, I will speak with them only judgments, only prophecies of God's judgment upon them, for I did not prophesy peace but only destruction, just as I heard from the Lord of Hosts.

13. **like clouds he will ascend**—Just as clouds ascend swiftly over the land, so will the enemy approach Eretz Israel very swiftly and ascend over this land, which is higher than all other lands.—[*Redak*]

Jonathan paraphrases: Behold, a king with his camp will ascend upon them like a cloud that ascends and covers the land.

and like the whirlwind—(*comme tourbillon in O.F.*).—[*Rashi*]

מחשבות אונך: טו כי קול מגיד מדן
ומשמיע און מהר אפרים: טז הזכירו
לגוים הנה השמיעו על־ירושלם
נצרים באים מארץ המרחק ויתנו
על־ערי יהודה קולם: יז כשמרי שדי
היו עליה מסביב כי־אתי מרתה נאם
יהוה

תרגום

טו אֲרֵי קָל נְבִיַיָא
דְמִתְנַבְּן עֲלֵיהוֹן דְיִגְלוֹן
עַל דִפְלָחוּ לְעֶגְלָא דִי
בְדָן וּמְבַשְּׂרֵי בְשׂוֹרַן
בִּישָׁן יֵיתוּן עֲלֵיהוֹן עַל
דְאִשְׁתַּעְבָּדוּ לְצַלְמָא
דַאֲקֵים מִיכָה בְּטוּרָא
דְבֵית אֶפְרָיִם: טז אַדְכָּרוּ
לְעַמְמַיָא הָא בַשְּׂרוּ עַל
יְרוּשְׁלֵם אֲמָרוּ מַשְׁרְיַת
עַמְמִין חֲטוּפִין כְּקַטוּפִין
אָתַן מֵאֲרַע רְחִיקָא
וִישָׁרוּן עַל קִרְוַיָא דְבֵית
יְהוּדָה וִירִימוּן עֲלֵיהוֹן קָלְהוֹן: יז כְּנָטְרֵי חַקְלָן הֲווֹ עֲלַהּ מְסַחוֹר סְחוֹר אֲרֵי עַל מֵימְרִי סָרִיבַת

רש"י

(יד) אונך. חמסך: (טו) כי קול מגיד מדן. ארי קל נבייא מתנבן עליהון דיגלון על דפלחו לעגלא דבדן ומבשרי בשורן בישן ייתון עליהון על דאישתעבידו לדמות דאקים מיכה דבית אפרים ואף על פי שכבר גלו העגלים מימות סנחריב עדיין עוונם קיים. גדולה היא עבירה שעוברת לפניה ולאחריה לפניה מימות אברהם שנאמר וירדוף עד דן (בראשית י"ד) כיון שהגיע לדן תשש כחו שעתידין בניו לעבוד שם עכו"ם ולאחריה בחורבן הבית שנאמר כי קול מגיד מדן: ומשמיע און. און. שבר: (טז) נוצרים. נותני מצור עליהם: (יז) שדי. כמו שדה: אותי מרתה. הקניטה כמו ממרים הייתם (דברים ט') מרגזין:

מהר"י קרא

ד"א אונך. לשון אונאה: (טו) כי קול מגיד מדן. שמעתי קול נבואה המגיד שהולכין בשבי בעון עגל שבדן: ומשמיע און מהר אפרים. וקול המבשר און על עגל שבבית אל שבהר אפרים. ד"א ומשמיע און. על פסל מיכה מהר אפרים: (טז) כשומרי שדי. שוכרי העיר ורואין אותן הבאין מארץ המרחק:

רוח מלא, בנבואה על ישראל: (יד) מחשבות אונך. און.

רד"ק

ובאותו פסוק כתבנו תשובת השאלה: ואונך. מענין עמל ואון ובאת הוי"ו נחה כמו עולתה ועולתה פעם נחה פעם נעה וענין תלין אינו לינת הלילה אלא השקידה על הדברים תמיד כי כן נמצא בלשון הקדש לשון לינה בזה הענין כמו ובהמרותם תלן עיני בצוארו ילין עז והדומים להם וי"ת עד אימתי יורכון ויתקיימין עבדי אתם דבגויך: (טו) כי קול מגיד מדן. אומר כי מדן יבא מי שיגיד ביאת האויב וזכר דן כי הוא גבול ארץ ישראל כמו שנא' מדן ועד באר שבע וכן הר אפרים ואון פי' עמל ורעה כמו עמל ואון והפסוק כפול בענין במלות שונות כי משמיע כמו מגיד וי"ת הפסוק כן ארי קל נבייא דמתנבן עליהון וגו' כבעמוד: (טז) הזכירו לגוים. ומה הוא הקול המגיד שאומר בעבור הגוים כי הנה השמיעו על ירושלם כי נוצרים באים וגר ולמ"ד לגוים כמו בעבור כלמ"ד אמרי לי אחי הוא והדומים להם ופירוש נוצרים חיל נבוכדנצר ונקראו על שמו וי"ת נוצרים כמו בוצרים בבי"ת שתרגם משרית עממיא חטופין כקטופין אתן מארע רחיקא והרגם לא תבצור לא תקטף: ויתנו על ערי יהודה קולם. כלומר השמיעו על ירושלם כי כבר נתנו על ערי יהודה קולם ובמהרה יגיעו לירושלם ופירוש נתינת הקול תקיעת השופרות והחצוצרות בחיל: (יז) כשמרי שדי. כמו שדים או שדות ובא בחסרון מ"ם כמו וקרע לו חלוני שהוא כמו חלונים וחשופי שת כמו וחשופים והדומים להם או היו"ד תמורת הה"א והוא כמו שדה אבל י"ה לשון רבים כנטרי חקלן ופירוש כשומרי שדי כמו שומרי השדות מהבהמות שלא יכנסו בו לרעות שצריך שיעמדו סביב השדה שלא תכנס בו הבהמה משום צד כן באו האויבים סביב ירושלם כי בכל ערי יהודה שהם סביבה חנו כי פירוש עליה על ירושלם ועליה ר"ל סביב לה בסמוך כמו ועליו מטה מנשה והדומים להם: כי אותי מרתה. אותי פירוש דברי על יד הנביאים כי דברו כמו עצמו וכן ממרים הייתם עם ה' פירש את פי ה' כי לשון מרי יקשר במלת את עם דבר כמו מריתם את פי ולא מרו את דברו כי ענין מרי הוא שנות והחליף הדבר והמצוה או יהיה פירוש אותי כמו בי כי יבא בקשר הבי"ת כמו כי מרו בך ימרו בי

מצודת דוד

(טו) קול מגיד מדן. קול שמועה מגיד מדן שהוא בקצה א"י ומשם תבא השמועה כי בא האויב ומהר אפרים משמיע הקול שבא העמל והשבר: (טז) הזכירו. כאלו הקול אומר הזכירו אלה לאלה בעבור העמים הבאים למלחמה להיות נשמרים מהם כי הנה המה נאספו לבא על ירושלים: נוצרים. בעלי מצור באים מארץ מרחק לצור ועל ערי יהודה נתנו קולם לאיימם ולהפחידם: (יז) כשומרי שדי. כשומרי שדות אשר יסבבום מסביב כן היו האויבים על ירושלים מסביב: כי אותי מרתה. כי הקניטה אותי במעשיה ולכן

מצודת ציון

מל' און ועם שהוי"ו נחה וכן ועולתה תקפץ פיה (איוב ה') שהוי"ו נחה עם כי הוא נעה בכ"מ: (טו) און. עמל: (טז) השמיעו. ענין אסיפה הבאה בהשמעת קול המאסף וכן וישמע שאול (ש"א ט"ו): נוצרים. בעלי מצור הצרים על העיר וכן ונצורה לב (משלי ז'): (יז) שדי. כמו שדה: מרתה. ענין מרד והקנטה:

Jonathan renders: Like watchers of fields. The intention is that the enemies will surround the city from all sides, camping in all Judean cities, just as watchmen stand around the fields on all sides to prevent animals from entering.—[*Redak*]

for she has rebelled against me—*She has provoked Me. Comp.* "(Deut. 9:24) *You have been rebellious* (מַמְרִים)," rendered by Targum as מְרַגְּזִין, *provoking* (not found in our editions).—[*Rashi*] In this manner, it is a transitive verb as it appears from אֹתִי, *Me.*

your iniquitous thoughts? 15. For a voice proclaims from Dan
and announces calamity from Mt. Ephraim. 16. Mention on
behalf of the nations, behold, announce concerning Jerusalem,
besiegers are coming from a distant land, and they have given
out their voice against the cities of Judah. 17. Like watchers of
a field they are against her round about, for she has rebelled
against Me, says the Lord.

above (3:10) 'did not return to Me with all her heart, but falsely.' Here too, he says further: 'How long will you harbor within you your iniquitous thoughts?'—[*Redak*]

your iniquitous thoughts—lit. thoughts of your iniquity, Heb. אוֹנֵךְ, *your injustice.*—[*Rashi*]

15. **For a voice proclaims from Dan**—Jonathan paraphrases: *'Behold the voice of the prophets prophesy about them that they will be exiled because they worshipped the calf that was in Dan, and people bringing bad tidings will come upon them because they subordinated themselves to the image that Micah erected on the mountain of the house of Ephraim.' Although the calves had already been exiled since the days of Sennacherib, their iniquity was still existing. Sin is harsh, for it destroys* (lit. breaks) *before it and after it; before it, since the days of Abraham, as it is stated:* "(Gen. 14:14) *And he pursued until Dan." As soon as he reached Dan, he grew faint* (lit. his strength was weakened), *for his children would, in the future, worship idols there, and after it, in the destruction of the Temple, as it is stated: "A voice proclaims from Dan."*—[*Rashi*]

These shrines, although in the northern kingdom, influenced the people of Judah to offer up sacrifices on high places instead of only in the Temple.—[*Daath Sofrim*]

Redak explains that the enemy would come from the direction of Dan and Mt. Ephraim, which are the border of Eretz Israel.

and announces calamity—Heb. אָוֶן, *a breach.*—[*Rashi*]

16. **Mention on behalf of the nations**—And what does the voice proclaim on behalf of the nations? Behold, announce concerning Jerusalem that besiegers are coming . . . —[*Redak*]

besiegers—Heb. נֹצְרִים, *those who will make a siege upon them.*—[*Rashi*]

Redak conjectures that Scripture alludes to the soldiers of Nebuchadnezzar, giving them this appellation from the last two syllables of his name. This could be rendered 'Nezzarites.' *Abarbanel* rejects this on the grounds that there is no reason to base their name on the second half of Nebuchadnezzar rather than on the first half.

17. **field**—Heb. שָׂדָי.—[*Rashi*]

Accordingly, the 'yod' is a substitute for the 'he' of שָׂדֶה. It is also possible that this is a plural form, short for שָׂדִים or שָׂדוֹת. Indeed,

יהוה: יח דרכך ומעלליך עשו אלה לך:
זאת רעתך כי מר כי נגע עד־לבך:
יט מעי ׀ מעי ׀ אוחולה קירות לבי
הומה־לי לבי לא אחריש כי קול שופר
שמעתי נפשי תרועת מלחמה:
כ שבר על־שבר נקרא כי־שדדה כל־
הארץ פתאום שדדו אהלי רגע

ה"א פעי. ברכות ח' ו: נ"א עשו בחולם קמץ בד"ק אוחילה קרי שמעת קרי ירידעתי

תרגום

אמר יי: יח אורחתך בישתא ועובדך מקלקליא גרמו אלין ליך דא בישתא ומרדא איתי עלך ירושלם עד דאתכר רשע לביך: יט אמר נביא מעי מעי ביבין לי נע מסך לבי המי לי לבי לא שתיק ארי קל צוחת קרנא שמעת נפשי יבבות עבדי קרבא: כ תברא על תברא יתשרע ארי אתבזיזת כל ארעא בתכיף חרובת ארעי זמן

רש"י

(יח) עשו אלה. לעשות אלה לך: (יט) אוחילה. לשון חיל ורתת: קירות. (אנסינא"ש בלע"ז): שמעת נפשי. מאחורי הפרגוד כאתגי בשורת קול מתרועת מלחמה: (כ) שבר על שבר. חרבות ירושלי' על גלות יכניה: רגע יריעותי.

רד"ק

וי"ת ארי על ממרי סריבת: (יח) דרכך ומעלליך. הדרך שהלכת בה והמעשים שעשית הם גרמו לך כל זה הרע שבא האויב להחריב ארצך: עשו. מקור והוא במקום עבר כאילו אמר עשה או עשו: זאת רעתך. רעתך גרמה כי מר וקשה הדבר הרע הבא עליך עד כי נגע עד לבך וי"ת דא בישתא ומרדא אייתי וגו' כבעמוד: (יט) מעי מעי אוחילה. הכפל כדרך הנוחים שכופלים דבריהם וכן ראשי ראשי. אוחילה. מענין חיל כיולדה אמר הנביא אצעק מכאב מעי כלומר שאחזני חיל וכאב במעי על הרעה הבאה לנו וכן קירות לבי אוחילה ואם תאמרו אצעק פעם ואחריש פעם הומה לי לבי: לא אחריש. לא אוכל להחריש כי לבי הומה לי תמיד: שמעת נפשי. אמר למה לא אוכל להחריש כי את נפשי שמעת קול שופר ואמר נפשי ולא אמר אזני כי עדיין לא שמעו אזניו כי עדיין לא בא האויב אבל נפשו שמעה בנבואה ידבר כנגד נפשו כלומר את נפשי גרמת לי שלא אוכל להחריש כי את שמעת קול שופר תרועת מלחמה וכתוב שמעתי ביו"ד ואחד הוא עם הקרי כי שמיעתו היא שמועת הנפש ומה שאמר קירות לבי הוא דרך השאלה לפי שבלב דפנות בחללים שיש בו וי"ת אמר נבייא וגו' כבעמוד: (כ) שבר על שבר. שבר השבטים בא בתחלה ועתה בא שבר יהודה: נקרא. ענין מקרא אע"פ שהוא באל"ף: שדדו אהלי. כנה הבתים החשובים והארמונים הגבוהים

מנחת שי

(יח) דרכך ומעלליך עשו אלה. כל הספרים הכתובים בפורק מוסיפים כי הוא מקור וצריך להיות בחולם וכוה מן הכתובים וא"ו בסוף מ"פ המסורת וס"פ ספר ירמיה כ"ב וכן הוא בספרים כ"י ודפוסים ישנים ובמכלול דף קנ"ב ומה שנרשם בגליון המכלול כנגד פסוק עשו אלה לך (יחזקאל כ"ג) הוא טעות ממתוקקים ול"ל (ירמיה ד') ועיין עוד מה שאני עתיד לכתוב בזה הענין בירמיה כ"ב נ"ס: (יט) מעי מעי. בהרבה מדוייקים אין פסיק אחרי מעי השני: אחולה. אחילה קרי: קירות לבי. במדרש קהלת רבתי פסוק כי ברב חלומות בענייתא דחזקיהו ר' הונא בשם ר"י אמר בקירות לבו הוא עיניו שנאמר מעי מעי אוחילה קירות לבי וגו' לבו כתיב ע"כ. והמימרא לי פורה אלא קא דייק מדכתיב לבו ועוד קשה דבעל המסורת לא חשיב ליה עם אלין דכתיב וא"ו בסוף תיבותא וקריין יו"ד לכן נראה דלא גרסינן ליה וגם בירושלמי פרק תפלת השחר ליתיה וכן כתב בעל אות אמת לבו כתיב יתר ע"כ. ויותר יש לתמוה על בעל מתנות כהונה שכתב כלשון הזה לבו כתיב כן דרך הספר להודיע לנו המסורת אף על פי שאין בו צורך לפי דרכו: שמעתי. יתיר יו"ד: (כ) שדדו אהלי. הש"ין בג' נקודות בכל ספרים שלנו וכן כתב רד"ק בשרשים אבל בעל פתח דברי כתוב ספרו כתבו בקמץ רחב שֻׁדְּדוּ:

מצודת ציון

(יח) ומעלליך. מעשיך: מר. מלשון מרירות: (יט) אוחילה. מל' חיל וחלחלה: קירות לבי. כתלי לבי ואמר כדרך השאלה לפי שהלב יש בו דפנות וחללים: (כ) נקרא. מל' מקרה ומה כי היא באל"ף: שדדה. נעשק': פתאום. ענין פתיאום רב: יריעותי.

מצודת דוד

כא עליה האויב מסביב: (יח) עשו אלה לך. ר"ל אלה הם גרמו לך מרכית סלרו' אלה: זאת רעתך. הפורענו' הזאת היא על רעתך כי המעורר ייסר לך: כי נגע. ר"ל קרוב' היא והגיעה אליך ונגע עד לבך: (יט) מעי מעי. כפל המלה כדרך הנוסים והזועקים מכאב וכן ראשי ראשי (מ"ב ד') ור"ל כמו' מכאב יש לי במעי מלפני דאגת הפורענו' הממשמשת לבא לכן אהיה מלא מחלחלה: קירות לבי. תגודל התוגה מקשקש לבי בקרבי וכאלו הלב מהמיים לי קול הומים: לבי לא אחריש. לא אוכל לשתוק ולהשתיק את לבי מהמייתו: שמעת נפשי. כנבואה שמעה נפשי היא קול שופ' ולהוסיף כאלו' אמר תרועת מלחמה. ר"ל שיבוא האויב ויריע בשופר כדרך הנלחמים: (כ) שבר על שבר נקרא. פורענות על פורענו' יבא במקרה רעה כי בראשונה גלו עשרת השבטים ועתה יגלה יהודה: כי שדדה. בזה יפרש מהו השב' על שבר ואמ' כי בראשונה שדדה כל הארץ היא ארץ עשרת השבטים ועתה פתאום שודדו אהלי וזהו כפל"ק: רגע. ברגע אחת שודדו יריעותי והוא

'kethib,' we render: I have heard, My soul, the sound of the shofar.—[*Redak*]

20. **Destruction upon destruction**—*The destruction of Jerusalem upon the exile of Jeconiah.*—[*Rashi*]

Redak explains: The destruction of the Tribes came first and now the destruction of Judah.

suddenly my tents have been plundered—He calls the palatial dwellings and the palaces 'tents,' denoting that they are no more than tents, easily conquered and plundered.—[*Redak*]

in a moment my curtains—*In a moment my curtains were plundered.*—[*Rashi*]

18. Your way and your deeds have done these to you. This is [because of] your evil that it is bitter, that it has reached to your heart. 19. My bowels, my bowels! I writhe in pain. The walls of my heart! My heart stirs within me. I cannot be silent, for you, my soul, have heard the sound of the shofar, the alarm of war. 20. Destruction upon destruction has occurred, for the entire land has been plundered; suddenly my tents have been plundered, in a moment my curtains.

It may also mean, she has rebelled against My word, or against Me.—[*Redak*]

18. **Your way and your deeds**—The way you have gone and the deeds you have done.—[*Redak*] I.e. the general direction in which you have gone and the involved deeds you have done, although you can devise devious excuses for them.—[*Daath Sofrim*]

have done these to you—*To do these to you.*—[*Rashi*] *Rashi,* obviously read עֲשׂוֹ instead of עָשׂוּ, as did *Redak*. This is the infinitive instead of the past tense. The intention is that your way and your deeds caused these calamities to come about, that the enemy has come to destroy the land.—[*Redak*]

This is [because of] your evil—Your evil has caused this bitter and dire calamity to befall you.—[*Redak*]

until it has reached to your heart—*Jonathan* paraphrases: until the wickedness of your heart is broken.

19. **My bowels, my bowels!**—The expression is repeated in the manner of one moaning in pain. Cf. II Kings 4:19.—[*Redak*]

I writhe in pain—Heb. אוֹחִילָה, *an expression of writhing in pain* (חִיל) *and shuddering.*—[*Rashi*] *Redak* in *Shorashim* suggests that the root is יחל, to hope. I give my bowels hope yet, although they are now in pain and my heart stirs.

the walls of my heart!—(*étançon in O.F.*), blocking wall, perhaps from late Latin, *intimus,* innermost.—[*Rashi*]

I writhe with the pain of the walls of my heart.—[*Redak*]

My heart stirs within me, I cannot be silent—I cannot cry once and then be silent because my heart constantly stirs within me, giving me no rest.—[*Redak*]

you, my soul, have heard—*From behind the curtain of heaven the tidings of the sound of the alarm of war reached me.*—[*Rashi*] My soul heard, but not my ears, for it has not yet come about, but my soul has already heard the voice of prophecy. The prophet speaks to his soul in the second person. You, my soul, have caused me to cry in pain and not to be able to remain silent, for you have heard the sound of the shofar, the alarm of war. This is according to the 'keri.' According to the

יְרִיעֹתָי׃ כא עַד־מָתַי אֶרְאֶה־נֵּס
אֶשְׁמְעָה קוֹל שׁוֹפָר׃ כב כִּי ׀ אֱוִיל עַמִּי
אוֹתִי לֹא יָדָעוּ בָּנִים סְכָלִים הֵמָּה וְלֹא
נְבוֹנִים הֵמָּה חֲכָמִים הֵמָּה לְהָרַע
וּלְהֵיטִיב לֹא יָדָעוּ׃ כג רָאִיתִי אֶת־הָאָרֶץ
וְהִנֵּה־תֹהוּ וָבֹהוּ וְאֶל־הַשָּׁמַיִם וְאֵין
אוֹרָם׃ כד רָאִיתִי הֶהָרִים וְהִנֵּה רֹעֲשִׁים
וְכָל־הַגְּבָעוֹת הִתְקַלְקָלוּ׃ כה רָאִיתִי
והנה

זְמַן חֲדָא כָּל קִרְוַי׃
כא עַד אֵימָתַי אֲנָא חָזֵי
סִמָן אֶשְׁמַע קָל קַרְנָא׃
כב אֲרֵי אִטְפַּשׁוּ עַמִּי
מִידַע דַּחֲלְתִּי לָא אֲלִיפוּ
בְּנִין טַפְשִׁין אִינוּן וְלָא
סוּכְלְתָנִין אִינוּן חַכִּימִין
אִינוּן לְאַבְאָשָׁא
וּלְאוֹטָבָא לֵית אִינוּן
יָדְעִין׃ כג חֲזֵיתִי יַת
אַרְעָא הָא צַדְיָא וְרֵקָנְיָא
אִסְתַּכַּלִית בִּשְׁמַיָּא וְהָא
לָא מְזַהֲרִין נְהוֹרֵיהוֹן׃
כד חֲזֵיתִי טוּרַיָּא וְהָא
זָיְעִין וְכָל רָמָתָא
אִתְפַּרְקָא׃ כה חֲזֵיתִי
והא

ת"א בנים סכלים. קדושין לו: קמץ בז"ק

רש"י

רגע שודדו יריעותי: (כא) עד מתי אראה. האסיפות האלה הנושאי' נס להקבץ לבוא להלחם: (כד) התקלקלו.

מהר"י קרא

(כד) ראיתי ההרים. ראיתי האבות והנה רועשים ואמהות נתקו ונזרקו ממקומן ועם קלקל בחצים (יחזקאל כ"א) חכרו

רד"ק

באהלים כאילו היו אהלים ויריעות נטויות שנקל לכבשם כמו האהלים כן הם שדדו פתאם ורגע: (כא) עד מתי. השומרים מנהגם לעמוד במגדלים הגבוהים ובהרים הרמים וכשרואין האויבים באים מרימים הנס כדי שיראוהו העם ויתקעו בשופר כדי שישמעו העם ויהיו נזהרים ואמר הנביא עד מתי יהיה זה הלא תשוב מחרון אפך על עמך ישראל. וענהו האל: (כב) כי אויל עמי. כי אילו היו חכמים ומכירין הדרך הטובה וידעו אותי כי אני המטיב להם והמריע לפי מעשיהם לא היו רואין נס ושומעים קול שופר: בנים סכלים. לפי שנקראו בני האל כמו שאמר בנים אתם לה' אלהיכם ואמר אלה הבנים סכלים המה ולא נבונים המה כלומר תבונתם וחכמתם אינה נחשבת תבונה וחכמה אלא סכלות כיון שלא ידעו את ה' כמו שאמר במקום אחר הנה בדבר ה' מאסו וחכמת מה להם וכן אמר ישעיהו הנביא ובילדי נכרים ישפיקו והחכמה השלמה אינה כי אם עם תורת ה' כמו שאמר כי היא חכמתכם ובינתכם לעיני העמים ואותה שאינם יודעים את ה' ולא עושים מצותיו הכמתם היא ערמה ותחבולה להרע לא להטיב אבל התורה מלמדת את האדם לעשות הטוב והישר: (כג) ראיתי. אמר הנביא ראיתי בנבואה את הארץ: והנה תהו ובהו. כתרגומו צדיא וחרובא כיון שהיא שממה ואין יושבין עליה הרי היא כתהו ובהו כמו בתחילת בריאתה שנאמר והארץ היתה תהו ובהו: ואל השמים. כמו ואת השמים וכן אספרה אל חק כמו אספרה את חק וירדפו אל מדין כמו את מדין והדומים להם ויונתן הוסיף הבטתי אסתכלית לשמיא וכל זה דרך משל מרוב הצרה כאילו קדרו השמים ורעשו ההרים והגבעות וכן ועוף השמים נדדו אמר דרך הפלגה מרוב חרבן הארץ כלו העופות משם ולא יעופו באותה הארץ: (כד) ראיתי. התקלקלו. ענין קלקול ידוע בדברי רז"ל. ואדוני אבי ז"ל פי' ענין קלות כלומר רעשו מרוב קלותם כי כבדותם יעמידם: (כה) ראיתי. אין האדם. האדם שהיו בארץ אינם והם ישראל:

מצודת דוד

כפל ענין במ"ש: (כא) עד מתי. ר"ל עד מתי תעמוד הגזירה במקומה ואראה במראה הנבואה כאלו האויב בא ונושא הנס לאסיפה וקול שופ' מתרועת מלחמה אשמעה בנבואה: (כב) כי אויל עמי. אמר המקום ה' למשיב על דבריו לו' הלא זה סוף דבריו' כי עמי אויל ואינם נותנים לב לדעת אותי: בנים וגו'. כפל הדבר במ"ש: להרע. לדברים לעשות הרע: לא ידעו. אינם נותנים לב לדברים לעשו' הטוב: (כג) ראיתי. זה מאמ' הנביא שאמ' לכן ראיתי במראה הנבואה את הארץ והנה היא תוהו ובוהו כי גלו אנשיה: ואין אורם. כאור שהיה בהם מאז הלך לו והיא משל על הצרה כי מי שהוא בצרה העולם חשך בעדו: (כד) והנה רועשים. הוא משל על

מצודת ציון

ענין וילון כמוי כאוהל: (כא) נס. כלונס ארוך: (כב) אויל. שוטה: סכלים. טפשי': (כג) תוהו. שממה: ובוהו. ענין ריקות וכן והארץ היתה תהו ובהו (בראשית א'): ואל השמים. כמו ואת השמים וכן אספרה אל חוק (תהלים ב'): (כד) רועשים. מל' רעש ותנועה חזקה: התקלקלו. ענין השחתה וכדרז"ל וכל

wisdom, it is only to do evil, not to do good.

23. **I saw the earth**—The prophet states that he saw the earth in a prophetic vision.—[*Redak*]

and behold, it was void and unformed—Since it is desolate without inhabitants, it is like the earth at the beginning of the Creation, as the Bible states: And the earth was void and unformed (Gen. 1:2).

and they had no light—This is a parable, depicting the indescribable troubles that would befall the land. It would be as though the heavens darkened and the fowl would cease to fly over the land.—[*Redak*]

24. **they were quaking**—This is symbolic of the destruction of the kings and the princes.—[*Metsudath David*]

moved to and fro—Heb. הִתְקַלְקָלוּ,

21. How long will I see the standard, will I hear the sound of the shofar? 22. For My people are foolish, they know Me not; they are foolish children, and they have no understanding. They are wise to do evil, but they know not to do good. 23. I saw the earth, and behold, it was void and unformed, and the heavens, and they had no light. 24. I saw the mountains, and behold, they were quaking, and all the hills moved to and fro. 25. I saw,

The prophet experiences pain as though they were his own property. —[*Daath Soferim*]

21. **How long will I see**—*these groups carrying the standard to come to wage war.*—[*Rashi*] *Redak,* however, explains:

The lookouts usually stand in high towers and on high mountains, and, when they see the enemy coming, they raise the standard so that the people should see and they sound the shofar so that they should hear and beware. The prophet asks God: How long will this be that Your anger will not turn back from Your people Israel?—[*Redak*] Others explain that the intention is the standard and the shofar of the enemy, carrying the standard and sounding the shofar on his march against Judah. How long will I see this scene in my prophetic visions indicating that the decree has not been revoked?—[*Abarbanel, Mezudath David*]

22. **For My people are foolish**—God replies: For My people are foolish. Were they wise, they would discern the good way and recognize that I am the One Who does good or bad to them according to their deeds. Then, they would neither see the standard nor hear the sound of the shofar.—[*Redak*]

they are foolish children—Indeed they are called My children, but these children are foolish and have no understanding, for their wisdom is not considered wisdom. The prophet states elsewhere (8:9): 'Behold, they have rejected God's word, and what wisdom have they?' Isaiah too, says: And with the ideas of the gentiles they satisfy themselves' (2:6). True wisdom is only God's Torah, as Moses states: 'For it is your wisdom and your understanding in the eyes of the people' (Deut. 4:6). Since they do not know the Lord and do not keep His commandments, their wisdom is but cunning and guile to do evil. The Torah, however, teaches one to do good.—[*Redak*]

Abarbanel explains that these are the words of the Prophet. He contrasts his vision with that of the people. He depicts how he sees very vividly that the enemy is coming, but the people of Judah are very different from him. They are very foolish, for they do not know me, and as they do not know their Creator, so they are foolish children in all their matters. If they have any

וְהִנֵּה אֵין הָאָדָם וְכָל־עוֹף הַשָּׁמַיִם
נָדָדוּ׃ כו רָאִיתִי וְהִנֵּה הַכַּרְמֶל הַמִּדְבָּר
וְכָל־עָרָיו נִתְּצוּ מִפְּנֵי יְהוָה מִפְּנֵי חֲרוֹן
אַפּוֹ׃ כז כִּי־כֹה אָמַר יְהוָה שְׁמָמָה
תִהְיֶה כָּל־הָאָרֶץ וְכָלָה לֹא אֶעֱשֶׂה׃
כח עַל־זֹאת תֶּאֱבַל הָאָרֶץ וְקָדְרוּ
הַשָּׁמַיִם מִמָּעַל עַל כִּי־דִבַּרְתִּי זַמֹּתִי
וְלֹא נִחַמְתִּי וְלֹא־אָשׁוּב מִמֶּנָּה׃ כט מִקּוֹל
פָּרָשׁ וְרֹמֵה קֶשֶׁת בֹּרַחַת כָּל־הָעִיר

תרגום

והא לית עמא שרי עלה
וכל עופא דשמיא
אטלטלו: כו חזיתי והא
ארעא דישראל דהות
מנצבא ככרמלא תבת
למהוי במדברא וכל
קרוהא צדיאה מן קדם
יי מן קדם תקוף רוגזיה:
כז ארי כדנן אמר יי צדו
תהי כל ארעא וגמירא
לא אעביד: כח על דא
תחרוב ארעא ויקבלון
נהורי שמיא מלעילא
על דגזרית במימרי
חשיבית בעצתי
אעבדינה ולא אתיבינה:
כט מקל פרשין ודנגדין
בקשתא גלו כל יתבי

מהר"י קרא

התקלקלו: (כו) ראיתי. שהיה מתחלת כרמל ועתה למדבר שממה: (כז) וכלה לא אעשה. באנשים לגמרי אלא יפורו בגלות:

רש"י

מנים: (כו) והנה הכרמל. ארץ הנטוע כל טוב ככרמל נהיה כמדבר. מדרש אגדה. ראיתי ההרים. אלו האבות. וכל הגבעות אלו אמהות כלומר זכותן תמה. אין האדם. זכות משה שנא' בו ענוו מכל האדם (במד' י"ב) והנה הכרמל. זה אליהו: (כז) וכלה לא אעשה. ביושביה כי אותיר פליטים שילכו בגולה: (כח) תאבל. תחרב: זמותי. ל' מחשבה: על כי דברתי הפורענות הזה ואקיימנה: ולא אשוב. ולא אנחם לחשוב מחשבות טובות עליהם: (כט) ורומה. כמו רמה בים (שמות ט"ו):

רד"ק

(כו) ראיתי הכרמל. הכרמל שהוא מקום תבואה ועץ פרי ראיתי אותו כמו המדבר: עריו. סמך הערים לכרמל שאמר עריו לפי שהערים סבת הישיבה בהם שדות וכרמים ועצי פרי והם נקראים בכלל כרמל: נתצו. ענין נתיצה והריסה ויונתן תרגם כמו הפך צדיא כמו שתרגם נצתו אולי היה לו' כן אבל אנחנו מצאנו נתצו התי"ו קודם לצד"י: (כז) כי כה אמר. וכלה לא אעשה. כמו שהבטחתים בתורה לא מאסתים ולא געלתים לכלותם: (כח) על זאת תאבל. תשחת וכן אבל פירוש נשחת: על כי דברתי זמותי. כי מה שדברתי אל הנביאים כאשר חשבתי לא נחמתי עד הנה ולא אשוב ממנה עוד כי כאשר חשבתי ודברתי כן יהיה על זאת ראוי שתאבל הארץ: וקדרו השמים. זה דרך משל לרוב הצרה כמו שפירשנו: (כט) מקול פרש ורמה קשת. לשון יחיד על רבים דרך כלל כמו ויהי לי שור וחמור ורומה קשת יורה החצי' בקשת אמר כשישמעו קול הפרשים והקשתות שיהיו מחנה רב וישמעו קולם מרחוק יברחו ויצאו מהערים להשגב במקומות הגבוהים: בורחת כל העיר. בורחים כל אנשי העיר וכן אמר

מצודת ציון

שמקלקלין ספולין (שבת ק"י): (כו) הכרמל. כן נקרא מקום שדות וכרמים וכן ונופל בשן וכרמל (ישעיה ל"ג): נתצו. מל' נתיצה והריסה: (כח) תאבל. ענין השחתה כמו אבל אמללה ארץ (שם): וקדרו. ענין חושך ושחרות וכן שמש וירח קדרו (יואל ב'): זמותי. ענין מחשבה כמו זממו אל תפק (תהלים ק"מ): נחמתי. ענין הפוך מחשבה: (כט) פרש. כן יקרא רוכב הסוס הרגיל בזה: ורומה. ענין השלכה וכן נושקי רומי קשת (שם ע"ח): בעבים.

מצודת דוד

אלדון השרים והגבורים: (כה) אין האדם. אין מי מבני אדם שם כי כלם גלו: נדדו. הלכו להם מן הארץ בעבור השממון: (כו) הכרמל המדבר. מקום הכרמל נתהפך להיות מדבר: וכל עריו. כל ערי הכרמל נתצו ונהרסו מפני ה' ומזו' ומפנ' מפני חרון אפו ולא במקרה תהיה כל זאת: (כז) וכלה. אבל לא אעשה כלה ביושביה: (כח) על זאת. על הדבר האמור תעשה אבל הארץ וחשכו השמים אשר ממעל: על כי וגו'. ר"ל כאמור זה תאבל הארץ וגו' על אשר דברתי מחשבתי לעשות לארץ שממה ולא נחמתי על הדבר ההיא ולא אשוב ממנה וכפל הדבר במ"ש: (כט) מקול פרש. מקול קבוצת הפרשים והמורים חצים בקשת

29. **From the voice of the riders and the archers**—This is actually a singular form, used as a collective noun to denote a group of riders and a group of archers. When they hear the voices of the riders and the archers, who comprise a large camp, they will flee from the cities to take refuge in the high places.—[*Redak*]

archers—Heb. רֹמֵה קֶשֶׁת, lit. *bow shooters. Comp 'Cast* (רָמָה) *into the sea'* (Exodus 15:1).—[*Rashi*]

the entire city flees—I.e. all the *people* of the city flee. He does not mean one city, but all the inhabitants of each city.—[*Redak*]

Jonathan renders: all the inhabitants of the land went into exile.

and behold, there were no people, and all the fowl of the
heavens wandered away. 26. I saw, and behold, the fruitful
field became a desert, and all its cities were destroyed because
of the Lord, because of His fierce anger. 27. For so says the
Lord: All the land shall be a desolation, but I will not make an
end. 28. For this shall the earth mourn, and the heavens above
shall darken, for that which I spoke as I had planned, I did not
regret and I will not turn back from it. 29. From the voice of
the riders and the archers, the entire city

they were uprooted and cast out of their place, Menahem associates it with: He shakes the arrows to and fro (קִלְקַל) (Ezekiel 21:26).—[*Rashi* from *Machbereth Menahem* p. 155]

Redak explains it to mean that they deteriorated. This is a common word in Rabbinic literature. His father explains it as an expression of lightness. They became light. I.e., they quaked because of their lightness, for their weight holds them in place.

25. **there were no people**—I.e., the people who were in the land, viz. Israel, are no longer there.—[*Redak*]

and all the fowl of the heavens—Those that frequent populated regions.

26. **and behold, the fruitful field**—Heb. *Karmel,* sometimes rendered: forest. *The land, planted with all good like a forest, has become like a desert. The Midrash Aggadah* states: '*I saw the mountains'—These are the Patriarchs. 'And all the hills'—These are the Matriarchs. That is to say that their merit was depleted. 'There were no people,'—This refers to Moses, about whom it is said: 'humbler than all the people'* (Num. 12:3). '*And behold the Karmel'—This is Elijah.*—[*Rashi* from obscure Midrashic source. See *Lev. Rabbah* 36:6.] This midrash is quoted also by *Ibn Nachmiash* and *Kara.*

and all its cities were destroyed—Heb. נִתְּצוּ. *Jonathan* renders: became desolate. This corresponds to נִצְּתוּ, with the letters reversed. Perhaps this was his reading, but all extant editions read נִתְּצוּ.—[*Redak*]

because of His fierce anger—This was not a happening, but an act of Divine retribution.—[*Mezudath David*]

27. **but I will not make an end**—*of its inhabitants, for I will leave over refugees who will go into exile.*—[*Rashi*]

This coincides with God's promise: 'I did not reject them, neither did I despise them to put an end to them' (Lev. 26:44).—[*Redak*]

28. **shall mourn**—*Shall be destroyed.*—[*Rashi*] Similarly, a mourner is one who has been destroyed, so to speak.—[*Redak*]

and the heavens above shall darken—This is symbolic of the dire straits in which they will find themselves.—[*Redak*]

בָּאוּ בֶּעָבִים וּבַכֵּפִים עָלוּ כָּל־הָעִיר
עֲזוּבָה וְאֵין־יוֹשֵׁב בָּהֵן אִישׁ׃
ל וְאַתְּי
שָׁדוּד מַה־תַּעֲשִׂי כִּי־תִלְבְּשִׁי שָׁנִי כִּי־
תַעְדִּי עֲדִי־זָהָב כִּי־תִקְרְעִי בַפּוּךְ
עֵינַיִךְ לַשָּׁוְא תִּתְיַפִּי מָאֲסוּ־בָךְ עֹגְבִים
נַפְשֵׁךְ יְבַקֵּשׁוּ׃
לא כִּי קוֹל כְּחוֹלָה

ת"א ואת שדוד. חגיגה ב טו: כי תקרעי. בבא בתרא ס טו: — ואת קרי — שמעתי

תרגום

אַרעָא עָלוּ לְמֶעֱרַק בְּחוּרשַׁיָא סְלִיקוּ לְאִטמְרָא בְּכֵיפַיָא כָּל קִרְוֵיהוֹן שְׁבִיקָן וְלֵית דְיָתֵיב בְּהוֹן אֱנָשׁ׃
ל וְאַתְּ הָא מִתְבַּזְזָא מָה אִית בִּיךְ חֵיל לְמֶעְבַּד אֲרֵי אִתְרְחֵיצְתְּ עַל לְבָשֵׁי צִבְעָנִין וְעַל דְמִתְקְנִין בְּתִיקוּנִין דִדְהַב אֲרֵי תְכַחֲלִין בִּצְדִידָא עֵינִיךְ לָא לַהֲנָאָה תִּתְקְנִין קְצוֹ בִיךְ רַחֲמַךְ מְקַטְלִין נַפְשֵׁךְ בְּעַן׃
לא אֲרֵי קָל כִּמְעַדְיָא שְׁמָעִית עָקָא כְּאִתְּתָא דִמְשַׁרְיָא לְמֵילַד בְּכוּר קָל כְּנִשְׁתָּא דְצִיּוֹן

רש"י

באו בעבים. ביערות עבים מקום סיבוך קוצים להטמן: ובכפים עלו. סלע מתורגם כיפיא: (ל) כי תלבשי שני. להתנאות ולמצוא רחמים לפני השודד: תקרעי בפוך. ל' קריעה שהפוך נראה כמרחיב קרע העין כך שמעתי וגם מנחם לא חלק במחברת קרע: פוך. לשון כחול: עוגבים. המשחקים עם הנשים בלדי מיני ניאוף כמו ותעגבה על פלגשיהם (יחזקאל כ"ג): נפשך יבקשו.

מהר"י קרא

(כט) באו בעבים. תרגום יונתן עלו למערק בחורשיא ומיכן תפשו חכמים את לשונם שקראו ליער אבא שאמרו מיניה וביה אבא ליזל ביה נרגא וא' מתחלף בע'. ור' מנחם פירש בעבים. בעובי היער: ובכפים. סלעים: (ל) ואת שדוד. כשתהית שדוד כמו שאמר למעלה אוי לנו כי שדדנו: מה תעשי. בבוא עליך האויב: כי תלבשי שני. וכי תקרעו בפוך עיניך. פתרונו כי תרחיבי בפוך עיניך: פוך. הוא כוחלא: מאסו בך עוגבים. אוהבים. אותם האומות שעגבת עליהן לשעבר הם בני מצרים ואשור וכשדים כמו שמצינו בספר יחזקאל אל בני אשור עגבת ויעדרת הוסיפה אל תזנותיה ותרא אנשי מחוקה על הקיר צלמי כשדים ותעגבנת עליהם. ועתה יהיו נהפכין עליך לאויבים דכתיב מאסו בך עוגבים נפשך יבקשו. וכן הוא אומר

רד"ק

וכל הארץ באו מצרימה והדומים לו ואינו אומר על עיר מיוחדת באמרו כל העיר אלא רוצה לומר כל אנשי עיר ועיר: באו בעבים. במקומות הגבוהים בעבים ע"ד הפלגה או פירוש בעבים ענין עובי רוצה לומר ביערים העבים והמסובכים באילנות להסתר שם וכן תירגם יונתן עלו למערק בחורשיא ותרגם יער חורשא: ובכפים עלו. בסלעים תרגום סלע כיפא: כל העיר עזובה. רוצה לומר כל העיר ועיר כמו שפירשנו לפיכך אמר ואין יושב בהן איש: (ל) ואת שדוד. י"א שהוא חסר כ"ף הדמיון ענינו ואת כשדוד ואין צורך לכל זה כי לכנסת ישראל ידבר פעם לשון נקבה פעם לשון זכר וכל אחד מהן נכון כמו שפירשנו בפסוק ותעשי הרעות: מה תעשי. כשיבא לך השוד והשבר מה תעשי כלומר במה תנצלי כי תלבשי עתה שני ותתיאשי מן הפורענות ולא תחושי לרעה העתידה לבא עליך ולא תכנעי והיה לך להכנע מפני האל וללבוש שקים כדרך הנכנע ושב מחטאתו לא תלבש שני ולעדות עדי זהב כמו שאמר עליהם ישעיהו הנביא והנה ששון ושמחה הרג בקר ושחוט צאן וגו' והיו אומרים עוד כרתנו ברית את מות ועם שאול עשינו חוזה שוט שוטף כי יעבור לא יבאנו וגו' והנה אתה רואה שהיו מתיאשים מן הפורענות והמשילם גם כן לזונה כמו שפירשנו וכמו שדרך הזונה ללבוש בגדים נאים ולהתיפות ולקרוע בפוך עיניה כדי שיחשקו בה החושקים כן כנסת ישראל היתה מתדמה במעשה העכו"ם לעבוד את אלהיהם וללבוש בלבושיהם להתגדל ולהתפאר בפניהם בבגדים נאים ובמרכבות נאות כדי שיאהבו אותם ויאמרו הרי היא כמוני ויאהבוה והנביא אומר לה מאסו בך עוגבים נפשך יבקשו אמר להפך בא מה שחשבתם כי אתם סלקתם בטחונכם מעלי ובטחתם בעכו"ם והתדמותם להם במעשיכם כדי למצא חן בעיניהם ויהיו חושקים בכם והנה מאסו בכם עד שיבקשו נפשתיכם להרג ולאבד: תקרעי. כתרגומו תכחלין ואמר בלשון קריעה כי היא קורעת עיניה מרוב התבדתה לכחול אותם: עוגבים. חושקים וכן ת"י קצו בך רחמך וכן ותעגב על מאהביה והדומים לו בזה הלשון ענין חשק: (לא) כי קול כחולה. חולה שם תואר בפל' טובה מענין

מנחת שי

(ל) ואתי שדוד. ואת קרי: כי תעדי. כן כתוב כי בלא וא"ו:

מצודת דוד

יברחו כל אנשי העיר: באו בעבים. יבואו להסתתר ביערי' העבי' והמסובכים באילנות: ובכפים עלו. יעלו בין הסלעי' להסתתר שמה: עזובה. מיושביה ולתוספת ביאור אמר ואין יושב בהן איש: (ל) ואת שדוד. אתה יהודה שסופך להיות שסוק ביד השטים: מה תעשי וגו'. ר"ל מה הועיל אשר תלבשי מלבושי תולעת שני אשר תקשטי עצמך בעדי זהב אשר תתמיד לכחול עיניך בכחל הפוך להיות כאשה יפה להלהיב לבות המנאפים: לשוא תתיפי. על חנם תשית עצמך יפה ומהודרת כי המוחשקים מאסו בך מעתה ומבקשים לקחת נפשך ממך והוא ענין משל לו' מה תתלי אל העכו"ם כשוחד ודורונות הנה כל זה לא יועיל לך כי נהפכו לך לאויבים: (לא) כי

מצודת ציון

מל' עב ור"ל ביערים עבים ומסובכים: ובכפים. תרגום של סלע הוא כיפא וכן חורי עפר וכפים (איוב ל'): (ל) שדוד. עשוק: שני. שני תולעת והוא מין לבע אדום: תעדי. עדי וקשוט: תקרעי. מרוב התמדה לכחול העינים נראה כאלו קורעת פתיחת בית העין: בפוך. היא הכחול שכוחלין בו העינים וכן ותשם בפוך עיניה (מ"ב ט'): לשוא. לחנם: תתיפי. מל' יפה: עוגבים. חושקים ואוהבי הניאוף כמו ותעגב על מאהביה (יחזקאל כ"ג):

words related to the root קרע, *to tear,* are all grouped together, this indicates that they all have the same definition.] Others explain that she tears, or irritates the eye by constantly painting it.—[*Redak*]

31. **like [that of] a travailing woman**—The prophet compares the daughter of Zion to a travailing woman who raises her voice to scream and wail.—[*Redak*] He further likens her to a woman giving

they came into the thickets, and they ascended among the boulders; every city is deserted, and no people are living in them. 30. And you, despoiled one, what can you do that you wear crimson, that you adorn yourself with golden ornaments, that you enlarge your eye with paint? In vain you beautify yourself; lovers despise you, they seek your life. 31. For a voice like [that of] a travailing woman

they came into the thickets—*Into the thick forests, a place intertwined with thorns, to hide.—[Rashi]*

Redak renders: Into the clouds, i.e. into the high places, compared to clouds, because of their height. *Jonathan,* however, renders: into the forests, agreeing with the first interpretation. Similarly, Rabbi Menahem [ben Helbo] renders: in the thickness of the forest.—[*Kara*]

and they ascended among the boulders—Heb. וּבַכֵּפִים. סֶלַע, *a rock, is translated into Aramaic as* כֵּפָא.—[*Rashi*]

*30. **despoiled one**—When you will be despoiled.—[*Kara*]

what can you do—when the enemy attacks you.—[*Kara*]

What do you expect to do when the enemy attacks you, that you wear crimson now, as though despairing of the impending doom and not humbling yourself before God and donning sackcloth as one who humbles himself and repents of his sin. You should neither wear crimson nor adorn yourself with golden ornaments. See Isaiah 22:13: 'And behold, joy and happiness, slaying cattle and slaughtering sheep, eating meat and drinking wine; "Let us eat and drink, for tomorrow we will die."' Also (28:15) For you have said, "We have made a treaty with death, and with the grave we have set a limit; when an overflowing scourge passes, it shall not come upon us, etc." Here we see that they despaired of the retribution.—[*Redak*]

that you wear crimson—*to beautify yourself and to gain clemency before the plunderer.*—[*Rashi*]

that you enlarge . . . with paint—Heb. תִּקְרְעִי, *an expression of tearing, for the paint appears as widening the opening of the eye. So have I heard, and Menahem did not differentiate in the group of* קרע.—[*Rashi*] [*Rashi* states that he heard this interpretation. It was probably from Rabbi Joseph Kara, who quotes Rabbi Menahem ben Helbo. It is known that Rabbi Joseph Kara was Rashi's contemporary and that Rashi incorporated many of his comments into his commentary. He was a nephew of Rabbi Menahem ben Helbo, who composed a work entitled פִּתְרוֹנִים, *interpretations,* where he defines many words of the Bible. This book is not found today. Then Rashi quotes Menahem ben Seruk, the author of the first Biblical lexicon, entitled Machbereth, in which he classifies the Hebrew roots according to their meaning. Since the

* For Rashi's commentary turn to page 221.

שמעתי צרה כמבכירה קול בת־ציון
תתיפח תפרש כפיה אוי־נא לי כי־
עיפה נפשי להרגים: ה א שוטטו
בחוצות ירושלם וראו־נא ודעו ובקשו
ברחובותיה אם־תמצאו איש אם־יש
עשה משפט מבקש אמונה ואסלח
לה: ב ואם חי־יהוה יאמרו לכן לשקר

תרגום

דמשתטחא ופרסא
ידהא אמרא וי כען לי
ארי משלהיא נפשי מן
קדם קטולין: א הליכו
בשוקי ירושלם נחזו כען
ודעו ובעו ברחובהא
אם תשכחון גבר דליה
עובדין טבין אם אית
עביד דין דקשוט בעי
הימנותא ואשבוק להון:
ב ואם בשמא דיי ימן
בכן לשקרא אינון
משתבעין

ת"א אוי נא לי. כס. שוטטו בחוצות. שבת קיט חגיגה ג יד: ואם חי ה'. פקידה שער פג: סבירין אכן

מהר"י קרא

ביחזקאל לכן נתתיה ביד מאהביה ביד בני אשור אשר עגבה עליהם. ואומר הנני מעיר את מאהביך את אשר נקעה נפשך מהם והבאתים עליך מסביב בני בבל: (לא) צרה כמבכירה. כיולדת בכור שהוא קשה לאם מכולן: צרה. אינו שם דבר אלא פעולה מצירה והוא צרה מגזרת צירים: תתיפח. לשון דאבון נפש שתרגומו מפחן נפש כלומר תדאב ותאבל על עצמה: תפרש כפיה. תשבר ידיה כמו פרשה ציון בידיה. כמו הלא פרש לרעב לחמך. ואומרת: אוי נא לי כי עיפה נפשי לחורגים. כמו מהורגים כמו [אמרי לי אחי הוא] שהל' במקום מ':

רש"י

מבקשים להרגך: (לא) כמבכירה. כאשה המבכרת תחלת לידתה: תתיפח. תייליל ותצעק גניחות (קונפלייג"ש בלע"ז) כמו ויפח חמס (תהלים כ"ז) ל' דיבור: אוי נא לי. כך אומרת

מנחת שי

ה (א) ודעו ובקשו. בספרים כ"י ודפוס יש קל הקו"ף כמשפט רוב הבנין בזה השורש כמ"ש בשרשים ור' יונה הביאו בספר הרקמה עם הקלין כמו קראו אלהו שבפ' הקודמת: (ב) לכן לשקר. סבירין אכן כמו אכן לשקר

רד"ק

חיל כיולדה ומשרשו ואמר דרך משל כי בת ציון תרים קול כמו האשה היושבת על משבר תחיל תזעק בחבליה ועוד הגדיל הענין והמשילם למבכירה והיא האשה היולדת ראשונה כי חבליה קשים מחבלי אשה אחרת ופירוש צרה שהיא צעקת צרה כמבכירה: תתיפח. מענין ויפח לקץ שהוא ענין העיון. תהגה ותהמה ותקונן על הרוגיה ואומרת אוי נא לי כי עיפה נפשי אמרה נפשי כנגד בת ציון אוי נא לי כי עיפה מסבול הצער הגדול לרוב הורגים שמצאוני וי"ת דמשתטחא ופרסא ידהא אמרה ווי כען לי וענין תפרש כפיה תשבר ידיה כמו פרשה ציון בידיה כי כן דרך המצטער לפרש כפיו אחת באחת לרוב הצער: (א) שוטטו. חפשו ובקשו והנה אמר דוד בספר תהלים נתנו נבלת עבדיך מאכל לעוף השמים בשר חסידיך לחיתו ארץ הנה כי היו בירושלם חסידים ועבדי האל ואיך אמר ירמיה אם יש עושה משפט מבקש אמונה ואסלח לה פירש אדוני אבי ז"ל כי ירמיה אמר בחוצות ירושלים ואמר ברחובותיה כי החסידים שהיו בירושלם היו מתחבאים בבתיהם ולא היו יכולים להתראות ברחובות ובחוצות מפני הרשעים ורז"ל פירשו כיון שנהרגו ע"י אויבים אף על פי שהיו רשעים וחייבי מיתה נתכפר להם במיתתן וקרי להו עבדיך וחסידך: אם תמצאו איש. ר"ל איש טוב וגדול במעשים וכן הלא איש אתה וכן ת"י אם תשכחון גבר דליה עובדין טבין: (ב) ואם חי ה'. כי ברוב הם נשבעים באלהים אחרים כמו שאמר וישבעו בלא אלהים ואם יהיה שישבעו בי להראות עצמן שהם יראי שמי ונשבעים

מצודת ציון

(לא) כמבכירה. יולדת בכור: תתיפח. ענין אמירה ודבור כמו ויפח חמס (תהלים כ"ז): תפרש. מל' פריסה ובקיעה כמו פרשה ציון בידיה (איכה א'): נא. עתה: עיפה. ענין יגיעה: להורגים. באה הלמ"ד במקום בעבור וכן פתח פיך לאלם (משלי ל"א) ור"ל בעבור האלם:

ה (א) שוטטו. ענין ההליכה אנה ואנה וכן משוט בארץ (איוב א'): בחוצות. בשוקים וכן וחוצות תשים לך בדמשק (מלכים א' כ'): ברחובותיה. מלשון רחוב: איש. ר"ל גדול ובעל מעש"ט

מצודת דוד

קול. שמעתי קול כקול חולה: צרה. צעקת צרה שמעתי כאשה המבכרת שחבליה חזקים: קול בת ציון. והוא הקול של עדת ציון אשר תרבה אמריה כדרך המקונן: תפרש כפיה. משברת כפיה זה בזה כדרך המצטער: אוי נא לי. צועקת מר ואומרת אוי עתה לי כי נפשי עיפה בעבור ההורגים אותנו:

ה (א) שוטטו בחוצות ירושלים. אנה ואנה וראו עתה בהם ותנו לב לדעת מעשה האנשים ובקשו ברחובותיה אם תמצאו שם איש ישר אם יש מי עושה משפט ומבקש אמונה ואסלח לה. אם תמצאו אף איש יחידי כזה אז אסלח לכל העיר:

(ב) ואם חי ה'. ואם יאמרו בשבועתם חי ה' לא הוא בעבור שהם מאמינים בו אבל באמת כבדולים להשבע בשקר כשבעי' בכ':

whether you will find a man—The term אִישׁ, *a man*, very often denotes a strong man, a man of courage. Jeremiah asserts that there are no courageous people who castigate the populace. There were, indeed, many righteous people, but they did not castigate the populace for their sins.

2. **And if they will say, "As the Lord lives . . ."**—Since many of them were wont to swear by pagan deities, the prophet says that, even if some people swear by the name of God to demonstrate that they fear Him, they nevertheless, swear falsely. God says that 'if they swear by

I heard, in pain as a woman bearing her first child, the voice of the daughter of Zion who will wail, will break her hands. "Woe is to me, for my soul is faint before the murderers."

5

1. Stroll in the streets of Jerusalem, and see now and know, and
seek in its squares, whether you will find a man, whether there
is one who performs justice, who seeks faith, and I will forgive
her. 2. And if they say, "As the Lord lives," they, nevertheless,
will swear falsely.

birth to her first child, when her labor pains are more severe than in subsequent births.—[*Redak, Kara*]

like a woman bearing her first child—Heb. כְּמַבְכִּירָה, *like a woman bearing her first child, the beginning of her birth.*—[*Rashi*]

who will wail—Heb. תִּתְיַפֵּחַ, *she will wail and cry out with sighs* (*konpljjnt in O.F.*). *Comp. 'who speak* (וִיפֵחַ) *violence'* (Psalms 27:12), *an expression of speech.*—[*Rashi*]

She moans and laments over those of hers who were slain.—[*Redak*]

will break her hands—She will press her hands together out of pain and anguish.—[*Kara, Redak, Mezudath David*]

"Woe is to me . . ."—*This is what she says.*—[*Rashi*]

1. **Stroll—search and seek.** It would appear from our verse that there were no righteous people in Jerusalem at the time of the destruction of the Temple. In Psalms 79:2, we read: 'They gave the corpses of Your servants as food for the fowl of the heavens, the flesh of Your pious ones to the beasts of the earth.' How then, does Jeremiah state that no righteous could be found in the streets or the squares of Jerusalem? Rabbi Joseph Kimchi states that there were indeed many righteous people in Jerusalem, but they feared to appear in the streets and in the squares because of the wicked. Our Sages state that, although those slain were wicked, and even liable to death, since they were slain, their death expiated their sins, and they were called 'God's servants and His pious ones' (*San.* 47a).—[*Redak*]

Abarbanel rejects both of these solutions. He rejects Rabbi Joseph Kimchi's solution because he sees no reason for the city to be destroyed if there were righteous men in the houses. Why should it be necessary for them to be in the streets? He rejects the Rabbis' solution as being the simple meaning of the verse since it would appear that there were, in fact, no righteous people at all in Jerusalem. Were all the priests wicked? Were there not the disciples of the prophets? He, therefore, resorts to another interpretation of our verse.

ישבעו: ג יהוה עיניך הלוא לאמונה
הכיתה אתם ולא־חלו כליתם מאנו
קחת מוסר חזקו פניהם מסלע מאנו
לשוב: ד ואני אמרתי אך דלים הם
נואלו כי לא ידעו דרך יהוה משפט
אלהיהם: ה אלכה־לי אל־הגדלים
ואדברה אותם כי המה ידעו דרך יהוה
משפט

ה"א אך דלים הם. פקרים מ"ג פו:

תרגום

משתבעין: ג יי הלא גלי
קדמך לאוטבא לעבדי
הימנותא רשיעיא
אלקיתא יתהון ולא
תבו שיציתינון סריבו
לקבלא אולפן אתקיפו
אפיהון מטינרא
סריבין למיהב:
ד ונא אמרית ברם
מדמסכנין אינון אטפשו
ארי לא אליפו למידע
אורחן דתקנן קדם יי
למעבד דין דקשוט
קדם אלההון: ה אהך לי
לות רברביא ואמליל
עמהון ארי אינון אליפו למידע אורחן דתקנן קדם יי למעבד דין דקשוט קדם אלההון

רש"י

ה (ג) ה' עיניך. הלא הם על בעלי אמונה להטיב ולמה בגדו אלה כך ואין מבקשין אמונה: הכיתה אותם. ולא נעשו חולים על המכה לשוב אל לבם לשוב מרעת': קחת. כמו לקחת: (ד) ואני אמרתי. הנביא אומר כן אך דלים הם מחכמה אלו שאני מדבר עמהם: נואלו. לשון אויל כתרגומו אטפשו: (ה) אלכה לי אל הגדולים. הם

מהר"י קרא

ה (ג) ה' עיניך הלא לאמונה. כשאתה נותן עיניך באדם לייסרו הלא לאמונה ואתה דן אותם במדת ייסורין וכל זה כדי שיתנו לב לשוב אצלך כשם שהוא אומר ויגל אזנם למוסר ויאמר כי ישובון מאון וצדיק שפוגעת בו מידת הדין נותן לב לחזור אליו. אלו: הכית אותם ולא חלו. לא נכנעו. לא חלו לשון חיל אחז: (ד) אך דלים הם. דלת העם עושין כן הם נואלו כי לא ידעו דרך ה'. אבל אם: (ה) אלכה לי אל הגדולים ואדברה אותם כי המה ידעי דרך ה'. אבל המה כולן יחדיו שברו עול הגדולים עם

מנחת שי

(ג) ולא חלו. יש ספרים ולא מגבעות דלעיל סימן ג' מסורה שמואל א' כ"ו:

רד"ק

בשמי לשקר הם נשבעים בשמי ואני היודע: (ג) ה' עיניך הלא לאמונה. אמר הנביא תמיה על זה הענין אמר דרך קריאה ה' עיניך הלא לאמונה כלומר השגחתך בעולם הלא לאמונה כלומר לדבר קיים לא לדבר בטל והנה הכית אותם על מעשיהם הרעים ולא חלו כלומר לא כאבו ולא הרגישו בעצמם כי אתה המכה אותם בעתם אם כן מה הועילה השגחתך בהם ודומה למה שאמר לשוא הכתי את בניכם מוסר לא לקחו וכן מה שאמר ישעיה הנביא על מה תכו עוד תוסיפו סרה: כליתם מאני קחת מוסר. הבאתם עד קרוב לכליה אף על פי כן מאנו קחת מוסר ואם נביאיך מזהירים אותם חזקו פניהם מסלע ולא בשו מפניהם ומאנו לשוב. לאמונה. ענין קיום כמו אמונה אומן במקום נאמן וי"ת ה' הלא גלי קדמך וגו' כבעמוד: (ד) ואני אמרתי. אמר הנביא נסיתי אותם בעניני התוכחה הקטנים והגדולים אמרתי כלומר חשבתי בעצמי כשתוכחתי העם ולא קבלו אמרתי אך דלים הם נואלו כי ברוב דלת העם אין להם דעת ובינה כמו הגדולים לפי שהם כורמים ויוגבים וכל עסקיהם עבודת האדמה ולא יתעסקו בדברי מוסר ובתורה ובחכמה לפיכך לא קבלו תוכחת כי נואלו ואין להם דעת כי לא ידעו דרך ה' משפט אלהיהם: (ה) אלכה לי אל הגדולים. כי לפי שהם גדולים ועשירים ואינם מתעסקים במלאכה יש להם פנאי ללמוד תורה וחכמה וברוב הם בעלי מוסר ודעת ולמדו תורה ומשפט אלהיהם ואולי תועיל בהם תוכחתי כי יבינו וישכילו

מצודת דוד

(ג) עיניך הלא לאמונה. הוא מאמ' הנביא אל מול ה' לומר הנה השגחתך בהם הלא היא על דבר המתקיים ולא על דבר בטל שאין בו תועלת: הכיתה אותם. בהשגחתך הכית אותם למען יוכרו לשוב להם: ולא חלו. לא נעשו חולים מן ההכאה ר"ל לא הרגישו שבא עליהם לעורר לבם לתשובה: כליתם. הבאתם קרוב אל הכליון ועכ"ז ממאנים לקחת מוסר: חזקו פניהם מסלע. הקשו פניהם יותר מן סלע ר"ל לא נכנעו אבל העיזו פניהם וממאנים לשוב: (ד) ואני אמרתי. כשהוכחתים ולא קבלו מוסר אמרתי בתחילה אין תבונה בהם ואך דלים המה מחכמה: נואלו. נפתו בדעתם כי לא ידעו דרך ה' וגו' שמביא פורעניות לגלות אוזן למוסר: (ה) אל הגדולים. בדבר החכמה: ואדברה אותם. אדבר עמהם

מצודת ציון

(ג) עיניך. ר"ל השגחתך: לאמונה. ענין דבר המתקיים וכן יתד במקום נאמן (ישעיה כ"ב): חלו. מל' חולי: כליתם. מלשון כליון: מאנו. מלשון מיאון: (ד) נואלו. ענין סכלות וטפשות כמו נואלו שרי צוען (שם י"ט): (ה) אותם. וכן כלא איש אתה (ש"א כ"ו):

engage in the study of the Torah, and who are immersed in ethics and the knowledge of God, will surely heed my reproof.

5. **I will go to the great ones**—*They will hearken. But I did not avail, and they too together broke the yoke of the Holy One, blessed be He, off them.*—[*Rashi*]

As mentioned above, *Redak* explains this verse literally, as referring to the wealthy classes, knowledgeable in God's law, from whom the prophet had expected response. The result was, however, that they together, all of them, despite their knowledge, broke off the yoke of the Torah.

3. O Lord, are not Your eyes upon faith? You smote them but they felt no pain, You consumed them, [but] they refused to receive correction. They have made their faces harder than a rock, they have refused to repent. 4. And I said, "But they are poor, they have become foolish, for they did not know the way of the Lord, the judgment of their God. 5. I will go to the great ones and speak with them, for they know the way of the Lord,

My name, they swear falsely by My name and I am aware of it.'—[*Redak*]

3. **O Lord, Your eyes**—*are they not on people with faith, to do good to them? Now why have these betrayed You, and they do not seek faith?*—[*Rashi*] I.e., You know whether they have faith in their hearts. You see that they have no faith, but are cunning and guileful. Therefore, you smote them.—[*Abarbanel*]

Others render: 'O Lord, are not Your eyes on permanence?' Your providence is on permanent things, not on things that do not last. If so, since You smote them for their sins and they felt no pain, what is the use of Your providence over them? This is parallel to 2:30. Also Isaiah (1:5) reproved the people for not taking their punishment to heart and for not receiving correction.—[*Redak, Mezudath David*]

You smote them—*and they did not become ill because of the blow to lay it to their heart to repent of their evil.*—[*Rashi*]

[*Rashi* apparently derives חָלוּ from חלה, *to be ill.* In that case, the accent should be on the last syllable.] *Redak,* therefore, derives it from the root חִיל, *to feel pain,* or as Isaiah da Trani explains it, *to fear.*

You consumed them—You brought them near to destruction, yet they refused to receive correction.—[*Redak, Mezudath David*]

to receive—Heb. קַחַת, *equivalent to* לָקַחַת, *to receive.*—[*Rashi*]

They have made their faces harder than a rock—When You sent Your prophets to reprove them, they made their faces harder than a rock and were not ashamed to disregard the prophets and refuse to repent.—[*Redak*]

4. **And I said**—*The prophet says so, "They are but impoverished of wisdom," these with whom I speak.*—[*Rashi*]

they have become foolish—Heb. נוֹאֲלוּ, *an expression of* אֱוִיל, *a fool, as the Targum renders:* אִשְׁפָּשׁוּ.—[*Rashi*]

Redak explains this more literally. The prophet says: I tested both the poor and the rich with my reproof. When I reproved the people and they did not respond, I thought that 'they are but poor,' and the poorer class is usually devoid of wisdom. They are not as learned and erudite as the wealthier classes since they devote their time to tilling the soil and dressing the vines, and they do not engage in the study of the Torah and religious ethics. The wealthier classes, however, who have time to

מִשְׁפַּט אֱלֹהֵיהֶם אַךְ הֵמָּה יַחְדָּו שָׁבְרוּ
עֹל נִתְּקוּ מוֹסֵרוֹת׃ ו עַל־כֵּן הִכָּם אַרְיֵה
מִיַּעַר זְאֵב עֲרָבוֹת יְשָׁדְדֵם נָמֵר שֹׁקֵד
עַל־עָרֵיהֶם כָּל־הַיּוֹצֵא מֵהֵנָּה יִטָּרֵף
כִּי רַבּוּ פִּשְׁעֵיהֶם עָצְמוּ מְשֻׁבוֹתֵיהֶם׃
ז אֵי לָזֹאת אֶסְלוֹחַ־לָךְ בָּנַיִךְ עֲזָבוּנִי
וַיִּשָּׁבְעוּ בְּלֹא אֱלֹהִים וָאַשְׂבִּעַ אוֹתָם

אסלח קרי וינאפו

תרגום

בְּרַם אִינוּן כַּחֲדָא מְרָדוּ
מִן אוֹרָיְתָא אִתְרַחֲקוּ מִן
אוּלְפָנָא׃ ו עַל כֵּן סְלֵקָה
בְּמַשִׁרְיָתֵיהּ יִסַּק עֲלֵיהוֹן
כְּאַרְיָא מֵחוּרְשָׁא
וְיִקְטְלִינוּן עַמְמַיָּא
דְתַקִּיפִין כְּדִיבֵי נִרְשָׁא
יְבַזְזוּנוּן שִׁלְטוֹנִין
דְחַסִּינִין כְּנִמְרָא בְּמָנִין
עַל קִרְוֵיהוֹן כָּל דְיִפּוֹק
מִנְהוֹן יִתְקְטִיל אֲרֵי
סַגִיאִין מָרְדֵיהוֹן תַּקִּיפִין
תְּיוּבָתְהוֹן׃ ז נְבִיָּא אֲמַר
לֵיהּ כְּנִשְׁתָּא דְיִשְׂרָאֵל
עַל אֵידָא אֶשְׁבּוֹק לְכוֹן
אֲנָא קְרֵיתִי לְכוֹן בְּנִין וְאִינוּן שְׁבַקוּ פּוּלְחָנִי
וּמְקַיְמִין בְּשׁוּם טַעֲוָתָא עוֹד שְׂבִעִית יַתְהוֹן

מהר"י קרא

הקטנים: (ו) על כן הכם אריה. זה נבוכדנצר: זאב ערבות. שדרכו לצאת לעת ערב שהוא רעב כל היום: ישדדם. אלו מדי ופרס: נמר. זה יון. כל הנמלט מאלו שנאמר למעלה: יטרף. ביד אדום: (ז) אי לזאת. לאיזו מכל חטאתיך אסלח לך: בניך עזבוני. והלכו לאלהים אחרים: וישבעו בלא אלהים. ונשבעים בשם ע"ז שאינן אלהים שציויתים ושם אלהים אחרים לא תזכירו: ואשביע אותם וינאפו. וכשהשבעתם מכל טוב סיד הם נעשין גדודין והולכין לבית הזונות וכן הוא אומר בסמוך איש אל אשת רעהו יצהלו שהשביעה מביאה

רש"י

ישמעו אך לא הועלתי וגם המה יחדו שברו עולו של הקב"ה מעליהם: (ו) אריה. מלכו' בבל: זאב. מלכות מדי: נמר. מלכות יון: יטרף. כשדים: זאב ערבות. לשון ערבה ושוחה זאב המדבר: שוקד. ממהר ומנחם חברו עם לשון שמירה כמו לשקוד על דלתותי (משלי ח) וי"ת לשון אריבה: (ז) אי לזאת אסלח לך. בתמיה שמא לזאת אסלח לך ומנחם פירש אי כמו אין אשר בניך עזבוני ואשביע אותם כל

מנחת שי

בגמ"א: (ו) ישדדם. כן כתוב בספרים מדוייקים ובהללו וכתב רד"ק בפירוש ובמכלול דף קפ"א ובשרשים שבא שלם ונקוד על דרך החסר כמו שהיה בחסרון הכפל יְשַׁדֵּם כי נקוד כשלם היה יְשָׁדְדֵם כמו ישמרם והוא מהקל ויתכן היותו מבנין פועל הכבד כדומה למרובע מן יְשׁוֹדֵד מלכותם (הושע י') ובא כמשפטו והוא הנכון עכ"ל. ולכל הלועזים קריאת השי"ן בקמ"ץ חטוף כמו ושדדו את בני קדם (ירמיה מ"ט) שדדה נינוה (נחום ג') ועיין בספר הדבקה אות י' ומ"ש בס"ד במזמור ט' על חנני: (ז) אסלוח. אסלח קרי: ואשבע. בכל ספרים כ"י בשי"ן שמאלית וכן פירש

רד"ק

לכה שאומר להם ותנה כשדברתי עמהם יחדיו שברו של התורה אע"פ שידעוה נתקו עולה מעליהם ותתקו מוסרותיה ואמר יחדו ר"ל כולם מצאתי' כן וכן ת"י ברם אינון כחדא מרדו וגו' כבעמוד: (ו) על כן הכם. על ששברו עול התורה מעליהם הכם אריה מיער המשיל האויב לאריה שיוצא מן היער לטרוף ולזאב שיוצא לעת ערב ובא סמוך לישוב כדי לטרוף הנמצא יחידי כי אינו בעל לב חזק כמו הנמר וכל שכן כאריה לפיכך ירא לצאת ברוב אלא לעת ערב לפיכך אמר זאב ערבות ואמר זאב ערבות ישדדם שלם נקוד על דרך החסר או הוא מבנין מרובע כמו ישודד מצבותיו ובא כמשפטו והוא הנכון האריה משל למלך כמו שהאריה מלך החיות הזאב משל לחיל והנמר לשרי החיל וכן תירגם יונתן סלק במשירתיה יסק עליהון וגו' כבעמוד ויש מפרשים ערבות כמו במדבר בערבה: נמר שקד. כמו שוא שקד שומר ענין השתדלות על הדבר והתמדה בו: מהנה. ר"ל מהערים: (ז) אי לזאת אסלח לך. מלת אי לשון קריאה והוא הפוך בלשון ערבי י"א מה טוב יש בך שאומר

מצודת ציון

עמהם: עול. כלי המונח על צואר בהמה החורשת: נתקו. ענין הפתק והפרדה: מוסרות. קשורי רצועות העול: (ו) ערבות. ענינו כמו מדבר וכן במדבר בערבה (דברים א'): ישדדם. ענין עושק הגזל: נמר. שם חיה מה: שוקד. ענין מהירות כמו כי שוקד אני (עיל א'): עצמו. חזקו: משובותיהם. ענין מרד וסירוב: (ז) אי.

מצודת דוד

דבר׳ הוכחתי כי המה ידעו וגו׳ שהפורענות לא לגלות עול למוסר: המה יחדו. סדלים עם הגדולים: שברו עול. ר"ל אינם רוצים להיות נכנעים למקום: נתקו. הפתיקו מעליהם מוסרי העול והוא כפל ענין במ"ש: (ו) על כן. בעבו׳ שאינם רוצים להיות נכנעים למקום לכן מסרם ביד האומות: הכם אריה מיער. זה משל על האומות: זאב ערבות. זאב היושב במדבר יעשוק נפשותם: שוקד. ממהר לבוא על עריהם להכחיתם: כל היוצא מהנה. מן הערים ההנה: יטרף. ע"י אחד מחיות ההם: עצמו. חזקו בדבר המרידה: (ז) אי לזאת. הנה הזונות אשר לזאת אסלח לך הלוא בניך עזבוני: בלא אלהים. בעכו"ם שאין בו ממש בו שאמינו ונשבעו בו: ואשביע. הני השבעתי אותם בכל טוב ומרוב טובה ותאוה הלכו שנו אל הזונות: ובית זונה. לבית זונה הלכו גדודים

the judgment of their God; but they together broke the yoke, burst the bands. 6. Therefore, a lion from the forest smote them, a wolf of the deserts spoils them, a leopard hastens upon their cities, anyone who comes out of them shall be torn to pieces, for their transgressions are many, their backslidings are increased. 7. Shall I forgive you for this? Your children have forsaken Me, and they swore by no-gods. Here I sated them

Alternatively, 'they together' denotes the poor and the wealthy.—[*Abarbanel, Mezudath David*]

6. **a lion**—The kingdom of Babylon.—[*Rashi*] *Kara* explains that this is Nebuchadnezzar. See above 4:7.

a wolf—*The kingdom of Media.*—[*Rashi*]

a leopard—*The kingdom of Greece.*—[*Rashi*]

shall be torn to pieces—*by Edom.*—[*Rashi* from *Lev. Rabbah* 13:2]

a wolf of the deserts—Heb. עֲרָבוֹת, *an expression of* (supra 2:6) עֲרָבָה וְשׁוּחָה, *plains and pits, a wolf of the desert.*—[*Rashi*]

hastens—Heb. שֹׁקֵד *Menahem* (p. 180) *associated it with an expression of watching. Comp.* (Prov. 8:34) *'To watch* (לִשְׁקֹד) *My doors daily.' And Jonathan rendered* it as *an expression of lying in wait.*—[*Rashi*]

Because they broke off the yoke of Torah, the lion from the forest smote them. He compares the enemy to a lion that comes out of the forest to tear its victims to pieces and to a wolf that comes out at evening time and comes near to civilization to attack anyone standing alone. The wolf is not as brave as the leopard and surely not as brave as the lion. He is therefore called זְאֵב עֲרָבוֹת, *a wolf of the evenings.* The lion represents the king, as the lion, who is the king of the beasts, the wolf represents the army, and the leopard the officers. This is *Jonathan*'s rendering.—[*Redak*]

who comes out of them—I.e. out of the cities.—[*Redak*]

7. **Shall I forgive you for this?**—*This is the rhetorical question, Shall I forgive you for this? and Menahem* (p. 22) *explains* אֵי *like* אֵין, *not.* For this I will not forgive you, *because your children have forsaken Me, when I sated them with all good.*—[*Rashi*]

Redak renders: What good is in you that I should say, 'For this I will forgive you'? I find no good in you, only many evils; your children have forsaken Me etc.' The prophet is addressing Jerusalem.

Others explain: אֵי as equivalent to אֵיכָה. How shall I forgive you for this?—[*Ibn Nachmiash*]

by no-gods—By pagan deities which have no power.—[*Mezudath David*]

וַיִּנְאָפוּ וּבֵית זוֹנָה יִתְגֹּדָדוּ: ח סוּסִים
מֻוזָּנִים מַשְׁכִּים הָיוּ אִישׁ אֶל־אֵשֶׁת
רֵעֵהוּ יִצְהָלוּ: ט הַעַל־אֵלֶּה לוֹא־אֶפְקֹד
נְאֻם־יְהוָה וְאִם בְּגוֹי אֲשֶׁר־כָּזֶה לֹא
תִתְנַקֵּם נַפְשִׁי: י עֲלוּ בְשָׁרוֹתֶיהָ
וְשַׁחֵתוּ וְכָלָה אַל־תַּעֲשׂוּ הָסִירוּ
נְטִישׁוֹתֶיהָ כִּי לוֹא לַיהוָה הֵמָּה: יא כִּי
בָגוֹד בָּגְדוּ בִּי בֵּית יִשְׂרָאֵל וּבֵית יְהוּדָה

טוּבָא וְאִינוּן הֲווֹ לְמֶהֱוֵי
זְנָאִין וּבֵית נַפְקַת בְּרָא
מִסְתַּיְעִין: ח סוּסְוָן
אֲגִירִיסִין אֲחֲרִין הֲווֹ גְּבַר
עַל אִתַּת חַבְרֵיהּ
מְצַוְּחִין: ט הַעַל אִלֵּין לָא
אַסְעַר לְאַיְתָאָה עֲלֵיהוֹן
בִּישְׁתָא אֲמַר יְיָ וְאִם מִן
עַמָּא דִכְדֵין עוֹבָדוֹהִי לָא
אִתְפְּרַע מִנְהוֹן כִּרְעוּתִי:
י סַקוּ בְּקִרְוָהָא וְחַבִּילוּ
וּגְמִירָא לָא תַעְבְּדוּן
פַּגַרוּ בִּרְנְיָתְהָא אֲרֵי לָא
בְעַנָא קֳדָם יְיָ בְּהוֹן:
יא אֲרֵי שִׁקְרָא שַׁקַּרוּ
בְּמֵימְרִי בֵּית יִשְׂרָאֵל

קמץ בז"ק מיוזנים קרי

רש"י

טוב. יתגודדו. יתקבצו גדודים: (ח) סוסים מיוזנים משכים היו. כסוסים אלו המזויינים בקושי אבר תשמיש בכל בקר היו משכים לאור בקר בהשכמה: יצהלו. ל' זה נופל על הסוסים מקול מהלות אביריו (לקמן ח) לשון להלה (אנווייזמיל"ט בלע"ז): (י) בשרותיה. לשון מישור ומנחם חברו לשון חומה עם אדלג שור (תהלים י"ח) אך לא יתכנו.

מהר"י קרא

לידי זנות. כמו: (ח) סוסים מיוזנים. לשון מזון: משכים היו איש אל אשת רעהו. כל אחד ואחד היה משכים לילך אל אשת חבירו. (י) עלו בשרותיה ושחתו. הנביא מכריז לאומות שיעלו בשרותיה וישחיתו הנטישת: שרותיה. כמו שרון. היא

רד"ק

לזאת אסלח לך כלומר בעבור זה הטובה ואינני מוצא בך טובה רק רעות רבות בניך עזבוני וגו' והקריאה כנגד ירושלם: ואשבע אותם וינאפו. על דרך וישמן ישורון ויבעט: יתגודדו. יתקבצו גדודים ולא ישובו איש מחברו וכן תירגם יונתן מסתייעין: (ח) סוסים מוזנים. כתיב בוי"ו וקרי ביו"ד ואותיות אה"וי מתחלפות והוא כמו הפוך מוזנים מן מזון אמר הנה הם כמו הסוסים שנתנו להם מזון רב בלילה והם שבעים בתאותם בבקר יצאו ויצהלו וצהלתם היא נתינת קולם ובשמחה אורי"ליר בלע"ז כן הם ינאפו בלילה עם נשי רעיהם וימלאו תאותם ובבקר יוצאים שמחים מתהללים ברעתם: אל אשת רעהו. בעבור אשת רעהו: משכים. שם וכן כטל משכים הולך כלומר בהשכמה בבקר: (ט) העל אלה. אם על אלה הרעות לא אפקוד אי אפשר שלא אענישם על הרעות הגדולות האלה וכפל הענין במלות שונות ואמר: ואם בגוי אשר כזה לא תתנקם נפשי. ונפשו הוא והוא נפשו וכן נשבע ה' בנפשו כמו בי נשבעתי ויונתן פי' בנפשי כלומר ברצוני תרגום ואם עמא דכדין עבדיהון לא אתפרע מנהון כרעותי: ואם בגוי אשר כזה. זה עם וי"ו השמוש ואם והבאים אחר זה בפרשיות האחרות אם בלא וי"ו השמוש בגוי שיהיה כזה העם או פירוש אם בגוי אשר כזה מעשיהם כתרגומו: (י) עלו בשרותיה. בחומותיה תרגום חומה שורא והכנוי לירושלם והצווי עלו ושחתו כנגד האויבים ויונתן תירגם בשרותיה בקרוהא: הסירו נטישותיה. הם שיני החומה ויונתן תירגם כמו ארמנותיה בירניתהא: כי לא לה' המה. עתה כבר היו לה' שאמר וגנותי על העיר הזאת להושיעה אבל עתה אין חומותיה לה' שיגן עליהם כי עם העיר עזבוהו והוא עזבה והתירה לאויב ויש מפרשים הסיר נטישותיה כמו ואת הנטישות הסר התז שהם סעיפי האילנות המתפשטים ובאמרו וכלה לא תעשו אינו אומר על החומה שהרי נתצוה כלה כמו שאמר ואת חומות ירושלם סביב נתצו כל חיל כשדים אלא פי' וכלה לא תעשו בעם: (יא) כי בגוד. לפיכך תקחו נקמתם מהם ובדין אני מצוה לכם

מנחת שי

כמתרגם והמפרשים: (ח) מוזנים. מיזנים קרי ביו"ד והכתיב בוא"ו כן הוא למערבאי:

מצודת דוד

יחד ולא יתבוששו אלה מאלה: (ח) סוסים מיוזנים. הם היו כמו הסוסים שנתנ' להם מזון הרבה בלילה והמה שבעים לתאותם כאשר ישכימו בבוקר ילאו ויצהלו וכן המה ימלאו תאותם וינאפו עם אשת רעיהם כל הליל' וכאשר ישכימו בבוקר יצהלו איש אל אשת רעהו מרוב שמחה והשגת תאות הלב: (ט) העל אלה. וכי על מעשים האלה לא אשגיח להפרע מהם בתמים: אשר כזה. אשר עושה כדבר הזה: (י) עלו בשרותיה. אתם האומות עלו בין שורות כרמי והשחיתו אותם אבל לא תכלו את הכל ר"ל שחתו בעם ואל תאבדו את כלם: הסירו נטישותיה. הסירו מהם הענפים הגדולים ר"ל הרגו הגדולים והשרים: כי לוא לה' המה. כי אינם עם ה' כי פשעו בו: (יא) כי בגוד וגו'. כי בגדו בי אלה כאלה

מצודת ציון

ענינו כמו אנה וכן אי הבל אחיך (בראשית ד'): ובית. כמו ולבית: יתגודדו. מלשון גדוד ומחנה: (ח) סוסים. כסוסים: מיוזנים. מלשון מזון: משכים. מלשון השכמה: יצהלו. ענין הרמת קול גדול וכן צהלו מים (ישעיה כ"ד): (ט) אפקוד. ענין השגחה וכן ופקוד גפן זאת (תהלים פ'): תתנקם. מלשון נקמה: (י) בשרותיה. מלשון שורה וידוע הוא כדרז"ל וכן בין שורותם יצהירו (איוב כ"ד):

they are the roots of the vineyard—to be associated either with the walls or with the plain. I say, therefore, that בְּשָׁרוֹתֶיהָ *is an expression of the rows of the vineyard. Jonathan, however, rendered* בְּשָׁרוֹתֶיהָ, *in her cities, and* נְטִישׁוֹתֶיהָ, *her palaces.—[Rashi]*

11. **have dealt treacherously with Me**—Therefore, you shall take your revenge from them, and I am right-

and they committed adultery, and they banded together in the
house of a harlot. 8. Like armed stallions, they would arise
early; they would neigh, each one over his friend's wife. 9. Shall
I not punish for these things? says the Lord, or for a nation
such as this shall My soul not wreak vengeance? 10. Ascend
upon its rows and destroy, but make no complete end; remove
its roots, for they are not the Lord's. 11. For the house of Israel
and the house of Judah have dealt treacherously with Me,

they banded together—*They gather in troops.*—[*Rashi*]

Although I sated you with all good, you have betrayed Me and committed adultery. This is reminiscent of 'And Jeshurun became fat and kicked' (Deut. 32:15). Not only did they commit adultery, but they banded together in the house of a harlot, none of them ashamed before his companions.—[*Redak*]

8. **Like armed stallions they would arise early**—*Like these stallions who are armed with erect membra, every morning they would arise at daybreak.*—[*Rashi*]

they would neigh—Heb. יִצְהָלוּ. *This too is an expression appropriate for horses. Comp.* (8:16) *'From the sound of the neighing* (מִצְהֲלוֹת) *of his steeds,' an expression of shouting* (*esjodement in O.F.*).—[*Rashi*] *Redak* (*Shorashim*) defines it as an expression of joy.

The prophet compares the people to stallions. They are fed at night, and they sate themselves with their lust in the morning. Similarly, the people would fornicate with their neighbors' wives at night, satisfying their lust, and in the morning, they would arise early, happy and boastful of their achievement. Hence, we render: Like well-fed stallions, they would arise early, each one would shout for joy over his neighbor's wife.—[*Redak*]

After reproving them for idolatry and murder, the prophet reproves them for immorality.—[*Abarbanel*]

9. **Shall I not punish for these things?**—Is it possible that I should not punish for these grave evils?—[*Redak*]

Daath Sofrim explains that, after they satisfy their sexual appetite at night with their own wives, they wake up in the morning, with a lust for their neighbors' wives, not that they actually committed the sin. Eventually, however, many were drawn into the sin itself. See *Num. Rabbah* 9:7–12.

shall My soul not wreak vengeance?—He and His soul are synonymous. He is His soul, and His soul is He. It may also be rendered: shall my desire not wreak vengeance? This follows *Targum Jonathan.*—[*Redak*]

10. **Ascend upon its rows**—Heb. בְּשָׁרוֹתֶיהָ, *an expression of a plain. Menahem* (p. 181) *associates it as an expression of a wall with* '(II Sam. 22:30) *I scale a wall* (שׁוּר),' *but* נְטִישׁוֹתֶיהָ (*cep in Prov.*) *do not fit—for*

נאם־יהוה׃ יב כחשו ביהוה ויאמרו
לוא־הוא ולא־תבוא עלינו רעה וחרב
ורעב לוא נראה׃ יג והנביאים יהיו
לרוח והדבר אין בהם כה יעשה להם׃
יד לכן כה־אמר יהוה אלהי צבאות
יען דברכם את־הדבר הזה הנני נתן
דברי בפיך לאש והעם הזה עצים

תרגום

וּבֵית יְהוּדָה אֲמַר יְיָ׃ יב כַּדִיבוּ בְּמֵימְרָא דַיְיָ וַאֲמַרוּ לָא מִן קֳדָמוֹהִי אַתְיָא עֲלָנָא טָבְתָא וְאַף לָא תֵיתֵי עֲלָנָא בִּישְׁתָא וּדְקַטְלִין בְּחַרְבָּא וּבְכַפְנָא לָא נֶחֱזֵי׃ יג וּנְבִיֵי שִׁקְרָא יְהוֹן לְלָמָא וּנְבוּאַת שִׁקְרֵיהוֹן לָא הִתְקַיַם דָא פּוּרְעֲנוּתָא תִתְעֲבִיד מִנְהוֹן׃ יד בְּכֵן כִּדְנַן אֲמַר יְיָ אֱלֹהִים צְבָאוֹת חֲלַף דְאִתְנַבִּיתוּן יַת פִּתְגָמָא הָדֵין הָא אֲנָא יָהֵיב פִּתְגָמֵי נְבוּאָתִי בְּפוּמָךְ תַּקִּיפִין כְּאֶשָּׁתָא וְעַמָּא הָדֵין סַלְּשִׁן

מהר"י קרא

ארץ כישור: (יב) כחשו בה'. בנביאי ה': ויאמרו לא הוא. אינו כן כמו שמתנבא עלינו אין אנו יראין ממה שהוא מתנבא שתבא עלינו רעה: (יג) והנביאים יהיו לרוח. דברי נביאיהם האמת בעיניהם לרוח. ללא כלום: והדיבר. שהם מתנבאין להם הם אומרים אין בהם לא מאת ה' הם מתנבאין נבואה זו. אבל בשבועה: כה יעשה להם. כמו שהם מתנבאין להם: (יד) יען דברכם את הדבר הזה הנני נותן את דברי בפיך לאש. שתהא נבואתי

רש"י

נטישותיה (לי"ש בלע"ז) שהם שרשי הכרם להיות נחשבים עם הקומות ולא עם המישור. ואני אומר שרותיה לשון שורות הכרם ויונתן תירגם בשרותיה בקירוהא ונטישותיה ברניתהא: (יב) ויאמרו לא הוא. לא מן קדמוהי אתיא עלנא טבתא: (יג) והנביאים יהיו לרוח. כתרגומו ונביי שקרא יהון ללמא כלומר הנבואה הניבאי' לנו נביאי שקר בשמו של הקדו' ב"ה דבריהם יהפכו להבל והדבור של קדושה שהם אומרים לנו בשם הקדוש ב"ה אינו בהם: כה יעשה להם. הנביא אומר לאומרים זאת כה יעשה להם כאשר אמר ה' לי ומה אמר ה' לי יען דברכם את הדבר הזה וגו': (יד) ואכלתם.

מנחת שי

(יב) לוא הוא. מתחלפת לא הוא וכן לוא נראה דסוף פסוק מתחלפת לא נראה המנס כמסו' פרשת ויקרא נמנו שניהם בנין ל"ב מלאים:

רד"ק

שתשחיתוה כי הם בגדו בי: (יב) כחשו בה' ויאמרו לוא הוא. פירוש לא הוא שישגיח עלינו ויראה במעשינו ואם נעשה כחפצנו לא תבא עלינו רעה בעבור זה וחרב ורעב לא נראה אע"פ שמפחידין אותנו נביאיו על זה שקר הם אומרים כי לא תבא להם נבואה מאת האל כי הוא אינו רואינו ואינו יודענו ועל הדרך הזה תירגם יונתן כדיבו במימרא דה' יאמרו וגו' כבעמוד: (יג) והנביאים. הנביא' שמפחידים אותם ואומרים שלום יהיה לכם יהיו לרוח כלומר כמוץ לפני רוח: והדיבר אין בהם. כיון שהדבר אין בהם כלומר רוח הקדש איך ידעו הם כך וכך אלא שהם סומכין בחלומותיהם או בקסמיהם ומבטיחים העם לטוב כדי שימצאו חן בעיניהם כשמיפין להם מעשיהם ואומרים לא תבא עליכם רעה ובעונש זה יכלו ויהיו לרוח: כה יעשה להם. על דרך כה יעשה לי אלהים וכה יוסיף כלומר כך וכך רעה יעשה להם וי"ת ונבייא שקרא יהון וגו' כבעמוד: (יד) לכן כה אמר. את הדבר הזה שאתם אומרים עלי לא הוא ולא נבואתי והנה דברי מגיעים אליך: הנני נותן דברי בפיך. והעם הזה עצים ואכלתם ובזה יכירו כי נבואתי מגעת א"יך שיתקיימו עליהם דברי לרעה כמו שאתה אומר ויהי דבריך להם כמו האש לעצים שתאכל אותם ומה שאמר דברכם כמדבר כנגד העם ואמר בפיך כמדבר כנגד הנביא הרי הוא כאומר אמור להם יען דברכם את הדבר הזה כי הנני נותן דברי בפיך לאש והעם הזה עצים ואכלתם ויונתן פירש דברכם כנגד הנביאים שתרגם חלף דאתנביתון ית פתגמא הדין:

מצודת ציון

נטישותיה. הם הענפים הגדולים המתפשטים למרחוק כמו ואת הנטישות הסיר התז (ישעיה י"ח): (יד) ואכלתם. ותשרפם וכן

מצודת דוד

כמו שבגד ישראל כן בגד יהודה: (יב) כחשו בה'. כחשו בהשגחת המקום: לוא הוא. ר"ל אין הוא משגיח: ולא תבוא עלינו רעה. כיהויאל ואין משגיח אין שכר ועונש: (יג) והנביאים. ר"ל דברי הנביאי' יהיו דומים לדברי רוח שאין בהם ממש: והדבר אין בהם. לא ה' דבר בם כי היו מכחישים דברי הנבואה: כה יעשה. כי היו מקללים את הנביאים לאמר להם כה יעשה ה' להם כפי הרעות אשר הם מתנבאים עלינו: (יד) יען. כעון אשר דברת' הדבר הזה להכחיש ההשגחה והנבואה: הנני נותן וגו'. דברי הנבואה אשר נתתי בפיך תהיה כאש השורף וסעם הזה יהיו נוח לנשרף כעלים: ואכלתם. דבר

So shall be done to them—This is similar to: 'So shall God do to me and so shall He continue,'' found frequently in the Scriptures. [This is a curse in which the details are not mentioned.] The intention is that so much bad should befall them.—[*Redak*]

14. **Therefore, so says the Lord God of Hosts**—Therefore, because you have spoken this word of denying God's prophecy and degrading His prophets, the Lord God of Hosts said to me: Behold, I put My words into your mouth as fire etc.—[*Ibn Nachmiash, Redak*]

and it shall consume them—Heb. וַאֲכָלָתַם.—[*Rashi*]

says the Lord. 12. They denied the Lord and said, "It is not
He, and no evil will befall us, neither will we see sword or
famine. 13. And the prophets shall become wind, for there is
no speech in them." So shall be done to them. 14. Therefore, so
says the Lord God of Hosts, because you have spoken this
word. Behold I put My words into your mouth as fire, and this
people [shall be wood] and it shall consume them.

fully commanding you to destroy the city, since they have dealt treacherously with Me.—[*Redak*]

12. **They denied the Lord**—They denied the Lord's providence.—[*Mezudath David*] *Jonathan* paraphrases: They denied the word of the Lord. In the worst times, the Jews did not deny God's existence. Even when they worshipped idols, they considered God as the God of gods. They did, however, deny His providence and His knowledge of earthly creatures.

I.e., He does not supervise over us, and he does not see our deeds. Therefore, if we do as we wish, no evil will befall us because of it.—[*Redak*]

neither shall we see sword or famine—Although His prophets wish to frighten us with their predictions of sword and famine, they are lying, for they receive no prophecy from God, since He neither sees us nor knows of our deeds.—[*Redak*]

13. **And the prophets shall become wind**—*As the Targum renders: And the false prophets shall become naught. That is to say: The prophecy that the false prophets prophesy for us in the name of the Holy One, blessed be He—their words shall turn to futility, and the speech of holiness that they say to us in the name of the Holy One, blessed be He, is not in them.*—[*Rashi*]

So shall be done to them—*The prophet says to those who say this, "So shall be done to them as the Lord said to me, and what did the Lord say to me? "Because you have spoken this word etc."*—[*Rashi*]

It appears that *Rashi* explains the entire two verses as a quotation of the people. They believe neither in the true prophets nor in the false prophets since they deny God's knowledge of what is transpiring in this world. At the end, the prophet concludes, "So shall be done to them." *Redak*, however, explains that the people deny God's prophets, who predict their doom. The prophet concludes with verse 13: And the prophets shall be for the wind etc. I.e., the prophets who predict that there will be peace shall be like chaff before the wind since there is no speech in them; i.e., God's speech is not in them for they are not endowed with the Divine Spirit, but rely on their dreams and their divinations and promise the people that all will be good, in order to please them and to flatter them. For this sin, they shall be like chaff before the wind.

בְּקַשְׁא וִיקַטְלוּנוּן: טו הָא
אֲנָא מַיְתִי עֲלֵיכוֹן עַם
מֵרְחִיק בֵּית יִשְׂרָאֵל אֲמַר
יְיָ עַם תַּקִּיף הוּא עַמָּא
דְמֵעָלְמָא הוּא עַמָּא לָא
הִידַע לִישָׁנֵיהּ וְלָא
תִשְׁמַע מָה דִימַלֵּיל:
טז בֵּית אֲזֵינֵיהּ כְּקִבְרָא
פְּתִיחַ כּוּלְהוֹן גִּבָּרִין:
יז וְיִבּוֹז חֲצָדָךְ וּמֵיכְלָךְ
יִקְטְלוּן בְּנָךְ וּבְנָתָךְ
יִשְׁבּוֹן עָנָךְ וְתוֹרָךְ יִבּוֹז
פֵּרֵי גוּפְנָךְ וְתֵינָךְ יְפַגֵּר
קִרְוֵי אַרְעָךְ כְּרִיכָתָא
דְאַתְּ רָחִיץ לְאִשְׁתֵּיזָבָא
בְּהוֹן מִן קֳדָם דְקַטְלִין
בְּחַרְבָּא: יח וְאַף בְּיוֹמַיָּא
הָאִינוּן

וַאֲכָלָתַם׃ טו הִנְנִי מֵבִיא עֲלֵיכֶם גּוֹי
מִמֶּרְחָק בֵּית יִשְׂרָאֵל נְאֻם־יְהוָה גּוֹי ׀
אֵיתָן הוּא גּוֹי מֵעוֹלָם הוּא גּוֹי לֹא־תֵדַע
לְשֹׁנוֹ וְלֹא תִשְׁמַע מַה־יְדַבֵּר׃
טז אַשְׁפָּתוֹ כְּקֶבֶר פָּתוּחַ כֻּלָּם גִּבּוֹרִים׃
יז וְאָכַל קְצִירְךָ וְלַחְמֶךָ יֹאכְלוּ בָּנֶיךָ
וּבְנוֹתֶיךָ יֹאכַל צֹאנְךָ וּבְקָרֶךָ יֹאכַל
גַּפְנְךָ וּתְאֵנָתֶךָ יְרֹשֵׁשׁ עָרֵי מִבְצָרֶיךָ
אֲשֶׁר אַתָּה בֹּטֵחַ בָּהֵנָּה בֶּחָרֶב׃ יח וְגַם

ת"א גוי איתן. סוטה מו: אשפתו כקבר. שם ח מב: ואכל קצירך. בבא קמא קיט:

רש"י

ותאכל אותם: (טו) איתן. תקיף: גוי מעולם הוא. מימי קדם התחיל למרוד כי בדור הפלג' בארץ שנע': (טז) אשפתו. מקום נרתק החצים: (יז) ירושש ערי מבצריך וגו'. הרי זה מקרא מסורס ירושש בחרב את ערי מבצריך אשר אתה בוטח בהנה: ירושש. ימסכן: בחרב. ע"י גייסות וכן הוא

מהר"י קרא

עליהם כמו שהאש עושה רושם בכל מקום שנופל: (טו) ולא תשמע מה ידבר. לא תבין מה ידבר: (טז) אשפתו. מלא חיצים ושמא תאמר מועטין הן בתוכו כב' וג' חיצין אינו כן אלא הרי רחב: כקבר פתו. וכולו מלא ושמא תאמר אין בהן כח לירות ת"ל כולם גבורים: אשפתו. כוב"ר בלע"ז: (יז) ואכל קצירך ולחמך יאכלו בניך ובנותיך. כלומר מה שראוי לאכל לבניך ולבנותיך: ירושש. לשון רש ונקלה וכן מתרושש והון רב: אשר אתה בוטח בהנה.

רד"ק

(טו) הנני מביא עליכם. בית ישראל קריאה: ממרחק. כי בבל היא רחוקה מארץ ישראל: גוי איתן. חזק שלא תוכל להלחם כנגדו: גוי מעולם הוא. מזמן רב הוא גוי זה חזק ושאר הגוים הם יראים אותו ולא תוכל להעזר עם גוי זולתו: גוי לא תדע לשונו. ולא תבין מה יאמר וזה יותר קשה מאויב שמבין אדם לשונו וכן אמרו בתורה בקללית גוי אשר לא תשמע לשונו: ולא תשמע. ולא תבין והענין כפול במלות שונות: (טז) אשפתו. כי חצי האשפה ימיתו כל מי שיגע בהם וכאלו כלם קבורים באשפה ואמר כקבר פתוח שמוכן להשחית בו המתים: כלם גבורים כי הם כלומדי מלחמה ואין לכם כפלט להנצל מידם: (יז) ואכל. לחבך כלל כל מאכל והאכילה הנזכרת בפסוק יש אכילה היא איכות המאכל ויש אכילת החרב כמו שתרגם יתתן ויבוז אוצרך וגו' כבעמוד: ירושש. ענין רש ושבר וענין הרישות נופל גם כן בהריסת הערים כמו כי תאמר אדום רששנו ונשוב ונבנה חרבות: בחרב. בעת החרב או טעם בחרב למעלה לבניך ולבנותיך כאלו אמר יאכלו בניך ובנותיך בחרב ומה שאמר בניך ובנותיך כי כמו כן יאכל האבות אלא שאמר בתורה ואכל פרי בטנך וזה להכאיב נפש האבות שישחטו בניהם לעיניהם והם הקטנים שמתים בעון אבותם: (יח) וגם בימים ההמה.

מנחת שי

(טו) כלם גבורים. במקצת ספרים מדוייקים מלא וא"ו וכן נמן מ"פ המסורת כי לא נמנה במספר ז' חסרים ביהושע סימן י' ובשיר השירים סימן ג': (יח) ירשש. חסר וא"ו ונמסר עליו במקצת ספרים ל"י לים וחסר וי"ם מלא: אתה בוטח. למערבאי מלא וא"ו ולמדנחאי חסר וכן מצאתי בכמה מדוייקים כ"י מלא ומסורת (משלי כ"ח) מסייע למדנחאי דאמרת כל נביאים חסר בר מן ב' וסי' אשר אתה

מצודת דוד

כעבודה תשרוף אותם ר"ל דבר הנבואה תבוא עליהם: (טו) הנני וגו' בית ישראל. ר"ל אתם בית ישראל הנני מביא עליכם וגו': גוי. הוא גוי חזק: גוי מעולם הוא. ר"ל מזמן רב הוא בממשלה ולכן יגבה לבו להשחית הכל: לא תדע. לא תבין לשונו ולזה תחשב כי לא יוכלו להתרצות אליהם בדברים: ולא תשמע. לא תבין וכפל הדבר במ"ש: (טז) אשפתו. נרתק חציו הוא כקבר פתוח ר"ל כמו קבר פתוח הוא מוכן לקבורה כן את מת כן חצי האשפה יביאו מות רבי' כי יגיחו במלחמה: כלם. כל אנשי המלחמה המה גבורים: (יז) ואכל. הגוי ההוא יאכל קציר שדך וכל מאכלך אשר היה למאכל לבניך ולבנותיך: ירושש. יעני ערי מבצריך אשר אתה בוטח בהנה להנצל בהן מפני האויב: בחרב. ר"ל בעת יבוא

מצודת ציון

ואש מפיו תאכל (תהלים י"ח): (טו) איתן. ענין חוזק כמו איתן מושבך (במדבר כ"ד): תשמע. ענין הבנה כמו כי שומע יוסף (בראשית מ"ב): (טז) אשפתו. הוא נרתק החצים כמו עליו תרנה אשפה (איוב ל"ט): (יז) ולחמך. כל המאכל קרוי בלשון לחם כמו

trees, he will destroy the fortified cities of your land on which you rely to seek refuge, before those who slay with the sword.—[*Redak*]

impoverish—Heb. יְרֹשֵׁשׁ, *he will impoverish.*—[*Rashi*]

with the sword—*With troops. Comp. 'And a sword will not pass in your land'* (Lev. 26:6).—[*Rashi*]

It may also be interpreted as 'at the time of war.' It may also refer to 'they shall devour your sons and your daughters,' meaning that they will slay them with the sword in the

15. Behold I bring upon you a nation from afar, O house of Israel, says the Lord; it is a mighty nation, it is an ancient nation, a nation whose language you will not know, and you will not understand what he will speak. 16. His quiver is like an open grave, all of them are mighty men. 17. And he will devour your harvest and your bread; they will devour your sons and your daughters; he will devour your flocks and your cattle; he will devour your vines and your fig trees; he will impoverish your fortified cities upon which you rely, with the sword.

When the fire consumes them, they will realize that the prophecy is true.—[*Redak*]

15. This is the interpretation of the allegory appearing in the preceding verse, that of the fire that will consume the people.—[*Abarbanel*]

from afar—For Babylon is far from Eretz Israel.—[*Redak*]

mighty—Heb. אֵיתָן, *strong.*—[*Rashi*]

This is such a mighty nation that you will be unable to oppose them.—[*Redak*]

it is an ancient nation—*From days of yore it began to rebel against Me, in the generation of separation in the land of Shinar.*—[*Rashi*]

This refers to the generation that built the tower and were then scattered all over the earth.

Others explain that this nation was mighty from ancient times, and all nations fear to oppose it.—[*Redak*] Moreover, its haughtiness will lead it to destroy the land.—[*Abarbanel, Mezudath David*]

a nation whose language you will not know—This is worse than an enemy whose language you understand. This is reminiscent of Moses' prophecy, 'A nation whose language you will not understand' (Deut. 28:49).—[*Redak*]

Since you do not understand his language, you will be unable to beg for clemency.—[*Abarbanel, Mezudath David*]

16. **His quiver**—Heb. אַשְׁפָּתוֹ, *the place of the arrow case.*—[*Rashi*]

an open grave—The arrows of the quiver slay everyone they hit, and it is as though all of them are buried in the quiver. It is called an open grave since it is prepared to kill its victims.—[*Redak*]

all of them are mighty men—I.e., all his soldiers are mighty men, and there is no refuge from their hands.—[*Redak*]

17. **And he will devour your harvest and your bread**—Bread denotes all food. The enemies eating the harvest etc. may be taken literally, that they will eat it, or it may be taken figuratively, that they will destroy it. Indeed, *Jonathan* renders: And he will spoil your harvest and your food, they will slay your sons and your daughters, they will capture your flocks and your herds, he will spoil your vines and your fig

בַּיָּמִים הָהֵמָּה נְאֻם־יְהוָה לֹא־אֶעֱשֶׂה
אִתְּכֶם כָּלָה׃ יט וְהָיָה כִּי תֹאמְרוּ תַּחַת
מֶה עָשָׂה יְהוָה אֱלֹהֵינוּ לָנוּ אֶת־כָּל־
אֵלֶּה וְאָמַרְתָּ אֲלֵיהֶם כַּאֲשֶׁר עֲזַבְתֶּם
אוֹתִי וַתַּעַבְדוּ אֱלֹהֵי נֵכָר בְּאַרְצְכֶם
כֵּן תַּעַבְדוּ זָרִים בְּאֶרֶץ לֹא לָכֶם׃ כ הַגִּידוּ
זֹאת בְּבֵית יַעֲקֹב וְהַשְׁמִיעוּהָ בִיהוּדָה
לֵאמֹר׃ כא שִׁמְעוּ־נָא זֹאת עַם סָכָל וְאֵין
לֵב עֵינַיִם לָהֶם וְלֹא יִרְאוּ אָזְנַיִם לָהֶם

תרגום

האינון אמר יי לא
אעביד עמכון גמירא׃
יט ויהי ארי תימרון חלף
מה עבד יי אלהנא לנא
ית כל אלין ותימר להון
כמא דשבקתון פולחני
ופלחתון לטעות פלחי
כוכביא בארעכון כן
תשתעבדון לעממיא
פלחי כוכביא בארעא
דלא דילכון׃ כ חוו דא
בבית יעקב ובשרוה
בדבית יהודה למימר׃
כא שמעו כען דא עמא
טפשא ולית ליה לב
דעינין להון ולא חזן
אודנין להון ולא שמעין׃
המן

ת"א שמעו נא. עקרים מד יח:

מנחת שי

כו ס ח כו דיעפיה ובאזן שלוש אמה כוסח (ירמיה י"ב): (יט) ואמרת אליהם. יש ספרים מלא יו"ד:

רד"ק

כשיבא האויב ויאכל זה וזה כמו שכתוב לא אעשה אתכם כלה כי אתן בלב האויב להשאיר להם פלטה: (יט) והיה כי תאמרו. מדבר כנגד העם כמו שדבר עד הנה. ושב לדבר כנגד הנביא שיענה להם תשובת השאלה כאשר עזבתם וגו' והשאלה והתשובה תהיה אחר שיבא האויב ויגלה העם: כן תעבדו זרים. מדה כנגד מדה אתם עבדתם אלהי נכר בארצכם תעבדו עם נכר בארץ לא לכם: (כ) הגידו. אומר לכל השומעים דברו שיאמרו להם זאת ההוכח' דבר חולגבול הים: (כא) שמע

מצודת ציון

וכתם עפל לחמו (ישעי' ס"ס): ירושש. מל' רש ועני: (יט) תחת.

מצודת דוד

עליך בחרב במלחמה: (יח) וגם בימים ההמה. שיכלו עליך צרות מרובות מ"מ לא אכלה הכל כי ישאר ממך שארית ללכת גולה:

(יט) כי תאמרו. אתם ההולכים גולה: תחת מה. בעבור מה עשה וגו' את כל אלה להיות מקצתם נהרגי' ומקצתם גולים: ואמרת. אתה ירמיה תאמר להם שבא מדה במדה כפי אשר עזבתם את ה' ועבדתם אלהי נכר בארצכם כן תהיו נעזבים מה' והלכו בגולה לארץ אחרת ותעבדו גויי הארץ ההיא: (כ) הגידו זאת. את האמור למטה: והשמיעוה. את הדבר הזה: (כא) עם סכל. עם טפש ואין להם לב משכיל: ולא יראו. נפלאות המקום: ולא ישמעו. פלאי מעשיו:

18. And also in those days, says the Lord, I will not make an
end to you. 19. And it will be that you will say, "For what
reason has the Lord our God done all these to us?" you shall
say to them: As you have forsaken Me and worshipped foreign
gods in your land, so shall you serve strangers in a land not
yours. 20. Tell this in the house of Jacob and make it heard in
Judah, saying: 21. Hearken to this, foolish people without
understanding; they have eyes yet they see not, they have ears

presence of the parents to cause them anguish. This means the small children who die for the sins of the parents.—[*Redak*]

Kara and *Mezudath David* render: He will eat your harvest and your bread which your sons and your daughters should eat.

18. **And also in those days**—Even in those days, when the enemy comes and destroys all your property, they will, nevertheless, not destroy you completely. I will inspire the enemies to leave over a remnant.—[*Redak*]

Lest they despair of having a remnant, God tells the prophet to encourage the people so that they should repent of their sins in order to be saved from annihilation.—[*Abarbanel*]

There will remain survivors who will go into exile.—[*Mezudath David*]

19. **And it shall be that you will say**—He now addresses the people as He did until now. Then He turns to the prophet: And you shall say to them etc. The question and the answer will be after the enemy attacks and the people are exiled.—[*Redak*]

"For what reason has the Lord done all these to us?"—That some of the people were slain and the survivors exiled.—[*Mezudath David*]

so shall you serve strangers—This is payment in kind. You worshipped foreign gods in your land; now you will serve strangers in a land not yours.—[*Redak*]

God reveals here that, although there were other sins as well, their doom was sealed because of idolatry. Since the Holy Land is dedicated to God's providence, worshipping strange gods there is more inappropriate than in any other land. Consequently, God tells them that, if they wish to worship idols, they should be exiled to another land and there worship them.—[*Abarbanel*]

20. **Tell this**—I.e. all those who hear the following reproof, tell it in the house of Jacob etc.—[*Redak*]

21. **they see not**—the wonders of the Omnipresent.—[*Mezudath David*]

וְלֹא יִשְׁמָעוּ׃ כב הַאוֹתִי לֹא־תִירָאוּ נְאֻם־
יְהוָה אִם מִפָּנַי לֹא תָחִילוּ אֲשֶׁר־שַׂמְתִּי
חוֹל גְּבוּל לַיָּם חָק־עוֹלָם וְלֹא יַעַבְרֶנְהוּ
וַיִּתְגָּעֲשׁוּ וְלֹא יוּכָלוּ וְהָמוּ גַלָּיו וְלֹא־
יַעַבְרֻנְהוּ׃ כג וְלָעָם הַזֶּה הָיָה לֵב סוֹרֵר
וּמוֹרֶה סָרוּ וַיֵּלֵכוּ׃ כד וְלוֹא־אָמְרוּ
בִּלְבָבָם נִירָא נָא אֶת־יְהוָה אֱלֹהֵינוּ

קמץ בז״ק

תרגום

כב הֲמִן קֳדָמַי לָא
תִדְחֲלוּן אֲמַר יְיָ אִם מִן
קֳדָם מֵימְרִי לָא תְזוּעוּן
דְשַׁוֵיתִי חָלָא תְּחוּמָא
לְיַמָא קְיָם עֲלַם וְלָא עָדֵי
לֵיהּ וּמִטַרְפִין וְלָא יָכְלִין
וְהָמַן גַלוֹהִי וְלָא עָדַן
לֵיהּ׃ כג וּלְעַמָא הָדֵין
הֲוָה לֵב סָטֵי וּמָרִיד עַל
דִסְטוֹ מִבָּתַר פּוּלְחָנִי
גְלוֹ׃ כד וְלָא אֲמָרוּ
בְלִבְּהוֹן נִדְחַל כְּעַן קֳדָם
יְיָ אֱלָהָנָא דִמְחֵית מְטַר
בכיר

ה״א האותי וגו׳. בכא בתרא ה מג עקידה שער ח: ולא אמרו. עקידה שם: אלהינו הנותן. עקרים פד:

רש״י

אומר והרב לא תעביר בארצכם (ויקר׳ כ״ו): (כב) האותי לא תיראו. הלא הים שאינו דואג מפני הפורענות ואינו מצפה לקבול שכר ירא מפני ואינו עובר הגבול אשר שמתי סביביו: תחילו. לשון פחד: ויתגעשו. גליו. ומרומם לעבור הגבול ולא יכלו לעבור: והמו גליו. שאון קול גדול:

מהר״י קרא

אותן ערי מבצר שאתה בוטח להנצל שם מפני השונאין הבאין עליך: (כב) האותי לא תיראו נאום ה׳. שאם תחטאו לפני יהיו בניכם גולין ואעפ״כ לא שמרתם ציווי והים לא ירא שאם לא ישמר ציווי שיהיו בניו גולין לפי שאין לו בנים אעפ״כ שומר ציווי שנאמר: אשר שמתי חול גבול לים חק עולם ולא יעברנהו. ואע״פ שהמו גליו כל כך שתוכל לומר עתה לא ישבר ציווי לא יעברנהו גליו: (כג) סרו וילכו. שסרו מאחרי ה׳ ילכו בשבי:

רד״ק

נא. מבואר הוא: (כב) האותי. איך לא תיראו מפני והנה יש לי שני עדים שלא תוכלו להכחיש כי האחד הוא בכלל העולם והאחד הוא בכם לבדכם אשר הוא בכלל העולם הוא דבר הים כי בראשית בריאת העולם היו המים מכסים הארץ כולה כי כן היה טבעם אחר כן אמרתי יקוו המים אל מקום אחד ותראה היבשה והנה בהקוות המים שהיו על פני כל הארץ אל מקום אחד היו שופעים על המקום ההוא נצבים כמו נד והיה להם לפי טבעם לרדת ולהתפשט על פני כל הארץ כבתחלה אלא שאני אמרתי לו עד פה תבא ולא תוסיף והאמירה היא הרצון ושמתי החול על שפתו גבול לו שלא יעברנהו והנה החול אין חומה נבוה שתעמוד בפני המים ולא עוד אלא שגלי הים מתגעשים והומין ובאים עד השפה כאלו יעברו עליה כפי טבעם ולא יוכלו לפי שאני מנעתי טבעם בזה ובזה תוכלו להכיר כי אני משגיח בתחתונים ועושה בהם כרצוני ואיך לא תיראו אותי ולא תחילו מפני ולא תעלו בדעתכם שאני יכול לעשות בכם כרצוני אם תעברו מצותי אם כן ראוי לקרוא אתכם עם סכל ואין לב שלא תבינו זה או אם תבינו ויש לכם לב להבין אם כן לבבכם סורר ומורה שאתם מכירים וכופרים כי הנה שמתי בכם עד כי בעשותכם רצוני אני נותן גשמיכם בעתם יורה במרחשון ומלקוש בניסן ונתנה הארץ את יבולה ועץ השדה יתן פריו ובימי הקציר לא ירד לכם מטר וזהו שאמר שבועות חקות קציר ישמור לנו ובהיותכם מיוחדים בין שאר האומות בזאת הברכה איך לא תשימו זה על לב כי אני משגיח עליכם ואיך תכחשו בי ותאמרו לא הוא ואם תאמר למה לא נתן להם לעדים האותות והמופתים הכתובים כמו קריעת ים סוף והירדן וזולתן משנוי הטבע שאי אפשר להם מבלתי מכוין ומשגיח היפך הטבע כרצונו נאמר כי כל האותות והמופתים יוכלו להכחיש בהם אם ירצו כי לא היו אלא פעם אחת בזמן אחד ואותם שלא היו בזמן ההוא יוכלו להכחיש בהם אם יהיו כופרים בתורה אבל זה העד היות החול גבול לים הוא חק עולם לא סר ולא יסור כל ימי היות עולם ובזה לא יוכלו להכחיש שהרי רואים בעיניהם ושומעים באזניהם רואים ביאת גלי הים עד השפה ולא יעבור החול שהוא שפה לים ושומעים התגעשות הגלים והמייתם כאלו בבאם יעברו הכל ויכסו פני הארץ זה דבר שלא יוכל אדם להכחיש: תחילו. מן חיל כיולדה: יעברנהו. הנו״ן נוספת כמו כל חיום יברכנהו: ויתגעשו. גליו שאומר בסוף ויעברנהו גם כן בנו״ן נוספת: (כג) ולעם. סרו וילכו. סרו מהדרך הטובה והלכו להם בשרירות לבם ות״י על דסטו מבתר פולחני גלו: (כד) ולא אמרו. נירא נא. נו״ן נא נקראת רפ״א אע״פ שמלת נירא נקראת

מנחת שי

(כד) ויורה. יורה קרי כן הוא שקלת מדויקים:

מצודת דוד

(כב) האותי. וכי לא תיראו ממני וכי לא תרעדו מפני: גבול לים. להיות גבול לים שעד החול יבוא: חק עולם. שהחק הזה הוא כל ימות עולם: ולא יעברנהו. אין מי הים עוברים את הגבול: ויתגעשו. אף כי ינידו בתנועה חזקה עכ״ז לא יוכלו לעבור הגבול: והמו גליו. אף כי ירומו גליו עד כי נשמע קול המייתם עכ״ז לא יוכלו לעבור הגבול וכ״ז הוא מפחד ה׳ ומהדר גאונו: (כג) ולעם הזה. אבל לעם הזה היה לב מעוות וממרה: סרו וילכו. סרו מה׳ והלכו להם: (כד) נירא נא. ר״ל אם עד הנה לא היה פחד אלהים לנגד עיניהם הנה עתה נשים על לב נירא אם

מצודת ציון

במקום: זרים. נכרים: (כב) תחילו. מלשון חיל ורעדה: חוק. דבר קבוע: ויתגעשו. ענין נדנוד ותנועה חזקה וכן ותגעש ותרעש הארץ (תהלים י״ח): יוכלו. מלשון יכולת: והמו. מלשון המיה: (כג) סורר. מעוות: ומורה. ענין מרי ומרד וכן בן סורר ומורה

yet they hear not. 22. Will you not fear Me? says the Lord, or,
do you not quake from before Me, for I made sand a boundary
for the sea, an everlasting ordinance, which it cannot pass, and
[its waves] toss themselves, yet they cannot prevail; and its
waves roar, but they do not pass it. 23. And this people had a
revolting and rebellious heart; they turned away and they were
gone. 24. And they did not say in their heart, "Let us now fear
the Lord our God,

22. **Will you not fear Me?**—*Does not the sea, which is not concerned about retribution and does not look forward to receiving reward, fear Me and not cross the boundary that I set around it?*—[*Rashi*]

do you not quake—Heb. תָחִילוּ, *an expression of fear.*—[*Rashi*]

and toss themselves—I.e. *its waves, and they lift themselves to cross the border but cannot cross.*—[*Rashi*]

and its waves roar—*A loud sound of roaring.*—[*Rashi*]

but they do not pass it—*The waves do not pass the border.*—[*Rashi*]

God brings two proofs of His providence, one involving the entire world, and one involving Israel alone. The proof involving the entire world is that of the sea. At the beginning of the Creation, the water covered the dry land. Then God ordered the water to gather in one place and form the seas. Since that time, the sand serves as a border for the sea, which the sea does not pass. Since the sea does not disobey God's orders, why should Israel? He continues in verse 24 to illustrate how the rain falls at the proper time, the early rain in Marcheshvan and the latter rain in Nissan. This is a blessing bestowed on Israel. Yet, you do not fear Me. He does not mention the miracles of the Bible, the splitting of the Red Sea and the Jordan, since those who did not witness them and who do not believe in the Bible could deny them. Instead, Scripture states constant miracles, which no one can deny.—[*Redak*]

23. **They turned away, and they were gone**—They turned away from the right path; therefore, they deserved to flee without strength before the enemies.—[*Abarbanel*]

הַנֹּתֵן גֶּשֶׁם וְיֹרֶה וּמַלְקוֹשׁ בְּעִתּוֹ
שְׁבֻעֹת חֻקּוֹת קָצִיר יִשְׁמָר־לָנוּ:
כה עֲוֹנוֹתֵיכֶם הִטּוּ־אֵלֶּה וְחַטֹּאותֵיכֶם
מָנְעוּ הַטּוֹב מִכֶּם: כו כִּי־נִמְצְאוּ בְעַמִּי
רְשָׁעִים יָשׁוּר כְּשַׁךְ יְקוּשִׁים הִצִּיבוּ
מַשְׁחִית אֲנָשִׁים יִלְכֹּדוּ: כז כִּכְלוּב מָלֵא

תרגום

בִּכִּיר וְלַקִּיש בְּעִדָּנֵיהּ
בִּזְמַן קְיָם שְׁבוּעַיָּא
דִבְזְמַן חַצְדָא נְטַר לָנָא:
כה חוֹבֵיכוֹן גְּרַמוּ אִלֵּין
לְכוֹן וְחֶטְאֵיכוֹן מְנַעוּ
טוּבָא מִנְכוֹן: כו אֲרֵי
אִשְׁתְּכַחוּ בְעַמִּי חַיָּבִין
בְּנִכְלִין אִשְׁרִין כִּדְ נַכָּאי
כִּלְבּוּשׁ צַיָּדִין דְּמָחֵי
וְקָטֵיל מִתְעַשְּׁתִין
לְחַבָּלָא נַפְשִׁין קָטְלִין:
כז כִּקְבִית פִּטְמָא דְמָלֵי

ת"א עונותיכם הטו אלה. תענית ג כג קדושין דף סג: | יורה קרי מלא ואו | עוף | עופא

מהר"י קרא

(כד) שבועות חקות קציר ישמר לנו. שומר לעולמו השבועה שכרת לנח זרע וקציר כלומר [חקות] שהקציר תלוי בו הוא יורה ומלקוש וקור וחום וקיץ וחורף יום ולילה כל זה שומר לנו שלא ישבתו לעולם אם תראו שהם פוסקין כוונותיכם הטו מכם את הטובה שניטלו ותנתו לשאר אומות: (כו) ישור כשך יקושים. רואים ומרגלים את בני אדם ללכוד אנשים כאותן שמושכין פחים ללכוד עופות: (כז) ככלוב מלא

רש"י

ולא יעברנהו. הגלים לא יעברו הגבול: (כד) יורה ומלקוש. כתרגום בכיר ולקיש: שבועות חוקות קציר. שבעה שבועות שחקק לנו בהן שתי חוקות קציר חק העומר וחק שתי הלחם: ישמר לנו. שיהא הקציר בזמנו: (כה) הטו אלה. הטו החוקות האלה מעליכם שאיני שומר' לכם ואתם כלים ברעב: (כו) ישור. יארוב וכן למען שוררי (תהלים כ"ז) לשון אשורנו ולא קרוב (במדבר כ"ד): כשך יקושים. כאשר ישוך היקוש שעושין ללכוד צביים ביער כשרגלו בא לתוכו והוא נושכו ומחזיקו ברגלו ונלכד וקורין (פי"ד בלע"ז): הציבו משחית. (ליגכ"ל בלע"ז) כך עושין אורבים על עיר או על דרך: הציבו. כמו מצב פלשתים (ש"א): (כז) ככלוב. הוא מקום שמפטמין בו עופות וכן תירגמו

רד"ק

מלעיל: הנותן גשם. ואחר כך פי' יורה ומלקוש בעתו אבל לפה שכתב ויורה בוי"ו השמוש הנותן גשם בשאר עתי השנה לצורך הגנות ולשתות ולשאר צרכי האדם והבהמות תתן גם כן יורה ומלקוש לצורך התבואה כל אחת בעתו: שבועות חקות קציר ישמר לנו. אותם שבועות מחקות קציר ישמור לנו שלא ירד מטר בימי הקציר שלא יפסיד הקציר וזהו חק הקציר ומשפטו וגם שתהיה רוח טובה נושבת בימי הקציר לזרות ולהבר הוא חק הקציר ומשפטו גם כן לפיכך אמר חקות ומה שאמר שבועות ולא אמר ימי הקציר לפי שאנו סופרים שבעה שבועות עד חג השבועות לפיכך תלה ימי הקציר בשבועות וי"ת בזמן קיים שביעיא דבזמן חצדא נטר לנא: (כה) עונותיכם. והיה לכם לאמר בלבבכם כי אלה הרעות הבאות עליכם עונותיכ' הטו אתכם שהרי כשהייתם עושים רצון האל היה נותן לכם גשם בעתו וכל דבריכם באים על תכונתם אם כן מי מנע הטוב מכם ומי הביא אליכם הרע אלא עונותיכם וחטאתיכם: (כו) כי נמצאו. ישור כשך יקושים. יבים כל אחד בדרכים אם יעבור אדם שיגזלו ממנו מה שעמו ויבים כאדם המניח יקושי' ומציב משחית ללכד העופות כן יביטו הם ויראו ויארבו והציבו משחי' אנשים ילכדו ולא עופות ומשחית יקרא הפח ש וכד העופות כן הם מציבים ומארבים מזה ומזה ללכוד אנשים ולגזול מהם מה שעמהם: ישור. יבים כמו אשורנו ולא קרוב: כשך. הוא כקיר כמו כרניח או תואר והוא כמו מניח מן וחמת המלך שככה שפירושו נחה ושך. הוא פעל יוצא ושככה פעל עומד: יקושים. שם כמו מוקשים וי"ת ארי אשתכחו בעמי חייבין וגו' כבעמיד: (כז) ככלוב מלא עוף. כלוב כלי עשוי מנסרין מגדלים בתם עופות ומפטמין אותם שם וכן ת"י כבית פיטמא ודומה לו והנה כלוב קיץ סל עשוי מנסרים והמשילם לכלוב מלא עוף כמו שהכלוב ממלאים אותו עופות כפי מה שהוא

מצודת ציון

(דברים כ"א): (כד) יורה. הוא המטר היורד על הזורעים המרוס הזרעים והאדמה: ומלקוש. היא המטר המאוחר היורד על הקשין ועל המלילות וכן ונתתי מטר וגו' יורה ומלקוש (שם י"א): שבועות. הוא מלשון מלא שבוע זאת (בראשית כ"ט): חקות. מלשון חק ודבר קבוע: (כו) ישור. ענין הבטה וראיה כמו למען שוררי (תהלים כ"ז): כשך. ענין הנחה וכן וישכו המים (בראשית ח') ות"א ונחו מיא: יקושים. הם מוקשים: משחית. הם מוקשים. הם משחית: ילכדו. יתפשו: (כז) ככלוב. מעשהו כעין סל העשוי לעופות ודומה לו כלוב קיץ (עמוס ח'):

מצודת דוד

ה' הנותן גשם וחוזר ומפרש שנותן יורה ומלקוש כי אם כזמ[נו] הצורך: שבועות חקות קציר. ר"ל החוק של שבועות ימי הקציר ישמר לנו שלא היה מוריד גשמים כה"י כל ימי הקציר הסוף סי' קללה וכמ"ש הלא קציר חטים היום אקרא אל ה' ויתן קולות ומטר (ש"א י"ב): (כה) הטו אלה. הטו מכם הידיעה והשלשה: מנעו הטוב, היא תכונת הכל המביא טובה: (כו) כי נמצאו בעמי רשעים. ומעשיהם הם המטמטמים את הכל: ישור. יביט לארוב על אנשים כאדם המניח הם יקושים ללכוד עופות כן הציבו הם פח משחית וילכדו אנשים לגזול הונם ולהרגם: (כז) ככלוב. כמו

make to catch deer in the forest, bites when his foot enters it and it bites him and holds onto his foot and he is caught, and they call this (piege in O.F.).—[Rashi]

Others render: As those who lay traps.—[*Redak*]

they stationed an ambush—(*Cambel in O.F.*) *So do those who lie in wait make for a city or on the road.*—[*Rashi*]

they station—Heb. הִצִּיבוּ, *like 'the garrison* (מַצַּב) *of the Philistines'* (I Sam. 14:4).—[*Rashi*] (In some editions this is omitted.)

27. **As a cage**—*That is a place*

Who gives rain, the early rain and the latter rain in its time, the weeks of the laws of harvest He keeps for us." 25. Your iniquities have brought these about, and your sins have withheld the good from you. 26. For wicked men are found in My people; they lie in wait as a trap bites; they station an ambush, they catch people. 27. As a cage is full,

24. **the early rain and the latter rain**—Heb. יוֹרֶה וּמַלְקוֹשׁ, *as the Targum renders:* בַּכִּיר וְלַקִּישׁ, *the early rain and the latter rain.*—[*Rashi*]

According to the 'keri,' 'the early rain and the latter rain' is an elaboration of 'Who gives rain.' According to the 'kethib,' however, the verse reads: 'Who gives rain, and the early rain and the latter rain.' The explanation is that God gives rain for the gardens, for the cattle, for drinking, and for other of man's necessities, and for the grain He gives the early rain and the latter rain, each in its time.—[*Redak*]

the weeks of the laws of harvest—*Seven weeks in which He ordained two ordinances of harvest, the ordinance of the omer, and the ordinance of the two breads.*—[*Rashi*]

Rashi refers to the ordinance of the offering of the *omer*, the barley offering, on the second day of Passover, and the offering of the two breads, the wheat offering on the festival of Shavuoth. These offerings correspond to the barley harvest and the wheat harvest.

He keeps for us—*that the harvest should be in its time.*—[*Rashi*]

Redak explains: Those weeks of the ordinances of harvest He keeps for us, that it does not rain during harvest season, lest the harvest be destroyed. That is the ordinance of the harvest and its custom. Also that a good wind should blow during the harvest season to facilitate the winnowing and the cleansing of the grain. He says: 'weeks of the ordinances of harvest,' rather than 'the days of harvest,' since we count seven weeks from Passover, the barley harvest, to Shavuoth, the wheat harvest. He, therefore, connects harvest to 'weeks.'—[*Redak*]

Kara renders שְׁבֻעֹת, as oaths. This alludes to God's oath to Noah that 'seeding and harvest, heat and cold, summer and winter, and day and night shall not cease' (Gen. 8:22).

25. **Your iniquities**—You should have thought that your iniquities have brought about the calamity that has befallen you, for when you followed God's will, the rains fell in the proper time and all your matters went along properly. If so, who withheld good from you and who brought evil upon you except your iniquities and your sins?—[*Redak*]

26. **For wicked men are found in My people**—It is their deeds that bring insensitivity to the heart.—[*Mezudath David*]

they lie in wait—Heb. יָשׁוּר. *Comp.* לְמַעַן שׁוֹרְרָי, *because of those who lie in wait for me* (Psalms 27:11), *an expression of 'I see him* (אֲשׁוּרֶנּוּ) *but not near'* (Num. 24:17).—[*Rashi*]

as a trap bites—*As a trap that they*

עוֹף כֵּן בָּתֵּיהֶם מְלֵאִים מִרְמָה עַל־כֵּן
גָּדְלוּ וַיַּעֲשִׁירוּ׃ כח שָׁמְנוּ עָשְׁתוּ גַּם עָבְרוּ
דִבְרֵי־רָע דִּין לֹא־דָנוּ דִּין יָתוֹם וְיַצְלִיחוּ
וּמִשְׁפַּט אֶבְיוֹנִים לֹא שָׁפָטוּ׃ כט הַעַל־
אֵלֶּה לֹא־אֶפְקֹד נְאֻם־יְהוָה אִם בְּגוֹי
אֲשֶׁר־כָּזֶה לֹא תִתְנַקֵּם נַפְשִׁי׃ ל שַׁמָּה
וְשַׁעֲרוּרָה נִהְיְתָה בָּאָרֶץ׃ לא הַנְּבִאִים

עופא כן בתיהון מלן
נכלין על כן סגיאו
ועתירו: כח עתרו אף
קנו נכסין אף עברו על
פתגמי אוריתא עבדו
דביש דין דקשוט לא
דיינין ואלו הוו דיינין דין
יתמא הוו מצליחין ודין
חשיביא בקושטא לית
אינון דיינין: כט העל אלין
לא אסער לאיתאה
עליהון בישא אמר
יי אם מן עמא דכדין
עובדוהי לא אתפרע
מנהון כרעותי: ל תימא ושנו הוו בארעא: לא נביי שקרא מתנבן שקר וכהניא מסיעין על

רש"י

יונתן כבית פוטמא ובלע"ז (פרג"ק): (כח) עשתו. לשון עשת שן (שה"ש ה) גוף עב ובלע"ז (אישפישיר"ט): עברו דברי רע. אם באה רעה או עבירה לידם לא נטו ממנה אלא עברו בה ועשאוה: לא דנו דין יתום. למען יצליחו: (ל) שמה. תמהון: ושערורה. דבר מגונה לכל ומהו דבר התמהון הנביאים נבאים שקר ואומרים הוו גוזלין ואונסין והכהנים שהם שופטי העם ונוגשיהם ירדו את העם על ידי הנביאים כלומר לאחריהם כמו (שמואל ב׳ ט"ו) והמלך עובר וכל העם עוברים על ידו (רודף) (ס"א דדוד) אחריו אף כאן על ידיהם אחריהם לעשות כדברי הנביאים:

מהר"י קרא

עוף. כלוב כלי הוא כמין סל ומפטמין שם עופות וכשמוציאין אלו מכניסין אלו ולכך הוא מלא בכל שעה: כן בתיהם מלאים מרמה. נכסים שקנו ברמאות: (כח) שמנו עשתו. עשתו עבתו כמו מעיו עשת שן: גם עברו דברי רע. תרגום אף עברו על פתגמי אוריתא עבדו דביש: דין לא דנו דין יתום ויצליחו. לא דנו אותו כעניין הזה שיוציאו אותו להצלחה. ד"א דין יתום. לא

רד"ק

ונותנים לתוכו מאכלם ומשקה ואוכלין שם תמיד כן בתי אלה הרשעים מלאים מרמה ר"ל ממון מקובץ ברמ׳ ובאין ומתעדנין בו: על כן גדלו ויעשירו. על כן שבא להם ממון זה בלי עמל ויגיעה גדלו בנכסים והעשירו: (כח) שמנו עשתו. על דרך משל כמו וישמן ישורון ויבעט כלומר הרבו בנכסים גם יש בו קצת המליצה כי העשירים ברוב הם שמנים ודשנים. עשתו זכו מן עשת שן כי השמן עור בשרו זך וכן תרגם יונתן עתרו אף קנו ניכסין: גם עברו דברי רע. לא דים בעשרם אלא הרבו לגזול ולחמוס עד שעברו כל דברי איש רע כלומר יותר הרעו לעשות משאר אנשים רעים עד שעברו עליהם ברעתם ויונתן תרגם אף עברו על פתגמי אוריתא עבדו דביש דין יתום לא דנו ופירוש דין יתום כלומר משפט היתום והאדם החלוש לא שפטו ולא לקחו משפטם מעושקיהם: ויצליחו. ואף על פי כן ויצליחו: ומשפט אביונים. כפל ענין במלות שונות: (כט) העל אלה. פירושו כתרגומו העל אילין לא אסער וגו׳ כבעמוד: (ל) שמה ושערורה נהיתה. שמה ענין תימה כמו כאשר שממו עליך רבים כלומר דבר תימה הוא מה שיהיה בארץ מרעות שעושין ודבר מנוף ולכלוך וזהו פירוש שערורה ענין מנוף ולכלוך כמו התאנים השוערים וכן תרגם יונתן שמה. תימה יש נוסחאות תיימא והוא לשון כליון כמו מתם תיימי מיא בדברי רז"ל יתרגום שערורה ושנו: (לא) הנביאים. עתה פירש מה היא השמה והשערורה שנהיתה בארץ נבאו בשקר לעם

מצודת דוד

הכלוב הוא מלא מן העופות כן בתיה׳ המה ממלאים מן המרמה: גדלו. בהון רב ולתוספת ביאור אמר ויעשירו: (כח) שמנו. נעשו שמנים ואחו בכסילו׳ רב: גם עברו. ר"ל גם כל דברי רע הבא לידם עבר עליהם: דין לא דנו. לא דנו דין אמת ואפי׳ דין יתום ואעפ"כ הצליחו ולא נפרעתי עדיין מהם: ומשפט. ר"ל ובעבו׳ כי הצליחו אחזו בדרכם ולא שפטו משפט האביונים אשר ילעקו מפני מנגשיהם: (כט) העל אלה. וכי על מעשים כאלה לא אשגיח להפרע בהם כתמיה: אשר כזה. אשר עושה הדבר הזה: (ל) שמה. דבר תמהון ומגונה נהיתה בארץ: (לא) הנביאים. נביאי הבעל: בשקר. בשם הבעל שהיא דבר שקר: והכהנים.

מצודת ציון

(כח) שמנו. מלשון שומן: עשתו. ענין לחות וכסילות כמו מעיו עשת שן (ש"ה ה׳): (ל) שמה. ענין תמהון: ושערורה. ענין דבר מגונה ומאוס וכן ראיתי שערורה (לקמן כ"ג): נהיתה.

them. Comp. '(II Sam. 15) *And the king was crossing and all the people were crossing on his hand,' stated concerning David, meaning 'after him. Here too, 'on their hands' means 'after them,' to do according to the words of the prophets.*—[*Rashi*]

[To avoid confusion, let it be stated that Rashi combines verses 30 and 31 and dwells on the expression עַל־יְדֵיהֶם, lit. *on their hands* in verse 31. He illustrated his point by quoting a verse in II Sam. That verse actually does not exist. *Rashi* perhaps means verse 18: And all his servants passed on beside him. *Rashi* ad loc., however, explains it to mean that they passed beside him. He stood and they passed by. Verse 23 reads: And the king passed over . . .

so are their houses full of deceit; therefore, they have become
great and they have become rich. 28. They have become fat,
they have become thick; also they transgress in deeds of wicked-
ness; they did not plead the cause of an orphan that they
prosper, and the judgment of the poor they did not judge.
29. Shall I not punish for these? says the Lord, or for such a
nation shall My soul not take vengeance? 30. An appalling and
horrible thing has come about in the land. 31. The prophets

where they fatten fowl, and so does Jonathan render it, like a fattening place, and in O.F. (frank).—[*Rashi*]

full of deceit—Full of property acquired through deceit.—[*Redak, Kara*]

therefore—I.e., since they acquired this property without toil, they became great with riches and have become rich.—[*Redak*]

28. **they have become thick**—Heb. עָשְׁתוּ, *an expression of 'a block* (עֶשֶׁת) *of ivory'* (Song 5:14), *a thick body, and in O.F. enboeront.*—[*Rashi*]

Redak explains: They have become sleek, for a fat person's skin is shiny and glossy.

This is symbolic of riches, like 'And Jeshurun became fat and kicked' (Deut. 32:15), symbolizing riches. *Jonathan,* too, renders: they became rich, they acquired property.—[*Redak*]

they transgressed in deeds of wickedness—*If evil or a sin came into their hand, they did not turn away from it, but transgressed it and committed it.*—[*Rashi*]

Redak explains: They surpassed the deeds of the wicked. They are not satisfied with their wealth, but they continue to rob and cheat until they surpass the deeds of the wicked.

Jonathan renders: Also, they transgressed the words of the Torah, they committed evil.

Ibn Nachmiash explains: They surpassed all limits in the deeds of the wicked.

they did not plead the cause of the orphan—*in order that they prosper.*—[*Rashi*]

that they prosper—And nevertheless, they prosper.—[*Redak*] *Ibn Nachmiash* explains it as a question: Shall they prosper?

Kara explains: They did not plead the cause of an orphan to bring out a satisfactory verdict that the orphan prosper. He suggests also: They did not plead, but had they pleaded, they would have prospered. This is similar to Jonathan's paraphrase: They do not judge truthfully, but had they judged the case of the orphan, they would prosper.

30. **An appalling . . . thing**—Heb. שַׁמָּה, *a wonder.*—[*Rashi*]

and horrible thing—Heb. וְשַׁעֲרוּרָה, *a disgraceful thing to all, and what is the appalling thing? The prophets prophesy falsely and say, "Rob and plunder," and the priests, who are the judges of the people and their overseers, govern the people on the hands of the prophets, that is to say, after*

נִבְּאוּ בַשֶּׁקֶר וְהַכֹּהֲנִים יִרְדּוּ עַל־יְדֵיהֶם
וְעַמִּי אָהֲבוּ כֵן וּמַה־תַּעֲשׂוּ לְאַחֲרִיתָהּ:
ו א הָעִזוּ ׀ בְּנֵי בִנְיָמִן מִקֶּרֶב יְרוּשָׁלַ͏ִם
וּבִתְקוֹעַ תִּקְעוּ שׁוֹפָר וְעַל־בֵּית הַכֶּרֶם
שְׂאוּ מַשְׂאֵת כִּי רָעָה נִשְׁקְפָה מִצָּפוֹן
וְשֶׁבֶר גָּדוֹל: ב הַנָּוָה וְהַמְּעֻנָּגָה דָּמִיתִי
בַּת

תרגום

יְדֵיהוֹן וְעַמִּי רְחִימוּ כֵּן וּמָה תַּעְבְּדוּן לְסוֹפָא: א גְּלוֹ בְּנֵי בִנְיָמִין מִגוֹ יְרוּשְׁלֵם אֲרֵי קָל צְוָחַת קַרְנָא אִשְׁתְּמַעַת בְּאַרְעָא וְעַל בֵּית בִּקְעַת כַּרְמַיָא וְקוּפוּ עַמְמַיָא סְמוֹתָא אֲרֵי בִישְׁתָא אִתְקְרִיאַת מִצְפּוּנָא וְתַבְרָא רַבָּא: ב יָאָתָה וּמְפַנְקְתָא אִיכְדֵין קַלְקֵילְתָּא יַת אוֹרְחָתִיךְ כְּדֵין בְּהֵיתַת כְּנִשְׁתָּא

מהר"י קרא

עשו שאם עשו הצליחו: (לא) ירדו על ידיהם. מסכימין על ידיהן: ירדו. לשון ממשלה כמו כי הוא רודה כלומר מאיימין על העם שישמעו לנביאי השקר:
ו (א) העיזו. התקבצו: בית הכרם. אילו ישראל דכתי׳ כי כרם ה׳ צבאות בית ישראל: שאו משאת. הכריזו ולאומות והניפו] יד להם כזה שמניף בכלונס והרימו קול להם ואמרו שיבאו על ישראל: (ב) הנוה והמעונגה. בת ציון שדימיתיה לשעבר לנוה ולמעונגה עכשיו יבאו אליה רועים ועדריהם:

רש"י

ו (א) העיזו בני בנימין. ללכת לעריהם לשמור מבצריה׳: בית הכרם. שם מקום הוא: שאו משאת. נס להקבץ ולהלח׳ על נפשיכם: (ב) הנוה והמעונגה דמיתי. החרבתי תירגמו יונתן לשון ונדמו נאות השלום (לקמן כ״ה)

רד"ק

יאמרו שלום יהיה לכם ובזה משים העם לדרך רע: נבאו בשקר והכהנים ירדו על ידיהם. ענין לקיחת מן רדה הדבש כלומר יקחו השחד לעות המשפט יקחו אותם על ידיהם כרודה הדבש בידו שהוא טוב וערב ויש מפרשים אותו ענין ממשלה מן כי הוא רודה לא תרדה בו ר״ל הכהנים רודים בעם על ידי הנביאי׳ ומצותם ומטים המשפט כרצונם: ועמי אהבו כן. ר״ל רוצים בכל זה לפי שהם כיפים להם כעשיהם הרעים: ומה תעשו לאחריתה. כלומר לאחרית שמה ושערורה שזכר כלומר אם השערורה יפה בעיניכם עתה מה תעשו לאחריתה כי תדעו כי מרה תהיה באחרונה: (א) העיזו. הניסו כמו שלח העז מקנך אמר לבני בנימן שהם בירושלם אתם בנימן נוסו והניסו את אשר לכם מקרב ירושלם כל שכן משאר עריכם כי אפילו ירושלם תלכד ומה שאמר העיזו הוא דרך נחמא כי אין להם מקום אנה ינוסו שם אלא כאומר אם יש לכם מקום שתנוסו נוסו והניסו מקרב ירושלם כי גם היא תלכד וירושלים היתה ליהודה ובנימן ומה שאמר לבנימן ולא אמר ליהודה כאדם שטחם על קרוביו תחלה כי הוא כואב עליהם יותר מכה שהוא כואב על אחרים והוא היה מענתות בארץ בנימן והם היו קרוביו בני משפחתו כמו שאמר לו עליהם כי גם אחיך ובית אביך גם המה בגדו בך וי״ת העיזו גלו: ובתקוע תקעו שופר. תקוע שם מקום הוא שנאמר וישלח יואב תקועה ואמר דרך צחות ובתקוע תקעו לשון נופל על לשון כמו ועקרון תעקר ואמר תקעו שופר להניס העם אל העיר: ועל בית הכרם שאו משאת. מגדל שבונים בכרם אחד נב״ה לשמור כל הכרמים אשר סביבותיו ואותו נקרא בית הכרם וכן הוא אומר ויבן מגדל בתוכו ואמר שישאו בו משאת שיראו הרחוקים הלהבה וינוסו ומשאת כמו כשיאין משואות בכשנה: נשקפה. נראתה ונגלתה עתה תבא: מצפון. היא בבל שהיא לצפון: (ב) הנוה והמעונגה דמיתי. פעל יוצא כמו אם היה מן הדגוש דמיתיך רעיתי כלומר דמיתי בת ציון לאשת הנוה והמעונגה והנה אני רואה שיבאו עליה רועים ועדריהם להחרידה ופירוש הנוה האשה השוכנת בנוה שלה שוקטת ומעונגה תוה תאר לנקבה במשקל דוה ורבי יהודה חיו״ג פירש

מצודת ציון

מלשון סיג: (לא) ירדו. ענין ממשלה כמו רדה בקרב אויביך (תהלי׳ ק״י): על ידיהם. בעבור כחם של הנביאים:
ו (א) העיזו. ענין אסיפה כמו העיזו אל תעמודו (לעיל ד׳): ובתקוע. שם מקום כמ״ש וישלח יואב תקועה (ש״ב י״ד): שאו. הרימו: משאת. ענינו להבת אש וכן וישאם דוד (ש״ב ה׳): נשקפה. ענין הבטה ורא״ה כמו וישקף אבימלך (בראשית כ״ו): (ב) הנוה. כמו הנאוה באל״ף והוא ענין יופי כמו נאוה כירושלים (ש״ה ו׳): והמעונגה. מלשון עונג ועידון: דמיתי. מלשון דמיון
ובימוסים: שאו משאת. הרימו להבת אש להיות נראה למרחוק: נשקפה. נראתה לבוא מבבל העומדת בצפון: ושבר גדול. הרעה

מצודת דוד

כסגי סבבל: ירדו. ימשלו בכח הנביאים כי הם המשילום: אהבו כן. להיות הם המושלי׳: ומה תעשו. הנביא יאמר להם ומה תעשו בבוא אחרית הדבר הוא גמול התשלומין וכי בידם להציל אתכם:
ו (א) העיזו. אתם בני בנימין האספו ללכת מקרב ירושלים כי האויב יכבשה ויהרוג עמה: ובתקוע. בעיר תקוע תקעו שופר להזהיר את העם להיות נכונים למלחמה (ונפי ששם העיר תקוע אמר תקעו שופר ל׳ נופל על לשון): ועל בית הכרם. דרך לבנות בית גבוה ומגדל בכרם אחד לשמור בו כל הכרמים אשר סביבו להזהיר את העם. (וגם שאו משאת הוא ל׳ נופל על לשון): ההוא תהיה שבר גדול: (ב) הנוה והמעוגגה וגו׳. אני דמיתי את

war. This is a play on words, Tekoa with *tekiath Shofar*.—[*Redak, Mezudath David*]

2. **The comely and the delicate one have I destroyed**—Heb. דָּמִיתִי. *Jonathan renders it as an expression related to* '(25:37) *And the dwellings of peace shall be destroyed* (וְנָדַמּוּ).' *Also,* '(47:5) *Ashkelon has been destroyed* (נִדְמְתָה).'—[*Rashi*]

Others render: I have likened the daughter of Zion to a woman dwelling peacefully in her place and is delicate.—[*Redak*]

have prophesied falsely, and the priests govern after them, and My people love to have it so. Now what shall you do in the end thereof?

6

1. Gather the sons of Benjamin from the midst of Jerusalem, and in Tekoa sound the shofar, and over Beth-hakerem raise a standard, for evil is visible from the north and a great calamity.

2. The comely and the delicate one have I destroyed,

and all the people passed over . . . The expression עַל־יָדוֹ is not found in that verse.]

31. He now elaborates on the appalling and disgraceful thing that came about in the land. The first thing is:

The prophets prophesied falsely—They tell the people that there will be peace, and thereby lead them to evil ways.—[*Redak*]

priests govern after them—*Redak* suggests other interpretations: (1) and the priests govern through them, i.e. through the prophets and their orders, and mislead the people to follow them. (2) And the priests take upon their hands; i.e., they take the bribes to pervert justice. *Ibn Nachmiash* elaborates that the priests are not ashamed to take the bribes by themselves. They do not send messengers to take them, but take them on their own hands from the litigants.

and My people love it so—They desire all this since the rulers make it appear attractive.—[*Redak*]

Now what shall you do in the end thereof?—I.e. at the end of the appalling and disgraceful thing. If you like this now, what will you do at the end when it will be as bitter as wormwood?—[*Redak, Ibn Nachmiash*]

1. **Gather the sons of Benjamin**—*to go to their cities to guard their fortifications.*—[*Rashi*]

Redak explains it as a direct address: Gather, O sons of Benjamin, from the midst of Jerusalem. You, sons of Benjamin, flee and let your belongings flee from Jerusalem, surely from your other cities, for even Jerusalem will be captured. This address is an exaggeration since they would have no place to flee. It is equivalent to saying, "If you have a place to flee, flee with all your belongings from Jerusalem, for that city, too, will fall to the enemy." Although Jerusalem belonged both to Benjamin and Judah, the prophet addresses Benjamin in particular, as one who laments over his kinsmen first, since he feels more pain for them.

and in Tekoa sound the shofar—In the city of Tekoa sound the shofar to arouse the populace to be ready for

* For Rashi's commentary turn to page 222.

בַּת־צִיּוֹן: ג אֵלֶיהָ יָבֹאוּ רֹעִים וְעֶדְרֵיהֶם
תָּקְעוּ עָלֶיהָ אֹהָלִים סָבִיב רָעוּ אִישׁ
אֶת־יָדוֹ: ד קַדְּשׁוּ עָלֶיהָ מִלְחָמָה קוּמוּ
וְנַעֲלֶה בַצָּהֳרָיִם אוֹי לָנוּ כִּי־פָנָה הַיּוֹם
כִּי־יִנָּטוּ צִלְלֵי־עָרֶב: ה קוּמוּ וְנַעֲלֶה
בַלַּיְלָה וְנַשְׁחִיתָה אַרְמְנוֹתֶיהָ: ו כִּי כֹה
אָמַר יְהוָה צְבָאוֹת כִּרְתוּ עֵצָה וְשִׁפְכוּ

דציון : ג לה ייתון
מלכין ומשריתהון יגדון
עלה משכנין סחור
סחור וסיעין גבר ית
חבריה : ד זמינו עלה
עבדי קרבא קומו ונסק
בטיהרא וי לנא ארי פנא
יומא ארי נגדו טולי
רמשא : ה קומו ונסק
בליליא ונחבל
בירניתהא : ו ארי כדנן
אמר יי צבאות קוצו
אעא וצברו על ירושלם

ת"א אוי לנו. תענית דף כח ס' זוהר פרשת בראשית ופרשת חיי שרה ופרשת אחרי מות: כי כה אמר. ספר הזוהר פרשת ואתחנן הפרש בין מאמר הנביא פעם כה אמר ה' צבאות ופעם כה אמר ה' אלהים :

קמץ בז"ק הה' רפה

רש"י

כדמתה אשקלון (לקמן מ"ז) : (ג) רועים ועדריהם. משל היא מלכים וחיילותיהם : רעו. אכלו : את ידו. את מקומו סביביו : (ד) קדשו. זמנו : אוי לנו. לעת פנות היום : כי פנה היום. כאש' פנה לעת ערב הליתו האור בבי' המקדש: (ו) כרתו עצה. לא מפיק ה"א והוא לשון עץ שאין לשון כריתה נופל על העצה ועצה האמור כאן לשון הרבה עצים

מהר"י קרא

(ג) רעו איש את ידו. רעו לשון מרעה ואחר הל' שתפס המקרא אליה יבאו רועים בו בלשון סיים רעו איש את ידו. כלומר שכל אחד ואחד מן האומות המתקבצין עליהן בזוו איש לו : איש את ידו. איש איש במקומו : (ד) קדשו עליה מלחמת. וזמינו. ואמרו איש לחבירו היאך נעשה עליה מלחמה אם נקום ונעלה בצהרים. אוי לנו שלא נגמר מלאכתנו לכבוש את העיר עד שיפנה היום: ינטו. ירכינו כמו ויט שכים ויענו האחרים בין ביום ובין בלילה נקום עליה ונשחיתה ארמנותיה:(ו) כרתו עצה.

מנחת שי

(ד) צללי ערב. במדוייקים הלמ"ד בשוא לבדו והצד"י בלא מאריך ויש ספרים שהצד"י במאריך ומה שכתב בעל מכלל יופי במקום הזה הוא לשון המכלול דף ל"ד ומה שעלה על לבי בענין זה כבר כתבתי בריש פרשת לך לך : (ו) כרתו עצה. לא מפיק ה"א וכן הוא למערבאי ודלא כמדנחאי. וקשה לי שלא נמנה עם הזוגים חד מפיק ה"א וחד לא מפיק דלא הבחינו אם עצה סוף פרשת שופטים

רד"ק

הנוה כמו נאוה באל"ף מן נאוו לחייך בתורים ענין יופי ונוי וכן ת"י ומפנקא. ואדוני אבי ז"ל פירש דמיתי כרתי כמו נדמו עמי : (ג) אליה. המשיל המלכים הבאים אליה להחריבה לרועים והעדרים הם חייליהם וצבאותם וכמו זה רבים במקרא והמשיל המלכים והמנהיגים לרועים והעם לצאן כמו הוי רועה אוילי ונתתי להם רועים כלבי והדומים להם וכן תרגם יונתן לה ייתון מלכים ומשריתהון : רעו איש את ידו. את מקומו וכן רועות על ידיהן כלומר מלך אחד או שר יצור על עיר או על ערים וכן האחר עד כלותם לכבוש את הארץ: (ד) קדשו עליה מלחמה. אומר איש לחברו מהרועים זמנו מלחמה על ציון כלומר אף על פי שרעו איש את ידו כולם זמנו עצמם למלחמה על ציון : קומו ונעלה בצהרים. ואמר בפסוק שאחריו קומו ונעלה בלילה זכר צהרים ולילה לפי שהם זמני הפגעים כמו שאמר מדבר באפל יהלך מקטב ישוד צהרים אמרו בזמנים קשים להם עולה עליהם אמר הנביא אוי לנו כי פנה היום כלומר בצהרים שאומרים אויבנו לרעה הוא לנו ולא לטובה כי צהרים קשה לרוב החום ועת יפה לרוב האורה ואנחנו נקח ממנו הרע ולא הטוב כי לנו חשך היום וזהו כי פנה היום כלומר האור פנה לו לדרכו והצללים הם נוטים ומתאשפים כי אין לנו אורה אלא חשכה : (ה) קומו. ארמנותיה. שהם חושבים להשגב בהם נשחיתה אותם : (ו) כי כה אמר ה'. כלומר מאת ה' היתה זאת כי הוא

מצודת דוד

בת ציון לאשה נאוה ומעונגה : (ג) אליה. אתה יבואו אליה רועים ועדריהם' ר"ל אנשים שפלים וגבוהים הם הכשדים אשר אינם יודעים לכבד המכובדים: תקעו. דרך לתקוע שפולי האוהל בארץ ע"י יתדות : רעו. ר"ל אתה רעו את מקומו שעמ' בו ר"ל כ"א מגדודי העכו"ם החריבו את המקום אשר יחנו שמה : (ד) קדשו. יזרזו אלו לאלו ויאמרו הזמינו עליה מלחמה קומו ונעלה עליה בצהרים והוא העת המוכן ביותר למלחמה : אוי לנו כי פנה היום. וכאשר לא יכבשו העיר ביומו ועל כי יהיה רב המלחמה לפתח העיר יתאוננו לומר אוי כי פנה היום ועדיין לא לכדנו העיר : כי ינטו צללי ערבי. הלא של ערב נטה כי כאשר קרבה השמש לבית מערבה לשקוע ינטו הצללים למרחוק ויתארכו ביותר והוא כפל ענין במ"ש : (ה) קומו. מרוב תאותם להשחיתם יאמרו קומו ונעלה בלילה ונשחית ארמנותיה ולא נמתין עד יאיר היום : (ו) כרתו עצה. כרתו העץ אשר סביבות ירושלים לתת' עם העפר כסוללה : ושפכו. דרך הכובשי

מצודת ציון

וסוללה : בת ציון. עדת ציון : (ג) תקעו. ענין תחיבה כדבר מה וכן ותקעתיו יתד (ישעיה כ"ב) : רעו. האכילו הצרעה : ידו. מקומו: (ד) קדשו. ענין הזמנה כמו הקדיש קרואיו (צפניה א') : קומו. ענין זריזות : בצהרים. הוא חצי היום : פנה. ענין הסבה : צללי. מלשון צל : (ה) ארמנותיה. מלשון ארמון ופלטרין : (ו) עצה. מלשון עץ:

of cutting is not appropriate for advice,' (עֵצָה), *and* עֵצָה *mentioned here is an expression of many trees, as* דָּגָה is an expression of many fish.—[*Rashi*] The word for 'tree' is עֵץ. עֵצָהּ, with a *'mappiq he'* denotes the feminine possessive, *her tree.* In this verse, however, since the Massorah states that there is no *mappiq he,* it cannot be explained in this manner. *Rashi,* therefore, considers the interpretation of עֵצָה as *counsel.* He rejects that, however, since the context of cutting does not apply to counsel, but to trees. *Rashi*'s conclusion, therefore, is that עֵצָה is a feminine noun denoting many trees, just as דָּגָה is a feminine noun denoting

O daughter of Zion. 3. Shepherds and their flocks shall come
to her, they have pitched tents around her, they feed bare, each
one in his place. 4. Prepare war against her, arise and let us go
up at noontime; woe is to us for the day has passed, for the
shadows of evening are stretched out. 5. Arise and let us go up
at night and let us destroy her palaces. 6. For so says the Lord
of Hosts: Cut the trees and cast

daughter of Zion—Community of Zion.—[*Targum Jonathan*]

3. **Shepherds and their flocks**—*Figurative of kings and their armies.*—[*Rashi, Redak* from *Jonathan*]

Mezudath David explains that the Chaldeans are compared to shepherds because of their coarse manners and their lack of respect for people whom respect is due.

they feed bare—Heb. רָעוּ, *they eat.*—[*Rashi*]

his place—Heb. יָדוֹ, lit. his hand, *his place around him.*—[*Rashi*]

I.e., each king or prince will besiege a city or a number of cities until the entire land has been conquered.—[*Redak*]

4. **Prepare**—Heb. קַדְּשׁוּ.—[*Rashi, Redak* from *Targum*]

Each shepherd says to his companions, "Prepare war against Zion." Although each one has fed bare in his place, they unite to wage war against Zion.—[*Redak*]

arise and let us go up at noontime—And in the following verse, 'arise and let us go up at night.' These are the two times of day when one is most vulnerable. The psalmist (91:6) too, mentions these times, 'From pestilence that goes about in the darkness, from destruction that spoils at noontime.' The prophet states that the time chosen by our enemies is good for them but bad for us, for the heat of noontime is very oppressive, and the light, although advantageous, is of little avail to us, for the day has become darkened to us.—[*Redak*]

woe is to us—*at the time the day declines.*—[*Rashi*]

for the day has declined—*When it declined to eventide, they ignited the Temple.*—[*Rashi* from *Taanith* 29a]

Others explain this as the plaint of the enemy. They wish to attack at noon, the most auspicious time for battle, but they fear that the day will decline and the shadows of evening will stretch out before they have accomplished their feat. They, therefore, decide to attack at night out of their strong desire to destroy Israel.—[*Kara, Mezudath David*]

5. **and let us destroy her palaces**—in which the people hope to seek refuge.—[*Abarbanel*]

6. **For so says the Lord of Hosts**—I.e., all this has come from the Lord, Who wishes to destroy the city and has inspired the enemies to march upon it.—[*Redak*]

Cut the trees—Heb. עֵצָה. *This is not a 'mappiq he,' yet it is an expression of a tree* (עֵץ) *for the expression*

על־ירושלם סללה היא העיר הפקד
כלה עשק בקרבה : ז כהקיר בור
מימיה כן הקרה רעתה חמס ושד
ישמע בה על־פני תמיד חלי ומכה :
ח הוסרי ירושלם פן־תקע נפשי ממך
פן־אשימך שממה ארץ לוא נושבה :
ט כה אמר יהוה צבאות עולל יעוללו

ביר קרי · כגפן

ת"א כהקיר בור. ברכות ס נו עירובין י קד: חמס ושוד. כלה מליצה דף כט:

תרגום

סליתא הא קרתא דאתפקידו לה חובהא כולהון אונסין בגוה : ז כנובא דמקיים מוהי כן אוריכו ואתקימו בגוה עבדי בישתא קל חטופין וביזוין משתמע בה קדמי תדירא על כן איתיתי עלה מרע ומחא : ח איתרדא ירושלם דלמא ירחק מימרי יתיך דלמא אשוינך צדיא בארע סדום דלא אתותבת : ט כדנן אמר יי צבאות אתבננא יתבזזון כמא דמהלכין על שולי גפן למקטף שארא דישראל ותתיב מחתך עליהון

מהר"י קרא

אילנותיה. היא העיר הפקד. ת"י היא קרתא דאיתפקידו בה חובהא : הפקד. לשון פקדון : (ז) כהקיר. לשון מקור : ביר. לשון בור כלומר כאשר ינבע הבור את מימיו שאינו פוסק כך הנביע רעתכם כמו שמפרש והולך חמס ושוד ישמע בה וגו' : (ח) פן

רש"י

כמו דגה לשון דגים הרבה: העיר הפקד. שכלה פקודתה: (ז) כהקיר. לשון מקור: ביר. כאר: כן הקרה רעתה. כן נובעת רעתם תמיד מוסיפים ומחדשים: חלי ומכה. ע"כ איתיתי עלה מרע ומחא: (ח) הוסרי. קבלי מוסר: פן תקע. פן תנתק הוקע לשון חיבור כמו והוקע אותם (במדבר כה) ויש לשון הסרת החיבור והרבה תיבות משמשות כן: (ט) עולל. (גרפלי"ר בלע"ז) לאחר שבצרו הכרם ונשארו עוללות והעניים באים ועוללים אותם כן יבוזו ויחזרו ויבוזו:

מנחת שי

מפיק וזה לא מפיק וכן מתורגם אם לא מתחיל יש אילנה וכאן מתורגם קולו אבא וי"ל דבפלוגתא לא קא מיירי : (ז) כהקיר. חלי המקרא לפסוקים כן מלתי

רד"ק

רוצה להשחיתה והעיר את רוחם לבא אליה וכאילו אמר להם כרתו עצה. עצה כמו עץ והה"א איננה לכינוי כי הוא רפה אמר כרתו עצים לעשות מהם דיק ולשפך סוללה על ירושלם והם האבנים שמשליכין בדיק וכדומה לו על העיר לנתוץ חומותיה ומגדליה ולדעת יונתן סוללה הוא תל גבוה שתרגום סוללה סליתא והוא ששופכין עפר ועצים תוך החפירות אשר סביב העיר עד שממלאים אותם מעפר ועצים תלים סביב לעיר על מלוי החפירות כדי לעלות מהם לחומה והוא הנקרא סוללה: העיר הפקד. היא העיר שהפקד עונה אעפ"י שהאריך לה הקב"ה לא יאריך לה עוד כי כלה עשק בקרבה בכל העיר ימצא אדם עשק בקרבה כלומר אפילו בתוך העיר עושקים אין צריך לומר חוץ לעיר בדרכים: (ז) כהקיר ביר. כהקיר מן מקור ביר כמו באר אמר כמו שהבאר מימיה נובעין תמיד בלי הפסק כן הקרה רעתה וזהו שאמר על פני תמיד ומה שאמר תמיד כלומר שאני רואה ומשגיח לעד לא כמו שהם אומרים אין ה' רואה אותנו: חלי ומכה. אמר חמס ושוד חלי ומכה ישמע בה שמחלים העניים ומכים אותם כמו שנאמר ופני עניים תטחנו או פירושו עונש החמס והשוד שהם עושים אני מביא עליהם חלי ומכה וכן ת"י כנובא דמקיים מוהי וגו' כבעמוד: (ח) הוסרי. פן תקע נפשי ממך. שאם לא תוסרי יפרד רצוני ממך שלא ארצה לך תקע נפשי ממך כמו ותקע כף ירך יעקב ענין הסרת הדבר ממקומו ושרשו קעע או יקע: לא נושבה. כאלו לא נושבה מעולם כך תהיה שממה וי"ת כארע דסדום דלא אתותבת : (ט) כה אמר ה'. עולל. מקור מן הדוכה למרובע כי שרשו עלל אמר כמו שמעללין הגפן אחר שבצרו אותה שישובו על העוללות הנשארות ויבצרו אותם כן יעשו האויבים כי שארית ישראל הוא כמו העוללות בגפן ועוד פירש ואמר השב ידך כבוצר על סלסלות כל אחד מהאויבים יאמר לחבירו השיב ידך לבוז ולשלול כמו שהוא בוצר ומשים בסלסלים ומשיב ידו פעם אחר פעם עד שיעולל הגפן כולה ויונתן פירש השב ידך דברי הנביא כנגד האל ותתיב מחתך עליהון כדקטיף על סלסלין. סלסילות. כמו סלים שרשו סלל והדגש לאות סלי

מצודת ציון

סללה. הוא תל העפר נמול העיר : הפקד. ענין השגחה כמו לא נפקד (לעיל ה') : (ז) כהקיר. ענין נביעה והוא מלשון מקור : ביר. כמו באר : ושוד. עושק : על פני. כמו לפני וכן לא יסיף וגו' ע"פ (שמות כ') : (ח) הוסרי. מלשון מוסר : תקע. ענין הסרה מן המקום וכן ותקע נפשי מהם (יחזקאל כ"ג) : (ט) עולל יעוללו. כן

מצודת דוד

העיר לשפוך תל עפר מול העיר ומשימים בה עלים ועולים עליה להלחם על העיר וכן וישפוך סוללה (יחזקאל כ"א) : הפקד כלה. רלה לומר שמקום השגחה בכל העיר ומלא עושק בקרבה : (ז) כהקיר ביר. כמו שהבאר שמימיו נובעים והולכים כן רעתם נובעת ואינה פוסקת : חמס ושוד. זעקת חמס ושוד נשמע בה לפני תמיד לכן אביא עליה חלי ומכה : (ח) הוסרי. קבלי מוסר פן תסיר נפשי ממך : ארץ לא נושבה. כאלו לא נתיישבה מעולם : (ט) עולל יעוללו כגפן. כמו הגפן אחר שבצרו אוסי

9. **thoroughly glean**—(*grappiller in French*). *After the vineyard has been gathered, and gleanings are left, and the poor come and glean them, so will they spoil and return and spoil.*—[*Rashi*]

Others explain that, after Nebuchadnezzar has sent the bulk of the people into exile, he will return to exile the remaining people.—[*Mezudath David*]

Others explain that after the exile

on Jerusalem a siege mound; that is the city whose sins have been visited upon her, everywhere there is oppression in its midst. 7. As a well lets its water flow, so has she let her evil flow; violence and spoil is heard therein before Me continually; sickness and wounds. 8. Be corrected, O Jerusalem, lest My soul be alienated from you; lest I make you a desolation, a land uninhabited. 9. So says the Lord of Hosts: They shall thoroughly glean

many fish. The intention is: Cut down the trees to erect a siege mound against the city.—[*Redak*]

It may also be rendered: Cut wood.—[*Targum Jonathan*]

a siege mound—Earth and wood are cast into the holes around the city to erect mounds upon which to stand in order to scale the wall of the city. This is *Jonathan*'s definition. This may also refer to the rocks that are cast from the bulwarks against the walls of the city.—[*Redak*] See *Rashi,* Isaiah 37:33.

that is the city whose sins have been visited upon her—Although God was patient with her until now, He will no longer be patient, for everywhere there is oppression in her midst.—[*Redak*]

the city whose sins have been visited upon her—Heb. הָפְקַד, *whose visitation has come.*—[*Rashi*]

there is oppression in its midst—I.e., even within the city there is oppression, surely on the roads.—[*Redak*]

7. **As . . . lets . . . flow**—Heb. כְּהָקִיר, *an expression of a spring.*—[*Rashi*]

a well—Heb. בַּיִר, *equivalent to* בְּאֵר.—[*Rashi*]

so has she let her evil flow—*So does their evil flow, constantly increasing and renewing.*—[*Rashi*]

before Me continually—I see this constantly, not as they say that 'the Lord does not see us.'—[*Redak*]

sickness and wounds—*Therefore, I brought upon her sickness and wounds.*—[*Rashi* from *Jonathan*]

Redak suggests: They cause sickness and wounds to the poor through their violence and spoil.

8. **Be corrected**—Heb. הִוָּסְרִי, *accept correction.*—[*Rashi*]

lest . . . be alienated—Heb. תֵּקַע, *lest it be pulled away.* יקע *is an expression of joining. Comp. 'and hang them up'* (וְהוֹקַע) (Num. 25:4), *and it is sometimes an expression of detaching. There are many words that are used in such a manner.*—[*Rashi*] I.e., there are many roots that have two opposite meanings.

I.e., if you do not accept correction, My desire will become detached from you. Comp. 'and the hollow of Jacob's thigh was strained (וַתֵּקַע), (Gen. 32:26).—[*Redak*]

a land uninhabited—I.e. like a land that was never inhabited. *Jonathan* paraphrases: like the land of Sodom, that was not inhabited.—[*Redak*]

כְּדְקָטֵיף עַל סַלְסְלִין:
י עַל מַן אֲמַלֵּיל וְאַסְהֵיד
דִּיקַבְּלוּן אוּלְפַן הָא
אִטְפְּשַׁת אוּדְנְהוֹן וְלָא
יָכְלִין לְמִיצַת הָא
פִּתְגָמָא דַּיְיָ הֲוָה לְהוֹן
לְחִיסוּדִין מִדְּלָא צָבַן
בֵּיהּ: יא וְיַת נְבוּאַת דַּיְיָ
בִּתְקוֹף מִן קֳדָם יְיָ

כַּגֶּפֶן שְׁאֵרִית יִשְׂרָאֵל הָשֵׁב יָדְךָ
כְּבוֹצֵר עַל סַלְסִלּוֹת: י עַל־מִי אֲדַבְּרָה
וְאָעִידָה וְיִשְׁמָעוּ הִנֵּה עֲרֵלָה אָזְנָם וְלֹא
יוּכְלוּ לְהַקְשִׁיב הִנֵּה דְבַר־יְהוָה הָיָה
לָהֶם לְחֶרְפָּה לֹא יַחְפְּצוּ־בוֹ: יא וְאֵת

ת"א הנה ערלה אזנם. שבת יד קה:

קמץ בז"ק

רש"י

השב ידך. אתה השונא השב ידך לשלול שנית כבוצר המשיב ידו על סלסלות המסלסל ומחפש העוללות וכן היה' משהגלה את יהויקים והרגו והמליך את יכניה חזר לסוף שלשה חדשי' והגלהו חזר לסוף עשתי עשרה שנה והגלה את צדקיהו. סלסלות (רביירקור"ש בלע"ז) כמו סלסלה ותרוממך (משליד) כך פירש דונש ומנחם פירש לשון (סלפליר"ש בלע"ז): (י) ואעידה. לשון התראה: ערלה. אטומה וכן כל לשון ערלה: לחרפה. מחרפין אותו: (יא) ואת חמת ה'

רד"ק

הורי ובסלסלות נכפלה גם כן פ"א הפעל: (י) על מי. ואעידה. ענין הזהרה כמו העד העיד בנו האיש ובא בלשון עדות כי המזהיר באחד מזהיר בו בפני עדים כדי שלא יכחיש בו אחר כן: ולא יוכלו להקשיב. הם עושים עצמם כאילו ערלה אזנם ואין בהם יכולת להקשיב: לחרפה. כי מה שהוא חרפה לאדם לא ירצה לשמעו כן היא להם דבר ה': (יא) ואת חמת. חמת ה' היוצאת על ישראל מלאתי מפנה עד שנלאתי

מהר"י קרא

תקע נפשי מכך. פן יעתק נפשי: (ט) כבוצר על סלסלות. כבוצר האומר לחברו חשב ידך וחרם סלסלות כמו סלסליה ותרוממך. כך פתר ר' מנחם חזקן. ומנחם בן סרוק פתר סלסלות כמו סל שחבוצר ענבים בוצר ומשים בסל. ודונש בן לברט השיבו ופתר סלסלות כמו סל החלות ושת לעקלקלות ועיקל משרים והוא פתר סלסלות. הם דליות הגפן: (י) הנה ערלה אזנם. [אטומה אזנם]: הנה דבר ה' היה להם לחרפה. כלומר לחרפה ולבושת יבואו לפי שאינן חפיצין בדבר ה': (יא) ואת חמת ה' מלאתי נלאתי הכיל. כלומר מנבואה מלאתי שאומרים לי שחמתו ישפוך על עולל בחוץ: ועל סוד בחורים. ת"י על

מנחה שי

בסלסלות כ"י: בוצר. ביר קרי והמלה מלעיל בספרי ספרדיין: (י) לא יחפצו בו. בספר אחד כ"י כתיב ולא בוא"ו וגם במקרא ישנה מויניציאה יש הערה מחילוף זה ובספרים אחרים כתוב לא בלא וא"ו: (יא) ואת חמת ה' מלאתי.

מצודת דוד

ונשאר עוללות מוזכים ללקט גם העוללות כן יהיה שארית ישראל כי יחזור האויב להגלות גם אותם: השב ידך. אתה האויב השב שנית ידך לקחת בגולה את הנשארים כמו הבוצר המשיב שנית ידו בסבור לחפש ולחפש אחר הענבים הנשארים מעיניו: (י) על מי אדברה. אל מי אדבר ואזהיר וישמעו אלי: ערלה אזנם. כאלו אזנם אטומה ולא יוכלו להקשיב אמרים: לחרפה. שמיעת דבר ה' יחשב להם לכלימה לכן לא יחפצו בו: (יא) ואת חמת ה'. החימה אשר אני רואה עליכם הנה מלאתי ממנה כי רבה היא:

מצודת ציון

נקרא סלסלות שאחר הבציר כמו לא תעולל אחריך (דברים כ"ד): כבוצר. כן נקרא אסיפת הענבים מן המחובר כמו כי תבצור כרמך (שם): על. בעבור: סלסלות. ענין נשמוש והפוש כמו סלסלה ותרוממך (משלי ד'): (י) על מי. אל מי: ואעידה. ענין אזהרה והתראה כי על פי רוב מתרין בעדים שלא יכחשו: ערלה. ענין אטום

like a vine the remnant of Israel; return your hand as a vintager over the branches. 10. To whom shall I speak and warn that they shall hearken? Behold, their ear is clogged, and they cannot listen; behold, the word of the Lord was a disgrace to them, they desire it not.

of the Ten Tribes, Nebuchadnezzar will come and exile the remaining two tribes.—[*Abarbanel*]

return your hand—*You, the enemy, return your hand to spoil a second time, like a vintager who returns his hand for the search, who looks and searches for the gleanings. And so it was when he exiled Jehoiakim and slew him, and crowned Jeconiah, he returned three months later and exiled him. He returned eleven years later and exiled Zedekiah.*—[*Rashi*]

the branches—Heb. סַלְסִלּוֹת (*reverchedures in O.F.*). *Comp.* '(Prov. 4:8) *Search for it* (סַלְסְלֶהָ) *and it will exalt you.*' *So did Dunash* (*Teshuvoth Dunash* p. 21) *explain it. Menahem* (*Machbereth* p. 126), *however, explains it as an expression of a basket* (סַל) (*paniers in O.F.*, baskets).—[*Rashi*] It appears from *Rashi* that *Dunash* interprets סַלְסִלּוֹת as 'searchings.' The same appears from *Rashi*, Prov. 4:8. Close scrutiny in *Teshuvoth Dunash*, however, yields the explanation of 'the branches.' Rabbi Joseph Kara, too, understands it in this manner. It is also curious that Dunash does not refer to the verse in Proverbs as Rashi states. Kara cites this interpretation in the name of Rabbenu Menahem the Elder, presumably R. Menahem ben Helbo, his uncle. Perhaps this name was inadvertently omitted from our editions of *Rashi*.

10. **To whom shall I speak**—Lit. upon whom shall I speak.—[*Mezudath David*]

and warn—Heb. וְאָעִידָה, *an expression of warning.*—[*Rashi*]

clogged—Heb. עֲרֵלָה, *clogged, and so is every expression of* עָרְלָה.—[*Rashi*]

and they cannot listen—They pretend that their ears are clogged and they cannot hear.—[*Redak*]

a disgrace—*They deride it.*—[*Rashi*] *Redak* explains that the word of the Lord was disgraceful to them; therefore they would not wish to hear it.

they desire it not—According to *Rashi*, we explain that they disgrace the word of the Lord since they do not desire to hear it.—[*Kara*] According to *Redak*, we explain that since it is disgraceful to them, they do not wish to hear it.

חמת יהוה מלאתי נלאיתי הכיל
שפך על־עולל בחוץ ועל סוד בחורים
יחדו כי־גם־איש עם־אשה ילכדו זקן
עם־מלא ימים: יב ונסבו בתיהם
לאחרים שדות ונשים יחדו כי־אטה
את־ידי על־ישבי הארץ נאם־יהוה:
יג כי מקטנם ועד־גדולם כלו בוצע בצע
ומנביא ועד־כהן כלו עשה שקר:

תרגום

אתמליתי לאיתי
לסוברא ולא יכילתי
למשפך על ינקין
בשוקא ועל סיעת
עולמין כחדא ארי אף
גבר עם אתא יתאחדו
סב עם דשבע יומין:
יב ויתפחרון בתיהון
לאוחרנין חקלן ונשין
כחדא ארי ארים ית
מחת גבורתי על יתבי
ארעא אמר יי: יג ארי
מזעיריהון ועד רבהון
כולהון אנסי ממון
ומספר ועד כהין כולהון
עבדי

הערי"ב ב׳ פסוקים לקמן ח י. ת"א שפוך על עולל. שבת קי קיט:

מהר"י קרא

סיעת עולימין: כי גם איש עם אשה ילכדו זקן עם מלא ימים. ודבר זה שלא ישאר כהן פלים. גורם: (יב) ונסבו בתיהם לאחרים. וכפני כת עתיד לשפוך חימה על הקטנים והגדולים: (יג) כי מקטנם ועד גדולם כולו בוצע בצע. בוצע לשון עושק.

רש"י

מלאתי. לכי מלא נבואה לבוא חמת ה׳ עליהם: הכיל. כמו להכיל (אסופרי"ר בלע"ז): שפוך על עולל. לשפוך על היונקים: בחוץ. בשוק: מלא ימים. קרוב למות והוא יותר על זקן: (יב) שדות ונשים יחדו. יוסבו לאחרים: (יג) בוצע בצע. אוסף ממון:

מנחת שי

יש פסיק בין ה׳ למלאתי כי מלא כל הארץ כבודו: (יג) כי מקטנם ועד גדולם. כל זה הענין הוא כתוב למטה סימן ח׳ עם שאר הפסוקים הבאים אחר זה במלות שונות למטה כתוב מקטון ועד גדול והנה מקטנם ועד גדולם. למטה כלה בה"א והנה כלו בוא"ו. למטה וירפו והנה וירפאו והוא חד מן ד׳ זוגים מן ב׳ ב׳ קדמאה מפיק א׳ ותנינא לא מפיק א׳ וסימן בד"ס א׳ ו׳. למטה את שבר בת עמי. והנה את שבר עמי:

רד"ק

לחכילה: שפוך על עולל. לשפוך החמה על עולל: בחוץ כלומר שיהרגו האויבים העוללים בחוצות בלי חמלה וכן נשפכה החמה על סוד בחורים יחדיו. ולא תועיל להם כחם. סוד ר"ל סיעה שמתחברים יחד בסוד אחד ובעצה אחת ולא יועילם כל זה: איש עם אשה. כלומר עם אשתו: זקן עם מלא ימים. כי לא יחמלו על זקן ומלא ימים הוא יותר מהזקן. ת"י ואת חמת ה׳ וית נבואת ה׳ בתקוף מן קדם ה׳ אתמליתי: (יב) ונסבו. שדות ונשים. וכן שדותיהם תתינת לאחרים: (יג) כי מקטנם. כמו שחטאו כולם כן ילקו כולם: מנביא. נביא השקר וי"ת ומספר ר"ל סופר מזהיר העם וכן כהן כהן

מצודת ציון

כמו עלי לב (לק׳ ס׳): להקשיב. ענין השמיעה והאזנה: (יא) נלאיתי. ענין עייפות ויגיעה כמו ונלאו מצרים (שמות ז׳): הכיל. ענין הסבלנה והחזקה כמו מרבה להכיל (יחזקאל כ"ג): עולל. ילדים רכים: בחוץ. בשוק: סוד. קבוצה הנאספת להעמיק סוד ועצה וכן בסוד עמקיב (לקמן ט׳): (יג) בוצע בצע. גוזלים הון וכן

מצודת דוד

נלאתי הכיל. נעשיתי עיף ויגע לסבול הלצר כלאותי שהחימה כיא לשפוך על קבוצת העוללים היושבים בחוץ מקום קבוצת העוללים: ועל סוד. על קבוצת בחורים על כלם יחדיו: ילכדו. ברשת החימה: מלא ימים. מי שנשלם ימיו והוא קרוב למות: (יב) ונסבו. ילכו מאתם ויסובבו לאומות: יחדיו. בפעם אחת: אטה את ידי וגו׳. להכות אותם בה והוא ענין מליצה: (יג) בוצע בצע. גוזלים הון מאחרים: ומנביא. מנביא השקר עד כהני הבמות:

money through dishonest means.—[*Daath Sofrim*]

and from prophet—*Redak* and *Mezudath David* identify this prophet with the false prophets or the prophets of Baal. *Jonathan* interprets it as ‘from a scribe,’ meaning that the scribes whose mission it was to admonish the people, were themselves guilty of dishonesty. *Daath Sofrim* identifies the prophet with the בְּנֵי הַנְּבִיאִים, mentioned throughout the Book of Kings as being the disciples of the great prophets such as Elijah and Elisha. These young men engaged in heavenly matters in order to attain the gift of prophecy. Apparently, they did not behave as young men of their pursuit were expected to behave.

to priest—Perhaps the reference is to the priests of the Baal, or even to the Levitical priests, since they too were evil.—[*Redak*]

I.e., exemplary conduct was expected of them.—[*Daath Sofrim*]

11. Therefore, I am full of the fury of the Lord, I am weary of containing it, to pour it out upon the babes in the street and upon the assembly of young men together, for a man with a woman shall be seized, an old man with one full of days.
12. And their houses shall be turned over to others, fields and wives together, for I will stretch out My hand over the inhabitants of the land, says the Lord. 13. For, from their smallest to their greatest, they all commit robbery, and from prophet to priest they all deal falsely.

11. **Therefore, I am full of the fury of the Lord**—*My heart is full of the prophecy of the coming of the fury of the Lord upon them.*—[*Rashi*]

containing—Heb. הָכִיל, *like* לְהָכִיל, *to contain* (*[à]souffrir in O.F.*) to tolerate.—[*Rashi*]

I am so full of God's fury upon Israel that I am too weary to contain it.—[*Redak*]

to pour it out upon the babes—*to pour it upon the sucklings.*—[*Rashi*]

in the street—*in the market.*—[*Rashi*]

I.e., that the enemies will ruthlessly slay the babes in the street.—[*Redak*]

and upon the assembly of young men—I.e., although they band together with one counsel, they will be unable to defend themselves against the enemy.—[*Redak*]

a man with a woman—I.e. a husband and a wife.—[*Redak*]

shall be seized—in the net of God's fury.—[*Mezudath David*]

one full of days—*I.e. one close to death, older than 'an old man.'*—[*Rashi*]

The enemies will have no pity even on the elderly and the dying.—[*Redak*]

Malbim pictures all these as one family. The babes are the youngest children, the young men are the grown children, the man and woman are the father and mother, the old man is the grandfather, and the one full of days is the great grandfather. The enemy will kill out entire families.

12. **And their houses shall be turned over to others**—They shall be taken away from them and given to the nations.—[*Mezudath David*]

fields and wives together—*shall be turned over to others.*—[*Rashi, Redak*]

The fact that no survivors will be left will cause their property to be turned over to others.—[*Kara*]

together—I.e. at one time.—[*Mezudath David*]

for I will stretch out My hand—I.e., I will stretch out My hand to strike you. This is an anthropomorphism.—[*Mezudath David*]

13. **For, from their smallest to their greatest**—Just as all of them sinned, so will all of them be punished.—[*Redak*]

commit robbery—I.e. they *rob money.*—[*Rashi*]

I.e. they are guilty of acquiring

יד וירפאו את־שבר עמי על־נקלה
לאמר שלום ׀ שלום ואין שלום׃
טו הבישו כי־תועבה עשו גם־בוש
לא־יבושו גם־הכלים לא ידעו לכן
יפלו בנפלים בעת־פקדתים יכשלו
אמר יהוה׃ טז כה אמר יהוה עמדו על־
דרכים וראו ושאלו ׀ לנתבות עולם
אי־זה דרך הטוב ולכו־בה ומצאו

תרגום:
עבדי שקר: יד ואסיאו
ית תבר כנשתא דעמי
בסלי שקריהון למימר
שלמא שלמא ולית
שלם: טו עליהון למבהת
ארי תועבתא עבדו אף
מבהת לית אינון בהתין
אף אתכנעא לית אינון
ידעין בכן יתרמון
קטילין בעדן דאסער
עליהון חוביהון יתקלון
אמר יי: טז כדנן אמר יי
קומו על אורחן וחזו
ושאילו לשבילין דמן
עלמא אידא אורחא
דתקנא והליכו בה
ואשכחו

מרגוע   קמץ בז"ק   ת"א הובישו. שם: ושאלו. עקידה. לקמן ח' י:

רש"י

(יד) על נקלה. קל הוא לנביאי השקר להוציא מפיה' ולומר שלו' יהיה לכם ובדבר זה מרפאין בדבור' את השבר העתיד לבא עליהן: (טו) הובישו. עליהן למבהת: הכלים. כמו להכלים: גם בוש לא יבושו. אינם

מהר"י קרא

(יד) על נקלה. דבר קל: (טו) בנפלים. ת"י יתרמון קטולין: (טז) ושאלו לנתיבות עולם. הם דורות הראשונים לאי זה דור

רד"ק

הבעל או מכהני הלוים כי גם הם היו רעים: (יד) וירפאו. נביאי השקר והכהנים רפאו את שבר עמי: על נקלה. כלומר על אמירה נקלה שאין בו ממש: לאמר שלום שלום ואין שלום. הם אמרו שלום והנה אין שלום כי הנה האויב בא יום יום: (טו) הובישו. פירוש בתמיה כשעשו תועבה הובישו לא הובישו: גם הכלים לא ידעו. פירוש לא הרגישו בכלימה שיכלימם אדם על רוע מעשיהם: לכן יפלו בנופלים. נביאי השקר וכהני הבעל יפלו בעת שיפלו שאר הנופלים מישראל וזה יהיה בעת פקודתם שאפקוד עליהם חטאתם והוא יום חורבן הבית והעיר: (טז) כה אמר ה' עמדו על דרכים. פירוש עמדו בדעתיכם על הדרך הטוב ועל הדרך הרע וראו בבינתכם ואמר זה כמו שאמר אליהו לעובדי הבעל עד מתי אתם פוסחים על שתי הסעיפים אם ה' הוא האלהים לכו אחריו וכן אמר להם הנה נביאי האמת אומרים לכם הוסרו ושובו מדרכיכם הרעים ואל תנתנו ביד אויב ונביאי השקר אומרים להם טוב הוא הדרך שאתם אוחזין לא תסורו ממנו וכה שהנביאי' מפחידים אתכם כי תנתנו ביד אויב אל תיראו כי שלום יהיה לכם ועתה בחנו בשכלכם איזה הוא הדרך הטוב גם שאלו בעבור נתיבות עולם כמו שאמר משה רבינו עליו השלום שאל אביך ויגדך כן אמר להם שאלו נתיבות עולם כלומר שאלו בעבור הדרכים אשר מעולם כלומר הדורות שעברו ותמצאו כי מי שאחז דרך האמת בא לו הטוב. ומי שאחז דרך שמידים אתכם נביאי השקר בא לו הרע לפי שאחז בדרך השקר משני פנים אלה תוכלו להכיר איזה הדרך הטוב ולכו בה או מדרך

מצודת דוד

(יד) וירפאו. הם מרפאים את שבר עמי ורעתם העתידה לבא ר"ל הם מוציאים מלבם דאגת הרעה הבאה: על נקלה. הם אמירה נקלה ומבוזה לאמר שלום תהיה ולא תבא הרעה וכזה המה מרפאים השבר אבל לא יהיה שלום והמה מכחשים: (טו) הובישו. ר"ל אכ"ם היה להם להנביאים והכהנים להיות נכלמים כאשר עשו דבר תועבה כדרך המתועבים אשר יכלמו אם נאה לידם דבר תועבה במקרה: גם בוש לא יבושו. רלה לומר עשו התועבה וגם לא יבושו בעבורה: גם הכלים לא ידעו. אינם יודעים מה היא כלימה וכפל הדבר במ"ש: לכן יפלו בנופלים. הנביאים והכהנים ההם יפלו בעת יפלו כל הנופלים ע"י האויבים: בעת פקדתים יכשלו. בעת שאזכור עליה' עונם לספרע מהם והוא בזמן החורבן אז יכשלו גם המה: (טז) וראו. העוברים והשבים ושאלו אותם על נתיבות העולם אי זה הדרך היותר טוב ולכו בה ואז תמצאו מרגוע ומנוחה והוא ענין מליצה לומר שאלו לחכמים והם יורו לכם דרך הטוב:

מצודת ציון

מוכר ביתו כולא כלא (משלי ט"ו): (יד) על. היא כמו עם: נקלה. מלשון קלון ובזיון: (טו) הובישו. מלשון בושה: תועבה. דבר איסור וגנאי: הכלים. מלשון כלימה: פקדתים. ענין זכרון: (טז) לנתיבו'.

said, "How long are you halting between two opinions? If the Lord is God, follow him, and if Baal, follow him." Here too, Jeremiah confronts the people with this ultimatum. The true prophets tell you to repent of your evil ways and you will not be delivered into the enemy's hands. The false prophets encourage you to continue on the way you are going and to ignore the threats of the true prophets. They assure you that there will be peace. Jeremiah exhorts the people to test the matter with their intelligence to determine which way is right. He tells them also to ask of the paths of old. Ask of the ways the earlier generations have traversed, and you will find that those who followed the true way prospered and those who followed the way the false prophets encourage you to follow,

14. And they healed the breach of My people easily, saying, "Peace, peace," but there is no peace. 15. They shall be put to shame since they have committed abomination. Neither are they ashamed nor do they know to feel disgrace. They will, therefore, fall among the slain; at the time I have visited upon them, they will stumble, says the Lord. 16. So says the Lord: stand on the roads and see, and ask of the paths of old, which is the good way, and go on it, and find

14. **easily**—*It is easy for the false prophets to pronounce with their mouths and to say, "You shall have peace," and with this thing they heal with their speech the breach destined to come upon them.*—[*Rashi*]

Redak renders: lightly, i.e. with an intangible word. *Mezudath David* renders: with disgraceful speech. *Jonathan* renders: with their false words.

"Peace, peace," but there is no peace—They say that there will be peace, but there is no peace, for the enemy draws nearer day by day.—[*Redak*]

Daath Sofrim asserts that the leaders did not intentionally mislead the people. They wished to save them from the panic of the impending invasion. They attempted to bribe the surrounding countries so that they should be friendly to Israel and not attack her. This solution, however, although generally acceptable, was, in this case, over simplistic. The prophet castigated them for engaging in these simple solutions instead of repenting.

15. **They should be ashamed**—Heb. הוֹבִישׁוּ, they *should be ashamed.*—[*Rashi* from *Jonathan*]

I.e., the prophets and the priests should, at least, have been ashamed of the abomination they committed as prominent people are ashamed if they are discovered committing an improper act.—[*Mezudath David*]

Redak explains this as a question: Were they not ashamed when they committed abomination?

to feel disgrace—Heb. הַכְלִים, like לְהַכְלִים.—[*Rashi*]

Neither are they ashamed—*They are not ashamed of their evil deeds.*—[*Rashi*]

They will, therefore, fall among the slain—The false prophets and the priests of Baal will fall when the other slain of Israel fall in battle. This will be when I visit their sins upon them, on the day of the destruction of the city and the Temple.—[*Redak*]

16. **So says the Lord: Stand on the roads**—I.e., in your speculation, stand on the road of good and on the road of evil, and seek to determine which is, indeed, the good road. In this, Jeremiah resembles Elijah, who told the people to choose between God and Baal, as in I Kings 18:21: And Elijah approached the entire people and

מַרְגּוֹעַ לְנַפְשְׁכֶם וַיֹּאמְרוּ לֹא נֵלֵךְ׃
יז וַהֲקִמֹתִי עֲלֵיכֶם צֹפִים הַקְשִׁיבוּ לְקוֹל
שׁוֹפָר וַיֹּאמְרוּ לֹא נַקְשִׁיב׃ יח לָכֵן
שִׁמְעוּ הַגּוֹיִם וּדְעִי עֵדָה אֶת־אֲשֶׁר־בָּם׃
יט שִׁמְעִי הָאָרֶץ הִנֵּה אָנֹכִי מֵבִיא רָעָה
אֶל־הָעָם הַזֶּה פְּרִי מַחְשְׁבוֹתָם כִּי עַל־
דְּבָרַי לֹא הִקְשִׁיבוּ וְתוֹרָתִי וַיִּמְאֲסוּ־

ת"א הנה אנכי. קדושין דף ח:

בה׳

תרגום

וְאַשְׁכְּחוּ נְיָח לְנַפְשְׁכוֹן
נַאֲמַרוּ לָא נֵיזֵיל׃
יז וַאֲקֵימִית עֲלֵיכוֹן
סָלְפִין קַבִּילוּ לְמִלֵּי
נְבִיָּא וַאֲמַרוּ לָא נְקַבֵּיל׃
יח בְּכֵן שְׁמַעוּ עַמְמַיָּא
וְדָעִי כְּנִשְׁתָּא דְיִשְׂרָאֵל
יַת חוֹבֵיהוֹן׃ יט שְׁמַעִי
אַרְעָא דְיִשְׂרָאֵל הָא
אֲנָא מַיְתֵי בִּישְׁתָּא עַל
עַמָּא הָדֵין תּוּשְׁלָמַת
עוֹבָדֵיהוֹן אֲרֵי לְפִתְגָמֵי
עַבְדֵי נְבִיַּיָּא לָא קַבִּילוּ
וְאוֹרָיְתִי וְקָצוּ בַהּ׃

למא

מהר"י קרא

השפיע הקב"ה טובה לדורות שהתקינו מעשיהן או לדורות שקלקלו מעשיהן הלא אם יורו אתכם ויאמרו לכם לדורות שהטיבו דרכיהם הטוב אף אתם אי זה דרך הטוב תלכו בה ומצאו מרגוע לנפשכם. ומשמאנו ללכת בהם: (יז) והקימותי עליכם צופים. הם הנביאים כדכתיב בן אדם צופה נתתיך ואמרתי לכם מעתה הואיל ואינכם רוצין ללכת בדרך הטוב: הקשיבו. לדברי הנביא שמכריז לכם שהאומות באין עליכם כצופה שעומד על המגדל ורואה חרב בא לעיר ותקע בשופר והזהיר את העם: ויאמרו לא נקשיב. כלומר לא נפל פחדם של אומות עליהם: (יח) לכן שמעו הגוים. הקבצו ובואו עליהם: ודעו עדה. את כנסת ישראל דעי לך את אשר יארע לכם לישראל: (יט) פרי מחשבהם. שילום מעשיהם. כי על כן:

רש"י

מתביישין ממעשיהם הרעים: (טז) **מרגוע.** מנוחה: (יז) **והקימותי עליכם צופים.** הוא שמעמידין אנשים על המגדלים בעת החירום איש צופה ורואה אם גייס בא לעיר תוקע בשופר ומזהיר את העם להחלץ ולבא על החומה אף אני העמדתי נביאים המשמיעים אתכם מן הפורענות הבאה להזהר ולתקן דרכיכ' שתנצלו והוא כשופר תקיעות הצופה הקשיבו לקול השופ' הזה והחלצו: והקימותי. פי' העמדתי להם ככר וכן תירגום יונתן ואקימית: **צופים.** (גיט"ש בלע"ז): (יח) **את אשר בם.** את הרעה אשר בידם: (יט) **פרי מחשבותם.** שכר מחשבותם: **ותורתי וימאסו בה.** הרי זה דוגמת עזי וזמרת יה ויהי לי לישועה (שמות ט"ו) שהיה לו לומר היה לי לישועה אף כאן היה לו לומר

רד"ק

השכל או מדרך הקבלה: ומצאו מרגוע לנפשכם. ובזה תמצאו מרגוע נפש ונחת רוח בשתי הסעיפים וכשאמרתי לכם זה אמרתם לא נלך ולא נחקיר על הדרכים כי מה שאנו אוחזין הוא טוב בעינינו: (יז) והקימותי. צופים. נביאי אמת שמזהירים אותם ואומרים להם הקשיבו לקול השופר ראו איך מבטיחין אתכם נביאי השקר על התהו שאומרים לכם שלום יהיה לכם ועתה הקשיבו לקול שופר שתוקעים סביבותיכם בשפר מפני האויב להניס העם. ויאמרו לא נקשיב וכן אמרו לא נחוש לכל זה כי אנחנו בירושלם נהיה בשלום וי"ת ואקימית עליהון וגו' כבעמוד: (יח) לכן שמעו הגוים. שאר העמים שמעו כי אני מזהיר בכם: ודעי עדה. ואת עדת ישראל דעי: את אשר בם. כמו שאמר ראי את עונך וזהו את אשר בם העונות אש־באנשיך מקטנם ועד גדולם וכן תרגם יונתן ודעי כנישתא דישראל ית חוביהון: (יט) שמעי הארץ. כי את עד ביני וביניהם ואמר הארץ ולא אמר השמים כי גם הם עדים לפי שהארץ תהיה חרבה בעונת: פרי מחשבותם. איני אומר שיענישם על המחשבה לבד אלא על מעשיהם שהם פרי מחשבותם שהם חושבים שאין אני רואה מעשיהם לפיכך הולכים אחר לבם למלאות תאותם: על דברי. כמו אל דברי וילך אלקנה הרמתה על ביתו כמו אל ביתו. ואאז"ל פירוש פרי מחשבותם המחשבות שאדם חושב ולא באו לידו על כן נמנע מעשותם עליהם אמר פרי מחשבותם אבל המחשבות שיבאו לידו ונמנע מעשותם מיראת שמים לא יצטרפו למעשים ויונתן תרגם פרי מחשבותם תושלמת עובדיהון: ותורתי וימאסו בה. כמו ואל תורתי לא הקשיבו כי על דברי ר"ל דברי הנביאים שמזהירים אותם ותורתי ר"ל תורת משה לא די שלא הקשיבו לה כשקוראים אותה

מצודת ציון

ענין שביל ודרך: מרגוע. מנוחה והשקט כמו וזאת המרגעה (ישעי' כ"ח): (יז) צופים. מביטים במקום גבוה: הקשיבו. ענ' האזנה:

מצודת דוד

ויאמרו. והם השיבו לא נלך לשאול כי דרכם ישרה בעיניהם: (יז) צופים. בזמן המלחמה הדרך להעמיד צופים לראות אם השונא בא וכשרוא' שהם באים תוקע בשופר להזהיר את העם ולאמר למשל לומר הנה העמדתי נביאים להזהירם על התשובה כי הצרה קרובה: לא נקשיב. לא נשמע לאזהרת הנביא: (יח) שמעו הגוים. אתם העכו"ם שמעו מה שאני מתרה בהם: ודעי עדה. כל עדה מעדת העובדי כוכבים ומזלות דעי את הרעה אשר בידם: (יט) שמעי הארץ. אתם יושבי הארץ שמעו מה שאני מתרה בהם: פרי מחשבותם. גמול מחשבתם: כי על דברי. כי אל דברי אשר

are a witness between us. He summons the earth rather than the heavens since the earth will become desolate because of Israel's sins.—[*Redak*]

Others render: You inhabitants of the earth, hearken to the warning I give My people Israel.—[*Mezudath David*]

the fruit of their thoughts—*the retribution for their thoughts*.—[*Rashi*]

This would appear to mean that God punishes for thoughts alone,

rest for your soul, and they said, "We will not go." 17. And I
have stationed lookouts over you. Hearken to the sound of the
shofar, and they said, "We will not hearken." 18. Therefore,
hearken, O nations, and know, O congregation, what is within
them. 19. Hearken, O earth, behold, I bring evil to this people,
the fruit of their thoughts, for they did not hearken to My
words, and they rejected My instruction.

met only with disaster. Hence, there are two ways of determining which road to follow, the philosophical approach and the traditional approach.—[*Redak*]

and find rest for your soul—By deciding this matter, you will find rest for your soul, and you will no longer be plagued by your doubts.—[*Redak*]

rest—Heb. מַרְגּוֹעַ.—[*Rashi*]

and they said, "We will not go"—When I said this to you, you said, "We will not go, and we will not delve into the matter. The way we are following suits us."—[*Redak*]

17. **And I have stationed lookouts over you**—*That is that they station men on the towers at the time of strife. A man looks and sees. If a troop is approaching the city, he sounds a shofar and warns the people to arm and to come on the wall. I, too, appointed prophets who inform you about the impending retribution to alert yourselves and to mend your ways, so that you be saved, and that is like the shofar sounded by the lookout. Hearken to the sound of this shofar and arm yourselves.*—[*Rashi*]

And I have stationed—Heb. וַהֲקִמֹתִי *This means: I have already stationed for them. And so did Jonathan render:* וַאֲקֵימִית *and I stationed.*—[*Rashi*]

lookouts—(*Badetes in O.F.*).—[*Rashi*]

Redak renders צֹפִים as *prophets.* I have appointed true prophets who warn you and announce, "Hearken to the sound of the shofar." See how the false prophets give you futile promises. They say that there will be peace, but now, hearken to the sound of the shofar all around you to warn the people to take refuge. But they said, "We will not hearken." For we in Jerusalem will have peace.—[*Redak*]

18. **Therefore, hearken, O nations**—Assemble and march upon them.—[*Kara*]

Hearken to what I warn Israel.—[*Redak, Ibn Nachmiash*]

and know, O congregation—And You, O congregation of Israel, know.—[*Redak, Kara, Targum*] *Mezudath David* renders: Each congregation of the gentiles, know.

what is within them—I.e. *the evil that is in their hands.*—[*Rashi*]

Know the iniquities of your men, from the smallest to the greatest.—[*Redak*]

19. **Hearken, O earth**—for you

* For Rashi's commentary turn to page 223.

כ לְמָא דְנַן קֳדָמַי
לְבוּנְתָא דְמִשְׁבָא תֵיתֵי
וְקָנֵי טַבְתָא מֵאֲרַע
רְחִיקָא עֲלָוָתְכוֹן לָא
לְרַעֲוָא וְנִכְסַת קוּדְשֵׁיכוֹן
לָא יִתְקַבְּלוּן קֳדָמָי׃
כא בְּכֵן כִּדְנַן אֲמַר יְיָ הָא
אֲנָא מַיְתֵי עַל עַמָא
הָדֵין תַּקְלָן וְיִתְקְלוּן
בְּהוֹן אֲבָהָן וּבְנִין כַּחֲדָא
שְׁגִיר וְקָרִיבֵיהּ יֵיבְדוּן׃
כב כִּדְנַן אֲמַר יְיָ הָא עַמָא
אָתֵי מִצְפּוּנָא וְעַמְמִין
רַבְרְבִין יֵיתוּן בִּגְלֵי
מִסְיְפֵי אַרְעָא׃ כג קַשְׁתָּן
וּתְרֵיסִין אֲחִידִין
אַכְזְרָאִין אִינוּן וְלֵית
לְהוֹן רַחֲמִין קָלְהוֹן
כְּיַמָא בְּאִתְרְגוּשֵׁיהּ וְעַל
סוּסְוָתָא רָכִיבִין מְסַדְּרִין

בָהּ׃ כ לָמָּה־זֶּה לִי לְבוֹנָה מִשְּׁבָא
תָבוֹא וְקָנֶה הַטּוֹב מֵאֶרֶץ מֶרְחָק
עֹלוֹתֵיכֶם לֹא לְרָצוֹן וְזִבְחֵיכֶם לֹא־עָרְבוּ
לִי׃ כא לָכֵן כֹּה אָמַר יְהוָה הִנְנִי נֹתֵן אֶל־
הָעָם הַזֶּה מִכְשֹׁלִים וְכָשְׁלוּ בָם אָבוֹת
וּבָנִים יַחְדָּו שָׁכֵן וְרֵעוֹ יֹאבֵדוּ׃ כב כֹּה
אָמַר יְהוָה הִנֵּה עַם בָּא מֵאֶרֶץ צָפוֹן
וְגוֹי גָּדוֹל יֵעוֹר מִיַּרְכְּתֵי־אָרֶץ׃ כג קֶשֶׁת
וְכִידוֹן יַחֲזִיקוּ אַכְזָרִי הוּא וְלֹא יְרַחֵמוּ
קוֹלָם כַּיָּם יֶהֱמֶה וְעַל־סוּסִים יִרְכָּבוּ

ואבדו קרי

רש"י

ותורתי מאסו בה ודרך המקראות לדבר כן: (כ) למה זה לי לבונה. אשר אתם מקריבים לפני אשר משבא באה: לא ערבו. לא נעמו: (כג) יחזיקו. יקחו כמו וישלח ידו

מהר"י קרא

דברי לא הקשיבו. כמו שנאמר למעלה ויאמרו לא נקשיב: (כ) וקנה הטוב. לקטרת ולפי שיש בקנה טוב ורע הוא אומר קנה הטוב:

מנחת שי

(כא) יאבדו. ואבדו קרי:

רד"ק

אליה' אלא גם מאסו בה שלא ירצו לקרותה ולשמעה כי בימי יאשיהו כשמצא חלקיהו ספר התורה ויקראו בה היה חידוש אצלם כי כבר שכחו אותה: (כ) למה זה לי לבונה. וקנה הטוב. שהיו מביאין אותם מארץ רחוק לקטרת כי לא היתה נמצאת בארץ ישראל ושאר סמני הקטרת היו נמצאים בה או זכר השני' והוא הדין אחרים והקטרת היתה באה להכשיר הקרבן ואם הקרבן אין נרצה לפני ולמה תטרחו להביא הכשרון שהוא הקטורת: (כא) לכן. אבות ובנים. שכן ורעו. זכר כן להודיע כי האב לא יוזהיר הבן אם ידע וכן אם הבן ידע לא יזהיר לאב וכן האיש עם שכנו ר"ל שהוא שוכן אצל ביתו וכן עם רעו שיש לו משא ומתן או שותפות עמו אין אחד מהם מתירא ומזהיר את חברו לפיכך יאבדו כולם כי כל אחד ירצה ברעת חברו: יאבדו. כתיב ואבדו קרי והענין אחד: (כב) כה אמר ה'. יעור. אני הוא המעיר אותו לבא מבבל אל ירושלם ארץ רחוקה לא יהיה בלתי הערה ויעור מבנין נפעל: (כג) קשת וכידון יחזיקו. כל אחד יחזיק בידו שני כלי זיין: כים יהמה. כגלי הים: ועל סוסים

מצודת דוד

ביד הנביאים לא הקשיבו וגם אל תורתי שנתתי ביד משה לא הקשיבו וימאסו בה: (כ) למה זה לי. מה נחת רוח יש לי בהקטרת הלבונה אשר תבוא משבא והקטרת' קנה הטוב הבא מארץ מרחק: לא לרצון. אינם לי לרצון: לא ערבו לי. לא ינעמו לי: (כא) מכשולים. דברים המכשילי': ורעו. חבירו הסמוך אצלו: יאבדו. כולם יאבדו יחד כי בבוא המכשול אל הבית כולם יכשלו בו ויאבדו: (כב) מארץ צפון. הוא בבל: יעור. יהיה נעור לבא מסוף הארץ ר"ל ממרחק: (כג) יחזיקו. יאחזו בידם להלחם בהם: ולא ירחמו. על הנופלים בידם: כים יהמה. כמו הים אשר הומה ע"י גליו המשמיעים בקול: ועל סוסים ירכבו. וימהרו לרדוף אחרי

מצודת ציון

(כ) לבונה. מין בושם: משבא. שם מדינה: וקנה. הוא קנמון מסממני הקטורת: ערבו. ענין נעימות ומתיקות כמו וערבה לי (לקמן ל"א): (כא) שכן. זה הדר עמו בבית: (כב) יעור. מלי התעוררות: מירכתי. מסוף וכן ולירכתי המשכן ימה (שמות כ"ו): (כג) וכידון. הוא כעין רומח וכן נטה בכידון (יהושע ה'): ערוך.

them to come from Babylon to Jerusalem. No one comes from such a distant land without being aroused.—[*Redak*]

23. **They will grasp**—Heb. יַחֲזִיקוּ, *they will take. Comp.* '(Exodus 4:4) *And he stretched out his hand and took it* (וַיַּחֲזֶק).' *Comp also* '(infra verse 24) *trouble grasped us* (הֶחֱזִיקָתְנוּ)' *held us.*—[*Rashi*]

Each one will grasp two weapons, a bow and a spear.—[*Redak*]

like the sea—Like the waves of the sea.—[*Redak*]

This will make them even more ominous.—[*Malbim*]

20. Why do I need the frankincense that comes from Sheba, and the good cane from a distant country? Your burnt offerings are not acceptable, and your sacrifices are not pleasant to Me.
21. Therefore, so says the Lord: Behold, I give this people stumblingblocks, and both fathers and sons together shall stumble upon them, a neighbor and his companion, and they shall perish.
22. So says the Lord: Behold, a people is coming from the northland, and a great nation will be aroused from the ends of the earth.
23. They will grasp bow and spear, they are cruel and have no compassion; their voice roars like the sea, and they ride on horses,

i.e. if one thought to commit a sin, although he did not, in fact, commit it. According to the Talmud (*Kiddushin* 40a), however, God does not account an evil thought as a deed. The Rabbis, therefore, interpret this verse to mean that God punishes for the fruit of their thoughts, meaning that if the thoughts produced fruit, i.e. if the deed was accomplished, God punishes for it. Otherwise, He does not punish for it. This is *Redak*'s interpretation. Further, he quotes his father who differentiates between one who thinks to commit a sin, but is never afforded the opportunity to commit that sin, and one who thought to commit a sin and refrained from doing so because of fear of God. In the latter case, it is not accounted as a deed. Jonathan renders: the payment for their deeds.

20. **Why do I need frankincense** —*that you offer up to Me, that comes from Sheba?*—[*Rashi*]

Sheba was located in the southwest of the Arabian peninsula. See I Kings 10:1.—[*Daath Mikra*]

and the good cane—Since some cane is good for incense and other cane is unsuitable, he states: the good cane.—[*Kara*]

These ingredients for the incense were imported from distant lands, not so the other ingredients, which were found in the Holy Land. It is also possible that these two ingredients are merely examples of all the ingredients. The incense served merely to make the sacrifice fit for acceptance. If the sacrifice itself was unacceptable, why go to the trouble to bring the incense?—[*Redak*]

are not pleasant—Heb. עָרְבוּ.—[*Rashi*]

21. **fathers and sons**—Neither will the fathers warn the sons nor the sons the fathers. Similarly, neighbors and friends will not warn each other. Therefore, they will all stumble and perish.—[*Redak*] This may mean that God will give them the opportunity to stumble upon sins. It may also mean that they will stumble upon disaster.—[*Alshich*]

22. **will be aroused**—I will arouse

עָרוּךְ כְּאִישׁ לַמִּלְחָמָה עָלַיִךְ בַּת־צִיּוֹן׃
כד שָׁמַעְנוּ אֶת־שָׁמְעוֹ רָפוּ יָדֵינוּ צָרָה
הֶחֱזִקַתְנוּ חִיל כַּיּוֹלֵדָה׃ כה אַל־תֵּצְאִי
הַשָּׂדֶה וּבַדֶּרֶךְ אַל־תֵּלֵכִי כִּי חֶרֶב
לְאֹיֵב מָגוֹר מִסָּבִיב׃ כו בַּת־עַמִּי חִגְרִי־
שַׂק וְהִתְפַּלְּשִׁי בָאֵפֶר אֵבֶל יָחִיד עֲשִׂי־
לָךְ מִסְפַּד תַּמְרוּרִים כִּי פִתְאֹם יָבֹא
הַשֹּׁדֵד עָלֵינוּ׃ כז בָּחוֹן נְתַתִּיךָ בְעַמִּי

ת"א כה עמי. גיטין כ: תצאו קרי תלכו קרי קמץ בפשטא מבצר

תרגום

אִינוּן כִּגְבַר עֲבִיד קְרָבִין עֲלָךְ כְּנִשְׁתָּא דְצִיוֹן׃ כד שְׁמַעְנָא יַת שִׁמְעֲהוֹן אִתְרַשְׁלָא יְדָנָא עָקָא אַחֲדַתְנָא הָא כְּחַבְלִין לְיָלֵדְתָּא׃ כה לָא תִפְקוּן לְחַקְלָא וּבְאוֹרְחָא לָא תְהָכוּן אֲרֵי חַרְבָּא דְסַנְאָה מְקַטְּלָא לְמִתְכַּנְשִׁין מִסְחוֹר סְחוֹר׃ כו כְּנִשְׁתָּא דְעַמִּי אֱסָרוּ סַקִּין וַחֲפוּ רֵישְׁכוֹן בְּקִטְמָא אֶבֶל כְּיָחִיד עֲבִידוּ לְכוֹן מִסְפֵּד בְּמָרַר אֲרֵי בִתְכֵיף יֵיתוֹן בָּזוֹזִין עֲלָנָא׃ כז בְּחִיר יְהַבְתָּךְ בְּעַמִּי כִּכְרַךְ

מהר"י קרא

(כה) מגור. כמו לא תגורו מפני איש: (כז) בחון נתתיך בעמי מבצר. מקרא מסורס הוא והוא כמו בחון מבצר נתתיך בעמי. ופתרון בחון חזק נתתיך בעמי: ותדע ובחנת את דרכם.

רש"י

ויחזק בו (שם ד) וכן צרה החזיקתני אחזתני: (כה) מגור. יראה. ל"א לשון אסיפה כמו מגורי אל חרב (יחזקאל כ"א) וכן תירגם יונתן: (כו) והתפלשי. התגלגלי: אבל יחיד. אבל של בן יחיד מי שאין לו אלא בן יחיד ומת: מספד תמרורים. לפי שהוא דבוק נקוד מספד בפתח ואינו נקוד מספד בצירי: עלינו. כביכול עלי ועליך: (כז) בחון נתתיך. לירמיה נאמר חזק נתתיך בתוכם ותדע ובחנת

מנחת שי

(כה) תצאי. תצאו קרי: תלכי. תלכו קרי:

רד"ק

ירכבו. כי לא יבאו רגלים לבד אלא אף רוכבי סוסים יהיו בהם רבים ומלחמתם יותר חזקה: ערוך כאיש למלחמה. כל אחד מהם יהיה ערוך בכלי זיין כמו איש אחד הנועד להלחם עם חברו מלחמה ערוכה שמגין עצמו בכלי זיין וברוב לא יהיו הרבים כל כך מזויינין וזה החיל יהיה כל אחד מהם ערוך למלחמה כאיש אחד ועל מי יבאו עליך בת ציון: (כד) שמענו את שמעו. שמע הגוי שזכר והנפרד מן שמעו שומע בפלס רומח ושמענו מאמר הנביא שכולל עצמו עם ישראל החרדים אל דבריו: (כה) אל תצאי. תלכי. תצאי תלכי כתיב ביו"ד הנקבה מדבר כנגד הכנסת תלכו תצאו קרי מדבר כנגד הפרטים והענין אחד: חרב. יש לאויב מבחוץ להכותכם אם תצאו: מגור. ופחד יש בכל סביבותיכם אם תצאו וי"ת מגור מסביב מקטלא למתכנשין מסחור סחור: (כו) בת עמי. והתפלשי באפר. התגוללי בתוך האפר וי"ת וחפו רישיכון: אבל יחיד. אבל אדם שמת לו בנו יחידו שהיא אבל קשה: מספד תמרורים. מספד סמוך לפיכך הוא פתוח מספד של מרירות ובמסרת ג' פתחין והסי' תמריא סמכין לרבתיא פירוש תמריא מספד תמרורי' סמיכין מספד בית האבל רמניא כמספד הדרימון: כי פתאום. מעתה התחילו לספוד כי לא תדעי עת בואו כי פתאום יבא עלינו: (כז) בחון. אמר לנביא אף על פי אתה

מצודת ציון

מסודר ומוכן: כאיש. ר"ל כגבור חיל: (כד) רפו. מלשון רפיון: החזקתנו. ענין אחיזה: חיל. חלחלה ורעד: (כה) מגור. ענין פחד כמו ויגר מואב (במדבר כ"ב): (כו) בת עמי. עדת עמי: חגרי. מלשון חגורה ואזור: שק. יריעת עבה: והתפלשי. ענין הכאוי והתגלגל בה וכן עפר התפלשי (מיכה א'): תמרורים. מל' מרירות: השודד. המעשק: (כז) בחון. ענין מגדל חזק וכן עופל ובחן (ישעי'

מצודת דוד

הנכנסים במלחמה: ערוך כאיש. ר"ל מהם ערוך ומוכן כאיש גבור חיל ללכת למלחמה עליך בת ציון: (כד) את שמעו. רלה לומר שמועת גבורתו: רפו ידינו. נחלשו רפיון וחלשים: צרה החזיקתנו. אחז אותנו צרה וחיל כיולדה: (כה) כי חרב לאויב. כי החרב אשר הוא להאויב מביא פחד מסביב: (כו) חגרי שק. דרך לאבל ואבילות: והתפלשי באפר. התגלגלי באפר ועשי לך אבל כאבל בן יחיד ומספד מר: השודד. זה בבל: (כז) בחון. אמר המקום לירמיה הלא נתתיך בעמי מחוזק כמגדל מבצר ולא תירא מהם להוכיח דרכם על פניהם: ותדע. וא"כ ידעת ובחנת את דרכם כי

The intention is that the mourning will be very intense as one mourns for his only son.—[*Redak*]

a bitter lamentation—Heb. מִסְפַּד תַּמְרוּרִים, lit. a lamentation of bitternesses. *Since it is the construct state, it is vowelized* מִסְפַּד *with a 'pattah,' and it is not vowelized* מִסְפֵּד *with a 'zere.'*—[*Rashi*]

27. **I have made you the strong one**—*This was said to Jeremiah. I have made you the strong one in their midst, and you shall know and test their way, that he tested them and they will not heed.* בָּחוֹן is an expression of strength. Comp. (Isa. 32:14) *rampart and tower* (בַּחַן),' also '(ibid. 23:13) *they erected its towers* (בְּחוּנָיו).'—[*Rashi*]

God says to the prophet:

equipped like a man for war, upon you, O daughter of Zion.
24. We have heard his report, our hands have become feeble,
trouble has grasped us, and pain, as a woman in travail. 25. Go
not forth into the field, and on the road do not go, for the
enemy has a sword; there is fear all around. 26. O daughter of
My people, gird yourself with sackcloth and roll in ashes; make
yourself a mourning [as] for an only child, a bitter lamentation,
for suddenly the plunderer will come upon us. 27. I have made
you the strong one and the fortress of My people,

equipped like a man for war—Each one will be armed with weapons like a man going alone to wage war. As a rule, armies were not that well equipped. In this case, however, each soldier will be equipped as though he himself were going to wage a battle with his opponent.—[*Redak*]

Malbim explains this as connected with 'they ride on horses.' I.e., each horse will be equipped like a man for war. A horse will not attack by accident, but will come upon you intentionally, O Daughter of Zion.

24. **We have heard his report**—The prophet includes himself among Israel, who listens to his words.—[*Redak*]

our hands have become feeble—We have despaired of doing anything. —[*Malbim*]

trouble has grasped us—at the time of the siege.—[*Malbim*]

and pain as a woman in travail—at the time the wall was broken. This is like the woman whose womb opens up, releasing its contents, for then the king and his soldiers fled at night.—[*Malbim*]

25. **Go not forth into the field**—I warn you not to go forth into the field.—[*Malbim*]

and on the road do not go—I.e., do not go on the road within the city. Instead, hide in the nooks and crannies.—[*Malbim*]

for the enemy has a sword—outside the city, to slay you if you go forth.—[*Redak, Malbim*]

there is fear—Heb. מָגוֹר.—[*Rashi*] There is fear all around if you go forth.—[*Redak*] *Malbim* explains: There is fear all around your dwelling for the city is ready to be broken into.

Another explanation: An expression of gathering. Comp. '(Ezekiel 21:17) *Gathered* (מְגוּרֵי) *to the sword.' And in this manner Jonathan renders it.*—[*Rashi*] *Jonathan* renders: For the sword of the enemy slays those gathered around.

26. **and roll**—Heb. וְהִתְפַּלְּשִׁי.—[*Rashi, Redak*] *Jonathan* renders: cover your head.

a mourning [as] for an only child—*A mourning for an only son; one who has only one son and he dies.*—[*Rashi*]

* For Rashi's commentary turn to page 223.

מִבְצָר וְתֵדַע וּבָחַנְתָּ אֶת־דַּרְכָּם:
כח כֻּלָּם סָרֵי סוֹרְרִים הֹלְכֵי רָכִיל נְחֹשֶׁת
וּבַרְזֶל כֻּלָּם מַשְׁחִיתִים הֵמָּה: כט נָחַר
מַפֻּחַ מֵאֵשְׁתַּם עֹפָרֶת לַשָּׁוְא צָרַף צָרוֹף

ורעים — מאש תם קרי

תקיף ותהודע ותחזי
להון ית אורחתהון:
כח כל רברביהון מרדין
מהלכין בנכילו כמא
דמערב נחש עם פרזלא
כולהון מחבלין אינון:
כט הא כמשב נפחין
דחריך בנואה דנורא כן
חשא קלהון דנבייא
דמתנבן להון תובו לאוריתא ולא תבו וכאברא דמתמסי בגו כורא כן הנאה בטילין

רש"י

את דרכם שהוכיחם והם לא ישמעו. בחון לשון חוזק כמו פופל וכחן (ישעיה ל"ב) הקימו בחוניו (שם כ"ח): (כח) סרי סוררים. שרים מן הדרך: הולכי רכיל. בין הנחושת והברזל מטילי איבה בין שני שרים שיש בהן כח להתגרות יחד כך שמעתי. ואני אומר הולכי רכיל הם וחזקים כנחשת וברזל להחזיק כזביהם. וי"ת רכיל זה לשון נוכל מהלכין בנכילו כמא דמערב נחש עם פרזלא. ונוכל הוא ל' מחשבה כמו ויתנכלו אותו להמיתו (ברא' ל"ז): (כט) נחר מפוח. משל הוא כשצורפים כסף נופחין במפוח ונותנין תמיד עופר' בתוך הכור ומועיל לצרוף אבל אתם באתי לצרוף אתכם המפוח נחר ונחרך מכח האש ותם העופרת כולו. נחר לשון חרה אפי (איוב ל"ב) ועצמי חרה מני חורב (שם ל') (איסר"ש

מהר"י קרא

שכשם שהאבן שמנסין בו את הזהב בחן את הזהב אם טוב ואם רע כך אני מודיע אותך את דרכם ומשתדע מעשיהן אתה בוחן את דרכם: (כח) והלכי רכיל נחשת וברזל. אומרים רכילות בין שני בני אדם שחוקין כנחשת וברזל כדי לעורר ביניהן מריבה: (כט) נחר מפוח. דבר שהנפח מנפח בו. גם מהמת האש: תם עופרת. כשזורקין העופרת באש. אבל ישראל: לשוא צרף צרוף ורעים לא נתקו. לשוא הנביאים מוכיחין אותם והם

רד"ק

אמר להם דברים קשים ומתנבא עליהם רעות אל תירא מהם כי בחון ומבצר נתתיך להם בחון פירושו מבצר כמו הקימו בחוניו וכן אמר לו בתחלת נבואתו הנה נתתיך היו' לעיר מבצר ולעמוד ברזל לפיכך אל תירא מהם והפש אחר דרכיהם וזהו שאמר ותדע ובחנת את דרכם ואמר ובחנת לשון נופל על לשון לפי שקראו בחון אמר ובחנת את דרכם ויונתן תרגם בחון בחיר: (כח) כלם סרי סוררים. סרי בסמ"ך כמו בשי"ן השרים הם שרי סוררים כלומר שעבדיהם סוררים והשרים כמו כן סוררים והעבדים הולכי רכיל לאדוניהם לחבל עניים באמ"י שקר והנה השרים עם העבדים נמשלים לנחשת וברזל שיעשו המלאכה כאחד כשהן מעורבין זה בזה והנחשת בזה המקום פירוש הברזל שקורין בלע"ז אצי"ר שמערבין אותו עם הברזל לעשות בו כלי אומנות כי לא יהתוך הברזל לבדו אלא עם זה הנחשת וכן פי' אדוני אבי כל נחושת הנחשת שבמקרא שמדבר לענין חוק וי"ת כל רברביהון מרדין וגו' בבעמוד: (כט) נחר מפוח. לפי שהמשילם לנחשת וברזל שעושה אותם הנפח כלי על ידי האש המשיל' עוד למלאכ' הצורף כשיתיך הכסף ישים העופרת עם הכסף כדי שלא יכלה הכסף האש והנופח נופח במפוח באש לצרף הכסף והמפוח הוא משל על הנביא הנופח הוא הנביא והמפוח הוא פיו וגרונו אמר כי המפוח נשרף מרוב התמדת הנופח בו והדבור הנביא הוא הנפיחה והעופרת תם ועדיין הכסף הרע לא נתך והם ישראל הרעים שמדבר אליהם הנביא השכם והערב תמיד עד שנחר גרונו ועדיין רעים לא נתכו ועודם בקשם והעופרת משל למעשה ההשתדלות וההתמדה בדברי משל ומליצת

מנחת שי

(כח) כלם סרי. בס"א נכתב בלדו נ"א שרי ע"כ. ובכל הספרים כתיב בסמ"ך וכן הוא במסורת וכ"כ רד"ק: משחיתים המה. יש מחלוקת בספרים ובמסורת במקומות מלא יו"ד קדמאה ובתראה וכ"כ ממסורת פרשת וירא ובקצת ספרים מלא יו"ד קדמאה וחסר יו"ד בתרא' וכן מצאתי במקר' ישנה כ"י בגליון נרא' לי חוקיה כנקדן שהוא חסר יו"ד בתרא' ע"פ המסורת ע"כ לשונו. ונוסח מסרה אלו כך היא משחיתים ח' ד' מנהון מלא דמלא וסימנהון משחיתים אותו בתוכו (שופטים כ') משחיתים לספיל החופה (ש"א כ') זרע מרעים בנים משחיתים. ועוד המה משחיתים (דברי הימים ב' כ"ז) וב' משחתים. כי משחתים אנחנו. וקדמתי עליך משחתים (ירמיה כ"ג) וב' כתיב משחיתם. וללמד עבדיכם המשחיתים את הארץ (ש"א ו') כלם משחיתים המה ע"כ. וברוך יודע האמת: (כט) מאשתם. מאש תם קרי והוא חד מן ט"ו מלין דכתיבין חדא מלה וקריין תרין מלין וסדורם בדברי הימים א' כ"ז כמ"ג:

מצודת דוד

מוכיח להוכיחם ולמן מי שומע: (כח) סרי סוררים. ר"ל הסריסים המיוחדים שבכל הסוררים ודוגמתו שיר השירים (ש"ה א') שר"ל השיר המיוחד שבכל השירים: הולכי רכיל. מדברי לה"ר: נחושת וברזל. ר"ל נכונים לאבד אנשים בכלי זיין העשוי מנחושת וברזל המורכב זה בזה שהוא חזק מאד וכן נאמר ברזל מצפון ונחושת (לקמן ט"ו): משחיתים המה. סוכנים זה את זה: (כט) נחר מפוח באש. דרך צורף כסף להסיר הסיג מניח הכסף בכור ועמו עופרת ומעמיד על האש ונופח במפוח עד יותך הכסף והעופרת ונשרף העופרת ונשאר הכסף נקי מבלי סיג ולזה אמר הנה המפוח נתייבש מן האש וגם העופרת כלה תם והנה כי נשרף הכל אבל להנם לצרף

מצודת ציון

ל"ב): ובחנת. מלשון בחינה: (כח) סרי סוררים. ענין סוות ועקום כמו סורר ומורה (דברים כ"א): הולכי רכיל. ענין לשה"ר כמו לא תלך רכיל (ויקרא י"ט): (כט) נחר. ענין יובש כמו חרה מני חורב (איוב ל'): מפוח. שם הכלי שמפיחים בו להבעיר האש: תם. ענין גמר וכליון: עופרת. מין מתכת: צרף צרוף. ענין

fire with a bellows in order to refine the silver. The bellows symbolizes the prophet. The blower is the prophet, and the bellows is his mouth and his throat. He says that the bellows becomes burned from its constant use. The prophet's speech is the blowing. The lead has been consumed, yet the impure silver has not yet been refined. I.e. the wicked of Israel, to whom the prophet speaks constantly, morning and evening. The lead is symbolic of the prophet's efforts to admonish the

and you shall know and test their way. 28. They are all extremely perverse, going tale bearing [like] copper and iron; they are all destructive. 29. The bellows is heated from the fire, the lead is consumed; in vain does the founder refine,

Although you speak harshly to them and prophesy their doom, fear them not for I have made you a tower and a fortress among them. This is reminiscent of '(1:18) And I, behold I have made you today into a fortified city and an iron pillar, and into copper walls.' Therefore, fear them not and search their ways. He uses the word וּבָחַנְתָּ, *'and you shall test,'* as a play on words with בָּחוֹן, *a strong one. Jonathan* renders: I have made you a chosen one in My people, like a fortress.—[*Redak*]

28. **extremely perverse**—*Turning away from the road.*—[*Rashi*]

The repetition denotes the most perverse.—[*Mezudath David*] I.e., even the perverse consider them perverse.—[*Ibn Nachmiash*]

Jonathan renders סָרֵי as שָׂרֵי, *princes,* yielding: princes of perverse ones. The servants are perverse, and the princes are likewise perverse.—[*Redak*]

going tale bearing—*between copper and iron. They introduce hatred between two princes who have the power to provoke one another. That is what I heard. But I say, they are tale bearers, and they are as strong as copper and iron to maintain their falsehood. Jonathan, however, renders this word* רָכִיל *as an expression of guile* (נוֹכֵל). *They go with guile as one mixes copper with iron.* נוֹכֵל *is an expression of plot. Comp.* '(Gen. 37:18) *And they plotted* (וַיִּתְנַכְּלוּ) *against him to slay him.'*—[*Rashi*]

Redak explains that the servants bear tales to their masters in order to harm the poor. The servants and their masters are compared to נְחשֶׁת וּבַרְזֶל, which, in this case, means 'steel and iron.' When they merge, they do their work as one. As mentioned, נְחשֶׁת, in this case, means steel, mixed with the iron to make it harder, and to give it the power to cut better. In all cases, נְחשֶׁת וּבַרְזֶל denote strength.—[*Redak* from his father]

they are all destructive—They kill each other.—[*Mezudath David*]

Others explain: Both copper and iron are destructive.—[*Malbim, Ibn Nachmiash*]

*29. **The bellows is heated**—*This is an allegory. When they refine silver, they blow with a bellows, and they always put lead into the crucible, which helps for the refining. But you—I have come to refine you. The bellows is heated and parched because of the fire, and the lead is completely consumed.* נָחַר *is an expression related to* '(Job 42:7) *My wrath has been kindled* (חָרָה),' '(ibid. 30:30) *And my bones are burned* (חָרָה) *with heat,'* (*esrast in O.F.*).—[*Rashi*]

Since he compared them to copper and iron, with which the smith creates a utensil through fire, he compares them further to the craft of the refiner. When he refines silver, he places lead with the silver in order that the fire should not consume it, and the refiner blows the

* For Rashi's commentary turn to page 223.

וְרָעִים לֹא נִתָּקוּ׃ ל כֶּסֶף נִמְאָס קָרְאוּ
לָהֶם כִּי־מָאַס יְהוָה בָּהֶם׃ ז א הַדָּבָר
אֲשֶׁר־הָיָה אֶל־יִרְמְיָהוּ מֵאֵת יְהוָה
לֵאמֹר׃ ב עֲמֹד בְּשַׁעַר בֵּית יְהוָה
וְקָרָאתָ שָּׁם אֶת־הַדָּבָר הַזֶּה וְאָמַרְתָּ
שִׁמְעוּ דְבַר־יְהוָה כָּל־יְהוּדָה הַבָּאִים
בַּשְּׁעָרִים הָאֵלֶּה לְהִשְׁתַּחֲוֺת לַיהוָה׃
ג כֹּה־אָמַר יְהוָה צְבָאוֹת אֱלֹהֵי יִשְׂרָאֵל
הֵיטִיבוּ דַרְכֵיכֶם וּמַעַלְלֵיכֶם וַאֲשַׁכְּנָה
אֶתְכֶם בַּמָּקוֹם הַזֶּה׃ ד אַל־תִּבְטְחוּ לָכֶם

תרגום

בְּעֵינֵיהוֹן מִלֵי נְבִיַיָא דְמִתְנַבַּן לְהוֹן לָא לַהֲנָאָה אֲלִיפוּנוּן סַלְפֵיהוֹן וְעוֹבָדֵיהוֹן בִּישַׁיָא לָא שְׁבַקוּ׃ ל הָא מִכְּסַף פְּסוּלָא מְרַחֲקִין לְהוֹן אֲרֵי רַחִיק יְיָ יָתְהוֹן׃ א פִּתְגָם נְבוּאָה כְהַנָה עִם יִרְמְיָה מִן קֳדָם יְיָ לְמֵימָר׃ ב קוּם בִּתְרַע בֵּית מַקְדְשָׁא דַיְיָ וְתִתְנַבֵּי תַמָן יָת פִּתְגָמָא הָדֵין וְתֵימַר קַבִּילוּ פִּתְגָמָא דַיְיָ כָּל דְבֵית יְהוּדָה דְעָלִין בִּתְרַעַיָא הָאִלֵין לְמִסְגַד קֳדָם יְיָ׃ ג כִּדְנַן אֲמַר יְיָ צְבָאוֹת אֱלָהָא דְיִשְׂרָאֵל אַתְקִינוּ אוֹרְחַתְכוֹן וְעוֹבָדֵיכוֹן וְאַשְׁרֵי יָתְכוֹן בְּאַתְרָא הָדֵין׃ ד לָא תִתְרַחֲצוּן לְכוֹן עַל פִּתְגָמֵי נְבִיֵי שִׁקְרָא דְאָמְרִין קֳדָם הֵיכְלָא דַיְיָ אַתּוּן פָּלְחִין

מהר"י קרא

לא שבו ולכך כסף נמאס קראו להם. ז (ד) אל תבטחו לכם. במה שאתם עולין לירושלים ג' פעמים בשנה ומעתה אתם רשאין לעבוד ע"ז. כי אם היטב תטיבו:

רש"י

בלע"ז): לשוא. על חנם צרף הצורף כי לא הועיל: ורעים לא נתקו. מדרכם הרעה כלומר יגעו הנביאים להוכיח ולא הועילו. נתקו. (פורלטאקיי"ץ בלע"ז). (כ"א) ורעים כמו רשעים (סא"א): (ל) כסף נמאס. שאינו נצרף בשום יגיעה:

מנחת שי

ז (ג) דרכיכם. בספ"ן רפ"ן וכן חברו שבסמוך:

רד"ק

לתחזירם למוטב. והנה לשוא צרף צרוף. צרוף שם תאר בשקל גדול. נחר מבנין נפעל ענין שרפה וכן וחרה נחשתה: מאשתם. כתיב מלה אחת וקרי תרין מלין: (ל) כסף נמאס. ואחר שלא נתקו מרעתם הנה הם ככסף נמאס וכן קראו אותם היודעים אותם ורעותם כי מאס ה' בהם כיון שלא נתקו מרעתם ואינן חוזרים למוטב: (א) הדבר. אמר בזה הענין הדבר אשר היה אל ירמיהו מה שלא אמר כן בפרשיות הקודמות אלא כה אמר ה' לפי שאמר לו זאת הנבואה בשער בית ה' לפיכך אמר הדבר אשר היה הדבר להודיע כי מה שעמד בשער בית ה' מאת ה' נאמרה לו דבר זה שיעשה כן: (ב) עמוד בשער בית ה'. הוא שער מזרחי כי הוא המיוחד שבשערים: הבאים בשערים האלה. שבעה שערים היו בעזרה שלשה בצפון ושלשה בדרום ואחד במזרח: (ג) כה אמר. ואשכנה אתכם. אעמידכם בשכונתכם במקום זה ולא תגלו ממנו וכמוהו החייתם כל נקבה העמדתם אותן בחיים: (ד) אל תבטחו לכם אל דברי השקר. לשון בטחון נקשר עם מלת אל ועם מלת על וצוה הפסוק הוא אל דברי ובפסוק

מצודת ציון

זקיקה והתכה: ורעים. הם הסיגים שהוא רע מול הכסף: נתקו. ענין העתק והסרה: ז (ג) היטיבו. מלשון טוב ותיקון וכן ותיטב את ראשה (מלכי' ב' ט'): ומעלליכם. מעשיכם:

מצודת דוד

את הכסף כי הסיגים הרעים לא נעתקו מן הכסף והנה מעורב בו כשהיה והיא למשל לומר הנה הנביאים מתייגעים להוכיח את העם ואינם מועילים כי עדיין עומדים במרדם: (ל) כסף נמאס. קראו שם ישראל כסף נמאס שא"א להפריד מהם את הסיגים הם המעשים המגונים: כי מאס ה' בהם. על אשר אינם עוזבים מעשיהם אשר לא טובים: ז (ג) ואשכנה. אשכין אתכם במקום הזה ולא תגלו ממנה:

and the wicked ones have not been separated. 30. Refuse silver have men called them, for the Lord has rejected them.

7

1. The word that came to Jeremiah from the Lord, saying:
2. Stand in the gate of the house of the Lord, and proclaim there this word, and say: Hearken to the word of the Lord, all Judah who come into these gates to prostrate yourselves before the Lord. 3. So said the Lord of Hosts, the God of Israel: Improve your ways and your deeds, I will allow you to dwell in this place. 4. Do not rely

people with allegories and figures to bring them back to improve their ways.

and the wicked ones have not been separated—*from their evil way. That is to say that the prophets toiled to reprove, but it did not avail them.* **Separated**—Heb. נִתָּקוּ (*furent de . . . in O.F.*). (*Another version:*) *and the wicked ones. This is like* רְשָׁעִים. (*In other versions, this is omitted*).—[*Rashi*]

30. **Refuse silver**—*which cannot be refined with any toil.*—[*Rashi*]

Since they have not been separated from their evil ways, they are like refuse silver, and those who know of their evil, indeed call them that, for the Lord has rejected them because of their failure to improve their ways.—[*Redak*]

1. **The word that came to Jeremiah**—This expression was not used in the previous prophecies. It is used here to tell us that Jeremiah's standing in the gate of the Temple was in compliance to a divine command.—[*Redak*]

2. **Stand in the gate of the house of the Lord**—That is the Eastern Gate, the main one.—[*Redak*]

who come into these gates—There were seven gates in the forecourt, three on the north, three on the south, and one on the east.—[*Redak* from *Middoth* 1:4].

to prostrate yourselves—I.e., do not think that with your coming here to prostrate yourselves your sins will be forgiven, for it is not so.—[*Abarbanel*]

3. **and I will allow you to dwell**—I will allow you to remain dwelling in this place and you will not be exiled therefrom.—[*Redak*]

4. **Do not rely on false words**—On

קֳדָם הֵיכְלָא דַיְיָ אַתּוּן
דָבְחִין, קֳדָם הֵיכְלָא דַיְיָ
אַתּוּן סָגְדִין תְּלָת זִמְנִין
בְּשַׁתָּא אַתּוּן מִתְחַזַן
קֳדָמוֹהִי : ה אֲרֵי אִם
אַתְקָנָא תְּתַקְנוּן יַת
אוֹרְחַתְכוֹן וְיַת עוֹבָדֵיכוֹן
אִם מֶעְבַּד תַּעְבְּדוּן דִין
דִקְשׁוֹט בֵּין גַבְרָא וּבֵין
חַבְרֵיהּ : ו גִיוֹר יָתוֹם
וְאַרְמְלָא לָא תוֹנִיסוּן וְדַם
זַכַּאי לָא תִשְׁדוּן בְּאַתְרָא
הָדֵין וּבָתַר פַּלְחֵי
טַעֲוָתָא לָא תְהָכוּן
לְאַבְאָשָׁא לְכוֹן : ז וְאַשְׁרֵי
יַתְכוֹן בְּאַתְרָא הָדֵין
בְּאַרְעָא דִיהָבִית
לַאֲבָהַתְכוֹן לְמִן עָלְמָא
וְעַד עָלְמָא : ח הָא אַתּוּן
מִתְרַחְצִין לְכוֹן עַל
פִּתְגָמֵי נְבִיֵי שִׁקְרָא בְּדִיל
דלא

אֶל־דִּבְרֵי הַשֶּׁקֶר לֵאמֹר הֵיכַל יְהוָה
הֵיכַל יְהוָה הֵיכַל יְהוָה הֵמָּה׃ ה כִּי אִם־
הֵיטֵיב תֵּיטִיבוּ אֶת־דַּרְכֵיכֶם וְאֶת־
מַעַלְלֵיכֶם אִם עָשׂוֹ תַעֲשׂוּ מִשְׁפָּט בֵּין
אִישׁ וּבֵין רֵעֵהוּ׃ ו גֵּר יָתוֹם וְאַלְמָנָה
לֹא תַעֲשֹׁקוּ וְדָם נָקִי אַל־תִּשְׁפְּכוּ
בַּמָּקוֹם הַזֶּה וְאַחֲרֵי אֱלֹהִים אֲחֵרִים לֹא
תֵלְכוּ לְרַע לָכֶם׃ ז וְשִׁכַּנְתִּי אֶתְכֶם
בַּמָּקוֹם הַזֶּה בָּאָרֶץ אֲשֶׁר נָתַתִּי
לַאֲבוֹתֵיכֶם לְמִן־עוֹלָם וְעַד־עוֹלָם׃
ח הִנֵּה אַתֶּם בֹּטְחִים לָכֶם עַל־דִּבְרֵי
השקר

ת"א היכל ה'. מיר לג:

רש"י

ז (ד) היכל ה'. היכל ה' וגו'. תלת זימנין בשתא אתון מתחזיין קדמוהי:

רד"ק

הנה אתם בוטחים הוא על: היכל ה' היכל ה' היכל ה' המה. אלו דברי השקר שאומרים להם נביאי השקר המתעים אותם או הם היו אומרים לנביא והוא ירמיהו והיו אומרים לו לא יחריב היכלו בעבור העון ולא החרב העיר הזאת ואמר שלשה פעמים היכל ה' לפי שהיו שלשה אולם והיכל ודביר כן פירש אדוני אבי ז"ל ופי' כי פסוק ארץ ארץ ארץ תשובת דבריהם אמר הרי ההיכלות שאתם אומרים לפני חשובים כמו הארץ כיון שאתם חוטאים לפני ומבזים ההיכלות וי"ת לא תתרחצון לכון וגו' כבעמוד. ויתכן כי הכפל לחזק כי כן מנהג הלשון לכפול המלות לחזק הענין פעם בשתי מלות פעם בשלש: עשו תעשו. מקור בוי"ו כמו בה"א: (ו) גר יתום. כמו שמש ירח בחסרון וי"ו החבור וזכר אלה והוא הדין לאחרים אלא זכר אלה לפי שהם עשוקים ברוב לחולשתם: במקום הזה. בכל מקום הוא רע ובמקום הזה הוא יותר רע שהוא מקום השכינה: לרע לכם. אתם רעים כי לרע לכם הוא הליכתכם אחרי אלהים אחרים כי בזמן שאתם עושים זה אתם נופלים לפני אויביכם: (ז) ושכנתי. למן עולם ועד עולם. למזמן רב שנתתיה לכם מימי אברהם נתתיה לכם עד עולם ר"ל כל ימי עולם אם ילכו בניכם בדרכי: (ח) הנה. לבלתי הועיל. כי אתם רואים כי אין תועלת באותם הדברים:

מנחת שי

(ד) היכל ה' היכל ה' היכל ה'. חד מן ג' פסוקים משולשים ועיין בירמיה סימן כ"ב במ"ג ובגנת אגוז ריש דף ל"ו:

מצודת דוד

(ד) אל דברי השקר. אל דבר שאין בו ממש שהם אומרים היכל ה' וגו' המה ר"ל הנה היכל ה' המה בתוכינו ולא יחריב ה' את היכלו ואמר ג' פעמים היכל ה' על האולם וההיכל והדביר שכולם נקראים בשם היכל ולזה אמר המה בלשון רבים כי שלשה המה: (ו) לרע לכם. אשר מעבודתכם תמשך לכם רע ולא טובה: (ז) ושכנתי. כאשר כן תעשו אז אשכין אתכם במקום הזה ולא בזולת זה: למן עולם. מאת בואכם שמה עד ימות עולם: (ח) על דברי השקר. הוא בטחון ההיכל שאין תועלת בבטחון הזה:

on false words, saying: The Temple of the Lord, the Temple of the Lord, the Temple of the Lord are they. 5. For if you improve your ways and your deeds, if you perform judgment between one man and his fellowman, 6. [if] you do not oppress a stranger, an orphan, or a widow, and you do not shed innocent blood in this place, and you do not follow other gods for your detriment, 7. I will allow you to dwell in this place, in the land that I gave your forefathers from days of yore to eternity.

8. Behold, you rely on false words,

words of no substance, for they say, "Is not the Temple of the Lord in our midst? God will never destroy His Temple because of the sins of the people, neither will He destroy His city. The expression, 'the Temple of the Lord' is mentioned three times, denoting the porch, the Temple, and the inner sanctum. Possibly, it is repeated for emphasis.—[*Redak*]

The Temple of the Lord, the Temple of the Lord etc.—*Three times a year you appear before Me.*—[*Rashi* from *Jonathan*] *Rashi* appears to quote *Jonathan* as explaining the three mentions of the Temple of the Lord as symbolic of the three appearances in the Temple. Our editions of Jonathan, however, read: Rely not on the words of the false prophets who say: You worship before the Temple of the Lord, you sacrifice before the Temple of the Lord, three times a year you appear before Him

5. **For if you improve your ways**—This denotes the observance of the positive commandments.—[*Abarbanel*]

6. **[if] you do not oppress**—I.e. if you observe the negative commandments.—[*Abarbanel*]

a stranger, an orphan—I.e. a stranger or an orphan. The same applies to others who are oppressed because of their weakness.—[*Redak*]

in this place—These are grave sins no matter where they are committed, but in this place they are still graver since here is the place of the Shechinah.—[*Redak*] Ibn Nachmiash words it as follows: There is no comparison between one who provokes the king in his palace and one who provokes him outside his palace.

for your detriment—Following the idols is for your harm, for when you commit idolatry, you will fall before your enemies.—[*Redak*]

7. **from days of yore to eternity**—When I gave it to you in Abraham's

הַשֶּׁקֶר לְבִלְתִּי הוֹעִיל׃ ט הֲגָנֹב ׀ רָצֹחַ
וְנָאֹף וְהִשָּׁבֵעַ לַשֶּׁקֶר וְקַטֵּר לַבָּעַל
וְהָלֹךְ אַחֲרֵי אֱלֹהִים אֲחֵרִים אֲשֶׁר לֹא־
יְדַעְתֶּם׃ י וּבָאתֶם וַעֲמַדְתֶּם לְפָנַי בַּבַּיִת
הַזֶּה אֲשֶׁר נִקְרָא־שְׁמִי עָלָיו וַאֲמַרְתֶּם
נִצַּלְנוּ לְמַעַן עֲשׂוֹת אֵת כָּל־הַתּוֹעֵבֹת
הָאֵלֶּה׃ יא הַמְעָרַת פָּרִצִים הָיָה הַבַּיִת
הַזֶּה אֲשֶׁר־נִקְרָא־שְׁמִי־עָלָיו בְּעֵינֵיכֶם
גַּם אָנֹכִי הִנֵּה רָאִיתִי נְאֻם־יְהוָה׃

תרגום

דלא לַהֲנָאָה׃ ט גנבין קָטולֵי נַפְשָׁן וְנַיְפִין וּמִשְׁתַּבְעִין לְשִׁקַר ומסקין בוסמין לְבַעְלָא וְאָזְלִין בָּתַר פָּלְחֵי כוכביא דלא יְדַעְתּוּן׃
י וְאָתַן אַתּוּן וְקַיְמִין קֳדָמַי בְּבֵיתָא הָדֵין דְאִתְקְרֵי שְׁמִי עֲלוֹהִי וְאָמְרִין אַתּוּן שֵׁיזִבְנָא בְּדִיל לְמֶעְבַּד יָת כָּל תּוֹעֲבָתָא הָאִלֵּין׃
יא הַכְּבֵית כְּנִישַׁת רַשִׁיעִין הֲוָה בֵיתָא הָדֵין דְאִתְקְרֵי שְׁמִי עֲלוֹהִי בְּעֵינֵיכוֹן אַף קֳדָמַי בֵּן גלי

פתח באתנח

מהר"י קרא

(ט) הגנוב רצוח. לאחר שאתם עוברין כל עבירות הללו ובאתם ועמדתם לפני בבית הזה ואמרתם נצלנו מעבירות שבידינו שביאתינו במקדש מגין עלינו מן העבירות נמצא שכל ביאתכם לפני במקדש אינו אלא לעשות את כל התועבות האלה: (יא) המערת פריצים היה הבית הזה, שמעתי שמערה אחת היתה בעזרת והיו נכנסין שם אנשי משמר בשעה שתמיד קרב ומתפללין על קרבן אחיהם שירצה וכשקלקלו הדורות הכניסו

רש"י

(ט) הגנוב רצוח וגו'. בתמיה וכי אלה תעשו ויועיל ההיכל לכם: (יא) המערת פריצים. היה בעיניכם הבית הזה בתמיה: הנה ראיתי. שכך הוא

מנחת שי

(ט) הגנב רצח ונאף. שלשתם חסרים וא"ו אחר ע"ין הפעל: ונאף. בס"ס בוא"ו בגעיא: (י) התועבת. במקצת ספרים מלא דמלא ותנה ע"פ המסורת דסוף פרשת אחרי מות נכון להיות חסר וא"ו שנייה: (יא) המערת. כתוב

רד"ק

(ט) הגנוב. התחשבו שתעשו מעשים רעים ותנצלו מעונשם בעבור שתבאו ותעמדו לפני בבית הזה כאשר אתם אומרים אחר שתעשו כל התועבות האלה ותבאו בבית הזה ואמרתם נצלנו ופי' אתם אומרים נצלנו בעבור שתשובו לעשות את כל התועבות האלה: (י) ובאתם, מפורש הוא: (יא) המערת פריצים. וכי תחשבו הבית הזה כמו מערת פריצים וכן הוא בעיניכם הבית הזה מה שתחשבו שאתם נצולים בבאכם אליו הוא כפל עונכם שתעיזו פניכם לבא אלי אחר עשותכם מה שמנעתי לעשותו אין זה אלא פריצות ועזות מצח וקשי לב שתעשו הפך רצוני ותבאו לפני זה מרד גדול והכעסה: גם אנכי הנה ראיתי. לא תחשבו כי אני לא אראה מחשבותיכם הרעות

מצודת ציון

(ח) לבלתי. ענינו כמו לא: הועיל. מל' תועלת: (י) נצלנו. מלשון הצלה: (יא) המערת. ענין חפירה בקרקע:

מצודת דוד

(ט) הגנוב. וכי תגנבו ותרצחו וגו': (י) ובאתם. אחר המעשים האלה תבאו אל ההיכל להתפלל שמה ותאמרו הנה בזה נצלנו מהעונש הראוי לבא על מעשים האלה: למען עשות. למען תשובו לחטוא ולעשות עוד המעשים האלה והיה בית ה' סיבה ועזר לעשות התועבות כחושבכם בו: (יא) המערת. האם חשבתם שהיה הבית הזה וגו' בעיניכם

see, therefore, that, when you come to Me, you do not come with sincerity, but you intend to continue with your sins. The analogy is to a cave where the robbers seek refuge outside the city, to avoid being apprehended.—[*Redak*]

Alshich explains this as an allusion to the generation of Josiah, whose repentance was insincere, and, as mentioned above (3:10), they would engrave pagan images behind their doors to conceal them from the king and his inspectors. Then they would go to the Temple to appear before God with the belief that he would take cognizance only of their appearance in the Temple. The prophet castigates them by saying that they make God's house a refuge from punishment as the robbers do by hiding in their cave.

of no avail. 9. Will you steal, murder, commit adultery, swear falsely, offer up to Baal, and follow other gods that you know not, 10. And will you not and stand before Me in this house, upon which My name is called, and say, "We are saved," in order to commit all these abominations? 11. Has this house upon which My name is called, become a cave of profligate men in your eyes? I, too, behold I have seen it, says the Lord.

days, I gave it to you to eternity on the condition that your children follow My ways.—[*Redak*]

8. **of no avail**—For you see that these words are of no use.—[*Redak*]

9. **Will you steal, murder, etc.**—*This is a question. Will you do all these, and should the Temple of the Lord avail for you?*—[*Rashi*]

Do you think that you can commit evil deeds and be saved from punishment because you come and stand before Me in this house as you say after you have committed all these abominations, and you come into this house and say, "We are saved." I.e., you say, "We are saved," in order to repeat these abominations.—[*Redak*]

The result is that the Temple is the cause of your sins.—[*Kara, Mezudath David*]

These words do not appear in the plural but as infinitives to indicate that the majority of the people were not guilty of these sins. The community was held responsible for the guilty individuals, however.—[*Daath Sofrim*] He illustrates from this verse, that, despite the sins of the people, they believed wholeheartedly in the efficacy of the Holy Temple, to the extent of believing that their appearance there and their worship there would expiate their sins.

Alshich conjectures that 'murder' alludes to the assassination of the prophet Zechariah, whose blood was still seething.

11. **Has . . . a cave of profligate men?**—*Was this house in your eyes? This is a question.*—[*Rashi*]

Rashi's intention is not clear. Perhaps he wishes to indicate that the clause, "upon which My name is called," is parenthetical, thus connecting, "this house" with "in your eyes." Perhaps also he wishes to tell us that the sentence is a question.

Do you think that this house is like a cave of profligate men? It, indeed, seems so since you believe that you will be saved by entering it. This, in fact, compounds your sin, since you have the audacity to come to My house after transgressing My commands. This is nothing but profligacy, brazenness, and obstinacy, that you disobey My wishes and then come before Me. This is rebellion and provocation.—[*Redak*]

behold I have seen—*that it is so in your eyes.*—[*Rashi*]

Do not think that I am unaware of your evil thoughts, for I am not like a human being, who can be deceived by outward appearances. I

יב כִּי לְכוּ־נָא אֶל־מְקוֹמִי אֲשֶׁר בְּשִׁילוֹ
אֲשֶׁר שִׁכַּנְתִּי שְׁמִי שָׁם בָּרִאשׁוֹנָה
וּרְאוּ אֵת אֲשֶׁר־עָשִׂיתִי לוֹ מִפְּנֵי רָעַת
עַמִּי יִשְׂרָאֵל׃ יג וְעַתָּה יַעַן עֲשׂוֹתְכֶם
אֶת־כָּל־הַמַּעֲשִׂים הָאֵלֶּה נְאֻם־יְהוָה
וָאֲדַבֵּר אֲלֵיכֶם הַשְׁכֵּם וְדַבֵּר וְלֹא
שְׁמַעְתֶּם וָאֶקְרָא אֶתְכֶם וְלֹא עֲנִיתֶם׃
יד וְעָשִׂיתִי לַבַּיִת ׀ אֲשֶׁר נִקְרָא־שְׁמִי
עָלָיו אֲשֶׁר אַתֶּם בֹּטְחִים בּוֹ וְלַמָּקוֹם

גְלֵי אֲמַר יְיָ : יב אֲרֵי
אֱזִילוּ כְעַן לְאַתְרָא בֵית
שְׁכִנְתִּי דִי בְשִׁלוֹ
דְאַשְׁרֵיתִי שְׁכִנְתִּי תַמָן
בְּקַדְמֵיתָא וַחֲזוֹ יָת
דַעֲבָדִית לֵיהּ מִן קֳדָם
בִּישַׁת עַמִי יִשְׂרָאֵל :
יג וּכְעַן חֲלָף דַעֲבַדְתּוּן
יָת כָּל עוֹבָדַיָא הָאִלֵין
אֲמַר יְיָ וּשְׁלָחִית לְוָתְכוֹן
יָת כָּל עַבְדֵי נְבִיַיָא
מַקְדִים וּמַלֵיל וְלָא
קַבֵּילְתּוּן וְאִתְנַבִּיאוּ לְכוֹן
וְלָא תַבְתּוּן : יד וְאַעְבֵּיד
לְבֵיתָא דְאִתְקְרֵי שְׁמִי
עֲלוֹהִי דְאַתּוּן רָחִיצִין
בֵּיהּ וּלְאַתְרָא דִיהָבִית
לְכוֹן

מהר"י קרא

שם ק"ז הוא שירמיה אמר המערת פריצים היה הבית הזה גם אנכי ה' הראיתי את אשר אתם עושין בו: (יב) כי לכו נא אל מקומי אשר בשילו אשר שיכנתי שמי שם בראשונה. ואע"פ שהיו נראין לפני שלש פעמים בשנה לא נשאתי לו פנים והחרבתיו מפני רעת עמי ישראל: (יד) ועשיתי לבית וגו'. ואברתם נצלנו בזכות שאנו עולין שם שלש פעמים בשנה לאתר שאתם

רד"ק

כי איני כמו בן אדם שיכול אחד לגנוב לבבו ולהראות לפניו מה שאין בלבו כי אני ראיתי לבבכם וראיתי כי בבאכם אלי אין לבבכם אלי אלא בלבבכם שתעשו עוד את התועבות אשר עשית' מתחילה ומה שאמר מערת כי כן דרך הפריצים בעשותם הרעות להאסף יחד חוץ לעיר באחת המערות להסתר שם מבני אדם ומה שתאברו כי לא אחריב ביתי בעבור מעשיהם כמו שאמר היכל ה' כמו שפירשנו' למעלה אלה הם דברי שקר: (יב) כי לכו נא. ראו מה עשיתי לו מפני רעת עמי ישראל שהחרבתי אותו וסלקתי שכינתי ממנו ונלה הארון

מנחת שי

במכלול דף ס"א בהמ"ס רפה וכה"ג בגעיא: (יב) כי לכו נא אל מקומי אשר בשילו. מלא יו"ד וכתיב וא"ו בסוף תיבה ע"פ המסורת בפסוק עד כי יבא שילה:

מצודת דוד

המערת הפריצים שבאשר יעשו התועבות ילכו להחבא במערה: גם אנכי. ר"ל כמו שיש הדבר הזה עם לבבכם לעשות התועבות על בטחונכם שהבית תציל אתכם כן אני רואה שכן הוא עם לבבכם ולא נכחד ממני: (יב) לכו נא אל מקומי. ר"ל התבוננו עתה אל המשכן אשר עמד בשילו: בראשונה. עד לא נבחר ירושלים: את אשר עשיתי לו. שהחרבתי אותו מפני רעת ישראל בימי עלי הכהן ולא חששתי עליו: (יג) השכם ודבר. אני משכים ומדבר ע"י הנביאים: ואקרא אתכם. לשוב אלי בתשובה: (יד) ועשיתי. ולכן אעשה לבית וגו':

מצודת ציון

פריצים. רשעים וקלי הדעת: (יג) עניתם. מל' מענה ותשובה:

12. For go now to My place that is in Shiloh, where I caused My name to rest at first, and see what I did to it because of the wickedness of My people Israel. 13. And now, because you have committed all these acts, says the Lord, and I spoke to you, going early and speaking, but you did not hearken, and I called you, but you did not respond. 14. And I will do to the house upon which My name is called, upon which you rely, and to the place

12. **For go now to My place that is in Shiloh**—Your belief that Jerusalem will not be destroyed because of the presence of the Temple is a false idea, for go now to My place that is in Shiloh, where Israel appeared before Me three times a year. Yet I did not favor them but destroyed the sanctuary because of the wickedness of My people Israel.—[*Kara*]

I.e. think about My place that was in Shiloh.—[*Mezudath David*]

at first—I.e. before I caused it to rest in Jerusalem.—[*Mezudath David*]

what I did to it—that I destroyed it and removed My Shechinah from there, and allowed the ark to be captured and stay with the Philistines. I did not have pity on My honor, since they defiled it. I will do the same to the Temple. Therefore, do not rely on words of falsehood, without substance.—[*Redak*]

13. **And now**—that your sin is greater than that of Shiloh because you should have learned a lesson from Shiloh.—[*Malbim*]

because you have committed all these acts—such as stealing and murdering, acts that were not committed in Shiloh.—[*Malbim*]

and I spoke to you going early and speaking—This too was not done in Shiloh.—[*Malbim*]

14. **And I will do**—Therefore, I will do to the house etc.—[*Malbim*]

upon which you rely—Since you rely on this house to sin.—[*Malbim*]

Although the sanctity of the Temple in Jerusalem is greater than that of the Tabernacle and it is situated opposite the Heavenly Temple, I will, nevertheless, not refrain from destroying it because of your sins.—[*Alshich*]

and to the place—I.e. to Jerusalem.—[*Mezudath David*]

Malbim explains: To the entire Eretz Israel.

אֲשֶׁר־נָתַתִּי לָכֶם וְלַאֲבוֹתֵיכֶם כַּאֲשֶׁר
עָשִׂיתִי לְשִׁלוֹ: טו וְהִשְׁלַכְתִּי אֶתְכֶם
מֵעַל פָּנָי כַּאֲשֶׁר הִשְׁלַכְתִּי אֶת־כָּל־
אֲחֵיכֶם אֵת כָּל־זֶרַע אֶפְרָיִם: טז וְאַתָּה
אַל־תִּתְפַּלֵּל ׀ בְּעַד־הָעָם הַזֶּה וְאַל־
תִּשָּׂא בַעֲדָם רִנָּה וּתְפִלָּה וְאַל־תִּפְגַּע־
בִּי כִּי־אֵינֶנִּי שֹׁמֵעַ אֹתָךְ: יז הַאֵינְךָ רֹאֶה
מָה הֵמָּה עֹשִׂים בְּעָרֵי יְהוּדָה וּבְחֻצוֹת
יְרוּשָׁלִָם: יח הַבָּנִים מְלַקְּטִים עֵצִים
וְהָאָבוֹת מְבַעֲרִים אֶת־הָאֵשׁ וְהַנָּשִׁים
לָשׁוֹת בָּצֵק לַעֲשׂוֹת כַּוָּנִים לִמְלֶכֶת

תרגום

לְכוֹן וְלַאֲבָהַתְכוֹן כְּמָא
דַעֲבָדִית לְשִׁילוֹ:
טו וְאַגְלֵי יַתְכוֹן מֵאַרְעָא
בֵּית שְׁכִנְתִּי כְּמָא
דְאַגְלֵיתִי יַת כָּל אֲחֵיכוֹן
יַת כָּל זַרְעָא דְיִשְׂרָאֵל:
טז וְאַתְּ לָא תְצַלֵּי עַל
עַמָא הָדֵין וְלָא תִתְחַנַן
עֲלֵיהוֹן בְּבָעוּ וּצְלוֹ וְלָא
תִבְעֵי מִן קֳדָמַי אֲרֵי לָא
בַעֲנָא קֳדָמַי לְקַבָּלָא
צְלוֹתָךְ: יז הֲלֵית אַתְּ
חָזֵי מָא דְאִינוּן עָבְדִין
בְּקִרְוַיָא דְבֵית יְהוּדָה
וּבְשׁוּקֵי יְרוּשְׁלֵם:
יח בְּנַיָא מְלַקְטִין אָעָא
וַאֲבָהָתְהוֹן מַדְלְקִין יַת
נוּרָא וּנְשַׁיָא לָיְשָׁן לִישָׁא
לְמֶעְבַּד כַּרְדוּטִין
לְכוֹכְבַת שְׁמַיָא וּלְנַסָכָא

ת"א ואתה אל תתפלל. ברכות דף כו תענית א ת סנהדרין יא לפ סוטה א' יד:

מהר"י קרא

עוברים כל העבירות הנזכרין למעלה כאשר עשיתי לשילו:
(יח) כוונים. אובלדי"ש בלע"ז: למלכת השמים. ת"י לכוכבת

רש"י

בעיניכם: (יד) כאשר עשיתי לשילו. בימי עלי:
(טו) כאשר השלכתי וגו'. עשרת השבטי': (יח) לעשות
כוונים. דפוס הכוכב: למלכת השמים. כוכב הגדול היו קורין מלכת השמים לשון מלכה וכן ת"י לכוכבת שמיא:

רד"ק

כמנו והיה עם פלשתים ולא חששתי לכבודי אחר שהיו הם מבזים אותו כן אעשה בבית הזה לפיכך אל תבטחו אל דברי שקר כאלו. ושלשת הפסוקים הבאים אחר זה הפסוק מבוארים הם: (טו) את כל זרע אפרים. עשרת השבטים שגלו וכנה אותם לאפרים לפי שהמלכות היתה לאפרים בימים שנחלקה המלכות ומשם ואילך נקראו עשרת השבטים בשם אפרים: (טז) ואתה. ואל תשא. ענין הגבהת הקול כמו וישא עשו את קולו: רנה. צעקה כמו ויעבר הרנה קומי רני: (יז) האינך. ובחוצות ירושלים. שלא יבושו להכעיסני בגלוי בשוק: וברחובות: (יח) הבנים. כל בני הבית מתעסקים בעבודה זו לשבר שיקבלו בעבודה: לעשות כונים. מיני מאכלים שהיו מכינים ומגישים למלאכת השמים וכן עשינו לה כונים וכן ואת כיון צלמיכם ואולי קראם כונים לפי שמכונין לבן ודעתן אליהם לעשותם ולתקנן היטב וי"ת כונים כרדוטין:

מצודה ציון

(טז) ואל תשא. ענין הרמת קול: בעדם. בעבורם: רנה. הוא ענין לשון תפלה: תפגע. ענין בקשה וכן ופגעו לי (בראשית כ"ג): (יז) האינך. האין אתה וכן אינך יודע איזה יכשר (קהלת י"א): ובחוצות. בשוקים: (יח) מלקטים. מל' לקיטה: מבערים. מדליקים: לשות. מלשון לישה והוא גלגול העיסה: בצק. עיסה כמו מלוש בלק עד חמלתו (הושע ז') ואמר בלק ע"ש סופו וכן אפיתי על גחליו לחם (ישעיה מ"ד): כונים. מין מאכל ויתכן שנקרא כן על כי עשאום בכונת הלב בתיקון רב וכן עשינו לה כונים להעציבה

מצודת דוד

ולמקום וגו'. הוא ירושלים: (טו) והשלכתי וגו'. לארץ אחרת: כל אחיכם. ומזור ומפרש את כל זרע אפרים והם בני עשרת השבטים וקראם על שם אפרים כי ירבעם שמלך בהם ראשונה היה מזרע אפרים: (טז) ואתה. לירמיה ידבר שלא יתפלל בעדם: ואל תשא וגו'. כפל הדבר במ"ש: כי אינני. כי אין אני שומע אליך: (יז) האינך. וכי אין אתה רואה מה המה עושים וגו': (יח) הבנים וגו'. ר"ל כ"א מהם מסייע לעבירה: לעשות כונים. לעשות מיני מאכלים להגיש מנחה למלכת שמים ר"ל לכוכב גדול שבשמים והוא

Redak defines them as a kind of food made to offer up to the stars. They are called כַּוָּנִים, since they are made with special devotion (כַּוָּנָה). *Jonathan* renders: כַּרְדוּטִין, *a special form. Daath Mikra* states that the word originates from the Assyrian, meaning 'cakes.' These were eight-pointed star cakes or cakes made in the shape of a young woman. Marcus describes them as half-moons.—[*Barzilai*]

to the queen of heaven—*The largest star they would call* מְלֶכֶת הַשָּׁמַיִם, *an expression of a queen* (מַלְכָּה), *and so did Jonathan render it*: לְכוֹכְבַת שְׁמַיָּא *to the female star of heaven*.—[*Rashi*] *Redak* defines it as מְלֶאכֶת הַשָּׁמַיִם, *the work of heaven*, meaning the stars. *Daath Mikra*

that I gave you and your forefathers, as I did to Shiloh.
15. And I will cast you away from My presence, as I cast all
your brothers, all the seed of Ephraim. 16. And you, pray not
on behalf of this people, neither lift up cry nor prayer, and
entreat Me not for I will not hear you. 17. Do you not see what
they are doing in the cities of Judah and in the streets of Jeru-
salem? 18. The sons are gathering wood, the fathers are kind-
ling fire, and the women are kneading dough to make star-
shaped cakes for the queen of

Alshich explains it as the temple site, holy from the time of the binding of Isaac. I will, nevertheless, destroy it.

as I did to Shiloh—*in the days of Eli.*—[*Rashi*] As mentioned above, the Tabernacle of Shiloh was destroyed on the day the ark was captured by the Philistines. See I Sam. 4, 5.

15. **And I will cast you**—I will exile you.—[*Targum*]

as I cast etc.—*the ten tribes.*—[*Rashi*]

all the seed of Ephraim—The ten tribes that were exiled. He calls them Ephraim because the throne was occupied by Ephraim when the kingdom was founded. From then on, the ten tribes were known as Ephraim.—[*Redak*]

I.e., the king, Jeroboam son of Nebat, who assumed the throne when the kingdom was divided, was an Ephraimite.—[*Ibn Nachmiash, Mezudath David*]

16. **And you**—God addresses the prophet.—[*Mezudath David*]

neither lift up—An expression of raising the voice.—[*Redak*]

I commanded you merely to stand in the gate of the temple and to reprove the people, not to pray for them.—[*Malbim*]

cry nor prayer—Not only shall you not pray on their behalf, but you shall not act as a cantor, uttering the prayers to which they respond.—[*Malbim*]

and entreat Me not—that I relent in your merit.—[*Malbim*]

for I will not hear you—I.e. I will not accept your prayers in any case.—[*Malbim*]

17. **Do you not see**—How can you pray for them? Do you not see what they are doing?—[*Malbim*]

what they are doing—I.e. the act itself.—[*Malbim*]

in the cities of Judah and in the streets of Jerusalem—They are committing these sins flagrantly.—[*Malbim*] They are not ashamed to provoke Me in public places.—[*Redak*]

18. **The sons are gathering wood**—All the members of the household are engaged in this worship for the reward they expect for it.—[*Redak*]

18. **star-shaped cakes**—Heb. כַּוָּנִים, *the shape of a star.*—[*Rashi*]

הַשָּׁמַיִם וְהַסֵּךְ נְסָכִים לֵאלֹהִים אֲחֵרִים
לְמַעַן הַכְעִסֵנִי: יט הַאֹתִי הֵם מַכְעִסִים
נְאֻם־יְהוָה הֲלוֹא אֹתָם לְמַעַן בֹּשֶׁת
פְּנֵיהֶם: כ לָכֵן כֹּה־אָמַר׀ אֲדֹנָי יֱהוִה
הִנֵּה אַפִּי וַחֲמָתִי נִתֶּכֶת אֶל־הַמָּקוֹם
הַזֶּה עַל־הָאָדָם וְעַל־הַבְּהֵמָה וְעַל־עֵץ
הַשָּׂדֶה וְעַל־פְּרִי הָאֲדָמָה וּבָעֲרָה וְלֹא
תִכְבֶּה: כא כֹּה אָמַר יְהוָה צְבָאוֹת אֱלֹהֵי
יִשְׂרָאֵל עֹלוֹתֵיכֶם סְפוּ עַל־זִבְחֵיכֶם

נִסְכִּין לְפָלְחֵי כּוֹכְבַיָא
בְּדִיל לְאַרְגָזָא קֳדָמַי:
יט הַקֳדָמַי דִי קָדָמַי
אִינוּן מְרַגְזִין אֲמַר יְיָ
הֲלָא לְאַבְאָשָׁא לְהוֹן
בְּדִיל דִיבְהֲתוּן
בְּעוֹבָדֵיהוֹן: כ בְּכֵן כִּדְנַן
אֲמַר יְיָ אֱלֹהִים הָא רוּגְזִי
וְחֶמְתִּי חָל בְּאַתְרָא
הָדֵין עַל אֲנָשָׁא וְעַל
בְּעִירָא וְעַל אִילַן חַקְלָא
וְעַל אִבָּא דְאַרְעָא וִישֵׁיצֵי
וְלָא יְהֵי חָיִם: כא כִּדְנַן
אֲמַר יְיָ צְבָאוֹת אֱלָהָא
דְיִשְׂרָאֵל עֲלָוָתְכוֹן
אוֹסִיפוּ עַל נִכְסַת
קוּדְשֵׁיכוֹן וַאֲכוּלוּ

ת"א עולותיכם ספו. מגילה כו:

רש"י

(כ) נתכה. יורדת ומגעת כמו ומטר לא נתך ארצה (שמו' ט) לא מטה: (כא) עולותיכם. שאתם מקריבים כליל טוב לכם שתוסיפו אותם על שלמיכם והקריבו אותם שלמי' ותאכלו הבשר שהרי אינם מקובלות לפני ולמה תפסידום:

מהר"י קרא

שמיא: (כ) נתכת. דווישטנפריד"א כמו ומטר לא נתך ארצה: (כא) עולותיכם ספו על זבחיכם ואכלו בשר. לשעבר בעשותכם רצוני אדם כי הקריב מכם קרבן אם עולה קרבנו היה כולה כלול לאישים ואני מקבלה לריח ניחח ואם זבח שלמים קרבנו איבורים למזבח חזה ושוק לכהנים ובשר לבעלים [ושניהם היו

רד"ק

למלכת השמים. חסר אל"ף ופי' כמו מעשה השמים כלומר לכוכבים ויש מפרשים למלכת השמים לשון מלוכה ר"ל לכוכב גדול שבשמים וי"ת לכוכבת שמיא: (יט) האותי. הם עושים להכעיסני וכי סבורים הם שהם מכעיסים אותי כי לא תחול בי מדת כעס ולא מדה א[ח]ת אינם מכעיסים אותי אלא עצמן כי עליהם יחול הכעס וחרון אף: למען בשת פניהם. שיבושו במעשיהם הרעים כי אני איני ראוי שאכעס במעשיהם אפילו החול בי שום מדה מה שלא תחול כי לא יזיקו לי מעשיהם הרעים ולא ייטיבו לי מעשיהם הטובים כמו שאמר אליהוא לאיוב אם חטאת מה תפעל בו ורבו פשעיך מה תעשה לו או מה מידך יקח לאיש כמוך רשעך ולבן אדם צדקתך וזה שאמר בתורה כעסוני בהבליהם הכעיסוני בפסיליהם דברה תורה כלשון בני אדם אבל הוא יתברך אין בו מדת כעס ולא מפחיתות המדות המצויות בבני האדם כמו הכעס וזולתו: (כ) לכן. אפי וחמתי. כי הם עשו להכעיסני והכעס יחול עליהם ואף וחמה ואמר נתכת לרוב מרוצתה לבא עליהם כדבר הנתך ובאמרו נתכת לשון נקבה וזכר גם כן אף שהוא לשון זכר כי כן הוא דרך לשון הקודש להיות זכר הפועל עם השם הדבוק בו יהיה ראשון או אחרון כמו ותדבר מרים ואהרן ותכתוב אסתר בת אביחיל ומרדכי היהודי והאבל תיא והוא גרי ביתי ואמהותי לזר תחשבוני: ובערה. אמר בערה ולא זכר האש לפי שהחמה ענין חמימות וטבע האש אשר באדם מוליד הכעס והחמה: (כא) כה אמר ה' צבאות. זכר העולות שהן כליל וזכר הזבחים שהם השלמים שמהם יאכלו הבעלים בשר ולא זכר חטאת ואשם כי לא היו מתודים מחטאתם ולא שבים ועוד כי במזיד היו חוטאים ואין על המזיד קרבן אלא היו מביאים עולות להראות עצמם שהם עובדים את ה' בנראה והשלמים היו מביאין לאכול בשר עם הראות במעשיהם עבודת האל ואמר מה לכם להביא זבחיכם ולהוסיף עוד עליהם עולות ותחשבו כי יהיו לרצון לי כמו שכתוב בהם ונרצה לו לכפר עליו וזה לא יהיה כי אם אין מעשיכם רצוין לפני עולות וזבחים ג"כ לא יהיו רצון: ספו. ענין תוספת שני שרשים בענין אחד יסף וספה וכן ספות חטאת על חטאת לספות עוד ואפשר גם כן ספו משרש יסף בשקל

מנחת שי

(יח) הכעסני. במקצת ספרים מלא יו"ד וצ"ע במסורת במאמר א' א':
(יט) מכעסים. במקצת ספרים חסר יו"ד קדמאה וע' מ"ש בספר זה סי' ל"ד:

מצודת דוד

השמש וכאלו מולך על כלם: והסך. ולהסך או נסכים וגו': למען הכעיסני. ר"ל יודעים הם שאין תועלה בעבידתם אבל כל מעשיהם להכעיסני: (יט) האותי. ר"ל וכי הכעס הוא בעבורי כלומר וכי מעשיהם מזיקים לי הלא הכעס יזיק להם כי יהיה להם לבושת ולכלימה: (כ) נתכת. ההיה נשפכת אל המקום הזה והוזר ומפרש על האדמה וגו': ולא תכבה. ר"ל לא תפסק החמה עד תכלה הכל: (כא) עולותיכם ספו וגו'. העולות שאתם מביאים שהמה כולה כליל הוסיפו אותם על זבחי שלמיכם ואכלו הבשר ר"ל הואיל ואין העולות

מצודת ציון

(לקמן מ"ד): למלכת השמים. הוא השמש וכן מקטרים למלכת השמים (שם): (כ) נתכת. ענין התכה והרקה כמו ותתך חמתי ואפי (שם): תכבה. מלשון כבוי: (כא) ספו. לשון הוספה:

offer up completely—it would be better for you to add them to your peace-offerings and sacrifice them as peace-offerings and eat the flesh, for they are not acceptable before Me. Why, then, should you lose them?—[*Rashi*]

It was customary for them to offer up burnt offerings, which were completely consumed by the fire, and peace-offerings, which were eaten by the owners, with the exception of the blood and fat that were offered up on the altar and the

the heaven and to pour libations to other gods, in order to
provoke Me. 19. Are they provoking Me? says the Lord. Are
[they] not [provoking] themselves for the shame of their faces?
20. Therefore, so says the Lord God: Behold, My wrath and
My fury reaches this place, upon man and upon beast, upon the
trees of the field and upon the produce of the soil, and it shall
burn and not be quenched. 21. So says the Lord of Hosts, the
God of Israel: Add your burnt offerings upon your sacrifices

identifies it with Ishtar, the chief goddess of the Assyrians and the Chaldeans. She was believed to be the planet Venus. Rather than ascribe queenship to this goddess, Scripture alters the word מַלְכַּת to מְלֶכֶת, to denote work or subservience, just as מֶלֶךְ is altered to מֹלֶךְ.

in order to provoke Me—The participation of the entire family in a project that one person could do is for no other reason than to provoke Me.—[*Malbim*]

They know that there is no use in their worship. They perform it only to provoke Me.—[*Mezudath David*]

19. **Are they provoking Me?**—Are they doing this to make Me angry? Do they really think that they can anger Me? For the trait of anger does not apply to Me, only to them, as do other character traits. Thus, the anger will fall upon them.—[*Redak*]

for the shame of their faces—that they be ashamed of their evil deeds, for it is not fitting that I become provoked from their deeds even if I were, indeed, affected by character traits. The truth is that nothing affects Me; neither do they anger Me with their evil deeds nor do they do good to Me with their good deeds. This is reminiscent of Elihu (Job 35:6ff), who reproved Job by saying, "If you sinned, what do you do to Him, and if your transgressions are many, what do you do to Him? If you have dealt righteously, what do you give Him, or what does He take from your hand? To a man like you is your wickedness, and to the son of man your righteousness." Although the Torah states (Deut. 32:21): They provoked Me with their futilities, this is an anthropomorphism.—[*Redak*]

reaches—Heb. נִתֶּכֶת, *falls and reaches. Comp.* '(Exodus 9:33) *and rain did not reach* (נִתַּךְ) *the earth,' did not reach.*—[*Rashi*] Others render: is poured upon this place.—[*Mezudoth*]

Through My anger, this place will be destroyed, wherever a man, beast, or plant is found.—[*Malbim*]

and it shall burn and not be quenched—Although illnesses are remedied by various foods and medications, when God's wrath is upon the vegetables as well as the animals, there is no remedy.—[*Malbim*]

21. **your burnt offerings**—*that you*

ואכלו בשר: כב כי לא-דברתי את-
אבותיכם ולא צויתים ביום הוציא
אותם מארץ מצרים על-דברי עולה
וזבח: כג כי אם-את-הדבר הזה צויתי
אותם לאמר שמעו בקולי והייתי
לכם לאלהים ואתם תהיו-לי לעם
והלכתם בכל-הדרך אשר אצוה
אתכם למען ייטב לכם: כד ולא שמעו
ולא-הטו את-אזנם וילכו במעצות

הוציאי קרי

תרגום

בסרא: כב ארי לא
מללית עם אבהתכון
ולא פקדתינון ביומא
דאפקית יתהון מארעא
דמצרים על עסקי עלון
ונכסת קודשין:
כג אלהין ית פתגמא
הדין פקדית יתהון
למימר קבילו למימרי
ואהוי לכון לאלהא
ואתון תהון קדמי לעם
ותהכון בכל אורחא
באפקיד יתכון בדיל
דייטב לכון: כד ולא קבילו
ולא ארכינו ית אודניהון
ואזלו בעצתהון
בהרהור לבהון בישא

ת"א כי לא וגו'. עקרים כג כח:

רש"י

(כב) **ביום הוציאי אותם.** תחלת תנאי לא היתה אלא אם שמוע תשמעו בקולי ושמרתם את בריתי והייתם לי

מהר"י קרא

לפני לרצון ועתה מאחר שאינכם עושין רצוני]: עולותיכם. שהם כליל: ספו על זבחיכם. שהוא נאכל. ואכלו הכל: (כב) כי לא דברתי את אבותיכם. על דברי עולה וזבח. לקובען חובה שאין כתוב שם קרבן לה' אלא אדם כי יקריב מכם קרבן אם עולה קרבנו אם זבח שלמים קרבנו: (כג) כי אם את הדבר הזה צויתי אותם לאמר שמעו בקולי. לקבוע דבר זה חובה (ועתה) צויתי משמע חובת הה"ד ושמעת ישראל

מנחת שי

(כב) הוציא. הוציאי קרי: אותם מארץ. במדוייקים מלא וא"ו וכן להוי פ"ש במסורת דירמיה כ"ג וכן לויתי אותם שבסמוך:

רד"ק

שבו רדו והציווי הזה אינו למצוה רצינית אלא כאומר לחברו עשה מה שתעשה כי לא יועילך: (כב) כי לא דברתי. ביום הוציאי אותם מארץ מצרים. יש מפרשים כי הוא המצוה הראשונה והוא מה שצוה אותם במרה שנאמר בו שם שם לו חק ומשפט והוא מה שאמרו רז"ל שבת ודינין במרה איפקוד ולא צוה על דבר עולה או זבח וי"ל גם כן כי עיקר המצוה לא היתה על דברי עולה וזבח אלא שמעו בקולי והייתם לי לעם ובזה התנאי נתן להם התורה ואין בכל עשרת הדברים שהם כלל התורה כלה זכר שלה וזבח ואף כשידבר על הקרבנות לא צוה להם שיקריבו קרבן אלא אדם כי יקריב מכם קרבן אם יעשה מדעתו יהיה כך וכך והתמידים שצוה בהם הוא לכבוד הבית והיו באין לצבור אבל ליחידים לא צוה להקריב קרבן כמו שצוה ליחידים לעשות משפט ושאר המצות ולא צוה ליחיד לעשות קרבן אלא אם כן יחטא בשוגג וצוה בשרפת האימורין להשיב החוטא אל לבו לכוף התאוות הבהמיות לפי שתולדתם מחלב ודם ויהיה נזהר שלא יהיה שוגג במצות כל שכן מזיד והתמידים גם בנין הבית לעבודה אפשר שהוא כמו שכתב מורה צדק רבינו משה ז"ל להעתיק הדעות הזרות ובנין ההיכלות שהיו לשם עכו"ם רצה להעתיקם לעבודת האל ושימחה שם עכו"ם מהם: (כג) כי אם. מבואר הוא: (כד) ולא שמעו. במועצות. פירוש בעצה שלהם לא בעצתי כמו שפירש בשרירות לבם הרע ושרירות פירוש הבטת לבם מענין ישר

מצודת ציון

(כב) על דברי. על ענין וכן ועל דבר כזבי (במדבר כ"ה): (כד) במעצות.

מצודת דוד

לרלון לפני למה תפסידו הבשר: (כב) כי לא דברתי וגו'. ביום שהוצאתים ממצרים לא דברתי עמהם אז על דבר עולה וזבח ואם היה עיקר הכולל; בעבור הבאת הקרבנות כי בזה הכל תלוי אף בזולת שמוע בקול ה' היה א"כ מהראוי להצוות עליה ביום שהוצאתים ממצרים: (כג) כי אם וגו' שמעו בקולי. רק הדבר הזה צויתים אז שמעו בקולי וגו' כמ"ש ועתה אם שמוע תשמעו בקולי וגו' (שמות י"ט) א"כ זה העיקר והבאת הקרבנות היא כאחד מכל המצות שאין נחת כהם בזולת שמוע בקול ה': והייתי לכם לאלהים. ר"ל אני בעצמי אשפיע לכם טובה בזולת אמצעי: ואתם וגו'. ולא אחליפכם באומה אחרת: למען ייטב לכם. ר"ל לא יבא לי תועלת מזה רק למען ייטב לכם: (כד) ולא שמעו. אף יוצאי מצרים לא שמעו וגו': במועצות. בעלתם מה שהלאה להם לגם הרע ר"ל מה שחמדו

vidual. The daily sacrifices were brought in honor of the Sanctuary. The individual, however, was never required to bring sacrifices unless he sinned inadvertently. The Torah ordained the burning of the fats on the altar to call to mind that one should eliminate his bestial desires which originate from the fat and the blood, and that he beware of sinning inadvertently, surely intentionally. The reason for the commandment to build a temple may be, as *Rambam* explains it, to wean the people from pagan ideas and to channel their desires to build temples to pagan deities into building a temple for the Almighty, thus ridding them of any attachment to paganism.—[*Redak*]

24. **but walked according to [their] own counsels**—*Abarbanel* explains this as an allusion to the sin of the

and eat flesh. 22. For neither did I speak with your forefathers
nor did I command them on the day I brought them out of the
land of Egypt, concerning a burnt offering or a sacrifice.
23. But this thing did I command them, saying: Obey Me so
that I am your God and you are My people, and you walk in all
the ways that I command you, so that it may be well with you.
24. But they did not obey nor did they incline their ear, but
walked according to [their] own counsels

breast and the leg that were awarded to the priests. They did not bring sin-offerings and guilt-offerings, since these are brought only if one repents of his sins and confesses them. Moreover, they are brought only for unintentional sins, not for intentional ones. They would, therefore, offer up only burnt offerings and peace-offerings, the burnt offerings to illustrate that they are faithful servants of the Lord, and the peace-offerings to benefit from the flesh at the same time. The prophet exhorts them to abandon the practice of bringing burnt offerings since they are not acceptable. It is better for them to bring only peace-offerings so that, at least, they would have some benefit from them.

Others explain this to mean: Do whatever you wish; it will be of no use.—[*Redak*]

22. **on the day I brought them forth**—*The beginning of the condition was only* (Exodus 19:5): *'If you hearken to My voice and keep My covenant, you shall be a peculiar treasure to Me.'*—[*Rashi*] This verse presents some difficulty. It seems that the prophet opposes the practice of animal sacrifice, as the Bible critics would have us believe. It is, however, absurd to think that Jeremiah would negate many portions of the Pentateuch. *Rashi*, therefore, takes this verse literally, to mean that on the day God brought them out of Egypt, He did not command them concerning sacrifices, but concerning obedience. Indeed, verse 23 matches Exodus 19:5 very closely. This is, therefore, the intention of the verse, that the first and primary command was to obey God and to keep His covenant.

Redak, too, suggests this explanation. He suggests also that the prophet alludes to the first commandments given in Marah (Exodus 15:25): 'There he gave them an ordinance and a statute, and there He tested them.' Concerning this verse, the Rabbis comment (*San.* 56b): The Sabbath and jurisprudence were ordained in Marah. Then He did not command them concerning burnt offerings or peace-offerings. To elaborate on *Rashi*'s explanation, he points out that in the Decalogue there is no mention of sacrifices. Even when the Torah does speak of sacrifices, it speaks of private sacrifices as voluntary, unlike the performance of justice, which is incumbent upon each indi-

בשררות לבם הרע ויהיו לאחור ולא
לפנים: כה למן־היום אשר יצאו
אבותיכם מארץ מצרים עד היום
הזה ואשלח אליכם את־כל־עבדי
הנביאים יום השכם ושלח: כו ולוא
שמעו אלי ולא הטו את־אזנם ויקשו
את־ערפם הרעו מאבותם: כז ודברת
אליהם את־כל־הדברים האלה ולא
ישמעו אליך וקראת אליהם ולא
יענוכה: כח ואמרת אליהם זה הגוי

תרגום

ואחזרו בפולחני קדל
ולא שויאו דחלתי
לקביל אפיהון: כה למן
יומא דנפקו אבהתכון
מארעא דמצרים עד
יומא הדין ושלחית
ליהכון ית כל עבדי
נבייא יום מקדים
ומשלח: כו ולא קבילו
למימרי ולא ארכינו ית
אודניהון וקשיאו ית
קדלהון אבאישו
מאבהתהון: כז ותמליל
עמהון ית כל פתגמיא
האלין ולא יקבלון מנך
ותתנבי להון ולא
יתיבונך: כח ותימר להון
בין עמא די לא שמעו
למימרא

רש"י

סגולה (שם י"ט): (כד) בשרירות לבם. כמראה לבם ל' אשורנו (במדבר כ"ד): (כה) יום השכם ושלוח. מידי

מהר"י קרא

ושכרת לעשות אשר ייטב לך וזה הוא שנאמר כאן למען ייטב לכם: (כד) בשרירות. תרגום בתרהור: (כו) ויקשו את ערפם. (גם לדור הזה): הרעו מאבותם. וכשם שהראשונים הקשו את

רד"ק

על אנשים למה שלבם פונה אליו ויש מפרשים תוקף לבם מענין שריר וקים בדברי רז"ל וי"ת תרהור לבהון: ויהיו לאחור. וכה היה עונשם שהיו לאחור ולא לפנים כלומר שהיה מארה במעשה ידיהם ולא ברכה וי"ת ואחזרו לפולחני קדל וגו' כבעמוד: (כה) למן היום. כי בכל דור ודור היו בהם פושעים ורוב הדורות היו רובם פושעים ואף על פי שהייתי מזהירם תמיד על ידי הנביאים: יום. כלומר יום ויום: השכם ושלוח. בכל בקר ובקר כי רוב ההזהרה תהיה בבקר קודם שילך אדם למלאכתו ושליח הייתי שולח בהשכמת הנביאים להזהירם: (כו) ולא הטו את אזנם. הרעו מאבותם. בכל דור ודור רובם הרעו מאבותם כמו מנשה ואמון שהיו אחרונים הרעו אשכח מן הראשונים: (כז) ודברת. ולא ישמעו. ידעתי כי לא ישמעו אליך ואפילו לא יענוכה כשתקרא להם אף על פי כן הזהירם: יענוכה. נכתב בו ה"א המבטא אחר כ"ף הנמצא וכן וחסידיך יברכוכה והדומין לו: (כח) ואמרת. מפיהם. אפילו מפיהם אבדה ונכרתה שלא יאמרו אמת בפיהם כל שכן בלבבם כי רוב בני אדם מדברים בפיהם מה שאין כן בלבבם להראות עצמן טובים ואינ' חפץ מי שנאמר עליו ודובר

מנחת שי

(כה) ושלח. מלא וא"ו אחר למ"ד: (כז) אליהם. א"ה מלא יו"ד שכן נמסר

מצודת דוד

והסתוו: ויהיו לאחור. הלכו לאחור ולא לפנים ר"ל בכל יום היו פוחתין והולכים בעבודת ה' ולא היו מוסיפים והולכים: (כה) למן היום וגו'. מאז ועד הנה המה פוחתים והולכים: יום השכם ושלוח. בכל יום אני משכים ומשלח: (כו) ולא שמעו אלי. אנשי הדור הזה: ויקשו את ערפם. הוא ענין מליצה כאלו נתקשה מפרק הערף עד שא"א להם להחזיר הפנים מול המקום ואמר במשל מכן אדם לחבירו שאינו רוצה להחזיר הפנים מול חבירו לשמוע דבריו: הרעו. עשו רעה' עוד יותר מאבותם: (כז) ודברת. אמר ה' לירמיהו כאשר תדבר אליהם את כל הדברים האלה ידעתי אשר לא ישמעו אליך ויכרתו להם ואם תקרא אליהם ידעתי אשר לא יענו לך: (כח) ואמרת אליהם. אז תאמר אליהם זה הגוי וגו' ר"ל אין אלה מבני ישראל אשר שמעו דבר ה' בסיני אבל כאלו הם גוי אחר אשר

מצודת ציון

מלשון מלה: בשרירות. ענין הבטה ולאיה כמו אשר שוררו אנשים (איוב ל"ו): לפנים. להלן מול הפנים: (כו) ויקשו. מלשון קשה: ערפם. הוא מול הפנים: (כז) יענוכה. מלשון ענייה ותשובה:

twice, once in the morning and once in the evening, both times accompanied by Jeremiah.—[*Pesikta Rabbathi* 34:9. See II Kings 17:13]

26. **they did worse than their fathers**—In each generation, most of them were worse than their fathers; e.g. Manasseh and Amon, who were the last kings, were worse than their predecessors.—[*Redak*]

27. **And when you will speak**—I know that they will not hearken to you, but nevertheless warn them.—[*Redak*]

28. **Then say to them**—Then you shall say to them that this nation is not of the children of Israel who heard the voice of the Lord their God on Mount Sinai, but they are like another nation, who did not

and in the view of their evil heart, and they went backwards and
not forwards. 25. Since the day that your fathers came forth
out of the land of Egypt until this day, I sent you all My ser-
vants the prophets, sending them day [after day] with every
fresh morn. 26. Yet they hearkened not to Me nor did they
incline their ear, but stiffened their necks; they did worse than
their fathers. 27. And when you will speak all of these words to
them and they will not hearken to you, and you call to them
and they will not answer you, 28. Then say to them: This is the
nation

golden calf, which the people built when they saw that Moses did not return from Mt. Sinai at the time he was expected.

They followed their own counsels, not Mine.—[*Redak*]

in the view—Heb. בִּשְׁרִרוּת, *in the view of their heart, an expression related to* '(Num. 24:17) *I see him* (אֲשׁוּרֶנּוּ).'—[*Rashi*]

Others render: in the stubbornness of their heart, derived from the Rabbinic formula שָׁרִיר וְקַיָּם, *valid and permanent*. *Jonathan* renders: the thought of their heart.—[*Redak*]

and they went backwards and not forwards—Their punishment was that they went backwards instead of forwards, that there was a curse in their work rather than a blessing. *Jonathan* renders: And they turned their back to My worship and did not put My fear before their faces.—[*Redak*]

Others render: They went backwards in their worship of God instead of going forward.—[*Mezudath David*]

Abarbanel explains this verse as referring to the worship of the calf, as mentioned above. You followed the stubbornness of your evil heart, the idolatrous thoughts you learned in Egypt, and therefore you were punished. That is the implication of 'backward and not forward.' Then the sacrifices were ordained to expiate their sins. In later generations, however, the sacrifices did not suffice since the sins became more and more serious. It was, therefore, necessary to send prophets daily to reprove them.

25. **Since the day**—For in every generation there were transgressors, in fact, many transgressors, although I warned them constantly through My prophets.—[*Redak*]

sending them day [after day] every fresh morn—*Every day sending them early* .—[*Rashi*]

He sent His prophets early in the morning, for most warnings were in the morning before the men went to work.—[*Redak*]

The Rabbis tell us that God sent two prophets daily, one in the morning and one in the evening. Others state that God would send a new prophet every day. He would appear

אֲשֶׁר לוֹא־שָׁמְעוּ בְּקוֹל יְהוָה אֱלֹהָיו
וְלֹא לָקְחוּ מוּסָר אָבְדָה הָאֱמוּנָה
וְנִכְרְתָה מִפִּיהֶם׃ כט גָּזִּי נִזְרֵךְ וְהַשְׁלִיכִי
וּשְׂאִי עַל־שְׁפָיִם קִינָה כִּי מָאַס יְהוָה
וַיִּטֹּשׁ אֶת־דּוֹר עֶבְרָתוֹ׃ ל כִּי־עָשׂוּ בְנֵי־
יְהוּדָה הָרַע בְּעֵינַי נְאֻם־יְהוָה שָׂמוּ
שִׁקּוּצֵיהֶם בַּבַּיִת אֲשֶׁר־נִקְרָא־שְׁמִי־
עָלָיו לְטַמְּאוֹ׃ לא וּבָנוּ בָּמוֹת הַתֹּפֶת
אֲשֶׁר בְּגֵיא בֶן־הִנֹּם לִשְׂרֹף אֶת־בְּנֵיהֶם

תרגום

למימרא דיי אלההון ולא קבילו אולפן פסקת הימנותא ואתמנעת מפומהון : כט תלישי על רברביך דיגלון וטולי על נגרין אליא ארי רחיק יי ורטיש ית דרא דעברו על מימריה : ל ארי עבדו בני יהודה דביש קדמי אמר יי שויאו שקוציהון בביתא דאתקרי שמי עלוהי לסאבותיה : לא ובנו במת תופת די בחילת בר הנום לאוקדא ית בניהון וית בנתיהון

ת"א אבדה האמונה. ספר הזוהר פרשת ויקרא: גזי נזרך. יומא ח פה סוטה ט מגילה ג' לא:

רש"י

יום כיום השכם ושלוח : (כט) גזי נזרך. תלשי שערך כמו ויגז שלוים (שם יט) ויגז את ראשו (איוב א) ל"א נזרך כתרך לשון גדולה וכן תרגם יונתן רברביך וכן חברו מנחם: ויטוש. ויעזוב: (לא) במות התופת. הוא המולך שהיה של נחשת ומסיקין אותו מתחתיו וידיו פשוטות וניסקות ונותנין את הילד על ידיו והוא נכוה ונוהם והכומרים מקישין בתופים שלא ישמע האב קול הבן ויכמרו רחמיו. תופת על שם

מהר"י קרא

ערפם גם לדור הזה ודברת אליהם את כל הדברים האלה ולא ישמעו אליך : (כט) גזי נזרך. תלשי כמו גוזי מבטן : נזרך. שעריך כמו זכו נזיריה : שפיים. דרכים : (לא) התופת. כמדומה לי שהוא לשון שחת ושאול כמו כי ערוך מאתמול תפתה וכן שמעתי שיש שם גומא אחת בירושלים צר מלמעלה ורחב מלמטה ולא מוצק תחתיה ואם יהיו מושלכין שם כל פגרי רשעי הדורות היא מקבלתן כמו שאמר למטה וקברו בתופת מאין מקום ובנו שם במה ושורפין את בניהם לע"ז : אשר לא צויתי. בתורתי לעובדני שיקריב אדם את בנו לפני כי אם כן

רד"ק

אמת בלבבו אבל אלה אפילו בפיהם אין אמת : (כט) גזי נזרך. גדול השער נקרא נזר לפי שהנזיר היה מגדל שערו וענין גזי נזרך כענין קרחי וגזי על בני תענוגיך והשליכי הנזר שהיה לך לפאר גזי אותו והשליכי בעפר לאבל ואמר לשון נקבה על הכנסיה וי"ת תלישי על רברבך דיגלון : את דור עברתו. הדור הזה ששפך עליהם עברתו וחמתו וי"ת ית דרא די עברו על מימריה : (ל) כי עשו. שמו שקוציהם. אחז ומנשה עשו זה כמו שכתוב ובני יהודה עמהם : (לא) ובנו. אשר לא צויתי ולא עלתה על לבי. לא היה רצוני בזה ולא צויתי להם שישרפו לי בניהם ובנותיהם ואם צויתי על בשר בהמה לשרוף לפני לא צויתי להם שישרפו בניהם ובנותיהם והם שורפים אותם לאל

מנחת שי

במסרה רבתא ערך א"ל שכל אליהם דירמיה מלאים ע"כ) : (כט) גזי נזרך. הגימל בקמץ חטוף מפני דגשות הזי"ן כמו רני ושמחי ועיין מ"ש בפרשת בראשית אל ביום אכלכם ממנו : והשליכי. בספרים מדוייקים הוא"ו בגעיה :

מצודת דוד

לא שמעו בקול ה' וכאלו לא למדו מעולם מוסר : אבדה האמונה. אמונת האל אבדה מלבותם וגם נכרתה מפיהם ולא יזכרו בה : (כט) גזי נזרך. לכן תלוש שער ראשך והשלך אותם והוא דרך לצער ולאבלות : ושאי. הרימי קול קינה על מקומות הגבוהות להיות נשמע למרחוק : ויטוש. עזב את הדור השפך עליו עברתו : (ל) שמו שקוציהם. עכו"ם המתועב שמו בבהמ"ק לטמא אותו : (לא) בבות התופת. במות של התופת אשר עמד בגיא בן הנום לשרוף על הבמות את בניהם וגו' (ולפי שהיו מקישין בתופים לבל ישמע האב בכיית הבן כשהוא נשרף ויכמרו רחמיו קראו בית הבמות תופת על שם

מצודת ציון

(כח) לקחו. ענין למוד : ונכרתה. ר"ל נפסקה : (כט) גזי. ענין תלישה כמו קרחי וגזי (מיכה א') : נזרך. גדול השער יקרא נזר כמו נזר אלהיו על ראשו (במדבר ו') : ושאי. ענין הרמה : שפים. כן נקראו מקומות הגבוהים : ויטש. ענין עזיבה כמו ויטוש משכן שלו (תהלים ע"ח) : עברתו. מלשון עברה וזעם : (ל) שקוציהם. מלשון שקץ ותועבה : (לא) במות. מלשון במה : בגיא. בעמק :

moni on our verse, *Aruch.* Also found in the addenda to *Tanhuma Buber, Va'ethhannan,* 2.]

The Midrash, in its entirety, reads as follows: Although all the pagan shrines were in Jerusalem, the Molech was outside Jerusalem. It was made as a hollow idol within seven rooms. If one would sacrifice fine flour, they would open one room for him. If he would sacrifice turtledoves or young pigeons, they would open two rooms for him. If he would sacrifice a lamb, they would open three rooms for him. If he would sacrifice a ram, they would open four rooms for him. If he would sacrifice a calf, they would open five rooms for him. If he would sacrifice an ox, they would open six

that did not hear the voice of the Lord their God and has not
received correction; out of their mouth faithfulness has disap-
peared, yea rooted out! 29. So tear off your diadem and cast it
off, and let lamentation sound out over the hillocks, for the
Lord has rejected and abandoned the generation of His wrath.
30. For the sons of Judah have done what is evil in My eyes,
says the Lord; they placed their abominations in the house
upon which My name is called, to pollute it. 31. And they have
built the high places of Topheth which are in the valley of Ben-
Hinnom, to burn their sons

hear His voice on Sinai and who has not received correction.—[*Abarbanel, Mezudath David*]

out of their mouth faithfulness has disappeared, yea rooted out!—They do not even speak the truth with their mouth, surely they do not feel it in their heart. Many people speak as though they are honest and faithful, although in their heart they are not. These people, however, do not even fein faithfulness with their mouth.—[*Redak*]

29. **So tear off your diadem**—Heb. גָּזִּי נִזְרֵךְ, *tear out your hair. Comp.* '(Num. 11:31) *And He caused quails to fly* (וַיָּגָז),' also '(Job 1:20) *And he shaved* (וַיָּגָז) *his head.*' *Another explanation is that* נִזְרֵךְ means 'your **diadem,' an expression of greatness, and so did Jonathan render:** רַבְרְבַיִךְ, ***your great ones, and so did Menahem classify it*** **(p. 83).—[*Rashi*]**

According to the first interpretation, נִזְרֵךְ is derived from נָזִיר, *a nazirite,* who lets his hair grow long. The prophet exhorts the people to tear out their hair in mourning.—[*Redak, Mezudath David*]

and abandoned—Heb. וַיִּטֹּשׁ.—[*Rashi*]

the generation of His wrath—This generation, upon whom He has poured His anger and His wrath. *Jonathan* renders: the generation that transgressed His word.—[*Redak*] *Jonathan,* apparently, understands עֶבְרָתוֹ as derived from עֲבֵרָה, *sin,* or *transgression.*

30. **they placed their abominations**—Ahaz and Manasseh did this, as it is written, (II Kings 21:4f., 23:12) 'and the sons of Judah followed them.'—[*Redak*]

31. **the high places of Topheth**—*That is Molech, which was of copper, and they would heat it up from underneath it with its hands spread out and heated. And they would place the child on his hands, and he would be burnt and moan, and the priests would beat drums so that the father should not hear his son's voice and take pity. It is called Topheth because of the drum* (תּוֹף), *Hinnom because of the child's moaning* (נְהָמַת).—[*Rashi* from *Yelam'denu,* a lost Midrash, quoted by *Redak, Abarbanel, Mezudath David,* II Kings 23:10, *Yalkut Shi-*

וְאֶת־בְּנֹתֵיהֶם בָּאֵשׁ אֲשֶׁר לֹא צִוִּיתִי
וְלֹא עָלְתָה עַל־לִבִּי: לב לָכֵן הִנֵּה־יָמִים
בָּאִים נְאֻם־יְהוָֹה וְלֹא־יֵאָמֵר עוֹד
הַתֹּפֶת וְגֵיא בֶן־הִנֹּם כִּי אִם־גֵּיא
הַהֲרֵגָה וְקָבְרוּ בְתֹפֶת מֵאֵין מָקוֹם:
לג וְהָיְתָה נִבְלַת הָעָם הַזֶּה לְמַאֲכָל
לְעוֹף הַשָּׁמַיִם וּלְבֶהֱמַת הָאָרֶץ וְאֵין
מַחֲרִיד: לד וְהִשְׁבַּתִּי | מֵעָרֵי יְהוּדָה
וּמֵחֻצוֹת יְרוּשָׁלִַם קוֹל שָׂשׂוֹן וְקוֹל

תרגום

בְּנוּרָא דְלָא פַקְדֵית
בְּאוֹרָיְתִי וְלָא כְעַוָא
קֳדָמַי: לב בְּכֵן הָא יוֹמַיָא
אָתַן אֲמַר יְיָ וְלָא יִתְאֲמַר
עוֹד תּוֹפַת וְחֵילַת בַּר
הִנוֹם אֱלָהֵין חֵילַת
קְטִילַיָא וְיִקְבְּרוּן בְּתוֹפֶת
מִבְּלִי אֲתַר: לג וּתְהֵי
נְבִילְתָא דְעַמָא הָדֵין
מְשַׁגְרָא לְמֵיכַל לְעוֹפָא
דִשְׁמַיָא וּלְבְעִירָא
דְאַרְעָא וְלֵית דְמָנִיד:
לד וְאֲבַטֵיל מִקִרְוַיָא
דְבֵית יְהוּדָה וּמִשׁוּקֵי
יְרוּשְׁלֵם קָל בִּיעַ וְקָל
חֶדְוָא

רש"י

התוף: הנם. על שם נהמת הבן: לא צויתי. במלות שיקריבו בניהם לקרבן ולא דברתי לאחד מן הנביאים וכשדברתי לאברה' לשחוט את בנו לא עלתה על לבי שישחוט אלא להודיע צדקו: (לג) ואין מחריד. את העופות מעל הפגרים:

מהר"י קרא

הבהמה מן הבקר ומן הצאן: (לג) ואין מחריד. לקוברו:

רד"ק

אחר ואינם מרחמים עליהם לרוב אהבתם העכו"ם וי"ת דלא פקידית באוריתי ולא רעוא קדמי ורז"ל פירשו אשר לא צויתי זה יפתח ולא עלתה על לבי זה מישע מלך מואב שנאמר ויקח את בנו הבכור ויעלהו לעולה ודעתם שהעלהו לשמים: (לב) לכן. וקברו בתופת מאין מקום. כי לא היה לפני זה מקום לקבורה: (לג) והיתה. אותם שלא יוכלו לקבור מאין מקום או שילאו הקוברים מרוב הרוגים: (לד) והשבתי. לחרבה תהיה הארץ.

מנחת שי

(לג) והיתה נבלת. בס"ם הוא"ו בגעיא וכן הוא בחילופים לבן אשר: (לד) ומחלות. ברוב ספרים כ"י מדוייקים הח"ת בגלא נקודות:

מצודת דוד

התופים ולהגיא קראו בן הנום על שם נהמת הבן): אשר לא צויתי. ר"ל לפני לא צויתי להקריב בנים ובנות: ולא עלתה על לבי. לשאול דבר כזאת: (לב) ולא יאמר עוד. אז לא יקרא עוד בית הבמו' בשם תופת והגיא בן הנום כ"א יקרא גי ההרגה כי שמה יפלו הרוגים רבים: וקברו. ההרוגים יקברו בתופת הרבה מאד עד שלא ימלא שם מקום לקבור עוד: (לג) והיתה נבלת העם. הנשארים אשר לא יקברו יהיה למאכל לעוף השמים וגו': ואין מחריד. לא יהיה מי להחרידם ללכת מן הנבלות: (לד) והשבתי וגו'. ר"ל לא ישמע עוד שמה קול ששון וגו' כי לחרבה תהיה ולא ישאר בה איש:

מצודת ציון

(לג) נבלת. כן נקרא גוף ההרוג: מחריד. מלשון חרדה ופחד: (לד) והשבתי. ענין בטול כמו שבת נוגש (ישעי' י"ד): ולחרבה. מלשון חורבן:

that it did not enter My mind to ordain an abominable worship of this sort.

32. **it shall no longer be called**—In those days, it will no longer be called Topheth or the Valley of the son of Hinnom, but the Valley of Slaughter since many people will fall there.—[*Mezudath David*]

for lack of room—For this was not used as a burial place prior to this time.—[*Redak*]

Redak, apparently, explains that this place will be used for burial for lack of room in other burial places. *Abarbanel* and *Mezudath David*, however, explain that it will be used as a burial place until it will be full and there will be no more room.

33. **and no one will frighten them**—I.e. no one will frighten *the fowl from the carcasses*.—[*Rashi*]

This is an example of punishment in kind. They devoted this valley for slaying their children. Therefore, fathers and sons will be slain there. Where they played music in honor of the sacrifice, there will be, instead, great mourning.—[*Abarbanel*]

34. **for the land shall be desolate**—and instead of joyous sounds,

and daughters with fire, which I did not ordain, neither did it
enter My mind. 32. Therefore, behold days are coming, says
the Lord, that it shall no longer be called Topheth or the Valley
of the son of Hinnom, but the Valley of Slaughter, and they
shall bury in Topheth for lack of room. 33. And the carcasses
of this people shall be for food for the fowl of the heaven and
for the beasts of the earth, and no one will frighten them.
34. And I will stop from the cities of Judah and from the streets
of Jerusalem the sound of mirth and the sound of

rooms for him. If he sacrificed his son, they would open all seven rooms for him. Its face was like that of a calf. Its hands were extended as one does to receive something from his friend. They would heat it with fire. Then the priests would take the child and place him in the hands of the Molech, where he would let out his soul. Why was it called Topheth and Hinnom? Topheth, because . . . and have pity on him and renege. Hinnom, because the child would moan (*nohem*), and his moans would ascend.

Ralbag and *Abarbanel* (II Kings 23:10) describe this as two fires between which the priests would pass the child.

According to the simple explanation, this valley belonged to a man named Hinnom, who left it to his sons or to one of them.—[*Redak* ibid.]

Rabbi Joseph Kara conjectures that Topheth is an expression denoting a pit. He reports that he heard that in Jerusalem there was a bottomless pit, narrow on top and wide at the bottom, into which the bodies of all the wicked of all generations would fit if they were cast therein. On that site, a high place was erected where people would burn their children as sacrifices to pagan deities.

Daath Mikra points out that Ahaz son of Jotham inaugurated this worship by passing his son through the fire (II Kings 16:3), and Hezekiah his son abolished it (II Chron. 31:1). Later, Manasseh his son reinstated it (II Kings 21:3, 6), and Josiah son of Amon abolished it (ibid. 23:10). It was probably reinstated after his death.

which I did not ordain—*with commandments that they offer up their children as sacrifices, and I did not speak to any of the prophets, and when I did speak to Abraham to slaughter his son, it did not enter My mind that he slaughter, but only to make his righteousness known.*—[*Rashi*]

Malbim explains: **which I did not ordain**—that such sacrifices be made to Me. Lest you think that I did not ordain it because I thought that no one would heed My command, but if I knew that they would obey, I would have ordained it, I tell you

שִׂמְחָה קוֹל חָתָן וְקוֹל כַּלָּה כִּי לְחָרְבָּה
תִּהְיֶה הָאָרֶץ׃ ח א בָּעֵת הַהִיא נְאֻם־
יְהוָה וְיוֹצִיאוּ אֶת־עַצְמוֹת מַלְכֵי־יְהוּדָה
וְאֶת־עַצְמוֹת שָׂרָיו וְאֶת־עַצְמוֹת
הַכֹּהֲנִים וְאֵת ׀ עַצְמוֹת הַנְּבִיאִים וְאֵת
עַצְמוֹת יוֹשְׁבֵי־יְרוּשָׁלָ͏ִם מִקִּבְרֵיהֶם׃
ב וּשְׁטָחוּם לַשֶּׁמֶשׁ וְלַיָּרֵחַ וּלְכֹל ׀ צְבָא
הַשָּׁמַיִם אֲשֶׁר אֲהֵבוּם וַאֲשֶׁר עֲבָדוּם
וַאֲשֶׁר הָלְכוּ אַחֲרֵיהֶם וַאֲשֶׁר דְּרָשׁוּם
וַאֲשֶׁר הִשְׁתַּחֲווּ לָהֶם לֹא יֵאָסְפוּ וְלֹא

תרגום

חֶדְוָא קָל חַתְנִין וְקָל כַּלִּין אֲרֵי לְחוּרְבָּא תְּהֵי אַרְעָא׃ א בְּעִדָּנָא הַהִיא אֲמַר יְיָ יַפְּקוּן יָת גַּרְמֵי מַלְכַיָּא דְבֵית יְהוּדָה וְיָת גַּרְמֵי רַבְרְבֵיהוֹן וְיָת גַּרְמֵי כַהֲנַיָּא וְיָת גַּרְמֵי נְבִיֵּי שִׁקְרָא וְיָת גַּרְמֵי יָתְבֵי יְרוּשְׁלֵם מִקִּבְרֵיהוֹן׃ ב וְיִשְׁטְחוּנוּן לָקֳבֵיל שִׁמְשָׁא וְסִיהֲרָא וּלְכֹל חֵילֵי שְׁמַיָּא דְרַחֲמוּנוּן וּדְפַלְחוּנוּן וְדִטְעוֹ בַתְרֵיהוֹן וְדִתְבְעוּנוּן וְדִסְגִידוּ לְהוֹן לָא יִתְכַּנְשׁוּן

תולדות אהרן

בעת ההיא. סנהדרין יא ו׳: לא יאספו יבמות ו רג׃

יוציאו קרי קמץ בטרחא

מהר"י קרא

ח (א) יוציאו את עצמות בלכי יהודה. מיכן שהקב"ה פורע

רש"י

ח (ב) ושטחום לשמש. והכשדים יסכנו לגור על העיר

מנחת שי

ח (א) ויוציאו. יתיר וא"ו כן מצאתי בספרים מדוייקים מספרד והוא חד מן י"ח מלין דכתובין וא"ו בריש תיבותא ולא קריין וסימן ומספר במסרה רבתא ובכמה ספרים ויוציאו כתיב וקרי יוציאו וככל אחד. ונראה שנוסחת רד"ק ויצאו כתיב וקרי יוציאו שכן כתוב בפירושו בספרים ישנים וכן העתיק בעל

רד"ק

ובבקום קול שמחה יהיה קול יללה קול בכי וצעקה: (א) בעת ההיא. ויוציאו. כתיב וקרי יוציאו והענין קרוב כי פירוש ויוציאו שיוציאו לא שיצאו מעצמם וזה הענין לא ספר הכתוב בחרבן ירושלם בספר מלכים שהוציאו הכשדים עצמות המלכים והשרים והכהנים והנביאים מיושבי ירושלם מקבריהם אלא הנביא שנבא עליהם שיהיה כך והיה כך ואף על פי שלא ספר הכתוב וזה יהיה העונש להם אחר מיתתם כמו שנאמר: (ב) אשר אהבום ואשר עבדום. וכן אמר על יהויקים כשהתנבא עליו ענ"ש ולא יהיה לו יושב על כסא דוד ונבלתו תהיה מושלכת לחורב ביום ולקרח בלילה וכן אמר בפושעי ישראל והיו מושלכים בחוצות ירושלם ורז"ל אמרו בעון חיים מתים נחטטים וסמכו זה בפסוק והיתה יד ה׳ בכם ובאבותיכם זה חטוטי שכבי והביאו גם זה הפסוק לא יאספו ולא יקברו והקשו אליו הפסוק הבא אחריו ונבחר מות מחיים כלומר לכה היה נבחר מות מחיים אם המתים נחטטים ואם היה עונש המתים היה להם כפרה וזה ונבחר מות אלא אם הוא עונש החיים ובעון החיים מתים נחטטים למה אמר ונבחר מות מחיים ופירש נבחר מות לרשעים שלא יחיו בעולם הזה ויחטאו ויפלו בגיהנם: לדומן. לזבל יהיו כלומר כי לעולם יהיו על פני האדמה כי לא יקברו ולרוב עמידתם על פני האדמה ירקבו וישובו עפר וזבל: (ג) ונבחר. המתים יהיה ענשם מה שאמר

מצודת ציון

ח (ב) ושטחום. ענין פרישה כמו משטח חרמים (יחזקאל כ"ו): צבא השמים. הם הכוכבים ומזלות: יאספו. ענין הכנסה

מצודת דוד

ח (א) יוציאו. האויבים הבאים יוציאום מקבריהם לבזותם: הכהנים. כהני הבעל: הנביאים. נביאי השקר: יושבי ירושלים. מיתר העם: (ב) ושטחום. ויפרשו אותם אל מול השמש וגו׳ לבזותם: אשר אהבום. לקבלם לאלהות: ואשר וגו׳. כפל הדבר במ"ש להתמדת הדבר: לא יאספו. לא יכניסום אל הקבר:

worshipped—A similar prophecy was pronounced upon Jehoiakim (infra 36:30): 'And he will have no one sitting on David's throne, and his corpse shall be cast to the heat by day and to the cold at night.' The same was prophesied concerning the wicked of Israel (infra 14:16): 'shall be cast in the streets of Jerusalem.' Our Sages state (*Yeb.* 63b): For the sins of the living, the dead are dug up, and they support this on the verse (I Sam. 12:15): 'the Lord's hand will be against you and against your fathers.' This alludes to digging up the dead. They quote our verse also, 'they shall neither be gathered nor buried.' They question this assertion, however, on the basis of the following verse, 'And death shall be chosen rather than life.' Why should death be chosen rather than life? If the punishment is for the dead, their sins would be expiated,

gladness, the voice of the bridegroom and the voice of the bride, for the land shall be desolate.

8

1. At that time, says the Lord, they will take out the bones of the kings of Judah and the bones of his princes and the bones of the priests and the bones of the prophets and the bones of the inhabitants of Jerusalem, from their graves. 2. And spread them before the sun and before the moon and before the entire host of the heavens, which they loved and which they worshipped and which they followed, and which they sought and to which they prostrated themselves; they shall neither be gathered nor

there will be cries and wailing.—[*Redak*]

Others explain that there will be no joyous sounds since no one will remain in the land.—[*Mezudath David*]

1. **they will take out**—This illustrates that God visits retribution on the wicked during their lifetime and after their death for the sin of idolatry.—[*Kara*]

the bones of the priests—the priests of Baal.—[*Mezudath David*]

the bones of the prophets—The false prophets.—[*Jonathan*]

Although this incident is not related in the narrative of the destruction in the Book of Kings, that the Chaldeans took the bones of the kings, the princes, the priests, the prophets, and the inhabitants of Jerusalem from their graves, since the prophet prophesied it, we know that it transpired, and that this was the punishment of the wicked after their death.—[*Redak*. See on following verse. Moreover, the fulfillment of this prophecy is mentioned in the Apocrypha (Baruch 2:21f).]

2. **And spread them before the sun**—*and the Chaldeans shall dwell when they besiege the city, in the graves of the princes, that were as beautiful as palaces.*—[*Rashi*]

Rashi alludes to the Talmudic narrative that the Moabites and the Ammonites, upon hearing the prophecy of the destruction of Jerusalem, encouraged Nebuchadnezzar to attack. When he replied that there would be no place for him and his armies to encamp outside Jerusalem, they replied, "Their graves are better than your palaces (*San.* 96b)." Thereupon, Nebuchadnezzar marched upon Jerusalem and stationed himself and his army in the graveyard and took out all the corpses.—[*Ibn Nachmiash*]

which they loved and which they

יִקָּבְרוּ לְדֹמֶן עַל־פְּנֵי הָאֲדָמָה יִהְיוּ׃
ג וְנִבְחַר מָוֶת מֵחַיִּים לְכֹל הַשְּׁאֵרִית
הַנִּשְׁאָרִים מִן־הַמִּשְׁפָּחָה הָרָעָה הַזֹּאת
בְּכָל־הַמְּקֹמוֹת הַנִּשְׁאָרִים אֲשֶׁר
הִדַּחְתִּים שָׁם נְאֻם יְהוָה צְבָאוֹת׃
ד וְאָמַרְתָּ אֲלֵיהֶם כֹּה אָמַר יְהוָה הֲיִפְּלוּ
וְלֹא יָקוּמוּ אִם־יָשׁוּב וְלֹא יָשׁוּב׃ ה מַדּוּעַ

יִתְכַּנְשׁוּן וְלָא יִתְקַבְּרוּן לְזִיבַל מְכַבַּד עַל אַפֵּי אַרְעָא יְהוֹן׃ ג וְיִתְרְעוּן בְּמוֹתָא מִדְּבַחַיָּא לְכָל שְׁאָרָא דְיִשְׁתָּאֲרוּן מִן זַרְעִיתָא בִישְׁתָּא הָדָא בְּכָל אַתְרַיָּא דְיִשְׁתָּאֲרוּן דְאַגְלֵיתִינוּן לְתַמָּן אֲמַר יְיָ צְבָאוֹת׃ ד וְתֵימַר לְהוֹן כִּדְנַן אֲמַר יְיָ הֲיִפְּלוּן וְלָא יְקוּמוּן אִם לְמֵיתַב גְּלֵי קֳדָמַי דְלָא יְתוּבוּן׃ ה מַה דֵין

ת"א ונבחר וגו'. שם: מדוע וגו'. סנהדרין יא קה:

רש"י

בקברי השרים שהיו נאים כפלטין: לדומן. לזבל: (ג) ונבחר מות מחיים. אע"פ שהם רואים את המתים נתונין כבזיון לרת החיים גדולה הימנו ויבחרו את המות: (ד) היפלו ולא יקומו. הטוב להם שיפילו את עצמם לנפילה שאין לה תקומה: אם ישוב ולא ישוב. לכשירצו לשוב מרעתם לא ישוב הקב"ה מגזירתו. ד"א אף אם ישובו בתשובה לא תתקיים בידם. כי ימהרו לשוב לרשעתם וכן

מהר"י קרא

מן הרשעים בחייהן ובמותם בעון ע"ז: (ב) לדומן. ת"י לזבל: (ד) היפלו ולא יקומו. כלומר אפשר היפלו לחנן לפני. שלא יקומו לפני אויביהם: אם ישובו. הם בתשובה אפשר שאני לא אשוב מחרוני הכל בתימה: (ה) מדוע שובבה העם הזה. כאשה זונה שכנאפת תחת בעלה ובעלה בא להשיבה מדרך הרע והיא נותנת כתף סוררת ושבת

רד"ק

שיהיו נחשים מקבריהם והחיים והם השארית הנשארים שלא יהרגו ויגלו יבחרו בגלותם מות מחיים כי יהיו ביד גוי נבל עבדים לעם אכזרים שלא ירחמו עליהם וטוב מותם מחייהם: בכל המקומות הנשארים. בכל מקום שיהיו הנשארים כמו הפוך הנשארים בכל המקומות אשר הדחתים שם כמו ותשם בפוך עיניה וכל הארץ באו מצרימה לשבר אל יוסף באו מצרימה אל יוסף לשבר לי יזעקו אלהי ידענוך ישראל לי יזעקו ישראל אלהי ידענוך והדומים להם שכתבנו בספר מכלל בחלק הדקדוק: (ד) ואמרת. היפלו ולא יקומו. טעמו דבק עם הפסוק הבא אחריו מדוע שובבה כלומר למה זה החזיקו כל כך במעשיהם הרעים ומאנו לשוב וכי נפלו בעונש מעשיהם שלא קמו אחר כן כלומר כמה פעמים נפלו בעונש מעשיהם ואחר כן בשובם קמו וכי סבורים הם שאם ישובו הם למוטב לא ישוב האל מחרון אפו עליהם היה שום פעם עד עתה שנפלו ולא קמו אחר כן או אם ישוב ישראל ממעשיו הרעים ולא ישוב האל מחרון אפו זה לא היה אם כן מדוע שובבה וי"ת היפלון ולא יקומון וגו' כבעבור: (ה) מדוע שובבה. בא הנה עם לשון נקבה כי רצונו על הכנסה כמו שפירשנו וכן וחטאת עמך העם אשר בקרבה יושבת לבטח שובבה ענין מרד וכן בנים שובבים משובה ישראל: העם הזה ירושלם. חסר הנסמך העם הזה עם ירושלם וכמוהו רבים כמו שפירשנו

מנחת שי

אכלל יופי אכל במקרא גדולה יש נמגוס כלשונו וצריך תיקון: (ג) בכל המקומות.

מצודת דוד

ולא יקברו. כפל הדבר במ"ש: לדומן. יהיו מונחים ע"פ האדמה דומה לדומן: (ג) ונבחר מות מחיים. הנשארים מן המיתה ההולכים בגולה יהיו בצרה גדולה עד שיבחרו המיתה: המשפחה הרעה. אשר עבדו לבעל: בכל המקומות הנשארים. הוא הפך כמו הנשארים בכל המקומות אשר הדחתים שם בגולה: (ד) היפלו. וכי בעונם יפלו ולא יוכלו לקום ר"ל וכי אין תשובה מועלת שיקומו מנפילתם: אם ישוב. וכי אם מי מהם ישוב בתשובה האם לא ישוב ה' מחרון אפו בתמיה (דרך המקרא כשאומר שני תמיהות זה אחר זה יאמר בראשונה ה"א התימה ובשניה מלת אם וכן המאום מאסת את יהודה אם בציון געלה נפשך (לקמן י"ד): (ה) מדוע. למה מרדה העם הזה מרידה מתמדת עד עולם: העם הזה ירושלים.

מצודת ציון

כמו ואין איש מאסף אותם (שופטים י"ט): לדומן. לזבל כמו כדומן ע"פ השדה (לק' ט'): (ג) הדחתים. מלשון דחיה: (ה) שובבה.

blessed be He, not return from His decree? Another explanation: If they repent, the repentance will not be permanent, for they will quickly return to their wickedness, and in this manner Jonathan rendered it: If to repent, it is revealed before Me that they will not repent.—[*Rashi*]

Redak connects this verse with the following one: Why has this people, Jerusalem, slid back a perpetual backsliding? I.e., why do they grasp tenaciously to their evil deeds and refuse to repent? Did they ever fall into the punishment for their deeds and not rise afterward? Although Israel fell many times, they rose by repenting. Do they think that if they repent, God will not return from His anger?

be buried; they shall be for dung on the surface of the earth.
3. And death shall be preferable to life for all the residue that remain of this evil family, which remain in all the places whither I have cast them out, says the Lord of Hosts.
4. And you shall say to them: So says the Lord: Shall they fall and not rise, if he repents, will He not return?

but if it is for the living, and because of their sins the dead will be dug up, why should death be chosen rather than life? Thereupon, the Sages reply that death is better for the wicked since they do not have the opportunity to sin and fall into Gehinnom.—[*Redak*]

Malbim explains the various types of worship denoted by the various synonyms used in this verse. There were some gods whom the people loved, for they attributed to them all types of plenty and bounty. There were others that they feared, attributing to them all types of illnesses and destruction. These two are depicted by: which they loved and which they worshipped, i.e. which they loved for the bounty they would bring and which they worshipped out of fear of illness and destruction. To appease these deities, they offered them both animal and human sacrifices. There were some whom they would seek as oracles, to learn of future events and of unknown facts and secrets, and others to whom they would prostrate themselves as a token of honor and exaltation. Still others they would follow to emulate their traits.

nor buried—They will not be buried at all.—[*Malbim*]

for dung—*For fertilizer.*—[*Rashi*]

Since they will never be buried, they will decay and fertilize the soil.—[*Redak*]

3. **And death shall be preferable to life**—*Although they see the dead being subjected to disgrace, the distress of the living is worse than that, and they will choose death.*—[*Rashi*]

The dead will be punished by being dug up from their graves, and the living, i.e. the survivors who will not be slain but who will be driven into exile, will choose death in exile to life, for they will be subjected to a cruel nation, to people who will show them no compassion. Consequently, death will be preferable to life.—[*Redak*]

of this evil family—I.e. those who worshipped Baal.—[*Mezudath David*]

which remain in all the places—In the Hebrew, the word order is inverted. This is not unusual in Scriptures.—[*Redak*]

This includes those remaining both in the Holy Land and in the Diaspora.—[*Malbim*]

4. **Shall they fall and not rise**—*Is it good for them to cast themselves into a fall from which there is no rising?*—[*Rashi*]

if he repents, will He not return?—*If they wish to repent of their wickedness, will the Holy One,*

שובבה העם הזה ירושלם משבה
נצחת החזיקו בתרמית מאנו לשוב:
ו הקשבתי ואשמע לוא־כן ידברו אין
איש נחם על־רעתו לאמר מה עשיתי
כלה שב במרצותם כסוס שוטף
במלחמה: ז גם־חסידה בשמים ידעה
מועדיה ותר וסוס ועגור שמרו את־

ת"א גם חסידה בשמים. עקרים מג : פתח באתנח קמץ בפשטא ה' במקום ו' במרוצתם קרי וסים קרי

תרגום

מתחסנין למיתב לפולחני עמא הדין יתבי ירושלם תבו למרד מן אוריתא ולא צבן למיתב אתקיפו בנכלין מסרבין למיתב:
ו אציתית וגלי קדמי לא כדכשר ממללין לית גבר דמתיב מן בישתיה למימר מה עבדית כולהון מסגן ברעות נפשיהון כסוסיא דנגר בקרבא:
ז אף חוריתא בשמיא ידעא זמנהא ושפנינא

רש"י

ת"י אם למיתב גלי קדמי דלא יתוכין: (ה) משובה נצחת. משובת עולם כמו נלה: החזיקו. אחזו: בתרמית. במרמה: (ו) לא כן. לא כדין כמו כן בנות צלפחד (במדבר ט): כלה שב במרוצתם. בדרך הראשון חוטאים וחוזרים וחוטאי'. מרוצתם (קורס"י בלע"ז): שוטף. (אישפרידי"ן בלע"ז): (ז) חסידה. (ציגוניא"ה בלע"ז): מועדיה. עת עברם אל איי הים מפני הצנה ועת בואם: שמרו. המתינו: ותור וסים ועגור. ושפנינא וכורכיא וסנוניתא. כורכיא (גרוא"ה

מהר"י קרא

מאחריו: משובה נצחת. מורדת לנצח: (ו) כולו שב במרוצתם. כשאנים הם לשוב אחרי ואצל מי הם שבים בדרך שהם רגילין לרוץ בו היא ע"ז: כסוס שוטף במלחמה. שאחר שתופס מרוצתו קשה הוא להשיבו: (ז) גם חסידה בשמים. עוף השמים: ידעה מועדיה. שהיא דרה על הים ויודעת אי זו שעה שבשוטטת בעולם שאינה יכולה להיות שם מפני קול הים וכן. ותור וסים. ארינדל"א בלע"ז: ועגור. גרואה בלע"ז:

מנחת שי

חבר וה"ו קדמאה עיין במסורת שמואל ב' י"ז: (ו) במרוצתם. במרוצתם קרי: (ז) וכוס. וסים קרי:

רד"ק

שפירשנו בחלק הדקדוק מספר כלל: משובה נצחת. פתח באתנח ופירוש עולמי' מן נצח: משובה. שם משובה ישראל האר: החזיקו בתרמית מאנו לשוב. ידמה כי לעולם ירצו להחזיק בה. בתרמית כמו מרמה: (ו) הקשבתי. מאמר הנביא כשאני הולך ביניהם אני מקשיב ומאזין להם אם אחד מדבר טוב ואם לא: כן. טוב וכשר כמו כן בנות צלפחד דוברות: אין איש נחם. נפעל עומד כי הוא קמוץ גם כלת אין מורה עליו: כלה שב במרוצתם. וכתוב במרצותם לשון רבות והכתוב דרך כלל והקרי דרך פרט כלם הולכים ושבים במרוצתם לעשות כסוס שוטף במלחמה ולרוב המרוצה אמר שוטף שהוא כמו נחל שוטף במרוצתי במלחמה וי"ת הקשבתי מאמר האל יתברך אציתית וגלי קדמי: (ז) גם חסידה. אפילו העופות שאין להם שכל בכח הדכיון שיש להם יש להם ידיעה להתרחק מן הנזק ולהתקרב אל הטוב ושומרים מנהגם וכח שגדלו עליו ועמי שיש להם שכל לא ידעו את משפט ה' שהיה להם לדעת מן השכל גם לשמרו לפי כח שהנהיגו אותם מורי התורה ומה שנחלו בו מן אבותם דור אחר דור ואמר להם ירמיהו זה כדרך שאמר ישעיהו ידע שור קונהו וחמור אבוס בעליו ועוד זכר חסידה וזכר בשמים לפי שהיא מקננת בישוב במגדלים הגבוהים ובמדבר בעצים הגבוהים כמו שאמר חסידה ברושים ביתה לפיכך אמר בשמים שהוא גובה האויר כמו שאמר גדולות ובצורות בשמים דרך נשר בשמים והחסידה מנהגה לשכון בימי הקור ותחורף במקום אחד ובימי הקיץ והחום במקום אחר וזהו מועדיה שאמר ולא תשנה מנהגה ועמי משנים משפט ה' שידעוהו בשכל אם ירצו וגדלו עליו אבותיהם והם אינם רוצים להחזיק בו: ותור וסוס ועגור. גם כן שמרו את עת באנה במקום אחד בזמן ידוע ובזמן אחר במקום ידוע לפי השתנות התקופות והזמנים ושומרות חקן ומנהגן ולא ישנוהו ולא כן עמי. חסידה פירשו רז"ל זו דיה

מצודת ציון

משובה. ענין מרידה והליכה בדרכי הלב: נצחת. מל' נלח ועולם: החזיקו. ענין אחיזה: בתרמית. ענין מרמה וכן שקר תרמיתם (תהלי' קי"ט): מאנו. מל' מיאון: (ו) הקשבתי. ענין האזנה: נחם. ענין חרטה והפוך מחשבה כמו פן ינחם העם (שמות י"ג): במרוצתם. ענין רדיפה ומהירת ההליכה: שוטף. ענין רדיפה ואמר בלשון שאלה מרדיפת המים: (ז) חסידה. שם עוף מה: מועדיה. ענין זמן כמו למועד אשוב אליך (בראשית י"ח): ותור. שם תורים ידוע: וסום ועגור. גם הם שמות עופות וכן כסוס עגור (ישעיה ל"ח): שמרו. המתינו כמו ואביו שמר את הדבר (בראש'

מצודת דוד

הסר הנסמך העם הזה עם ירושלים ורבים כמוהו: החזיקו. אוחזים במרמה וממאנים לשוב כאלו אין תשובה מועלת: (ו) הקשבתי. אני מקשיב ושומע אשר לא ידברו כן לומר שממאנים לשוב בעבור כי חושבים שאין תשובה מועלת אבל גם עתה אין איש מהם מתחרט על הרעה שעשה לאמר מה עשיתי הלא סכנתי בנפשי: כלה שב. ר"ל לא די שאין מי מתחרט אלא אפי' כלם כאיש אחד שב לרוץ במרוצתם שרצו מאז כמו שהיו רודפים מאז אחר הרעות כן הם רודפים גם עתה: כסום. כמו הסוס הרודף במלחמה כנחל שוטף ועם כי הוא בנפשו כן הם רודפים אחר הרעות עם כי מאבדים נפשם בזה: (ז) גם חסידה בשמים. אפי' עוף החסידה הפשט באויר השמים אשר איננה ברשות אדם הלא תדע זמניה מתי תלך ומתי תשוב כי דרכה לעוף בזמן הקור לארצות החמים ובזמן הקיץ תשוב לארצות הקרים: שמרו. גם המה בלכתם לארצות החמים ממתינים את עת בואם ולא יקדימו ולא יאחרו: ועמי וגו'. ר"ל העופות ההם

Isaiah's reproof: '(Isa. 1:3) An ox knows his owner and a donkey his master's crib.' He mentions the stork in the heavens since in populated areas the stork makes its nest at the tops of lofty towers, and in the forests on the tops of high trees as in Psalms 104:17: 'The stork, the fir-trees are her house.' He, therefore, states, 'in the heaven,' meaning 'in the high atmosphere,' as in Deut. 1:28: cities great and fortified in the

5. Why has this people, Jerusalem, slid back a perpetual back-
sliding? They have held on to deceit, they refuse to repent. 6. I
hearkened and heard, they do not speak properly; no man
regrets his wickedness, saying, "What have I done?" Each one
turns away in his course, as a frightening horse into battle.
7. Even the stork in the heaven knows her seasons, and the
turtledoves and the crane and the swallow await

5. **Why has this people slid back**—Heb. שׁוֹבְבָה, the feminine form, referring to כְּנֶסֶת, the people.—[*Redak*]

this people, Jerusalem—*Jonathan* renders: this people, the inhabitants of Jerusalem. *Redak* renders: this people, the people of Jerusalem.

a perpetual backsliding—Heb. מְשֻׁבָה נִצַּחַת, *a perpetual backsliding, like* נֶצַח, *perpetual.*—[*Rashi*]

They have held—Heb. הֶחֱזִיקוּ.—[*Rashi*]

to deceit—Heb. בַּתַּרְמִית.—[*Rashi*]

they refuse to repent—It is as though they wish to hold onto deceit forever and not to repent.—[*Redak*]

This nation is like an adulterous woman who plays the harlot. When her husband seeks to bring her back to the proper way, she turns her shoulder to him.—[*Kara*]

6. **I hearkened and heard**—When I go among the people, I hearken to hear whether any of them speaks properly.—[*Redak*]

not . . . properly—Heb. לֹא כֵן, *not right Cf.* '(Num. 27:7) *The daughters of Zelaphhad speak properly* (כֵּן).'—[*Rashi*]

"What have I done?"—This is the first essential of repentance, for the sinner to realize the evil of his way and to regret his sins.—[*Sha'arei Teshubah* 1:1]

Each one turns away in his course—lit. in their course. *In the first way. They sin and repeatedly sin.* מְרוּצָתָם *is korse in O.F.*—[*Rashi*]

like a frightening—*effaye in French.*—[*Rashi*]

Others render: like a fast running horse. Since he runs so fast, he is compared to a running stream (נַחַל שׁוֹטֵף).—[*Redak*]

Jonathan renders this verse as the words of God: I hearkened, and it is revealed before Me.—[*Redak*]

*7. **Even the stork**—(*Cigogne in French*).—[*Rashi*]

her seasons—*The time they pass to the islands of the sea because of the cold, and the time of their return.*—[*Rashi*]

Even birds who have no intelligence, know by instinct that they must stay away from harm and stay near things that will benefit them. They keep their custom and pursue the way they were raised. Yet, My people, who have intelligence, do not know God's ordinance, which they should have known by their intelligence. They should also have kept it as the teachers of the Torah have led them. This is reminiscent of

* For Rashi's commentary turn to page 224.

עֵת בֹּאָנָה וְעַמִּי לֹא יָדְעוּ אֵת מִשְׁפַּט
יְהוָה׃ ח אֵיכָה תֹאמְרוּ חֲכָמִים אֲנַחְנוּ
וְתוֹרַת יְהוָה אִתָּנוּ אָכֵן הִנֵּה לַשֶּׁקֶר
עָשָׂה עֵט שֶׁקֶר סֹפְרִים׃ ט הֹבִשׁוּ
חֲכָמִים חַתּוּ וַיִּלָּכֵדוּ הִנֵּה בִדְבַר־יְהוָה
מָאָסוּ וְחָכְמַת־מֶה לָהֶם׃ י לָכֵן אֶתֵּן אֶת־
נְשֵׁיהֶם לַאֲחֵרִים שְׂדוֹתֵיהֶם לְיוֹרְשִׁים
כִּי מִקָּטֹן וְעַד־גָּדוֹל כֻּלֹּה בֹּצֵעַ בָּצַע
מִנָּבִיא וְעַד־כֹּהֵן כֻּלֹּה עֹשֶׂה שָּׁקֶר׃

תרגום

וְכוּרְכְיָא וְסנוּנִיתָא נַטְרִין
יַת עִדָן מֵיעַלְהוֹן וְעַמִּי
לָא הֲווֹ יָדְעִין לְמֶעְבַּד
יַת קְיָמָא דַייָ׃ ח אֵיכְדֵין
תֵּימְרוּן חַכִּימִין אֲנַחְנָא
וְעַל אוֹרַיְתָא דַייָ אֲנַחְנָא
רְחִיצִין בְּכֵן הָא לְשִׁקְרָא
עֲבִיד סְפַר קוֹלְמוֹס
דִּשְׁקַר לְזַיָּפָא׃ ט בְּהִיתוּ
חַכִּימַיָּא אִתְּבָרוּ
וְאִתְאֲחִידוּ הָא בְּפִתְגָמָא
דַייָ קְצוּ וְחוּלָק
בְּחוּכְמְתָא לֵית לְהוֹן׃
י בְּכֵן אֶתֵּן יַת נְשֵׁיהוֹן
לְאוֹחֲרָנִין חַקְלָתְהוֹן
לְיָרוֹתִין אֲרֵי מִן זְעֵירָא
וְעַד רַבָּא כּוּלְהוֹן אָנְסִי
מָמוֹן מִסָּפַר וְעַד כָּהֵן

קמץ בז"ק ה' במקום ו' ה' במקום ו'

רש"י

בלע"ז) כנוית (ארונדל"י בלע"ז):(ח) אכן הנה לשקר. הנה חכמתכם לשקר בכם לרפאותכם על נקלה: **עשה עט שקר סופרים.** נביאיכם: (ט) **הובישו חכמים.** כמותכם

מהר"י קרא

(ח) איכה תאמרו חכמים אנחנו ותורת ה'. אנו תופשין. אבל כל נביא ונביא שכתב ספר תוכיחה עלינו: לשקר עשה. ולשוא כתבו. שהרי בתורת ה' אנו הולכין: עט שקר סופרים. הם כל התוכחות הכתובין עלינו: (ט) הובישו חכמים חתו וילכדו וחכמת מה להם. שחכמת התורה אינה אלא להשיב את האדם מדרך הרע ומאחר שאינו שב מדרכו הרעה כה הנאה יש לו מן החכמה שלכד: (י) שדותיהם ליורשים. ליורשיהם

רד"ק

לבנת ולמה נקרא שמה חסידה שעושה חסידות עם חברותיה כלומר במזונות שמחלקה להם ויש מפרשים שהיא שקורין לה ציגוניא: ותור. ידוע: וסוס כתוב. בוי"ו וקרי ביו"ד וכן נמצא כתוב ביו"ד וקרי בוי"ו כסים עגור כן אצפצף ת"י וכורכיא ובדברי רבותינו ז"ל קם ריש לקיש צוח כי כרוכיא ופירש רש"י ז"ל גרוא"ה בלע"ז: ועגור. ת"י וסנוניתא ובדברי רבותינו ז"ל איסת סנונית על הגשר ופירש רבינו האי קטא"ף בערבי והוא הדרור שקורין בלע"ז רונדונ"א ויש מפרשים הוא העוף המצפצף מלות מעטות כלשון בני אדם כשמלמדין אותו גיי"ם בלע"ז: (ח) איכה תאמרו חכמים אנחנו. בחכמות החיצונות ועוד תורת ה' אתנו כלומר אצלנו היא כתובה: אכן הנה לשקר עשה עט. אם תורת ה' אתכם מה תועיל אם לא תקייכו אותה מי שעשה הקולמוס לכתוב אותה לחנם עשה אותו וכן שקר סופרי' הסופרים כתבו אותה לחנם כי אחרי שאין אתם מקיימין אותה הרי היא כאילו אינה כתובה. לשקר. להנם כמו אך לשקר שמרתי: (ט) הובישו. כי שקר עשו כשיראו שלא תועיל להם הכמתם אז בכח יהיה להם בשת פנים ויראו כי אם התעסקו בתורה וקיימו אותה היתה מועילה להם להצילם כהרעות הבאות עליהם ואחר שבדבר ה' מאסו ולא רצו ללמוד התורה ולעשותה מה הכמה להם לא תועיל ההכמה מבלי התורה וחכמת סמוך למלת מה כלומר כה מועיל ממה שיש להם חכמה אם אין להם התורה: (י) לכן אתן. ליורשים. כלומר למי שיחזיקהו בהם בגלות כאילו הם יורשים: כי מקטון ועד גדול. כל זה הענין הוא כתוב למעלה עם שאר הפסוקים הבאים אחר זה במלות שונות כי כל הכופל ענין ישנה במלות לכעלה מקטנם ועד גדולם והנה מקטון ועד גדול למעלה כלו בוי"ו והנה כלה בה"א ואחד הוא:

מצודת דוד

יודעים דרך מנהג העולם ועמי לא ידעו משפט והנהגת המקום ב"ה שמשלם לאיש כמפעלו: (ח) ותורת וגו'. כלה לומר יודעים אנו את התורה: אכן. באמת הנה לחנם עשה העושה את הקולמוס לכתוב ספר תורה ולחנם היו הסופרים שכתבו את התורה הואיל ואינכם מקיימים אותה: (ט) הובישו חכמים. הם המחזיקים עלמם לחכמים הלא יבושו בעת יחתו וילכדו ברעה ולא יצילו נפש' בחכמתם: וחכמת מה להם. ר"ל מה היא החכמה שבידם הלא בחכמת התורה מאסו ואף לא יוכלו להציל נפשם בחכמה א"כ במה יתפארו: (י) לאחרים. לעם אחר: ליורשים. כל מי מהעכו"ם שירצה לרשת: כלה בוצע בצע. כלם גוזלים הון: מנביא. נביא השקר: כהן. כהן הבעל:

מצודת ציון

ל"ז): (ח) איכה. כמו איך: לשקר. על חנם: עט. קולמוס כמו עט סופר מהיר (תהלים מ"ה): (ט) הובישו. מלשון בושה: חתו. ענין שבר ופחד: (י) בוצע בצע. גוזל הון:

that their wisdom will be of no avail to them. Then they will be ashamed and realize that if they had occupied themselves with the study of the Torah and the observance of its commandments, it would help extricate them from their distress. Now, however, since they rejected the word of the Lord and did not wish to learn the Torah and observe its commandments, their wisdom will be of no avail to them.—[*Redak*]

10. **to others**—I.e. to another people.—[*Mezudath David*]

their fields to those who possess them—When they go in exile, others

the time of their coming, but My people do not know the ordinance of the Lord. 8. How do you say, "We are wise, and the Law of the Lord is with us"? Verily, behold it is in vain, he made a false scribes' pen. 9. Wise men were ashamed, they were broken and caught; behold they rejected the word of the Lord, now what wisdom have they? 10. Therefore, I will give their wives to others, their fields to those who possess them for from the smallest to the greatest, they all commit robbery, from prophet to priest, they all deal falsely.

heavens.' Also, '(Prov. 30:19) The way of the eagle in the heavens.' The stork is a migratory bird, that sojourns in the winter in one place and in the summer in another. That is the meaning of 'her seasons.' She does not change her habits, but My people change God's ordinance, which they know through their intelligence and which they know through the tradition they received from their parents.—[*Redak*]

8. **How do you say, "We are wise, and the Law of the Lord is with us"?**—How do you say, "We are erudite in secular knowledge and the Lord's Torah is written with us"?—[*Redak*]

Verily, behold it is in vain—*Behold your wisdom is in vain within you to heal you lightly.*—[*Rashi*]

he made a false scribes' pen—I.e. *your prophet.*—[*Rashi*]

Rashi explains that the people claim to be wise and to possess God's Torah. To this, the prophet retorts that the wisdom is of no use; it but heals their woes lightly, and that the Torah they claim to possess is forged by their prophet.

Redak explains that the prophet retorts: Verily, behold in vain he made a pen, also the scribes are in vain. You claim to have the Torah. The truth is that the one who made the pen did so in vain. Also, the scribes who wrote the Torah did so in vain. Since you do not keep the Torah, it is as though it was not written, and its writing is of no use.

Kara explains that the entire verse is the statement of the people. How do you say, "We are wise, and the instruction of the Lord is with us. Verily, behold he dealt falsely, the pen of the scribes is false"? The people claim that they are wise and that they keep the Torah. They claim that every prophet who wrote reproof against them dealt falsely, and that the pen of the scribes that wrote against them is false. The prophet questions how they can make such a statement.

9. **Wise men were ashamed**—I.e. wise men *like you. And what is the shame? Behold, they rejected the word of the Lord, now what wisdom have they?*—[*Rashi*]

They are ashamed when they see

יא וַיְרַפּוּ אֶת־שֶׁבֶר בַּת־עַמִּי עַל־נְקַלָּה
לֵאמֹר שָׁלוֹם ׀ שָׁלוֹם וְאֵין שָׁלוֹם׃
יב הֹבִשׁוּ כִּי תוֹעֵבָה עָשׂוּ גַּם־בּוֹשׁ לֹא־
יֵבֹשׁוּ וְהִכָּלֵם לֹא יָדָעוּ לָכֵן יִפְּלוּ
בַנֹּפְלִים בְּעֵת פְּקֻדָּתָם יִכָּשְׁלוּ אָמַר
יְהוָה׃ יג אָסֹף אֲסִיפֵם נְאֻם־יְהוָה אֵין
עֲנָבִים בַּגֶּפֶן וְאֵין תְּאֵנִים בַּתְּאֵנָה

ת״א אסף אסיפם. מגילה ד׳ לא: — חסר א׳ קמץ בז״ק

תרגום

כולהון עבדי שקר׃
יא ואסיאו ית תבר
כנשתא דעמי בסלי
שקריהון למימר שלמא
שלמא ולית שלם׃
יב עליהון למבהת ארי
תועבה עבדו אף מבהת
לית אינון בהתין
ואתכנעו לית אינון
ידעין בכן יתרמון
קטילין בעדן דאסער
עליהון חוביהון יתקלון
אמר יי׃ יג שיצאה
אשיצינון אמר יי
ויסופון כמיסף ענבין
מגפן וכנבלא מתינא וכטרף מאילן על דיהבית להון אוריתי מסיני ועברו עלה׃

מהר״י קרא

לא נאמר שגם בניהם ימותו אבל נכרים יקחו שדותיהם וירשום : (יג) אסף אסיפם נאום ה׳ אין ענבים בגפן. כל כך שאפילו הטובים לא ישארו בישראל וישראל נקראו גפן שנאמר גפן ממצרים תסיע והוא הדין : ואין תאנים בתאנה. וישראל נקראו האינה שנאמר כביכורה בתאינה בראשיתה ראיתי אבותיכם : והעלה נבל. וכל שכן שהרשעים יבולו כלומר ימותו כל כך לא יותר דבר: והעלה נבל. לשון כמש (פלייסטי״ש בלע״ז)

רש״י

ומה הבוש׳ הנה כדברי ה׳ מאסו וחכמת מה להם: (יא) וירפו. כמו וירפאו : (יב) הובישו . בושת וכלימה תבוא להם : גם בוש לא יבושו. אינם מתביישים במעשיהם הרעים לתת לב לשוב : (יג) אסוף אסיפם . לשון כלייה כמו אסוף אסף כל מעל פני האדמה (צפניה א׳) : אין ענבים בגפן. כמו וכנובלת מתאנה (ישעי׳ לד) כאלה נובלת עליה (שם א׳) :

מנחת שי

(יב) הבשו כי תועבה . בספרים מדוייקים חסר וא״ו וחסר יו״ד כתברו שלמעלה הבשו חכמים ונמסר עליהם ב׳ חסר דחסר : לא יבשו . חסר וא״ו אחר הבי״ת

רד״ק

(יא) וירפו . למעלה וירפאו באל״ף נעה והנה וירפו בבעלי הה״א והענין אחד ענין רפואה למעלה את שבר עמי והנה את שבר בת עמי : (יב) הובישו . פירשנוהו למעלה כי פירושו בתמיה . למעלה גם הכלים והנה הכלם כבנין נפעל ומפורש הוא והכלים שהוא מבנין הפעיל פירש למעלה עם שאר הפסוקים ולמעלה בעת פקדתיכ פירשנו פקדתי אותם והנה בעת פקדתם שם והענין אחד : (יג) אסף אסיפם נאם ה׳ . שניהם לשון כליון אסף מקור כן ואספת נפשך ונפש ביהך אסיפם מן יחדו יסופו אלא שמלת אסיפם מבנין הפעיל והוא יוצא ויסופו מבנין הקל והוא עומד הכל יכלה עד שלא ימצאו ענבים בגפן ולא תאנים בתאנה וזכר אלו שני המינים כי הם עיקר הפירות ואותם שירבה אדם מהם יותר משאר הפירות כמו שאמר בברכה איש תחת גפנו ותחת תאנתו ואמר בקללה יאכל גפנך ותאנתך : והעלה נבל . אפילו העלה יבול טרם זמנו כדי להרבות רעתם : ואתן להם יעברום . מה שנתתי להם רוב הפירות וברכתי פרי אדמתם יעברו מהם שיאכלום האויבים מ״ם יעברום במקום מהם וכן חוקתני ותוכל הזקת מטני תמלאמו נפשי תמלא מהם בני יצאוני יצאו ממני והמפרשים פירשו בעבור שנתתי להם תורה ומצוה ועברו עליהם בעונש זה אסיפם וכן דעת יונתן והתרגם

מצודת ציון

(יא) וירפו. מל׳ רפואה: בת עמי. עדת עמי: על. כמו עם : נקלה. מלשון קלון ובזיון : (יב) תועבה. דבר איסור וגנאי: והכלם. מלשון כלימה : פקדתם. ענין זכרון : (יג) אסף אסיפם . ענין כליה כמו אסף אדם ובהמה (צפניה א׳) : נבל ענין כמישה כמו ועלהו לא

מצודת דוד

(יא) וירפו . הם מרפאים את שבר בת עמי ורעתם שעתידה לבא ר״ל הם מוציאים מלבם דאגת הרעה הבאה : על נקלה עם אמירה נקלה ומבוזה לאמר שלום תהיה ולא תבא הרעה ובזה כמה מרפאים שברם אבל לא יהיה שלום והמה מכחשים : (יב) הובישו . ר״ל עכ״פ היה להם להנביאים והכהנים להיות נכלמים כאשר עשו דבר התועבה כדרך החטאים אשר יכלמו אם בא לידם דבר תועבה במקרה : גם בוש וגו׳ . ר״ל עשו התועבה וגם לא יבושו בעבורה : והכלם וגו׳ . אינם יודעים מה היא כלימה וכפל הדבר במ״ש : לכן יפלו . הנביאים והכהנים ההם יפלו בעת יפלו כל הנופלים ע״י האויבים : בעת פקידתם . בעת שאזכור עליהם עונם להפרע מהם והוא בזמן המורכן אז יכשלו גם המה : (יג) אסף אסיפם . אכלה אותם מן העולם : אין ענבים בגפן . כאילו הגפן לא ישאר ענבים ר״ל לא יותר דבר : בתאנה . כאילו תאנה : והעלה נבל . גם העלים יכמשו

11. And they healed the breach of My people easily, saying, "Peace, peace," but there is no peace. 12. They shall be put to shame since they have committed abomination. Neither are they ashamed nor do they know to feel disgrace. They will, therefore, fall among the slain; at the time I have visited upon them, they will stumble, says the Lord. 13. I will utterly consume them, says the Lord. There shall be no grapes on the vine, nor figs on the fig tree;

will take possession of their fields as though they were the rightful heirs.—[*Redak*]

11. **And they healed**—Heb. וַיְרַפּוּ, *similar to* וַיְרַפְּאוּ.—[*Rashi*] Indeed, that is the reading above 6:14. There it is conjugated as a verb ending with 'aleph,' and here it is conjugated as a verb ending with 'he.'—[*Redak*]

12. **They shall be put to shame**—*Shame and embarrassment shall come upon them.*—[*Rashi*]

Neither are they ashamed—*They are not ashamed of their evil deeds to take heart to repent.*—[*Rashi*]

Redak explains this verse as a question: Were they ashamed since they committed abomination? Neither were they ashamed nor did they know to feel disgrace.

13. **I will utterly consume them**—*This is an expression of destruction. Comp.* '(Zeph. 1:2) *I will utterly consume* (אָסֹף אָסֵף) *everything from upon the face of the earth.*'—[*Rashi*]

There shall be no grapes on the vine—*Nothing will be left over.*—[*Rashi*]

I.e., I will utterly destroy them to the extent that there will be no grapes on the vine nor any figs on the fig tree. He mentions these fruits in particular since they were the major fruits, and most people accumulated large quantities of them, more than of other fruits. Compare the expression, 'each man under his

והעלה נבל ואתן להם יעברום: יד על־
מה אנחנו ישבים האספו ונבוא אל־
ערי המבצר ונדמה־שם כי יהוה
אלהינו הדמנו וישקנו מי־ראש כי
חטאנו ליהוה: טו קוה לשלום ואין
טוב לעת מרפה והנה בעתה: טז מדן
נשמע נחרת סוסיו מקול מצהלות
אביריו רעשה כל־הארץ ויבואו

יד על מה אנחנא יתבין
אתכנשו וניעול לקרוין
כריכן ונשתוק תמן ארי
יי אלהנא איתי עלנא
תבר ואבהתנא ואשקנא
כס דלוט ביש כרישי
חיון ארי חבנא קדם יי:
טו סוברנא לשלם ולית
טב ולעדן סליחות חובין
והא פורענות חטאין:
טז על די פלחו לעגלא
דבדן מלך במשריתיה
יסק עליהון ויגלי יתהון
כקל פסיעות גברוהי
יזועון כל יתבי ארעא

ת"א מדן נשמע. סנהדרין יא לו:

ה' במקום א'

רש"י

ואתן להם יעברום. כל זאת תהיה להם על כי נתתי להם חוקים ועברו עליהם: (יד) ונדמה שם. ונדום שם נשב שם דומים ואבלים: מי ראש. כס דלווט כיש כרישי חיון ראש פתניס הוא חרס שבשיניו: (טז) מדן נשמע. על דפלחו לעגלא דבדן: נחרת סוסיו. עטישות נחיריו: מצהלות אביריו. צהלות משחק סוסיו ומלינו במקום אחר

מהר"י קרא

מפני: ואתן להם יעברום. כלומר מפני שנתתי להם תורתי ומצותי והם עברו עליהם: (יד) ונדמה שם. ת"י ונשתוק תמן כאלם שאין לו פתחון פה: כי ה' אלהינו הדימנו. השתיקנו פ"א אם אנו אומרים על מה אנחנו יושבים האספו ונבוא אל ערי המבצר גם שם לא נמלט אלא נדמה שם. כמו הדמין תתעבדון: כי ה' אלהינו הדימני. שיברנו: וישקנו מי ראש. ת"י כס דילווט ביש כרישי חיון: (טז) מדן. שהוא תחילת ארץ ישראל נשמע נחרת סוסיו: מקול מצהליו אביריו. גם

רד"ק

הפסוק כן שיצאה אשצינון אמר ה' וגו' כבעמוד: (יד) על מה אנחנו יושבים, בכפרים ובערי המישור כבפוחים ועל מה עזר יש לנו: ונדמה. ענין שתיקה כלומר אין לנו להתלונן ולהתרעם על מה באה עלינו הצרה כי ה' אלהינו הדימנו כי חטאנו לו ונדמה שרשו דמה והוא מן הקל ממשקל ישם וישרק מה אקוב ידמו כאבן. ולדעת אדוני אבי ז"ל שרשו נדמה הדמינו שרשו דמם מבנין הפעיל והה"א בשוא ופתח ויהיה ענין שתיקה כלומר הוא השתיקנו שאין לנו רשות להתלונן כי חטאנו לו ואיך נעיז פנינו לנגדו או יהיה ענין כריתה כמו ידמו לשאול ונדמו נאות השלום: וישקנו מי ראש. סם המות מסחיטת עשב לפיכך אמר כי ועניינו כתרגומו ואשקנא כס דלוט ביש כרישי חיון והפסוק מאמר הנביא בלשון ישראל: (טו) קוה לשלום. מקור כלומר ואם נקוה לשלום כהאויב ואין טוב ואיננו השלום שהוא טוב: לעת מרפה. בה"א כמו באל"ף אם קוינו לעת רפואה ממכאוב הצרות: והנה בעתה. צרות גדולות שמכאיבים ושמכעיסים אותנו וי"ת ולעידן סליחות חובין והא פורענות חטאין כענין רפאה נפשי כי חטאתי לך: (טז) מדן נשמע. לפי שהיה קצה ארץ ישראל זכרו וי"ת על דפלחו לעגלא די בדן מלך במשריתיה יסק עליהון ויגלה יתהון: נחרת סוסיו. עטישת סוסיו ונקראת העטישה כן על שם הנחירים שהם נקבי האף: מקול מצהלות אביריו. על הסוסים אמר אביריו ומצהלות ענין השמעת קול הסוסים בצהלות ושמחה כמו שנאמר על הסוס וישיש בכח וי"ת

מנחת שי

בספרים מדוייקים: (יד) מי ראש. באל"ף ובכתיבים עם פירוש הרי"א וגם בס"א כ"י כתוב ר"ש בוא"ו ושעותא הוא דלא אשתכח בוא"ו רק מנכמו מנכי רוש בלחוד דהאזינו: (טו) קוה לשלום וגו'. עיין מה שאכתוב בסימן י"ד בפסוק הדומה לזה: (טז) מדן נשמע נחרת. בס"ס הנו"ן בלא מאריך והחי"ם

מצודת דוד

ור"ל לא ישאר שארית מה: ואתן להם יעברום. אזמין להם אויבים אשר יעברו אותם מן העולם: (יד) על מה וגו'. כשיבא האויב יאמרו יושבי השדות על מה אנחנו יושבים בשדות להיות נמסרים ביד האויב הבא: ונדמה שם. כאומר אבל קרוב הדבר שגם בערי המבצר נהיה נכרתים ואנו מודים כי ה' הכרית אותנו ואין עלה נגד גזרת המקום: וישקנו. הוא השקה אותנו מים המסמים מעשב מר ר"ל המקום הכין לנו פורעניות ולא על חנם כי באמת חטאנו לה' ונגמל הרע: (טו) קוה לשלום. הם יקוו לשלום ולא יהיה טוב כי לא יבא השלום: לעת מרפא. יקוו לעת מרפא והנה בא בעתה ורעד: (טז) מדן. כאשר יהיה האויב בדן בקצה גבול ארץ ישראל יהיה נשמע נחרת סוסיו: מקול מצהלות. מהרמת קול גבוריו

מצודת ציון

יבול (תהלים א'): יעברום. ענין העברה מן העולם: (יד) ונדמה. הדמנו. ענין כריתה כמו אל תדמו בנפשך (לקמן כ"א): ראש. שם עשב מר וכן שורש פורה ראש ולענה (דברים כ"ט): (טו) מרפא. מל' רפואה ושם הוא בה"א: בעתה. מל' בעת ופחד: (טז) נחרת. הקול היוצא מנחיריו הם נקבי האף וכן הוד נחרו אימה (איוב ל"ט): מצהלות. ענין הרמת קול גדול כמו אל אשת רעהו יצהלו (לעיל

good came—The peace, which is good, did not come.—[*Redak*]

for a time of healing—If we hoped for a time of healing of the pains of our distress.—[*Redak*]

but behold, terror—Grave troubles that cause us pain and anger. *Jonathan* renders: And [we hope] for the forgiveness of sins, but there is retribution for sins. This is similar to '(Psalms 41:5) Heal my soul for I have sinned against You.'—[*Redak*]

*16. **From Dan is heard**—*Because they worshipped the calf that was in Dan.*—[*Rashi* from *Targum Jonathan*] I.e. because they worshipped . . . the king with his camp will

* For Rashi's commentary turn to page 225.

even the leaves will be withered, for what I gave them they transgressed. 14. Why do we sit still? Gather together, and let us go to the fortified cities, and there let us sit in silence, for the Lord our God has silenced us, and has given us poisoned water to drink because we have sinned against the Lord. 15. We hoped for peace, but no good came; for a time of healing, but behold, terror. 16. From Dan is heard the snorting of their horses, at the sound of the neighing of their stallions the whole land quakes; they come

vine and each man under his fig tree.'—[*Redak*]

even the leaves will be withered—Heb. נָבֵל, *an expression of withering* (*fletrit in French*). *Comp.* '(Isa. 34:4) *and as a withered fig* (וּכְנֹבֶלֶת) *from a fig tree.' Also,* '(ibid 1:30) *like an elm whose leaves are wilting* (נֹבֶלֶת).'—[*Rashi*]

Even the leaves will wither before their time. This will be to increase the evil that will befall them.—[*Redak*]

for what I gave them they transgressed—*All this shall befall them because I gave them statutes and they transgressed them.—[Rashi*]

This follows *Jonathan. Redak,* however, renders: and what I gave them shall pass away from them. I.e., all the produce that I gave them and that I blessed them with will pass away from them; the enemies will devour them.

Malbim explains that the prophet puts his words into the mouths of different speakers. He debates with the people, and God enters the conversation. God says: (אָסֹף) I will cause them to gather, to take counsel, and the purpose will be (אֲסִיפֵם) to utterly consume them.

The people reply: There are no grapes on the vine, and there are no figs on the fig tree. There is no food with which to refresh ourselves.

God replies: For what I gave them they transgressed. How can I give them grapes and figs? They transgressed what I gave them, viz. the Torah and the commandments.

14. **Why do we sit still?**—I.e., why do we sit still in the villages and in the towns of the plains as though we were secure? What help have we?—[*Redak*]

and there let us sit in silence—*And let us be silent there. Let us sit there silent and mournful.*—[*Rashi*]

Redak explains: Let us be silent; i.e., we have no right to complain to God for the trouble that has come upon us, for the Lord our God has silenced us, i.e. He has not given us the right to complain, and he has given us poisoned water because we have sinned against the Lord.—[*Redak*]

Others render: and there let us meet our doom! For the Lord our God has doomed us (to death) because we have sinned against the Lord.—[*Rabbi Joseph Kimchi*]

15. **We hoped for peace, but no**

ויאכלו ארץ ומלואה עיר וישבי בה׃
יז כי הנני משלח בכם נחשים צפענים
אשר אין־להם לחש ונשכו אתכם
נאם־יהוה׃ יח מבליגיתי עלי יגון עלי
לבי דוי׃ יט הנה־קול שועת בת־עמי
מארץ מרחקים היהוה אין בציון אם־
מלכה אין בה מדוע הכעסוני

תרגום

ייתון ויבזון ארעא
ומלואה קרוא ודיתבין
בהון׃ יז ארי הא
אנא מגרי בכון עממין
קטולין כחיון חורמנין
דלית להון לחשא
ויקטלון יתכון אמר יי׃
יח על דהוו מלעיגין
לקבל נביא דמתנבן
להון דנא והיתאתא
איתי עליהון מן קדם
חוביהון עליהון אמר
נביא לבי דוי׃ יט הא
קל צוחת כנשתא דעמי
מארעא רחיקא נביא אובח יתהון השכינתא דיי לית בציון אם מלכא לית בה מא דין מרגזין

מהר"י קרא — ב' טעמים

הוא קול שאון: (יז) כי הנני משלח בכם נחשים צפעונים אשר אין להם לחש. ת"י עמבין קטולין כחויין חורמנין דלית להון לחישא שאין לחישת האדם מועיל להם שכשהנחש מזקין תעשה צפעוני אוטם אזנו שלא ישמע לחישת בני אדם וכן כת' וכפתן חרש יאטם אזנו: (יח) מבליגיתי. לשון חוזק ותיבה אחת היא כמו המבליג שוד על עז ופתרונו כשאני בא לחזק את עצמי על יגון אין לבי נותן להבליג את עצמי עליו מפני שעלי: לבי דוי. על שאני שומע: (יט) קול שועת בת עמי מארץ מרחקים. ומתרעמין על מדותיו של הקב"ה ואומרים הה' אין בציון אם

רש"י

סוסים נקראים אבירים מדהרות דהרות אביריו (שופטים ה) לשון סוס דוהר (נחום ג) ויונתן תרגם מקל פסיעות גברוהי: (יז) נחשים צפעונים. לסוף שבעים שנה נעשה אפע ואוטם אזנו שלא ישמע לקול חבר המלחש שנאמר כמו פתן חרש יאטם אזנו (תהלים נ"ח) היא שנא' אשר אין להם לחש: (יח) מבליגיתי עלי יגון. כמו הבלגתי ושם דבר הוא(מישאיטיגמנ"ך בלע"ז)כלו' אם אמרתי אבליגה ואתאפק על יגוני: עלי לבי דוי. מקול נבואות הנגלות אלי בפורעניו' הבאות: (יט) הנה קול שועת בת עמי. אני שומע שסופן לצעוק בארץ מרחקי' ולמה כל זאת הלא ה' בציון ואם

מנחת שי

בזוא לבדו וכמוהו קוד נהרו אימה (איוב ל"ט): (יט) מרחקים. המ"ם בפתח וכן תראינה ארץ מרחקים (ישעיה ל"ג): היהוה. האל"ף נחה וכן במסורת כל לשון אדנות עם מא"ה מפיח בר מן חד הה' אין בציון מכלול דף נ':

רד"ק

מקל פסיעות גברוהי: (יז) כי הנני משלח בכם. פירוש כתרגומו הא אנא מגרי בכון עממין קטולין כחיון חורמנין דלית להון לחישא ויקטלון יתכון אמר ה': (יח) מבליגיתי עלי יגון. ענין התחזקות כמו ואבליגה מעט ורבי יונה פירש המלה הזאת מורכבת מפועל ופועלת כי מהפועל אומר מבליגי ומהפועלת מבליגיתי והורכבה המלה משניהם ופי' אמר הנביא אנשים ונשים המחזקים אותי עלי יגון אומר להם שלא אוכל להתחזק כי עלי לבי דוי ור' אחי רבי משה פירש המלה שם מבליגית בשקל מרבית שהיה בתשלומו מרביתי ובמשקלו מבליגיתי אמר הנביא התחזקי על יגון כלומר שארצה להתחזק על יגוני לא אוכל כי עלי לבי דוי ומה שאמר עלי לבי דוי על צרתי בוסף על צרת ישראל שאני מוכיחם ולא ישמעו לי וזהו שאמר עלי: (יט) הנה קול שועת בת עמי בארץ מרחקים. צועקים מפחד האויב הבא מארץ מרחקים ואומרים השם אין בציון אם מלכה אין בה אם כן איך יבא עלינו הלא ה' שכינתו בציון ומלך יש בציון וא"ך ישלוט בה האויב והאל משיבה מדוע הכעיסוני איך יחשבו להנצל בהיותי בציון והם הכעיסוני בפסיליהם בהבלי נכר רוצה לומר בהבלי אל נכר. מרחקים. המ"ם בפתח: הי"י. האל"ף נחה וי"ת השם אין בציון נבייא אוכח יתהון וגו'

מצודת ציון

ה'): אביריו. מלשון אביר וחזק: (יז) משלח. ענין גרוי והשסה כמו ושן בהמות אשלח בם (דברים ל"ב): צפעונים. מין נחש רע: ונשכו. מלשון נשיכה וכן אם ישוך הנחש בלא לחש (קהלת י'): (יח) מבליגיתי. ענין התחזקות כמו ואבליגה מעט (איוב י'): דוי. מלשון מדוה וחולי: (יט) שועת. צעקת:

מצודת דוד

רעשה כל הארץ: ומלואה. הדברים שבארץ מלאה מהם: עיר. יאכלו כל עיר והיושבים בה: (יז) משלח בכם. אגרה בכם נחשים רעים אשר אין מועיל להם לחש והם ישכו אתכם ר"ל לא תוכלו לגלות את האויב בדברים רכים ותחנונים: (יח) מבליגיתי. ר"ל אם אמרתי אתחזק על היגון לבל אתמיד בה אבל לא אוכל כי עלי לבי דוי: (יט) הנה קול. ר"ל איך לא ידוה לבי הלא הגליות בעיני כאלו כבר נעשה וכאלו אני שומע קול צעקת בת עמי מארץ מרחקים אשר הלכו שם בגלות והלא בידם היה לתקן הדבר כי האם אין ה' בציון

from a distant land, and they say, "Is the Lord not in Zion? Is not her King therein? If so, how can he come upon us? Is not God's Presence in Zion, and is He not the King there? How, then, can the enemy rule over it?" God replies: "Why have they provoked Me with their graven images, with their strange vanities?"

and devour the land and its produce, the city and those that dwell therein. 17. For behold, I am sending you serpents, adders which cannot be charmed, and they shall bite you, says the Lord. 18. Were I to suppress my grief, my heart is sick within me. 19. Hark the voice from a distant land, the cry of the daughter of My people; is the Lord not in Zion? Is not her King therein? Why have they provoked Me

ascend upon them and exile them. —[*Targum Jonathan,* quoted by *Redak*]

The simple explanation is that from Dan, the border of Eretz Israel, is already heard the snorting of the enemies' horses.—[*Redak. Kara*]

17. **serpents, adders**—*After seventy years, the snake becomes a* צֶפַע, *which shuts its ear so that it will not hear the voice of the charmer who charms him, as it is stated:* '(Psalms 58:5) *Like a deaf asp that shuts up its ear.' That is the meaning of 'that cannot be charmed.'*—[*Rashi*]

Jonathan paraphrases it as figurative of the nations that will attack them: For behold, I incite against you peoples that kill like destructive serpents that cannot be charmed, and they will kill you, says the Lord.—[*Redak*] These enemies cannot be appeased.—[*Mezudath David*]

Malbim explains this verse as God's reply to the people: What you think that Dan is like a serpent is now the very opposite; I send adders against you, which are worse than serpents, and they will bite you yourselves, not your horses.

18. **Were I to suppress my grief**—Heb. מַבְלִיגִיתִי, *my suppression, and it is a noun,* (*mes estenimenc in O.F.*). *That is to say, if I said, "I will suppress and keep in my grief.*—[*Rashi*]

my heart is sick within me—*From the voice of the prophecies that are revealed to me of the coming retributions.*—[*Rashi*]

Rabbi Jonah explains מַבְלִיגִיתִי as a combination of masculine and feminine. The meaning is: Those men and women who seek to strengthen me—I say to them that I cannot be strengthened for my heart is sick within me.—[*Redak* from *Sepher Haschoraschim*]

Others explain: Were I to suppress my grief, I would be unable, for upon me my heart is sick. I.e., in addition to the troubles of the people, my heart is sick with my own troubles, that I reprove the people and they do not heed my reproof.—[*R. Moses Kimchi,* quoted by *Kara*]

19. **Hark the voice . . . the cry of the daughter of My people**—*I hear that eventually they will cry from a distant land, but why is all this necessary? Is not the Lord in Zion? If they return to Him, He will allow Himself to be found by them.*—[*Rashi*]

Redak explains that they cry from the fear of the enemy who comes

בפסליהם בהבלי נכר: כ עבר קציר
כלה קיץ ואנחנו לוא נושענו: כא על־
שבר בת־עמי השברתי קדרתי
שמה החזקתני: כב הצרי אין בגלעד
אם־רפא אין שם כי מדוע לא עלתה
ארכת בת־עמי: כג מי־יתן ראשי מים

ת"א הצרי אין בגלעד. תענית ח ד: פתח באתנח ועיני

קדמי בצלמניהון
בפולחן טעותא:
כ אמרת כנשתא
דישראל עדא זמנא
שלים קבא ואנחנא לא
מתפרקין: כא אמרית
ירושלם על תבר
כנשתא דעמי אזדעזעית
אתחפיאו אפי אכרום
אוכמין כקדרא
אשתממו אחדתני:
כב אמר ירמיה נביא
דלמא לא אית בי
עובדין טבין למבעי על בית ישראל הלא מחמיד הויתי לאולפניה דאליה נביא דמגלעד
דפתגמוהי אינון אסותא ארי על דלא תבו בכן לא סליקת אסו למחת כנשתא דעמי: כג מי

רש"י

ישובו אליו ימלא להם: (כ) עבר קציר כלה קיץ. קוינו לעזרת מצרים ולא כאשר אמרנו יעבור הקציר ויהיו פנויין ויבואו והנה עבר זמן הקציר באייר וזמן הקיץ בתמוז ולא באו: (כא) קדרתי. לשון שחרות ואופל: שמה. תמהון: החזיקתני. אחזתני: (כב) הצרי אין בגלעד. שהצרי בא משם כמו שנאמר עלי גלעד וקחי צרי (לקמן מ"ו) כלומר וכי לא היו להם אנשים צדיקים ממי ללמוד וייטיבו דרכיהם: ארוכת. רפואה (איינפלאשטר"א בלע"ז):

מהר"י קרא

מלכה אין בה והקב"ה עתיד להשיב כנגדן: מדוע הכעיסוני. בפסלים בהבלי נכר: (כ) עבר קציר כלה קיץ. כל זה עתיד להתרעם בגלות ולומר עברו עיתים רחוקות ואנחנו לא נושענו: (כא) שמה. שממה: (כב) הצרי אין בגלעד אם רופא אין שם. משל ודימוי הוא שדימה הנביא לסבות אליו מליצת הדבר וכן עלה בדעתו לומר שנודע שבעולם במקום שיש סממני רפואה ואין שם רופא מה הנאה יש לאנשי המקום שסמנין יש שם הואיל ואין שם רופא או אפילו יש שם רופא ואין שם צרי וסממני רפואה מה מועיל לאנשי המקום שיש שם רופא אומן מאחר שאין שם סמני רפואה אבל בגלעד שצרי מצוי שם שמועיל לרפואה כענין שנא' והנה ארחת ישמעאלים באה מגלעד וגמליהם נשאים נכאת וצרי ולוט וגם רופאים מצוין שם הרופאים הולכין אחריהם ועתה במקום שיש שם רופא וגם סממני רפואה כמו בגלעד שמצוי שם רופא וצרי אם חולים מתים שם מחמת חוליים יש לתמוה בדבר מדוע לא עלתה ארוכתם הלא צרי ורופא מצויין שם אף כאן יש לתמוה על בת עמי מאחר שהקב"ה מצוי ביניהם והנביאים שמזהירין אותם בכל יום על התשובה והתשובה נמשלת לרפואה בכל מקום. כי מדוע לא עלתה ארוכת בת עמי: (כג) מי יתן ראשי מים. כל זה מן התרעומות

רד"ק

כבעמוד: (כ) עבר קציר. קציר הוא זמן שיושע אדם בו מפני הבצרות ואדם שמח בבא הקציר כמו שכתוב כשמחת בקציר וכן זמן הקיץ אדם שמח בפירות הקיץ ואומר זה דרך משל כלומר עברו הזמנים שחשבנו להושע בהם ולא נושענו: (כא) על שבר. הוא מאמר הנביא על עצמו שהשבר לשבר ישראל ויונתן פירש שהיא מאמר ירושלם שתרגם אמרת ירושלם על תבר כנשתא וגו' כבעמוד ואכרום פי' מן נתכרכמו פניו: (כב) הצרי אין בגלעד. אמר דרך משל אם אין צרי בגלעד אם רופא אין עם לרפאות עמי ממכתו וגלעד היה מקום הצרי כמו שאמר גם כן עלי גלעד וקחי צרי והיא רפואה לחלאים קשים כמו נשיכת הנחש וזולתו כלומר לא יהיה להם שלום מזאת הצרה וכי אין חסיד ביניהם שיכפר האל בעדו: ארוכת. רפואת וי"ת אמר ירמיהו נבייא וגו' כבעמוד: (כג) מי יתן. מי יתן שיהיה ראשי כלי מים ויזוב דרך עיני בבכי וכן תהיה עיני מקור דמעה שלא יפסק: את חללי בת עמי. מי שבוכים עליו נעשה כפעול לבכי ואם לא ישיננו כן דרך לשון העברי

מנחת שי

(כ) לוא נושענו. מלא וא"ו והאל"ף במקצת ספרים כ"י ודפוסים ישנים וכן

מצודת דוד

וגו' ולמה א"כ לא התפללו אליו לבטל הגזרה ומדוע הוסיפו עוד להכעיסני בפסיליהם בהבלי אל נכר הם העכו"ם: (כ) עבר קציר. אמרו אנו לתשועה והיא מתאחרת לבא כי כבר עבר הקציר וכבר כלה זמן הקיץ ועדיין לא נושענו ר"ל זה זמן רב אנו בתוחלת ממושכ': (כא) על שבר. על הפורעניות העתידה לבא השברתי גם אני: קדרתי. השחיר תארי והתמהון אחז אותי: (כב) הצרי אין בגלעד. וכי אין בגלעד צרי לרפאות בו החולי הלא שם הוא מקום הצרי וכי אין שם רופא לדעת אופן הרפואה ומדוע לא נתרפאה בת עמי ר"ל וכי אין בידם תורה ומצות וכי אין להם חכמים להורותם הדרך ומדוע א"כ לא החזירום למוטב לבטל את הגזרה: (כג) מי יתן. הלואי

מצודת ציון

(כ) כלה. מל' כליון: קיץ. הוא עת בשילת התאנים ליבשם וכן כשלג בקיץ (משלי כ"ו): (כא) השברתי. מל' שברון: קדרתי. ענין שחרות וחושך כמו שמש וירח קדרו (יואל ב'): שמה. תמהון ובלבול כמו ונשמו הכהני' (לעיל ד'): החזיקתני. ענין אחיזה: (כב) הצרי. הוא גוף המוזכר בסממני הקטורת והוא שרף אילן והוא מיוחד לרפואה וכן קחו צרי למכאוב (לקמן נ"א): ארוכת. ענין רפואה כמו הנני מעלה לה ארוכה (לקמן ל"ג): (כג) מי יתן. ענינו כמו הלואי וכן מי יתן

where there are both balm and physicians, it is surprising if many sick people die of their ailments. The same applies to my people. Since God is found among them, Who is analogous to the physician, and the prophets admonish them daily to repent—repentance is analogous to balm—why, then, has the spiritual health of my people not been restored?

23. **O that my head were (full of) waters**—O that my head were a vessel full of water which would flow

with their graven images, with their strange vanities? 20. The
harvest is past, the summer is ended; and we are not saved.
21. For the wound of the daughter of my people, I am wound-
ed (with grief); I mourn, (and) dismay has taken hold of me.
22. Is there no balm in Gilead? Is there no physician there?
Why then, has the health of the daughter of my people not been
restored? 23. O that my head were (full of) waters

20. **The harvest is past, the summer is ended**—*We looked forward to the aid of Egypt, but it did not come. We said, "Let the harvest pass, and they will be free, and they will come." Now behold, the time of harvest has passed in Iyar, and the summer season in Tammuz, and they have not come.*—[*Rashi*]

Redak explains that the harvest season is a joyous time when people expect to be saved from hunger, as is the summer season, when people rejoice with the summer fruits. The people say: These joyous times have passed, when we expected to be saved, but we were not saved.

21. **For the wound of the daughter of my people**—Lit. for the breach. For the impending doom destined to come upon my people, I, too, am wounded with grief.—[*Mezudath David*] This follows *Redak,* who explains this as Jeremiah's statement. *Jonathan,* however, paraphrases: Said Jerusalem: For the breach of the congregation of my people, I am startled.

I mourn—Lit. I am darkened, *an expression of blackness and darkness.*—[*Rashi*]

My countenance has become darkened, and dismay has taken hold of me.—[*Mezudath David*] *Jonathan* renders: My face was covered; it became black as a pot.

dismay—Heb. שַׁמָּה, *wonder.*—[*Rashi*]

has taken hold of me—*Has held me.*—[*Rashi*]

22. **Is there no balm in Gilead**—*For balm comes from there, as it is said:* '(infra 46:11) *Go up to Gilead and take balm.' That is to say, "Did they not have any righteous men from whom to learn so that they should improve their ways?"*—[*Rashi*]

Is there no righteous man in whose merit God should forgive them?.—[*Redak*]

the health of—lit. *the cure of,* (*emplâtre in O.F.*), plaster, dressing.—[*Rashi*]

Jonathan paraphrases: Said Jeremiah the prophet, "Have I no good deeds that I should be able to supplicate for the house of Israel? Did I not covet the teachings of Elijah the prophet who was from Gilead, and whose words were a cure? Surely, because they did not repent, there was no cure for the wound of the congregation of my people

Kara explains the symbol of balm and physicians in Gilead. It is known that where there are medicines, but no physician to apply them, the medicines are useless. Likewise, where there are physicians but no medicines, the physicians can accomplish nothing. Where there are both, however, as in Gilead,

וְעֵינִי מְקוֹר דִּמְעָה וְאֶבְכֶּה יוֹמָם וָלַיְלָה
אֵת חַלְלֵי בַת־עַמִּי׃ ט א מִי־יִתְּנֵנִי
בַמִּדְבָּר מְלוֹן אֹרְחִים וְאֶעֶזְבָה אֶת־עַמִּי
וְאֵלְכָה מֵאִתָּם כִּי כֻלָּם מְנָאֲפִים עֲצֶרֶת
בֹּגְדִים׃ ב וַיַּדְרְכוּ אֶת־לְשׁוֹנָם קַשְׁתָּם
שֶׁקֶר וְלֹא לֶאֱמוּנָה גָּבְרוּ בָאָרֶץ כִּי

מרעה

ת"א וידרכו . מקדם שער כב :

תרגום

יְהֵן רֵישִׁי כְּנַחַל דְמִין
וְעֵינַי כְּמַבּוּעָא דִמְעִין
וְאֶבְכֵּי יְמָם וְלֵילֵי עַל
קְטִילֵי כְּנִשְׁתָּא דְעַמִּי :
א מִי יִתְּנִינַנִי בְּמַדְבְּרָא
בֵּית מִבָּתַת עֲדֵי אוֹרְחִין
וְאֶשְׁבּוֹק יַת כְּנִשְׁתָּא
דְעַמִּי וְאֶהַךְ מִלְוָתְהוֹן
אֲרֵי כוּלְּהוֹן נָאֲפִין סִיעַת
שַׁקְרִין : ב וְאַלִּיפוּ יַת
לִישָׁנְהוֹן פִּתְגָמֵי שְׁקַר
דְמַן אִינוּן כְּקַשְׁתָּא
נְכִילָא וְלָא לְהֵימָנוּתָא

רש"י

ט (א) עצרת בוגדים. כנסיות בוגדים: (ב) וידרכו. לשון זה נופל בהזמנת הקשת לירות חץ וקשת היא (ארקוליסט"א בלע"ז) וברגלי' דורכין אותה לכך קורא אותה דריכה והנביא המשיל לשונם לקשת שקר שדרכו לשונם קשת

מהר"י קרא

שישראל עתידין להתרעם בפלותן והקב"ה משיב בו בלשון כנגדן . מי יתנני במדבר מלון אורחים ואעזבה את עמי ואלכה מאתם כי כולם מנאפים.ואני יוסף ב"ר שמעון ראיתי בפתרוני הפותרים הצרי אין בגלעד. שפותרין מקרא זה.על אליהו שהיה מתושבי גלעד וגם על בתו של יפתח ואין הדבר מתיישב על אופניו כלל כל עיקר לפי פשוטו של מקרא שאם כדברי הפותרים שגלעד זה אליהו כשאתה מגיע לפורענות של מצרים על חיל פרעה נכה מלך מצרים שהיה על נהר פרת בכרכמיש שהכה נבוכדנצר מלך בבל בשנה הרביעית ליהויקים בן יאשיה ואתה קורא שם בפרשה עלי גלעד וקחי צרי בתולת בת מצרים לשוא הרבית רפואות תעלה אין לך . ועתה יש להשיב וכי מה טיבה של מצרים לילך אל אליהו שהיה מתושבי גלעד שהוא מקנתר את האומות לעלות אצל אליהו ועוד בשנה הרביעית ליהויקים כבר עברו כמה שנים שנסתלק אליהו בסערה השמים על כן נתתי את לבי ליישב המקראות על יישובן ועל פשוטן :

ט (א) מי יתנני במדבר . אתם צועקים הה' אין בציון אם מלכה אין בה ומתאבלים לומר מי יתן ראשי מים ואני משיב תשובה כנגדכם הלואי מי יתן שלא שיכנתי שמי הציון ביניכם מפני רעתכם שנוח היה לי שהייתי שרוי במדבר ואעזבה את עמי ואלכה מאתם משהייתי שוכן בציון ביניכם ואתם מכעיסין אותי על פני כמו שמפרש והולך : כי כולם מנאפים . וכל העניין וראייה לדברי שמקרא זה תשובה הוא שהקב"ה הוא משיב לישראל . מיסודו של ר' אליעזר הקלירי שייסד בקינתו ופץ כי יתנני במדבר למדת שהקב"ה אמר מקרא זה ולא ירמיה : עצרת בוגדים . קבוצת בוגדים : (ב) כי מרעה אל רעה יצאו . משעושין רעה זו יוצאין לעשות רעה אחרת ואחרי כל רעתם אילו היו שבים אלי עדיין הייתי מקבלם אלא משיצאו מרעה אל רעה אותי לא ידעו : וידרכו . לשון רכילות כמו כל דורך בה לא ידע שלום וכן הדריכני באמיתך כלומר הרגילו לשונם בדברי שקר: וידרכו את לשונם קשתם שקר. לשונם דומה לקשת רמיה אשר יבטח

רד"ק

וכן אמר ויבך אותו אביו וכן ולבכותה וכן נעשה זה תשבוש בלשון אחר וזולתי העברי לפי שבעבורו נעשה הבכי הרי הוא כאילו מקבל הפעולה : (א) מי יתנני . מלון אורחים . במדבר ישבתי. מלון לעוברי אורח שילינו שם בלילה ואמר הנביא שיתאו' להיות שוכן באותו המלון שלא יראה עוד את ישראל כי לא יוכל לראות רעתם : עצרת בוגדים. שהם נעצרים יחד לדבר בגד ושקר וכן ת"י סיעת שקרין ואדוני אבי ז"ל פירש מלות בוגדים כן יורש עצר זה יעצר בעמי : (ב) וידרכו. מבנין הפעיל משפטו וידריכו וכמוהו בא וידבקו גם המה : לשונם. היא קשת דרוכה וחציהם דבר שקר ודבר מר : ולא לאמונה גברו בארץ. מה שהם מתגברים ומתחזקים על ההלשים לא לאמת' שישפטו משפט אמת ושימנעו העושקים : כי מרעה אל רעה יצאו. יש לפרשו על המעשים יוצאים ממעשה רע למעשה רע ר"ל כי כל ימיהם במעשה רע עוסקים עתה בזה ועתה בזה ובכל זה לא נתנו אל לבם שעה אחת לדעת את ה' ויש לפרשו על העונש ברעת אויב זה יוצאים לרעת אויב אחר או לוקים שנה זו בשדפון ושנה זו בירקון או בארבה ועם כל זה לא נתנו

מנחת שי

נפנה במסורת פרשה ויקרא עם ל"ה מלאים בקריאה : (כג) חללי בת עמי. במקצת ספרים הגיהו חללי וכ"כ רד"ק בשרשים והגה הללי חרב בלמ"ד בשוא לבדו. את חללי [illegible] בת עמי הלמ"ד בשוא ופתח והחי"ת מעמדת בגעיה עכ"ל ולפ"ד זהו תלוי במנהג הספרים כמ"ש בריש פרשת לך לך וטעם המלה מירכא :

מצודת דוד

והיה ראשי מלא מי בכי ועיני היה מקור הנובע דמעה והייתי אז בוכה יומם ולילה על חללי בת עמי : ט (א) מי יתנני במדבר. מי יתן לי לאורחי להיות במדבר מקום מלון להולכי אורח : ואעזבה. אז הייתי עוזב את עמי ואלכה מאתם אל מלון המדבר : עצרת. קבוצת אנשים בוגדים : (ב) וידרכו. הזמינו את לשונם שהיא להם לקשת להרוג אנשים ממרחק כמו שדורכין בקשת אותם הזמינו לדבר שקר ולפי שהמשילם לקשת אמר לשון הדרכה הנופל בקשת : ולא לאמונה גברו בארץ. מה שמחזקתן מתגברים על קלתם אין דעתם למען תחזק ידם לעשות אמונה : כי

מצודת ציון

והיה לכבס וגו' (דברים כ') : מקור. מעיין : את חללי בת עמי. על חללי וכן ויתנכלו אותו (בראשית ל"ז) ת"א ואשיכו עלוהי : ט (א) מלון. מקום לנון : אורחים. הולכי אורח : עצרת. קבוצת וכן קראו עצרה (יואל א') : (ב) וידרכו. הדרך לדרוך ברגל

generation and the generation of the desert that made the golden calf and worshipped it. Here, God states that He wishes to take His presence away from Israel because of their sins. The question is why are they different from the generation of the desert, who made the golden calf. The reply is that that generation had four merits: (1) they did not change their names; (2) they did not change their language; (3) they did not commit adultery; and (4) they were not tale-bearers. Jeremiah's generation,

and my eyes a fountain of tears, that I might weep day and night for the slain of the daughter of my people.

9

1. O that I had in the desert a wayfarers' lodging-place, that I might leave my people and go away from them! For they are all adulterers, a company of traitors! 2. They have directed their tongue treacherously (as) their bows, and they have grown strong in the land not for the sake of truth; for

through my eyes as tears, and that my eyes be a fountain of tears that does not run dry.—[*Redak*]

Jonathan paraphrases: O that my head be like a stream of water and my eyes like a flowing fountain.

Kara sees this as the plea of Israel in exile, who will complain to the Almighty. He will reply to them: O that I had in the desert . . . for they are all adulterers, a company of traitors!

1. **O that I had in the desert a wayfarers' lodging-place**—A lodging-place where travelers can stay overnight. The prophet states that he would desire to live in such an inn, so as not to see Israel any longer, for he cannot bear to see their wickedness.—[*Redak*]

a company of traitors—*Companies of traitors.*—[*Rashi*] I.e. people who join together to speak treachery and falsehood. This follows Jonathan. Rabbi Joseph Kimchi, explains: a government of traitors.

Kara interprets this as God's reply to the people. They complain, "Is the Lord not in Zion? Is not her King therein." They mourn, "O that my head were full of water and my eyes a fountain of tears." And I reply, "O that I had not caused My Name to rest in Zion among you, because of your wickedness! It would have been better for Me had I dwelt in the desert and I would leave My people and go away from them, rather than to dwell in Zion among you when you provoke Me," as he continues in the following verses. This follows R. Eleazar Hakalir in *Kinot for the Ninth of Av,* (Not found in our editions. See *Kinot for the Ninth of Av,* p. 94.).

2. **They have directed**—Lit. trodden. *This expression is appropriate for the preparation of the bow to shoot an arrow, and a bow* (קֶשֶׁת) *is* (*arbalete in French*)*, and they tread it with their feet. Therefore, he calls it treading, and the prophet compared their tongue to a treacherous bow, for they directed their tongue like a treacherous bow.*—[*Rashi*]

Redak renders: They prepared their tongue—it is like a trodden bow—and their arrows are words of falsehood and bitterness.

Alshich explains that God wishes to differentiate between Jeremiah's

מֵרָעָה אֶל־רָעָה ׀ יָצָאוּ וְאֹתִי לֹא־יָדָעוּ
נְאֻם־יְהֹוָה׃ ג אִישׁ מֵרֵעֵהוּ הִשָּׁמֵרוּ וְעַל־
כָּל־אָח אַל־תִּבְטָחוּ כִּי כָל־אָח עָקוֹב
יַעְקֹב וְכָל־רֵעַ רָכִיל יַהֲלֹךְ׃ ד וְאִישׁ
בְּרֵעֵהוּ יְהָתֵלּוּ וֶאֱמֶת לֹא יְדַבֵּרוּ לִמְּדוּ
לְשׁוֹנָם דַּבֶּר־שֶׁקֶר הַעֲוֵה נִלְאוּ׃
ה שִׁבְתְּךָ בְּתוֹךְ מִרְמָה בְּמִרְמָה מֵאֲנוּ
דַעַת־אוֹתִי נְאֻם־יְהֹוָה׃ ו לָכֵן כֹּה אָמַר
יְהֹוָה צְבָאוֹת הִנְנִי צוֹרְפָם וּבְחַנְתִּים

ת"א למדו לשונם. סוטה מו יבמות סג: קמץ בתביר קמץ בטרחא כי

סְקִיפוּ בְּאַרְעָא אֲרֵי
מִבִּישְׁתָּא לְבִישְׁתָּא נְפַקוּ
וּמִידַע דַחַלְתִּי לָא אֲלִיפוּ
אֲמַר יְיָ׃ ג גְּבַר מֵחַבְרֵיהּ
אִסְתַּמְרוּ וְעַל כָּל אֲחָא
לָא תִתְרַחֲצוּן אֲרֵי כָּל
אֲחָא מִכְמַן כָּמַן וְכָל
רָחִים בִּנְכִילוּ מְהַלֵּךְ׃
ד וּגְבַר בְּחַבְרֵיהּ
מְשַׁקְּרִין וְקוּשְׁטָא לָא
מְמַלְּלִין אֲלִיפוּ לִישָּׁנְהוֹן
פִּתְגָמֵי שְׁקַר אִיטַּפְּשׁוּ
טְעוּ׃ ה יָתְבִין בְּבֵית
כְּנִשְׁתְּהוֹן וּמִשְׁתַּעַן עַל
עֲוָיָתְהוֹן בִּנְכִילוּ מְסָרְבִין
לְמִידַע דַחַלְתִּי אֲמַר יְיָ׃
ו בְּכֵן כִּדְנַן אֲמַר יְיָ
צְבָאוֹת הָא אֲנָא מַיְתֵי
עֲלֵיהוֹן עָקָא וְצָרֵיף

רש"י

כשקר: מרעה אל רעה. מעבירה אל עבירה: (ג) עקוב יעקב. ארוב יארוב: (ד) העוה נלאו. יגעו וטרחו לעוות את דרכם. העוה כמו הכבד את לבו (שמות ח') להעוות: (ה) שבתך בתוך מרמה. כשהן יושבים חושבין מחשבות מרמה ובמרמה החליפו יראתי ומאנו דעת אותי: במרמה. בשביל המרמה: (ו) הנני צורפם. ביסורין: מפני בת

מהר"י קרא

בה הדורך וכשהוא דורכה היא נשברת ביד בעליה אף הם בפיו שלום את רעהו ידבר ובקרבו ישים ארבו כמו שמפרש והולך איש מרעהו השמרו ובכל הענין: (ו) הנני צורפם. על ידי האומות: ובחנתים. על ידי גלות:

רד"ק

לבם לשוב ממעשיהם הרעים ולדעת את ה': (ג) איש מרעהו. עקוב יעקב. ענין התרמית והערמה כמו ויעקבני זה פעמים ויעקב העי"ן בשו"א לבדו וכל שאר יעקב שום בר נש העי"ן בשו"א ופתח: (ד) ואיש. יהתלו. דגש הלמ"ד לתפארת הקריאה מפני התפסק: למדו לשונם. הרגילו כמו פרא למוד מדבר: העוה נלאו. להתעוות ולעשות מעשה עול ובא על דרך תאונים הלאת: (ה) שבתך. אמר האל יתברך מה יועיל שבתך בתוך מרמה כלומר בתוך עם מרמה שלא תוכל להשיבם אליך: במרמה. כל כך גדלו במרמה עד שמאנו לדעת אותי לא יוכלו להניח דרכם הרעה וי"ת יתבין בבית כנישתהון וגו' כבעמוד: (ו) לכן. הנני צורפם. בצרות שאביא עליהם אראה אם ישארו

מנחת שי

ט (ג) ואתי לא ידעו. בספרים מדוייקים חסר וא"ו אחר האל"ף גם לא נזכר במסורת בכלל המלאים: לא ידעו. הדל"ת קמוצה שגם התביר והטרחא לפעמים יש להם דין הפסק כמ"ש המכלול שקל פָּעֲלוּ ומי שכתב לא ידעו בשוא הדל"ת לא ידע בין ימינו לשמאלו והוא גם כן אחד מן ה' קמצין במסורת: (ג) איש מרעהו השמרו. בנביאים עם הרי"א כת"י ואיש בוא"ו אמנם בשאר ספרים כתוב איש בלא וא"ו: יעקב. העיין בשוא לבדו וכל שאר יעקב שום בר נש בשוא ופתח: (ד) יהתלו. בדגש הלמד לתפארת מכלול שקל

מצודת דוד

מרעה וגו'. כי יוצאים מעבירה אחת אל עבירה שנית ואינם נותנים לב לדעת אותי ולעשות אמונה: (ג) השמרו. היו נשמרים זה מזה לבל תגלות מסתרי לבבו: ועל כל אח. על שום אח: עקוב יעקב. יעקם ויעוות דרכו מול אחיו: רכיל יהלוך. מדבר רכילות על רעהו: (ד) ואיש. כל איש מהתל ומלעיג ברעהו: למדו. הרגילו את לשונם לדבר שקר כי מתמידים בזה: העוה נלאו. כאלו נתייגעו לעות דרכם כי הרבה עוות עשו והוא ענין מליצה: (ה) שבתך בתוך מרמה. ר"ל המרמה מקפת אותך מסביב וכאלו א"א לך להפרד ממנו ובעבור עסקם במרמה ממאנים לדעת אותי כי המרמה נוח להם מלדעת את ה': (ו) צורפם ובחנתים. כדרך הכסף שצורפים

מצודת ציון

על הקשת למתחו היטב לירות כמרחוק: (ג) עקוב יעקב. ענין עקום ועוות וכן העקוב למישור (ישעיה מ'): (ד) יהתלו. ענין לעג כמו הנה התלת בי (שופטים ט"ז): למדו. ענין הרגל כמו פרא למד מדבר (לעיל ב'): העוה. מל' עוות ועקום: נלאו. ענין יגיעה כמו ונלאתי כלכל (לקמן כ'): (ו) צורפם. ענין זקוק:

Redak explains that God addresses the prophet: Of what use is your habitation among a deceitful people, since you cannot bring them back to you?

in deceit—Since they have grown into deceit to the extent that they refuse to know Me and they cannot abandon their evil way. *Jonathan* paraphrases: They sit in their synagogue and discuss their sins deceitfully. With deceit, they refuse to know My fear, says the Lord.—[*Redak*]

6. **I will refine them**—*with torments.*—[*Rashi*]

With the troubles I will bring upon them, I will see whether dross

they proceed from evil to evil, and they do not know Me, says
the Lord. 3. Let each one beware of his neighbor, and do not
trust any brother; for each brother forges plans, and every
neighbor spreads slander. 4. Indeed, they deceive one another
and do not speak the truth; they have taught their tongue to
speak lies, they commit iniquity (until) they are weary. 5. Your
habitation is in the midst of deceit; because of deceit they refuse
to know Me, says the Lord. 6. Therefore, thus says the Lord of
Hosts, I will refine them and test them,

however, possessed only two of these admirable traits, viz. they did not change their names and they did not change their language. As regards adultery, however, although Moses' generation also committed adultery in Shittim, in Jeremiah's time they were all adulterers. As regards talebearing, too, they were a company of traitors. No one could trust the other. Then he goes on to elaborate that 'they have directed their tongue treacherously.'

from evil to evil—*From sin to sin.*—[*Rashi*]

I.e., all their lives they engage first in one evil deed and then in another, and with all this, they do not take out any time to know the Lord. It is also possible to explain that because of their sins they proceed from the evil inflicted by one enemy to the evil inflicted by another one, or that one year they are punished with blast and one year with yellowing or locusts, and, in spite of this, they do not set their heart on repenting of their evil deeds.—[*Redak*]

3. **Let each one beware of his neighbor**—Let them beware of revealing their secrets to their neighbors.—[*Mezudath David*]

forges plans—*He lays traps.*—[*Rashi*] He disregards his brotherhood and plans to trap his brother.—[*Abarbanel*]

and every neighbor spreads slander—I.e., he spreads slander against his own neighbor.—[*Mezudath David*]

4. **Indeed, they deceive one another**—This follows *Targum Jonathan. Mezudath David* explains that each one mocks the other.

they have taught their tongue—I.e., they have accustomed their tongue. —[*Redak*]

they commit iniquity (until) they are weary—*They wearied themselves and toiled to pervert their way.* הַעֲוֵה *is like* '(Exod. 8:11) *and making heavy* (וְהַכְבֵּד) *his heart,' to commit iniquity.* —[*Rashi*]

5. **Your habitation is in the midst of deceit**—*When they sit, they devise plans of deceit, and with deceit they have exchanged fear of Me and refused to know Me.*—[*Rashi*]

because of deceit—Heb. בְּמִרְמָה.—[*Rashi*]

כי־איך אעשה מפני בת־עמי: ז חץ
שוחט לשונם מרמה דבר בפיו שלום
את־רעהו ידבר ובקרבו ישים ארבו:
ח העל־אלה לא־אפקד־בם נאם־יהוה
אם בגוי אשר־כזה לא תתנקם נפשי:
ט על־ההרים אשא בכי ונהי ועל־נאות
מדבר קינה כי נצתו מבלי־איש עובר

תרגום

להון ובתר להון ארי איבדין אעביד מן קדם חובי כנשתא דעמי: ז כגיר די מחרף לישנהון נכלין מחשב בפומהון שלמא גבר עם חבריה מסללין ובמעוהי משוי כמנהיה: ח העל אלין לא אסער לאיתאה עליהון בישתא אמר יי אם מן עמא דקבלין עובדוהי לא אתפרע מנהון כרעותי: ט על טוריא אנא מרים קלי ובכי ומצוח ועל דירות מדברא אליא ארי צדיאו מבלי אנש דעבר ולא אשתמע קל בעירא בארעהון מעופא

ת"א חץ שחוט. חולין ל ערכין טו: על ההרים. ברכות נו שבת קמה: שחוט קרי ולא

מהר"י קרא

כי איך אעשה. מפני עון בת עמי מאחר שאני מזהירם לשוב אלי ואינן שבים: (ז) חץ שחוט. תרגום גיר דמחרף ופתרונו כגיר די מחרף: ובקרבו. תירגם יונתן ובמעוהי:

רש"י

עמי. מן קדם חובי כנשתא דישראל: (ז) חץ שחוט לשונם. משוך כמו זהב שחוט (מלכים א י') וכן ושחטה שטים (הושע ה)(טריי"ש בלע"ז) ליטנא אחריגא לשון שחיטה ממש (טרא"נקא"ט בלע"ז) וכן חברו מנחם וכן תירגם יונתן כגיר די מחרף: ובקרבו. תירגם יונתן ובמעוהי: (ט) על ההרים. על חורבן ההרים: ועל נאות מדבר. נוה רועים שבמדברות. נאות לשון נוה וכן נאות אלהים (תהלים פג) וכן לביתך נאוה קודש (שם לג): נצתו. לשון ציה וכן

מנחת שי

(ז) שוחט. שחוט קרי ויש אם למקרא ולמסורת שזה בא להיות שוחט לאחרים ונמלא שחוט כי ליה תלתא קטיל כדאיתא בערכין פרק ג'. כלי יקר סוף פרשת קרח:

רד"ק

סיגים או אם ישובו כסף נבחר מפני הצרות: כי איך אעשה. מפני בת עמי. כי איך אעשה שלא אצרפם מפני שהיא בת עמי לא אוכל שלא אצרפם כי איך אניחם ברעתם והם נקראים עמי וי"ת איבדין אעביד מן קדם חובי כנישתא דעמי: (ז) חץ שוחט. כן כתיב וקרינן שחוט והכתיב ר"ל כמו שוחט שהוא הורג כן הורגים הם בני אדם בלשונם הרע שהם הולכי רכיל והקרי שחוט ר"ל נמשך אפיל"ט בלע"ז רוצה לומר שהוא נמשך על המשחות לחדדו וי"ת כגיר די מחריף. כמו סכינא חריפא בדברי רבותינו ז"ל שפירשו מחודד ודק החתיכה ומת שפי' בו ג"כ לשון משיכה הוא ג"כ מדברי רבותינו ז"ל שאמרו התיז את הראש בבת אחת פסולה ואמרו מנא הני מילי אמר קרא חץ שחוט לשונם ואמר תנא דבי ישמעאל ושחט אין ושחט אלא ומשך וכן הוא אומר זהב שחוט ואמר חץ שחוט לשונם מרמה דבר ואדוני אבי ז"ל פירש שחוט שם תאר כמו שוחט וכן במשקלו אדם עשוק בדם נפש כמו עושק: מרמה דבר. כל אחד מהם ידבר מרמת לחברו ומפרש מה היא המרמה בפיו שלום את רעהו: (ח) העל אלה. מבואר הוא: לא אפקוד בם. והשנים הראשונים אין כתוב בם והענין אחד: (ט) על ההרים. נאות מדבר. ההרים מקום מרעה הצאן והעזים ברוב או זכר הרים להשמיע קולו למרחוק וכן נאות מדבר רוצה לומר אהלי המדבר כי נאות מדבר פירושו אהלים ומשכנים כמו נדמו נאות השלום וכן בוי"ו נוה משלח ונעזב נות כרות רועים ואמר מדבר כי יש מדבר שיש בו מקום מרע' כמו וינהג את הצאן אחר המדבר ותרגם אונקלוס בתר שפר רעיא דמדברא וכן על פני דרך המדבר ואמר הנביא בראותו חרבן הארץ שישא בכי ונהי לקינה במקומות המרעה כי נחרבו מבלי איש עובר אין צריך לומר שאין אהלים תקועים לרועים אלא אפילו איש אין עובר שם לרעות מקנה ולא נשמע קול מקנה כי כלם נדדו הלכו בשבי ובאמרו מעוף השמים הוא דרך גוזמא להפליג הדבר או נאמר זה לענין חרבן הארץ כמשמעו כי רוב העופות לא ישכנו במדבר כי אם במקומות שימצאו זרע ופירות ופרחי האילנות: נצתו. ענין חרבן וכן נצתו כמדבר ושרשו יצת

מצודת ציון

ובחנתים. מל' בחינה: (ז) שחוט. משוך כמו זהב שחוט (מ"א י'): ארבו. מל' מארב: (ח) אפקד. ענין השגחה כמו פקדו נא והלא (ש"א י"ד): (ט) ונהי. ענין יללה כמו יודעי נהי (עמוס ה'): נאות. ענין מדור כמו בנאות דשא (תהלים כ"ג): מדבר. לפעמים יאמר ל' מדבר על מקום המרעה כמ"ש הצאן הסנה

מצודת דוד

אותו בכור להסיר הסיג ולבחון הכסף הטובה היא אם רעה כן אביא עליה' פורעניו' למרק ולהסיר מהם סיגי העון: כי איך אעשה וגו'. ר"ל אם אניחם להיות מעוקשים בעון הלא המה עדת עמי וראוי ס המה להיות עם קדוש ואם אעשה עמהם כלייה הנה המה עדת עמי ורחמי עליהם ולכן אצרפם ביסורים למרק מהם העון למען ישארו מנוקים מעון: (ז) חץ שחוט לשונם. נדמה לשונם לחץ הנמשך על יתר הקשת כי בלה"ר הורגים למרחוק כמו חצי הקשת: מרמה דבר. כ"א מדבר מרמה כי בפיו ידבר שלום עם רעהו ובקרב לבו ישים מארב עליו: (ח) העל אלה. וכי על מעשים כאלה לא אשגיח בם להפרע מהם: אם בגוי. וכי בגוי אשר וגו': (ט) על ההרים. על חורבן ההרים אשא קול בכי ויללה: ועל נאות מדבר. על חורבן אהלי הרועים אשר במדבר ארים קינה כי נעשו

sion of a dwelling. Comp. '(Psalms 83:13) *the dwellings* (נְאוֹת) *of God'; also* '(ibid. 93:5) *to Your house, the dwelling* (נָאֲוָה) *of sanctity.'*—[*Rashi*]

The mountains are, as a rule, the pastureland for the sheep and the goats. He, therefore, mentions the mountains. Or, perhaps it is because the voice carries there over long distances. Likewise, he mentions the dwellings of the wilderness, meaning the tents of the shepherds in the pastures of the wilderness. The prophet, upon perceiving the des-

for what else can I do because of (the wickedness of) the daughter of My people? 7. Their tongue is a deadly arrow, it speaks deceit; each one speaks peaceably with his mouth to his neighbor, but in his heart he lays a trap for him. 8. Shall I not punish them for these things, says the Lord, shall I not avenge Myself on a nation such as this? 9. I will take up weeping and wailing for the mountains, and a lamentation for the dwellings of the wilderness, because they are withered and without any one passing through,

will remain or whether they will become as pure silver because of the troubles.—[*Redak*]

because of the daughter of My people—*Because of the sins of the congregation of Israel.*—[*Rashi from Jonathan*] How can I refrain from refining them? Since they are My people, I cannot allow them to remain in their evil state.—[*Redak*]

7. **Their tongue is a deadly arrow**—Heb. שָׁחוּט, *drawn. Comp.* '(I Kings 10:16) *malleable gold* (שָׁחוּט).' *Also,* '(Hos. 5:2) *And the extent of their turning away* (וְשַׁחֲטָה)' (*tirer in French*), pulling. *Another explanation is that it is actually an expression of slaughter* (*tranchant in French*, cutting). *In this manner Menahem classified it* (*Machbereth Menahem* p. 172), *and in this manner Jonathan rendered it:* כְּגִיר דִּי מְחָדַּךְ, *like a sharpened arrow.*—[*Rashi*] *Redak* differentiates between the *keri* and the *kethib*. According to the *keri* שָׁחוּט, the word is passive, meaning 'drawn,' i.e. an arrow drawn over the grindstone to sharpen it. Hence, a sharpened arrow, as *Jonathan* renders it. According to the *kethib*, שׁוֹחֵט, the word is active, a slaughtering arrow, or a deadly arrow. Rabbi Joseph Kimchi explains the *keri* also as being active since we find the פָּעוּל form sometimes substituted for the פּוֹעֵל, giving it the active sense.—[*Redak*] Rabbi Joseph Kimchi apparently agrees with Menahem. Jonathan, however, appears to explain the word like *Redak*, drawn. This may be Rashi's interpretation, although it is possible that Rashi means that the arrow is placed in the bow and drawn to be shot. Rashi's association of *Jonathan* with Menahem, however, is very difficult. See Lexicon Chaldaicum Authore Ellia Levita. *Shem Ephraim* explains that it is the sharpened arrow that slaughters.

it speaks deceit—I.e., each one speaks deceitfully, as Scripture proceeds to explain.—[*Redak*]

but in his heart—lit. in his midst. *Jonathan renders: in his innards.*—[*Rashi*]

9. **for the mountains**—I.e. *for the destruction of the mountains.*—[*Rashi*]

for the dwellings of the wilderness—*The dwelling of the shepherds in the wilderness.* נְאוֹת *is an expres-*

* For Rashi's commentary turn to page 225.

ולא שמעו קול מקנה מעוף השמים
ועד־בהמה נדדו הלכו: י ונתתי את־
ירושלם לגלים מעון תנים ואת־ערי
יהודה אתן שממה מבלי יושב:
יא מי־האיש החכם ויבן את־זאת ואשר
דבר פי־יהוה אליו ויגדה על־מה
אבדה הארץ נצתה כמדבר מבלי
עבר: יב ויאמר יהוה על־עזבם את־

דשמיא ועד בעירא
אטלטלו גלו: י ואתן
ית ירושלם לנגרין
מדור ירודין וית קרויא
דבית יהודה אתן לצדו
מבלי יתיב: יא מן גברא
דחכים ויסבר ית דא
ודאתמלל מן קדם יי
עמיה ויחוינה על מן
חרובת ארעא צדיאת
כמדברא מבלי יתיב:
יב ואמר יי על די שבקו
ית אוריתי דיהבית
קדמיהון

ת"א ועד בהמה. (תענית כט): מי האיש. נדרים פא ב"מ פה:

רש"י

נכתה: נדדו הלכו. סופן לילך. חמשים ושתים שנה לא עבר איש ביהודה מגלות צדקיהו עד פקודת כורש מלך פרס חמשים ושתים שנה היו ורמז לדבר ועד בהמה השכונה בגימטריא נ"ב והחשבון מכוון במסכת מגילה [נ"ל יומא י' כד]: (י) לגלים. דגורין: (יא) מי האיש החכם. שיבין זאת ומי הנביא אשר דבר פי ה' אליו ויגידה. ומי יגיד על

מהר"י קרא

חץ מחודד והוא מגזר' דוב שכול שפתרונו משכל: (י) לגלים. לשון גל: (יא) ויבן את זאת. לאחרים כלומר אם ישב אדם משתומם על כך על מה עשה ה' ככה לארץ הזאת שנדדו כולם מעוף השמים ועד בהמה אם נצתה הארץ כבלי איש עובר ולא שמעו קול מקנה. זה היא נוהג שבעולם שאדם גולה ממקומו ומוליכין בשביה את מקניהו עמו. אבל כאן כה חרי האף הגדול שמעוף השמים ועד בהמה נדדו הלכו דבר זה אין לך חכם בעולם שיוכל לידע ולהבין לאחרים מהו הדבר אלא יבין: אשר דבר פי ה' אליו. ויגידה לכל התמיהין על כך וכך יאמר

דצונך לידע: על מה אבדה הארץ. כל כך שנצתה במדבר מבל עובר: (יב) ויאמר ה' על עוזבם את תורתי. והזקף שראיתי בתיבת ויבן את זאת והו' של ואשר דבר פי ה' אליו גרמו לי שעמדתי על פתרון זה שהזקף מעמד את התיבה לבד ומפרידה כחבירתה ועושה אותה סוף מלה והו' שבתיבת ואשר מלמדנו שאין זה אותו חכם שדיבר ממנו למעלה אלא

רד"ק

ובדברי רז"ל ר' יהודה אומר חמשים ושתים שנה לא עבר איש ביהודה שנאמר על ההרים וגו' מעוף השמים ועד בהמת נדדו הלכו בהמה בגימטריא נ"ב הוו ר' יוסי אומר שבע שנים נתקיים בה גפרית שנאמר גפרית ומלח שרפה כל ארצה: (י) ונתתי. לגלים. גלי אבנים מהבתים והחומות שנהרסו: מעון תנים. משכן התנים ובגורם ות"י תנין ירודין: (יא) מי האיש החכם ויבן את זאת. יבין מדעתו והנביא יגיד התשובה והשאלה כמו שנאמרה מפי ה': (יב) ויאמר ה'. לפניהם. לא

מצודת דוד

שממה ואין איש עובר שם ולא נשמע קול מקנה כי האויב שללם לעצמו: נדדו הלכו. נדדו ממקומם והלכו להם כי רוב העופות ישכנו במקום אנשים כי שם ימצאו פירות ופרחי אילנות וזרעים למאכלם וכאשר יהיה שממה ילכו להם והבהמות יקחם האויב:

מצודת ציון

במדבר (ש"א י"ז): נצתו. מלשון ציה ושממה: (י) לגלים. ענין תל ולגור כמו עד הגל הזה (בראשית ל"א): מעון. מדור כמו למעון קדשו (ד"ה ב' ל'): תנים. מין נחש: (יא) נצתה. מלשון

(י) לגלים. כי ינתצו הבתים ויהיו גלי אבנים: מבלי יושב. כי כלם ילכו בגלות: (יא) ויבן את זאת. האמור למעה על מה אבדה וגו': ואשר דבר. ר"ל ומי האיש אשר ה' דבר בו הוא הנביא: ויגידה. ויגיד מדעתו בעבור מה אבדה הארץ ונעשה שממה כמדבר מבלי מי עובר שמה ר"ל מהו הדבר העיקר בדבר החורבן וכאומר אין מי בהם יגיד זאת: (יב) ויאמר ה'. המקום בעצמו אמר שהעיקר הוא על אשר עזבו את תורתי וגו' ר"ל שלא למדו את התורה ולכן לא שמעו בקולי בכל הדברים ולא הלכו בדרך התורה לקיים מצותיה כי אם עסקו בתורה היה המאור שבה מחזיר אותם למוטב אבל בעבור שלא עסקו בה

will understand this, and who is the prophet to whom the mouth of the Lord has spoken, that he may declare it? And who will declare why the land is ruined and all this retribution has come?—[*Rashi*]

I.e., who is the man so wise to understand this through his own intelligence and who is the prophet who knows the answer because the Lord has revealed it to him?—[*Redak*]

12. **And the Lord said:**—I.e. the Lord said to them, for the Torah is neither in heaven nor on the other side of the sea.—[*Redak*]

because they have forsaken—They did not learn the Torah, and, therefore, they have not hearkened to My voice, in all that I commanded them, nor have they walked in the way of the Torah to keep its commandments. Had they studied the Torah, its light would have caused them to

and the lowing of the cattle is not heard; both the fowl of the
heavens and the beast have fled and are gone. 10. And I will
make Jerusalem heaps (of ruin), a lair of jackals; and I will
make the cities of Judah a desolation, without inhabitant.
11. Who is the man so wise that he can understand this? And
who is he to whom the mouth of the Lord has spoken, that he
may declare it? Why is the land ruined (and) withered like a
wilderness, without anyone passing through? 12. And the Lord
said: (It is) because they have forsaken

tined desolation of the pastureland, announces that he will take up weeping and wailing in the place of pasture, for they will become withered and without anyone passing through. Not only will there be no tents pitched there, but there will not even be any one passing through to graze cattle, and the lowing of the cattle will not be heard since all will have been driven into exile.—[*Redak*]

both the fowl of the heavens—This may be interpreted as an exaggeration to illustrate the extent of the desolation, or it may be interpreted literally, since most fowl do not live in desolate places, but where they can find seeds, fruits and blossoms of trees.—[*Redak*]

have fled and are gone—I.e. *they are destined to go. For fifty-two years no one passed through Judah; from the exile of Zedekiah until the order of Cyrus, king of Persia, were fifty-two years. An allusion to the matter 'and the beast* (בְּהֵמָה)*' amounts to fifty-two, and the computation is exact, in Tractate Megillah* [should read: *Yoma* 54a].—[*Rashi*]

Perhaps Rashi means that the computation of the years is consistent with the chronology delineated in Tractate *Megillah* 11b, that the exile of Zedekiah was eighteen years after the vanquishing of Jehoiakim, which was seventy years prior to Cyrus' proclamation.

2	=	ב
5	=	ה
40	=	מ
5	=	ה
52		

Rabbi Yose says: For seven years, the verse '(Deut. 29:22) Brimstone and salt, all her land was burnt,' was fulfilled in Israel (ibid.).—[*Redak*]

10. **heaps**—*Jonathan* renders דְגוֹרִין, *heaps*.—[*Rashi*] Our editions read: יַגָּרִין.

I.e., heaps of stones from the houses and the walls that were demolished.—[*Redak*]

a lair of jackals—For the house will be demolished, and become heaps of ruins, where jackals will make their lair.—[*Mezudath David*]

Some explain תַּנִּים as a type of snake.—[*Mezudath Zion*]

11. **Who is the man so wise**—*who*

תורתי אשר נתתי לפניהם ולא־שמעו
בקולי ולא־הלכו בה: יג וילכו אחרי
שררות לבם ואחרי הבעלים אשר
למדום אבותם: יד לכן כה־אמר יהוה
צבאות אלהי ישראל הנני מאכילם
את־העם הזה לענה והשקיתים מי־
ראש: טו והפיצותים בגוים אשר לא
ידעו המה ואבותם ושלחתי אחריהם
את־החרב עד כלותי אותם: טז כה
אמר יהוה צבאות התבוננו וקראו

תרגום

קדמיהון ולא קבילו
למימרי ולא הליכו בה:
יג ואזלו בתר הרהור
לבהון ובתר בעליא
דאליפינון אבהתהון:
יד בכן כדנן אמר יי
צבאות אלהא דישראל
הא אנא מיכל עקא על
עמא הדין מרר כגידין
ואשקינון כס דלוט
כרישי חיון:
טו ואבדרינון ביני
עממיא דלא ידעו אינון
ואבהתהון ואגרי
בתריהון דקטלין
בחרבא עד דאשיצי
יתהון: טז כדנן אמר יי
צבאות אסתכלו וקרו

מהר"י קרא

שני בני אדם הן וכמה שתמיה החכ' מגיד לו הנביא: (יד) לענה. אשינ"ץ דושטור"א בלע"ז: (טו) התבוננו וקראו למקוננות. יכה תאמרו להם מהרנה ותשאנה עלינו נהי כדי שתרדנה עינינו דמעה.

רש"י

מה אבדה הארץ ובא כל הפורענות הזה: (יד) לענה. עשב שאפילו שאין בדעתו של אדם לבכות כששומע

מנחת שי

(יד) מי ראש. באל"ף כמ"ש למעלה סימן ח': (טו) והפצותים. במקצת ספרים מדוייקים חסר יו"ד אחר פ"א ונמסר עליו ב' חד חסר וחד מלא ע"כ. ועיין פ"ב ביחזקאל י"א: אשר לא ידעו. כן כתיב ולא תטעה לדברי מי שאומר פ"א

רד"ק

בשמים היא ולא מעבר לים היא: (יג) וילכו. שרירות. פירשנוהו למעלה: למדום אבותם. הרגילו בהם האבות וראו אבותם עובדים אותם ועבדום הם גם כן אחריהם והאבות הם הרורות הרשעים שעברו: (יד) לכן. מאכילם. בא הכנוי קודם הידיעה שהוא את העם הזה כמו ותראהו את הילד אשר לא יעבדו אותו את נבוכדנצר והדומים להם שכתבנו בספר מכלול בחלק הדקדוק ממנו והמשיל הצרות ללענה ורוש והם סמי המות ובארו מי רוש לפי שהוא מי סחיטת העשב שקורין ריש גם יש שהוא מראש הפתן ואמרו כי לפיכך נקרא ראש כי ברוב עושין אותו מראש הפתן: (טו) והפיצותים. עד כלותי אותם. רובם: (טז) כה אמר. התבוננו. בפורענות הקרוב לבא ומעתה

מצודת ציון

ים ושממה: (יג) שרירות. ענין ראיה כמו אשר שורריו אנשים (איוב ל"ו): למדום. ענין הרגל כמו פרה למוד מדבר (לעיל ב'): (יד) לענה. שם עשב מר: מי ראש. מי סחיטת ראש וה"א שם עשב מר: (טו) והפיצותים. ענין פזור: כלותי. מלשון כליה:

מצודת דוד

כאו לכל אלה השמים ואבדה הארץ בעונם: (יג) שרירות לבם. מה שלבם רואה וחמד: אשר למדום אבותם. אשר הרגילום אבות': (יד) הנני מאכילם וגו'. רלה לומר אביא עליהם צרות שונות: (טו) והפיצותים. אפזר אותם בארצות עכו"ם אשר לא הכירו מעולם גם המה גם אבותם: ושלחתי. אל המקומות אשר ינוסו ויפזרו שנה ושנה שמה אשלח את חרב האויב עד אכלה אות': (טז) התבוננו. תנו לב להבין בהרעה הזאת המיוחדת לבא ומעתה קראו למקוננות

14. **with wormwood**—*Bitter grass.*—[*Rashi*]

poisonous water—*Snake venom.*—[*Rashi*]

It is also possible that both of these are poisonous plants. If רוש is snake venom, it is called רוש because it is extracted from the head (ראש) of the snake.—[*Redak*]

15. **until I have consumed them**—I.e., until I have consumed the majority of them.—[*Redak*]

My Law, which I set before them, and have not hearkened to
My voice, nor walked by it. 13. But they have followed the
view of their own heart, and after the Baalim, which their
fathers taught them (to worship). 14. Therefore, so thus said
the Lord of Hosts, the God of Israel: Behold, I will
feed them—this people—with wormwood, and will give them
poisonous water to drink. 15. I will scatter them among the
nations, whom neither they nor their fathers have known; and I
will send the sword after them, until I have consumed them.
16. Thus said the Lord of Hosts: Consider and call

repent, but since they did not study the Torah, they came to all their sins, causing the land to be desolate.—[*Mezudath David*]

The Rabbis (*Nedarim* 81a, *Baba Mezia* 85b) explain this as follows: This matter was asked of the sages, the prophets, and the ministering angels, and they did not explain it, until the Holy One, blessed be He, explained it Himself, as it is stated: Because they have forsaken My Torah etc. That is apparently synonymous with 'and have not hearkened to My voice.' This is also synonymous with 'nor walked by it.' Said Rav Yehudah in the name of Rav: This comes to say that they did not recite a blessing on the Torah at the beginning. *Ran* explains that the Talmud deviates from the simple explanation since, were it so that no one studied the Torah, it would have been obvious, and it would not be hidden from the sages and the prophets. The Talmud, therefore, deduces that they indeed studied the Torah, but they did not study it for its own sake but for their own interests. Consequently, they did not consider it important enough to warrant the recitation of a blessing. This is the meaning of 'nor walked by it.' I.e., they did not proceed with the Torah according to its proper intention and devotion.—[*Ran*, quoting *Rabbenu Yonah* in *Megillath Setharim*]

Rashi explains that the words, 'which I set before them,' allude to the formula of the blessing, 'and gave us His Torah,' which we recite every morning. This intimates that they did not recite this blessing.

Apparently, the intention is that their lack of devotion in their studies led them to follow the view of their hearts and eventually to follow the Baalim. Had they learned the Torah for its sake, they would never have come to that state.

13. **which their father taught them**—I.e., to which their fathers accustomed them. They witnessed their fathers worshipping these idols and emulated them. The fathers were the wicked generations that were before them.—[*Redak*]

למקוננות ותבואינה ואל־החכמות
שלחו ותבואנה: יז ותמהרנה ותשנה
עלינו נהי ותרדנה עינינו דמעה
ועפעפינו יזלו־מים: יח כי קול נהי
נשמע מציון איך שדדנו בשנו מאד
כי־עזבנו ארץ כי השליכו משכנותינו:
יט כי־שמענה נשים דבר־יהוה ותקח
אזנכם דבר־פיו ולמדנה בנתיכם נהי

לאליתא ויתין
ולחכימתא שלחו וייתין
יז ויותן ויטלן עלנא
אליא וישגרן עיננא
דמעין וגלגלי עיננא
יגרון מיא: יח ארי קל
אליא אשתמע מציון
אכדין אתבזזנא
בהיתנא לחדא ארי
חריבת ארעא ארי
צדיאה בירניתהא:
יט ארי שמעא נשיא
פתגמא דיי ותצית
אודניכון למלי נביוהי
ואליפנא לבנתיכון
אליא ואתתא לחברתה

ת"א ולמדנה בנותיכם. פ"ק כח: חסר א' קמץ בז"ק

רש"י

מר: מי ראש. ארס נחש: (יח) כי השליכו משכנותינו.

מהר"י קרא

קול המקונן נוטה לו לבו לבכות: (יח) כי עזבנו ארץ. וכי השליכו אויבינו משכנותינו: (יט) כי שמענה נשים דבר ה' וגו'. כלומר שעתידין הדברים ליגע שתהיו צריכות לקונן לפיכך למדנה בנותיכם נהי ואשה רעותה קינה. כשיגיע הדבר

רד"ק

קראו למקוננות בפתח הלמ"ד ר"ל המקוננות הידועות: ואל החכמות. שהן חכמו' בדברי הספד וקינה: ותבואינה. הראשון בתנועת האל"ף בסגול והשני ותבואנה בהעלם האל"ף בתנועה ושני המשקלים נמצאים בנחי העין בספרת: (יז) ותמהרנה ותשנה. בהעלם האל"ף מהמכתב: עלינו. מאמר הנביא בכלל ישראל: ותרדנה עינינו דמעה. כלומר לקול נהיין והספדן נבכה ופי' דמעה בדמעה כי תרדנה פעל עומד ותרב הבכי דמה הענין כאילו העין נתכת ויורדת בדמעה וכן עיני ירדה מים וי"ת וישגרן עיננא דמעין: ועפעפינו. הם אישוני העינים וכפל הענין במלות שונות וי"ת וגלגלי עיננא יגרון מיא: (יח) כי קול נהי נשמע מציון. וכן נשמע משאר המקומות אלא קודם שנכבשה ציון היו חושבים להשגב בציון וירושלם שאם תשאר להם ירושלם עוד היו לבנות שאר הערים שנכבשו ולחזור לישובן כמו שעשו בימי סנחריב שכבש הכל זולתי ירושלם וכיון שנשארה ירושלם נשאר הכל ולא גלו ולא עזבו ארץ ישראל אבל כיון שנכבשה ירושלם אין עוד תקנה ואז היה קול הנהי נשמע ואומרים איך שדדנו בושנו מאד: כי עזבנו ארץ. ארץ בקמץ בזקף והוא אחד מי"ד ארץ שהם זקפין קמצין: כי השליכו משכנותינו. כאילו משכנותינו השליכו אותנו חוצה או בא על דרך ולא תקיא הארץ אתכם ואין בשת גדול מזה שיצא אדם מוכרח מביתו לפיכך בושנו מאד: (יט) כי שמענה. כי המספד והנהי בנשים ברוב כי הן רכות הלב יותר כן

מנחת שי

ידמוע: (יז) ותשנה. בס"ן שמאלים: (יח) כי השליכו. כל הקורא וכי כו"ו אינו אלא טועה: (יט) בנותיכם. מתחלפת חסר וא"ו:

מצודת דוד

הם הנשים היודעות לספוד ולקונן על המתים: ותבואינה. אליכם לעורר קינות ויללות: ואל החכמות. הן הבקיאות לומר לסדר אמרי אבלות לוח ויגון להדאיב נפשו' השומעים: (יז) ותמהרנה. הן המקוננות יהרימו קול יללה למען יתעוררו לבכינו: ותרדנה עינינו דמעה. יזלו מים. ישפכו מי דמעת הבכי וכפל הדבר במ"ש: (יח) כי קול. כי מציון נשמע קול יללה שאומרים איך שדדנו ובשנו מאד כי חשבנו להשגב בציון ועתה לא כן היה כי עזבנו ארץ נחלתינו כי השליכו משכנותינו את היושבים בהם חוצה וכענין שנאמר ולא תקיא הארץ אתכם וגו' כאשר קאה וגו' (ויקרא י"ח): (יט) דבר ה'. באמר שהפורעניות מעותדות לבא: ותקח וגו'. כפל הדבר במ"ש: נהי. דברי יללה: ואשה רעותה. ואשה תלמד את רעותה

מצודת ציון

(טז) למקוננות. מל' קינה: (יז) ותשנה. כמו ותשאנה בא"ל"ף: ותרדנה. מלשון ירידה: ועפעפינו. הוא אישון העין: יזלו. מל' זולה ונשיפה: (יח) שדדנו. ענין עושק: משכנותינו. מלשון משכן ומקום מדור: (יט) ותקח. ר"ל תקבל: רעותה. חברתה:

dath David, however, render: Our dwellings have cast us out. It is as though our dwellings have cast us out. Comp. '(Lev. 28:18) And the land shall not vomit you.' There is no greater shame than that of a person being compelled to leave his dwelling. Therefore, we are very much ashamed.—[*Redak*]

19. **the word of the Lord**—that the retribution is destined to befall you.—[*Mezudath David*]

and teach your daughters a lamentation—As above, the women

for the (hired) women mourners that they may come; and send
for the skillful women, and let them come. 17. O let them make
haste and raise a wailing over us, so that our eyes may shed
tears, and our eyelids gush with water. 18. For a sound of
wailing is heard from Zion: 'O how we are ruined! We are very
much ashamed, because we have left the land, because they
have cast down our dwellings!' 19. Indeed hear, O women, the
word of the Lord, and let your ear receive the word of His
mouth; teach your daughters a lamentation,

for the (hired) women mourners—Heb. לַמְקוֹנְנוֹת. The *pattah* under the *lammed* takes the place of the definite object, indicating that these women were well-known.—[*Redak*]

Since women are more emotional than men, they are chosen for this profession.—[*Ibn Nachmiash*]

for the skillful women—I.e. for the women who are skillful in eulogy and lamentation.—[*Redak*]

Malbim explains that the skillful women are those who know how to keep the living from dying in the calamity.

17. **over us**—The prophet includes himself with the people.—[*Redak*]

so that our eyes may shed tears—lit. and our eyes shall come down with tears. It will be as though our eyes are dissolving and running down in tears. At the sound of the mourning women, we will burst into tears and our eyelids will gush with water.—[*Redak*]

and our eyelids—Heb. וְעַפְעַפֵּינוּ. This is the usual translation, following *Ibn Ganach* (*Sepher Haschoraschim*). *Targum Jonathan* and *Redak*, however, interpret it as the pupil of the eye.

18. **For a sound of wailing is heard from Zion**—The wailing is heard from other places as well, but before Zion was conquered, the people expected to take refuge there, for if Zion and Jerusalem were left, they would be able to rebuild the other cities that were already conquered and resettle them, as they did in the time of Sennacherib, who conquered the entire land except Jerusalem. Since Jerusalem was left, everyone remained and they did not go into exile. In this case, however, since Jerusalem was conquered, there was no more hope. Then there was a cry from Zion, "O how we are ruined!"—[*Redak*]

they have cast down our dwellings—Heb. הִשְׁלִיכוּ מִשְׁכְּנוֹתֵינוּ. Our dwellings *have cast out their inhabitants. We can also explain: For the enemies have cast our dwellings to the ground.*—[*Rashi*]

Kara follows the second interpretation. *Jonathan, Redak,* and *Mezu-*

וְאִשָּׁה רְעוּתָהּ קִינָה: כ כִּי־עָלָה מָוֶת
בְּחַלּוֹנֵינוּ בָּא בְּאַרְמְנוֹתֵינוּ לְהַכְרִית
עוֹלָל מִחוּץ בַּחוּרִים מֵרְחֹבוֹת: כא דַּבֵּר
כֹּה נְאֻם־יְהוָֹה וְנָפְלָה נִבְלַת הָאָדָם
כְּדֹמֶן עַל־פְּנֵי הַשָּׂדֶה וּכְעָמִיר מֵאַחֲרֵי
הַקּוֹצֵר וְאֵין מְאַסֵּף: כב כֹּה אָמַר יְהוָֹה
אַל־יִתְהַלֵּל חָכָם בְּחָכְמָתוֹ וְאַל־
יִתְהַלֵּל הַגִּבּוֹר בִּגְבוּרָתוֹ אַל־יִתְהַלֵּל
עשיר

תרגום

עֲנוּיָא: כ אֲרֵי סְלֵיק
מוֹתָא בְּחַרְבְּנָא עַל
בְּכַרְנָוָתָנָא לְשֵׁיצָאָה
יָנְקִין מִשּׁוּקָא עוּלֵימִין
מִרְחוֹבִין: כא אִתְנַבֵּי
כִּדְנַן אֲמַר יְיָ וְתִתְרְמֵי
נִבְלַתָא דֶאֱנָשָׁא כְּזִיבַל
מִבַדַּר עַל אַפֵּי חַקְלָא
וּכְעָמִירָא מִבָּתַר חָצְדָא
וְלֵית דִּמְכַנֵּשׁ: כב כִּדְנַן
אֲמַר יְיָ לָא יִשְׁתַּבַּח
שְׁלֹמֹה בַּר דָּוִד חַכִּימָא
בְּחוּכְמְתֵיהּ וְלָא יִשְׁתַּבַּח
שִׁמְשׁוֹן בַּר מָנוֹחַ גִּבָּרָא
בִּגְבוּרְתֵּיהּ וְלָא יִשְׁתַּבַּח
אַחְאָב בַּר עָמְרִי עַתִּירָא

ת"א עולל מחוץ. ב"ק כ: אל יתהלל. ערכין י פקרא ספר עו:

רש"י

את שוכניה'. ויש עוד לומ' כי השליכו האויבי' את משכנותינו לארץ: (כ) להכרית עולל מחוץ. מן השוק כמו וחוצות תשים לך בדמשק (מלכים א' כ'): (כב) אל יתהלל חכם. אל תתהללו לומר חכמים אנחנו הנה בדברי מאסתם וחכמת מה לכם אם השכלתם וידעתם אותי אז תתהללו בחכמתכם:

מהר"י קרא

תדעו לקונן ותהיו מזומנות: (כא) וכעמיר מאחרי הקוצר. וכעמיר שזורק קוצר מאחריו: (כב) אל יתהלל חכם בחכמתו. למעלה בענין אומר אתם תאמרו חכמים אנחנו ותורת ה' אתנו למדנו שהיו מתהללין בחכמתן אע"פ שלא היו מקיימין מה שחכמה מלמדן כמו שהנביא מקנתרן הנה בדבר ה' מאסו וחכמת מה להם וחזר הנביא והותם על הדבר הזה ומשיב להם השיבה: אל יתהלל חכם בחכמתו. אדם שלמד תורה ואינו מקיים מה שכתוב בה אין הילולו בכך שלמדה אלא גנאי הוא לו שלמדה ואינו מקיים מה שכתב בה כמו שמפרש למעלה הובישו חכמים חתו וילכדו הנה בדבר ה' מאסו וחכמת מה להם שאין החכמה מזהיר את האדם על הליסור אלא בשביל המעשה דכתיב ושמעת ישראל ושמרת לעשות: אל יתהלל הגבור בגבורתו ואל יתהלל עשיר בעשרו. שהחכמה והגבורה

רד"ק

האנשים: (כ) כי עלה. הארמון הוא הבית הגבוה ובהסגר שערי הארמון אין דרך לחכנס בו אלא שיעלה הנכנס בו דרך החלונים וזה דבר רחוק כי הסה גבוהים לפיכך לא יסגרו חלוני הארמון אלא יהיו פתוחים תמיד ואמר דרך משל כי עלה מות בחלונינו בא בארמנותינו כלומר כי באה לנו הצרה פתאום שלא היינו נשמרים ממנה ואע"פ שהיו נביאי האמת אומרים זה אלינו תמיד לא היינו שומעים אליהם ולא עלה על לבנו שתהיה ואם תהיה שתהיה גדולה כזאת: עולל מחוץ. כי דרך העוללים לשחוק בשוק והבחורים ברחובות והנה הם נכרתים משם: (כא) דבר כה נאם ה'. אמר האל לנביא דבר ואמור כה נאם השם כמו כה אמר ה' אלא שנאם הוא שם המאמר: כדומן. כבר פירשנוהו למעל': וכעמיר מאחרי הקוצר. ששכחו הקוצר ונשאר מאחריו ואין מאסף אותו כן יהיו פגרית' כנשכחי' על פני השדה ואין קובר אותם: (כב) כה אמר ה'. אם יש בכם חכמים אל יתהללו בחכמתם כי לא תועילם כיון שלא ידעו את ה' ולא הלכו בדרכיו חכמת מה להם וכמו שאמר חכמים המה להרע וכן אם יש בכם גבורים אל יתהללו בגבורתם כי לא

מנחת שי

(כב) אל יתהלל עשיר. בדפוס יגן כתיב וא"ו בוא"ו וכן מלאתי בס"א כ"י זכל אלן דכתיב הכי טעי דבמסרה רבתא נמסר כ"ב ישירהין וא"ו וגיס להון זוגא ומאן דמשיב בהדייהו מהי תלת הוא וא"ו יתהלל הגבור:

מצודת דוד

קינה: (כ) כי עלה וגו'. אף כי סגרנו שערי הארמון לבלי תת לבא האויב הממית הנה עלה דרך החלונות ודרך שם בא אל הארמנות ור"ל לא הועלנו בכל התחבולות והתחכמות למנוע האויב: להכרית. והיה בדעתו להכרית קבוצת העוללים מן החוץ שהוא מקום ששוחקים שם התינוקות כי הרג כלם ואין מי ישחק בחוצות: בחורים. וכן הכרית הבחורים מן הרחובות ששם מנהגם ללכת תמיד: (כא) דבר

מצודת ציון

(כ) בארמנותינו. מל' ארמון ופלטרין: עולל. כן יקראו ילדים רכי' כמו עוללי' שאלו לחם (איכ' ד'): מחוץ. משוק: (כא) נבלת. כן נקרא פגר המת: כדומן. כזבל: וכעמיר. כן נקרא אגודת שבלי התבואה כמו ושכחת עומר (דברים כ"ד): מאסף. ענין הכנסה: (כב) יתהלל. מל' הלול והתפארות:

כה. מאמר ה' אל הנביא כה דבר אל ישראל נאם ה' וגו': נבלה. הנה פגרי אדם יפלו על הארץ כמרבית הזבל על פני השדה וכמרבי' עומרי התבואה המושלכים מאחרי הקוצר אשר דרכו לעשות עמרים ומניחם ע"פ השדה והסולך להכין לקציר עוד: ואין מאסף. אין מי יכניס את ההרוגים אל הקבר כי הנשארים יתפחדו לצאת ממקום מחבואם: (כב) אל יתהלל חכם. כי לא יוכל להציל נפשו בחכמתו והגבור לא יוכל להציל נפשו בגבורתו והעשיר לא יפדה נפשו בעשרו ואם כן אין להם להתהלל באלו כי לא יבא להם אז תועלת

retorts to them, "Let not the wise man boast of his wisdom." If a man learns Torah and does not keep it, he deserves no praise for his learning. On the contrary, it is a disgrace for him that he learned it and does not practice it. Above, he castigates them, "Wise men were ashamed, behold they were broken and caught; behold they rejected the word of the Lord, now what wisdom have they?" The Torah commands that we study in order to practice, as it is written (Deut. 6:3): And you shall hearken, O Israel, and observe to do.—[*Kara*]

and each to her neighbor a dirge. 20. For death has penetrated
our windows, it has entered our palaces; to cut off the infants
from the streets, and the young men from the squares.
21. Speak: Thus says the Lord: Indeed, the carcasses of men
shall fall like dung on the open field, and like sheaves after the
reaper, with none to gather them! 22. Thus says the Lord: Let
not the wise man boast of his wisdom, nor the strong man boast
of his strength, nor

were taught to recite lamentations since they are more emotional than men.—[*Redak*]

and each to her neighbor a dirge—So that they should be prepared to lament when the time comes.—[*Kara*]

20. **For death has penetrated our windows**—A palace is a tall edifice which cannot be entered, once the portals are closed, except by climbing through the windows. This, however, is very rare since the windows are high above the ground. They are, therefore, seldom shut. The prophet states allegorically, that 'death has penetrated our windows, it has entered our palaces.' I.e., it has taken us by surprise, for we did not beware of it. Although the true prophets constantly warned us, we paid them no heed and it did not enter our mind that the invasion would take place, and even if it would take place, we did not expect it to reach such proportions.—[*Redak*]

from the streets—Heb. מִחוּץ, *from the street. Comp.* '(I Kings 20:34) *And you shall make yourself streets in Damascus.*'—[*Rashi*]

and the young men from the squares—It is customary for the children to play in the streets and for the young men to frequent the squares.—[*Redak*]

21. **Speak: Thus says the Lord**—God commands the prophet to speak and to tell the people, "Thus says the Lord, etc."—[*Mezudath David*]

and like sheaves after the reaper—Like sheaves that the reaper forgot, and they remained behind him, with no one to pick them up and gather them in, so will your carcasses be left forgotten in the fields with no one to bury them.—[*Redak*]

Kara renders: like a sheaf that the reaper cast behind him.

22. **Let not the wise man boast**—*Do not boast, saying, "We are wise." Behold, you have rejected My words, so what wisdom do you have? If you understand and know Me, then you can boast of your wisdom.*—[*Rashi*]

Above (8:8), he stated, "How do you say, 'We are wise, and the Law of the Lord is with us?'" This indicates that the people boasted of their wisdom although they did not practice its teachings, as the prophet taunts them, (8:9), "Behold they rejected the word of the Lord; now what wisdom have they?" Here the prophet concludes this matter and

עָשִׁיר בְּעָשְׁרוֹ: כג כִּי אִם־בְּזֹאת יִתְהַלֵּל
הַמִּתְהַלֵּל הַשְׂכֵּל וְיָדֹעַ אוֹתִי כִּי אֲנִי
יְהוָה עֹשֶׂה חֶסֶד מִשְׁפָּט וּצְדָקָה בָּאָרֶץ
כִּי־בְאֵלֶּה חָפַצְתִּי נְאֻם־יְהוָה: כד הִנֵּה
יָמִים בָּאִים נְאֻם־יְהוָה וּפָקַדְתִּי עַל־

ת"א בזאת יתהלל. עקרים מ"ב פכ"ד ומ"ג פ"ה : פסה חסד . עקדה שער לו :

בְּעוּתְרֵיהּ: כג אֱלָהֵין בְּדָא
יִשְׁתַּבַּח דְמִשְׁתַּבַּח
דְחַכִּים וְאַלִּיף לְמִידַע
דְחַלְתִּי אֲרֵי אֲנָא יְיָ
עָבֵידְנָא חִסְדָא וְדִין
דִקְשׁוֹט וְזָכוּ בְּאַרְעָא אֲרֵי
בְּאִלֵּין רַעֲוָא קֳדָמַי אֲמַר
יְיָ: כד הָא יוֹמַיָא אָתַן
אֲמַר יְיָ וְאַסְעַר עַל כָּל
עַמְמַיָא פַּלְחֵי כוֹכְבַיָא
וְעַל בֵּית יִשְׂרָאֵל דְדָמַן

רש"י

(כג) השכל. כמו הככד (כרלמית ה) (הנטלייג"ט בלע"ז): (כד) על כל מול בערלה. על כל מול שיש לו ערלה אפי'

מהר"י קרא

והעושר אין עומדין לו לאדם להציל מיד חדיין אלא אם בא להתהלל: (כג) בזאת יתהלל המתהלל השכל וידע אותי. מי שלמד השכל והחכמה על מנת לידע אותי כי בדבר הזה יש קבול שכר כשם שמפרש והולך: כי אני ה' עושה חסד. לשומרי מצותי: כי באלה חפצתי. בבני אדם שמלמדין את החכמה על מנת ללמוד לשמור ולעשות ולא כבני אדם הכתיבין למעלה המתהללים לימר חכמי' אנחנו ותורת ה' אתנו ובדבר ה' מאסו: (כד) ופקדתי על כל מול בערלה. על הנימולים עם הערלים:

רד"ק

תועילם להצילם מן המות או מן השבי וכן אם יש בכם עשיר אל יתהלל בעושרו כי לא יפדהו מן החרב כי הוא ועושרו יאבדו וזכר אלו התכונות השלש כי החכם ינצל פעמית רבות בתחבולותיו ובערמתו וכן הגבור ינצל בגבורתו ובכחו וכן העשיר יפדה נפשו מיד האויב בעשרו כן מנהג העולם ברוב ואמר להם הנביא כי לא ינצלו באלה השלש שדרך העולם להנצל בהם אלא במה ינצלו אותם שינצלו: (כג) השכל וידוע אותי. פירוש בהשכל אותי וידוע אותי והשכל האל הוא שישכיל כי הוא אחד קדמון ואינו גוף והוא בורא הכל ומשגיח על הכל ומנהיג כל העולם בחכמתו עליונים ותחתונים וידיעת האל הוא ללכת בדרכיו לעשות חסד משפט וצדקה כי כן עושה אותם הוא בארץ. כלומר עם בני העולם וההולך בדרכיו הוא יודע אותו כמו שאמר אביך הלא אכל ושתה ועשה משפט וצדקה אז טוב לו כי דן דין עני ואביון אז טוב לו הלא הוא הדעת אותי נאם ה' הנה כי מעשה המשפט והצדקה הוא ידיעת האל ובזה נצולו דניאל וחבריו שגלו בחרבן הארץ עם גלות יהודה ונצלו מן הקלון והבזיון שהיה מגיע לשאר השבוים והיו נכבדים וגדולים בארץ גלותם לפי שהיו צדיקים וחסידים ולא היה להם דרך להנצל מן הגלות כי איך ישארו בארץ ג' או ד' או אפילו י': כי אם בזאת. בזאת התכונה שתהיה לו תכונה נפשית להשכיל ולדעת אותי ומה שאמר כי אני ה' טעם למה שאמר וידוע אותי כי בכלל וידוע אותי עשות חסד ומשפט וצדקה כמו שפירשנו לפיכך פי' ואמר כי אני ה' עושה חסד אלה הם דרכי ומדותי שאני מתנהג בהם בעולמי: באלה חפצתי. שיעשה אותם האדם וחי בהם ומה שאמר בארץ והסדו וצדקתו גם כן בשמים כמו שאמר ה' בהשמים חסדך אמר בארץ לפי שחסדו וצדקתו בארץ גלויה לבני אדם כלם ומה שבשמים אינו גלוי כי אם לחכמים הנה פירשתי לך שני הפסוקים האלה לפי ענין הפרשה דבקים בעניניה באר היטיב והחכמים אשר ראינו ספריהם פירשו אלה שני הפסוקים לענין נאות אבל לא הדביקום לענין הפרשה. והחכם רבי אברהם ב"ר חייא המכונה צאחי"ב אלצירט"א פירש אלו שלש התכונות בחכמה יקנה האדם החכמה ויקרא חכם וכשיהיה מוסיף על קנינו ומתגבר בה נקרא גבור והמעדיף על זה נקרא עשיר ואשר מגיע אל עומק החכמה נקרא משכיל והכתר על ראש החכמות והמגדל הבנוי עליהם הוא דעת אלהים שאין האדם ראוי להתהלל כי אם בה כמה שאמר כי אם בזאת יתהלל המתהלל בידיעת האל ובלמוד תורתו אשר היא חסד ומשפט וצדקה בה ראוי שיתהלל המתהלל. והחכם הגדול מורה צדק רבי משה בר מימון זצ"ל פי' כן ואמר תחלה כי שם החכמה נופל בלשון עברי על ארבעה ענינים נופל על השגת האמיתיות אשר תכלית כונתם השגתו יתברך שמו אמר והחכמה מאין תמצא ונופל על ידיעת המלאכות איזו מלאכה שתהיה וכל חכם לב בכם וכל אשה חכמת לב וניפל על קנות מעלות המדות וזקניו יחכם בישישים חכמה ונופל על הערמה וההתחכמות הבה נתחכמה לו ולפי זה הענין אמר ויקח משם אשה חכמ' ומזה הענין חכמים המה להרע ואפשר שיהיה ענין החכמה מורה על הערמה שיכוש המחשבה פעמי' יהי' החכמה ההיא וההתחכמו' ולקנות מעלות שכליות או לקנות מעלות מדות אמר שאין שלימות הקנין ולא שלימות בריאות הגוף ולא שלמות המדות הטובות אין כל זה שלמות שראוי להתפאר ולהתהלל בו והשלמות שראוי להתהלל בו הוא ידיעת האל יתברך שהיא החכמה האמיתית ופי' גם כן שלשת השמות חסד ומשפט וצדקה חסד הוא ההפלגה בגמילות הטובה וכולל שני ענינים האחד לגמול טוב למי שאין לו חק עליו כלל והשני להטיב למי שראוי לך להטיב לו יותר ממה שהוא ראוי וצדקה הוא היושר לתת לכל אחד כפי הראוי לו ומשפט לדון בכה שראוי על הנכון יהיה נקמה או יהיה טוב ואמר שאין ראוי לאדם להתהלל לא בחכמה ולא בגבורה ולא בעושר כי אם בהשכל וידוע האל שהיא החכמה והגבורה ולא בזה לבד אלא גם בידיעת מדות האל ותאריו' והם לעשות חסד משפט וצדקה כמו שאני עושה אותם והוא ית' לפי המציאו הכל נקרא חסיד ולפי שרחמיו על הענניים ר"ל הנהגתו בב"ח בכחותיה' יקרא צדיק ולפי מה שיתחדש בעולם מן הטובות והרעות כפי מה שמחייב אותם הדין הנמשך אחר החכמה יקרא שופט והוסיף עוד ואמר בארץ להודיע כי השגחתו ג"כ בארץ כפי מה שהוא כמו שמשגיח בשמים כפי מה שהם: (כד) הנה ימים באים. קריבים לבא וזכר אלה האומ' בעבור ישראל כי אלו הם אשר הרעו לישראל

מצודת דוד

מאלה: (כג) כי אם בזאת יתהלל המתהלל. המשבח את עצמו ישבח את עצמו בזאת והוא ומפרש במה שהשכיל וידוע אותי אשר אני ה' ואין עוד מלבדי ואני הוא העושה חסד לאוהבי ולשומרי מצותי ואני הוא העושה משפט להפרע מן הרשעים ואני הוא העושה צדקה לקבל את השבים ולהסיר מעליהם המשפט ולא שיש ח"ו פועל טוב ופועל רע כי בכל אלה חפצתי אני לתת לכל אחד כגמולו והמשכיל את זאת ראוי להתהלל בעצמו כי בזה יבא לו תועלת רב: (כד) הנה ימים באים. זהו בעת ההתגברות י"כ: ופקדתי. אשגיח לענש ולהביא גמול: על כל מול בערלה. מלות על כל עומדת במקום שתים על כל מול ועל כל אשר בערלה ר"ל על ישראל ועל העכו"ם:

מצודת ציון

(כד) ופקדתי. ענין השגחה: מול. מלשון מילה: בערלה.

24. **Behold, days are coming**—I.e., days are approaching. He mentions the following nations because they have dealt harshly with Israel. Moreover, because these nations were conquered by Nebuchadnez-

the rich man boast of his riches. 23. But let him that boasts
exult in this, that he understands and knows me, for I am the
Lord Who practices kindness, justice and righteousness on the
earth; for in these things I delight, says the Lord. 24. Behold,
days are coming, says the Lord, when I will punish

23. **But let him that boasts exult in this, that he understands and knows Me**—He who learns understanding and wisdom with the intention of knowing Me, for in this there is reward, as the prophet proceeds to elaborate.—[*Kara*]

that he understands—lit. understanding, Heb. הַשְׂכֵּיל, *like* (Exod. 8:11) *'making heavy* (הַכְבֵּד)*,'* (*Enteliant in O.F.*).—[*Rashi*]

Redak renders: By understanding and knowing Me. Understanding God consists of knowing that He has always existed, that He is incorporeal, that He created everything, guides everything, and leads the entire world, both heavenly and earthly beings, with His wisdom. Knowing God consists of going in His ways, to practice kindness, justice, and righteousness on the earth, i.e. with the inhabitants of the earth. One who follows His ways is said to know Him. We find a similar verse below (22:16): 'Did not your father eat and drink and practice justice and righteousness? Then it was good for him. He pleaded the cause of the poor and the impoverished, then it was good. Is that not knowledge of Me? said the Lord.' This illustrates that practicing kindness, justice, and righteousness constitutes knowledge of the Lord. Through this, Daniel and his companions, who were exiled with the exile of Judah, were saved from the disgrace that befell the other captives, and they were highly esteemed in the land of their captivity since they were righteous and pious. They had no way of being spared exile, because it was impossible for three, four, or even ten people to remain alone in Eretz Israel.—[*Redak*]

exult in this—I.e., let him exult in this character, to understand and to know Me.—[*Redak*]

that I am the Lord Who practices kindness, justice, and righteousness—This is the explanation of 'knows Me,' for knowing the Lord consists of practicing kindness, justice, and righteousness. He, therefore, elaborates on the matter and states, 'for I am the Lord, Who practices kindness, justice, and righteousness, for these are My ways and My traits, with which I deport Myself in My world.—[*Redak*]

for in these things I delight—that a man practice them and live with them. He states that He performs kindness, justice, and righteousness on earth, although He performs kindness in the heaven as well, as is stated: '(Psalms 36:6) O Lord, Your kindness is in the heavens,' he states here only that God practices kindness on the earth since that is manifest to human beings. His kindness in heaven, however, is known only to the wise.—[*Redak*]

כָּל־מוּל בְּעָרְלָה׃ כה עַל־מִצְרַיִם וְעַל־
יְהוּדָה וְעַל־אֱדוֹם וְעַל־בְּנֵי עַמּוֹן וְעַל־
מוֹאָב וְעַל כָּל־קְצוּצֵי פֵאָה הַיֹּשְׁבִים
בַּמִּדְבָּר כִּי כָל־הַגּוֹיִם עֲרֵלִים וְכָל־בֵּית
יִשְׂרָאֵל עַרְלֵי־לֵב׃ י א שִׁמְעוּ אֶת־
הַדָּבָר אֲשֶׁר דִּבֶּר יְהוָה עֲלֵיכֶם בֵּית
יִשְׂרָאֵל׃ ב כֹּה ׀ אָמַר יְהוָה אֶל־דֶּרֶךְ
הַגּוֹיִם אַל־תִּלְמָדוּ וּמֵאֹתוֹת הַשָּׁמַיִם

תרגום

עוֹבָדֵיהוֹן לְפַלְחֵי
כּוֹכְבַיָא : כה עַל מִצְרָאֵי
וְעַל יְהוּדָה וְעַל אֱדוֹמָאֵי
וְעַל בְּנֵי עַמּוֹן וְעַל
מוֹאֲבָאֵי וְעַל כָּל מַקְפֵי
פָּתָא דְשָׁרָן בְּשִׁכּוּנִין
בְּמַדְבְּרָא אֲרֵי כָל
עַמְמַיָא עַרְלִין בִּבְשַׂרְהוֹן
וְכָל בֵּית יִשְׂרָאֵל עַרְלִין
בְּלִבְּהוֹן : א קַבִּילוּ יָת
פִּתְגָמָא דְמַלֵּיל יְיָ
עֲלֵיכוֹן בֵּית יִשְׂרָאֵל :
ב כִּדְנַן אֲמַר יְיָ מֵאוֹרְחַת
עַמְמַיָא לָא תֵילְפוּן
וּמֵאָתְוָן דְמִשְׁתַּנִּין
בִשְׁמַיָא

ת"א ערלי לב. נדרים לא : אל תלמדו. שבת קנו סוכה כט עקידה שער לו :

קמץ בז"ק

מהר"י קרא

(כה) על כל קצוצי פאה. קצוצי לשון קצה :
י (ב) ומאותות השמים אל תחתו. הם חמה ולבנה וכוכבים ומזלות שנקראו אותות דכתיב והיו לאותות ולמועדים אל תחתו מהם אע"פ שאתם רואים כי יחתו הגוים מהמה ועושין

רש"י

ערלת לב וכ"ש על העכו"ס: (כה) על מצרים וגו'. שכיני ארץ ישראל היו ולקו אחריה בסמוך לה כמ"ש (ביחזקאל כ"ח) ומפ' כס"ע : קצוצי פאה. לשון קצה המוקצין בפאת מדבר :

י (ב) אל דרך הגוים אל תלמדו. ולא מאותות השמים אל תחתו מחמה לוקה וממאורות לוקין :

רד"ק

ועוד כי אלו האומות החריב נבוכדנצר וגם הוא וזרעו לקו באחרונה לפי שהרעו לישראל יותר מדאי : על כל מול. אלו ישראל שהם מולים ועל אשר בערלה אלו האומות שזוכר ועל שוכר עומד במקום שנים : (כה) על מצרים ועל יהודה. כי ישראל מלכות אפרים החריב מלך אשור כבר ויהודה החריב נבוכדנצר וכל שאר הגוים שזכר : ועל כל קצוצי פאה היושבי' במדבר. זה קדר וממלכות חצור אשר הכה נבוכדנצר כמו שהתנבא ירמיהו ונבואתו כתובה בסוף הספר ופירוש קצוצי פאה שוכנים בקצה הפאה כלומר רחוקים במדבר והדבר הרחוק יקרא קצה ויקרא פאה כי קצה ופאה רחוקי הגבול בכל דבר וקצה וקצץ בענין אחד : כי כל הגוים. עתה פי' מול ופי' בערלה אמר כל העכו"ם שהם ערלים ומול אמר על ישראל כי אף על פי שהם מולי בשר הם ערלי לב וראויין ליענש ולא אמר על העכו"ם שיהיו ענושים בעבור הערלה כי לא נצטוו עליה אלא בעבור ישראל אמר כלומר הרי שבו ככל הגוים שהם ערלים שלא נבדלו מן האומות במילתם אלא שיבדלו מהם גם כן במעשיהם וכיון שמעשיה' כמעשה העכו"ם והם ערלי לב לא הועילם מילת הבשר והרי הם כאילו לא מלו כי מילת הבשר נתנה לברית ולאות להיות סגולה מכל העמים לעבוד את ה' כמו שאמר לברית עולם להיות לך לאלהים ולזרעך אחריך תחתם אות בבשרם למען יזכרו תמיד כי הם נבדלי' מן האומו' והואיל והתערבו בגוים ולמדו ממעשיהם הרי הם כהם כאילו הפרו הברית והאות ואינו להם לאלהים כי בחרו תחתיו לאלהי' אחרים לפיכך אמר אחר זה אל דרך הגוים אל תלמדו וגו' : (א) שמעו. מבואר הוא: (ב) כה אמר ה' אל דרך הגוים. כמו את דרך הגוים וכמוהו אספרה אל חק ה' וירדפו אל מדין אמר אל תלמדו דרך העכו"ם כיון שאתם מולים לאות ולברית ביני וביניכם שמרו את דרכי ולא דרכי העכו"ם : ומאותות השמים אל תחתו. ואם תאמר נעבוד הכוכבים כדרך העכו"ם כי הם שולטים בארץ ואותותם נראים להטיב ולהרע כמו השמש שיש לו ממשל בארץ בתבואות ובפירות כמו שכתוב וממגד תבואות שמש ואם נעבוד אותו ירבו תבואותינו ואם לא נעבדנו ירע לנו ויחסרו תבואותינו ונירא גם כן מקדרותו שהוא סימן רע לעולם אל תחתו ממנו ומזולתו מן הכוכבים כי הם עבדי עושי דברי ואם תעבדו האדון לא תצטרכו אל העבד ואם תעבדו העבד יכעס האדון וישלח מארה בתבואותיכם הפך מחשבתכם : כי יחתו הגוים מהמה. אע"פ שיחתו העכו"ם מהמה אתם אל תחתו כי אם תעבדוני אין להם רשות להרע לכם ולא תזיק לכם קדרותם ואם הם דרך הנהגתם בעולם יהי' קיום העולם ולפעמי' יבא הפסד בפרטים בדרך מהלכם והו לשאר העמים כמו שאמר אשר חלק ה' אלהיך אותם לכל העמים אם להטיב אם להרע ואתכם לקח אם תעבדוהו בלב שלם יצילכם מכל נזק משפטי

מצודת ציון

סד שלא נמול : (כה) קצוצי. ענין חתוך כמו וקצץ פתילים (שמות ל"ט) ור"ל נפרדים וכאלו הם קצוצים אלה מאלה : פאה. ענין עבר וצד וכן על ארבע הפאות (שם כ"ה) : ערלי לב. אטומי לב כאלו מכוסה בשומן :
י (ב) ומאותות. מלשון אות וסימן : תחתו. ענין פחד ושבר :

מצודת דוד

(כה) על מצרים. עתה מפרש מי הם המקבלים העונש ונגמול לנפול ביד נבוכדנצר : וקצוצי פאה. הנפרדים ומפוזרים בהעבר הסוף היושבים במדבר : כי כל הגוים וגו'. ר"ל כי כמו שכל העכו"ם המה ערלי בשר כן כל בית ישראל ערלי לב בלבי שמוע בקול ה' ולכן בדין הוא שילקו ישראל עם העכו"ם :
י (ב) אל דרך וגו'. אל תלמדו ללכת על דרך העכו"ם לעבוד אל הפסילים הנעשים למזלות השמים : ומאותות. ר"ל אל תחשבו שבעבור עבודתם תהיו נצלים מהרעות אשר יורו עליהם מחברות הכוכבים ולקיות המאורות כי אין לכם לפחוד מאלה כי העכו"ם יפחדו מהם כי הם נתונים תחת מערכת השמים ולא כן אתם כי אתם

you worship the master, you will not need the servants, but if you worship the servant, the master will become incensed and send a blight upon your grain, contrary to your thoughts.—[*Redak*]

every circumcised one with his uncircumcision. 25. Egypt,
Judah, Edom, the children of Ammon, Moab, and all those
cast off to the corners, who dwell in the desert, for all the
nations are uncircumcised, and all the house of Israel are of
uncircumcised hearts.

10

1. Hearken to the word that the Lord spoke about you, O
house of Israel. 2. So says the Lord: Of the way of the nations
you shall not learn, and from the signs of the heaven

zar, and later, he and his seed were punished because they were too harsh to Israel.—[*Redak*]

every circumcised one for his uncircumcision—*Every circumcised one who has a foreskin, even an uncircumcised heart, and surely I will punish the heathens.*—[*Rashi*]

Redak renders: Every circumcised one and everyone who has a foreskin. This refers to the Jews and the gentiles. The circumcised ones are the Jews, and those who have a foreskin are the gentiles, mentioned in the following verse.

25. **Egypt etc.**—*These were the neighbors of Eretz Israel, and they were punished shortly after her, as it is written in Ezekiel* (29), *and explained in Seder Olam* (ch. 26).—[*Rashi*]

Judah—Since Israel, the kingdom of Ephraim, was already destroyed by the king of Assyria, and Judah and all the nations mentioend were destroyed by Nebuchadnezzar.—[*Redak*]

cast off to the corners—Heb. פְּאָה, *an expression of an end, those cast off to the corner of the desert.*—[*Rashi*]

2. **Of the way of the nations you shall not learn**—This follows the Targum. *Redak* renders: The way of the nations you shall not learn.

Rashi comments: Of the way of the nations you shall not learn—*and then, from the signs of the heavens you will not be dismayed, from the eclipse of the sun or the eclipse of the luminaries.*—[*Rashi*]

Since you are circumcised as a sign between Me and you, observe My ways and not the ways of the nations.—[*Redak*]

and from the signs of the heavens be not dismayed—If you say, "Let us worship the stars as the heathens do, for they rule the earth, and their signs appear to do good and to do harm, as the sun, which has control over the earth as regards the grain and the produce . . . If we worship it, our grain will increase, and if we do not worship it, it will harm us and we will suffer a shortage of grain. We must also fear the eclipse of the sun, which is an evil omen for the world," do not fear the sun or the other stars, for they are My servants, who execute My word. If

בשמיא לא התברון ארי
מתברין עממיא מנהון:
ג ארי גזירת עממיא
למא אינון צרי אעא
מחורשא קיץ ליה עובד
ידי נגר בחציבא:
ד בכספא ובדהבא חפי
ליה במסמרין ובמקבן
מתקיף ליה דלא יתטלי:
ה עובד נגיד זקיפין
אינון ולא ממללין
אתנטלא יתנטלון ארי
לית בהון רוחא להלכא
לא תדחלון מנהון ארי

אל-תחתו כי-יחתו הגוים מהמה:
ג כי-חקות העמים הבל הוא כי-עץ
מיער כרתו מעשה ידי-חרש במעצד:
ד בכסף ובזהב ייפהו במסמרות
ובמקבות יחזקום ולוא יפיק: ה כתמר
מקשה המה ולא ידברו נשוא ינשוא
כי-לא יצעדו אל-תיראו מהם כי-

רש"י

(ג) **חרש.** אומן: **מעצד.** דולדוייר"א בלע"ז: (ד) **במסמרות.** קלו"ש בלע"ז: **ובמקבות.** קורנס מרטי"ל בלע"ז: **יפיק.** יכרע ברכיו לשון פוקה (שמואל א כ"ה) ופיק ברכים (נחום ב'): (ה) **כתומר מקשה.** מקיש אותם בקורנס עד שזוקף לו קומה כדקל: **אל תיראו מהם.** אם תפרשו מהם כי לא

מהר"י קרא

אותן אלהית אתם אל תיראו מהם ולא תחתו מ־ם: (ג) **במעצד.** ברד"א בלע"ז: (ד) **יחזקום ולא יפיק.** יחזקום שלא ימוטו: (ה) **כתומר.** [פירש ר' מנחם ב"ר חלבו] כתומר מצוייר צורת אדם שעושין להפחיד העופו' שלא יאכלו הפירו': **מקשה.** בטדי"ץ בלע"ז כמו מקשה תעשה המנורה: **אל תיראו מהם כי לא ירעו.** ואם תאמר אע"פ שאינן מריעין יש בהם כח להיטיב והריני

רד"ק

הכוכבים וגם העכו"ם לא תועילם עבודתם להם כי האחרון ראוי ליעבד לא העבד לפיכך לא תצילם עבודתם אות' מנזקם: (ג) **כי** חקות העמים. ראו אל מה הביאם עבודה זו כי מעבודת הכוכבים באו אל עבודת אלילים כי יאמרו להם כהניהם צלם חזה נעשה במקום השמש ולכבודו והעובדו כאילו עובד השמש כמו צלם הזהב שעשה נבוכדנצר לשמש וכן יעשו הצלמים לשאר הכוכבים ואלו הם חוקות ששמו להם לחק כהני הצלמים והרגילו אותם בזה הדעת עד שארכו השני' בזה הדעת עד שיחשבו התמון כי זה אליל מטיב ומריע וזה הוא הבל ודבר שאין בו ממש כי האליל הזה עץ הוא ומיער כרתו העושה אותו והוא מעשה ידי הרש שתקנו במעצד והוא שקורין אותו דולדויי"א בלע"ז וזה אליל אין לו פעולה בעצמו ואיך ייטיב ואיך ירע כאשר יחשבו אלה הסכלים וזה הבל שאין כמוהו: (ד) **בכסף ובזהב ייפהו.** לפי שהוא עץ חופה אותו בכסף ובזהב כדי שיהיה יפה ונאה בעיני הרואי' ויכנס בלבם לעבדו: **יחזקום.** פסי הכסף וזהב יחזקו אותם על העץ במסמרות והמקבות שיכו בהם עליהם עד שלא יפיק כלומר שלא יצא מתכונתו ולא יכשל מענין ופיק ברכי' ויש לפרשו מענין והפק לרעב ויהיה זה פעל עומד רוצה לומר שלא יצא ממקומו: (ה) **כתמר מקשה.** כמו התמר שהוא שוה אין בגופו עוות כי ענפיו הם למעלה וכל גופו שוה וכן מעשה מקשה שוה כן הצל עומד זקוף שוה בדמות אדם ולא ידברו כי אין בקרבם רוח מניעה כל שכן מדברית וזהו שאמר נשא ינשא אם יסיעום ממקו' למקו' ינשאו כי הם לא יצעדו ברגליהם ואחר שהם כך אל תבטחו בהם ואל תיראו מהם כי לא ירעו: וגם היטב אין אותם. אין עמם כח להטיב. תומר כמו תמר וכן בא בחולם והיא יושבת תחת

מנחת שי

י (ה) נשוא ינשוא. כל"ג ס"א במקרא חסר וא"ו והין כלחוד מלא:

מצודת דוד

מיוחדים להשגחת המקום ב"ה וכמ"ש אשר חלק וגו' לכל העמים וגו' ואתכם לקח ה' וגו' (דברים ד): (ג) **כי חקות.** אשר חקות העמים הכל הוא גם לתועלת כמה שטועים לורה ללבא השמים ואליו יעבדו: **כי עץ.** ר"ל אף אם היה הכח ביד לבא השמים להפך הרעה לטובה ע"י העבודה להם מ"מ הכל הוא לעבוד את הלורה כי הלא הוא עץ בעלמא הנכרת מן היער והוא מעשה ידי אומן בכלי המעלד: (ד) **ייפהו.** מייפה את הלורה כחפוי בכסף וזהב ומחזיק עליו החפוי ע"י המסמרות ובהכאות המקבות: **ולא יפיק.** למען לא יהיה נכשל ר"ל שלא יתקלקל להפרד הלפוי ממנו: (ה) **כתומר מקשה המה.** ר"ל אין הפרש בין אלה הלורות ובין לורת אילן תמר הנעשה בהקשת הקורנס ממתכת כי גם המה כמוהו ולא יוכלו לדבר כמוהו: **נשא ינשוא.** מהלוכך לשאתו על כתף כי לא ילעדו בעלמם א"כ הואיל וכן אין לך הבל גדול מזה: **אל תיראו מהם.** ר"ל ואתם ישראל אל תיראו אף מלבא השמים עלמם כי אין בידם לעשות לכם

מצודת ציון

(ג) **כי.** אשר: **חוקות.** ענין דבר קבוע: **חרש.** אומן: **במעצד.** שם כלי גדול עשוי לחתוך בו וכן חרש ברזל מעלד (ישעיה מ"ד): (ד) **במסמרות.** כיתדות וכן ובברזל לרוב למסמרים (דה"א כ"ב): **ובמקבות.** הוא הפטיש כמו ותשם המקבת בידה (שופטים ד') ויקרא כן ע"ש שראשו אחד חד לנקוב בו האבנים: **יפיק.** ענין כשלון וכן ופיק ברכים (נחום ב'): (ה) **מקשה.** ענין הקשת בקורנס וכן מקשה אחת (שמות כ"ה): **נשוא ינשוא.** מלשון משא

Sam. 25:31) *a stumblingblock* (פוּקָה),' '(Nahum 2:11) *and tottering* (וּפִיק) *of the knees*.'—[*Rashi*]

Redak explains: that it should not lose its shape. He suggests also: that it should not slip from its place.

5. **Like a palm tree they are beaten**—*He hammers them with a hammer until it has an upright stature like a palm tree*.—[*Rashi*]

As a palm is even—there are no uneven parts on its trunk for its branches are above—so is a beaten article even, and so does the idol stand upright like the images of a man, but they do not speak.—[*Redak*]

they are carried for they do not step—They have no power to move, surely they cannot speak. Conse-

* For Rashi's commentary turn to page 227.

be not dismayed, for the nations are dismayed from them.
3. For the statutes of the peoples are vanity, for it is but a stock
that one cut from the forest, the handiwork of a carpenter with
a small axe. 4. With silver and gold he beautifies it, with nails
and with sledge hammers they strengthen them so that it does
not bend. 5. Like a palm tree they are beaten, and they do not
speak; they are carried for they do not step; fear them not for

for the nations are dismayed by them—Although the nations are dismayed by them, you shall not be dismayed, for if you worship Me, they have no right to harm you, neither will their eclipse harm you. Although sometimes they do harm individuals, that applies only to other nations, but if you worship God wholeheartedly, He will save you from the harm caused by the heavenly bodies. Even the nations will find that worshipping the heavenly bodies is of no avail, for it is proper to worship the master rather than the servant.—[*Redak*]

3. **For the statutes of the peoples**—See what the worship of the heavenly bodies led to, for the worship of the stars brought them to worship idols, for their priests taught them that a certain idol represented the sun and that it was made in his honor, and that he who worships the idol is accounted as worshipping the sun. We find an instance of this in Daniel 3, that Nebuchadnezzar erected a golden idol to represent the sun. Similarly, they would erect idols to represent other stars. These are the statutes that the pagan priests instituted for them. They became so accustomed to this belief that the populace finally believed that the idols had power to do good or harm. This was obviously vanity, a thing without substance, for the idols were but stocks cut from the forest, the handiwork of a carpenter with a small axe. Since this idol cannot move by himself, how can he benefit or harm?—[*Redak*]

a carpenter—Heb. חָרָשׁ, *a craftsman.*—[*Rashi*]

a small axe—*Dolodojjre in O.F.*—[*Rashi, Redak*] *Jonathan*, too, renders חֲצִינָא, an axe. *Mezudath Zion* defines it as a large axe.

4. **With silver and gold he beautifies it**—Since it is made of wood, he plates it with silver that it should appear beautiful and attract worshippers.—[*Redak*]

with nails—*clous in French.*—[*Rashi*]

and with sledge hammers—*A hammer, marteau in French.*—[*Rashi*]

they strengthen them—They strengthen the silver and gold plates on the wood with nails and sledge hammers, with which they fasten them onto the wood.—[*Redak*]

it does not bend—Heb. יָפִיק, *it does not kneel with its knees. Comp.* '(I

לֹא יָרֵעוּ וְגַם־הֵיטֵיב אֵין אוֹתָם: ו מֵאֵין
כָּמוֹךָ יְהוָה גָּדוֹל אַתָּה וְגָדוֹל שִׁמְךָ
בִּגְבוּרָה: ז מִי לֹא יִרָאֲךָ מֶלֶךְ הַגּוֹיִם כִּי
לְךָ יָאָתָה כִּי בְכָל־חַכְמֵי הַגּוֹיִם וּבְכָל־
מַלְכוּתָם מֵאֵין כָּמוֹךָ: ח וּבְאַחַת יִבְעֲרוּ
וְיִכְסָלוּ מוּסַר הֲבָלִים עֵץ הוּא: ט כֶּסֶף
מְרֻקָּע מִתַּרְשִׁישׁ יוּבָא וְזָהָב מֵאוּפָז
מַעֲשֵׂה

ת"א מלך הגוים. להר ברלהית. משפטים:

תרגום

לָא מַבְאֲשִׁין וְאַף לְאֵיטָבָא לֵית אִינוּן יָדְעִין: ו לֵית בַּר מִנָּךְ יְיָ רַב אַתְּ וְרַב שְׁמָךְ בִּגְבוּרְתָא: ז מַן לָא יִדְחַל מִן קֳדָמָךְ מַלֵּךְ עַל כָּל עַמְמַיָא אֲרֵי דִילָךְ הִיא מַלְכוּתָא אֲרֵי בְּכָל חַכִּימֵי עַמְמַיָא וּבְכָל מַלְכְוָתְהוֹן לֵית בַּר מִנָּךְ: ח וּבְחֲדָא יְחוּבוּן עַמְמַיָא פָּלְחֵי כּוֹכְבַיָא עַל דְאִטְפְּשׁוּ עַל דְפָלְחוּ לְטַעֲוָתָא דְלָמָא אִינוּן: ט בְּסַפָּא דִמְחַפַּן מֵאַפְרִיקָא מַיְתַן וְדַהֲבָא מֵאוֹפִיר עוֹבַד נַגַר וִידֵי קֵינֵי תִּכְלָא וְאַרְגְוָנָא לְבוּשְׁהוֹן עוֹבַד חַכִּימִין

רש"י

ירעו לכם: וגם היטיב אין אותם. אם תעבדום. היטיב כמו להטיב: (ז) לך יאתה. לך נאה: (ח) ובאחת יבערו. עכו"ם ומה היא האחת מוס' הבלים של עץ שלהם ויתייסרו עליו. יבערו לשון שטות וכן ויכסלו: (ט) מרוקע. מרודד:

מהר"י קרא

הולך אחריהם כדי שיטיבו לי ת"ל וגם היטיב אין אותם: (ו) מאין כמוך ה' גדול אתה וגדול שמך בגבורה. ובידך כח להרע לעוברי מצותיך ולהיטיב לשומרי מצותיך *): כי לך יאתה. היראה: מאין כמוך. שיכול להרע ולהיטיב: (ח) ובאחת יבערו ויכסלו. כל החכמים שעושין להם פסל וכל תמונה אם חכמים הם [לייפותו] אם בכסף וזהב ייפהו במסמרות ובמקבות יחזקנו ולא יפיק בער וכסיל הוא בדבר זה שאין יכול להטיל בו רוח כשם שמפרש והולך נבער כל אדם מדעת וגו' כי שקר נסכו ולא רוח בם אבל הקב"ה אינו כן דכתיב לא כאלה חלק יעקב כי יוצר הכל הוא ופת' יוצר של אדם מבחוץ ויוצר רוח אדם בקרבו נמצא שיצר את הכל וכשתבדוק בפרשה זו תמצא שכל דבר שמגנה בע"ז באותו דבר עצמו מקלס להקב"ה.

מנחת שי *ל"ב מאין כמוך ה'. המ"ס יתירה. העתק מהנדפס

(ז) יראך. ביו"ד האיתן לבד ופ"א הפעל נעלמת מהמכתב ונמשכת היו"ד בגעיה להורות על יו"ד הנפקדת. רד"ק: (ט) לורף. טעה המדפיס לרף חסר כי אינו

רד"ק

תומר. ינשוא הפוך כי הראוי ינשאו וכן נשוא לשוא צריך כמו נשאו: (ו) מאין כמוך. ממה שאנו רואי' ויודעים שאין כמוך לא בעליונים ולא בתחתונים ידענו כי גדול אתה וגדול שמך בגבורה ואמר אתה ואמר שמך להודיע כי הוא שמו ושמו הוא: (ז) מי לא יראך. ביו"ד האיתן לבד ופ"א הפעל נעלמת מהמכתב ונמשכת היו"ד בגעיא להורות על יו"ד הנפקדת אמר מי לא יראך לפי שאמר אל תיראו מהם אמר אות' אין ראוי לירא מהם אבל אתה מי לא ייראך אפילו העכו"ם העובדים האלילים ראוי להם שיראוך כי אתה מלך עליהם: כי לך יאתה. המלוכה לא לאחר כלומר ראויה היא לך וליחס אותה אליך לא לאחר כי בכל חכמי הגוים ובכל מלכותם אומרים מאין כמוך ואינם עובדים הכוכבים אלא להיותם אמצעיים בינך ובינם ואמר חכמי הגוים כי הם יודעים כי הפסל אינו כלום ואם יעבדו הכוכבי' לא יעבדום אלא מפני שהם משרתיך להיותם אמצעיים אף על פי כן הם חוטאים כי אין צריך אמצעי בין האל ובין האדם כי רם ה' ושפל יראה אבל ההמון חושבים כי הפסילים מטיבים ומריעים מפני שהורגלו בעבודתם ואמר ובכל מלכותם כי המלכי' ברוב הם חכמי' גם יש עמהם חכמים יודעי' ומכירי' כי מלכות בן אדם הוא כלות נפסקת ואין מלכות קיימת כי אם לה': (ח) ובאחת. חכמי העכו"ם כאחת יבערו ויכסלו שהם מייסרים העם לעבוד הפסילים שהם הבלים ועץ כי הוא מרוקע בכסף וזהב ואין לו פעולה בעצמו כי הוא עשוי מן השפל שבנמצאות והוא הדומם כי הנמצאות שלשה חי צומח דומם: (ט) כסף מרוקע. מן וירקעו את פחי הזהב והם מרקעין הפסים לחפות בו פסל העץ ליפותו ועוד מטריחים עצמם להביא כסף

מצודת ציון

וסכל: ירעו. מלשון רעה: אותם. עמהם וכן והדבר אותך (יחזק' כ'): (ז) יאתה. ענין רלוי כמו ויאותו הכהנים (מלכים ב' י"ג): (ח) יבערו. מלשון בער ושוטה וכן איש בער לא ידע (תהלי' ל"ב): ויכסלו. מלשון כסיל: מוסר. ענין תוכחה: (ט) מרוקע. מרודד לעשות טסים וכן ועשו אותם רקועי פחים (במדבר י"ז): מתרשיש.

מצודת דוד

רעה וגם אין עמהם לעשות טובה למי מהם כי הכל בא לכם בהשגחת המקום: (ו) מאין כמוך. ממה שאנו רואים שאין כמוך ה' לכן גדול אתה על כל צבא השמים: בגבורה. במה שאתה מתגבר עליהם לבטל הוראתם. (ז) מי לא ייראך. מי לא יפחד ממך אתה מלך לכל העמים עם שהם נתונים תחת ממשלת השמים: כי לך יאתה. כי לך נתרלה דבר היראה: כי בכל חכמי וגו'. כי היראה ממך תקועה בלב כל חכמי וגו' ממה שהם רואים שאין כמוך אף בצבא השמים (אבל יחשבו שגם להם מועיל העבודה): (ח) ובאחת. בדבר אחת הם כולם בוערים וכסילים: מוסר הבלים. במה שהם מיסרים ומוכיחים את העם לעבוד להבלי הפסילים כי הלא עץ הוא ומה א"כ יעבדו וכ"ל אף לפי טעותם שמועיל עבודה לצבא השמים הנה זה בודאי כסילות לחשוב שגם יועיל העבודה לצורה מעץ: (ט) כסף מרוקע. טסי כסף יובא מתרשיש לצפות בהם את הצורה והזהב יקחו מאופז לייפות בו את הצורה: מעשה חרש. כל

8. **But with one thing they are brutish**—I.e. *the heathens, and what is that one thing? Their vanities of wood for which they will be punished, and they will be punished for it* יִבְעֲרוּ *is an expression of foolishness, so is* וְיִכְסָלוּ.—[*Rashi*]

9. **Silver beaten into plates**—Heb. מְרֻקָּע.—[*Rashi*]

They beat the plates to deck the wooden idol to beautify it. Moreover, they make great effort to bring fine silver from Tarshish and gold from Uphaz, far away places, and

they will do no harm, neither is it in them to do good. 6. There
is none like You, O Lord; You are great, and Your name is
great with might. 7. Who will not fear You, O King of the
nations, for it befits You, for among all the wise men of the
nations and among all their kingdom there is none like You.
8. But with one thing they are brutish and foolish, the vanities
for which they will be punished are but wood. 9. Silver beaten
into plates is brought from Tarshish, and gold from Uphaz,

quently, do not trust in them, neither shall you fear them, for they will neither harm you nor benefit you.—[*Redak*]

Kara renders: like a beaten scarecrow. *Daath Mikra*: like a scarecrow in a cucumber garden.

neither is it in them to do good—*if you worship them.* הֵיטֵיב *is like* לְהֵיטִיב, *to do good.*—[*Rashi*]

6. **There is none like You**—This follows *Targum Jonathan. Redak* renders: From [what we see that] there is none like You, O Lord, [neither among the heavenly creatures nor among the earthly creatures, we know that] You are great, and that Your name is great with might.

and Your name is great with might—I.e., You have the power to harm those who transgress Your commandments and to benefit those who keep Your commandments.—[*Kara*]

The expressions, 'You' and 'Your name' are interchangeable, indicating that God and His name are synonymous.—[*Redak*]

7. **Who will not fear You**—Since he stated above, 'fear them not,' he proceeds to state that only the idols should not be feared, but God should be feared even by the heathens, since He is the King over them.—[*Redak*]

for it befits You—*It is proper for you.*—[*Rashi*]

I.e., the kingship befits you, and it is to be attributed to You and to no other, for among all the wise men of the nations and in their entire kingdom, all state that there is none like You, and they worship the stars only as intermediaries. He mentions the wise men of the nations since they know that the idols are meaningless, and if they do worship the stars, they worship them only as God's servants who serve as intermediaries. Nonetheless, they sin, for there is no necessity of an intermediary between God and man, for the Lord is high, and he sees the lowly. The populace, however, believed that the idols themselves had power to do good or bad, since they had become accustomed to worshipping them. He mentions 'and in their entire kingdom,' since the kings were unusually wise men and they had wise men to advise them. They, therefore, know that man's kingdom is transient, and that the only everlasting kingdom is God's.—[*Redak*]

Kara explains: fear befits You.

מַעֲשֵׂה חָרָשׁ וִידֵי צוֹרֵף תְּכֵלֶת וְאַרְגָּמָן
לְבוּשָׁם מַעֲשֵׂה חֲכָמִים כֻּלָּם: י וַיהוָה
אֱלֹהִים אֱמֶת הוּא־אֱלֹהִים חַיִּים וּמֶלֶךְ
עוֹלָם מִקִּצְפּוֹ תִּרְעַשׁ הָאָרֶץ וְלֹא־
יָכִלוּ גוֹיִם זַעְמוֹ: יא כִּדְנָה תֵּאמְרוּן לְהוֹם
אֱלָהַיָּא דִּי־שְׁמַיָּא וְאַרְקָא לָא עֲבַדוּ

ת״א כדנה תאמרון . זוהר בראשית סוטה כח : פתח באתנח יאבדו

כּוּלְהוֹן :
י וַיָי אֱלֹהִים קְשׁוֹט הוּא אֱלָהּ קַיָם וּמַלַךְ עָלְמִין מֵרוּגְזֵיהּ תְּזוּעַ אַרְעָא וְלָא יָכְלִין עַמְמַיָא לְסוֹבָרָא רוּגְזֵיהּ:
יא דְנָא פַּתְשֶׁגֶן אִגַרְתָּא דִשְׁלַח יִרְמְיָה נְבִיָא לְוַת שְׁאָר סָבֵי גָלוּתָא דִי בְּבָבֶל וְאִם יֵימְרוּן לְכוֹן כַּשְׂדָאֵי דְאַתּוּן בֵּינֵיהוֹן פְּלָחוּ לְטַעֲוָתָא בֵּית יִשְׂרָאֵל כְּדֵין תְּתִיבוּ וּכְדֵין תֵּימְרוּן לְהוֹן טַעֲוָן דְאַתּוּן פָּלְחִין לְהוֹן טַעֲוַת דְלֵית בְּהוֹן צְרוֹךְ אִינוּן מִן שְׁמַיָא לָא יָכְלִין לְאַחֲתָא מִטְרָא וּמִן

רש״י

(י) וה׳ אלהים אמת. למה כי הוא אלהי׳ חיים ומלך עולם לכך יכול לאמת דבריו אבל בשר ודם אומר לעשות ומת או תשש כחו או יורד מנכסיו ואין בידו לקיים: (יא) כדנה תאמרון. אגרת היא ששלח ירמיה ליכניה וגלותו בגולה

מהר״י קרא

[בע״ז הוא אומר כי לא ירעו וגם היטיב אין אתם ובו בלשון מקלס להקב״ה] מאין כמוך ה׳ מי לא ייראך מלך הגוים. בע״ז הוא אומר ובאחת יבערו ויכסלו מוסר הבלם עץ הוא שאין בו ממש ובאותו דבר עצמו מקלס להקב״ה. וה׳ אלהי׳ אמת הוא אלהים חיים. בע״ז מגנה למעלה אל תיראו מהם כי לא ירעו ובה במדה הוא מקלס להקב״ה. מקצפו תרעש הארץ ולא יכילו גוים זעמו: (יא) כדנה תאמרון להום. כמו שת״י דנא פתשגן איגרתא דשלח ירמיה נבייא לוות שאר שבי גלותא די בבבל אם יימרון לכון עממייא דאתון ביניהון פלחו לטעוותא בית ישראל כדין תתיבון וכדין תימרון להום טעון דאתון פלחון להון טעון דלית בהון צרוך אינון. מן שמיא לא יכילו לאחתא מטרא ואף כן ארעא לא יוכלון לאצמיחא פירין אינון ופלחיהון יאבדו מן ארעא וישתיצון מן תחות שמייא אלה. ובלשון שמגנה ע״ז דכתיב שמייא וארקא לא עבדו בו בלשון זה מקלס להקב״ה בצידו עושה ארץ בכחו

רד״ק

טוב מתרשיש וזהב מאופז אעפ״י שהם רחוקים מאלה המקומות ועוד לובשים אותם בתכלת וארגמן מרוקם במלאכת החכמים במלאכה וכל זה להראות בעיני ההמון יפים ושיכנס בלבם ידאתם ושיאמינו בהם ויעבדום: (י) וה׳ אלהים אמת. אלה האלהי׳ שעושין לעבדם הם שקר והם מתים כי אינם אלהי׳ ואין יכולת בהם אבל ה׳ אלהים אמת שהוא אדון על כל האלהים והם הכוכבים הוא לבדו אמת אלהים ויכול על הכל וישופט הכל ואשר זולתו אינם אמת אע״פ שהם אלהים כי אין כחם אלא ממנו והוא לבדו היכול האמיתי והשופט האמיתי שאין כחו והנהגתו תלוים ביד אחר: הוא אלהים חיים. הוא החי האמתי שאין חייו תלוין באחר כי חייו ממנו וכל החיי׳ זולתו חייהם ממנו ואמר חיים בלשון רבים כמו אלהים קדושים הוא דרך כבוד והוא מלך עולם ותכירו זה כי מקצפו תרעש הארץ ולא יכילו גוים זעמו ואין יכולת בהם שינצלו ממנו כשיקצוף עליה׳ ולא יכלו להכיל ולסבול זעמו ורעש הארץ הוא משל לחרבן יושבי הארץ איזה גוי שיהיה ויוכלו להכיר כי מאתו הוא שמודיע אותם תחלה קודם בא הפורעני׳ ביד עבדיו הנביאי׳: תרעש הארץ. נוכל לפרש גם כן כמשמעו שתשקע עיר ויושביה פעמי׳ ברעש הארץ: (יא) כדנה תאמרון להום. זה מאמר האל שלח ירמיהו לבבל בני הגולה שיענו זה לכשדים כשיאמרו להם שיעבדו אלהיהם יענו אותם אלהיא די שמיא וארקא לא עבדו יאבדו מן ארעא ומן תחות שמיא אלה וכתב להם המאמר הזה בלשון ארמי שיאמרו אותו לכשדים בלשונם ומה שאמר כדנה תאמרון להום שהוא אזהרה להם לישראל ג״כ בלשון ארמי כדי שלא לחלוק בפסוק שיהא חציו עברי וחציו ארמי ואמר להום בכ״ם כי פעמים בא כן בכ״ם כמו שנמצא בעזרא וכן אמרין להום אע״פ שברוב יבא בנו״ן: אלה. לשון עברי ולשון ארמי ג״כ מצאנוהו בעזרא אלה מניא בכתוב הוא אלה וקרי אל ואל ואלה אחד ואמר אלה כמו הארצות האל לפי שהם נראין לבני האדם אע״פ שהם גבוהים: וארקא. פי׳ ארץ ובדברי רז״ל ארבע שמות נקראו לה כנגד ארבע תקופותיה ארץ תבל ארקא ארחה וי״ת הפסוק כן כבעמוד ולא האריך בלשון הארמי כי עדיין לא הפסיק הענין עד ה׳ צבאות שמו הכל הוא מענה שיאמרו להם בני ישראל כי אנחנו לא

מנחת שי

מן ד׳ חסרים בישעיה סימן מ״ח : (י) יכלו. בספרים כ״י מדוייקים ודפוסים ישנים חסר יו״ד וכן נמסר עליו ב׳ חסר וחברו אבר לא י כ ל ו המים (ירמיה ג) : (יא) אלהיא די. היו״ד דגושה : ומן תחות. בנביאים עם פירוש הרי״א

מצודת דוד

הפסל נעשה ממעשה חרש וידי צורף הטן עשה החרש והלפוי עשה ידי צורף: לבושם. בגדי הפסילים מתכלת וארגמן : מעשה חכמים כולם. כל הלבושים המה מעשי חכמים וכאומר ואיך יעסקו חכמים בדבר שטות כזה : (י) וה׳. אבל ה׳ אלהים אמת הוא אלהים חיים ר״ל הוא חיי כל הברואים והוא מלך מושל על כל העולם: מקצפו תרעש. כל יושבי הארץ וכל העכו״ם לא יסבלו זעמו כי כל אשר יחפוץ יעשה ואין ערוך אליו בכל צבא השמים: (יא) כדנה. כן אמר הנביא לישראל שיאמרו אל האומות העובדים לצבא השמים: אלהים. האלהים אשר לא עשו את השמים ואת הארץ יהיו נאבדים מן הארץ ומתחת השמים האלה שעשה המקום ב״ה ר״ל מהלאוי שיהיה נאבד

מצודת ציון

שם מקום: מאופז. מין זהב טוב וכן בכתם אופז (דניאל י׳): תכלת וארגמן. שמות מיני צבעים חשובים: (י) מקצפו. מלשון קצף וזעם: תרעש. ענין תנועה והכדה: יכילו. ענין סבל כמו ומי יכילנו (יואל ב׳): (יא) כדנה. כזאת: להום. להם ומלאנו בלשון ארמי המ״ם במקום הנו״ן כמו וכן אמרין להום (עזרא ה׳): אלה. כזה

Although the beginning of the verse, 'so shall you say to them,' could have been written in Hebrew, it was written in Aramaic in order not to separate one verse by writing it in two languages.—[*Redak*]

Jonathan paraphrases: This is the contents of the letter the prophet Jeremiah sent to the other elders of the exile who were in Babylon: And if the Chaldeans among whom you are say to you, "Worship idols, O

the work of a craftsman and the hands of a smith; their raiment is blue and purple, all of them the work of experts. 10. But the Lord God is true; He is a living God and the King of the world; from His anger the earth quakes, and the nations cannot contain His fury. 11. So shall you say to them, "The gods who did not make the heavens and the earth,

they dress the idols with blue and purple, embroidered by experts. They do all this to show the people how beautiful the idols are and to encourage them to worship them and to believe in them.—[*Redak*]

the work of a craftsman and the hands of a smith—The entire idol was manufactured by a craftsman and the hands of a smith. The wooden idol itself was made by a carpenter, and the silver and gold plate that decked it was made by a smith.—[*Mezudath David*]

all of them the work of experts—All the raiment of the idol was the work of experts. Now, how can people with such talents engage in such foolish things?—[*Mezudath David*]

10. **But the Lord God is true**—*Why? Because He is a living God and the King of the world. Therefore, He can make His words come true. A flesh and blood person, however, plans to do something and dies or becomes weak or loses his property, and has no ability to execute his plans.*—[*Rashi*]

These gods that the pagans make for their worship are false, and they are dead, for they are not gods and they have no ability. But the Lord God is true, for He is the Lord over all the gods, i.e. over the stars, He alone is the true God, has power over everything, and judges all. The others, even though they can be called gods, are not true, since their power comes from Him, and He is the All-powerful and the true Judge, for His power and His guidance are not dependent on another.—[*Redak*]

He is a living God—He is the true live one since His existence is independent of others, for His life is from Him, and the life of all others is also from Him. The plural form is used here as a form of honor, similar to the plural of majesty.—[*Redak*]

from His anger the earth quaked—You will recognize this since the earth will quake from His anger, and the nations will not be able to contain His fury. This may be figurative of the destruction of any land. This will be obviously His doings since He notified the nation of their impending doom through His prophets. It may also be interpreted literally, that a city with its inhabitants sinks into the ground when the earth quakes.—[*Redak*]

11. **So shall you say to them**—*This is a letter that Jeremiah sent to Jeconiah and those exiled with him in exile, to reply to the Chaldees in Aramaic, a reply if they tell them to worship idols.*—[*Rashi*]

יאבדו מארעא ומן תחות שמיא אלה:
יב עשה ארץ בכחו מכין תבל
בחכמתו ובתבונתו נטה שמים:
יג לקול תתו המון מים בשמים ויעלה
נשאים מקצה *ארץ ברקים למטר

עשה · הארץ קרי

ת"א המון מים. ברכות נט מגלה טו: ברקים למטר. ברכות נט:

תרגום

ארעא לא יכלין לצמחא פרין אינון ופלחיהון ייבדו מארעא וישתיצון מן תחות שמיא אלין: יב וכרנא תימרון להון אנחנא פלחין לדעביד ארעא בחילי שכליל תבל בחוכמתיה בסוכלתנותיה תלא שמיא: יג לקל מתניה רכפת דמיין בשמיא

מהר"י קרא

מכין תבל בחכמתו ובתבונתו נטה שמים: (יג) לקול תתו המון מים בשמים. על ידי קול נותן המון מים בשמים: ויעלה נשיאים מקצה הארץ. שהעננים שותין ממי אוקיינוס דכתיב ויעלה נשיאי' מקצה הארץ ומששותין היכנו מעלין אותן לרקיע כדי להורידן לארץ וכה פתרונו לקול תתו הכון מים בשמים על ידי שמעלה נשיאים מקצה הארץ: ויוצא רוח מאוצרותיו. להוליך את העננים לכל אשר יצום על פני תבל ארצה שיוריד

רש"י

להשיב לכשדים ארמית תשובה אם אומרים להם לעבוד עכו"ם: (יב) נטה. (טונדי"ם בלע"ז): (יג) לקול תתו. בעת בא קול שהוא נותן המון מים בשמים: נשיאים.

מנחת שי

כתוב פ ו פ ת ו ח ופעום הוא: (יג) מקלה * ארץ. הארץ קרי:

רד"ק

בעבוד אלה האלהות שלא עשה שמים וארץ אלא אלהים שעשה ארץ בכחו הם יבינו העברי ויאמרו להם בלשון ארמי אבל פתח הדברים שלח להם ירמיה בלשון ארמי וכן פי' יונתן בזה הענין עשה ארץ בכחו כדין תימרון להום אנחנו פלחין לדעביד ארעא בחילי' ואמת הוא שלא עבדו ישראל ע"א משגלו וכה שהשתחוו לצלם שהעמיד נבוכדנצר אנוסים היו ואעפ"כ היו ענושים בזה בימי המן לולא שרחם עליהם האל כמ"ש מפני מה נתחייבו ישראל שבאותו הדור כליה מפני שהשתחוו לצלם: (יב) עשה ארץ בכחו. למי שעשה הארץ בכחו אנחנו עובדים וזכר בכחו על הארץ לפי שהגלגלים רצין עליה סביב תמיד בכח שאין לו הפסק הבא מאתו יתברך ובאותו הכח עומדת הארץ תלויה בינתים לא תזוז אילך ואילך אפילו כחוט השערה כמו שכתוב תולה ארץ על בלימה לא ידע אדם במה אלא שהחכם מתבונן כי מכח הסבוב היא עומדת בנתים בלא שום סמיכה אף על פי שיש טעם אחר כי בטבעה הוא שתעמוד באמצע לפי שהיא כבדה אף על פי כן האל שם בה זה הטבע וכחו הוא הכל: מכין תבל בחכמתו. תבל הוא מקומות הישוב מן הארץ והכין אותם האל בחכמתו בנהרות נמשכים ובמעיינות נוזלים שלא יתכן הישוב מבלעדיהם ויצמח בהם כל עשב וכל עץ פרי הצריכים לישוב אדם ובהמה וכל התועלות הנמצאות בה הכל עשה בחכמה: ובתבונתו נטה שמים. שנטע אותם כאהל לשבת וימתחם כאהל לשבת תחתיו כמו שאמר ויתחם כאהל לשבת והאהל הוא כחצי כדור ואין אנו משיגים מן השמים אלא חצי כדור אשר על הארץ אלא שאנחנו מתבוננים שיש חצי כדור אחר כי עגולים הם ונטיתם ומהלכם ומרוצתם ממזרח למערב וממערב למזרח הכל נעשה בתבונתו שלא תושג: (יג) לקול תתו. וכן אנחנו עובדים אותו לקול תתו המון מים בשמים והוא האויר הנקרא רקיע כי ידענו כי הוא הנותן מטר כמו שאמר הנותן מטר על פני ארץ ולא האלילים. כמו שאמר היש בהבלי הגוים מגשימים אם השמים יתנו רביבים הלא אתה הוא אלהינו והנה אנחנו ישראל שאנו חלק ה' יתברך ועמו מודים בו כי בידו לעשות כל זה שזכר לא יתנו השמים המטר כי אין בהם כח אלא הוא נותן אותם בהם אחר שיעלה נשיאים מקצה הארץ כמו שאמר ואד יעלה מן הארץ והשקה את כל פני האדמ' והמים לא יעלו מן הארץ אלא איד הוא שיעלה מן הארץ שמעלה אותו האל בנובע ששם בו והאל יתנהו מים באויר בכח שנתן בו וז"ש לקול תתו המון מים בשמים: ויעלה נשיאים. וי"ו ויעלה כוי"ו וירד מעשות החטאת והעולה שפי' אחר שירד מעשות העולה נשא ידיו על העם ויברכם וכן הן אתה קצפת ונחטא אחר שחטאנו קצפת וכן ויעלה נשיאים אחר שמעלה נשיאים נותן המים כי בעבור במקום מיוחד שבו ישוב האיד מים ובאמרו מקצה הארץ זה מאמר הפלוסופים שאומרי' שהאדים עולים מפאתי צפון ודרום זה מקצה הארץ הפאות הרחוקו' מן הישוב: ארץ. כתיב הארץ קרי והענין אחד: ברקים למטר עשה. ועוד פלא גדול עושה בירידת המטר שיורידי' ברקי' עם המטר והברק אש ואין המים מכבין אותו ובזה שאמר לקול תתו הוא נחיכת התחלת המטר שמשמעת קול וכן אמר כי קול המון הגשם:

מצודת ציון

לשון ארמי כלשון עברי וכן אלה מאלה (שם): (יב) תבל. שם המקומות המיושבות מבני אדם: (יג) לקול. באה הלמ"ד במקום בעבור וכן פתח פיך לאלם (משלי ל"א): תתו. מלשון נתינה: המון. מלשון המייה ושאון: ויעלה. באה הוי"ו במקום אז וכן ואם נקבה תלד וטמאה שבועים (ויקרא י"ב) ור"ל אז טמאה: נשיאים. עננים ע"ש שמנשאי' עלמן למעלה וכן מעלה נשיאים (תהלי' קל"ה):

מצודת דוד

אמם שם אלהות בכל המקומות שבהם אלהי האמתי כי אם לבם בהמקומות האלה (ולפי שכן לוה לו' להאומות אמר בלשון ארמי לשון שמכירים בו האומות ולזה פתח ואמר כדנה תאמרון להום ג"כ בלשון ארמי): (יב) עשה ארץ בכחו. עתה בא לגמור דבריו שאמר וה' אלהי' אמת וגו' ואמר הוא העושה ארץ בכחו: מכין תבל. המקומות המיושבות מכין בהם בחכמתו כל הדברים הנצרכים שמה: נטה שמים. אמר בלשון שאלה מנטיית אוהל: (יג) לקול תתו. בעבור נתינתו קול המיית מים באויר השמים אז מעלה את העננים לרום השמים: מקצה הארץ. ר"ל כאשר שמה נראים למראית העין שהם בשפולי הרקיע בקלה הארץ אז מעלה אותם אל מול המקום אשר ירצה להמטיר שמה: ברקים. לעת בוא המטר מבריק ברקים ואין

a tent to dwell.' The tent is like a half sphere, for, although we know that the heavens encompass the earth on all sides, we see only a half sphere. All this was done with God's understanding, which cannot be grasped.—[*Redak*]

13. **At the sound of His giving**—*At the time the sound comes that He is giving a multitude of water in the heavens.*—[*Rashi*]

clouds—Heb. נְשִׂאִים, *clouds.*—[*Rashi*]

We worship Him also at the sound of His giving a multitude of water in the heavens, i.e. in the

shall perish from the earth and from beneath these heavens.
12. Who made the earth with His strength, He prepared the world by His wisdom, and with His understanding He stretched out the heavens.
13. At the sound of His giving a multitude of waters in the heaven, and He brought up clouds from the end of the earth, He made lightning for the rain,

house of Israel," so shall you reply and so shall you say to them: The deities you worship are deities that have no power. They cannot bring down rain from the heavens, neither can they cause produce to grow from the earth. They and their worshippers will perish from the earth and will be destroyed from beneath these heavens.

Although this reply continues until the end of verse 16, Scripture did not wish to include a long Aramaic section and continued the reply in Hebrew. The Jews would understand the reply in Hebrew and translate it to the Chaldees.—[*Redak*]

earth—Heb. אַרְקָא. This is synonymous with אֶרֶץ. The Rabbis account for the four names of the earth: אֶרֶץ, תֵּבֵל, אֲדָמָה, אַרְקָא, as corresponding to the four seasons.—[*Redak* from *Gen. Rabbah* 13:12]

12. **Who made the earth with His strength**—*Jonathan* paraphrases: And so shall you say to them: We worship Him Who made the earth with His strength, completed the world with His wisdom, and with His understanding hung up the heavens. Accordingly, this is a continuation of the reply they are to give the Chaldeans. Indeed, we do not find that the Jews in Babylonian exile worshipped idols. The only time they worshipped idols was when Nebuchadnezzar erected his golden idol and coerced everyone to prostrate himself before it. Although they were coerced to worship it, they were, nevertheless, threatened with annihilation during the time of Haman, only that God showed compassion on them and spared them (*Megillah 12a*).—[*Redak*]

Redak goes on to explain that the matter of making the earth with His strength alludes to the power of gravity by which the earth hangs suspended in space and does not deviate from its orbit.

he prepared the world with His wisdom—I.e., He prepared places for settlement in the world by preparing rivers and streams without which the world would be unable to exist. He prepared all vegetables and fruit trees required for consumption by man and beast. All this He did with His infinite wisdom.—[*Redak*]

Others explain this verse as a continuation of verse 10. Verse 11, comprising the reply to the Chaldeans is an interpolation.—[*Mezudath David*]

He stretched out—*Tendre in French*.—[*Rashi*]

He stretched them out like a tent under which to dwell, as in Isaiah 40:22: 'And He spread them out like

עָשָׂה וַיּוֹצֵא רוּחַ מֵאֹצְרוֹתָיו׃ יד נִבְעַר
כָּל־אָדָם מִדַּעַת הֹבִישׁ כָּל־צוֹרֵף
מִפָּסֶל כִּי שֶׁקֶר נִסְכּוֹ וְלֹא־רוּחַ בָּם׃
טו הֶבֶל הֵמָּה מַעֲשֵׂה תַּעְתֻּעִים בְּעֵת
פְּקֻדָּתָם יֹאבֵדוּ׃ טז לֹא־כְאֵלֶּה חֵלֶק
יַעֲקֹב כִּי־יוֹצֵר הַכֹּל הוּא וְיִשְׂרָאֵל

תרגום

ומסיק ענגין מסיפי
ארעא ברקין לזמן
מטרא עבד ומפיק
רוחין מבית גנזוהי׃
יד אתברו כל פלחי
כוכביא מלמידע חכמתא
בהית כל קיני מלמעבד
צלם ארי שקרא אתכונון
ולא רוחא בהין׃ טו למא
אינון עובד תולעבא
בעדן דאסער עליהון
חוביהון ייבדון׃ טז לא
כאלין חולקיה דיעקב

ת"א הבל המה . תענית ה סנהדרין לב זוהר בראשית : בעת פקודתם . סנהדרין קב :

רש"י

סניס : ברקים . (פלנדורי"ש בלע"ז) : (יד) נבער . לשון איש בער (תהלים לב) וכן נבערו הרועים. כמו : נסכו . כ' מסכה: (טו) בעת פקודתם. כשאפקד עליהם:

מהר"י קרא

את הגשמי' לארץ: (יד) נבער כל אדם מדעת. למעלה נאמ' עשה ארץ בכחו וגו' ובדבר זה נבער כל אדם מדעת מלעשות ארץ בכחו ומלהכין תבל בחכמתו ולנטות שמים בתבונתו : הוביש כל צורף מפסל . כל צורף שעושה פסל משעושה אותו יכול לתתבייש לפי שאינו יכול להטיל בו רוח ונשמה כשם שמפרש והולך כי שקר נסכו ולא רוח בם : (טו) בעת פקדתם יאבדו . פירוש שיפקוד הקב"ה על עושיהם יאבדו עושיהם: (טז) לא

רד"ק

ויוצא רוח מאוצרותיו. זכר המטר וזכר הרוח כי בסבת הנשיאים שמעלה מן הארץ יהיה המטר ויהיה הרוח כי שני אידי' הם שעולים מן הארץ שקורא אותם נשיאים לנשואתם מעל הארץ האחד לח והוא הנקרא אד וממנו יהיה המטר והאחד יבש וממנו יהיה הרוח והוא הנקרא קיטור וכה שאמר באוצרותיו לפי שהיא מרחפת ואינה נראית כדבר הנתון באוצר : (יד) נבער כל אדם מדעת . מדעת חכמתו שעושה הדברים בחכמה: הוביש כל צורף מפסל . וכל צורף יבוש לפסלו שלא יוכל לעשות זה וקורא אותו אלוה יש לו להוביש כי שקר נסכו לשקר חפה אותו בזהב כי לא יועיל כלום אלא להטעות העם והוא שקר : ולא רוח בם . באלילים והוא נסך וחיפה אותם בזהב ובכסף ללא צורך: נסכו . ענין כסוי וחפוי כמו המסכה הנסוכה ואת קשות הנסך : (טו) הבל . בעת פקודתם יאבדו . כמ"ש למעלה יאבדו מארעא ופקודתם היא פקידת בבל שפקד האל עליה עונה והחריבוה מדי ופרס ואז בא פקידת האלילים ג"כ שאבדו מאלהותם ומעבודתם כמו שאמר כרע בל קורס נבו היו עצביה' לחיה ולבהמה וגו' כלומר ששברו אותם ונשאו על הבהמות ר"ל הכסף והזהב שבהם: (טז) לא כאלה חלק יעקב . לא כמו אלה האלילים שהם חלקם אין חלק יעקב כאלה כי יוצר הכל הוא וישראל שבט נחלתו ואנחנו לא נעבוד בלתו כי הוא יוצר הכל ואין זולתו נוצר ונברא ובחר ישראל לנחלה שיעבדוהו ויהיה הוא חלקם והם נחלתו וחלקו ואע"פ שגלינו לא עזבנוהו

מנחת שי

(טו) מעשה תעתעים . יש ספרים שכתוב בהם תעתועים מלא וא"ו וטועים בם כי הם שנים חסרים במסורת ותלוי בירמיה ל"א :

מצודת דוד

ממטר מכה אותם : ויוצא . הוא מוליא את הרוח ממקום אוצרו : (יד) נבער . כל אדם העובד הפסל הוא נבער מהיות בו דעת וכל צורף העושה הפסל יקבל בושה מן הפסל כאשר כי בקר המסכה בנסך ואין באחד מהם רוח החיוני : (טו) מעשה תעתעים . המה מעשי ידי התועים מדרך השכל : בעת פקדתם . בעת יגיע המקום להפרע מהם אז יאבדו מבלי תקומה : (טז) לא כאלה . לא כהפסילי' האלה הוא אלהי יעקב הנתון לחלקו : כי יוצר הכל הוא . לא כהפסילים בהמה מעשי ידי אדם כי חלק יעקב הוא היוצר את הכל : וישראל . ואת ישראל בחר להיות כ"א משבטיו שבט נחלתו : ה'

מצודת ציון

(יד) נבער . מלשון בער ושוטה : מדעת . מהיות בו דעת וכן וימאסך ממלך (ש"א ט"ז) ור"ל מהיות מלך : הוביש . מלשון בושה : נסכו . הפסל הנעשה ביציקת המתכת וכן אלהי מסכה (שמות ל"ד) : (טו) תעתועים . מל' תועה : פקודתם . ענין השגחה :

He chose Israel as His inheritance to worship Him and that He be their portion and they His inheritance and His portion. Although we have gone into exile, we have not forsaken Him. Because we forsook Him in our land, we were exiled from it. Now we recognize and acknowledge Him, that He is the Lord of Hosts, the Lord of both the heavenly and the earthly hosts. It is fitting to worship the Lord, rather than His hosts, the heavenly bodies. Jeremiah sent all this to the elders of the exile, who went with Jeconiah to Babylon, that they should reply to

and He took wind out of His treasuries. 14. Every man is
brutish without knowledge; every smith is put to shame by his
graven image, for his molten images are false, without spirit in
them. 15. They are vanity, a work of delusion; at the time of
their visitation they shall perish. 16. Not like these is Jacob's
portion, for He is the One Who formed everything, and Israel is

upper atmosphere called שָׁמַיִם, for we know that He gives the rain, not the pagan deities. We know that He brings the rain up to the heavens since there is no water there. He brings it up into the clouds.—[*Redak*]

14. **brutish**—Heb. נִבְעַר. *Comp.* '(Psalms 92:7) *a brutish* (בַּעַר) *man*'; *also,* '(infra 10:21) *the shepherds have become brutish* (נִבְעֲרוּ),' *here.*—[*Rashi*]

Every man is brutish, unable to grasp God's knowledge and wisdom with which He performs all these wonders.—[*Redak*]

Others explain: Every man is brutish, not possessing the knowledge to perform such wonders.—[*Kara*]

Still others explain: Every man who worships idols is brutish without knowledge.—[*Mezudath David*]

every smith is put to shame—Every smith is put to shame by his graven image, which cannot perform these wonders, yet he calls it a god.—[*Redak*]

his molten images—Heb. נִסְכּוֹ, *an expression of* מַסֵּכָה, *a molten image.*—[*Rashi*]

Others interpret it as 'a covering.' His covering is false. He covered it with gold for nought, for it is of no avail. It was covered with gold to mislead the people.—[*Redak*]

and there is no spirit in them—I.e., there is no spirit of life in the idols. Therefore, their gold covering is of no use.—[*Redak*]

15. **a work of delusion**—They are the work of those straying from common sense.—[*Mezudath David*]

at the time of their visitation—*When I will visit retribution upon them.*—[*Rashi*]

This is a repetition of v. 11, 'shall perish from the earth and from beneath these heavens.' Their visitation is the visitation of Babylon, when Persia and Media destroyed it. Then the Babylonian deities were destroyed, and their worship was discontinued. See Isaiah 46:1: 'Bel squats; Nebo soils himself; their idols were to the beasts and to the cattle; what you carry is made a load, a burden for the weary.' The intention is that the Persians broke the idols into pieces and carried the silver and gold on their beasts of burden.—[*Redak*]

Kara explains: When God will visit retribution on their worshippers, the worshippers will perish.

16. **Not like these is Jacob's portion**—Not like these idols, who are the portion of the heathens, is Jacob's portion, for He is the One Who formed no one but Him, for He formed everything, and without Him nothing was created or formed.

שֵׁבֶט נַחֲלָתוֹ יְהוָה צְבָאוֹת שְׁמוֹ׃
יז אִסְפִּי מֵאֶרֶץ כִּנְעָתֵךְ יוֹשֶׁבֶתי בַּמָּצוֹר׃
יח כִּי־כֹה אָמַר יְהוָה הִנְנִי קוֹלֵעַ אֶת־
יוֹשְׁבֵי הָאָרֶץ בַּפַּעַם הַזֹּאת וַהֲצֵרוֹתִי
לָהֶם לְמַעַן יִמְצָאוּ׃ יט אוֹי־לִי עַל־שִׁבְרִי
נַחְלָה מַכָּתִי וַאֲנִי אָמַרְתִּי אַךְ זֶה חֳלִי

יושבת קרי מלעיל — ואשאנו

תרגום

אֲרֵי דִבְרָא כוּלָא הוּא וְיִשְׂרָאֵל שִׁבְטָא דְאַחְסַנְתֵּיהּ יְיָ צְבָאוֹת שְׁמֵיהּ׃ יז כְּנוֹשִׁי מֵאַרְעָא סְחוֹרְתִיךְ דְיָתְבָא בְּתוּקְפָא בְּקִרְוִין כְּרִיכָן׃ יח אֲרֵי כִדְנַן אֲמַר יְיָ הָא אֲנָא מַיְתֵי עָקָא עַל עַמָּא הָדֵין וּכְמָה דְשָׁדַן אַבְנָא בְּקַלְעָא כֵּן אֲבַדֵּר יָת יָתְבֵי אַרְעָא בְּזִמְנָא הָדָא וְאָעִיק לְהוֹן בְּדִיל דִיקַבְּלוּן פּוּרְעָנוּת חוֹבֵיהוֹן׃ יט וַי לִי עַל תַּבְרִי סְמַרְעָא מַחְתִי וַאֲנָא אֲמָרֵית בְּרַם דֵין מַרְעִי וְאֶסוֹבְרִינֵיהּ׃

מהר"י קרא

כאלה חלק יעקב. כבר מפורש למעלה: (יז) אספי מארץ כנעתך. אספי בעיר סוחרתך שיש לך חוצה לעיר שעתידה שיצורו עליה במצור: (יח) הנני קולע את יושבי הארץ. [משליך את יושבי הארץ] אל ארץ אחרת כזה שקולע את האבן מתוך הקלע למרחוק לכן אני אומר להם לכל אחד מהם לאסוף את שללו בתוך העיר: והצרותי להם למען ימצאו. כתרגומו בדיל דיקבלון פורענות חוביהון: (יט) נחלה מכתי. [לשון] חולי שאין לך בכל התוכחות קשה כתוכחת גלות לפיכך מדמה אותה הנביא למכת חולי: ואני אמרתי אך זה חלי ואשאנו. כשאני אומר הריני נושא וסובל חלי זה שהקב"ה מטיל עלי ואני חוזר ורואה המכה שכל כך היא אנושה שאיני יכול לסובלה שהיא דומה לאהל ששודד וכל מיתריו נתקו. שכל זמן שהאהל נטוי ומיתריו עומדין בני אדם השרויין בתוכו יוצאין ממנו אף כאן משעה שאהלי שודד הוא אוהל בת ציון דכתיב באהל בת

רש"י

(יז) אספי מארץ כנעתך. התחילי כנוסי מארעא סחורתיך כמו כנען בידו מאזני מרמה (הושע יב) ומנחם פירש כנעתך ל' הכנעה ושפלות ואספי לשון שחייה שחי והשפילי יותר משפלות ארץ את הכנעתך את ירושלי' היושבת עתה במצור: (יח) קולע. כזה שהוא זורק אבן בקלע: למען. אשר ימצאו שכר פעולתם: (יט) נחלה. לשון חולי: ואשאנו.

מנחת שי

(יז) יושבתי. יושבת קרי: (יח) והצרותי להם. מלעיל הטעם בר"ש ועיין מ"ש בפרשת סימן מ': (יט) נחלה. התי"ו בגעיא לבדו רד"ק ועיין מ"ש בתהלים סימן

רד"ק

ובעבור שעזבנוהו בארצינו גלינו ממנה וזה אנחנו מכירים ומודים ה' צבאות שמו שהוא אדון צבאות מעלה ומטה והאדון ראוי לעבוד לא הכוכבים שהם צבאותיו כל אלה הדברי' שלח ירמיה הנביא לזקני ישראל אשר בגלות בבל שגלו ראשונה עם יהויכין שיענו הדברים האלה לכשדים אם ירצו לפתותם בעבודת אלילי'. והחכם הכוזרי פירש בעת פקודתם יאבדו אם תפקדם ותחפש עליהם יהיה לאפס כדבר המזויף שאם יחפשו עליו יהיו מוצאים התחבולה אבל הענין האלהי כל אשר תחפש עליו תמצא כזהב: (יז) אספי מארץ כנעתך. יאמר כנגד בבל אל תתגאו עתה על ישראל בשביל שגלו ביניכ' כי לא בצדקתכ' ולא תאמרו להם שיעבדו אליליכ' בעבור שאתם עתה מושלים באומות כי הנה ה' אומר לך בבל אספי מן הארץ כנעתך החכנעה שהיית מכנעת העמים אספי אותה ההכנעה כי לא תכניעי עוד וענין אספי כענין אסוף ידך וי"ת כנושי מארעא סחורתך פירש כנעתך מן כנעניה נכבדי ארץ: ישבת במצור. את שאת יושבת במקום חזק ואת חשבת שלא תשלום בך אומה. מצור ענין חוזק כמו ותבן צור מצור לה וכת"י דיתבא בתוקפא בקירון כריכן וי"מ כן ובנית כצור ופי' את שאת עתידה לשבת במצור. יושבתי כתיב בתוספת י' כמו אהבתי לדוש וקרי יושבת והענין אחד: (יח) כי כה אמר ה'. קולע. כמו שמשליכין אבן בקלע ישלכו כל גוי וגוי ממקומו ויגלו כולם לא ישראל בלבד לפיכך אל תרחיבי פה עליהם וכן נבא עליהם ירמיהו לאדום ולמואב וכן השאר כמה שכתוב בפעם הזאת כי כלם לקו על ידי נבוכדנצר ואחר כך לקה הוא ונלכד בבל בתחלת מלכות בן בנו: והצרתי להם למען ימצאו. אשר דברתי ע"י עבדי הנביאים למען ידעון כי מאתי הכל. והצרתי ענין צרה וצוקה. והחכם ראב"ע פירש כן כי ה' יביא עליהם קולעים ויצר להם מקומם הטעם להיות' נחברי' במקום אחד למען ימצאו אותם הקולעים. ואדוני אבי ז"ל פירש סמוך לפסוק הבא אחריו למען ימצאו צרות עד שיאמר כל א' מהם אוי לי על שברי כי ישראל לוקין. והצרתי מלעיל הטעם בר"ש וי"ת ואעיק להון בדיל דיקבלון חוביהון: (יט) אוי לי על שברי. אמר הנביא לפי שדבר בפורענות יושבי הארץ ר"ל שאר האומות העתידה לבא אמר בין כך ובין כך אוי לי על שברי כי ישראל לוקים תחלה: נחלה מכתי. החי"ת בשו"א לבדו נחלה פירש נכאבת כלומר מכה קשה היא וחשבתי שזה חלי שאוכל לסבול

מצודת ציון

(יז) אספי. ענין הכנסה כמו ואין איש מאסף אותם (שופטים י"ט): כנעתך. ענין סחורה כמו והגור נתנה לכנעני (משלי ל"א): במצור. ענין מבצר ע"ש שאין לכבשה בלא מצור וכן ערי מצור (דה"ב ח'): (יח) קולע. ענין השלכת אבן בכלי המיוחד לזה וכן ויקלע ויך את הפלשתי (ש"א י"ז): והצרותי. מלשון צר ומצוק: (יט) נחלה. מל'

מצודת דוד

צבאות שמו. כי הוא מושל על צבאות מעלה ומטה: (יז) אספי. אתה היושבת בירושלים הבצורה אספי סחורתך מן הארץ אל תוך העיר לבל ישללם האויב הבא ואמר כמהתל בהם וכאומר וכי תתחזקו במשגב העיר נהפך בה גם אתם: (יח) הנני קולע. ר"ל גם אתם לא תשארו בה כי בפעם הזאת אשליך נהלאה מן העיר את יושבים כאדם המשליך אבן בקלע וכאומר אל תחשבו שתתחזקו עתה במשגב העיר כמו אז כבלא עליכם מחריב כי בפעם הזאת לא תתחזקו עוד: והצרתי להם. אביא עליהם צרות למען ימצאו הגמול הראוי: (יט) אוי לי וגו'. זהו מאמר הנביא המתאונן על שבר ישראל: נחלה מכתי. המכה הבאה עלי יש בה חולי רב: ואני אמרתי. מתחלה

tined to be conquered, I lament over Israel since they will be first.—[*Redak*]

grievous—Heb. נַחְלָה, *an expression of sickness* (חֳלִי).—[*Rashi*]

and I will bear it—Heb. וְאֶשָּׂאֶנּוּ. *Jonathan renders: And I will bear it* (*[à]souffrir lui in O.F.*), to tolerate it.—[*Rashi*]

The wound that will come upon

the tribe of His inheritance; the Lord of Hosts is His name."
17. Gather in from the land your merchandise, you who sit in
the fortified cities. 18. For, so says the Lord: Behold, I will
sling the inhabitants of the land this time, and I will bring
troubles to them that they may find. 19. Woe is to me for my
hurt, my wound is grievous, and I said, "This is but an illness,
and I will bear it."

the Chaldeans if they attempt to seduce them to worship pagan deities. The *Khuzari* explains: **At the time of their test, they shall perish.** If you put them to the test and examine them, they will become nought, like a forged document, which, if tested, will be discovered to be counterfeit (*Khuzari*, conclusion).—[*Redak*]

17. **Gather in from the land your merchandise**—Heb. כִּנְעָתֵךְ. *Hide, gather in from the land your merchandise. Comp.* '(Hos. 12:8) *The trafficker* (כְּנַעַן) *in his hand are deceitful scales.' Menahem explains* כִּנְעָתֵךְ *as an expression of humility* (הַכְּנָעָה) *and lowliness. And* אִסְפִּי *is an expression of bending down. Bend down and humble yourself more than the lowliness of the earth, you Jerusalem, that dwells now in a fortified city* (*Machbereth* p. 107).—[*Rashi*]

According to the first interpretation, the prophet is addressing Jerusalem also. He exhorts them to bring in their merchandise from the land into the fortified city to prevent the enemy from spoiling it. He is speaking to them sarcastically, as though asking them, "Do you think you will be able to save yourselves by hiding in the fortified city?"—[*Mezudath David*]

18. **sling**—*as one slings a stone with a slingshot.*—[*Rashi*]

As one slings a stone with a slingshot, so will all the nations be exiled from their places, not only Israel. Therefore, Babylon, do not open your mouth wide against them. So did Jeremiah prophesy about Edom, Moab, and other nations, who were destined to be conquered by Nebuchadnezzar, and finally, during the reign of his grandson, Belshazzar, Babylon would be vanquished.—[*Redak*] Note that this follows *Redak*'s explanation of the previous verse, that the prophet is addressing Babylon. According to *Rashi*, however, he is addressing Jerusalem, and telling them that, lest they expect to be saved within the fortifications of Jerusalem as they were during the siege of Sennacherib, they should know that God will sling them at this time, and they will not find refuge in Jerusalem.—[*Mezudath David*]

that—*they may find their just deserts.*—[*Rashi*]

19. **Woe is to me for my hurt**—The prophet, complaining over the troubles of Israel, says, "Woe is to me for my hurt."—[*Mezudath David*]

Although all the nations are des-

וְאֶשָּׂאֶנּוּ׃ כ אָהֳלִי שֻׁדָּד וְכָל־מֵיתָרַי
נִתָּקוּ בָּנַי יְצָאֻנִי וְאֵינָם אֵין־נֹטֶה עוֹד
אָהֳלִי וּמֵקִים יְרִיעוֹתָי׃ כא כִּי נִבְעֲרוּ
הָרֹעִים וְאֶת־יְהוָה לֹא דָרָשׁוּ עַל־כֵּן
לֹא הִשְׂכִּילוּ וְכָל־מַרְעִיתָם נְפוֹצָה׃
כב קוֹל שְׁמוּעָה הִנֵּה בָאָה וְרַעַשׁ
גָּדוֹל מֵאֶרֶץ צָפוֹן לָשׂוּם אֶת־עָרֵי
יְהוּדָה שְׁמָמָה מְעוֹן תַּנִּים׃ כג יָדַעְתִּי

תרגום

כ ארעי חרובת וכל קרוי
אתבזיזא עמי גלו
וליתינון לית דמתח עוד
משכני ומקים יריעתי׃
כא ארי אטפשו מלכיא
ואולפן מן קדם יי לא
תבעו על כן לא יצלחון
וכל עמהון יתבדרון׃
כב קל בשורתא הא אתיא
ותברא רבא מארע
צפונא לשואה ית קרויא
דבית יהודה לצדו מדור
ירודין׃ כג ידענא יי ארי
לא לאנשא אורחיה ולא
לגבר

קמץ בז"ק

רש"י

ת"י ואסוברניה (אשופרילו"י בלע"ז)׃ (כ) יצאוני. יצאו ממני ירושלים אומרת כן׃ (כא) הרועים. המלכים׃ לא השכילו. לא הצליחו במלכותם כמו בכל אשר יפנה ישכיל

מהר"י קרא

ציון שפך כאש חמתו׃ (כ) וכל מיתרי נתקו. הם גלות יהויקים ואנשי כנסת הגדולה גלות יכניה שגלו י"א שנה עד שלא חרב הבית ומשעה ששודד האוהל׃ בני יצאוני ואינם. יצאו ממני׃ אין נוטה עוד אהלי. שמגלות צדקיהו לא העמידו מלך עד היום׃ (כא) כי נבערו הרועים. הם מלכי ישראל ומלכי יהודה שהדיחו את ישראל מאחרי ה'׃ על כן לא השכילו. פת' על אשר לא השכילו דבר זה גרם שכל מרעיתם נפוצה׃

רד"ק

אותו ולא אוכל כי אהלי שדד׃ (כ) אהלי. המשיל ירושלים לאהל וערי יהודה כמיתרים לאהל׃ בני יצאוני. כי העם כבנים לנביא שמיסר אותם כאב המיסר את בנו אם ישמעו אליו׃ יצאני. יצאו ממני כלומר שגלו עם יהויכין וכן חוקתני ותוכל חוקת ממני׃ אין נוטה עוד אהלי. אם אומר עוד יהיה מלך שיטה האהל ששדד ראיתי כי אינני ואין מקום יריעת האהל שנפלו כי האהל עשוי כיריעות׃ (כא) כי נבערו הרועים. לפיכך אין נוטה עוד האהל והרועים הם יהויכין וצדקיהו שהיו מלכים והמלך יקרא רועה וכן תרגם יונתן ארי אטפשו מלכיא׃ לא השכילו. לא הצליחו כמו ויהי דוד לכל דרכיו משכיל והדומין לו ויהויכין וצדקיהו בעבור שלא דרשו את ה' כמו יאשיהו על כן לא הצליחו במלכות כמו שהצליח הוא כמ"ש עליהם ועל מרעית' נפוצה הצאן שהיו רועים והם ישראל נפוצו בגלות׃ (כב) קול שמועה. הקול שאנחנו שומעים ורעש גדול בשמועת מבהילות כמו הרעש בא מארץ צפון כלומר ששמענו שנסע נבוכדנצר ממקומו זה היה הקול אבל לא היו אומרים לאיזה מקום יבא ואמר הנביא שראה בנבואה כי יבא לשום את ערי יהודה שממה׃ (כג) ידעתי ה'. פירושו כמו שפי' אדוני אבי ז"ל כי על נבוכדנצר נאמר שהיה דעתו על בני עמון כמו שאמר כי עמד מלך בבל על אם הדרך כי הוא היה דעתו על בני עמון בנסעו ממקומו וכאשר היה על אם הדרך והיה לשני דרכים האחת לבני עמון והאחת לירושלם עמד בדעתו כאילו חוזר בו מדעתו שהיה בתחילה והאל החליף רוחו ושנה את קסמיו לבא אל ירושלם בעבור צדקיהו שעבר על שבועתו וחלל

מנחת שי

קל"ג׃ (כ) יצאני ואינם. יש ספרים שהוא"ו בגעיא׃

מצודת דוד

הסכתי שאך זה חלי במנמא ואוכל לשאתו ולסבלו וכאו' אבל לא כן הוא וקלר לדבר המוכן׃ (כ) וכל מיתרי נתקו. כל חבלי האוהל נמתקו ממקומ' והוא משל על חורבן ירושלים וכסמ"ק׃ בני יצאוני. בני יצאו ממני ואין א"כ מי עוד לנטות אהלי ומקים יריעות האוהל׃ (כא) כי נבערו הרועים. הרי העם נשתטו׃ לא השכילו. לא הצליחו על כי המצליח נראה שעשה דרכיו בהשכל׃ וכל מרעיתם. כל לאן מרעיתם נפוצו הנה והנה. ר"ל בני העם הלכו בגולה ואמר דבריו כאלו כבר נעשה כי כן ראה במראה הנבואה׃ (כב) מארץ צפון. היא בבל׃ מעון תנים. להיות מדור לתנים השוכנים במקו' שממון׃ (כג) ידעתי ה'. זהו מאמר בני יהודה שיאמרו אתה ה' הן ידעתי כי לא היה לאדם מכל בני יהודה את הדרך שלאוי לו

מצודת ציון

חולי׃ ואשאנו. מלשון משא וסבל׃ (כ) שדד. ענין עושק׃ מיתרי. חבלי האוהל וכן יתריס לחים (שופטים ט"ז)׃ נתקו. נפתקו ממקומם׃ ומקים. מלשון הקמה׃ יריעותי. ענין וילון׃ (כא) נבערו. מלשון בער ושוטה׃ השכילו. ענין הצלחה וכן ויהי דוד לכל דרכיו משכיל (ש"א י"ח)׃ מרעיתם. מלשון מרעה ור"ל לאן מרעיתם׃ נפוצה. ענין פיזור׃ (כב) ורעש. ענין תנועה והכאה׃

22. **Hark! a report**—The sound of the report that we hear and the great tumult that is reported, frightened us. We heard that Nebuchadnezzar had left his place. This was the report. But we did not hear where he

20. My tent has been spoiled, and all my cords have been broken; my children have left me and they are not here. No one pitches my tent anymore, or sets up my curtains. 21. For the shepherds have become brutish, and they did not seek the Lord; therefore, they have not prospered, and all their flocks have been scattered. 22. Hark! A report, behold it comes, and a great tumult from the northland, to make the cities of Judah a desolation, a lair of jackals. 23. I know,

me is very grievous, whereas, in the beginning, I thought it was a minor ailment.—[*Mezudath David*]

20. **My tent has been spoiled**—He likens Jerusalem to a tent and the cities of Judah to the cords of the tent.—[*Redak*]

They are the exile of Jehoiakim and the Men of the Great Assembly, and the exile of Jeconiah who went into exile eleven years before the destruction of the Temple, and from the time that the tent was spoiled . . .—[*Kara*]

have left me—Heb. יְצָאוּנִי, *have left me,* lit. have gone out from me. The suffix נִי is not the direct object, me, but the adverbial phrase, from me. *Jerusalem says this.*—[*Rashi*]

This is the exile of Jeconiah.—[*Redak*]

Others explain that the prophet refers to the people as his children since he instructed them as a father instructs his son.—[*Redak*]

No one pitches my tent anymore—If I say that there will be another king who will pitch my tent that has been spoiled, I see that there is none.

and no one sets up the curtains of my tent.—[*Redak*] Since Zedekiah, Israel has had no king to this very day.—[*Kara*]

21. **For the shepherds**—*The kings.*—[*Rashi*]

This refers to Jehoiachin and Zedekiah, who were kings, and the kings are referred to as shepherds.—[*Redak*]

Kara explains that these are the kings of Israel and Judah who misled the people from following God.

Mezudath David takes it as a reference to the princes of Israel.

they have not prospered—Heb. לֹא הִשְׂכִּילוּ, *they have not prospered in their kingdom. Comp.* '(Prov. 17:8) *To all that he turns, he will prosper* (יַשְׂכִּיל).'—[*Rashi*]

Jehoiachin and Zedekiah, since they did not seek the Lord as Josiah had done, did not prosper in their reigns as he had prospered. Instead, all their flocks are scattered, i.e., all Israel has been exiled.—[*Redak*]

and they did not seek the Lord—*Jonathan* paraphrases: They did not seek instruction from the Lord.

their flocks—Heb. מַרְעִיתָם, lit. their pasture, *the flocks of their pasture.*—[*Rashi*]

יְהוָה כִּי לֹא לָאָדָם דַּרְכּוֹ לֹא־לְאִישׁ
הֹלֵךְ וְהָכִין אֶת־צַעֲדוֹ: כד יַסְּרֵנִי יְהוָה
אַךְ בְּמִשְׁפָּט אַל־בְּאַפְּךָ פֶּן־תַּמְעִטֵנִי:
כה שְׁפֹךְ חֲמָתְךָ עַל־הַגּוֹיִם אֲשֶׁר לֹא־
יְדָעוּךָ וְעַל מִשְׁפָּחוֹת אֲשֶׁר בְּשִׁמְךָ
לֹא קָרָאוּ כִּי־אָכְלוּ אֶת־יַעֲקֹב וַאֲכָלֻהוּ
וַיְכַלֻּהוּ וְאֶת־נָוֵהוּ הֵשַׁמּוּ: יא א הַדָּבָר

תרגום

לגבר דאזיל ומתקין ית פסיעתיה : כד איתי עליהון יסורין יי קבל כדין חשוך לא יתקף רוגזך בהון דלמא יזערון: כה שפוך חימתך על עממיא דלא אליפו למידע דחלתך ועל זרעיתא דבשראי די בפולחן שמך לא תבעו ארי שליטו בדבית יעקב ובזו נכסהון ושיציאונון וית מדורהון אצדיאו: א פתגם נבואה

מהר"י קרא

(כג) ידעתי ה' כי לא לאדם דרכו . אמר הנביא רבונו של עולם ידוע אני שלא יעלה ללב אדם לתתן דרכו ולהחריב את ירושלים אם לא שמעו שמאתך נהיה הדבר : ולא לאיש הולך והכין את צעדו . פת' אין לך מלך ומושל בעולם שיתן אל לבו ללכת להכין את צעדו לבא ולהחריב את ירושלים כי מי הוא זה ערב את לבו להחריב את נוהו של הקב"ה אם לא שאתה קורא להם ומצוה אתה להחריבו כענין שאמר בתחילת הספר כי הנני קורא לכל משפחות ממלכות צפונה נאום ה' : (כד) יסרני ה' אך במשפט אל באפך פן תמעיטני . כראות הנביא שהקב"ה מכריז לאומות לבוא לירושלים להחריב נוהו ולהפיץ את ישראל בארצות ואין לך תוכחת חימה כתוכחת גלות. התחיל לבקש מלפניו על עמו. אמר לפניו רבש"ע בבקשה ממך יסרני בכל מידות יסורין של משפט שאתה רוצה ובלבד שלא תייסרני על ידי האומות שהיא תוכחת של אף כלומר עשה לנו ככל הטוב בעיניך אך במכה של אומות אל תרדה אותנו בה לפי שהיא רידוי של אף וזהו הוא אל באפך פן תמעיטני שכשישראל מסורין ביד האומות. האומות ממעטין אותן כענין שנאמר ואכלה אתכם ארץ איביכם . על מי תשפוך אפך וחמתך על הגוים אשר לא ידעוך : (כה) כי אכלו את יעקב ואכלוהו ויכלהו. לא כזה שאוכל ומותיר אלא כזה שאוכל ומכלה את הכל ואינו משאיר כלום :

רש"י

(משלי י"ז):מרעיתם.לשון מרעיתם:(כג) לא לאדם דרכו. כי יצר הרע שברחת בו מטהו מן הדרך . דבר אחר ידעתי ה' כי לא לאדם דרכו אין ביד כל אדם כח להצליח דרכו ואם לא על פיך אין כח ביד אויב להחריב ביתך : (כד) אך במשפט . ביסורים : במשפט . (יוסטיל"א בלע"ז) : אך במשפט . ת"י כרם בדין חסוך : אל באפך . פן תהא כלייה : (כה) אכלו . (דיורידנו"ש בלע"ז) וכן ואכלוהו :

רד"ק

את השם ואמר הנביא ידעתי ה' כי לא לאדם בקמץ הלמ"ד לידיעה לאדם הידוע והוא נבוכדנצר : לא לאדם דרכו . כלומר אינו ברשותו כי אתה תשנה רצונו : לא לאיש הולך . וכן לא לאיש הולך בעולם שהולך בדרך אין לו דרכו להכין צעדו כי לא ידע מה יבואנו ואין התכנה בידו כמו שאמר דוד מה' מצעדי גבר כוננו ודרכו יחפץ : (כד) יסרני ה' אך במשפט . פירושו כמו שפירש רבי יונה כי הנביא מדבר בלשון ישראל בל' יחיד דרך כלל ואמר בראותו נבוכדנצר בא לארץ יהודה לשום הכל שממה אמר ידעתי כי זה מוסר שאתה מיסר אותנו טוב שתיסרני אך במשפט כפי שנוכל לסבול אל באפך פן תמעיטני כי אם תיסרני באפך תמעיטני מהיות גוי וכן ת"י איתי עליהון יסורין וגו' כבעמוד וכן ויסרתיך למשפט ונקה לא אנקך : (כה) שפוך חמתך . אם יש לך אף וחמה שפוך אותם אל הגוים אשר לא ידעוך ועל משפחות הממלכות אשר בשמך לא קראו כי ישראל אף על פי שחטאו לפניך לא יצאו מתחת רשותך מכל וכל ולא נתערבו עם עם אחר אלא הם נבדלים מכל העכו"ם ומחזיקים ברוב המצות וקוראים בשמך ומתפללין לפניך ואע"פ שאין לבם נכון ישובו עוד בתשובה כי לא אבדה תקותם מהם ועוד היום יש בהם חסידים : משפחות . כמו גוים כי האומה תקרא משפחה כמו ואם משפחת מצרים לא תעלה : כי אכלו . ואף על פי שהם שבט אפך על ישראל אתה קצפת מעט והם עזרו לרעה וראויין הם ליענש ועליהם שפוך חמתך : ואת נוהו השמו . כתרגומו וית מדוריהון אצדיאו ויתכן לפרש כי על בית המקדש אמר ודבר על העתיד : (א) הדבר . לאמר שיאמרו אותו לאיש יהודה ומהו הדבר שיאמרו שמעו את דברי הברית הזאת ודברי הברית הם כתובי'

מצודת ציון

מעון . מדור : תנים . מין נחש : (כג) צעדו . מענין פסיעות והלוך כמו ויהי כי צעדו (ש"ב ו') : (כד) במשפט . ר"ל במשפט הראוי לגלות עון למוסר וכן ויסרתיך למשפט (לקמן ל') : (כה) אכלו ואכלוהו . ענין אכלון . מלשון כליון : נוהו . ענין מדור כמו יוזרה על נוהו (איוב י"ח) : השמו . מלשון שממון :

מצודת דוד

להלוך בו : לא לאיש . לא יתלה ביכלתו איש ההולך ומכין את צעדו ללכת בדרך הישר אבל הלכו כפי הזדמן ומקרי : (כד) יסרני ה'. אבל מכ"ז יסרני ה' : אך במשפט . ר"ל שיהיו היסורין בדרך משפט יסורין לבד כהלים לגלות עון למוסר אבל אל תיסרני באפך בדרך שמתנקם פן תהיה ממעט והולך עד לא ישאר ממני מאומה : (כה) שפוך . על האומות הוא מהראוי לשפוך עליהם חמתך לעשות כלה נקם: אשר לא ידעוך . אינם רוצים לדעת אותך ולקרוא בשמך : כי אכלו את יעקב ואכלוהו . ר"ל פעם אחר פעם : ויכלוהו ואת נוהו השמו . גם כלו אותו גם השמו את נוהו וזהו הכפל :

completely destroy you.'—[*Redak*] According to *Rabbi Jonah Ibn Ganah* and *Redak*, the concept of justice denotes 'with a measure,' not with intolerable severity. The prophet surely does not supplicate God not to chastise the people more severely than they deserve. He supplicates Him to chastise them with a measure, not with the complete severity of His wrath, lest they be diminished from nationhood. Rashi, too, explains in a similar manner:

25. **Pour out Your wrath**—If You

* For Rashi's commentary turn to page 228.

O Lord, that man's way is not his; neither has the man who goes, to prepare his step. 24. Chasten me, O Lord, but with a measure, not with Your wrath, lest You diminish me. 25. Pour out Your wrath upon the nations that do not know You and upon the families that have not called in Your name, for they have devoured Jacob and consumed him and destroyed him, and have wasted his dwelling.

was going. Then the prophet told us that he was coming to make the cities of Judah desolate.—[*Redak*]

23. **man's way is not his**—*For the evil inclination that You created in him leads him astray from the way. Another explanation is: I know, O Lord, that man's way is not his; not every man has the power to make his way prosper, and if it were not for Your command, the enemy would have no power to destroy Your Temple.*—[*Rashi*]

Rabbi Joseph Kimchi interprets this verse as an allusion to Nebuchadnezzar, who had intended to march against Ammon. As Ezekiel states (21:26): 'For the king of Babylon stands at the parting of the way,' for his intention was to march on Ammon when he left his place, but when he came to the parting of the way, and there were two roads, one to Ammon and one to Jerusalem, God changed his mind and his divination so that he should march on Jerusalem in order to punish Zedekiah for transgressing his oath and profaning God's name. Concerning this, the prophet states: I know, O Lord, that *the* man's way is not his. Since the *lammed* is vowelized with a *kamatz,* the definite article is meant. *The man* refers to Nebuchadnezzar. I know that the man's way is not under his control, for You will change his intention.—[*Redak*]

neither has the man who goes to prepare his step—The man who goes on his way does not have control over his own way to prepare his step, for he does not know what will befall him. This is reminiscent of King David's statement (Psalms 37:23): 'From the Lord are man's steps planned,' and He desires his way.'—[*Redak*]

24. **Chasten me**—Rabbi Jonah (*Sepher Haschoraschim* p. 528) explains that the prophet speaks for the people in the singular as for one person. When he sees that Nebuchadnezzar is coming to the land of Judah to make the land a waste, he supplicates God saying, "I know that this is the chastening that You are chastening us. It is good that You chasten us, but with a measure, as much as we can tolerate, not with Your wrath, lest You diminish me, for if You chasten me with Your wrath, You will diminish me from being a nation. *Jonathan,* too, renders: Bring upon them chastisements, but with mild judgment. The prophet expresses the same idea below (46:28:) 'And I will chastise you with a measure, and I will not

* For Rashi's commentary turn to page 228.

אֲשֶׁר־הָיָה אֶל־יִרְמְיָהוּ מֵאֵת יְהוָה
לֵאמֹר: ב שִׁמְעוּ אֶת־דִּבְרֵי הַבְּרִית
הַזֹּאת וְדִבַּרְתָּם אֶל־אִישׁ יְהוּדָה וְעַל־
יֹשְׁבֵי יְרוּשָׁלָםִ: ג וְאָמַרְתָּ אֲלֵיהֶם כֹּה־
אָמַר יְהוָה אֱלֹהֵי יִשְׂרָאֵל אָרוּר הָאִישׁ
אֲשֶׁר לֹא יִשְׁמַע אֶת־דִּבְרֵי הַבְּרִית
הַזֹּאת: ד אֲשֶׁר צִוִּיתִי אֶת־אֲבוֹתֵיכֶם
בְּיוֹם הוֹצִיאִי־אוֹתָם מֵאֶרֶץ־מִצְרַיִם
מִכּוּר הַבַּרְזֶל לֵאמֹר שִׁמְעוּ בְקוֹלִי

דַהֲוָה עִם יִרְמְיָה מִן
קֳדָם יְיָ לְמֵימַר:
ב קַבִּילוּ יָת פִּתְגָמֵי
קְיָמָא הָדֵין וּתְמַלְּלוּן עִם
אֱנָשׁ יְהוּדָה וְעַל יָתְבֵי
יְרוּשְׁלֶם: ג וְתֵימַר לְהוֹן
כִּדְנַן אֲמַר יְיָ אֱלָהָא
דְיִשְׂרָאֵל לִיט גַבְרָא דְלָא
יְקַבֵּיל יָת פִּתְגָמֵי קְיָמָא
הָדֵין: ד דְפַקֵּדִית יָת
אֲבָהָתְכוֹן בְּיוֹמָא
דְאַפֵּקִית יָתְהוֹן מֵאַרְעָא
מִצְרַיִם מִכּוּרָא דְפַרְזְלָא
לְמֵימַר קַבִּילוּ לְמֵימְרִי
וְתַעְבְּדוּן יָתְהוֹן כְּכֹל
דאפקיד

מהר"י קרא

יא (ג) ארור האיש אשר לא ישמע וגו׳. והנביא ענה אחריו אמן. יאע״פ שכתב מקרא זה ואען ואומר אמן ה׳ בסוף הענין קבלת שבועה היא לארור האיש אשר לא ישמע דברי הברית הזאת שהקב״ה השביע בארור האיש אשר לא ישמע את דברי הברית הזאת האמור בענין והנביא עונה אחריו אמן: (ד) אשר צויתי את אבותיכם. זה פתרונו דברי הברית שאני מבקש לחשביעכם אינם דברי הברית חדשה שיהא בדעתי עכשיו לכרות עמכם ברית חדשה אלא דברי הברית שאני משביע עליכם לשומעם. הם דברי הברית אשר צויתי את אבותיכם ביום הוציאי אותם מארץ מצרים. הם דברי תוכחות האמורים בפרשת והיה כי תבוא שכן הוא אומר בסוף הענין אלה דבר הברית אשר צוה ה׳ את משה ושמעי היאך נידעת,

רד"ק

בתורת משה ברכות וקללות אם תשמעו אם לא תשמעו וכתב בסוף אלה דברי הברית אשר צוה ה׳ את משה לכרות את בני ישראל בארץ מואב מלבד הברית אשר כרת אתם בחורב ובחורב אמר ויקח ספר הברית ויקרא באזני העם ויאמרו כל אשר דבר ה׳ נעשה ואמר ויקח משה את הדם ויזרוק על העם ויאמרו כל אשר דבר ה׳ נעשה ונשמע ונאמר ויאמר הנה דם הברית אשר כרת ה׳ עמכם על כל הדברים האלה ודברי הברית הם שישמעו לקול ה׳ ויעשו מצותיו והוא יהי׳ להם לאלהים והם יהיו לו לעם ובאמרו הזאת כמו שכתוב בתורה: (ב) ודברתם. אתם ונביאי האמת האחרים עמך כי היה צפניה שנתנבא בימי יאשיהו ואולי היו אחרי׳. אמר לו שיאמרו דברי הברית לאיש יהודה וליושבי ירושלם וזכר להם הברית לפי שהברית הוא דבר קיום אפי׳ בין אדם לחברו אם יעשו תנאים ביניהם יעשו ברית לקיים התנאי׳ ביניהם כל שכן בין האל ובין בני האדם שראוי לקיים הברית: אל איש יהודה. כולל לכלם כאחד וכן הל׳ לומר לשון יחיד על רבים דרך כלל כמו ויהי לי שור וחמור ואיש ישראל נגש ורבים כמוהם: ועל יושבי ירושלים. כמו ואל יושבי ירושלם וכן וילך אלקנה הרמתה על ביתו כמו אל ביתו ותתפלל על ה׳ כמו אל ה׳ והחוזים להם וי״ת ודברהם ותמללינון נראה שהיה קורא ודברתם בקמ״ץ התי״ו ואנחנו מצאנו בכל הספרים המדויקי׳ ודברתם בפתח התי״ו: (ג) ואמרת. עוד תאמר אליהם הדברים בקללה בארור כמו שנאמרה בתורה בסיני ובערבות מואב תדבר להם עד ל׳ ארור אולי יפחדו וישובו: (ד) אשר. ביום הוציאי. בהר סיני בעת שהוצאתים מארץ מצרים כי לחמשים יום שיצאו ממצרים נעשה זה הברית: ביום. פי׳ במקום עת וזמן כמו והיה ביום ההוא שרש ישי והרה אפי בו ביום ההוא: מכור הברזל. שהיו

מנחת שי

יא (ב) ודברתם. יונתן תרגם ותמללינון מראה שהיה קורא ודברתם בקמץ התי״ו ואנחנו מצאנו בכל הספרים המדוייקים ודברתם בסגול התי״ו כל זה לשון רד״ק ואולם בספרים שלנו מתורגם ותמללון: ועל יושבי ירושלם. בדפוס ישן כתיב ואל ובנוסח אחר על כי ע״פ המסורת כתוב ועל עיין במסרה גדולה בערך ישב: (פ ז ח מ):

מצודת דוד

יא (ב) שמעו. אתה ושאר הנביאים שעמו ר״ל אמו לב להבין את דברי הברית הזאת כלומר הברית הידוע המוזכר בתורה והם הברכות והקללות שבערבות מואב אשר כרת עליהם ברית כמ״ש אם אלה דברי הברית וגו׳ (דברים כ״ח): ודברתם. אתם הנביאים תדברו דברי הברית אל אנשי יהודה ואל יושבי ירושלים: (ג) אשר לא ישמע. אשר לא ירצה לשמוע: (ד) מכור הברזל. ר״ל מגלות

מצודת ציון

יא (ב) שמעו. ענין הבנה: איש יהודה. אנשי יהודה וכן ואיש ישראל כמו (ש״א י׳): ועל יושבי ירושלם. ואל יושבי ירושלים: (ג) ארור. ענין קללה: (ד) מכור. הוא הכלי שצורפין בו הזהב

who renders: And you shall speak *them,* meaning the words of the covenant. He deduces that Jonathan's reading was: וְדִבַּרְתָּם, unlike our editions. We do not find that reading in *Targum Jonathan.*—[*Minchath Shai*]

3. **And you shall say to them**– You shall further tell them thes things with a curse just as the covenant was given at Sinai and in the plains of Moab, perhaps they will be frightened and repent.—[*Redak*]

who will not hearken—I.e. who will not wish to hearken.—[*Mezudath David*]

4. **Which I have commanded your forefathers**—The covenant I am tell-

11

1. The word that came to Jeremiah from the Lord, to say:
2. Hearken to the words of this covenant, and you shall speak
to the men of Judah and to the inhabitants of Jerusalem.
3. And you shall say to them, So said the Lord God of Israel:
Cursed be the man who will not hearken to the words of this
covenant, 4. Which I commanded your forefathers on the day I
took them out of the land of Egypt, out of the iron furnace,
saying: Hearken to My voice

have wrath and fury, pour it out upon the nations that do not know You and upon the families that did not call in Your name, for Israel, although having sinned before You, have not left Your jurisdiction completely, and they have not become assimilated with any other nation. They are still a distinct nation, adhering to most of the commandments, calling in Your name and praying to You. Although they are not wholeheartedly with You, there is still hope that they will repent, and even today, there are many pious people among them.—[*Redak*]

1. **The word that came to Jeremiah**—*Abarbanel* interprets this as a prophecy that came to Jeremiah from God through intermediaries, unlike Moses' prophecy, which came to him directly from God. Although Jeremiah resembled Moses in many ways, e.g. the length of his prophetic career, his designation before birth, and his refusal to accept his calling, he, nevertheless, did not attain the level of prophecy attained by Moses. His prophecy, therefore, reached him through intermediaries.

2. **Hearken to the words of this covenant**—As explained above, these were the words the prophet was instructed to say to the people. *Abarbanel* explains that the prophet was instructed to call to the people to hear the words of 'this covenant.' They would think that he meant a new covenant and would come to listen attentively. Then he would tell them that he meant the covenant of the Torah. *Mezudath David* explains that the prophets, Jeremiah, Zephaniah, and their colleagues, should hearken to the words of the covenant, i.e. they should set their hearts to understand the words of the covenant of the Torah, the blessings and the curses.

and you shall speak—You and the other true prophets with you, for Zephaniah prophesied during Josiah's reign, and perhaps there were other prophets at that time (cf. 7:25, Commentary Digest). A covenant is an agreement even between people; if they make stipulations, they make a pact to make them binding. It is surely fitting to do so between God and men.—[*Redak*]

Redak quotes *Targum Jonathan,*

וַעֲשִׂיתֶם אוֹתָם כְּכֹל אֲשֶׁר־אֲצַוֶּה
אֶתְכֶם וִהְיִיתֶם לִי לְעָם וְאָנֹכִי אֶהְיֶה
לָכֶם לֵאלֹהִים׃ ה לְמַעַן הָקִים אֶת־
הַשְּׁבוּעָה אֲשֶׁר־נִשְׁבַּעְתִּי לַאֲבוֹתֵיכֶם
לָתֵת לָהֶם אֶרֶץ זָבַת חָלָב וּדְבַשׁ כַּיּוֹם
הַזֶּה וָאַעַן וָאֹמַר אָמֵן׀ יְהוָה׃ ו וַיֹּאמֶר
יְהוָה אֵלַי קְרָא אֶת־כָּל־הַדְּבָרִים
הָאֵלֶּה בְּעָרֵי יְהוּדָה וּבְחֻצוֹת יְרוּשָׁלִַם
לֵאמֹר שִׁמְעוּ אֶת־דִּבְרֵי הַבְּרִית הַזֹּאת
וַעֲשִׂיתֶם אוֹתָם׃ ז כִּי הָעֵד הַעִדֹתִי
בַּאֲבוֹתֵיכֶם בְּיוֹם הַעֲלוֹתִי אוֹתָם
מֵאֶרֶץ מִצְרַיִם עַד־הַיּוֹם הַזֶּה הַשְׁכֵּם

מלעיל

תרגום

דְּאַפְקֵיד יָתְכוֹן וּתְהוֹן
קֳדָמַי לְעַם וַאֲנָא אֱהֵוֵי
לְכוֹן לֶאֱלָהּ׃ ה בְּדִיל
לְקַיָּמָא יָת קְיָמָא
דְּקַיֵּמִית לַאֲבָהָתְכוֹן
לְמִתַּן לְהוֹן אַרְעָא עָבְדָא
חֲלַב וּדְבַשׁ כְּיוֹמָא הָדֵין
וַאֲתֵיבִית וַאֲמָרִית אָמֵן
יְיָ׃ ו וַאֲמַר יְיָ לִי אִתְנַבֵּי
יָת כָּל פִּתְגָמַיָּא הָאִלֵּין
בְּקִרְוַיָּא דְּבֵית יְהוּדָה
וּבְשׁוּקֵי יְרוּשְׁלֶם לְמֵימַר
קַבִּילוּ יָת פִּתְגָמֵי קְיָמָא
הָדֵין וְתַעְבְּדוּן יָתְהוֹן׃
ז אֲרֵי אַסְהָדָא אַסְהֵדִית
בַּאֲבָהָתְכוֹן בְּיוֹמָא
דְּאַסֵּקִית יָתְהוֹן מֵאַרְעָא
דְּמִצְרַיִם וְעַד יוֹמָא הָדֵין
מַקְדִּים וּמַסְהִיד לְמֵימַר
קַבִּילוּ

ת"א למען הקים. סוטה יא

מהר"י קרא

עם אבותיכם מיום העלותי אותם מארץ מצרים ועד היום הזה העידותי באבותיכם על דברי הברית לקיים ככל הכתוב בדברי הברית הזאת כשם שמספר והולך כי העד העידותי באבותיכם ביום העלותי אותם מארץ מצרים ועד היום הזה.

רש"י

יא (ה) אמן ה'. יהא ארור: (ז) העד העידותי. לי

מנחת שי

(ד) ועשיתם אותם. ברוב ספרים מדוייקים מלא וא"ו וכן נכון כי לא נמנה בהאי ספרא ריש סימן כ"ג במנין החסרים:

רד"ק

הם במצרף הצרוף כמו שצורפין הכסף והזהב בכור: ועשיתם אותם. המצות והוא שמעו בקולי המצות שיצום: (ה) למען. ואען ואמר אמן ה'. אמת יהיה זה שיהא ארור מי שלא ישמע אל דברי הברית וה' לשון קריאה ותפלה כלומר ה' כן יהיה: (ו) ויאמר. הוסיף עוד והזהירו לקרא אליהם את כל הדברים ופי' לו כימה שאמר אל איש יהודה שלא ימתין להם עד שיבאו לירושלם אלא שילך הוא בערי יהודה ויקרא באזניהם כל הדברים ויאמר להם בל' ארור ויתרה בהם אולי ישובו וכן מה שיאמר לישבי ירושלים יאמר להם בחוצות בפרהסיא כנגד כל העם: (ז) כי העד. באבותיכם התרתי כשהעלתי אותם מארץ מצרים וכן בכל דור ודור עד היום הזה השכם והעד ששלחתי להם הנביאים להתרות בכל בקר ובקר בכל יום ויום תמיד:

מצודת ציון

כמו וכור לזהב (משלי י"ז): (ה) הקים. מל' קיום: זבת. ענין נטיפה כמו זב עמקך (לק' מ"ט): (ו) ובחוצות. בשוקים: (ז) העד העדותי. ענין התראה כי ע"פ רוב מתרין בעדים לבל יכחשו:

מצודת דוד

שם בלרוף הלרות כמו שלורפין זהב בכור סברזל: לאמר שמעו וגו'. ר"ל אשר תכלית הברית ההוא וגו' לאמר שמעו בקולי ועשיתם את המלות ככל אשר וגו': והייתם לי לעם. ולא אחליפכם באומה אחרת: (ה) למען הקים. ר"ל וזהו לתועלתם למען הקים וגו': זבת. מתוך רבוי חלב ודבש זב ויורד בארץ וכת חלב ודבש: כיום הזה. שהנכם היום בארץ: ואען. אמר ירמיה עניתי ואמרתי אמן ה' כן יאומן הדבר היאמר ארור האיש אשר לא ישמעו וגו': (ו) את כל הדברים. אשר אני אומר אליך: ועשיתם אותם. עשו המלות אשר בעבורם כרתי הברית: (ז) כי העד העדותי. מאז הזהרתי על זה באבותיכם ביום העלותים ממצרים ומשם והלאה עד היום הזה:

and do them, according to all that I will command you, and
you shall be to Me for a people, and I will be to you for a God.
5. In order to establish the oath that I swore to your fore-
fathers to give them a land flowing with milk and honey as of
this day. And I replied and said, "Amen, O Lord." 6. And the
Lord said to me: Proclaim all these words in the cities of Judah
and in the streets of Jerusalem, saying: Hearken to the words of
this covenant and you shall do them. 7. For I warned your
forefathers on the day I brought them up from the land of
Egypt until this day, warning early every morning,

ing you about is not a new covenant that I intend to make with you now, but the covenant I made with your forefathers when I took them out of Egypt.—[*Kara*]

and do them—I.e. perform the commandments.—[*Redak*]

This was the aim of the covenant, viz. that you hearken to My voice and perform My commandments. —[*Mezudath David*]

5. **"Amen, O Lord"**—*that he be cursed.*—[*Rashi*]

'Amen' means, 'it shall be true,' in this case, that he who does not hearken to the words of the covenant shall be cursed.—[*Redak*]

Jeremiah's response is to the curse in verse 3, although the explanation of the covenant follows it.—[*Kara*]

6. **And the Lord said to me**—God continues to exhort the prophet to proclaim all these words and that he shall not wait until he comes to Jerusalem, but he shall proclaim it in the cities of Judah, and when he arrives in Jerusalem, he shall proclaim it in the streets, in public. He shall announce the curse and warn them, perhaps they will repent.—[*Redak*]

7. **For I warned**—Heb. הַעִידֹתִי, *an expression of warning.*—[*Rashi*]

Rashi's intention is that it is an expression of warning rather than an expression of testimony as the root usually denotes.

I warned your forefathers when I brought them up out of Egypt, and so throughout every generation until

וְהָעֵד לֵאמֹר שִׁמְעוּ בְּקוֹלִי׃ ח וְלֹא
שָׁמְעוּ וְלֹא־הִטּוּ אֶת־אָזְנָם וַיֵּלְכוּ אִישׁ
בִּשְׁרִירוּת לִבָּם הָרָע וָאָבִיא עֲלֵיהֶם
אֶת־כָּל־דִּבְרֵי הַבְּרִית־הַזֹּאת אֲשֶׁר־
צִוִּיתִי לַעֲשׂוֹת וְלֹא עָשׂוּ׃ ט וַיֹּאמֶר יְהוָה
אֵלָי נִמְצָא־קֶשֶׁר בְּאִישׁ יְהוּדָה
וּבְיֹשְׁבֵי יְרוּשָׁלִָם׃ י שָׁבוּ עַל־עֲוֺנֹת
אֲבוֹתָם הָרִאשֹׁנִים אֲשֶׁר מֵאֲנוּ
לִשְׁמוֹעַ אֶת־דְּבָרַי וְהֵמָּה הָלְכוּ אַחֲרֵי
אֱלֹהִים אֲחֵרִים לְעָבְדָם הֵפֵרוּ בֵית־
יִשְׂרָאֵל וּבֵית יְהוּדָה אֶת־בְּרִיתִי אֲשֶׁר

תרגום

קבילו למימרי: ח ולא
קבילו ולא ארכינו ית
אודנהון ואזלו גבר
בהרהור לבהון בישא
ואיתיתי עליהון
פורענותא על דלא
קבילו פתגמי קימא
הדין דפקדית למעבד
ולא עבדו: ט ואמר יי
לי אשתכח דמרדו
בסימרי אנש יהודה
ויתבי ירושלם: י תבו
לחובי אבהתהון קדמאי
דסריבו לקבלא ית
פתגמי ואינון טעו בתר
פלחי כוכביא
למפלחהון אשניאו בית
ישראל ובית יהודה
ית קימי דגזרית ית
אבהתכון

רש"י

התראה: (ח) ואביא עליהם את כל דברי הברית. האלות האמורות בברית על הדברים אשר צויתי

מהר"י קרא

(ז) השכם והעד לאמר שמעו בקולי: (ח) ולא שמעו ולא הטו את אזנם. ואביא עליהם את כל דברי הברית הזאת. אשר לא שמעו בקולי. וכשם שנענשו אבותיכם על שלא שמעו בקול אלה דברי הברית הזאת אף אתם איש יהודה ויושבי ירושלים ששבתם על עונות אבותיכם הראשונים אשר מאנו לשמוע את דברי כמו

רד"ק

(ח) ולא שמעו. את כל דברי הברית. הקללות שהן תנאי הברית אם לא ישמעו זהו שאמר אשר צויתי לעשות ולא עשו צויתי להם לקיים דברי הברית ולא קיימו ובכלל קיום הברית עשה ולא תעשה וקיום הברית קורא מעשה: (ט) ויאמר ה' אלי נמצא קשר. יראה מן הדומה כי נבואה זו נאמרה בימי יהויקים וזהו שאמר נמצא קשר כלומר מרדו בי אחר ששבו בימי יאשיהו: (י) שבו על עונות אבותם הראשונים. דור אמון ומנשה ואחז וכל הפסוקי' עד מה לידידי מבוארי' הם ופי' והלכו ערי יהודה וכן וכל הארץ באו מצרימה ופסוק ואתה אל תתפלל פירשנוהו למעלה ולמעלה אמר כי אינני שומע אותך והנה אמר כי אינני שומע בעת קראם אלי הוסיף לומר כי אפי' הם יקראו אלי לא אשמע אליהם אלא אנקם מהם כל כך הרבו לעשות הרע בעיני להכעיסני שלא אוכל למלט אותם מהפורענות:

מנחת שי

(ט) נמצא קשר. במאריך הנו"ן בס"ס: (י) שבו. בספר אחד ספרדי נכתב בלדו טעמו מלמיל גם בספר אחד קדמון כתוב עליו מלעיל אבל ש ט ו מלרע עיין מ"ש בפרשת בהעלתך: על עונת. חסר וא"ו אחר הנו"ן גם במסורת נחשב ריש סימן ט' לא בא במספר המלאים בליבנא: אבותם הראשונים. ברוב ספרים מדוייקים מלא וא"ו וכן דינו כי לא נמנה במסורת עם החסרים דנביאים וכתובים:

מצודת דוד

השכם והעד. אני משכים ומתרה ע"י הנביאים לאמר שמעו בקולי: (ח) ולא שמעו. והם אינם שומעים: וילכו איש. כ"א הולך במה שלבו הרע מראה אותו ומתאוה לה: ואביא. ולכן אביא עליהם את כל דברי הברית הזאת והם הקללות הנזכרות בברית: אשר צויתי לעשות. יען אשר צויתי אותם לעשות מצותי והם לא עשו: (ט) נמצא קשר. נמצא אגודת מרד באנשי יהודה וגו': (י) שבו. חזרו על עונות אבות' וגו' כי אחזו בדרך הזה: והמה. ועוד הוסיפו המה ללכת אחרי אלהים אחרים: הפרו. א"כ כולם יחד הפרו הם

מצודת ציון

השכם. מל' השכמה ור"ל בזריזות: (ח) בשרירות. כמראות: (ט) קשר. ענינו אגודת מרד כמו ותקרא קשר קשר (מ"ב יא): באיש. כמו באנשי: (י) מאנו. מל' מיאון: הפרו. בטלו:

saying: Hearken to My voice. 8. But they did not hearken,
neither did they bend their ears, and they went, each man
according to the view of his evil heart, and I brought upon them
all the words of this covenant that I commanded to do, and
they did not do. 9. And the Lord said to me: A conspiracy has
been found among the men of Judah, and among the inhabi-
tants of Jerusalem. 10. They have returned to the iniquities of
their first forefathers, who refused to hearken to My words, and
they followed other gods to worship them; the house of Israel
and the house of Judah broke My covenant that

this day, constantly sending prophets every morning to warn them.—[*Redak*]

8. **But they did not hearken**—They do not hearken.—[*Mezudath David*]

He apparently explains this as a present tense. Others, however, explain it in its simple sense, as a past tense, referring to all the past generations.—[*Abarbanel*]

and I brought upon them—This is the prophetic past, since the curses had not yet been brought upon them.—[*Abarbanel, Mezudath David*]

And I brought upon them all the words of this covenant—*The curses stated in the covenant for the things that I commanded to do and they did not do.*—[*Rashi*]

that I commanded to do—I.e., that I commanded to fulfill. The fulfillment of the covenant includes both mandatory and prohibitory commandments. This fulfillment is considered a deed.—[*Redak*]

9. **A conspiracy has been found**—It appears that this prophecy came to him during Jehoiakim's reign. God, therefore, tells him that a conspiracy has been found; i.e., the people have rebelled against God after having repented during Josiah's reign.—[*Redak*]

10. **They have returned to the iniquities of their first forefathers**—I.e.

כרתי את־אבותם: יא לכן כה אמר
יהוה הנני מביא אליהם רעה אשר
לא־יוכלו לצאת ממנה וזעקו אלי
ולא אשמע אליהם: יב והלכו ערי
יהודה וישבי ירושלם וזעקו אל־
האלהים אשר הם מקטרים להם
והושע לא־יושיעו להם בעת רעתם:
יג כי מספר עריך היו אלהיך יהודה
ומספר חצות ירושלם שמתם מזבחות
לבשת מזבחות לקטר לבעל:
יד ואתה אל־תתפלל בעד־העם הזה
ואל־תשא בעדם רנה ותפלה כי
אינני שמע בעת קראם אלי בעד

תרגום

אבהתכון: יא בכן כדנן אמר יי הא אנא מיתי עליכון בישתא דלא יכלון לאשתזבא מנה ויצלון קדמי ולא אקבל צלותהון: יב ויהכון אנש קרויא דבית יהודה ויתבי ירושלם ויבעון מן טעותא דאינון מסקין בוסמין להן האם יכלן למפרקהון בעידן בישתהון: יג ארי סגין קרויכון הואה דחלתכון דבית יהודה ומנין שוקי ירושלם שויתון אגורין לבהתא ואגורין לאסקא בוסמין לבעלא: יד ואת לא תצלי על עמא הדין ולא תתחנן עליהון בבעו ובצלו ארי לא כבעוא קדמי בעידן דאת מצלי עליהון קדמי בעידן

ת"א לצאת ממנה. יבמות סג:

מהר"י קרא

כן הפרתם בית ישראל ובית יהודה את בריתי אשר כרתי את אבותיכם: (יא) לכן כה אמר ה' הנני מביא עליהם. על בית ישראל ועל בית יהודה. רעה אשר לא יוכלו לצאת ממנה. או ילכו: (יב) ערי יהודה וישבי ירושלים וזעקו אל האלהים אשר הם מקטרים להם: (יג) כי מספר עריך היו אלהיך יהודה. כביכול כאדם המשחק שרואהו שטועה בדבר שאין בו ממש ומשחק בו ואומר לו קרא בקול גדול כי אלהים הוא אף כאן מאחר שמספר עריך כלומר שרבים הם במספר עריך אם הם אלהים הם יקומו ויעזרוכם: (יד) ואתה אל תתפלל. כלומר על מה ישא בעדם רנה ותפלה שום

רש"י

לעשות ולא עשו: (יב) ערי יהודה. מערי יהודה: (יד) רנה

מנחת שי

(יב) והלכו ערי יהודה. כוה"ו נגעיה נס"ס:

רד"ק

(יד) בעד רעתם. על רעתם וכן בעד השלח יפלו והדומים להם

מצודת ציון

(יד) בעד. בעבור: תשא. ענין הרמת קול: רנה. היא ענין תפלה:

מצודת דוד

הברית כמו בית ישראל כן בית יהודה: (יא) אשר לא יוכלו. בכח הזדון: וזעקו אלי. להושיע למו: (יב) ערי יהודה. אנשי ערי יהודה: והושע. אבל לא יוכלו להושיע להם בעת בא עליהם הרעה: (יג) בספר. כחשבון מספר הערים כן מספר הפסילים: ומספר. כמספר שוקי ירושלים כמספר הזה עשיתם מזבחות לבושת היא העכו"ם אשר היא לבושת לעובדים על כי צועקים אליה ואינה עונים: (יד) ואתה. לירמיה אמר שאל יתפלל בעדם: כי אינני וגו'. ר"ל אף אם הם עצמם היו קוראים ומתפללים אלי בעבור הרעה הבאה לספירם מעליהם ומבלי תשובה וחרטה על העונות אינני שומע להם וכ"ש שהם אינם מתפללים לפני ואיך א"כ אשמע לך מה שאתה

I made with their forefathers. 11. Therefore, so says the Lord:
Behold, I bring upon them evil which they shall be unable to
escape, and, although they shall cry out to Me, I will not heed
them. 12. And they shall go [from] the cities of Judah and the
inhabitants of Jerusalem and cry out to the gods to whom they
burn incense, and they shall not save them at the time of their
misfortune. 13. For as many as your cities were your gods, O
Judah, and as many as the streets of Jerusalem you have made
altars for the shameful thing, altars to burn incense for the
Baal. 14. And you, do not pray for this people, neither shall
you lift up cry nor prayer, for I do not hearken at the time they
call out to Me because of their misfortune.

to the iniquities of the generations of Amon, Manasseh, and Ahaz.—[*Redak*]

11. **upon them**—I.e. upon the house of Israel and the house of Judah.—[*Kara*]

which they shall be unable to escape—I.e. with physical strength.—[*Mezudath David*]

12. **And they shall go the cities of Judah**—*From the cities of Judah.*—[*Rashi*]

Redak renders: And the inhabitants of the cities of Judah shall go. Jonathan: And the people of the cities of Judah.

13. **For as many as your cities were your gods**—So to speak, like a person mocking his companion who believes in a thing that has no substance. He mocks him and says, "Cry out loud, for he is a God." Here, too, since your gods are so many, if they are gods, let them help you.—[*Kara*]

for the shameful thing—This is a pejorative for the idols. See above 3:24.

רעתם: טו מה לידידי בביתי עשותה
המזמתה הרבים ובשר־קדש יעברו
מעליך כי רעתכי אז תעלזי: טז זית
רענן יפה פרי־תאר קרא יהוה שמך:

ת"א מה לידידי. מנחות נג: זית רענן. כרכות נו מנחות נג:

לקול

בעובדן בישתהון: טו מה
לעמא דהוה חביב
קדמי שבקו פולחן בית
מקדשי עבדו עצה
לחטאין סגיאין מערבין
בשר שקוצין עם בשר
קודשא יגלון סניך מן
קדם בשתיך בכן
הויתא תקיפא: טז הא
כאילן זיתא דשפיר בריוה ויאי בחזויה וסוכיה מטלן באילניא כן רבי יי שמיך

רש"י

ותפלה. בכעו וכללו: (טו) מה לידידי בביתי. מה לעם סגולתי לבא עוד בביתי: עשותה המזמתה. לעשות היא מזמת עלת הטאים שלה: הרבים. שבהם: ובשר קודש יעברו מעליך. אף המילה בטלו מבשרם שעל ידה הי' מקודשים לי: כי רעהכי אז תעלוזי. כשאת' עוברין פרי תאר קרא ה' שמך. לשעבר כשהייתם מקיימין את התורה

מהר"י קרא

אוהב שלי והם עוברים על מה שכתוב בתורה כמו שמספר והולך: (טו) עשותה המזמתה. כלומר חושבין מחשבות און ועושין אותם: ובשר קודש יעברו מעליך. שפרקו ברית מילה מעליהם ולא עוד אלא שכל אחד ואחד מהן שמה באיד חבירו שנאמר: כי רעתכי או תעלזי. ומאחר שעושין את כל אלה מה לידידי בביתי. על מה יבא שום ידיד שיש לי להתפלל בביתי בעד העם הזה ולישא בעדם רנה ותפלה: (טז) זית רענן יפה הייתם דומין לזית רענן שצילו נאה ופריו הדור ועכשיו כשאתם

רד"ק

רבים: (טו) מה לידידי בביתי. אמר הנביא מה לידידי בביתי קרא האל ידידי לפי שהוא היה מאוהבי האל אמר מה לו עוד בביתי ר"ל בבית המקדש כלומר להשרות שכינתו שם: עשותה המזמתה הרבים. בעשות כנסת ישראל התועבה את רבים כלומר עם אלהים אחרים כמו שאמר למעלה כי מספר עריך היו אלהיך יהודה וכיון שהיא הניחה אל אחד ועשתה מזמה את הרבים ועבדה אותם מה לי לידידי בביתי ואמר בביתי כמו שאמר לידידי כי ידיד הנביא הוא ולא ידידם וכן בית המקדש בית הנביא הוא ולא ביתם: ובשר קדש יעברו מעליך. חוזר לכנסת ישראל ואומר לה את מקרבת קרבנות לרבים שהם אלהים אחרי' ובשר קדש בשר מזבח ה' שהוא קדש אותן קרבנות הקדש עוברים מעליך כאילו אינם מוטלים עליך לעשותם: כי רעתיכי אז תעלזי. ולא שיש לך בושת ורוע לב מזה כי בעת שתעשי הרעות אז תעלזי ותשמחי וי"מ ובשר קדש כמו ואנשי קדש וכמו יבא כל בשר להשתחות שפירושו בני אדם כלומר החסידים אנשי קדש עברו מעליך לפיכך את עושה הרעות: המזמתה. הכפל לחזק הענין וכן ישועתה עזרתה: רעתיכי. היו"ד נוספת כיו"ד נעוריכי תחלואיכי וי"ת הפסוק כן מה לעמא דהוה חביב וגו' כבעמוד. ובמדרש בשעה שחרב בית המקדש מצאו הקב"ה לאברהם עומד בבית המקדש ואמר לו מה לידידי בביתי אמר לו על עסקי בני באתי אמר לו בניך חטאו וגלו אמר לו ושמא בשוגג חטאו אמר לו עשותה המזמתה אמר לו שמא מיעוטם חטאו אמר לו הרבים אמר לו היה לך לזכור בשר המילה אמר לו ובשר קדש יעברו מעליך אמר לו שמא אם המתנת להם היו חוזרים בתשובה אמר לו כי רעתיכי אז תעלוזי אמר לו שמא חס ושלום אין להם תקנה אמר לו זית רענן וגו': (טז) זית רענן. המשילה לזית לפי שהוא רענן כל זמן וכל ימות השנה עליו לחים: יפה פרי תאר. פי' יפה פרי ויפה תאר ויפה שזכר עומד במקום שנים ר"ל שפריו יפה ותארו יפה אמר לכנסת ישראל מתחלת קרא ה' שמך זית רענן כשהיית עושה רצונו היית כמו זית רענן לא

מנחת שי

(טז) שמך. י"ס שכתוב בהם שְׁמֵךְ ונטלים בפיפוסן: המולה. נכתב בוא"ו עם דגש כלמ"ד רד"ק בפי' וכשרשים אבל קול המלה כקול מחנה דיים יחזקאל בלא וא"ו וכן במסורת המולה ב' א' מלא וא' חסר:

מצודת דוד

מתפלל עליהם: (טו) מה לידידי בביתי. ישראל שהיו מקדם עם סגולתי מה להם לבא בבית המקדש ולעשות שמה המזמות הרבים מאד: ובשר קדש. ר"ל הקרבנות שאתה מקריב שמה יעברו ממך כי אינני חפץ בהם: כי רעתכי. בעת תעשו הרעות אז תשמחו ולא תדאג עליהם ומה לי א"כ בהקרבנות ולמ' תבואו לבית המקדש:
(טז) זית רענן. אל מול המקדש אמר הנה מאז קרא ה' שמך זית רענן שהוא אילן מפואר: יפה. כך נמלא היופי של פרי בעל תואר

מצודת ציון

(טו) לידידי. אהובי: המזמתה. ענין מחשבה רע כמו זמה היא (ויקרא יח): רעתכי. מל' רעה: תעלוזי. ענין שמחה כמו יעלזו חסידים (תהלים קמ"ט): (טז) רענן. רטוב ומלוחלח כמו דשנים ורעננים יהיו (שם צ"ב): תואר. מהודר: המולה. ענין המייה

Temple, He found Abraham standing in the Temple, and He said to him, "What has My beloved to do in My house?" He replied, "I have come concerning my children." He said, "Your children have sinned and have been exiled." He said to Him, "Perhaps they have sinned inadvertently." He replied, "They perform evil design." He asked, "Perhaps only the minority has sinned?" He replied, "The many." He said to Him, "You should remember the covenant of the circumcision." He replied, "The holy flesh they remove from you." He asked Him, "Perhaps if You had waited for them, they would have repented." He replied, "For with evil, then you rejoice." He replied, "Perhaps, God forbid, there is no hope for them?" He replied, "A leafy olive tree fair with goodly fruit . . ."—[*Redak* and *Yalkut Shimoni* from *Men.* 53b]

16. **A leafy olive tree**—He com-

15. What has My beloved to do in My house, [seeing that] the
many perform evil design, and the holy flesh they remove from
you, for [with] your evil then you rejoice. 16. A leafy olive-tree
fair with goodly fruit, has the Lord called your name;

15. **What has my beloved to do in My house**—*What reason has My treasured people to come anymore into My house?*—[*Rashi*]

[seeing that] . . . perform evil design—*That she does the evil design of her sinful plans.*—[*Rashi*]

the many—*of them.*—[*Rashi*]

and the holy flesh they remove from you—*Even the circumcision through which they were hallowed to Me, they have abolished from their flesh.*—[*Rashi*]

for [with] your evil, then you rejoice—*When you commit a transgression, you rejoice.*—[*Rashi*]

To simplify the matter, *Rashi* explains the verse as the words of God. He asks, "What has My people, who were beloved to Me, to do in My house, seeing that many of them perform evil design and sin intentionally? Also, they have ceased to perform the precept of circumcision, and they rejoice in all their evil deeds.

Mezudath David explains the verse similarly. However, he interprets, 'the holy flesh' as the flesh of the sacrifices. The holy flesh that you sacrifice there will be removed from you, since I do not accept it.

Rabbi Joseph Kara explains that God is addressing the prophet. He says: What has any beloved of Mine to do in My house, praying for this people? They plan evil designs and execute them. They have abolished the covenant of circumcision, and they rejoice at their companions' misfortune.

Redak explains that the prophet is addressing God. He says: What has my Beloved to do in my house? What does God have to do any longer in the Temple, to cause His presence to rest there? Since the congregation of Israel commits abominations with many strange deities, as is mentioned above, that they had as many deities as they had cities. Since they worshipped many gods, what does my Beloved have to do in my house? He calls the Temple, 'my house,' since God is his Beloved, not the Beloved of the people, and the Temple is his house, not the house of the people.

and the holy flesh they remove from you—God turns now to Israel and addresses them. You offer up flesh to many gods, but the holy flesh that is on My altar you neglect to offer up. You have neglected the sacrificial service as though it is not incumbent upon you.

for [with] your evil, then you rejoice—You have no shame or remorse from your sins, but when you commit the evils, you rejoice. Others explain: And holy people pass away from you. I.e., the righteous and the pious are no longer with you; therefore, you commit these sins.

The Midrash explains in the following manner: When the Holy One, blessed be He, destroyed the

לְקוֹל ׀ הֲמוּלָּה גְדֹלָה הִצִּית אֵשׁ עָלֶיהָ
וְרָעוּ דָּלִיּוֹתָיו: יז וַיהוָה צְבָאוֹת הַנּוֹטֵעַ
אוֹתָךְ דִּבֶּר עָלַיִךְ רָעָה בִּגְלַל רָעַת בֵּית־
יִשְׂרָאֵל וּבֵית יְהוּדָה אֲשֶׁר עָשׂוּ לָהֶם
לְהַכְעִסֵנִי לְקַטֵּר לַבָּעַל: יח וַיהוָה

ת"א לקול המולה. (תענית כח): דגש אחר שורק הודיעני

תרגום

בְּעִמְסַיָא וּכְדֵי דַעֲבַרְתְּ
עַל אוֹרָיְתָא מַשְׁרְיַת
עַמְמִין דִּתְקִיפִין
כְּאֶשָּׁתָא יֵיתוּן
עֲלַהּ וְיִתְּבָרוּן
לְהוֹן סוּכְּכָן: יז וַיְיָ
צְבָאוֹת דְּקַיֵּם יָתִיךְ גְּזַר
לְאַיְתָאָה עֲלַהּ בִּישָׁא
בְּדִיל חוֹבֵי בֵית יִשְׂרָאֵל
וּבֵית יְהוּדָה דַּעֲבַדוּ
לְהוֹן לְאַרְגָּזָא קֳדָמַי לְאַסָּקָא בּוּסְמִין לְבַעְלָא: יח וַיְיָ אַלְפַנִי
ואליפית

מהר"י קרא

עובדין את תורתי הריני עושה לכם כמו שעושין לאילן שפוסק מלעשות פירות שאין בעליו נהנין ממנו מה עושין לו משברין דליותיו לצורך האש. כמו כן אני עושה לכם: לקול המולה גדולה. הריני מכריז לקול שאון במלכות שיהיו נאספין עליכם ויציתו בכם את האש: קול המולה. פת' קול שאון המון. כמו קל המולה כקול מחנה: ורעו. לשון שבירה כמו תרועם בשבט ברזל: דליותיו. ברני"ש בלע"ז: (יז) וה' צבאות הנוטע אותך. כביכול כאדם שנוטע אילן ויומים רבים יתן פריו וכל זמן שיתן פריו חביב לבעליו ומשפוסק מלעשות פרי הוא נותן לב לקוצצו אף אתם בתחילה נטע אתכם הקב"ה נטיעה בארץ עד שלא תינתשו ממנו לעולם ומשעשיתם הרע בעיניו נתן לב לעקור אותה נטיעה שנמשלת לשעבר זית רענן יפה פרי תואר: (יח) וה' הודיעני. שרוצה לעקור אותה נטיעה: ואדעה. פתרונו

רש"י

עבירה אתם עושים: (טז) לקול המולה. ל' שאון עם רב שיחה עליהם: ורעו דליותיו. ורצצו את ענפיו: (יח) וה' הודיעני. כך אמר הנביא הקב"ה הודיעני את

רד"ק

יבול עלהו ר"ל שהצלחה היתה תמידה עמך ואת היית עושה מעשים טובים ויפים דומים לפרי זית אשר בדשנו והוא שמנו יכבדו אלהים ואנשים: לקול המולה גדולה. ועתה גרמו עליך עונך להביא גוים רבים ישמעו קול המולתם שהיא גדולה ועל ידם הצית אש עליה כאילו אמר עליך כי כן דרך המקרא לדבר בפסוק אחד לנכח ושלא לנכח כמו שמעו עמים כולם כי יבש מאלים אשר חמדתם וה' הודיעני אז הראיתני והדומים להם רבים: ורעו דליותיו. ואותם הגוים ישברו דליות הזית שהיית נמשלת בו. ואדוני אבי ז"ל פירש עליה כמו עלה זית ר"ל הצית אש בעליה פי' בעלי הזית שהיו רעננים ולחים עתה יצית אש בהם וכנה הזית בל' נקבה ואף על פי שהוא ל' זכר כמ"ש רענן דליותיו והנה מצאנו גפן בל' זכר גפן בוקק ומצאנוהו בל' נקבה לגפן אדרת כן יהיה זית כמוהו ועוד לפי שהמשיל בו כנסת ישראל שהוא בל' נקבה זכר הזית שהוא משל לה גם כן בל' נקבה כאילו זכר הכנסה ואחר כך שב לדבר בלשון זכר בל' עצמו ואמר דליותיו: המולה כתיב בו' עם הדגש וכמוהו מעטים נמצאו באותיות אהו"י עם הדגש וזכרנום בספר מכלל מחלק הדקדוק ממנו ופי' המולה כמו מלה כמו אין מלה בלשוני וכן קול חמלה כקול מחנה ופי' הצית הבעיר כמו ויצת אש בציון והדומים לו ורעו פי' וישברו כמו ירעוך קדקד ורעו את ארץ אשור בפתחיה: דליותיו. פי' ענפיו וקראו בזה הל' ר"ל בל' ארוממך ה' כי דליתני שפירושו רוממתני וזכר הענפים הנה בזה הל' ר"ל שאפי' הענפים הרמים ישברו והוא משל על ירושלים ובית המקדש וי"ת הפסוק כן הא כאילן זיתא וגו' כבעמוד: (יז) וה' צבאות הנוטע אותך. לפי שהמשילה לזית אמר עליה ל' נטיעה כלומר שהשכינך בארץ טובה כמו שעשה לך טובה בעשותה טובה כן דבר עתה עליך על ידי הנביאים שעתיד לבא אליך בגלל רעת בית ישראל ובית יהודה על בית ישראל דבר רעה ובאה להם ועליך גם כן דבר רעה ותבא לך: (יח) וה' הודיעני. פי' אאו"ל הודיעני שהיו חושבים להאכילני

מצודת ציון

וכן קול המולה (יחזקאל א'): הצית. מל' הלהב והבערה: ורעו. ענין שבירה כמו ירעוך קדקוד (לעיל ב'): דליותיו. ענפים גדולים כמו לפנות דליותיו אליו (יחזקאל י"ז): (יז) בגלל. בעבור

מצודת דוד

מסודר: לקול המולה. אבל עתה לעת בוא קול המייה גדולה של חיל הכשדים הבאים למלחמה אז הקב"ה בעצמו יהיה המצית והמבעיר אש עליה וישברו ענפיו ולפי שהמשילו לזית אמר ל' הנופל באילן: (יז) הנוטע אותך. הבונה הבית והשכין בה שכינתו הוא גזר הרעה ולא באה בכח הזרוע של הכשדים (ועל כי המשילו לזית אמר לשון נטיעה הנופל באילן): רעת. היא הבעל: עשו להם. הם עצמם למען הכעיסני לקטר לבעל: (יח) וה' הודיעני. ה' הודיע לי הרעה הבאה לכן ידעתיו: אז. כשהודיע לי הרעה אז

to the sound of a great tumult, He has kindled fire upon it, and
they have broken its branches. 17. And the Lord of Hosts Who
planted you spoke evil concerning you, about the evil of the
house of Israel and the house of Judah, which they did to them
to provoke Me, to burn sacrifices to Baal. 18. And the Lord

pares them to an olive tree, since it is always leafy and its leaves are green throughout the year.—[*Redak*]

to the sound of a great tumult—And now, because of your sins, many nations will come upon you, and a great tumult will be heard. Through them, fire will be kindled upon 'it.' The intention is 'He has kindled upon you,' but it is not unusual for Scripture to change from second to third person.—[*Redak*]

to the sound of a great tumult—Heb. הֲמוּלָּה, *an expression of the tumult of a large multitude that will come upon them.*—[*Rashi*]

and they have broken its branches—Heb. וְרָעוּ דָּלִיּוֹתָיו.—[*Rashi*]

Those nations shall break the branches of the olive tree to which Israel is compared.—[*Redak*]

Rabbi Joseph Kimchi renders: And He shall kindle fire with its leaves, meaning the leaves of the olive tree.

and they have broken its branches—**Heb.** דָּלִיּוֹתָיו, **the high, raised up** branches, symbolic of Jerusalem and the Temple.—[*Redak*]

Jonathan renders: Like an olive tree, beautiful in form and beautiful in appearance, whose branches give shade among the trees, so did the Lord exalt your name among the peoples, but when you transgressed the Torah, a camp of peoples, strong as fire, will come upon you, and a mingling of nations shall join them.

17. **Who planted you**—Since he compares them to an olive tree, he continues the metaphor with the expression of planting. I.e., just as the Lord established you in the good land when you did good, so did He speak concerning you to the prophets, that evil is destined to befall you because of the evil deeds of the house of Israel and the house of Judah. He predicted evil to the house of Israel and it has already befallen them. Now He predicts evil to the house of Judah, and it will befall them.—[*Redak*]

18. **And the Lord let me know**—*So said the prophet, "The Holy One, blessed be He, let me know their retribution."*—[*Rashi*]

Rabbi Joseph Kimchi explains: He let me know that they were plotting to poison me, as is mentioned in the following verse. He says: He let me know, and I knew." Then I knew, for I did not know before this, since it did not enter my mind. I did no evil to them. I castigate them for their own benefit.—[*Redak*]

הוֹדִיעַנִי וָאֵדָעָה אָז הִרְאִיתַנִי
מַעַלְלֵיהֶם׃ יט וַאֲנִי כְּכֶבֶשׂ אַלּוּף יוּבַל
לִטְבוֹחַ וְלֹא־יָדַעְתִּי כִּי־עָלַי ׀ חָשְׁבוּ
מַחֲשָׁבוֹת נַשְׁחִיתָה עֵץ בְּלַחְמוֹ
וְנִכְרְתֶנּוּ מֵאֶרֶץ חַיִּים וּשְׁמוֹ לֹא־יִזָּכֵר
עוֹד׃ כ וַיהוָה צְבָאוֹת שֹׁפֵט צֶדֶק בֹּחֵן
כְּלָיוֹת וָלֵב אֶרְאֶה נִקְמָתְךָ מֵהֶם כִּי

תרגום

נַלְפִּית בְּכֵן אַחֲזֵיתַנִי
עוֹבָדֵיהוֹן׃ יט וַאֲנָא
כְּאִימַר בְּחִיר
דִלְנִכְסְתָא מְתוּבַל וְלָא
יְדַעִית אֲרֵי עֲלַי חֲשִׁיבוּ
עֵשְׁתּוֹנִין בִּישִׁין אָמְרִין
נִרְמֵי סַמָּא דְמוֹתָא
בְּמֵיכְלֵיהּ וּנְשֵׁיצֵינֵיהּ
מֵאַרְעָא דְיִשְׂרָאֵל וּשְׁמֵיהּ
לָא יִדְּכַר עוֹד׃ כ וַיְיָ
צְבָאוֹת דַּיָּין קְשׁוֹט גְּלַן
קֳדָמוֹהִי כּוּלְיָן וְלִבָּא אֶחֱזֵי
פּוּרְעָנוּת דִּינָךְ מִנְּהוֹן

ת"א ככבש אלוף. פסחים מ״ד עט״ו:

רש"י

פורענותם: (יט) **ואני ככבש אלוף.** אשר יובל לטבוח: **יובל.** יובא. לפי שאני מודיעם הרעה הם אומרים להרגני. **ככבש אלוף** דונש ויהודה בן קוריש פתרוהו ככבש ופר אשר יובל לטבח ואלוף כמו שגר אלפיך (דברים כ"ח) ואף על פי שלא נאמר ואלוף יש לנו כיוצא בו שמש ירח עמד זבולה (חבקוק ג') כסוס עגור כן אצפצף (ישעיה ל"ח) ומנחם פתר ככבש אלוף כבש גדול (עיין בתהלים כ"ה בפרש"י) ויונתן מסייעו שתירגם כאימר בחיר: **נשחיתה עץ בלחמו.** נרמי סמא דמותא במיכליה: (כ) **אראה נקמתך מהם.**

מהר"י קרא

משידעת שהוא רוצה לעקרה [באותה שנה הודיעני מפני מה הוא רוצה לעוקרה] כשם שהוא כפורש בעניין בגלל רעת בית ישראל ובית יהודה וזה הוא: אז הראיתני מעלליהם. וכל כך כדי שלא אריב כנגד מידת הדין: (יט) **ואני ככבש אלוף. פתר** בו מנחם ככבש מלומד להובילו לבית המטבחים ופתר אלוף לשון ליכוד כמו אאלפך חכמה. ודונש השיבו היכן ראית מימיך שילמד איש שורו ואיש שיהו לילך לבית המטבחים אלא פת' אלוף לשון שור כמו שגר אלפיך אם תאמר אם כן היה למקרא לומר ואני ככבש ואלוף יש לך הרבה תיבות במקרא שחסירין ו' ופתרונו כאילו כתובין ו' כמו כסים עגור כן אצפצף שפתרונו כסים ועגור ורבים כיוצא בו במקרא. וכן אמר ירמיה אני בתומי הלכתי ככבש ושור זה שמוליכין אותו לטבח והוא אינו מכיר שלטבח הוא יובל שם כן לא ידעתי שגם עלי חשבו מחשבות: **נשחיתה עץ בלחמו.** ת"י אמרין איתו ונרמא סמא דמותא במיכליה:

רד"ק

סם המות כמו שאמר בפסוק שאחר זה אמר **הודיעני נא ואדעה** אז ידעתי כי לא הייתי יודע כי לא היה עולה על לבי כי אני לא הרעותי להם אם אני מוכיח אותם לטובת' אני עושה: **אז הראיתני מעלליהם.** כי בזה הראיתני מעלליהם הרעי' אם לי היו רוצי' לעשות כן ק"ו לאחרים ואמר הודיעני ואמר הראיתני שלא לנכח ולנכח כאחד וכמוהו רבים במקרא כמו שכתבנו למעלה: (יט) **ואני ככבש אלוף.** כמו ואלוף חסר ו' התחבור וכן שמש ירח ראובן שמעון והדומים להם ואלוף הוא שור כמו אלופינו מסובלי' וכן במשקל אחר שגר אלפיך וי"ת כאימר בחיר פי' אלוף תאר לכבש שהיה נבחר כמו אלוף תימן אמר הנביא אני הייתי עמהם קודם שהודיעני האל זה כמו הכבש או השור שיובילו אותו לבית המטבחיים לטבח אותו והוא כשמוליכין אותו אינו יודע כי לשוחטו מוליכין אותו כן אני היו מוליכין אותי קרובי ומיודעי לאכול עמהם לא הייתי יודע כי להמיתני מוליכין אותי והנה אם לא הודיעני האל היו כמיתים אותי ומה היו חושבים עלי ואומרים נשחיתה עץ בלחמו ופי' כתרגום נרמי סמא דמותא במיכליה ואמר נשחיתה במקום נשימה כי התשומה הזאת היתה השחתה. ועץ פי' עץ כות כלומר עץ שהוא סם המות וכן ויורהו ה' עץ אמרו שהוא עץ מר והיה נס בתוך נס: **בלחמו.** במאכלו כי לחם כלל לכל מאכל: **מארץ חיים.** כן העה"ז וי"ת מארעא דישראל: **לא יזכר עוד.** פירש בחיים וכפל הענין במ"ש: (כ) **וה' צבאות שופט צדק.** שפטני מהם כי אתה שופט בצדק: **בוחן כליות ולב.** כי אתה בחנת לבם וכליות' והודעתני מחשבותם כדי שאשמר מהם:

מצודת דוד

גילה לי מעשיהם אשר לא טובים ובגמול תבא הרעה: (יט) **ואני.** ר"ל לא מדעתי אני הולך לנבאות עליהם הרעה כי יד ה' היתה חזקה עלי ללכת אליהם ולנבאות ואני ככבש ואלוף אשר כל אחד מהם יובא לטבוח שלא מרצונו כי אין חפצי לנבאות עליהם רעה: **ולא ידעתי.** ולא אדע מה שבעי בזה אשר המה חשבו עלי מחשבות רעות ואומרי' נשחית מאכלו בעץ הממית ר"ל נשים סם המות במאכלו ובזה נכרית אותו מארץ חיים כי ימות ומינו ולא יזכר עוד שמו: (כ) וה' צבאות.

מצודת ציון

כמו כי בגלל הדבר הזה (דברים טו): (יח) **מעלליהם.** מעשיהם: (יט) **אלוף.** כמו ואלוף ותחסר הוי"ו והוא הפר כמו שגר אלפיך (דברים ז'): **יובל.** יובא כמו יובל שי (ישעיה י"ח): **לטבוח.** לשחוט: **עץ בלחמו.** כמו בעץ לחמו ועץ מין עץ שהיא סם המות ועליו נאמר ויורהו ה' עץ (שמות ט"ו) והיה נס בתוך נס כמ"ש רז"ל: **בלחמו.** כל מין מאכל קרוי בשם לחם: (כ) **בוחן.** מל' בחינה ונסיון: **כליות.** כשם מקום העצה: **גליתי.** מל' גלוי:

no longer be remembered—I.e., let him no longer be remembered among the living.—[*Redak*]

20. **And the Lord of Hosts is a just Judge**—Plead my cause that I have against them because You are a just Judge.—[*Redak*]

Who searches the kidneys and the heart—For You searched their heart and kidneys and informed me of their plot, so that I should beware of them.—[*Redak*]

Let me see Your vengeance against them—*He cursed the people of Anathoth.*—[*Rashi*]

I supplicate You that I remain alive until after You have wrought vengeance upon them.—[*Redak*]

let me know, and I knew, then You showed me their deeds.
19. And I was like a lamb and a bull, [that is] brought to the slaughter, and I did not know that they had devised plans about me, "Let us destroy his food with wood, and let us cut him off from the land of the living, and let his name no longer be remembered." 20. And the Lord of Hosts is a just Judge, Who searches the kidneys and the heart, "Let me see Your vengeance against them, for

19. **And I was like a lamb [and] a bull**—*that will be brought to the slaughter.*—[*Rashi*]

brought—Heb. יוּבַל. *Since I let them know of the evil, they plan to kill me.*—[*Rashi*]

like a lamb [and] a bull—Heb. כְּכֶבֶשׂ אַלּוּף. *Dunash and Judah son of Kudish* (Karish) *interpreted it 'as a lamb and a bull, brought to the slaughter. And* אַלּוּף is like '(Deut. 28:4) *the offspring of your cattle* (אֲלָפֶיךָ).' *Although it was not stated* וְאַלּוּף, *we find similar cases, e.g.* '(Habukkuk 3:11) *The sun [and] the moon* (יָרֵחַ) *stood on high,*' '(Isaiah 38:14) *Like a crane [and] a swallow* (עָגוּר) *so I chirp.' And Menahem interpreted* כְּכֶבֶשׂ אַלּוּף: *a large lamb* (see Psalms 58:9, *Rashi* ad loc.), *and Jonathan supports him, since he renders like a choice lamb.*—[*Rashi* from *Machbereth Menahem* p. 26, *Teshuvoth Dunash* pp. 46,47] The intention is that he was like a choice lamb, designated for slaughter; not like a lean lamb, which is not used for slaughtering.—[*Rabbenu Tam*]

The prophet says: Before God informed me of their plot, I was like an innocent lamb, led to the slaughter. Just as the lamb or the bull knows nothing of his master's plans when he leads him to the slaughterhouse, so was I unaware of the plans of my friends and my kinsmen when they called me to eat with them.—[*Redak*]

Let us destroy his food with wood—*Let us put poison into his food.*—[*Rashi* from *Jonathan*]

The intention is that they would put poisonous wood into his food. This resembles the episode of Marah (Exodus 15:25) when Moses cast a stick of poisonous wood into the water and, by a miracle, the water became sweet.—[*Redak*]

his food—Heb. לַחְמוֹ, lit. his bread. This term is often used to denote all food.—[*Redak, Mezudath Zion*]

It may also be rendered: Let us put poisonous wood into his food, rendering נַשְׁחִיתָה like נָשִׁיתָה. It may also mean: Let us sink poison into his food, deriving נַשְׁחִיתָה from שַׁחַת, *a pit,* for one who wishes to poison someone sinks the poison deeply into the food lest it be detected by the intended victim.—[*Ibn Nachmiash*]

from the land of the living—From this world. *Jonathan* renders: From Eretz Israel.—[*Redak*]

אֵלֶיךָ גִּלִּיתִי אֶת־רִיבִי׃ כא לָכֵן כֹּה־
אָמַר יְהוָה עַל־אַנְשֵׁי עֲנָתוֹת
הַמְבַקְשִׁים אֶת־נַפְשְׁךָ לֵאמֹר לֹא
תִנָּבֵא בְּשֵׁם יְהוָה וְלֹא תָמוּת בְּיָדֵנוּ׃
כב לָכֵן כֹּה אָמַר יְהוָה צְבָאוֹת הִנְנִי
פֹקֵד עֲלֵיהֶם הַבַּחוּרִים יָמֻתוּ בַחֶרֶב
בְּנֵיהֶם וּבְנוֹתֵיהֶם יָמֻתוּ בָּרָעָב׃
כג וּשְׁאֵרִית לֹא תִהְיֶה לָהֶם כִּי־אָבִיא
רָעָה אֶל־אַנְשֵׁי עֲנָתוֹת שְׁנַת פְּקֻדָּתָם׃

תרגום

ארי קדמך אמרית ית
עלבני׃ כא בכן כדנן
אמר יי על אנשי
דבען למקטלך דאמרין
לא תתנבי בשמא דיי
ולא תמות בידנא׃
כב בכן כדנן אמר יי
צבאות האנא מסער
עליהון עולימיהון
יתקטלון בחרבא
בניהון ובנתיהון ימותון
בכפנא׃ כג ושארא לא
יהי להון ארי איתי
בישתא על אנשי
ענתות שנת סועכן
חוביהון

רש"י

את אנשי ענתות היה מקלל׃ (כג) אל אנשי ענתות. כמו על אנשי ענתות׃

מנחת שי

(כב) ובנותיהם. מתחלפת חסר וא"ו בתר נו"ן׃

רד"ק

אראה נקמתך. כלומר שלא אמות עד שאראה שתקח נקמת מהם׃ כי אליך גליתי את ריבי. אין לי אח וקרוב לגלות את ריבי כי הם חשבו להמיתני׃ אליך גליתי את ריבי. ואתה תקח משפטי מהם ובאמרו גליתי דברה תורה כלשון בני אדם כי גלוי וידוע לפניו וכת"י גליתי אמרית׃ (כא) לכן. ולא תמות בידינו. ואיך אמר ירמיהו וה' הודיעני והרי היו אומרים לו על פניו כי ימיתוהו אם יתנבא אלא שירמיהו לא היה חושש למה שהיו אומרי' בפניו כי חשב כי זה דרך הפחד והגזים כי לא יתכן שימיתוהו בגלוי ולא היה מפחד מזה אך שיכתוהו בסתר על ידי סם זה היה יכול להיות כי היה דבר שלא היה נודע כי יש סם שמאכיל אותו שלא ימות מיד אלא עד שמנה או עשרה ימים ואם ימות על הדרך הזה לא היו אומרים כי על ידי סם המות מת׃ (כב) לכן כה אמר ה'. הבחורים ימותו בחרב. הבחורים שיבטחו בגבורתם ויצאו להלחם ימותו בחרב׃ בניהם ובנותיה' ימותו ברעב. בעיר וזכר הבנים ולא האבות כי האבות אם ישנו דבר מאכל יאכלו הם כי חייהם קודמי' לחיי בניהם ולא עוד אלא שיאכלו בשר בניהם ובנותיהם מפני הרעב׃ (כג) ושארית. אנשי ענתות ילקו יותר משאר ישראל לפי שהיה להם להחזיק יד ירמיהו שהם קרוביו ובני עירו והם היו אומרי' להמיתו אם ינבא בשם ה'׃ שנת פקדתם. שנת החרבן שהיתה שנת תשע עשרה לנבוכדנאצר שפקד האל עליהם את עונם והחרבה הארץ וגלו הנשארי' מן החרב ומן הרעב ואמר כי אנשי ענתות לא תהי' להם שארית ואף על פי שנגזרה עליהם גזרה שלא תהיה להם שארית בעת שחלה עליה' הגזרת ולכדו האויבי' את העיר עשו תשובה והיתה להם שארית וכן ארז"ל וכן מצאנו בשוב גלות בבל אנשי ענתות מאה ועשרים

מצודת ציון

(כב) פוקד. ענין זכרון׃ (כג) ושארית. ענין שיור׃

מצודת דוד

אבל אתה ה' לבאות הלא אתה שופט צדק ובוחן לדעת מחשבות כליות ולב ותדע שאין שמחה בלבי בהנבאות להם הרעה׃ אראה. לכן אראה הנקמה שתקח מהם׃ כי אליך. לכך אליך אני מגלה את הריב שיש לי עמהם אבל לא סוכתתים ע"ז להודיעך שאני יודע מחשבותם׃ (כא) המבקשים. אשר הם מבקשים לקחת את נפשך׃ לאמר. אשר אומרים לך לא תנבא בשם ה' ואז לא תמות בידינו׃ (כב) פוקד. אזכור עליהם עונם להשיב גמול׃ הבחורים. ההולכי' במלחמה׃ בניהם. הקטנים׃ (כג) שנת פקודתם. השנה אשר אזכור עליהם עונם להשיב גמול׃

when the enemy captured the city, the Rabbis tell us that the men of Anathoth repented, and they did have a remnant. Indeed, we find that when they returned from Babylonian exile, the men of Anathoth were one hundred and twenty-eight (Ezra 2:23).—[*Redak* and *Yalkut Shimoni* from *Pesikta d'Rav Kahana*, pp. 160f.]

to You, I have revealed my cause. 21. Therefore, so says the
Lord of Hosts concerning the men of Anathoth, who seek your
life, saying, "You shall not prophesy in the name of the Lord,
and you shall not die by our hand." 22. Therefore, so says the
Lord of Hosts: Behold, I will visit retribution upon them; the
young men shall die by the sword: their sons and daughters
shall die through hunger. 23. And they shall have no remnant,
for I will bring misfortune upon the men of Anathoth in the
year of their remembrance.

to You I have revealed my cause—I have no kinsmen to whom to reveal my cause for they have plotted to kill me. I have, therefore, revealed my cause to You, and You execute judgment against them. The expression of revealing his cause to God is anthropomorphic, for God knows everything. *Jonathan,* in fact, renders: I said.—[*Redak*]

21. **and you shall not die by our hand**—Now, how did Jeremiah state that God informed him of the plot if the people of Anathoth openly threatened him with death if he continue to prophesy in the name of God? The answer is that he considered it a mere threat that they would kill him in public, and he had no fear of that. That they should poison him was still possible, but he was completely unaware of such a plot.—[*Redak*]

22. **the young men shall die by the sword**—The young men, who rely on their strength, and will go forth to wage war, will die by the sword.—[*Redak*]

their sons and daughters—who will remain within the city, will die from hunger. He does not mention the fathers, since they will be the ones to eat any food obtainable, according to the Rabbinic maxim: Your life comes before your fellow's. Moreover, they will eat the flesh of their children because of the famine.—[*Redak*]

23. **And they shall have no remnant**—The men of Anathoth shall be punished more severely than the rest of Israel since they should have supported Jeremiah, being his neighbors and his kin. Instead, they threatened to kill him if he would prophesy in God's name.—[*Redak*]

upon the men of Anathoth—Heb. אֶל־אַנְשֵׁי עֲנָתוֹת, lit. to the men of Anathoth. *Like* עַל־אַנְשֵׁי עֲנָתוֹת, *upon the men of Anathoth.*—[*Rashi*]

in the year of their visitation—The year of the destruction, which was the nineteenth year of Nebuchadnezzar's reign, when God visited upon them their punishment for their iniquity, the land was devastated, and the survivors went into exile. The prophet states that the men of Anathoth will have no survivors. Although this was decreed upon them, when the time came for the decree to be executed,

יב א צַדִּיק אַתָּה יְהוָה כִּי אָרִיב אֵלֶיךָ
אַךְ מִשְׁפָּטִים אֲדַבֵּר אוֹתָךְ מַדּוּעַ דֶּרֶךְ
רְשָׁעִים צָלֵחָה שָׁלוּ כָּל־בֹּגְדֵי בָגֶד׃
ב נְטַעְתָּם גַּם־שֹׁרָשׁוּ יֵלְכוּ גַּם־עָשׂוּ
פֶרִי קָרוֹב אַתָּה בְּפִיהֶם וְרָחוֹק
מִכִּלְיוֹתֵיהֶם׃ ג וְאַתָּה יְהוָה יְדַעְתָּנִי
תראני

חוֹבֵיהוֹן׃ א זַכָּאי אַתְּ
יְיָ מַלְמִידַן לְקַבָּלָא
פִּתְגָמָךְ בְּרַם שְׁאֵילַת
דִּינִין אֲנָא שָׁאֵיל מִן
קֳדָמָךְ מָה דֵּין אוֹרְחַת
רַשִׁיעַיָּא מַצְלְחָא שְׁלַן
שַׁלְוָא כָּל מְשַׁקְרֵי שְׁקָר׃
ב קַיַּמְתִּינוּן אַף תְּקִיפוּ
עֲתָרוּ אַף קְנוֹ נִכְסִין
קָרִיבִין פִּתְגָמֵי אוֹרַיְתָךְ
בְּפוּמְהוֹן וּרְחִיקָא
דַּחֲלְתָךְ מִכּוּלְיָתְהוֹן׃
ג וְאַתְּ יְיָ כּוּלָּא יְדִיעַ וּגְלֵי

ת״א צדיק אתה ה׳. סנהדרין לו פקדה שער לו עקרים מ״ד פס״ו:

רש״י

יב (א) צדיק אתה ה׳ כי אריב אליך. כשאתווכח עמך ידעתי כי תצדק בדבריך אך חסן אני לדבר משפטים אותך להודיעני דרכך: מדוע דרך רשעים צלחה. שנתת גדולה לנ״כ הרשע ותצליחהו להחריב ביתך. דבר אחר על אנשי ענתות היה צועק וקורא תגר: שלו. ל׳ שלוה: (ג) ואתה ה׳ ידעתני. גם על אנשי הענתות

מהר״י קרא

יב (א) צדיק אתה ה׳ כי אריב אליך. יודע אני שכל משפטיך צדק מה להריב להשיב על משפטיך מאחר שכל משפטיך דיני אמת איני כאדם שרב את יוצרו אלא כאדם אשר יקשה ממנו משפט ושאלו מרבו. וזה הוא: אך משפטי׳ אדבר אותך. כלומר אל תדינני כמתווכח עם רבו אלא כשואל דין מרבו וכת״י ברם שאילת דינין אנא שאל מן קדמך: מדוע דרך רשעים צלחה. הם רשעי ענתות הנזכרין למעלה: שלו. לשון שלוה כמו ישליו אוהביך: (ב) קרוב אתה בפיהם ורחוק מכליותיהם. כתרגומו פתגמי אוריתך בפומהון ורחיקא דחלתך מכוליתהון: (ג) ואתה ה׳ ידעתני. פתרוני אתה יודע מה הם עושין לי כמו וירא אלהים את בני ישראל וידע אלהים שפת׳

רד״ק

ושטונה: (א) צדיק אתה ה׳ כי אריב אליך. שאריב אליך כלומר שאם אומר שאריב אליך. לא יתכן שאתה צדיק ואין לי לחלוק בזה: אך משפטי׳ אדבר אותך. אך אדבר עמך כאדם הנשפט על חברו ונושא ונותן בטעות הנידונין כי אני נבוך בזה: מדוע דרך רשעים צלחה. כי היו בישראל רשעי׳ מצליחין וכת״י זכאי את ה׳ מלמידן וגו׳ כבעמוד: (ב) נטעתם. משל על הצלחתם שהיא קיימת והולכת וגדלה ובאמרו נטעתם הראה כי טובת הרשעי׳ תבא להם מאת האל לא שהיה להם דרך מקרה וכן אמר בתורה ומשלם לשונאיו אל פניו להאבידו כתרגומו: שרשו. מבנין פעל הכבד אשר על דרך המרובע וכן בל שורש בארץ גזעם: קרוב אתה בפיהם. אם יקראוך בתפלה או יזכרוך בשבועה לשקר הוא כי אתה רחוק מכליותיה׳ ואינם חושבי׳ כי בידך טובתם ושאתה המטיב והמריע וי״ת קריבין פתגמי אוריתך וגו׳ כבעמוד: (ג) ואתה ה׳ ידעתני תראני. ואתה

מנחת שי

יב (ג) גם עשו פרי. הפ״א רפה:

מצודת דוד

יב (א) צדיק. אמר הנביא ידעתי ה׳ שאתה צדיק בדבר אשר אריב אליך אך אדבר עמך דברי ויכוח וכאומר עכ״ז אתווכח למען דעת את הטעם והסבה לא על היותי מסופק אם צדיק אתה בדינך: מדוע. וזהו דברי מדוע דרך רשעים מצלחת וכל הרשעי׳ הבוגדים יושבים בשלוה ואמר זה כראותו בנבואה מרבית ממשלת נבוכדנצר: (ב) נטעתם. מיד כשנטעתם נשרש גזעם ר״ל שתאום כא׳ לשם הגדולה: ילכו. והם הולכים ומתפשטים ועושים פירות מרובות ר״ל בנים ובני בנים יורשים המלוכה והממשלה: קרוב אתה בפיהם. גם כי בפיהם מראים עצמם יראים את האל זהו מן השפה ולחוץ אבל רחוק אתה ממחשבות כליותיהם ולא יאמינו בך באמת: (ג) ידעתני. הלא ידעת אותי ותראה לבי ובחנת אותה אם היא אתך להאמין בך ר״ל

מצודת ציון

יב (א) משפטים. ענין ויכוח: צלחה. מלשון הצלחה: שלו. מל׳ שלוה: בוגדי בגד. ענין סרוב ומרד: (ב) מכליותיהם.

thoughts, and they do not believe in His retribution, there is no hope that they will repent.

Abarbanel explains that this verse refers to Nebuchadnezzar, as *Rashi* explains it in his first interpretation. Since Nebuchadnezzar did not inherit the throne, but was the first of the dynasty, it is said that the Lord planted him. Then he begot children and grandchildren who succeeded him on the throne. This is symbolized as taking root and producing fruit. The prophet asks God why they merited this success, since they are not of the pious of the nations, for 'You are near in their mouths, but far from their thoughts.'

3. **But You, O Lord, have known**

12

1. You are right, O Lord, when I contend with You, but I will argue with You. Why has the way of the wicked prospered, all who deal with treachery have peace? 2. You have planted them, they have even taken root, they have even produced fruit. You are near in their mouths but far from their thoughts.
3. But You, O Lord, have known me,

1. **You are right, O Lord, when I contend with You**—*When I debate with You, I know that you will be right in Your words, but I wish to argue with You so that You will let me know Your way.*—[*Rashi*]

Redak explains: To contend with You is impossible, for You are just, and I cannot disagree on this point, but I will speak with You like a person who debates with his friend, who discusses the arguments on both sides of the question for I am perplexed in this matter.

Why has the way of the wicked prospered?—*That You have given greatness to Nebuchadnezzar the wicked, and you have made him succeed in destroying Your house? Another explanation is that he was crying and complaining about the men of Anathoth.*—[*Rashi*] *Metsudath David* follows the first explanation, and *Rabbi Joseph Kara* follows the second one. *Redak* explains simply that among the Jews there were wicked men who were prosperous.

have peace—Heb. שָׁלוּ, *an expression of* שַׁלְוָה, *peace.*—[*Rashi*]

5. **You have planted them**—This symbolizes their prosperity, which is stable and becomes progressively greater and greater. This word indicates that they have not gained prosperity by chance, but that God Himself has given it to them.—[*Redak*]

You are near in their mouths—If they call upon You in prayer or mention You in an oath, it is false, for You are far from their thoughts, and they do not think that their success is in Your hand, and that it is You Who brings success or misfortune upon them. *Jonathan* renders: The words of Your Torah are close to their mouths, but fear of You is far from their thoughts.—[*Redak*]

Although they appear outwardly to fear You, that is merely lip service, but You are far from their thoughts, and they do not believe in You wholeheartedly.—[*Mezudath David*]

Malbim explains that Jeremiah contends with God that it is unfair that the wicked have children, and these children remain alive. You cannot say that God waits for them to repent, for a wicked man can be expected to repent only if he believes in Divine retribution, but cannot control his desires. In this case, however, since God is far from their

תִּרְאֵנִי וּבָחַנְתָּ לִבִּי אִתָּךְ הַתִּקֵם כְּצֹאן
לְטִבְחָה וְהַקְדִּשֵׁם לְיוֹם הֲרֵגָה: ד עַד־
מָתַי תֶּאֱבַל הָאָרֶץ וְעֵשֶׂב כָּל־הַשָּׂדֶה
יִיבָשׁ מֵרָעַת יֹשְׁבֵי־בָהּ סָפְתָה בְהֵמוֹת
וָעוֹף כִּי אָמְרוּ לֹא יִרְאֶה אֶת־
אַחֲרִיתֵנוּ: ה כִּי אֶת־רַגְלִים | רַצְתָּה

תרגום

קֳדָמָךְ דְּאַתְּ בָּסַר
לִבְבִיָא דְרָעַן בִּדְחַלְתָּךְ
רַשִׁיעַיָא אַתְקֵינִינוּן כְּעָנָא
לְנִכְסְתָא וְזַמְנִינוּן לְיוֹם
קְטוֹלֵי: ו עַד אֵימָתַי
תֶּחֱרוּב אַרְעָא וְעִשְׂבָא
דְּכָל חַקְלָא יִיבַשׁ מֵחוֹבֵי
רַשִׁיעַיָא דְיָתְבוּן בַּהּ סָף
בְּעִירָא וְעוֹפָא אֲרֵי
אֲמַרוּ לָא גְלֵי קֳדָמוֹהִי
סוֹפָנָא: ה דְנָא תְיוּבְתָּא
לְיִרְמְיָה נְבִיָא עַל

מהר"י קרא

ידע בצרתם וכן יודע צדיק נפש בהמתו שפתרונו יודע מה היא צריכה ומספיק לה אף כאן ידעתני ידעת בצרות נפשי: תראני. פי' ראה עניי ועמלי: ובחנת לבי אתך. שאיני כמותם שקרוב אתה בפיהם ורחוק מכליותיהם אלא לבי ופי שוין: התיקם כצאן לטבחה. בה במדה שמדדו לי כענין שנאמר למעלה ואני ככבש אלוף יובל לטבוח: והקדישם ליום הרגה. הזמינם: (ד) עד מתי תאבל הארץ וגו'. פתרונו עד מתי אתה מכלה את שאינן חוטאין בעון החוטאין שבעון אנשי ענתות עתידה הארץ שתחרב ועץ השדה ייבש וספתה בהמה ועוף מרעת יושבי בה כלה את החוטאין והנח אותן שלא חטאו וכל העניין הזה מלמד קטגורייא על אנשי ענתות: כי אמרו לא יראה את אחריתינו. כך אמרו אנשי ענתות אחרית שהוא מתנבא עלינו ושארית לא תהיה להם תוכחת זו לא תהא בימיו של נביא עד כאן דבריו של ירמיהו ששאל אך משפטים אדבר אותך מיכן ואילך תשובת שהשיבו הקב"ה וזו היא תשובתו: (ה) כי את

רש"י

העומדים עלי עזרתני כי אתה ידעתני: התקם כצאן לטבחה. נתקם מן החיי' למות (דישטאקאלו"ש בלע"ז) כמו עד התיקנו אותם מן העיר (יהושע ח'): והקדישם. הזמינם: (ד) עד מתי תאבל הארץ ועשב כל השדה ייבש. עד כאן דברי הנביא ורה"ק משיבתו מרעת יושבי בה ספתה בהמות ועוף: תאבל. תחרב: ספתה. (פוניד"א בלע"ז): כי אמרו. יושבי הארץ הזאת: לא יראה את אחריתנו. אין גלוי לפניו מה יהיה בסופינו: (ה) כי את רגלים

מנחת שי

(ד) ישבי בה. במקצת ספרים כ"י ודפוסים ישבים מלא ביו"ד:

רד"ק

ראה אותי במה שאני: ובחנת לבי אתך. בחנת לבי שהוא אתך לא כלבם שאתה רחוק ממנו אם כן למה הם בטוב ואני ברע: התיקם כצאן לטבחה. כמו עד התיקנו אותם מן העיר אמר אלו השלוי' הרשעים התיקם ממקום רבצם לרעתם כצאן לטבחה: והקדישם. והזמינם: ליום הריגה. ליום שיהיה בו הרג רב והוא יום החרבן הזמינם לחרב ולא יהיה להם מקום להנצל מן ההרג ואז יודע לעולם כי רשעתם גרמה להם אבל עתה יש מבוכה בהצלחה: (ד) עד מתי תאבל הארץ. עד מתי יהיה זה שהוקדשו אלה ליום הריגה כשתאבל הארץ והוא יום החרבן: ועשב כל השדה ייבש. זה על דרך הפלגה וכן ספתה בהמות ועוף ומפני מה תאבל ותשחת הארץ מרעת יושבי בה כי אמרו הדין נותן שלא ינצלו אלה הרשעים השלוי' מיום הריגה כי הם אומרי' בשלותם לא יראה אחריתנו אם יאמרו להם נביאי האמת האל יביא אחריתכם לרע אע"פ שאתם שלוי' עתה והם אומרי' לא יראה האל אחריתנו כי אינו משגיח בנו ובמעשינו. ואינו יודע מה אחריתנו: ספתה. ענין כליון כמו האף תספה צדיק עם רשע אלא שהוא פעל יוצא וזה פעל עומד והנה שאל ירמיהו על הצלחת הרשעי' ולא השיבו האל: (ה) כי את רגלים. פי' אאז"ל כי זה הפסוק תשובת שאלתו

מצודת ציון

מל' כליות: (ג) התיקם. ענין העתקה: והקדישם. ענין הזמנה כמו קדשו קהל (יואל ב'): (ד) תאבל. ענין השחתה כמו אבלה נבלה הארץ (ישעיה כ"ד): ספתה. ענין כליון כמו אסף אסיפם (לעיל ח'): אחריתנו. מלשון אחרית וסוף: (ה) רצתה. מלשון

מצודת דוד

מכיר אני בעצמי שנגלה לך תעלומות לב וא"כ יודע אתה שרחוק אתה מכליותיהם כי אין דבר נעלם ממך: התיקם. לכן העתיקם מהצלחתם אל הטבחה כצאן הזה והזמינם ליום הרגה: (ד) עד מתי זהו תשובת המקום כאומר הלא הוא העומד להיות רעועה מדות על ישראל להיות שבט אפי כי עד מתי תהיה הארץ נשחתה ועשב יבשה בסבת רשעת יושבי בה וכלתה בהמה ועוף כי לא תרבינה בארץ בגמול פשעם באומרים שאני איני רואה אחריתם לדעת מה יהיה בסופם וכאומר וכי כן תהיה הארץ נשחתה עד עולם לכן יבוא נ"כ ויגלה אותם מארצם וימורק עונם וישובו אל ארצם ותהיה אז ארץ חמדה כמאז: (ה) כי את רגלים רצתה. לפי שירמיה לא היה עדיין מכיר בסופו מרבית רשעת בני יהודה וירושלים לכן אמר לו

interpretation also, the following verses illustrate the wickedness of the people of Judah, to convince the prophet of the necessity of the exile.

Rabbi Joseph Kara, as mentioned above, explains that the prophet asks why the people of Anathoth, who dealt wickedly with him, were prospering? He proceeds to ask:

[3] **But You, O Lord, have known me**—I.e., You know what they are doing to me; You know the pain of my soul.

You shall see me—I.e., You shall see my affliction and my toil.

and You shall try my heart with You—that I am not like them, for You are near to them in their mouths but far from their thoughts, but I am sincerely with You.

5. **For if you have run with footmen and they wearied you**—*Your kin, the priests like you and the men of your city come to kill you.*—[*Rashi*]

with footmen—Heb. רַגְלִים (*pieton in O.F*), pedestrian.—[*Rashi*]

* For Rashi's commentary turn to page 230.

You see me, and You try my heart with You. Draw them out
like sheep to the slaughter, and prepare them for the day of
slaughter. 4. How long will the land mourn and the grass of all
the field dry out?" Because of the evil of its inhabitants, beasts
and fowl are ended, for they said, "He will not see our end."
5. For if you have run with footmen

me—*Also, concerning the men of Anathoth You have aided me, for You have known me.*—[*Rashi*]

Draw them out like sheep to the slaughter—*Draw them out of life to death* (*détache les in French*, separate them, cut them off). Comp. '(Joshua 8:6) *until we have drawn* (הִתִּיקֵנוּ) *them from the city.'*—[*Rashi*]

and prepare them—Heb. וְהַקְדִּישֵׁם, *prepare them.*—[*Rashi*] This is not related to hallowing as one may think. This root is often used in the sense of preparing. *Jonathan*, too, interprets the word in this manner, followed by *Redak* and *Mezudoth*.

4. **How long will the land mourn and the grass of all the field dry out?**—*Up to here are the prophet's words, and the Holy Spirit replies to him, "Because of the evil of its inhabitants, beasts and fowl are ended.*—[*Rashi*]

will ... mourn—*Be waste.*—[*Rashi*]

ended—(*finira in French*, will terminate).—[*Rashi*]

for they said—I.e., *the inhabitants of this land* have said.—[*Rashi*]

"He will not see our end."—*It is not revealed to Him what will be at our end.*—[*Rashi*]

This follows *Rashi*'s first interpretation, that Jeremiah's question is about the success of Nebuchadnezzar. He prays that the enemy will be drawn to death like sheep to the slaughter. He asks how long the land will be desolate and the grass will be dry. God replies that all this is because the Israelites have denied God's knowledge of their end. He continues to elaborate upon the wickedness of the people of Judah, pointing out to the prophet that even his own kinsmen dealt treacherously with him, surely the princes of Judah. For this reason, Nebuchadnezzar was sent to conquer the land. This will be explained further in the following verses.

Mezudath David, following *Abarbanel*, likewise explains that the prophet questions God's reason for making Nebuchadnezzar prosper. God replies: How long will the land mourn and the grass of all the field dry out; because of the evil of its inhabitants, beasts and fowls are ended, for they said, "He will not see our end"? Should the land remain desolate forever, and shall all the beasts and fowls end because of the sins of the inhabitants of the land, who say, "God does not know what our end will be"? Rather, let Nebuchadnezzar conquer the land and exile its inhabitants in order to expiate their sins, and then let them return to the land. According to this

וַיַּלְאוּךָ וְאֵיךְ תְּתַחֲרֶה אֶת־הַסּוּסִים וּבְאֶרֶץ שָׁלוֹם אַתָּה בוֹטֵחַ וְאֵיךְ תַּעֲשֶׂה בִּגְאוֹן הַיַּרְדֵּן: ו כִּי גַם־אַחֶיךָ וּבֵית־אָבִיךָ גַּם־הֵמָּה בָּגְדוּ בָךְ גַּם־

המה

בעותיה נביא את דמי לגברא דרהט עם רגלאה ולאי ואיכדין את מדמי למרהט כל קביל סוסותא בבקעתא ובארעא שלמא את סתקפט ונפיל ואיכדין את מדמי למעבד כל קביל חיות ברא די ברום ירדנא ואם על טבון דאנא מוטב לנבוכדנאצר מלכא דבבל רגלאה נביא את חזי וסתקפיה ומן פון דאחוינך מה דאנא עתיד למעבד לאבהתך צדיקיא דמן עלמא דרהטו כסוסותא למעבד עובדין טבין קדמי ואף אמרית להון דאיתי על בניהון ברכן ונחמן הא כסיא דנחתין שטוף לירדנא: ו וראף ירמיה בעי עליהון רחמין ארי ית אחך ובית אבוך אף אינון

רש"י

רצתה וילאוך. קרוביך הכהני' כמותיך ואנשי עירך באים להורגך: **את רגלים**. עם רגלים (פיאוניד"ש בלע"ז): **ואיך תתחרה את הסוסי'**. לרוץ את הסוסים כלומר ומה קרוביך הכהנים באים להרגך כל שכן שיקומו להרגך שרי יהודה וזהו קלפי עליהם וזו היא הגללת האויב וכן ת"י דנא תיובתא וגו'. ומדרש רבותינו אם על שכר שלא פסיעת שרך כ"כ לכבודי בימי מרודך אתה תמה שהרביתי גדולתו כל כך מה תתמה עוד כשתראה שילום שכר שאשלם לצדיקים שרצו לפני כסוסים: **תתחרה**. (אאטיר"ש בלע"ז): **ובארץ שלום אתה בוטח**. עם הלאוך: **ואיך תעשה בגאון**. שרי יהודה. וגאון הירדן משל הוא לפי שהוא מקום אריות ונמרים וכן למדנו יונתן בהרבה מקומות וכאן תירגם ואיכדין את מדמי למעבד לקבל חיות ברא די ברום ירדנא והנה כאריה יעלה מגאון הירדן (לקמן ס') ת"י בשתי מקומו' כאריא דסליק מרום ירדנא: (ו) **קראו אחריך**

מהר"י קרא

רגלים רצתה וילאוך ואיך תתחרה את הסוסים. דומה אתה לזה שמתפאר לרוץ עם הסוסים ובא רגלי אחד והלאהו במרוצתו וקידמו אמרו לו הרואים אתה היית מתפאר. את רגלים רצתה וילאוך ואיך תתחרה את הסוסים. אף אתה: בארץ שלום אתה בוטח ואיך תעשה בגאון הירדן. פת' כשאני שולחך בארץ יהודה ובנימין שהיה לך לבטוח בהן שהרי אחיך אנשי ענתות יושבין עמך אתה מקטרג עליהן שמבקשין את נפשך אם הייתי שולחך בגאון הירדן הם ראובן וגד שישבו להם בעבר הירדן עד שלא גלו כל שכן שהיית מלמד עליהן קטגירייא כמו שמפרש והולך: (ו) כי גם אחיך ובית אביך בגדו בך. הם אנשי ענתות המבקשים את נפשך: גם המה

רד"ק

שלא יהרהר אחר מדות הקב"ה אמר ועל מה ששאלתני אני משיבך זה המשל כי אני רואה אותך שרצת עם רגלים כמותך והלאוך כי רצו יותר ממך ולא היה בך יכולת להשיגם והלאוך במרוצתם להשיגם: ואיך תתחרה את הסוסים. ואיך תתערב עם הסוסים לרוץ עמהם וזה פי' המשל הנה אתה בין בני אדם כמותך ואינך יודע דעתם ויסודת' שהרי אמרו להאכילך סם המות ולא ידעת ולא הרגשת בהם אם לא הודעתיך ואתה איך תרצה לדעת דעתי וסודותי בהנהגת העולם בהצלחת הרשעים ודעת הצדיקים בעה"ז לפיכך שתוק ואל תהרהר אחר מדותי והוסיף לו עוד על המשל לדבר לו על הענין עצמו וכלל בו מראש הפסוק ענין עצמו ואמר לו אני רואה אותך חלוש ונלאה בשליחותי וצריך שתחזק עצמך ולבך כי אני רואה כי רצת את רגלים כמותך והם אנשי ענתות שהם בני משפחתך ובמדרגה אחת עמך לענין גדולה והם הלאוך והפחידוך להמיתך ואיך תתחרה את הסוסי' כשתלך לירושלי' שהם שרים גדולי' וגם המלך שם איך תתנהג עמם צריך אתה שתתחזק שלא תפחד מהם ותדבר להם שליחותי בלא מורא והוסיף לו עוד ואמר ובארץ שלום אתה בוטח פי' אתה בוטח באנשי ענתות שהיה ראוי שתהיה לך ארץ שלום והיה לך לבטוח בהם שיצילוך מיד המבקשי' להרע לך. כי הם קרוביך ובני עירך ומדרך העולם שהקרובי' ובני עיר אחת שנתגדלו ביחד להגן זה על זה ושיתאהבו האחד על חברו עד שיתמסרו למות על אהוביה' או קרוביהם ואתה לא תוכל לעשות זה כי הם מערימי' אליך להמיתך: ואיך תעשה בגאון הירדן. כלומר במקום שמתגאין גלי הירדן והוא משל על שרי יהודה וירושלם והמשילו' לגאון הירדן לפי שהיא הנהר שבתוך ארץ ישראל כי פרת בגבול ארץ ישראל הוא ויתכן לפרשו על נבוכדנאצר שעתיד להעמיד חיילותיו בארץ ישראל מעבר לירדן ואמר לו לירמיה ואם אתה מפחד מהם שהם מעטי' איך תעשה במי שהוא דומה לגאון הירדן ויונתן גם כן פי' הפסוק לפי תשובת השאלה מיושב על הענין וכן תרגומו דנא תיובתא לירמיה וגו' כבעמיד: (ו) כי גם. בגדו בך. כי היית בוטח בהם ואמרו להאכילך סם המות:

מצודת דוד

במשל הנה התחברת לרוץ יחד עם אנשים הולכי רגל כמותך והנה המה הלאוך כי נפשית עיף ויגע לרוץ כמוהם: **ואיך תתחרה**. איך תתערב להדמות לרוץ יחד עם רוכבי סוסים ור"ל הנה אנשי ענתות המה קרוביך וכמה מהרעות עשו עמך עד שתפחד מפניהם ומה עוד תלאה אם תתחבר עם אנשי ירושלים ושריהם כי אז תכיר ברשעתם כפלים מבני ענתות ולאומר ועל כי גדלה רעתם מהצורך הוא להמשיל את כ"כ לבוא עליהם ולהשחיתם: **ובארץ שלום**. עתה בא לפרש המשל ואמר בהיותך בארץ שלום בענתות עם קרוביך וכי אתה בוטח בהם שלא יעשו עמך רעה ואיך א"כ תעשה בהיותך בגאון הירדן שהוא מעון אריות ור"ל איך העמוד מול אנשי ירושלים ושרים: (ו) **בגדו בך**. והמה לך לאויבים: **קראו וגו'**. אספו קבוצת אנשים

מצודת ציון

רילם ורדיפת ההליכה: **וילאוך**. ענין עייפות כמו ומה הלאתיך (מיכה ו'): **תתחרה**. ענין הדמות והתערב כמו אל תתחר במרעים (תהלים ל"ז): **בגאון**. ענין גבהות ורוממות ורצה לומר ככר המעולה הסמוך לירדן שם היה מקום האריות כמו שנאמר

'the enemies of' Israel. [This is a euphemism for Israel.]

will you compete—(*aastir in O.F.*).—[*Rashi*]

6. **have dealt treacherously with you**—For you trusted them, and they plotted to poison you.—[*Redak*]

and they wearied you, how will you compete with horses, and in the peaceful land which you trust, how will you do in the heights of the Jordan? 6. For, even your brethren, and your father's household, they too have dealt treacherously with you,

how will you compete with horses—*to run with the horses. That is to say, if even your brethren the priests come to kill you, surely the princes of Judah will rise up against you to kill you. This is* the reason for *My anger against them, and this is* the reason for *the success of the enemy. And so did Jonathan render: This is the reply etc. And, according to the Midrash of our Rabbis* (*Sanhedrin* 96a): *If you are amazed about the reward for the three steps that Nebuchadnezzar ran in My honor in the days of Merodach-baladan, why I gave him so much greatness, how much more will you be amazed when you see the payment of reward that I will pay the righteous who ran before Me like horses!*—[*Rashi*] *Jonathan*'s paraphrase of this verse matches the Talmudic explanation, rather than *Rashi*'s. It is, therefore, possible that the words, 'And so did *Jonathan* render: This is the reply etc.' should follow the Talmudic explanation. The story of the three steps Nebuchadnezzar ran in God's honor, is told by the Talmud (ad loc.). In II Kings 20:12, it is stated: 'At that time, Berodach-baladan the son of Baladan, the king of Babylonia, sent letters and a gift to Hezekiah for he heard that Hezekiah had been ill.' Because Hezekiah was ill and recovered should he send him letters and a gift? Yes, '(II. Chron. 32:31) To enquire of the wonder that was in the land,' for Rabbi Jonathan said: That day that Ahaz died was only two hours, and when Hezekiah became ill and recovered, the Holy One, blessed be He, restored those ten hours to the day, as it is written: '(Isaiah 38:8) Behold I return the shade of the steps that it went down on the steps of Ahaz by the sun backwards ten steps, and the sun returned ten steps on the steps that it had descended.' He said to them, "What is this?" They replied, "Hezekiah was ill and recovered." He said, "Is there such a man, and I should not want to send him a greeting? Write to him, 'Greetings to King Hezekiah, greetings to the city of Jerusalem, greetings to the great God.'" Nebuchadnezzar was Baladan's secretary. He was not there at the time. When he came, he said, "How did you write?" They replied, "This is how we wrote." He said to them, "You call Him the great God and you write to Him at the end?" He proceeded, "Write in this manner, 'Greetings to the great God, greetings to the city of Jerusalem, greetings to King Hezekiah.'" They said to him, "He who reads the letter shall be the messenger." He ran after him. When he had run three steps (in our editions of the Talmud, *four*), Gabriel came and stopped him. Said Rabbi Johanan: Had Gabriel not come and stopped him, there would have been no hope for

הֵמָּה קָרְאוּ אַחֲרֶיךָ מָלֵא אַל־תַּאֲמֵן
בָּם כִּי־יְדַבְּרוּ אֵלֶיךָ טוֹבוֹת׃ ז עָזַבְתִּי
אֶת־בֵּיתִי נָטַשְׁתִּי אֶת־נַחֲלָתִי נָתַתִּי
אֶת־יְדִדוּת נַפְשִׁי בְּכַף אֹיְבֶיהָ׃
ח הָיְתָה־לִּי נַחֲלָתִי כְּאַרְיֵה בַיָּעַר נָתְנָה
עָלַי בְּקוֹלָהּ עַל־כֵּן שְׂנֵאתִיהָ׃ ט הַעַיִט
צָבוּעַ נַחֲלָתִי לִי הַעַיִט סָבִיב עָלֶיהָ

ת"א ידידות נפשי. מנחות נ"ג : נחלתי כאריה. תענית טז זבחים קי"ח (מגלה פ"ב) : נתנה עלי. (תענית כ"ט) :

תרגום

שקרו בך אף אינון אמרו עלך מילין בישין לא תהימן בהון ארי ימרון עלך פתגמין טבין : ז שבקית ית בית מקדשי רטישית ית אחסנתי ומסרית ית עמא דהוה חביב קדמי ביד סנאוהי : ח הות קדמי אחסנתי כאריא בחורשא סליקת עלי אתרגושתה על כן רחיקתה : ט כעופא דמתבדר כן אתבדרת אחסנתי קדמי וכעופא

מהר"י קרא

קראו אחריך. וחרפוך בפה מלא: (ז) עזבתי את ביתי וגו'. עונותיה גרמו לי את כל זה לפי שהיתה לי נחלתי: (ח) כאריה ביער. כאריה בבהמות יער שמשכיל את הכל: נתנה עלי בקולה. רבים עשוקין הזעיקה עלי שצעקת העשוקים שהם עושקים באה עלי על כן שנאתיה: (ט) העיט צבוע נחלתי לי העיט סביב עליה. פת' נחלתי ישראל גרמו בעונם שדומין לי

רש"י

מלא. קבוצת אנשים: (ז) ידידות נפשי. עם סגולתי: (ח) נתנה עלי בקולה. עלתה לפני צעקת חמסיה: (ט) העיט צבוע. הה"א תמוהה לכך הוא נקוד פתח הכי הם עוף צבוע מגואל בדם שאר העופות נאספים עליו. דבר אחר העיט צבוע עוף אחד שהוא צבוע וכל העופות נאספים עליו לאוכלו שסונאים אותו: **העיט סביב עליה**. שמא עוף שמים הם אלו החיילות הגדודים הקלים אשר

רד"ק

קראו אחריך מלא. קבוץ כלומר התקבצו אחריך ליראך ולבהלך אם תתנבא להם וכן מלא רעים קבוץ רעים שיתקבצו אחרי האריה: אל תאמן בם. אם יקרבוך וידברו אליך טובות אל תאמן בם כי שקר הם דוברי' כי דעתם כדי שתקרב אצלם ותהיה בבתיהם לאכול ולשתות עמהם ודעתם להאכילך או להשקותך סם המות וי"ת ודאת ירמיה בעי עליהון רחמין וגו' כבעמוד,ורבי' האי פירש מלא מן המלות שמפרשין איתן בהפכן כלומר חסר בכל דבר כמו שאומרים לסמיא סגי נהור, ואדוני אבי ז"ל פי' מלא מן אשר מלאו לבו אומרים עליך שלא בפניך שאין לך שום יראה בעולם שהם אומרי' לך לא תנבא בשם ה' ולא תמות בידינו ואתה מוסיף עוד להנבא ולא תפחד מן המיתה: (ז) עזבתי את ביתי. אמר האל כאדם הנוהם על אבדתו: את ביתי. זה בית המקדש נחלתי זה ישראל כמו שאמר יעקב חבל נחלתו: ידידות נפשי. אהבתיה אהבת עזה ועתה בעונותיה נתתיה בכף אויביה: (ח) היתה. כאריה ביער. כששואג האריה ביער ונותן קולו וישמעו העוברים ושבים הקול יעזבו דרך היער או הסמוך לו כן עזבתי אני את נחלתי כי היתה לי כמו האריה ביער השואג בליל' ונתינת קול' ושאגת' היא צעקת העשוקי' מפני החמס או נתינת קול עובדי עכו"ם בבתי האלילי' כמ"ש במעשה אליהו עם אחאב ויקראו בשם הבעל מהבקר ועד הצהרים לאמר הבעל עננו ואומר ויקראו בקול גדול: על כן שנאתי'. ונתשתי' כי נלאתי נשוא עוד מעשי' הרעי': (ט) העיט. שניה' הה"א בפתח כי היא לשאל' ופי' א"א ז"ל הפ' כן העיט צבוע בדם חללי' יהי' סביב על נחלתי שבחרתי לי ואחר שישבע העיט יבאו כל חיות השד' לאכול כמו שנאמר לכו אספו כל חית השד' התיו לאכלה אמר לעופות אחר שתשבעו אתם לכו אספו כל חית השד' בעבור כי כן מנהג העופות יבאו על החללים תחל' כי הם יראו בעופפ' כמו

מצודת ציון

הנה כאריה יעלה מגאון הירדן (לקמן מ"ט): (ו) מלא. ענין קבוץ כמו קראו מלאו (לעיל ד'): (ז) נטשתי. ענין עזיבה: ידידות. ענין אהבה: (ט) העיט. הוא שם עוף הדורס וכן וקץ עליו העיט (ישעיה י"ח): צבוע. ר"ל בעל גוונים וכראה כלבוע:

מצודת דוד

לרדוף אחריך: אל תאמן בם. שהמה אוספים אותך עם שמדברים עמך דברים טובים ורכים ומסה תקח לאיש לרשעת כל העם הזה ומוסב למעלה לומר בעבור כ"ז נתתי הנה ביד כ"כ לסיום מסה זעמי: (ז) עזבתי. לכן עזבתי את בית המקדש: נחלתי. הם ישראל כמ"ש יעקב חבל נחלתו (דברים ל"ב): את ידידות נפשי. את ישראל שהיו אהובים לפני מסרתים ביד האויב וכפל הדבר כמ"ש: (ח) כאריה ביער. עדת ישראל היו לפני כאריה ביער הטורף כל בשר כי כן המה טורפים ומאבדים זה את זה: נתנה עלי. מדברת למולי בקול רם וברמות רוח: (ט) העיט צבוע. וכי ישראל המה לפני כעיט הצבוע בעלת גוונים שהנוהג לכל העופו' וקבולת העופות הדורסים תחלה סביב עליה לאכלה ועוד יוסיפו לגרז זה את זה

gative. Therefore, it is vowelized with a 'pattah.' Are they like a speckled bird of prey, stained with blood, around which other birds gather? Another explanation: Is . . . a speckled bird of prey— One bird is speckled, and all the birds gather around it to eat it because they hate it.—[Rashi]

Are there birds of prey around her?—*Are these armies fowl of the heavens, the swift troops that are around her?—[Rashi]*

Redak explains: Are there birds of

they too have called a gang after you; do not believe them
although they speak cordially to you. 7. I have abandoned My
House, I have forsaken My inheritance; I have delivered My
soul's beloved into the hand of her enemies. 8. My inheritance
was to Me like a lion in the forest; she raised her voice against
Me; therefore, I hated her. 9. Is My inheritance to Me a
speckled bird of prey? Are there birds of prey around her?

have called a gang after you—Heb. קָלֵא, *a group of men.*—[*Rashi*]

I.e., they have gathered after you to frighten you if you prophesy against them.—[*Redak*]

Others explain: they too have called after you and have reviled you aloud.—[*Kara, Isaiah da Trani*]

Others render: They too have called, "Fearless!" after you. Since you show no fear and continue to prophesy, they say about you, in your absence, that you are fearless.—[*Rabbi Joseph Kimchi*]

Rav Hai explains it as a pejorative, to be explained in the opposite sense of the word. Whereras קָלֵא means 'full,' they use it in the sense of 'lacking,' i.e., imperfect in all ways. *Ibn Nachmiash* suggests: full of foolishness, full of stupidity.

do not believe them—If they are friendly with you and speak cordially to you, do not believe them, for they are lying. They intend to befriend you so that you will eat in their house and they will poison you.—[*Redak*]

7. **I have abandoned My House**—God says this like a person lamenting a loss.—[*Redak*]

My inheritance—Israel.—[*Redak, Mezudath David*]

My soul's beloved—*My treasured people.*—[*Rashi*]

I loved her deeply, and now, because of her iniquities, I have delivered her into the hand of her enemies.—[*Redak*]

8. **she raised her voice against Me**—*The cry of her violent deeds has ascended before Me.*—[*Rashi*]

When a lion roars in the forest, and the passersby hear his voice, they leave the road of the forest and even the road near the forest. So have I forsaken My inheritance, for they were like a lion in the forest that roars at night. The raising of the voice is figurative of the cries of the oppressed or the shouts of the idolaters in the pagan temples, as we find in the episode of Elijah with Ahab, '(I Kings 18:26) And they called in the name of Baal from morning to noon, saying, "O Baal, answer us!" And in verse 28, 'And they called aloud."

therefore, I hated her—and uprooted her, for I am weary of bearing her evil deeds any longer.—[*Redak*]

Jonathan renders: I have rejected her.

9. **Is ... a speckled bird of prey?**—*The 'he' is that of the interro-*

לְכוּ אִסְפוּ כָּל־חַיַּת הַשָּׂדֶה הֵתָיוּ
לְאָכְלָה׃ י רֹעִים רַבִּים שִׁחֲתוּ כַרְמִי
בֹּסְסוּ אֶת־חֶלְקָתִי נָתְנוּ אֶת־חֶלְקַת
חֶמְדָּתִי לְמִדְבַּר שְׁמָמָה׃ יא שָׂמָהּ
לִשְׁמָמָה אָבְלָה עָלַי שְׁמֵמָה נָשַׁמָּה
כָּל־הָאָרֶץ כִּי אֵין אִישׁ שָׂם עַל־לֵב׃
יב עַל־כָּל־שְׁפָיִם בַּמִּדְבָּר בָּאוּ שֹׁדְדִים
כִּי חֶרֶב לַיהוָה אֹכְלָה מִקְצֵה־אֶרֶץ
וְעַד־קְצֵה הָאָרֶץ אֵין שָׁלוֹם לְכָל־בָּשָׂר׃

דִמְשַׁהֲדֵי כֵּן יִתְכַּנְשׁוּן
עֲלָהּ דְקַטְלִין בְּחַרְבָּא
מִסְחוֹר סְחוֹר מַלְכֵי
עַמְמַיָא וּמַשִׁרְיָתֵיהוֹן
יֵיתוּן עֲלָהּ לְמִבְזָהּ׃
י מַלְכִין סַגִיאִין קְטָלוּ
עַמִי דוּשִׁישׁוּ יַת אַחְסַנְתִּי
יְהָבִין יַת אַחְסָנַת
חֶמְדָתִי לְמַדְבַּר צָדוּ׃
יא שַׁוְיוּהָא לְצָדוּ
אִתְאַבְּלַת קֳדָמַי חֲרוּבַת
צְדִיאַת כָּל אַרְעָא אֲרֵי
לֵית אֱנָשׁ דִמְשַׁוֵי דַחֲלְתִּי
עַל לִבָּא׃ יב עַל כָּל
נִגְרִין בְּמַדְבְּרָא אֲתוֹ
בָזוֹזִין אֲרֵי חַרְבָּא קֳדָם יְיָ
מְקַטְלָא מִסְיָפֵי אַרְעָא
וְעַד סְיָפֵי אַרְעָא לֵית

חס׳ בצירי

רש״י

סביביה: התיו. בואו: (י) רועים רבים. ראשי גייסות של חיל כ״כ כמ״ש למעלה אליה יבואו רעים ועדריהם (לעיל ו׳): בוססו. ל׳ מרמס וכן והיו כגבורים בוסים כטיט חוצות (זכריה י׳): חלקת. (קנפני״א בלע״ז): (יא) אבלה שמתאבלין עלי כשהם בגלות כדי שאושיעם: נשמה כל הארץ. כל הדברים חללו תלויין בדבר זה: כי אין איש שם על לב.

מהר״י קרא

לעיט לעוף שמתגולל בדם הנבילה וכסבורין שאר עופות שהוא עצמו נבילה ומתקבצין עליו לאוכלו אף נחלתי לפי שנגואלו בדם נקי ששפכו. לפיכך: לכו אספו כל חית השדה אתיו לאכלה. כלומר אתם הנביאים אספו את האומות והכריזו להם שיבואו לאכול את ישראל: (י) רועים רבים. עמים רבים: חלקת חמדתי. שדה חמדתי: (יא) שמה לשמה אבלה עלי שממה.

רד״ק

שאמר באשר חללי׳ שם הוא והחיות רואות העופות צבועי׳ כדם החללים ויסורו ממקום׳: התיו. הה״א תמורת אל״ף אתיו אקח׳ יין שיבו אתיו וענינו כמו באו והחיות הן משל על האומות שבאו עם נבוכדנאצר להחריב לירושלי׳ כאילו עשו להם אות והריכו להם נס שיבאו והוא משל העיט הצבוע לחיות והוא דבר הנבואה: (י) רעים רבים. מלכי גוים שבאו עם נבוכדנאצר והמלך כמו הרועה לצאן וכת״י מלכין סגיאין קטלו עמי: כרמי. ישראל כמו שאמר כי כרם ה׳ צבאות בית ישראל: בססו. רמסו: (יא) שמה. נבוכדנאצר ואף על פי שלא זכרו תחלה זכר רועים רבים והוא היה בראש והוא שם החלקה לשממה: אבלה עלי שממ׳. שם תאר כנסת ישראל שהיא שממה התאבלה עלי על שממותי׳ לאמר שאני השימותיה: כי אין איש שם על לב. למה התרבה כי אין איש מהם שם על לב דברי ותוכחותי שהייתי מוכיח אותם ע״י הנביאים ולא שמו על לבם ולא שמעו אליה׳ וי״ת תרי לית אנש דמשוי דחלתי על לבא: (יב) על כל שפים במדבר. מקו׳ מרעה הבהמות יקרא מדבר כמו שפירש ושפים הם המקומות הגבוהי׳ כמו הרים וגבעות גם לשם שהוא כן הישוב באו שדדי׳: חרב לה׳ אכלה. כמו אוכלת אמר בזה ובזה כמו אש אכלה אבל ברוב יאמר על משקל פעלת והתרגום הוא אכילת החרב כמו וחרבי תאכל בשר כזה וכזה תאכל חרב: מקצה ארץ ועד קצה הארץ. כי גם בשאר המקומות תהיה כי בכל׳ פשטה יד נ״נ וחרבו הוא לה׳ כי הוא העיר את חרבו עליה׳

מצודת דוד

לומר אספו החיות אשר יבואו גם המה לאכלה כי כן כל האומות שונאים את ישראל ומזרזים אלה לאלה לכלותם: (י) רועים רבים. עכשיו יפרש אמריו ויאמר רועים וגו׳ ר״ל מלכי האומות משחיתים את ישראל: בוססו. רמסו חלקת שדי ר״ל החריבו ארצי: נתנו וגו׳. את החלקה החמודה לי שמו להיות מדבר שממה: (יא) שמה. ר״ל המחריב שם את ארצי לשממה והנה הארץ השוממה מתאבלת לפני: נשמה. ר״ל עכ״ז לא ארחם ותהיה נשמה כל הארץ כי אין בה איש שם על לב להתחרט מטוען לשוב אלי: (יב) על כל שפים. על כל המקומות הגבוהים שבמדבר באו שודדי׳: כי חרב לה׳. חרב מלחמ׳

מצודת ציון

התיו. ענין ביאה כמו שובו אתיו (שם כ״א): (י) בוססו. ענין רמיסה כמו בוססו מקדשך (שם ס״ג): חלקת. ענין אחוזת שדה כמו ואכלה את החלק (עמוס ז׳): (יא) עלי. ר״ל לפני: נשמה. מלשון שממון: (יב) שפים. מקומות הגבוהים: אכלה. ענין כרת

11. **He has made it**—The antecedent is Nebuchadnezzar; although he was not mentioned before, Scripture does mention many shepherds, of whom he was the head, and he made the field into a waste.—[*Redak*]

12. **On all rivulets**—Heb. שְׁפָיִם. This translation follows *Targum Jonathan.*

Redak renders: On all the high places in the pastureland; i.e. on the hills and the mountains. Although this region is settled, the plunderers will come there.—[*Redak*]

from one end of the land to the other end of the land—Nebuchadnezzar's armies spread to other countries as well as Judah, and his sword was the sword of the Lord,

Go, gather all the beasts of the field; come to eat. 10. Many
shepherds have destroyed My vineyard, they have trampled My
field; they have made My delightful field into a desert waste.
11. He has made it a waste; the wasted one mourns before Me;
the entire land is waste because no one lays it to his heart.
12. On all the rivulets in the pastureland have plunderers come,
for the sword of the Lord consumes from one end of the land to
the other end of the land; there is no peace for any flesh.

prey speckled with the blood of carcasses around My inheritance that I chose for Myself?

Go, gather all the beasts of the field—After the birds of prey have gorged themselves, all the beasts of the field come to devour the remains. Accordingly, he says to the fowl, "After you are sated, go, gather all the beasts of the field." The birds usually are the first to spot the carcasses since they see them from above. When the beasts see the birds speckled with the blood of the carcasses, they leave their lairs to partake of the feast.—[*Redak*]

come—Heb. הֵתָיוּ.—[*Rashi*] The 'he' is instead of an 'alef,' like in the word אֵתָיוּ. The beasts represent the nations that accompanied Nebuchadnezzar in his destruction of Jerusalem. It is as though they signaled them and raised a standard that they should come. This is symbolized by the speckled birds of prey attracting the beasts. It is a prophecy.—[*Redak*]

Rabbi Joseph Kara explains that God's inheritance, Israel, is like a speckled bird of prey because of their sins. The bird of prey wallows in the blood of a carcass, and the other birds mistake him for a carcass and gather around him to devour him. So is My inheritance; they have become stained with the innocent blood that they have shed.

Therefore, Go, gather all the beasts of the field; come to eat—You prophets, gather the nations and announce to them that they come and consume Israel.

10. **Many shepherds**—*The commanders of the troops of Nebuchadnezzar's army, as it is stated above* (6:3): *'Shepherds and their flocks shall come to her.'*—[*Rashi*]

Redak identifies them as the kings of the nations allied with Nebuchadnezzar, for the king is to his nation as the shepherd is to his flock. *Jonathan,* too, renders: Many kings have slain My people.

My vineyard—This refers to Israel. Cf. Isaiah 5:7: For the vineyard of the Lord of Hosts is the House of Israel.—[*Redak*]

they have trampled—Heb. בֹּסְסוּ, *an expression of trampling. Cf.* (Zech. 10:5) *'And they shall be like mighty men trampling* (בוֹסִים) *the mire of the streets.'*—[*Rashi*]

My field—Heb. חֶלְקָתִי, (*campagne in French*), *countryside.*—[*Rashi*]

יג זָרְעוּ חִטִּים וְקֹצִים קָצָרוּ נֶחְלוּ לֹא
יוֹעִלוּ וּבֹשׁוּ מִתְּבוּאֹתֵיכֶם מֵחֲרוֹן אַף־
יְהוָה: יד כֹּה אָמַר יְהוָה עַל־כָּל־שְׁכֵנַי
הָרָעִים הַנֹּגְעִים בַּנַּחֲלָה אֲשֶׁר־הִנְחַלְתִּי
אֶת־עַמִּי אֶת־יִשְׂרָאֵל הִנְנִי נֹתְשָׁם מֵעַל
אַדְמָתָם וְאֶת־בֵּית יְהוּדָה אֶתּוֹשׁ
מִתּוֹכָם: טו וְהָיָה אַחֲרֵי נָתְשִׁי אוֹתָם

ת"א כל שכני. ברכות ח: קמץ בז"ק אשוב

תרגום

שְׁלָמָא לְכָל בִּשְׂרָא:
יג לָא תְהוֹן דָמִין לִדְזָרְעוּ
חִטִּין עַל בַּיְר וְלָא
מִשְׁתַּכְּחִין לִמְכְנַשׁ אֱלָהֵין
כּוּבִין וּמְעַלַלְתְּהוֹן לֵית
לְהוֹן הֲנָאָה וְתִבְהֲתוּן
בְּעוֹבָדֵיכוֹן בְּמֵיתֵי
עֲלֵיכוֹן תְּקוֹף רוּגְזָא דַיְיָ:
יד כִּדְנַן אֲמַר יְיָ עַל כָּל
מַגִירַיָא בִּישַׁיָא דְמַנְזְקִין
בְּאַחְסַנְתָּא דְאַחְסֵנִית
יַת עַמִּי יַת יִשְׂרָאֵל הָא
אֲנָא מְטַלְטֵיל לְהוֹן
מֵעַל אַרְעֲהוֹן וְיַת דְבֵית
יְהוּדָה אֲטַלְטֵיל
מִבֵּינֵיהוֹן: טו וִיהֵי בָּתַר דְאֲטַלְטֵל יַתְהוֹן אֲתוּב בְּמֵימְרִי וַאֲרַחֵים עֲלֵיהוֹן וְאֲתֵיבִינוּן גְּבַר

מהר"י קרא

לעשות תשובה ודבר זה גורם לכל הדברים הללו: (יג) זרעו חטים. בעונותיכם נמשלתם לזה שזורע חטים בשדה בור שזורע אל קוצים שאין מועיל לו זריעתו אף אתם עונותיכם גורמים שאתם יגיעים ואומות העולם אוכלין: (יד) על כל שכני הרעים. שם האומות השוכנים סביבות ארץ ישראל: הנני נותשם מעל אדמתם. הנני מגלה ונותש את האומות מעל ארמת עצמן כדי שיטעמו טעם גלות כשם שטעמו ישראל: ואת בית יהודה אתוש מתוכם. כלומר את בית יהודה אתוש מתוך האומות שגלו ביניהם לפי שאמר למעלה עזבתי את ביתי וגו' בו בלשון שהכה חזר וריפא ואמר על כל שכיני הרעים הנוגעים בנחלה: (טו) והיה אחרי נתשי אותם אשוב ורחמתים. פת'

רש"י

עלי. לפני: (יג) זרעו חטים וקוצים קצרו. התפללו ולא נתקבלה תפלתם למה לפי שלא נרו להם ניר תשובה ומעשים טובים לכך זרעו אל קוצים. ספר שנקוד בו זרעו בחיר"ק הזיי"ן שיבוש הוא: נחלו. לשון חולי נחלו במכאובם ולעקתם לפני ולא יועילו: מתבואותיכם. ממעשיכם: (יד) שכיני הרעים. מצרים עמון ומואב

מנחת שי

(יג) זרעו חטים. כתב רש"י ספר שנקוד בו זֶרְעוּ בחירק הזי"ן שיבוש הוא. נחלו. כתי"ם בשוא לבדו וכן חברו על פי המסורת ולא נחלו על

רד"ק

והנביא התנבא על אחת מהן טרם בא לה הפורענות כמ"ש בזה הספר וזהו שאמר אין שלו' לכל בשר: (יג) זרעו חטים וקוצים קצרו. אמר הנביאי' זורעי' חטי' בכם ישראל שאתם נקראים חלקתי כמו שאמר למעלה והנה הנביאים זרעו בחלקה חטי' הם דברי הנבואה. וקוצי' קצרו. כי לא צמחו להם בחלק' כי אם קוצים אלו הם מעשי' רעים שדומין לקוצים: נחלו לא יועילו. ונחלו הנביאים על זה כי לא הועילו מעשיה': ובשו מתבואתיכם. היה להם לנביאי' בשת מתבואותיכם שהיו מיחלים שיהיו חטי' והיו קוצים ונחלו הנביאים על זה מחרון אף ה' מפחד' מחרון אף ה' העתיד לבא עליכם מפני מעשיכם הרעים ואמר ירמיהו משל זה על החלק' כמו שאמר ישעיהו משל דומה לו על הכר' שאמר ויטעהו שורק ויקו לעשות ענבי' ויעש באושים וישראל הם שנקראו כרם ה' וחלקת ה'. וא"א ז"ל פירש זרעו ישראל חטי' והוא משל על הממון הרב שהיו שולחים למלכי מצרים שיהיו להם לעזרה וישעו לעזרתם מפני מלך בבל ובטחונ' על משענת קנה רצוץ זהו וקוצי' קצרו נחלו ולא יועילו נחלו מרוב ממון שנתנו ולא היה להם בו שום תועלת ופי' ובשו מתבואותכ' צווי כלו' יש לכם ליבוש מתבואותיכ' שהם קוצי' וי"ת לא תהון דמין לדזרעו חטין וגו' כבעמוד: (יד) כה אמר ה' על כל שכני הרעי'. הם פלשתים ועמון ומואב וצור וצדון ואדום שהיו שכני' לא"י והיו מריעי' להם ואמר שכני כי ישראל הם חלקתו וכרמו והנה הם שכניו: הנוגעים. פי' להרע וכן כל הנוגע בחם הנוגע באיש הזה כתרגומו דינזק וכן הנגעים דמנזקין: הנני נתש'. גם הם יגלו כמו עמי לפיכך אל ישמחו לגלות: ואתוש מתוכם. אות' שגלו מביניה' אתוץ מתוכם בשובי שבות עמי: (טו) והיה

מצודת ציון

ואכדון וכן ואכלי תאכל כשר (דברים ל"ב): (יג) נחלו. מלשון חולי: יועילו. מלשון תועלת: (יד) הנגעים. ר"ל לנסרע וכן הנוגע באיש הזה (בראשית כ"ו): נותשם. אתוש. ענין עקירה כמו רפואה מועלת: ובושו. אמר הנביא כנגדם לאוי היה לכם שתבושו מהתבואותיכם שהדבר עלה שהם כמארה מחרון אף ה' ולא במקרה:

מצודת דוד

הסוכן מה' היא תאכל ותאבד מקלה וגו' ולכל בשר לא יהיה שלום כי ר"ל יעורר מלחמות על כל האומות ויכבוש את כלם: (יג) זרעו חטים. ר"ל עוד אמלא כסם אלי לעב וכאשר יזרעו חטים יקצרו קוצים כי תצמיח קוצים: נחלו. מעקת רעבון נחלו ולא ימצאו (יד) שכני הרעים. שכני א"י הרעים הנוגעים לרעה בנחלת ישראל: הנני נותשם. אעקור אותם מאדמתם ללכת גולה: ואת בית

sending to the kings of Egypt so that they should aid them against Babylon, and their reliance on the support of the splintered reed, namely Egypt. In this way he interprets 'they sowed wheat, but they reaped thorns'; i.e., there was no result from the money they paid Egypt. They became ill from the vast amount of money they paid Egypt, which was of no avail.

14. **My wicked neighbors**—*Egypt, Ammon and Moab, Tyre and Sidon, who were neighbors of Eretz Israel and were inflicting harm upon them.*—[*Rashi*]

Redak adds the Philistines and Edom to the list. See ch. 47,

13. They sowed wheat, but they reaped thorns; they have
become ill to no avail. Be ashamed of your increase, because of
the fierce anger of the Lord. 14. So says the Lord: Concerning
all My wicked neighbors who touch the inheritance that I have
given My nation, Israel, to inherit, behold I uproot them from
upon their land, and the house of Judah I will uproot from their
midst. 15. And it shall come to pass, that after I uproot them,

for He inspired the sword to attack them, and the prophet prophesies concerning each one of these nations further on in this Book. In this way, there will be no peace for any flesh.—[*Redak*]

13. **They sowed wheat, but they reaped thorns**—*They prayed, but their prayer was not accepted. Why? Because they did not plow for themselves a furrow of repentance and good deeds. Therefore, they sowed seeds resulting in thorns. A book in which* זרעו *is vowelized with a 'chirik' under the 'zayin,' is erroneous.*—[*Rashi*] If it is written זִרְעוּ, the meaning is 'sow,' the imperative form. This is not appropriate here.

they have become ill—Heb. נֶחְלוּ, *an expression of illness. They have become ill with their pain and their cry before Me, but they did not avail.*—[*Rashi*]

of your increase—*Of your deeds.*—[*Rashi*]

Other exegetes interpret this verse literally. I will decree a famine upon you. You will sow wheat, but thorns will grow. You will become ill from hunger, but no remedy will avail you. Be ashamed of the curse in your grain since it is obvious that it is due to God's fierce anger upon you.—[*Kara, Mezudath David, Abarbanel*]

Redak explains that God refers to the prophets. The prophets have sown in Israel, God's field, words of prophecy, likened to wheat, but the result was only that the people committed evil deeds, compared to thorns.

they have become ill because they did not avail—The prophets became ill because their efforts did not avail.—[*Redak*]

they were ashamed of your increase—The prophets suffered shame from your increase, from the results of their efforts, that they hoped to reap wheat and, instead, reaped thorns, and the prophets became ill because of fear of the fierce anger of the Lord that is destined to come upon you because of your deeds. Jeremiah expressed this prophecy in the form of an allegory of a field, similar to Isaiah's allegory of the vineyard, wherein he states: '(Isaiah 5:2) And he planted it with the choicest vines . . . and he hoped to produce grapes, but it produced wild berries.' Israel is called both the vineyard of the Lord and the field of the Lord.—[*Redak*]

Redak proceeds to quote his father, Rabbi Joseph Kimchi, who explains the passage as an allusion to the vast tribute that Israel was

אָשׁוּב וְרִחַמְתִּים וַהֲשִׁבֹתִים אִישׁ
לְנַחֲלָתוֹ וְאִישׁ לְאַרְצוֹ: טז וְהָיָה אִם־
לָמֹד יִלְמְדוּ אֶת־דַּרְכֵי עַמִּי לְהִשָּׁבֵעַ
בִּשְׁמִי חַי־יְהוָה כַּאֲשֶׁר לִמְּדוּ אֶת־עַמִּי
לְהִשָּׁבֵעַ בַּבָּעַל וְנִבְנוּ בְּתוֹךְ עַמִּי:
יז וְאִם לֹא יִשְׁמָעוּ וְנָתַשְׁתִּי אֶת־הַגּוֹי
הַהוּא נָתוֹשׁ וְאַבֵּד נְאֻם־יְהוָה:
יג א כֹּה־אָמַר יְהוָה אֵלַי הָלוֹךְ וְקָנִיתָ

תרגום

לְאַחְסַנְתֵּיהּ וּגְבַר לְאַרְעֵיהּ: טז וִיהֵי אִם מֵילַף יֵילְפוּן. מֵאוֹרְחַת כְּנִשְׁתָּא דְעַמִּי לְקַיָּמָא בִשְׁמִי קַיָּם הוּא יְיָ כְּמָא דְאַלִּיפוּ יַת עַמִּי לְקַיָּמָא בְּשׁוּם טַעֲוָתָא וְיִתְקַיְּמוּן בְּגוֹ עַמִּי: יז וְאִם לָא יְקַבְּלוּן אוּלְפַן וְאֶטַלְטֵל יַת עַמָּא הָדֵין טַלְטוּל דְאָבְדַן אֲמַר יְיָ: א כִּדְנַן אֲמַר יְיָ לִי אֱזֵיל וְתִזְבּוֹן לָךְ

רש״י

וגור ולידון שהיו שכני ארץ ישראל ומזיקין אותם: (טו) **אשוב ורחמתים**. כלן לקו סמוך לחורבן בית וכולם נאמר ושבתי את שבות בספר זה: (טז) **אם למוד ילמדו**. אם יתגיירו: **ונבנו**. לשון בנין:

מהר״י קרא

והיה אחרי נותשי אותם את האומות מאדמת עצמן אשוב וריחמתים. וכן דרכו של הקב״ה כשנותש את האומות איש מארצו ואיש מנחלתו לאחר זמן יפקדם ושב שבותם. כענין שנאמר בישעיה באחרית הימים ושבתי את שבות בני עמון וכן ושבתי את שבות מואב, אף כאן והיה אחרי נתשי את האומות אשוב ורחמתים ואחר כך והשיבותים איש לנחלתו ואיש לארצו: (טז) והיה אם למוד ילמדו. האומות: את דרכי עמי להשבע בשמי חי ה׳. שיתגיירו עצמן: כאשר למדו את עמי להשבע בבעל. בעוד שהיו עמי בינותם: ונבנו בתוך עמי. כעניין שאמר ישעיה ונלוה הגר עליהם ונספחו על בית יעקב וכן זכריה הוא אומר ונלוו גוים רבים אל ה׳ ביום ההוא והיו לי לעם: (יז) ואם לא ישמעו. ללמוד את דרכי עמי ונתשתי את הגוי ההוא:

רד״ק

אשוב ורחמתים. כמו שנבא עליהם ירמיה כשנבא על גלות׳ נבא ג״כ על שוב׳ כמ״ש והשבתי את שבות מואב ואמר ואחרי כן אשיב את שבות בני עמון ואמר כי כששבו יהודה ובנימין מגלות בבל שבו גם הם: (טז) והיה. את דרכי עמי. הדל״ת מעמדת בגעיא והמסרה לית געיא: בשמי חי ה׳. כי מעת ששבו ישראל מגלות׳ לא עבדו עכו״ם ולא נשבעו בבעל ואם הם ילמדו דרכם בזה ובזה הוא בטול עכו״ם: כאשר למדו. כי באמת ישראל לא למדו לעבוד עכו״ם כי אם משכניהם: ונבנו בתוך עמי. כי הרבה נתגיירו מהם בשוב׳ מגלות׳ ושכנו בתוך בני ישראל. ונבנו. יהיה להם בנין ביניהם כלומר עמידה וקיום וכן ת״י ויתקימון: (יז) ואם. ואבד. שלא ישובו עוד לארצם ומ״ש בנבואת בני עמון ואחרי כן אשיב את שבות בני עמון אית׳ שלמדו דרכי ישראל או עדיין לא שבו כדברי רבי יהושע במחלקתו של רבן גמליאל בברכות: (א) כה אמר ה׳. ענין האזור אפשר שהיה ממש ועשה כן ירמיהו מה שציוהו האל והחכם הגדול מורה צדק רמב״ם כתב כי בחלו׳ של נבואה היה כל המעשה הזה ומה שאמר לו ובמי׳ אל תביאהו לא אדע בו טעם עדין ואם ר״ל שלא יכבסהו אחר שחגרו ימים אלא יחגרהו עם הזיעה למה לא אמר לא תכבסהו ושאר הענין מפורש ופירש בנקיקי הסלע בחור הסלע וי״ת בשעיעות כיף גלי ומה שאמר שילך לנהר פרת לטמנו שם לפי שהוא גבול

מנחת שי

שבר יוסף (עמוס ו) ועיין מ״ש בעמוס שם: (טז) את דרכי. הדל״ת מעמדת בגעיה והמסורת עליו לית בגעיה רד״ק בפירוש ושרשים וכן מצאתי בס״ס:

מצודת דוד

יהודה. וגם בית יהודה אעקור מתוכם ולפי שהאומות ההם שוכנים סביבות א״י לכן אמר אתוש מתוכם: (טו) **אשוב ורחמתים**. את כל הנתושים אף מן האומות: (טז) **אם למוד ילמדו**. אם האומות ילמדו דרכי עמי להאמין בה׳ ולהשבע בו לומר בשבועתם חי ה׳ כאשר בתחלה למדו הם את עמי להשבע בבעל: **ונבנו**. אז יהיו בנוים ומתקיימים: **בתוך עמי**. ר״ל דומים ושוים לעמי: (יז) **ואם לא ישמעו**. ללמוד מעמי אמונת ה׳: **ונתשתי**. אז אעקור שוב את העכו״ם ההוא: **נתוש ואבד**. יהיה נעקר ואבוד עד עולם:

מצודת ציון

לנתוש ולנתוץ (לעיל א׳): (טז) ונבנו. מלשון בנין:

returned from exile, but they will return when the Messiah comes and the Jews will return from exile.—[*Redak, Ibn Nachmiash*]

1. **So said the Lord**—This entire episode concerning the girdle may be understood to have actually occurred, that Jeremiah did as God had commanded him. Maimonides, however, interprets it as a prophetic vision (*Guide to the Perplexed,* vol. 2, ch. 45a).—[*Redak*]

I will return and have pity on them, and I will restore them,
each one to his inheritance and each one to his land. 16. And it
shall be, if they learn the ways of My people to swear by My
name, "As the Lord lives," as they taught My people to swear
by Baal, they shall be built up in the midst of My people.
17. And if they do not heed, I shall uproot that nation, uprooting and destroying, says the Lord.

13

1. So said the Lord to me: Go and buy

49:7–22. God calls them 'My neighbors,' because Israel is His field and His vineyard. Therefore, they are 'His neighbors.'—[*Redak*]

15. **I will return and have pity on them**—*They all suffered close to the destruction of the Temple, and concerning each one it is stated in this Book, "I will return the exile of . . ."*—[*Rashi*]

Just as Jeremiah prophesied concerning their exile, so did he prophesy concerning their return. Cf. 48:47, 49:6. He says that when Judah and Benjamin returned from Babylonian exile, they too returned from exile.—[*Redak*]

It is usual that God restores the nations He uproots, as we find in the Book of Isaiah, that, at the end of days, He will restore the captivity of Ammon and the captivity of Moab. Here too, He will have pity on the nations and restore them, each one to his inheritance and each one to his land.—[*Kara*]

16. **if they learn**—*If they proselytize.*—[*Rashi*]

If the nations learn the ways of My people to believe in God and to swear by Him, saying, "As the Lord lives," in their oath, as they previously taught My people to swear by Baal.—[*Mezudath David*]

Since Israel returned from the Babylonian exile, they did not worship idols and they did not swear by Baal. Now, if the neighboring nations learn these two things from them, that means the abolition of idolatry.—[*Redak*]

as they taught My people—For Israel learned idolatry only from her neighbors.—[*Redak*]

they shall be built up in the midst of My people—For many of them proselytized when they returned from exile and dwelt among the Jews. The intention of 'being built up' is that they will remain permanently among the Jews.—[*Redak*]

17. **uprooting and destroying**—I.e., they will never again return to their land. The later prophecies of the return of Ammon and Moab refer only to those who will learn the ways of Israel. According to Rabbi Joshua (*Ber.* 28a) who disagreed with Rabban Gamliel, the Ammonites and the Moabites have not yet

לך אזור פשתים ושמתו על־מתניך
ובמים לא תבאהו: ב ואקנה את־
האזור כדבר יהוה ואשם על־מתני:
ג ויהי דבר־יהוה אלי שנית לאמר:
ד קח את־האזור אשר קנית אשר על־
מתניך וקום לך פרתה וטמנהו שם
בנקיק הסלע: ה ואלך ואטמנהו בפרת
כאשר צוה יהוה אותי: ו ויהי מקץ
ימים רבים ויאמר יהוה אלי קום לך
פרתה וקח משם את־האזור אשר
צויתיך לטמנו־שם: ז ואלך פרתה
ואחפר ואקח את־האזור מן־המקום
אשר־טמנתיו שמה והנה נשחת
האזור לא יצלח לכל: ח ויהי דבר־

תרגום

לך זרז דכתן ותשויניה
על חרצך ובמיא לא
תעליניה: ב וזבינית ית
זרזא כפתגמא דיי
ושויתיה על חרצי:
ג והוה פתגם נבואה
מן קדם יי עמי תנינות
למימר: ד סב ית זרזא
די זבינתא די על חרצך
וקום אזיל לפרת וטמרהי
תמן בשעיעות כיף גלי:
ה ואזלית וטמרתיה
בפרת כמה די פקיד יי
יתי: ו והוה מסוף יומין
סגיאין ואמר יי לי קום
אזיל לפרת וסב מתמן
ית זרזא די פקדתך
למטמריה תמן:
ז ואזלית לפרת וחפרית
ונסיבית ית זרזא מן
אתרא דטמרתיה תמן
והא אתחביל זרזא
לית ביה צרוך לכל
מדעם: ח והוה פתגם
נבואה

ת"א שנית לאמר. עקדה שער רפ:

רש"י

יג (א) אזור. (פורזונ"ט בלע"ז): ובמים לא תביאהו. לככנסו כשיהא מלא זיעה כדי שימהר לירקב: (ז) לא יצלח

מהר"י קרא

יג (א) ושמתו על מתניך. ומשהיה דבוק על מתניך כל כך שקלט זיעה אל תביאהו במים לכבסו מן הזיע אלא קחנו בעוד שיש בו הזיעה וטמניהו בנקיק הסלע: (ז) והנה נשחת

רד"ק

ארץ ישראל. ר"ל כי כשיצאו מארץ ישראל לבבל ישחת גאונ': (ז) לא יצלח לכל. לשו' דבר כמו כל מלאכה לא תעשו שום

מנחת שי

יג (ז) לא יצלח לכל. מה שכתוב במק"ג כן בספר מוגה ר"ל שכן כתיב לא בלא וה"ו:

מצודת דוד

יג (א) אזור. חגורה של פשתן: ושמתו על מתניך. למען ימלא זיעה ויפסל להרקיב: ובמים לא תביאהו. לא תכבסו לנקותו מן הזיעה: (ג) שנית. כדבר האזור: (ד) פרתה. לנהר פרת: וטמנהו שם. תטמינו שם בנקיק הסלע: (ה) בפרת. אצל נהר פרת: (ז) ואחפור. כי כסהו בעפר ממעל: נשחת. נתקלקל ונרקב: לא יצלח לכל. לא היה ראוי לשום דבר:

מצודת ציון

יג (א) אזור. חגורה: מתניך. חלציך: (ד) וטמנהו. ענין הסתרה: בנקיק הסלע. בקע הסלע הכולם וכן ובנקיקי הסלעים (ישעיה ז'): (ו) מקץ. מסוף: (ז) ואחפור. מלשון

or that they were corrupted by the idol worship of the Assyrians and the Babylonians from the land bounded by the Euphrates.—[*Daath Mikra*]

in the cleft of a rock—*Daath Mikra* explains that the intention is to hide it in a small cave in the mountain, large enough for a person or persons to enter. It was probably the cave near the spring of Al-farah, which is always moist, and which would promote the decay of the linen girdle. Isaiah da Trani, too, notes that he put it in a moist place to hasten its decay.

yourself a linen girdle and put it on your loins, and do not put it in water. 2. And I bought the girdle according to the word of the Lord, and I put [it] on my loins. 3. And the word of the Lord came to me a second time, saying: 4. Take the girdle that you bought and rise, go to Perath and hide it there in the cleft of a rock. 5. And I went and hid it in Perath, as the Lord had commanded me. 6. And it came to pass at the end of many days, that the Lord said to me: Arise, go to Perath and take from there the girdle which I commanded you to hide there. 7. And I went to Perath, and I dug and took the girdle from the place where I had hidden it, and behold, the girdle was rotten; it was of no use for anything. 8. And the word of the Lord came

a girdle—(*pourceint in O.F.*).—[*Rashi*]

and put it on your loins—so that it become full of sweat and hasten to decay.—[*Mezudath David*]

and do not put it in water—*to wash it when it will be soaked with sweat, in order that it hasten to decay.*—[*Rashi*]

Abarbanel adds that water strengthens linen, thereby retarding its decay from the sweat with which it is soaked. Although *Abarbanel* identifies his commentary with *Rashi*'s, it is difficult to reconcile these two explanations. *Rashi,* apparently, explains that the girdle was not to be washed, lest it be cleansed of the sweat and fail to decay but God did not forbid its being dipped in water. According to *Abarbanel,* however, wetting it in any way was forbidden, since this would strengthen the fibers.

3. **a second time**—I.e. a second time concerning the matter of the girdle.—[*Mezudath David*]

4. **to Perath**—All classical commentators identify this with the Euphrates River. This symbolizes that when the Jews would be exiled from their borders and cross the Euphrates into Babylon, their pride would be destroyed.—[*Redak, Abarbanel*]

Modern exegetes, however, question God's commanding the prophet to go such a long distance to the Euphrates, also the description of the rocky terrain, which does not fit most of the banks of the Euphrates. They identify Perath with the town Haparah, mentioned in Joshua 18:23. This is known today as 'En-al-farah, approximately five kilometers from Anathoth and approximately nine kilometers northeast of Jerusalem. Perhaps this location was chosen because of the similarity of its name to Perath, the Euphrates. This indicated that the Jews who were corrupted would eventually be exiled to Babylon, which is bounded by the Euphrates,

יהוה אלי לאמר: ט כה אמר יהוה
ככה אשחית את־גאון יהודה ואת־
גאון ירושלם הרב: י העם הזה הרע
המאנים | לשמוע את־דברי ההלכים
בשררות לבם וילכו אחרי אלהים
אחרים לעבדם ולהשתחות להם ויהי
כאזור הזה אשר לא־יצלח לכל: יא כי
כאשר ידבק האזור אל־מתני איש
כן הדבקתי אלי את־כל־בית ישראל
ואת־כל־בית יהודה נאם־יהוה להיות
לי לעם ולשם ולתהלה ולתפארת ולא
שמעו: יב ואמרת אליהם את־הדבר

נבואה מן קדם יי עמי למימר: ט כדנן אמר יי כדין אחביל ית תקוף אנש יהודה וית תקוף יתבי ירושלם דהוה סגי: י עמא הדין דעובדיהון בישין דסריבו לקבלא ית פתגמא דאזלין בתר הרהור לבהון וטעו בתר טעות פלחי כוכביא למפלחהון ולמסגיד להון ויהון כזרנא הדין דלית בהון צרוך לכל מדעם: יא ארי כמא דמדבק זרנא בחרצא דגברא כן קרבית לפולחני ית כל בית ישראל וית כל בית יהודה אמר יי למהוי קדמי לעם ולשום ולחושבחא ולרבו ולא קבילו: יב ותימר להון ית פתגמא הדין כדנן

רש"י

לכל. אינו ראוי לכלום: (י) ויהי כאזור הזה. גאונם

מהר"י קרא

האזור. מחבת שלא כובס מן הזיעה: (יא) להיות לי לעם. וכח

רד"ק

מלאכה כל חלב וכל דם שום חלב ושום דם: (י) המאנים. שם תאר האחד מאן בצר"י לפיכך הוא בקבוץ האלו"ף בשו"א ופת"ח: ויהי כאזור. ופי' ויהיה גאונ' שזכר את גאון יהודה ואם גאון ירושלים: (יב) ואמרת. כל נבל מלא יין. אמור להם ג"כ זה המשל והנבל היה להם כלי חרש והנבל היה להם משל לשני דברים האחד כי כמו שהנבל ימלא יין וכו' כלומר ימלא בתוכו ושהוא נבלע בדפניו כן יהיו מלאי' שכרון מכל צד והשכרון הוא משל לרב הצרות כי כמו שהשכור שאין בו דעת לא ידע מה יעשה כן מי שתכפוהו הצרות הוא נבהל ונדה' ולא ידע מה יעשה והדבר השני שנמשלו בנבל כי כשיכ' אדם נבל בנבל

מצודת דוד

(ט) ככה. כמו שהשחתה האזור כן אשחית את גאון וגו': הרב. המרובה מאד: (י) העם הזה. ר"ל לפי שהעם הזה הרע הם הממאנים לשמוע דבר ה': בשרירות לבם. כמה שלבם מראה להם ומתאוים לה: ויהי. לכן יהיה העם הזה כאזור הזה: (יא) כי כאשר ידבק. ר"ל הנה המשלתי' לאזור כי כמו האזור דבוק הוא למתני איש כן וגו': ולשם. ולהיות להם הדבר הזה לשם טוב וגו': ולא שמעו. והם לא שמעו אל דברי ולכן יהיו נשחתים כאזור הזה: (יב) את הדבר הזה. והוא כה אמר ה' וגו': כל נבל. כל אחד יהיה מלא יין: ואמרו. וכשיאמרו

מצודת ציון

הסירים והכרים: לכל. ר"ל לשום דבר וכן לא תעשה כל מלאכה (שמות כ') ור"ל שום מלאכה: (ט) גאון. מלשון גאות ורוממות: (י) המאנים. מל' מאון וסרוב: בשררות. במראי': (יא) ולתהלה.

Although all the details were symbolic, God explained only two of them, the meaning of the girdle and the meaning of its decay.—[*Abarbanel*]

12. **And you shall say this word to them**—When the Judeans saw Jeremiah's deeds or his words, how he bought the girdle and hid it, and how it rotted away, they ridiculed him, saying that he was drunk. Therefore, immediately following the episode of the girdle, God commanded him to tell them that every bottle would be filled with wine and that they are the drunk

to me, saying: 9. So said the Lord: So will I destroy the pride of
Judah and the great pride of Jerusalem. 10. This evil people,
who refuse to hearken to My words, who follow the view of
their heart, and they followed other gods to worship them and
to prostrate themselves to them; and it shall be like this girdle,
which is of no use for anything. 11. For, just as the girdle clings
to a man's loins, so have I caused the entire house of Israel and
the entire house of Judah to cling to Me, says the Lord, to be
My people, and for a name and for praise and for glory, but
they did not hearken. 12. And you shall say this word to them:

9. **So will I destroy**—I.e., just as the girdle has been destroyed, so will I destroy the pride of Judah etc.—[*Mezudath David*]

the pride of Judah—The might of the people of Judah.—[*Targum Jonathan*]

Pride and might are often compared to a girdle. See Psalms 18:40, 65:7.—[*Isaiah da Trani*]

10. **and it shall be like this girdle**—*Their pride shall be like this rotten girdle.*—[*Rashi, Redak*]

who refuse—lit. the refusers.—[*Redak*]

11. **For, just as the girdle clings**—In this respect, I have likened them to a girdle, for just as the girdle clings etc.—[*Mezudath David*]

and for a name—I.e., that this thing shall be to them for a good name.—[*Mezudath David*]

The details of the allegory may be interpreted as follows: The girdle represents the Jewish people, which clung to God as a girdle clings to the loins of its wearer. Moreover, just as a girdle is a garment indicating importance, so was Israel caused to cling to the Almighty 'for a name and for praise and for glory.' God commanded the prophet to buy the girdle symbolizing that Israel is one of God's possessions, as in *Avoth* 6:10. It was to be made of linen, פִּשְׁתִּים in Hebrew, to indicate that, although they were downtrodden and humbled in Egypt, they were, nevertheless, destined to expand (פשה) in the Promised Land. He commanded him to put the girdle on his loins since the girdle symbolized the Jewish people and the prophet the Almighty, and just as the Almighty acquired the Jewish people and caused them to cling to Him, so did the prophet purchase the girdle and put it on his loins so that it should cling to him. The command not to put the girdle in water symbolized the splitting of the Red Sea, when the Israelites were led through the sea without touching the water. He symbolized further that, when they left their land, their clinging to God ceased. He did this by removing the girdle and taking it to the Euphrates, where it decayed.

הַזֶּה כֹּה־אָמַר יְהוָה אֱלֹהֵי יִשְׂרָאֵל כָּל־
נֵבֶל יִמָּלֵא יָיִן וְאָמְרוּ אֵלֶיךָ הֲיָדֹעַ לֹא
נֵדַע כִּי כָל־נֵבֶל יִמָּלֵא יָיִן׃ יג וְאָמַרְתָּ
אֲלֵיהֶם כֹּה־אָמַר יְהוָה הִנְנִי מְמַלֵּא אֶת־
כָּל־יֹשְׁבֵי הָאָרֶץ הַזֹּאת וְאֶת־הַמְּלָכִים
הַיֹּשְׁבִים לְדָוִד עַל־כִּסְאוֹ וְאֶת־הַכֹּהֲנִים
וְאֶת־הַנְּבִיאִים וְאֵת כָּל־יֹשְׁבֵי יְרוּשָׁלִָם
שִׁכָּרוֹן׃ יד וְנִפַּצְתִּים אִישׁ אֶל־אָחִיו
וְהָאָבוֹת וְהַבָּנִים יַחְדָּו נְאֻם־יְהוָה לֹא־
אֶחְמוֹל וְלֹא־אָחוּס וְלֹא אֲרַחֵם
מֵהַשְׁחִיתָם׃ טו שִׁמְעוּ וְהַאֲזִינוּ אַל־

תרגום

אֲמַר יְיָ אֱלָהָא דְיִשְׂרָאֵל כָּל גְרַב יִתְמְלֵי חֲמַר וְיֵימְרוּן לָךְ הֲמִידַע לָא הֲוֵינָא יָדְעִין אֲרֵי כָּל גְרַב יִתְמְלֵי חֲמַר׃ יג וְתֵימַר לְהוֹן כִּדְנַן אֲמַר יְיָ הָא אֲנָא מְמַלֵּי יַת כָּל יָתְבֵי אַרְעָא הָדָא וְיַת מַלְכַּיָא דְיָתְבִין לְדָוִד עַל כּוּרְסוֹהִי וְיַת כָּהֲנַיָא וְיַת נְבִיַיָא דְשִׁקְרָא וְיַת כָּל יָתְבֵי יְרוּשְׁלֵם עָקָא וִיהוֹן דָמָן לְרַוְיָא׃ יד וְאֶגְרֵינוּן גְבַר בְּאָחוּהִי וַאֲבָהָן וּבְנִין כַּחְדָא אֲמַר יְיָ לָא אֶחְמוֹל וְלָא אֵיחוּס וְלָא אֲרַחֵם מִלְחַבָּלוּתְהוֹן׃ טו קַבִּילוּ וְאַצִּיתוּ לָא תִתְרַבְרְבוּן אֲרֵי

ת"א שמעו והאזינו. סוטה ה מדרש רבה פ' ראה :

מהר"י קרא

שהיה לי לעם יהיה לי לשם ולתהלה : (יב) כל נבל ימלא יין. סתם כל נבל למלאותו יין הוא עשוי : (יג) שכרון. זה הוא כוס התרעלה : (יד) ונפצתים איש אל אחיו.

רש"י

יהיה כאזור הזה הנרקב : (יב) נבל. כלי חרס הוא ועשוי להכניס בו יין : (יד) ונפצתים איש אל אחיו. אכה זה על זה עד שישברו לחתיכות דקות כמו ככלי יוצר תנפצם (תהלים ב') ונפץ את עולליך (שם קל"ז) וכן כל ניפוץ שבמקרא : והאבות והבנים. אנפץ

מנחת שי

(יב) הידע לא נדע. חילוף מסורת אני רואה איכא דמסרי הידוע ב' מלא וא' חסר וסימן הידוע נדע דמקץ ודין דהכא ואידך הידע תדע כי בעלים מלך נהאי סיפרא סימן מ' ואיכא דמסרי ב' חסר וא' מלא ותרפי מסראתא לא מסייעי הי ניכו המלא והחסר וניחא לי למימר דמסרא בתרייתא ספי עדיפא דנסחי דיקי נקטי כוותא דאורייתא מלא כמ"ש שם ודירמיה חסרים : (יג) ואת הנביאים. י"ס חסר יו"ד קדמאה : שכרון. בכ"ף :

רד"ק

ינפצו שבריו וכן כתיב ל' נפוץ בנבלי' כמ"ש ונבליהם ינפצו כן יהיה מריבת ביניה' על רוב צרותיה' אפי' האבות עם הבני' ינופצו איש באחיו והנה ישחתו על ידי האויבים ועל ידי עצמ' : (טו) שמעו. אל תגבהו. לא תתגאו ותחשבו עצמכם כי המוסר והחכמה עמכם ואינכם צריכים לשמוע מוסר האל על ידי

מצודת ציון

ענ' הלול ושבח : (יב) נבל. נאד היין וכן ונבל יין (שמואל א' א') : (יד) ונפצתים. ענין השיבור עם הקילון וכן ונפוץ הכדים (שופטים ז') : איש אל אחיו. ר"ל זה אל זה וכן ואת כל מלכי הצפון וגו' איש אל אחיו (לקמן כ"ה) : אחום. ענין חמלה כמו יחוס על דל (תהלים ע"ב) וכפל הדבר במלות שונות : (טו) והאזינו. הטו

מצודת דוד

אליך וכי לא נדע אשר כל נבל דרכו למלאותו יין : (יג) הנני ממלא וגו'. ר"ל דברי המה למשל לומר כמו הנאד על שהוא ראוי ליין דרכו למלאותו יין כן אמלא את כל יושבי ארץ יהודה וגו' שכרון ר"ל יהיו מבולבלים מהצרות כמו השכור המבולבל ביינו כי כן ראוי להם וכן יהיה : היושבים לדוד. ר"ל זרע דוד היושבים על כסא המלוכה : הכהנים. כהני הבעל : הנביאים. נביאי השקר : (יד) ונפצתים. אשבר אותם זה אחר זה כסמוך לו : (טו) אל תגבהו. אל תהיו גבהי לב לבלי הכנע למקום : כי ה' דבר. שאל

15. **Do not be proud**—and think highly of yourselves that you do not need to hearken to God's reproof through His prophets. You shall not do that.—[*Redak*]

Do not be haughty, but humble yourselves before God.—[*Mezudath David*]

Therefore, you the kings and princes of Judah, the priests and the prophets, hearken to the word of the Lord and be not proud.—[*Abarbanel*]

So said the Lord God of Israel: Every bottle will be filled with wine. And they will say to you, "Do we not know that every bottle is filled with wine?"
13. And you shall say to them: So said the Lord: Behold, I will fill all the inhabitants of this land and the kings who sit upon David's throne, and the priests and the prophets, and all the inhabitants of Jerusalem with drunkenness.
14. And I will dash them one against the other, and the fathers and the sons together, says the Lord. I will neither pity, nor will I spare, nor will I have compassion not to destroy them.
15. Hearken and give ear, do not

ones, for they would be intoxicated with their troubles, not the prophet. —[*Abarbanel*]

12. **bottle**—Heb. נֶבֶל. *This is an earthenware vessel, and it is used to hold wine.*—[*Rashi*]

And they will say to you—I.e., and when they say to you, "Do we not know that every bottle will be filled with wine?" . . .—[*Mezudath David*]

13. **Behold, I will fill etc.**—My words are a parable, meaning that, just as a bottle is destined to be filled with wine, so will I fill all the inhabitants of the land of Judah etc. with drunkenness. They will be confused by the troubles that befall them, even as the drunkard is confused by his wine, for so is befitting for them, and so will it be.—[*Mezudath David*]

who sit on David's throne—I.e. David's descendants who occupy the royal throne.—[*Mezudath David*]

the priests—I.e. the priests of Baal.—[*Mezudath David*]

the prophets—I.e. the false prophets.—[*Jonathan, Mezudath David*]

14. **And I will dash them one against the other**—*I will dash one against the other until they break into small pieces. Cf.* '(Psalms 2:9) *Like a potter's vessel shall you shatter them* (תְּנַפְּצֵם),' '(ibid. 137:9) *And dash* וְנִפֵּץ *your babes;' and so is every expression of* נִפּוּץ *in Scripture.*—[*Rashi*]

and the fathers and the sons—*I will dash one against the other.*—[*Rashi*]

Redak explains that the bottle becomes filled with wine, and its walls, too, absorb much wine. This symbolizes that the people will be permeated from all sides with drunkenness. Just as the drunkard is confused and perplexed, so will the people be confused and perplexed by the multitude of troubles that befall them. Also, just as the wine bottles, when dashed one against the other, are shattered into tiny pieces, so will the people of Judah be dashed against each other. I.e., the many troubles will bring about discord and strife among them, even between fathers and sons. Hence, they will be destroyed both by the enemies and by one another.

תִּגְבָּהוּ כִּי יְהוָה דִּבֵּר: טז תְּנוּ לַיהוָה
אֱלֹהֵיכֶם כָּבוֹד בְּטֶרֶם יַחְשִׁךְ וּבְטֶרֶם
יִתְנַגְּפוּ רַגְלֵיכֶם עַל־הָרֵי נָשֶׁף וְקִוִּיתֶם
לְאוֹר וְשָׂמָהּ לְצַלְמָוֶת יְשִׁית לַעֲרָפֶל:
יז וְאִם לֹא תִשְׁמָעוּהָ בְּמִסְתָּרִים תִּבְכֶּה
נַפְשִׁי מִפְּנֵי גֵוָה וְדָמֹעַ תִּדְמַע וְתֵרַד

ת"א במסתרים תבכה׳ חגיגה ה עקרים מ"ד פכ"ז: ושית קרי עיני

אֲבֵי בְסִימְרָא דַיְיָ גְּזֵירָתֵּן: טז הָבוּ קֳדָם יְיָ אֱלָהֲכוֹן יְקָרָא עַד לָא תֵיתֵי עֲלֵיכוֹן עָקָא וְתִהְוֹן דָּמַן לִדְמְהַלְּכִין בְּקַדְבְּלָא וְעַד לָא יִתְנַגְּפוּן רַגְלֵיכוֹן עַל טוּרֵי קְבַל וְתִסְבְּרוּן לִנְהוֹר וִיהֵי עֲלֵיכוֹן חֲשׁוֹךְ לְנֵיהוֹר וְהָא כִּדְבְקַבְלָא תְּהוֹן מְהַלְּכִין אִתּוּן: יז וְאִם לָא תְקַבְּלוּן אוּלְפַן כַּד בְּסִתְרָא תִבְכֵּי נַפְשִׁי מִן קֳדָם דְּיַעְדֵּי מִנְּכוֹן יְקָרְכוֹן וּמִדְמַע תִּדְמַע וְתִשְׁגַּר עֵינַי דִּמְעִין

רש"י

ושית קרי

זה אלא זה: (טז) יתנגפו. יכשלו (אלופי"ר בלע"ז): הרי נשף. הרי החשך בלכתם בגולה: ושית לערפל. כמו ולשית את האור לערפל: (יז) מפני גוה. מפני גדולה שלכם שתתבטל. ד"א מפני גאותה של מלכות שמים

מהר"י קרא

ושברתים כזה שמכה כלי נבלי חרש זה בזה ושניהם נשברים: (טז) תנו לה' אלהיכם כבוד. זו תשובה כמו שים נא כבוד ותן לו תודה: בטרם יחשיך ובטרם יתנגפו רגליכם על הרי נשף. מקרא זה דומה לאחד שהיה מהלך במדבר לעת ערב והיה מהלך לאט אמר אחד שראהו מהלך לאט רוץ במרוצה בעוד שהוא יום עד שלא יחשיך היום ויתנגפו רגליך על הקוצים ועל הברקנים אף כאן אמר להם לישראל בעוד שהיה ירושלים יושבת בשלוותה ועריה סביבותיה. תנו לה' אלהיכם כבוד. בטרם יחשיך עליהם עול המלכיות. ובטרם יתנגפו רגליכם על הרי נשף. פת' בטרם תהיו גולין שהן דומין להרי חושך שההולך בהם נוקף רגליו וכן בזכריה היא אומר והנה ארבע מרכבות יוצאות מבין שני הרים וההרים הרי נחשת: יתנגפו. לשון נגיף כמו פן תגוף באבן רגליך וכן ולאבן נגף ואם תאמר מאחר שידמה את המלכיות לחשך אין לו חשך שאין לו קץ ואין לך יום קרוב לו לכך נאמר וקויתם לאור ושמה לצלמות ושית לערפל: (יז) ואם לא תשמעוה במסתרים תבכה נפשי. אני

רד"ק

נביאיו לא תעשו זה: (טז) תנו לה' אלהיכם כבוד. ואל תבוזוהו שלא לשמוע דבריו אלא תנו לו כבוד: בטרם יחשיך. יחשיך עליכם השמש כלומר שידמה לכם היום כלילה מרוב הצרות: ובטרם יתנגפו רגליכם על הרי נשף. על הרי חשך. נשף פי' לילה ואמר הרי כשתחשבו להשגב בהרים כן תחשבו להשגב בעזר מצרי' או על ההרי' עצמ' יתנגפו רגליכ' כמי שהולך בחשך שתגוף רגלו באבן כמו שנבא עליה' ישעיהו משא בהמות נגב כמו שפירשנו: וקויתם לאור. על ידי מצרי': ושמה לצלמות. האל ישית אותה התקוה לצלמות: ושית לערפל. כפל ענין במ"ש ישית כתיב פירש כמו ישית וקרי ושית והוא מקור והענין אחד: (יז) ואם לא תשמעוה. אמר הנביא אם לא תשמעו זאת הנבואה שאני אומר לכם מפי האל יתברך במסתרי' תבכה נפשי כי אני רואה אחריתכם ובכיית הנפש במסתרים היא הדאגה: מפני גוה. מפני גאותכ' שאין אתם רוצים להשפיל עצמכם לשמוע דבר ה' כמו שנאמר להם ואל תגבהו: גוה. כמו גאה וי"ת מן קדם דיעדי מנכון יקרכון:

מנחת שי

(טז) יחשך. במסורת ב' חד מלא וחד חסר וכספרים כ"י ודפוסים ישנים זהו החסר והמלא הוא גם חשך לא יחשיך ממך (תהלים קלט) ושניהם החי"ת בשוא לבדו: ישית. ושית קרי: (יז) במסתרים תבכה־נפשי. כ"ב במרכא: מפני גוה. כה"א רפה: עיני דמעה. בס"א יען כתוב בלדו

מצודת דוד

תגבהו: (טז) תנו וגו'. הכבדו לה' והכניעו עצמיכם לפניו: בטרם יחשיך. עד לא יחשיך עליכם אור היום בעבור מרבית הצרות: יתנגפו רגליכם. יוכו רגליכם באבני מכשול כשתלכו גולה על הרי חושך: וקויתם לאור. כאשר תקוו שיהיה לכם הרוחה מה אז ישים אותה המקום לצלמות ויהיה מושם לערפל וכפל הדבר במלי' שונו': (יז) ואם לא תשמעוה. אם לא תקבלו אמרי הנה תבכה נפשי במסתרים במקום שהיא בחדרי הגוף כי רואה אני הרעה המוצאת אתכם: מפני גוה. מפני הגאוה שיש בכם ולא אבו להכניע אל

מצודת ציון

אוזן לשמוע: (טז) יתנגפו. ענין הכאה וכן פן תגוף באבן רגליך (שם צ"א): נשף. ענין חושך כמו אך הושך ישופני (שם קל"ט): לצלמות. צלו של מות והוא חשכת הקבר: ושית. ענין שימה כמו ישת חושך סתרו (שם י"ח): לערפל. עב הענן: (יז) גוה. כמו גאה וכאם סוי"ו במקום האל"ף וכן כי השפילו והאמר גוה (איוב

that the Almighty Himself, so to speak, weeps in a hidden place called מִסְתָּרִים, because of the pride of Israel or the pride of the kingdom of Heaven, as above. *Kara* contends that the expression 'the Lord's flock' at the end of the verse indicates that Jeremiah is the speaker. Otherwise, it would say, 'My flock.' See *Sefer Ha-ikarim,* Section 4: Chapter 23.

and my eye shall weep sore and run down with tears—My soul weeps in secret, but my eye weeps openly, for I see that the Lord's flock has been

be proud, for the Lord has spoken. 16. Give the Lord your
God honor before it becomes dark, and before your feet
stumble on the dark mountains, and you shall hope for light,
but He will make it into darkness, and making it into a thick
cloud. 17. And if you do not hearken to it, in secret my soul
will weep because of your pride and my eye shall weep sore and

for the Lord has spoken—that you shall not be proud.—[*Mezudath David*]

16. **Give the Lord your God honor**—and do not despise Him by disregarding His words, but give Him honor.—[*Redak*]

Give Him honor by repenting of your sins.—[*Kara*]

before it becomes dark—Lit. before He makes it dark; i.e. before He darkens the sun, before the troubles befall you that will make the day appear dark as night.—[*Redak*]

and before your feet stumble—Heb. יִתְנַגְּפוּ, (*achopper in French*), *to stumble.*—[*Rashi*]

Others render: before your feet are bruised.—[*Mezudath Zion*; *Redak, Shorashim*]

the dark mountains—Heb. נֶשֶׁף *the dark mountains when they go into exile.*—[*Rashi*]

I.e., repent before you go into exile and the enemies lead you barefoot on the mountains that will appear to you as mountains of darkness.—[*Ibn Nachmiash*]

Redak explains this as symbolic of the aid they expected to receive from Egypt. Just as one hopes to gain refuge in the mountains, so do you think to gain refuge with the aid of Egypt. Then you will bruise your feet on these very mountains, as one who walks at night bruises his feet on stones.

and you will hope for light—through Egypt.—[*Redak*]

and He will make it into darkness—I.e., God will make your hope into darkness.—[*Redak*] Heb. צַלְמָוֶת. See above 2:6 for derivation.

and making it into a thick cloud—Heb. וְשִׁית, *like* וְלָשִׁית, *and to make the light into a thick cloud.*—[*Rashi*] The *Kethib* is יָשִׁית, He shall make it into a thick cloud.—[*Redak*]

17. **And if you do not hearken to it**—The prophet says: If you do not hearken to this prophecy, which I am telling you in the name of God, my soul will weep in secret for I see your end. Weeping in secret denotes worry.—[*Redak*]

because of your pride—*Because of your greatness which will be curtailed. Another explanation: Because of the pride of the kingdom of Heaven that will be given over to the idols of Babylon.*—[*Rashi* from *Hagigah* 5b]

The first explanation follows *Jonathan.* Others explain: Because of your pride, that you refuse to humble yourselves to obey the word of the Lord, as he said above: Do not be proud.—[*Redak, Kara, Mezudath David*]

The Rabbis (*Hagigah* 5b) explain

עֵינִי דִּמְעָה כִּי נִשְׁבָּה עֵדֶר יְהוָה׃
יח אֱמֹר לַמֶּלֶךְ וְלַגְּבִירָה הַשְׁפִּילוּ שֵׁבוּ
כִּי יָרַד מַרְאֲשֹׁתֵיכֶם עֲטֶרֶת
תִּפְאַרְתְּכֶם׃ יט עָרֵי הַנֶּגֶב סֻגְּרוּ וְאֵין
פֹּתֵחַ הָגְלָת יְהוּדָה כֻּלָּהּ הָגְלָת

תרגום

אֲרֵי אִשְׁתְּבִי עַמָא דַיְיָ׃
יח אֱמַר לְמַלְכָּא
וּלְמַלְכְּתָא אִמְאִיכוּ תִּבוּ
אֲרֵי גְלָא יְקָרְכוֹן מִנְכוֹן
נְפַל כְּלִיל תּוּשְׁבַּחְתְּכוֹן׃
יט קִרְוֵי דָרוֹמָא
אִתְאַחִידוּ וְלֵית
דְפָתַח גְלוֹ דְבֵית יְהוּדָה
כּוּלְהוֹן גְלוֹ שְׁלֵימָא
אִתְקַבְּלוּ תוּשְׁלֵימַת

רש"י

שתכתן לאלילים של כשדים: (יח) למלך ולגבירה. יהויכון ואמו: ירד מראשותיכם. (ווסטריקא"ץ בלע"ז) עלייתכם כמו שנאמר (מלכים ב' כ"ד) ויצא אליו יהויכין הוא ואמו ועבדיו וכולם הוליכם בגולה: (יט) ערי הנגב סוגרו. לפני הבאים עליהם מן הצפון ערי ארץ ישראל סגורות מאימת נבוכדנצר: הגלת שלומים. לאילהם יהויכון כי לשלום יצא ויגלהו. ל"א שלומים (גרדונאמינ"ץ)

מהר"י קרא

אמרתי לכו שמעו והאזינו אל תגבהו אם תשמעוה מוטב ואם לא תשמעוה במסתרים תבכה נפשי מפני גאונכם הגורם לכם שאתם מאנתם לשמוע את דברי כשם שאמר לבעלה כך אשחית את גאון יהודה ואת גאון ירושלים הרב העם הזה הרע המאנים לשמוע את דברי וכן הוא אומר בזה הענין שמעו והאזינו אל תגבהו. ותדע שירמיה על עצמו אמר [מקרא זה] במסתרים תבכה נפשי שכן בסוף המקרא הוא אומר כי נשבה עדר ה' ואם הקב"ה אמרו כביכול שיש בכיה לפניו היה למקרא לומר כי נשבה עדרי: (יח) אמור למלך ולגבירה השפילו שבו. הוא יהויכין ואמו בענין שנא' במלכים ויצא יהויכין מלך יהודה אל מלך בבל הוא ואמו ושריו: כי ירד מראשותיכ' זהו עטרת תפארתכ'. וכת [ירד] מראשותיכ': (יט) ערי הנגב סוגרו ואין פותח. אלו ערי יהודה ובנימין היושבין בדרומה של ארץ ישראל. סוגרו ואין פותח. פתרוני מאין יוצא ובא כמו שנאמר בצור משא צור הלילו אניות תרשיש כי שדד מבית מבוא. שפת' שודד צור מיהכנס עוד אדם. אף כאן סוגרו ואין פותח. נשמו מעובר ושב. ואע"פ שנשמו הערים מעובר ושב. עשה הקב"ה ברחמיו שהגלה יהודה כלה: הגלת שלומים. זה גלית יכניה שהוגלה הוא ואמו

מנחת שי

כצ"ל עיני פ"כ ואין כן בספרים שלנו: (יט) הגלת שלומים. כרוב המדוייקים

רד"ק

ודמוע תדמע. נפשי תבכה במסתרים יעיני תדמע בגלוי כי אני רואה שנשבה עדר ה' שהיה האל להם רועה ועתה נפש' כי לא שמעו לו והניח' ביד שובים: והרד. כל כך תדמע עיני עד שתרד בדמע: (יח) אמר למלך ולגבירה. זה הצווי אינו לאדם מיוחד אלא לכל כי שיתי' וכן ראה ריח בני קול אומר קרא אמרו לנמהרי לב והדומי' להם והמלך והגבירה הם יהויכין ואמו שהם גלו ראשונים עם הגבורי' והחרש והמסגר: השפילו שבו. כאילו אמר שבו בשפל. כי השפילו פעל עומד כמו כי השפילו ותאמר גוה או יהיה פעל יוצא ופירושו השפילו כסאכ' ושבו על הקרקע: כי ירד מראשותיכם. בפלם כמלכותיכם האחד מראשה בפלם ממלכה והוא שם לרשות ולממלכה ואמר ירד ואמר מראשותיכם ל' רבים ר"ל שום רשות לא נשאר לכם אלא הכל יורד כי אף בגלות' לא נהוג בהם מנהג מלכים שהרי נתנו יהויכין בית הכלא כאחד העם: עטרת תפארתכם. כפל הענין במ"ש ואמר ירד ל' זכר ומראשותיכם ועטרת ל' נקבה ר"ל דבר מראשותיכם וכן כי יהיה נערה יעשה מלאכה אשר כמוהו לא נהיתה והדומים לו ובזה נוכל לתקן גם ל' רבוי' אבל ענין טוב הוא מה שכתבנו בו: (יט) ערי הנגב. ת"י קרוי דרומא ועל ערי יהודה אומר כי חלק יהודה היה בדרו' ארץ ישראל כמ"ש וזכר בזה הל' כפני הפ' הבא אחריו שזכר צפון הבאים מצפון כי המחרי' והמגלים יבאו מצפון: סגרו ואין פותח. ר"ל חרבו כי העיר החרבה אין יוצא ואין בא אין סוגר ואין פותח ובאמרו סוגר ר"ל שלא יכנס אדם שם וכן אמר בזה הל' בחרבן הארץ בנבואת ישעיהו סגר כל בית מבוא: הגלת יהודה כלה.

מצודת ציון

כ"כ) וסוא ענין רוממות: ודמוע. הוא דמעת הבכי: נשבת. מלשון שביה: (יח) ולגבירה. היא המלכה: מראשותיכם. מל' ראש וכ"ל גדולתכם: (יט) שלומים. מל' שלם והכל:

מצודת דוד

המקום: ודמוע תדמע. מלבד בכיית הנפש עוד דמוע תדמע וחזר ופי' ותרד עיני דמעה בעבור שנשבה עדר ה' הם ישראל עם מרעיתו וצאן ידו: (יח) אמור. ה' אמר אל הנביא אמור למלך ולמלכה אשתו השפילו שבו ר"ל שבו במקום שפל מוטה לארץ ואל תשבו על כסאות: כי ירד מראשותיכם. ר"ל גדולתכם והוד ופירש עטרת תפארתכם: (יט) ערי הנגב. הם ערי יהודה שהמה בדרום א"י: סגרו ואין פותח. ר"ל כלא הם חרבים ולכן סוגרו ואין מי פותח כי הואיל ואין שם אדם מי יפתח בערי העיר: הגלת יהודה כלה.

Also, because the prominent citizens were exiled with Jehoiachin, and the entire nation was destined to be exiled shortly afterward.—[*Redak*]

she was exiled peacefully— *Jehoiachin will not wage war, but he will come out peacefully, and he will exile them. Another interpretation:* שְׁלוֹמִים (*gueredon in O.F.*), *reprisal. That is to say: she was exiled as the recompense for their iniquity. And Jonathan rendered in this manner: the recompense of their sins was received.—[Rashi]*

Kara explains like *Rashi*'s first interpretation. He points out that Scripture contrasts the exile of Jeconiah with the exile of Zedekiah. The exile of Jeconiah was peaceful, whereas the exile of Zedekiah was involved with much fighting and bloodshed.

run down with tears, for the Lord's flock has been captured.
18. Say to the king and to the queen-mother, "Sit in a low
place, for your greatness has come down, the crown of your
glory." 19. The cities of the South are shut up and there is none
to open [them]; all of Judah has been exiled, she was exiled

captured. God was their Shepherd, but now He has forsaken them since they did not obey Him, and he has delivered them into the hands of their captors.—[*Redak*]

the Lord's flock—*Jonathan* renders: The Lord's people.

18. **Say to the king etc.**—This is not a command to any particular individual, but for anyone it may be.—[*Redak*]

to the king and to the queen-mother—*Jehoiachin and his mother.* —[*Rashi*]

They were the first to be exiled with the mighty warriors and the craftsmen and the sentries of the gates. See II Kings 24:14–16.—[*Redak*] Jehoiachin's mother was named Nehushta the daughter of Elnathan of Jerusalem (II Kings 24:8).

Jonathan renders: Say to the king and the queen. *Abarbanel* takes this to mean Zedekiah and his wife, the queen. This appears to be *Mezudath David's interpretation as well.*

Sit in a low place—Put away your thrones and sit on the ground.—[*Redak, Mezudath David*]

your greatness has come down—Heb. מַרְאֲשֹׁתֵיכֶם (*Vostremjjevec in O.F.*), *your ascent, as it is stated:* '(II Kings 24:12) *And Jehoiachin . . . came out to him* (sic), *he and his mother and his servants,' and he led all of them in exile.*—[*Rashi*]

The word is derived from ראש, *a head.* It is a term used for any governing position. It appears in the plural form, denoting that they will be left with no governing position whatever, for Jehoiachin was imprisoned like the humblest of the populace.—[*Redak*]

19. **The cities of the South are shut up**—*before those coming upon them from the north.* I.e., *the cities of Eretz Israel are shut up because of fear of Nebuchadnezzar.*—[*Rashi*]

Also, Judah was the southern part of Eretz Israel; hence, the cities of the South were the cities of Judah. They are called 'cities of the South' in contrast to 'those coming from the north,' mentioned in the following verse.—[*Redak, Mezudath David*]

Archaelogical discoveries in Arad indicate that the Chaldeans besieged even the southernmost cities of Judah, the cities of the Negev.—[*Daath Mikra*]

are shut and there is none to open them—This is equivalent to 'no one leaves and no one comes.' They are desolate; therefore, no one opens them and no one closes them.—[*Kara, Redak, Mezudath David*]

all of Judah has been exiled—Although not all of them were exiled until the exile of Zedekiah, since the king was exiled, it was counted as though the entire nation was exiled.

שְׁלוֹמִים: כ שְׂאִי עֵינֵיכֶם וּרְאִי הַבָּאִים
מִצָּפוֹן אַיֵּה הָעֵדֶר נִתַּן־לָךְ צֹאן
תִּפְאַרְתֵּךְ: כא מַה־תֹּאמְרִי כִּי־יִפְקֹד
עָלַיִךְ וְאַתְּ לִמַּדְתְּ אֹתָם עָלַיִךְ אַלֻּפִים
לְרֹאשׁ הֲלוֹא חֲבָלִים יֹאחֱזוּךְ כְּמוֹ אֵשֶׁת
לֵדָה: כב וְכִי תֹאמְרִי בִּלְבָבֵךְ מַדּוּעַ

עוֹבָדֵיכוֹן: כ זְקִיפוּ
עֵינֵיכוֹן וַחֲזוֹ דְאָתָן
מִצִּפּוּנָא אָן עַמָּא
דְאִתְמְסַר לִיךְ עַם
תּוּשְׁבַּחְתִּיךְ: כא מָה
תֵּימְרוּן אֲרֵי יִסְעַר עֲלַךְ
חוֹבִיךְ וְאַתְּ אַלֵיפְתְּ יַתְהוֹן
לְמֶעְבַּד בִּישִׁין עֲלַךְ הֲווֹ
בְרַבְרְבִין קַדְמוֹן אוּלָא הֲלָא
עָקָא וְחַבְלִין יְחַדוּנִיךְ הָא
כְּחַבְלִין לְיָלִידְתָּא:
כב וַאֲרֵי תֵימְרִין בְּלִבִּיךְ

שאו קרי וראו קרי למדת קרי

רש"י

בלע"ז) כלומר תשלום עונש וכן ת"י איתקבלו תושלמת חוביהון: (כ) שאו עיניכם וראו. את הכשדים עליכם מצפון: איה העדר נתן לך. אחר שיגלו יאמר לירושלים כן: (כא) מה תאמרי כי יפקוד. הקב"ה עליך: למדת אותם עליך אלופים לראש. שלחתם אליהם מלאכים לכשדיים להביא משם עכו"ם שלהם לעבדם כמו שכתוב (ביחזקאל כ"ג) ותעגבה עליהם למראה עיניה ותשלח

מהר"י קרא

ותחרש והמסגר שגלו כולן גלות של שלים ולא הגלת חרב חרג ואבדן כשם שגלה גלות צדקיהו: (כ) שאו עיניכם וראו. אתם ראו דורו של צדקיהו שאו עיניכם וראו חיל כשדים הבאים מצפון להכרית מכם אדם ובהמה וכשיבואו עליך צדקיהו ולא ישאירו בכל חילך שריד אז יכולין לומר לך איה העדר נתן לך: (כא) מה תאמרי כי יפקוד עליך. הקב"ה כל משפחות ממלכות צפונה לבוא עליך: ואת למדת אותם עליך אלופים לראש. כענין שנאמר ותרא אנשי מחוקה על הקיר צלמי כשדים חקוקים בששר ותעגב עליהם למראה עיניה ותשלח

מנחת שי

פלה וא"ו: (כ) שאי. שאו קרי: וראי. וראו קרי: (כא) ואת למדת. בספרי ספרים כתוב לִמַּדְתִּי ביו"ד ומסורת עליו יתיר יו"ד ובספרים כתובי יד מדוייקים כתוב בלא יו"ד גם לא נמנה במסורת ריש מלכים עם אלין דכתיבין יו"ד בסוף תיבותא ולא קרי' ואלת למדתי דהכא הוא בירמיה ב' בפסוק מה תיטבי. ומסרה זו מלאתיה גם במקרא כ"י במלכים ב' ד' ולא נזכר פזה כלום: יאחזוך. ראיתי בקצת ספרים חלוקים זה פזה בנקודת החי"ת פי בצירי ופי בסגול ופי בחטף פתח ובמדוייקים בחטף סגול וכ"כ רד"ק בכי' ובשרשים:

רד"ק

ואף על פי שלא הגלת כלה עד צדקיהו כיון שגל' מלכם והוא יהויכין הרי היא כאילו גלתה כולה כי סופה לגלות בקרוב והגדולים שבהם גלו עם יהויכין: הגלת שלומים. כפל ענין במ"ש כי שלומים כמו כלם ר"ל שלמים וכן מוסר שלומנו עליו כמו מוסר כלנו וי"ת רבוי מלת שלומים וכלל בו שני ענינים גלו שלימא אתקבלו תושלמת עובדיכון: הגלת. משפטה הגלתה כמו והרצת את שבתותיה הרצתה: (כ) שאי עיניכם. כתוב שאי וראי כנגד הכנסת כמו תכלית הפ' ושני הפסוקים הבאים אחריו וקרי שאו וראו כנגד הרבים הפרטים ולפי דעתי כי שאו וראו אמר למלך ולגביר' שזכר כי להם היה העדר כי הם הרועי' ומה שזכר בל' נקבה הוא כנגד כניסת השרי' הגדולי' שגלו עם יהויכין החרש והמסגר שגם להם הוא העדר והם בכלל הרועי' אמר שאו עיניכם וראו הבאים מצפון ראו הכשדי' הבאי' מצפון להגלותכם: איה העדר נתן לך. ראי העדר שנתן לך להיות רועה עליהם והיו צאן תפארתך איה הם עתה כי לא תרעם עוד: (כא) מה תאמרי כי יפקוד עליך. יפקוד האויב עליך כלומר שיבא עליך להגלותך ולהחריבך מה תאמרי אז וי"ת ארי יסער עלך חובך ר"ל יפקוד האל אבל לענין הפסוק נראה מה שפירשנו שהרי אומר ואת למדת אותם ע' יך אלופים לראש ואמר מה תאמרי כי יפקוד עליך האויב כי את למדת אותם להיות עליך אלופים ולהיות לך לראש כי אחז שלח למלך אשור עבדך ובנך אני עלה והושיעני מכף מלך ארם ומכף מלך ישראל הקמים עלי אמר את גרמת לך שיגלוך אלה ויחריבוך כי את הרגלת אותם עליך כי רחוקים היו מארצך מה תאמרי כשיבאו להחריבך כי כבר באו להושיעך: הלא חבלים יאחזוך. כשתראי זה יאחזו אותך חבלים כמו אשת לידה האשה העומדת ללדת וזה הענין יתחפך כי נאמר צירים וחבלי' יאחזוך: יאחזוך. החי"ת בחט"ף סגו"ל: לדה. יתכן שיהיה שם כמו מלידה ומבפן ויהיה אשת סמוך גם אפשר שיהיה לדה תואר כמו וכה אין ללידה ויהיה אשת מוכרת כמו אשת יפת תואר: (כב) וכי תאמרי. נגלו שוליך הבגד הם התחתונים וכשיהפכו

מצודת דוד

כל יהודה גלה: הגלת שלומים. ר"ל גלות שלימה כי כשגלה יכניה נשארו רבים מהשרים וכל עם הארץ לכן אמר פתה בגלות צדקיה יהיה גלות שלימה כי יגלו כולם: (כ) שאו עיניכם. אתם המלך והגבירה שאו עיניכם וראו חיל כשדים הבאים מצפון: איה העדר. איה עם יהודה שניתן לך להיות להם לרועה ומלך והיה לאן תפארתך שלא ילכו בגולה: (כא) מה תאמרי. כמה תגלל כאשר האויב ישגיח בך לקחת אותך בשבי: ואת למדת. אתה כעצמך הרגלת את הכשדים להיות עליך אלופים להיות ראשים עליך כי על שהראית חזקים לשלוחי מרודך בלאדן מלך בבל את כל בית נכותו הסית לבם אותם להלחם בישראל פעם בפעם לקחת הסגולות: חבלים יאחזוך. בבוא האויב יאחזו אותך חבלים ומכאובי' כמו אשה הכורעת ללדת: (כב) וכי

מצודת ציון

(כא) יפקוד. ענין השגחה: למדת. ענין הרגל וכן פרה למד מדבר (לעיל ב'): אלופים. שרים וכן מפריד אלוף (משלי ט"ז): חבלים. מכאובי

See the flock which was given you to be the shepherd over them, and they were the sheep of your glory. Where are they now, for you no longer pasture them?—[*Redak*]

22. **And if you say in your heart**—*Mezudath David* renders: Now will

The prophet says, "You caused them to exile you and destroy you, since you accustomed them to be over you, for they were far from your land. What will you say when they come to exile you, since they already came to save you?—[*Redak*]

peacefully. 20. Lift your eyes and see those coming from the North. Where is the flock that was given you, the sheep of your glory? 21. What will you say when He visits upon you, when you accustomed them to be princes over you at your head? Will not pangs seize you like a woman in confinement? 22. And if you say in your heart, "Why

Others render: She was exiled completely.—[*Redak, Mezudath David*]

20. **Lift your eyes and see**—*those coming upon you from the North.*—[*Rashi*]

The 'kethib' is in the feminine singular, referring to the nation; the 'keri' is in the masculine plural, referring to the individuals. I feel that the plural form is addressed to the king and the queen-mother, mentioned above, for the flock was given to them, they being the shepherds. The 'kethib' is addressed to the gathering of the great princes who were exiled with Jeconiah and the craftsmen and the sentries of the gate, for the 'flock was given to them,' and they were included among the shepherds.—[*Redak*]

Kara explains: See, you generation of Zedekiah. Lift your eyes and see the army of Chaldees coming upon you from the North to cut off from you both man and beast, and when they come upon you, O Zedekiah, and they will not leave over any remnant among your entire army, then they will be able to say to you, "Where is the flock that was given you?"

Where is the flock that was given you—*After they are exiled, this will be said to Jerusalem.*—[*Rashi*]

As mentioned above, according to *Redak*, this will be said to Jehoiachin and his mother, or to the officers and the craftsmen and gate sentries, and according to Kara, to Zedekiah.

21. **What will you say when He visits**—I.e., *when the Holy One, blessed be He visits upon you?*—[*Rashi*]

when you accustomed them to be princes at your head—*You sent emissaries to the Chaldees to bring their idols from there to worship them, as it is written in Ezekiel (23:16): 'And she lusted for them to the sight of her eyes, and she sent emissaries to them, to the Chaldees.' Another explanation of 'you accustomed them to be princes over you': Hezekiah who showed the emissaries of Merodach-baladan his entire treasure-house (Isaiah 39:2, II Kings 20:13).*—[*Rashi*]

Redak explains: What will you do when he, the enemy, visits upon you; i.e., when he comes to exile you and to destroy your land, what will you say? For you accustomed them to be princes over you at your head. 'Ahaz sent messengers to Tiglath-pileser the king of Assyria, saying, "I am your servant and your son. Come up and save me from the hand of the king of Aram and from the hand of the king of Israel who have risen up against me (II Kings 16:7).'

קראני אלה ברב עונך נגלו שוליך
נחמסו עקביך: כג היהפך כושי עורו
ונמר חברברתיו גם-אתם תוכלו
להיטיב למדי הרע: כד ואפיצם כקש
עובר לרוח מדבר: כה זה גורלך מנת-
מדיך מאתי נאם-יהוה אשר שכחת
אותי

ת"א היהפך כושי. שבת כ"ז:

תרגום

מא דין ארעוני כל אלין על דסגיאו חובך אתגליאת בהתתיך אתחזי קלניך: כג האפשר דישני הנדואה משכיה ונמרא שלטירקמתיה אף אתון תיכלון לאוטבא דהויתון מלפין למעבד בישין: כד ואבדרינון כקשא דעבי מן קדם רוחא למדברא: כה דין עדביך וחולק אחסנתיך.

מהר"י קרא

מלאכים אליהם כשדימה וגו': (כב) ברוב עונך. נגלו שולי בגדיך ונגלה ערותך: נחמסו עקביך. לשון גילוי כמו ויחמס כגן שוכו: (כג) היהפוך כושי עורו. נכלומר כשם שאי אפשר לכושי להפוך עורו] שהוא שחור ללבן ולא לנמר לשנות חברבורותיו להיעשות כולו [בגוון אחד] גם אתם אי אפשר לכם שתוכלו להיטיב לאחר שלמדתם הרע ללכת בדרכי האומות: הרע. כמו להרע. בעון זה: (כד) ואפיצם כקש עובר: (כה) זה גורלך מנת מדיך. שכר זה לפעלה זו יען שכחת אותי. ותבטחי

רש"י

מלאכים אליהם כשדימה. ד"א למדת אותם עליך אלופים חזקיהו שהראה לשלוחי מרודך בלאדן את כל בית נכאתה (ישעיה ל"ט): (כב) שוליך. שיפולי הבגדים (טי"ש אורלא"ש בלע"ז) כשמפשיטין את האשה דרך בזיון מהפכין חלוקה מלמטה למעלה: נחמסו עקביך. נגזרו דרכיך נחמסו. כמו ויחמס כגן שוכו (איכה ב'): עקביך. (פרלי"ש בלע"ז) פסקו עוברי דרכים: (כג) כושי. שם אדם שחור וקורין (מא"ר בלע"ז): ונמר. (ליאפר"ש בלע"ז): חברבורותיו. הנמר מנומר הוא והם החברבורות (טק"ש בלע"ז) ואי אפשר שיהפכו: הרע. כמו להרע: (כה) מנת מדיך. חלק מדותיך מדה כנגד מדה:

רד"ק

למעלה הנה הם נגלי' והלובש נגלה וכן אמר וגלותי שוליך על פניך והנה אחר שיהפכו השולים העקבים נגלי': נחמסו. כמו נגלו וכן ויחמוס כגן שוכה ויגלה וזה הוא משל על כנסת ישראל שהיתה נסתרת תחת כנפי האל ונכבדת בארצה ועתה היא גולה והוסר סתרה מעליה והנה היא גלויה ונגלה קלונה לעין כל בארצות נכרי': (כג) היהפוך. כי דבר טבעי הוא השחרות בכושי ואינו דבר מקרה ולא יסור ממנו לעולם וכן החברבורות בנמר כן הרשע לא יוכל לסור מכם כאילו הוא טבעי בכם כ"כ למדת' והרגלתם עצמכם במעשה הרע עד ששב אצליכם דבר טבעי: למדי. כמו למוד כדבר מורגל: הרע. מקור כמו ואם הרע תריע. וי"ת כושי הנדואה: חברבורותיו. כתמיו וי"ת שלטי רקמתיה: (כד) ואפיצם. לפיכך אפיץ אותם מהרה בקלות כקש עובר לרוח מדבר פי' כקש שהוא עובר מהרה בעבור הרוח שנושבת בו כן אפיצ' במדבר כלומר ארציאם מריחם למקום רחוק כמו המדבר גם יש מהבר בין ירושלם ובבל: (כה) זה גורלך מנת מדיך. כמו מדותיך או יהיה מדה מחובר בלשון זכרים ובל' נקבות כמו ארבע פנותיו ויקובץ בלשון זכרים כמו שער הפנים כן יאמר כן מדת מדות ויאמר מדים וממנו מדיך ופי' במדה שמדדת מדדתי לך את שכחת אותי ואני שכחתי אותך פנית אלי עורף ולא פני' ואני הסתרתי פני ממך והיית

מצודת ציון

יולדה וכן חבלי יולדה (הושע י"ג): (כב) קראוני. מלשון מקרה: שוליך. הם התחתיות הבגד כמו על שולי המעיל (שמות כ"ח): נחמסו. ענין הסרה כמו ויחמס כגן שכו (איכה ב'): עקביך. עקבי הרגל: (כג) כושי. הם השחורים: ונמר. הם חיה: חברבורותיו. ענין כתמים וכן חבורה תחת חבורה (שמות כ"א) כי במקום המכה נראה כעין כתם: למדי. ענין הרגל: (כד) ואפיצם. ענין פזור: (כה) גורלך. חלקך לפי שעל פי רוב חולקים בגורל יקרא חלק בשם גורל: מנת. גם זה ענין חלק כמו מנת שועלים

מצודת דוד

תאמרי. וכי תוכל להרהר בלבבך מדוע קרה לי הגרוע הזאת הלא בעבור רוב עונך בא לך בזיון רב כאשה זונה שמפשיטין חלוקה ומהפכין מלמטה למעלה דרך בזיון ומגלים שולי החלוק בהגבהתם כלפי מעלה: נחמסו עקביך. עקבי רגליך נתגלו והוסרו מנן הכסות שעליהם ר"ל קבלת בזיון הרבה ולפי שהמשילה לזונה אמר ל' הנופל בזונ' שמפשיטין חלוקה ומוליכין אותה ערומה ויחיפ': (כג) היהפוך. האם יוכל הכושי להפוך עורו משחרות ללובן האם יוכל הנמר להפוך הכתמים שבעורו לבל יהיו בו הכתמים הלא הוא דבר שא"א כי שמה דבר טבעי בהם: גם אתם. כן גם אתם תוכלו להיטיב מפני הסרגל הרע שאתם מורגלים ונעשה אצליכם כדבר טבעי ור"ל כמו שאין בכושי והנמר יכול להשתנות כן גם אתם והוא ענין גוזמא והפלגה כלומר בקושי רב תשתנו ממעשיכם: (כד) ואפיצם. לכן אפזרם בעכו"ם במהירות רב כמו הקש העובר ממקומו בקלות ע"י הרוח הבא מפאת המדבר שאין שם דבר לעמוד בפני הרוח ולעכבו: (כה) זה גורלך. זה הגמול יהיה חלקך וזהו המנה הניתן לך מאתי

tween Jerusalem and Babylon.—[*Redak*]

25. **the portion of your measures**—*The portion of your measures, a measure for a measure.*—[*Rashi*]

With the measure that you meted out, I meted out to you. You forgot Me, and I forgot you. You turned your back to Me, and I hid My face from you, and you shall be

have these befallen me? For the greatness of your iniquity were your skirts uncovered, your steps cut off. 23. Will a Cushite change his skin, or a leopard his spots? So will you be able to improve, you who have become accustomed to do evil. 24. And I will scatter them like straw that passes with the wind, to the desert. 25. This is your lot, the portion of your measures, from Me, says the Lord, for you have forgotten

you say in your heart. . . ? The intention is that the answer is obvious and that there is no reason to ask.

your skirts—*The skirts of the garments* (*tes ourlets in French*), *your hems. When a woman is stripped in a humiliating way, they turn her chemise upside-down.*—[*Rashi*]

your steps cut off—Heb. נֶחְמְסוּ, *your ways are cut off.* נֶחְמְסוּ *is like* '(Lam. 2:6) *And He cut off* (וַיַּחְמֹס) *like a garden His dwelling.*'—[*Rashi*]

your steps —(*traces in O.F.*) *Travelers have stopped.*—[*Rashi*]

Redak renders: Your heels uncovered. After the hems are turned up, the heels are uncovered. [Jonathan, too, renders: your disgrace was seen.] This is figurative of the people of Israel, who were hidden under the wings of God and who were the most honored among the nations, and now they wander about without shelter. Their disgrace is, therefore, revealed to all the nations.

Because of your great iniquity, you are utterly disgraced like a prostitute, who is disgraced by stripping her of her chemise, pulling it off from the bottom to the top, thus revealing the hems, and taking off her shoes, to lead her naked and barefoot. Since Scripture compares her to a harlot, it gives an example of the disgrace meted out to a harlot.—[*Mezudath David*]

23. **a Cushite**—Heb. כּוּשִׁי, *the name of a black man, who is called Maure in French, a Moor.*—[*Rashi*]

or a leopard—*léopard in French.*—[*Rashi*]

his spots—*The leopard is spotted, and they are the spots* (*taches in French*), *and it is impossible for them to change.*—[*Rashi*]

The blackness of a Cushite is natural, not incidental, and cannot change, neither can the spots of a leopard. So can the wickedness not be removed from you as though it was a natural thing. So have you become accustomed to evil deeds that they have become natural to you.—[*Redak*]

This is an exaggeration, meaning that it will be very difficult to change your ways.—[*Mezudath David*]

to do evil—Heb. הָרֵעַ, *like* לְהָרַע, *to do evil.*—[*Rashi*]

24. And I will scatter them—Therefore, I will scatter you swiftly and easily like straw that passes quickly because of the wind that blows it. So will I scatter them in the desert. I.e., I will take them out of their cities to a distant place like a desert. Also, there is a desert be-

אותי ותבטחי בשקר: כו וגם־אני
חשפתי שוליך על־פניך ונראה
קלונך: כז נאפיך ומצהלותיך זמת
זנותך על־גבעות בשדה ראיתי
שקוציך אוי לך ירושלם לא תטהרי
אחרי מתי עד: יד א אשר היה דבר
יהוה אל־ירמיהו על־דברי הבצרות:
ב אבלה יהודה ושעריה אמללו קדרו

מן קדמי אמר יי דשבקת
פולחני ואתרחיצת על
שקרא: כו ואף אנא
אגלי בהבת חובך על
אפך ויתחזי קלניך:
כז טפשותיך ושטותיך
ועצת חטאי נקותיך
על רמתא בחקלא גלי
קדמי שקוציך ווי ליך
ירושלם לא תדכין עד
כען ליך ארכא יומין
סגיאין: א דהוה פתגם
נבואה מן קדם יי עם
ירמיה על עסקי
בוצרתא: ב אתאבלו
דבית יהודה וקרויהון

רש"י

(כו) חשפתי שוליך. גיליתי שיפולי בגדיך להפכם על פניך: (כז) מצהלותיך. כצהלת סוסים נואפים: אחרי מתי. תטהרי עוד:

יד (א) דברי הבצרות. שיביא עליהם רעב ומנחם חברו לשון מבצר כמו ומבצר משגב חומותיך (ישעיה כ"ה): (ב) ושעריה. עריה: וצוחת ירושלים.

מהר"י קרא

על עזרת האומות שהם עזרת שקר: (כו) וגם אני חשפתי שוליך. פתרונו הנני מעיר את חיל כשדים עליך אשר למדת אותם עליך אלופים לראש והפשיטוך את בגדיך ולקחו כלי תפארתך ולקחו כל יגיעך ועזבוך ערום ועריה ונראה ערות זנותך וזה הוא גם אני חשפתי שוליך על פניך ונראה קלונך. ואף נבואה זו אמרה יחזקאל אלא שלא אמורה שניהם בלשון אחד: (כז) לא תטהרי אחרי מתי עוד. פת' לא תטהרי עוד אחרי שהזהרתיך ימים רבים לומר מתי תשובי מדרכך ואת לא שבת. מעתה לא תטהרי עוד:

יד (א) על דברי הבצרות. אלו שני בצרות שבאין מחמת עצירת מטר. וכאן סתם הנביא את דבריו שלא פירש באי זה דור באו אלו שני בצרות מה שלא מצינו כן בכל מקום שיסתמו הנביאים את דבריהם כל כך שכל שני רעבון שבא לעולם בימי הדורות בכל רעב ורעב פירשו הכתובים באי זה דור בא לעולם כמו רעב שבא בימי אברהם וכן רעב שבא בימי יצחק וכן בימי דוד וכן בימי אלישע. וכאן הזכיר שני בצרות ולא פירש באי זה דור באו לעולם. ירמיה ראה שני בצרות באין לעולם וסדר עליה' תפלה כמו שאתה קורא בענין הכתוב (אם) [אינני] שומע אל רנתם וכי יעלו עולה ומנחה אינני רוצם כי בחרב וברעב ובדבר אנכי מכלה אותם. אמור מעתה באי זה דור אירעו שלשה שפטים הללו חרב ורעב ודבר. אם תאמר בימי יאשיהו הלא עליו נאמר בשלום תמות. ואם תאמר בגלות יכניה אי אפשר לומר כן. שגלות יכניה כולן גלו

רד"ק

לאכול ומצאוך צרות רבות ורעות וזה גורלך ומנתך מאתי: (כו) וגם אני. מבואר הוא: (כז) נאופיך. כבר פירשנו כי כל ענין הנאוף הוא משל לע"א: ומצהלותיך. שהיית שמחת על מעשיך הרעים: לא תטהרי אחרי מתי עוד. לא תטהרי אחרי שנטמאת ואם תאמרי שתטהרי מתי עוד כיון שלא תטהרי קודם שתגלי וי"ת לא תדכין עד כען ליך ארכא יומין סגיאין:

(א) אשר היה. הבצרות. האחד בצרת וי"ם זה לעת"ת בצרה חבי"ת שרש ופירושו יוקר המאכל והוא הרעב ובמשקל אחר ובשנת בצורת והוא מל' לא יבצר מהם ענין מניעה כי הרעב מפני מניעת הגשמים ובאמרו בלשון רבי' בצרות ר"ל יוקר מעות ויוקר פירות והיה דבר ה' אליו קודם היות הבצרות כי יהיה ואמר לו בנבואה כך: (ב) אבלה יהודה. ענין השחתת

מצודת דוד

מדה כמדה על אשר שכחת אותי ובטחת בעכו"ם שהיא שקר לכן אשכחך גם אני: (כו) וגם אני חשפתי שוליך. ר"ל על כי זנית אחרי העכו"ם לכן אביא עליך בזיון רב כדרך שמבזין את הזונה ולפי שהמשיל אותה לזונה אמר ל' בזיון הזונה שמפשיטין מלבושה ומהפכין מלמטה למעלה ומגלים שולי המלבוש בהגבהתם כלפי מעלה על פניה: ונראה קלונך. בזיונך יהיה נראה לכל: (כז) נאופיך. מרבית הניאוף שלך והרמת קול שמחה על קלות ראש ומחשבות זנותך ר"ל הנה כל אלה עדיין הם עמך ולא עזבתם: שקוציך. העכו"ם המתועב כשקץ: לא תטהרי. ר"ל אינך רוצה לטהר אחר שנטמאת כי קשה לך לפרוש מן הטומאה ואם תאמרי שתטהרי עדיין אמרי אחרי מתי עוד תטהרי וכי אחר שתלך בגולה: יד (א) על דברי. על ענין מניעת הגשמים: (ב) אבלה יהודה.

מצודת ציון

יסיו (תהלים ס"ג): מדיך. מלשון מדה: (כו) חשפתי. ענין גלוי כמו וחשופי שת (ישעיה כ'): שוליך. תחתיות הבגד: קלונך. מל' קלון ובזיון: (כז) נאופיך. ענין זנות: ומצהלותיך. ענין הרמת קול שמחה של קלות וכן איש אל אשת רעהו יצהלו (לעיל ה'): זמת. ענין מחשבה רעה: שקוציך. מל' שקץ ותעוב: מתי. ענין השאלה על הזמן וכן מתי תנחמני (תהלים קי"ט):

יד (א) על דברי. על ענין וכן על דבר פעור (במדבר כ"ה): הבצרות. ענין מניעה כמו לא יבצר מהם (בראשית י"א) ור"ל מניעות הגשמים וכן ובשנת בצורת (לקמן י"ז): (ב) אמללו.

1. **concerning the droughts**—Heb. הַבַּצָּרוֹת, *that He would bring famine upon them, and Menahem* (*Machbereth* p. 47) *classified it as an expression of fortification* (מִבְצָר) *like* '(Isaiah 25:12) *And the fortress of* (וּמִבְצַר) *the strength of your walls.'*—[*Rashi*]

2. **Judah mourns**—This is an expression of destruction. *Jonathan,* however, renders: The people of Judah mourns.—[*Redak*]

and her cities—Heb. וּשְׁעָרֶיהָ, lit. her gates.—[*Rashi* after *Jonathan*]

Some, indeed, render: gates. *Redak* sees here a parallel to '(Lam.

Me, and you have trusted in falsehood. 26. And I also have uncovered your skirts over your face, and your disgrace has been seen. 27. Your adulteries and your neighings, and the thoughts of your harlotry; on hills in the field have I seen your abominations; woe to you, Jerusalem, you shall not become purified. After when shall it ever be?

14

1. The word of the Lord that came to Jeremiah concerning the droughts. 2. Judah mourns, and her cities are cut off; they have become blackened

devoured, and many evil troubles will befall you. This is your lot and your portion from Me.—[*Redak*]

and you have trusted in falsehood—You have trusted pagan deities. Therefore, I have forgotten you.—[*Mezudath David*]

Others explain: You have trusted in the false help of the nations.—[*Kara*]

26. **have uncovered your skirts**—*I have uncovered the hems of your garments upon your face.*—[*Rashi*]

Since you have played the harlot by straying after idolatry, I will bring great disgrace upon you in the manner they disgrace a harlot. Since he compares her to a harlot, he depicts her disgrace in a manner a harlot is disgraced, namely that they strip her of her chemise and pull the bottom over her face, thereby exposing the hems of the chemise when it is lifted over her face.—[*Mezudath David*]

I will inspire the army of the Chaldees whom you accustomed to be heads over you, and they will strip you of your garments and take your beautiful vessels and everything you toiled for, and they will leave you naked and bare so that your disgrace will be exposed to all. Ezekiel, too, said this same prophecy, but in a different manner.—[*Kara*]

27. **Your adulteries**—We have already explained that adultery is an allegory representing idolatry.—[*Redak*]

your neighings—*like the neighing of adulterous horses.*—[*Rashi*]

I.e. your joyous shouts of levity and the thoughts of your harlotry are still with you; you have not abandoned them.—[*Mezudath David*] See above 5:8.

You rejoiced in your evil deeds.—[*Redak*]

After when—*will you ever become purified?*—[*Rashi*] Mss. read: *After I have done this, when will you ever be purified?*

Redak renders: You will not become purified after you have become contaminated, and if you say that you will become purified, when will it ever be, since you will not become purified before you are exiled?

לארץ וצות ירושלם עלתה:
ג ואדיריהם שלחו צעוריהם למים
באו על־גבים לא־מצאו מים שבו
כליהם ריקם בשו והכלמו וחפו
ראשם: ד בעבור האדמה חתה כי
לא־היה גשם בארץ בשו אכרים חפו
ראשם: ה כי גם־אילת בשדה ילדה

תרגום

חרובא אתחפיאו אפיהון אכרוב אוכמין כקדרא אתרטישו לארעא וצוחת יתבי ירושלם סליקת: ג ותקיפיהון שלחו תנוקיהון למיא אתו על פצידיא ולא אשכחו מיא תבו מניהון ריקן בהיתו ואתכנעו וחפו רישיהון: ד בדיל חובי יתבי ארעא אתברו ארי לא הוה מטרא בארעא בהיתו אכריא וחפו רישיהון: (ה) ארי אף אילתא במדברא ילידת ושבקא ארי לא

צ׳ ועירא צעיריהם קרי מלרע

מהר״י קרא

תגלת שלומים ועליו נאמר כתאנים הטבות האלה כן אכיר את גלות יהודה ואומר ויגל יהויכין בבלה ואת אם המלך ואת נשי המלך ואת סריסיו ואת אילי הארץ הוליך גולה מירושלים בבלה אלא מעתה [אתה] למד אין לך דור שמתו בחרב וברעב ובדבר אלא דורו של צדקיה. למדת שבדורו של צדקיהו באו אלו שני בצורת: (ג) באו על גבים. אלו מי גשמים המכונסין בבורות: (ד) בעבור האדמה חתה. ת״י בדיל חובי יתבי ארעא אתברו: בושו אכרים. אלו זורעי אדמה הרי שחרש חרע ואין גשמים יורדין שתרוה הארץ והולידה והצמיחה מה מועיל לו זריעתו שזרע: (ה) כי גם אילת בשדה ילדה ועזוב

רש״י

לעקת ירושלים כמו מרחם הרים יצווחו (שם מ״ב): (ג) על גבים. בורות שהמים מתכנסים בהם: שבו כליהם ריקם. שלא ירד מטר: וחפו. לשון כסוי: (ד) אכרים. (בוביר״ש בלע״ז): (ה) ילדה ועזוב. את וולדה לבקש

מנחת שי

יד (ג) לצוריהם. צעיריהם קרי: (ד) היה גשם. בא מלרע שלא כמנהג וכן:

רד״ק

כמו אבל תירוש אמלל יצהר וי״ת אתאבלו דבית יהודה: ושעריה אמללו. על דרך כל שעריה שוממין ר״ל אין יוצא ואין בא בהם או ששבתו הזקנים משבת בשערים כמו שאמר זקנים משער שבתו וי״ת וקרויהון חריבא: קדרו לארץ. השערים על דרך משל או פי׳ יושבי השערים על דרך ישבו לארץ ידמו וי״ת אתחפיאו אפיהון אכרום אוכמין כקדרא אתרטישו לארעא: וצוחת ירושלם עלתה. על דרך ותעל שועת העיר השכימה ר״ל יושבי העיר ירושלם: (ג) ואדיריהם. הגדולים ששלחו צעיריהם חוץ לעיר לראות אם ימצאו מים באו על החפירות שדרך למצא בהם מים המתכנסי׳ שם מי גשמים או שיחיה שם מקו׳ מים לעומק המקום והנה לא מצאו מים לפיכך היה להם בשת ששבו כליהם רקי׳ כלומר שבו ריקם כמו שנאמר באיוב בשו כי בטח ופירש שבו כליהם שבו עם כליה׳ או פי׳ שבו על הכלי׳ כלומר ע״י משיב וכן אפוד ירד־בידו. לבלתי באו הכלים: צעוריהם. כתיב וחקרי ביו״ד ושניהם נכונים במשקל חשמות אלא שהקרי יותר מבואר כי נמצא צעיר ביו״ד ולא נמצא צעור בו״ו: (ד) בעבור האדמה חתה. בעבור טעם לסוף הפסוק שעליו למה חפו ראשם בעבור שהאדמה חתה ונשברה כי לא היה גשם בארץ או טעם בעבור לסוף הפ׳ הזה שאמר בשו אכרי׳ חפו ראשם: היה. מלרע: בארץ. ר״ל בארץ ישראל: אכרים. הם עובדי השדות: (ה) כי גם אילת. אפי׳ האילת ילדה העפרי׳ ועזבה אותם מחסרון מרעה כי לא היה דשא ועזבה ילדיה לבקש מרעה בארץ אחרת ולא חששה על ילדיה אף על פי שהיא רחמנית והלכה לתחיות את נפשה: ועזוב. מקור

מצודת ציון

ענין כליהם כמו כי אמלל אני (תהלים ו׳): קדרו. ענין שחרות והושך כמו שמש וירח קדרו (יואל ב׳): וצוחת. מלשון צוחה ולעקה: (ג) ואדיריהם. מלשון אדיר וחזק ור״ל השרים: צעיריהם. ענין קטן ושפל וכן לעיר אנכי נבזה (תהלים קי״ט): גבים. בורות כמו ולחשוף מים מגבא (ישעיה ל׳): וחפו. ענין כסוי וכן ופני המן חפו (אסתר ז׳): (ד) חתה. ענין שבר כמו ולדקתי לא תחת (ישעיה נ״א): אכרים. הם עובדי האדמה כחורשים וכדומה וכן

מצודת דוד

הם יהודה תאבל: ושעריה. שערי יהודה ככלתם ונשתמו להתדמות לשחרות הארץ והוא ענין מליצה לומר שהיה לער כעולם על מניעת הגשמים: וצוחת ירושלים. עם כי הוא שרתי במדינות נחסר לחמה ומימה ולעקת אנשיה עלתה למעלה: (ג) ואדיריהם. השרים שלחו נעריהם לבקש מים לשתות והמה באו על הבורות ולא מלאו בהם מים והחזירו את כליהם כשהם ריקים מבלי מים: בושו. ולזה בושו הנערים וגם נכלמו וכסו ראשם דרך לער ואבל על שלא מלאו מים להביא לאדוניהם: (ד) בעבור. על כי נשברה ונשחתה האדמה כי לא היה גשם בארץ לכן בושו עובדי האדמה וכסו ראשם כי לריק היה יגיעם: (ה) אילת בשדה. נקבת

also possible that it is a reason for the end of the preceding verse.—[Redak]

Jonathan renders: Because of the sins of the inhabitants of the land, they were broken.

farmers—Heb. אִכָּרִים, (*bubirs [?] in O.F.*).—[*Rashi*] [The nearest known word is the Latin *buris*, bent wood of the plow.] This refers to the tillers of the fields.—[*Redak*] *Abarbanel* interprets אִכָּרִים like כָּרִים, *lambs*. It is as though the lambs mourn and cover their heads, for there are no more lambs.

5. **the hind of the field**—Not only are the domesticated animals effected by the drought, but also the hinds of the field.—[*Abarbanel*]

has borne and abandoned—*her*

to the ground, and the cry of Jerusalem has risen. 3. And their mighty ones have sent their youths for water. They have come upon pits and have found no water; their vessels have returned empty; they have been ashamed and confounded and have covered their heads. 4. Because the earth was broken for there was no rain on the earth, farmers were ashamed; they covered their heads. 5. For also the hind in the field has borne

1:4) All her gates are desolate.' I.e., no one passes through the gates, or that the elders who sat in the city to judge are no longer there.

to the ground—Allegorically speaking, the gates have become blackened down to the ground. Or, those who sit in the gate will sit on the ground. Cf. Lam. 2:10, The elders of the daughter of Zion sit on the ground and remain silent. *Jonathan* renders: Their faces were covered with blackness like a pot, they were dashed to the ground.—[*Redak*]

and the cry of Jerusalem—Heb. צִוְחַת, *the cry of Jerusalem. Comp.* '(Isaiah 42:11) *from the mountain peaks they shall shout* (יִצְוָחוּ).'—[*Rashi*]

I.e., the cry of the inhabitants of Jerusalem.—[*Jonathan, Redak*]

Although she was the princess of provinces, she had neither bread nor water, and the cry of her inhabitants ascended on high.—[*Mezudath David*]

3. **And their mighty ones**—When the prominent people sent their youths outside the city to find water, the latter came upon pits where rain water is usually stored, or with the hope of finding an underground spring, but they found no water. Therefore, they returned shamefacedly with empty vessels.—[*Redak*]

upon pits—*Pits in which the water is usually gathered.*—[*Rashi*]

their vessels have returned empty —*for no rain has fallen.*—[*Rashi*]

Redak considers rendering: 'They have returned with their vessels empty,' or, 'their vessels have returned empty,' i.e., the vessels have returned through the one who brought them back. The latter coincides with *Jonathan, Mezudath David,* however, renders: They have returned their vessels empty. [This is not grammatically correct.]

and have covered—Heb. חָפוּ, *an expression of covering.*—[*Rashi*]

They covered their heads out of anguish and mourning, being unable to bring back water for their masters.—[*Mezudath David*] Covering the head is a sign of mourning. See Lev. 13:45, *Targum Onkelos*; Esther 6:11.

4. **Because the earth was broken** —This is a reason for the statement at the end of the verse, 'farmers were ashamed, they covered their heads.' I.e., they were ashamed and covered their heads because the earth was broken for there was no rain. It is

ועזוב כי לא־היה דשא: ו ופראים
עמדו על־שפים שאפו רוח כתנים כלו
עיניהם כי־אין עשב: ז אם־עונינו ענו
בנו יהוה עשה למען שמך כי־רבו
משובתינו לך חטאנו: ח מקוה ישראל
מושיעו בעת צרה למה תהיה כגר
בארץ

הוו דתאין דעשבא: ו בעדרין קמו על נגדין שתן רוחא כירודין קמא עיניהון ארי לית עשבא: ז אם חובנא אסהידו בנא יי עביד בדיל שמך ארי סגיאין תיובתנא קדמך חבנא: ח סבור ישראל פרקיה בעדן עקא למה

ת"א אם עונינו. סוטה לט: מקוה ישראל. מקוה פסוק ל (יומא פה):

יחול

רש"י

לה מרעה: על שפיים. יבלי מים (כיבייר"ש בלע"ז): (ז) ענו בנו. העידו בנו: עשה למען שמך. עשה מה שתעשה עמנו למען שם גדול שילא לך שאתה מושל בכל ואנחנו עמך ולאן מרעיתך ולא נאה שתתן שם גלהוכך לפסילים. ומדרש אגדה למען שמך המשותף בשמינו: (ח) מקוה. תוחלת:

מלרע

מהר"י קרא

כי לא היה דשא. כשתדשא הארץ דשא ועשב מזריע זרע ואינה *) יולדת היא יולדת מצד זה לפי שמרחמת על בנה ואינה רוצה להרחיק ממנו אבל כשיבש חציר וכלה דשא וירק לא היה היא יולדת כאן ועוזבת בניה לדרוש אחר כל ירוק: (ו) ופראים עמדו על שפיים. שפיים מדברות שהם גדילים בו בשעה שעשב מצוי ועכשיו שאין עשב מצוי להם פינו את מקומם ועמדו על שפיים הם נאות דשא ואף שם כלו עיניהם כי אין עשב: (ח) מקוה ישראל. פתרונו תקוותן של ישראל וכן ת"י סבור ישראל כלומר שבך מקוים שתושיע אותם בעת צרה: למה תהיה כגר בארץ. שאינו נותן לב על הרעה שתבוא על

*) אולי צ"ל ואילה אמנם בכל סכ"י כתוב ואינה וצ"ע

רד"ק

במקום עבר כאילו אמר ועזבת וכן והחיות רצוא ושוב כאילו אמר רצו ושבו: (ו) ופראים. שפים. חסר י' הרבי' מהמכתב וכבר פירשנו שפירושו המקומות הגבוהי' ועמידת' שם לראות כשם אם יראו עשבי' בשום מקום וילכו שם ושאיפת הרוח פירש בפ' פרא למוד מדבר שם אמר על הפרא שאיפת רוח בלא סמיכה אל אחר והנה סמך אותם אל התנים נראה כי עקר השאיפה היא בתנים וכן הוסיף המתרגם שם ואמר כירודא ובאמרו שאפו רוח ר"ל כי לא היה להם הנאה בעמדם על השפי' אלא שאיפת הרוח: כלו עיניהם. בראותם כי אין עשב כאילו כלו עיניהם מרוב הביטם למרחוק ולא ראו עשב וזה היה בעונש עונותיהם בישוב ובמדבר ושאר הגוים היה להם שובע וזה היה להם בעמים לאות לקבל עונש עונותיהם מאת האל כמו שאמר והיו בך לאות ולמופת: (ז) אם עונינו ענו בנו. אמר הנביא בראותו בנבואה הרעה שיהיה אומר לאל וכולל עצמו בכלל ישראל ואע"פ שהוא לא היה בו עון אמר אם עונינו ענו בנו ה' עשה למען שמך וכן אמר משה רבינו וסלחת לעונינו ולחטאתנו ונחלתנו. אמר אם עונינו ענו בנו העידו בנו כי בחיות מניעת הגש' בארצנו ולא בארצות הגוים הם העידו בנו כי עליהם אנו לוקי' ואף על פי כן עשה למען שמך הנקרא עלינו: כי רבו משובותינו לך חטאנו. אמת כי הדין עליך להענישנו כי רבו משובותינו שמרדנו בך בכמה דברים בעבוד אלהים אחרים ובהרבות החמס ובשמוע לנביאי השקר ולא לנביאי האמת לפיכך אמר כי רבו ואעפ"כ עשה למען שמך הנקרא עלינו שאנו נקראים עם ה': עונינו. חסר י' הרבי': (ח) מקוה ישראל. כי אע"פ שסרו מדרכיך לך הם מקוים ובכל דור ודור אתה מקוה ישראל ואתה מושיעו בעת צרה אע"פ שהצרה תבא להם בעונם אתה תושיע' ותרחם עליהם גם כן עתה בזמן הזה תושיעם ורחם עליהם ולא יכלו ברעב: למה תהיה כגר בארץ. במקומות רבים דברה תורה בענין הבורא

מנחת שי

(ה) היה דשא. דכסמוך מכלול שקל פעל ועיין מ"ש במלכים א' י"ו וצ"ע ממניינא דמסורת: (ז) אם עונינו ענו בנו. כתב רד"ק חסר יו"ד הרבים וגם המכלול יופי העתיק דבריו וכן מצאתי במקרא ישנה מהדפוס אבל בכל אחר ספרים שלפני מלא וכן מסור עליו לית ומלא:

מצודת דוד

הפיל אשר בשדה כשילדה הולד עוזבה אותו והלכה לה כי לא היה לה דשא למאכלה ולזה הלכה מולדה לבקש מרעה באחר אחרת: (ו) עמדו על שפים. על מקומות הגבוהות לראות משם אולי ימצאו דשא: שאפו רוח. על כי לדפו לבקש מרעה שאפו את האויר כי כן דרך הכלים מהרס: כתנים. מנע התנים היא לשאוף הרבה את האויר: כלו עיניהם. המלפה לדבר ואינו משיגו קרוי כליון עינים בלשון המקרא: (ז) אם עונינו. ובעבור הצרה הזאת התפלל הנביא ואמר אם עונינו העידו בנו לקטרג עלינו: עשה למען שמך. עשה עמנו לדקה למען שמך לבל יחולל בעמים כי פן יאמרו זהו מבלתי יכולת ה' להושיע לעמו: כי רבו. כי באמת מרדנו הרבה וחטאנו לך ואין אנו ראוים לתשועה לכן עשה למען שמך: (ח) מקוה ישראל. אתה תקותם של ישראל כי לך יקוו ואתה הוא המושיעם בעת בוא

מצודת ציון

ונפלתי כך אכר ולמדו (לקמן נ"א): (ו) ופראים. הוא חמור הבר: שפים. מקומות גבוהים: שאפו. ענין המשיכה אל בית הבליעה וכן בתאוות נפשה שאפה רוח (לעיל ב'): רוח. האויר: כתנים. מין נחש: (ז) ענו. העידו כמו לא תענה (שמות כ'): משובותינו. ענין מרד כמו שובבה המה הזה (לעיל ח'): (ח) מקוה. מלשון תקוה:

that You rule over all and that we are Your people and the flock of Your pasture, and it is not fitting that You give Your victorious name to the idols. And the Midrash Aggadah explains: for the sake of Your name that is inherent in our name.—[*Rashi*]

I.e., our name, Israel, meaning the prince of God. The source of *Rashi*'s Midrash is obscure. Perhaps, *Rashi* refers to *Yerushalmi Taanith* 2:6. That source is, however, based on Joshua 7:9. See Commentary Digest ad loc.

8. **hope**—Heb. מִקְוֵה.—[*Rashi*]

Although they have turned away from Your ways, they hope to You, and in every generation, You are the

and abandoned, for there was no grass. 6. And wild donkeys stood by the rivulets, they gasped for air like jackals, their eyes failed for there is no herbage. 7. If our iniquities have testified against us, O Lord, do for Your name's sake, for our backslidings have increased; we have sinned to You. 8. O hope of Israel, his Savior at time of trouble, why should you be like a stranger

offspring, to hunt for pastureland for herself.—[*Rashi*]

Even the hind of the field, known to have compassion on her fawns, has abandoned them because of lack of pasture, and has gone to refresh herself.—[*Redak*]

for there was no grass—When the land is grassy and full of herbs, the hind gives birth in a grassy spot since she does not wish to leave her offspring, but when the grass is dry, and there is no herbage, she gives birth here and leaves her offspring to search for forage.—[*Kara*]

6. **by the rivulets**—Heb. שְׁפָיִם, *rivulets of water* (*riveyres in O.F.*).—[*Rashi*]

Redak explains it as 'high places.' The wild donkeys stand there to overlook the entire surrounding area for grass, and then they go to obtain it.

they gasped for air like jackals—This has been explained above (2:24). The wild donkey ascends to the top of the hill to seek food, but derives only the pleasure of breathing the fresh air.—[*Redak*]

Mezudath David explains that they gasp for air because they are out of breath from running all around the area, searching for food.

their eyes failed—When they saw that there was no grass, it was as though their eyes failed from exerting them by looking all around the area for grass. This famine was a punishment for their sins both in settled areas and in the desert. Since all other peoples had sufficient food, it was obviously a punishment for their sins.—[*Redak*]

7. **have testified against us**—Heb. עָנוּ.—[*Rashi*]

When the prophet perceived the impending trouble through his prophecy, he prays to God for Israel's sake and includes himself with them. Although he did not sin, he says, "If our sins have testified against us, O Lord, do for Your name's sake." Moses, too, prayed in this manner, when he said, "And you shall forgive our iniquity and our sin and take us for Your heritage" (Exodus 34:9). Since rain is scarce only in our country and not in any other country, it is as though our iniquities are testifying against us that we are suffering because of them. Nevertheless, do for Your name's sake, for Your name is called upon us.—[*Redak*]

do for Your name's sake—*Do what You will do with us for the sake of the great name that has spread about You*

בָּאָרֶץ וּכְאֹרֵחַ נָטָה לָלוּן: ט לָמָּה תִהְיֶה
כְּאִישׁ נִדְהָם כְּגִבּוֹר לֹא־יוּכַל לְהוֹשִׁיעַ
וְאַתָּה בְקִרְבֵּנוּ יְהוָה וְשִׁמְךָ עָלֵינוּ
נִקְרָא אַל־תַּנִּחֵנוּ: י כֹּה־אָמַר יְהוָה
לָעָם הַזֶּה כֵּן אָהֲבוּ לָנוּעַ רַגְלֵיהֶם לֹא
חָשָׂכוּ וַיהוָה לֹא רָצָם עַתָּה יִזְכֹּר עֲוֺנָם
ויפקד

ת"א נדהם. סוטה לט:

תרגום

יֵיחוּל רוּגְזָךְ עֲלָנָא וַאֲנַחְנָא כְּתוֹתָבִין בְּאַרְעָא וּכְעָדֵי אוֹרְחָא דִסְטָא לְמִבָּתָא: ט לְמָה יֵיחוּל רוּגְזָךְ עֲלָנָא וַאֲנַחְנָא מְטַלְטְלִין וּשְׁבִיקִין וְאַתְּ גִבַּר יָכִיל לְמִפְרַק וְאַתְּ שְׁכִינְתָּךְ בֵּינָנָא יְיָ וּשְׁמָךְ עֲלָנָא אִתְקְרֵי לָא תִשְׁבְּקִינָנָא: י כִּדְנַן אֲמַר יְיָ לְעַמָּא הָדֵין כְּמָא דִרְחִימוּ כֵּן אִתְפְּרַע מִנְהוֹן לְאַגְלָוּתְהוֹן מֵאֲרַע בֵּית שְׁכִנְתִּי וּכְמָה דַהֲווֹ מְעָרְבִין לְפוּלְחַן טַעֲוָתָא וּמִבֵּית מַקְדְּשִׁי רַגְלֵיהוֹן לָא

מהר"י קרא

האדמה: וכאורח נטה ללון. שם ואינו חושש מה רעה תהיה בעיר: (ט) למה תהיה כאיש נדהם. כאיש שמניח את מקומו ונד ממקום למקום: כגבור לא יוכל להושיע. למה אתה אינך מראה את גבורתך על האומות כשם שהראית לשעבר ותחריש על מה שהם עושים לנו כביכול כגבור זה שאינו יכול להושיע: ואתה בקרבנו ה' ושמך עלינו נקרא אל תניחנו. פתרונו ח"ו שיהיו שני המדות הללו שאמרתי נוהגות בך שמה שאמרתי שאתה כאיש נדהם חס ושלום אינו כן אלא ואתה בקרבנו ה'. ומה שדימיתיך לגבור שלא יוכל להושיע אינו כן אלא שמך מעולם עלינו נקרא [ואתה בקרבנו ה'] שאתה גבור ורב להושיע את ישראל ביום צרתם וכשם שהושיעם לשעבר גם עכשיו אל תניחני. למדנו שמתפלל הנביא על שתי גזירות על הרעב שבא לעולם ועל האומות שמצירין לישראל. והקב"ה משיבו על שתיהן. על שהתפלל על הגלות משיבו: (י) כה אמר ה' לעם הזה כן אהבו לנוע. מה אתה קובל על הגלות אם הם גורמים לעצמם גלות בעונם ואני מעיד בהם יום השכם ושלות שיגלו בעונם. והם: רגליהם לא חשכו. מלחשוא. ומה אני יכול [לעשות] להם אם הם גולים הרי הזהרתים והם לא שבו

רש"י

(ט) נדהם. (דקרו"ך בלע"ז) מושך ידו מן המלחמה וי"א (רקרואנ"ך בלע"ז): ושמך עלינו נקרא. לפיכך אין כבודך בכך: הניחנו. פי' כמו תעזבנו: (י) כן אהבו לנוע. כן כמה שגזרתי עליהם גולה אהבו שם

רד"ק

כל' בני אדם ויחסה אותו בראות ובשמע ובריח וביד וברגל כדברי בני אדם והכל דרך משל להבין בני אדם ובכל מקום רחקו אונקלוס מתרגם התורה ויונתן בן עוזיאל מתרגם ספרי הנביאים רחוק מעל הבורא יחסי התארים וענין הפסוק גם כן ואשר אחריו הסב יונתן הדבר הנאמר על האל על ישראל ראה להרחק מעליו יתברך אפי' דרך דמיון ותרגם כן סבר ישראל וגו' כבעמוד: (ט) למה תהיה כאיש נדהם. למה יחול רוגזך עלנא וגו' כבעמוד. ופשט הפסוקים כן הוא למה תהיה כגר בארץ כי מי שהוא גר בארץ ואינו כאזרחי הארץ וכתושביה אינו חושש בענין הארץ מה יהיה בה כ"א הוא בה היום לא יהיה בה למחר וכל שכן האורח שנטה בעיר ללון בה לבד כי הוא עובר אורח שאינו חושש בטובתה וברעתה ואתה דומה להם בענין הזה בהסתירך פניך מהארץ ולא תחוש לצרתה ולך הארץ ואנחנו גרים בה ותושבים עמך או אתה דומה בענין הזה כאיש נדהם ונבהל לא ידע מה לעשות או כגבור אמר כגבור כי בידו התשועה ויש עת שלא יוכל להושיע בגבורתו: ואתה בקרבנו ה'. ואיך תוכל להעלים עיניך מצרותינו: ושמך עלינו נקרא. כי אנחנו נקראים על שמך עם ה' לפיכך אל תניחנו. ובדרש שמך משותף בשמינו ישראל. נדהם פירושו לפי מקומו נבהל. וא"א ז"ל כתב כי מפרש אותו מן הערבי למי שהוא מכוסה לב מחלי מדהום: (י) כה אמר ה'. כן אהבו לנוע. כמו שאהבו הם לנוע כן אעשה עמהם כי הם הולכי' למצרי' ולאשור לבקש מהם עזר מאויביה' ולא בטחו בי ורגליהם לא חשכו מלכת אע"פ שהיו מוכיחים אותם הנביאים כמו שאמר להם ועתה מה לך לדרך מצרים לשתות מי שיחור ומה לך לדרך אשור לשתות מי נהר ואף על פי כן לא מנעו רגליהם מלכת וכיון שאהבו לנוע אני אניעם

מצודת ציון

וכאורח. הולך דרך: (ט) נדהם. ענינו כמו נבהל ואין לו דומה: הנחנו. מלשון הנחה ועזיבה: (י) לנוע. מלשון נע ונד: חשכו. ענין מניעה כמו ולא חשכת (בראשית כ"ב): רצם. מלשון רצוי:

מצודת דוד

לזה למה עתה תהיה כגר בארץ שאינו חושש בטובת הארץ כי כמו כן אינך חושש על רעבון הארץ: נטה ללון. הנוטה ללון במלון שאינו חושש בטובתה וכאלו הדבר כמ"ש: (ט) כאיש נדהם. כאיש נבהל שאינו חושש בשום דבר בעבור הבהלה אשר החזיקתהו: כגבור לא יוכל להושיע. דרך הגבור מאמד ומשער כחו עד כמה הוא וכאשר יבין כי הדבר אשר הדבקתהו הוא רב מכחו ולא יוכל להושיע אז מושך ידו ולא יעשה עוד גבורות וכאומר וכי אתה מאלה הוא כן: ואתה. הלא אתה שוכן בקרבנו ושמך נקרא עלינו כי אנו נקראים עם ה' ולכן אל תעזבנו לבל יחולל שמך כי יאמרו הגוים מבלי יכולת העלים עין מעמו: (י) לעם הזה. על טעם הזה: כן אהבו לנוע. כמו שהם נעים עתה מפני הרעב נבקש מאכל בארצות אחרות כן אהבו מאז להיות נעים ולא חשכו רגליהם מללכת פעם למצרים פעם

Your anger fall upon us, when we are wandering and forsaken, and You are mighty, able to save...? The simple explanation, however, is as mentioned above.—[*Redak*]

and Your name is called upon us—*Therefore, by doing this, it is no longer honor for You.*—[*Rashi*]

We are called by Your name, the people of the Lord, therefore, do not forsake us. According to the *derash*, Your name is inherent in our name, Israel (*Yerushalmi Taanith* 2:6).—[*Redak*]

forsake us—Heb. תַּנִּחֵנוּ. *Its explanation is like* תַּעַזְבֵנוּ, *forsake us.*—[*Rashi*]

10. **So have they loved to wander**—*So, just as I have decreed upon them exile* (*to Egypt and Babylon*

in the land, and like a wayfarer who turns aside to lodge?
9. Why should You be like a man overcome, like a mighty
man, unable to save? For You are in our midst, O Lord, and
Your name is called upon us; forsake us not. 10. So says the
Lord to this people: So have they loved to wander, they have
not kept their feet back; therefore, the Lord did not accept
them; now He will remember their iniquity

hope of Israel, and You are his Savior in time of trouble. Although the trouble is a result of their sins, You save them and are compassionate to them. Now too, at this time, save them and have compassion on them and do not let them perish from hunger.—[*Redak*]

like a stranger in the land—who is not concerned with the evil that will befall the land.—[*Kara, Mezudath David*]

and like a wayfarer who turns aside to lodge—who is unconcerned with the evil that will befall the city.—[*Kara, Mezudath David*]

The wayfarer is even less concerned than the stranger, since he is here today and not tomorrow. You are like them in this respect when You hide Your face from the land and do not concern Yourself with the misfortunes befalling it. Yet, in reality, the land is Yours, and we are the strangers who have become inhabitants with You.—[*Redak*]

9. **overcome**—(décrû in O.F.) diminished, waned, *who withdraws his hand from the battle, and some say* (*recroyant in O.F.*), tiring out, resigned.—[*Rashi*]

Redak renders: stupified. His father: One whose heart is clogged from illness, after the Arabic cognate.

Rabbi Joseph Kara interprets it as a wanderer, who leaves his home to wander from place to place.

like a mighty man, unable to save—Like a mighty man, who can usually save in battle, but who is sometimes unable to do so. In this case, You are like a stupified man, or a mighty man, who cannot save us.—[*Redak*]

Why do You not display Your might to the nations as You have done in the past? You remain silent to all they are doing to us as though You were a mighty man who cannot save.—[*Kara*]

In many instances, Scripture speaks of God anthropomorphically, ascribing to Him vision, hearing, smell, hands, and feet. In all these places, Onkelos, the translator of the Torah, and Jonathan, the translator of the Prophets, paraphrase in a manner to avoid anthropomorphism. Here, too, *Jonathan* paraphrases these two verses as referring to Israel rather than to the Deity: Why should Your anger fall upon us, when we are but like strangers in the land and like a wayfarer who turns aside to lodge? Why should

וְיִפְקֹד חַטֹּאתָם׃ יא וַיֹּאמֶר יְהוָה אֵלַי
אַל־תִּתְפַּלֵּל בְּעַד־הָעָם הַזֶּה לְטוֹבָה׃
יב כִּי יָצֻמוּ אֵינֶנִּי שֹׁמֵעַ אֶל־רִנָּתָם וְכִי
יַעֲלוּ עֹלָה וּמִנְחָה אֵינֶנִּי רֹצָם כִּי בַּחֶרֶב
וּבָרָעָב וּבַדֶּבֶר אָנֹכִי מְכַלֶּה אוֹתָם׃
יג וָאֹמַר אֲהָהּ ׀ אֲדֹנָי יְהוִה הִנֵּה הַנְּבִאִים
אֹמְרִים לָהֶם לֹא־תִרְאוּ חֶרֶב וְרָעָב לֹא־
יִהְיֶה לָכֶם כִּי־שְׁלוֹם אֱמֶת אֶתֵּן לָכֶם
בַּמָּקוֹם הַזֶּה׃ יד וַיֹּאמֶר יְהוָה אֵלַי שֶׁקֶר
הַנְּבִאִים נִבְּאִים בִּשְׁמִי לֹא שְׁלַחְתִּים

מַנְעוּ וּקְדָם יְיָ לָא רַעֲוָא
בְּהוֹן כְּעַן יִסְעַר עֲלֵיהוֹן
חוֹבֵיהוֹן וְיִתְפְּרַע
שְׁנְיָתְהוֹן׃ יא וַאֲמַר יְיָ
לִי לָא תְצַלֵּי עַל עַמָּא
הָדֵין לְטָבָא׃ יב אֲרֵי
יְצוּמוּן לָא רַעֲוָא קֳדָמַי
לְקַבָּלָא צְלוֹתְהוֹן וַאֲרֵי
יִסְקוּן עֲלָתָא וּמִנְחָתָא
לָא רַעֲוָא קֳדָמַי בְּהוֹן
בְּחַרְבָּא וּבְכַפְנָא
וּבְמוֹתָא אֲנָא מְשֵׁיצֵי
יַתְהוֹן׃ יג וַאֲמָרִית קַבֵּל
בָּעוּתִי יְיָ אֱלֹהִים הָא
נְבִיֵּי שִׁקְרָא אָמְרִין לְהוֹן
לָא תֶחֱזוֹן דְּקַטְלִין
בְּחַרְבָּא וְכַפְנָא לָא יְהֵי
לְכוֹן אֲרֵי שְׁלָם דִּקְשׁוֹט
אֶתֵּן לְכוֹן בְּאַתְרָא הָדֵין׃
יד וַאֲמַר יְיָ לִי שִׁקְרָא

מהר"י קרא

מדרכיתם ועל שהתפללת עליהם על שני בצרות. בבקשה ממך: (יא) אל תתפלל בעד העם הזה לטובה: (יב) כי יצומו אינני שומע

רד"ק

ואגלם בין העמים ואם תאמר מה תשובה היתה זאת לדברי ירמיה כי הוא היה מתפלל על הרעב. נאמר כי אע"פ שהיה מניעת גשמים אם היו יכולין לצאת לארצות הגוים להביא תבואה לא היה הרעב כל כך גדול אבל האויבים היו באים עליהם בכל יום ולא היו יכולים לצאת לפיכך היה רעב חזק לפיכך השיב לו האל על שלום האויבים בהם ויגלו אותם ובין כך הרעב והחרב עליהם לפיכך אמר עתה יזכור עונם כלומר עתה קודם הגלות יזכור עונם ברעב ויפקוד חטאתם בחרב: (יא) ויאמר ה'. לטובה. לפי שהתפלל על מקצתם לרעה והם רצו להמיתו ואמר אראה נקמתך בהם ואמר התיקם כצאן לטבחה והקדיש' ליום הרגה לפיכך אמר לו לטובה אל תתפלל עליהם: (יב) כי יצומו. כשיקראו צום ויתענו ויתפללו אינני שומע אל רנתם פי' אל צעקתם כמו קומי רני בלילה ואמר אל רנתם והוא לא הזכיר תפלה וצעקה אלא הצום לפי שאין צום בלא תפלה וצעקה: רצם. ירצה אותם כלומר עולותם ומנחתם לא יהיו לרצון לפני: (יג) ואמר. מה יוכל ישראל לעשות אם הנביאים מפתים אותם ואומר' להם לא תראו חרב ורעב: שלום אמת. שלום של קיימא: (יד) ויאמר ה'. חזון שקר. כי לא ראת

מנחת שי

(יג) הנה הנבאים. בספרים מוגהים חסר יו"ד קדמאה ומלא יו"ד בתראה וכן כולם שבפרשה ויש חילופים אחרים בספרים ולא נביא אני ולא בן נביא: (יד) שקר הנבאים. כן כתיב: ואלול. ואליל קרי: ותרמות. ותרמית קרי: מתנבאים לכם. במקצת ספרים כתוב להם וברוב דפוסים ישנים וספרים כתובי

מצודת דוד

לאסור לבקש מהם עון'. וכאומר לכן יענשו גם עתה: לא רצם. אינו מרוצה להם והנה עתה יזכור את עונם וישלם הגמול: (יא) לטובה. להסיר עמהם: (יב) כי יצומו. אף אם בעלמם יצומו לא אשמע אל תפלתם אשר יתפללו ביום הצום ואף אם יעלו עולה ומנחה אינני מרוצה להם כל עוד שאוחזים במעשיהם: כי בחרב. אלא אכלה אותם בחרב וגו': (יג) ואומר אהה. אמרתי אוי לי מדוע יכלו הלא אין להם אשם כי הנה נביאי השקר מטעים אותם ואומרים להם לא תראו חרב וגו' ולזה חושבים שמעשיהם מרוצים לה' ומהראוי להביא העונש על הנביאים ההם לבד: שלום אמת. שלום מתמיד ומתקיים: במקום הזה. כי לא תגלו ממנו: (יד) שקר וגו'. ר"ל הלא יש להם לדעת אשר המה מתנבאים בשקר כי מעולם לא שלחתים ולא צויתי אותם שום לואת אף לא דברתי אליהם דבר מבלי שליחות וא"כ אין בידם לתת שום אות ומופת ובמה מחזיקים אותם לנביאים:

מצודת ציון

ויפקוד. ענין זכרון: (יב) יצומו. ענין תענית: רנתם. ענין תפלה: (יג) אהה. ענינו כמו הוי: (יד) חזון. מראה החלום וכן

burnt offering or a meal offering, I will not accept them.—[*Mezudath David*]

Redak notes that there is no fast without prayer. Therefore, He mentions their prayer without previously mentioning that they will pray.

13. **And I said**—What can Israel do if the prophets mislead them and tell them that they will see neither sword nor famine?—[*Redak*]

They believe that their deeds are acceptable to God. It is, therefore, fitting that only the prophets receive the punishment, not the people.—[*Mezudath David*]

a true peace—I.e. a lasting peace.—[*Redak, Mezudath David*]

14. **are prophesying lies**—They should have known that they are prophesying lies, since I never sent them, neither did I give them any

and visit their sins [upon them]. 11. And the Lord said to me:
Do not pray for this people for good. 12. If they fast, I will not
hearken to their prayer, and if they offer up a burnt offering or
a meal offering, I do not accept them, but I will utterly destroy
them with the sword and with famine and with pestilence.
13. And I said, "Ah, O Lord God, behold the prophets say to
them, 'You will see no sword, neither will you have a famine, I
will give you a true peace in this place. 14. And the Lord said
to me: The prophets are prophesying lies in My name; I did not
send them

—Warsaw edition), *they loved it there to go into exile to worship distant idols.*—[*Rashi*] Mss. yield: *they loved to go into exile.* Warsaw edition reads: *to worship their distant idols.*

The intention is that God will exile them just as they loved to wander, according to *Rashi,* to worship foreign deities, and, according to *Redak,* to enlist aid from Egypt or Assyria. The connection between the prophet's prayer to save the people from the drought and God's reply that they will be exiled is obscure. The probable meaning is that the famine would not have been so severe had they been able to leave the country and purchase foodstuffs from their neighbors. Since the enemies were coming every day, however, it was impossible to leave. This situation intensified the famine. Therefore, God replied to him concerning the enemies' rule over them, that they would exile them, and meanwhile they would be plagued by the famine and the sword. He, therefore, says: Now He will remember their iniquity. I.e., now, before the exile, God will remember their iniquity with the famine, and visit upon them their sins with the sword.—[*Redak*]

Abarbanel objects to this explanation as not being relevant. He explains that, since they loved to wander to Egypt and Assyria for aid, they will be punished with famine. The matter of the remembrance and the visitation is explained in the following verses, where God forbids the prophet to pray for that generation.

11. **Do not pray for this people for good**—Since he had prayed for some of them for evil for they had planned to kill him, and he beseeched God, '(11:20) Let me see Your vengeance against them,' and '(12:3) Draw them out like sheep to the slaughter, and prepare them for the day of slaughter,' God specifies, 'Do not pray for this people for good,' implying that he might pray for evil to befall them.—[*Redak*]

12. **If they fast**—Even if they themselves fast, I will not hearken to the prayer they offer up on their fastday, and even if they offer up a

וְלֹא צִוִּיתִים וְלֹא דִבַּרְתִּי אֲלֵיהֶם חֲזוֹן
שֶׁקֶר וְקֶסֶם וֶאֱלוּל וְתַרְמוּת לִבָּם הֵמָּה
מִתְנַבְּאִים לָכֶם׃ טו לָכֵן כֹּה־אָמַר
יְהוָה עַל־הַנְּבִאִים הַנִּבְּאִים בִּשְׁמִי
וַאֲנִי לֹא־שְׁלַחְתִּים וְהֵמָּה אֹמְרִים
חֶרֶב וְרָעָב לֹא יִהְיֶה בָּאָרֶץ הַזֹּאת
בַּחֶרֶב וּבָרָעָב יִתַּמּוּ הַנְּבִאִים הָהֵמָּה׃
טז וְהָעָם אֲשֶׁר־הֵמָּה נִבְּאִים לָהֶם יִהְיוּ
מֻשְׁלָכִים בְּחֻצוֹת יְרוּשָׁלַ͏ִם מִפְּנֵי ׀
הָרָעָב וְהַחֶרֶב וְאֵין מְקַבֵּר לָהֵמָּה
הֵמָּה נְשֵׁיהֶם וּבְנֵיהֶם וּבְנֹתֵיהֶם

תרגום

אָמְרִין נְבִיֵי שִׁקְרָא דְמִתְנַבַּן בִּשְׁמִי לָא שְׁלַחְתִּינוּן וְלָא פַקֵדְתִּינוּן וְלָא מַלֵלִית עִמְהוֹן נְבוּאַת שְׁקַר וְאוּלְפַן וְכַדְבִין וּרְשַׁע לִבְּהוֹן אִינוּן מִתְנַבַּן לְכוֹן׃ טו בְּכֵן כִּדְנַן אֲמַר יְיָ עַל נְבִיֵי שִׁקְרָא דְמִתְנַבַּן בִּשְׁמִי וַאֲנָא לָא שְׁלַחְתִּינוּן וְאִינוּן אָמְרִין חַרְבָּא וְכַפְנָא לָא יְהֵי בְּאַרְעָא הָדָא בְּחַרְבָּא וּבְכַפְנָא יְסוּפוּן נְבִיֵי שִׁקְרָא הָאִינוּן׃ טז וְעַמָא דְאִינוּן מִתְנַבַּן לְהוֹן יְהוֹן מִטַרְפִין רְמַן בְּשׁוּקֵי יְרוּשְׁלֵם מִן קֳדָם כַּפְנָא וְחַרְבָּא וְלֵית דִקְבַר לְהוֹן אִינוּן נְשֵׁיהוֹן בְּנֵיהוֹן וּבְנָתֵיהוֹן ואשפוך

רש"י

אל רנתם וכי יעלו עולה ומנחה אינני רוצם כי בחרב וברעב ובדבר אנכי מכלה אותם: (יד) וקסם ואליל. אליל לשון אין כמו רופאי אליל כולכם שפתרונו לשון אל ואין:

מהר"י קרא

להיות גולים לעבוד עכו"ם רחוקות: (יד) ואליל. לשון אל דבר שאינו:

ואליל קרי ותרמית קרי כך נמצא בספרים מדויקים

מנחת שי

יד שאלו לידי כתוב לכם וכן תרגמו מתנבאין לכון גם החכם לוחאנו כתב שכן עיקר: (טו) על הנבאים. כן כתיב: הנבאים ההמה. כן כתיב:

רד"ק

זו בנבואה והם אומרים כי בנבואה ראו אותה: וקסם ואליל ותרמית לבם. קסם כתב החכם הגדול רמב"ם ז"ל כי יש אנשי' שישפע אליהם הכח השכלי בכח המדמה עד שידברו עתידות ויחלמו חלומות צודקות ומזה הכת היו נביאי הבעל ומפני זה היו מאמינים בהם ויקרא זה הענין קסם ויקרא בעליו קוסם ר"ם כי חוזה בכוכבי' יקרא קוסם: ואלול ותרמות. כתוב בוי"ו וקרי בי' והענין אחד ואליל הוא דבר שאינו וזה שהם אומרים חרב ורעב לא יהיה זהו דבר שאינו כי באמת יהיה הרעב והחרב: תרמית לבם. מרמה חושבים בלבם כיון שחושבים אותנו שאני צודקי' בדברינו כמו שנסו אותנו בקצת העתידות נאמר להם שלא יפחדו מדברי ירמיה כי אנחנו ראינו בנבואה כי לא ראינו חרב ורעב וגיפה להם מעשיה' כדי שנהיה נכבדי' בעיניהם ונאהבי' להם וזהו תרמית לבם שהם חושבים לרמות העם בדבריהם: מתנבאים לכם. אמר לכם וכלל הנביאי' עמהם כמו שהוא היה כולל עצמו בכלל ישראל כאומר כי רבו משובותינו וגו': (טו) לכן. יתמו הנביאים ההמה. ר"ל ראשונה ילקו הם בחרב וברעב בעבור שהם החטיאו את ישראל: (טז) והעם. אע"פ שהיו מטעי' אותם נביאי השקר היה להם לבחון בין נביאי האמת לנביאי השקר כי נביא האמת מעמיד

מצודת ציון

הבין בכל חזון (דניאל א'): וקסם. זה ראיית הכוכבים: ואליל. ענינו דבר שאין בו ממש וכן רופאי אליל (איוב י"ג): ותרמית. ענין ערמה כמו כי שקר תרמיתם (תהלים קי"ט): (טו) יתמו. יכלו מן העולם:

מצודת דוד

חזון שקר. ר"ל א"כ היה לכם לדעת שהם מתנבאים או כחזון שקר מה שראו בחלום הלילה מדמיונות כוזבות או כמעשה הקסם מה שראו בכוכבים או מה ששמעו מן החרטומים שהם דבר שאין בהם ממש כלל או בערמת לבם ידברו שקרים: (טו) לכן וגו'. הוא"ל והנביאים מתנבאים מאחת מאלה: (טז) מפני הרעב. אשר ימותו מפני הרעב והחרב: ואין מקבר. כי ירבו מאד ולא

15. **Therefore . . . Those prophets shall perish by the sword and the famine**—They shall be the first to perish by the sword and the famine since they led the people to sin.—[*Redak*]

16. **And the people**—Although they were misled by the false prophets, they should have been able to distinguish between true prophets and false ones since the true prophet bases his words on Mosaic Law, whereas the false prophets praise idol worship, which is a direct negation of Mosaic Law. Although they sometimes make correct predictions, the people should have attributed this to psychic powers rather than to prophecy, since their words are in support of idolatry, a negation of the Torah. Even if they show signs and wonders, they are, nevertheless,

neither did I command them, nor did I speak to them. A false vision, divination, a thing of nought, and the deceit of their heart they prophesy to you. 15. Therefore, so says the Lord concerning the prophets who prophesy in My name although I have not sent them, and they say, "Sword and famine shall not be in this land." Those prophets shall perish by the sword and the famine. 16. And the people to which they prophesy, shall be cast in the streets of Jerusalem because of the famine and the sword, and no one will bury them, they, their wives, their sons, and their daughters,

command, nor did I speak to them even without a mission. Hence, they have no sign or wonder to verify their prophecy. Why then should they be thought of as prophets?—[*Mezudath David*]

A false vision—For they did not see it through prophecy, yet they claim that they did.—[*Redak*]

divination—Maimonides writes that there are some people whose intellect combines with their imagination, and they are able to predict the future and dream true dreams. The prophets of Baal were of this group. Therefore, many people believed in them. This talent is called divination, and those who practice it are called diviners. [Perhaps in today's language, psychics, or clairvoyants]. Others define this as star-gazers.—[*Redak*]

a thing of nought—Heb. אֱלִיל, *an expression of* אַל, *not, a thing which is not.*—[*Rashi*]

Their prediction of peace, saying that there will be no sword or famine, is a thing of nought, for there will, indeed, be sword and famine.—[*Redak*]

the deceit of their heart—Since the people believe us, since we have predicted some future events, let us tell them not to fear Jeremiah's prophecies for we have seen prophetic visions and we did not see any sword or famine. Let us, therefore, praise their deeds so that we will gain their esteem and love. This is meant by 'the deceit of their heart,' for they intended to deceive the people.—[*Redak*]

Malbim classifies these false prophets into four categories. One group prophesied by 'the false vision,' the product of their imagination. The second group by 'divination' through star-gazing or lots. The third group by 'the thing of nought,' the reply of the teraphim, or oracles, which are of no value. Others misled the people by 'the deceit of their heart,' (i.e. by) intentional lies, prophecies fabricated by the prophet.

to you—God includes the true prophets with the people, just as Jeremiah included himself with the people when he said, "Our backslidings have increased."—[*Redak*]

ושפכתי עליהם את-רעתם: יז ואמרת
אליהם את-הדבר הזה תרדנה עיני
דמעה לילה ויומם ואל-תדמינה כי
שבר גדול נשברה בתולת בת-עמי
מכה נחלה מאד: יח אם-יצאתי
השדה והנה חללי-חרב ואם באתי
העיר והנה תחלואי רעב כי-גם-נביא
גם-כהן סחרו אל-ארץ ולא ידעו:

ואשפוך עליהון ית
בישתהון: יז ותימר
להון ית פתגמא הדין
ישגבן עיני דמען לילי
ויֹמם ולא ישתקן ארי
תברא רבא אתברת
מלכות כנישתא דעמי
מחא מסרעא להדא:
יח אם נפקית לחקלא
והא קטילי חרבא ואם
עלית לקרתא והא
מסרעי כפנא ארי אף
ספר אף כהן אתפניאו
לסחורתהון על די מה
בארעא ולא בקרו:
המרטש

רש"י

(יז) נחלה מאד. לשון חולי: (יח) סחרו. סבבו לבקש הגלה: אל ארץ ולא ידעו. אל ארץ אחרת ולא היו יודעין בה עד הנה:

מהר"י קרא

(יח) סחרו אל ארץ ולא ידעו. פת' כלומר שיהיו גולין אל ארץ

רד"ק

אותם על תורת משה ונביאי השקר מיפי' להם ע"ז שהוא בטול התורה ואף על פי שהם צודקי' בקצת דבריה' בעתידות היה לכם להזיק זה בקס' לא בנבואה כיון שדבריהם לבטול הורה והיא עבו"ם שאפי' יעשו אותות ומופתים אמרה תורה יומת כי דבר סרה וקיום האותות והמופתים אמר הכ' הטעם כי מנסה ה' אלהיכם אתכם: ואין מקבר להמה. זה יהיה עונש עונם מוסף על היסורים והמיתה: נשיהם. כי היו נשמעות לדברי שקר יותר מן האנשי': ובניהם ובנותיהם. הקטנים בעונש אבותיה' כי כן הוא המשפט מאת האל יתברך שהוא אל אמונה ואין עול: (יז) ואמרת. אתה תאמר להם זה הדבר שאתה בוכה ומצטער על שברם שאתה רואה שיבא עליהם בנבואה ותאמר להם שאתה רואה ג"כ חללי חרב מבחוץ ותחלואי הרעב מבפני' וזה להפחיד' אולי ישבר לבם ויכנעו בשמעם את הדברי' האלה: בתולת בת עמי. עד שתגלה היא כמו הבתולה שלא ידעה איש ולא שלט עליה וכן היא דומה לבתולה כלומר שלא שלטו עליה הגוים להגלותה מארצה עד עתה ותהיה נכנעת להם בגלותה כמו הבתולה כשנבעלה: מכה נחלה. מכה קשה בחולי גדול: (יח) אם. תחלואי רעב. שם תואר על משקל ותעלולים יכשלו בם וזכר החולי' מפני הרעב ולא זכר המתים ברעב כי החולי' היו רבים מהמתי': כי גם נביא גם כהן. נביא מנביאי השקר כהן מכהני הלוים שהיו בהם רעים כמו שאמר כי גם אחיך ובית אביך גם המה בגדו בך: סחרו אל ארץ ולא ידעו. סבבו ללכת לגלות אל ארץ אחרת ולא ידעו לא הרגישו בעצמם לך שגלו כי אף על פי שהיה מתנבא על הנביאי' שיתמו בחרב וברעב מהם גלו עם יהויכין כמ"ש שהיו מתנבאים שם בגולה ואמר גם ר"ל גם הם שהם גדולי העם כי גלו עם יהויכין

מנחת שי

(יז) מכה נחלה. כתי"ת כגול לבדו. ברפים: (יח) והנה חללי חרב. הלמ"ד רפוא

מצודת דוד

יספיקו לקברם: הכה. הם יהיו מושלכים ונשיהם וגו': ושפכתי. אשלם להם גמול רעתם: (יז) הדבר הזה. והוא הן תרדנה עיני דמעה מבלי הפסק: כי שבר. רואה אני בנבואה כי שבר גדול וגו': בתולת בת עמי. קראה בתולה כי עוד לא כבשה שום מלך כבתולה שלא באה ברשות הבעל: נחלה מאוד. כאובה ביותר: (יח) והנה חללי חרב. והנה מושלכים חללי חרב: והנה תחלואי רעב. שוכבי' חולים מעקת הרעבון: כי גם נביא. ר"ל וכדין הוא כי עשו הרע

מצודת ציון

יכלו כמו תם הכסף (בראשית מ"ז): (יז) תדמינה. ענין שתיקה והפסק כמו אל דמי לכם (ישעיה ס"ב): בת עמי. עדת עמי: נחלה. מלשון חולי: (יח) חללי. הרוגים: תחלואי. מלשון חולי: סחרו. ענין סבוב ועפ"ז נקרא התגר בשם סוחר כי מסבב אחר הסחורה

around to go into exile although they did not realize that they were going into exile. These were the ones who went into exile with Jeconiah,

and I will pour out upon them their evil. 17. And you shall say
this word to them: May my eyes run down with tears day and
night and not be silent, for the virgin daughter of my people is
broken with a great breach, a very grievous blow. 18. If I go
out to the field, behold the slain of the sword, and if I go into
the city, behold those ill with famine, for even the prophet and
even the priest have gone around to a land [which] they had not
known.

put to death, '(Deut. 13:4) For the Lord your God tests you to know whether you love the Lord your God with all your heart and with all your soul.'—[*Redak*]

their evil—I.e. the recompense for their evil.—[*Mezudath David*]

17. **this word**—I.e. starting from 'May my eyes run with tears.'—[*Mezudath David*]

You tell them this word, that you are weeping and grieving for the breach that you see coming upon them and tell them that you see people slain by the sword lying outside the city, and those dying of hunger lying in the city. Perhaps this will frighten them and bring humility into their hearts.—[*Redak*]

the virgin daughter of my people—Before the exile, she was like a virgin, never possessed by a man and never ruled over by a man. So was Israel likened to a virgin, since, until now, she had not been conquered by any nation to exile her from her land. Now, when she will go in exile, she will be compared to the virgin who has been possessed by a man.—[*Redak*]

very grievous—Heb. נַחְלָה, *an expression of illness* (חֳלִי).—[*Rashi*]

a very grievous blow—A very serious blow accompanied by severe illness.—[*Redak*]

18. **ill with famine**—He does not mention those who died from the famine, for the ill greatly outnumbered the dead.—[*Redak*]

even the prophet—I.e. the false prophets.—[*Redak*] *Jonathan* renders: scribe.

even the priest—These are the Levitic priests, for there were many wicked among them, e.g. those who plotted to assassinate Jeremiah.—[*Redak*]

have gone around—*They have gone around to seek rescue.*—[*Rashi*]

to a land [which] they had not known—*To another land about which they did not know until then.*—[*Rashi*]

Others explain that the prophets and priests truly deserved their punishment since they had gone around all over the land to recite their 'prophecy' although they did not know the word of God, for they prophesied falsely.—[*Mezudath David*]

Others explain that even the most esteemed of the population, the prophets and the priests, went

יט הֲמָאֹס מָאַסְתָּ אֶת־יְהוּדָה אִם־בְּצִיּוֹן
גָּעֲלָה נַפְשֶׁךָ מַדּוּעַ הִכִּיתָנוּ וְאֵין לָנוּ
מַרְפֵּא קַוֵּה לְשָׁלוֹם וְאֵין טוֹב וּלְעֵת
מַרְפֵּא וְהִנֵּה בְעָתָה׃ כ יָדַעְנוּ יְהוָה
רִשְׁעֵנוּ עֲוֺן אֲבוֹתֵינוּ כִּי חָטָאנוּ לָךְ׃
כא אַל־תִּנְאַץ לְמַעַן שִׁמְךָ אַל־תְּנַבֵּל

תרגום

יט הֲמִרְחַק רְחֶקְתָּא יַת
דְּבֵית יְהוּדָה וְאִם יַתְבֵי
צִיּוֹן רַחִיק מֵימְרָךְ מָה
בֵין אַלְקֵיתָנָא וְלֵית לָנָא
אַסָא סַבַּרְנָא לִשְׁלָם
וְלֵית טַב וּלְעִדָּן סְלִיחַת
חוֹבִין וְהָא פוּרְעָנוּת
חַטָאִין׃ כ יְדַעְנָא יְיָ
חוֹבָנָא וְחוֹבֵי אֲבָהָתָנָא
אֲרֵי חַבְנָא קֳדָמָךְ׃
כא לָא תְרַחֲקִינָנָא בְּדִיל
שְׁמָךְ לָא תְנַבֵּל אֲתַר

מהר"י קרא

אחרת: (יט) המאס מאסת את יהודה. בראות הנביא תוכחות הללו שהקב"ה גוזר על ישראל אמר לפניו רבונו של עולם המאום מאסת את יהודה בנוגע שבעולם אדם הכועס על עבדו ומואס בו מכדי מכה שיש בה מרפא. אבל אתה לאחר שאי אפשר דבר זה שלא תמאס ביהודה ולא בציון הגאל נפשך [שכן] כתבת לנו בתורתך ואף גם זאת בהיותם בארץ אויביהם וגו' מדוע הכיתנו ואין לנו מרפא: (כא) אל תנבל. ירושלים

רש"י

(יט) אם בציון געלה נפשך. על מנת שלא לשוב עליה כי אם דעתך לשוב מדוע הכיתה באין מרפא: (כא) למען

מנחת שי

לגדו פרשים ועיין מ"ש לעיל סימן ח': (יט) קוה לשלום וגו'. למעלה בפרשה אסוף אסיפם כתוב מקצת פסוק זה ויש ביניהם שינוי מעט הראשון עת וזה ולעת

רד"ק

החרש והמסגר באמרו סחרו לפי שההולך דרך רחוקה אי אפשר שלא יסוב הדרכים כי אין כל הדרך דרך ישרה וי"ת ארי אף ספר וגו' כבעמוד: (יט) המאוס מאסת. חזר הנביא להתפלל עוד ואף על פי שאמר לו האל אל תתפלל בעד העם הזה על מקצת העם שב להתפלל: אם בציון. אם ביושבי ציון כתרגומו כי לא דבר עד עתה על החרבן אלא על צרת היושבי' בה: הכיתנו. מכת רעב: ואין לנו מרפא. כי אין כמר: קוה לשלום. מקור אם נקוה שלום מהאומות שכנינו ונלך ונשבור בר בארצ': ואין טוב. שום טובה לא יבא לנו משום צד: ולעת מרפא. מצרת הרעב ומצרת האויב: והנה בעתה. והנה אנחנו נבעתי' מצרת שניהם ויונתן תרגם ולעדן סליחת חובין והוא פורענות חטאין ובקצת זה הפסוק הוא כתוב למעלה בפרשה אסף אסיפם ויש ביניהם שנוי מעט הראשון לעת וזה ולעת הראשון מרפה בה"א וזה מרפא באל"ף: (כ) ידענו. ידענו רשענו וידענו ג"כ עון אבותינו: כי חטאנו לך. אנחנו והם ותדין עליך לפקוד עלינו עונם ועונינו כי אחזנו מעשיהם הרעים בידינו וזכר בפסוק המרדים והוא שאמר רשענו וזכר הזדונות והוא שאמר עון וזכר ג"כ השגגות והוא שאמר כי חטאנו לך: (כא) אל תנאץ. אף על פי כן למען שמך עשה ואל תנאץ: אל תנבל כסא כבודך. אל תפילהו לארץ כי כסא כבודך הוא ירושלים אל תפילהו ותנבלהו בהיות יושביה נעזבים אין פונה אליהם: זכור. כלומר זכור ברית אבות ואותו הברית אל תפרידהו אתנו וכן תרגם יונתן יעול דוכרן קיים אבהתנא קדמך

מצודת ציון

לקטוסה: (יט) געלה. ענין מאוס כמו וגעלה נפשי אתכם (ויקרא כ"ו): בעתה. חרדה ורתת: (כא) תנאץ. ענין בזיון וכן נאצו כל תוכחתי (משלי א'): תנבל. ענין הורדה והשפלה כמו ונבל נובל

מצודת דוד

כי גם נביא השקר וכהן הבעל סבבו מעיר אל עיר לנבאות לעם ולא ידעו מה מדבר ה' כי נבאו בשקר: (יט) המאוס. אמר הנביא וכי מאסת את יהודה וכי תעבה נפשך בציון מדוע הכיתנו ואין למלא רפואה על המכה: קוה. כאשר קוינו לשלום ולא הובא שמה טובים וכאשר נקוה לעת רפואה והנה בא עוד חרדה: (כ) ידענו. מכירים אנו בהרשענו אנחנו וגם מכירים אנו בעון אבותינו כי כלנו חטאנו לך כמוהם כמוהם: (כא) אל תנאץ. עכ"ז אל תבזה אותנו למען שמך לבל יחולל בעמים כאומרם מקוצר יד עוז עמו: אל תנבל.

19. Have You indeed rejected Judah? Has Your soul despised
Zion? Why have You smitten us and we have no cure? We hope
for peace, but there is no good, and for a time of healing, but
behold, there is terror. 20. We know, O Lord, our wickedness,
the iniquity of our forefathers, for we have sinned to You.
21. Do not condemn us for Your name's sake, do not disgrace

the craftsmen and the gate keepers. They will go around on the tortuous roads.—[*Redak*]

19. **Have You indeed rejected Judah**—The prophet resumes his prayer to God; although God admonished him not to pray for the people, he prays for a part of them. —[*Redak*]

or has Your soul despised Zion—*with the intention of never returning, for, if You have in mind to return, why have You smitten us without a cure?* —[*Rashi*]

This refers to the inhabitants of Zion who were dying of hunger, as *Jonathan* renders: or has Your word rejected the inhabitants of Zion? Now Scripture discusses the troubles of the inhabitants, not the destruction of the city.—[*Redak*]

You smitten us—with a blow of famine.—[*Redak*]

and we have no cure—I.e., we have no rain.—[*Redak*]

We hope for peace—If we hope for peace with our neighbors, and we go to them to purchase food.—[*Redak*]

but there is no good—We derive no benefit in any way.—[*Redak*]

and for a time of healing—I.e. for a time of rescue from the distress of the famine and the enemy.—[*Redak*]

and behold, there is terror—We are terrified by both. *Jonathan* renders: and for a time of forgiveness of sins, and behold, retribution for sins.—[*Redak*]

Rabbi Joseph Kara explains: When the prophet sees the retributions God has decreed upon Israel, he petitions God, "O Lord of the world, have You indeed despised Judah? It is customary in the world that if one is incensed against his slave and rejects him, he strikes him a blow that can be healed. But with You, since it is impossible that You have rejected us or that Your soul has despised us, for the Torah states: 'And, in spite of this, when they were in the land of their enemies, I have neither rejected them nor despised them . . .' (Lev. 26:44). Why then have You smitten us and we have no cure? See *Yalkut Shimoni* from *Pesikta Rabbathi*, 32:3.

20. **We know**—We know our wickedness, and we know also the iniquity of our forefathers.—[*Redak*]

for we have sinned—We have sinned as well as our forefathers, and Divine justice requires that You visit their iniquities upon us since we continue to sin as they did. He mentions all types of sins: wickedness, meaning rebellious transgressions, iniquities, meaning intentional transgressions, and also sin, meaning unintentional transgressions.—[*Redak*]

21. **for Your name's sake**—Al-

בֵּית כּוּרְסֵי יְקָרָךְ יֵיעוּל
דוּכְרָן קְיָם אֲבָהָתָנָא
קֳדָמָךְ לָא תְשַׁנֵּי קְיָמָךְ
עִמָּנָא׃ כב הָא לֵית צְרוֹךְ
בְּטַעֲוַת פָּלְחֵי כוֹכְבַיָּא
לְאַחָתָא מִטְרָא וְאִם
שְׁמַיָּא לָא יִתְּנוּן רְסִיסִין
אֱלָהֵין עַל מֵימְרָךְ הֲלָא
אַתְּ הוּא יְיָ אֱלָהָנָא
וּנְסַבַּר קֳדָמָךְ אֲרֵי אַתְּ
עֲבַדְתְּ יָת כָּל אִלֵּין׃
א וַאֲמַר יְיָ לִי אִם יְקוּם
מֹשֶׁה וּשְׁמוּאֵל לְמִבְעֵי
מִן קֳדָמַי לָא רַעֲוָא קֳדָמַי
בְּעַמָּא הָדֵין שַׁלַּח מֵאַרַע

כִּסֵּא כְבוֹדֶךָ זְכֹר אַל־תָּפֵר בְּרִיתְךָ
אִתָּנוּ׃
כב הֲיֵשׁ בְּהַבְלֵי הַגּוֹיִם מַגְשִׁמִים
וְאִם־הַשָּׁמַיִם יִתְּנוּ רְבִבִים הֲלֹא אַתָּה־
הוּא יְהוָה אֱלֹהֵינוּ וּנְקַוֶּה־לָּךְ כִּי־אַתָּה
עָשִׂיתָ אֶת־כָּל־אֵלֶּה׃
טו א וַיֹּאמֶר יְהוָה
אֵלַי אִם־יַעֲמֹד מֹשֶׁה וּשְׁמוּאֵל לְפָנַי
אֵין נַפְשִׁי אֶל־הָעָם הַזֶּה שַׁלַּח מֵעַל־
פני

ת"א היש בהבלי. עקדה שער פ:

רש"י

שמך. שנקראת רחום: כסא כבודך. בית המקדש. ומדרש אגדה ישראל החקוקים בכסא כבודך: (כב) ואם השמים יתנו רביבים. מאיליהם אם לא על פיך בתמיה כל תמיהה הכפולה הראשונה בה"א והשנייה באם כגון המחנים אם במבצרים (במדבר י"ג) הטובה היא אם רעה (שם) המאום מאסת אם בציון געלה נפשך (כאן) אף כאן היש בהבלי העכו"ם ואם השמים:

טו (א) משה ושמואל. שניהם נזקקו לבקש רחמים על ישראל ומתחלה החזירום למוטב ואחר כך התפללו

מהר"י קרא

שנקרא כסא כבוד. שנאמר כסא כבוד מרום מראשון: זכור אל תפר. זכור לאבותינו לאברהם ליצחק וליעקב אל תפר מאתנו בריתך שכרת עמהם: (כב) היש בהבלי הגוים מגשימים. הם הפסילים הבל המה מעשה תעתועים: ואם השמים יתנו. על ידם רביבים. הם טיפת מטר: הלא אתה הוא ה' אלהינו. המגשים והנותן רביבים כבר עשית את כל אלה. וכל זה מתפלל על דברי הבצרות שהזכיר למעלה:

טו (א) אם יעמוד משה ושמואל לפני אין נפשי אל העם הזה. פתרונו תפלה זו שאתה מתפלל על ישראל כענין זה שאתה שואל ומתפלל עליהם לא יתפללו עליהם אפילו משה ושמואל. אפילו אם יעמדו משה ושמואל לפני להתפלל בעד העם הזה כענין זה שאתה מתפלל עליהם לא הייתי נענה להם אתה מניח אותם והולכין וחוטאין ואתה חוזר להתפלל עליהם ולא היה לך ללמוד ממשה רבך שכשחטאו ישראל בעגל אתה

רד"ק

לא תשני קימך עמנא: (כב) היש. למי נצעק על המטר אלא לך: בהבלי הגוים מגשימים. פי' נותנין גשם: ואם השמים יתנו רביבים. אפילו השמים והוא הרקיע שנותנים המטר כי השמים הם נותנין המטר זולתך זה אינו שהרי אתה עוצר' כשתרצה שלא יתנו מטר א"כ אין נתינת המטר ברשות' וברצונ' וכן אתה פותחן כשתרצה הלא אתה הוא ה' אלהינו הנותן מטר לפיכך עלינו שנקוה לך שתתן מטר: כי אתה עשית את כל אלה. מניעת הגשמים אתה עשית אותה שעצרת השמים שלא יתנו מטר והארץ שלא תתן את יבולה וזהו שאמר את כל אלה וכן אמר בנבואת זכריה כי זרע השלום הגפן תתן פריה והארץ תתן את יבולה והשמים יתנו טלם והנחלתי את שארית העם הזה את כל אלה הנה אמר את כל אלה על מניעת השמי' שלא יתנו מטר והארץ שלא תתן את יבולה: (א) ויאמר ה' אלי. למה תרבה בתפלה לפני כי אם יעמוד משה ושמואל לפני בתפלה שהיו גדולים ממך אם יעמדו הם לפני אין נפשי אל העם הזה. נפשי ר"ל רצוני כמו אל תתנני בנפש צרי וזכר משה ושמואל שהיו לוים ונביאי' והגדול שבנביאים אחר משה רבינו היה שמואל וכן אמר משה ואהרן בכהניו ושמואל

מנחת שי

הראשון מרפה בה"א וזה מרפה באל"ף: (כב) יתנו רביבים. י"ס מלא דמלא ומסרה עליהם רביבים ב' א' חסר וא' מלא וסימנהון וימנעו רבבים ירמיה ג' חסר יו"ד קדמאה. היש בהבלי הגוים מגשימים. והוכן של מדוייקים שניהם חסרים ולמסר עליהם ב' חסר וכן נמסר במסרה גדולה שלנו:

מצודת דוד

אל תוריד כסא כבודך להיות מחולל בפי העמים וכפל הדבר במ"ש: זכור. הברית שכרת עמנו להיות לך לעם ואל תפר היום את הברית: (כב) היש. כלומר אל מי נזעק בעבור הגשם וכי יש מי בהבלי העכו"ם הם הפסילים: מגשימים. מורידים גשמים: ואם השמים. וכי מערכת השמים נותנים רביבים מעצמם מבלי גזירת המקום: הלא אתה תה'. הם מערכות השמים וא"כ אתה הוא המוריד את הגשם ולכן נקוה לך לבדך שאתה הורידו: את כל אלה. הם מערכות השמים וא"כ לא אשר תחפוץ תעשה ולא ימרו את פיך: טו (א) אם יעמוד. ר"ל בתפלה ובקשה: משה ושמואל. משה או שמואל ר"ל אף שהיתה תפלתם מקובלת לפני מ"מ אם

מצודת ציון

ישועתו (דברים ל"ב): תפר. ענין בטול: (כב) בהבלי. מלשון הבל והם הפסילים: מגשימים. מלשון גשם: רביבים. כן נקרא הגשם הדק כמו וכרביבים עלי עשב (שם): ונקוה. מלשון תקוה: טו (א) נפשי. ענין רצון כמו אם יש את נפשכם (בראשית כ"ג):

פירוש ט"ס

forth its produce. That is the intention of 'all of these.' The identical expression is found in the prophecy of Zechariah (8:12), used in this context.—[*Redak*]

1. **Moses and Samuel**—*Both were needed to beg mercy for Israel, but first they induced them to repent, and afterwards they prayed on their behalf, but they had no idea of turning away My wrath until they had induced them to repent. Moses—'*(Exodus 32:27) *Let each man put his sword*... (v. 20) *and he scattered it on the surface of the water etc.' And afterwards,* '(v. 30) *I will ascend to*

the throne of Your glory. Remember, do not break Your covenant with us. 22. Are there among the vanities of the nations those who give rain? Does the heaven give raindrops? Is it not You, O Lord our God? Now let us hope for You, for You have done all these.

15

1. And the Lord said to me: If Moses and Samuel stand before Me, I have no desire for this people, send [them] away from

though we are guilty, do not condemn us for Your name's sake.—[*Redak*]

the throne of Your glory—*The Temple. And* according to *Midrash Aggadah, Israel who is engraved on the throne of Your glory.*—[*Rashi* from obscure Midrashic source]

Redak and *Kara* see Jerusalem as the throne of God's glory. Jeremiah beseeches God not to overturn Jerusalem, the throne of His glory. Do not disgrace it or cast it down, for when its inhabitants are forsaken, no one turns to them.—[*Redak*]

Remember—I.e., remember the covenant of the Patriarchs and do not break it with us. *Jonathan* renders: May the remembrance of the covenant of the Patriarchs come before You. Do not break Your covenant with us.—[*Redak*]

22. **Are there among the vanities of the nations those who give rain?**—To whom shall we cry for rain except You? Are there among the vanities of the nations those who give rain?—[*Redak*]

This refers to the pagan deities, which are vanity.—[*Kara, Mezudoth*]

Does the heaven give raindrops?—*by itself, except by Your command? This is the interrogative form. In every double question, the first* question *is preceded by a 'he' and the second one with* אִם, *like* '(Num. 13:19) *Are they in open cities* (הַבְּמַחֲנִים) *or in fortresses* (אִם בְּמִבְצָרִים)?' '(Ibid. 13:19) *It is good* (הֲטוֹבָה) *or bad* (אִם רָעָה)?' '(verse 19) *Have You indeed rejected* (הֲמָאֹס) *Judah, or has Your soul despised* (אִם . . . גָּעֲלָה) *Zion?' Here, too, 'are there among the vanities of the nations those who give rain? Does the heaven . . .?'*—[*Rashi*]

Even the heavens that give rain, do they give it without You? That is not so, for You hold back the rain when You wish that they should not give it. Hence, the giving of the rain is in Your power and dependent upon Your will, and You open the heavens when You wish. 'Is it not You, O Lord our God? We will, therefore hope for You.'—[*Redak*]

for You have done all these—Holding back the rain You have done, for You have shut up the heavens so that they should not give rain and the earth should not give

פני ויצאו׃ ב והיה כי־יאמרו אליך
אנה נצא ואמרת אליהם כה־אמר
יהוה אשר למות למות ואשר לחרב
לחרב ואשר לרעב לרעב ואשר
לשבי לשבי׃ ג ופקדתי עליהם ארבע
משפחות נאם־יהוה את־החרב
להרג ואת־הכלבים לסחב ואת־עוף
השמים ואת־בהמת הארץ לאכל
ולהשחית

תרגום

בית שכנתי ויגלון׃
ב ויהי ארי יימרון לך
לאן נגלי ותימר להון
כדנן אמר יי דלמותא
למותא ודלחרבא
לחרבא ודלכפנא
לכפנא ודי לשביא
לשביא׃ ג ואסער עליהון
ארבע פורענון בישן
אמר יי ית דקטלין
בחרבא למקטל וית
כלביא לגררא וית עופא
דשמיא וית בעירא
דארעא למיכל ולחבלא׃
ואתנינון

ת״א הנה גלה . כ״כ ח׃

מהר״י קרא

[מוצא] בתחילה שאמר להם שימו איש חרבו על ירכו והרגו איש את אחיו וגו׳ וכתיב ויקח את העגל אשר עשו וישרף משהחזירן למוטב מה כתיב שם ויהי ממחרת ויאמר משה אל העם אתם חטאתם חטאה גדולה ועתה אעלה אל ה׳ אולי אכפרה בעד חטאתכם . ואף שמואל לא תפס אותה מידה שאתה תופס שכשבאו ישראל ואמרו לו התפלל בעד עבדיך אל ה׳ אלהינו ולא נמות כי יספנו על כל חטאתינו רעה . מה שמואל משיבן ויאמר שמואל אל העם אל תיראו אתם עשיתם את הרעה הזאת אך אל תסורו מאחרי ה׳ ועבדתם את ה׳ בכל לבבכם ולא תתורו אחרי התוהו ומשתעבדו את ה׳ בכל לבבכם ותסירו את אלהי הנכר מקרבכם גם אנכי חלילה לי מחטוא לה׳ מחדול להתפלל בעדכם . ולפי שבתחילה החזירו אותם למוטב ואחר כך באו להתפלל עליהם שמעתי להם אבל אם יעמדו להתפלל עליהם עד שלא חזרו בתשובה לא הייתי שומע להם גם לך אינני שומע כשאתה מתפלל עליהם בעוד

רש״י

עליהם ולא עלה בלבם להשיב אפי עד שהחזירום למוטב • משה. שימו איש חרבו וגו׳ (שמות ל״ב) ויזר על פני המים וגו׳ (שם) ואחר כך אעלה אל ה׳ אולי אכפר׳. שמואל במצפ׳ ויסירו בני ישראל את הבעלים (שמואל א׳ ז׳) ואח״כ קבצו את כל ישראל המצפתה ואתפלל עליכם (שם) אתה אינך יכול להשיבם אלי לכך אל תתפלל עליהם : נפשי . רצוני : (ב) אשר למות וגו׳. כל המאוחר בפ׳ קשה מחבירו חרב קשה ממות מיתת חרב מנוולת ומיתה על מטתו אינה מנוולת וכה״א (תהלים קט״ז) יקר בעיני ה׳ המותה לחסידיו רעב קשה מחרב. שזה מצטער וזה אינו מצטער וכה״א טובי׳ היו חללי חרב מחללי רעב שבי כולהו איתנהו בגוה : (ג) ופקדתי. לשון מינוי ופקידות : לסחוב. לגרר וכן

רד״ק

בקוראי שמו ונאמר כי נאמן שמואל לנביא לה׳ ונאמר ולא הפיל מכל דבריו ארצה ; שלח מעל פני ויצאו . שלחם מעל פני ויצאו ואמר הצווי כנגד ירמיהו כאילו אמר אם בידך לשלחם טוב שתשלחם משתתפלל עליהם ; (ב) והיה כי יאמרו. אשר למות . אמרו רז״ל כל המאוחר בפסוק זה קשה מחברו חרב קשה ממות איבעית אימא סברא האי קא מנוול והאי לא מנוול ואיבעית אימא קרא יקר בעיני ה׳ המותה לחסידיו רעב קשה מחרב סברא האי קא מצטער והאי לא מצטער קרא טובי׳ היו חללי חרב מחללי רעב שבי קשה מכולם כלהו איתנהו ביה : (ג) ופקדתי . משפחות . על דרך השאלה כלומר ארבע מיני פורעניות ; לסחוב . כי דרך הכלבים לגרר הנבלה באכלם אותה :

מצודת ציון

שלח . ענין שילוח וגרושין כמו הן ישלח (לעיל ג׳) : (ב) אנה. להיכן וכן אנה אעלה (שמואל ב׳ ב׳) : (ג) ופקדתי. ענין מינוי ונזכרות : משפחות . אמר כן בדרך השאלה : לסחוב . ענין גרירה

מצודת דוד

מי מהם יתפלל בעד העם הזה אין רצוני עליהם להיות מרוצה להם: שלח. אמור להם בנבואה שאמרתי לגרשם מארצי ויצאו מפניה ; (ב) אנה נצא . להיכן נלך ולתכלית מה : אשר למות . מי שראוי למות בפועו במיתת דבר יומן למיתה : ואשר לחרב וגו׳ . כל אחד יעונש כדבר הראוי לו : (ג) ופקדתי . אמנה עליהם : ארבעה משפחות . ר״ל ארבעה מיני עונשין : לסחוב . דרך הכלבים לגרר

before My face and let them go forth. 2. And it shall be if they
say to you, "Where shall we go?" you shall say to them, "So
said the Lord: Such as are for death, to death, and such as are
for the sword, to the sword, and such as are for famine, to
famine, and such as are for captivity, to captivity." 3. And I
will appoint over them four families, says the Lord, the sword
to slay and the dogs to drag and the fowl of the heaven and the
beasts of the earth to devour

the Lord, perhaps I will atone.' Samuel in Mizpah— '(I Samuel 7:4, 5) *And the children of Israel removed the Baalim,' and afterwards, '"Gather all Israel to Mizpah, and I shall pray to the Lord on your behalf* (sic).''' *But you cannot bring them back to Me, therefore do not pray for them.*—[*Rashi*]

2. **And it shall be if they say to you**—after they have left their land.—[*Abarbanel*]

"Where shall we go?"—What will be the use of our going forth?—[*Abarbanel, Mezudath David*]

Such as are for death, to death—*Each* calamity *mentioned later in this verse is harsher than the one preceding it. The sword is harsher than death. Death by the sword is defacing, whereas death in bed is not defacing. And so he says:* '(Psalms 116:15) *Precious in the eyes of the Lord is the death of His Saints.' Famine is harsher than the sword, for this one is agonizing whereas the other is not agonizing. And so Scripture states:* '(Lam. 4:9) *Better are those who die from the sword than those who die from famine.' Captivity*—all sorts of death are in it.—[*Rashi, Redak* from *Baba Bathra* 8b]

Death, in this case, means death from pestilence.—[*Mezudath David*]

3. **And I will appoint**—Heb. וּפָקַדְתִּי, *an expression of appointment and designation.*—[*Rashi*]

four families—This is a borrowed term, meaning four types of retribution.—[*Redak, Mezudath David*]

to drag—Heb. לִסְחֹב, *to drag. Cf.* (infra. 49:20) '*If* the young of the sheep *do not drag them* (יִסְחָבוּם).'—[*Rashi*]

וּלְהַשְׁחִית׃ ד וּנְתַתִּים לְזַוְעָה לְכֹל
מַמְלְכוֹת הָאָרֶץ בִּגְלַל מְנַשֶּׁה בֶן־
יְחִזְקִיָּהוּ מֶלֶךְ יְהוּדָה עַל אֲשֶׁר־עָשָׂה
בִּירוּשָׁלִָם׃ ה כִּי מִי־יַחְמֹל עָלַיִךְ
יְרוּשָׁלִַם וּמִי יָנוּד לָךְ וּמִי יָסוּר לִשְׁאֹל
לְשָׁלֹם לָךְ׃ ו אַתְּ נָטַשְׁתְּ אֹתִי נְאֻם־יְהוָה
אָחוֹר תֵּלֵכִי וָאַט אֶת־יָדִי עָלַיִךְ
וָאַשְׁחִיתֵךְ נִלְאֵיתִי הִנָּחֵם׃ ז וָאֶזְרֵם
בְּמִזְרֶה בְּשַׁעֲרֵי הָאָרֶץ שִׁכַּלְתִּי

ד ואתנינון לזיע לכל
מלכות ארעא על דלא
תבו כמנשה בר יחזקיה
מלכא שבטא דבית
יהודה על דאסגי
למעבד בירושלם׃
ה ארי מן יחוס עלך
ירושלם ומן ידוי עלך
ומן יזור למשאל לשלמא
לך׃ ו את שבקת פולחני
אמר יי לאחורא
אסתחרת וארים ית
מחת גבורתי עלך
ואחבלינך על דהוית
יכלא למיתב ולא תבת׃
ז ובמא דדכן במדיריא
כן אבדר ית עמי בקרוי

ת"א לזעוה. סנהדרין ק"ב:

לזעות קרי

רש"י

אם לא יסחבום (לקמן מ"ט): (ד) **לזועה.** מגזרת לא קם ולא זע (אסתר ה') וכמוהו גאות מגזרת גאה אחד (ישעיה ס"ו): **לכל ממלכות הארץ.** כל השומע רעה הבאה עליהם יזוע: (ה) **ינוד.** יקונן: **ומי יסור.** אליך לנטות מדרכו אליך לשאול לך לשלום: (ו) **נלאתי הנחם.** כמה פעמים חשבתי להשחית ונחמתי על הרעה עתה נלאיתי הנחם. הנחם (דפורפנשי"ר בלע"ז): (ז) **במזרה.** נפה שקורין

מהר"י קרא

שאינך משיבם מדרכם הרעה: (ד) **לזועה.** מגזרת לא קם ולא זע כלומר זעים וחרדים מפני ממלכות הארצות: (ה) **כי מי** יחמול עליך ירושלים. מי מן הממלכות שיחמול עליך: **ומי. הם:** ינוד לך. כשאסתיר פני ממך: ומי. הם יפנה **יסור לשאול:** (ו) **את נטשת אותי.** סדר המקראות כולן נשמעין לשעבר וכן הילוכן את נטשת אותי על כן אחור תלכי: (ז) **ואזרם במזרה.**

רד"ק

(ד) **ונתתים לזועה.** כתיב וקרי לזעוה והענין אחד אלא שהם שני שרשים והם ענין התנועה: **בגלל מנשה.** כי הוא הנהיג את יהודה במעשים רעים ודם נקי שפך עד שמלא ירושלים חללים כמו שכתוב ות"י על דלא תבו כמנשה בר חזקיהו: (ה) **כי מי. ינוד לך.** כמו לנוד לו ולנחמו ענין נחמת האבל וספור הצרות עמו ובא בזה הלשון לפי שהמנחמין נדין ממקומן זה מפה וזה מפה לנחם האבל אמר מי יחמול ומי ינוד לך ומי יסור לשאול לשלום לך כי את גרמת חרבנך שנטשת אותי לפיכך תלכי אחור ולא לפני: (ו) **את. נלאתי הנחם.** כמה פעמים נחמתי על הרעה אשר דברתי לעשות להם ולא עשיתי נלאתי על זה לא אוכל עוד להנחם אלא אפרע מהם: (ז) **ואזרם.** כמו שזורים התבואה במזרה כן אזרם בשערי הארץ כלומר בגלותם אפיצם בכל ערי הארץ ואמר בשערי במקום בערי כי דרך השער נכנסין ויוצאין בעיר

מנחת שי

טו (ד) לזועה. לזעוה קרי: (ו) נלאיתי. י"ס נלאתי חסר יו"ד:

מצודת דוד

סכילות ממקום למקום: **לאכול ולהשחית.** סוף לאכול הנבילות והכותה להשחית ברמיסת הרגל: (ד) **לזועה לכל ממלכות.** כלם יחרדו ויזועו פלא יקרה להם כמקרם: **בגלל מנשה.** ר"ל בעבור שאחזו במעשה מנשה וגו': **על אשר וגו'.** בעבור אשר עשה מעשיו בירושלים בפרסום לכן למדו ממנו ואחזו בהם: (ה) **כי מי יחמול.** ר"ל אין מי יחמול עליך ואין מי ינודד בראש עליך כדרך המנחמים לנחמך כבוא הצרה עליך ואין מי יסור לנטות מדרכו לבוא אליך לשאול בשלומך: (ו) **את נטשת אותי.** על כי עזבת אותי ותלכי לאחור לפרוש ממני לכן אטה את ידי עליך להכות בך ולהשחיתך: **נלאיתי הנחם.** הנה רבות פעמים גזרתי עליך השחתה ואח"ז נחמתי ועתה נלאתי להנחם על הרעה: (ז) **ואזרם.** אפזרם בכל ערי הארץ כהמפזר תבואה במזרה שאין כלם נופלים במקום אחד: **שכלתי.**

מצודת ציון

ומשיכה כמו סחוב והשלך (לקמן כ"ב): (ד) **לזועה.** ענין רתת וחרדה כמו והיה רק זועה (ישעיה כ"ח): **בגלל.** בעבור כמו בגלל הדבר הזה (דברים ט"ו): (ה) **יחמול.** מלשון חמלה ורחמים: **ינוד.** מלשון נדידה: (ו) **נטשת.** עזבת: **ואט.** מלשון נטיה: **נלאיתי.** ענין עייפות ויגיעה כמו ונלאו מצרים (שמות ז'): **הנחם.**

and who will turn aside—*to you, to turn aside from his road to you, to ask of your welfare?—[Rashi]*

Since you brought all this upon yourself, no one will console you, for you have forsaken Me. Therefore, you shall go backwards, and not forwards.—[*Redak*]

6. **You have forsaken Me**—Since you have forsaken Me and have gone backwards to move away from Me, I will stretch out My hand over you to strike you and destroy you.—[*Mezudath David*]

I am weary of repenting—*Many times I planned to destroy but repented of the evil. Now I am weary of repenting.* Heb. הִנָּחֵם *(Dporpnser in O.F.).—[Rashi]*

7. **with a sieve**—*A sieve called* (*van*

and to destroy. 4. And I will make them a horror to all the kingdom of the earth because of Manasseh the son of Hezekiah, king of Judah, for all that he did in Jerusalem. 5. For, who will have pity on you, O Jerusalem, and who will lament over you, and who will turn aside to ask of your welfare? 6. You have forsaken Me, says the Lord. You shall go backwards, and I have stretched out My hand over you and destroyed you. I am weary of repenting. 7. And I winnowed them with a sieve in the cities of the earth; I bereft,

Dogs customarily drag a carcass when they eat it.—[*Redak, Mezudath David*]

4. **a horror**—Heb. לְזַעֲוָה, *from the same root as* '(Esther 5:9) *And he neither rose nor quaked* (זָע).' *Similarly,* גַּאֲוָה, *pride, from the root* '(Isa. 16:6) *Have become very proud* (גֵּא).'—[*Rashi*]

to all the kingdoms of the earth—*Anyone who hears the evil that has befallen you will shudder.*—[*Rashi*]

They will fear that the same thing will happen to them.—[*Mezudath David*]

Others explain that Israel will quake before the other kingdoms of the earth.—[*Kara*]

because of Manasseh—He led Judah to commit evil deeds, and he shed innocent blood until he filled Jerusalem with the slain, as in II Kings 21:16. *Jonathan,* however, renders: Since they did not repent as Manasseh son of Hezekiah.—[*Redak*]

The intention is that Manasseh was very wicked. He led the people into idolatry with the intention of changing the face of the Jewish people. Although he repented of his sin of idolatry, he left his impression upon the people, who followed his early practices. They were punished for following Manasseh's sins. Had they repented as he had done, they would have been forgiven. See *Daath Soferim,* also II Kings 21, Commentary Digest.

for all that he did in Jerusalem—Since he instituted idolatry in public, the populace learned to emulate his ways and adhered to them.—[*Mezudath David*] The Rabbis tell us that Manasseh placed an image in the Temple whereas Ahaz had placed one in the attic, but feared rebellion if he would place it in the Temple proper. Also, Ahaz was ashamed to look Isaiah in the face, whereas Manasseh assassinated him. See Commentary Digest II Kings 21.

5. **For, who will have pity on you, O Jerusalem**—Which of the kingdoms will have pity on you?—[*Kara*]

will lament—Heb. יָנוּד.—[*Rashi*] Lit. who will wander for you. This refers to the consolation of the mourners, for people come to their house, each one wandering from his own home to come and console the mourners.—[*Redak*]

אבדתי את־עמי מדרכיהם לוא שבו:
ח עצמו־לי אלמנותו מחול ימים
הבאתי להם על־אם בחור שדד
בצהרים הפלתי עליה פתאם עיר
ובהלות: ט אמללה ילדת השבעה

ארעא תכלית אבדית
ית עמי מאורחתהון לא
תבו: ח סגיאת קדמי
ארמלתהון מחל ימין
איתיתי עליהון על
סיעת עולימיהון באזין
כד בטיהרא איתיתי
עליהון משרין בתקיף
וחבילא קרניהון:
ט צדיאת ארעהון סבלי

ת"א עצמו לי (יבמות טו): ילדת השבעה. גיטין פח זוהר פרשת פקודי:

אלמנותיו קרי — נפחה

מהר"י קרא

כזה שזורה את המוץ במזרה: (ח) עצמו לי אלמנותיו. פתרונו רבו לי אלמנותיו מחול ימים. עצמו מגזירת רב ועצום: הבאתי להם על אם. זו ירושלם. שהיא אם לכל ערי ישראל: בחור. זה נבוכדנצר: שודד בצהרים. שאין אדם יכול להסתיר מפניו. שבפני שודד לילה אדם יכול להטמן מפניו אבל בפני אדם השודד בצהרים אין אדם יכיל להטמן ולהחבא. ודקדקתי בסדר המקראות וכל הענין נשמע לשעבר וכן הליכן. את נטשת אותי נאם ה' אחור תלכי. תנו דעתכם שמיום שנטשתם אותי בימי יהויקים בכל יום ויום את הולכת לאחור ולא לפנים. ואט את ידי עליך ואשחיתך. כענין שנאמר ביהויקים וישלח ה' בו את גדודי כשדים ואת גדודי ארם ואת גדודי מואב ואת גדודי בני עמון וישלחם ביהודה להאבידו: ואזרם במזרה בשערי הארץ. שבימי יהויקים גלו דניאל וחבריו ורבים משרי יהודה: שכלתי אבדתי את עמי. לפי שמדרכיהם לא שבו: עצמו לי אלמנותיו מחול ימים. שמיום שפשעתם בי רבו חלליכם ותרבו אלמנותיכם. והבאתי את יהויקים ואת יהויכין ואת החרש ואת המסגר: הפלתי עליה פתאום עיר. אנשי עיר מלך בבל ובבהלות: (ט) אומללה יולדת חשבעה. פי' אשה שילדת ר בנים אומללה [מהם] שהבנים מתים כלומר ירושלים שהיתה רבת עם ישבה לה בדד מהם לפי שיש מהם שגלו ויש מהם

רש"י

(וו"ן בלע"ז) כזה שהוא זורה שעורין שלא יהיו כלן גולין למקום אחד: (ח) עצמו לי. רבו לפני אלמנותיו: על אם. על ירושלים שהיא עיר ואם בישראל: בצהרים. הכל יהא גלוי לפניו כל גנזי מטמונים: הפלתי עליה פתאום עיר. השכנתי עליהם פתאום גייסות של עיר ובהלות רבות. ויש פותרים עיר לשון שונא כמו ויהי ערך (שמואל א' כ"ח) ופשריה לערך (דניאל ג'): (ט) אמללה יולדת השבעה. שומרון וכנסיה של עשרת שבטים שעמדו מהם ז' משפחות מלכים רשעים כבר אומללה וגלתה: ושאריתם. אלו יהודה וקצת בנימין שנשתיירו בישראל לחרב אתן. אלו הן שבע משפחות ירבעם בן נבט וביתו בעשא וביתו עמרי וביתו יהוא וביתו מנחם וביתו פקח וביתו הושע

מנחת שי

(ח) אלמנותו. אלמנותיו קרי: (ט) בלה שמשה. בא קרי:

רד"ק

וכן אמר לכל באי שער עירו וכת"י בקרוי ארעא וכן תרגם במקומות רבי' בשעריה בקרותא ואמר ואזרם על עשרת חשבטים שגלו וכן שכלתי אבדתי אומר עליהם ואף על פי כן שבט יהודה שראו כל זה מדרכיה' הרעי' לא שבו ואמר שכלתי כי בניו היו: (ח) עצמו לי. יבא זה הלשון בענין הכמות והאיכות ואמר לי ר"ל כי אני מצר עליהם ורבו אלמנותיו בעיני: אלמנותו, כתוב בלא יו"ד וקרי ביו"ד וימצאו רבים כמוהו וזה היה בימי אחז שהרג פקח בן רמליהו ביהודה מאה ועשרים אלף ביום אחד ונשארו הנשים אלמנות: הבאתי להם על אם בחור שודד בצהרי'. על קהלת בחורים הבאתי שודד בצהרי' כלומר כי לא באו בלילה כגנבי' אלא בצהרים ולא הועילה לבחורים גבורתם: אם. ר"ל קהלה או משפחה כמו שנקראת אום ואומה: בחור. על דרך כלל כמו בחורים וכן שש מאות רכב בחור וכן ת"י איתיתי עליהון וגו' כבעמוד: הפלתי עליה פתאום עיר ובהלות. עליה על האם שזכר הפלתי עיר ר"ל חרבן הערים. ובהלות כמו פתאום כמו ויבהילו להביא את המן מהרוהו ללכת פתאום וכאילו אמר הפלתי עליה פתאו' ובהלות עיר והכפל לחזק הענין כמו פתע פתאום. ואדוני אבי ז"ל פירש עיר שונא מן ויהי עריך וי"ת איתיתי עליהון משירין וגו'. כבעמוד: (ט) אמללה יולדת השבעה. יולדת בנים רבים והיא כנסת ישראל ושבעה ענין רבוי במקומות לא חשבון מכוון וכן עד עקרה ילדה שבעה. שבע יפול צדיק וקם. שבע כחטאתיכ':

מצודת ציון

ענין הסוך מחשבה כמו פן ינחם העם (שם י"ג): (ז) ואזרם. ענין פזור כמו ואתכם אזרה בגוים (ויקרא כ"ו): במזרה. הוא הכלי שזורין בו התבואה וכן ברחת ובמזרה (ישעיה ל'): בשערי, בערי וכן באחד שעריך (דברים י"ז): שכלתי. ענין מיתה כמו מחוץ תשכל חרב (שם ל"ב): (ח) עצמו. ענין רבוי כמו בעם עצום (תהלים ל"ה): אם. כן תקרא עיר גדולה אשר הקטנות סביב לה וכן עיר ואם בישראל (ש"ב כ'): בחור. נבחר וגבור: שודד. עושק: הפלתי. ענין השכנה והניח כמו נופלים בעמק (שופטים ז'): עיר. ענין שונא כמו ויהי ערך (ש"א כ"ח): ובהלות. מלשון בהלה ופחד: (ט) אומללה. ענין כריתה כמו אומלל אני (תהלים

מצודת דוד

אף כי שכלתי אותם והאבדתים עכ"ז לא שבו מדרכיהם ולא לקחו מוסר: (ח) עצמו לי. האלמנות שבהם המה מרובים בעיני יותר מחול ימים. ר"ל אין אני עושה בהם כמתנקם להיות הכל נחשב לפני למעט כי אדרבה נחשב לפני להרבה ואין בזה שמחה לפני: הבאתי להם. שלחתי עליהם וחוזר ומפרש על אם ר"ל על ירושלים הבאתי קבוצת בחורים להיות שודד אותם בעת צהרים למען יראה למלא כל גנזי המטמוניות: הפלתי. השכנתי עליה פתאום קבוצת שונאים ועדת עם המבהילות: (ט) אומללה. כבר גלתה שומרון ועשרת השבטים שגדלה שבעה משפחות מלכים רשעים והם ירבעם בן נבט וביתו בעשא וביתו עמרי וביתו יהוא וביתו מנחם וביתו פקח

upon her suddenly the destruction of the cities and hurriedly.

Kara places this passage, commencing with verse 6, as referring to the reign of Jehoiakim. He explains the entire passage in the past tense, as follows:

[6] **You have forsaken me, says the Lord, you have gone backwards—** Think into this matter, that since you have forsaken Me, every day you are going backwards and not forwards.

and I stretched out My hand over

* For Rashi's commentary turn to page 233.

I destroyed My people; they have not returned from their ways.
8. His widows are to Me more numerous than the sand of the
seas; I have brought to them upon the mother a chosen one
who will rob them at midday; I have cast upon her suddenly a
city and terrors. 9. She who bore seven has been cut off,

in French), like one who winnows barley, so that they should not all be exiled to one place.—[*Rashi*]

Just as grain is winnowed with a sieve, so will I winnow them in the cities of the land. I.e., in their exile, I will scatter them throughout all the cities of the earth. The word שַׁעֲרֵי, lit. gates, is used instead of עָרֵי, cities, since people enter and leave a city through its gates. *Jonathan,* too, renders: in the cities of the earth. Scripture states: I winnowed them, in reference to the Ten Tribes. I bereft, I destroyed My people, also refers to that kingdom. Nevertheless, the tribe of Judah, which saw all that, did not return from their evil ways.—[*Redak*]

8. **are to Me more numerous**—*His widows are more to Me.*—[*Rashi*]

I am troubled about them, and they are in My eyes more than the sand of the seas. This refers to the time of Ahaz, when Pekah son of Remaliah slew one hundred twenty thousand Judeans in one day (II Chron. 28:6). All the wives of the soldiers remained widows.—[*Redak*]

Abarbanel quotes a commentator who explains: To Me, His widows are heavier than the sand of the seas. I.e., the distress of the widows of Judah weighs heavily upon Me, even more than the sand of the seas.

upon a mother—*Upon Jerusalem, which is a city and a mother in Israel.*—[*Rashi*] I.e., Jerusalem was a metropolis about which smaller towns were clustered.—[*Mezudath Zion*] See II Sam. 20:19.

Kara explains that Jerusalem was the mother of all the cities of Israel.

a chosen one—Nebuchadnezzar. —[*Kara*]

Redak renders: I have brought to them, upon the congregation of youths, a robber at midday.

at midday—*Everything will be exposed before him, all their hidden treasures.*—[*Rashi*]

They did not come upon them at night like thieves, but at midday, and the youths' might did not avail them.—[*Redak*]

I have cast upon her suddenly a city—*I caused the troops of a city and many terrors to rest upon her. Some interpret* עִיר as 'an enemy.' Cf. '(I Sam. 28:16) And has become [the supporter of] your adversary (עָרֶךָ).' '(Dan. 4:16) And its interpretation to your adversaries (לְעָרָךְ).'—[*Rashi*] [The quotation from Daniel appears in Rashi as Dan. 3. In II Sam. 28:16, it appears in Rashi as Dan. 3:49. Accordingly, the copyist must have had an edition in which Chapter 3 continued through the first sixteen verses of our Chapter 4. In early editions, this verse is 4:19, Chapter 4 commencing three verses before our division. Saadiah Gaon had this division and it was also adopted by the Christians].

Redak renders: I brought about

נָפְחָה נַפְשָׁהּ בָּאָה שִׁמְשָׁהּ בְּעֹד יוֹמָם
בּוֹשָׁה וְחָפֵרָה וּשְׁאֵרִיתָם לַחֶרֶב אֶתֵּן
לִפְנֵי אֹיְבֵיהֶם נְאֻם־יְהוָה׃ י אוֹי־לִי
אִמִּי כִּי יְלִדְתִּנִי אִישׁ רִיב וְאִישׁ מָדוֹן
לְכָל־הָאָרֶץ לֹא־נָשִׁיתִי וְלֹא־נָשׁוּ־בִי
כֻּלֹּה מְקַלְלַונִי׃ יא אָמַר יְהוָה אִם־לֹא

בא קרי ה׳ במקום ואו שרותך

שְׁמָא הֲווֹ לְמִפַּחַת נְפַשׁ
גְּלָא יְקָרְהוֹן בְּחַיֵּיהוֹן וְעַד
דְּאִינוּן קַיְמִין בְּהִיתוּ
וְאִתְכְּנַעוּ וּשְׁאָרְהוֹן
לְחַרְבָּא אֶמְסַר קֳדָם
בַּעֲלֵי דְבָבֵיהוֹן אֲמַר יְיָ׃
י וַי לִי אִמִּי אֲרֵי יְלִדְתִּינִי
לְמֶהֱוֵי גְּבַר דִּין וֶאֱנָשׁ
מַצּוּ לְכָל יָתְבֵי אַרְעָא
לָא רְשֵׁן בִּי וּמָא דַאֲנָא
דְּשֵׁינָא לָא תְּבַע מִנְּהוֹן
כּוּלְּהוֹן מְלַטְטִין לִי׃
יא אֲמַר יְיָ אִם לָא סוֹפֵךְ

רש״י

ויכיהו: נפחה נפשה. לשון דאבה נפשה מתורגמינן ודאבון נפש (דברים כ״ח) ומפחן נפש: בעוד יומם. בלא זמנה מהרו ליפול כך נדרש במסכת גיטין. ובמדרש רבי תנחומא דרשו כלפי ירושלים ומונה שבעה רשעים יהורם יהואש אחז מנשה אמון יהויקים צדקיהו אך יש למנות עוד רחבעם אביה אמציה אחזיה: וחפרה. לשון בושת: (י) אוי לי אמי. ירמיה היה מתאונן על עצמו שהיו שונאין אותו בני עירו על דברי תוכחותיו: ואיש מדון. איש מריבה כמו לא ידון רוחי (בראשית ו׳): לא נשיתי. כמו לא תהיה לו כנושה (שמות כ״ב): כלה מקללוני. איני רב עמהם על עסקי ממון שיש לי עליהם

מהר״י קרא

שנהרגו: נפחה נפשה: כמו מפח נפש: באה שמשה בעוד יומם. כלומר שקעה אורה אפילו בעוד יום: ושאריתם לחרב אתן. זה דורו של צדקיה ולפי ששלח ירמיה לומר להם קשות חללו היה מתאונן על עצמו ואמר אוי לי אמי כי ילדתני איש ריב ואיש מדון לכל הארץ ושמא תאמר נשיתי בהן או הם נשו בי ולכך מריבים עמי לכך נאמר לא נשיתי ולא נשו בי ואעפ״כ: (י) כלו מקללוני. מקללים אותי וכל זה שאני הולך בשליחותך: (יא) אמר ה׳ אם לא שריתיך לטוב. בשבועה אשאירך לטוב:

רד״ק

נפחה נפשה. ענין דאבון כמו מפח נפש: באה שמשה בעוד יומם. על דרך משל מרוב הצרות כמו שאמר גם כן על הצרות חשך השמש בצאתו. באה כתוב בא קרי והשמש ימצא לשון זכר ולשון נקבה: בושה וחפרה. כפל ענין במ״ש: ושאריתם. השארית שלא יכלו בגלות אתן לחרב ויש לפרש ושארית׳ בניה׳ כמו שם ושאר: (י) אוי לי אמי. איש ריב ואיש מדון. כי כלם מריבים עמי ומדון כמו ריב: לא נשיתי ולא נשו בי. לא נשיתי בהם שאהיה תובע הלואתי מהם ויקללוני בעבור זה וגם הם לא נשו בי שיהיו תובעים הלואתם ממני ולא ארצה לתת להם ובעבור זה יקללוני אין שום דבר מכל זה רק ששונאי׳ אותי מפני שאני מוכיח אותם לטובת׳: כלה מקללוני. הורכבה המלה משני שרשים מן קלל ומן קלה כי הם שני ענינים הקללה הוא הפך הברכה והקלון הוא הפך הכבוד וכן אמר הנביא כלה מקללני ומקלני והורכבו שניהם כאחד ואמר במלה אחת שני ענינים לקצר הלשון ולצחותו והומרה ה״א קלה בוי״ו כמנהג התחלפה במקומו ולולי שהחליפוה וקראו למ״ד הפעל בקריאה לא היה נכר במלה ענין קלה: (יא) אמר ה׳. אמר לי האל כשהייתי מתרעם עליהם שסופי יהיה לטוב: אם לא. כענין שבועה כמו אם לא שויתי והומכתי אם לא כאשר דמיתי כן

מנחת שי

(י) מקללוני. במקצת ספרים בלמ״ד בקמץ ועיין דקדוקו במכלול דף ע״ט וכפל רב פעלים בחלק הורים כתב שבמסורת עליו ליה ופתח בס״ף: (יא) שרותך. שריתיך קרי:

מצודת דוד

ויכיהו שופט בן אלה וכיוצא: נפחה נפשה. היה לה דאבון נפש: באה שמשה. שקעה שמשה כשהיה עוד היום גדול ר״ל הושפלה גדולתה במסירות בלא זמנה: בושה וחפרה. והיא יושבת בגולה בבושה ובכלימה: ושאריתם. השארית הנשארה מעדת ישראל הם יהודים ובנימין אתן גם אותם לחרב לפני אויביהם: (י) אוי לי אמי. ירמיה היה מתאונן והסב הדבור מול אמו ואמר אוי לי אמי אשר ילדתני להיות איש ריב ומדון לכולם כי יריבו עמדי על שאני מוכיחם: לא נשיתי. לפעמים מריבים עם המלוה על שהוא נוגש כסף ההלואה ולפעמים מריבים עם הלוה על שאינו משלם ההלואה אבל אני לא הלויתי להם ולא הם הלוו לי ועכ״ז כלם מקללים ומבזים אותי: (יא) אמר ה׳. אמר הנביא ה׳ אמר לי מה אתה חושש על קללתם הריני נשבע אם לא השאיר אותך לטוב כל המקללים אותך ימותו וילכו בשבי ואתה תשאר לטובה: אם לא. הריני נשבע אם לא בעת בא הרעה והצרה אפגיע בו את לב האויב הוא לנבוזראדן להפגיע בך ולהלות פניך לבא עמו לבבל ולא יקחך בשבי ביד חזקה כמ״ש אם

מצודת ציון

ו׳): נפחה נפשה. ענין דאבון נפש וכן ותקותם מפח נפש (איוב י״א): באה. ענין שקיעה כמו כי בא השמש (בראשית כ״ח): וחפרה. ענין כלימה וכן וחפרה הלבנה (ישעיה כ״ד): ושאריתם. מלשון שארית ושיור: (י) מדון. ענין מריבה כמו ישתוק מדון (משלי כ״ו): נשיתי. ענין הלואה כמו לא תהיה לו כנושה (שמות כ״ב): מקללוני. הוא מלשון קללה ומלשון קלון ובזיון: (יא) אם לא. הוא ענין לשון שבועה וגזם ולא אמר והרי הוא כאדם האומר אם לא כן הוא יהיה כזאת וכזאת וכן אם לא בתים רבים (ישעיה ה) ורבים

a man of quarrel and a man of contention—For they all quarrel with me.—[*Redak*]

and a man of contention—Heb. וְאִישׁ מָדוֹן, *a man of quarrel, Cf.* '(Gen. 6:3) *Let My spirit not contend* (יָדוֹן).'—[*Rashi*]

I have not lent—Heb. נָשִׁיתִי, *Cf.* (Exodus 22:24) *You shall not be to him as a creditor* (כְּנֹשֶׁה).'—[*Rashi*]

Sometimes people quarrel with the creditor because he exacts the payment of the loan from them and sometimes they quarrel with the debtor if he is delinquent in his payments. But I did not lend money

her soul grieves, her sun sets when it is still day. She is ashamed and confounded. And her remnant I shall deliver to the sword before their enemies, says the Lord.
10. Woe is to me, my mother, that you bore me, a man of quarrel and a man of contention to the whole land. I have not lent, nor have they lent to me. Yet, they all curse me.
11. Said the Lord: Verily, I will

you and destroyed you—This alludes to '(II Kings 24:2) And the Lord incited against him bands of Chaldeans and bands of Moabites and bands of the children of Ammon, and He incited them against Judah to destroy it.'

9. **her soul grieves**—Heb. נָפְחָה, נַפְשָׁהּ, *an expression of 'her soul grieves.' We translate* '(Deut. 28:65) *And grieving of the soul* (וְדַאֲבוֹן נָפֶשׁ)' *as* וּמַפְּחַן נְפַשׁ.—[*Rashi*]

when it is still day—*Before its time, they hastened to fall. In this manner it is expounded in Tractate Gittin.* [See *Gittin* 88a].—[*Rashi*]

The Rabbis explain that God hastened to exile Judah in order that the exile of Zedekiah should still find the craftsmen and the gate sentries, explained by the Sages as the greatest scholars of the age. The exile of Zedekiah was accelerated in order that the exile of Zedekiah still find the scholars exiled with Jeconiah still alive in Babylon. Had they come later, they would not have had any teachers to teach them the Torah.

And in the Midrash of Rabbi Tanhuma (*Tanhuma Buber, Vayetze* p. 153) *it is expounded as referring to Jerusalem, and he counts seven wicked men: Jehoram, Jehoash, Ahaz, Manasseh, Amon, Jehoiakim, and Zedekiah. But there are yet to count Rehoboam, Abijah, Amaziah, and Ahaziah.*—[*Rashi*] Surprisingly, Zedekiah is listed among the wicked kings. His only wickedness was that 'he did not humble himself before Jeremiah the prophet from the mouth of the Lord' (II Chron. 36:12). The Chronicler continues, '(v. 13) Also he rebelled against King Nebuchadnezzar, who had adjured him by God, and he stiffened his nape and strengthened the temptation of his heart from returning to the Lord God of Israel.'

The reference is to Jeremiah 38, wherein the prophet commanded Zedekiah to surrender to the Chaldeans, and he would be spared, whereas if he would continue to battle against them, the city would be destroyed. Zedekiah was afraid to do so and disobeyed the command of Jeremiah. With this one exception, Zedekiah is considered a righteous king. He was called Shallum because he was perfect in his deeds (*shalem, perfect*) (*Horioth* 11a). A further account of Zedekiah's righteousness appears in II Kings 24:19, Commentary Digest.

10. **Woe is to me, my mother**—*Jeremiah was complaining about himself, that his townsmen hated him because of his castigations.*—[*Rashi*]

שֵׁרוֹתִךָ לְטוֹב אִם־לוֹא ׀ הִפְגַּעְתִּי בְךָ
בְּעֵת רָעָה וּבְעֵת צָרָה אֶת־הָאֹיֵב׃
יב הֲיָרֹעַ בַּרְזֶל ׀ בַּרְזֶל מִצָּפוֹן וּנְחֹשֶׁת׃
יג חֵילְךָ וְאוֹצְרוֹתֶיךָ לָבַז אֶתֵּן לֹא בִמְחִיר
וּבְכָל־חַטֹּאותֶיךָ וּבְכָל־גְּבוּלֶיךָ׃

שריתיך קרי מלא ואו

תרגום

יהא לטב אם לא ייתון
ויבעון מנך בעדן דאיתי
עליהון סנאה ויעיק
להון בעדן דעקא׃
יב מלך דתקיף כברזלא
יסק לסעיר מלך דתקיף
כברזלא וכנחשא יתי
מצפונא עלה למתברא׃
יג נכסיכון ובית גנזיכון
לבזא אמסר לא בדמין
בחובין דהויתון

והעברתי

מהר"י קרא

אם לא הפגעתי בך. פתרונו שאפגיע בך בעת רעה ובעת צרה את האויב. ישראל שהם אויבים לך עכשיו יבאו בעת צרתם ויבקשו ויפגיעו מכך לדרוש בעדם את ה׳ להתפלל בעדם וכן היה הדבר. דכתיב בשלוח אליו המלך צדקיהו את פשחור דרוש נא בעדינו את ה׳ כי נבוכדנצר מלך בבל בא עלינו. וכן כשנהרג גדליה בן אחיקם וישמעו כל שרי החיילים ויוחנן בן קרח ויאמרו אל ירמיה הנביא תפל נא תחנתנו לפניך והתפלל בעדינו אל ה׳ אלהיך. וזה הוא אם לא הפגעת בך: (יב) הירוע ברזל ברזל. וכי מה יכולין לעשות לך בתמיה הירוע ישראל אפילו אם הם קשין כברזל. לירמיה שהוא קשה מהם שקשה כברזל וכנחושת דכתיב ואני הנה נתתיך היום לעיר מבצר ולעמוד ברזל ולחומת נחשת: מצפון. ועוד שנבוכדנצר יבא מצפון לרועעו: הירוע. לשון שבירה: (יג) חילך וכל אוצרותיך

רש"י

ולא להם עלי והרי כל העם מקללני: (יא) שריתיך. השארתיך לשון שארית וכן פתרו מנחם אבל דונש פתרו אותו לשון התרה ושריתיך כמו (דניאל ה׳) משרי קטרין ופתרון שריתיך כן הוא שנאמר הנה פתחתיך היום מן האזיקים (לקמן מ׳) כלומר ביום אשר הקים ה׳ את דברו נאמר לו ועתה הנה פתחתיך היום מן האזיקים אשר על ידיך אם טוב בעיניך לבא אתי בבלה וגם ישראל בקשו ממנו שיתפלל בשבילם כאשר נאמר לו התפלל בעדינו אל ה׳ אלהינו כי נשארנו מעט מהרבה (לקמן מ"ב): אם לא. לשון שבועה: הפגעתי בך בעת רעה. את האויב כשתבא עליהם הרעה יפגעו בך שתבקש רחמים עליהם כגון לצדקיה אמר לו דרש נא בעדנו את ה׳ וגו׳ (לקמן כ"א) ד"א נבוזראדן יבקש מאתך אם טוב בעיניך לבא אתי בבלה (לקמן מ׳): (יב) הירוע ברזל ברזל מצפון. אומר אני ברזל הבא מצפון קשה משאר ברזל וכן פתרונו הם נמשלו לברזל הולכי רכיל נחשת וברזל (לעיל ו׳) ובירמיה נאמר נתתיך לעמוד ברזל ולחומת נחשת (לעיל א׳) ושלו חזק משלהם כי נ"כ מצפון יבא כדבריו עליהם: הירוע. הירוצץ ברזל שלהם את שלך ד"א הירוצץ פרעה הבא בעזרתכם שהוא קשה כברזל את נ"כ שהוא ברזל הבא מצפון ונחשת ות"י נוטה לצד זה: (יג) חילך. לשון ממון: ואוצרותיך. לישראל הוא אומר: ובכל חטאותיך. ולמען כל חטאתיך תהי זאת לך: ובכל גבולך. אשר העמדת עכו"ם בכלן:

מנחת שי

(יג) ואוצרותיך. י"ס ואוצרותיך מלא וא"ו גם אחר רי"ש וי"ס חסר־דחסר:

רד"ק

היתה: שרותיך. כמו שריתך וחירק התי"ו במקום סגול וכן תי"ו ותפוצותיכם חירק התי"ו במקום סגול ואל"ף שאר נעלם מהמכתב וכן וגם כל שרית ישראל כמו שארית ושאריתך ענינו אחריתך כלומר מה שישאר לך מהוכן בבא רעת׳ וכן ת"י אם לא סופך יהא לטב: אם לא הפגעתי בך בעת רעה ובעת צרה את האויב. בעת רעת ישראל וצרתם אפגיע בך את האויב והוא נבוזראדן יפגע בך שתעשה הטוב והישר בעיניך אם לשבת אם ללכת כמו שכתוב. הפגעתי בפעל יוצא כלומר איטיבנו שיפגע בך ויבקש מכך שתעשה איזה דבר שתרצה ויש לפרש הפגעתי ענין פגיעת החרב ויהיה הפסוק חלוק אם לא שריתיך יאמר כנגד הנביא אם לא הפגעתי בך יאמר כנגד ישראל כי גם לפירוש הראשון יאמר חילך ואוצרותיך כנגד ישראל. ויש מפרשים שאריתך התרתיך מן משרה קטרין כמו שאמר לו נבוזראדן הנה פתחתיך היום מן האזיקי׳ אשר על ידך. שרותך כתוב בוי"ו וקרי ביו"ד והענין אחד והאותות אהו"י מתחלפות: (יב) הירוע. מן תרועם בשבט ברזל ענין שבר אמר הישבר ברזל ברזל אם ברזל אחד יחתוך ברזל אחר אם הברזל ההוא מעורב עם הנחשת והוא הברזל החזק שקורין בלע"ז אצייר"ו ר"ל יחשבו שהם יוכלו לעמוד בפני נבוכדנאצר כי אם הם ברזל נבוכדנאצר הוא ברזל ונחשת: מצפון. כי בבל צפונית לארץ ישראל כמו שנאמר מצפון תפתח הרעה: (יג) חילך. לא במחיר. כל כך יהיו בוזזי׳ רבים כי לא ימכר ולא יותן במחיר השלל אלא כל אחד ואחד יבוז לעצמו: וכל חטאתיך. ובעבור

מצודת ציון

כמוהו: שריתך. מלשון שארית ובא בחסרון אל"ף וכן גם כל שרית ישראל (דה"א י"ב): הפגעתי. ענין בקשה כמו ופגעו לי (בראשית כ"ג): (יב) הירוע. ענין שבירה כמו ורעו דליותיו (לעיל י"א): (יג) חילך. מלשון חיל ועושר כמו וישראל עושה חיל (במדבר כ"ד): לבז. מלשון בזה ושלל: מחיר. ענין דמי הדבר וערכו כמו

מצודת דוד

טוב בעיניך לבא אתי בוא ואשים את עיני עליך (לק׳ מ): (יב) הירוע. וכי אפשר שהברזל מהמערכות שלך ישבר ברזל המערכות שבא מצפון שהברזל חזק מאד ונחושת מעורב בו המחזיק עוד יותר וכן נאמר הולכי רכיל נחושת וברזל (לעיל ו׳) ר"ל וכי תחשוב שאתה תתגבר במלחמה מול נ"כ הלא מאד יחזק ממך: (יג) לבז אתן. לו אתן

Nebuchadnezzar who comes from the north is stronger, compared to iron and copper.

13. **Your wealth**—*An expression of money.*—[*Rashi*]

and your treasures—*He is addressing Israel.*—[*Rashi*]

not for a price—There will be so many plunderers that the plunder will not be sold for a price, but everyone will plunder for himself.—[*Redak*]

and for all your sins—*And because of all your sins, this will befall you.*—[*Rashi*]

and throughout all your boundar-

leave you over for good; verily I will cause [them] to beg you in
time of famine and in time of distress, with the enemy. 12. Will
iron break iron from the north and copper? 13. Your riches
and your treasures I will give for plunder, not for a price, and
for all your sins and throughout all your boundaries.

to them, neither did they lend to me. Nevertheless, they curse me and deride me.—[*Mezudath David*]

11. **I leave you over**—Heb. שְׂרִיתִךָ *I leave you over, an expression of a remnant. In this manner, Menahem* (*Machbereth* p. 181) *interpreted it, but Dunash* (*Teshuvoth Dunash* p. 36) *interpreted it as an expression of release. And* שְׂרִיתִךָ *is like* '(Dan. 5:12) *And untying* (וּמְשָׁרֵא) *knots,' and the interpretation of* שְׂרִיתִךָ *is so, as it is stated* (below 40:4): *'Behold I have released you from the chains that are on your hand.' That is to say, on that day that the Lord fulfilled His word, it was said to him, 'And now, behold I have released you today from the chains that are on your hand, if it pleases you to come with me to Babylon. And also, Israel begged him to pray for them, as it was said to him:* '(below 42:4) *Pray on our behalf to the Lord our God, for we remain few from many.'*—[*Rashi*]

Redak explains שְׂרִיתִךָ as a noun, *your end.* Verily, your end will be for good. This is in accordance with *Jonathan.*

Verily I will—Heb. אִם לֹא, lit. if not, *an expression of an oath.*—[*Rashi*]

I will cause [them] to beg you in time of evil—*with the enemy. When evil befalls them, they will beg you to supplicate God for mercy upon them, for example, Zedekiah said to him,* '(below 21:2) *Beseech God now on our behalf etc.' Another explanation: Nebuzaradan will beg you,* "(below 40:4) *If it pleases you to come with me to Babylon."*—[*Rashi*]

Redak suggests: Verily, I will make the enemy strike you. This is addressed to Israel, although the beginning of the verse is addressed to the prophet.

12. **Will iron break iron from the north**—*I say that iron that comes from the north is harder than other iron, and this is its interpretation: They were compared to iron,* '(above 6:28) *Going tale bearing like copper and iron.' And concerning Jeremiah it is stated*: '(above 1:18) *I have made you . . . into an iron pillar and into copper walls,' and his is stronger than theirs, for Nebuchadnezzar will come upon them according to his words.*—[*Rashi*]

Will .. break—*Will their iron break yours? Another explanation: Will Pharaoh who comes in your aid, who is as hard as iron, break Nebuchadnezzar, who is iron that comes from the north and copper? Targum Jonathan is inclined toward this direction.*—[*Rashi*]

Redak explains that although Israel is strong, compared to iron,

יד וְהַעֲבַרְתִּי אֶת־אֹיְבֶיךָ בְּאֶרֶץ לֹא
יָדָעְתָּ כִּי־אֵשׁ קָדְחָה בְאַפִּי עֲלֵיכֶם
תּוּקָד: טו אַתָּה יָדַעְתָּ יְהוָה זָכְרֵנִי
וּפָקְדֵנִי וְהִנָּקֶם לִי מֵרֹדְפַי אַל־לְאֶרֶךְ
אַפְּךָ תִּקָּחֵנִי דַּע שְׂאֵתִי עָלֶיךָ חֶרְפָּה:
טז נִמְצְאוּ דְבָרֶיךָ וָאֹכְלֵם וַיְהִי דְבָרְךָ
לִי לְשָׂשׂוֹן וּלְשִׂמְחַת לְבָבִי כִּי נִקְרָא

ג"א והעבדתי למדנחאי תיקר קרי דברך קרי שמך

פלחין לטעותא
ובכל תחומיכון:
יד ותשתעבדון לבעלי
דבביכון בארעא דלא
ידעתון ארי קידום
תקיף כאשתא נפק מן
קדמי ברגז עליכון יחול:
טו אתגלי קדמך יי יעול
דוכרני ופקדני לאוטבא
לי ואתפרע על בעלי
דבבי אתפרע לי מרדפי
לא תתן ארכא לעולבני
גלי קדמך דקבלית
חסודין על מימרך:
טז קבלית לפתגמך וקימתינון והוה מימרך לי לביע ולחדות לבי ארי אתקרי שמך עלי

רש"י

(טו) אל לארך אפך תקחני. ת"י לא תתן ארכא לעולבני אל תקח את ריבי להניח לארך אפך אלא מהר והנקם לי: שאתי. כמו סבלתי: עליך. בשבילך: (טז) נמצאו דבריך ואכלם. לתאוה מתחילה והיו לי לששון כי דמיתי

מהר"י קרא

לבז אתן. לא שיתנו לך מחירם. ולמה: ובכל חטאתיך ובכל גבוליך. ת"י ובחובין דהויתון פלחין לטעותא בכל תחומיתון: (יד) והעבדתי. אותך: את אויביך. שתהיו עובדין את אויביכם: (טו) אתה ידעת ה'. מה הם עושים לי והנקם לי מרודפי: אל לארך אפך תקחני. פתרונו לא תמשך נקמתי מהם כשם שאתה נוהג לחיות מאריך אפך ולהיות תולה ברשעים

לזמן מרובה. אלא בזמן קרוב הנקם לי מהם: דע שאתי עליך חרפה. שכל מה שהם מחרפין אותי אינו אלא מפני שאני הולך בשליחותך אליהם. ואע"פ שאני יודע שכשאלך בשליחותך אליהם. דברי יהיו גורמין לי חרפה וקלס אעפ"כ. נמצא דבריך ואוכלם. פת' קיבלתם: (טז) ויהי דבריך לי לששון ולשמחת לבבי. ולא מפני שהייתי [שמח] להנבא פורענות על ישראל שהרי מתעצב אני כשאני רואה הפירענות שעתיד לבוא עליהם כשם שמפרש בסמוך לא ישבתי בסוד משחקים ואעלוז מפני ידך בדד ישבתי אלא שנקרא שמך עלי שאתה ה' אלהי צבאות ופת' אדון כל חבריות לכך אני מקבל עלי ללכת בשליחותך:

רד"ק

מה יהיה זה בעבור כל חטאתיך: ובכל גבולך. הם חטאתיך כי לא במקום אחד לבד אלא בכל גבוליך הם במותיך שהם חטאתיך וזה ענין עד עולם תוקד ונאמר אחר זה בפרשת חטאת יהודה במלות שונות במקצת: (יד) והעברתי. ברי"ש פירוש אעביר אותך אל אויביך בארץ אשר לא ידעת: את אויביך. כמו אל אויביך וכן והראה את הכהן כמו אל הכהן ונראה כי יונתן היה קורא והעבדתי בדל"ת כי כן תרגם ותשתעבדון לבעלי דבביכון אבל אנחנו קראנו והעברתי ברי"ש וכן נמצא בספרי' המדויקים הראוי לסמוך עליהם ובפרשת חטאת יהודה והעבדתיך בדל"ת: קדחה. פעל עומד פירוש בערה: (טו) אתה ידעת. כלומר ידעת מה שעושים לי בה שאומרים על המוכיח' אותם: אל לארך אפך תקחני. אם תאריך אפך עליהם אל תקחני כלומר אל תמיתני כדי שאראה נקמתך מהם וי"ת לא תתן ארכא לעולבני: דע שאתי עליך חרפה. כלומר הראת להם שידעת ולא נעלם מכך: (טז) נמצאו. כשנמצאו לי דבריך בנבואה קבלתים ברצון כמו שאוכל אדם הדבר הערב לו לפיכך אמר ואכלם: כי נקרא שמך עלי. בזה אני שמח מאד שיאמרו עלי נביא השם ושאר הנביאים יקראו נביאי הבעל: ויהי דבריך.

מנחת שי

(יד) והעברתי. ברי"ש וכן נמצא במדויקים הראויים לסמוך עליהם ובפרשה חטאת יהודה שבסמוך והעבדתיך ונראה כי יונתן היה קורא גם זה בדל"ת שתרגם ותשתעבדון כ"כ רד"ק וגם אני מצאתי ס"א שזה כתוב בדל"ת וקרי ברי"ש: בארץ לא ידעת. בנביאים עם פירוש ברי"א כתוב אשר לא ידעת וטעה המדפיס בין זה ובין מה שבסמוך בפ' חטאת יהודה: קדחה. הקו"ף במאריך: (טז) ויהי דבריך. דברך קרי והוא חד מן ח' כתובים דבריך וקריין דברך וסימנהון במ"ג אור דל"ת

מצודת דוד

בבז ולא יקח בעדם מחיר ר"ל לא ישאיר אותך בארץ במחיר האוצרות שיקח כי יקחם דרך בזה: ובכל חטאותיך. ר"ל יהיה בכל הטאתיך שחטאת לה' ובכל גבוליך חטאת מבלי מקום נעדר: (יד) והעברתי. אעביר אותך מארצך ללכת עם אויביך בארץ אשר לא ידעת מאז: כי אש. אש החרון תבער באפי ועליכם תשרוף ר"ל עליכם אשפוך אש החרון: (טו) אתה ידעת ה'. את הרעה שעושים לי אנשי ענתות: זכרני ופקדני. זכור כי והשגיח עלי ועשה לי נקמה מרודפי: אל לארך אפך תקחני. ר"ל אל תניחני לאריכת אפך בנקמתי אבל מהרה חושה תנקום נקמתי מהם: דע. תן לב לדעת מה שאני נושא וסובל חרפה בעבורך כמה שאני מתנבא בשמך: (טז) נמצאו דבריך. כשהרתה עלי רוח הנבואה ונמצאו לי דברך הבלתים בשמחה כאוכל דבר מה לתאוה ותזר ופירש ויהי דברך לי

מצודת ציון

סקנה מאותך במחיר (ש"ב כ"ד): (יד) קדחה. ענין הבערה כמו הן כלכם קודחי אש (ישעיה נ'): תוקד. ענין שריפה כמו ותוקד עד שאול (דברים ל"ב): (טו) ופקדני. ענין השגחה: שאתי.

words were found and I ate them,' i.e. I accepted them.—[*Kara*]

Malbim explains: Although You are long suffering when they sin against You, do not be patient with them concerning what they do against me, for You should know that with this they are humiliating You by denying Your prophecy and thereby increasing their sins daily. Also, through this You must demonstrate Your power to them lest Your name be profaned.

16. **Your words were found and I ate them**—*eagerly at the beginning, and they were a joy for me, for I*

14. And I will cause [you] to pass over to your enemies in a land that you do not know, for a fire burns in My nostril; it shall be kindled against you.
15. You know, O Lord, remember me and think of me, and avenge me of my pursuers. Take me not to Your long sufferring, know, I bore disgrace for Your sake.
16. Your words were found and I ate them, and Your word was to me a joy and a rejoicing of my heart, for Your name was called

ies—*For you erected idols in all of them.*—[*Rashi*]

14. **And I will cause you to pass over**—Heb. וְהַעֲבַרְתִּי. This is the reading of reliable editions of the Bible. *Jonathan,* however, renders: And you shall be subservient to your enemies. He, apparently, read וְהַעֲבַדְתִּי, *and I will make you serve your enemies.*—[*Redak*] Rabbi Joseph Kara, too, follows *Jonathan. Minchath Shai* cites editions in which it is written וְהַעֲבַדְתִּי, but the *keri* is וְהַעֲבַרְתִּי.

Abarbanel explains: And I will cause your enemies to pass over to a land that you do not know. I.e., your enemies will penetrate your land even to places unknown to you.

to your enemies—Heb. אֶת, instead of אֶל.—[*Redak*] [Obviously, this explanation must be given only according to the reading וְהַעֲבַרְתִּי, but according to the reading וְהַעֲבַדְתִּי, we can render simply: And I will cause you to serve your enemies. Also, according to *Abarbanel,* this is unnecessary.

Malbim understands this as an allusion to the Judeans' going to Egypt. Even there, I will give you over to your enemies, the Chaldeans, who will go to Egypt, and there the sword of Nebuchadnezzar will overtake you again.

it shall be kindled against you—even after the destruction.—[*Malbim*]

15. **You know**—what they are doing to me, what they say of those who reprove them.—[*Redak*]

Take me not to Your long suffering—*Jonathan renders: Do not grant a reprieve for my humiliation. Do not take my cause to leave it for Your long suffering, but hasten and avenge me.*—[*Rashi*]

Redak renders: If You are long suffering, take me not. I.e., if You are patient with them and do not punish them immediately, do not take me from the world before I have seen my revenge upon them.

know, I bore disgrace for Your sake—I.e. show them that You know, and that it is not hidden from You.—[*Redak*]

I bore—Heb. שְׂאֵתִי, *like* סָבַלְתִּי, *I bore.*—[*Rashi*]

for Your sake—Heb. עָלֶיךָ, *for You.*—[*Rashi*]

All that they humiliate me is only because I follow Your mission to them, and although I know that, when I go on Your mission, I will bring humiliation on myself, 'Your

שִׁמְךָ עָלַי יְהוָה אֱלֹהֵי צְבָאוֹת: יז לֹא־
יָשַׁבְתִּי בְסוֹד־מְשַׂחֲקִים וָאֶעְלֹז מִפְּנֵי
יָדְךָ בָּדָד יָשַׁבְתִּי כִּי־זַעַם מִלֵּאתָנִי:
יח לָמָּה הָיָה כְאֵבִי נֶצַח וּמַכָּתִי אֲנוּשָׁה
מֵאֲנָה הֵרָפֵא הָיוֹ תִהְיֶה לִי כְּמוֹ אַכְזָב

תרגום

יְיָ אֱלֹהִים צְבָאוֹת: יז לָא
יְתֵיבִית בְּסִיעַת מְשַׁבְּחִין
וְלָא חֲדִיתִי מִן קֳדָם
מֵימְרָךְ פְּרֵישׁ יְתֵיבִית אֲרֵי
נְבוּאָה דִלְוָט מַלֵיתָנִי:
יח לְמָה הֲוָה כֵיבִי
לְאַפְרַשׁ וּמַחָתִי תַקִיפָא
לְמִסְרְבָא לְאִתַּסָאָה לָא
יְהֵי מֵימְרָךְ לִי כִּדְבִין
קְמַבּוּעַ דְמַיִין דְפָסְקִין

מהר"י קרא

(יז) לא ישבתי בסוד משחקים ואעלוז. כי מפני שאני שלוח אליהם לדבר קשות בדד ישבתי: ידך. נבואתך: כי זעם מלאתני. ת"י ארי נבואה דלווט מליתני: (יח) למה היה כאבי נצח. מה נשתניתי מכל הנביאים שהיו ממשה עד עכשיו שחזון שחזו. לימים רבים ולעתים רחוקים נתנבאו. ואני כל הנבואות שניבאתי לפורענותם של ישראל כולן אירעו בימי. שהרי נבואתי *) על גלות יהויקים ועל גלות יהויכין וכולן גלו בימיו ותוכחתי ונבואתי דומה למכה שהיא אנושה שאדם מצפה וסבור לרפואה והיא ממאנת להרפא. היו אש"פ בלע"ז: תהיה לי כמו אכזב. הרפואה שאני מצפה לה שתבוא דומה לי לגבים שאדם הולך לשאוב משם מים וכשבא לשם כיזבו מימיו ופסקו להם אף אני כשאני מקוה לעת שתרפא המכה מכאב הכאב

*) בכ"י ג"כ נבואתו כ"ל

רש"י

שישמעו אלי עתה: (יז) מפני ידך. מפני נבואה הבאה לי מאתך: ישבתי. יחידי ומשתומם באבילות כי נבואת זעם מלאתני בחורבן ביתך: (יח) אנושה. חולה כמו ויאנש ויחלה בבנה של בת שבע: היו תהיה לי. אתה הוי לי: כמו אכזב. כאדם שמבטחו נפסק ממנו שאתה מניחני להעטר בידם. אכזב מקור פוסק (פייליי"ן בלע"ז):

מנחת שי

ומ"ש שם נמלאו דבריך והכלם ב' בפסוק ר"ל הגיין דפסוק: (יז) ואעלז. במקצת ספרים הפי"ן בחטף סגול ובמדוייקים בשוא לבדו וחסר וא"ו אחר למ"ד: (יח) למה היה. כתב רד"ק למה בדגש ומלעיל על הה"א והוא חד מן הה' מל"ל. ובמסורה ס' דגש לא"ה וסימנהון בתהלים מ"ג במ"ג ומ"ש שם שהם סמוכים לאח"ע צריך להגיה לא"ה. וכן צ"ל בלוית חן פ"ו מהספר התשיעי עיין בסוף ספר מכלול על הנם מה וקל להבין: לא נאמנו. כאל"ף בחטף סגול ברוב הספרים:

רד"ק

כתוב ביו"ד וקרי דברך בלא יו"ד לשון יחיד כמו שאמר ויהי והכתוב דרך פרט והקרי דרך כלל: (יז) לא ישבתי בסוד משחקים. כי דברך הוא שמחת לבבי ובאמרו לבבי ר"ל שמחת השכל אבל שמחה אחרת לא היתה שמחה שהיא שמחת הגוף שאשב בסוד' ובקהל' כשהם משחקים ואשמח עמהם וזה לא היה לי אפי' לחברה לא היה לי עמהם אלא בדד ישבתי כי אני מתבודד בביתי: מפני ידך. ר"ל מפני יד הנבואה כמו היתה עלי יד ה' וכן תרגם יונתן מן קדם מימרך פריש יתיבית וכן תרגם כי זעם מלאתני ארי נבואה דלוט מליתני ויש לפרש מפני ידך מכתך כמו הנה יד ה' הויה והמכה והזעם והכאב הוא בוזתם אותו וקללם אותו עד שהיו מכים אותו כמו שכתוב: (יח) למה היה. למה בדגש ומלעיל על הה"א והוא אחד מן החמשה: נצח. עולמי ותמידי שלא יפסק לי בכל יום ויום אני במריבה וכאילו מכתי מאנה הרפא ולשון מאנה נאמר על דרך מליצת השיר כי אין למכה רצון למה היה זה ומה עון יש בי: היו תהיה לי כמו אכזב. והנה אתה תהיה לי כמו אכזב ר"ל כמו מקור אכזב וכמו מים לא נאמנו שיבטח אדם שימצא מים ויכזבו כלומר יפסקו והנה לא נאמנו והענין אחד כפול במלות שנות ובאמרו אכזב זכר התאר ולא זכר המתאר כן דרך הכתוב במקומות כמו כעדר הקצובות ומאכלו בריאה ואמר המשל כנגד האל בעבור שאמר לו בתחילת נבואתו ואני הנה נתתיך היום לעיר מבצר ולעמוד ברזל ולחומות נחשת וגו' והנה הם מחרפים ומכים אותי ואף על פי שאמר לו ונלחמו אליך היה דעתו שבמלחמה ההיא לא תהיה תמידית אלא שיהי' לה הפסק ובראותו כי לא היה הפסק נתרעם על האל ואמר למה היה כאבי נצח היו תהיה לי כמו אכזב: אנושה. כמו אנושה מכותיה. וכאב אנוש ר"ל חזקה וכבדה. ואכזב האל"ף נוספת והוא תואר כמו כזב והוא במשקל ארבע ויונתן הוסיף לא יהי מימרך לי כדבין כמבוע דמיין דפסקן מוהי:

מצודת ציון

מלשון משא וסבל: (יז) בסוד. ענין קבוץ כי להמתיק סוד מתקבלין הראויים לו וכן ועל סוד בחורים (לעיל ו'): משחקים. מל' שחוק ושמחה: ואעלוז. ענין שמחה: בדד. יחידי כמו איכה ישבה בדד (איכה א'): זעם. כעס ותרון: (יח) נצח. לעולם ר"ל זמן רב: אנושה. כאובה ביותר כמו אנוש חלי (איוב ל"ד): מאנה. מלשון מיאון: אכזב. ענין הפסק ומזיבה כמו אשר לא יכזבו מימיו:

מצודת דוד

לשמוע וגו' על כי נקרא שמך עלי אהם ה' וגו' ר"ל שמחתי היה על כי בא עלי שפע הנבואה להיות נקרא נביא ה': (יז) לא ישבתי. אמר שקבלתי הנבואה לא ישבתי בקבוצת משחקים לשמוח עמהם: מפני ידך. מפני הנבואה הבאה לי מידך ישבתי בדד ויחידי כדרך המתאבל כי מלאת אותי נבואות זעם הם הייעודים הרעים מחורבן הבית והגלות העם: (יח) כאבי נצח. ר"ל זה זמן רב אורבים עלי אנשי ענתות: ומכתי אנושה. המכה שעלי היא כאובה מאד ר"ל הם מכאיבים אותי ביותר: מאנה הרפא. ממאנת לקבל רפואה ר"ל אינם חוזרים מרעתם: היו תהיה לי. אתה הוית לנגדי כמו מקור מים הנפסק ועוזב סגניעם ולתוספת ביאור אמר מים לא נאמנו שאין מתקיים ומתמיד כי כמו כן הגלה ממני סעודה ובצלה מן

brought me joy, which is a prerequisite to prophecy.

for Your name was called upon me—through an awakening from above, but I did not have joy before the prophecy. On the contrary,

[17] **I did not sit in the council of musicians**—so that—**I rejoice**—so that the prophecy come upon me through joy, but

because of Your hand—i.e. Your prophecy,

I sat in seclusion—constantly

for You filled me with—a prophecy of fury and retribution.

18. **Why was my pain perpetual**—Why do the men of Anathoth lie in wait for me all this time?—[*Mezudath David*]

grievous—Heb. אֲנוּשָׁה, *sick. Comp.*

* For Rashi's commentary turn to page 234.

upon me, O Lord God of Hosts. 17. I did not sit in the council
of merrymakers, nor did I rejoice; because of Your hand I sat in
seclusion, for You filled me with fury. 18. Why was my pain
perpetual, and my wound grievous? It has refused to heal; you
are to me as a failing spring,

thought that now they would listen to me.—[*Rashi*]

When I found Your words in my prophecy, I accepted them willingly, like a person who eats a tasty morsel.—[*Redak*]

for Your name was called upon me—With this I am very happy, to be called a prophet of God, while the other prophets are called prophets of Baal.—[*Redak*]

17. **I did not sit in the council of merrymakers**—for Your word is the joy of my heart. I.e., it is an intellectual joy for me, but I had no physical joy, that I should sit among the merrymakers and rejoice with them. I did not even join their company, but I sat in seclusion at home—[*Redak*]

because of Your hand—*Because of the prophecy that came to me from You.*—[*Rashi*] We find prophecy called 'the hand of the Lord' very often in Scripture, especially in the Book of Ezekiel. This is *Jonathan*'s translation. It is also possible to explain: because of Your wound. I.e., because his neighbors would deride him and curse him until they would strike him and wound him.—[*Redak*]

I sat—*alone and bewildered by mourning, for You filled me with a prophecy of fury concerning the destruction of Your House.*—[*Rashi*]

Abarbanel explains that Jeremiah alludes to the false prophets, who would sit together and make merry. He states that he never sat in such a group to make merry, because of his sad prophecy.

I.e., *after* receiving his sad prophecy, he did not rejoice.—[*Mezudath David*]

Malbim explains that the prophets would always prepare themselves for prophesying by calling musicians to play before them so that they should be happy. In that way, the Shechinah would rest on them and they would prophesy. Jeremiah, however, always prophesied gloomy prophecies and was, therefore, unhappy and unprepared for prophecy. When God wished to convey His prophecy to him, He would send down His word, which inherently brought joy upon its recipient. Through this word, the prophet became joyful, as one who drinks wine, and he was thereby prepared to continue his prophecy. After the prophecy, however, he returned to his unhappy state. He, therefore, states:

[16] **Your words were found**—I found them as someone finds an article in the street without effort. I did not prepare myself for the prophecy.

and I ate them—I was like a hungry person, who finds bread and eats it eagerly.

and Your word was to me a joy and a rejoicing of my heart—The words

מים לא נאמנו׃ יט לכן כה־אמר יהוה
אם־תשוב ואשיבך לפני תעמד ואם־
תוציא יקר מזולל כפי תהיה ישבו
המה אליך ואתה לא־תשוב אליהם׃
כ ונתתיך לעם הזה לחומת נחשת
בצורה ונלחמו אליך ולא־יוכלו לך כי־
אתך אני להושיעך ולהצילך נאם־

יהוה

מוהי׃ יט בכן כדנן אמר
יי אם תתוב ואתיבינך
קדמי תשמש ואם תתיב
חשיביא למהוי צדיקיא
בענת מימרי תקים
יתובון אינון לפתגמך
ואת לא תתוב למטעי
בתריהון׃ כ ואתנינך
לעמא הדין כשור דנחש
כריך ויגיחון לקבלך
ולא יכלון לך ארי
בסעדך מימרי למפרקך
ולשיזבותך אמר יי׃
ואשזבנך

ת"א אם תשוב. ב"מ פ"ה עקדה שער לה:

רש"י

מים לא נאמנו. לסמוך עליהם: (יט) לכן. בעבור שאני סובל הצרות האלה: כה אמר ה'. לי: אם תשוב. אתה ישראל ע"י ואשיבך אני אליו אמר לי לפני תעמד: ואם תוציא יקר מזולל. אם תוציא אדם הגון מאדם רשע שתחזירנו למוטב: כפי תהיה. שאני גוזר גזירה ואתה מבטלה: ישובו המה אליך ואתה לא תשוב אליהם. יתובון אינון לפתגמך ואתה לא תתוב למטעי בתריהון:

מהר"י קרא

כתחזק והולך והרפואה דוכה: לבים שלא נאמנו. פת' לבורות כי ס שלא עמדו כימיהן אלא פסקו והלכו להם: (יט) אם תשיב ואשיבך לפני תעמוד. ירמיה אמר להם לישראל אם תשובו בתשובה על ידי שאצליח כל כך בשליחותי אליכם שאשיבך בתשובה שכר הרבה אני נוטל על כך ומהו השכר זה הוא לפני תעמוד שבלשון הזה אמר לו הקב"ה אתה ירמיה: אם תוציא. צדיק מרשע: כפי תהיה. ויהיו דבריך מקובלין כאילו אני בעצמי דברתי אליהם: ישובו המה אליך ואתה לא תשוב אליהם. שכן דרך העולם עד שלא יקבל אדם תוכחה המזהיר המוכיח הולך אצל הנזהר המסרב לקבל תוכחה והולך ושב אצלו עד שמקבל תוכחתו כשנכנס תוכחתו בלבו ושב מרשעו הנזהר הולך אצל המזהיר אף כאן משקיבלו תוכחתך ישובו המה אליך ואתה לא תשוב אליהם. כלומר הם יחזרו אליך ואתה לא תצטרך לשוב אליהם:

רד"ק

(יט) לכן כה אמר ה' אם תשוב ואשיבך לפני תעמוד. אמר לו האל דברת כנגדי דברים אשר לא כן באמרך היו תהיה לי כמו אכזב והנה חטאת לי ועתה אם תשיב בתשובה לפני ותתחרט על כה שאמרת אני אשיבך בתשובה ואסלח לך ותעמוד לפני כבתחילה והעמידה לפני ה' היא התפלה וההודאה לפניו וקבול הנבואה כמו שאמר אם יעמוד משה ושמואל לפני ואברהם עודנו עומד לפני ה' ולא יאמר זה הלשון אלא בנביא: ואם תוציא יקר מזולל כפי תהי'. ואם תטריח עצמך עליה' להחזיר' למוטב ותוציא יקר מזולל שתוכל להשיב הרשעים שהם זוללים להשיבם טובים ויקרים כפי תהיה מה שתגזור ותאמר יתקיים כאילו אני אומר אותו כמו שאמר בשמואל הנביא ולא הפיל מכל דבריו ארצה וי"ת רעות מימרי תקיים ויש מפרשים כפי תהי' כמאמרי תהי' כמו שאמרתי לך לעיר מבצר ולחומת נחשת: ישובו המה אליך ואתה לא תשוב אליהם. אבל זה השמר לך שלא תשוב לרעתם בהשתדלותך עמהם שמא יטעוך ברוב טענותם זה תשמר לך השתדל עמהם שישובו המה אליך והשמר שלא תשוב אתה אליהם: (כ) ונתתיך. אמר לא אהיה לך כמו אדם אכזב אלא כמו שאמרתי לך בתחילה כן אעשה שאתנך לעם הזה לחומת נחשת בצור': ונלחמו אליך ולא יוכלו לך. כי אני לא אמרתי שמלחמתם אליך תהיה לזמן ואת' לא הבינות היטב דברי אלא כמו שהבטחתיך כן אקיים כי לא יוכלו לך להכיתך אבל הם ילחמו אליך בין בדברים בין במכות ובין בבזיון כל זמן שתוכיחם וכל זה הטורח תסבול להשיבם אלי כי אם לא תשוב כולם אי אפשר שלא תשוב מקצתם כמו שראינו שאמרו מקצתם כשרצו להמיתו אבותיו השרים אין לאיש הזה משפט מות כי בשם ה' אלהינו דבר אלינו ואם תטרח בזה ולא

מצודת דוד

סקמים עלי: (יט) לכן כה אמר ה'. שלא יקופח שכרי וכן אמר אם אתה ישראל תשוב לה' ואני אשיבך ר"ל תשובתך תהיה ע"י בגמול זה הבטיחני לומר לפני תעמוד עד עולם ולא תפסוק הנבואה ממך ואם תוציא את מי מן הזוללות להיות אדם יקר או תהיה כפי כי מתקיים גזרתך כמו גזרתי: ישובו המה אליך. זהו דבר הפשרות שהמה ישובו אליך להיות כדברים כמותך ואל תדאג לילך אליהם בשליחות כי סן תלמוד ממעשיהם להיות כמוהם כי תהיה בטוח מזה: (כ) ונתתיך. אתן אותך מול העם הזה להיות חזק כחומת נחושת

מצודת ציון

(ישעיה כ"ח): נאמנו. ענין דבר המתקיים כמו יתד במקום נאמן (שם כ"ב): (יט) יקר. מכובד וחשוב: מזולל. ענין הרכיה האכילה ורדיפת התאוה וכן זולל וסובא (דברים כ"א): (כ) בצורה. חזקה:

evil when you contend with them. Perhaps they will mislead you with their many arguments. Therefore, be careful to strive with them that they return to you, but beware that you do not return to them.—[*Redak*]

20. **And I will make you**—I will not be like a failing spring as you have complained, but as I have promised you originally, so will I fulfill My promise, that I will make you for this nation into a fortified copper wall.—[*Redak*]

and they shall fight against you but they shall not prevail against you—I did not say that their fight against you would be for a short time; you misunderstood Me. As I promised

water that is not faithful.
19. Therefore, so said the Lord: If you return, I will return you, you will stand before Me, and if you take the precious out of the vile, you shall be as My mouth. Let them return to you, but you shall not return to them.
20. And I will make you for this nation into a fortified copper wall, and they shall fight against you but they shall not prevail against you, for I am with you to redeem you and to save you, says the Lord.

'(II Sam. 12:15) *And he became mortally ill* (וַיֵּאָנַשׁ),' *mentioned concerning Bath-sheba's son.*—[*Rashi*]

Kara notes that, whereas other prophets prophesied occurrences in the distant future, Jeremiah prophesied what would happen in his time. He prophesied the exile of Jehoiakim and the exile of Jehoiachin, both of which took place during his lifetime. He complains, "Why was my pain perpetual and my wound grievous? It has refused to heal. It is like a man who hopes his wound will heal but it does not."

19. **Therefore**—*Because I suffer from these troubles.*—[*Rashi*]

so said the Lord—*to me.*—[*Rashi*]

If you return—*You, Israel, through me, and I will return you to Him, He said to Me, "You will stand before Me."*—[*Rashi*]

Redak explains that God takes the prophet to task for his complaint. You said false words to me when you said that I was like a failing spring. You sinned against Me. Now if you completely repent before Me and regret what you said to Me, I will return you in repentance and I will forgive you, and you shall stand before Me as before. Standing before God includes prayer and thanksgiving before Him, as well as the reception of prophecy.—[*Redak*]

and if you take precious out of the vile—*If you take a pious man from a wicked man,* i.e. *if you bring him to repentance.*—[*Rashi*]

If you make a great effort to lead them to repentance and you take the precious out of the vile; i.e., if you are able to bring the wicked, who are vile, to be good and precious.—[*Redak*]

Others render: If you take a precious man out of a glutton.—[*Mezudath Zion* and *Mezudath David*]

Whatever you decree and say, will be fulfilled just as if I had said it. We find a similar statement regarding the prophet Samuel, '(I Sam. 3:19) And did not let any of his words fall to the ground.' *Jonathan* renders: You will fulfill My will. Others render: You will be like My statement, as I said to you, that you would be a fortified city and a copper wall.—[*Redak*]

Let them return to you, but you shall not return to them—*Let them return to your word, but you shall not return to stray after them.*—[*Rashi* from *Jonathan*]

But beware of returning to their

יְהוָה׃ כא וְהִצַּלְתִּיךָ מִיַּד רָעִים וּפְדִתִיךָ
מִכַּף עָרִצִים׃ טז א וַיְהִי דְבַר־יְהוָה אֵלַי
לֵאמֹר׃ ב לֹא־תִקַּח לְךָ אִשָּׁה וְלֹא־יִהְיוּ
לְךָ בָּנִים וּבָנוֹת בַּמָּקוֹם הַזֶּה׃ ג כִּי־כֹה
אָמַר יְהוָה עַל־הַבָּנִים וְעַל־הַבָּנוֹת
הַיִּלּוֹדִים בַּמָּקוֹם הַזֶּה וְעַל־אִמֹּתָם
הַיֹּלְדוֹת אוֹתָם וְעַל־אֲבוֹתָם הַמּוֹלִדִים
אוֹתָם בָּאָרֶץ הַזֹּאת׃ ד מְמוֹתֵי

תרגום

כא וְאֲשֵׁיזְבִנָךְ מִיַד
מִבְאֲשִׁין וְאֶפְרְקִנָךְ מִיַד
תַּקִיפִין׃ א וַהֲוָה פִתְגָם
נְבוּאָה מִן קֳדָם יְיָ עִמִי
לְמֵימָר׃ ב לָא תִסַּב לָךְ
אִתְּתָא וְלָא יְהוֹן לָךְ בְּנִין
וּבְנָן בְּאַתְרָא הָדֵין׃
ג אֲרֵי כִדְנַן אֲמַר יְיָ עַל
בְּנִין וְעַל בְּנָן דְמִתְיַלְדִין
בְּאַתְרָא הָדֵין וְעַל
אִמְהָתְהוֹן דִילְדִין יָתְהוֹן
וְעַל אֲבָהַתְהוֹן דְמוֹלְדִין
יָתְהוֹן בְּאַרְעָא הָדָא׃
ד מְמָת מְמַרְעֵי כַפַּן
ימותון

מנחת שי

טז (ג) הילודים. במדוייקים מלא וא"ו וכן במסורת ג' ב' חסר וחד מלא וסימנהון וכל העם הילודים במדבר דיהושע ואלה שמות הילודים לו בירושלם (שמואל ב' ה') הילודים במקום ע"כ. כך היא הגירסא הנכונה והמסרה כתובה ביהושע ה' בס"ג פוטעית ומה שכתוב שם בירושלם דדברי הימים לא יסכן להיות כענין זה דהתם כתיב ואלה שמות **הַיִּלּוֹדִים** (דברי הימי' א' י"ד)

רד"ק

תחוש לחרפתם וגדופם תקבל שכר מאתי: (כא) והצלתך מיד רעים: מכף ערצים. שרוצי' להכיתך: (א) ויהי דבר ה'. (ב) לא תקח לך אשה. יש הנה מבוכ' למה צוהו האל שלא יקח אשה ולא יוליד בנים ובנות לפי שנגזרה גזרה על הבנים ועל הבנות הילודים במקום הזה שימותו ברעב וכי לא הי' כדאי ירמיה שיחיו בניו בזכותו והנה הקטני' אינם מתים אלא בעון אבותיה' וירמיהו לא היה לו עון שימותו בניו בעונו ועוד אע"פ שנגזרה גזירה שימותו בחרב וברעב הגזרה על קצתם ולא על כלם כי גם גלות נגזר עליהם והנה נאמר בנבואת יחזקאל על ירושלים הנה נותרת בה פליטה המוצאים בנים ובנות ועוד שגם על האבות ועל האומות גזר שימותו ולא כתו כלם שהרי גלו מהם וכענין הזה נאמר בנבואת יחזקאל אם בנים ואם בנות יצילו המה לבדם ינצלו ולמה לא הצילו האבות הצדיקים את בינהם שהרי הם כמות' כי אין לבנים הקטנים חטא שימותו בעבורו אלא כשהם מתים בעון אבותיהם מתים ואם האבות הם צדיקי' למה ימותו הבנים ובה שאני רואה בזה הוא כי במקום הזה ר"ל בענתות ובענתות נאמר לו נבואה זו והזהירו שלא יקח אשה ולא יוליד בנים ובנות שם כי נגזרה גזרה על הבנים והבנות הנולדים בענתות וכן אמר למעלה על אנשי ענתות ושארית לא תהיה להם כי אביא רעה על אנשי ענתות שנת פקדתם הנה אמר כי לא תהיה שארית לאנשי ענתות אבל בירושלים תהיה שארית ופלט' כמו שנאמר בנבואת יחזקאל והנה נותר' בה פלט' המוצאים בנים ובנות וכיון שנגזרה גזרה זו על אנשי ענתות כלם אם יהיו לירמיהו שם בנים ובנות יסופו בכלל האחרים כמו שנאמר כי עד צדק ישוב משפט כמו שפירשנו במקומו כי יסוף צדיק אחד בתוך אלפים אנשים חייבים כמ"ש ללוט פן תספ' בעון העיר וכ"ש מי שאין לו זכות מעצמו כמו הבנים והבנות ואילו היו לירמיהו בנים ובנות בענתות והיה מוציאם מענתות טרם בא הגזרה לא היו נספים עם האחרים אלא שלא היו מניחין אותן קרוביהן בני ענתות כי לא היו מאמינים בנבואה לפיכך אמר לו האל שלא יהיו לו שם בנים ובנות כי יסופו בעון העיר ואפי' היה ירמיהו עצמו בענתות שמא לא ינצל בין כלם וכה שאמר המה לבדם ינצלו זהו כשיהיו שלשה צדיקים בעיר אחת כמ"ש נח דניאל ואיוב בתוכה לא אמר צדיק אחד לבד אלא כשהם שלשה או יותר ינצלו כי יצטרפו זכיות שלשתן להצילם ואם יהיו עשרה הם בצדקתם יצילו כל העיר כמ"ש ונשאתי לכל המקום בעבורם ואם ינצלום מכיתה אפשר שלא יצילום בגלות או בעונש אחר ומה שנאמר בשיר של פגעים יפול מצדך אלף ורבבה מימינך אליך לא יגש לא יקרה זה לכל צדיק אלא לכי שההשגחה בו תמיד לא תסור ממנו כמ"ש בו כי בי חשק ואפלטהו אשגבהו כי ידע שמי. ואף על פי שנגזרה גזרה על אנשי ענתות שלא תהיה להם שארית היתה להם שארית שעשו תשובה בעת כבוש הארץ כי מצאנו בשוב גלות בבל אמר אנשי ענתות מאה ועשרים ושכנה אף על פי כן האל צוה לירמיהו על מה שהיתה גזרתם תחלה ולא גלה תשובתם לירמיהו לפי שאמר לו ה' כי גזרתם קשה עד שצוהו האל שלא יקח אשה במקום ההוא: (ג) כי כה. הילודים. שם תאר וכן הילודי' במדבר: (ד) ממותי. שם בפלס כמבואי עיר מבוקעה ובלא מ"ם נוספת מותי חלאים תמות והוא קבוץ מן מות ר"ל מיתת תחלואים ימותו ותחלואים

מצודת ציון

יוכלו. מלשון יכולת: (כא) ופדיתיך. מלשון פדיון: מכף. מיד: עריצים. חזקים כמו גבור עריץ (לקמן כ'): טז (ד) התחלואים. מלשון חולי: לדומן. לזבל:

מצודת דוד

בלורה ועם כי ילחמו עליך לא יוכלו לך כי אני אושיעך: (כא) מיד רעים. הם אנשי ענתות: מכף עריצים. המחזיקים מתך בכח הזרוע וכפל הדבר במלות שונות:
טז (ב) ולא יהיו וגו'. למען לא יהיו לך בנים וגו': (ג) המילידים. המעבירים אותם: (ד) ממותי תחלואים. מיתת תחלואי רעב ימותו כמ"ש ואם באתי העיר והנה תחלואי רעב (לעיל י"ד):

remembrance.' Hence, there was a decree on the people of Anathoth that they would have no remnant, but Jerusalem would have a remnant and people would escape, as in the aforementioned prophecy of Ezekiel. Since this decree was made on the people of Anathoth, if Jeremiah would beget children there, they would perish among the others, as in Psalms 94:15: 'For to righteousness, judgment will return,' as we explained there, that one righteous man may perish among thou-

21. And I will save you from the hand of the wicked, and I will redeem you from the hand of the terrible.

16

1. And the word of the Lord came to me saying: 2. You shall take no wife, and you shall have no sons or daughters in this place 3. For so said the Lord regarding the sons and the daughters born in this place and regarding their mothers who bear them and their fathers who beget them in this land.

you, so will I fulfill My promise, that they will be unable to kill you, but they will fight against you with words, with blows, and with humiliation as long as you reprove them. And all this toil you shall bear in order to bring them back to Me, for even if all of them do not repent, some of them will. Indeed, we see that when they wished to kill him, the princes said, "This man is not worthy of death for he has spoken to us in the name of the Lord our God" (below 26:16). And if you make great effort to do this and ignore their humiliations, you will be rewarded.—[*Redak*]

21. **from the hand of the terrible**—Heb. עָרִיצִים. The strong are called עָרִיצִים because people fear them.—[*Redak* in *Shorashim*] *Jonathan* and *Mezudath Zion* render: the mighty.

I will save you from the terrible men who wish to kill you.—[*Redak*]

2. **You shall take no wife**—There is quite some difficulty in God's command to Jeremiah not to marry or beget children in this place because they will die of hunger. Was not Jeremiah worthy that his children be saved in his merit? Young children die only because of the sins of the parents, and Jeremiah had no sins for which his children should die. Moreover, although there was a decree that they die by the sword and through famine, that decree was upon some of them, not all of them, for exile too was decreed upon Jerusalem, yet Ezekiel states: '(14:22) Still, behold, there are left therein some that escape, who shall be carried forth, both sons and daughters.' Moreover, the decree was also on the fathers and mothers, yet many of them survived to go into exile. Now the children are like the parents. They do not die except for the parents' sins. Consequently, if the parents are righteous enough to be spared death, why should the children die?

It appears to me that 'this place' refers to Anathoth. In Anathoth this prophecy came to him, and God warned him not to marry or beget children there, for there was a decree on the sons and daughters born in Anathoth. See above (11:23): 'And they shall have no remnant, for I will bring misfortune upon the men of Anathoth in the year of their

תַּחֲלֻאִים יָמֻתוּ לֹא יִסָּפְדוּ וְלֹא יִקָּבֵרוּ
לְדֹמֶן עַל־פְּנֵי הָאֲדָמָה יִהְיוּ וּבַחֶרֶב
וּבָרָעָב יִכְלוּ וְהָיְתָה נִבְלָתָם לְמַאֲכָל
לְעוֹף הַשָּׁמַיִם וּלְבֶהֱמַת הָאָרֶץ׃ ה כִּי־
כֹה ׀ אָמַר יְהוָה אַל־תָּבוֹא בֵּית מַרְזֵחַ
וְאַל־תֵּלֵךְ לִסְפּוֹד וְאַל־תָּנֹד לָהֶם כִּי־
אָסַפְתִּי אֶת־שְׁלוֹמִי מֵאֵת הָעָם־הַזֶּה
נְאֻם־יְהוָה אֶת־הַחֶסֶד וְאֶת־הָרַחֲמִים׃
ו וּמֵתוּ גְדֹלִים וּקְטַנִּים בָּאָרֶץ הַזֹּאת לֹא
יִקָּבֵרוּ וְלֹא־יִסְפְּדוּ לָהֶם וְלֹא יִתְגֹּדַד

יְמוּתוּן לָא יִסְתַּפְּדוּן וְלָא
יִתְקַבְּרוּן לִזְבַל מְבַדַּר
עַל אַפֵּי אַרְעָא יְהוֹן
וּבְחַרְבָּא וּבְכַפְנָא יְסוּפוּן
וּתְהֵי נְבֵלַתְהוֹן מְשַׁגְרָא
לְמֵיכַל לְעוֹפָא דִשְׁמַיָא
וּלְבְעִירָא דְאַרְעָא׃
ה אֲרֵי כִדְנַן אֲמַר יְיָ לָא
תֵעוֹל לְבֵית מַרְזְחָא וְלָא
תְהָךְ לְמִסְפַּד וְלָא תְנַגֵי
לְהוֹן אֲרֵי כְנַשִׁית יָת
שְׁלָמִי מִן עַמָא הָדֵין אֲמַר
יְיָ יָת חִסְדָא וְיָת רַחֲמַי׃
ו וִימוּתוּן רַבְרְבִין
וְזַעְרִין בְּאַרְעָא הָדָא
לָא יִתְקַבְּרוּן וְלָא יִסְפְּדוּן
לְהוֹן וְלָא יִתְחַבְּמוּן וְלָא
יִמְרְטוּן

ת"א לא יספדו. סנהדרין מו: בית מרזח. ב"ב י (מ"ק יג:)

רש"י

טז (ה) **בית מרזח.** משתה. בספרי בפרשת בית פעור ראיתי חזרו לעשות להם מרזיחין אבל רבותינו פירשו מרזח אבל: **תנוד.** תקונן: **כי אספתי את שלומי וגו'.** כשהיה אברהם אביהם עושה צדקה ומשפט נתתי לזרעו חסד ורחמים שנאמר ה' אלהיך לך וגו' (דברים ז') ונתן לך רחמים (שם י"ג) הם הפכו ללענה משפט וצדקה לארץ הניחו (עמוס ה') אף אני הזרתי ואספתי אלי את חסדי ואת רחמי: **אספתי.** (אטולי"ר בלע"ז) כמו אסף אלהים את חרפתי (בראשית ל'): (ו) **ומתו גדולים וקטנים.** ואחר שהכל מתים מה לך לספוד: **ולא יתגודד ולא יקרח להם.** דרך האבלים להתגדד ולשרוט בשרם ולקרוח קרחה

מהר"י קרא

טז (ה) בית מרזח. מר וזח זה אבל:

רד"ק

ר"ל בחלי רעב ימותו כמ"ש למעלה ואם באתי לעיר והנה תחלואי רעב וכן ת"י ממרעי כפן ימותו ואם לא יהיה זה פי' כזה ירצה לומר מיתת תחלואי' ימותו כל בני אדם מתים בחולי אם **לא** ימותו בחרב אלא כך פי' כמו שת"י: **לא יספדו ולא יקברו**, כי כל אחד יהיה טרוד בעצמו לא יהיה פנאי לספוד ולקבור: (ה) **כי כה.** בית מרזח. בית אבל כן פירשו רז"ל וכן וסר מרזח סרוחים. וא"א ז"ל פי' כי מרזח הוא ל' הרמת קול בין לבכי בין לשמחה וכן הוא בל' ערבי מרזח: **ואל תנוד להם.** בהולם ועניינו פירשנו למעלה: **כי אספתי את שלומי מאת העם הזה.** השלום והחסד והרחמים שהייתי נותן לעם הזה לקחתי אותם מאתם ואספתי אותם אלי וכיון שאספתי אני שלומי מהם לא תדרוש אתה בשלומם לא באבלם ולא בשמחתם: (ו) **ומתו.** ולא יתגודד ולא יקרח להם. ואף על פי שהוא אסור לישראל לעשותו כמ"ש לא תתגודדו ולא תשימו קרחה בין עיניכם למת אולי הם היו עושין כמנהגי הגוים כמו שהיו עושים עבירות אחרות כמנהג הגוים ואמר כי לא יהיה להם פנאי לעשות הדברים שעושים על מת לא דברי אבל ולא דבר נחמה:

מנחת שי

ונמסר עליו לית ומלא: (ה) ואל תנד. במקצת ספרים כתוב תנוד כוה"ו שורק ובמקצתם חנ"ר בג' נקודות וכב"א כ"י נכתב בלא וי"ו ונראה

מצודת דוד

לא יספדו. כי יהיו טרודים בצרתם: **ולא יקברו.** כי ירבו מאד ולא יספיקו לקברם ויהיו מושלכים ע"פ האדמה כזבל: **למאכל וגו'.** מוטיל ולא יקברו: **ולבהמת הארץ.** ר"ל לחית הארץ כי חיה בכלל בהמה: (ה) **כי כה אמר וגו'.** ר"ל כי כן אמר לי ה' וגו' למען היות לאות: **בית מרזח.** לבית אבל לנחמו: **ואל תנוד.** דרך המנחמים לנוד בראש: **כי אספתי.** ר"ל זה להם לאות אשר כליתי מהם את שלומי ולא אעשה עמהם חסד ולא ארחם עליהם: (ו) **לא יקברו.** בעבור הרבוי: **ולא יספדו.** בעבור טרדות הצרות: **ולא יתגודד.** לא ישרטו בבשרם ולא יקרחו שער ראשם כי יהיו מבולבלים בצרתם

מצודת ציון

(ה) **בית מרזח.** בית אבל וכן סר מרזח סרוחים (עמוס ו'): **תנוד.** מל' נדידה: **להם.** עליהם: **אספתי.** ענין כליון כמו אסף אסיפם (לעיל ח'): (ו) **יתגודד.** ענין שריטת הבשר כמו ויתגודדו כמשפטם (מ"א י"ח): **יקרח.** ענין מריטת השער כמו קרחי וגוזי (מיכה

one will be able to bury them, and they will be as dung on the face of the ground.—[*Mezudath David*]

5. **house of mourning**—Heb. מַרְזֵחַ, *feasting. In Sifrei, in the section dealing with Beth-peor (Balak), I saw: They returned to make feasts* (מַרְזֵיחִין) *for them, but our Rabbis explained* מַרְזֵחַ *as 'a mourner.'*—[*Rashi* from *Kethuboth* 69b] The Talmud derives the word from מַר וְזָח, *bitter and upset*.—[*Kara*]

6. **And large and small shall die**—*And since everyone will die, why should you lament?*—[*Rashi*]

and they shall not cut their flesh

* For Rashi's commentary turn to page 235.

4. Deaths of sicknesses shall they die; they shall neither be lamented nor buried; they shall be as dung on the face of the ground, and with the sword and with famine shall they perish, and their carcasses shall be for food for the fowl of the heaven and for the beasts of the earth. 5. For so said the Lord: Do not go into a house of mourning, neither go to lament, nor bemoan them, for I have gathered in My peace from this people, says the Lord, the lovingkindness and the mercies. 6. And large and small shall die in this land, they shall not be buried, and men shall not lament for them and they shall not cut their flesh,

sands of guilty ones, as it is said regarding Lot, '(Gen. 19:15) Lest you perish for the iniquity of the city.' This is surely so regarding young children, who have no merits of their own. Now, if Jeremiah had sons and daughters in Anathoth and took them out before the execution of the decree, they would not perish with the others, but their kin, the people of Anothoth, who did not believe in prophecy, would not let him take them out. Therefore, God exhorted him not to beget any sons or daughters in Anathoth, for they would perish for the iniquity of the city, and even if Jeremiah himself were in Anathoth, perhaps he would not be saved among all the wicked people. Although Ezekiel says, "(14:16) They alone will be saved," that is only if there are three righteous men in the city, such as Noah, Daniel, and Job, as he mentions before, 'and Noah, Daniel, and Job within it.' If there are three or more righteous men, their combined merits will save them. If there are ten, they will save the entire city, as we find in the chapter of Sodom, in which God promises Abraham, "And I will forgive the entire place for their sake" (Gen. 18:26). And if they save them from death, perhaps they do not save them from exile or from other punishments. Although the Psalmist (91:7) states: 'A thousand shall fall from your side and ten thousand from your right, it will not touch you,' that applies only to a righteous man over whom divine Providence hovers constantly and does not leave him, as the Psalm concludes: '(v. 14) For he desires Me, and I will therefore deliver him. I will strengthen him for he knows My name.'

4. **Deaths of sicknesses**—I.e., deaths of sicknesses caused by the famine, as above 14:18. This follows *Jonathan.* Otherwise, what does Scripture tell us? Everyone who does not die by the sword, dies from sickness.—[*Redak, Mezudath David*]

they shall neither be lamented nor buried—Everyone will be occupied with his own troubles and will not have time to lament or bury the dead.—[*Redak*]

They will be so numerous that no

ולא יקרח להם: ז ולא־יפרסו להם על־
אבל לנחמו על־מת ולא־ישקו אותם
כוס תנחומים על אביו ועל־אמו:
ח ובית־משתה לא־תבוא לשבת אותם
לאכל ולשתות: ט כי כה אמר יהוה
צבאות אלהי ישראל הנני משבית

תרגום

ימרטון להון: ז ולא
יפרסון להון על אבלא
לנחמותהון על מיתא
ולא ישקון יתהון כס
תנחומין גבר על אבוהי
ועל אמיה: ח ובית
אסחרותא לא תיעול
לאסחרא עמהון למיכל
ולמשתי: ט ארי כדנן
אמר יי צבאות אלהא
דישראל

מהר"י קרא

(ז) ולא יפרסו להם על אבל לנחמו על מת. כשם שמבריין את האבל: יפרסו. כמו הלא פרוס לרעב לחמך והוא לשון בציעה שאד׳ בוצע ככר ולמה כל הדברים הללו לפי שלא ישאר אדם שיעשהו לאחר שכבר נאמר למעלה ומתו גדולים וקטנים בארץ הזאת:

רש"י

בראשם ומכל מקום לישראל אסור ולא הזכירו כאן אלא לדוגמת אבל: (ז) ולא יפרסו. ל׳ שבירה כמו (דניאל ה׳) מנא מנא תקל ופרסין שמברין את האבלים ברחבה ופורסין להם ברכת המוציא. כי הוא יברך הזבח (שמואל א׳ ט׳) תירגם יונתן ארי הוא פריס כל מזונא: ולא ישקו אותם וגו׳. הרי טעם למה שאמרתי אל תלך לספוד: (ח) ובית משתה. אשר אמרתי לך למעלה לא תבא זה הטעם הנני משבית מן המקום הזה וגו׳:

מנחת שי

היה הנקדן הָגָד ע"כ. וגם רד"ק כתב שהוא כחולם: (ח) לשבת אותם. במקצת ספרים מדוייקים מלא וא"ו וכן נכון כי לא נמנה עם המנחים

רד"ק

(ז) ולא יפרסו. בסמ"ך כתוב וענינו כמו פרשה ציון בידיה פרישת הידים באבל והכות כף אל כף. ופי׳ לא יפרסו ולא יתגודדו על המתים ולא יתנחמו מן החיים. וא"א ז"ל פי׳ ולא יפרסו כמו שפורסין ובוצעין הלחם לאבל כשמברין אותו וזהו שאמר לנחמו על מת ואמר על אביו ועל אמו לשון יחיד והפסוקי׳ לשון רבים ר"ל כל אחד על אביו ועל אמו וכן ת"י גבר על אבוהי ועל אימיה: (ח) ובית משתה. הפסוקים האלה מבוארים

מצודת ציון

א׳): (ז) יפרסו. מלשון פריסה ושבירה כמו פרוס לרעב לחמך (ישעיה נ"ח): כוס. ר"ל כוס יין: (ח) משתה. ענין סעודה כמו עשה משתה (אסתר א׳): לשבת. מלשון ישיבה: אותם.

מצודת דוד

ולא יחישו על מתיהם (ועם כי אסרה התורה לשרוט שריטות ולעשות קרחה על מת מ"מ דרכם היה לעשות כן אשר לא כדת): (ז) ולא יפרסו לחם. לא יפרסו פריסת המוציא עליהם בעבור הבראת האבל לנחמו על מת (כי סעודה הראשונה אין האבל אוכל משלו ומברכין אותו משל אחרים): ולא ישקו. כי הדרך הוא להשקות האבלים כוס תנחומים אבל אז יהיו טרודים בצרתם ולא יעשו הדברי׳ הראוים על אביו. לכל אחד על אביו ועל אמו: (ח) ובית משתה. לבית משתה נשואין לא תבא לשבת עמהם לאכול ולשתות וזה למען היות לכם למופת ואות: (ט) הנני משבית. אבטל ואמנע מן המקום הזה וגו׳: לעיניכם ובימיכם. היא היא וכפל הדבר במ"ש: קול

cut off from this place etc.—[*Rashi*] This apparently follows *Rashi*'s first definition of מַרְזֵחַ. See above v. 5.

You shall not go to a wedding feast to sit with the celebrants to eat and drink, in order that you be a sign that I will cut off all joy.—[*Mezudath David*]

nor shall they tear their hair for them. 7. And they shall not break [bread] for them in mourning, to console him for the dead, neither will they give them to drink a cup of consolation for his father or for his mother. 8. And to a house of feasting you shall not go to sit with them, to eat and to drink. 9. For so said the Lord of Hosts, the God of Israel: Behold, I will cut off

nor shall they tear their hair for them—*It is the custom of mourners to cut and tear their flesh and to tear their hair out of their head. In any case, it is forbidden for Jews, but he mentions it here only as an example of mourning.*—[*Rashi*]

Redak conjectures that the Jews mentioned in this prophecy emulated the gentiles in this practice just as they committed other sins by following pagan customs. The prophet tells them that they will not have time to perform their usual customs for the dead, neither the mourning nor the consolation.

7. **And they shall not break [bread] for them**—Heb. יִפְרְסוּ, *an expression of breaking. Comp.* '(Dan. 5:25) *Mene Mene Tekel Upharsin,* (*divided*). *This alludes to the practice of giving a meal to the mourners in the city square and they break for them* the bread upon reciting *the blessing of 'hamotzi.'* '(I Sam. 9:13) *For he will bless the sacrifices,' Jonathan renders: He will break* (פָּרֵיס) *bread.*—[*Rashi*] It appears from *Rashi* that the root פרס primarily means 'to break' or divide. Since it is used in conjunction with breaking bread at the beginning of a meal upon the recitation of the 'hamotzi,' it was extended to mean 'to bless.' Hence, the connection to the blessing on the sacrifice. See *Rashi* ad loc. Accordingly, we may render in *Rashi,* and they recite for them the blessing of 'hamotzi.' The allusion here is to the first meal a mourner eats after the burial of his close kinsman. He may not eat his own food, but a meal given him by a close friend or neighbor. In this case, there will be no one to give them the customary repast.

Redak suggests that the reference is to clasping the hands together and clapping them as though breaking them. He renders: They will not break [their hands] for them. See Lam. 1:17.

to console him—I.e., to console each one.—[*Redak*]

neither will they give them to drink etc—*This is the reason for what I said, Neither go to lament."*—[*Rashi*]

Although it is customary to give the mourners a cup of wine to console them, then they will be so preoccupied with their own troubles that they will be unable to do so.—[*Mezudath David*]

for his father or for his mother—I.e., for each one, for his father or for his mother.—[*Redak* from *Jonathan*]

8. **And to a house of feasting**—*that I said to you above, "You shall not go," this is the reason: Behold, I will*

מִן־הַמָּקוֹם הַזֶּה לְעֵינֵיכֶם וּבִימֵיכֶם
קוֹל שָׂשׂוֹן וְקוֹל שִׂמְחָה קוֹל חָתָן וְקוֹל
כַּלָּה: י וְהָיָה כִּי תַגִּיד לָעָם הַזֶּה אֵת
כָּל־הַדְּבָרִים הָאֵלֶּה וְאָמְרוּ אֵלֶיךָ עַל־
מֶה דִבֶּר יְהוָה עָלֵינוּ אֵת כָּל־הָרָעָה
הַגְּדוֹלָה הַזֹּאת וּמֶה עֲוֺנֵנוּ וּמֶה
חַטָּאתֵנוּ אֲשֶׁר חָטָאנוּ לַיהוָה אֱלֹהֵינוּ:
יא וְאָמַרְתָּ אֲלֵיהֶם עַל אֲשֶׁר־עָזְבוּ
אֲבוֹתֵיכֶם אוֹתִי נְאֻם־יְהוָה וַיֵּלְכוּ אַחֲרֵי
אֱלֹהִים אֲחֵרִים וַיַּעַבְדוּם וַיִּשְׁתַּחֲווּ לָהֶם
וְאֹתִי עָזָבוּ וְאֶת־תּוֹרָתִי לֹא שָׁמָרוּ:
יב וְאַתֶּם הֲרֵעֹתֶם לַעֲשׂוֹת מֵאֲבוֹתֵיכֶם
וְהִנְּכֶם הֹלְכִים אִישׁ אַחֲרֵי שְׁרִרוּת לִבּוֹ־
הָרָע לְבִלְתִּי שְׁמֹעַ אֵלָי: יג וְהֵטַלְתִּי

דְיִשְׂרָאֵל הָא אֲנָא מְבַטֵל
מִן אַתְרָא הָדֵין לְעֵינֵיכוֹן
וּבְיוֹמֵיכוֹן קָל חֶדְוָא וְקָל
חֶדְוָא קָל חֲתָנִין וְקָל
כַּלָן: י וִיהֵי אֲרֵי תְחַוֵי
לְעַמָא הָדֵין יָת כָּל
פִּתְגָמַיָא הָאִלֵין וְיֵימְרוּן
לָךְ עַל מָה גְזַר יְיָ עֲלָנָא
יָת כָּל בִּישְׁתָא רַבְּתָא
הָדָא וּמָה חוֹבָנָא וּמָה
סוּרְחָנָנָא דְחַבְנָא קֳדָם
יְיָ אֱלָהָנָא: יא וְתֵימַר
לְהוֹן עַל דִשְׁבַקוּ
אֲבָהָתְכוֹן פּוּלְחָנִי אֲמַר
יְיָ וּטְעוֹ בָתַר טַעֲוַת
עַמְמַיָא וּפְלַחוּנוּן וּסְגִידוּ
לְהוֹן וּפוּלְחָנִי שְׁבַקוּ וְיָת
אוֹרַיְתִי לָא נְטַרוּ:
יב וְאַתּוּן אַבְאֶשְׁתּוּן
לְמֶעְבַּד מֵאֲבָהַתְכוֹן וְהָא
אַתּוּן אָזְלִין גְבַר בָּתַר
הִרְהוּר לִבֵּיהּ בִּישָׁא
בְּדִיל דְלָא לְקַבָּלָא
לְמֵימְרִי: יג וְאַטְלְטֵל
יתכון

רד"ק

קמץ בז"ק

עד לכן הנה ימים באים: (י) על מה דבר ה'. מה בסגול והוא אחד מכ"ד מה שהם בסגול וכל דסמיך לת"ע דכר' במ"ז: עוננו. בלא יו"ד וכן חטאתנו לשון יחיד: (יב) ואתם הרעותם. והוא מן הדין פוקד עון אבות על בני' כשאוחזין מעשה אבותיהם בידיהם: (יג) והטלתי. ענינו והשלכתי. ועבדתם שם אלהים אחרים יומם ולילה. כתרגומו ותפלחון תמן וגו' כבעמוד:

מנחת שי

בכאי ביפרא סימן כ"ג: (י) ומה עוננו ומה חטאתינו. כי דכתיב עונינו חטאתינו ביו"ד טעו דבספרי דיקי בלא יו"ד וכן כתב הקמחי:

מצודת דוד

חתן. קול שמחת חתן: (י) ואמרו אליך. ואם יאמרו אליך: על מה. בעבור מה: (יא) ואותי עזבו. לא האמינו כי בלכם ולא שמרו מורתי: (יב) הרעותם. עשיתם הרע עוד יותר מאבותיכם: והנכם. והנה אתם הולכים כל איש אחר מה שלבו הרע מראה לו ומתאוה לה: לבלתי שמוע אלי. ר"ל כל עקר התאוה היא לבל שמוע אלי: (יג) והטלתי. לכן אשליך אתכם וגו': אשר לא ידעתם. מאז גם

מצודת ציון

ממסס: (ס) משבית. ענין בטול כמו שבת נוגש (ישעיה י"ד): (יב) שרירות. ענין ראיה והבטה: לבלתי. כמו לבלי: (יג) והטלתי. ענין השלכה כמו ויטילו את הכלים (יונה א'):

on the children,' which is true only if they continue after the sins of the fathers.—[*Redak*]

Malbim, following his explanation of the preceding verses, explains:

But you have done worse than your fathers—for you know the Torah.

and behold, you are going, each one after the view of his evil heart not to hearken to Me—You do not wish to hearken to the words of the Torah although you know it. You go after the view of your heart, seeking excuses and heretic reasons not to observe the commandments. Hence, your fathers, because they did not hearken to Me, they followed the view of their hearts, but you, on the contrary, because you went after the view of your heart, you do not hearken to Me. Their wickedness was due to ignorance and error,

from this place in your presence and in your days a voice of mirth and a voice of gladness, a voice of a bridegroom, and a voice of a bride. 10. And it shall be, that you shall tell this people all these things, and they shall say to you, "For what did the Lord speak about us all this great evil, and what is our iniquity and what is our sin that we have sinned to the Lord our God?" 11. And you shall say to them, "Because your fathers have forsaken Me, says the Lord, and they followed other gods and worshipped them and prostrated themselves before them, but they forsook Me, and did not keep My Torah. 12. And you have done worse than your fathers, and behold, you are going, each one after the view of his evil heart, not to hearken to Me. 13. And I will cast

in your presence and in your days—This cutting off will last for a long time, throughout that entire generation until the end of the seventy years of the Babylonian exile.—[*Malbim*]

a voice of a bridegroom—The voice of the rejoicing of a bridegroom.—[*Mezudath David*]

Malbim explains: the voice of the bridegroom even without mirth and joy.

10. **For what did the Lord speak about us etc.**—Why are we worse than all the preceding generations? All of them sinned, e.g. the generation of Manasseh, yet no calamity befell them.—[*Malbim*]

and what is our iniquity etc.—We have sinned neither intentionally nor unintentionally.—[*Malbim*]

11. **And you shall say to them**—that there is a vast difference between them and their fathers, for their fathers had forgotten the Torah completely and committed all these sins because they did not know the Torah. They were like children captured by gentiles, who knew nothing of their background.—[*Malbim*]

Because your fathers forsook Me etc. and they followed others gods—All this was because

they forsook Me and did not keep My Torah—They did not keep the Torah at all. Since they did not know the Torah, they forsook God and worshipped other gods.—[*Malbim*]

Mezudath David explains: They did believe in Me in their heart and did not keep My Torah.

12. **And you have done worse than they**—It is, therefore, proper that you be punished for your fathers' sins, according to '(Exodus 20:5) Who visits the iniquity of the fathers

אֶתְכֶם מֵעַל הָאָרֶץ הַזֹּאת עַל־הָאָרֶץ
אֲשֶׁר לֹא יְדַעְתֶּם אַתֶּם וַאֲבוֹתֵיכֶם
וַעֲבַדְתֶּם־שָׁם אֶת־אֱלֹהִים אֲחֵרִים
יוֹמָם וָלַיְלָה אֲשֶׁר לֹא־אֶתֵּן לָכֶם חֲנִינָה׃
יד לָכֵן הִנֵּה־יָמִים בָּאִים נְאֻם־יְהוָה וְלֹא־
יֵאָמֵר עוֹד חַי־יְהוָה אֲשֶׁר הֶעֱלָה אֶת־
בְּנֵי יִשְׂרָאֵל מֵאֶרֶץ מִצְרָיִם׃ טו כִּי אִם־
חַי־יְהוָה אֲשֶׁר הֶעֱלָה אֶת־בְּנֵי יִשְׂרָאֵל
מֵאֶרֶץ צָפוֹן וּמִכֹּל הָאֲרָצוֹת אֲשֶׁר
הִדִּיחָם שָׁמָּה וַהֲשִׁבֹתִים עַל־אַדְמָתָם
אֲשֶׁר נָתַתִּי לַאֲבוֹתָם׃ טז הִנְנִי שֹׁלֵחַ

תרגום

יַתְכוֹן מֵעַל אַרְעָא הָדָא
לְאַרְעָא דְלָא יְדַעְתּוּן
אַתּוּן וַאֲבָהָתְכוֹן
וְתִפְלְחוּן תַּמָן לְעַמְמַיָא
פָּלְחֵי טַעֲוָתָא יְמָם וְלֵילֵי
דְלָא יְהֵי לְכוֹן רַחֲמִין׃
יד בְּכֵן הָא יוֹמַיָא אָתַן
אֲמַר יְיָ וְלָא יְהוֹן מִשְׁתָּעַן
עוֹד בִּגְבוּרְתָּא דַיְיָ
דְאַסִיק יַת בְּנֵי יִשְׂרָאֵל
מֵאַרְעָא דְמִצְרָיִם׃
טו אֱלָהֵן יְהוֹן מִשְׁתָּעַן
בִּגְבוּרְתָּא דַיְיָ דְאַסִיק
יַת בְּנֵי יִשְׂרָאֵל מֵאַרְעָא
צִפּוּנָא וּמִכָּל מְדִינָתָא
דְאַגְלֵינוּן לְתַמָן
וַאֲתִיבִינוּן לְאַרְעֲהוֹן
דִיהָבִית לַאֲבָהָתְהוֹן׃
טז הָא אֲנָא שָׁלַח לְעַמְמִין
קְטוֹלִין

ת"א לכם חנינה. סנהדרין לב: תי ה'. שם פו עקרה. שער מב: אשר העלה. פקרים מ"ג פי"ו:

רש"י

(יג) ועבדתם שם את אלהים אחרים. ת"י ותפלחון למן לעממיא פלחי טעוותא יממ ולילי: (יד) לכן. ל' שבועה אע"פ שבגדתם כי שבועה היא בידי שאגאול אתכם: ולא זה

מהר"י קרא

(טו) כי אם חי ה' אשר העלה את בני ישראל מארץ צפון ומכל הארצות. לפי שנאמר למעל' והטלתי אתכם מעל הארץ הזאת. חזר ורפא כאן והשיבותים על אדמתם אשר נתתי לאבותם: (טז) הנני שולח לדייגים רבים נאם ה' ודיגום. כלומר היה סכריז לאומות שיבואו עליהם ויהיו שובים אותם חוץ מארצם כדייגים הללו שבעלים דגים בחרכם מן הים ליבשה.

רד"ק

חנינ'. רחמים כלומר לא ירחמו עליכם האויבים אלא יעבדו בכם בפרך: (יד) לכן הנה ימים באים. זו היא עתידה והיה הנביא אומר להם נחמה זו אחר פורענות והיה האל שולח להם בזה הענין על ידי נביאיו פורענות ונחמה כדי שלא יאמרו אבדה תקותינו כי אף על פי שיפרע מהם על מעשיהם הרעים עוד באחרית הימים תהיה להם התקומ': ולא יאמרו עוד חי ה'. כשישבע אדם ויאמר חי ה' ודרך העולם לסמוך על הזכרת ה' דבר ממעשיו או מנפלאותיו כמו שאמר צדקיהו חי ה' אשר עשה לנו את הנפש הזאת וכן היו אומרים חי ה' אשר העלה את בני ישראל מארץ מצרים ואמר הנה ימים באים שלא יאמר כי אם חי ה' אשר העלה וגו' וזה יהיה בימות המשיח בקבוץ גליות: (טו) אשר הדיחם. המדיחים והם מלכי אשור המגלים אותם ות"י לא יהון משתען עוד בגבורתא דה' דאפיק ית בני ישראל וגו' כבעמוד. והענין הזה מחלוקת בדברי רבותינו זכרונם לברכ' י"א שלא יזכרו יציאת מצרים כל עיקר ויש אומרים שיזכרו אלא שיהא שעבוד גליות עיקר ויציאת מצרים טפל לו: (טז) הנה שולח לדוגים. כתיב בוי"ו כמו עמדו עליו דוגים וקרי לדיגים ביו"ד והענין אחד הוא תואר לצדי הדגים:

מנחת שי

(טו) והשבתים. מתחלפים הספרים במילוי וחיסור יו"ד אחר השי"ן וא"ו אחר

מצודת ציון

חנינה. מלשון חן: (יד) העלה. מלשון עליה: (טו) הדיחם. מל' דחיה: והשיבותים. מלשון השבה: על אדמתם. אל אדמתם:

מצודת דוד

אתם גם אבותיכם: את אלהים אחרים. ר"ל את האומות המודים אלהים אחרים: אשר וגו'. על אשר לא אתן לכם חן בעיני האומות לכן תעבדו אותם יומם ולילה ולא תמלאו מנוח: (יד) לכן. ר"ל כוחיל והצרות יהיו מרובות כ"כ לכן תהיה הגאולה ממנה חשובה עד מאד כי אז לא יאמר עוד מי כשבועתו חי ה' אשר העלה וגו' מארץ מצרים: (טו) כי אם. כי אז יאמרו כשבועתם חי ה' אשר העלה וגו' מארץ צפון ומשאר ארצות אשר הדיחם שמה כי הגאולה ההיא תהיה חשובה יותר לפי מרבית הצרות שיסבלו בגולה ויזכירו יותר בזה הגאולה: והשיבותים. כן יאמרו כשבועתם חי ה' אשר העלה וגו' ואשר השיבותי אותם על אדמתם (וזהו מאמר המקום כמדבר בעדו אבל הם יאמרו והשיב אותם אשר נתן וגו' וכמדברים בעדם):(טז)הנני

Jonathan renders: Then days will come, says the Lord, when they will no longer speak of the might of the Lord Who brought up the children of Israel from the land of Egypt, but they will speak of the might of the Lord Who brought up the children of Israel from the northland and from all the provinces where He had driven them etc. There is a dispute between the Sages whether the departure from Egypt will be mentioned after the Messiah has come, but it will be secondary to the final redemption, or whether it will no longer be mentioned.—[*Redak*]

you off this land to a land that you and your fathers did not know, and you shall serve there other gods day and night, for I will show you no favor. 14. Therefore, behold days are coming, says the Lord, and it shall no longer be said, "As the Lord lives, Who brought up the children of Israel from the land of Egypt," 15. But, "As the Lord lives, Who brought up the children of Israel from the northland and from all the lands where He had driven them," and I will restore them to their land that I gave to their forefathers. 16. Behold I will send

whereas your wickedness is due to your being overly wise, thinking that you know better than the Torah.

13. **and you will serve there other gods**—*Jonathan paraphrases: And you will serve there nations that worship idols day and night.*—[*Rashi, Redak*]

Abarbanel and *Malbim* interpret it literally. Since you worshipped idols in your land willingly, you will now be coerced to worship them in the land of your captivity. See above 10:11, Commentary Digest. It appears that the Jews did not worship idols in Babylon. Hence, *Jonathan*'s paraphrase.

for I will show you no favor—I.e., the enemies will show you no mercy but will force you to work hard.—[*Redak*]

14. **Therefore**—*An expression of an oath. Although you betrayed Me, I have an oath that I will redeem you.*—[*Rashi*]

This is a future prophecy. The prophet tells them this consolation after telling them the retribution. This was customary that God would send a prophet to tell them retribution and then consolation, lest they say that they have no more hope, for although He will punish them for their evil deeds, at the end of days they will rise again.—[*Redak*]

and it shall no longer be said—*Our Rabbis expounded: Not that the departure from Egypt shall be uprooted from its place, but the final redemption will be the most important and the departure from Egypt secondary to it.*—[*Rashi* from *Ber.* 12b]

When one swears, it is customary to say, "As God lives," and to combine with the mention of God's name one of His deeds or His wonders. Comp. below 38:16: 'And King Zedekiah swore to Jeremiah in secret, saying, "As the Lord lives, Who made this soul for us . . ." It was customary for the people to swear, "As the Lord lives, Who brought up the children of Israel from the land of Egypt." Days will come, however, when people will no longer swear in this manner, but will say, "As the Lord lives, Who brought up the children of Israel from the northland and from all the lands etc." This will be in the Messianic era.—[*Redak*]

לדוגים רבים נאם יהוה ודיגום ואחרי
כן אשלח לרבים צידים וצדום מעל
כל הר ומעל כל גבעה ומנקיקי
הסלעים: יז כי עיני על כל דרכיהם
לא נסתרו מלפני ולא נצפן עונם
מנגד עיני: יח ושלמתי ראשונה משנה
עונם וחטאתם על חללם את ארצי
בנבלת שקוציהם ותועבותיהם מלאו

לדיגים קרי

תרגום

קטולין אמר יי ויקטלונון
ובתר כן אשלח לסניאין
צידין ויצדונון מעל כל
כל טור ומעל כל רמתא
ומשקיפי כיפיא: יז ארי
קדמי גלן כל אורחתהון
לא מסתרן מן קדמי ולא
מטמרן חוביהון
מלקביל מימרי: יח ואשלם להניינין
כקדמאין על חד תרין
חוביהון וחטאיהון על
דאחילו ית ארע בית
שכנתי בנבלת
שקוציהון ותועבתהון
מלו

רש"י

יאמר עוד וגו'. רבותינו דרשו לא שתעקר יציאת מצרים ממקומה אלא גאולה אחרונה עיקר וי"מ טפל לה: (טז) ודיגום. מה הדייג שולהו מתוך מקום גדולו אף אלו יוליכו אותם בתוך העיר ומה עסקו של דג משנלכד הוא מת כך הביא עליהם הורגים ואח"כ אשלח ציידים לנשארים ולבורחים מן החרב אל ההרים והגבעות ולצוד להגלותם בשבי: (יח) משנה עונם. את ששנו על עונם לעשות

מהר"י קרא

נבוכדנצר שהגלם לבבל: ואחרי כן אשלח לרבים ציידים. מעל כל הר ומעל כל גבעה. אלו האומות השוכנים סביבות ארץ ישראל שהיו רודפין אחרי ישראל בכל מקום שהיו נמלטין ומסגירין איתן [לאויב]: (יח) ושלמתי ראשונה משנה עונם וחטאתם. פתרונו בתחילה עד שלא יבאו ימי הגאולה אני אפרע מהם על עון וחטאת שבידם שהוא כפול ואחר כך אני

רד"ק

ודיגום. משפטו והדגום כמו מדוע אלי רבות משפטו הרבות אמר עתה הנני שולח לדיגים כלומר שיעיר את רוחם לבא כאילו שלח להם שיבואו והמשל כמשל צידת הדגים וכמשל צידת החיות והעופות ומשל הדגים הוא על המתים בחרב כי הדגים מתים בצידתם כשיעלו אותם מן המים ומשל החיות הוא על הגולים כי צדי החיות והעופות יצודו אותם חיים ולא ימותו בצידתם אם לא ימותון אחרי כן וכן ת"י לדיגים לעמין קטולין ויקטלינון: (יז) כי עיני. לא כמו שהם אומרים אין ה' רואה אותנו: (יח) ושלמתי ראשונ'. בתחלה אפרע מהם על חלל הארץ שהיא ארץ טהורה והם טמאו' כי לא תסבול הארץ תועבות ומעשים רעים כמו שאמר אלהי נכר הארץ ואמר ויורם את משפט אלהי הארץ ואמר ולא תקיא הארץ אתכם בטמאכם אותם כאשר קאה את הגוי אשר לפניכם כי אפי' לא צויתים ולא הזהרתים על התועבות כמו שלא צויתי ולא הזהרתי הגוים שהיו בה מקדם אף על פי כן הארץ לא סבל' אותם התועבות והקיא' אותם כי אף על פי שהגוים לא נצטוו הרי נתן בהם האל שכל ובינה ומדרך השכל יש להשמר מכל התועבות ומלעבוד אלהים אחרים עץ ואבן כל שכן ישראל שנצטוו שהוא מן הדין שתקיאם הארץ לפיכך בתחלה יפרע מהם על חלול הארץ ומה שאמר משנ' עונם ר"ל עונותיהם ועונות אבותיהם כמ"ש פוקד עון אבות על בנים והוא כשאוחזין מעשה אבותיה' בידיהם כמ"ש לשונאי וי"ת ואשלם לתניינין כקדמאין על חד תרין חוביהון וחטאיהון על דאחילו ית ארע בית שכנתי ומה שאמר בנבלת שקוציה' וגלוליה' ר"ל שיעור שקוציהם וגלוליה' ועל הדרך הזה נאמר והשלכתי עליך שקוצים ונבלתיך כי

מנחת שי

כ"מ: לדוגים. לדיגים קרי: (יז) לא נסתרו. כן כתיב לא בלא וא"ו ברוב ספרים: (יח) ותועבותיהם. בקצת ספרים מדוייקים מלא וא"ו גם אחר כ"ף וכן נכון כי כן הוא מ"ג' מלאים שנמסרו ביחזקאל י"ג:

מצודת דוד

שולח. חוזר לדבר ולומר הנה הגלות יהיו מאד ובתחלה אשלח לדיגים רבים וגו' ר"ל ציידי הדגים: ודיגום. יצודו הדגים ור"ל בתחלה יקחו האומות בשבי את המלאים בתוך העיר כדיגים שהם צדים הדגים במקום גדולם ומאסף כלם ברשתו: ציידים. הם ציידי החיות: מעל כל הר. ר"ל ילכדו גם הבורחים על ההרים כדרך הצייד הרודף בהרים לצוד החיות: ומנקיקי. הבורחים על שני הסלעים: (יז) כי עיני. משגיח אני על דרכיהם: לא נסתרו וגו'. כפל הדבר במ"ש וכפל עוד ואמר ולא נצפן וגו' וזהו לחזוק הענין: (יח) ושלמתי ראשונה. טרם בוא הגאולה אשלם להם בתחלה על מה ששנו בעון אבותם לכפלם עוד: בנבלת. במה שהעמידו בה עכו"ם המאוסים כנבלת השקץ: ותועבותיהם. עם

מצודת ציון

(טז) לדיגים. צדים את הדגים: ודיגום. ר"ל יצודו דגים וכן מולל ישוללו (לעיל ו') ור"ל ילקטו השוללות: ומנקיקי. כן יקרא חן הסלע הסגולה וכן נקיק הסלע (לעיל י"ג): (יז) נצפן. ענין הסתרה כמו יצפון לישרים (משלי ב'): (יח) משנה. מלשון שנים

17:16), and a priest was sent for who 'would teach them the law of the God of the land' (v. 27). Also, God warns Israel, 'so that the land should not vomit you out when you contaminate it as it vomited out the nation that was before you' (Lev. 18:28). Even if I had not warned them or commanded them concerning these abominations, as I did not warn or command the nations that were before them, the land would not tolerate these abominations as it did not tolerate them when committed by those nations and it vomited them out, for even though they were not commanded, God gave them intelligence to understand to beware

for many fishers, says the Lord, and they will fish them, and afterwards I will send to many hunters and they will hunt them from upon every mountain and upon every hill, and from the clefts of the rocks. 17. For My eyes are on all their ways, they were not hidden from before Me, neither was their iniquity hidden from before My eyes. 18. And I will pay first the doubling of their iniquity and their sin, for their profaning My land; with the carcass of their detestable things and their abominations they filled My heritage.

16. **Behold I will send for many fishers**—He resumes the prophecy of the destruction and the exile, telling that the troubles will become very severe, commencing with the sending for many fishers who will fish them etc.—[*Mezudath David*]

and they will fish them—*Just as the fisher takes it*—i.e. the fish—*from its habitat, so will these capture them within the city, and just as the manner of a fish, that when he is caught he dies, so will I bring killers upon them, and afterwards I will send hunters for the survivors and for those who flee from the sword to the mountains and the hills, and they will hunt them to exile them in captivity.*—[*Rashi*]

Thus, *Rashi*, also *Redak*, explains that the fishers symbolize the killers and the hunters the captors of the survivors. Rabbi Joseph Kara explains that the fishers symbolize Nebuchadnezzar who would capture the Jews in their land and carry them off in captivity, just as the fisher takes the fish out of the water and deposits them on dry land. The hunters are the neighboring peoples who would pursue the Jews wherever they would flee and deliver them to the enemies.

Malbim explains that the fishers are those who capture the bulk of the people, as a fisher catches many fish in his net. The hunters are those who pursue the remaining people, who flee to the mountains and the hills and hide in caves.

17. **For My eyes**—Not as they say, "The Lord does not see us (Ezekiel 8:12)."—[*Redak*]

18. **the doubling of their iniquity**—*Because they repeated their iniquity to do the iniquities of their fathers. And Jonathan renders in this manner: And I will recompense the second ones like the first ones double.*—[*Rashi*]

First I will punish them for their profaning My land, which is a pure land, but they are unclean, for the land will not tolerate abominations and evil deeds, as we find in many places in the Torah and in the Prophets. In Deut. 31:16, the idols are referred to as 'the strange gods of the land.' We find also that when the kingdom of Israel was exiled to Assyria and the country was repatriated by other nations, that these peoples were attacked by lions because 'they did not know the law of the God of the land' (II Kings

אֶת־נַחֲלָתִי: יט יְהוָֹה עֻזִּי וּמָעֻזִּי וּמְנוּסִי
בְּיוֹם צָרָה אֵלֶיךָ גּוֹיִם יָבֹאוּ מֵאַפְסֵי־
אָרֶץ וְיֹאמְרוּ אַךְ־שֶׁקֶר נָחֲלוּ אֲבוֹתֵינוּ
הֶבֶל וְאֵין־בָּם מוֹעִיל: כ הֲיַעֲשֶׂה־לּוֹ
אָדָם אֱלֹהִים וְהֵמָּה לֹא אֱלֹהִים: כא לָכֵן
הִנְנִי מוֹדִיעָם בַּפַּעַם הַזֹּאת אוֹדִיעֵם
אֶת־יָדִי וְאֶת־גְּבוּרָתִי וְיָדְעוּ כִּי־שְׁמִי
יְהוָֹה: יז א חַטַּאת יְהוּדָה כְּתוּבָה בְּעֵט

תרגום

מְלוֹ יַת אַחְסַנְתִּי: יט יְיָ תּוּקְפִּי וְרוּחְצָנִי וּמְשֵׁיזְבִי בְּעִדָּן עָקָא לָךְ שְׁמַע גְּבוּרְתָךְ עַמְמִין יֵיתוֹן מִסְיָפֵי אַרְעָא וְיֵימְרוּן בְּרַם לְשִׁקְרָא פְּלַחוּ אֲבָהָתָנָא לְלָמָא וְלֵית בְּהוֹן הֲנָאָה: כ הַאֶפְשַׁר דְיַעְבֵּד לֵיהּ אֱנָשׁ דַחֲלָן וְאִינוּן טַעֲוָן דְלֵית בְּהוֹן צְרוֹךְ: כא בְּכֵן הָא אֲנָא מְחַוֵי לְהוֹן בְּזִמְנָא הָדָא אֲחַוֵינוּן יַת פּוּרְעָנוּתִי וְיַת מְחַת גְּבוּרְתִּי וְיִדְעוּן אֲרֵי שְׁמִי יְיָ: א חוֹבֵי בֵית יְהוּדָה כְּתִיבִין בְּעֵט

רש"י

עונות אבותיהם ויונתן תירגם כן ואשלם להניינין כקדמאין על הד תרין: (יט) ה' עוזי ומעוזי ומנוסי. (אנטיפוימא"ש בלע"ז) ומנחם חברו ל' פלא כמו נתת ליראיך נס להתנוסס (תהלים ס') וכן ה' נסי (שמות ז) ודונש פתר אותו ל' מנוס ממש: אליך גוים יבאו. סוף העכו"ם לשוב אליך ולעבדך שכם אחד ויאמרו איך עשו להם אלהים והמה לא אלהים: מאפסי. כמו מקצה: נחלו. ל' נחלה: מועיל. ל' תועלת: (כא) כי שמי ה'. כמשמעו מושל ושליט לקיים גזרתי: יז (א) בעט ברזל. משל הוא כלומר חקוקה בשיקוע ואין

קמץ בז"ק

מהר"י קרא

נואלם. והם ישובו לומר: (יט) ה' עוזי ומעוזי. וכשיבא אותו היום שתהיה אתה ה' עוזי ומעוזי ומנוסי ביום צרה. אז. אליך גוים יבאו מאפסי ארץ ויאמרו אך שקר נחלו אבותינו: (כא) לכן הנני מודיעם בפעם הזאת. כלומר בתחלה עד שלא אושיעם מצרתם אני נפרע מהם בפעם הזאת ואודיעם את ידי ואת נבדתי. שאני כייסרם על ידי האומות כדי שיכירו את ידי ואת גבורתי וידעו כי אני ה'. ואחר כך אני גואלם: יז (א) חטאת יהודה כתובה בעט ברזל. חטאתכם שנזכרת

רד"ק

עבודת השקוץ דבר כעור וכנו' הוא מ"ש ארצי ונחלתי הארץ הראוי' לי להשרות בה שכינתי וכן אמר ותבאו ותטמאו את ארצי ונחלתי שמתם לתועב' כי היא מקודשת מכל הארצות לפעם ידוע אצל מביני מדע: (יט) ה' עזי ומעזי ומנוסי. אמר הנביא דרך קריאה אתה ה' שאתה עזי מאלו הנלחמים עמי ואנוס אליך ביום צרתי אלה שאני מוכיחם על העכו"ם אינם רוצים לשוב מדרכם הרעה וידעתי כי יבא זמן שאפילו הגוים הרחוקים ישובו ויבאו אליך מאפסי ארץ יבאו אליך במקום הזה ויאמרו אך שקר נחלו אבותינו והבל וזה יהי' בימות המשיח ובאמרו נחלו שעבדו עכו"ם דור אחר דור נחל' לבנים מאבות: ואין בם מועיל. פי' באלהים אחרים כי אין בהם שיהיה מועיל שום תועלת: (כ) היעשה לו. אלהים. לא יעשו משפט אלהים שיענם בקראם אליהם ויעזרום מצרתם. זה יאמרו הגוים כשיבאו אליך ויתודו על עונם ויתמהו איך היתה עולה על דעתם זאת האמונה: (כא) לכן. אמר לו האל לכן הנני מודיעם לאלה שאינם רוצים לשוב כי בפעם הזאת אודיעם את ידי: וידעו כי שמי ה'. כמו כי אני ה'. כי הוא שמו ושמו הוא: (א) חטאת יהודה. ידמה כי חטאתם היא כתובה וחרושה על

מצודת דוד

תועבותיהם מלאו את נחלתי וכפל הדבר במ"ש: (יט) ה' עוזי ומעוזי. אמר הנביא אתה ה' חזקי וכפל המלה לחזק הענין: ביום צרה. כשבא לרה אני נס אליך להמלט והוא ענין מליצה לומר אז אבטח בך: אליך. הן ידעתי שסוף הדבר יהיה שהגוים מקצות הארץ יבואו אליך להאמין בך ויאמרו האלילים אשר נחלו אבותינו להיות להם לאלהים אך המה שקר והבל ואין בהם תועלת: (כ) היעשה. וכי ראוי שאדם במעשה ידיו יעשה לעצמו אלהים הלא בני אדם עצמם אינם אלהים ואיך יהיו מעשה ידיהם טובים מהם: (כא) לכן. אמר במקום ה' הואיל וכן יהיה לעתיד לכן הנני מודיעם עתה אבל בפעם הזאת בגאולה העתידה אודיעם את כח ידי ואת גבורתי ואז ידעו אשר שמי ה' המורה על היכולת המוחלט ולא יהיו עוד נבוכים בדבר כמו שהיו נשבר בגאולות הראשונות: יז (א) חטאת יהודה. מוסב למעלה לומר הנה בסוף גם האומות

מצודת ציון

וכפל: חללם. מלשון חלל: שקוציהם. מלשון שקץ ושרץ: (יט) עוזי ומעוזי. ענין חוזק: ומנוסי. מלשון ניסה ובריחה: מאפסי. מקצות כי בקצות הארץ כאלו אפס וכלה: מועיל. מלשון תועלת: יז (א) בעט. בקולמוס כמו לשקר עשה עט (לעיל ח): בצפורן.

do not perform the function of gods, to answer those who call upon them to help them from their straits. When the nations come to You to confess their sins, they will wonder how they ever thought of such a religion.—[*Redak*]

21. **Therefore**—God replies to the prophet, "Therefore, behold I will let them know." I will let those who refuse to repent know that "this time I will let them know My power."—[*Redak*]

1. **The sin of Judah**—Although the time will come when even the gentiles will forsake their idols and believe in God, Judah's sin is still preserved in their heart as though it

19. O Lord, Who are my power and my strength and my refuge
in the day of trouble, to You nations will come from the ends of
the earth and say, "Only lies have our fathers handed down to
us, emptiness in which there is nothing of any avail! 20. Can a
man make gods for himself, and they are no gods?" 21. There-
fore, behold I let them know; at this time I will let them know
My power and My might, and they shall know that My Name
is the Lord.

17

1. The sin of Judah is written with a pen of

of these abominations and of worshipping gods of wood and stone. Surely Israel, who was commanded to beware of these acts, deserved to be vomited out by the land. Therefore, first God will visit retribution for the profanation of the land.—[*Redak*]

19. **O Lord, Who are my power and my strength**—The prophet addressed God: You, Who are my power against those who fight with me.—[*Redak*]

and my refuge—Heb. וּמְנוּסִי, (*mon vantement in French*), *my boast. Rashi* probably derives it from an expression of raising, the root being נסס, see *Shorashim, Redak.* Were that the case, however, there should be no 'vav,' and the 'sammech' should be punctuated with a 'dagesh.' *And Menahem* (*Machbereth* p. 123) *classified it as an expression of a wonder. Cf.* '(Psalms 60:6) *You have given those who fear You a wonder to be wondrous* (נֵס לְהִתְנוֹסֵס).' *Similarly,* '(Ex. 17:15) *The Lord is my miracle* (נִסִּי).' *And Dunash* (*Teshuvoth Dunash* p. 21) *interpreted it as an expression of actual refuge.* —[*Rashi*] Dunash's interpretation is accepted by *Redak* and *Mezudath Zion* and is supported by *Targum Jonathan.* I will flee to You on the day of My trouble.—[*Redak*]

to You nations will come—*Eventually, the heathens will come to you and worship You of one accord, and they will say, "How did they make gods for themselves, and they are no gods?"*—[*Rashi*]

from the ends of—*Like* מִקְצֵה, *from the end of.*—[*Rashi*]

handed down—Heb. נָחֲלוּ, *an expression of an inheritance.*—[*Rashi*]

avail—Heb. מוֹעִיל, *an expression of use* (תּוֹעֶלֶת).—[*Rashi*]

The people I reprove for worshipping idols do not wish to repent of their evil way, and I know that there will come a time when even the distant nations will come to You in this place and say, "Only lies have our fathers handed down to us, emptiness in which there is nothing of any avail!" This will take place in the Messianic era.—[*Redak*]

20. **and they are no gods**—They

בַּרְזֶל בְּצִפֹּרֶן שָׁמִיר חֲרוּשָׁה עַל־לוּחַ
לִבָּם וּלְקַרְנוֹת מִזְבְּחוֹתֵיכֶם: ב כִּזְכֹּר
בְּנֵיהֶם מִזְבְּחוֹתָם וַאֲשֵׁרֵיהֶם עַל־עֵץ
רַעֲנָן עַל גְּבָעוֹת הַגְּבֹהוֹת: ג הֲרָרִי

דִּבְרַזֶל בְּטַפַּר שָׁמִיר
חֲרִיתִין עַל לוּחַ לִבְּהוֹן
וּלְקַרְנַת אֱגוֹרֵיכוֹן:
ב כְּאַדְכָּרָא בְּנֵיהוֹן
אֱגוֹרֵיהוֹן וַאֲשֵׁירֵיהוֹן
תְּחוֹת כָּל אִילַן עֲבוֹף וְעַל
רָמָתָא מְנַטְלְתָא: ג עַל

ת"א כזכר בניהם. סנהדרין ס"ג:

רש"י

נוחה למחוק. ומדרש אגדה בעט ברזל בצפורן שמיר על ידי ירמיה שנקרא עמוד ברזל ועל ידי יחזקאל שנאמר לו (יחזקאל ג') כשמיר חזק מצור נתתי מצחך: חרושה. חקוקה כזה שהוא חורש בעומק: על לוח לבם. שאינם שוכחין ככו"ם שלהם: (ב) כזכור בניהם מזבחותם. כזכירת בניהם כן היתה להם זכירת מזבחותם כאדם שיש לו גיעגועין על בנו: ואשריהם. חסר על עץ רענן: על עץ. כמו אצל וכת"י תחות כל אילן עבוף: (ג) הררי בשדה.

מהר"י קרא

לפני כאילו כתובה בעט ברזל ובצפורן שמיר אינה מניחני שלא אפרע מהן. וכן ישעיה הוא אומר הנה כתובה לפני כי אם שלמתי ושלמתי אל חיקם: חרושה על לוח לבם ולקרנות מזבחותיכם. מחשבתם שחרושה על לוח לבם לקטר לע"ז עושים לקרנות מזבחותיהם. וכן הוא אומר במקום אחר הוי חושבי און ופועלי און על משכבותם לאור הבוקר יעשוה: (ב) כזכור בניהם מזבחותם. כאדם שכל שעה שזוכר את בנו מחבבו כך הם מחבבים לקטר על מזבחותם שבנו לע"ז וכן פרשו רבותינו כאדם שיש לו געגועין על בנו *) זהו מדרש חכמינו. ופשוטו של מקרא כשזוכרין בניהם מזבחותם שעשו לע"ז מיד הולכין ומקטרין עליהם לע"ז: (ג) הררי בשדה. ת"י על דפלחתון על טוריא בחקלא. ור' מנחם ב"ר חלבו פת'. ההרים שאתם עובדין עליהן לזרים יהו שפלים כשדה. ודומה לו ציון שדה

*) נוסחת הכ"י על אביו והנחתו הגהנו פה כלשון הנדפס כי כן גם לשון רש"י.

רד"ק

לוח לבם שלא תוכל להמחק מלבם כאילו היא כתובה וחרושה בעט ברזל כי הדבר שיכתוב האדם בו וחוקק באבן הוא דבר קיים לעולם כמ"ש בעט ברזל ועופרת לעד בצור יחצבון ומה שזכר עופרת כי ימלא אדם חקוק הכתובה בעופרת כדי שלא ישברו צדי החקוק והפסד צורת הכתיבה ופי' בצפורן כמו בעט כי לפי שהאדם חוקק בצפרניו דמה עט ברזל שאדם חוקק בו לצפורן או נקרא צפורן וכה"א במדרש נטל צפורן של ברזל וחקק בו: ושמיר. פירושו הברזל החזק כמו שקרא האבן החזק שמיר באמרו כשמיר חזק מצור נתתי מצחך ותרגם ירושלמי מצור החלמיש שמיר טינרא ויש לפרש כי שמיר אמר על האבן החזק ובי"ת בצפורן במקום שנים כאילו אמר בשמיר כלומר כתובה בעט ברזל ובצפורן שמיר כי אחר שאמר הכלי שיכתוב בו צריך שיאמר הדבר שיכתוב עליו ואף על פי שאמר על לוח לבם הוא שמיר וחזק שהמשילו במקום אחר לאבן שנא' והסירותי את לב האבן ותכונת הפסוק כן הוא כתובה בעט ברזל בצפורן ברזל והיא כתובה בשמיר ובאבן חזק כי הוא חרושה על לוח לבם ולוח לבם הוא השמיר וי"ת בעט בצפורן תהיה הבי"ת שקוראים בי"ת העזר ובי"ת בשמיר תהיה ב"ת כלי ופי' חרושה כמו חרותה מן חרות על הלוחות: ולקרנות מזבחותיכם. בכ"ה אף על פי שאמר לבם לשון נסתר ואחר כך אמר מזבחותיכם לשון נוכח כן הוא דרך המקרא במקומות רבים אמר וכן חטאתיכם חרושה בקרנות מזבחותיכם כי הם החטאת ולמ"ד ולקרנ' במקום בי"ת כלמ"ד לפניכם לחרב הרגתי לפצעי ישבת לכסא והדומים להם: (ב) כזכור. אמר זכירת מזבחותם ואשריהם והספור עליהם הוא ערב עליהם כזכר בניהם שהם חביבים עליהם וזוכרים אותם תמיד לאהבתם אותם וי"מ כזכר ענין הקטרה כמו אזכרתה לה' כלומר שהיו מעבירים בניהם באש והראשון נכון וי"ת כאדכרא בניהון אגוריהון: על עץ רענן. טעמו דבק עם מזבחותם. לא עם אשריהם כי עץ רענן היא האשרה ופי' על סמוך כמו ועליו מטה מנשה וזבחת עליו את עולותיך והדומים להם כי האשרה היא העץ שהיו נוטעים לעבדו או שהיו מניחים הצורה שהיו עובדים תחת האילן ועליו נאמר בכל מקומות תחת כל עץ רענן והיו בונין מזבחותם סמוך לאותו אילן שהיו מקריבין עליו קרבנות לעכו"ם הנעבדה תחת האילן או לאילן עצמו וכן היו בונין מזבחות על ההרים הרמים ועל הגבעות הגבוהות שהיו עובדים שם אלהיהם כמ"ש: על גבעות. חסר וי"ו השמוש כמו שמש ירח ראובן שמעון והדומי' להם ואני תמה מהמתרגם שתרגם על עץ רענן תחות כל אילן עבוף איך תרגם מלה בהפכה כי על ותחת שני הפכים: (ג) הררי בשדה. לפי שהיו עובדים על ההרים קרא ישראל הררי אמר דרך קריאה אתה הררי ומלת בשדה אע"פ שהטעם עמד בה פירושה שהיא דבוקה עם חילך אמר אתה הררי בשדה חילך וכל אוצרותיך לבז אתן כלומר שיוציאו השוללים הבזה בשדה

מנחת שי

יז (ג) על גבעות. פה שכתוב בס"ג כן בס' מוגה ר"ל שכתוב על בלא וא"ו וא"ו חס"פ

מצודת דוד

יעזבו הפסילים ויאמינו בה' והנה יהודה עדיין עתה חטאתם חמורה בלבם כאלו כתובה שמה בקולמוס מברזל ובצפורן משמיר ויחקק בחוזק ובעומק רב: חרושה. הרושם בעומק המחרישה: על לוח לבם. הם דפנות הלב כי הוא עשוי כענין דפנות ולוחים ואמר כדרך שאלה: ולקרנות. גם בקרנות מזבחותיכם חקוק וחרות חטאת' כי על הקרנות ההם יתמידו לזרוק דם לעכו"ם וכאומר בין במחשבת הלב בין במעשה שמור הדבר אצליכם: (ב) כזכור. כמו שיתמידו לזכור בניהם כן זוכרים מזבחותם ואשריהם: על עץ רענן. סמוך לעץ רענן ומוסב על המזבחות שהעמידום סמוך לעץ רענן ועל הגבעות הגבוהות: (ג) הררי. ר"ל אתה יהודה העובדים לעכו"ם העומדים על ההרים הנה חילך יוציאו השוללים ויחלקו

מצודת ציון

והוא שם האצבעות ממעל וכן ועשתה את צפרניה (דברים כ"א) ולפי שדרך האדם לחרות בצפרניו קרא לעט בלשון צפורן כדרך שאלה: שמיר. כן נקרא ברזל החזק וכן כשמיר חזק מצור (יחזקאל ג'): חרושה. חקוקה בעומק כחרישה: לוח. נסר ודף כמו ואת כל לחותיה (שם כ"ז): ולקרנות. הם הבליטות שבארבע זויות המזבח וכן ועשית קרנותיו (שמות כ"ז) והלמ"ד הוא במקום בי"ת וכן ישבת לכסא (תהלים ט'): (ב) ואשריהם. הוא אילן הנעבד: רענן. ענין לחות ולחלוחית כמו כשמן רענן (שם נ"ב): (ג) הררי.

iron, with a diamond point, engraved on the tablet of their heart and on the horns of your altars. 2. As they remember their children, [so do they remember] their altars, and their *asherim* by the green trees upon the high hillocks.

were written there with a pen of iron and with a point of the hardest iron.—[*Mezudath David*]

with a pen of iron—*This is an allegory. That is to say that it is deeply engraved, and cannot be erased. And the Midrash Aggadah* explains: *with a pen of iron, with a diamond point, preserved by Jeremiah, called 'an iron wall,' and by Ezekiel, to whom it was said:* '(3:9) *As a diamond, harder than flint have I made your forehead.'*—[*Rashi* from obscure Midrashic source]

diamond—Heb. שָׁמִיר. This may also be the hardest iron. It may also be the hard stone upon which the sins are engraved. The tablet of their heart is like hard stone.—[*Redak*]

point—Heb. צִפֹּרֶן, a nail. This is a pen or a stylus. It is called thus because it scratches like a fingernail.—[*Redak*]

engraved—Heb. חֲרוּשָׁה, lit. plowed. *Engraved like one who plows deeply.*—[*Rashi*] *Redak* explains חֲרוּשָׁה as a byform for חֲרוּתָה, the usual word for 'engraved.'

on the tablet of their heart—*that they do not forget their idolatry.*—[*Rashi*]

and on the horns of your altars—The thought that is engraved on the tablet of their heart, to burn incense to pagan deities, they execute on the horns of your altars.—[*Kara*]

The shift from third person to second person is not unusual in Scriptures.—[*Redak*]

2. **As they remember their children, [so do they remember] their altars**—*Like the remembrance of their children, so was the remembrance of their altars to them, like a man who longs for his son.*—[*Rashi* from *San.* 63b]

and their asherim—*which are by the green trees.*—[*Rashi*]

by . . . trees—Heb. עַל, *like* אֵצֶל, *by. And Jonathan renders in this manner: under every green tree.*—[*Rashi*] *Redak* questions this Targum, since עַל, *on,* and תַּחַת, *under,* are direct opposites.

Redak interprets this statement to mean that the altars were near every green tree. The *asherim* were trees themselves. The *asherim* were deities which the pagans worshipped, or perhaps the idols were erected under the *asherim.* Nearby stood an altar upon which sacrifices were offered to that deity, either to the tree or to the idols under it. In this manner, they erected altars on all mountains and hills.—[*Redak*]

Ramban, Deut. 16:21, explained that the *asherah* was a tree planted outside the pagan shrines to direct the worshippers there.

Abarbanel renders the verse literally, and their *asherim* on the green trees. The *asherim* were crescents attached to the trees. These images were worshipped.

upon the high hillocks—*Redak* renders: and on the high hillocks. *Jonathan,* too, renders in this

בשדה חילך כל־אוצרותיך לבז אתן
במתיך בחטאת בכל־גבוליך׃
ד ושמטתה ובך מנחלתך אשר נתתי
לך והעבדתיך את־איביך בארץ
אשר לא־ידעת כי־אש קדחתם באפי
עד־עולם תוקד׃ ה כה ׀ אמר יהוה
ארור הגבר אשר יבטח באדם ושם
בשר

תרגום

דפלחתון על מוריא בחקלא נכסיכון וכל בית גנזיכון לבזא אמסר כתובין דהויתון פלחין לטעותא בכל תחומיכון׃ ד ואיתי סנאה על ארעכון ותהי צדיא כשמטתא ובכון אעביד פורענות דינין עד דאגלי יתכון מאחסנתכון דיהבית לכון ותשתעבדון לבעלי דבביכון בארעא דלא ידעתון ארי קדום תקיף כאשתא נפק מן קדמי ברגז עד עלמא ייחול׃ ח כדנן אמר יי ליט גברא דאתרחיץ באנשא וישוי בשרא בתקוניה ומן

מהר"י קרא

תחרש׃ (ד) ושמטתה. בעון שלא שמרתם שביתת הארץ בעוד שהייתם יושבים בארצכם תהיו משמיטין כשתהיו גולין חוצה לארץ. ששם בין האומות לא יהיה לכם שדה וכרם לחרוש ולזרוע׃ ובך. אביא צרות עד שאגרש אותך מנחלתך אשר נתתי לך וכן ת"י ואיתי סנאה על ארעכון ותהי צדיא בשמיטתא ובכון אעביד פורענו' דינן עד דאגלי יתכון מעל ארעכון דיהבית לכון׃(ה) ארור הגבר אשר יבטח באדם. שזורע וחורש בשביעית׃ ושם בשר זרועו. אלו איברים שחורשים וזורעין לו את שדהו׃

רש"י

ירושלים היושבת בהר המישור כל סביב העיר מישור שדה ול' הררי כמו ערבי (ישעיה י"ג) על שם שיושב בערבה (אינטיינד"ש בלע"ז) יושבי ההר(ס"א יושבת ההר)׃ חילך. כמו ממונך׃ במותיך בחטאת. במותיך עשויות בחטא לשם עכו"ם בכל גבוליך׃(ד)ושמטתה. על כרחך תשמט את ארצך את אשר לא שבתה בשבתותיכם שאמרתי לכם ושבתה הארץ (ויקרא כ"ה)׃ ובך. אנקם מאמת נחלתך אשר נתתי לך שלא עשית רצוני להשמיטם. ד"א ובך מנחלתך ובך אנקם מנחלתך שאגלה אותך ממנה׃ כי אש קדחתם באפי. יקדתם בנחירי׃ (ה) אשר יבטח באדם. בחרישו וקצירו לומר אזרע בשביעית ואוכל׃ זרועו. כמו עזרו וכן תרגם יונתן

מנחת שי

שאין גראה כן מתרגום וכן מצאתי בס"א כ"י ועל׃ (ג) חילך כל אוצרותיך. במקצת ספרים כ"י כתוב וכל כוא"ו ובספרים אחרים בלא וא"ו וזהו מה שכתב על זה במקרא גדולה יפה ר"ל שנכון לעשות כן בלא וא"ו וכ"כ רד"ק חסר וא"ו השמוש כמו שמש ירח׃ אוצרותיך. חלוקים הספרים זה מזה אם חסר וא"ו קדמאה או נראה או אם הוא מלא דמלא או חסר דחסר׃ (ד) והעבדתיך. בדל"ת ולמעלה בפסוק אוי לי אמי ברי"ש פ"ט׃

רד"ק

לחלוק שם השלל׃ חילך. ממונך׃ כל אוצרותיך. חסר וי"ו השמוש כמו שמש ירח ראובן שמעון והדומים להם׃ במותיך בחטאת. כמו הפוך כאילו אמר בחטאת במותיך שהם בכל גבוליך כלומר למה יהיה כל חילך וכל אוצרותיך לבז בעבור חטאת במותיך וכמוהו רבים תיבות שהן הפוכות בטעם כמו מקום שם קבר שטעמו מקום קבר שם ומספד אל יודעי נהי כמו ויודעי נהי אל מספד והדומים להם רבים וכן ת"י הפוך בחובין דהויתון פלחין לטעותא בכל תחומיכון׃ (ד) ושמטתה ובך. פי' ושמט' והשמטה תהיה בך שתשמט מנחלתך לפי שלא שמטת אותה בהיותך בה וי"ת ואייתי סנאה על ארעכון ותהא צדיא משמטתא ובכון אעביד פורענות דינין׃ והעבדתיך. בדל"ת ולמעלה בפרשת אוי לי עמי והעברתי ברי"ש׃ קדחתם. הבערהם למעלה קדחה בכאן קרחתם. למעלה עליכם בכאן עד עולם׃ (ה) כה אמר ה'. לפי שהיו ישראל בוטחים במצרים

מצודת ציון

מלשון הר׃ חילך. עושרך׃ לבז. לבזה ושלל׃ במותיך. מל' במה׃ (ד) ושמטתה. מלשון השמטה ועזיבה כמו שמוט כל בעל משה ידו (דברים ט"ו)׃ קדחתם ותוקד. ענין הבערה ושריפה כמו אש קדחה באפי. עליכם תוקד (לעיל ט"ו)׃ (ה) ארור. ענין קללה׃ הגבר. האיש׃ בשר. ר"ל אדם שהוא בשר׃ זרועו. חזקו׃

מצודת דוד

ביושבים בשדה במקום אשר יחנו עליך וכל האוצרות הטמונות אתן אותם לבזה׃ במותיך. ר"ל בעבור במותיך העשוים בחטאת לעכו"ם העומדים בכל גבוליך מקום אחד לא נעדר׃ (ד) ושמטתה. תעזוב את האדמה מלעבדה בחרישה וזריעה׃ ובך. ר"ל לא מרצונך תעזוב עבודתה אלא בך תהיה העזיבה כי תהיה נעזב מנחלתך וגו' ולא תהיה שמה לעבדה וזה בגמול שלא שמטו בשביעית׃ והעבדתיך. ר"ל אכל אתה תעבוד אדמת האויב בארץ אשר לא ידעת מאז׃ כי אש. הבערתם חמתי ותשרוף עד עולם ר"ל אכעס עליכם זמן מרובה׃ (ה) אשר יבטח באדם. ר"ל ולא ימלאו עזר ממלכי האדמה כי ארור הגבר וגו'׃ ושם. ומשים חזקו ובטחונו בבשר

until I drive you out of your heritage.

for you have kindled fire in My nostrils—Heb. קְדַחְתֶּם.—[*Rashi*]

that shall burn forever—I.e., I will be angry with you for a long time.—[*Mezudath David*]

5. **who trusts in man**—*In his plow-*

3. You, who sit upon the mountain in the field, I will give your substance, all your treasures for a spoil! Your high places are made for sin within all your borders. 4. And you shall release, and [I will avenge Myself] of you because of your heritage that I gave you, and I will make you serve your enemies in the land that you did not know, for you have kindled fire in My nostrils that shall burn forever. 5. So says the Lord: Cursed is the man who trusts in man and makes

manner. *Minchath Shai* conjectures that his edition read: וְצַל, as he found in mss.

3. **You, who sit upon the mountain in the field**—*Jerusalem that is situated on the mountain of the plain. All around the city is a fielded plain. The structure of* הֲרָרִי *is like* עַרְבִי, called so *because he dwells in the plain* (עֲרָבָה), (*montanyers in O.F.*), *mountain dwellers* (*other versions: a mountain dweller*).—[*Rashi*]

your substance—Heb. חֵילְךָ, lit. your strength, *like* מָמוֹנְךָ, *your money.*—[*Rashi*]

Redak renders: You, who worship idols on the mountains! In the field I will give your substance, all your treasures for a spoil. You, Israel, who worship idols on the mountain! I will give your substance, all your treasures to the enemy in the field, that they will take the spoil out into the field to divide it there.

all your treasures—To be explained as: and all your treasures. —[*Redak, Jonathan*]

Your high places are made for sin—*Your high places are made in sin for the purpose of idolatry within all your borders.*—[*Rashi*]

Redak explains the verse as in reversed order: For the sin of your high places within all your borders. I.e., I will give your treasures to your enemies because of the sin of your high places etc.

4. **And you shall release**—*Perforce you will release your land for the time that it did not rest on your Sabbaths, which I said to you,* "(Lev. 25:2) *And the land shall rest a Sabbath for the Lord.*"—[*Rashi*]

of you—*I will avenge Myself of you because of your heritage that I gave you, that you did not perform My will to release it. Another explanation: even of you, from your heritage: I will avenge Myself of you from your heritage, that I will exile you from it.*—[*Rashi*]

Redak renders: **And you shall release, even of yourself and from your heritage**—You shall release, and that release shall be of you from your heritage, since you did not release the land while you dwelt there.

Kara renders: **And you shall release**—the fields, for in the lands of your exile you will not have fields and vineyards to plow and to sow.

and upon you from your heritage—I will bring troubles upon you

בשר זרעו ומן־יהוה יסור לבו: ו והיה
כערער בערבה ולא יראה כי־יבוא
טוב ושכן חררים במדבר ארץ מלחה
ולא תשב: ז ברוך הגבר אשר יבטח
ביהוה והיה יהוה מבטחו: ח והיה
כעץ ׀ שתול על־מים ועל־יובל ישלח
שרשיו ולא ירא* כי־יבא חם והיה

ת״א והיה כערער . אבות ח : ברוך הגבר . פסה יא עקדה שער נח : כעץ שתול . אבות ט בכורות נה פקדה ש׳ נח :

יראה קרי

תרגום

מימרא דיי יעדי לביה: ו ויהי כעבוביתא במישרא ולא יחזי ארי ייתי טבא וישרי בלא ולד במדברא בארע סדום דלא אתיהבת: ז בריך גברא דאתרחיץ במימרא דיי ויהי מימרא דיי רוחצניה: ח ויהי כאילן דשתיל על מבוע דמין ועל נגרין ישלח שורשוהי ולא יחזי ארי ייתי חוקא ויהון טרפוהי

מנחת שי

(ח) ירא . יראה קרי :

רש״י

רהגליה : ומן ה׳ יסיר לבו . שהבטיחו וצויתי את ברכתי לכם (שם) כך שמעתי : (ו) כערער . כעץ יחידי ל׳ ערירי (בראשי׳ ט״ו) ויש אומר (דגהשטי״ה בלע״ז) ומנחם פי׳ בם עץ מעצי היער וערער שמו וכן פי׳ כערער במדבר עץ אחד מעצי היער : בערבה . לשון מישור : חררים . יובש כמו חרה מני חורב (איוב ל׳) : ארץ מליחה . ארץ שהיא מליחה ולא תהא מיושבת : (ח) ולא יראה . העץ כי יבא שריפה כמו וחרה נתושתה: ארץ מלחה ולא תשב. שאינה מיישבת.

מהר״י קרא

זרועו . הבטחתו : ומן ה׳ יסור לבו . שציוהו לשמט בשביעית והבטיחו שכרו בצידו . דכתיב וצויתי את ברכתי לכם בשנה הששית . ולפי שהזכיר למעלה עון שמיטות כתב סמוך לה עונשן : (ו) והיה כערער בערבה . ערער יחיד כמד״א פנה אל תפלת הערער כלומר כאילן העומד יחיד בערבה במדבר וכל הרוחות שבעולם באות ונושבת בו ועוקרות והופכות אותו על פניו : ולא יראה כי יבא טוב . לא יראה בשנים הטובות שהבטחתי לשומרי שמיטות דכתיב וזרעתם את השנה השמינית ואכלתם מן התבואה ישן עד השנה התשיעית עד בוא תבואתה תאכלו ישן : חררים . אילנות של להבת והוא לשון ו׳ זו של ולא תשב כמו ו׳ של ויהי לי לישועה. שפתרונו היה לי לישועה : (ז) ברוך הגבר אשר יבטח בה׳ . ששומר מצותיו ומשמט בשביעית : והיה ה׳ מבטחו . שוכר הבטחתי שהבטחתי וציויתי את ברכתי לכם ושובת בשביעית : (ח) כעץ שתול על מים . שבריח מים יפריח : ועל יובל ישלח שרשיו . יובל הם יבלי מים : ולא יראה כי יבא חום . איני מתירא שייבש כשיבוא הום : ובשנת בצורת . אלו עצירת גשמים : לא ידאג ולא יביש

רד״ק

ובאשור אמר זה : ומן ה׳ יסור לבו . כי אם לא יסיר לבו מה׳ אינו רע אם יבטח באדם שיעזרהו והיתה כונתו כי בעזרת האל יוכל האדם לעזרו לא זולתו : (ו) והיה כערער בערבה . ת״י כעכוביתא במישרא ופירש רב האי ז״ל עכבית הוא קוץ כבחוץ ובכפנים פרי נאכל ונקרא ערער : ולא יראה . על דרך השאלה: כי יבא טוב . הוא הבשר : ושכן חררים במדבר . שהעץ הוא ישכון במקום שהוא חררים וזהו במדבר במקום שלא יפרה שם מפר מרוב החום וחררים ענין שרפה ודלקה מרוב היביבית כן ועצמי חרה כמו חרב וחרה נחשת׳ נחר כמפוח חררים עב בשקל חצרים וכפל הענין במ״ש ואמר ארץ מלחה ולא תשב ומלחה תאר לארץ שלא תצמיח ונגזרה מן הישוב וכן ברית מלח ברית נגזרה וכן ארץ פרי למלחה ות״י כארע סדום דלא אתיהבת והמשיל האדם שיסיר בטחונו מהאל כזה העץ שאינו מתלחלח אלא עומד ביובש כל זמן ואע״פ שאין מת כן האדם הרע יהיה ברע כל ימיו ויבחר מותו מחייו : (ז) ברוך הגבר . והיה ה׳ מבטחו . אם יבטח בו הוא יהיה מבטחו ולא יירא מכל רע : (ח) והיה. על מים. שלא יצמא לעולם : ועל יובל. ועל פלגי מים ישלח שרשיו שאפי׳ שרשיו שיתפשטו במקום רחוק יהיו על פלגי מים : ולא יראה . על דרך השאלה כלומר אפי׳ כשיהיה חום בעולם לא יחוש כמנו כי על מים הוא שתול ולא יוכל החום ליבשו ואפי׳ עליו יהיה רענן שלא יפול כשאר העצים שנובלין עליהם בימות הגשמים ואפי׳ יהיה שנת בצורת שימנעו

מצודת דוד

ודם ומסיר לבו מבטוח בה׳ : (ו) והיה. הבוטח באדם יהיה כערער הגדל בערבה : ולא יראה . אינו רואה כבוא טובה בעולם והם הגשמים ור״ל לא עליו יהיו הגשמים : ושכן חררים . שוכן בם ביבשות מרוב החמימות במדבר : ארץ מלחה . והיא ארץ בצורה מלוחה ואינה מיושבת והוא כפל ענין במ״ש : (ז) והיה ה׳ מבטחו . ר״ל כמו בוטח בו כן יהיה לו למבטח ולעזרה : (ח) והיה כעץ שתול . יהיה ממולא בטוב כאילן הנטוע אצל המים ובדליו מתפשטים אצל פלגי מים : ולא יראה . ר״ל לא ירגיש כבוא הום ובדרך הומיל

מצודת ציון

(ו) כערער . שם עץ מדברי וכן כערער במדבר (לקמן מ״ח) : בערבה . ענינו כמו מדבר : חררים . ענינו יובש כמו נחר מפוח (לעיל ו׳) : מלחה . מלשון מלח : (ח) שתול . נטוע כמו שתולים בבית ה׳ (תהלים צ״ב) : יובל . פלגי מים כמו על יבלי מים (ישעיה מ״ד) : ישלח . ענין התפשטות וכן תשלח קציריה (תהלים פ׳) : חום.

an expression of burning from the great heat.—[*Redak*]

salt-sodden soil—*Land that is salty and will not be settled.*—[*Rashi*]

The term 'salty' is used to depict land that cannot produce vegetation, as in other places in Scripture. *Jonathan* renders: And he will dwell without offspring in the desert, in the land of Sodom that was not inhabited. Scripture likens the man who takes his trust away from God to a tree that receives no moisture, but remains dry all the time although it does not die from the dryness. So will the wicked man remain all his life until he prefers death to life.—[*Redak*]

7. **Blessed is the man . . . the Lord shall be his trust**—If he trusts in the

flesh his arm, and whose heart turns away from the Lord. 6. He shall be like a lone tree in the plain, and will not see when good comes, and will dwell on parched land in the desert, on salt-sodden soil that is not habitable. 7. Blessed is the man who trusts in the Lord; the Lord shall be his trust. 8. For he shall be like a tree planted by the water, and by a rivulet spreads its roots, and will not see when heat comes, and its leaves shall be

ing and his harvest, saying, "I will sow during the seventh year and I will eat."—[*Rashi, Kara*]

his arm—*Like 'his help,' and so did Jonathan render: his trust.*—[*Rashi*]

This refers to the limbs with which a person plows and sows his field.—[*Kara*]

and whose heart turns away from the Lord—*Who promised him,* "(Lev. 25:21) *And I will command My blessing to you." This is what I heard.*—[*Rashi*]

I.e., he disregarded what God had commanded him to release the fields during the sabbatical year and His promise to send His blessing in the sixth year to last over the sabbatical year.—[*Kara*]

Others explain that the prophet was addressing Israel because she trusted in Egypt and Assyria for aid.—[*Redak, Abarbanel*]

and whose heart turns away from the Lord—Had he not turned his heart away from the Lord, there would be no sin in trusting in man if he believed that man could help him only with God's help.—[*Redak, Abarbanel*]

6. **like a lonely tree**—Heb. עַרְעָר, *like a lonely tree, an expression of* '(Gen. 15:2) *Childless* (עֲרִירִי), *and some say* (*dégât in O.F.*) *laid waste, and Menahem* (*Machbereth Menahem* p. 137) *explained: The name of a tree of the forest trees, and its name is ar'ar, and this is the explanation of* (*infra 48:6*) *Like an 'aro'er in the desert,' one of the trees of the forest.* —[*Rashi*] Note the difference between our presentation of *Rashi* and *Rashi* in printed editions. We have emended *Rashi* to agree with *Machbereth Menahem.* Without this emendation, *Rashi* does not make sense.

Redak in *Sefer Hashorashim* identifies it as the tamarisk or the juniper. He quotes Rav Hai, who defines it as a tree producing fruit, covered with thorns, perhaps the prickly pear.

in the plain—Heb. בָּעֲרָבָה, *an expression of a plain.*—[*Rashi*]

and will not see—The following terminology is borrowed from living creatures.—[*Redak*]

when good comes—I.e. rain.—[*Redak*]

parched land—Heb. חֲרֵרִים, *aridness. Comp.* '(Job 30:30) *Became dry* (חָרָה) *from heat.*'—[*Rashi*]

The tree will dwell in a place of parched land, the desert where no rain falls because of the heat. חֲרֵרִים is

עָלֵהוּ רַעֲנָן וּבִשְׁנַת בַּצֹּרֶת לֹא יִדְאָג
וְלֹא יָמִישׁ מֵעֲשׂוֹת פֶּרִי: ט עָקֹב הַלֵּב
מִכֹּל וְאָנֻשׁ הוּא מִי יֵדָעֶנּוּ: י אֲנִי יְהוָה
חֹקֵר לֵב בֹּחֵן כְּלָיוֹת וְלָתֵת לְאִישׁ
כִּדְרָכוֹ כִּפְרִי מַעֲלָלָיו: יא קֹרֵא דָגַר

תרגום

עֲבוּף וּבִשְׁנַת בַּצּוֹרְתָא לָא יְהַר וְלָא יִפְסוֹק מִלְּמֶעְבַּד פֵּרִין: ט נְכִיל לִבָּא מִכּוּלָא וְתַקִּיף הוּא מַן יְדַעִינֵיהּ: י אֲנָא יְיָ חָקַר לִבָּא בְּחַר כּוּלְיָתָא וּלְמִתַּן לֶאֱנָשׁ כְּאוֹרְחָתֵיהּ כְּפֵירֵי עוֹבָדוֹהִי: יא הָא כְּקוֹרָאָה דִּמְכַנֵּשׁ בֵּעִין

ת"א עקוב הלב. עקידה שער י: קורא דגר. חולין קמ:

קמץ בז"ק כדרכיו קרי

סהר"י קרא

מעשות פרי. שהמים שהוא גדל עליהם מגדלין את פירותיו: והיה עלהו רענן. מרובה בעליו שלו כן הבוטח בה' לא ימוט לעולם: (ט) עקוב הלב מכל ואנוש. הלב עקוב ואנוש מכל צדדין שאינו בוטח בה': מי ידענו. לפרסמו לעולם לומר לב זה בטח בי ולב זה לא בטח בי: (י) כי אני ה' חוקר לב בוחן כליות ולתת לאיש כדרכיו וכפרי מעלליו. לפרע מזה שלא בטח בי וליתן שכר לזה שבטח בי. אנוש אנפר"ם בלע"ז. ואדם שאינו בוטח למה הוא דומה לעוף ששמו [קורא. שאסף ביצים שלא ילד: (יא) קורא. עוף ששמו] קוקו בלע"ז *): דגר. לשון אסיפה כמו חמרים דמתרגמ' דגורין וכן ובקעה ודגרה בצילה ומה דרכה של אותו עוף שאוסף בצים שאינם שלו ויושב עליה' ימחמכן עד שאפרוחין נבקעין מהם כיון שיוצאין לאויר העולם ורואין שאינן דומין לו מניחין והולך לו אף אדם שגוזל והומס את הבריות ועושה עושר ולא במשפט בחצי ימיו יעזבנו: ובאחריתו יהיה נבל. **) כמו שעשה נבוכדנצר אשר הרחיב

רש"י

חום: בצורה. ל' רעב (פאמנ"א בלע"ז). ל"א בצורת לשון מבצר וכן חברו מנחם: לא ידאג. לא יפחד: (ט) עקוב הלב. מלא תואנה ועקובה מכל רעה: ואנוש. לשון חולי וחליו הוא זה: מי ידענו. הוא כמו מי ידענו אני ה' חוקרו: (יא) קורא דגר. (קוק"ו גלוגל"ע בלע"ז): ולא

*) נ"ב ודומה לו כאשר ירדוף הקורא בהרים. העתק מהמדפס. **) נ"ב נבל לשון בזיון כמו אל תנבל כסא כבודך כי נבלה עשה בישראל. העתק מהמדפס.

מנחת שי

(י) כדרכו. כדרכיו קרי:

רד"ק

נשמים לא ידאג מפני זה כי היא על מים ואמר ידאג על דרך השאל': ולא ימיש מעשות פרי. כי אפי' בשנת בצורת יהיה בלחותו ויתן פריו בעתו כן האדם הטוב אשר יבטח בה' לא יסור טובו לעולם ואפי' בשעה ששאר בני אדם בצרה הוא יהיה בטוב כמ"ש בשש צרות יצילך ובשבע לא יגע בך רע וכן האדם הטוב שילמדו בני אדם חכמתו ומעשיו הטובים והעלה הוא משל למכונו ועשרו שיהנו בני אדם ממנו: (ט) עקוב הלב. לפי שדבר על הבטחון שהוא רב כשישים בטחונו באדם וזה תלוי בכונת הלב כמ"ש ומן ה' יסור לבו כמו שפירש לפיכך דבר בכונת הלב ואמר כי הלב עקוב יותר מכל דבר כלומר מרמה כי יוכל אדם להראות בפיו ובמעשיו טוב ויהיה לבו רע ומי ידע זה בלתי האל לפיכך אמר מי ידענו. ואמר אני ה' חוקר לב והמרמה תלויה בלב לא בפה ובמעשה כי אף על פי שתהיה לפעמים המרמה בפה שיאמר דברים שהכונה בהם על שני פנים או יעשה מרמה בידיו הכל היא בכונת הלב לפיכך אמר מכל כי אין דבר מרמה כמו הלב: ואנוש הוא. ענין כאב ושבר כמו אנוש כאבי אנושה מכתי ויאמר על דרך השאלה בכאב הלב בינון או בדאגה או בעסקים רעים או במחשבה לפיכך אמר ואנוש הוא ואמר חרפה שברה לבי ואנושה: (י) אני ה' חוקר לב בחן כליות. וזכר כליות כי הכליות יועצות והלב גומר: ולתת. בפרשה זו ולתת בוי"ו כפרי בלא וי"ו ולמטה בפ' חנמאל בן שלום בהפך לתת בלא וי"ו וכפרי בוי"ו והסימן וכלו ופי' ולתת. אמר אני ה' חוקר לב וכן בידי גם כן לתת לאיש כדרכיו: כדרכו. לשון יחיד כתיב וקרי כדרכיו לשון רבים והענין אחד כי זה דרך כלל וזה דרך פרט או הוא ג"כ ככתוב לשון רבים ויו"ד הרבים חסרה מהמכתב: (יא) קורא דגר. לפי שאמר לתת לאיש כדרכיו אמר אל תתמה על הרשע שהוא מצליח בנכסים

מצודת ציון

מלשון חמימות: עלהו. העלין: רענן. ענין לחות: בצורת. ענין מניעת הגשמים וכן על דברי הבצרות (לעיל י"ד): ידאג. מל' דאגה: ימיש. ענין הסרה כמו לא ימוש עמוד הענן (שמות י"ג): (ט) עקוב. ענין עקום ועוות וכן כל אח עקוב יעקב (לעיל ט'): ואנוש. ענין מכאוב חזק כמו אנוש חצי (איוב ל"ד): (י) חוקר. ענין חפוש ודרישה: בוחן. מלשון בחינה ונסיון: מעלליו. מעשיו: (יא) קורא. שם עוף וכן כאשר ירדוף הקורא בהרים (ש"א

מצודת דוד

הוא נטוע אצל המים שמאלחלחים אותו: והיה עלהו רענן. העלים שבו יהיו רטובים: ובשנת בצורת. בשנה שיהיה מניעת גשמים: לא ידאג. הוא ר"ל לא יזיק לו: ולא ימיש. לא יסור מלגדל פירות ור"ל וכן יהיה הבוטח בה' שלא יחסר לו שום דבר ולא ידאג מהצרות המתרגשות בעולם: (ט) עקוב הלב. עם כי לב האדם הוא מעוקם ומשוש יותר מכל איבריו ויש לו מכאוב חזק ר"ל דעה נפסדת להטוב מי הוא היודע תעלומות לבו אם הוא בוטח באמת או לא: (י) אני ה'. ר"ל אולם אני ה' חוקר לב האדם ובוחן מחשבות הכליות לדעת מה היא נמשך לתת לכל איש כדרכי לבו וכפרי מעלליו הם מחשבות הלב ודרכיו וכפל הדבר במ"ש: (יא) קורא דגר. כמו עוף הקורא ממשיך אחריו אפרוחי' בצפצוף הקול והוא לא ילדם שהוא דבר שאין מתקיים כי כשיגדלו יכירו שהוא לא ילדם ויעזבו אותו כן

green, and in the year of drought will not be anxious, neither
shall it cease from bearing fruit. 9. The heart is deceitful above
all things, and when it is sick, who will recognize it? 10. I, the
Lord, search the heart, test the kidneys, to give everyone
according to his ways, according to the fruit of his deeds.
11. The cuckoo calls

Lord, the Lord will be his trust, and he will not fear any calamity.—[*Redak*]

8. **drought**—Heb. בַּצֹּרֶת, *an expression of hunger, (famine in French). Another interpretation:* בַּצֹּרֶת *is an expression of fortification (*מִבְצָר*), and in this manner, Menahem (Machbereth Menahem* p. 47) *classified it.*—[*Rashi*]

The tree is depicted as a living creature that does not see when heat comes and is not anxious in the year of drought.—[*Redak*]

neither shall it cease from bearing fruit—For, even during the year of drought it will remain moist and will bear fruit in its time. So will it be with the righteous man, who places his trust in the Lord. The goodness the Lord bestows upon him will never leave him, and, even when others suffer want, he will enjoy plenty. This is the righteous man from whom others learn wisdom and the practice of good deeds. The leaves symbolize his possessions and his wealth from which others will benefit.—[*Redak*]

The fruit symbolizes his children.—[*Abarbanel*]

9. **The heart is deceitful**—*Full of pretext and deceit of all evil.*—[*Rashi*]

Since he spoke of trust in God and the evil of placing one's trust in man, and this depends upon the intention of the heart, he proceeds to discuss the intention of the heart. He states that the heart is more deceitful than anything, for a person may appear good with his speech and his deeds, and in his heart he may be evil, and who can know this except God? Therefore, the verse concludes, 'Who will recognize it?'—[*Redak*]

and when it is sick—Heb. וְאָנֻשׁ, *an expression of sickness, and this is its sickness.*—[*Rashi*]

who recognizes it?—*He thinks, "Who recognizes it?" I, the Lord, search it.*—[*Rashi*]

Others explain: if the heart is sick with unhappiness, who recognizes it? Only the Lord.—[*Redak*]

to give everyone—Lit. and to give. I, the Lord, search the heart, and it is in My hands to give everyone according to his ways.—[*Redak*]

Mezudath David renders: In order to give everyone etc.

11. **The cuckoo calls**—Heb. קֹרֵא דָגָר. (*Coucou glousse in French*). *This cuckoo draws after it chicks that it did not lay.*—[*Rashi*]

דָגָר—*This is the chirping which the bird chirps with its voice to draw the chicks after it, but those whom the cuckoo called will not follow it when*

וְלֹא יָלָד עֹשֶׂה עֹשֶׁר וְלֹא בְמִשְׁפָּט בַּחֲצִי יָמָו יַעַזְבֶנּוּ וּבְאַחֲרִיתוֹ יִהְיֶה נָבָל׃ יב כִּסֵּא כָבוֹד מָרוֹם מֵרִאשׁוֹן מְקוֹם מִקְדָּשֵׁנוּ׃ יג מִקְוֵה יִשְׂרָאֵל יְהוָה

קמץ בז"ק ימיו קרי

ת"א כסא כבוד. פסחים ה נד נדרים לט:

דְלָא דִילֵיהּ וּמְשַׁחֲין אֶפְרוֹחִין דִבְתְרוֹהִי לָא יְהַכוּן בֵּן כָּל גְבַר רַשִׁיעַ דְקָנֵי נִכְסִין דְלָא בְדִינָא בִּפְלָגוּת יוֹמוֹהִי שָׁבִיק לְהוֹן וּבְסוֹפֵיהּ מִתְקְרֵי רַשִׁיעָא׃ יב פּוּרְעֲנוּתָא תִתְעֲבֵיד מְנֵיהּ מִן קֳדָם דְשַׁבְנְהֵיהּ עַל כּוּרְסֵי יְקָרָא בִּשְׁמֵי מְרוֹמָא עֵיל מִן אוּלָא מְקַבִּיל אֲתַר בֵּית מַקְדְשָׁנָא׃ יג סְבוּר יִשְׂרָאֵל יְיָ כָּל דִשְׁבַקוּ

רש"י

ילד. הקורא הזה מוסך אחריו אפרוחים שלא ילד: דגר. הוא ליפלוף שמלפלף העוף בקולו למשיך אפרוחין אחריו ואלו שהקורא דגר לא ילכו אחריו משיגדלו שאינם מינו כך עושה עושר ולא במשפט: יהיה נבל. מתקרי רשיעא: (יב) כסא כבוד וגו'. לפי שבא לומר כל עוזביך יבושו מתחיל בקילוסו של מקום ומדבר לפניו אתה שכסא כבוד ומרו' מראשי' בריאת עולם ומכוון כנגד מקדשנו: (יג) מקוה ישראל ה'. יושב עליו לפיכך כל עוזביך יבושו: וסורי בארץ יכתבו.

מהר"י קרא

כשאול נפשו והוא כמות ולא ישבע ויאסוף אליו כל הגוים והחריב כסא כבוד מרום מראשון מקום מקדשנו. ובבוא עת פקודתו גם הוא שיבא דריוש עליו ויהרגהו יבאו אליו כולם שאספם אליו וישאו עליו משל ויאמרו הוי המרבת עושר ולא במשפט וסופו שבניח הכל כאן כשם שאמר חבקוק הלא אלה כולם עליו משל ישאו ומליצה חידות לו ויאמר הוי המרבה לא לו עד מתי ומכביד עליו עבטים: (יג) מקוה ישראל. פתרונו

רד"ק

איך לא יתן לו האל כדרכיו כי תדע כי הרשע שאין עשרו במשפט לא יעמוד לו אלא יצא מידו בחצי ימיו והבשילו לקורא והוא עוף שקוראין בלע"ז פרני"ז והוא רובץ על ביצי עוף אחר ומחמם אותם והביצים ההם לכשיבקעו ויצאו האפרוחים לא יהיו כמו בניו שילכו אחריו אלא יעזבוהו ולא יכירוהו אלא אחרי מי שהיא להם א"כ גם הרשע שעשה עושר ולא במשפט בחצי ימיו יעזבנו או ימות הוא ויעזוב עשרו לאחרים ולא ישלים ימיו עם העושר שעשה ויהיה נבל באחריתו כלומר נופל מת טרם זמנו או יאבד העושר מידיו בחצי ימיו ויהיה נבל ופחות באחריתו וכן ת"י הפסוק הוא כקוראה די מכנש בעין דלא דיליה וגו' כבעביד: ימו. כתוב בלא יו"ד הרבים וקרי ימיו ביו"ד הרבים וכמוהו יחתו מריבו עלו בשמים ירעם: (יב) כסא כבוד. פירש הגאון רב סעדיה דבק עם סוף הפ' שלמעלה ממנו כאילו אמר יהיה נבל מכסא הכבוד כלומר מושלך וי"ת פורענותא תתעביד מניה וגו' כבעמוד ורבותינו פירשו על בית המקדש שאמרו שבעה דברים נבראו קודם שנברא העולם ואחד מהם מקום בית המקדש שנא' כסא כבוד מרום מראשון מקום מקדשנו מראשון עד שלא נברא העולם ועוד אמרו שבית המקדש מכוון כנגד כסא הכבוד שנאמר כסא כבוד מרום מראשון מקום מקדשנו וזה הדרך דרכו המפרשים ואמרו בספר יצירה והיכל קדש מכוון באמצע ואני הארכתי בזה הענין בפי' תהלים במזמור שיר המעלות זכור ה' לדוד והענין הוא טוב אלא שאין ענינו דבק עם הפ' שלפניו ושלאחריו והחכם רבי שמואל בן תבון הדביקו לענין הפ' שאמר אני ה' חוקר לב בוחן כליות וגו' ופירש כסא כבוד בחסרון כ"ף הדמיון כאילו אמר ככסא כבוד וכמוהו רבים ופירש הענין כן בא הנביא להודיע שהשם יתברך שכן במקדש כמו שיושב בכסא כבוד מרום שהוא השמים העליונים שקראו ישעיהו הנביא גם כן כסא רם ונשא כן קראו ירמיה מרום ואמר שהוא מראשון כלומר מקדם כמ"ש נכון כסאך כאז אמר כמו שהשמים שהם כסא ה' והם כסא כבודו מעידים על מציאותו ועל כבודו כן מקום מקדשנו מעיד ומורה על עצם מציאותו שהשכין אורו וכבודו בו ולא יחשוב ההושב שהיות הש"י על כסא רם ונשא והוא השמים ימנעהו מלדעת את אשר בארץ ומלהשגיח בשפלים ובהעניש הרעים על רשעם כי מקום מקדשנו הוא עדות וראיה שהוא רואה בשפלים וחוקר לבותם וכליותם כי הוא שוכן במקדשנו ושכנו ושבתו בשמים ונראת בו אורו וכבודו ואחר שהוא שוכן בו והוא נמצא בתוכנו מן ההכרח להאמין שהשם רואה אותנו ופוקד את מעשינו ובוחן את לבבינו וכליותינו לטוב ולרע וזה הוא שהוסיף ואמר מקוה ישראל וגו' וענין וסורי בארץ יכתבו כלומר הסורים אשר בעמו שהם סרים מהשם יתברך ומעבודתו יכתבו בארץ לשוב לעפר כבהמות לא יהיה בהם חלק נשאר שיכתב בשמים כבני עליה וזה מפני שעזבו מקור מים חיים היא השם יתברך ע"כ לא יחיו אך ימותו כבהמות וזה הפי' הוא נכון לענין הפרשה: (יג) מקות

מנחת שי

(יא) ימו. ימיו קרי: (יג) וסורי. יסורי קרי:

מצודת דוד

הוא המקבץ עושר ולא במשפט יושר כ"א בעלמת הגב כי העושר הזה לא יתקיים בידו ובחצי ימיו יעזוב העושר ההוא ובסוף ימיו יהיה לא:שים עלמת לבי ויהיה מוחזק לנבל: (יב) כסא כבוד. כמו כסא הכבוד והוא שמי מרום כמ"ש השמים כסאי (ישעיה ס"ו): מראשון. הסוכן לך מקדם כמ"ש נכון כסאך מאז (תהלים צ"ג): מקום מקדשנו. ר"ל כן הוא מקום מקדשנו. כי כמו שהשכינה היא בשמים כן היא בבית המקדש: (יג) מקוה ישראל ה'. לכן מסלאוי שתקות ישראל יהיה אל ה' הואיל ונטעת בבינתך ביניהם: כל עוזביך. כל

מצודת ציון

כ"ו): דגר. ענין לפלוף העוף להמשיך האפרוחים אחריו כמו ודגרה בצלה (ישעיה ל"ד): עושה. ענין אסיפה כמו ויעשו ישראל טובה חיל (במדבר כ"ד): ובאחריתו. בסופו: נבל. פחות ונבזה: (יב) כסא. כמו ככסא ותחסר כ"ף הדמיון וכן יישיב נגה (תהלי י"ז) ומבפסו כנגה: מרום. השמים העליונים: מראשון. מאז מקדם: (יג) מקוה.

but has not laid, so it is he who gathers riches but not by right; he shall leave them in the midst of his days, and at his end he stands dishonored.
12. As a Throne of Glory, exalted from the beginning, so is the place of our Sanctuary.
13. The Lord who is the source of the hopes of Israel,

they grow up for they are not of its kind. So is one who gathers riches but not by right.—[*Rashi*]

Thus, *Rashi* identifies the *kore* with the cuckoo, which calls chicks of other birds, only to have them desert him when they grow up. *Redak,* however, identifies the *kore* as the partridge, as does *Rashi* himself in I Sam. 26:20. Since the prophet stated: to give everyone according to his ways, he proceeds to explain that, although sometimes a wicked man prospers, do not be surprised. He is like the partridge that gathers eggs of other birds, explaining דָגַר as 'gathers,' sits on them, and hatches them. When they hatch, however, they realize that they are not of the same species and desert their adopted parents. The same is true of the wicked man who amasses wealth not by right. He will lose it in the midst of his days.

he stands dishonored—*He is called wicked.*—[*Rashi* from *Jonathan*]

Either he dies young, thus leaving his wealth and being dishonored at his death, or he loses his wealth in the midst of his days, standing dishonored for the rest of his life.—[*Redak*]

12. **As a Throne of Glory**—*Since he wishes to state: All that forsake You shall be shamed, he commences with the praise of the Omnipresent, and says before Him, 'You, Whose Throne of Glory is exalted from the beginning of the Creation of the world and is directed opposite our Sanctuary.*—[*Rashi*]

13. **The Lord Who is the source of**

כָּל־עֹזְבֶיךָ יֵבֹשׁוּ יְסוּרַי בָּאָרֶץ יִכָּתֵבוּ
כִּי עָזְבוּ מְקוֹר מַיִם־חַיִּים אֶת־יְהוָה:
יד רְפָאֵנִי יְהוָה וְאֵרָפֵא הוֹשִׁיעֵנִי
וְאִוָּשֵׁעָה כִּי תְהִלָּתִי אָתָּה: טו הִנֵּה־
הֵמָּה אֹמְרִים אֵלָי אַיֵּה דְבַר־יְהוָה
יָבוֹא נָא: טז וַאֲנִי לֹא־אַצְתִּי מֵרֹעֶה
אחריך

וסורי קרי

פּוּלְחָנָךְ יִבְהֲתוּן וְרַשִׁיעַיָא דַעֲבַרוּ עַל מֵימְרָךְ בְּגֵיהִנָם אִינוּן עֲתִידִין לְמִפַּל אֲרֵי שְׁבָקוּ פּוּלְחָנָךְ יְיָ דִּבְדִילֵיהּ אַתְּ מַיְתֵי עֲלֵיהוֹן יְקָרָא כְּמַבּוּעַ דְּמַיִין דְּלָא פָסְקִין טוּהִי: יד אַסֵּנִי יְיָ וְאֶתַּסֵי פְּרוּקְנִי וְאֶתְפְּרַק אֲרֵי תוּשְׁבַּחְתִּי אַתְּ: טו הָא אִינוּן אָמְרִין לִי אָן דְּאִתְנַבֵּיתָא בִּשְׁמָא דַיְיָ יִתְקַיַּם כְּעַן: טז וַאֲנָא לָא עַכְּבֵית עַל מֵימְרָךְ מִלְאִתְנַבָּאָה עֲלֵיהוֹן לְאוֹתָבוּתְהוֹן לְדַחַלְתָּךְ

מהר"י קרא

תקותן של ישראל ה׳: כל עוזביך יבושו. אלו האומות שעוזבים אותך: וסורי בארץ יכתבו. הרשעים שסרו מאחרי כשאני מדבר בשליחותך אליהם. בארץ יכתבו. פתרונו בארץ יהקקו כלומר יהיו נגזרין למיתה ויהיו נקברים בארץ. ויונתן תרגם בגיהנם אינון עתידין למיפל. כי עזבו את ה׳ שהוא דומה למקור מים חיים אשר לא יכזבו מימיו כך כל הבוטח [בו] לא יבוש: (יד) רפאני ה׳ וארפא. על שראה נבוכדנצר מחריב את בית המקדש אומר כך כשירפא את שבר עמו ואת מחץ מכתו: (טו) הנה המה אומרים אלי. כלו׳ שאני מתנבא להם שאומות עתידין לבוא עליהם ולהגלותם הם משיבין אותי: איה דבר ה׳ יבא נא. כלומר אם יבא עלינו אנו עומדין כנגדם מי הוא שיחת עלינו: (טז) ואני לא אצתי מרועה אחריך. כלומר לא מהרתי [לבקש ממך] שתשימני עליהם לנביא רועה להתנבאות עליהן נבואה של פורענות ואני לא מהרתי לבקש לפניך על איתי פורענות שיבא. כלומר אם הם מתאוים לראותו איה

רש"י

אותם שסרים מדברי שאינם שומעים שליחותי בקברות תחתיות ארץ יכתבו: (יד) כי תהלתי אתה. כך אני מתהלל ומתפאר לומר שאתה מושיעי תהלתי. (ווינטנל"א בלע"ז): (טו) איה דבר ה׳. הפורענות שאתה מתנבא: (טז) ואני לא אצתי. לא מהרתי לזרוך להביאם מהיות

רד"ק

ישראל. ענינו לשון קריאה אתה שאתה מקוה ישראל ומבטח לכל הבוטחי׳ בך כל עוזביך שאין להם בטחון בך יבשו ממבטחם בבשר ודם כמו שהקדים שהיו בוטחים באדם ואמר עוד וסורי בארץ יכתבו והסורים ממך כמ״ש ומן ה׳ יסור לבו בארץ יכתבו לא יהיה להם חלק בך כיון שעזבוך אלא יכתבו בארץ כמו הבהמות שלא ישאר מהם דבר שיהיה להם חלק בך: כי עזבו מקור מים חיים את ה׳. וזהו מדה כנגד מדה שהם עזביך שאתה מקור מים חיים שלא יפסקו כן הדבקים בך לא תפסוק טובתם לא בזה ולא בבא והם שעזבוך ושמו בטחונם בבשר ודם שהוא חלק הארץ כן יכתבו הם בארץ ולא בשמים. מקוה ענין תקוה וכן ת״י סבור ישראל ויש מפרשין כמו מקוה מים כלומר שאתה מקום טהרה לישראל והראשון נכון: וסורי. יסורי כתיב כלומר אותם שיסורו ממך וקרי וסורי והוא תאר מנחי העי״ן בשור״ק כמו סורי הגפן נכריה גולה וסורה נחלץ חשים והדומים להם והכנוי לנביא כלומר סורי מכני שהם סרים מהשם כי אני דבק בהשם והם סרים ממני ועוזבים את ה׳ ועל הדרך הזה אמר ככל אשר צוך משה עבדי אל תסור ממנו כי ממנו יטב אל משה ור״ל מדרכו הטוב וכן אמר ירמיה וסורי ר״ל הסורים ממני כלומר מדרכי התשובה שאני דבק באל ואפשר שיהיה וסורי כמו סורים ויהיה חסר מ״ם הרבים כמו וקרע לו חלוני שהוא כמו חלונים והדומים להם: (יד) רפאני ה׳: הוא בקש רפואה מן המכה והכאב כמו שאמר למה היה כאבי נצח ומכתי אנושה והכאב והמכה כמו שפירשנו הוא הבזוי והקללה: כי תהלתי אתה. אני מתהלל בך שתצילני מידם: (טו) הנה המה. דבר ה׳. שאתה אומר שתחרב הארץ יבא נא כי אין אנחנו מאמינים כי ה׳ דבר להחריב עירו: (טז) ואני לא אצתי. לא דחקתי עצמי

מצודת ציון

מלשון תקוה: וסורי. מלשון הסרה: מקור. מעין: (טו) נא. עתה: (טז) אצתי. ענין מהירות כמו ולא אץ לבא (יהושע י׳):

מצודת דוד

שעוזבים אותך ובוטחים באדם לא יהיה סוף שיבושו: וסורי. הסרים ממני והוא מאמר הנביא כדבר האל: בארץ יכתבו. כספר יכתבו לרדת בתחתיות הארץ בעמקי השאול על כי עזבו מקור הנובע מים חיים וחוזר ומפרש את ה׳ שמשפיע הטובה בכל עת כמקור הנובע: (יד) רפאני. אמר הנביא כשאתה תרפא אותי אהיה נרפא ולתוספת ביאור אמר הושיעני מן הקמים עלי ואז אהיה נושע ר״ל אין ביד מי להושיע לי זולתך: כי תהלתי אתה. בך אני מתהלל לומר שאתה אלהי ישעי: (טו) הנה המה. הקמים עלי אומרים אלי בלעג איה דבר ה׳ יבא עתה ונראה אם האמת אתך כי יחשבו שמלבי אני בודאם לבהלתי אותם: (טז) ואני. אבל אני לא מהרתי ממה בהיה אחריך רועה לרעות צאן עמך ולנבאות להם וכמ״ש בתחלת נבואתו שאמר

Let it come now—We do not believe that God spoke to destroy His city.—[*Redak*]

Thereby, they wish to accuse me of being a false prophet and to condemn me to death.—[*Malbim*]

16. **But I did not hasten**—*I did not hasten to urge You to bring them, because I am a good shepherd, who goes after You to beg mercy for them.*—[*Rashi*]

Others render: But I was not eager

all that forsake You shall be shamed, and they who turn away from me shall be marked out on the earth that they have forsaken the source of living waters, the Lord. 14. Heal me, O Lord, then shall I be healed; help me, then I shall be helped, for You are my praise! 15. Behold, they say to me, "Where is the word of the Lord? Let it come now." 16. But I did not hasten since I was a shepherd

the hopes of Israel—*sits upon it. Therefore, all that forsake You shall be shamed.*—[*Rashi*]

and they that turn away from me shall be marked on the earth—*Those who turn away from my words, who do not hearken to my message, will be marked out in the nether graves of the earth.*—[*Rashi*]

The Midrash (*Tanhuma, Ki theze* 2, Buber 3) explains these verses in a most interesting manner, connecting verses 11 and 12, as follows: This partridge brings other eggs from other birds and sits on them until they emerge from their shells and become chicks, and they climb upon him and pluck his feathers . . . When he wishes (goes out—Buber) to fly (to flee—*Yalkut*), he cannot, for his feathers have been plucked. If a beast or a reptile finds him, he eats him up. Who caused this? Because he stole (raised—Buber) eggs that were not his. So will it be with the nations of the world and the Moabites and the Ammonites who stretched out their hands upon His Throne of Glory and destroyed His Temple and exiled Israel. The Holy One, blessed be He, will obliterate their remembrance, as is stated: '(Zephaniah 2:9) Therefore, as I live, says the Lord of Hosts, the God of Israel, that Moab shall be like Sodom etc.' *Tanhuma Buber* and *Yalkut* read: And stretched out their hands upon the 'Throne of Glory, exalted from the beginning, the place of our Sanctuary,' and destroyed it and burned His Temple.

Kara interprets this as referring to Nebuchadnezzar, whose lust was not sated until he conquered many nations and destroyed the Holy Temple. Ultimately, he was dishonored. See Habakkuk 2.

14. **Heal me**—The prophet petitions God to heal him from his pain and his wound (supra 15:18), meaning the curses and humiliation he was subjected to.—[*Redak*]

save me and I shall be saved—Save me from those who rise up against me. Then, I will be saved, since no one can save me but You.—[*Mezudath David*]

for You are my praise—I praise myself and boast with You, saying that You are my Savior.—[*Rashi*]

my praise—Heb. תְּהִלָּתִי (*vantance in O.F.*), *boast.*—[*Rashi*]

15. **Behold, they say to me**—Those who rise up against me say sarcastically . . .—[*Mezudath David*]

"Where is the word of the Lord?—*The retribution which you prophesy.*—[*Rashi*]

אַחֲרֶיךָ וְיוֹם אָנוּשׁ לֹא הִתְאַוֵּיתִי אַתָּה
יָדָעְתָּ מוֹצָא שְׂפָתַי נֹכַח פָּנֶיךָ הָיָה׃
יז אַל־תִּהְיֵה־לִי לִמְחִתָּה מַחֲסִי אַתָּה
בְּיוֹם רָעָה׃ יח יֵבֹשׁוּ רֹדְפַי וְאַל־אֵבֹשָׁה
אָנִי יֵחַתּוּ הֵמָּה וְאַל־אֵחַתָּה אָנִי הָבִיא
עֲלֵיהֶם יוֹם רָעָה וּמִשְׁנֶה שִׁבָּרוֹן שָׁבְרֵם׃
יט כֹּה־אָמַר יְהוָה אֵלַי הָלֹךְ וְעָמַדְתָּ
בְּשַׁעַר בְּנֵי־*עָם אֲשֶׁר יָבֹאוּ בוֹ מַלְכֵי

תרגום

וּלְיוֹם בִּישׁ דְּאַתְּ מַיְתֵי
עֲלֵיהוֹן לָא חֲמֵידִית אַתְּ
גְּלֵי קֳדָמָךְ אַפָּקוּת
שִׂפְוָתִי גְּלֵי קֳדָמָךְ הֲוָה׃
יז לָא יְהֵי מֵימְרָךְ לִי
כְּדִבִין רְחִיצְנִי אַתְּ בְּעִדַּן
עָקָא׃ יח יִבְהֲתוּן רָדְפַי
וְלָא אֶבְהֵית אֲנָא
יִתַּבְּרוּן אִינוּן וְלָא
אִתְכְּלֵם אֲנָא אַיְתֵי
עֲלֵיהוֹן יוֹם בִּישׁ וְעַל
חַד תְּרֵין תְּבָרָא תַּבְּרִינוּן׃
יט כִּדְנַן אֲמַר יְיָ לִי אֱזֵיל
וּתְקוּם בִּתְרַע בְּנֵי עַמָּא
דְּיָעֲלוּן בֵּיהּ מַלְכַיָּא

ת״א ומשנה שברון. חגיגה טז:

* הי׳ בצירי העם קרי

רש״י

רועה טוב מחזר אחריך לבקש עליהם רחמים: ויום אנוש. חולי של פורענותם לא התאויתי וי״ת ואנא לא עכבית על מימרך מלהתנבאה עליהון לאותבותהון לדהלתך ולפי התרגו׳ יהיה אלתי ל׳ עכוב כלומר לא עכבתי מלומר להם שליחותיך ולהכנס אליך אם היו שומעים אלי: מוצא שפתי נוכח פניך היה, להשיב את המתך מהם: (יז) אל תהיה לי למחתה. אל יהי שליחותיך לי למחתה: (יח) יבושו רודפי.

מהר״י קרא

דבר ה׳ יבא נא אני איני כתאוה לראותו כמו שמפרש והולך ויום אנוש לא התאויתי: אתה ידעת מוצא שפתי נכח פניך היה. שאני מתפלל עליהם לטובה שלא יבא הפורענות: נכח פניך היה. כלומר גלוי לפניך: (יז) אל תהיה לי למחתה. אל יהיו דבריך שאני מתנבא להן בשמך למחיתה שהם מחתים אותי ומביישין אותי כשאני מדבר בשמך אליהם: מחסי אתה. ביום צרתי: רעה. שהם מריעים לי כשאני הולך אצלם בשליחותך: (יח) יבושו רודפי. אלו רשעי הדור שהיו רודפין אותו כשהיה מוכיחן:

רד״ק

ולא דאגתי מזה הדבר שאהיה רועה אחריך כלומר שאהי׳ נביא: ויום אנוש לא התאויתי. כי ידעתי כי יום אנוש יהיה לי יום הנבואה אבל אתה הכרחת אותי. יום אנוש יום חזק וכבד: מוצא שפתי. שאמרתי לך הנה לא ידעתי דבר כי נער אנכי וי״ת ואנא לא עכבית על מימרך מלאתנבאה עליהון וגו׳ כבעמוד: (יז) אל תהיה לי למחתה. כלומר אל תרים לי בנבואתי שאהיה מחתת לפניהם: מחסי אתה ביום רעה. ביום שחושבים עלי רעה אתה מחסי וכן תעשה תמיד שלא אחת לפניהם כמו שהבטחתני: (יח) יבשו רודפי. הבא עליהם אחר שהם אומרים יבא נא הביא אותו עליהם: ומשנה שברון שברם. ומשנה איננו סמוך כי הוא נקוד סגול והוא כמו ושברון שני וכן ומשנה כסף כמו וכסף שני ור״ל בשברון שני שברון אחר שברון ולא ר״ל שנים לבד באמרו משנה אלא שברון אחר שברון כמה פעמים וכן ושוב מול את בני ישראל שנית כמו שפירשנו: (יט) כה אמר ה׳. עם. כתיב וקרי העם ואחד הוא אלא שהכתוב חסר ה״א הידיעה: אשר יבאו בו. תחלת קרא בשער שנכנסין ויוצאין בו מלכי יהודה כי להם ראוי להוכיח העם ולשמור את יום השבת ומ״ש בשער בני העם לקרא באזני העם הנכנסים והיוצאים באותו

מנחת שי

(יז) אל תהיה לי. היו״ד בצירי ונמסר עליו לית: מחסי אתה. החי״ת בגעיא ופתח והוא חד מן ח׳ רפין בליעא עיין שרשים שרש חסה: (יח) ומשנה. בכמה ספרים הנו״ן בצירי ובמסורת ג׳ וחברו ומשנה כסף וגם רד״ק כתוב כי הוא נקוד סגול: (יט) הלך ועמדת. * חסר וא״ו בעקלם מדוייקים וכן משפטו

מצודת דוד

הנה לא ידעתי דבר כי נער אנכי (לעיל א׳): ויום אנוש לא התאויתי. ואף אחר שהלכתי לנבאות שלא כרצוני לא הייתי מתאוה לנבאות עליהם שיבא יום אנוש היא זמן הגלות: אתה ידעת. כי כן היה: מוצא שפתי. מה שהתפללתי עליהם הלא היה מלפניך וכאומר הלא לא רציתי לנבאות להם ובכוא אלי נבואת פורעניות התפללתי עליהם והמה חושבים שמלבי אני בודאם משנאתי בם: (יז) אל תהיה. לכן שאלתי אל תהיה לי הנבואה למכשול ולמחתה הלא מעולם אתה מחסי בעת רעה לזה הושיעני גם עתה: (יח) יבושו רודפי. בעת ילכו גולה: יחתו. הם ישברו ביד האויב: ומשנה שברון. שבר כפול ר״ל שבר על שבר שברם: (יט) בשער בני העם. בשער שמצויים שם בני העם והוא השער אשר מלכי

מצודת ציון

אנוש. ענין מכאוב רב: התאויתי. מל׳ תאוה: נכח. נגד: (יז) למחתה. ענין שבר וכן ולדקתי לא תחת (ישעיה נ״א): (יח) ומשנה. ענין

first, he prayed for their good, but after they humiliated him and abused him considerably, he changed his tactics and prayed for their retribution.—[*Ibn Nachmiash*]

May they be shamed when they go into exile.—[*Mezudath David*]

May they be broken—by the hand of the enemy.—[*Mezudath David*]

and with a second destruction—I.e. a destruction after a destruction, repeated destructions.—[*Redak*]

19. **the gate of the children of the people**—The gate frequented by many of the people.—[*Mezudath David*]

You shall announce My admonition to all the people found in that gate.—[*Redak*]

in which the kings of Judah

after You, and I did not desire the woeful day, You know it. What came out of my lips was before Your face. 17. Let it not be to me for a ruin; You are my shelter on a day of evil.
18. May my pursuers be shamed, but let me not be shamed; may they be broken, but let me not be broken; bring upon them a day of evil, and with a second destruction destroy them.
19. So said the Lord to me: Go and stand in the gate of the children of the people, in which the kings of Judah come,

to be a shepherd after You; i.e., I was not eager to become a prophet. —[*Redak, Mezudath David*]

and . . . the woeful day—*The illness of their retribution I did not desire. Jonathan renders: And I did not hamper Your word from prophesying concerning them to return them to fear You. According to the Targum,* אָצְתִּי *is an expression of hampering. That is to say, I did not hesitate from telling them Your message and to return them to you if they would hearken to me.*—[*Rashi*]

What came out of my lips was before Your face—*to return Your wrath from them.*—[*Rashi*] You know that what came out of my lips was before Your face, that I pray for their good, that the calamity not befall them.—[*Kara*]

Redak, following the interpretation of the beginning of the verse, explains: **and I did not desire the woeful day**—I knew that the day I would prophesy would be a woeful day for me, but You coerced me to prophesy.

What came out of my lips—that I said, "I am a youth."—[*Redak*]

17. **Let it not be to me for a ruin**—*Let not Your mission be to me for a ruin.*—[*Rashi*]

Let Your words, which I prophesy to them in Your name, not be a ruin to me, for the people ruin me and humiliate me when I speak to them in Your name.—[*Kara*]

You are my shelter on a day of evil—You are my shelter on a day of my trouble, on a day they plot evil against me, when I go to them with your message.—[*Kara*]

May You always be my shelter, that I not be broken before them.—[*Redak*]

Ibn Nachmiash asserts that because of this prayer, Nebuzaradan was kindly disposed toward Jeremiah, as below 40:4.

18. **May my pursuers be shamed**—I.e. *the men of Anathoth alone.*—[*Rashi*]

Bring upon them what they demanded, since they said, "Let it come now," bring it upon them.—[*Redak*]

Although it was previously stated that Jeremiah prayed for their good, it is possible that he prayed for the people in general, but not for his pursuers. It is also possible that, at

יהודה ואשר יצאו בו ובכל שערי
ירושלם: כ ואמרת אליהם שמעו דבר
יהוה מלכי יהודה וכל־יהודה וכל
ישבי ירושלם הבאים בשערים
האלה: כא כה אמר יהוה השמרו
בנפשותיכם ואל־תשאו משא ביום
השבת והבאתם בשערי ירושלם:
כב ולא־תוציאו משא מבתיכם ביום
השבת וכל־מלאכה לא תעשו
וקדשתם את־יום השבת כאשר
צויתי את־אבותיכם: כג ולא שמעו
ולא הטו את־אזנם ויקשו את־ערפם

תרגום

דבית יהודה ודיפקון ביה ובכל תרעי ירושלם: כ ותימר להון קבילו פתגמא דיי מלכיא דבית יהודה וכל דבית יהודה וכל יתבי ירושלם דעלין בתרעיא האילין: כא כדנן אמר יי אסתמרו בנפשתכון ולא תטלון מטול ביומא דשבתא ותעלון בתרעי ירושלם: כב ולא תפקון מטול מבתיכון ביומא דשבתא וכל עבידתא לא תעבדון ותקדשון ית יומא דשבתא כמא דפקדית ית אבהתכון: כג ולא קבילו ולא ארכינו ית אודניהון ואקשיאו ית קדלהון בדיל דלא למשמע
ובדיל

רש"י

אנשי ענתות לבדם: (כג) ולא שמעו. אבותיכם למה שצויתים:

מנחת שי

פ"ס במסורת דסוף פרשת וילך: בני *עם. בעם ק': (כ) ואמרת אליהם. במקצת ספרים מדוייקים מלא יו"ד וכן כתוב במסרה גדולה ודירמיה ודישעיה

רד"ק

שער כי לא מלכי יהודה לבד היו נכנסים ויוצאים בו כי גם העם שהיו שוכנים סמוך לאותו שער היו נכנסין ויוצאין בו ואמר לו שיקרא אחר כן בכל שערי ירושלם כדי להזהיר כל העם ומה שאמר לו לקרוא בשערים לפי שהיו מכניסין ומוציאין דרך השערי' בשבת ולא הזהירם אלא בהכנסה והוצאה דרך השערי' חוץ לעיר כי בעיר לא היו חייבים כי ירושלם דלתותיה נעולות בלילה ואין חייבין עליה משום ר"ה לפיכך אמר והבאתם בשערי ירושלם לבלתי הביא משא בשערי העיר הזאת ואמר ולבלתי שאת משא ובא בשערי ירושלים ומה שאמר ולא תוציאו משא מבתיכם ביום השבת ר"ל חוץ לעיר ומה שזכר ההבאה יותר מן ההוצאה לפי שירושלם היה כרך גדול ובכרך המביאים משא הם יותר מן המוציאים כי מביאים בני הכפרים לעיר תבואה ופירות וכן ממכר וכ"כ בספר עזרא כשהוכיחם נחמיה על השבת אמר ומביאים ירושלם ביום השבת ואמר ויסגרו הדלתות ואמר אשר לא יפתחום עד אחר השבת ומנערי העמדתי על השערים לא יבא משא ביום השבת הנה לא הזהירם אלא מחוץ לעיר לא בתוך העיר כי לא היו חייבים בהכנסה והוצאה מבתיהם בתוך העיר לפי שירושלים היו דלתותיה נעולות בלילה ואין חייבין עליה משום ר"ה ומה שאמר שמעו דבר ה' מלכי יהודה ולא היה

מצודת ציון

כפל: (כג) ויקשו. מלשון קשה: ערפם. מלשון אחורי הפנים:

מצודת דוד

יהודה באים ויוצאים בו: ובכל. וכן תלך ותעמוד בכל שערי ירושלי': (כא) השמרו בנפשותיכם. ר"ל היו נשמרים בדבר שיש בו שמירת נפשותיכם ואל תשאו משא ביום השבת להביא אותה בשערי ירושלים מן החוץ: (כב) ולא תוציאו וגו'. אל החוץ: וכל מלאכה. ושום מלאכה: וקדשתם. מבלי לחללו בדבר הנאסר בשבת: (כג) ולא שמעו. אבל הם האבות לא שמעו למצותי: ויקשו את ערפם. הוא ענין משל כאלו נתקשה ערפם עד שלא יוכלו לחזור פניהם ולשמוע: ולבלתי קחת מוסר. לא החזירו פניהם למען לא יקבלו מוסר ותוכחה

until after the Sabbath. And of my youths I appointed a watch over the gates that no burden enter on the Sabbath day.' Hence, we see that the only violation of Sabbath law was in carrying in and out of the gates, not in carrying from the houses into the street. That is because the city gates were closed at night. Therefore, the city streets did not constitute a public domain. Mention of 'kings' of Judah although there was but one king, refers to the princes who were destined to occupy the throne after their father's death.—[*Redak*]

Ibn Nachmiash conjectures that

and out of which they go, and in all the gates of Jerusalem.
20. And you shall say to them: Hearken to the word of the Lord, O kings of Judah and all of Judah and all the inhabitants of Jerusalem, who come into these gates.
21. So said the Lord: Beware for your souls and carry no burden on the Sabbath day, nor bring into the gates of Jerusalem.
22. Neither shall you take a burden out of your houses on the Sabbath day nor shall you perform any labor, and you shall hallow the Sabbath day as I commanded your forefathers.
23. But they did not hearken, neither did they bend their ear[s], and they hardened their nape

come—for it is fitting for them to reprove the people for profaning the Sabbath.—[*Redak*]

He was to announce to the entire populace, not only to the kings, for all the people who lived near that gate would come and go through it.

and in all the gates of Jerusalem—He should make the same announcement in all the gates of Jerusalem to warn the people. He was commanded to announce it in the gates since the people were accustomed to carry burdens from outside the city into the gates of the city and from the city through the gates outside the city. This constituted a violation of Sabbath law. He did not mention carrying within the city, since the city gates were locked at night, conferring upon the city the status of a private domain. There was therefore no prohibition of carrying articles through the street as there usually is when the street has the status of a public domain.—[*Redak*]

21. **nor bring into the gates of Jerusalem**—I.e. to bring from outside Jerusalem into the gates.—[*Redak*]

22. **Neither shall you take a burden out of your houses**—I.e. you shall not take any burden out of your houses through the gates of the city. The emphasis is placed on the bringing in rather than on the carrying out of burdens, since Jerusalem was a large city, and it was more usual to bring grain and produce from the villages than to carry it out. A similar situation is found in Nehemiah 13, where it is mentioned only that they would bring produce to Jerusalem on the Sabbath. No mention is made of carrying out since it was unusual. As mentioned above, he admonished them only not to bring in or carry out of the city, not to refrain from carrying within the city. In verse 19, he states, 'And when the shadows commenced to fall in the gates of Jerusalem before the Sabbath, I commanded and the portals were closed, and I commanded that they not open them

* For Rashi's commentary turn to page 236.

לְבִלְתִּי שׁוֹמֵעַ וּלְבִלְתִּי קַחַת מוּסָר׃
כד וְהָיָה אִם־שָׁמֹעַ תִּשְׁמְעוּן אֵלַי נְאֻם־
יְהוָה לְבִלְתִּי ׀ הָבִיא מַשָּׂא בְּשַׁעֲרֵי
הָעִיר הַזֹּאת בְּיוֹם הַשַּׁבָּת וּלְקַדֵּשׁ אֶת־
יוֹם הַשַּׁבָּת לְבִלְתִּי עֲשׂוֹת־בָּהּ* כָּל־
מְלָאכָה׃ כה וּבָאוּ בְשַׁעֲרֵי הָעִיר הַזֹּאת
מְלָכִים ׀ וְשָׂרִים יֹשְׁבִים עַל־כִּסֵּא דָוִד
רֹכְבִים ׀ בָּרֶכֶב וּבַסּוּסִים הֵמָּה וְשָׂרֵיהֶם
אִישׁ יְהוּדָה וְיֹשְׁבֵי יְרוּשָׁלִָם וְיָשְׁבָה
הָעִיר הַזֹּאת לְעוֹלָם׃ כו וּבָאוּ מֵעָרֵי־
יְהוּדָה וּמִסְּבִיבוֹת יְרוּשָׁלִַם וּמֵאֶרֶץ
בִּנְיָמִן וּמִן־הַשְּׁפֵלָה וּמִן־הָהָר וּמִן־הַנֶּגֶב

* בו קרי

ת"א ביום השבת, בילק יב הוריות ד (שבת ד שבועות לב):

וּבְדִיל דְלָא לְקַבָּלָא
אוּלְפָן: כד וִיהֵי אִם קַבָּלָא
תְקַבְּלוּן לְמֵימְרִי אֲמַר יְיָ
בְּדִיל דְלָא לְאַעָלָא מְטוֹל
בְּתַרְעֵי קַרְתָּא הָדָא
בְּיוֹמָא דְשַׁבְּתָא
וּלְקַדָשָׁא יָת יוֹמָא
דְשַׁבְּתָא בְּדִיל דְלָא
לְמֶעְבַּד בֵּיהּ כָּל
עֲבִידְתָּא: כה וְיֵעֲלוּן
בְּתַרְעֵי קַרְתָּא הָדָא
מַלְכִין וְרַבְרְבִין יָתְבִין
עַל כּוּרְסֵי דָוִד רָכְבִין
בִּרְתִיכִין וּבְסוּסָוָן אִינוּן
וְרַבְרְבָנֵיהוֹן אֱנָשׁ יְהוּדָה
וְיָתְבֵי יְרוּשְׁלֵם וְתִתֵּב
קַרְתָּא הָדָא לְעָלַם:
כו וְיֵיתוֹן מִקִרְוַיָא דְבֵית
יְהוּדָה וּמִסַחֲרָנֵי יְרוּשְׁלֵם
וּמֵאֲרַע שִׁבְטָא בִנְיָמִן וּמִן
שְׁפֵילְתָּא וּמִן טוּרָא וּמִן
דָרוֹמָא מַיְתָן עֲלָוָן וְנִכְסַת
קוּדְשִׁין

רד"ק

אלא מלך אחד ר"ל המלך ובניו ולפי שהיו עתידים למלוך אחר האב קראם מלכים: (כד) עשות בה כל מלאכה. בה כתיב וקרי בו ושניהם נכונים כי ימצא שבת לשון זכר ולשון נקבה לשון נקבה ברוב ולשון זכר כל שומר שבת מחללו ומה שאמר ובאו בשערי העיר הזאת ר"ל ובאו ויצאו כמו שאמר אשר יבאו בו מלכי יהודה ואשר יצאו בו ובמה שצוה להזהירם על השבת והיו כמה עברות אחרות בידם ואף ע"א לפי ששמירת שבת עיקר גדול באמונת האל בחדוש העולם ובאמונה באותות ובמופתים ובקיום כל התורה וכל המשמר השבת באמונה ישרה לא בבהר' הוא חוטא בשאר המצות וארז"ל כל המשמר שבת כהלכת' אפי' עובד עכו"ם כדור אנוש מוחלין לו שנאמר אשרי אנוש יעשה זאת ובן אדם יחזיק בה כל שומר שבת מחללו אל תקרי מחללו אלא מחול לו והמצוה הראשונה שנצטוו ישראל קודם מתן תור' הוא שבת ואתה רואה כמה גדולה שמירת שבת שהרי תלה חרבן ירושלם בשמירת שבת ומפרש והצתי אש בשערים ואכלה ארמנות ירושלי' לכדו רז"ל רמז ואמרו אין הדלקה מצוי' אלא בבית שיש בו חילול שבת ואמרו מאי לא תכבה בשעה שאין בני אדם מצוים לכבותה והנה הפרשה מבוארת וענין פ'

מנחת שי

מלא בספרים מדוייקים: (כג) שומע. שמיע ק': (כד) בה. בו ק': (כו) מבאים. ברוב הספרים, חסר יו"ד קדמאה ומלא יו"ד בתראה: ומביאי. ברוב הספרים חסר יו"ד אחר הבי"ת וכן הוא במסורת מן מלין דחסר יו"ד בליש' ביאה וקשה לי למה לא נמנה במסורה זו מלת מבאים שבפסוק:

מצודת דוד

מן הביאים: (כד) אם שמוע. אם אתם תשמעון אלי לבלי הביא וגו' ולקדש השבת לבלי עשות בו שום מלאכה: (כה) ובאו. אז יבואו בשערי וגו': על כסא דוד. ר"ל על כסא המלוכה מוסב על מלכים: ברכב. במרכבה העשוי לרכוב בה: ובסוסים. הסוסים המרכבה: המה. המלכים: איש יהודה. אנשי יהודה מיתר העם: וישבה. תהיה מיושבת באנשים: (כו) ובאו. יבאו אנשים מערי יהודה וגו': ומן השפלה. מן הערים היושבים בעמק: ומן הנגב. היושבים בפאת הדרום: מביאים. והמה יהיו מביאים עולה וזבח

מצודת ציון

(כו) השפלה. העמק:

not to hearken and not to receive instruction. 24. And it shall be if you hearken to Me, says the Lord, not to bring any burden into the gates of this city on the Sabbath day and to hallow the Sabbath day not to perform any labor thereon, 25. Then shall there enter into the gates of this city kings and princes sitting on David's throne, riding in chariots and with horses, they and their princes, the men of Judah and the inhabitants of Jerusalem, and this city shall be inhabited forever. 26. And they shall come from the cities of Judah and from the environs of Jerusalem and from the land of Benjamin and from the lowland and from the mountain and from the Negev,

Jeremiah repeated this admonition during the reign of each king who reigned during his career as prophet.

25. **Then shall there enter**—The intention is that then there shall enter and leave as in verse 19. He commanded the prophet to reprove the people particularly about the Sabbath precept since it is fundamental in belief in God and in the Creation of the world, also in belief in miracles and in the observance of the entire Torah, to the extent that if one observes the Sabbath with the proper faith, he is not apt to sin by infracting other precepts. Moreover, the Rabbis state that if one observes the Sabbath properly, even if he worships idols like the generation of Enosh, he is forgiven (*Shabbath* 118b).—[*Redak*]

sitting on David's throne—This refers to the kings.—[*Mezudath David*]

and with horses—that draw the chariots.—[*Mezudath David*]

they—the kings.—[*Mezudath David*]

the men of Judah—I.e. the rest of the populace.—[*Mezudath David*]

26. **And they shall come**—I.e., people shall come from the cities of Judah etc.—[*Mezudath David*]

and from the lowland—From the cities of the valley.—[*Mezudath David*]

מְבִאִים עֹלָה וְזֶבַח וּמִנְחָה וּלְבוֹנָה
וּמְבִאֵי תוֹדָה בֵּית יְהוָה: כז וְאִם־לֹא
תִשְׁמְעוּ אֵלַי לְקַדֵּשׁ אֶת־יוֹם הַשַּׁבָּת
וּלְבִלְתִּי ׀ שְׂאֵת מַשָּׂא וּבֹא בְּשַׁעֲרֵי
יְרוּשָׁלִַם בְּיוֹם הַשַּׁבָּת וְהִצַּתִּי אֵשׁ
בִּשְׁעָרֶיהָ וְאָכְלָה אַרְמְנוֹת יְרוּשָׁלִַם
וְלֹא תִכְבֶּה: יח א הַדָּבָר אֲשֶׁר הָיָה
אֶל־יִרְמְיָהוּ מֵאֵת יְהוָה לֵאמֹר: ב קוּם
וְיָרַדְתָּ בֵּית הַיּוֹצֵר וְשָׁמָּה אַשְׁמִיעֲךָ
אֶת־דְּבָרָי: ג וָאֵרֵד בֵּית הַיּוֹצֵר וְהִנֵּהוּ
עֹשֶׂה מְלָאכָה עַל־הָאָבְנָיִם: ד וְנִשְׁחַת

והנה הוא קרי

תרגום

קוּדְשִׁין וְקוּרְבְּנִין וּלְבוּנְתָא וּמַעֲלֵי תוֹדְתָא לְבֵית מַקְדְּשָׁא דַיְיָ: כז וְאִם לָא תְקַבְּלוּן לְמֵימְרִי לְקַדָּשָׁא יָת יוֹמָא דְשַׁבַּתָּא וּבְדִיל דְלָא לְמִטַּל מְטוּל וּמֵיעַל בְּתַרְעֵי יְרוּשְׁלֵם בְּיוֹמָא דְשַׁבְּתָא וְאַדְלֵיק אֶשָּׁתָא בְּתַרְעָהָא וּתְשֵׁיצֵי בִּירָנְיַת יְרוּשְׁלֵם וְלָא תִטְפֵי: א פִּתְגָם נְבוּאָה דַהֲוָה עִם יִרְמְיָה מִן קֳדָם יְיָ לְמֵימָר: ב קוּם וְתֵיחוּת לְבֵית פַּחְרָא וְתַמָּן אַשְׁמְעִינָךְ יָת פִּתְגָמָי: ג וּנְחָתֵית לְבֵית פַּחְרָא וְהָא הוּא עֲבִיד עֲבִידְתָּא עַל סַדְנָא: ד וְאִתְחַבַּל מָנָא

הכלי

ת"א והלתי אש. שבת קיט: בית היוצר. סוטה יא:

רש"י

(כז) ובא. כמו ולבוא: יח (ג) על האבנים על סדנא.

מהר"י קרא

יח (ג) על האבנים. אלו דפוסות של יוצר כלי חרס שעושה

רד"ק

היוצר ג"כ מבוארת ועניינה כי ההשגחה בבני אדם והיכולת ביד האל וכל שכן ישראל שהשגחתו תמיד עליהם לפיכך אמר כן אתם בידי בית ישראל: (ג) והנהו. כתוב מלה אחת וקרי והנה הוא שתי מלות והענין אחד: האבנים. כלי היוצר שעושה עליו

מנחת שי

יח (ג) והנהו. והנה הוא ק' ועיין מ"ש הרמב"ע בס' לחות דף קמ"ט:

מצודת דוד

וגו' ומהם יהיו מביאים קרבן תודה אל בית ה': (כז) ואם לא תשמעו אלי. מה שצויתי לקדש את יום השבת ולבלתי שאת משא ולבא עמה בשערי ירושלים: והצתי. אז אבעיר אש בשערים ותשרף הארמנות ולא תכבה עד תשרוף הכל:

יח (ב) בית היוצר. לבית אומן חרס: (ג) עושה מלאכה. עושה מלאכתו בחומר אשר בידו על האבנים והוא הכלי המיוחד לכך: (ד) ונשחת הכלי. נתקלקל הכלי אשר היה עושה בחומר כשהי' ביד היוצר כשעשה הכלי: ושב. וחזר היוצר ועשה מהחומר ההוא

מצודת ציון

(כז) והצתי. ענין הבערה: ואכלה. ותשרוף וכן כמאכלת אש (ישעיה כ"ט): ארמנות. היכלות ופלטרין: תכבה. מלשון כבוי:

יח (ב) קום. הוא ענין זרוז: (ג) האבנים. כן שם הכלי המיוחד ליוצר חרס לעשות עליו מלאכתו ודומה לו ורואיתן על

11) explains that, although the implement is called אָבְנָיִם, lit. two stones, it was made of wood, not stone. It was called *avnaim* because of its resemblance to millstones. *Daath Mikra* has illustrations of these implements found in Megiddo. He explains that the bottom stone had a pivot in the middle, and the upper stone had a hole into which the pivot would fit. The potter would rotate the bottom stone with his feet, thus rotating the upper stone along with it. With the upper stone he would shape the clay. Although Ibn Janach saw only

bringing burnt offerings and sacrifices and meal-offerings and
frankincense, and those bringing thanksgiving offerings to the
house of the Lord. 27. And if you will not hearken to Me to
hallow the Sabbath day and not to carry burdens and to come
into the gates of Jerusalem on the Sabbath, I will kindle a fire in
her gates, and it will consume the palaces of Jerusalem, and it
will not be quenched.

18

1. The word that came to Jeremiah from the Lord, saying:
2. Rise and go down to the house of the potter, and there I will
let you hear My words. 3. So I went to the house of the potter,
and behold, he was doing work on the wheels.

bringing burnt offerings—Since the Temple will not be destroyed, they will come with sacrifices.—[*Malbim*]

sacrifices—Heb. זֶבַח. This usually refers to peace-offerings.

and frankincense—This is brought with the meal offering, as in Lev. 2:1.

and those bringing thanksgiving offerings—to thank God for His miracles.—[*Malbim*]

27. **and to come**—Heb. וּבֹא, *like* וְלָבֹא.—[*Rashi*]

I.e., and to come with it.—[*Mezudath David*]

I will kindle a fire—Note the importance of the Sabbath, that Scripture depends the destruction of Jerusalem on whether the Jews keep the Sabbath. The Rabbis (*Shabbath* 119b) deduce from here that fires are usual only in a house where the Sabbath is profaned. Then it will break out when there is no one to quench it.—[*Redak*]

1. **The word**—This chapter illustrates Divine Providence and power over mankind and especially over Israel.—[*Redak*]

2. **Rise and go down**—Since, after all the evil decrees, God revealed to the prophet that if they observe the Sabbath, He would repeal the decree, He calls him to the house of the potter to illustrate His words graphically.—[*Malbim*]

3. **on the wheels**—*Jonathan* renders: *on the wheel.* (*Formes in French*).—[*Rashi*]

These are the forms of a maker of earthenware, with which the potter makes large and small vessels. אָבְנָיִם (*formes* in French).—[*Kara*]

Redak in *Shorashim* describes it as having the shape of a mill, consisting of two flat circular wooden blocks, the larger one below and the smaller one lying atop it. These were the implements used by the potters of the East. He quotes this description from Rabbi Jonah Ibn Janach. Ibn Janach (*Sepher Haschoraschim*, p.

הכלי אשר הוא עשה בחמר ביד
היוצר ושב ויעשהו כלי אחר כאשר
ישר בעיני היוצר לעשות: ה ויהי דבר־
יהוה אלי לאמור: ו הכיוצר הזה לא־
אוכל לעשות לכם בית ישראל
נאם־יהוה הנה כחמר ביד היוצר כן
אתם בידי בית ישראל: ז רגע אדבר
על־גוי ועל־ממלכה לנתוש ולנתוץ
ולהאביד: ח ושב הגוי ההוא מרעתו
אשר דברתי עליו ונחמתי על־הרעה
אשר חשבתי לעשות לו: ט ורגע

מנא דהוה עביד דטינא
ביד פחרא ותב ועבדי
מן אוחרן כמא דכשר
בעיני פחרא למעבד:
ה והוה פתגם נבואה
מן קדם יי עמי למימר:
ו הכפחרא הדין הלא
יוכלא קדמי למעבד
לכון בית ישראל אמר
יי הא כמא דטינא ביד
פחרא כן אתון חשיבין
קדמי בית ישראל:
ז זמן אמליל על עמא
ועל מלכותא למעקר
ולתרעא ולאבדא:
ח ויתוב עמא ההוא
מבישתיה דגזרית
עלוהי ואיתוב מן
בישתא דחשבית
למעבד ליה: ט וזמן

ת"א הנה כחומר. ברכות לב סוטה נג (ברכות יד): רגע אדבר. עקדה שער לו:

מלא וא"ו

רש"י

(פרומא"ש בלע"ז): **(ד) אשר הוא עושה בחומר.** אשר הוא עושה מן החומר נשחת ביד היוצר בעודו לח ומקרא מסורס הוא: **(ח) מרעתו אשר דברתי עליו.** מעבירות שבידו אשר

מהר"י קרא

בהם היוצר כלים קטנים וגדולים. אבנים פירש בלע"ז:

רד"ק

הכלים מחומר אשר בידו וי"ת סדנא ובספר השרשים הארכתי בפירושו עוד: (ד) ישר. פעל עבר כי הוא חציו קמוץ וחציו פתח: (ח) ברעתו אשר דברתי. פי' מרעתו אשר דברתי עליו בעבורם להרע לו אחר כן אמר ורגע אדבר וגו': (ט) לבנות

מנחת שי

(ד) עשה בחומר ביד היוצר. בני"ת כן פירשו המפרשים וכן מוגה בספרים מדוייקים: (ה) אלי לאמור. חד מן ג' מלא וא"ו: (ז) לנתוש ולנתוץ. התיי"ן

מצודת דוד

כלי אחר משונה מן הראשון כפי אשר יכשר בעיניו: (ו) הכיוצר. וכי לא אוכל לעשות עמכם כדרך שעושה היוצר עם החומר שעושה ממנו כלי אחר אחר שנשחת הראשון: הנה כחומר. כאשר כמו שהחומר הוא ביד היוצר לעשות בו מה שירצה כן אתם בידי: (ז) רגע אדבר. כרגע אחת אגזור על אומה מהעכו"ם כליון ואבדון בעבור רעתם: (ח) ושב. יחזור בו הגוי ההוא מהרעה אשר

מצודת ציון

האבנים (שמות א') שהוא המיוחד אל היולדת: (ד) בחומר. טיט: (ז) לנתוש. ענין עקירה: ולנתוץ. ענין כתיתה ושבירה וכן לנתוש ולנתוץ ולהרוס (לקמן א'): (ח) ונחמתי. ענין הפוך

4. And the vessel that he was making of clay was spoiled in the potter's hand, and he made it again another vessel, as it had pleased the potter to make. 5. And the word of the Lord came to me, saying: 6. As this potter can I not do to you, O house of Israel? says the Lord. Behold, as clay in the potter's hand, so are you in My hand, O house of Israel. 7. One instant I may speak concerning a nation and concerning a kingdom, to uproot and to demolish and to destroy. 8. And when that nation repents of its evil for which I spoke concerning it, I will repent of the evil that I thought to do to it.

wooden ones, archaeologists have discovered stone implements of this sort.

4. **that he was making of clay**—That he was making of the clay was spoiled in the potter's hand while it was still wet, and this is an inverted verse.—[*Rashi*]

This allegory consists of two parts: (1) that the first vessel was completely destroyed and demolished, and (2) that this destruction was temporary, for he made another vessel from the clay.—[*Malbim*]

and he made it again another vessel—Not a vessel of another shape, but—

as it had pleased the potter to make—I.e., as it has pleased him to make originally.—[*Malbim*] This is the past tense.—[*Redak*]

6. **As this potter can I not do to you, O house of Israel?**—I.e., in accordance with these two allegories.—[*Malbim*]

7. **One instant I may speak**—Just as in the second allegory, the breaking of the vessel was very temporary, and only in order to make another vessel, so was the decree temporary and only so that the nation repent.—[*Malbim*]

8. **of its evil for which I spoke concerning it**—*Of its sins for which I spoke concerning it.*—[*Rashi*]

This may also be translated: And when that nation repents because of its evil that I spoke concerning it. I.e., if the nation repents only because of fear of the evil I decreed against it, its repentance nevertheless helps to repeal the decree.—[*Malbim*]

to uproot and to demolish—(*dépayser [?] in French*). This appears to be in the wrong place. It

* For Rashi's commentary turn to page 237.

אֲדַבֵּר עַל־גּוֹי וְעַל־מַמְלָכָה לִבְנוֹת
וְלִנְטוֹעַ׃ י וְעָשָׂה הָרַעָה בְּעֵינַי לְבִלְתִּי
שְׁמֹעַ בְּקוֹלִי וְנִחַמְתִּי עַל־הַטּוֹבָה אֲשֶׁר
אָמַרְתִּי לְהֵיטִיב אוֹתוֹ׃ יא וְעַתָּה אֱמָר־
נָא אֶל־אִישׁ יְהוּדָה וְעַל־יוֹשְׁבֵי
יְרוּשָׁלַםִ לֵאמֹר כֹּה אָמַר יְהוָה הִנֵּה
אָנֹכִי יוֹצֵר עֲלֵיכֶם רָעָה וְחֹשֵׁב עֲלֵיכֶם
מַחֲשָׁבָה שׁוּבוּ נָא אִישׁ מִדַּרְכּוֹ הָרָעָה
וְהֵיטִיבוּ דַרְכֵיכֶם וּמַעַלְלֵיכֶם׃ יב וְאָמְרוּ
נוֹאָשׁ כִּי־אַחֲרֵי מַחְשְׁבוֹתֵינוּ נֵלֵךְ וְאִישׁ

תרגום

אֲמַלֵיל עַל עַמָא וְעַל מַלְכוּתָא לְמִבְנֵי וּלְקַיָמָא׃ י וְיַעְבֵּיד דְבִישׁ קֳדָמַי בְּדִיל דְלָא לְקַבָּלָא לְמֵימְרִי וְאֵיתוּב מִן טַבְתָא דַאֲמָרִית לְאֵיטָבָא לֵיהּ׃ יא וּכְעַן אֱמַר כְּעַן לֶאֱנָשׁ יְהוּדָה וּלְיָתְבֵי יְרוּשְׁלֵם לְמֵימַר כִּדְנַן אֲמַר יְיָ הָא אֲנָא בָרֵי עֲלֵיכוֹן בִּישָׁא וּמְחַשֵׁב עֲלֵיכוֹן מַחְשְׁבָא תּוּבוּ כְעַן גְבַר מֵאוֹרְחֵיהּ בִּישְׁתָא וְאַתְקִינוּ אוֹרְחָתְכוֹן וְעוֹבָדֵיכוֹן׃ יב וַאֲמָרוּ תִּבְנָא מִבָּתַר פּוּלְחָנָךְ אֲרֵי בָתַר עֲשָׁתוּנָנָא נְהָךְ וּגְבַר הרהור

הרע קרי

מהר"י קרא

(יא) אמר נא אל איש יהודה. אע"פ שאני יוצר עליכם רעה וחושב עליכם מחשבה רעה אעפ"כ: שובו. עדיין: איש מדרכו הרעה והטיבו דרכיכם ומעלליכם. גם אני אנחם על הרעה שדיברתי לעשות כמו יוצר הזה כשנשחת הכלי אשר

רש"י

בשבילו דברתי עליו: לנתוש ולנתוץ. (אשרפורק"י בלע"ז): ונחמתי. והשבתי מחשבה אחרת: (יב) ואמרו נואש. וידעתי שהם יאמרו לך על דבריך שאין חוששין

מנחת שי

רפין: ולהאביד. הוא"ו בגעיא: (י) הרעה. הרע ק': (יא) יוצר עליכם. אין לשמוע לעלת מי שחשב לומר יועץ במקום יוצר: והיטיבו דרכיכם.

רד"ק

ולנטוע: פי' וכן עשיתי שבניתים ונטעתים ואחר כך עשה הרע ונחמתי והוצרכנו לפי' הזה לפי שצריך להפריש בין שתי המדות האלה כי הרעה לא תחול אם יעשו תשובה אבל הטובה תחול על כל פנים כיון שיעדה האל אבל לא תעמוד אם יעשו הרעה כמ"ש ירמיהו לחנניה בן עזור ויש רמז בענין הזה כי ברעה אמר חשבתי ובטובה אמר אמרתי: (י) להיטיב אותו. כמו להטיב לו וכן את מי הגדת מלין כמו למי: (יא) ועל יושבי. כמו ואל יושבי וכן והתפלל על ה' כמו אל ה': יוצר עליכם רעה. מחדש ואמר בזה הלשון לפי שזכר בפרשת יוצר כלי חרש שהוא מחדש הכלים ועוש' כלי זה ואחר כך כלי אחר חדש שלא ידמה לראשון כן אחדש עליכם רעה אחר רעה: (יב) ואמרו נואש. וכשתאמר

מצודת ציון

מחשבה: (יא) יוצר. בורא ומחדש: ומעלליכם. מעשיכם: (יב) נואש. מלשון יאוש ועזיבת הדבר כמו ותאמרי נואש (לעיל

מצודת דוד

בעבורה גזרתי עליה האבדון: ונחמתי. אז בהרגע ההיא אני מתנחם על הרעה ולא אביאנה: (יא) איש יהודה. אנשי יהודה: ועל יושבי. ואל יושבי: יוצר. בורא עליכם רעה וחושב להפרע

כה מהם לכן שובו עתה כל איש מדרכו וגו': (יב) ואמרו נואש. ידעתי שיאמרו אנו מתייאשים מדרכי המקום אלא נלך אחר

11.. .. **I am devising evil upon you**—Heb. יוֹצֵר, *forming.* This expression is used because it coincides with יוֹצֵר, *a potter,* who makes new vessels, and makes first one vessel and then another unlike the first. So will I devise against you one evil after another.—[*Redak*]

12. **But they shall say, "We despair**—*I know that they will say to you regarding your words that they do not heed them.*—[*Rashi*]

9. And at one instant I may speak concerning a nation and concerning a kingdom, to build and to plant, 10. And it will do what is evil in My eyes, not to hearken to My voice, I will repent of the good I said to benefit it. 11. And now, say now to the men of Judah and to the inhabitants of Jerusalem, saying, So said the Lord: Behold I am devising evil upon you, and I am laying plans against you. Return now, each one from his evil way and improve your ways and your deeds. 12. But they shall say, "We despair, but after our thoughts we will go, and we will do

should be in the preceding verse. The Warsaw edition reads: *for which I spoke concerning it to uproot and to demolish* (*dépayser in French*). See above 1:10.

9. **to build and to plant**—And so I did, that I built and planted them, and if then they deal wickedly, I will repent. It is necessary to explain in this manner because there must be a difference between a favorable prophecy and an unfavorable one, that in the case of an unfavorable prophecy, repentance helps to avoid the evil completely, whereas, in the case of a favorable prophecy, the good must come about in any case, only that if the people become wicked, it does not remain. This is illustrated in the episode of Jeremiah and Hananiah son of Azzur. The latter prophesied that in two years the Lord would restore the vessels of the Temple and return those exiled with Jeconiah. Thereupon, Jeremiah announced, "(infra 28:9) The prophet who prophesies for peace, when the prophet's word comes, the prophet whom God truly sent will be known." I.e., if a prophet prophesies favorably, his prophecy must be realized. Otherwise, he is surely a false prophet. There is an allusion to this principle in the wording of our chapter. Concerning evil, Scripture states: that I thought to do, and concerning good, Scripture states: that I said to benefit it.—[*Redak*]

This distinction between favorable and unfavorable prophecies is in accordance with *Rambam, Introduction to Mishnah Commentary. Abarbanel* and *Ibn Nachmiash disagree and maintain that God may repent of the prophecy in either case. Consequently, the truth of any prophet cannot be tested by the failure of his prophecy to be realized. Abarbanel* maintains that the truth of the prophet is tested only by wonders which he claims will come about. If they fail to come about, he is judged as a false prophet. The episode of Hananiah son of Azzur is explained differently, as will be discussed there.

שְׁרִרוּת לִבּוֹ־הָרָע נַעֲשֶׂה׃ יג לָכֵן כֹּה
אָמַר יְהוָה שַׁאֲלוּ־נָא בַּגּוֹיִם מִי שָׁמַע
כָּאֵלֶּה שַׁעֲרֻרִת עָשְׂתָה מְאֹד בְּתוּלַת
יִשְׂרָאֵל׃ יד הֲיַעֲזֹב מִצּוּר שָׂדַי שֶׁלֶג
לְבָנוֹן אִם־יִנָּתְשׁוּ מַיִם זָרִים קָרִים
נוֹזְלִים׃ טו כִּי־שְׁכֵחֻנִי עַמִּי לַשָּׁוְא יְקַטֵּרוּ

הִרְהוּר לִבֵּיהּ בִּישָׁא
נַעֲבֵיד׃ יג בְּכֵן כִּדְנַן
אֲמַר יְיָ שְׁאִילוּ כְעַן
בְּעַמְמַיָא מַן שְׁמַע
כְּאִלֵּין שְׁנוּי עֲבָדַת
לַהֲדָא כְּנִשְׁתָּא דְיִשְׂרָאֵל׃
יד הָא כְּמָה דְלֵית אֶפְשַׁר
דְּיִפְסוֹק מֵי תַלַג דְּנָחֵית
עַל חַקְלֵי לִבְנָן כֵּן לָא
יִפְסְקוּן מְטַר נָחֲתִין
וּמֵי מַבּוּעַ נָבְעִין׃ טו אֲרֵי
שְׁבַקוּ פוּלְחָנִי עַמִּי לָא

רש״י

להם: (יג) שערורית. דבר גנאי: (יד) היעזוב מצור שדי שלג לבנון. היעזוב אדם הצריך לשתות מים הנוזלים מצור שבשדות הבאים משלג הלבנון שהוא נקי: אם ינתשו מים זרים. או אם יעזבו מים חיים נובעים שהם זרים עד הנה מכל אדם והם קרים. זרים הם נובעים וזה יוכיח אני קרתי ושתיתי מים זרים (ישעיה ל"ז) ומנחם חבר זרים עם לא זורו ולא חובשו (שם א') לשון מימי תרופה ונתן טעם לדבריו ואמר כי אם בקש לדבר בלשון זרם היה מכפיל את המ"ם והיה מוסיף יו"ד מ"ם והיה אומר זרומים לרבות המים ולהיותם זרמים: שדי. כמו שדה: קרים. (פריווד"ש בלע"ז): נוזלים. (קורנ"י בלע"ז) ועוד יש לפתרו אם ינתשו להיות מים זרים נמאסים המי' שהם קרים נוזלים: (זרים. ללשון ראשון היא לשון זרם ללשון שני הוא לשון זרות כלומר מים מאוסים): (טו) כי. כן עשו עמי אשר שכחוני ולשוא יקטרו: שבילי עולם. שבילים המתוקנים אמרו

מהר״י קרא

הוא עושה בחומר ביד היוצר ושב ויעשהו כלי אחר כאשר יישר בעיניו לעשות כמו כן כשרגע אדבר על גוי ועל ממלכה לנתוש ולנתוץ ושב הגוי ההוא מרעתו. גם אני נחמתי על הרעה אשר דברתי לעשות לו. לכן אמר אל איש יהודה שובו נא ואם יאמרו נואש כי אחרי מחשבותינו נלך ואיש אחרי שרירות לבו הרע נעשה: (יג) לכן כה אמר ה' שאלו נא בגוים מי שמע כאלה וגו'. אם נעשה בכל האומות דבר כיעור כמו שנעשה בישראל ומפרש והולך מה שערורית זהו: (יד) היעזוב מצור שדי שלג לבנון. כלומר היעזב אדם מים החיים היוצאין מן הצור וישתה מים רעים היוצאים מן שלג לבנון הנמצאים בשדה או ינתוש אדם מים קרים נוזלים וישתה מים זרים בתמיה: (טו) כי שכחוני עמי. שיש באלהותי ומכמרין לשוא שאין

רד״ק

להם זה חם יאברו לך נואש כלומר נואש לבנו מהלוך אחרי ה': (יג) לכן. שערורי'. ענין לכלוך וטנוף ומי שמע. כזה שיניח אדם טהור וילך אחרי גלול וטנוף וי"ת שנוי כלומר דבר משונה עשתה והמשיל משל ואמר: (יד) היעזוב מצור שדי שלג לבנון. היעזוב אדם המים היוצאים מצור שדה וזכר שדה לפי שהם נמצאים אתו בשדה ומזומנים לו ולא יצטרך ללכת אחריהם לרחוק לשתות מהם אבל אם הם בשדה ונוזלים מצור שהם קרים היעזוב אדם אותם משתותם בימי החום באבת לא יעזוב אותם ואני לישראל טוב כמים קרים על נפש עיפה ואני מזומן וקרוב אליהם בכל קראם אלי ואיך עזבוני ושכחוני עמי והמשיל עוד משל אחר קרוב לזה כי המים הקרים והטובים יביאום בני אדם מרחוק דרך צנורות מתחת הארץ עד לעיר או קרוב לעיר מרוב חשיבותם וקראם זרים לפי שהם באים ממקום זר ורחוק ואותן מים אם ינתשו באמת לא ינתשו ואני רחוק מהם לפי מעלתי וקרוב אליהם להטיב להם אם ישמעו אלי ואיך נטשוני ושכחוני עמי: ינתשו. בתי"ו כמו בטי"ת שהיא נטישה ועזובה כי הטי"ת והתי"ו ממוצא אחד ויבאו בענין אחד כמו טעה ותעה וכן ונטשתי אתכם ואת העיר אשר נתתי לכם ולאבתיכם מעל פני כענין ונתשתי בתי"ו וי"ת הפ' כן כמא דלית איפשר דיפסקון מי תלג וגו' כבעמוד: (טו) כי שכחוני. ויכשילום. חסר

מנחת שי

בספרים הטובים מלא יו"ד אחר ה"א ואחר טי"ת: (יד) אם ינתשו. בתי"ו כמו בטי"ת רד"ק: (טו) שבילי עולם. במדוייקים כתוב ש ב י ל י ביו"ד ואין כאן ק' וכתיב כלל אבל רד"ק כתב שבולי בוא"ו וקרי שבילי ביו"ד וכן הוא בקצת

מצודת דוד

מחשבותינו: ואיש וגו'. נעשה כל איש כפי מה שמראה לו לבו הרע ומתאוה לה: (יג) מי שמע כאלה. מי מהגוים שמע כדברים כאלה ומי נלך בשרירות הלב: שערורית. דבר מגונה עשתה הרבה מאד בתולת ישראל המיוחדת אלי כבתולה בבית אביה המיוחדת למי שישאנה: (יד) היעזוב. וכי מהראוי לעזוב מים היורדים מן הצור אשר בשדה הבאים מהפשרת השלג אשר בלבנון שלא המים ההם המה מתוקים וקרים וטובים לרוות הצמאון: אם ינתשו. וכי מהראוי לנטוש ולעזוב מים הזרים מאנשים הבאים ממרחק במלאכת הצנורות והמה קרים ומטפטפים מעצמם ובקל יוקח מהם ואיך מי יעזבם ור"ל וכי מהראוי לעזוב את המקום המשפיע בכל עת חכמה והשכל בלבות הדורשים אותו: (טו) לשוא

מצודת ציון

כ'): שרירות. ענין ראיה והבטה: (יג) שערורית. ענין דבר מגונה ומכוער כמו שמה ושערורה (לעיל ה'): (יד) מצור. מסלע. לבנון. שם יער בארץ ישראל: ינתשו. כמו ינטשו בטי"ת כי דטלנ"ת מתחלף וכמו שיבואו בענין אחד טעה ותעה ונטישה היא ענין עזיבה כמו כי לא יעזוב (ש"א י"ב): זרים. מל' זר ונכרי: קרים. מלשון קור וצנה: נוזלים. מלשון הזלה והשפה כמו יזל

make it plural.] But זר has nine definitions, and none is closer to its interpretation than this, and the following is the interpretation of the verse. 'Shall one abandon the water of the snow of Lebanon that flows from a rock of the field,' that goes slowly on the sand of the earth? Should anyone who finds water of the snow of Lebanon leave it? Is it pleasing to its finder to leave it when it is for everlasting life, refreshing the soul and reviving the spirit and relieving the body? 'Is it proper to abandon and destroy a spring of water designated for healing? Faith-

each one the view of his evil heart. 13. Therefore, so said the Lord: Ask now among the nations, who heard of anything like these? The virgin of Israel committed a very disgraceful thing. 14. Shall one abandon [water flowing] from rocks of the field [that comes from] the snow of Lebanon? Shall strange cold flowing water be abandoned? 15. For My people have forgotten Me; they burn incense to vanity;

I.e. we despair of following the Lord.—[*Redak*]

the view of his evil heart—Heb. שְׁרִרוּת. See above 3:17 for other definitions.

13. **Who heard of anything like these?**—Which people heard anything like these, that they should say, "We will follow the view of our heart"?—[*Mezudath David*]

Who heard of such things, that a person should reject a clean thing only to choose filth and contamination?—[*Redak*]

disgraceful thing—Heb. שַׁעֲרֻרִת.—[*Rashi*] *Redak* defines it as a filthy, contaminated thing.

14. **Shall one abandon from rocks of the field the snow of Lebanon**—*Shall a man who needs to drink abandon water that flows from the rock in the fields that comes from the snow of the Lebanon, which is clean?*—[*Rashi*]

Shall strange cold ... water be abandoned?—*Or shall flowing spring water, which was strange to all people until now, and it is cold, be abandoned?* זָרִים *means flowing, and this proves it:* '(2 Kings 19:24) *I dug and drank strange water* (זָרִים). *Menahem, however, classified with* '(Isaiah 1:6) *they have not been sprinkled* (זֹרוּ), *neither have they been bandaged,' an expression of curative water, and he gave a reason for his statement, and he said that if he wished to speak with an expression of* זֶרֶם, *a stream, he would double the 'mem,' and he would add 'yud' 'mem,' and he would say* זרוּמִים *because of the plural number of* מַיִם, *water, and because they are streams* (זְרָמִים).—[*Rashi* from *Machbereth Menahem* p. 18] Our editions of *Machbereth Menahem* read: מַיִם זָרִים (Jer. 18:14) are curative waters. Some commentators compare מַיִם זָרִים to '(Habakkuk 3:10) a stream of water (זֶרֶם מַיִם),' '(Psalms 77:18) The clouds dripped water like a stream (זֹרְמוּ),' but it is incorrect to interpret [it] in that manner, because the letters of זֶרֶם are all three of them radicals, and if he wished to speak with an expression of זֶרֶם, he would double the 'mem' and say, זְרָמִים, and he would leave זרם, because the entire word is radical, and he would add 'yud' 'mem' to make the 'stream' plural to become זְרָמִים. But when you do this to מַיִם זָרִים, [i.e. to classify it as curative water] the 'zayin' 'resh' are found to be the radicals, and the rest is like the rest of the language, [i.e. it follows the rule of the rest of the language, adding 'yud' 'men' as a suffix to

* For Rashi's commentary turn to page 237.

ויכשלום בדרכיהם שבולי עולם
ללכת נתיבות דרך לא סלולה:
טז לשום ארצם לשמה שרוקת עולם
כל עובר עליה ישם ויניד בראשו:
יז כרוח־קדים אפיצם לפני אויב ערף
ולא־פנים אראם ביום אידם: יח ויאמרו
לכו ונחשבה על־ירמיהו מחשבות כי

ת"א לכו ונחשבה. פקדס סער כח: שבילי קרי· שריקת קרי

תרגום

להנאה אסיקו בוסמין ואטעיאונון באורחתהון בישתא משבילין תקנן דמן עלמא למיזל באורחן דלא תקנן בשבילין דלא מכבשין: טו לשואה ארעהון לצדו אשתממות עלם כל דיעבר עלה יבלי ויניד ברישיה: יז כבידור רוח קדומא כן אבדרינון קדם בעלי דבביהון קדל ולא אפין אחזינון ביום תברהון: יח ואמרו אתו ונחשב על ירמיה

רש"י

שהם מכשול כדי ללכת: דרך לא סלולה. לא כבושה: (טז) שריקות. העובר על חרבות שראה כבר בבניינים טובות רגיל לשרוק: ישום. יתמה: (יז) עורף ולא פנים. כשיברחו מפני האויב: אראם. ולא אושיעם: (יח) ויאמרו

מהר"י קרא

בו מכש: ויכשילום. הם כשילים את עצמן בדבר שהולכין בדרכיהם הרעים שמניחין שבילי עולם ללכת נתיבות דרך לא סלולה וגורמים לעצמם לשום ארצם לשמה שריקות עולם: (יז) כרוח קדים אפיצם. במלך שהוא חזק כרוח קדים שהוא קשה מכל הרוחות: עורף ולא פנים אראם. כביכול כאדם שכועס על חבירו. וכשהוא רואה אותו אינו רואה אותו אלא לאחורי העורף ואינו נוטה אליו פנים: (יח) ויאמרו לכו ונחשבה על ירמיה מחשבות. אמר ירמיה כשאני הולך ומוכיחן הם

מנחת שי

כפרים: (טז) שרוקת. שריקת ק׳: (יז) כרוח קדים. בכ"ף וכן במסורת כרוח קדים ב׳ וסימן כרוח קדים עזה כל הלילה כרוח קדים תשבר אניות תרשיש ע"כ. ולא קא חשיב דין משום דליתיה בכ"ף וכן נראה מהתרגום ורד"ק והלפודי פ׳ י"ד וכתב המתורגמן ערך רוח ברוב העולם טועין וקורין בכ"ף ועיין מה שכתוב ביחזקאל ט"ו אל"ל וכדמי כניך:

רד"ק

המכשילים וכן ויגד ליעקב ויגד המגיד והמכשילים הם נביאי השקר: שבילי עולם. חסר לעזוב שבילי עולם כלומר הם המכשילים השבילים שדרכו אבותיהם הצדיקי׳ מעולם וללכת נתיבו׳: דרך לא סלולה. כי דרכם היא דרך לא דרוכה כי חרשה היא כמו שאמ׳ חדשי׳ מקרוב באו: שבולי. כתי׳ בוי"ו וקרי שבילי ביו"ד והענין אחד אבל המשקלים אינם אחד וחסרון מלת לעזוב וימצאו כמות רבים כי כן דרך הכ׳ לחסר מלים שיובן ענינם מהכ׳ ותחס עליך שחסר נפשי או עיני ותכל דוד והדומים להם רבים כמו שכתבנו בספר מכלל: (טז) לשום. הם גורמין בדרכיה׳ הרעים לשום ארצם לשמה: שריקות עולם. כתיב בוי"ו וקרי ביו"ד שריקות ר"ל שישרוק עליהם כל עובר וזה יהיה לעולם כלומר זמן רב: ישם ויניד בראשו. יתמה בלבו ויניד בראשו כאדם התמה: (יז) כרוח. כמו רוח קדים שהיא חזקה ומפיצה הקש והדברים הדקים כן אפיצם לפני האויב שיברחו לפניו הנה והנה ערף ולא פנים: אראם. מדה כנגד מדה כמו שהם פנו אלי ערף ולא פנים כן אפנה להם ערף ולא פנים אראם כי אפנה אליהם כלומר כשיבא יום אידם אסתיר פני מהם ולא אראם בפנים להושיעם רק ראיית ערף שהוא הסתרת פנים והשלכה אחר גו: (יח) ויאמרו. אלה הם דברי ירמיהו שאמר

מצודת ציון

מים מדליו (במדבר כ"ד): (טו) שבילי. נתיבות. ענינם אחד ענין אורח ומעגל: סלולה. ענין משמוש התמידות וכן ואורח ישרים סלולה (משלי ט"ו): (טז) שריקות. ענין השמעת קול בקבוץ השפתיים כברואים דבר חשוב שנחרב וכן שרקו ויניעו ראשם. (איכה ב׳): ישום. ענין תמהון כמו פנו אלי והשמו (איוב כ"א): ויניד. מלשון נדוד והנעה: (יז) אפיצם. ענין פזור כמו ויפץ העם (שמות ה׳): עורף. הוא אחורי הפנים והצואר: אידם. ענין שבר ומקרה

מצודת דוד

יקטרו. המה מקטירים לבעל השמים שאין תועלת בעבודתם: ויכשלום בדרכיהם שבילי עולם. ר"ל שבילי העולם הם המכשילים אותם בדרכיהם כי בראותם דרכי הטבע בעולם שהכוכבים ממשלותם פועלים בדברים השפלים אלה שבילי עולם הם יכשילום בדרכיהם לחשוב שכל טובתם תלוי בעבודת השמים ולכן היו מקטרים להם וזהו שאמר ללכת נתיבות וגו׳ ר"ל ללכת בנתיב דרך אשר איננה סלולה שלא תשמשו בה להסיר המכשול שלא חקרו בדבר לדעת שהכל ביד ה׳ ואין מהראוי לעבדם עבודות אלהות: (טז) לשום. וזהו הוא סבה לשום ארצם לשממה: שריקת עולם. זמן רב ישרקו על חורבנה ושממותה: ישום. יתמה על השממון ויניד בראשו כדרך המתמיה: (יז) ברוח. כמו רוח קדים שהיא העזה שברוחות המפזר דברים הנפזרים כן אפזרם בנוסם מפני האויב: עורף וגו׳. ביום בוא אידם אסתיר פני מהם ואראה להם העורף ואחז במשל מאדם המהפך פניו מאדם השנאוי לו ור"ל לא אשגיח עליהם להושיעם: (יח) ויאמרו. כשאמרתי להם הנבואה הזאת אמרו אלו לאלו נחשבה על ירמיה מחשבות מה לעשות עמו לבל נשמע לדבריו האלה: כי

light materials, so will I scatter them before the enemy hither and thither.—[*Redak*]

upon their back and not their face—*when they flee from before the enemy, I will look upon them and I will not save them.*—[*Rashi*]

Others explain: **My back and not My face will I show them on the day of their misfortune.** I.e., I will hide My face from them. I will not heed their misfortune. This is called הֶסְתֵּר פָּנִים, *hiding the countenance*. This is payment in kind. Just as they turned their backs to Me, so will I turn My back to them, so to speak.—[*Redak, Mezudath David, Abarbanel*]

and the ancient paths caused them to stumble in their ways, to walk [in] paths, [on] a way that is not trodden. 16. To make their land waste, a perpetual hissing, everyone who passes it will be astonished and shake his head. 17. Like an east wind I will scatter them before the enemy; I will look upon their back and not their face on the day of their misfortune. 18. And they said, "Come, let us devise plots against Jeremiah,

ful water prepared for life, and upon which life depends, is it good that it should be destroyed and abandoned? 'For My people have forgotton Me; they burn incense to vanity.' Now how have My people forgotten Me and forsaken the paths of life and abandoned the source of spring water? They have become foolish for they neither know nor understand.

ancient paths—*The proper paths they said that they are a stumbling-block, in order to go—*

[on] a way that is not trodden down—Heb. סְלוּלָה.—[*Rashi*]

I.e., they claimed that the old paths, the ways of the Torah, traversed by their forefathers, brought them obstacles. They, therefore, adopted new ways, ways they were unaccustomed to, namely the ways of the gentiles.

Abarbanel explains in a similar manner: **and the paths of the world caused them to stumble in their ways etc.**—The paths of the world, both the orbits of the planets and the stars, and the natural phenomena of the lower world caused them to believe that the stars in their orbits had power over the lower world and that their success depended on the heavenly bodies. Consequently, they began to worship them. This was a new way, a way that was not trodden. 'The ways of the world' may also mean 'the ways of the nations of the world.' These ways caused them to stumble since they were attracted to follow them.

Redak asserts that the verse is elliptical. It is to be explained as follows: And they (the false prophet) caused them to stumble in their ways [and to forsake] the ancient paths upon which their righteous forefathers had trodden. This follows Targum Jonathan.

a way that was not trodden —I.e., a new lifestyle to which they were unaccustomed.—[*Redak*]

16. **To make their land a waste** —With their evil ways, they cause their land to become a waste.—[*Redak*]

hissing—*One who passes by ruins that he already saw with good buildings is accustomed to whistle.*—[*Rashi*]

a perpetual hissing—This hissing will go on for a long time.—[*Redak*]

will be astonished——Heb. יִשֹּׁם, *will wonder.*—[*Rashi*]

and shake his head—as a manifestation of his bewilderment.—[*Redak*]

17. **Like an east wind**—which is strong and scatters straw and other

כִּי לֹא־תֹאבַד תּוֹרָה מִכֹּהֵן וְעֵצָה
מֵחָכָם וְדָבָר מִנָּבִיא לְכוּ וְנַכֵּהוּ בַלָּשׁוֹן
וְאַל־נַקְשִׁיבָה אֶל־כָּל־דְּבָרָיו׃
יט הַקְשִׁיבָה יְהוָה אֵלָי וּשְׁמַע לְקוֹל
יְרִיבָי׃ כ הַיְשֻׁלַּם תַּחַת־טוֹבָה רָעָה
כִּי־כָרוּ שׁוּחָה לְנַפְשִׁי זְכֹר ׀ עָמְדִי
לְפָנֶיךָ לְדַבֵּר עֲלֵיהֶם טוֹבָה לְהָשִׁיב
אֶת־חֲמָתְךָ מֵהֶם׃ כא לָכֵן תֵּן אֶת־

תרגום

מְחַשְּׁבָן אֲרֵי לָא תִפְסוֹק אוּרַיְתָא מִכָּהֵין וּמְלַךְ מֵחַכִּים וְאוּלְפַן מִסָּפַר אָתוּ וּנְסָהֲדִינֵיהּ סָהֲדָן דִּשְׁקַר וְלָא נְצִית לְכָל פִּתְגָמוֹהִי׃ יט גְּלֵי קֳדָמָךְ יְיָ דִּינִי וּשְׁמַע קֳדָמָךְ עוּלְבָּנִי׃ כ הַאֶפְשַׁר לְשַׁלָּמָא חֲלַף טַבְתָא בִּישְׁתָא אֲרֵי כְרוּ פַּחַת לְמִקְטְלֵי יֵעוֹל דּוּכְרַן מֵקָמַי קֳדָמָךְ לְמַלָּלָא עֲלֵיהוֹן פִּתְגָמִין תַּקְנִין לַאֲתָבָא יָת חֲמָתָךְ מִנְּהוֹן׃ כא בְּכֵן הַב יָת בניהון

רש"י

לכו וגו'. ירמיה היה קובל על אנשי ענתות ואומר שאומרי' כן: תורה מכהן. שעל הכהנים להורות תורה שנאמר יורו משפטיך ליעקב (דברים ל"ג): ודבר מנביא. דברי נבואה: ונכהו בלשון. ונסהדיניה סהדון דשקר:

מהר"י קרא

אומרים איש לרעהו לכו ונחשבה עליו מחשבות רשע כדי שימות ושמא תאמר אם ימות זה על ידינו היכן נמצא כזה איש שיהיה כהן וחכם ונביא הרבה כהנים יודעי תורה עומדין במקומן הרבה חכמים והרבה נביאים. לכך נאמר לא תאבד תורה מכהן ועצה מחכם ודבר מנביא: לכו ונכהו בלשון. סוף מקרא זה מפרש את ראשו כשהוא אומר לכו ונחשבה על ירמיה מחשבות. לא פירש מה הם המחשבות וכאן פירש מה הן. ונכהו בלשון. נגרה אותו בעיני השרים. ונאמר עליו אין איש הזה מתנבא על המקום הזה כי אם לרעה כדי שיהרג בידם: ואל נקשיבה אל כל דבריו. לעשותם. ויונתן תרגם. לכו ונכהו בלשון איתו ונסהדיניה סהדין דשקר. לפיכך היה מתפלל: (יט) הקשיבה ה' אלי ושמע לקול יריבי. שאומרים לכו ונחשבה.

רד"ק

כנגד האל כלומר אני אוכיחם בדבריך והם אומרים איש לאחיו לכו ונחשבה על ירמיהו: לכו. ענין זרוז כמו לכו נא אנסכה בשמחה לכו נא ונוכחה לכו ונכהו בל' והדומי' להם: מחשבות. ר"ל מחשבות רעות להמיתו: כי לא תאבד תורה מכהן. כלומר מה אנו חסרים אם ימות כי לא תאבד בעבור זה התורה כי שאר הכהנים יודעים אותה וכן יש אתנו חכמים בעלי עצה וכן יש אתנו נביאים שיאמרו לנו דברי נבואה ולא יהיו כמו זה שאינו מתנבא עלינו כי אם רע: ונכהו. שנלשין עליו למלך בדברים רעים כדי שימיתהו: ואל נקשיבה אל כל דבריו. כלומר אל דבריו שאומר לנו אל נקשיב. ואמר ירמיהו: (יט) הקשיבה. הם אומרים שלא יקשיבו לי אתה הקשיבה אלי כלומר לתפלתי. ושמע לקול יריבי. כלומר לדבריהם שמדברים עלי: (כ) הישולם. כי כרו שוחה לנפשי. סם המות שרצו להשקותו שהוא כמו שכורים שוחה לאדם להפילו בה בלא ידיעתו והנה הם משלמי' לי רעה תחת טובה כי אני דברתי עליהם טובה לפניך והתפללתי עליהם עד העת ההיא שגלית לי שרצו להמיתני: (כא) לכן. מעתה אני רשאי להתפלל עליהם לרעה כיון שחשבו להמיתני: והגרם. נאמר לשון הגרה בחרב כפני הדם הנגר וכן יגרהו על

מצודת דוד

לא תאבד. כאומרים מה נהיה הסרים במיתתו הלא לא תאבד ממוס' מיתר הכהנים (על הכהן ללמד תורה וכמ"ש כי שפתי כהן וגו' ותורה יבקשו מפיהו (מלאכי ב') ולא תאבד העלה מהחכמים אחרים אשר יש עמנו ודבר נבואה לא תהיה נאבדת מיתר הנביאים אשר לא יתנבאו רעה כמותו) : לכו ונכהו. לכן נכהו נפש בלשון כי נדבר עליו מלשינות לפני המלך והוא יכנו נפש : ואל נקשיבה. אז לא נשמע כמו כל הדברים שדבר הוא כי אין מי בנביאים לדבר דברים כמותו : (יט) הקשיבה ה' אלי. מה באני מתפלל עליהם טובות ולעומת זה שמע קול המריבים עמדי אשר יתיעצו עלי : (כ) הישולם. וכי מן הראוי שיבולם רעה תחת טובה כי חפרו בור ללכדני ר"ל חושבים עלי מחשבות רעות : זכור. תן דעתך לזכור פה עמדי לפניך בתפלה לבקש עליהם טובה להעביר את חמתך מהם : (כא) לכן. הואיל ומשלמים רעה תחת טובה : והגרם.

מצודת ציון

רע כמו הלא איד לעול (איוב ל"א) : (יח) לכו. הוא ענין זרוז : נקשיבה. ענין שמיעה והאזנה : (כ) כרו. חפרו כמו בור כרה (תהלים ז') : שוחה. בור כמו שוחה עמוקה (משלי כ"ב) : (כא) תן. ענין מסירה : והגירם. ענין הזלה ושפיכה וכן יגירהו על ידי

19. **Hearken, O Lord, to me**—They say, "Let us not listen to all his words." But You, O Lord, I beseech You to listen to me, i.e. to my prayer.—[*Redak*]

and hear the voice of those who quarrel with me—Listen to the words they speak about me.—[*Redak*]

20. **for they have dug a pit for my life**—The poison they attempted to give him was like a pit into which he would fall unknowingly. With this, they are paying evil for good, for I spoke good for them and interceded with You to spare them until the attempt on my life.—[*Redak*]

The Rabbis tell us that they accused him of adultery with a married woman.—[*Abarbanel* from *Baba Kamma* 16b. See below v. 22.]

21. **Therefore**—Since they attempted to kill me, I may pray for their doom.—[*Redak*]

for the Torah shall not be lost from the priest, neither counsel from the wise man, nor speech from the prophet. Come, let us strike him with the tongue, and let us not listen to all his words."
19. Hearken, O Lord, to me, and hear the voice of those who quarrel with me.
20. Shall evil be paid instead of good, for they have dug a pit for my life. Remember when I stood before You to speak good for them, to bring back Your wrath from them.
21. Therefore, deliver

*18. **not speech from the prophet**—I.e. *words of prophecy.*—[*Rashi*]

What will we lose if Jeremiah dies? The Torah will not be lost, for there are many other priests who know it, and there are many wise men who can give counsel. Also, we have many prophets who will prophesy for us, and they will not be like this one, who prophesies only evil.—[*Redak*]

and let us not listen to all his words—Let us not listen to the many words he says to us.—[*Redak*]

Then we will not hear all his words, for there is no prophet like him.—[*Mezudath David*] Perhaps this is *Redak*'s intention.

Let us not listen to all his words—when he seeks to justify himself.—[*Malbim*] Perhaps this is *Redak*'s intention. The word נַקְשִׁיבָה, rather than נִשְׁמְעָה makes this interpretation more likely than that of *Mezudath David.*

Abarbanel questions how the people who sought to kill Jeremiah were concerned with the Torah being lost and with prophecy being lost. Also, the meaning of 'Let us not listen to all his words.' If they kill him, he can no longer say anything to them to which they could possibly listen. He, therefore, explains that the people were concerned with ridding themselves of Jeremiah's reproof and his prophecy of doom. They were certain that Jeremiah would not cease to function as a priest, wise man, or prophet. 'They said, "Come, let us devise plots against Jeremiah, for the Torah shall not be lost from the priest."' I.e., Jeremiah the priest will not cease his Torah instruction to the people. Once he reproves us concerning idolatry, once concerning immorality, once concerning Sabbath observance, for it is the function of the priest to teach Torah. If he is not teaching us Torah, he will seek to advise us in matters, contrary to our custom, for counsel will not be lost from the wise man. When he does not reprove us and does not advise us on political matters, he will prophesy his prophecies of doom. While they were conferring among themselves what to do to rid themselves of Jeremiah, some suggested, "Let us strike him on his tongue." I.e., let us sever his tongue so that he will be unable to speak to us. Others, thinking this too severe, to maim the priest of God, suggested, "Let us not hearken to all his words." Let us just ignore him and not listen to him.

* For Rashi's commentary turn to page 237.

בְּנֵיהֶם לָרָעָב וְהַגִּרֵם עַל־יְדֵי־חֶרֶב
וְתִהְיֶנָה נְשֵׁיהֶם שַׁכֻּלוֹת וְאַלְמָנוֹת
וְאַנְשֵׁיהֶם יִהְיוּ הֲרֻגֵי מָוֶת בַּחוּרֵיהֶם
מֻכֵּי־חֶרֶב בַּמִּלְחָמָה׃ כב תִּשָּׁמַע זְעָקָה
מִבָּתֵּיהֶם כִּי־תָבִיא עֲלֵיהֶם גְּדוּד
פִּתְאֹם כִּי־כָרוּ שִׁיחָה לְלָכְדֵנִי וּפַחִים
טָמְנוּ לְרַגְלָי׃ כג וְאַתָּה יְהוָה יָדַעְתָּ אֶת־
כָּל־עֲצָתָם עָלַי לַמָּוֶת אַל־תְּכַפֵּר עַל־
עֲוֺנָם וְחַטָּאתָם מִלְּפָנֶיךָ אַל־תֶּמְחִי
וְהָיוּ מֻכְשָׁלִים לְפָנֶיךָ בְּעֵת אַפְּךָ
עשה

שוחה קרי ויהיו קרי

ת"א כרו שוחה. ב"ק סז: בעת אפך. ב"ב ט:

תרגום

בְּנֵיהוֹן לְכַפְנָא וְתַבְּרִינוּן
יְדֵי קָטוֹלֵי חַרְבָּא וִיהוֹן
נְשֵׁיהוֹן תַּכְלָן וְאַרְמְלָן
וְגֻבְרֵיהוֹן יְהוֹן קְטִילֵי
מוֹתָא עוּלֵימֵיהוֹן מְמַעְנֵי
חַרְבָּא בִּקְרָבָא׃
כב תִּשְׁתְּמַע צְוָחְתָא
מִבָּתֵּיהוֹן אֲרֵי תַיְתֵי
עֲלֵיהוֹן מַשִׁרְיָן בִּתְכֵיף
אֲרֵי כְרוֹ פַּחַת לְמִקְטְלִי
וְקוּלְיוֹצְלוּ לְפָרְסַת רִגְלָי׃
כג וְאַתְּ יְיָ יְדִיעַ וּגְלֵי
קֳדָמָךְ יָת כָּל
אִתְמְלוֹכֵיהוֹן עֲלַי
לְמִקְטְלִי לָא תְּכַפַּר עַל
חוֹבֵיהוֹן וְחַטָּאֵיהוֹן מִן
קֳדָמָךְ לָא יִתְמְחוֹן וִיהוֹן
מִתַּקְּלִין דָּמִן קֳדָמָךְ
בְּעִדָּן פּוּרְעָנוּת רוּגְזָךְ
אִתְפְּרַע

מהר"י קרא

על ירמיה כחשבות: (כא) והגירם. מגרה בהם בני אדם אוכלי חרב והוא לשון מגרה. ד"א והגירם לשון זריקה ושפיכה כמו מים המוגרים במורד: (כג) וחטאתם מלפניך אל תמחי. כלומר אל תמח מה שעושין לי: בעת אפך עשה בהם. מה שאתה עתיד לעשות להם לא בעת רצון כדי שתרחם עליהם. אלא כדי שלא תרחם עליהם:

רש"י

(כא) והגירם. (הורידם על ידי חרב) לשון עיני נגרה (איכה ג') כמים המוגרים (מיכה א'): על ידי חרב. ע"י גייסות: ואנשיהם. של האלמנו' יהיו הרוגי מלאך המות: (כב) כי כרו שוחה. שחשדוהו מאשת איש שנ' (משלי כ"ג) כי שוחה עמוקה זונה: (כג) אל תמחי. אל תהי מחויה ולפי שהיא לשון נקבה נתן בו יו"ד ואף היא יתירה כיו"ד של ותזני בם (יחזקאל ט"ז):

מנחת שי

(כב) שיחה. שוחה קרי: טמנו לרגלי. הקמץ במדוייקים לא בשורק: (כג) והיו. ויהיו קרי:

רד"ק

ידי חרב: שכולות. מבניהם: ואלמנות. מאנשיהם שיהיו הרוגי מות כלומר שימותו בדבר והבחורים שדרכם לצאת במלחמה יהיו מוכי חרב במלחמה: (כב) תשמע זעקה. כי הזעקה תהיה כשיבא הרע פתאם: כי כרו שוחה. כתוב ביו"ד וקרי בוי"ו שוחה והשיחה והפחים הוא סם המות שחשבו להאכילו: (כג) ואתה. אל תמחי. כמו אל תמחה היו"ד במקום ה"א למ"ד הפעל כמו צור ילדך תשי: והיו מוכשלים. כתיב וקרי ויהיו והענין אחד: בעת אפך עשה בהם. על דרך ויחר אפי בהם

מצודת ציון

חרב (תהלים ס"ג): שכולות. מי שמתו בניו קרוי שכול: (כב) גדוד. לכאות עם: ופחים. מלשון פח ורשת: טמנו. ענין הצפנה: (כג) תמחי. מלשון מחייה ומחיקה:

מצודת דוד

שפוך דמיהם ע"י חרב האויב: שכלות ואלמנות. שכולות מבניהם ואלמנות מבעליהן: ואנשיהם. אנשי האלמנות יהיו מתים ע"י הרג ולא במיתת עצמן: במלחמה. כי דרך הבחורים ללכת במלחמ': (כב) זעקה. זעקת שבר: פתאום. בל ידעו להזהר מהם: כרו שוחה. חפרו בור ללכדני בו ר"ל יעלו עלי ריבות: ופחים. הטמינו רשתות ללכוד רגלי והוא כפל הדבר במ"ש: (כג) עצתם עלי למות. אשר המה מתיעצים עלי להמיתני: אל תמחי. אל תמחק חטאתם מלפניך כי יהיו כתובים לזכרון למען יקבלו גמול: ויהיו וגו'. אף בעת ילכו לפניך בדרך מלותיך יבוא להם מכשול למען לא יוכלו לעשות כהוגן: בעת אפך. בזמן שאתה כועס אז עשה בהם נקם למען יהיה הרבה מלהכיל:

suspected him of intimacy with a harlot. Hence the expression, 'they dug a pit,' alluding to the expression in Proverbs. Verse 23 means that they cast him into a pit of mud to kill him.

Redak explains that the 'pit' and the 'snares' represent the poison they intended to feed him.

23. **all their plan against me for death**—I.e. how are they plotting to kill me.—[*Mezudath David*]

let not be erased—Heb. אַל תֶּמְחִי, *let it not be erased. And because it is a feminine gender, he placed a 'yud' therein. This too is superfluous, as the 'yud' of* '(Ezekiel 16:17) *And you played the harlot* (וַתִּזְנִי) *with them.'*—

their children to the famine and spill their blood by the sword, and let their wives be bereaved and widows, and their husbands slain by death, their youths struck by the sword in battle.
22. May an outcry be heard from their houses, for You shall bring a troop upon them suddenly, for they dug a pit to seize me and they hid snares at my feet to trap me.
23. And You, O Lord, know all their plan against me for death; do not atone for their iniquity, and let not their sin be erased from before You, and let them be made to stumble before You; at the time of Your anger do it to them.

and spill their blood—Heb. הַגִּרֵם. (*Bring them down by the sword,*) *an expression of* '(Lam. 3:49) *My eye runs* (נִגְּרָה).' '(Micah 1:4) *Like water that runs* (מֻגָּרִים).'—[*Rashi, Abarbanel*]

Others render: and spill their blood by the sword—[*Redak, Mezudoth*]

by the sword—*By troops.*—[*Rashi*] Rashi understands חֶרֶב as 'those who wield the sword.' It is found very often in the Scriptures to mean armies or war. *Redak,* however, takes it literally, to mean that their blood will be shed by the sword. So *Mezudath David.*

bereaved—of their children.—[*Mezudath David*]

and their husbands—I.e. the husbands *of the widows shall be slain by the angel of death.*—[*Rashi*] *Rashi*'s intention is to eliminate the apparent tautology of the expression 'slain by death.' The reason for mentioning the angel of death is, however, obscure. Others interpret this expression to indicate that they will be slain and not die from natural causes.—[*Mezudath David*]

Redak renders: slain by pestilence.

their youths—who customarily go out to war, will be struck by the sword in battle.—[*Redak*]

22. **May an outcry be heard**—People cry out when calamity strikes them suddenly.—[*Redak*]

suddenly—It will strike them suddenly so that they will be unable to beware of it.—[*Mezudath David*]

for they dug a pit to seize me—The Rabbis (*Baba Kamma* 16b) interpret this to mean *that they suspected him of* intimacy with *a married woman, as it is stated:* '(Prov. 23:27) *For a harlot is a deep pit* (שׁוּחָה).'—[*Rashi*] The Talmud states that a married woman who commits adultery is no less a harlot than a single woman. Therefore, this opinion is not contradicted by the verse in Proverbs. The evidence that they suspected him of intimacy with a married woman is the wording of verse 23, in which the prophet mentions 'their plan against me for death.' Intimacy with a harlot is not a capital offense. Even a priest who commits this sin is liable only to flogging. Others maintain that they

עֹשֶׂה בָהֶם׃ יט א כֹּה אָמַר יְהֹוָה הָלֹךְ
וְקָנִיתָ בַקְבֻּק יוֹצֵר חָרֶשׂ וּמִזִּקְנֵי הָעָם
וּמִזִּקְנֵי הַכֹּהֲנִים׃ ב וְיָצָאתָ אֶל־גֵּיא בֶן־
הִנֹּם אֲשֶׁר פֶּתַח שַׁעַר הַחַרְסוּת וְקָרָאתָ
שָּׁם אֶת־הַדְּבָרִים אֲשֶׁר־אֲדַבֵּר אֵלֶיךָ׃
ג וְאָמַרְתָּ שִׁמְעוּ דְבַר־יְהֹוָה מַלְכֵי
יְהוּדָה וְיֹשְׁבֵי יְרוּשָׁלִָם כֹּה־אָמַר יְהֹוָה
צְבָאוֹת אֱלֹהֵי יִשְׂרָאֵל הִנְנִי מֵבִיא רָעָה
עַל־הַמָּקוֹם הַזֶּה אֲשֶׁר כָּל־שֹׁמְעָהּ
תִּצַּלְנָה אָזְנָיו׃ ד יַעַן אֲשֶׁר עֲזָבֻנִי

אִתְפְּרַע מִנְהוֹן׃ א כִּדְנַן
אֲמַר יְיָ לִי אֱזֵיל וְתִזְבּוֹן
זְלוֹעַ דַּחֲסַף פֶּחָר וְתִדְבַּר
עִמָּךְ מִסָּבֵי עַמָּא וּמִסָּבֵי
כָהֲנַיָּא׃ ב וְתִפּוֹק לְחֵילַת
בַּר הִנּוֹם דִּקְדָם תְּרַע
קַלְקַלְתָּא וְתִתְנַבֵּי תַמָּן
יָת פִּתְגָמַיָּא דַאֲמַלֵּיל
עִמָּךְ׃ ג וְתֵימַר קַבִּילוּ
פִּתְגָמָא דַיְיָ מַלְכַיָּא
דְבֵית יְהוּדָה וְיָתְבֵי
יְרוּשְׁלֶם כִּדְנַן אֲמַר יְיָ
צְבָאוֹת אֱלָהָא דְיִשְׂרָאֵל
הָא אֲנָא מַיְתֵי בִישְׁתָּא
עַל אַתְרָא הָדֵין דְּכָל
דְּיִשְׁמְעִינַהּ יִצְלְּן
אוּדְנוֹהִי׃ ד חֲלַף דִּשְׁבָקוּ
פולחני

החרסית קרי

רש"י

יט (א) בקבוק. צלוחית: יוצר חרש. כלומר של יוצר שהוא של חרש: ומזקני העם. הוליך עמך ומזקני העם מוסב על הלוך ומזקני העם עמך: (ב) שער החרסית. שער האשפות ששם זורקין חרסים הנשברים וכן ת"י תרע קלקלתא: (ג) תצלנה. (סינטני"ר בלע"ז) לשון מצלתים

מהר"י קרא

יט (א) וקנית בקבוק. כד של חרס וכשתלך לקנותו קח עמך מזקני העם ומזקני הכהנים: (ב) שער החרסית. ששם עושין כלי חרס: (ג) תצלנה אזניו. לשון המון הוא כמו בצלצלי

רד"ק

ואכלם: (א) כה אמר ה'. בקבוק יוצר חרש. מיוצר חרש תקנה הבקבוק כי יש בקבוק מעץ או מזכוכית או משאר מתכות וי"ת הפך המלות ותרגם זלוע דחסף פחר וחסרון המ"ם ימצא כמוהו אלחנן בן דודו בית לחם כמו מבית לחם: ומזקני העם ומזקני הכהנים. פי' תוליך עמך הזקנים כדי להשמיעם הנבואה ולשבר לעיניהם הבקבוק להיות להם למופת כמו שאומר ושברת את הבקבוק לעיני האנשים ההולכים אתך וכן ת"י ותדבר עמך מסבי עמא והפרשה מבוארת זולתי מעט ממנה שצריכה באור: (ב) אשר פתח שער החרסית. משער החרסית יוצאים לגיא בן הנם ות"י די קדם תרע קלקלתא וקלקלתא הוא בדברי רז"ל אשפה ולדעתי הוא השער הנזכר בספ' עזרא ואת שער האשפו'. ורז"ל פירשו שהוא שער משערי העזרה שהוא שער מזרחי אמרו שבעה שמות נקרא לו שער סור ששם היו טמאים פורשי' הדא הוא דכתיב סורו טמא שער היסוד ששם היו מיסדים ההלכה שער החרסית שהוא מכוון כנגד זריחת החמה היך מה דתימא האומר לחרס ולא יזרח שער האיתון שהוא משמש כניסה ויציאה ושער התוך שהוא ממוצע בין שני שערים שער חדש ששם חדשו סופרים את ההלכה שער העליון שהוא למעלה מעזרת ישראל: החרסות. בוי"ו כתיב וקרי ביו"ד החרסית ואחד הוא: אשר אדבר אליך. הדברים שאני מדבר עתה אליך והם כן ואמרת עד והסך נסכים לאלהים אחרים: (ג) הצלנה אזניו. ענין תנועת הרעשה והוא מבנין נפעל ותאמר זה הלשון באזנים ובשפתים כמו לקול צללו שפתי:

מנחת שי

יט (א) הלך וקנית. בספרים מוגהים חסר וא"ו וכן ראוי ע"פ המסורת דסוף פרשת וילך: בקבק. בית ראשונה רפה: (ב) החרסות. החרסית קרי:

מצודת דוד

יט (א) בקבוק. צלוחית מן יוצר חרס: ומזקני וגו'. מוסב על הלוך. ור"ל הלוך אתה וגם מזקני העם וגו' ילכו עמך: (ב) אשר פתח. אשר מול פתח: שער החרסית. הוא שער האשפות הנזכר (בנחמיה ג') ששם זורקים חרסים הנשברים: אשר אדבר אליך. הוא האמור במקרא שלאחריו: (ג) כל שומעה. כל השומע הרעה ההיא ירעשו אזניו מתנועת הרעד: (ד) יען.

מצודת ציון

יט (א) בקבוק. כן שם הכלי שפיו צר על כי בעת ישפך ממנו נשמע כעין קול בקבק וכן ובקבק דבש (מ"א י"ד): יוצר חרש. אומן חרס: (ב) גיא בן הנם. כן שם המקו': (ג) תצלנה.

some distance from the Ben Hinnom Valley, especially if it is the gate of the Israelites' Court. See *This is Jerusalem* by Menashe Har-el, where he states that the gate known today as the Dung Gate is not the Dung Gate of Biblical times, which was at the southern tip of the Cheesemongers' Valley, near the Ben-Hinnom Valley.

that I will speak to you—I.e. the words I speak to you now, commencing here and extending to verse 13.—[*Redak*]

3. **his ears will tingle**—Heb. תִּצַּלְנָה, (*tinter in French*), *an expression*

19

1. So said the Lord: Go and buy a potter's earthen jug, and
[take] along some of the elders of the people and some of the
elders of the priests. 2. And you shall go out to the Ben-
Hinnom Valley which is at the entrance of the Harsith Gate,
and you shall call there the words that I will speak to you.
3. And you shall say: Hearken to the word of the Lord, O kings
of Judah and inhabitants of Jerusalem: So said the Lord of
Hosts, the God of Israel: Behold I am bringing evil upon this
place, which whoever hears, his ears will tingle. 4. Because they
forsook Me

[*Rashi*] The irregular form of תֻּמָּחִי is puzzling. *Rashi* identifies it as the passive, *let not be erased.* Since it is the third person singular, and חַטָּאתָם is of feminine gender, it should appear as תִּמָּחֶה, as indeed it appears in Nehemiah 3:37. To account for the presence of the 'yud,' *Rashi* suggests that it is placed in the word because it is feminine. This does not, in fact, account for the 'yud,' since it is suffixed to a verb only in the second person, not in the third. It would appear that Rashi quotes the verse of Ezekiel to illustrate that it appears as a suffix to a verb although it is superfluous. In fact, the verse of Ezekiel is in the second person, in which case, it is the usual form. In our verse, however, the verb is in the third person. Such a form is not found elsewhere.

1. **a jug**—Heb. בַּקְבֻּק.—[*Rashi*]

The Hebrew word בַּקְבֻּק denotes a narrow-necked jug, which emits a sound resembling 'bak-buk' when it is being emptied.—[*Mezudath Zion; Redak, Shorashim*]

potter's earthen—*That is to say, of a potter, which is of earthenware.*—[*Rashi*]

Redak renders: an earthen potter's jug. You shall buy the jug from an earthen potter, for there are also wooden and metal jugs.

and some of the elders of the people—*take along with you. 'And of the elders of the people' refers back to 'Go,' and some of the elders of the people with you.*—[*Rashi*]

You shall take along some of the elders of the people to recite the prophecy before them and to break the jug in their presence as a symbol thereof, as in verse 10.—[*Redak*]

2. **the Harsith Gate**—*The Dung Gate, where broken pottery is cast, and Jonathan rendered in this manner* תְּרַע קִלְקַלְתָּא.—[*Rashi*]

Both according to Targum, that it is the Dung Gate, and according to Yerushalmi, that it is the gate to the Israelites' Court in the Temple, it is

וַיְנַכְּרוּ אֶת־הַמָּקוֹם הַזֶּה וַיְקַטְּרוּ־בוֹ
לֵאלֹהִים אֲחֵרִים אֲשֶׁר לֹא־יְדָעוּם הֵמָּה
וַאֲבוֹתֵיהֶם וּמַלְכֵי יְהוּדָה וּמָלְאוּ אֶת־
הַמָּקוֹם הַזֶּה דַּם נְקִיִּם: ה וּבָנוּ אֶת־
בָּמוֹת הַבַּעַל לִשְׂרֹף אֶת־בְּנֵיהֶם בָּאֵשׁ
עֹלוֹת לַבָּעַל אֲשֶׁר לֹא־צִוִּיתִי וְלֹא
דִבַּרְתִּי וְלֹא עָלְתָה עַל־לִבִּי: ו לָכֵן הִנֵּה־
יָמִים בָּאִים נְאֻם־יְהוָה וְלֹא־יִקָּרֵא
לַמָּקוֹם הַזֶּה עוֹד הַתֹּפֶת וְגֵיא בֶן־הִנֹּם
כִּי אִם־גֵּיא הַהֲרֵגָה: ז וּבַקֹּתִי אֶת־עֲצַת

תרגום

פּוּלְחָנִי וְסָאִיבוּ יַת
אַתְרָא הָדֵין וְאַסִּיקוּ בֵיהּ
בּוּסְמִין לְטַעֲוַת פַּלְחֵי
כּוֹכְבַיָּא דְלָא יַדְעוּנוּן
אִינוּן וַאֲבָהַתְהוֹן וּמַלְכַיָּא
דְבֵית יְהוּדָה וּמְלוֹ יַת
אַתְרָא הָדֵין דַּם זַכָּאִין:
ה וּבְנוֹ יַת בָּמַת בַּעְלָא
לְאוֹקָדָא יַת בְּנֵיהוֹן
בְּנוּרָא עֲלָוָן לְבַעְלָא
דְלָא פַקֵּדִית בְּאוֹרַיְתִי
וּדְלָא שְׁלָחֵית בְּיַד
עַבְדֵי נְבִיַּיָא וְלָא רַעֲוָא
קֳדָמַי: ו בְּכֵן הָא יוֹמַיָּא
אָתָן אֲמַר יְיָ לָא יִתְקְרֵי
לְאַתְרָא הָדֵין עוֹד תּוֹפֶת
וְחֵילַת בַּר הִנּוֹם אֱלָהֵין
חֵילַת קְטִילַיָּא:
ז וָאֲקַלְקֵיל יַת מְלַךְ אֱנָשׁ

ת"א לא צויתי. תענית ד עקרים מ"ג פ"ד:

מהר"י קרא

שמע ועל שם שמוציא קול נקרא צלצל וכן מצילות הסוס הוא
צלצל שתולין לו לסוס בין עיניו ומוציא קול ועושין לנוי.
ופתרון תצלנה. תהמנה: (ה) ובנו את במות הבעל לשרוף את
בניהם באש. אשר לא צויתי. דבר זה אפילו לעבודתי שיקריב אדם את בנו לפני: (ז) ובקותי. והריקותי לשון ריקם ודומה

רש"י

(ד"ה א' ט"ו) בצלצלי שמע (תהלים ק"נ): (ד) וינכרו.
עשאוהו נכרי לפני: (ז) ובקותי. ורוקנתי ל' בוקה ומבוקה

רד"ק

(ד) וינכרו. כמ"ש אלהי נכר הארץ כי לא יסבול המקום ההוא עכו"ם: (ה) אשר לא צויתי. פירשתיו בפרשה גזי נזרך וי"ת דלא פקדית באוריתא ודלא שלחית ביד עבדי נבייא ולא רעוא
קדמי: (ז) ובקותי. ענין ריקות כמו בוקק הארץ וי"ת ואקלקיל:

מצודת ציון

ענין תניעת הכנף וכן לקול צללו שפתי (חבקוק ג'): (ד) וינכרו.
ענ' נכר וזרות: (ז) ובקותי. ענין ריקות כמו הבוק תבוק הארץ
(ישעיה כ"ד) והוא ל' נופל על לשון בקבוק:

מצודת דוד

בעבור אשר עזבו אותי: וינכרו. עשה את המקום הזה נכרי וזר
ממני ר"ל לא הקריבו שם לפני כאלו לא היתה אלי: ויקטרו בו.
אבל קטרו בו לאלהים אחרים: המה וגו'. מוסב על ויקטרו בו
לומר שגם המה קטרו גם אבותיהם וגו': דם נקים. דמי הילדים
שהקריבו לפני העכו"ם: (ה) עולות לבעל. להיות עולות לבעל: אשר לא צויתי. אף לפני לא צויתי להקריב בנים ובנות: ולא
דברתי. אף דבור בעלמא מבלי צווי ואזהרה: ולא עלתה וגו'. לאמור דבר כזאת: (ו) ולא יקרא. אז לא יקרא: התופת. בית
הבמות נקראו תופת לפי שהיו מקישים שם בתופים לבל ישמע האב בנהימת הבן כשהוא נשרף ויכמרו רחמיו: בן הנם. הגיא שעמד
בו בית הבמות קראו בן הנם ע"ש נהימת הבן כנשרף: גיא ההרגה. כי יפלו שם הרוגי' רבים: (ז) ובקותי. ארוקן עצתם ר"ל לא ימלאו

Torah, neither did I send through My servants, the prophets, nor do I have any desire for it. See above 7:31, for the Midrashic interpretation of this verse.

6. **Topheth**—Derived from תֹּף, *a drum.* The priests would beat a drum to drown out the cries of the children.—[*Mezudath David*] See above 7:31.

Ben-Hinnom Valley—Hinnom denotes the moaning of the children (נְהִימָה). For this, too, see above.—[*Mezudath David*]

7. **And I will frustrate**—Heb. וּבַקֹּתִי, lit. *and I will empty, an expression similar to* '(Nahum 2:11) *She is empty and void* (בּוּקָה וּמְבוּקָה),' *and because of the jug* (בַּקְבֻּק) *about which he is speaking, he adopted this expression.*—[*Rashi*]

This is a play on words peculiar to Jeremiah's prophecies. Compare the prophecy of the girdle and of the potter who destroys the form he has made and makes another form out of the clay.—[*Kara*]

The counsel mentioned here is the plot against the prophet mentioned in the preceding chapter.—[*Kara*]

and they estranged this place and burnt incense therein to other
gods, which they had not known, they, their forefathers, and
the kings of Judah, and they filled this place with the blood of
innocent people. 5. And they built the high places of Baal to
burn their children with fire as burnt offerings to Baal, which I
did not command, neither did I speak nor did it enter My mind.
6. Therefore, behold days are coming, says the Lord, when
this place will no longer be called Topheth or Ben-Hinnom
Valley, but the Valley of Slaughter. 7. And I will frustrate the
counsel of

similar to 'cymbals' (מְצִלְתַּיִם) (Neh. 12:27), *'with loud-sounding cymbals'* (בְּצִלְצְלֵי שָׁמַע) (Psalms 150:5).—[*Rashi*]

4. **and they estranged**—*They made it strange before Me.*—[*Rashi*]

They made this place strange to Me by discontinuing My worship as though it were not My place.—[*Mezudath David*]

Others explain: They estranged it by worshipping gods that do not belong there but are strangers there, as in Deut. 31:16, 'the gods who are strange in the land.' The Holy Land does not tolerate idol worship.—[*Redak*] *Abarbanel* identifies 'this place' as Jerusalem. *Daath Soferim* and *Daath Mikra,* however, identify it as the Topheth, where human sacrifice was practiced. Others render: They delivered this place. I.e., they were instrumental in delivering this place, namely Jerusalem, over to the Chaldeans through their sins. Accordingly, the word וַיְנַכְּרוּ is derived from נִכֵּר as in I Sam. 23:7.—[*Ibn Nachmiash*]

and burnt incense to other gods—Instead of offering up sacrifices to Me, they burnt incense to other gods.—[*Mezudath David*]

they, their forefathers, and the kings of Judah—I.e., they, their forefathers, and the kings of Judah offered up incense to strange gods.—[*Abarbanel, Mezudath David*]

Malbim explains simply: which they, their forefathers, and the kings of Judah had not known. They have no excuse that they follow the custom of their ancestors.

the kings of Judah—I.e., the wicked kings of Judah, viz. Ahaz, Manasseh, and Amon.—[*Daath Mikra*]

blood of innocent people—I.e. the blood of innocent children. Thus, the two horrendous crimes of idolatry and murder were combined in the Ben-Hinnom Valley.—[*Abarbanel*]

5. **which I did not command**—I never commanded that such a sacrifice be offered in My worship.—[*Mezudath David*] *Jonathan* renders: which I did not command in the

יְהוּדָה וִירוּשָׁלִַם בַּמָּקוֹם הַזֶּה וְהִפַּלְתִּים
בַּחֶרֶב לִפְנֵי אֹיְבֵיהֶם וּבְיַד מְבַקְשֵׁי
נַפְשָׁם וְנָתַתִּי אֶת־נִבְלָתָם לְמַאֲכָל
לְעוֹף הַשָּׁמַיִם וּלְבֶהֱמַת הָאָרֶץ׃
ח וְשַׂמְתִּי אֶת־הָעִיר הַזֹּאת לְשַׁמָּה
וְלִשְׁרֵקָה כֹּל עֹבֵר עָלֶיהָ יִשֹּׁם וְיִשְׁרֹק
עַל־כָּל־מַכֹּתֶהָ׃ ט וְהַאֲכַלְתִּים אֶת־
בְּשַׂר בְּנֵיהֶם וְאֵת בְּשַׂר בְּנֹתֵיהֶם
וְאִישׁ בְּשַׂר־רֵעֵהוּ יֹאכֵלוּ בְּמָצוֹר
וּבְמָצוֹק אֲשֶׁר יָצִיקוּ לָהֶם אֹיְבֵיהֶם
וּמְבַקְשֵׁי נַפְשָׁם׃ י וְשָׁבַרְתָּ הַבַּקְבֻּק
לְעֵינֵי הָאֲנָשִׁים הַהֹלְכִים אוֹתָךְ׃

תרגום

יהודה ויתבי ירושלם
באתרא הדין וארמינון
בחרבא קדם בעלי
דבביהון וביד דבען
למקטלהון ואתן ית
נבלתהון משגרא למיכל
לעופא דשמיא ולבעירא
דארעא׃ ח ואשוי ית
קרתא הדא לצדו
ולאשתממו כל דיעבר
עלה יכלי ויניד על כל
מחתהא׃ ט ואוכלינון
ית בשר בניהון וית
בשר בנתהון וגבר נכסי
קריביה יבזון בצירא
ובעקתא דיעיקון להון
בעלי דבביהון ודבען
למקטלהון׃ י ותתבר
זלוע לעיני גבריא
דאזלין

רד"ק

(ח) מכותה. חסר יו"ד הרבים מהמכתב :

רש"י

(נחום ב') ועל שם בקבוק שהוא מדבר בו לקח לשונו כן :
(ט) ובמצוק. לשון צרה כמו צוקה :

מהר"י קרא

לו נפן בוקק ישראל. וזה לשון תפש אחר הבקבק שציוהו לקנות . וכן כשאמר לו וקנית לך אזור פשתים ואחר כך אמר כאשר ידבק האזור וכן על היוצר חרס אמר הנה אנכי

יוצר עליכם רעה וכן בכל מקום הלשון נופל על הלשון : ובקותי את עצת יהודה וירושלים . העצות והמחשבות הם

מצודת דוד

אלה להצלה : למאכל וגו' . כי לא יקברו : (ח) לשמה . לתמהון ולסיום שורקין עליה : (ט) במצור . בסבת המצור יהיו חסרים

מצודת ציון

(ח) לשמה . לתמהון : ולשרקה . ענין השמעת קול בקיבוץ השפתים דרכו לעשותו כשרואים דבר חשוב שנחרב : ישום . יתמה : (ט) במצור . ענין הקפת גייסות סביבות העיר לכבשה

ולהצר להם : ובמצוק . יציקו . מלשון צוקה וצרה : (י) אותך . עמך :

Judah and Jerusalem in this place, and I will hurl them down by
the sword before their enemies and into the hand of those who
seek their lives, and I will give their carcasses for food to the
fowl of the heavens and to the beasts of the earth. 8. And I will
make this city into a waste and a hissing; everyone who passes
by it shall be astonished and hiss concerning all her plagues.
9. And I will feed them the flesh of their sons and the flesh of
their daughters, and each one will eat the flesh of his friend, in
the siege and the straits that their enemies and those who seek
their lives will inflict upon them. 10. And you shall break the
jug before the eyes of the men who go with you.

From the context, it appears that he is referring to ways of escaping from the enemies when they attack. So *Abarbanel* and *Mezudath David.*

9. **And I will feed them**—As payment in kind for sacrificing their children to Baal, they will be forced to eat them because of their intense hunger.—[*Abarbanel*]

10. **And you shall break**—After explaining to the prophet the meaning of the jug, God commands him to break it before all those accompanying him.—[*Abarbanel*]

יא וְאָמַרְתָּ אֲלֵיהֶם כֹּה־אָמַר יְהוָה
צְבָאוֹת כָּכָה אֶשְׁבֹּר אֶת־הָעָם הַזֶּה
וְאֶת־הָעִיר הַזֹּאת כַּאֲשֶׁר יִשְׁבֹּר אֶת־
כְּלִי הַיּוֹצֵר אֲשֶׁר לֹא־יוּכַל לְהֵרָפֵה עוֹד
וּבְתֹפֶת יִקְבְּרוּ מֵאֵין מָקוֹם לִקְבּוֹר׃
יב כֵּן־אֶעֱשֶׂה לַמָּקוֹם הַזֶּה נְאֻם־יְהוָה
וּלְיוֹשְׁבָיו וְלָתֵת אֶת־הָעִיר הַזֹּאת
כְּתֹפֶת׃ יג וְהָיוּ בָּתֵּי יְרוּשָׁלַםִ וּבָתֵּי מַלְכֵי
יְהוּדָה כִּמְקוֹם הַתֹּפֶת הַטְּמֵאִים לְכֹל
הַבָּתִּים אֲשֶׁר קִטְּרוּ עַל־גַּגֹּתֵיהֶם לְכֹל
צְבָא הַשָּׁמַיִם וְהַסֵּךְ נְסָכִים לֵאלֹהִים

תרגום

דְאָזְלִין עִמָּךְ׃ יא וְתֵימַר לְהוֹן כִּדְנַן אֲמַר יְיָ צְבָאוֹת כְּדֵין אֶתְבַּר יָת עַמָּא הָדֵין וְיָת קַרְתָּא הָדָא כְּמָא דְמִתְּבַר יָת מָנָא דְפַחֲרָא דְלָא אֶפְשַׁר לְאִתַּסָּאָה לֵיהּ עוֹד וּבְתוֹפֶת יִקְבְּרוּן מִבְּלִי אֲתַר לְמִקְבַּר׃ יב כֵּן אַעֲבֵיד לְאַתְרָא הָדֵין אֲמַר יְיָ וּלְיָתְבוֹהִי וּלְמִתַּן יָת קַרְתָּא הָדָא כְּתוֹפֶת׃ יג וִיהוֹן בָּתֵּי יְרוּשְׁלֵם וּבָתֵּי מַלְכַיָא דְבֵית יְהוּדָה כְּאֲתַר תּוֹפֶת דִמְסָאַב לְכָל בָּתַּיָא דְאַסִּיקוּ בּוּסְמִין עַל אֶגָּרֵיהוֹן לְכָל חֵילֵי שְׁמַיָא וְנַסִּיכוּ נִסְכִין לְטַעֲוַת פַּלְחֵי כוֹכְבַיָא׃

ה׳ במקום א׳

מהר״י קרא

שאמרו למעלה לכו ונחשבה על ירמיה מחשבות של מות: (יא) ובתופת יקברו מאין מקום לקבור. שמעתי שיש בתופת מקום חלל צר מלמעלה ומלמטה רחב לא מוצק תחתיה וכל כך רחב תחתיה שאפילו יהיו נקברים שם כל רשעי דור ודור משנברא העולם עד עכשיו לכולם היה להם מקום לקבר שם שכל כך הוא עמוק וזהו ובתופת יקברו מאין מקום לקבור שמתוך שתהיה כל העיר וגם סביבות העיר מלאים קברים ולא ימצאו מקום לקבור יקברו בתופת: (יב) ולתת את העיר הזאת כתופת. שאף תמלא העיר קברים:

רש״י

(יא) אשר לא יוכל להרפה. אהעס קאי אבל העיר אעשה לתופת ואטהר לעתיד): (יב) העיר הזאת כתופת. כולה מליאה הרוגים כמו התופת שהורגין את הילדים למולך:

מנחת שי

(יג) כמקום התפת. בכ״ף וכן נמסר עליו לית ר״ל לית כוותיה בקריאה בכ״ף ואילו בבי״ת טובא הוו: לכל צבא. י״ס לכל צבא והרוב כחולם:

רד״ק

(יא) כאשר ישבור. פי׳ כאשר ישבור איש וכן אם יחרש בבקרים החורש: להרפה. בה״א כמו באל״ף ובא בדרך השאלה כמו וירפא את מובח ה׳ ההרום: ובתפת יקברו. אע״פ שהוא מקום עכו״ם שלהם: (יג) כמקום התופת. אשר טמאו יאשיהו: הטמאים. טעמו אל בתי ירושלים ובתי מלכי יהודה: לכל הבתים. פי׳ בעבור כל הבתים כלו׳ מה שאני אומר שיהיו בתי ירושלם ובתי מלכי יהודה כמקו׳ התפת על הבתים אשר קטרו

מצודת ציון

(יא) ככה. כן: היוצר. אומן חרס: להרפה. היא מלשון רפואה. ועם כי הוא בה״א ור״ל לתקנו ואמר בלשון שאלה וכן

מצודת דוד

ממאכל ויאכלו בשר בניהם וגו׳: (יא) ככה אשבר. כמו שנשבר הבקבוק כן אשבר וגו׳: כאשר ישבור וגו׳. ר״ל כשבירת כלי יוצר אשר ישבור מי שאין למלאת תקנה לעשותו שלם כן ישבר העם והעיר מבלי תקנה: ובתופת. ההרוגים יקברו בתופת הרבה מאד עד שלא ימלא שם מקום לקבור עוד: (יב) כן אעשה. כמו שאמרתי כן אעשה וגו׳: כתופת. ר״ל מלאה הרוגים כתופת שהיא מלאה מהרוגי הילדים המומתים לעכו״ם: (יג) והיו וגו׳. ר״ל הם יהיו מקום קברות ההרוגים כמקום התופת: הטמאים. מוסב על הבתים לומר הבתים הטמאים יהיו כתופת וחוזר ומפרש מי הם

11. And you shall say to them: So said the Lord of Hosts: So will I break this people and this city, as one breaks the potter's vessel, which can no longer be repaired, and in the Topheth they will bury without place to bury.
12. So will I do to this place, says the Lord, and to its inhabitants, and to make this city like the Topheth.
13. And the houses of Jerusalem and the houses of the kings of Judah shall be like the place of the Topheth, the unclean ones, of all the houses on whose roofs they offered up incense to all the host of heaven and poured libations to other gods.

11. **So will I break**—as the jug was broken.—[*Mezudath David*]

(which can no longer be repaired—*This refers to the people, but the city I will make like the Topheth and purify it in the future.*)—[*Rashi*]

Unlike the clay in the potter's hand, which can be formed into a different shape, the finished jar cannot be repaired.—[*Malbim*]

and in the Topheth they will bury—although it is their shrine.—[*Redak*]

without place to bury—They will bury so many corpses in Topheth until there is no longer any room to bury any more.—[*Mezudath David*]

Kara writes: I heard that in the Topheth there is a hollow place, narrow on top and wide on the bottom. It is so wide and deep that even if all the wicked of all generations were buried there, there would be room to bury them. They will bury them in Topheth because there will be no other burial place. The entire city will be full of graves, as well as the environs of the city. They will, therefore, be compelled to bury the dead in the Ben-Hinnom Valley, called Topheth.

12. **this city like the Topheth**—*All of it will be full of the slain just as the Topheth, where they slay the children for Molech.*—[*Rashi, Mezudath David*] Or, just as there was a constant fire in the Topheth, so will Jerusalem be burnt.—[*Isaiah da Trani*]

13. **like the place of Topheth**—that Josiah contaminated.—[*Redak*]

the unclean ones—I.e. the unclean houses of Jerusalem and the unclean houses of the kings of Judah.—[*Redak*]

of all the houses etc.—The unclean houses are those upon whose roofs they offered up incense to the host of heaven and poured libations to other gods.—[*Mezudath David, Abarbanel*]

Redak suggests: Because of all the houses etc. Another explanation: I refer to all the houses etc.

אֲחֵרִים: יד וַיָּבֹא יִרְמְיָהוּ מֵהַתֹּפֶת אֲשֶׁר
שְׁלָחוֹ יְהוָה שָׁם לְהִנָּבֵא וַיַּעֲמֹד בַּחֲצַר
בֵּית־יְהוָה וַיֹּאמֶר אֶל־כָּל־הָעָם: טו כֹּה־
אָמַר יְהוָה צְבָאוֹת אֱלֹהֵי יִשְׂרָאֵל הִנְנִי
מֵבִי* אֶל־הָעִיר הַזֹּאת וְעַל־כָּל־עָרֶיהָ
אֵת כָּל־הָרָעָה אֲשֶׁר דִּבַּרְתִּי עָלֶיהָ כִּי
הִקְשׁוּ אֶת־עָרְפָּם לְבִלְתִּי שְׁמוֹעַ אֶת־
דְּבָרָי: כ א וַיִּשְׁמַע פַּשְׁחוּר בֶּן־אִמֵּר
הַכֹּהֵן וְהוּא־פָקִיד נָגִיד בְּבֵית יְהוָה
אֶת־יִרְמְיָהוּ נִבָּא אֶת־הַדְּבָרִים הָאֵלֶּה:
ב וַיַּכֶּה פַשְׁחוּר אֵת יִרְמְיָהוּ הַנָּבִיא וַיִּתֵּן
אֹתוֹ עַל־הַמַּהְפֶּכֶת אֲשֶׁר בְּשַׁעַר בִּנְיָמִן
הָעֶלְיוֹן אֲשֶׁר בְּבֵית יְהוָה: ג וַיְהִי

*מביא קרי נ״א אל

יד וַאֲתָא יִרְמְיָה מִתּוֹפֶת
דִּשְׁלָחֵיהּ יְיָ תַּמָּן
לְאִתְנַבָּאָה וְקָם בְּדָרַת
בֵּית מַקְדְּשָׁא דַּייָ וַאֲמַר
לְכָל עַמָּא: טו כִּדְנַן
אֲמַר יְיָ צְבָאוֹת אֱלָהָא
דְּיִשְׂרָאֵל הָא אֲנָא מַיְתֵי
עַל קַרְתָּא הָדָא וְעַל כָּל
קִרְוַהָא יָת כָּל בִּישְׁתָּא
דְּגְזָרִית עֲלַהּ אֲרֵי
אַקְשִׁיאוּ יָת קְדָלְהוֹן
בְּדִיל דְּלָא לְקַבָּלָא יָת
פִּתְגָמָי: א וּשְׁמַע פַּשְׁחוּר
בַּר אִמֵּר כָּהֲנָא וְהוּא
מְמַנָּא סְגַן כָּהֲנַיָּא בְּבֵית
מַקְדְּשָׁא דַּייָ דְּיִרְמְיָה
מִתְנַבֵּי יָת פִּתְגָמַיָּא
הָאִלֵּין: ב וְאַלְקֵי פַשְׁחוּר
יָת יִרְמְיָה נְבִיָּא וִיהַב
יָתֵיהּ לְכִיפְּתָא דִּבְתְרַע
שִׁבְטָא בִנְיָמִין עִלָּאָה
דִּי בְּבֵית מַקְדְּשָׁא דַּייָ:
ג וַהֲוָה בְּיוֹמָא דְּבַתְרוֹהִי
ואפיק

מנחת שי

(טו) מבי. מביא קרי:

רש״י

כ (ב) המהפכת. שם מקום בית אסורים וי״ת לכיפתא

מהר״י קרא

כ (ב) המהפכת. בית הסהר:

רד״ק

על גנותיהם אני אומר: (טו) כה אמר ה׳ צבאות אלהי ישראל. אדון צבאות בעלה ומטה ואצביא עליכם צבא מטה: אלהי ישראל. אף על פי שהם חוטאים לפני ועבדו אלהים אחרים אלהיהם אני כי כלם לא פשעו בי ומקצת הפושעים יחזרו בהם: הנני מבי. חסר אל״ף למ״ד הפעל מהמכתב: ועל כל עריה. ערי יהודה כי כלם היו נסמכות אל ירושלם כי היא האם: (א) פקיד. נגיד הפקיד הגדול שהוא נגיד על כלם ות״י ממנ׳ סגן כהניא: (ב) על המהפכת. יש מפרשים שהוא בית הסוה׳ וא״א ז״ל פירש כלי שהוא עשוי שני עצים ועושין בנתים בית צואר ומכניסין שם צוארי האסורין וי״ת לכיפתא: בשער בניב׳

מצודת דוד

מהכתים ואמר לכל העמים אשר קטרו וגו׳: (יד) לתנבא. הנבואה האמורה למעלה: (טו) ועל כל עריה. הערים הסמוכי׳ לה: כי הקשו. לבל יוכלו להסך אלי פניהם והוא ענין מלילה:
כ (א) פקיד נגיד. ממונ׳ ושר היה בבית ה׳: את ירמיהו. מוסב על וישמע: (ב) המהפכת. הוא שם של בית הסוהר: בשע־

מצודת ציון

ויכפא את מזכח ה׳ (מ״א י״ח): (טו) הקשו. מלשון קשה: ערפם. הוא אחורי הפנים והצואר:

the discipline of the people congregating in the Temple court. He considered Jeremiah a subversive element, and therefore, struck him and imprisoned him.

Daath Soferim points out that Pashhur was descended from a prominent priestly family, mentioned in Ezra 2:37. Because of his prominence, he dared attack the prophet of God without fear of punishment. His son, Gedaliah, too, followed in his father's footsteps (38:4) and accused Jeremiah of weakening the war effort.

2. **And Pashhur struck Jeremiah the prophet**—Whether he beat him mercilessly or struck him on the cheek to humiliate him is not clear. *Daath Soferim* conjectures on the basis of the Targum, וְאַלְקֵי, that he sentenced him to be flogged for dis-

14. And Jeremiah came from the Topheth where the Lord had sent him to prophesy, and he stood in the court of the house of the Lord and said to all the people. 15. So said the Lord of Hosts, the God of Israel: Behold, I am bringing upon this city and upon all her cities all this evil that I spoke concerning her, for they stiffened their necks not to hearken to My words.

20

1. And Pashhur son of Immer the priest—he was the chief officer in the house of the Lord—heard Jeremiah prophesying these things. 2. And Pashhur struck Jeremiah the prophet and placed him in the prison that is in the upper gate of Benjamin, which is in the house of the Lord.

14. **And Jeremiah came from the Topheth**—Scripture relates that when Jeremiah returned from the Topheth where he had gone to prophesy concerning the jug, he stood in the Temple court and recited his prophecy in the name of God to all the people congregated there.—[*Abarbanel*]

15. **the Lord of Hosts**—The Lord of the hosts of heaven and earth. I will mobilize the hosts of the earth against you.—[*Redak*]

the God of Israel—Although they sin before Me and worship other gods, I am still their God, for not all of them have rebelled against Me, and some of the transgressors may repent.—[*Redak*]

and upon all her cities—I.e., all the cities near Jerusalem.—[*Mezudath David*]

Redak explains: all the cities of Judah, which depended upon Jerusalem, the mother city.

He recited this prophecy so that all the people should know what he had prophesied before the elders.—[*Abarbanel*]

Since God had commanded him to perform a deed in conjunction with his prophecy, he knew that this prophecy would definitely be fulfilled, that the decree had been sealed with no more possibility of being revoked. This is discussed by Ramban (Gen. 12:6).—[*Malbim*]

for they stiffened their necks—It is as though they stiffened their necks, making it impossible to turn their faces around to hearken to Me.—[*Mezudath David*] Therefore, their verdict was sealed.—[*Malbim*]

1. **the chief officer**—He was in charge of all the priests in the Temple and according to *Jonathan,* he was the assistant to the High Priest.—[*Redak*]

Daath Mikra conjectures that Pashhur's position was to preserve

מִמָּחֳרָת וַיֹּצֵא פַשְׁחוּר אֶת־יִרְמְיָהוּ מִן־
הַמַּהְפָּכֶת וַיֹּאמֶר אֵלָיו יִרְמְיָהוּ לֹא
פַשְׁחוּר קָרָא יְהוָה שְׁמֶךָ כִּי אִם־מָגוֹר
מִסָּבִיב: ד כִּי־כֹה אָמַר יְהוָה הִנְנִי
נֹתֶנְךָ לְמָגוֹר לְךָ וּלְכָל־אֹהֲבֶיךָ וְנָפְלוּ
בְּחֶרֶב אֹיְבֵיהֶם וְעֵינֶיךָ רֹאוֹת וְאֶת־כָּל־
יְהוּדָה אֶתֵּן בְּיַד מֶלֶךְ־בָּבֶל וְהִגְלָם
בָּבֶלָה וְהִכָּם בֶּחָרֶב: ה וְנָתַתִּי אֶת־כָּל־
חֹסֶן הָעִיר הַזֹּאת וְאֶת־כָּל־יְגִיעָהּ וְאֶת־

תרגום

וְאַפִּיק פַּשְׁחוּר יָת יִרְמְיָה
מִן כִּיפְתָּא וַאֲמַר לֵיהּ
יִרְמְיָה לָא פַּשְׁחוּר רַבִּי
יְיָ שְׁמָךְ אֱלָהֵין יִתְכַּנְשׁוּן
עֲלָךְ דְקַטְלִין בְּחַרְבָּא
מִסְחוֹר סְחוֹר: ד אֲרֵי
כִדְנַן אֲמַר יְיָ הָא אֲנָא
מְסַר לָךְ לְתָבַר לָךְ וּלְכָל
רַחֲמָךְ וְיִתְקַטְלוּן בְּחֶרֶב
בַּעֲלֵי דְבָבֵיהוֹן וְעֵינָךְ
חָזְיָן וְיָת כָּל דְבֵית יְהוּדָה
אֶמְסַר בְּיַד מַלְכָּא דְבָבֶל
וְאַגְלֵינוּן לְבָבֶל וְיִמְחִינוּן
בְּחַרְבָּא: ה וְאֶתֵּן יָת כָּל
עוּתַר אַרְעָא הָדָא וְיָת
כָּל עֲמָלַהּ וְיָת כָּל
ליאותה

רש״י

(ארוולו״ר בלע״ז): (ג) מגור. יראה: **לא פשחור קרא ה׳ שמך וגו׳.** לא נקרא שמך פשחור אלא בשביל דבר זה כלומר פשח שחור כמו אילן שנפשח וכן ויפשחני (איכה ג׳) וכן אמר לו לא פשחור קרא שמך שלשון פשחור משמע אדם גדול ובן חורין פשהור אלא לכך נקרא שמך פשחור פשח שחור. דבר אחר פשח סחור רבים סביבותיך להרוג וללשון זה מגור הוא לשון אסיפה כמו מגורי אל חרב (יחזקאל כ״א): (ה) חוסן. ממון:

מהר״י קרא

(ג) לא פשחור קרא ה׳ שמך. אמר ירמיה לפשחור כמדומה אתה ששמך [פשהור] משמע לטובה פירוש פש ובן חורין. לא כי אלא לרעה משמע פשחור (פחור) [סחור] לשון ויפשחיני יזהו מגור מסביב: (ה) כל חוסן. כל תוקף הוא מלך צדקיה

רד״ק

העליון. השער הזה היה בחלק בנימן כי בית המקדש היה מקצתו בחלק יהודה ומקצתו בחלק בנימן: (ג) לא פשחור קרא ה׳ שמך. אמר קרא ה׳ שמך לפי שהוא היה מחזיק עצמו כנביא ואומר כי ה׳ קרא לו כי שלום יהיה להם לפיכך אמר לו ירמיהו אשר נבאת להם בשקר ואמר לו ירמיהו אתה אומר כי קרא ה׳ שמך ודבר עמך לא קרא ה׳ אותך בשם פשחור כי אם מגור מסביב לא תהיה בטוח כמו שאתה אומר אלא פחד יהיה לך מכל סביבותיך ומגור ראוי לקרא שמך כי מגור יהיה לך: (ד) כי כה אמר ה׳. נתנך למגור. היה לו לומר נותן מגור לך ולכל אוהביך אלא כך אמר לו במקום שאתה עתה בנבואתך מבטח לך ולכל אהביך שבוטחים בדברי שקר שאתה אומר להם תהיה להם במקום מבטח למגור ולפחד וגם אתה תפחד עמהם: (ה) ונתתי. חוסן. ענין חוזק ותוקף כמו והיה החסון לנעורת וחסון הוא כאלונים וחוסן ר״ל האוצר הטוב והיקר וכן חוסן

מצודת ציון

כ (ג) מגור. ענין אסיפה וקבוץ כמו אוגר בקיץ (משלי י׳): (ה) חוסן. ענין חוזק ועל העושר יאמר שהוא המחזק

מצודת דוד

בנימין. כן נקרא שם השער: העליון. העומד בגובה ההר: (ג) לא פשחור וגו׳. ר״ל לא נקרא שמך פשחור כי אם לאום שאסיפת גייסות יקיפו אותך מסביב כי פשחור הוא כמו פש סחור ופש הוא ענין רבוי כמו ופשו פרשיו (חבקוק א׳) וסחור הוא תרגומו של סביב: (ד) למגור. לאסיפת הגייסות: לך. אותך אתן ולכל אוהביך: ועיניך רואות. כשיפלו בחרב: והכם. מהם יכה בחרב: (ה) ואת כל יקרה. כל הדברים היקרים הנמצאים

lon—I.e., he will exile some of them.—[*Abarbanel, Mezudath David, Malbim*]

and strike them—I.e., and strike some of them.—[*Abarbanel, Mezudath David, Malbim*]

Malbim suggests: And he will strike them in Babylon. See below v. 6.

5. **the wealth**—Heb. חֹסֶן, *money*.—[*Rashi*]

Lit. strength. Wealth and treasures are called חֹסֶן because they represent a person's strength in time of need.—[*Redak*]

her toil—This, too, denotes the wealth acquired through toil.—[*Mezudath Zion*]

Rabbi Joseph Kara renders: **her strength**—I.e. King Zedekiah and the princes.

her toil—I.e. the people.

3. And it came to pass on the next day that Pashhur released Jeremiah from the prison, and Jeremiah said to him, "Not Pashhur did the Lord call your name, but Magor Missaviv.
4. For so said the Lord: Behold I will make you a terror to yourself and to all your friends, and they shall fall by the sword of their enemies with your eyes seeing, and all of Judah I will deliver into the hand of the king of Babylon, and he shall exile them to Babylon and strike them with the sword. 5. And I will
give all the wealth of this city and all her toil and

turbing the peace in the Temple Court. This punishment was meted out to any priest who violated the rules of the Temple.

3. **Magor**—*Terror.—[Rashi]*

Not Passhur did the Lord call your name etc—*Your name was not called Pashhur except for this matter, that is to say:* פָּשַׁח שָׁחוֹר, *cut off and black like 'a tree that was cut off* (נִפְשַׁח)' (*Shevi'ith* 4:6, *Orlah* 1:5). *Also,* '(Lam. 3:11) *And He cut me off* (וַיְפַשְּׁחֵנִי).' *And so he said to him, "Not Pashhur did He call your name, for the expression of Pashhur means a great man and the son of nobles, Pashhur. Pash* denotes expansion and *hur* nobility. *But for this reason your name was called Pashhur, Pashah shahor.* 'Pashah' means 'cut off,' and 'shahor' means 'black.' *Another explanation: Pashah sehor. Many will be around you to slay* you. *Now according to this explanation,* מָגוֹר *is an expression of gathering, like* '(Ezekiel 21:17) *Gathered* (מְגוּרֵי) *to the sword.'—* [*Rashi*]

Mezudath David explains פַּשְׁחוּר as 'a large gathering of troops around.' פָּשׁ denotes multiplicity. Cf. '(Habakkuk 1:8) And his riders will be many (פָּשׁוּ).' סְחוֹר is the Aramaic for 'around.' Hence, 'Pashhur' and 'Magor Missaviv' are synonymous. He, too, interprets מָגוֹר as 'a gathering.' So *Targum Jonathan.*

Redak explains that, as mentioned below in verse 6, Pashhur pretended to be a prophet. He claimed that God had called him and told him that there would be peace. To this, Jeremiah retorts, "Not Pashhur did the Lord call your name—as you claim—but Magor Missaviv." You shall not be secure, as you claim, but you shall be surrounded by terror, and it is fitting to call you Magor, for you will have terror.

4. **Behold I will make you a terror etc.**—It would seem that the verse should read: I will make terror for you and for all your friends. The meaning is that, instead of your being the reliance and security for all your friends, who believe your prophecies, you will be a terror for them, and you yourself will be terrorized along with them.

As above, *Mezudath David* renders: Behold I will give you to the gathering of troops, you and all your friends.

and he shall exile them to Baby-

כָּל־יְקָרָהּ וְאֵת כָּל־אוֹצְרוֹת מַלְכֵי
יְהוּדָה אֶתֵּן בְּיַד אֹיְבֵיהֶם וּבְזָזוּם וּלְקָחוּם
וֶהֱבִיאוּם בָּבֶלָה׃ ו וְאַתָּה פַשְׁחוּר וְכֹל
יֹשְׁבֵי בֵיתֶךָ תֵּלְכוּ בַּשֶּׁבִי וּבָבֶל תָּבוֹא
וְשָׁם תָּמוּת וְשָׁם תִּקָּבֵר אַתָּה וְכָל־
אֹהֲבֶיךָ אֲשֶׁר־נִבֵּאתָ לָהֶם בַּשָּׁקֶר׃
ז פִּתִּיתַנִי יְהוָה וָאֶפָּת חֲזַקְתַּנִי וַתּוּכָל
הָיִיתִי לִשְׂחוֹק כָּל־הַיּוֹם כֻּלֹּה לֹעֵג לִי׃

תרגום

לְיָאוּתַהּ וְיָת כָּל אוֹצְרֵי
מַלְכַיָא דְבֵית יְהוּדָה
אֶמְסַר בְּיַד בַּעֲלֵי
דְבָבֵיהוֹן וְיִבְזוּנוּן
וְיִשְׁבּוּנוּן וְיוֹבְלִינוּן
לְבָבֶל׃ ו וְאַתְּ פַּשְׁחוּר
וְכָל יָתְבֵי בֵיתָךְ תְּהָכוּן
בְּשִׁבְיָא וּלְבָבֶל תְּתוּבַל
וְתַמָן תְּמוּת וְתַמָן
תִּתְקְבַר אַתְּ וְכָל רַחֲמָיךְ
דְאִתְנַבֵּיתָא לְהוֹן
בְּשִׁקְרָא׃ ז שַׁבֵּישְׁתַּנִי יְיָ
וְאִשְׁתַּבֵּישִׁית תַּקִיפְתַּנִי
וִיכָלְתְּ לִי הֲוֵיתִי לְלַעֵיב
כָּל יוֹמָא כּוּלְהוֹן מְחַיְכִין

ת"א ואתה פשחור. (כלאים לג):

רש"י

(ז) פתיתני. ללכת בשליחותך: חזקתני. הכבדת עלי ידך החזק' ללכ' על כרחי: ותוכל. ונלחת: כולה. כל העם לועג

ת' במקום ואו

מהר"י קרא

והשרים: יגיעת. תהמון: יקרה. חדרה: (ז) פתיתני ה' ואפת. שידלתני בדברים שאלך בשליחותך שאמרת לי בתחל' הספ' ונלחמו עליך ולא יוכלו לך כי אתך אני נאם ה' להצילך. כי יפתה תרגום ארי ישדל: פתיתני. פתרונו לסוף נשתדלתי שקיבלתי עלי לילך בשליחותך: ואפת. אפוראס"ש בלע"ז: חזקתני. מסרב הייתי בתחלה ללכת בשליחותך דכתיב ואמר אהה ה' אלהים הנה לא ידעתי דבר ותכריחני שאלך על כרחי כדכתיב אל תאמר נער אנכי: ותוכל. שהיה כח בידך להכריחני לילך בשליחותך על כרחי וכשאני הולך בשליחותך אצלם הייתי לשחוק כל

רד"ק

ויקר יקחו וכן הנפעל ממנו לא יאצר ולא יחסן וקרא האוצר חוסן לפי שהאוצר חוזק האדם ותוקפו לעת צרה: (ו) ואתה. אתה וכל אהביך. ולמעלה אמר על אהביו שיפלו בחרב אויביה' והנה אומר שיקברו בבבל ר"ל אותם שימלטו מחרב ירושלים ילכו בשבי בבל ושם ימותו ויקברו והקללה הוא שיקברו בארץ טמאה לפיכך אמר ושם תקבר כי אחר שאמר ושם תמות ידוע הוא ששם יקבר אלא דרך קללה זכר לו הקבורה שיקבר בארץ טמא' ומה שאמר בכל פסוק מהם כל אהביך ר"ל רבים מאהביך כי יבא כל בענין הזה כמו וכל הארץ באו מצרימה רצה לומר רבים מהארץ וכמוהו רבים: (ז) פתיתני. לפי שהכה אותו פשחור ונתן אותו במהפכת צעק חמס מתוך צערו ואמר פתיתני ה' כאדם המפתה חברו כי אני הייתי מונע עצמי מן שליחותך ואמרתי אהה ה' אלהים הנה לא ידעתי דבר כי נער אנכי ואתה פתיתני ואמרת לי אל תאמר נער אנכי: ואפת. ואני הייתי נפתה לדבריך: חזקתני ותוכל. היית חזק ממני בטענה ויכלת לי ועשיתי שליחותך והנה הייתי לשחוק כל היום כי הם שוחקים ולועגים לי: כלה. אומר על ישראל דרך כלל. ואפת מבנין נפעל ויהיה בתשלומו אפתה על משקל אבנה

מנחת שי

כ (ז) הייתי לשחוק. מלא וא"ו ועם כ"ש להאריך בזה אכתבנו מה הספר בסימן

מצודת דוד

כה: אתן. אל כי האריך והפסיק מזו ואמר אתן וכן דרך המקרא: (ו) אשר נבאת. כי השמור אמר שהוא נביא ונבא בשקר: (ז) פתיתני. אתה ה' פתית אותי ללכת בשליחותך: ואפת. קבלתי הפתוי: חזקתני. חזקת אותי בדברים כאמרך אל תירא מפניהם (לעיל א') והנה בזה יכלת לפתות אותי: הייתי לשחוק.

מצודת ציון

וכן חוסן ויקר יקחו (יחזקאל כ"ב): יגיעה. גם הוא יאמר על הטורח הבא ביגיעה ועמל: ובזזום. ענ' בזה ושלל: (ז) פתיתני.

speak for I am a youth." And You enticed me and said, "Say not, 'I am a youth.'"—[*Redak*]

You overcame me—*You made Your strong hand heavy upon me to go against my will.*—[*Rashi*]

and You prevailed—*And You were victorious.*—[*Rashi*]

Redak explains: You were stronger than I with your argument and You prevailed over me. Consequently, I accepted Your mission, and now I am a laughing-stock, for everyone mocks me.

everyone—Lit. all of it. *All the people mock me.*—[*Rashi*]

Others render חֲזַקְתַּנִי: You encouraged me.—[*Mezudath David, Abarbanel*]

In this complaint, Jeremiah said nothing derogatory about the Lord. He merely cried out because of his pain. In this way, this complaint differs from that of 15:18.—[*Redak*]

all her precious things, and all the treasures of the kings of Judah I will deliver into the hand of their enemies, and they shall plunder them and take them and bring them to Babylon.
6. And you, Pashhur, and all those who dwell in your houses shall go into captivity, and you shall come to Babylon and there you shall die and there you shall be buried, you and all your friends to whom you have prophesied falsely.
7. You enticed me, O Lord, and I was enticed, You overcame me and You prevailed. I have become a laughing-stock; everyone mocks me.

her beauty—Heb. יְקָרָהּ.

Abarbanel renders: **her strength**—I.e. her weapons and defense materials.

her toil—the work of her artisans and craftsmen.

her precious things—the money and precious things found in the possession of the merchants.

6. **And you . . . and you and all your friends**—In verse 4, Jeremiah prophesies that Pashhur's friends will fall by the sword and here he says that they will be taken in captivity to Babylon and die and be buried there. *Redak* reconciles this difficulty by explaining that those who will escape the sword of the Babylonians will be taken captive to Babylon, where they will die and be buried. Verse 4 is to be understood as 'and to many of your friends.' He cites many examples of this usage of כָּל. See on v. 4.

you shall be buried—You shall be buried in the unclean soil of Babylonia, not in the Holy Land.—[*Redak*]

The Rabbis teach us (*Tanhuma, Va'yehi* 3) that those who die and are buried in the Holy Land will be resurrected before those who are buried outside the Holy Land. They will be resurrected forty years before those buried in the Diaspora, and will merit to enjoy the Messianic era (*Etz Yosef*).

The Midrash proceeds with another advantage of being buried in Eretz Israel, for those who die in the Diaspora will suffer both from death and burial, making it seem like two deaths (See *Etz Yosef*).

to whom you have prophesied falsely—Pashhur was obviously one of the false prophets who prophesied, "Peace, peace," but there was no peace" (supra 6:14, 8:11).—[*Ibn Nachmiash*]

7. **You enticed me**—*to go on your mission.*—[*Rashi*]

Since Pashhur struck him and had him imprisoned, he cried out in complaint about the injustice done him. He cried because of his pain and said, "You enticed me, O Lord," like a man who entices his friend, for I hesitated to accept the mission and said, "(I:6) Alas, O Lord God! Behold I know not to

ח כִּי־מִדֵּי אֲדַבֵּר אֶזְעָק חָמָס וָשֹׁד אֶקְרָא
כִּי־הָיָה דְבַר־יְהוָה לִי לְחֶרְפָּה וּלְקֶלֶס
כָּל־הַיּוֹם׃ ט וְאָמַרְתִּי לֹא־אֶזְכְּרֶנּוּ וְלֹא־
אֲדַבֵּר עוֹד בִּשְׁמוֹ וְהָיָה בְלִבִּי כְּאֵשׁ
בֹּעֶרֶת עָצֻר בְּעַצְמֹתָי וְנִלְאֵיתִי כַּלְכֵל
וְלֹא אוּכָל׃ י כִּי שָׁמַעְתִּי דִּבַּת רַבִּים

כִּי: ח אֲרֵי בְּזִמַן דַּאֲנָא מִתְנַבֵּי אֲנָא מָרִים קָלִי בָּכֵי וּמְצַוַּח וְעַל חֲטוֹפִין וּבִזּוּזִין אֲנָא מִתְנַבֵּי אֲרֵי הֲוָה פִּתְגָמָא דַיְיָ לִי לְחִסוּדִין וּלְלַעַג כָּל יוֹמָא: ט וַאֲמָרִית לָא אַדְכְּרִינֵיהּ וְלָא אֲמַלֵּיל עוֹד בִּשְׁמֵיהּ וַהֲווֹן פִּתְגָמוֹהִי בְּלִבִּי כְּאֶשָּׁתָא בְּעָרָא שָׁמְפִין יַת גַּרְמַי וּלְאֵיתִי לְסוֹבָרָא וְלָא יְכֵילִית: י אֲרֵי

קמץ בז"ק

מהר"י קרא

היום: (ח) כי מדי אדבר. בשמך אזעק על חמס ושוד. שעושין לי: כי היה דבר ה' לחרפה ולקלס כל היום. שאני רואה שהן מחרפין אותי: (ט) ואמרתי לא אזכרנו ולא אדבר עוד בשמו. אף דבר זה אי אפשר לפי שהנבואה בלבי כאש בוערת וכופה אותי לאומרה בעל כרחי. והנבואה נודמת שאני: עצור בעצמותי. כל זמן שאני כובשה שלא לאומרה. עצור. דשטטריינ"ט בלע"ז. לפיכך: ונלאתי כלכל. הנבואה ולא אוכל להעלימה ומפני מה הייתי רוצה לכובשה שאמרתי לא אזכרנו ולא אדבר עוד בשמו: (י) כי שמעתי דבת רבים מגור מסביב. שאמרו [תגידו לנו] מה פורענות דבר ירמיה על המקום הזה:

רש"י

לי: (ח) מדי אדבר. בכל עת שאדבר אליה' אני צריך לזעוק ולהרים קול ואיני קורא אליה' טובה כי אם נביאו' חמס ושוד: כי היה דבר ה' לי. לפיכך דברו לי חרפה שהם מחרפים אותי: ולקלס. לדבור כמו וקלסה: (ט) ואמרתי לא אזכרנו. אם אמר לי לבי שלא אלך בשליחותך עוד: והיה בלבי. הנבואה: כאש בוערת. ועל כרחי אני צריך לילך: עצור בעצמותי. וכנוס בעצמותי האש: בלכל. לסבול האש: (י) כי שמעתי. אני אמרתי שלא אזכרנו לפי

מנחת שי

פ"ח בכ"ד: (ט) ונלאיתי. ברוב ספרים מלא יו"ד אחר אל"ף: כלכל. כ"ף ראשונה דגושה והאחרונה רפה ודומה לו וטמתי כדכד (ישעיה נ"ד) כמו שכתבתי שם וכן כתבו המדקדקים והמסורת מנה אותם בכלל הזוגים עיין במקרא גדולה דניאל ה' ובקצת ספרים מדוייקים כ"ף ראשונה בפתח:

רד"ק

ובחסרון למ"ד הפעל אפת כמו תגל ערותך ויקר אלהים והדבר הזה אשר דבר ירמיה לא היה דבר שלא כהוגן כנגד האל אלא דברי צער על עצמו לפיכך לא חשב לו אלה הדברים באלה הפסוקים לעון כמו שחשב לו לעון מה שאמר למעלה היו תהיה לי כמו אכזב כי אותו הדבר היה דבר חטא כנגד האל לפיכך אמר לו אם תשוב ואשיבך כמו שפירשנו: (ח) כי מדי. בכל עת שאדבר בדברי נבוא' וכן מדי עברו והיה מדי צאתם והתרומי' להם: אזעק. אמר אני זועק ומרים קולי להם להוכיחם והנה חמס ושוד אקרא שהם אומרים לי דברי חמס ושוד עד שיכוני ואצרך לקרא חמס על דבריהם הרעים שאומרים לי כי היה דבר ה' לי לחרפה ולקלס: כל היום. כל הימים שאדבר דבר ה' הוא לי לחרפה ולקלס שהם מחרפים אותי עליו וקלס ענינו לעג ובוז וכן וקלסה לכל הארצו' וי"ת ארי בזמן דאנא מתנבא אנא מרים קלי בכי ומצוח ועל חטופין ובזוזין אנא מתנבי ארי הוה פתגמא דה' לי לחסודין וללעג כל יומא: (ט) ואמרתי. ואם אחשב בלבי שלא אזכרנו עוד ושלא אדבר בשמו עוד לא אזכרנו להם ולא אדבר עוד בשמו להם כי אני נבזה עליו: והיה בלבי כאש בוערת. היה דבר ה' בלבי כאש בוערת. שאשתדל בכל כחי להוציאם וכן כמו אם היה אש עצור בעצמותי שאשתדל להוציאו בכל כחי כן דבר ה': ונלאיתי כלכל. נלאתי לכלכלו ולא אוכל לסבלו בקרבי כמו אם היה אש ואני על כרחי מוציאו בשפתי ואמרו להם ואמר בוערת ואמר עצור כי האש ימצא זכר ונקבה כי אש יצאת מחשבון ובפסוק אחר זכר ונקבה תאכלהו אש לא נפח. כלכל. ענין סבל וכן מי מכלכל את יום בואו: (י) כי שמעתי דבת רבים. לה"ר שאומרים עלי: מגור מסביב. מפחידים אותי מסביב זה מכאן וזה מכאן וי"ה מגור ל' אסיפה דמתכנשין מסחור סחור כמו יגורו עלי עזים יגורהו בחרמו ומה הם אומרים עלי זה לזה:

מצודת ציון

מלשון פתוי והסתה: ותוכל. מל' יכולת: (ח) מדי. ענינו כמו מתי וכן מדי דברי בו (לקמן ל"א): חמס. ענין הסרת הזכר והוא מלשון וחמסו מקניך (לעיל י"ג): ושוד. עושק הגוף: ולקלס. ענין לעג כמו וקלסה לכל הארצות (יחזקאל כ"ב): (ט) עצור. כנוס ומאוסף כמו עוצר בוגדים (לעיל ט'): ונלאיתי. ענין עייפות ויגיעה כמו העוה נלאו (שם): כלכל. ענין הסבלה והחזקה כמו ומי מכלכל את יום בואו (מלאכי ג'): אוכל. מלשון יכולת: (י) דבת. ענין אמירה וע"ס רוב יאמר על האומרים הרעה

מצודת דוד

עתה הנה הייתי לשחוק וכולם מלעיגים עלי: (ח) כי מדי אדבר. עתי שאדבר דברי נבואה אני זועק על הרעה הנעשה לי ואקרא בקול החמס והשוד הבא לי בעבור': להרפה. המה מחרפים אותי כל הימים בעבור דבר הנבואה: (ט) ואמרתי. פעמים רבות אמרתי בלבי לא אזכיר בפניהם שם ה' על פי ולא אדבר עוד נבואה בשמו: והיה בלבי. אבל הנבואה היה בלבי כאש בוערת וכנוס בעצמותי: ונלאיתי. נעשיתי נלאה ועיף לסבול בי הנבוא' ולא יכולתי להתאפק בבלי לאמרה: (י) כי שמעתי. אע"פ ששמעתי

8. For whenever I speak, I cry out; I call out violence and spoil,
for the word of the Lord has been scorn and mockery for me all
day long. 9. Should I say: I will not mention Him, and I will no
longer speak in His name, it would be in my heart like a burn-
ing fire, confined in my bones, and I wearied to contain it but
was unable. 10. For I heard the slander of many,

8. **Whenever I speak**—*Every time I speak to them, I must cry out and raise my voice, and I do not proclaim good for them but prophecies of violence and spoil.*—[*Rashi*]

for the word of the Lord has been . . . for me—*Therefore, they spoke to me with scorn, for they scorn me.*—[*Rashi*]

and mockery—Heb. וּלְקֶלֶס *for speech. Comp.* '(Ezekiel 22:4) *and mockery* (וְקַלָּסָה).'—[*Rashi*] *Rashi*'s intention here is obscure.

Others explain: I call out complaining of the words of violence and spoil they say to me until they strike me, and I must call out to complain of their speech against me, for the word of the Lord has been scorn and mockery for me all day long.—[*Redak*] *Kara* explains similarly: I call out to complain about the violence and spoil they commit against me. Or: I shout "violence and spoil!"—[*Abarbanel*]

all day long—All the days that I speak the word of the Lord, it is scorn and mockery to me, for they scorn me and mock me for it.—[*Redak*]

9. **Should I say: I will not mention Him**—*If my heart said to me not to go on Your mission anymore.*—[*Rashi*]

If I think that I will no longer mention Him and that I will no longer speak to them in His name, for I am despised by Him.—[*Redak*]

it would be in my heart—I.e. *the prophecy.*—[*Rashi*]

The word of the Lord was in my heart like a burning fire, that I strive with all my might to take it out. Similarly, if there were a fire confined in my bones, that I would surely strive to rid myself of it, so is the word of the Lord.—[*Redak*]

like a burning fire—*And against my will I must go.*—[*Rashi*]

confined in my bones—*And* as if *the fire were confined in my bones.*—[*Rashi*]

to contain—*To endure the fire.*—[*Rashi*]

I wearied to contain the prophecy, and to conceal it.—[*Kara*]

10. **For I heard**—*I said that I would not mention Him because I heard the speech of many, those who whisper about me.*—[*Rashi*]

Others render: Although I heard the slander of many. I could not contain the prophecy although I heard the slander of many, who were

* For Rashi's commentary turn to page 239.

מגור מסביב הגידו ונגידנו כל אנוש
שלמי שמרי צלעי אולי יפתה ונוכלה
לו ונקחה נקמתנו ממנו: יא ויהוה אותי
כגבור עריץ על כן רדפי יכשלו ולא
יכלו בשו מאד כי־לא השכילו כלמת
עולם לא תשכח: יב ויהוה צבאות בחן
צדיק ראה כליות ולב אראה נקמתך

תרגום

שמעית מלי סגיאיא
דמתכנשין מסחור
סחור הוו ונחויניה כל
אנש שלמי כמנין
לאבאשא לימאים יטעי
ונכול ליה ונתפרע
פורענותנא מניה:
יא ויי מימריה בסעדי
כגבר תקיף על כל רדפי
יתקלון ולא יכלון למיקם
יבהתון לחדא ארי לא
יצלחון ותתחפינון
אתכנעות עלם דלא
תתנשי: יב ויי צבאות

רש"י

שמעתי דבת רבים אלו שמתלחשים עלי: מגור. לשון אסיפה וכן ת"י: הגידו. עליו עדות שקר: ונגידנו. ונעידנו ומנחם פירש הגידו ונגידנו כמו (דברים י"ד) לא תתגודדו וכן חבר להלק יגיד רעים (איוב י"ז) ל' השחתה כמו גודו אילנא (דניאל ג') ודונש פתר אותו לשון הגדה ממש וכה פתרונו הגידו עליו דברי שקר ונגידנו למלך ויש לנו כמו נגידנו דברים רבים במקרא אשר לא יכון פתרונו כי אם עד אשר יהלקון לשתי וניבות או לשלש כמו ולא יכלו דברו לשלום (בראשית ל"ו) בני יאלוני (לעיל י'): שומרי צלעי. מלפים שברי: אולי יפותה. לשמוע לנו ולטעות אחרינו: (יא) כי לא השכילו. לא הצליחו בעלתם:

מהר"י קרא

תגידנו. פת' ונגידה בית המלך שהוא מתנבא על המקום הזה לרעה. ולא תאמר שהאנשים החושבים עלי לרעה זה רחוקים לי אינו כן אלא אותם האנשים קרובי הם ואנשי שלומי והם שהי' לי לשמור צלעי ואעפ"כ אומרים עלי נוציא דבר מפיו שהוא לרעה על המקום הזה: אולי יפותה. ויאמר נבואה של רעה על המקום הזה ועל ידי כן נוכלה לו ונקחה נקמתנו ממנו: (יא) וה' אותי כגבור עריץ. (יב) וה' צבאות בוחן צדיק. אין פתרונו שהקב"ה בוחן צדיק אלא פתרונו בוחן על בוריו של דבר. לפי שאתה רואה כליות ולב ובוחן צדיק. שלא כמדת הקב"ה מדת בשר ודם. בנוהג שבעולם אם יהיה ריב בין אנשים ונגשו אל המשפט שישפוט אותם פעמים שטענתם שקולה. ומתוך שכל

רד"ק

הגידו ונגידנו. פי' הגידו דבר שקר עליו ונגידנו למלך כמ"ש לכו ונכהו בל': כל אנוש שלמי שומרי צלעי. אותם שהייתי חושב שהם אנשי שלומי הם שומרים ומצפים מתי אהיה צולע ונכשל בשום דבר: אולי יפתה ונוכלה לו. אולי יפתה לדברינו שיאכל וישתה עמנו ונקח' נקמתינו לפי שנשקהו סם המות וי"ת מאים יטעי: (יא) וה' אותי. הם חושבים להמיתני וכזה לא אפחד כי ה' הבטיחני ואמר אלי ונלחמו אליך ולא יוכלו לך והוא עמי כגבור עריץ שיהיה עמי שלא אפחד או פי' ונתן אות כמו גבור עריץ לעמוד כנגדם ות"י וה' מימריה בסעדי כגבור תקיף: בשו מאד כי לא השכילו. ענין הצלחה כמו ויהי דוד לכל דרכיו משכיל והוא עבר במקום עתיד יבשו מאד כי לא השכילו כלו' יהיה להם בשת שלא יצליחו במעשיה' ובמחשבותם עלי ואותה הבושת תהיה כלימה שלא תשכח כי יהיו לקללה בפי האנשי' לעול' ולא יוכלו. חסר וי"ו שהוא במקו' יו"ד פ"א הפעל מהמכתב: (יב) וה' צבאו' בוחן צדיק. אותו שהוא צדיק. לעיני בני אדם לא ידעו בו אם תוכו כברו וה' צבאות בוחן אותו אם לבו בסתר כמו מעשיו בגלוי ימלהו כצדקו ואם לאו יגלהו ויפרסמהו לעיני האנשי' שידעו מי הוא כלומר שיכשילהו

מצודת דוד

דברי רבים אסיפת אויבים מסביב שאומרים אלו לאלו הגידו עליו עדות שקר ונגיד הדבר ההיא לפני המלך: כל אנוש. כל איש ואיש אשר הכרתים שהם אוהבי ואנשי שלומי המה מצפים על תקלתי להיות צולע ופוסח והוא ענין מליצה: אולי יפותה. מאמרם אולי יפות' לדברינו ונוכל' לו שידבר דבר שיהיה בעבורו חייב מיתה ואז נקחה את נקמתינו ממנו: (יא) וה' אותי. הנה עכ"ז היה ה' עמי לעזר' כגבור חזק על כן כשלו רודפי ולא יוכלו לי לעשות עמי רעה: בושו מאוד. נתביישו מאד כי לא הצליחו בעצתם וכלימת עולם תהיה זאת להם ולא תשכח: (יב) וה' צבאות. ואתה ה' צבאות הבוחן את הצדיק לדעת מעשיו ורואה מחשבות כליות ולב בטוח אני אשר בעיני אראה נקמתך מהם: כי אליך. לכך אליך אני מגלה הריב שיש להם עמדי ולא גליתי למי לבקש ממנו עזר:

מצודת ציון

כמו דבת הארץ (במדבר י"ג): מגור. ענין אסיפה: שומרי. ענין תקוה ולפוי כמו ואביו שמר את הדבר (בראשית ל"ז): צלעי. ענין הגר ופסח ויאמר על המכשול והתקלה וכן ובצלעי שמחו (תהלים ל"ה): יפותה. מלשון פיתוי והסתה: ונוכלה. מלשון יכולת: (יא) אותי. עמי וכן ואדבר אותך (יחזקאל ב'): עריץ. חזק כמו אל נערץ (תהלים פ"ט): השכילו. ענין הצלחה על כי המצליח נדמה בעיני הבריות שעשה מעשיו בהשכל וכן ויהי דוד לכל דרכיו משכיל (ש"א י"ח): (יב) בוחן. מלשון הבחנה:

teous. He tests him whether his heart is as righteous as the deeds he performs in public. If not, He reveals his true character to the public. I.e., He brings stumbling-blocks before him to cause him to stumble in his deeds.—[*Redak*]

Let me see Your vengeance—Since You see the kidneys and the heart and know that I am just, not

a gathering around; tell and let us tell about him; everyone who was friendly with me awaits my destruction. Perhaps he will be enticed and we will prevail against him, and we will wreak vengeance upon him. 11. But the Lord is with me as a mighty warrior. Therefore, my pursuers shall stumble and did not prevail. They were very much ashamed for they not succeed, a perpetual shame that will not be forgotten. 12. And the Lord of Hosts tests the righteous, He sees the kidneys and the heart. Let me see Your vengeance

plotting against me and awaiting my destruction.—[*Abarbanel, Mezudath David*]

Perhaps he will be enticed—*to listen to us and to stray after us.*—[*Rashi*]

Abarbanel quotes *Rashi* to read: **Perhaps he will be enticed**—*to err like us.*

and we will prevail against him—*to bring him to commit idolatry.*

Redak explains: Perhaps he will be enticed to eat and drink with us, and we will take our revenge from him by giving him poison to drink.

Kara explains: Perhaps we will entice him to say evil prophecies about this place, and, thereby, we will prevail against him and wreak vengeance upon him.

Or, we will entice him to say something for which he will be liable to death.—[*Abarbanel, Mezudath David*]

11. **But the Lord is with me**—Nevertheless, the Lord was with me to aid me like a mighty warrior. Therefore, my pursuers stumbled and could not prevail against me.—[*Mezudath David*]

for they did not succeed—Heb. הִשְׂכִּילוּ. *They did not succeed with their plan.*—[*Rashi*] Lit. they did not understand. Since a successful person appears to have succeeded because of his superior intelligence, this word is used in that context.—[*Mezudath David*]

a perpetual shame that will not be forgotten—Let the failure of their plot be a perpetual shame to them, a shame that will never be forgotten.—[*Mezudath David*]

Redak explains the verse in the prophetic past. They plot to kill me, but I fear it not, for the Lord already promised me, "And they will fight with you and not prevail against you," and He is with me like a mighty warrior that I should not fear. Or, He gave a signal like a mighty warrior, to stand up against them.

May they be very much ashamed for they shall not succeed—with their deeds and plots against me, and may that shame be a perpetual shame that will not be forgotten.—[*Redak*]

12. **And the Lord of Hosts tests the righteous**—The Lord of Hosts tests him who appears to be righ-

מֵהֶם כִּי אֵלֶיךָ גִּלִּיתִי אֶת־רִיבִי׃ יג שִׁירוּ
לַיהוָה הַלְלוּ אֶת־יְהוָה כִּי הִצִּיל אֶת־
נֶפֶשׁ אֶבְיוֹן מִיַּד מְרֵעִים׃ יד אָרוּר הַיּוֹם
אֲשֶׁר יֻלַּדְתִּי בּוֹ יוֹם אֲשֶׁר־יְלָדַתְנִי אִמִּי
אַל־יְהִי בָרוּךְ׃ טו אָרוּר הָאִישׁ אֲשֶׁר
בִּשַּׂר אֶת־אָבִי לֵאמֹר יֻלַּד־לְךָ בֵּן זָכָר
שַׂמֵּחַ שִׂמְּחָהוּ׃ טז וְהָיָה הָאִישׁ הַהוּא
כֶּעָרִים אֲשֶׁר־הָפַךְ יְהוָה וְלֹא נִחָם
וְשָׁמַע זְעָקָה בַּבֹּקֶר וּתְרוּעָה בְּעֵת

תרגום

בְּהוֹן קְשׁוֹט גַּלְיָן קֳדָמוֹהִי
כּוּלְיָן וְלִבָּא אַחֲזֵי פּוּרְעָנוּת
דִּינָךְ מִנְּהוֹן אֲרֵי קֳדָמָךְ
אֲמָרֵית יָת עוּלְבָּנִי׃
יג שַׁבַּחוּ קֳדָם יְיָ אוֹדוּ
קֳדָם יְיָ אֲרֵי שֵׁיזֵיב יָת
נְפַשׁ מִסְכְּנָא מִיַּד מַבְאֲשִׁין׃
יד לִיט יוֹמָא דְּאִתְיְלִידִית
בֵּיהּ יוֹמָא דִּילֵדַתְנִי בֵּיהּ
אִמִּי לָא יְהֵי בְּרִיךְ׃
טו לִיט גַּבְרָא דְּבַשַּׂר
יָת אַבָּא לְמֵימַר אִתְיְלִיד
לָךְ בַּר דְּכַר חַדָּאָה
חַדְיֵהּ׃ טז וִיהֵי גַּבְרָא
הַהוּא כְּקִרְוַיָּא דַּהֲפַךְ יְיָ
בְּרוּגְזֵיהּ וְלָא אִתּוֹתַבָא
וְיִשְׁמַע צְוָחְתָא בְּצַפְרָא
וְיַבָּבָא בְּעִדָּן טִיהֲרָא׃

מהר"י קרא

אחד ואחד צדיק בריבו אינהדיין יכול להבחין מי זכאי ומי חייב לפי שאינו יכול לדון דינין שבלב אבל אתה לך נאה לקרותך בוחן צדיק לפי שאתה רואה כליות ולב ואתה יודע שהדין עמי. בבקשה ממך תראני נקמתך מהם כי אליך גליתי את ריבי:

רש"י

(יד) ארור היום אשר ילדתי בו. (פוח"י אינייניר"מבלע"ז) היא שעת הריון ועל ידי אונס שמש חלקיהו אביו מטתו ביום שהיה בורח מפני מנשה שהיה הורג את הנביאים ושמש מטתו וברח: (טו) שמח. מ"ם דגושה שהוא לשון משמח אחרי' שמח את אביו בבשורתו: (טז) כערים אשר הפך. סדום ועמורה: ולא נחם. משגזר עליהם חורבן

רד"ק

במעשיו: (יג) שירו לה'. אמר זה כנגד החסידים אשר היו בירושלם: כי הציל. שגלה לו שלא יאכל ולא ישתה עמהם כי היו רוצים להמיתו: (יד) ארור היום. ממרירו' נפש' יקללו הצדיקי' יום הולדם בו ואף על פי שלא תשיגהו קללה כי כבר עבר וכן אמר איוב יאבד יום אולד בו וגו' והוסיף הענין במ"ש ואמר יום אשר ילדתני אמי: (טו) ארור האיש אשר בשר את אבי. ואף על פי שהיה מקלל ממרירות נפשו יש לתמוה איך היה מקלל המבשר כי אם הוא היה בחיי' תשיגהו קללה ואולי היה איש טוב המבשר והיה לירמיהו עון על קללו אותו ואמרו כי נודע לו כי פשחור בן אמר היה המבשר: שמח שמחהו. באמת שמחהו כשאמר לו כי בן זכר נולד לו כי בני אדם שמחים לבן זכר ודואגים על הנקבה ואם היה יודע אבי סופי שיהיו ימי בעמל ויגון לא היה שמח בי: (טז) והיה. ושמע זעקה בבקר. זעקת מקרוביו ומאוהביו בבקר כלומר בתחלת היום. וכן ישמע תמיד עד עת צהרים. וכן מכאן ואילך כל היום אלא זכר צהרים לפי שהאור הולך ומוסיף מהבקר עד עת הצהרים ותהיה קללתו מוספת והולכת כי התרועה יותר מהזעקה והתרועה תהיה לשמחה כמו לא ירונן ולא ירועע יתרועעו אף ישירו ותהיה

מצודת ציון

(יג) מרעים. רשעים: (טז) נחם. ענין הפוך מחשבה: ותרועה.

מצודת דוד

(יג) שירו לה'. ומעתה אתם אנשי הצדק שירו לה' והללו אותו אשר הציל מיד המרעי' את נפש האביון ועל נפש עצמו אמר:

(יד) ארור היום. ממרירת לב על כי רבים קמו עליו קלל ימיו' יום מולדתו כפי המורגל בפי קשי המזל: יולדתי בו. הוא יום ההריון המיוחס גם לאב וכא"ש לאביך זה ילדך (משלי כ"ג): אשר ילדתני אמי. זה יום הלידה המיוחס לבד לאם: (טו) ארור האיש וגו'. הואיל ולמפרע לא היתה הבשורה טובה בודאי לא היה המבשר איש טוב כי דרך איש טוב לבשר טובה כמ"ש איש טוב זה ועל בשורה טובה יבוא (ש"ב י"ח): שמח שמחהו. אמר בתמיה וכי למפרע היתה שמחה: (טז) והיה האיש ההוא. זה המבשר: כערים וגו'. הם סדום ועמורה: ולא נחם. משגזר עליהם הפיכה לא חשב מחשבה אחרת לבטל הגזרה: ושמע. המבשר הזה ישמע מאוהביו

turned—Namely *Sodom and Gemorrah.*—[*Rashi*]

and did not repent—*Since He decreed destruction upon them, he did not think another thought to rescind His decree.*—[*Rashi*]

and let him hear an outcry in the morning—I.e. in the beginning of the day, and so on until noon.—[*Redak*]

and a scream at noontime—And so on all day long. The curse becomes more intense as it goes on, for a scream is more intense than an outcry. The word תְּרוּעָה is sometimes used for a shout of joy and sometimes for a scream of anguish.—[*Redak*]

Malbim explains: The one who brought the glad tidings was

from them for to You I have revealed my cause. 13. Sing to the
Lord, praise the Lord, for He has saved the soul of the poor
from the hand of evildoers. 14. Cursed be the day in which I
was begotten; the day in which my mother bore me shall not be
blessed. 15. Cursed be the man who brought the news to my
father, saying, "A male child has been born to you," making
him glad. 16. And that man shall be like the cities that the Lord
overturned and did not repent, and let him hear an outcry in
the morning and a scream at noontime.

they, I beg You to let me see Your vengeance upon them.—[*Kara*]

13. **Sing to the Lord**—Here he addresses the pious in Jerusalem.—[*Redak*]

for He has saved etc—by revealing to him that they were plotting to poison him so that he should not join them at their repast.—[*Redak*]

14. **Cursed be the day in which I was begotten**—Heb. יֻלַּדְתִּי, (*engendrer* or *engenrer in O.F.*). *That is the time of conception, and through compulsion Hilkiah his father performed the marriage act by day, for he was fleeing from before Manasseh, who was slaying the prophets, and he performed the marriage act and fled.*—[*Rashi* from *Gen. Rabbah* 64:5]

15. Cursed be the man etc.—Although Jeremiah was cursing out of the bitterness of his heart, it is astonishing that he should curse the man who brought the news of his birth to his father, for if he was still living, the curse would fall upon him, and perhaps he was a good man. Jeremiah would, consequently, have committed a sin by cursing him. The Rabbis tell us that Jeremiah knew that it was Pashhur who had brought the news to Hilkiah of Jeremiah's birth.—[*Redak* and *Ibn Nachmiash* from obscure Midrashic source]

Malbim writes that Manasseh killed him for bringing joy to Hilkiah. He renders: Cursed was the man etc. This is apparently his own conjecture.

making him glad—Heb. שַׂמֵּחַ שִׂמְּחָהוּ, lit. he made him glad. *The 'mem' is punctuated with a 'dagesh,' which is an expression of making others glad, for he made his father glad with his news.*—[*Rashi*]

The intention is that the words שַׂמֵּחַ שִׂמְּחָהוּ belong to the 'piel' conjugation, making it a transitive verb, unlike שָׂמַח, of the 'kal' conjugation, which is an intransitive verb, meaning 'he was glad.'

Indeed, he made him glad, for people are glad of the birth of a boy but worried about a girl. Had my father known that I would end in such an unfortunate situation, he would have not rejoiced.—[*Redak*]

16. **like the cities that . . . over-**

יז לְנִי דְלָא אֲמִיר עֲלַי
דְמִיתֵית מִמְעִין וַהֲוָת
לִי פוּן אִמִי קִבְרִי וַהֲוֵית
כִּדְלָא הֲוֵית׃ יח לְמָה
דְנַן מִבִּטְנָא נְפַקִית
לְמֶחֱזֵי עָמָל וּדְוָן וְסָפוּ
בִּבְהָתָא יוֹמָי׃ א פִּתְגַם
נְבוּאָה דַהֲוָה עִם יִרְמְיָה
מִקֳדָם יְיָ כַּד שְׁלַח
לְוָתֵיהּ מַלְכָּא צִדְקִיָּה
יַת פַּשְׁחוּר בַּר מַלְכִּיָּה
וְיַת צְפַנְיָה בַר מַעֲשֵׂיָה
כַּהֲנָא לְמֵימַר׃ ב צַלֵי
כְעַן עֲלָנָא קֳדָם יְיָ אֲרֵי
נְבוּכַדְרֶצַר מַלְכָּא דְבָבֶל

צָהֳרָיִם׃ יז אֲשֶׁר לֹא־מוֹתְתַנִי מֵרָחֶם
וַתְּהִי לִי אִמִּי קִבְרִי וְרַחְמָה הֲרַת עוֹלָם׃
יח לָמָּה זֶּה מֵרֶחֶם יָצָאתִי לִרְאוֹת עָמָל
וְיָגוֹן וַיִּכְלוּ בְּבֹשֶׁת יָמָי׃ כא א הַדָּבָר
אֲשֶׁר־הָיָה אֶל־יִרְמְיָהוּ מֵאֵת יְהוָה
בִּשְׁלֹחַ אֵלָיו הַמֶּלֶךְ צִדְקִיָּהוּ אֶת־
פַּשְׁחוּר בֶּן־מַלְכִּיָּה וְאֶת־צְפַנְיָה בֶן־
מַעֲשֵׂיָה הַכֹּהֵן לֵאמֹר׃ ב דְּרָשׁ־נָא
בַעֲדֵנוּ אֶת־יְהוָה כִּי נְבוּכַדְרֶאצַּר מֶלֶךְ־

לא מפיק ה'

רש"י

לא חשב מחשבה אחרת לבטל גזרתו: (יז) **אשר לא מותתני**. מלאך המות מרחם והרי זה מן המקראות קלרי דכור: **הרת עולם**. הריון של עולמית: (יח) **עמל ויגון**. חורבן בית המקדש:

מהר"י קרא

(יז) ורחמה הרת עולם. שיהיה לי הרחם הריון של עולם כדי שלא יצאתי ממנו:
כא (ב) כי נבוכדנצר. נלחם עלינו אולי יעשה ה' אתנו ככל נפלאותיו. כמו שעשה כבר לחזקיה כשצר סנחריב מלך אשור על העיר הזאת: ויעלה מעלינו. נבוכדנצר גם הוא

רד"ק

לאבל ולצער כמו למה תריע רע וכן ותרועת בעת צהרים: (יז) אשר לא מותתני מרחם. מותתני מבנין מרובע אומר על איש למה לא המיתו קודם צאתו מרחם או אמר על האל כמ"ש איוב כי לא סגר דלתי בטני: ותהי לי אמי קברי. שאם מותתני קודם צאתי מרחם היתה לי אמי קברי: ורחמה הרת עולם. רחם אמי למה לא היתה לי להריון עולם ממני הרה בסמיך הרת כמו סן שנה שנת שלומים שפה שפת היאור ובאמרו הרת ל' נקבה ורחם מן הדומה ל' זכר מעם הנקבות על האם שתהיה הרת עולם ממני שאהיה לעולם ברחמה: (יח) למה זה. מבואר הוא וכן הפ' הבאה אחריו מבוארת: (ב) נלחם

מנחת שי

(יז) ורחמה הרת עולם. הה"א נחה ועיקרה במפיק מכלול דף ל"ג וירושים ומסורה וכן הוא בספרים כתובי יד מדוייקים ודפוסים ישנים עוד נמסר במסרה גדולה רחמה ד' וגו' וא' ורחמה הרת עולם לא מפיק ה"א:
כא (ב) דרש נא בעדנו את. ברוב הספרים חסר יו"ד אחר דל"ת:

מצודת דוד

זעקת לרה ותרועת יללה: (יז) **אשר לא מותתני מרחם**. ר"ל לזה אני מקלל יום הלידה והמבשר כי למה מי שבידו להמית לא המית אותי עודי ברחם והיתה לי א"כ אמי לקבר לפי שעה ורחמה היה לי הריון עד עולם עד המיתה: (יח) **למה זה מרחם יצאתי**. ר"ל למה יצאתי מעלמי כדרך הנולד חי: **לראות עמל ויגון**. התולדה הזאת היתה לרעתי לראות עמל ויגון והנה ימי כלים בבושת כי כל הימים מביישים אותי הקמים עלי:
כא (ב) **דרש נא**. עתה דרש בתפלה בעבורינו אל ה': **ככל נפלאותיו**. כמו כל הנפלאות הרגיל לעשות מאז: **ויעלה**.

מצודת ציון

ענין זעקת יללה כמו נפשו ירעה לו (ישעיה ט"ו): (יז) מרחם הוא מקום הולד: הרת. מלשון הריון: (יח) עמל. ענין יגיעה: ויכלו. מלשון כליון:
כא (ב) ויעלה. ענין סלוק כמו העלות הענן (במדבר ט'):

17. That he did not put me to death from the womb, that my mother should be my grave and her womb a perpetual pregnancy. 18. Why did I come forth out of the womb to see toil and grief, and my days end with shame?

21

1. The word that came to Jeremiah from the Lord when King Zedekiah sent him Pashhur son of Milchiah and Zephaniah son of Maasiah the priest, saying: 2. Please petition the Lord for us, for Nebuchadrezzar king of

destroyed 'like the cities that the Lord overturned.' So was he and all his destroyed by Manasseh.

17. **That he did not put me to death**—I.e. that *the angel of death* did not put me to death *from the womb, and this is one of the verses with brief language.*—[*Rashi*]

The subject is either 'man,' or 'god.' The latter interpretation would be analogous with Job's lamentation, '(3:10) Who did not shut the doors of my [mother's] womb.'—[*Redak*]

that my mother should be my grave—Had he put me to death before I emerged from the womb, my mother would have been my grave.—[*Redak*]

a perpetual pregnancy—Heb. הֲרַת עוֹלָם, *a pregnancy of eternity.*—[*Rashi*]

18. **Why did I come forth out of the womb**—Why did I come out by myself in the manner of a child born alive?—[*Mezudath David*]

toil and grief—*The destruction of the Temple.*—[*Rashi*]

and my days end with shame—My assailants are constantly deriding me and humiliating me.—[*Mezudath David*]

Malbim explains:

[17] **For he did not put me to death from the womb**—Manasseh put him to death because he knew of my conception, but did not report it to the king so that he could kill me from the womb by giving my mother a potion so that she should abort me, for Manasseh endeavored to annihilate the seed of the prophets.

[18] **Why have I come forth**—Since my very birth transpired under a bad sign, why did I come forth from the womb—to be destined to a life of trials and tribulations?

1. **the priest**—This title belongs to both Pashhur and Zephaniah. Pashhur son of Milchiah is mentioned among the priests in Neh. 11:10, 12. He is likely the one mentioned below 38:1. Zephaniah the priest is mentioned also in 29:25, 29, and 37:3. He was apparently the priest of second rank who was brought by Nebuzaradan to Riblah and dispatched there by order of

בָּבֶל נִלְחָם עָלֵינוּ אוּלַי יַעֲשֶׂה יְהוָה
אוֹתָנוּ כְּכָל־נִפְלְאֹתָיו וְיַעֲלֶה מֵעָלֵינוּ׃
ג וַיֹּאמֶר יִרְמְיָהוּ אֲלֵיהֶם כֹּה תֹאמְרֻן
אֶל־צִדְקִיָּהוּ׃ ד כֹּה־אָמַר יְהוָה אֱלֹהֵי
יִשְׂרָאֵל הִנְנִי מֵסֵב אֶת־כְּלֵי הַמִּלְחָמָה
אֲשֶׁר בְּיֶדְכֶם אֲשֶׁר אַתֶּם נִלְחָמִים בָּם
אֶת־מֶלֶךְ בָּבֶל וְאֶת־הַכַּשְׂדִּים הַצָּרִים
עֲלֵיכֶם מִחוּץ לַחוֹמָה וְאָסַפְתִּי אוֹתָם
אֶל־תּוֹךְ הָעִיר הַזֹּאת׃ ה וְנִלְחַמְתִּי אֲנִי
אִתְּכֶם בְּיָד נְטוּיָה וּבִזְרוֹעַ חֲזָקָה וּבְאַף
וּבְחֵמָה וּבְקֶצֶף גָּדוֹל׃ ו וְהִכֵּיתִי אֶת־
יוֹשְׁבֵי הָעִיר הַזֹּאת וְאֶת־הָאָדָם וְאֶת־
הַבְּהֵמָה בְּדֶבֶר גָּדוֹל יָמֻתוּ׃ ז וְאַחֲרֵי־

תרגום

מְגִיחַ קְרָבָא בָנָא מָאִים
יַעֲבֵד יְיָ עִמָנָא כְּכָל
פְּרִישָׁתֵיהּ וְיִסְתַּלַק
מִנָנָא׃ ג וַאֲמַר יִרְמְיָה
לְהוֹן כְּדֵין תֵּימְרוּן
לְצִדְקִיָה׃ ד כִּדְנַן אֲמַר
יְיָ אֱלָהָא דְיִשְׂרָאֵל הָאֲנָא
מְסַחַר יַת מָאנֵי קְרָבָא
דִבְיֶדְכוֹן דְאַתּוּן מְגִיחִין
קְרָבָא בְהוֹן עִם מַלְכָּא
דְבָבֶל וְעִם כַּשְׂדָאֵי
דְצַיְרִין עֲלֵיכוֹן מִבָּרָא
לְשׁוּרָא וַאֲכַנֵשׁ יַתְהוֹן
לְגוֹ קַרְתָּא הָדָא׃
ה וַאֲגִיחַ אֲנָא עִמְכוֹן בְּיַד
מְרַמְמָא וּבִדְרַע תַּקִיפָא
וּבִרְגַז וּבְחֵמָה וּבְתְקוֹף
רָב׃ ו וְאֶמְחֵי יַת יָתְבֵי
קַרְתָּא הָדָא וְיַת אֱנָשָׁא
וְיַת בְּעִירָא בְּמוֹתָא
סַגִיאָה יְמוּתוּן׃ ז וּבָתַר
כן

רש"י

כא (ד) הנני מסב את כלי המלחמה. יש בכם היודעים להשביע את השרים של מעלה הממוני' על הפורעניות להציל איש איש מן הרעה שהוא ממונה עליה ובכך אתם בוטחים הנני מיסב את השררה של זה לזה ולא תדעו על מי תשביעו: ואספתי אותם. כלי מלחמה אל תוך העיר הזאת שאשחית אתכם בדבר על ידי מלאך המות

מהר"י קרא

כמו שעשה בסנחריב דכתיב ויצא מלאך ה' ויך במחנה אשור וגו': (ד) הנני מיסב את כלי המלחמה אשר בידכם. אשר אתם סבורים להלחם בם עם מלך בבל ועם הכשדים כלומר מה שאתם סבורים שאני נלחם בעדכם במלך שאתם סבורים שאני כלי מלחמתכ' להלחם בעדכם על מלך בבל שאתם אומרים אולי יעשה אותנו ה' ככל נפלאותיו ויעלה מעלינו. אינו כן אלא מיסב אני את פני מכם ומחזק את בבל הנלחם בכם. ואספתי אותם אל תוך העיר הזאת. (ה) ונלחמתי אני אתכם ביד

רד"ק

עלינו. קמוץ כי הוא בינוני: (ג) כה תאמרון. חסר וי"ו המשך: (ד) הנני מסב. כאילו כלי המלחמה אשר בידכם יהיו בידם שלא יהיה לכם כח לחלחם כנגדם: ואספתי אותם. הכשדי': (ה) ונלחמתי. הכשדים ילחמו אתכם מחוץ ואני אלחם אתכם

מצודת ציון

(ד) מסב. מל' סביב: את מלך. אל מלך: הצרים. מל' מצור: ואספתי. ענין הכנסה כמו ואין איש מאסף אותם (שופטים י"ט):

מצודת דוד

ויסתלק מעלינו: (ד) הנני מסב. אסבב מכם את כלי המלחמה לתתם אל מלך בבל וגו' ר"ל לא תצליחו עם כלי המלחמה כאילו הם לקוחים מכם ונתונים בידם להלחם עמהם: ואספתי. אני אכניס את הכשדים אל העיר ולא תוכלו למנעם: (ה) ונלחמתי. ר"ל אגביר הכשדים עליכם כאלו אני נלחם עמכם: ביד נטויה. אחז כמשל מגבור הנלחם ונוטה ידו מול האויב: (ו) את יושבי העיר. ומוזר ומפרש ואת האדם ואת הבהמה: בדבר. רוצה לומר

5. **And I will wage war**—The Chaldeans will wage war against you from outside, and I will wage war against you with a great pestilence, with which I will smite you and your livestock.

one *of the heavenly princes. And in this manner it is explained in the chapter* (v. 6): *'with a great pestilence they shall die.'*—[*Rashi*]

Redak explains: And I will gather the Chaldeans, so *Mezudath David.*

Babylon is waging war against us; perhaps the Lord will do to us like all His wonders, and he will withdraw from us." 3. And Jeremiah said to them, "So shall you say to Zedekiah, 4. So said the Lord God of Israel: Behold I turn back the weapons of war that are in your hand[s], with which you are waging war against the king of Babylon and against the Chaldeans who are besieging you from outside the wall, and I will gather them into this city. 5. And I will wage war with you with an outstretched hand and with a strong arm, and with anger and with fury and with great wrath. 6. And I will smite the inhabitants of this city and the people and the beasts; with a great pestilence they shall die.

Nebuchadnezzar. See II Kings 25:18, 20–21; Jer. 52:24, 26, 27.—[*Daath Mikra*]

2. **will do for us like all his wonders**—as He did for Hezekiah when Sennacherib, king of Assyria, besieged this city.—[*Kara*]

Perhaps he will perform wonders for us as He was wont to do in days of yore.—[*Mezudath David*]

This prophecy came to Jeremiah when the city was already under siege. Then Zedekiah sent emissaries to him, begging him to petition God to perform wonders for them so that Nebuchadnezzar would withdraw. Neither Zedekiah nor his people had repented of their sins, but they begged Jeremiah to pray, thinking that their future depended upon him and that God would relent even if they did not repent of their sins.—[*Abarbanel*]

4. **Behold I turn back the weapons of war**—*There are some among you who know how to adjure the heavenly princes in charge of retribution, that each one save them from the evil he is in charge of, and you rely on that. Behold, I will transfer one's authority to another one, and you will not know whom to adjure.*—[*Rashi* from unknown Midrashic source]

Kara explains that they considered God as their weapons of war. This was illustrated by their petition to Jeremiah. Thereupon, God replies, "I will turn My face—your weapons of war—away from you and I will strengthen the king of Babylon, and gather the weapons into the city.

Redak explains simply that they would have no power to wage war, thus making their weapons useless, as though they were in the hands of the Chaldeans.

and I will gather them—I.e. *the weapons of war, into this city, that I will destroy you with pestilence through the angel of death, who is*

כֵן נְאֻם־יְהוָה אֶתֵּן אֶת־צִדְקִיָּהוּ מֶלֶךְ־
יְהוּדָה ׀ וְאֶת־עֲבָדָיו ׀ וְאֶת־הָעָם וְאֶת־
הַנִּשְׁאָרִים בָּעִיר הַזֹּאת מִן־הַדֶּבֶר ׀ מִן־
הַחֶרֶב וּמִן־הָרָעָב בְּיַד נְבוּכַדְרֶאצַּר
מֶלֶךְ־בָּבֶל וּבְיַד אֹיְבֵיהֶם וּבְיַד מְבַקְשֵׁי
נַפְשָׁם וְהִכָּם לְפִי־חֶרֶב לֹא־יָחוּס עֲלֵיהֶם
וְלֹא יַחְמֹל וְלֹא יְרַחֵם׃ ח וְאֶל־הָעָם הַזֶּה
תֹּאמַר כֹּה אָמַר יְהוָה הִנְנִי נֹתֵן לִפְנֵיכֶם
אֶת־דֶּרֶךְ הַחַיִּים וְאֶת־דֶּרֶךְ הַמָּוֶת׃
ט הַיֹּשֵׁב בָּעִיר הַזֹּאת יָמוּת בַּחֶרֶב
וּבָרָעָב וּבַדָּבֶר וְהַיּוֹצֵא וְנָפַל עַל־
הַכַּשְׂדִּים הַצָּרִים עֲלֵיכֶם יְחִיֶה וְהָיְתָה־

תרגום

כֵּן אֲמַר יְיָ אֶמְסַר יַת
צִדְקִיָּה מַלְכָּא שִׁבְטָא
דְבֵית יְהוּדָה וְיַת עַבְדוֹהִי
וְיַת עַמָּא וְיַת דְאִשְׁתְּאָרוּ
בְּקַרְתָּא הָדָא מִן מוֹתָא
וּמִן חַרְבָּא וּמִן כַּפְנָא
בְּיַד נְבוּכַדְרֶאצַּר מַלְכָּא
דְבָבֶל וּבְיַד בַּעֲלֵי
דְבָבֵיהוֹן וּבְיַד
דְבָעַן לְקַטָּלְהוֹן
וְיִמְחִינוּן לְפִתְגָם דְחֶרֶב
לָא יְחוּס עֲלֵיהוֹן וְלָא
יַחְמוֹל וְלָא יְרַחֵם׃
ח וּלְעַמָּא הָדֵין תֵּימַר
כִּדְנַן אֲמַר יְיָ הָאֲנָא יָהֵיב
קֳדָמֵיהוֹן יַת אוֹרַח חַיֵּי
וְיַת אוֹרַח מוֹתָא׃
ט דְיָתֵיב בְּקַרְתָּא הָדָא
יִתְקְטֵיל בְּחַרְבָּא
וּבְכַפְנָא וּבְמוֹתָא וּדְיִפּוֹק
וְיִשְׁתְּמַע לְכַשְׂדָּאֵי
דְצַיְרִין עֲלֵיכוֹן וִיחֵי וּתְהֵי
לֵיהּ

ת"א היושב בעיר. סנהדרין לז:

וחיה קרי

רש"י

שהוא מן השרים העליונים וכן מפורש בענין בדבר גדול ימותו: (ט) והיתה לו נפשו לשלל. כאדם השולל שלל

מהר"י קרא

נשוית. (ט) והיתה לו נפשו לשלל. בהצלת נפשו כאילו נדמה לו כאילו מצא שלל:

רד"ק

בדבר גדול שאכה אתכם ואת בהמתכם: (ז) מן הדבר מן החרב. מחרב המלחמה בהלחמה על העיר אתן אותם ביד נבוכדנצר כשיכבוש העיר ואף צדקיהו ועבדיו שברחו: והכם לפי חרב. מי שירצה להמית יכות ומי שירצה להגלות יגלה: לא יחוס עליהם ולא יחמול ולא ירחם. שהרי שחט בני צדקיהו לעיניו וכן בשדים ובזקנים לא חמל: (ט) הצרים עליכם יחיה. כתיב וקרי וחיה והענין אחד: והיתה לו נפשו לשלל. לרוחה כאילו שלל אותה:

מנחת שי

(ז) לא יחוס. לא כתיב בלא וא"ו וכן הוא במ"ג עם פסוקים שכתוב בהם לא ולא ולא באמצע פסוק: יחוס. בשורק לא בחולם: (ט) יחיה. וחיה קרי:

מצודת דוד

שהכללם תהיה שימותו בדב׳ גדול: (ח) נותן לפניכם. ר"ל מפרש אני לפניכם באיזה ענין תמלאו חיים ובאיזה ענין תשיג אתכם המיתה: (ט) בחרב וגו׳. ר"ל באחד מאלה: ונפל. ישכון אל הכשדים לסיום סר למשמעתם: וחיה. ישאר חי וילוים נפשו

מצודת ציון

(ז) יחוס. ענין חמלה כמו וחוסה עלי (נחמיה י"ג) וכפל הדבר כמ"ש: (ח) נותן. ענין אמירה כמו ולא נתן הסכם (איוב ט׳): את דרך. את ענין: (ט) ונפל. ענין השכנה וחניה כמו אל הכשדים אתה נופל (לקמן ל"ז): לשלל. ענין בזה:

7. And afterwards, says the Lord, I will deliver Zedekiah, the king of Judah and his servants and the people and those remaining in this city, from the pestilence, from the sword, and from the famine, into the hand of Nebuchadrezzar, the king of Babylon and into the hand of your enemies and into the hand of those who seek your lives, and he shall strike them by the edge of the sword; he will not spare them, neither will he pity nor show compassion. 8. And to this people you shall say: So said the Lord: Behold I place before you the way of life and the way of death. 9. Whoever abides in this city shall die by the sword or by famine or by pestilence, but whoever goes forth and defects to the Chaldeans who are besieging you, shall live, and he will have

7. **from the pestilence, from the sword**—From the sword of the war, when it fights against the city, I will deliver them into the hand of Nebuchadnezzar, when he conquers the city, and also Zedekiah and his servants, who fled.—[*Redak*]

and he shall strike them by the edge of the sword—Those he wishes to kill, he will kill, and those he wishes to exile he will exile.—[*Redak*]

by the edge of the sword—Heb. לְפִי חָרֶב, lit. by the mouth of the sword. That is the sharp edge.—[*Redak, Shorashim*] *Jonathan* renders לְפִתְגַם דְחַרְבָא, *by the word of the sword.* It is as though the sword decrees death on its victims. See *Nefesh Hager,* vol. 1, p. 8. The author obviously forgot our verse.

he will not spare them, neither will he pity nor show compassion—For he slew Zedekiah's sons before his very eyes, and he had no pity on the princes or the elders.—[*Redak*]

8. **Behold I place before you**—I am explaining to you in which way you will remain alive and in which way you will die.—[*Mezudath David*]

9. **and he will have his life as a prey**—*As a man who plunders booty,*

לוֹ נַפְשׁוֹ לְשָׁלָל: י כִּי־שַׂמְתִּי פָנַי בָּעִיר
הַזֹּאת לְרָעָה וְלֹא לְטוֹבָה נְאֻם־יְהוָֹה
בְּיַד מֶלֶךְ־בָּבֶל תִּנָּתֵן וּשְׂרָפָהּ בָּאֵשׁ:
יא וּלְבֵית מֶלֶךְ יְהוּדָה שִׁמְעוּ דְּבַר־
יְהוָֹה: יב בֵּית דָּוִד כֹּה אָמַר יְהוָֹה דִּינוּ
לַבֹּקֶר מִשְׁפָּט וְהַצִּילוּ גָזוּל מִיַּד עוֹשֵׁק
פֶּן־תֵּצֵא כָאֵשׁ חֲמָתִי וּבָעֲרָה וְאֵין
מְכַבֶּה מִפְּנֵי רֹעַ מַעַלְלֵיהֶם: יג הִנְנִי
אֵלַיִךְ יֹשֶׁבֶת הָעֵמֶק צוּר הַמִּישֹׁר נְאֻם־

מעלליכם קרי

תרגום

ליה נפשיה לשיזבא:
י ארי חל רוגזי בקרתא
הדא לבישא ולא לטבא
אמר יי בידא דמלכא
דבבל תתמסר ויוקדינה
בנורא: יא ולבית מלך
שבטא דבית יהודה
קבילו פתגמא דיי:
יב בית דוד כדנן אמר
יי דינו לצפרא דינא
ושיזיבו אניסא מיד
דאנים ליה דלמא ידלק
כאשתא רוגזי וישיצי
ולא יהי חיים מן קדם
בישות עובדיכון:
יג האנא שלח רוגזי עלך
דיתבא בתוקפא בקרוין

ת"א בית דוד. שבת י סנהדרין ז:

רש"י

וחוטפו והולך לו כן תהיה לו נפשו גולה מן המיתה מן ההורגים: (י) פני. כתרגומו רוגזי: (יב) מיד עושק. טעמו למטה שאינו שם דבר אלא שם הגזלן העושק את אחרים: ואין מכבה. שלא ימלט לכם שריד: (יג) יושבת העמק. ירושלים היא בתוך עמק. דבר אחר שהעמיק

מהר"י קרא

(יג) יושבת העמק. בת ירושלים היושבת בעמק: ומי יבא במעונותינו. בסלע צור המישור. ציון היושבת על הסלע מישור האומרים מי יוכל לרדת עלינו לחזיק לנו בעמק. ומי

מנחת שי

(יב) מעלליכם. מעלליכם קרי והוא חד מן תרין מלין כתבין ה"א וקריין כ"ף ואידך ותשב עליה ם מתשבה (ירמיה מ"ט):

רד"ק

(יא) ולבית מלך יהודה. חסר תאמר כמ"ש למעלה ואל העם הזה תאמר וסמך על המבין בחסרונו וזה מנהג המקרא במקומות רבים ופירושו ולבית לו ולבניו ושריו שהם בני משפחתו: (יב) בית דוד. זכר דוד לפי שהוא היה עושה משפט כמ"ש ויהי דוד עושה משפט וצדקה לכל עמו וכן היה ראוי שיעשו בניו ובני ביתו שילמדו ממעשיו הטובים: דינו לבקר משפט. לבקר קודם שתתעסקו באכילה ושתיה וכדבר מצרכיכם תשבו במקום הדין לדון כל מי שיבא לצעוק וכן אמר במשה רבינו ע"ה וישב משה לשפט את העם מן הבקר: והצילו גזול מיד עושק. מיד כי שעושק אותו וגוזלו והגוזל הוא מי שחוטף מיד חברו או לוקח מידו או מביתו בחוקה ועושק מי שבא ממון חברו לידו בפקדון או בהלואה או שכירות ואין רוצה לתתו לו מי שגוזל כל שכן שעושק לפיכך אמר והצילו גזול מיד עושק כי הגוזל גוזל ועושק: מעלליהם. כתיב בה"א לנפתרים וקרי בכ"ף מעלליכם לנמצאים כמ"ש דינו והצילה (יג) הנני אליך. אמר כנגד ירושלם וקראה יושבת העמק לפי שהיא גבוהה וסביבותיה עמק והיא יושבת בעמק וכן קראה צור המישור כי היא צור והר וסביבותיה מישור ואמר לה הנני אליך לפי שיושביך מתגאים ואומרים מי יחת עלינו ומי

מצודת דוד

כאלו גולה לעצמו מיד ההורגים: (י) שמתי פני. שמתי מחשבותי בעיר הזאת להרע לה וגו': (יא) ולבית מלך יהודה. מוסב על מלת תאמר האמור בתחלת הענין וכאומר ולבית וגו' תאמר שמעו וגו': (יב) דינו לבקר. הוא ענין דרך זריזו: גזול. הנגזל: עושק. הגזלן העושק את הגזלה: כאש חמתי. ר"ל כמו האש כשיוצא' הולכת ושורפת מעלמה כן תבער בהם חמתי ולא ימלא מי יכבנה. ר"ל אין מי ימחה בידי: מפני רוע מעלליכם. מוסב על ובערה: (יג) הנני אליך. הנה אני אליך להלך לך אתה ירושלים היושבת בתוך העמק כי סביב ירושלים בסמוך לה היה עמק והיא על הסלע ממעל: צור המישור. היושבת על הצור אשר במישור: מי יחת עלינו. מי ירד עלינו למלחמה ומי וגו' כאומר שלא יפיל

מצודת ציון

(יב) דינו. מלשון דין: מעלליכם. מעשיכם: (יג) צור. סלע: המישור. מל' ישר ושוה: יחת. ענין ירידה כמו אליך נחתו כי

rescue the robbed from the hand of an oppressor, for the robber robs and oppresses.

with no one to extinguish [it]—*that no one of you will escape as a survivor.*—[*Rashi*]

your deeds—Although the 'kethib' is מַעַלְלֵיהֶם, *their deeds,* referring to the people, the 'keri' is מַעַלְלֵיכֶם, *your deeds,* referring to the royal family, who were negligent in their execution of justice.—[*Redak*]

13. **Behold I am against you**—He addresses Jerusalem.—[*Redak*]

O dweller of the valley—*Jerusalem is in the midst of a valley. Another explanation: That the Holy One, blessed be He, devised a deep plot against you to destroy you.*—[*Rashi*]

Jerusalem is situated on a mountain surrounded by a valley, thus situated in the midst of the valley. God addresses them in such a harsh

his life as a prey. 10. For I have set My anger against this city
for evil and not for good, says the Lord; it shall be delivered
into the hand[s] of the king of Babylon, and he shall burn it
with fire. 11. And to the house of the king of Judah: Hear the
word of the Lord. 12. O house of David, so said the Lord:
Execute justice in the morning and rescue the robbed from the
hand of the robber, lest My fury go forth like fire, and it burn
with no one to extinguish [it], because of the evil of your deeds.
13. Behold I am against you, O dweller of the valley, rock of
the plain, says

and he seizes and goes away, so will his life be plundered from death by the slayers.—[*Rashi*]

10. **My anger**—Heb. פָּנַי, *as the Targum,* רוּגְזִי, *My anger.*—[*Rashi*]

Mezudath David renders: I set My thought against this city.

11. **And to the house of the king of Judah**—The words, 'you shall say,' are missing. This is true in many cases, where Scripture relies on the reader's understanding to insert the missing words. The king's house is composed of his sons and his priests, who are his kin.—[*Redak*]

12. **O house of David**—He mentions David, who was conscientious in his performance of justice, as Scripture states: '(II Sam. 8:15) And David administered justice and charity for all his people,' and so should his sons and his household learn to emulate his good deeds.—[*Redak*]

Execute justice in the morning—In the morning, before you occupy yourselves with eating and drinking and with your personal needs, sit in the courthouse to judge anyone who comes to plead with you. Moses, too, sat to judge the people 'from morning until evening.'—[*Redak*]

from the hand of the robber—Heb. עוֹשֵׁק. *Its accent is below*—that is at the end of the word—*for it is not a noun*—denoting robbery—*but a noun denoting the robber who robs others.*—[*Rashi*] *Rashi* wishes to differentiate between עֹשֶׁק and עוֹשֵׁק. The former is the abstract noun denoting robbery, whereas the latter is the noun derived from the verb, meaning, the one who robs.

This translation follows *Jonathan. Redak,* however, differentiates between גּוֹזֵל and עוֹשֵׁק. The former denotes one who seizes something from someone's hand or takes it from his hand or his house by force. עוֹשֵׁק is one who receives his friend's property as a depository, a loan, or for hire, and refuses to return it. [This may be rendered: an oppressor, since he deprives his friend of his property and thereby oppresses him.] One who robs will surely oppress, hence the expression: and

יְהוָה הָאֹמְרִים מִי־יֵחַת עָלֵינוּ וּמִי יָבוֹא
בִּמְעוֹנוֹתֵינוּ׃ יד וּפָקַדְתִּי עֲלֵיכֶם כִּפְרִי
מַעַלְלֵיכֶם נְאֻם־יְהוָה וְהִצַּתִּי אֵשׁ
בְּיַעְרָהּ וְאָכְלָה כָּל־סְבִיבֶיהָ׃ כב א כֹּה
אָמַר יְהוָה רֵד בֵּית־מֶלֶךְ יְהוּדָה וְדִבַּרְתָּ
שָּׁם אֶת־הַדָּבָר הַזֶּה׃ ב וְאָמַרְתָּ שְׁמַע
דְּבַר־יְהוָה מֶלֶךְ יְהוּדָה הַיֹּשֵׁב עַל־
כִּסֵּא דָוִד אַתָּה וַעֲבָדֶיךָ וְעַמְּךָ הַבָּאִים
בַּשְּׁעָרִים הָאֵלֶּה׃ ג כֹּה ׀ אָמַר יְהוָה
עֲשׂוּ מִשְׁפָּט וּצְדָקָה וְהַצִּילוּ גָזוּל מִיַּד
עָשׁוֹק וְגֵר יָתוֹם וְאַלְמָנָה אַל־תֹּנוּ אַל־

דְּרִיכָן אֲמַר יְיָ דְּאָמְרִין
מַן יֵחוּת עֲלָנָא וּמַן
יֵעוֹל בְּבִירָנְיָתַנָא׃
יד וְאַסְעַר עֲלֵיכוֹן כְּפֵירֵי
עוֹבָדֵיכוֹן אֲמַר יְיָ
וְאַדְלֵיק אֶשָּׁתָא בְּקִרְוָהָא
וּתְשֵׁיצֵי כָּל סַחְרָנַהָא׃
א כִּדְנַן אֲמַר יְיָ חוּת
לְבֵית מְלַךְ שִׁבְטָא דְבֵית
יְהוּדָה וּתְהַנְבֵּי תַמָּן יָת
פִּתְגָמָא הָדֵין׃ ב וְתֵימַר
קַבֵּיל פִּתְגָמָא דַיְיָ מְלַךְ
שִׁבְטָא דְבֵית יְהוּדָה
דְּיָתֵיב עַל כּוּרְסֵי דָוִד
אַתְּ וְעַבְדָךְ וְעַמָּךְ דְּעָלִין
בְּתַרְעַיָא הָאִלֵּין׃ ג כִּדְנַן
אֲמַר יְיָ עֲבִידוּ דִינָא
וּצְדַקְתָּא וְשֵׁיזִיבוּ אֲנִיסָא
מִיַּד דְּאָנֵים לֵיהּ וְגִיּוֹר
יְתַם וְאַרְמְלָא לָא תוֹנוּן

רש"י

הקב"ה עלה עליך להחריבך: צור המישור. הר שכל סביביו מישור: מי יחת עלינו. מי יהנה עלינו כמו כי שם ארם נחיתם (מלכים ב' ו'): כב (ג) אל תונו. זו אונאת דברים:

מהר"י קרא

יבא במעונותינו בסלע. הנני עליכם להשמידכם: (יד) נאום ה'. שאני מושל בהרים ובמעמקים: והצתי אש ביערה. בביהמ"ק:

רד"ק

יבא במעונותינו הנני אבא אליך ונלחמתי אתך: יחת. שרשו נחת ולולי התי"ת שהיא גרונית היתה דגושה ופירש ירד ויחנ' וכן ותנחת עלי ידך ותרגום וירד ונחת ואמר בל' ירידה לענין המלחמה שהיא בעמק ובמישור כמ"ש או במלחמה ירד ונספ': (יד) ופקדתי. ביערה. הכנוי לירושלם ר"ל הערים אשר סביבותיה המשילם ליער לענין האש כמו כאש תבער יער וכת"י ביערה בקרוהא: (א) כה אמר ה' רד בית מלך יהודה. בהר הבית נאמרה לו נבואה זו לפיכך אמר רד ואף על פי שזאת הנבואה כבר אמרה בית דוד כה אמר ה' דינו לבקר משפט אמר לו עוד שיאמר אותה להם עוד בבתיהם ושיבטיחם ההבטחה ותשובה אם ישמעו: (ב) בשערים האלה. בשערי העזרה כמ"ש בסמוך ובאו בשערי הבית הזה או יהיה פי' הבית הזה בית המלך לפי שאמר רוכבים ברכב ובסוסים ולא יכנס אדם רוכב בשערי העזרה: (ג) כה אמר ה'. מיד עשוק. תואר בפלס

מנחת שי

כב (ג) יתום. בלא וא"ו בתחלת הפלג: אל תנו. ברוב הספרים חסר וכן נמסר עליו לית חסר: אל תחמסו. באיזה ספרים כתוב ואל בוא"ו וכס"א

מצודת דוד

בצורה וחזקה ומי יערב לבו לגשת אלינו למלחמה ומי יכבוש אותה: (יד) ופקדתי. אשגיח עליכם להשיב כגמול מעשיכם: ביערה. הם ערי יסודה: ואכלה. תשרף הכל: כב (ב) אתה ועבדיך. גם אתה שומע גם עבדיך וגו' ישמעו: בשערים האלה. שערי בית המלך: (ג) גזול. הנגזל:

מצודת ציון

(תהלים ל"ח): במעונותינו. מלשון מעון ומדור כמו ה' מעון אתה היית (שם צ'): (יד) ופקדתי. ענין השגחה: והצתי. ענין הבערה כמו באש יצתו (ישעיה ל"ג): ואכלה. ענין שריפה כמו מאכלת אש (שם ט'): כב (ג) תונו. ענין אונאת דברים וכן וגר לא תונה (שמות כ"ב):

to the gates of the Temple court as in verse 4, or it may refer to the gates of the king's palace, for, no one would enter the Temple gates riding a horse or a chariot as is mentioned in that verse.—[*Redak*]

3. **do no wrong**—*This means taunting with words.*—[*Rashi*]

The word אוֹנָאָה, *wronging,* is used for two kinds of mistreatment, אוֹנָאַת מָמוֹן, *wronging with money,* as in Lev. 25:14, where it denotes overreaching, either overcharging a purchaser or underpaying a seller.

It is also used to denote אוֹנָאַת דְּבָרִים, *wronging with words,* as in Lev. 25:17. There it denotes taunting one who is vulnerable because of his lineage or his past actions. The latter is the more serious offense, and the prophet is castigating the royal family for their guilt in this field.

the Lord, those who say, "Who will encamp upon us, and who will come into our dwellings?" 14. And I will visit upon you according to the fruit of your deeds, says the Lord, and I will ignite a fire in her forest, and it will consume all her surroundings.

22

1. So said the Lord: Go down to the house of the king of Judah and speak this word there. 2. And say: Listen to the word of the Lord, O king of Judah, who sits on the throne of David, you and your servants and your people who come in these gates.
3. So said the Lord: Perform justice and charity, and rescue the robbed from the hand of the robber, and to a stranger, an orphan, and a widow do no wrong,

manner because of their arrogance, for they would say, "Who will encamp upon us, and who will come into our dwellings?" Behold I will come upon you and wage war against you.—[*Redak*]

Who will encamp upon us—Heb. יֵחַת, *who will encamp upon us. Comp.* '(II Kings 6:9) *For there the Arameans are encamped* (נְחִתִּים).'—[*Rashi*]

Redak renders: Who will come down and camp upon us? *Jonathan,* too, renders in this manner. Since the battle took place in the valley, the expression of going down is used.

in our dwelling places—*Jonathan* renders: בְּבִרְנְיָתָנָא. This may be interpreted as palaces, towers, or fortresses.

14. **And I will visit . . . in her forest**—The reference is to Jerusalem. The cities surrounding Jerusalem resemble a forest in that they will be burnt as a forest burns. *Jonathan,* too, renders: in her cities.—[*Redak*]

Kara renders: **says the Lord**—Who rules over the moutains and the valleys.

And I will ignite a fire in her forest—This refers to the Temple. [See II Kings 19:23, Isaiah 37:24, where the Temple is compared to the Lebanon forest.]

1. **Go down to the house of the king of Judah**—Since this prophecy was given to him on the Temple Mount, the expression, 'go down' is used. Although this prophecy was already conveyed to them (21:12), God commanded him to repeat it when they were in their houses and that he should promise them good if they would heed his words.—[*Redak*]

2. **in these gates**—This may refer

תַּחְמֹסוּ וְדָם נָקִי אַל־תִּשְׁפְּכוּ בַּמָּקוֹם
הַזֶּה׃ ד כִּי אִם־עָשׂוֹ תַּעֲשׂוּ אֶת־הַדָּבָר
הַזֶּה וּבָאוּ בְשַׁעֲרֵי הַבַּיִת הַזֶּה מְלָכִים
יֹשְׁבִים לְדָוִד עַל־כִּסְאוֹ רֹכְבִים בָּרֶכֶב
וּבַסּוּסִים הוּא וַעֲבָדָו וְעַמּוֹ׃ ה וְאִם לֹא
תִשְׁמְעוּ אֶת־הַדְּבָרִים הָאֵלֶּה בִּי
נִשְׁבַּעְתִּי נְאֻם־יְהוָה כִּי־לְחָרְבָּה יִהְיֶה
הַבַּיִת הַזֶּה׃ ו כִּי־כֹה אָמַר יְהוָה עַל־
בֵּית מֶלֶךְ יְהוּדָה גִּלְעָד אַתָּה לִי רֹאשׁ

תרגום

וְלָא תֵינְסוּן וְדַם זַכָּאי לָא
תִישְׁדוּן בְּאַתְרָא הָדֵין׃
ד אֲרֵי אִם מֶעְבַּד
תַּעְבְּדוּן יַת פִּתְגָמָא הָדֵין
וְיֵעֲלוּן בְּתַרְעֵי בֵיתָא
הָדֵין מַלְכִין יָתְבִין לְדָוִד
עַל כּוּרְסוּהִי רָכְבִין
בִּרְתִיכִין וּבְסוּסָוָן הוּא
וְעַבְדוֹהִי וְעַמֵּיהּ׃ ה וְאִם
לָא תְקַבְּלוּן יַת פִּתְגָמַיָא
הָאִלֵּין בְּמֵימְרִי קַיֵּמִית
אֲמַר יְיָ אֲרֵי לְחוּרְבָא
יְהֵי בֵיתָא הָדֵין׃ ו אֲרֵי
כִדְנַן אֲמַר יְיָ עַל בֵּית
מַלְכָּא דְבֵית
יְהוּדָה אִילוּ אַתְּ חֲבִיב
קֳדָמַי מִבֵּית מַקְדְּשָׁא
דְרָם בְּרֵישׁ טוּרַיָא אִם

ועבדיו קרי

מהר"י קרא

כב (ו) כה אמר ה' על בית מלך יהודה גלעד אתה לי ראש הלבנון אם לא אשיתך מדבר. פת' אילו היית חביב [עלי] כגלעד שהוא משובח שבלבנון שמשם ראשי בשמים באין לעולם כענין שנאמר והנה ארחת ישמעאלים באה מגלעד

רש"י

(ו) גלעד אתה לי וגו'. אילו את חביב קדמי כבית מקדשא דרם כריש טוריא אם לא אשוינך מדברא: גלעד אתה. בית אפילו אעפ"כ אתה גורם בעונותיך שאשים אותך שממה ויונתן

מנחת שי

בלא וא"ו והולם יש לתמוה שלא נמנה פסוק זה עם ה' פסוקים שכתוב בהם אל אל וסימנם במסרה גדולה: (ד) כי אם עשו תעשו. ד' כתיבין וא"ו בסוף וסימנם דרכיך ומעלליך עשו אלה (ירמיה ד') כי אם היטב תיטיבו וגו' אם עשו תעשו משפט (ירמיה ז') כי אם עשו תעשו את הדבר הזה. ביד אל גוים עשו יעשה לו (יחזקאל ל"א) ובפרשת וילך הככלת עשו נמסר עליו ד' ג' כתיבין ה"א וא' וא"ו וסימן הככלת עשו. נמצא עשה כיום הזה סוף פרשת ויחי. עשה ספים (תהלים ק"ח) עשה צדקה ומשפט (משלי כ"א) קדמאה כתוב וא"ו ע"כ. והמגיה נתקשה מאד במסורת אלו ובסוף דבריו כתב ולא ידענא מה למימר ביה ולדידי חזי לי דהכי מסרתא לא פליגן אהדדי ותרווייהו איתנהו דמאי דנמסר בפרשת וילך מיירי מהנהו דמיינין דילהון בווא ומאת ג' מנהון כה"א וחד בוא"ו ומסרה דהכא מהנהו דמיינין דילהון בקמץ וכולהון בוא"ו ומשום הכי לא חשיב הכו עשה אלה לך בזנותך (יחזקאל כ"ג) ודכוותיה סוכה דלא דמיין לאינך דאינון בקמץ וכתיבין בה"א והנהו לא מיירי לא הכא ולא התם בפרשת וילך והכי כולהו ריהטן ומיברכן שפיר ולא קשיין כלל: ועבדו. ועבדיו קרי: (ו) אם לא אשיתך וגו' ערים לא נושבה. י"ם שכתוב לוא מלא וא"ו ואל"ף ובדפוס ישן הראשון שבפסוק מלא והשני חסר. אמנם ברוב ספרים מדוייקים שניהם בלא וא"ו גם לא נמנו במסורת במנין המלאים: נושבה. נושבו קרי:

רד"ק

קרוב נדול וענינו כמו עושק: (ד) כי אם עשו תעשו. עשו מקור בוי"ו במקום ה"א למ"ד הפעל: ועבדו. כתיב בלא יו"ד הרבוי והענין אחד וכמוהו רבים: (ה) ואם לא. מבואר הוא: (ו) כי כה אמר ה'. גלעד אתה לי ראש הלבנון. אמר על בית מלך יהודה שהוא ראש ממלכת ישראל אתה היית לי כמו גלעד כי גלעד עיר אחת בעבר הירדן וכל הארץ ההיא ארץ סיחון ועוג וכל הבשן היתה נקראת על שמה ארץ הגלעד כי היא ראש להם וכן היית אתה לי ראש כמלכ' ישראל כי ציון וירושלם ראש לכל ארץ ישראל וכן היית ראש הלבנון שנקראת ג"כ ארץ ישראל בשם הלבנון כמ"ש ההר הטוב הזה והלבנון ועתה אשיתך מדבר ואשית הערים אשר סביבותיך כאלו לא נושבו: אם לא. ענין שבועה כמו אם לא שויתי ודוממתי אם

מצודת ציון

תחמסו. ענין עושק: (ו) אשיתך. ענין שימה כמו שתו

מצודת דוד

עושק. הגזלן: אל תונו. זהו אונאת דברים של עגמת נפש: אל תחמסו. אל תעשו לקח המס וזהו עושק הממון: (ד) ובאו. אז יבואו בשערי הבית וגו': לדוד. ר"ל מי מזרע דוד ישב על כסאו למלוך על ישראל: ברכב. במרכבה הראויה למלך: ובסוסים. המושכים את הרכב: הוא וגו'. גם הוא יבא בשער הבית הזה גם עבדיו ועמו יבואו עמו: (ה) כי לחרבה וגו'. ואין מי יבוא בשעריו: (ו) גלעד אתה לי. אם אמנם אתה בעיני כגלעד אשר כל ארץ סיחון ועוג וכל הבשן היו נקראים על שמה כמ"ש ויבואו וגו' אל ארץ הגלעד (יהושע כ"ב) כי כן הוא ציון וירושלים מקום בית המלך כי היא סעיף החשובה שבכל א"י ולתוספות ביאור אמר ראש

do no violence, and shed no innocent blood in this place.
4. For if you will do this thing, there will come into the gates of
this house kings descended from David, sitting on his throne,
riding in chariots and with horses, he and his servants and his
people. 5. But if you do not hearken to these words, I swear by
Myself, says the Lord, that this house will become a waste.
6. For so said the Lord concerning the house of the king of
Judah: You are [as] Gilead to me, O head of

Perhaps the mention of the stranger suggests Lev. 19:33, Exodus 22:20, both of which refer to wronging with words by reminding a proselyte of his heathen origin.

Here, he repeats 21:11f. before the king. Also, he admonishes him concerning wronging the stranger, the orphan, and the widow, and concerning bloodshed.—[*Abarbanel*]

4. **the gates of this house**—This may refer to the Temple or to the king's palace.—[*Abarbanel*]

sitting on his throne—This denotes that they will occupy the throne with great pomp, riding in chariots with horses. This imples the perpetuation of the kingdom of the Davidic dynasty, the city of Jerusalem, and the Temple.—[*Abarbanel*]

5. **But if you do not hearken**—If you do not hearken to My words, do not rely on the Temple of the Lord, for I have sworn by Myself that this house will become a waste. This alludes both to the Temple and to the house of David, which represents the kingdom.—[*Abarbanel*]

6. **You are [as] Gilead to Me etc.**—Even *if you are as dear to Me as the Temple, which is high on the mountain peaks, I swear that I will make you a desert.*—[*Rashi* from *Jonathan*]

You are [as] Gilead—*The Temple from which balm and healing emanate to the whole world.*—[*Rashi*]

Redak explains that God compares the royal house to Gilead, the principal city of the eastern bank of the Jordan, on whose name the entire region of Sihon and Og and the entire Bashan was called the land of Gilead. Similarly, you were the head of the entire kingdom of Israel, for Zion and Jerusalem are the capital of the entire land of Israel. The Holy Land is known also as the Lebanon. He, therefore, calls the head of the kingdom the head of the Lebanon. Now I will make you a desert and the cities around you as though they had never been inhabited.

that I will surely—Heb. אִם לֹא, an expression of an oath.—[*Mezudath David*]

הַלְּבָנ֑וֹן אִם־לֹ֤א אֲשִֽׁיתְךָ֙ מִדְבָּ֔ר עָרִ֖ים
לֹ֥א נוֹשָֽׁבָה׃ ז וְקִדַּשְׁתִּ֤י עָלֶ֙יךָ֙ מַשְׁחִתִ֔ים
אִ֖ישׁ וְכֵלָ֑יו וְכָֽרְתוּ֙ מִבְחַ֣ר אֲרָזֶ֔יךָ וְהִפִּ֖ילוּ
עַל־הָאֵֽשׁ׃ ח וְעָֽבְרוּ֙ גּוֹיִ֣ם רַבִּ֔ים עַ֖ל
הָעִ֣יר הַזֹּ֑את וְאָֽמְרוּ֙ אִ֣ישׁ אֶל־רֵעֵ֔הוּ עַל־
מֶ֨ה עָשָׂ֤ה יְהֹוָה֙ כָּ֔כָה לָעִ֥יר הַגְּדוֹלָ֖ה
הַזֹּֽאת׃ ט וְאָ֣מְר֔וּ עַ֚ל אֲשֶׁ֣ר עָזְב֔וּ אֶת־
בְּרִ֛ית יְהֹוָ֖ה אֱלֹהֵיהֶ֑ם וַיִּשְׁתַּחֲו֛וּ לֵאלֹהִ֥ים
אֲחֵרִ֖ים וַיַּֽעַבְדֽוּם׃ י אַל־תִּבְכּ֣וּ לְמֵ֔ת

תרגום

לָא אֲשַׁוִינָךְ מַדְבְּרָא
קִרְוִין דְלָא אִתְיְתִבָא:
ז וְאַזְמִין עֲלָךְ מְחַבְּלִין
גְבַר וְזֵינֵיהּ וְיִקְטְלוּן
שְׁפַר גִּבָּרָךְ כְּמָא דְקַצְצִין
אָעֵי חוּרְשָׁא וְרָמָן לְנוּרָא:
ח וְיֶעְבְּרוּן עַמְמִין סַגִיאִין
עַל קַרְתָּא הָדָא וְיֵימְרוּן
גְבַר לְחַבְרֵיהּ עַל מָה
עֲבַד יְיָ כְּדֵין לְקַרְתָּא
רַבְּתָא הָדָא: ט וְיֵימְרוּן
עַל דִשְׁבָקוּ יַת קְיָמָא
דַיְיָ אֱלָהָהוֹן וּסְגִידוּ
לְטַעֲוַת פַּלְחֵי כוֹכְבַיָא
וּפַלְחוּנוּן: י לָא תִבְכּוּן
עַל

ת"א אל תבכו. מ"ק כז:

נושבו קרי

רש"י

המקדש שממנו אורי ורפואה לכל העולם: (ז) וקדשתי. וזמנתי: וכרתו מבחר ארזיך. לפי שדמהו ללבנון נופל כאן הלשון הזה: (י) אל תבכו למת. ליהויקים שימות לפני הצער כשיסחבוהו להגלות: בכו להולך. ליהויכין

מהר"י קרא

תרגם אילו את חביב קדמי [כבית מקדשא דרם] בריש טוריא אם לא אשוינך מדברא: (ז) וקדשתי עליך. ואיזמן עלך: (י) אל

רד"ק

לא בתים רבים והדומים להם: נושבה. כתיב בה"א על הארץ דרך כלל וקרי נושבו על הערים ויונתן פי' גלעד בית המקדש ותרגם הפסוק כן ארי כדנן אמר ה' על בית מלך שבטא וגו' כבעמוד: (ז) וקדשתי. אזמן עליך משחיתים שישחיתו בתיך: איש וכליו. ר"ל וכלי כפצו להפיל הבית: מבחר ארזיך. ר"ל קירוי הבתים הספונים כמ"ש למטה בענין וספון בארז וכן כי ארזה ערה אמר על קירות הבתים הספונים בארז: והפילו על האש. כמ"ש וישרוף את בית ה' ואת בית המלך וגו' וי"ת ואזמן עלך מחבלים וגו' כבעמוד: (ח) ועברו. מבואר הוא וכן ואמרו: (י) אל תבכו למת. למי שיכות מבית דוד שזכר

מצודת דוד

הלבנון ר"ל ראש לכל א"י הנקראת כל' לבנון כמ"ש ההר הטוב הזה והלבנון (דברים ד'): אם לא. הוא ענין לשון שבועה כאדם האומר אם לא כן הוא יהיה כזאת וכזאת וגזם ולא אמר וכן אם לא בתים רבים (ישעיה ה') ורלה לומר עם כל החשיבות הריני נשבע שאשים אותה כמדבר וכערים אשר לא נתיישבו מעולם: (ז) וקדשתי. אזמין עליך אנשים משחיתים כל איש יבוא עם כלי מלחמתו: וכרתו. ר"ל יהרגו השרים והגבורים ולפי שאמר ראש הלבנון אמר לשון הנופל בעלי היער: (ח) על העיר. סמוך להעיר: על מה. בעבור מה: (ט) ואמרו. רעיהם ישיבום לומר על אשר עזבו וגו': (י) אל תבכו למת. אין ראוי לבכות על מי מהמלכים שמת בארצו

מצודת ציון

עלי (תהלים ג'): נושבו. מלשון ישיבה: (ז) וקדשתי. ענין

the Lebanon, that I will surely make you a desert, cities not
inhabited. 7. And I will prepare for you destroyers, each one
with his weapons, and they will cut your choice cedars and cast
them upon the fire. 8. And many nations will pass by this city,
and they will say each one to his friend, "For what [reason] did
the Lord do so to this great city?" 9. And they will say,
"Because they forsook the covenant of the Lord their God, and
they prostrated themselves to other gods and worshipped
them." 10. Weep not for the dead,

7. **And I will prepare**—Heb. וְקִדַּשְׁתִּי, *and I will prepare.*—[*Rashi* from *Targum, Redak, Mezudath Zion*]

and his weapons—Heb. וְכֵלָיו, lit his utensils. *Jonathan* renders: his weapons. *Redak* renders: his weapons of destruction. Cf. Ezekiel 7:2. Each one will come with his weapons of destruction to destroy the house.

and they will cut your choice cedars—*Since he compares him to the Lebanon, this expression is appropriate.*—[*Rashi*] *Rashi* follows *Targum Jonathan,* who interprets this verse figuratively: And I will prepare for you destroyers, each one with his weapons, and they will slay your choice mighty men, as they cut down the trees of the forest and cast them into the fire.

Redak, however, explains that the 'cedars' are the roofs of the houses covered with cedar wood.

10. **Weep not for the dead**—

וְאַל־תָּנֻדוּ לוֹ בְּכוּ בָכוֹ לַהֹלֵךְ כִּי לֹא
יָשׁוּב עוֹד וְרָאָה אֶת־אֶרֶץ מוֹלַדְתּוֹ׃
יא כִּי־כֹה אָמַר־יְהוָה אֶל־שַׁלֻּם בֶּן־
יֹאשִׁיָּהוּ מֶלֶךְ יְהוּדָה הַמֹּלֵךְ תַּחַת
יֹאשִׁיָּהוּ אָבִיו אֲשֶׁר יָצָא מִן־הַמָּקוֹם
הַזֶּה לֹא־יָשׁוּב שָׁם עוֹד׃ יב כִּי בִּמְקוֹם
אֲשֶׁר־הִגְלוּ אֹתוֹ שָׁם יָמוּת וְאֶת־הָאָרֶץ

תרגום

עַל מִיתְוְלָא תִדְווּן עֲלוֹהִי
בְּכוּ מִבְכָּא לִדְגָלֵי אֲרֵי
לָא יְתוּב עוֹד וְיֶחֱזֵי יַת
אַרְעָא דְיַלְדוּתֵיהּ׃
יא אֲרֵי כִּדְנַן אֲמַר יְיָ עַל
שַׁלּוּם בַּר יֹאשִׁיָּה מַלְכָּא
שִׁבְטָא דְבֵית יְהוּדָה
דִמְלַךְ תְּחוֹת יֹאשִׁיָּה
אֲבוּהִי דִגְלָא מִן אַתְרָא
הָדֵין לָא יְתוּב לְתַמָּן
עוֹד׃ יב אֱלָהֵין בְּאַתְרָא
דְאַגְלִיאוּ יָתֵיהּ תַּמָּן
יְמוּת וְיַת אַרְעָא הָדָא לָא

ת״א בכו בכו ב״ב קיו:

מהר״י קרא

תבכו למת. זה יהויקים כמו שמפרש למטה בענין כה אמר ה׳ אל יהויקים בן יאשיהו מלך יהודה לא יספדו לו הוי אחי והוי אחות קבורת חמור יקבר סחוב והשלך: בכו בכו להולך. זה צדקיה שלא שב עוד וראה את ארץ מולדתו: (יא) אל שלום בן יאשיהו. זה צדקיה שנשתלמה מלכות בית דוד בימיו:

רש״י

ולצדקיהו. אמור מעתה חביבה מיתתו של יהויקים שנאמר בו ונבלתו תהיה מושלכת לחורב ביום ולקרח בלילה (לקמן ל״ו) מחייו של יהויכין שנאמר בו וארוחתו ארוחת תמיד וגו׳ (לקמן נ״ב): (יא) אל שלום. הוא צדקיהו וכן נקרא (בדברי הימים א׳ ג׳) והרביעי שלום וקראו רביעי למלכות בבני יאשיהו שבתחלה מלך יהואחז ואחר כך יהויקים ואחריו יהויכין ואחריו צדקיהו: אשר יצא. ואף על פי שלא יצא

מנחת שי

(יב) כי במקום. חד מן כ׳ פסוקים מטעין דלית בהון את וסימן בריש פרשת חיי

רד״ק

והוא יהויקים שמת בדרך כשהוציאו אותו מירושלם להגלותו אמר אל תבכו לו כיון שמת טוב הוא בשיגלה ויחיה חיי צער ובזיון כמו יהויכין ואמר בעבור יהויקים אל תבכו ואל תנודו לו כי טובה היא לו מיתתו אלא למי ראוי שתבכו לבכי שהולך בגלות כי לא ישוב עוד וראה את ארץ מולדתו וזהו יהויכין שהגלו אותו לבבל ושם מת והיה בבית הכלא ל״ז שנה לו ראוי לבכות ודרשו רז״ל אל תבכו למת יותר מדאי ואל תנודו לו יותר מכשיעור הא כיצד שלשה לבכי שבעה להספד שלשים לגהוץ ולתספורות ואמר בכו בכו להולך בלא בנים בכו מקור בוי״ו במקום ה״א למ״ד הפעל: (יא) כי כה אמר ה׳ אל שלום בן יאשיהו. שלום הוא יהויכין ושני שמות היו לו ואע״פ שהית בן בנו בני בנים הרי הם כבנים לפי שאמר בכו בכו להולך פי׳ מי הוא ההולך והוא לא שב עדיין משגלה ומת בבבל ורז״ל פי׳ כי שלום הוא צדקיהו והחכם רבי אברהם בן עזרא פירש כי

מצודת ציון

הזמנה כמו קדשו מלחמה (יואל ד׳): (י) תנודו. ענין הנעה:

מצודת דוד

ונקבר בקברי אבותיו: ואל תנודו לו. כן דרך המקונן להניע ראשו דרך אבל וצער: בכו בכו להולך. אבל בכו על ההולך מארצו בשבי ובמקרא שלאחריו יפרש מי הוא: כי לא ישוב. על כי לא ישוב עוד לארצו ולא יראה ארץ מולדתו כי שם בגולה ימות ויקבר: (יא) כי כה. כי כן אמר ה׳ על שלום וגו׳. הוא צדקיהו וכן נקרא (דה״א ג׳) ובדרז״ל: המולך וגו׳. לפי שלא בא לו המלוכה מאחת יכניה שמלך לפניו כ״א מאחת יאשיהו אביו לכן אמר המולך תחת יאשיהו אביו אשר יצא בשבי לבבל:

neither bemoan him; weep for him who goes away, for he will return no more, nor see his native land.
11. For so said the Lord concerning Shallum son of Josiah, king of Judah, who ruled instead of Josiah his father, who left this place; he shall not return there again.
12. For, in the place where they exiled him, there he will die, and this land

Namely, for Jehoiakim, who will die before the gate, when they drag him into exile.—[*Rashi*]

neither bemoan him—I.e. do not shake your head in bemoaning him as is customary.—[*Mezudath David*]

weep for him who goes—*For Jehoiachin and for Zedekiah. Deduce from here that Jehoiakim's death, concerning which it is stated:* '(infra 36:30) *And his carcass shall be cast to the heat by day and to the cold at night,' is preferable to the life of Jehoiachin, about whom it is stated:* '(52:34) *And his meals, regular meals etc.'*—[*Rashi*]

Do not weep for the dead, for Jehoiakim, who died when he was led out of Jerusalem into exile. Since he died, it was better for him than it was for Jehoiachin, who was led into exile and lived a life of disgrace, for he will never again return and see his native land. He remained in prison thirty-seven years. For him it is proper to weep and lament. The Rabbis explain: Weep not for the dead more than is necessary, neither bemoan him more than the prescribed time. How so? Three days of weeping, seven days for eulogy, thirty days for abstinence from cleaning clothes and cutting hair. Weep for one who goes away without children (*Moed Katan* 27b).—[*Redak*]

11. **concerning Shallum**—*That is Zedekiah, and that is what he was called in I Chron.* (3:14): *'the fourth Shallum.' And he called him the fourth, meaning the fourth to assume the kingship of Josiah's sons, for first Jehoahaz reigned, then Jehoiakim, and after him Jehoiachin, and after him Zedekiah.*—[*Rashi* from *Horioth* 11b]

The Rabbis account for this name as based on Zedekiah's righteousness. He was perfect (מְשֻׁלָּם) in his deeds. Another reason given is that the kingdom of the house of David was completed (שָׁלְמָה) in his time.

הַזֹּאת לֹא־יִרְאֶה עוֹד׃ יג הוֹי בֹּנֶה בֵיתוֹ בְּלֹא־צֶדֶק וַעֲלִיּוֹתָיו בְּלֹא מִשְׁפָּט בְּרֵעֵהוּ יַעֲבֹד חִנָּם וּפֹעֲלוֹ לֹא יִתֶּן־לוֹ׃ יד הָאֹמֵר אֶבְנֶה־לִּי בֵּית מִדּוֹת וַעֲלִיּוֹת מְרֻוָּחִים וְקָרַע לוֹ חַלּוֹנָי וְסָפוּן בָּאָרֶז וּמָשׁוֹחַ בַּשָּׁשַׁר׃ טו הֲתִמְלֹךְ כִּי אַתָּה מְתַחֲרֶה בָאָרֶז אָבִיךָ הֲלוֹא אָכַל

תרגום

יֶחֱזֵי עוֹד׃ יג וַי דִבְנֵי בֵיתֵיהּ בְּלָא קְשׁוֹט וְעִלִּיתֵיהּ בְּלָא דִינָא בִּדְחַיֵי בְּחַבְרֵיהּ מַפְלַח סַגַּן וְאַגְרֵיהּ לָא יְהַב לֵיהּ׃ יד דַאֲמַר אֶבְנֵי לִי בָּתִּין דִמְשַׁחַן וְעִלִּין מְרַוְחָן וּפָצִים לֵיהּ חַרְכִּין וּמְטַלֵּל בְּכִיוּרֵי אַרְזַיָא וּמְצַיַּר בְּסַמְמָנִין׃ טו הַאַתְּ מְדַמֵּי לְמֶהֱוֵי כְמַלְכָּא קַדְמָאָה אֲבוּךְ הֲלָא אֲכַל וּשְׁתָא וַעֲבַד

ת"א הוי בנה. זוהר תזריע: הלא אכל. עקרים מ"ג פ"ה:

רש"י קמץ בז"ק

עדיין מתנבא עליו כאלו יצא: (יג) הוי בונה ביתו. על יהויקים הוא אומר שהוא היה רשע וסוף הענין מוכיח לכן כה אמר ה' אל יהויקים: (יד) בית מדות. בית גדול כמו אנשי מדות (במדבר י"ג) שיש בהן מה למדוד: וקרע לו. והרחיב לו. אחרים הגיהו וקרע לו ופתח לו וכן ותקרעי בפוך (לעיל י"ד) קרעת שמים ירדת (ישעיה ס"ג) כולן לשון פתיחה: וספון בארז. מסכך הגג בארזים: ומשוח בששר. ומצייר בסממנים ת"י בששר צבע הוא ממין הציורים. ל"א ומשיח בששר כמו הוט המשחה (אלייגא"ס אנשינופל"א בלע"ז): (טו) התמלוך. התאריך ימים על שאתה מתחרה להכביד ממשלתך להודיע שאתה מלך:

מהר"י קרא

(יג) הוי בונה ביתו בלא צדק. פרשה זו נאמרה על יהויקים: (יד) בית מדות. בתים גדולים: וקרע לו חלוני. כדרחיב לו חלונות ודומה לו ותקרעי בפוך עיניך שפת' והרחיבי בפוך עיניך: וספון בארז. ת"י ומטליל בכיורי ארזיא: (טו) התמלך כי אתה מתחרה בארז. האיש כמוך ראוי למלכות בפני שאתה

רד"ק

שלום הוא יהואחז כי במצרים מת וכבר בארתי כל זה הענין בספר מלכים ובספר דברי הימים: (יג) הוי בונה ביתו. זה נאמר על יהויקים שהיה בונה בתים אל תבכו למת כמו שפירשנו ואחר שפירש ההולך פירש הבית שבנה בתים ועליות בגזל ובחמס וכן זכרו בפי' בסוף הפרשה לכן כה אמר ה' אל יהויקים: ברעהו יעבד חנם. היה שוכר הפועל במלאכת הבתים ולא היה נותן לו שכרו וזהו חנם והוסיף לפרש ואמר ופעלו לא יתן לו ופעלו שם מן ואת פעל ה' לא יביטו ואמר פעלו הצ"ן בקמץ חטף כמו מן תאר מה תארו ובא זה בחולם הפ"א כמו שבא מן תאר ותארו מן בני אדם ופי' שכר פעלתו לא יתן לו וזהו חנם שאמר וכן לא תלין פעולת שכיר שכר פעלתו. וא"א ז"ל פירש ופעלו פעל לו שם כאילו אמר ופעלו שעבד עמו לא יתן לו שכרו: (יד) האומר אבנה לי. אמר לבנות ובנה: בית מדות. גדולות וכל אנשי מדות: ועליות מרוחים. מן ורוח לשאול ענין הרחבה ויתכן להיות כרוחים מענין רוח כלומר שיכנס בהם הרוח עשוים לימי הקיץ וי"ש וקרע לו חלוני ופי' פתח לו חלונים כתרגומו ופצים ליה חרכין חלוני כמו חלונים וכן על דברי חזי כמו חזים ואירגים חורי וחשופי שת והרומי' להם: וספון בארז. פי' בית כדו' שוכר הוא מקורה בקורות ולוחות ארזים ועוד הוא משוח בששר פי' מצוייר במיני צבעונים חכר אחד מהם שמציירין בו ביחוד והוא ששר נקרא בערבי צנגפר"ר ובלע"ז מיני"ו: ספון. מקורה כמו חלקת מחוקק ספון. אתם יושבים בבתיכם ספונים בארז בקמץ האל"ף בזקף. ומשוח שם התאר בפלס קרוב רחוק ונקרא מעשה הציור בזה הלשון לפי שהוא במשיכת היד על הדבר כמו המשיח: (טו) התמלוך. ותחשב לעמוד במלכותך בעבור זאת ההנאה שאתה נהנה בבתים הנאים הבנוים בחמס: מתחרה בארז. מתערב בארז

מנחת שי

(יג) בלא צדק. במקצת ספרים כתובי יד והדפוסים ישנים הבי"ת בגעיא: ופעלו לא יתן לו. במקצת ישנה מוגייה הפ"א בחטף קמץ ולפי דעתי טעו בלשון רד"ק כמו המוטעה במקצתו שלנו שכתב ואחר פעלו הפ"א בקמץ חטף וגו'. ונראה לי שצריך להגיה והחולם במקום ואחר ועיין בשרשים ובכלל יופי ומשם תבין שזו היא כוונת רד"ק וכן בכל הספרים הפ"א בחולם והפ"א כתוב ז"ה וגם במסורת ופעלו ב' וחברו ופעלו לנילון (ישעיה סוף סימן ל'): (טו) התמלך. הת"ו נסמכת בשוא והפ"א בשו"א ופתח כן כתב רד"ק בשרשים וכן מצאתי כתוב

מצודת דוד

(יג) הוי בונה. יש להתאונן על זה שבונה ביתו בלא צדק ועליות בבית בנה בלא משפט כי עבד ברעהו חנם כי לא הקדים לו שכרו ואף אחר העבודה לא נתן לו שכר פעולתו ועל יהויקים הוא אומר כמפורש בסוף הענין: (יד) בית מדות. ר"ל מדות גדולות וכן אנשי מדות (במדבר י"ג): מרווחים. להיות ריוח גדול בין חדרי העליה שיכנס בם הרוח בימי הקיץ: וקרע לו חלוני. כדי להתענג בזמן החום פתח לעשות חלונות רבות כביכו: וספון בארז. וכיסה הכתלים בלוחות ארז: ומשוח בששר. ועל הלוחות היה משוח בשיד ששר והוא מין צבע: (טו) התמלוך. וכי סבור אתה שמלוכך לזמן מרובה אשר אתה מתכלכל ונלחץ באלו ארזים לנכת בהם על שהם מתקיימים לזמן מרובה ור"ל למה לך בית חזק כ"כ

מצודת ציון

(יג) ועליותיו. מל' עליה והם החדרים שהמה ממעל: ופעלו. ר"ל שכר הפעולה: (יד) מרווחים. מל' ריוח: וקרע. ענין פתיחה וכן ותקרעי בפוך עיניך (לעיל ד'): חלוני. כמו חלונים וכפלם סמ"ס: וספון. ענין קירוי הכתלי' ובסוים כמו ויספון את הבית גבים (מ"א ו'): ומשוח. ענין טיחה ולכיסה: בששר. הוא מין צבע השיר וכן מחוקים בששר (יחזקאל כ"ג): (טו) מתחרה. ענין

15. **Shall you reign**—*Will you live long that you contend to make your rule oppressive to let all know that you are a king?*—[*Rashi*]

Do you expect to remain on the throne for a long time, to enjoy the beautiful houses of cedar that you have built through dishonesty and violence?—[*Redak*]

Jehoiakim's construction of sturdy cedar houses, capable of standing many years, indicate that he expected to remain on the throne for many years. The prophet, there-

he will no longer see. 13. Woe to him who builds his house without righteousness and his upper chambers without justice, who makes his fellowman work without wages and his hire he does not give him. 14. Who says, "I will build myself a wide house with spacious upper chambers, and he cuts out windows for himself, and it is ceiled with cedar and painted with vermilion. 15. Shall you reign, for you compete with the cedar? Your father—did he not eat

13. **Woe to him who builds his house**—*He is saying this about Jehoiakim, who was a wicked man, and the end of the section proves this: 'Therefore, so said the Lord about Jehoiakim.'*—[*Rashi*]

As mentioned above, Jehoiakim is meant by 'the dead.' After the Scripture identifies the one 'who goes away,' it returns to identify 'the dead.' Jehoiakim built his palace by robbing and cheating.—[*Redak*]

who makes his fellowman work without wages—He would hire workers to build his houses and not pay them their wages.—[*Redak*]

and his hire he does not give him—Heb. וּפֹעֲלוֹ, lit. his labor, meaning the hire for his labor. Rabbi Joseph Kimchi renders: his laborer. And his laborer—he does not give him [his hire].

14. **Who says, I will build myself**—Who says, "I will build," and he builds.—[*Redak*]

a wide house—Heb. בֵּית מִדּוֹת, lit. a house of measures, *a large house. Cf.* '(Num. 13:32) *Men of great stature* (אַנְשֵׁי מִדּוֹת),' *who have what to measure.*—[*Rashi*]

Redak explains that the implication is 'house of *large* measures.'

spacious upper chambers—Heb. מְרֻוָּחִים. This may also be translated: airy upper chambers, made for summer use.—[*Redak*]

and he cuts out . . . for himself—Heb. וְקָרַע, lit. he tears. *And he widens for himself.* (Some emend: *And he opens for himself.*) Comp. '(supra 4:30) *that you enlarge* (וַתִּקְרְעִי) . . . *with paint.' Also* '(Isaiah 63:19) *Had You rent* (קָרַעְתָּ) *the heavens, had You descended.' They are all an expression of opening.*—[*Rashi*] Rabbi Joseph Kara does indeed interpret it as an expression of widening. He, however, cites only the first verse, which speaks of painting the eye to give the impression that it is larger. *Rashi,* however, quotes the second verse as well. This is more likely to be interpreted as an expression of opening, rather than 'widening.' Moreover, *Rashi*'s conclusion appears to support the emendation. See also *Rashi* (above 4:30). *Redak,* too, interprets it as an expression of opening. He bases this on *Targum Jonathan.*

windows—Heb. חַלּוֹנָי, same as חַלּוֹנִים.—[*Redak*]

and ceiled with cedar—*He covers the roof with cedars.*—[*Rashi*]

* For Rashi's commentary turn to page 242.

ושתה ועשה משפט וצדקה אז טוב
לו: טז דן דין עני ואביון אז טוב הלא
היא הדעת אתי נאם יהוה: יז כי אין
עיניך ולבך כי אם על בצעך ועל דם
הנקי לשפוך ועל העשק ועל
המרוצה לעשות: יח לכן כה אמר
יהוה אל יהויקים בן יאשיהו מלך
יהודה לא יספדו לו הוי אחי והוי אחות

תרגום

דין דקשוט וזכו בכן טב
ליה: טז דן דין מסכן
וחשוך בכן הוה טב
הלא היא דעתא
דרעינא בה אמר יי:
יז ארי לית עינך ולבך
אלהין על ממונא למינס
ועל דם זכאי למשפך
ועל עושקא ועל
דברעות נפשך למעבד:
יח בכן כדנן אמר יי על
יהויקים בר יאשיה מלך
שבטא דבית יהודה לא
יספדון ליה וי על אחי
וי על אחת לא
יספדון ליה וי

מהר"י קרא

מתגאת בבניינים של ארז בתמיה: הלא. אביך יאשיהו. אכל ושתה ועשה משפט וצדקה: (טז) הלא הוא הדעת אותי. שאני רוצה בהן: (יז) ועל המרוצה. לרוצץ דלים:

רש"י

אביך. יאשיהו שהתנהג בענוה הלא אכול ושתה וראה טוב כל ימי חייו: (יז) על בצעך. לגזול ממון: המרוצה. רצוץ דלים ועושק יוכיח עליו כי עשוק ורצוץ תמיד סמוכין

מנחת שי

ספרים מדוייקים: (טז) הלא היא. בכמה ספרים כתוב הלוא מלא וא"ו והלי"ף המגה במ"ג נמסר וירמיה כולהון מלא במ"ג חסר וזה אחד מהם: היא. כן כתוב בספרים מדוייקים ביו"ד ומה שכתוב במסורת ג' ר"ל ג' הלא היא הכתובים במקרא וכימן בסוף פרשת דברים במ"ג ודהתם כתוב הלא בה"א ותלת הוה פוה"ו

רד"ק

כלומר בבנין הארזים אתה מתערב ונאחז להגאתך: אביך הלא אכל ושתה ועשה משפט וצדקה. כלומר איני תופש אותך בהנאותיך אם היית עושה משפט וצדקה כי אביך יאשיהו אכל ושתה בדרך המלכים ונהג בטובתו וכיון שעשה משפט וצדקה אז טוב לו והיה בטוב כל ימיו אבל אתה נהגת בטובת העה"ז בדרך רעה שבניניך שאתה נהנה בהם אינם ביושר ובמשפט כי אם בעשק וכן מאכלך ומשקך ושאר הנאותיך הם בחמס כמו שאמר כי אין עיניך ולבך כי אם על בצעך וגו' ויש אומרים כי יהויקים היה מתענה תמיד והיה סבור כי התעניות היו תשלום מעשיו הרעים לפיכך אמר לו אביך הלא אכל ושתה ועשה משפט וצדקה וי"ת האת מדמי למהוי כמלכא קדמאה ר"ל דוד שהיה המלך הראשון ואתה לפי שאתה מזרעו אתה חושב להיות כמוהו אין זה כי דוד עשה משפט וצדקה וקרא דוד ארז כי היה כארז בלבנון: (טז) דן דין עני. הלא היא הדעת אותי נאם ה'. פי' אותו בפ' כה אמר ה' אל יתהלל חכם וגו' וי"ת הלא היא דעתא דרעינא אמר ה': (יז) כי אין. בצעך. אחר חמדתך בממון: המרוצה. ענין שבר כמו את מי עשקתי ואת מי רצותי ואם אינו משרשו כי ימצא זה הענין בנחי העי"ן כמו לא יכהה ולא ירוץ והעשק בממון והמרוצה בגוף שהיה עושק שכר שכיר כמ"ש והיה מכה אותם ומכריחים לעבודתו וזהו המרוצה שאמר וגם היה שופך דם נקי ועל כל זה אמר בד"ה ותועבותיו אשר עשה והנמצא עליו הנם כתובים על ספר מלכי ישראל ויהודה ועל זה הספר אמר שמדבר על ישראל ויהודה ועל מלכיהם: (יח) לכן. הוי אחי והוי אחות. הספד הקרובים כמ"ש הוי אדון והוי הודו הוא' הספד העם ואיך יספדו על המלך אלא זכר ל' הספד שהקרובים סופדים על האיש הוי אחי ועל האשה הוי אחות או אמר הוי אחות על אשת יהויקים ואף על פי שלא נזכרה: הודו. כחו והדרו ר"ל מלכותו כמו שת"י וי על מלכותי

מצודת ציון

כדבוק והתערב וכן ואיך תתחרה את הסוסים (לעיל י"ב): (יז) בצעך. ענין חמדת הממון כמו מה בצע (בראשית ל"ו): העושק. הגזל: המרוצה. מלשון רצוץ ושבירה וכן את מי רצותי (ש"א י"ב): (יח) הוי. הוא ענין לשון יללה: הודה. ענין הדר

מצודת דוד

וכי תחשב בו לאורך ימים: אביך. הוא יאשיהו: הלא אכל ושתה. יתכן שהיה יהויקים מסגף עצמו במאכל ובמשתה ועשה הרע וחשבו שהסגוף יכפר על רעתו ולזה אמר הלא אביך התענג במאכל ובמשתה ועשה משפט וצדקה ובעבור זה היה טוב לו כי לא עשה הרע ולא היה לו לורך אל הסגוף: (טז) דן. היה דן דין עני ואביון ובעבור זה היה טוב לו כי הלא זהו הדעת אותי כי בזה מדבק במעשי לרחם על העניים כמוני: (יז) כי אין עיניך. ר"ל אכל בסגוף שלך אין נחת כי אין מחשבתך כ"א על חמדת הממון ותסגף עצמך למען תכוסף העבירה ולעשותה טוב: ועל המרוצה לעשות. ר"ל לרוצץ דלים ואביונים: (יח) לא יספדו לו. כאשר ימות לא יספדו עליו קרוביו לומר הוי כי אחי היה וקרובותיו לא תספדנה לומר הוי כי הייתי לו

The oppression denotes his failure to pay his hired workers, and the crushing denotes his practice to strike them and coerce them to work. Also, he shed innocent blood. The Chronicler (II 36:8) refers to this as 'all his abominations which he committed and that which was found on him, behold they are written in the Book of the Chronicles of the kings of Israel and Judah.' The reference could only be to our Book, which deals with Israel and Judah and their kings.—[*Redak*] See Commentary Digest, II Kings 24:5.

18. **Therefore ... "Hoe, brother!" or "Hoe, sister!"**—This is the lament of the relatives. "Hoe, lord!" or "Hoe, his glory!" is the lament of the people for their

and drink and perform justice and righteousness? Then it was
well with him. 16. He judged the cause of the poor and needy,
then it was good. Is not that the knowledge of Me? says the
Lord. 17. For your eyes and your heart are on nothing but
your gain and on innocent blood to shed and on the oppression
and on the crushing to do. 18. Therefore, so said the Lord
about Jehoiakim, king of Judah: They will not lament him,
[saying], "Hoe, brother!" or "Hoe, sister!"

fore, asks him, "Will you really rule so long, that you have attached yourself to the cedars?—[*Mezudath David*]

Redak and *Mezudath David* render: that you attach yourself to the cedars.

your father—*Josiah, who demeaned himself with humility, did he not eat and drink and enjoy pleasure all the days of his life?*—[*Rashi*]

I would not blame you for your pleasures if you performed justice and righteousness, for your father Josiah ate and drank in kingly manner and enjoyed his bounty, but since he performed justice and righteousness, it was well for him, and he enjoyed his bounty all his life. But you are enjoying the bounty of this world unjustly, for your buildings with which you enjoy this world are not built with justice and righteousness, but with oppression. Likewise, your eating, your drinking, and your other pleasures are derived through violence, as is stated further, "For your eyes and your heart are on nothing but your gain . . ." Others explain that Jehoiakim would constantly engage in fasts in order to expiate his sins. Therefore, God tells him, "Your father—did he not eat and drink and perform justice and righteousness?" [The fasts are of no avail without sincere repentance.] *Jonathan* renders: Do you think to be like the first king? Your father—did he not eat and drink and perform true and just judgment? Then it was well with him. He sees David as the 'father' in this verse, i.e. the first king of the dynasty. Do you think to be like him because you are his descendant? No, it is not so. David performed true and just judgment. He calls David the cedar because he was like a cedar in Lebanon.—[*Redak*]

16. **Is not that the knowledge of Me?**—See above 9:23. *Jonathan* renders: Is not that the knowledge which I desire?

17. **on your gain**—*to steal money.*—[*Rashi*]

I.e., your thoughts are only on your desire to acquire wealth.—[*Redak*]

the crushing—Heb. הַמְּרוּצָה, *the crushing of the poor, and* עֹשֶׁק, *oppression proves it, for 'oppressed' and 'crushed' are always juxtaposed in the language of the Scriptures. Cf.* '(I Sam. 12:3) *Whom did I oppress or whom did I crush*?'—[*Rashi*]

לֹא-יִסְפְּדוּ לוֹ הוֹי אָדוֹן וְהוֹי הֹדֹה׃
יט קְבוּרַת חֲמוֹר יִקָּבֵר סָחוֹב וְהַשְׁלֵךְ
מֵהָלְאָה לְשַׁעֲרֵי יְרוּשָׁלִָם׃ כ עֲלִי
הַלְּבָנוֹן וּצְעָקִי וּבַבָּשָׁן תְּנִי קוֹלֵךְ וְצַעֲקִי
מֵעֲבָרִים כִּי נִשְׁבְּרוּ כָּל-מְאַהֲבָיִךְ׃
כא דִּבַּרְתִּי אֵלַיִךְ בְּשַׁלְוֹתַיִךְ אָמַרְתְּ לֹא

אשמע

על מַלְכָּא יְיָ עַל מַלְכוּתֵיהּ: יט כְּמָה דִמְשַׁגְרָן יָת נְבֵלַת חֲמָרָא כֵּן יְשַׁגְרוּן יָת נְבִילְתֵיהּ יִתְגְרַר וְיִשְׁתְּדֵי לְהַלְאָה לְתַרְעֵי יְרוּשְׁלֵם: כ סְקִי לְבֵית מַקְדְשָׁא וּצְוַחִי וּבְתַרְעֵי טוּר בֵּיתָא אֲרִימִי קָלִיךְ וּצְוַחִי עַל מְגִיזָתָא אֲרֵי אִתְּבָרוּ כָּל רַחֲמָךְ: כא וּשְׁלָחִית לְוָתִיךְ יָת כָּל עַבְדֵי נְבִיַּיָא כַּד הֲוֵית יָתְבָא

ה"א קבורת חמור. סנהדרין פב קד:

כצ"ל

רש"י

כל' מקרא וכן את מי עשקתי ואת מי רצותי (שמואל א יב): (יח) והוי הודה. הוי על תפארתו: (יט) קבורת חמור יקבר. כמה דמשגרן ית נבלת חמרא כן ישגרון ית נבלתיה. ישגרון יסחבון: (כ) עלי הלבנון וצעקי. סקי לבית מקדשא וצוחי: ובבשן תני קולך. על הבשן שיחרב וי"ת ובתרעי טור ביתא ואיני יודע לפרש היאך נופל לשון בשן בשערי הר הבי' אם לא בשביל הדלתו' שעושין מאלוני הבשן והוא שם מקום או לשון בשן מקום בקעה רחבה כן היקף הר הבי' מגרש ריוח לכ"ה: וצעקי מעברים. וצוחי על מגיזת' והם לשון מקום: (כא) בשלותיך. כשהיתה בשלוה:

מהר"י קרא

(יט) קבורת חמור יקבר. מה דרכו של חמור כשמת גוררין אותו חוץ לעיר אף נבלתו של יהויקים סחיב והשלך בהלאה לשערי ירושלי': (כ) עלי הלבנון וצעקי. כשינתן יהויקים ביד נבוכדנצר על אותו היום נאמר עלי הלבנון וצעקי כלומר אז יכול יהויקים להתאונן על בתי ארזים שהיה מתחרה בהן לבנותן על בניינים שבנה מאלוני הבשן: וצעקי מעברים כי נשברו כל מאהביך. פתרונו כשינתן יהויקים ביד נבוכדנצר אם יזעק לפרעה מלך מצרים שהמליכו תחת יאשיהו אביו מה מועילו לו כבר לקח מלך בבל מנחל מצרים עד נהר פרת כל אשר היתה למלך מצרים. וכן הוא אומר כשינתן יהויקים ביד נבוכדנצר לא הוסיף עוד פרעה מלך מצרים לצאת מארצו כי לקח מלך בבל מנחל מצרים עד נהר פרת כל אשר היתה למלך מצרים וכן הוא אומר ביחזקאל בן אדם את זרוע מלך מצרים שברתי חה הוא כי נשברו כל מאהביך. וכן כל מה שאתה מוצא בפרשה זו אתה מוצא ביהויקים כאן הוא אומר כי אין עיניך ולבך כי אם על בצעך ועל דם נקי לשפוך ולהלן בספר מלכים הוא אומר וגם

רד"ק

והה"א במקום וי"ו הכנוי כה"א אהלה והדומים לו: (יט) קבורת חמור. ר"ל כמו שהחמור לא יקבר כן לא יקבר הוא כי מה הוא קבורת החמור שיסחבו אותו וישליכוהו לאשפה כן יסחבו נבלת יהויקים וישליכו אותו בהלאה לשערי ירושלם כי כשהיו מוליכים אותו בגלות בפעם השנית והכשדים לא הניחוהו להקבר: (כ) עלי הלבנון. אמר כנגד כנסת ישראל ראוי אם יש לך עזר מכל מאהביך שהם אשור ומצרים שהיית בוטחת בהם וסלקת בטחונך כמני עתה כבא שברך צעקי להם אם יושיעוך כי גם להם בא שבר כי מלך אשור נשבר ומצרים גם כן נשברו על ידי נבוכדנאצר בימי יהויקים כמ"ש ולא הוסיף עוד מלך מצרים לצאת מארצו כי לקח מלך בבל מנחר מצרים עד נהר פרת כל אשר היה למלך מצרים ואף על פי שאחר זמן בימי צדקיהו אמר וחיל פרעה יצא ממצרים וגו' באחרונה נצח נבוכדנאצר והחריב מצרים ואמר על דרך משל עלי הלבנון ר"ל עלי להר הלבנון וכן ובבשן ר"ל ובהר הבשן כי מן ההרים ישמע קול הצועק למרחוק: וצעקי. בקמץ העי"ן מפני הזקף והצד"י מפוארת בקמץ חטף: מעברים. מכל עבר ומכל צד גם כן צעקי וראי כי לא יועילוך כי נשברו כל מאהביך וי"ת סקי לבית מקדשא וצוחי ובתרעי טור ביתא הרימי קליך תרגם לבנון בית מקדשא כמו שת"א ההר הטוב הזה והלבנון ובית מקדשא וכן פירשו רבותינו זכרונם לברכה ואמרו ולמה נקרא ביהמ"ק לבנון שהיה מלבין עונותיהם של ישראל אבל ובבשן שתרגום ובתרעי טור ביתא לא ידעתי טעם אולי כנה הר הבית בשם בשן לפי שהבשן היה מקום מרעה הבהמות ובבית המקדש גם כן היה תמיד בהמות לקרבן: (כא) דברתי אליך בשלותיך. אמר בלשון רבים כי היו להם שלוות רבות כשהיו מעשיהם טובים וכאשר החלו להרע והיו בשלות' הוכיח' האל על ידי הנביאי' ולא הועיל: מנעוריך.

מנחת שי

וקרי בחירק: (כ) ולעקו. פ"א הפעל בחטף קמץ והעי"ן בקמץ רחב כן כתב ר' יונה בספר הרקמה וכן כתב רד"ק בפירוש ובמכלול דף י"ס ובשרשים וכן הוא במקלת

מצודת דוד

לאחות: הוי אדון. עבדיו לא יספדו לומר הוי כי אדון היה לנו הוי על הודו והדרו ר"ל על מלכותו שאבדה ממנו במותו: (יט) קבורת חמור יקבר. ר"ל שכמו שלא יקבר החמור כשימות כדרך אבל יעזבוהו שם כן יהיה ענין יהויקים כי יוליכוהו בגולה וימות בדרך ויהיה לו קבורה כמו שיש אל החמור, ר"ל כמו שאין לו לחמור כן לא יהיה לו: סחוב והשלך. יהיה מגורר ומושלך להלן לשערי ירושלים מחוץ להם ולא יקבר כלל: (כ) עלי הלבנון. עלי על הר הלבנון ולעקי למען יהיה נשמע הקול למרחוק: ובבשן. על הר הבשן הרימי את קולך ולעקו מכל עבר וככל לד: כל מאהביך. האומות שהיו לך לעזרה והם אשור ומצרים גם המה נשברו ע"י כ"כ ומעתה לא תמלא עוזרים: (כא) בשלותיך. עוד היית יושבת בשלוה דברתי אליך לשוב אלי ואתה אמרת לא אשמע: זה דרכך. כן דרכך

מצודת ציון

ויופי: (יט) סחוב. ענין גרירה ומשיכה על הקרקע וכן ואם סכלכים לסחוב (לעיל ט"ו): מהלאה. להלן ולרחוק: (כ) מעברים. מלשון עבר ולד: (כא) בשלותיך. מלשון שלוה:

21. **in your peaceful times**—Heb. בְּשַׁלְוֹתַיִךְ, *when you lived in peace*.—[*Rashi*]

The plural form is used because they had many times of peace when their deeds were good. When they commenced to commit evil deeds and they were still living in peaceful

they will not lament him, "Hoe, lord!" or "Hoe, his glory!"
19. A donkey's burial shall he be buried, dragged and tossed
past the gates of Jerusalem. 20. Ascend to the Lebanon and
cry, and on the Bashan give forth your voice, and cry for
Avarim for all your lovers have been broken. 21. I spoke to
you in your peaceful times. You said, "I will not heed."

monarch. The prophet tells us that for a man it was customary to lament, "Hoe, brother!" and for a woman, "Hoe, sister!" This may also allude to Jehoiakim's wife although she is not mentioned.—[*Redak*]

Others explain: When he dies, his kinsmen will not lament him, saying, "Hoe, brother!" Neither will his kinswomen lament him, saying, "Hoe, sister!" I was to him a sister. —[*Abarbanel, Mezudath David*]

"Hoe, his glory!"—*Woe for his glory.*—[*Rashi*]

Redak interprets הֹדֹה as *his might and his glory,* following *Jonathan,* who renders: Woe to his kingdom!

19. **A donkey's burial**—*As they drag the carcass of a donkey, so will they drag his carcass.* The word יְשַׁגְּרוּן used by *Targum Jonathan* means, *they will drag.*—[*Rashi* from *Jonathan*]

Just as it is customary to drag a donkey's carcass outside the city, so will the carcass of Jehoiakim be dragged past the gates of Jerusalem. —[*Kara*]

Just as a donkey is not buried, so will he not be buried, for the donkey's burial is to be dragged and tossed into a dungheap; so will they do to Jehoiakim's carcass, and they will throw him outside the gates of Jerusalem, for he died outside Jerusalem when they were leading him into exile the second time, and the Chaldeans did not permit his burial.—[*Redak*]

*20. **Ascend the Lebanon and cry**—*Go up to the Temple and cry.*—[*Rashi* from *Targum Jonathan*]

for all your lovers have been broken—All your allies have been defeated by Nebuchadnezzar. The king of Assyria was broken, and the king of Egypt, too, was broken in the days of Jehoiakim, as Scripture states: '(II Kings 24:7) And the king of Egypt no longer went out of his land, for the king of Babylonia had taken from the river of Egypt until the Euphrates River, all that belonged to the king of Egypt.' Although afterwards in the times of Zedekiah, '(below 37:5) And Pharaoh's army left Egypt, and the Chaldees who were besieging Jerusalem heard their report, and they withdrew from Jerusalem,' later Nebuchadnezzar vanquished Egypt and laid their land waste.—[*Redak*]

Kara takes 'Lebanon' and 'Bashan' as figurative of the houses Jehoiakim had built from the cedars of Lebanon and the terebinths of Bashan. The prophet tells him that he will then lament over these houses that he had built.

* For Rashi's commentary turn to page 242.

אֶשְׁמָע זֶה דַרְכֵּךְ מִנְּעוּרַיִךְ כִּי לֹא־
שָׁמַעַתְּ בְּקוֹלִי׃ כב כָּל־רֹעַיִךְ תִּרְעֶה־
רוּחַ וּמְאַהֲבַיִךְ בַּשְּׁבִי יֵלֵכוּ כִּי אָז
תֵּבֹשִׁי וְנִכְלַמְתְּ מִכֹּל רָעָתֵךְ׃ כג יֹשַׁבְתְּי*
בַּלְּבָנוֹן מְקֻנַּנְתְּי* בָּאֲרָזִים מַה־נֵּחַנְתְּי
בְּבֹא־לָךְ חֲבָלִים חִיל כַּיֹּלֵדָה׃ כד חַי־
אָנִי נְאֻם־יְהוָה כִּי אִם־יִהְיֶה כָּנְיָהוּ בֶּן

תרגום

שְׁלֵוְיָא אֲמַרְתְּ לֵית אֲנָא
מְקַבְּלָא אוּלְפַן דָא
אוֹרְחָתִיךְ מִנְעוּרַיִךְ אֲרֵי
לָא קַבֵּילְתְּ לְמֵימְרִי׃
כב כָּל פַּרְנָסַךְ יִתְבַּדְּרוּן
לְכָל רוּחַ וְרַחֲמַךְ בְּשִׁבְיָא
יְהָכוּן אֲרֵי בְּכֵן תִּבְהֲתִין
וְתִתְכַּנְעִין מִכָּל בִּישָׁתִיךְ׃
כג דְיָהֲבָא בְּבֵית מַקְדְּשָׁא
בֵּינֵי מַלְכַיָא מְרַבְיָא
בְנָהָא מָה תַּעְבְּדוּן
בְּמֵיתֵי לִךְ עָקָא וְזִיעַ הָא
כְּחֶבְלִין לְיָלֵידְתָּא׃
כד קַיָם אֲנָא אֲמַר יְיָ

ישבת קרי מקננת קרי נחנת קרי

מהר"י קרא

דם הנקי אשר שפך וימלא את ירושלים דם הנקי: (כב) כל רועיך תרעה רוח. אלו מלכי יהודה: ומאהביך בשבי ילכו. אלו מלכי מצרים. שנסמכו עליהם יהויקים וצדקיהו. שכן מצינו שצר נבוכדנצר על מצרים תשא המונה ושלל שללה ובז ביזה ואז כשראו שמלכי מצרים שאתם נסמכין עליהם הולכין בשבי לפני נבוכדנצר. אז תבושי ונכלמת מכל רעתך. וכן הוא אומר בישעיה הוביש על עם לא יועילו לכו: (כג) יושבת בלבנון מקוננת בארזים. אתה יהויקים שעסקת כל ימיך לבנות בתי ארזים ולשבת בהן ולהרים בארזי הלבנון הרמים והנשאים כלומר בניינים הגבוהים כמו שאמר למעלה אבנה לי בית מדות ועליות מרווחים. ודימה את העליות לקן המיושב על ארז גבוה זה הוא מקוננת בארזים. וכל מה שעסקת כל ימיך לבנות לך קן של ארזים: מה נחנת בבא לך חבלים. מה חן תמצא בהן. לכך נאמר. (כד) חי אני נאום ה' כי אם יהיה כניהו בן יהויקים מלך יהודה חותם על ימיני. פת' אילו היה חביב

רש"י

(כב) כל רועיך. כל מלכיך: תרעה רוח. רוח קדים תרועם: (כג) מקוננת בארזים. עושה קנך במגדלות בתי ארזים לבנות בתי מדות: מה נחנת. מה מצאת חן בשביל גובה מגדלייך בעיני שודדך בבא לך חבלים של לידה ומנחם פתר נחנת לשון חניה אבל דונש פתר אותו לשון חן:

מנחת שי

ספרים מדוייקים והוא"ו נמחליך וי"ס שהלד"י נשו"א לבדו: (כב) ומאהביך. כ"ע נס"ס נמחליך נוא"ו: (כג) ישנתי נלננון. יתיר יו"ד: מקננתי. יתיר יו"ד: נחנת. ברוב ספרים כתיב וקרי גלא יו"ד וכן משמע מדברי רד"ק שכתב ישנתי מקננתי י' יתירה נכתב לא נמסטא ועל ונחנת לא כתב מאומה מזה ונספר מכלול כתב שכמוא השני אינו מתנועע אלא הוא נח מפני דגש הכ' הסמוכה לו רולה לומר כי אין דגש אחר שוא נע ונמסורת ריש ספר מלכים נמסר הסימן מן מלין דכתיבין יו"ד נסוף תיבותא ולא קריין ונמסורת כ"י מלאתי כתוב נהדיא ישנתי נלננון מקננתי נארזים כ' נפסוק ועיין מה שכתבתי נרות ע' ורחלה

רד"ק

רוצה לומר דור המדבר שהיה להם כימי הנעורים כי תחלת הכנס האומ' בעבודת האל ובמצותיו היה הדור ההוא וכן פי' חסד נעוריך: (כב) כל רעיך תרעה רוח. כתרגומו כל פרנסיך ר"ל מלכי אשור ומצרי' שהיו להם כפרנסים וכרועים. אותם תרעה רוח. תאכלם הרוח כלומר שישברו קל מהרה כאילו הרוח הדיחה אותם ותירגם יונתן יתבדרון לכל רוח: כי אז תבושי. כשיכל' בטחונך: (כג) יושבתי בלבנון מקוננתי בארזי'. יושבתי מקוננתי ביו"ד יתרה בכתב לא במבטא ונמצאת יתרת גם במבטא אהבתי לדוש מלאתי משפט ושתי המלות האלה אמרו שהן מורכבות יושבתי מן ישבת ויושבת מקוננתי מן מקננת ומקוננות וטעם התרכבה רוצה לומר שיושבת וקוננת מקדם וגם עתה את יושבת ומקוננת כי עדיין היו בארץ שהיא מיוחסת ללבנון וזכר לבנון וארזים לפי שהיו בתי הגדולים בירושלם ספונים בארז כבית המלך כמו שאמר על יהויקים וספון בארז: מה נחנתי. עקרו נחננת והוא מענין חן ומה יבצא לשני פני' למעלת הדבר ולחסרונו למעלה כמו מה רב טובך מה יקר חסדך אלהים ולחסרון מה אנוש כי תזכרנו ובזה יתפרש לשני הפנים למעלה כלומר מה חן ומה ופי היה לך כשבאו לך החבלים והצרות האלה ולחסרון אמר מה חן הוא אשר נשאר לך מכל אשר בנית וקוננת בארזים בבא לך החבלים: (כד) חי

מצודת ציון

(כב) תרעה. מנין שביר' כמו תרועם בשבט ברזל (תהלי' ב'): ונכלמת. מל' כלימה וחרפה: (כג) מקוננת. מנין מדור כמו ודרור קן לה (תהלים פ"ד) ואמר בלשון שאלה: נחנת. מל' חן: חבלים. מכאובים: חיל. חלחלה: (כד) כניהו. הוא יכניה והוא יהויכין: חותם.

מצודת דוד

מאז בהריתיך לי לעם כי מעולם לא שמעת בקולי: (כב) כל רועיך. אשור ומצרי' שהיו רועים ומנהיגים אותך תשבר אותם הרוח ועל"כ יאמר כי הוא ישברם ומאהביך הם אשור ומצרים וכפל הדבר במ"ש: כי אז. כאשר ילכו המה בשבי תבושי מכל רעתך אשר עזבת את ה' ובטחת עליהם: (כג) יושבת בלבנון. את ירושלים היושבת בלבנון ועשר ופירש מקוננת בארזים. ר"ל יושבת בבתי עצי ארזי הלבנון: מה נחנת. מהו החן אשר תמצא בזה בבוא לך מכאובים וחיל

Menahem interpreted נֵחַנְתְּ *as an expression of camping, but Dunash interpreted it as an expression of grace.*—[*Rashi*]

Menahem (*Machbereth* p. 13, p. 91) interprets it as an expression of camping, rendering: Where will you camp? *Dunash* (*Teshuvoth Dunash* pp. 64f.) questions the use of מָה for 'where?' He, therefore, interprets it as an expression of grace (חֵן). *Rabbenu Tam* questions the idea that the towers should find favor in the eyes of those who bring the birthpangs. He prefers: What grace have you found with your fortified towers to drive off the enemy from you?

24. **As I live**—Since he mentioned Jehoiakim, he now speaks of

* For Rashi's commentary turn to page 243.

This is your way since your youth, for you did not hearken to My voice. 22. All your shepherds shall be broken by the wind, and your lovers shall go into captivity, for then you shall be ashamed and confounded because of all your evil. 23. You, who abide in the Lebanon, who nest in the cedars, how gracious shall you be when pangs come to you, the pain of a woman in travail? 24. As I live, says the Lord, though Coniah the son of

times, the Lord would castigate them through His prophets, but to no avail.—[*Redak*]

since your youth—The youth of the Jewish people is the generation that was freed from Egypt and wandered for forty years in the desert, for that was the nation's initiation into God's service. See above 2:2.—[*Redak*]

for you did not hearken to My voice—From the very beginning, you did not hearken to My voice.—[*Mezudath David*]

22. **All your shepherds**—*All your kings.*—[*Rashi*]

This refers to the kings of Judah.—[*Kara*]

Redak interprets this as a reference to the kings of Assyria and Egypt, who were to Judah as leaders and shepherds.

shall be broken by the wind—Heb. תִּרְעֶה רוּחַ, lit. the wind shall break. *The east wind shall break them.*—[*Rashi*]

Redak renders: The wind shall devour them. They shall quickly break as though the wind had driven them. *Jonathan* renders: They shall be scattered to every direction (רוּחַ).

and your lovers shall go into captivity—These are the kings of Egypt, upon whom Jehoiakim and Zedekiah depended, for so we find that Nebuchadnezzar besieged Egypt, 'and he spoiled her spoil and plundered her booty (Ezekiel 29:19),' and then, when you see the kings of Egypt upon whom you depend, going off into exile, you will be ashamed and confounded because of all your evil.—[*Kara*]

23. **You, who abide in the Lebanon, who nest in the cedars**—Heb. יֹשַׁבְתְּ, מְקֻנַּנְתְּ. These peculiar forms are meant as a combination of the present and past tenses: You who abide now and who abided before this in the Lebanon. You who nest now and who nested before this in the cedars, for they were still in the land compared to the Lebanon.—[*Redak*]

who nest in the cedars—*For you placed your nest in the towers of the cedar houses to build wide houses.* —[*Rashi*]

The houses of the wealthy were ceiled with cedar as were those of Jehoiakim.—[*Redak*]

how gracious shall you be—Heb. נֵּחַנְתְּ. *What grace have you found because of the height of your towers, in the eyes of your plunderers, when birth pangs come upon you. And*

יְהוֹיָקִים מֶלֶךְ יְהוּדָה חוֹתָם עַל־יַד
יְמִינִי כִּי מִשָּׁם אֶתְּקֶנְךָּ: כה וּנְתַתִּיךָ בְּיַד
מְבַקְשֵׁי נַפְשֶׁךָ וּבְיַד אֲשֶׁר־אַתָּה יָגוֹר
מִפְּנֵיהֶם וּבְיַד נְבוּכַדְרֶאצַּר מֶלֶךְ־בָּבֶל
וּבְיַד הַכַּשְׂדִּים: כו וְהֵטַלְתִּי אֹתְךָ וְאֶת־
אִמְּךָ אֲשֶׁר יְלָדַתְךָ עַל הָאָרֶץ אַחֶרֶת
אֲשֶׁר לֹא־יֻלַּדְתֶּם שָׁם וְשָׁם תָּמוּתוּ:
כז וְעַל־הָאָרֶץ אֲשֶׁר הֵם מְנַשְּׂאִים אֶת־

אֲרֵי אִם יְהֵי כָנְיָה בַר
יְהוֹיָקִים מַלְכָּא שִׁבְטָא
דְבֵית יְהוּדָה כִּגְלַף
דְעִזְקָא עַל יַד יְמִינִי אֲרֵי
מִתַּמָן בְּמֵימְרִי אַגְלֵינָךְ:
כה וְאֶתְּנִינָךְ בְּיַד דְבָעַן
לְמִקְטְלָךְ וּבְיַד דְאַתְּ
דָחִיל מִן קֳדָמֵיהוֹן וּבְיַד
נְבוּכַדְנֶצַּר מַלְכָּא דְבָבֶל
וּבְיַד כַּשְׂדָאֵי:
כו וַאֲטַלְטֵיל יָתָךְ וְיָת
אִמָּךְ דִילִדְתָּךְ לַאֲרַע
אוֹחֲרֵי דְלָא אִתְיְלֵידְתּוּן
תַּמָן וְתַמָּן תְּמוּתוּן:
כז וּלְאַרְעָא דְאִינוּן מִטְעַן
יַת נַפְשֵׁיהוֹן לְמֵתַב תַּמָּן

רש"י

(כד) הותם על יד ימיני. חקוק והתום בתוך בשר זרועי: אתקנך. אנתקך לשון התיקס כלאן לטבהה (לעיל י"ב) עד התיקנו אותס (יהושע ח') והנו"ן יתירה בו ומדרש אגדה במקוס שנתק נתקן שעשה תשובה בבבל ונשאל הקב"ה על שנשבע כתבו את האיש הזה ערירי (כאן) ונולד לו זרובבל בבבל ונאמר לו על פי הנביא ביום ההיא אקחך זרובבל בן שאלתיאל עבדי ושמתיך כחותס (לקמן סוף מ"ג) כלפי שאמר לאביו אס יהיה הותס על יד ימיני אנתקנו: (כו) והטלתי. לשון הטלכה: (כז) מנשאים את נפשם. לשון תנחומים

מהר"י קרא

כניהו כחותם של טבעת שאדם משים על יד ימינו משם הייתי מנתקו ומשליכו בעבורך: (כה) ונתתיך. כניהו ביד מבקשי נפשך: (כו) והטלתי אתך ואת אמך. כענין שנאמר במלכים ויגל יהויכין בבלה ואת אם המלך וימלוך את מתניהו דודו: (כז) ועל הארץ אשר הם מנשאים את נפשם. כמו מתנשא

רד"ק

אני. כיון שדבר על יהויקים דבר גם כן על יהויכין בנו וקראו כניהו לפחיתות: הותם על יד ימיני. הטבעת שחותמים בה הכתבים נקרא חותם וכן שיכני כחות' חותמך ופתילך והטבעת ההוא לא תסיר מיד האדם לא ביום ולא בלילה לפיכך אמר כי אפילו יהיה כניהו ככו החותם על יד הימין שלא יוסר ממנה משם אסירך ואתקנך: אתקנך. שרשו נתק ודגש התי"ו מור' חסרון הנו"ן והנון האחרונה נוספת כנו"ן יברכנהו יצרנהו ויש דרש על הנו"ן היתרה אמרו שבמקו' שנתק שם נתקן כי בבית האסורים עשה תשובה וקבלו הקדוש ברוך הוא ונולד לו בן בבית האסורים ומשל בן בנו זרובבל בן שאלתיאל ביהודה וישב על כסא דוד ואמר לו ושמתיך כחותם כנגד כה שאמר לאביו אם יהי' כניהו חותם על יד ימיני כי משם אתקנך: (כה) ונתתיך. כל אלו ביד שאמר לענין אמרם וכן אשר הציל אתכם מיד מצרי' ומיד פרעה אשר הציל את העם מתחת יד מצרים זה הכפל ג"כ לחזק לענין ההוא ופירוש ביד מבקשי נפשך שלא יחכלו עליך: אשר אתה יגור מפניהם. שלא יהיה לך כח לעמוד כנגדם: וביד נבוכדנצר מלך בבל. שהוא מלך עז וקשה כמו שנאמר עליו עלה אריה מסבכו ומשחית גוים נסע ממקומו: וביד הכשדים. שהם גוי עז וקשה אשר לא ישא פנים כמו שנאמר עליהם הגוי המר והנמהר: (כו) והטלתי. כמו והשלכתי וכן ויטילו את הכלים ובאמרו אשר ילדתך ר"ל שהיה דומה לה במעשים רעים לפיכך היה אומר ושם אמו במלכים שהיה הבן דומה לאם: על הארץ אחרת. בידיעת המתואר בלא ידיעת התאר כמו הגפן נכריה הכבש אחד תדור אחד: אשר לא ילדתם שם. שלא תמצאו שם בני משפחה שירחבו עליכם: ושם תמותו. גם זו קללה כלומר בארץ טמאה ימותו: (כז) ועל הארץ. כמו ואל הארץ ורבים כמוהו: אשר הם מנשאים את נפשם. שהיו מבטיחים אותם נביאי השקר שישובו הגולים עתה מהרה כמו שאמר הנה כלי בית ה' מושבים מבבל עתה מהרה וגו' ובעבור זה היו מנשאי' את נפשם ובוטחים על שקר

מנחת שי

ופכה ושמת: (כד) אתקנך. הס"ו כדגש לחסרון נו"ן פ"א כפעל והנו"ן נוספת ומפני ההפסק בא מלפיל ודגש קל בכ"ף ע' בספר ההרכבה אות אל"ף ובמדרש חזית פסוק שימני כחותם ובפסיקתא משם אתקנך ר' חמא בר חנינא אמר משם אני נותק מלכות בית דוד. ד"א אנתקך אין כתיב כאן אלא אתקנך בתשובה. ד"א ממקום נתיקתו תהא תקנתו ע"כ. ויתכן לומר שהוא מורכב משני שרשים נתק ותקן והטעם שאמר לנתק יכניה ואח"כ אמר לתקנו ע"י בנו שאלתיאל אשר יצא ממנו זרובבל שבנה הבית ונהג שררה בישראל. לויה חן שער ז' פ' א': (כה) וביד נבוכדראצר מלך בבל ביד הכשדים. בס"א כ"י מלאתי נסוב וביד

מצודת דוד

כיולדה ר"ל וכי בעבור זה המלה הן בעיני האויב: (כד) חותם. כמו טבעת שחותמים בו אגרות הנתון תמיד על יד הימין ואינו מוזזה ממנה ואחז כמשל כדרך הנהוג בבן אדם: משם אתקנך. מכ"ז אסיר אותך מן היד ולפי שהמשילו לטבעת שחותמין בו אמר לשון הנופל בטבעת ורלה לומר אף באתה מזרע דוד מ"מ אמזכך: (כה) ונתתיך ביד וגו'. כפל הדבר פעמים רבות במ"ש להגדיל הענין ולהפחידו: (כו) והטלתי אותך. אשליך אותך: אשר ילדתך. אשר גדלה אותך ללכת בדרך רעה: (כז) ועל הארץ. ואל הארץ:

מצודת ציון

כן נקראת הטבעת שחותמים בה האגרות וכן חותמך ופתילך (בראשית ל"ח): אתקנך. ענין העתקה והסרה: (כה) יגור. ענין פחד כמו ויגר מואב (במדבר כ"ב): (כו) והטלתי. ענין השלכ' כמו ויטילו את הכלים (יונה א'): ילדתך. ענין גדול ואמון וכן יולדו על ברכי יוסף (בראשית נ'): (כז) מנשאים.

is an expression of consolation, that their soul lifts itself to console itself and to say, "We will again return to our land."—[*Rashi*]

The false prophets would assure them that the exiles would return very soon, as he says, "Behold, the vessels of the house of the Lord will be restored from Babylon now quickly etc. (27:16)." Because of

Jehoiakim, king of Judah, be a signet on My right hand, from
there I will remove you. 25. And I will deliver you into the
hand[s] of those who seek your life and into the hand[s] of those
you fear and into the hand[s] of Nebuchadrezzar, king of
Babylon, and into the hand[s] of the Chaldees. 26. And I will
cast you and your mother who bore you, to another land where
you were not born, and there you shall die. 27. But to the land
to which they long

his son Jeconiah. Here he is called Coniah as a sign of denigration.—[*Redak*]

a signet—*Engraved and sealed in the flesh of My arm.*—[*Rashi*]

Others define this as the seal on a signet ring, which is worn constantly, both day and night. God says, "Though Coniah . . . would be a signet on My right hand, which is never removed, from there I will remove you."—[*Redak, Kara*]

Malbim calls to our attention that in the prophecy of Haggai (2:23), God says , "On that day I will take you, Zerubbabel, and I will make you like a signet," for the King Messiah will be like a signet ring on God's right hand, so to speak. Just as the name of the owner of the ring is engraved on his signet ring, through which he makes himself known, so will God's name be known in the world through the King Messiah, through whom His miracles will be known. He says here that, though, in the future, Coniah will be the signet on My right hand, for the Messiah will spring from his seed, now I will remove him from there.

into the hand[s] of . . . and into the hand[s] of etc.—The repetition is to intensify the power of the sentence, as follows.—[*Redak*]

into the hand[s] of those who seek your life—I.e. people who will not have pity on you.

into the hand[s] of those you fear—And you will not be able to stand up before them.

and into the hand[s] of Nebuchadnezzar king of Babylon—a powerful and harsh king, as above 4:7, where he is likened to a lion.

and into the hand[s] of the Chaldees—a strong and harsh nation, called by Habakkuk (1:6), 'the bitter and hasty nation.'—[*Redak*]

26. **And I will cast**—Heb. וְהֵטַלְתִּי, *an expression of throwing.*—[*Rashi*]

who bore you—This is stated because he resembled her in his evil deeds. For this reason, the king's mother is always mentioned in Kings, since he resembled her in his deeds.—[*Redak*]

where you were not born—and you will not find relatives who will show you clemency.—[*Redak*]

and there you shall die—This too is a curse, that they will die in an unclean land.—[*Redak*]

27. **they long**—Heb. מְנַשְּׂאִים אֶת־נַפְשָׁם, lit. they raise their souls. *This*

נַפְשָׁם לָשׁוּב שָׁם־שָׁמָּה לֹא יָשׁוּבוּ׃
כח הַעֶצֶב נִבְזֶה נָפוּץ הָאִישׁ הַזֶּה כָּנְיָהוּ
אִם־כְּלִי אֵין חֵפֶץ בּוֹ מַדּוּעַ הוּטְלוּ הוּא
וְזַרְעוֹ וְהֻשְׁלְכוּ עַל־הָאָרֶץ אֲשֶׁר לֹא־
יָדָעוּ׃ כט אֶרֶץ אֶרֶץ אָרֶץ שִׁמְעִי דְּבַר־
יְהוָה׃ ל כֹּה אָמַר יְהוָה כִּתְבוּ אֶת־
הָאִישׁ הַזֶּה עֲרִירִי גֶּבֶר לֹא־יִצְלַח בְּיָמָיו

תרגום

לְתַמָן לָא יְתוּבוּן׃ כח בְּסִירָא חֲלָשָׁא מְטַלְטְלָא גַבְרָא הָדֵין כָּנְיָהוּ כְּמָנָא דְלֵית צְרוֹךְ בֵּיהּ מָה דֵין אִטַּלְטְלוּ הוּא וּבְנוֹהִי וְאִתְגְּלִיאוּ לְאַרְעָא דְלָא יְדָעוּ׃ כט מֵאַרְעֵיהּ אַגְלוֹהִי לְאַרְעָא אוּחֲרֵי אַרְעָא דְיִשְׂרָאֵל קַבִּילִי פִּתְגָמֵי דַיְיָ׃ ל כִּדְנַן אֲמַר יְיָ כְּתוּבוּ יָת גַּבְרָא הָדֵין דְּלָא וְלַד גַּבְרָא דְלָא

ת"א ארץ ארץ. חולין קכו: ערירי. סנהדרין לו:

רש"י

שנפשם מתנשאה להתנחם ולומר עוד נשוב לארצנו: (כח) העצב נבזה. תמיה הוא שמא דמות קבר ונבזה האיש הזה שהושלך מעל פני כמי שאין חפץ בו: נפוץ. נשבר כמו ככלי יוצר תנפצם (תהלים ב') ואחרים הגיהו העצב כמו העצבים מעצבין את הקטן במסכת שבת כלומר האתה נבזה ונפוץ בעיניך כעולל קטן שמעצבין אותו (מילולי"ר בלע"ז) אין זה כדי: הוטלו. הושלכו. לשון השלכה שאין לה הקימה כמו כי יפול לא יוטל (שם ל"ז): (כט) ארץ ארץ. ד"א ארץ ארץ ארץ. ארץ שהוא ארץ שבארצו' השוב' שבכולן. מארצו גלה אל ארץ אחרת ואת ארץ ישראל שמעי דבר ה'. ד"א ארץ ישראל שלש ארצות היו בה יהודה ועבר הירדן והגליל: (ל) גבר אשר לא יצלח בימיו. כתבוהו:

מהר"י קרא

לאמר אני אמלוך: (כח) העצב נבזה נפוץ. חכמים פתרוהו ככלי של מימי רגלים שלאחר שנשבר אדם משליכו לחוץ: נפוץ. נשבר ופת' הכלי נבזה ונשבר הוא שאדם משליכו לחוץ האיש הזה כניהו. אם כלי הוא אין חפץ בו. שאדם מואס בו ומשליכו: מדוע הוטלו הוא וזרעו והושלכו אל הארץ אשר לא ידעו. ומפרש בצידו ומה הוא הדבר זה הוא הטעם שממרום נגזר עליו שלא יצליח מזרעו איש יושב על כסא דוד ומושל עוד ביהודה: (כט) ארץ ארץ ארץ. אמר ג' פעמים כנגד ג' גליות שגלו על ידי נבוכדנצר: (ל) כתבו את האיש הזה ערירי. מן המלכות ולא ערירי מן הבנים כמו שמפרש והולך: גבר לא

רד"ק

המלך יהויכין ושאר הגולים: (כח) העצב נבזה. הה"א ה"א השאלה לפיכך היא פתוחה אמר אם כניהו הוא כמו עצב נבזה ועצב הוא מן עצבים שהיא שם לאלילים והעצב הוא נבזה ומשליך אותו המכיר בו שהוא הבל אין בו תועלת משליך אותו ומשביר אותו וזהו שאמר נפוץ כמו ונפוץ הכדים כי בהשליך אדם הכלי ישבר ויתנפצו שבריו ויתפזרו וכן כלי שאין חפץ בו ישליכנו האדם חוץ מביתו: הוטלו. כמו הושלכו הוא וזרעו והנה היה לו זרע בגלותו והרי אמר עליו ערירי ואפשר שהיו לו בני' בצאתו בגולה ומתו בבבל והנה הוא ערירי וכפל הענין ואמר הושלכו אחר שאמר הוטלו והענין אחד לחזק הדבר כי כן דרך המקרא לכפול הענין במלות שונות לחזק הדבר: (כט) ארץ ארץ ארץ. כבר כתבתי בפסוק היכל ה' היכל ה' היכל ה' מה שפירש בו אדוני אבי ז"ל ויתכן לפ' כי הכפל לחזק הענין כי כן מנהג הלשון פעם בשתי מלות כמו כל הקרב הקרב נחמו נחמו עמי והדומים להם ובשלש מלות כמו ארץ ארץ ארץ היכל ה' היכל ה' היכל ה' עוה עוה עוה אשימנה והקריאה לארץ ר"ל לאנשי הארץ שהרי אמר כתבו וכן וכל הארץ באו מצרים' וי"ת מארעי' אגלוהי לארע אוחרי ארעא דישראל קבילי פתגמא דה': (ל) כה אמר ה' כתבו. זה הצווי כצווי ראה ריח בני טולו טולו והדומים להם: ערירי. אם היו לו בנים ימותו בחייו ואם לא היו לו לא

מנחת שי

פנדיו וטעמים הוא: (כח) הוטלו. בכמה ספרים הוטלו הטי"ת בחטוף פתח: (כט) ארץ ארץ ארץ. חד מן ג' פסוקים משולשים בקריאה וסימן נמסר כתן במסרה גדולה:

מצודת דוד

מנשאים את נפשם. מלפים ומרוממים ומבטיחים את נפשם: שמה. ר"ל לא יהיה כן כי לא ישובו שמה: (כח) העצב נבזה וגו'. וכי זה כניהו דומה הוא לצלם נבזה ומפוץ וכי הוא ככלי שאין בו צורך ומדוע א"כ הוטלו מארצם הוא וזרעו וגו': אשר לא ידעו. עד הנה: (כט) ארץ ארץ ארץ. ר"ל ארץ שהיא ארץ מיוחדת בכל הארצות ועולה על כולן: (ל) האיש הזה. הוא כניהו: ערירי. שיהיה ערירי ר"ל נשחת ונחרב ולתוספת ביאור אמר שיהיה גבר אשר לא יצליח

מצודת ציון

ענין הרמה ור"ל מבטיחים: (כח) העצב. כן נקרא הצלם הנעבד כמ"ש עצבי הגוים (תהלים קל"ה) וזהו לפי שמעצב לב עובדיו לזעק אליו ואינו עונה ובדרך מליצה קרא כן לכל הצלמים: נפוץ. ענין שבירה וכליה כמו ונפוץ הכדים (שופטים ז'): חפץ. ענין רצון וצורך וכן שחפץ לשדי כי תצדק (איוב כ"ב): הוטלו. הושלכו: (ל) ערירי. ענין השממה וחורבן כמו ערו ערו עד היסוד (תהלים קל"ז): גבר. איש:

'(Gen. 27:27) See, the odor of my son . . .' and other similar instances.—[*Redak*]

childless—If he had children, they will die, and if he had no children, he will never have any.—[*Redak*] See v. 28, v. 24.

a man who will not prosper in his days—*Inscribe him.*—[*Rashi*] I.e., inscribe him as a man who will not prosper in his days.

The intention is that he will live all his days in captivity.—[*Redak*]

Rabbi Joseph Kara explains that he will be childless of the kingdom, i.e., his children will not occupy the throne after him, not literally childless. He will not prosper in his days

to return there, there they shall not return. 28. Is this man, Coniah, a despised, shattered image, or a vessel in which there is no use? Why were he and his seed cast away, thrown to a land they know not? 29. O land, land, land, hearken to the word of the Lord. 30. So said the Lord: Inscribe this man childless, a man who will not prosper in his days,

this, Jehoiachin and the other exiles relied on the falsehoods of the prophets.—[*Redak*]

28. **Is . . . a despised . . . image**—*It is a rhetorical question. Is this man a broken and despised image, that he was cast away from My face like a vessel in which there is no use?*—[*Rashi*]

shattered—Heb. נָפוּץ, *broken. Cf.* '(Psalms 2:8) *Like a potter's vessel you shall shatter them* (תְּנַפְּצֵם).' [*Others annotated:* הֶעָצֵב *is like 'the idols* (הָעֲצַבִּים).' *'We may swathe* (מְעַצְּבִין) *an infant' in Tractate Shabbath* 22:6. *That is to say, 'Are you despised and broken in your eyes like a small infant who is being swathed* (*emmailloter in French*)? *This one is not worthy.*]—[*Rashi*]

This annotation was apparently added to *Rashi* at some later date by a copyist. The derivation from הָעֲצַבִּים is not clear, since this word is used in Scripture only in the sense of 'idols,' which has no connection to the definition of the word in this verse according to the annotators.

Abarbanel derives it from עֶצֶב, *sadness.* Is this man, Coniah, a sad, despised, scattered person. I.e., is he a poor, wretched person, wandering from one country to another?

a vessel in which there is no use—Such vessels are usually cast out of the house.—[*Redak*]

cast away—Heb. הוּטְלוּ, *thrown, an expression of throwing that has no restoration. Comp.* '(Psalms 37:24) *If he falls, he will not be cast off* (יוּטָל).'—[*Rashi*]

he and his seed—Although he was to be inscribed childless, perhaps he had children when he was driven into exile, and they subsequently died in Babylon.—[*Redak*]

thrown—Heb. הָשְׁלְכוּ, synonymous with הוּטְלוּ, repeated for emphasis.—[*Redak*]

29. **O land, land, land**—*He was exiled from his land to another land, and you, the land of Israel, hearken to the word of the Lord. Another explanation:* **O land, land, land**—*A land that is a land among lands, the most esteemed of all of them. Another explanation: Eretz Israel had three lands in it: Judea, Transjordania, and Galilee.*—[*Rashi*] The first explanation follows *Targum Jonathan. Redak* explains that the repetition is merely for emphasis. The prophet is addressing the *people* of the land.

30. **Inscribe**—This type of command resembles the command of

כי לא יצלח מזרעו איש ישב על־כסא
דוד ומשל עוד ביהודה: כג א הוי
רעים מאבדים ומפצים את־צאן
מרעיתי נאם־יהוה: ב לכן כה־אמר
יהוה אלהי ישראל על־הרעים הרעים
את־עמי אתם הפצתם את־צאני
ותדחום ולא פקדתם אתם הנני פקד
עליכם את־רע מעלליכם נאם־יהוה:
ג ואני אקבץ את־שארית צאני מכל
הארצות אשר־הדחתי אתם שם
והשבתי אתהן על־נוהן ופרו ורבו:

תרגום

יצלח ביומוהי ארי לא
יצלח מזרעיה גבר יתיב
על כורסי דוד ועביד
שולטן על דבית יהודה:
א וי פרנסיא דמאבדין
ומבדרין ית עם דאתקרי
שמי עלוהי אמר יי:
ב בכן כדנן אמר יי
אלהא דישראל על
פרנסיא דמפרנסין ית
עמי אתון בדרתון ית
עמי וטלטילתינון ולא
תבעתון יתהון האנא
מסער עליכון ית בישות
עובדיכון אמר יי:
ג ואנא אכניש ית שארא
דעמי מכל מדינתא
דאגליתי יתהון לתמן
ואתיב יתהון לאתריהון
ויפשון

רש"י

כג (א) הוי רועים. מלכי יהודה: (ב) ולא פקדתם

מהר"י קרא

יצלח בימיו. האיש הזה לא יצלח בימיו להושיב בנו על כסאו תחתיו שהרי נבוכדנצר העבירו מן המלכות והגלהו לו ולנשיו ולאמו והחרש והמסגר עמו והמליך את צדקיהו דודו תחתיו וזה הוא כי לא יצלח מזרעו יושב על כסא דוד ומושל עוד ביהודה: כג (א) הוי רועים מאבדים ומפצים את צאן מרעיתי. הם מלכי ישראל ומלכי יהודה שהדיחו את ישראל עד

רד"ק

יהיו לו: לא יצלח בימיו. כי כל ימי חייו היה בשבי: כי לא יצלח. וגם בזה לא תהי' לו הצלח' שיהי' מזרעו מושל ביהודה והנה זרובבל שהית בן בנו היה מושל ביהודה אלא כמו שאמרו רז"ל שעשת תשובת בבית האסורי' ואמרו רבותינו ז"ל גדולת תשובה שמקרעת גזר דינו. של אדם שנאמר כתבו את האיש הזה ערירי וכיון שעשה תשובה נהפך לו גזר דין לטוב' ואמר לו אקחך זרובבל בן שאלתיאל עבדי ושמתיך כחותם כי בך בחרתי ועוד אמרו א"ר יוחנן גלות מכפרת על הכל שנאמר כתבו את האיש הזה ערירי ובתר דגלה כתיב ובני כניהו אסיר בנו שאלתיאל בנו וגו': (א) הוי רועים. אמר על מלכי יהודה הרעים אמר להם הוי אתם מאבדים ומפיצים את צאן מרעיתי כלו' שאני הייתי רועה אותם כשהיו שומעים לקולי ואחר שהייתם אתם רועים אותם נהגתם אותם בדרך רעה ואבדתם והפיצותם אותם בגלות: (ב) לכן. ולא פקדתם אותם. ולא השגחת' עליה' אנה הם ומה הם עושים אם טוב ואם רע והיה לכם לדעת כי בעון הוא שהם נדחים וגולי' ובעונש שלא פקדתם אות' הנני פוקד עליכם את רוע מעלליכם: (ג) ואני אקבץ. אם על גלות בבל אמר יהיה פירש ולא ייראו עוד זמן רב או יהיה

מנחת שי

כג (ג) והשבתי. בספרים מדוייקים חסר יו"ד בתר ש"ן וחסר וא"ו בתר בי"ת:

מצודת דוד

בכל ימיו כי בימיו לא יצליח איש מזרעו לשבת על כסא המלוכה ולמשול ביהודה כי בשגלה הוא לא נתנה המלוכה לזרעו כ"א לצדקיה דודו ולא היה לזרעו ממשלה אף בימיו אבל לאחר מותו היה ממשלה לזרובבל שהיה מזרעו:
כג (א) הוי רועים. יש להתאונן על המלכים הרעים אשר במעשיהם מאבדים ומפזרים את העם ללכת גולה בארצות אויביהם: צאן מרעיתי. הם ישראל שאני להם לרועה: (ב) אתם הפצותם. ר"ל בעוניכם נפזרו בין האומות ונדחו בארצות האויב: ולא פקדתם אותם. לא השגחתם עליהם להישירם בדרך הישר: פוקד עליכם. אזכור עליכם רוע מעשיכם להשיב עליכם גמול: (ג) ואני אקבץ. וכחסדי אקבץ את שארית וגו' כי רובם יכלו ומעט ישארו: והשיבותי.

מצודת ציון

כג (א) ומפצים. ענין פיזור כמו ויפץ העם (שמות ה'): מרעיתי. מלשון מרעה: (ב) ותדחום. מלשון דחיה: פקדתם. ענין זכרון והשגחה: מעלליכם. מעשיכם: (ג) נויהן. מדורם כמו נוה שאנן (ישעיה ל"ג): ופרו. יעשו פירות ר"ל יולידו בנים:

know where they were and what they were doing, whether good or evil. You should have known that because of their iniquity they would be driven away into exile. Now, as a punishment for not taking care of them, I will visit upon you the evil of your deeds.—[*Redak*] This is a play on words. The word for 'you have not taken care' (לֹא פְקַדְתֶּם) and the word for 'visit' (פֹּקֵד) stem from the same root (פקד).

3. **And I will gather**—If the reference is to the return from the Babylonian exile, the words 'and they shall no longer fear' in verse 4 are to be interpreted to mean that they will not fear enemies for a long time. It

for no man of his seed shall prosper, sitting on the throne of David or ruling anymore in Judah.

23

1. Woe to the shepherds who destroy and scatter the flocks of My pasture! says the Lord. 2. Therefore, so says the Lord God of Israel concerning the shepherds: You who pasture My people, you have scattered My flocks and have driven them away and have not taken care of them; behold, I will visit upon you the evil of your deeds, says the Lord. 3. And I will gather the remnant of My flocks from all the lands where I have driven them, and I will restore them to their dwellings and they shall be fruitful and multiply.

to seat his heir on the throne, for Nebuchadnezzar removed him from the throne and exiled him and his wives and his mother, the craftsmen and the gatekeepers with him, and crowned his uncle Zedekiah in his stead.

for no man of his seed shall prosper—In this, too, no man of his seed shall prosper, namely tht no one will occupy the throne of David nor rule in Judah. Although we find that Zerubbabel, his great grandson, did rule over Judah upon the return of the exiles, the Rabbis (*Pesikta d'Rav Kahana* p. 163a) state that this was because Jehoiachin repented while in prison. They state further: Repentance is great, for it nullifies a person's sentence, as it is stated: 'Inscribe this man childless.' But since he repented, his sentence was revoked and turned to the good, and he said to him, "I will take you, Zerubbabel, and I will make you a signet" (Haggai 2:23). They state further: Said Rabbi Johanan: Exile expiates all sins, as it is said: "Inscribe this man childless," and after he was exiled, it is written: '(I Chron. 3:17) And the sons of Jeconiah, Assir, Shealtiel his son'—[*Redak*] See above verse 24.

1. **Woe to the shepherds**—*The kings of Judah.*—[*Rashi, Redak*]

He addresses the evil kings of Judah. He says to them: Woe that you are destroying and scattering the flock of My pasture. That is to say, I would lead them if they listened to My voice. Now that you are leading them, you have led them in evil ways and caused them to be lost and scattered in exile.—[*Redak*]

Kara adds the kings of Israel to the evil kings of Judah. Both were instrumental in bringing exile upon their people.

2. **and have not taken care of them**—*You were not careful to watch them.*—[*Rashi*]

You did not watch over them to

ד וַהֲקִמֹתִי עֲלֵיהֶם רֹעִים וְרָעוּם וְלֹא־
יִירְאוּ עוֹד וְלֹא־יֵחַתּוּ וְלֹא יִפָּקֵדוּ נְאֻם־
יְהוָה: ה הִנֵּה יָמִים בָּאִים נְאֻם־יְהוָה
וַהֲקִמֹתִי לְדָוִד צֶמַח צַדִּיק וּמָלַךְ מֶלֶךְ
וְהִשְׂכִּיל וְעָשָׂה מִשְׁפָּט וּצְדָקָה בָּאָרֶץ:
ו בְּיָמָיו תִּוָּשַׁע יְהוּדָה וְיִשְׂרָאֵל יִשְׁכֹּן
לָבֶטַח וְזֶה־שְּׁמוֹ אֲשֶׁר־יִקְרְאוֹ יְהוָה

ת"א וזה שמו. כ"כ פה: מלעיל

תרגום

וְיִפְשׁוּן וְיִסְגוּן: ד וַאֲקִים עֲלֵיהוֹן פַּרְנְסִין וִיפַרְנְסוּנוּן וְלָא יִדְחֲלוּן עוֹד וְלָא יִתַּבְּרוּן וְלָא יְזוּעוּן אֲמַר יְיָ: ה הָא יוֹמַיָא אָתַן אֲמַר יְיָ וַאֲקִים לְדָוִד מְשִׁיחַ דְּצַדִּיקַיָא וְיִמְלוֹךְ מַלְכָּא וְיַצְלַח וְיַעְבֵּד דִּין דִּקְשׁוֹט וְזָכוּ בְּאַרְעָא: ו בְּיוֹמוֹהִי יִתְפָּרְקוּן דְּבֵית יְהוּדָה וְיִשְׂרָאֵל יִשְׁרוּן לְרַחְצָן וְדֵין שְׁמֵיהּ דִּיהוֹן קָרַן לֵיהּ יִתְעַבְּדָן לָנָא זָכְוָן מִן

מהר"י קרא

שגלו בעונם: (ד) ולא יחתו ולא יפקדו. ולא יחסרו כמו ולא נפקד ממנו איש: (ה) ועשה משפט וצדקה בארץ. לא כיהויקים שנאמר לו אביך הלא אכל ושתה ועשה משפט וצדקה אבל אתה אין עיניך ולבך כי על בצעך ועל דם הנקי לשפוך: (ו) וזה שמו אשר יקראו ה' צדקנו. פת' ה' שופטנו מן האומות אשר הרעו לנו. צדק האמור כאן הוא משפט כד"א ושפטו את העם משפט צדק וכת"י ודין שמיה דיהון קרן ליה יתעבדון לנא

רש"י

אותם. לא נזהרתם לשומרם: (ד) ולא יפקדו. ולא יחסרו לשון ולא נפקד ממנו איש (במדבר ל"א): (ה) והשכיל. ויצליח: (ו) ה' צדקנו. ה' מצדיק אותנו

מנחת שי

נוכן. בספרים מדוייקים חסר יו"ד כתר וה"ו: (ד) והקמתי עליהם. בספרים מדוייקים חסר דחסר וכן נכון ע"פ המסורת שאין זה מן ג' מלא דמלא וסימן נמסר ביחזקאל סוף סימן ס"ז ולא מן ו' חסרים וא"ו וסימן נמסר בפרשת בחקתי וכן הוא: (ה) והקמתי לדוד. בשמוך: (ו) אשר יקראו. בספרי ספרד האל"ף נגעיה כמוהו רבים כמ"ש בסוף מאמר המחריך: יקראו. אל ירוץ הקורא לקרות יקראו בשורק כמ"ש באיוב דפוס שאם ירוץ יכשל: וזה שמו אשר יקראו ה' | צדקנו. כתב ן' עזרא בריש פרשת יתרו כי שם המשיח ה' צדקנו כמו שקרא משה למזבח ה' נסי. והגאון אמר כי השם דבק עם מלת יקראו וגם המשיח הוא צדקנו והנה הוא מטעה בעל הטעמים שגם סרתא במלת יקראו וגו' עיין שם וגם מה שכתב בפרשת ויצלא על פסוק אל אלהי ישראל וכן פירש רד"ק כאן וגם בירמיה ל"ג על פסוק אשר יקרא לה ה' | צדקנו. ולכן יבין כי גם' | יראה וכו' | נסי וכו' | צדקנו בשני המקומות וכו' | שמה דסוף יחזקאל בכולם יש פסוק אחר מלת ה' ובפסוק ויקרא לו אל אלהי ישראל יש טפחא במלת אל וכן בפסוק ויקרא לו ה' שלום (שופטים ו') יש טפחא בה' וזו חכמה מפוארה מבעל הטעמים להורות לנו כי גם שלכולם בשם ה' יקראו המשכילים יחידו ויבינו כי נשגב ה' לבדו ולא הנקראים בשמו וכן בבראשית רבה פרשת ל"ט משה ניסן של ישראל וגו' ופי' הוא ניסו של משה הקב"ה שנאמר ויקרא לו ה' נסי. דוד רועו של ישראל וגו' פי' הוא רועו של דוד הקב"ה שנאמר ה' רועי לא אחסר. ירושלם אורו של עולם פי' הוא אורה של ירושלם הקב"ה דכתיב והיה לך ה' לאור עולם. ובמדרש איכה רבתי על כי רחק ממני מנחם בענין שמו של משיח אמר ר' לוי טבא למדינתא דשמה כשם מלכה ושם מלכה כשם אלהיה טבא למדינתא דשמה כשם מלכה ו זיב ושם העיר מיום ה' שמה ושם מלכה כשם אלהיה שנאמר וזה שמו אשר יקראו ה' צדקנו. ועיין מה שכתבתי בפרשת שמות על משה משה ובפרשת כי משא על פסוק ויקרא בשם ה' ובסוף יחזקאל ובב"ר פ' ס"ד סימן ד' ויפה תואר שם וגם בב"ר סוף פ' ע"ט על פסוק ויקרא לו אל אלהי ישראל ובקהלת רבה ובראב"ן שם ובכוזרי בקדש סוף פ' י"ח מחלק המנורה ופ' כ"א מחלק סתרי התורה ודרך אמונה מאמר ב' סוף שער ד' ופ' ב' דמגלה ושם' שם וגור אריה

רד"ק

כמשמעו לעולם והוא אומר על קבוץ זה הגלות כמו הפרשה הבאה אחריו והוא הנכון: (ד) והקימותי. ורעום. ירעו אותם כמו הרועה הטוב: ולא יפקדו. לא יחסרו כמו ולא נפקד ממנו איש: (ה) הנה ימים באים. צמח צדיק. זהו המשיח וקראו צמח שיהי' צאתו בעולם כצאת צמח השדה שהיא רבבה כן בהיות צדיק יהיו עמו צדיקים רוב העולם כמו שאמר יפרח בימיו צדיק ואמר והוכיח עמים רבים: ומלך מלך. אמר הכפל לחזק הפעולה כי בזכור הפעול' השם נזכר עמה ובזכור אחריה השם הוא לחזק כמו למען בצוע בצע מספיר עליו ספר כל בוגדי בגד וכן ומלך מלך כי באמרו ומלך ידענו שהוא מלך והוסיפו מלך היא לחזק המלכות שתהי' מלכותו בכל הארץ לא בישראל לבד כמו שאמר עליו וישלו מים ועד ים ומנהר עד אפסי ארץ: והשכיל. הצליח וכת"י ויצלח וכן ויהי דוד לכל דרכיו משכיל ואחרים זולתו: (ו) בימיו. וזה שמו אשר יקראו ה' צדקנו. יקראו ישראל יקרא המשיח בזה השם ה' צדקנו לפי שבימיו יהיה צדק ה' לנו קיום תמיד לא יסור וזו הקריאה על דרך הקריאה שקרא משה רבינו עליו השלום למזבח ה' נסי וקרא יעקב למזבח אל אלהי ישראל כל אחד לפי ענינו הנמצא בו וכן ושם העיר מיום ה' שמה וי"ת דיהוון קרן ליה וגו'

מצודת ציון

(ד) יחתו. ענין שבר ופחד: יפקדו. ענין חסרון כמו אשר רעותם לא פקדו (שם ל"ד): (ה) והשכיל. ענין הצלחה כמו ויהי דוד לכל

מצודת דוד

אשיב אותם אל מדורם ושמה ירבו: (ד) והקמותי. אני אקים לכם רועים כשרים ושם ירעו אות' להנהיגם בדרך טובה: ולא ייראו. ולכן לא יראו עוד מן האומות ולא ישברו ולא יהיו נחסרים: (ה) והקמותי לדוד. אקים לדוד מזרעו צמח צדיק זהו מלך המשיח: ומלך מלך. מלך ימלוך על ישראל והצליח ויעשה משפט וצדקה: (ו) בימיו. בימי המשיח תושע גם יהודה גם ישראל ישכון במרגוע לבטח לא כמו בבית שני שלא חזר כ"א יהודה: וזה שמו. של המשיח אשר יקראו אותו

ly unknown, that he will be a righteous king, not like Jehoiakim and Zedekiah. Also, that there will be but one king, no longer the separate kingdoms of Judah and Israel.

6. **In his days**—I.e. in the days of the Messiah.—[*Mezudath David*]

Judah shall be saved and Israel shall dwell safely—unlike the days of the Second Temple, when only Judah was restored.—[*Mezudath David*]

that he shall be called—Lit. that he shall call him, viz. that Israel shall call the Messiah.—[*Redak*]

The Lord is our righteousness—

4. And I will set up shepherds over them and they shall pasture them, and they shall no longer fear nor shall they be dismayed, nor shall [any of them] be missing, says the Lord. 5. Behold, days are coming, says the Lord, when I will set up of David a righteous shoot, and he shall reign a king and prosper, and he shall perform judgment and righteousness in the land. 6. In his days, Judah shall be saved and Israel shall dwell safely, and this is his name that he shall be called, The Lord is our righteousness.

may also be taken as a reference to the Messianic era and interpreted literally. *Redak* is inclined to accept the second interpretation, which places these verses into the same era as the following section. *Ibn Nachmiash* and *Abarbanel* also interpret this passage in like manner.

4. **And I will set up . . . and they shall pasture them**—They will pasture them as the good shepherd does.—[*Redak*]

I.e., they will have good leaders, who will lead them on the proper way.—[*Mezudath David*]

Unlike the many years of the exile, when they had neither king nor prince, I will set up rulers over them, who will rule them properly.—[*Abarbanel*]

and they shall no longer fear—This refers to the Messianic era, when the Jews will no longer fear the nations. Unlike the days of the Second Commonwealth, when they were subordinate, sometimes to Persia, sometimes to Greece, and sometimes to Rome, thus always living in fear, they will then fear no nation.—[*Abarbanel*]

5. **of David**—In the Second Commonwealth, the kings were not of the Davidic dynasty. Consequently, this passage could not possibly refer to that era, but to the Messianic Era.—[*Abarbanel*]

a righteous shoot—This refers to the Messiah. He is called a shoot to indicate that his emergence into the world will resemble that of a shoot, which sprouts among myriads of other shoots. So will it be in Messianic times, when the Messiah reveals himself, that the majority of the world's population will be righteous men. Comp. '(Psalms 72:7) In his days, a righteous man shall blossom.' Also, '(Isaiah 2:4) And reprove many nations.'—[*Redak*]

This verse is also reminiscent of Isaiah's (11:1) And a shoot shall spring forth from the stem of Jesse.'—[*Abarbanel*]

and he shall reign a king—The double expression is for emphasis.—[*Redak*]

Abarbanel explains that the intention is that the king will be of the house of David, that he will emerge as from under the ground, previous-

צדקנו: ז לכן הנה-ימים באים נאם-
יהוה ולא-יאמרו עוד חי-יהוה אשר
העלה את-בני ישראל מארץ מצרים:
ח כי אם-חי-יהוה אשר העלה ואשר
הביא את-זרע בית ישראל מארץ
צפונה ומכל הארצות אשר הדחתים
שם וישבו על-אדמתם: ט לנבאים
נשבר לבי בקרבי רחפו כל-עצמותי
הייתי כאיש שכור וכגבר עברו יין

תרגום

מן קדם יי ביומוהי:
ז בכן הא יומיא אתן
אמר יי ולא יהון משתען
עוד בגבורתא דיי
ודאסיק ית בני ישראל
מארעא דמצרים:
ח אלהין יהון משתען
בגבורתא דיי דאסיק
ודאיתי ית זרעא דבני
ישראל מארע צפונא
ומן מדינתא דאגליתינון
לתמן ויתבון על ארעהון:
ט מן קדם נביי שקרא
אתבר לבי במעי זעו
כל גרמי הויתי כגבר
רוי וכגברא דמשתטי
מן קדם חמריה מן קדם
יי

ת"א ימים באים. ברכות יב קידושין סט עקדה בשער מב (ברכות ד) : חי ה'. נדרים יב קדושין סט:

רש"י

בימיו של זה: (ט) לנביאים נשבר לבי בקרבי. לדברי הנביאים האומרים שלום יהיה לכם נשבר לבי: רחפו. הולכים ונעים ככנפי לפור המרחף על קנו. (טרנבליר"ש בלע"ז): מפני ה'. שאני שומע ממנו גזירה רעה זאת:

רד"ק

כבעמוד: (ז) לכן. אלה שני הפסוקים נאמרו למעלה אלא שיש ביניהם שנוי מעט בקצת המלות כי כן דרך המקרא לכפול מלין או פסוקים בס"ש והענין אחד והכפל בכ"מ לחזק הענין וכבר פירשנו אלו הפסוקים למעלה במקומם: (ט) לנביאים. בעבור נביאי השקר שהם מטעי' ישראל כי לולי הם שהם אומר' שהם נביאים ודבר ה' אתם היו ישראל שבים בתשובה בתוכחות נביאי האמת אבל הם מטעים אותם ואומרים להם עשו איש כתאות לבו כי דבר ה' לנו שלא תבא עליכם רעה: רחפו. התנודדו וכן כן הכבד מרחפת על פני המים: וכגבר עברו יין. עבר עליו היין כלומר שגבר עליו ונשתכר ואינו יודע מה יעשה כן הייתי מפני ה' שהוא מחולל על ידי הנביאים

מצודת דוד

ישראל: ה' צדקנו. ה' ילדיק אותנו בימיו של זה: (ז) לכן וגו'. הואיל והגאולה ההוא תהיה חשובה כ"כ לכן לא יאמרו עוד בשבועת' חי ה' אשר העלה וגו' מארץ מצרים: (ח) כי אם. כי אז יאמרו בשבועתם חי ה' אשר העלה וגו' מארץ לפונה מאשר הרלות וגו', כי הגאולה ההיא יזכר יותר בפי האנשים לפי מרבית ההשיבות: הדחתים. הדחתי אותם (וזהו מאמר המקום כמדבר בעדו אבל הם יאמרו הדיח אותנו שם וכמדבר בעדם): וישבו. וכן יאמרו בשבועתם חי ה' אשר העלה וגו' והמה יושבים על אדמתם: (ט) לנבאים. בעבור נביאי השקר נשבר לבי בקרבי וכל עלמותי נעים ונדים ואני מבולבל כגבר כאיש שכור וכגבר אשר היין עבר עליו להתחזק ממנו ובלבל מוחו: מפני ה'. ר"ל כל הלער הזה

מהר"י קרא

זכוון מן קדם ה' ביומוהי: (ט) רחפו כל עצמותי. כמו על גוזליו ירחף: לנביאים נשבר לבי בקרבי. מפני נביאי השקר: הייתי כאיש שיכור וכגבר עברו יין. שאני שומע כפי הקב"ה שבעון שבלאה כנאפים את הארץ עתידה הארץ שתתאבל ויבשו נאות מדבר:

מנחת שי

פ' ויצלח ובעל הטורים סוף פרשת וירא על פ' ירמיה: **ולא יאמרו עוד**. ובמקלת ס"ס ולא **יאמרו עוד** ס"א **יאמרו עוד**: (ח) מארץ לפונה. אין לנו לסמוך על מסורת שבמ"ג שדברים סותרים זה את זה כמ"ג נמסר ה' חסר בירמיה וכן נמסר כאן וגם בסימן ג' וכשאציין עליהם בכתובים תמלא ג' מהם מלאים וב' חסרים ולא עוד אלא שבסימן ג' בפסוק הלך וקראת מסור עליו במס"ק ה' בסיפרא ולית חסר ואולם המוסכם מרוב ספרים המדוייקים כי כלם מלאים וכן מלאתי מסורת כ"י האומרת לפונה ה' בסיפרא ולא חילקה ביניהם בלום ממלוי וחיסור: (ט) עברו יין. בספרים מדוייקים מלרע הטעם בר"ב וכן הוא

מצודת ציון

דרכיו משכיל (ש"א י"ח): (ט) לנביאים. הלמ"ד היא במקום בעבור כמו פתח פיך לאלם (משלי ל"א): רחפו. ענין תנועה ותנודה

7. Therefore, behold days are coming, says the Lord, when
they shall no longer say, "As the Lord lives, Who brought up
the children of Israel from the land of Egypt," 8. But, "As the
Lord lives, Who brought up and Who brought the seed of the
house of Israel from the northland and from all the lands where
I have driven them, and they shall dwell on their land."
9. Because of the prophets my heart is broken within me, my
bones shake, I was like a drunken man and like a man whom
wine has overcome,

The Lord will vindicate us during this one's days.—[*Rashi, Mezudath David*]

Redak explains: God's righteousness will be with us forever. He draws a parallel between this and Moses' altar called "The Lord is my miracle,' and Jacob's altar, 'God is the God of Israel.'

7f. See above 16:14f., where the same verses appear with few changes.

Since the future redemption will be so much greater than the redemption from Egyptian bondage, the latter will not be given the importance it was given previously, but will be secondary to the later redemption when mentioned in oaths.—[*Mezudath David*]

8. **where I have driven them**—These are the words of God, not of the one swearing, who would say, ". . . where He has driven us."—[*Mezudath David*]

9. **Because of the prophets my heart is broken within me**—*Because of the words of the prophets who say, "You shall have peace," my heart is broken.*—[*Rashi*]

Because of the false prophets who mislead Israel and tell them to follow their desires, for they are endowed with prophecy and perceive this message, that no evil will befall the people.—[*Redak*]

shake —Heb. רָחֲפוּ, *sway like the wings of a bird who hovers over his nest,* (*trenblent in O.F.*) *tremble.*—[*Rashi*]

and like a man whom wine has overcome—lit. whom wine has passed over. I.e., like a man whom wine has overpowered and he has become drunk, not knowing what to do. So was I because of the Lord,

מִפְּנֵי יְהוָה וּמִפְּנֵי דִּבְרֵי קָדְשׁוֹ׃ י כִּי
מְנָאֲפִים מָלְאָה הָאָרֶץ כִּי־מִפְּנֵי אָלָה
אָבְלָה הָאָרֶץ יָבְשׁוּ נְאוֹת מִדְבָּר וַתְּהִי
מְרוּצָתָם רָעָה וּגְבוּרָתָם לֹא־כֵן׃ יא כִּי־
גַם־נָבִיא גַם־כֹּהֵן חָנֵפוּ גַּם־בְּבֵיתִי
מָצָאתִי רָעָתָם נְאֻם־יְהוָה׃ יב לָכֵן
יִהְיֶה דַרְכָּם לָהֶם כַּחֲלַקְלַקּוֹת בָּאֲפֵלָה
יִדַּחוּ וְנָפְלוּ בָהּ כִּי־אָבִיא עֲלֵיהֶם רָעָה
שנת

תרגום

יְיָ וּמִן קֳדָם פִּתְגָמֵי קוּדְשֵׁיהּ׃ י אֲרֵי וְגָאִין אִתְמְלִיאַת אַרְעָא אֲרֵי מִן קֳדָם מוֹמֵי דִשְׁקַר חֲרוּבַת אַרְעָא יְבִישׁוּ דִירָנַת מַדְבְּרָא וְעַל דִסְגַן בְּרָעוּת נַפְשֵׁיהוֹן בִּישְׁתָא תֵיתֵי עֲלֵיהוֹן וְגִבְרַהוֹן לָא יַצְלְחוּן׃ יא אֲרֵי אַף סָפַר אַף כָּהֵן גְנִיבוּ אוֹרְחַתְהוֹן אַף בְּבֵית מַקְדְשִׁי גַלְיָן קֳדָמַי בִּישַׁתְהוֹן אֲמַר יְיָ׃ יב בְּכֵן תְּהֵי אוֹרְחַתְהוֹן לְהוֹן כְּמַשְׁרוּעִין בְּקִבְלָא יִתְקְלוּן וְיִפְּלוּן בַּהּ אֲרֵי
איתי

ת"א מפני אלה. קידושין יג שבועות לט:

פתח במקום קמץ מלעיל

מהר"י קרא

(י) ותהי מרוצתם רעה. כלומר לרע ירוצו: וגבורתם לא כן. לא נכונה: (יב) לכן יהיה דרכם להם. אפילו ביום: כחלקלקות באפילה. חלקלקות פת' כמו במקום חלק שאדם מחליק שם רגליו כשהוא מהלך במקו' אפילה ואינו נזהר על אותו חלק ונופל שם אם ידיחוהו שם שאינו יכול לעמוד על רגליו ונופל מפני כמה דברים. אחת שהוא מקום חלק ואחת שהוא מקום אפילה ומי יוכל לעמוד כפני שני דברים הללו ובבא הדיחה שמדיחין אותו ואינו יכול לעמוד כל עיקר וזה הוא ידחו ונפלו בה:

רש"י

(י) מפני אלה. שבועת שקר: אבלה. חרבה: מרוצתם. (קורס"א בלע"ז) וי"ת ל' רצון: לא כן. לא כדין: (יא) גם נביא גם כהן. אפי' אלו שהכל למידין מהם: גם בביתי מצאתי רעתם. שהעמידו דמות בהיכל: (יב) כחלקלקו'. ארץ חלקה שהרגל מחלקת בה והאדם נופל: כחלקלקות באפלה. כשלון על כשלון חלקלקות באור יש כשלון אפלה

מנחת שי

בדפוסים ראשונים: (יב) ידחו. מלעיל שלא כמנהג מכלול דף קנ"ו:

רד"ק

האלה: ומפני דברי קדשו. שהם מחוללים על פיהם שהם אומרים כי דברי ה' הם מה שהם אומרים: (י) כי מנאפים. איך יוכלו ליפות מהם מעשיהם והנה מנאפים מלאה הארץ ועוד כי מפני אלה אבלה הארץ ומפני שבועות שקר נשחתה הארץ אלו שתי הרעות הם ברוב אנשי הארץ ואיך יוכלו נביאי השקר להטעותם כי לא תבא עליהם רעה והנה הם רואים בעיניהם כי רוב א"י נשחתה מפני רוב מעשיהם הרעים: נאות מדבר. מקום מרעה הבהמות: ותהי מרוצתם רעה. זריזותם ומרוצתם הם לרעה כי לא ירוצו לדבר מצוה ולעבודת האל אלא לרעה: וגבורתם לא כן. וכן גבורתם אינה לדבר אמת: כן. פירושו אמת כמו כן בנות צלפחד דוברות שהיה להם להתגבר על נביאי השקר ולמנעם מלספר חלומותם ודברי שקריהם והם מתגברים על נביאי האמת ואומרים להם שלא יתנבאו בשם ה' כמו שאמרו לירמיהו לא תתנבא בשם ה' ולא תמות בידינו וי"ת מרוצ:ם ענין רצון וכן תרגם ועל דמסגן ברעות נפשהון בישתא תיתי עליהון וגבריהון לא יצלחון: (יא) כי גם נביא גם כהן חנפו. בצרי בגזרת פעל ופי' נביא וכהן כתרגומו ארי אף ספר אף כהן ר"ל ספר מזהיר העם כי נבואה ענין דבור ויש מהם דבור רוח הקדש ויש מהם דבור דברי שקר כדברי נביאי השקר וכן מזהיר העם מדבר להם לפי דעתו דברים להזהירם וכהן הוא מכהני הלוים כמ"ש גם בביתי מצאתי רעתם: חנפו. ענין רשע וכשוא פנים ות"י גניבו ארחתהון: גם בביתי. כי גם בבית המקדש היו עובדים ומזבחים לאלהים אחרים: (יב) לכן יהיה. כחלקלקות באפלה. כמו דרכים חלקלקות שתמעד רגל ההולך בהם כל שכן כשתהיה אפלה שלא יראה אנה יסמוך ואנה ילך: ידחו ונפלו בה. כאילו ידחה אותם דוחה מאחריהם כי על פנים יפלו בה

מצודת ציון

כמו על גוזליו ירחף (דברים ל"ב): (י) אלה. ענין שבועה כמו ושמעה קול אלה (ויקרא ה'): אבלה. ענין השממה כמו על כן תאבל הארץ (הושע ד'): נאות. ענין מדור כמו בנאות דשא (תהלי' כ"ג): מדבר. לפעמים יאמר לשון מדבר על מקום המרעה הסמוך למדבר כמ"ש הצאן הסגה במדבר (ש"א י"ז): מרוצתם. מל' ריצה ומהירות ההליכה: כן. נכון ואמת כמו לא כן בדיו (ישעיה ט"ז): (יב) כחלקלקות. מלשון חלק: באפלה. ענין חושך: פקודתם.

מצודת דוד

סוא עלי מפני ה' שהיה מחולל ע"י הנביאים האלה ומפני דברי קדשו שהמה מחוללים על פיהם: (י) כי מנאפים. כי על ידיהם מלאה הארץ נאוף וזנות: כי מפני אלה. בעבור שבועת שוא השמה כסנתם תשחת הארץ וייבשו מדורי המדבר מקום מרעה הצאן: מרוצתם. מה שהם רצים לעשות בזריזות הוא רק לרעה ולא לטובה: וגבורתם. הגבורת הלב שבהם איננה על דבר נכון ואמת: (יא) נביא. זה נביא שקר: כהן. זה כהן הבעל: חנפו. מחניפים לבני אדם ואינם אומרים האמת: גם בביתי. בבהמ"ק מצאתי רעתם כי היו מזבחים בה לאלהים אחרים: (יב) דרכם להם. ר"ל יוכשלו בדרכם כמו ההולך באפלה במקום חלק שהוא נוח שימעדו רגליו: ידחו.

their evil—*For they placed an image in the Temple.*—[*Rashi*]

For even in the Temple they would worship and sacrifice to other gods.—[*Redak*]

Redak takes this passage as an indication that it is the Levitical priests, who performed the Temple service, that are meant in this verse.

12. **like slippery places**—*Smooth ground upon which the foot slips and the person falls.*—[*Rashi*]

like slippery places in the dark—*Stumbling upon stumbling.* On *slip-*

because of the Lord and because of His holy words. 10. For the
land is full of adulterers, for because of oaths the land mourns,
the dwellings in the wilderness are dried out, and their eager-
ness was evil and their power not right. 11. For both prophet
and priest are false; even in My house have I found their evil,
says the Lord. 12. Therefore, their way shall be for them like
slippery places in the dark; let them be thrust and fall therein,
for I will bring evil upon them,

Who is profaned by these prophets. —[*Redak*]

and because of His holy words—which are profaned by these prophets, who claim to have the words of the Lord.—[*Redak*]

Abarbanel understands this to mean that Jeremiah was upset by the fact that he would lose control of his faculties when the spirit of prophecy would come upon him, while the false prophets would experience nothing of this sort. They would prophesy although engaged in physical pleasures such as adultery.

10. **For the land is full of adulterers**—How can they praise the people's deeds, when the land is full of adulterers and because of false oaths the land mourns? These two evils have spread throughout most of the inhabitants of the land. How then can the false prophets mislead the people to believe that no evil will befall them when they see with their own eyes that most of the land has been destroyed because of their evil deeds?—[*Redak*]

Abarbanel explains that these were the sins of the prophets.

Ibn Nachmiash interprets 'adulterers' figuratively, meaning idolators, since idolatry is frequently represented by the prophets by 'adultery.'

not right—*Not according to the law.*—[*Rashi*] Heb. לֹא כֵן. They do not use their might for matters of truth. Instead of using their power to stop the false prophets from telling their dreams and their lies, they overwhelm the true prophets and tell them not to prophesy, as they did to Jeremiah, when they threatened him with death.—[*Redak*]

Jonathan renders: And their mighty men shall not prosper.

11. **both prophet and priest**—*Even these, from whom everyone learns.*—[*Rashi*]

Jonathan renders: For even the scribe, even the priest. 'The scribe' denotes one who admonishes the people. נָבִיא denotes 'speaker,' either one who speaks with divine inspiration or one who speaks lies like the false prophets, and also the teacher of the people who speaks to them to admonish them. The 'priests' are the Levitic priests who served in the Temple.—[*Redak*] *Mezudath David* defines it as a priest of Baal.

are false—Heb. חָנֵפוּ, an expression of wickedness and flattery.—[*Redak*]

even in My house have I found

שְׁנַת פְּקֻדָּתָם נְאֻם־יְהוָה׃ יג וּבִנְבִיאֵי
שֹׁמְרוֹן רָאִיתִי תִפְלָה הִנַּבְּאוּ בַבַּעַל
וַיַּתְעוּ אֶת־עַמִּי אֶת־יִשְׂרָאֵל׃ יד וּבִנְבִאֵי
יְרוּשָׁלִַם רָאִיתִי שַׁעֲרוּרָה נָאוֹף וְהָלֹךְ
בַּשֶּׁקֶר וְחִזְּקוּ יְדֵי מְרֵעִים לְבִלְתִּי־שָׁבוּ
אִישׁ מֵרָעָתוֹ הָיוּ־לִי כֻלָּם כִּסְדֹם וְיֹשְׁבֶיהָ
כַּעֲמֹרָה׃ טו לָכֵן כֹּה־אָמַר יְהוָה צְבָאוֹת
עַל־הַנְּבִאִים הִנְנִי מַאֲכִיל אוֹתָם לַעֲנָה
וְהִשְׁקִתִים מֵי־רֹאשׁ כִּי מֵאֵת נְבִיאֵי
יְרוּשָׁלִַם יָצְאָה חֲנֻפָּה לְכָל־הָאָרֶץ׃

תרגום

אַיְתֵי עֲלֵיהוֹן בִּישְׁתָא
שְׁנַת סְעוֹרַן הוֹבֵיהוֹן
אֲמַר יְיָ׃ יג וּבִנְבִיֵי שֹׁמְרוֹן
חֲזֵיתִי רְשַׁע מִתְנַבַּן
בְּשׁוּם טַעֲוְתָא וּמַטְעַן
יַת עַמִּי יַת יִשְׂרָאֵל׃
יד וּבִנְבִיֵי יְרוּשְׁלֵם חֲזֵיתִי
שְׁנוּ זַנְאִין וּמְהַלְכִין
בְּשִׁקַר וּמִתְקְפִין יַד
מִבְאֲשִׁין בְּדִיל דְלָא
לְמֵיתַב גְבַר מִן בִּישְׁתֵיהּ
הֲווֹ קֳדָמַי כּוּלְהוֹן כִּסְדוֹם
וְיָתְבָהָא כַּעֲמוֹרָה׃
טו בְּכֵן כִּדְנַן אֲמַר יְיָ
צְבָאוֹת עַל נְבִיֵי שִׁקְרָא
הָאֲנָא מַיְתֵי עֲלֵיהוֹן עָקָא
מְרַר כְּגִידִין וְאַשְׁקֵינוּן
כָּס דִלְוָט בִּישׁ כְּרֵישֵׁי
חִיוִין אֲרֵי מִן נְבִיֵי
יְרוּשְׁלֵם נְפַקִית חַנֻפְּתָא

רש"י

בלא חלקלקות יש כשלון: (יג) ובנביאי שומרון ראיתי תפלה. קודש נגלו: (יד) ובנביאי ירושלם. אני רואה עתה: שערורה. דבר מגונה: וחזקו ידי מריעים. אומרים לרשעי' שלום יהיה לכם: לבלתי שבו. שלא ישובו

רד"ק

ולרוב מחירות הנפיל' זכר בה שלש סבות חלקות הדרך והאפלה והדחיה: ידחו. מלעיל שלא כמנהג נחי הלמ"ד:

(יג) ובנביאי שומרון. תפל'. כמו נביאיך חזו לך שוא והפל ולא נתן תפלה ענין דבר גרוע שאין לו טעם: הנבאו בבעל. כי אחאב עבד את הבעל וקמו נביאי שקר רבים מתנבאים בבעל שהיו ד' מאות וחמשים איש בימי אחאב שהרג' אליהו ואחרי כן קמו אחרים שהרג יהוא והם היו מתעים את ישראל עד שגלו בעתם אבל בירושלים לא קמו נביאי הבע' ולא עבדו לבעל מלכי יהודה כי אם מנשה ואחרי כן שב בתשוב': הנבאו. חסר ת"ו התפעל ומשפטו התנבאו: (יד) ובנביאי ירושלי'. לא התנבאו בבעל אבל היתה בהם דרך רעה: שערורה. פירש רשע ולכלוך: נאוף. כמ"ש בצדקיהו ובאחאב וינאפו את נשי רעיה': והלוך בשקר. שהיו אומרים כי דבר ה' בהם: וחזקו ידי מרעים. שהיו אומרים להם שלום יהי' לכם לפיכך לא היו שבים מרעת': לבלתי שבו. שלא שבו כלומר הם גרמו להם שלא שבו וכן לבלתי תקריב שלא להקריב לבלתי ראו אומרים מה שלא ראו: כסדום. כאנשי סדום: ויושביה כעמורה. ויושבי ירושלים כאנשי עמורה כלומר הנביאים כעם והעם כנביאים ברשע ובמעשים רעים: (טו) לכן. מאכיל אותם לענה. אביא עליהם צרה מרה כלענה וכמי ראש והוא סם הכות: חנופה. רשע ונשוא פנים שהם

מנחת שי

(טו) חנפה. הנו"ן בשלש נקודות והפ"א בדגש:

מצודת דוד

יהיו נדחים ממקומם ויפלו בדרך: כי אביא. כזה יפרש לאשית המקרא לומר המכשול יהיה כי אביא הרעה: פקודתם. זכרון פעולותיהם לשלם עליהם גמול: (יג) ובנביאי שומרון. ר"ל כמו שמאז ראיתי בנביאי שומרון דבר גרוע מבלי טעם וזהו מה שנבאו בשם הבעל והתעו את עמי ללכ' בדרך רעה: (יד) ובנביאי ירושלי'. ר"ל כן אני רואה בנביאי ירושלים דבר מגונה וזהו שהמה שטופים בניאוף והולכים בדרך שקר ומחזקים ידי רשעים לבל ישובו מרעתם כי מנבאים להם לשלום: כלם. כל בני יהודה: ויושביה. יושבי ירושלים: (טו) הנני מאכיל וגו'. ר"ל אביא עליהם לחץ מרורות וגדולות: כי מאת וגו'. על ידיהם יצאה חנופה לכל הארץ ר"ל

מצודת ציון

ענין זכרון: (יג) תפלה. ענין דבר גרוע מבלי טעם וכן ולא נתן תפלה לאלהים (איוב א'): ויתעו. לשון תועה: (יד) שערורה. ענין דבר מגונה כמו שמה ושערורה (לעיל ה'): נאוף. ענין זנות: מרעים. רשעים: (טו) לענה. מין עשב מר: והשקיתים. ענין שתייה: מי ראש. מי סחיטת עשב מר ששמו ראש כמו וישקנו מי

wormwood and poisonous water.—[*Redak*]

falseness—Wickedness and flattery, for they would praise their deeds and favor them not to reprove them.—[*Redak*]

to all the land—To all the inhabitants of the land.—[*Redak*]

the year of their visitation, says the Lord. 13. And in the
prophets of Samaria I saw unseemliness; they prophesied by
Baal and misled My people Israel. 14. And in the prophets of
Jerusalem I saw a horrible thing, committing adultery and
going with falseness, and they encouraged evil-doers, that none
returns from his evil; all of them were to Me as Sodom and her
inhabitants as Gemorrah. 15. Therefore, so said the Lord of
Hosts concerning the prophets: Behold I will feed them worm-
wood and give them poisonous water to drink, for from the
prophets of Jerusalem has falseness emanated to the whole
land.

pery places in the light there is stumbling. In *the dark without slippery places, there is stumbling.*—[*Rashi*]

13. **And in the prophets of Samaria I saw unseemliness**—*before they were exiled.*—[*Rashi*]

unseemliness—Heb. תִּפְלָה, something improper that has no reason. —[*Redak*]

they prophesied by Baal—Because Ahab worshipped Baal, and many false prophets arose, prophesying by Baal, for there were four hundred and fifty men in Ahab's time slain by Elijah. Later, others arose and were slain by Jehu. These prophets misled Israel until they were exiled because of their iniquity. In Jerusalem, however, no prophets of Baal arose, and the kings of Judah did not worship Baal, except Manasseh who later repented.—[*Redak*]

14. **And in the prophets of Jerusalem**—*I now see.*—[*Rashi*]

a horrible thing—Heb. שַׁעֲרוּרָה, *a shameful thing.*—[*Rashi*]

Redak renders: wickedness and contamination. See above 18:13.

committing adultery—As below (29:23), concerning Ahab and Zedekiah, 'and they committed adultery with their friends' wives.'—[*Redak*]

and going with falseness—For they said that the Lord had spoken to them.—[*Redak*]

and they encouraged evil-doers —*They say to the wicked, "You shall have peace."*—[*Rashi*]

Therefore, the people did not repent of their evil deeds.—[*Redak*]

that none returns—*So that the evil-doers would not return each one from his evil.*—[*Rashi*]

as Sodom—As the people of Sodom.—[*Redak*]

and her inhabitants as Gemorrah —And the inhabitants of Jerusalem like the inhabitants of Gemorrah. I.e., as the prophets so was the people, and as the people, so were the prophets in wickedness and evil deeds.—[*Redak*]

15. **feed them wormwood**—I will bring upon them trouble as bitter as

טו כֹּה־אָמַר יְהוָה צְבָאוֹת אַל־תִּשְׁמְעוּ
עַל־דִּבְרֵי הַנְּבִאִים הַנִּבְּאִים לָכֶם
מַהְבִּלִים הֵמָּה אֶתְכֶם חֲזוֹן לִבָּם יְדַבֵּרוּ
לֹא מִפִּי יְהוָה׃ יז אֹמְרִים אָמוֹר לִמְנַאֲצַי
דִּבֶּר יְהוָה שָׁלוֹם יִהְיֶה לָכֶם וְכֹל הֹלֵךְ
בִּשְׁרִרוּת לִבּוֹ אָמְרוּ לֹא־תָבוֹא עֲלֵיכֶם
רָעָה׃ יח כִּי מִי עָמַד בְּסוֹד יְהוָה וְיֵרֶא
וְיִשְׁמַע אֶת־דְּבָרוֹ מִי־הִקְשִׁיב דְּבָרִי
וַיִּשְׁמָע׃ יט הִנֵּה ׀ סַעֲרַת יְהוָה חֵמָה

יצאה

דברו קרי

ת"א הנה סערת. חגיגה יג:

תרגום

לכל יתבי ארעא:
טו כדנן אמר יי צבאות
לא תקבלון לפתגמי
נביי שקרא דמתנבן
לכון מטען אינון לכון
רשע לבהון ממללין לא
במימרא דיי: יז אמרין
בנבואת שקריהון
לדמרגזין קדמי מליל יי
שלמא יהא לכון וכל
דאזיל בהרהור לביה
אמרין לא תיתי עליכון
בישתא: יח ארי לא
קמו ואתגלי להון רז
מן קדם יי ולא חזו ולא
שמעו ית פתגמוהי ולא
אציתו למימרה ולא
קבילו: יט הא מזופיתא
מן

רש"י

המריעים איש מרעהו: (יז) וכל הולך בשרירות לבו וגו'. ולכל הולך בשרירות לבו וגו': (יח) מי עמד בסוד ה'. וישמע את הנגזר מלפניו אותו שהקשיב דבר תורתו

מהר"י קרא

(יח) כי מי עמד בסוד ה'. כלומר הנביא העומד בסוד ה': וירא וישמע. את דבר ה' ומי ששמע מגיד לעמו. אבל מי בכם נביאי השקר שהקשיב דבר ה' וישמע: (יט) הנה. אני רואה: סערת ה' חמה יצאה וסער מתחולל. היכן. על ראש רשעים

מנחת שי

(יז) וכל הלך בשררות. מלא הלך חסר וא"ו בספרים כ"י מדויקים והדפוסים ישנים גם בא"ג לא נמנה עם המלאים בנביאים: (יח) דברי. דברו ק':

רד"ק

מיפים להם מעשיהם ונושאים פניהם שלא להוכיחם: לכל הארץ. לכל יושבי ארץ יהודה: (טז) כה אמר. על דברי הנביאים. כמו אל דברי וכן וילך אלקנה הרמתה על ביתו ונתן הספר על אשר לא ידע ספר כמו אל: מהבילים. מפתים אתכם לדברי הבל לאמר שלום יהיה לכם כי החזון שהם אומרים מלבם הוא לא כפי ה': (יז) אומרים אמור. המקור הוא ברוב קודם הפעל וכאשר יבא אחרי הפעל הוא לחזק הפעולה כמו ויברך ברוך אתכם והדומים לו: וכל הולך בשרירות לבו. כמו ולכל הולך ולמ"ד למנאצי שוכר עומדת במקום שנים: (יח) כי מי עמד. כי מי מהם שעמד בסוד השם רוצה לומר בסוד הנבואה ואיך יאמרו כי דבר השם אתם: וירא. פי' במראה הנבואה: וישמע. הראשון בשוא הוי"ו והשני בפתח הוי"ו: (יט) הנה סערת ה' חמה יצאה. עבר במקום עתיד כדרך הנבואות במקומות רבים כי דבר ה' הנבוא' קיים כאילו נעשה והנבואה הזאת עתיד' ליםות המשיח כי אז יכלו הרשעים כלם ואמר זה הענין על דבר נביאי השקר הרשעים כי כבר אמר כי יעשה משפט בהם כמ"ש הנני מאכיל אותם לענה ואמר אף על פי שאין האל עשה משפט ברשעים כלם הנה ימים באים שתצא סערת ה': חמה יצאה. כחמת תצא אותה הסערה מלפני האל ותחול על הרשעים עד כלותם: וסער מתחולל.

מצודת ציון

לבם (לעיל ה'): (טז) מהבלים. מלשון הבל: חזון. ענין ראיה. ופ"ה רוב יאמר על מראה הנבואה: (יז) למנאצי. ענין בזיון כמו כי נאצו האנשי' את מנחת ה' (ש"א ב'): וכל. כמו ולכל: בשרירות. ענין ראיה ר"ל מה שהלב רואה וחומד: (יח) בסוד. ר"ל מקום כששפעת הנבואה: הקשיב. ענין האזנה וקבלה: (יט) סערת. רוח סערה: חמה. כמו בחמה: מתחולל. מלשון חיל וחלחלה:

מצודת דוד

כולם מחניפים ליצרם למלאות תאותם: (טז) על דברי. אל דברי: מהבלים. אומרים לכם דברי הבל: חזון לבם. מראות לבם ידברו כי לא ראו בנבואה רק בודים מלבם: (יז) אומרים אמור. רגילים הם לומר להרשעים המנאצים אותי ה' דבר שלום יהיה לכם: וכל הולך. ולכל ההולך בשרירות לבו אמרו וגו': (יח) כי מי עמד. נתן טעם למה לא ישמעו אליהם באמרו כי מי מאלה עמד בסוד ה' לקבל נבואה ומי ראה מראות הנבואה ומי מהם שמע את דברו כי בהיות' רשעים אינם ראויים לנבואה: מי הקשיב. אמנם מי שהקשיב דברו כירמיה שהקשיב בקול ה' ועשה מצותיו הוא השומע הנבואה ולא הרשעים האלה: (יט) חמה יצאה. תצא בחמה עבר במקום עתיד: וסער מתחולל. הסער הזה הוא מלא מחלחלה ורעד והוא יחיה

denied God's word, but followed their own heretic thoughts, the prophets would say, "No evil shall befall you." In verse 18, he elaborates on the theory that there is no prophecy. 'For who stood in the council of the Lord and will see and hear His word?' It is impossible for a man to stand and to know the counsel of the Lord, for it is impossible for him to see or hear God's message, for spirit cannot be perceived by the physical eye, neither can a spiritual message be heard by the physical ear. 'Who hearkened to His word and heard?' Even a *bath-kol,* a heavenly voice, heard from a distance, is impossible, for the human ear cannot hear a spiritual voice. In this way, Jeremiah

16. So said the Lord of Hosts: Do not hearken to the words of
the prophets who prophesy for you; they mislead you. The
vision of their heart they speak, not from the mouth of the
Lord. 17. They say to those who despise Me, "The Lord has
spoken, 'You shall have peace,'" and [to] everyone who follows
the view of his heart they say, "No evil shall befall you."
18. For who stood in the council of the Lord and will see and
hear His word? He who hearkened to His word and listened.
19. Behold a storm from the Lord has gone forth [with] fury,

16. **Do not hearken**—He warns the people not to heed the false prophets.—[*Malbim*]

they mislead you—Heb. מְהַבְּלִים, from the root הֶבֶל, *futility*. They entice you with futile words, saying that you shall have peace, for the vision they tell you is from their own heart, not from the mouth of the Lord.—[*Redak*]

Others interpret simply: They tell you words of futility.—[*Mezudath David, Malbim*]

The vision of their heart they speak—Sometimes people tell lies in the name of the Lord. The statement itself, however, is not futile but is of some use. In this case, however, these prophets speak both lies and futile words.—[*Malbim*]

Jonathan renders: The wickedness of their hearts they speak.

17. **They say**—They constantly say to the wicked who despise Me, "You shall have peace."—[*Mezudath David*]

and everyone who follows the view of his heart—*And to everyone who follows the view of his heart etc.*—[*Rashi, Redak, Mezudath David*]

18. **For who stood in the council of the Lord**—*and will hear what is decreed by Him? He who hearkened to the word of His Torah and listened to His commandments, but not these wicked men. The first* expression of שְׁמִיעָה *in the verse is actual hearing; the latter* expression of שְׁמִיעָה *is an expression of acceptance.*—[*Rashi*]

The intention is that these prophets, who did not obey God's commandments surely did not stand in His council and were surely not permitted to see visions of prophecy or to hear words of prophecy. Only Jeremiah and those like him, who hearkened to the word of the Lord are endowed with the spirit of prophecy.—[*Mezudath David*]

Malbim explains that the false prophets addressed two groups, one who believed in prophecy, but despised God, and one who denied the possibility of prophecy. These denied that there was any contact between God and man. To the former the prophet would say, "The Lord spoke, 'You shall have peace.'" To the latter, whom Scripture calls 'everyone who follows the view of his heart,' i.e. those who

יֵצֵאָה וְסַעַר מִתְחוֹלֵל עַל רֹאשׁ רְשָׁעִים
יָחוּל׃ כ לֹא יָשׁוּב אַף־יְהוָה עַד־עֲשֹׂתוֹ
וְעַד־הֲקִימוֹ מְזִמּוֹת לִבּוֹ בְּאַחֲרִית
הַיָּמִים תִּתְבּוֹנְנוּ בָהּ בִּינָה׃ כא לֹא־
שָׁלַחְתִּי אֶת־הַנְּבִאִים וְהֵם רָצוּ לֹא־
דִבַּרְתִּי אֲלֵיהֶם וְהֵם נִבָּאוּ׃ כב וְאִם־
עָמְדוּ בְּסוֹדִי וְיַשְׁמִעוּ דְבָרַי אֶת־עַמִּי
וִישִׁבוּם מִדַּרְכָּם הָרָע וּמֵרֹעַ מַעַלְלֵיהֶם׃
כג הַאֱלֹהֵי מִקָּרֹב אָנִי נְאֻם־יְהוָה וְלֹא

מִן קֳדָם יְיָ בִּרְגַז נָפְקַת
וְעַלְעוֹל מִשְׁתַּגַשׁ עַל
רֵישׁ רַשִׁיעִין יָחוּל׃
כ לָא יְהוּב רוּגְזָא דַייָ
עַד דְיַעְבֵּד וְעַד דִיקַיֵם
מַחְשְׁבַת רְעוּתֵיהּ בְּסוֹף
יוֹמַיָא תִסְתַּכְּלוּן בַּהּ
אִסְתַּכָּלָא׃ כא לָא שְׁלָחִית
יַת נְבִיֵי שִׁקְרָא וְאִינוּן
רְהַטִין לְאַבְאָשָׁא וְלָא
מַלֵלִית עִמְהוֹן וְאִינוּן
מִתְנַבָּן שְׁקַר׃ כב וְאִלוּ
קָמוּ אִתְגְלֵי לְהוֹן רָז מִן
קֳדָם יְיָ וְאַשְׁמָעוּ פִּתְגָמַי
יַת עַמִי וַאֲתִיבִינוּן
מֵאוֹרְחַתְהוֹן בִּישְׁתָא
וּמִבִּישׁוּת עוֹבָדֵיהוֹן׃
כג אֲנָא אֱלָהָא בְּרֵית

קבץ בשרחא

רש"י

ישמע למלותיו ולא הרשעי' האלה. שמיעה הראשונה שבמקרא זה שמיעה ממש שמיעה האחרונה קבלה: (יט) מתחולל. השוכן מהזר לשכון ועל ראש רשעים ישכון: (כ) מזמות. לשון מחשבה: (כב) ואם עמדו בסודי וישמיעו דברי וגו'. היה להם להשמיע דברי ותורתי את עמי ולא להטעות' בה מעלי: (כג) האלהי מקרוב. שאיני רואה אלא בסמוך

מהר"י קרא

יהול. והמה. מתנבאים המה לשלום: (כ) באחרית הימים התבוננו בה בינה. כשתבא אליכם הרעה אז תדעו עם מי האמת או עמי שאני מתנבא לכם לרעה או עם נביאי השקר שמתנבאים לכם לשלום. ד"א באחרית. הימים תתבוננו. על מה עשה ה' ככה לכם: (כא) לא שלחתי. את נביאי השקר והם רצו: (כב) ואם עמדו בסודי. כלומר אילו עמדו בסודי עתה ישמיעו דברי את עמי כדי להשיבם מדרכם הרעה: (כג) האלהי מקרוב אני. פתרונו וכי כה שאדם עושה בגלוי במפרסם כל כך אני רואה ואין אני רואה כשאדם מרחיק את עצמו כמני להסתיר במסתרים ולעשות במחשך מעשהו ואם יסתר איש במסתרים ואני לא אראנו הלא את השמים ואת הארץ אני מלא:

רד"ק

כפל הענין לחזק הדבר וי"ת בהפרש מעט בינידם שתרגם סערה מזופיתא והרגם וסער מהחולל ועלעול משתגש וענין מתהולל ויהול ענין נפילה ותניה כמו יחילו על ראש יואב: (כ) לא ישוב. באחרית הימים. זהו בימות המשיח ואז תתבוננו בזאת הנבואה כי עד אות' הימים הרי אתם כאלו אינכם מתבוננים בה לפי שאינכם רואים כליון הרשעים ובאמרו בינה אחר תתבוננו הוא לתוספת ביאור ולחזק הפעולה כמו קצף ה' על אבותיכם קצף ויצם דוד צום למען טבוח טבח והדומים להם ובאמרו תתבוננו ולא אמר יתבוננו רמז לתחיית המתים בימות המשיח: (כא) לא שלחתי את הנביאים. אלה נביאי השקר אני לא שלחתי אותם: והם רצו. כהרו לומר לעם דברי' אשר בדו מלבם בשמי: (כב) ואם עמדו בסודי. ואם הוא כמו שהם אומרים שעמדו בסודי ודבר הנבואה באה להם מאתי ישמיעו את דברי אל עמי לא דבר שקר וישיבום מדרכם הרעה לא שיחזיקו ידי מרעים. וי"ו וישמיעו כוי"ו וטמאה שבעים כנדהה ונתתי גשמיכם והדומים להם שהוא לתנאי כלומר אם יהיה זה יהיה זה: (כג) האלהי מקרוב. כמו אלהים אחרים שיאמר עליהם חדשים מקרוב באו וכי אינני אלהי מרחיק הלא מבריאת עולם ידעוני בני אדם כי אני אלהי עולם ואינני כמו

מנחת שי

(כא) לא שלחתי את הנבאים. במקצת מדוייקים חסר יו"ד קדמאה וכן נכון ע"פ המסורה דסיפרא פי' כ"ו: (כב) וישמעו. במקצת ס"ס הקדמונים חסר יו"ד וכן נמסר עליו לית וחסר:

מצודת דוד

אל ושוכן על ראש הרשעים האלה הם נביאי השקר: (כ) לא ישוב וגו'. לא ישוב מהם חרון אפו עד יעשה ויקיים מחשבות לבו: באחרית הימים. ר"ל אם יתמהמה הנה בסוף הימים כשתתקיים ההבונו בה בינה שלא שב ה' מחרון אפו עם כי נתארך הזמן: (כא) והם רצו. במהירות רב כאלו היו שלוחים בדבר: והם נבאו. מלבם ולא שמעו ממני: (כב) ואם עמדו בסודי. ר"ל אם היא כדבריהם שעמדו בסודי לקבל נבואה היה ראוי שישמיעו לעמי את דברי אשר דברתי בתורתי ולהשיבם מדרכם הרע ולא להכשילם ביד בעבירה: (כג) האלהי מקרוב אני. ר"ל וכי אינני רואה ומשגיח אלא בסמוך לי ולא את התחתוני' שהמה רחוקי' ממכון שבתי בשמי':

מצודת ציון

יחול. ישכון כמו יחולו על ראש יואב (ש"ב ג'): (כ) הקימו. מל' קיום: מזמות. מחשבות כמו זממה שדה (משלי ל"א): באחרית. בסוף: (כא) רצו. מלשון מרוצה ומהירות ההליכה: (כב) וישיבום.

announces that He never sent them and that their prophecy is entirely false.

22. **And if they stood in My council, they should have let My people hear My word etc.**—*They should have let My people hear My words and My Torah, rather than cause them to stray away from Me.*—[*Rashi*]

23. **Am I a God from near**—*that I do not see but what is close to Me, and have I no power to judge the lower creatures that are far from Me and do I not know of their deeds?*—[*Rashi*]

yea, a whirling storm, on the heads of the wicked it shall rest.
20. The Lord's anger shall not return until He executes it and
until He fulfills the plans of His heart. At the end of days, you
shall consider it perfectly. 21. I did not send the prophets, yet
they ran; I did not speak to them, yet they prophesied.
22. And if they stood in My council, they should have let My
people hear My words, so that they bring them back from their
evil way and from the evil of their deeds. 23. Am I a God from
near, says the Lord, and not

exposes the false prophets, who preach their false prophecy to those who believe in prophecy and deny prophecy to those who do not believe in it.

19. **a whirling**—Heb. מִתְחוֹלֵל an expression of shuddering and quaking.—[*Mezudath David, Mezudath Zion*] *Rashi,* however, renders: A *resting* storm, a storm which *seeks to rest, and it shall rest on the heads of the wicked.*—[*Rashi*] *Redak,* too, explains this in that manner.

According to *Malbim,* this is directed against the two groups mentioned above. Although the prophets have assured them that they will have peace and that no harm will befall them, God's fury has already gone forth. That is the storm of the Lord which whirls and whirls until it rests on the heads of the wicked.

20. **the plans of**—Heb. מְזִמּוֹת, *an expression of thought.*—[*Rashi*]

at the end of days—This denotes the Messianic era. Then you will consider this prophecy, for, until those days, you do not consider it since you do not witness the destruction of the wicked. The use of the second person rather than the third, denotes the resurrection of the dead that will take place at that time. Therefore, he addresses his own generation, who will be present at the end of days.—[*Redak*]

Rabbi Joseph Kara explains 'the end of days' as the time the prophecy will be fulfilled. When evil befalls you, you will consider whether the truth is with me, who prophesies evil, or with the false prophets, who prophesy peace for you. Another explanation: You will consider why God did this to you.

21. **I did not send the prophets**—I did not send these false prophets.—[*Redak*]

yet they ran—They hastened to tell the people the prophecy that they fabricated.—[*Redak*] They hastened as though they were sent on an errand.—[*Mezudath David*]

Jonathan renders: Yet they run to do evil.

yet they prophesied—They prophesy what they themselves have fabricated.—[*Mezudath David*]

According to *Malbim,* this is directed toward those who believe in prophecy, yet despise the Lord. To them, the prophets preach that God has assured them of peace. God

אֱלֹהֵי מֵרָחֹק: כד אִם־יִסָּתֵר אִישׁ
בַּמִּסְתָּרִים וַאֲנִי לֹא־אֶרְאֶנּוּ נְאֻם־יְהוָה
הֲלוֹא אֶת־הַשָּׁמַיִם וְאֶת־הָאָרֶץ אֲנִי
מָלֵא נְאֻם־יְהוָה: כה שָׁמַעְתִּי אֵת אֲשֶׁר־
אָמְרוּ הַנְּבִאִים הַנִּבְּאִים בִּשְׁמִי שֶׁקֶר
לֵאמֹר חָלַמְתִּי חָלָמְתִּי: כו עַד־מָתַי
הֲיֵשׁ בְּלֵב הַנְּבִאִים נִבְּאֵי הַשָּׁקֶר
וּנְבִיאֵי תַּרְמִת לִבָּם: כז הַחֹשְׁבִים
להשכיח

ה"א אם יסתר. זכר תג:

עָלְמָא מִבְּרֵאשִׁית אֲמַר יְיָ אֲנָא אֱלָהָא עֲתִידְנָא לְחַדָּתָא עָלְמָא לְצַדִּיקַיָּא: כד אִם יְדַמֵּי גְּבַר לְאִטַּמָּרָה כַּד בְּסִתְרָא קֳדָמַי הֲלָא גְּלֵי אֲמַר יְיָ הֲלָא יַת שְׁמַיָּא וְיַת אַרְעָא יְקָרִי מְלֵי אֲמַר יְיָ: כה שְׁמִיעַ קֳדָמַי יַת דְּאָמְרִין נְבִיֵּי שִׁקְרָא לְמֵימַר פִּתְגָם נְבוּאָה בְּחֶלְמָא אִתְחֲזָא לִי: כו עַד אֵימָתַי אִית בְּלִבְּהוֹן דִּנְבִיֵּי שִׁקְרָא דְּמִתְנַבָּן שְׁקַר וּמִתְנַבָּן רְשַׁע לִבְּהוֹן: כז דִּמְחַשְּׁבִין לְאַנְשָׁאָה יַת

רש"י

לי ואין בי כח לשפוט את התחתונים שהם רחוקים ממני ואיני יודע במעשיהם: (כד) **אם יסתר איש**. זהו כפל תמיהה האלהי מקרוב כדרך כל התמיהות הכפולו': (כו) **עד מתי**. ינבאו שקר וכי יש בלבם של הנביאים הללו הנבאים

מנחת שי

(כד) הלוא את השמים. לפי המסורת מלא וא"ו ואל"ף וכן הוא בספרים

רד"ק

אלהים חדשים אלא **אשר לא יראו ולא ישמעו כי אני רואה** מעשה בני אדם ושומע דבריהם ואני שומע דברי **הנביאים** הנבאים בשמי לשקר וי"ת אנא אלהא ברית עלמא וגו' כבעמוד: (כד) **אם יסתר**. **אני מלא**. כמו וכבוד ה' מלא את המשכן כלומר שהיה ממלא את המשכן כי נאמר זה על האור שנברא כי אני מלא ר"ל אני ממלא כלומר כי בכ"מ אני וזה דרך משל כי הוא יתברך איננו גוף שיהיה ממלא מקום אלא ר"ל כי הנשחתו בכ"מ בשמים ובארץ ות"י יקרי מלי: (כה) **שמעתי**. **חלמתי חלמתי**. הפעל לחזק הענין והיו אומרים שהוא חלום של נבואה: (כו) **עד מתי היש בלב**. ר"ל היש לעולם כמ"ש עד מתי: **נבאי השקר**. כבנין נפעל: **ונביאי תרמית לבם**. כמו מרמה כלומר הם הנביאים מהתרמית שחושבים בלבם לא שבה אליהם הנבואה: (כז) **החושבים להשכיח את עמי שמי**. כי הם מונעים אותם לשמוע אל נביאי האמת המדברים בשמי

מצודת ציון

מלשון השבה: **מעלליהם**. מעשיהם: (כו) **ונביאי**. הוא"ו במקום אבל: **תרבית**. ענין ערמה כמו שקר תרמיתם (תהלים קי"ט): (כז) **החושבים**. מלשון מחשבה:

מצודת דוד

(כד) **אם יסתר**. הלא אף אם יסתר איש במקום נסתר וכי אני לא אראה אותו: **הלא וגו' אני מלא**. א"כ במקום שנסתר שם אני: (כה) **שמעתי**. ר"ל הואיל ואין נסתר ממני לכן שמעתי מה שמנבאים בשמי שקר שאומרים כל היום חלמתי חלמתי ומחזיקים חלומתם שפשוט הדמיוני כחלום נבואה: (כו) **עד מתי**. יהיה השטות והטעו' הזה: **היש בלב**. וכי יש בלבם מה שאומרים תדיר שחלום הדמיוני הוא כחלום הנבואה: **ונביאי הרמית לבם**. אבל הם נביאי הרמית לבם כי יודעים המה שאין ערך לחלום הדמיוני עם חלום הנבואי ובערמת הלב ידברו בפיהם שדומים הם: (כז) **החושבים**. אבל יחשבו לסבב לעמי שישכחו שמי ע"י חלומותם אשר יתמידו לספר זה

who prophesy falsely really believe that their dreams are prophetic?

But they are prophets of the deceit of their hearts—They realize that a dream is not related to a prophetic vision, but they are deceitful.—[*Abarbanel, Mezudath David*]

deceit—Heb. תַּרְמִת, *an expression of* מִרְמָה, *deceit*.—[*Rashi*]

27. **Who think**—But all their intention is to cause My people to forget My name. I.e., they pretend to be prophets with the bad intention of making My people forget My name through the dreams they tell, just as their forefathers forgot My name through the Baal.—[*Abarbanel, Mezudath David*]

Through their dreams, they prevent the people from listening to the true prophets who speak in My name, as their forefathers who worshipped Baal were wont to do, for the prophets of Baal would prophesy to them in the name of Baal, and they gradually forgot My name. So

a God from afar? 24. Can a man hide in secret places that I
should not see him? says the Lord. Do I not fill the heavens and
the earth? says the Lord. 25. I heard what the prophets said,
those who prophesy in My name falsely, saying, "I have
dreamed, I have dreamed." 26. How long [will this be]? Is it in
the heart of the prophets who prophesy lies? But they are
prophets of the deceit of their hearts, 27. Who think

Rabbi Joseph Kara explains this verse in a similar manner: Do I see only what a person does in public, but not what a person does when he draws himself far away from Me to hide in secret places and to do his deeds in the dark? Do I not fill the heavens and the earth?

Redak renders: Am I a recent God? Am I not a God from days of yore? Did people not know Me from the Creation of the world that I am an eternal God, not like the new gods who neither see nor hear, but I see people's deeds and hear their speech, and I hear the words of the prophets who prophesy falsely in My name,

Jonathan paraphrases: I am God Who created the world from the beginning, says the Lord; I am God Who is destined to renew the world for the righteous.

Malbim explains that this passage is directed toward those who deny the existence of prophecy. To this, God replies: Am I a God from near? Can I speak only to those in the upper worlds who are near to Me, and not to earthlings, who are far from Me? Am I subject to the concept of near and far?

Is not My Shechinah both in heaven and on earth?

24. **Can a man hide in secret places**—*This is a repetition of the question, 'Am I a God from near,' according to the manner of all double questions.*—[*Rashi*] See above 14:22.

Do I not fill the heavens and the earth?—This is figurative, for God is incorporeal. The intention is that God's providence fills the heaven and the earth. *Jonathan* renders: Does not My glory fill the heaven and the earth?

25. **I heard**—Since no one can hide from Me, I heard what the prophets say falsehoods in My name, that they say, "I have dreamed, I have dreamed." They represent a simple imaginative dream as a prophetic vision.—[*Mezudath David, Redak*]

I have dreamed, I have dreamed—The repetition is for emphasis.—[*Redak*]

26. **How long [will this be]?**—That *they will prophesy falsely? Do these prophets who prophesy falsely have in their heart to execute their thoughts that they are thinking to cause My people to forget My name etc.?*—[*Rashi*]

Others render as follows:

How long will this foolishness and error continue? Do the prophets

לְהַשְׁכִּיחַ אֶת־עַמִּי שְׁמִי בַּחֲלוֹמֹתָם
אֲשֶׁר יְסַפְּרוּ אִישׁ לְרֵעֵהוּ כַּאֲשֶׁר שָׁכְחוּ
אֲבוֹתָם אֶת־שְׁמִי בַּבָּעַל׃ כח הַנָּבִיא
אֲשֶׁר־אִתּוֹ חֲלוֹם יְסַפֵּר חֲלוֹם וַאֲשֶׁר
דְּבָרִי אִתּוֹ יְדַבֵּר דְּבָרִי אֱמֶת מַה־לַתֶּבֶן
אֶת־הַבָּר נְאֻם־יְהוָה׃ כט הֲלוֹא כֹה
דְבָרִי כָּאֵשׁ נְאֻם יְהוָה וּכְפַטִּישׁ יְפֹצֵץ

יַת עַמִּי שְׁמִי בְּחֶלְמְהוֹן
דְּמִשְׁתָּעַן גְּבַר לְחַבְרֵיהּ
כְּמָה דִּשְׁבַק אֲבָהָתְהוֹן
יַת פּוּלְחַן שְׁמִי וּמְקַיְמִין
בְּשׁוּם טַעֲוָתָא׃ כח נְבוּאָה
דְּעִמֵּיהּ חֶלְמָא יִשְׁתָּעֵי
חֶלְמָא וּדְפִתְגָּמַי עִמֵּיהּ
יְמַלֵּיל פִּתְגָּמַי קְשׁוֹט
הָא כְּמָה דְּפָרִישׁ בֵּין
תִּבְנָא לְעִבּוּרָא כֵּן פָּרִישׁ
בֵּין צַדִּיקַיָּא לְרַשִׁיעַיָּא
אֲמַר יְיָ׃ כט הֲלָא כָּל
פִּתְגָּמַי תַּקִּיפִין כְּאֶשָּׁתָא
אֲמַר יְיָ וּכְפַטִּישָׁא

ת״א יספר חלום. ברכות נה: דברי כאש. ברכות כב. סוכה נב. תענית ד חגיגה כו קידושין ל (נדרים לז): וכפטיש. שבת פח סוטה נב סנהדרין לד:

רש״י

שקר לקיים מחשבותם שהם חושבים להשכיח את עמי שמי וגו׳: תרמית. לשון מרמה: (כח) יספר חלום. יספרנו לשון חלום כשאר חלומות ולא יחזיקנו בדברי נבואה: מה לתבן את הבר. מה ענין שקר אצל אמת: את הבר. עם הבר: (כט) הלא כה דברי כאש. לא היה להם לטעות ולדמות חלומותם לומר שהם נבואה כי דבר נבואה כשבאה בפי הנביא בגבורה היא באה בו כאש בוערת כענין שנאמר ותהי בלבי כאש בוערת (לעיל כ) ואומר ויד ה׳ עלי חזקה (יחזקאל ג׳): וכפטיש. (פי״ק כלע״ז) וים אומר (מרטיי״ל

מהר״י קרא כצ״ל

(כח) מה לתבן את הבר. כשם שהבר משובח מן התבן כך דברי הנביאים אמת ומשובחין מדברי נביאי השקר כשם שמפרש בסמוך: (כט) הלא כה דברי כאש. שכשם שהאש בכל מקום שהוא הולך עושה רושם: וכפטיש יפוצץ סלע. כן יהיה דברי אשר יצא מפי לא ישוב אלי ריקם כי אם עשיתי את אשר חפצתי. דברי מתקיימין אבל דברי נביאי השקר אינן

רד״ק

כמו שהיו עושים אבותם כשהיו עובדים הבעל שהיו נביאי הבעל מתנבאים להם בבעל ושכחו שמי כן עתה שוכחים שמי בחלומות נביאי השקר וי״ת כמה דשבקו אבהתהון וגו׳ כבעניד: (כח) הנביא. אמר איך תשוו חלום החולם עם הנבואה הבאת בחלום כי החולם יספר חלומו ואם יזדמן שיהיה בו דבר אמת מעט הוא כי החלומות מדמיון המחשבות בהקיץ והמחשבות בעתידות לא יצדיקו רובם וכ״א וחלומות השוא ידברו: ואשר דברי אתו ידבר דברי אמת. ידבר דבר שהוא אמת אם יהיה דברי בחלום לנביא ידבר דברי דברי אמת אין בו שקר כלל א״כ דברי החולמים הם כמו התבן והתבן אין בו הנאה כי אם למאכל הבהמות או למלאכה והבר הוא מאכל לבני אדם אם כן איך ישוו ביניהם מה לתבן את הבר ואמר בחלום יספר ובנבואה ידבר כי מספר החלום אין דבריו אלא ספור דברים שראה בחלומו כמו שיספר דברים ששמע אין לשכל בהם חלק כי אם בכח המדמה אבל דברי חלום הנבואה נאמר עליהם ידבר כי הם בכח הדברי ר״ל השכלי עם כח המדמה וי״ת הא כמה דפריש בין תבנא לעבורא כן פריש בין רשיעיא לצדיקיא. ורז״ל אמרו וכי מה ענין בר ותבן אצל חלום אמר רבי יוחנן כמה שאי אפשר לבר בלא תבן כך אי אפשר לחלום בלא דברים בטלים: (כט) הלא כה דברי. דברי החולמים הם בטלים כמו שתראו כי הם אומרים שלום שלום ואין שלום אבל דברי הוא כאש שתצא והשרף את אשר תמצא וכן הוא כפטיש יפוצץ סלע לא יעמוד

מנחת שי

מדוייקים: (כז) איש לרעהו. י״ס בכתוב כתב איו אל רעהו ובטלים במיעוטן:

מצודת דוד

לזה להיות כל עסקם בזה: בבעל. בהתמדת עבודת הבעל: (כח) הנביא וגו׳. ר״ל מהראוי שהנביא אשר אתו חלום פשוט ודמיוני יספרנו כדרך סיפור חלום בעלמא: ואשר דברי אתו. ומי אשר בחלום אדבר בו הוא ידבר דברי ויאמת אותם. ר״ל חלום כזה יוכל לספר כדרך סיפור נבואה: מה לתבן. מה ענין לתבן להדמותו עם הבר. ר״ל מה ענין חלום דמיוני להדמותו עם חלום נבואי: (כט) הלא כה דברי. הלא החלום אשר הוא דברי באה כחוזק רב וכהרגשה יתירה כאש הבוערת וכפטיש המפוצץ את הסלע שהוא

מצודת ציון

(כח) לתבן. קש: הבר. כן נקרא התבואה וכן לשבור בר (בראשית מ״ג): (כט) וכפטיש. הוא המקבת כמו עושים כל האמן (לקמן כ׳): יפוצץ. ענין השבר לחתיכות רבות וכן ויתפוצצו הררי עד (חבקוק ג׳):

Abarbanel and *Mezudath David* concur with *Rashi* that the prophetic dream is accompanied by strong sensations. It is only by these sensations that a prophet is conscious of his prophecy and is certain that it is not an ordinary dream. Maimonides, too, subscribes to this theory.

Redak explains that the dreams are of no consequence, whereas the words of prophecy are fulfilled, resembling a fire that goes forth and burns, and a hammer that shatters a rock. *Kara,* too, explains in this manner.

The Talmud explains this verse as referring to the various facets of Torah. Words of Torah are likened to fire in that they are not subject to ritual contamination. Even one who is ritually unclean may study the Torah (*Berachoth* 22a).

The second segment of the verse is interpreted to mean that, just as a

to cause My people to forget My name with their dreams that they tell, one to another, as their forefathers forgot My name through Baal. 28. The prophet who has a dream, let him tell a dream, and who has My word, let him tell My word as truth. What has the straw to do with the wheat? says the Lord. 29. Is not My word so like fire? says the Lord, and like a hammer that shatters a rock?

is it now, that they forget My name through the dreams of the false prophets.—[*Redak*]

28. **let him tell a dream**—*Let him tell it as vain talk like other dreams, and let him not presume it as words of prophecy.*—[*Rashi*]

I.e., it is proper that the prophet who has a simple imaginative dream tells it as a mere story.—[*Abarbanel, Mezudath David*]

and who has My word—I.e., he who has received a prophetic message from Me through a dream shall recount it as a true prophecy.—[*Abarbanel, Mezudath David*]

What has the straw to do with the wheat?—*What has falsehood to do with truth?*—[*Rashi*]

What has an imaginative dream to do with a prophetic dream?—[*Abarbanel, Mezudath David*]

Jonathan paraphrases: Just as there is a difference between straw and wheat, so is there a difference between the righteous and the wicked. The Rabbis explain: Just as it is impossible to have wheat without straw, so is it impossible for a dream not to have vain words.—[*Redak* from *Ber.* 55a]

with the wheat—Heb. אֶת־הַבָּר, like עִם־הַבָּר.—[*Rashi*]

Redak appears to explain this verse as referring to those who hear the dreams being told and do not distinguish between dreams and prophecies. The Lord reproaches them for their failure to distinguish between the two. He says: How can you confuse the ordinary dream with prophecy that comes through a dream? A prophet who has a dream will tell it as a dream, and if some of it is true, it is a small part of it, for a dream is a product of one's imagination. However, if one experiences a prophetic dream, he will recite it as 'My word,' words of truth. The difference between the two is like the difference between straw, useful only as fodder, and wheat, useful for human consumption.

29. **Is not My word so like fire?**—*They should not have erred to compare their dreams to say that they are prophecy, for the prophetic word, when it comes to a prophet, it comes into him with force like a burning fire, as the matter is stated* (supra 20:9): *'And it was in my heart like a burning fire,' and* (Ezekiel 3:14): *'And the hand of the Lord became strong upon me.'*—[*Rashi*]

and as a hammer—Heb. פַּטִּישׁ (*pic in French*), *a pick. And some say* (*marteau in French*), *a hammer.*—[*Rashi*]

סלע׃ ל לכן הנני על־הנבאים נאם־יהוה
מגנבי דברי איש מאת רעהו׃ לא הנני
על־הנבאים נאם־יהוה הלקחים
לשונם וינאמו נאם׃ לב הנני על־נבאי
חלמות שקר נאם־יהוה ויספרום
ויתעו את־עמי בשקריהם ובפחזותם
ואנכי לא־שלחתים ולא צויתים

תרגום

דמפגע ביפא: ל בכן הא אנא שלח רוגזי על נביי שקרא אמר יי מגנבין פתגמי גבר מן חבריה: לא בכן הא אנא שלח רוגזי על נביי שקרא אמר יי דמתנבן כרעות לבהון ואמרין כן אמר: לב הא אנא שלח רוגזי על דמתנבן חלמא דשקר אמר יי ומשתען ומטען ית עמי בשקריהון ובבקרותהון ואנא לא שלחתינון ולא

מהר״י קרא

מתקיימין: (ל) לכן הנני על הנביאים נאום ה׳ מגנבי דברי איש מאת רעהו. שהיה חנניה בן עזור שולח שלוחיו לשער העליון ששם היה ירמיה מתנבא לשמוע את דבריו זלפי נביאות ירמיה היה חנניה מתנבא לישראל בשקר בשער התחתון כדי שיאמינו לו כשהוא מתנבא להם דברים אחרים: (לא) הלוקחין לשונם וינאמו נאם. המרגילים את לשונם לומר כוביהם בלשון נאם ה׳: (לב) ובפחזותם. לועז ווש״ת:

רש״י

בלע״ז): (ל) מגנבי דברי איש מאת רעהו. יש להם מרגלים אצל נביאי האמת ושומעין שנכון שלהם שאם מתנבאים בו ואומרין נבואות שקר באותו לשון כמו שעשה חנניה בן עזור שמע את ירמיה מתנבא בשוק העליון הנני שובר את קשת עילם והוא ניבא בשוק התחתון שברתי את עול מלך בבל (לקמן כ״ח) כמה שכתבו רבותינו בסנהדרין: (לא) הלוקחים לשונם. המלמדים לשונם לומר שקריהם בלשון נאם ה׳ כנביאי האמת למען יאמינו בהם: (לב) ובפחזותם. לשון תמהון (איסטורדיזו״ן בלע״ז):

מנחת שי

כאשר שכחו. י״דמשתעין אשר בקריאה וסי׳ נמסר ביונה סי׳ א׳ במ״ג: (ל) לכן הנני על הנבאים. במקצת ספרים מדוייקים חסר יו״ד קדמאה וכן חברו שבסמוך הנני על הנבאים ומסורת הסיפרא סי׳ כ״ו מוכחת שאין אלו מן המלאים אמנם י״ם שזה השני דלא פסוק כתוב הנבאם ומסור עליו ג׳ כתיבין כן:

רד״ק

דבר לפני דברי לבטלו כי את אשר דברתי אעשה ולא יפול דבר: (ל) לכן הנני על הנביאים. כלומר הנני עליהם לכלותם וכן ת״י הא אנא שלח רוגזי וכן תירגם כל אלה הנני אשר בפרשה ואמר שלשה פעמים הנני כי שלשה חלקים היו נביאי השקר באותו הזמן היו בהם נביאים שהיו שומעים דברי נביאי האמת בנבואת אומות העולם כמו שהתנבא ירמיה על האומות והיו הולכים לעם ואומרים להם כה אמר השם לעמון ועניין הנבואה כמ״ש ירמיה בביתו לתלמידיו כדי שיאמינו העם להם באמרם להם בשם ה׳ שלום יהיה לכם ועל אלה אמר מגנבי דברי איש מאת רעהו ועל זה ארז״ל המתנבא מה שלא נאמר לו הא לחברו נאמר כגון חנניה בן עזור דקאי ירמיה בשוק העליון ואמר כה אמר ה׳ צבאות הנני שובר את קשת עילם ראשית גבורתם נשא חנניה ק״ו בעצמו ומה עילם שלא בא אלא לעזור את כשדים אמר הקב״ה הנני שובר את קשת עילם כשדים עצמן על אחת כמה וכמה אתא איהו לשוק התחתון ואמר כה אמר ה׳ אלהי ישראל שברתי את עול מלך בבל והקשו על זה ואמרו האי לחברו לא נאמר כיון דאתיהיב ק״ו כמאן דאתמר ליה דמי והחלק השני היו בהם נביאים שהיו בעלי ל׳ צח ומתק שפתים ועליהם נאמר הלוקחים לשונם וינאמו נאם היו אומרים לעם דברי שלום בשם ה׳ והיו מראים פניהם בפתק דבריהם כדי שישמעו להם וע״ז אמרו רז״ל המתנבא מה שלא שמע והחלק השלישי נביאי חלומות שקר שהיו אומרי׳ כי חלומותיה׳ נבואה והיו אומרים אותה לעם בשם ה׳: (לא) הנני. הלוקחים לשונם. המחליקי׳ לשונם. וכן חשתו ברוב לקחה בחלק שפתיה תדיחנו כמ״ש במתק שפתיה תדיחנו: (לב) הנני על נבאי. מבנין נפעל: ובפחזותם. ובקלותם כלומר בקלות דעתם וכן

מצודת ציון

(לא) הלוקחים. ענין למוד והרגל כמו הטתו ברוב לקחה (משלי ז׳): וינאמו נאם. הוא ענין אמירה והוא לשון שהנביאים רגילים בו: (לב) ויתעו. מל׳ תועה: ובפחזותם. ענין קלות הדעת וכן אנשים

מצודת דוד

דבר המורגש מאד כן הוא חלום הנביאי ולא כן חלום הדמיוני כי הרגשתה קלה מאד: (ל) לכן הנני וגו׳. ר״ל הואיל ויש הפרש רב בין הלום נביאו לחלום דמיוני וכזדון לכם יאמתו חלום דמיוני כחלום נביאי לכן כמו שהנני מוכן להביא פורעניות על הנביאים אשר גונבים דברי וגו׳ ר״ל שהיו שומעים דברי נביאי האמת והיו מגידים אותם מעצמם ואמרו שאליהם נאמרו וכאלו יגנבו דברי הנבואה מן הנביא האמיתי: (לא) הנני וגו׳. וכמו שהנני מוכן להביא פורעניות על הנביאים המלמדים לשונם נמסר לדבר אחות: וינאמו נאום. ר״ל שבודים שקרים מלבם ויאתיקו ממדיהם וידברום במקום נבואה ובלשון הנביאים כאלו היה דבר ה׳: (לב) הנני על נבאי חלומות. ר״ל כמו כן הנני מוכן להביא פורעניות על המנבאים חלומות שקר. כלומר שאומרים חלום דמיוני כאלו הוא חלום נביאי כי בזדון ידברו ואינם מוטעים: ויספרום. מתמידים לספרם כאלו היה דבר ממש: ויתעו. והמה מתעים את עמי בחלום הדמיוני שהיא דבר שקר: ובפחזותם. בקלות דעתם יפתו את העם להאמין בחלומותם הדמיוני: ואנכי וגו׳. אמר כמתרעם על הנפתים להם ואמר הלא אנכי מעולם

Babylon.' " They questioned this identification since that prophecy was not said even to his colleagues. They replied that since one may infer a major premise from a minor one, it is as though it was said to him.

31. **those who train their tongues**— Heb. הַלֹּקְחִים, *who teach their tongues to say their falsehoods with the expression, "Says the Lord," like the true prophets, so that they should believe them.*—[*Rashi*]

32. **with their bewilderment**—

30. Therefore, behold I am against the prophets, says the Lord,
those who steal My words from one another. 31. Behold I am
against the prophets, says the Lord, those who train their
tongues and say, "He says," 32. **Behold I am against those who**
prophesy with false dreams, says the Lord, and they tell them and mislead My people with their falsehoods and with their bewilderment, but I neither sent them nor commanded them,

hammer shatters a stone into many fragments, so are the words of Torah interpreted in many various manners, all of which are valid (*Sanhedrin* 34a). Also, every word that emanated from the mouth of the Holy One, blessed be He, at Mount Sinai, spread out into seventy languages (*Shabbath* 88b). Another interpretation is that the Torah has the power to shatter the evil inclination even if it is as hard as a rock. I.e., by studying the Torah, one gains inspiration to combat his evil inclination that entices him to sin (*Kiddushin* 30b). See *Yalkut Shim'oni.*

30. **behold I am against the prophets**—Lit. behold I am on the prophets; i.e. I am against them to destroy them. *Jonathan* renders: Behold I send My wrath upon the false prophets.—[*Redak*]

those who steal My words from one another—*They have spies* who spy *upon the true prophets, who listen to their expression with which they prophesy and say false prophecies with that same expression, as Hananiah son of Azzur did. He heard Jeremiah prophesying in the upper marketplace, "Behold I break the bow of Elam,' and he prophesied in the lower marketplace, "I have broken the yoke of the king of Babylon* (28:2)," *as our Rabbis wrote in Sanhedrin* 89a.—[*Rashi*]

Redak explains that there were three types of false prophets at that time. There were those who would listen to the true prophets prophesying to the nations of the world, as Jeremiah would prophesy concerning the nations. Then they would go to the people and say to them, "So said the Lord to Ammon. . . ," repeating the prophecy as Jeremiah gave it over to his disciples, so that the people should believe them when they tell them, "You shall have peace." Concerning them, the prophet says, "Those who steal My words from one another." Concerning this group the Rabbis say, "One who prophesies what he did not hear but was said to his colleague, such as Hananiah son of Azzur, for Jeremiah was standing in the upper marketplace . . . Hananiah deduced a major premise from a minor one. If concerning Elam, who came only to aid the Chaldeans, the Holy One, blessed be He, said, "Behold I break the bow of Elam," how much more would He say so concerning the Chaldeans themselves!" He came to the lower marketplace and stated, "So said the Lord God of Israel, 'I have broken the yoke of the king of

והועיל לא־יועילו לעם־הזה נאם־
יהוה: לג וכי־ישאלך העם הזה או־
הנביא או־כהן לאמר מה משא יהוה
ואמרת אליהם את־מה־משא
ונטשתי אתכם נאם־יהוה: לד והנביא
והכהן והעם אשר יאמר משא יהוה
ופקדתי על־האיש ההוא ועל־ביתו:
לה כה תאמרו איש על־רעהו ואיש אל־
אחיו מה־ענה יהוה ומה־דבר יהוה:
לו ומשא יהוה לא תזכרו־עוד כי המשא

תרגום

פקדתינון נהנאה לא
יהנון לעמא הדין אמר
יי: לג וארי ישאלינך
עמא הדין או ספר או
כהין למימר מה נבואתא
בשמא דיי ותימר להון
כדין נבואתא וארטוש
יתכון אמר יי: לד וספר
וכהן ועמא דימר
נבואתא בשמא דיי
ואסער על גברא ההוא
ועל ביתיה: לה כדין
תימרון גבר לחבריה
וגבר לאחוהי מה אתיב
יי ומה מליל יי:
לו ונבואה בשמא דיי
לא תדכרון עוד ארי
נבואתא תהי לגבר

רש"י נ"א אל

(לג) מה משא ה'. לשון שחוק לפי שנבואותו להם למשא: ואמרת אליהם את מה משא ונטשתי וגו'. אומרים לכם מה המשא אתם למשא להקב"ה והוא אומר שיטוש וישליך אתכם מעל זרועותיו משמים ארץ, כך שמעתי: ונטשתי. ועזבתי: (לו) כי המשא יהיה לאיש דברו.

מהר"י קרא

(לג) מה משא ה'. שדומה עליו נבואתו של הקב"ה כמשא אף אתה הקהה את שיניו והשיב לו לפי שאילתו: ואמרת אליהם את מה משא. כלומר אתם עליו למשא ומה דרכו של אדם כשמשוי עליו משליכו מעליו אף אני לפי שאתם עלי [למשא]. ונטשתי אתכם נאם ה': (לו) כי המשא יהיה לאיש דברו. אחר הלשון שהוא הופך את הנבואה למשא יארע לו. הוא הפך את

רד"ק

אנשים רקים ופוחזים: (לג) וכי ישאלך. האל יתברך שהוא חוקר לב ובוחן כליות ידע את לבבם כי כשהיו אומרים משא ה' היה דעתם וכונתם ענין כבדות ומשא כמו תחת משאו לפיכך אמר לירמיהו הנביא שיזהירם שלא ישאלו דבר ה' בל' משא: או הנביא. נביאי שקר. וי"ת ספר וכבר פירשנוהו: או כהן. מכהני הלוים: את מה משא. תאמר להם את שאלתם ששואלים מה משא ומה תאמר ונטשתי אתכם זו תהיה תשובת שאלתם ות"י ותימר להון כדין נבואתא וארטוש יתכון: (לד) והנביא. מבואר הוא: (לה) כה. איש על רעהו. כמו אל רעהו וכן וילך אלקנה הרמתה על ביתו כמו אל ביתו: מה ענה ה'. כמו מה דבר וכן וענית ואמרת ויען איוב הראשון: (לו) ומשא ה'. כי המשא יהיה לאיש דברו. לכל איש מהם יהיה המשא דברו

מצודת דוד

לא שלחתים ולא צויתי אותם שום צווי ומעולם לא הועילו לעם הזה בשום דבר וא"כ אין בידם לתת שום אות ומופת וגם היטיב אין עמהם וכמה א"כ מהזיקים אותם לנביאים: (לג) וכי ישאלך. אמר המקום לירמיה אם ישאלך העם הזה או נביא הבקר או כהן הבעל לאמר מה משא ה' ר"ל מה דבר ה' ובדרך לעג אמרו לשון משא לפי שהיה להם למשא ולטורח כבד: ואמרת. אז תאמר אליהם את מה משא ר"ל את מה שיאות לעשות במשא אעשה לכם ומוזר ופירוש ונטשתי אתכם כאדם העוזב ומשליך את המשא הכבידה עליו: (לד) ופקדתי. במקרא שלפניו אמר שהנביא ישיב להם דרך אוגאת דברים שהמקום יעזוב את ישראל כעונם וישליכם כאדם המשליך משא כבידה וכזה אמר העון הזה אזכור להשיב גמול ביחוד על האיש המדבר ועל ביתו: (לה) כה תאמרו. בלשון הזה תאמרו וגו': מה ענה ה' וגו'. ר"ל אם תשאלו על הנבואה תאמרו מה ענה ה' ואם תשאלו על מה שדבר מבלי שאלה תאמרו מה דבר ה': (לו) ומשא. לשון משא לא תזכרו עוד: כי המשא יהיה לאיש דברו. ר"ל דברי הנבואה שהם כאלו למשא

מצודת ציון

רקים ופוחזים (שופטים ט'): והועיל. מלשון תועלת: (לג) משא. כן תקרא הנבואה: ונטשתי. ענין עזיבה: (לד) ופקדתי. ענין זכרון: (לה) על רעהו. אל רעהו: ענה. מלשון עניה ותשובה על

reply?"—If you ask what the Lord replied to a question, you shall use this expression. If you ask what the Lord spoke unrelated to a question, you shall say, "What did the Lord speak?"—[*Mezudath David, Abarbanel*]

Redak renders: What did the Lord declare? *Jonathan,* however, appears to follow the first interpretation.

***36. But "the burden of the Lord" you shall no longer mention**—I.e., the expression מַשָּׂא ה׳ you shall no longer mention in conjunction with prophecy.—[*Mezudath David*]

* For Rashi's commentary turn to page 245.

and they have not availed this people, says the Lord. 33. Now
if this people or the prophet or priest asks you, saying, "What is
the burden of the Lord?" And you shall say to them, "What
burden? And I will forsake you, says the Lord." 34. And the
prophet and the priest and the people who will say, "The
burden of the Lord," I will visit retribution upon that man and
upon his household. 35. So shall you say each one to his friend
and each one to his brother, "What did the Lord reply?" or
"What did the Lord speak?" 36. And "the burden of the Lord"
you shall no longer mention, for the burden

Heb. וּבְפַחֲזוּתָם, *an expression of wonder* (*estordisoun in O.F.*).—[*Rashi*] *Rashi*'s intention is not clear. Perhaps these prophets would feign astonishment at their remarkable dreams to convince the people that they were prophetically inspired.

Others explain this to mean 'their frivolousness, their lightheadedness.'—[*Redak, Mezudoth*]

This was the third group of false prophets, those who would represent their dreams as prophecy, as mentioned above (verses 25–29).—[*Redak*]

and they have not availed this people—They were never of any use to this people. On the contrary, they led them away from the word of the Lord.—[*Malbim*]

Since I neither sent nor commanded them, nor did they ever help this people, they have no sign or wonder, nor have they ever done any good. If so, how can they regard themselves as prophets?—[*Mezudath David*]

33. **or the prophet**—I.e. the false prophets. *Jonathan*, however, renders: the scribe. This has already been explained above (v. 11).—[*Redak*]

or a priest—of the Levitical priests (*Redak*) or the idolatrous priests.—[*Mezudath David*]

"What is the burden of the Lord?"—*This is an expression of derision, for his prophecy is a burden to them.*—[*Rashi*] The expression מַשָּׂא ה' is a legitimate expression meaning 'God's prophecy.' The people of Jeremiah's generation, however, chose this expression when asking the prophet what he had to prophesy because it had a double meaning, also meaning 'the burden of the Lord.' They used it in derision of the prophecy, which they considered a burden.

God, Who knows people's thoughts, knew that their intention was, 'What is the burden of the Lord,' for prophecy was burdensome to them. He, therefore, enjoined the prophet to warn them against using this expression.—[*Redak, Mezudath David*]

35. **"What did the Lord**

יִהְיֶה לְאִישׁ דְּבָרוֹ וַהֲפַכְתֶּם אֶת־דִּבְרֵי
אֱלֹהִים חַיִּים יְהוָה צְבָאוֹת אֱלֹהֵינוּ׃
לז כֹּה תֹאמַר אֶל־הַנָּבִיא מֶה־עָנָךְ יְהוָה
וּמַה־דִּבֶּר יְהוָה׃ לח וְאִם־מַשָּׂא יְהוָה
תֹּאמֵרוּ לָכֵן כֹּה אָמַר יְהוָה יַעַן אֲמָרְכֶם
אֶת־הַדָּבָר הַזֶּה מַשָּׂא יְהוָה וָאֶשְׁלַח
אֲלֵיכֶם לֵאמֹר לֹא תֹאמְרוּ מַשָּׂא יְהוָה׃
לט לָכֵן הִנְנִי וְנָשִׁיתִי אֶתְכֶם נָשֹׂא

תרגום

דמקים פתגמי רעותיה ואתון מדמן לבטלא ית פתגמי אלהא קימא דיי צבאות אלהנא: לז כדין תימר לנביא מה אתיבך יי ומה מליל יי: לח ואם נבואה בשמא דיי תימרון בכן כדנן אמר יי חלף דאמרתון ית פתגמא הדין נבואה בשמא דיי ושלחית לותכון למימר לא תימרון נבואתא מקדם יי: לט בכן האנא שלח רוגזי וארטוש יתכון מרטש

מהר"י קרא

הנבואה לקרותה בלשון משוי. אף תהיה לו למשא ולפורענות. וזה הוא: (לט) לכן הנני ונשיתי אתכם נשא. לשון נענוע גיד הנשה שנשה את מקומו והלך לו. ופתרונו והניעותי אתכם בהנעה:

רש"י

אע"פ שאתם מהפכין את המשא לגנאי משא דבר ה' לאיש דברו ולאיש עצתו הוא מגלהו ואתם מהפכין אותו לל' משאוי זו לא שמעתי כן והיא עיקר אבל כך שמעתי כי המשאוי יהיה משאוי של פורעניות למי שאומרו השואל מה משא. ע"א משא ה' לשון נבואה הוא והיה הנביא השקר שואל לנביא האמת לאמר לו את דבר הקב"ה בלשון שבא הסיגנון אליו והסיגנון לא היה מפרש הדיבור כל כך והיה הנביא השקר מהפך הפירוש לצד אחר והיה מדבר בדוגמות נביא האמת כדי שיאמינו בו וכן עשה חנניה בן עזור לכן הוא אומר אל תשאלו משא ה' את לשון הסיגנון אלא מה דבר ומה ענה. את פי' הדבר שאלו לנביא אמת לאמר לכם מה הקב"ה אומר ולהיכן נוטין את דבריו: **כי המשא יהיה לאיש דברו**. סיגנון שתם הקב"ה אמרו שהם לאיש עצתו שאינו חשוד להפכו ואתם שואלים אותו כדי להפכו והפכתם את דברי הקב"ה וז"ש למעלה מגנבי דברי איש מאת רעהו (כאן) גם זה לשון מיוסר: (לז) **כה תאמר אל הנביא**. כשאתם באים לשאול דברי מאת הנביא: (לט) ונשיתי. לשון גיד הנשה (בראשית ל"ב) ולשון ונשתה גבורתם (לקמן נ"א) קופץ ומטלטל ממקום למקום:

מנחת שי

(לח) ואם משא ה'. חד מן ד' פסוקים דאית בהון שם הקדוש ד' פעמים וסימן

רד"ק

כלומר בדברו לבד יאמר משא שמשמע נבואה אך בלבו הוא לי כבדות וזה שאמר והפכתם את דברי אלהים חיים כלומר בלבבכם תהפכו אותם מנבואה לכבדות: ה' צבאות. כי הוא אדון צבאות מעלה וצבאות מטה ובידו להביא עליכם מה שדבר: אלהינו, כלומר אלהינו הוא ולא אלהיכם שאין אתם מאמינים בו. וא"א ז"ל פירש כי דברו של אדם היא נשיאות שפתיו כמ"ש ובל אשא את שמותם על שפתי כלומר וכראוי נקראת הנבואה משא שהיא נשאת בפי הנביא אלא שאתם הופכים דברי אלהים חיים ותחשבו משא ענין כבדות: (לז) כה. מבואר הוא: (לח) ואם. מבואר הוא: (לט) לכן הנני ונשיתי

מצודת ציון

(לט) ונשיתי. נשא. ענין הסרה והעתקה כמו נשתה גבורתם (לקמן נ"א):

מצודת דוד

כשאלה: על הנביא שה' דבר בו על כי לא יוכל לכבוש הנבואה לבלי להגידה כאלו היתה למשא עליו וכמ"ש ואמרתי וגו' ולא אדבר עוד בשמו והיה בלבי כאש וגו' ונלאתי כלכל (לעיל כ') וגם בעבור זה יתכן נקראת בשם משא לבד מה שנקראת כן על כי נשאת בפי הנביא: והפכתם. אבל אתם מהפכים את דברי וגו' היא את המשא לומר שהיא למשא על השומעים ולא כן היא: (לז) כה תאמר אל הנביא. ר"ל ואף אם תשאלו את הנביא עצמו עם כי נמולו כאלו למשא על כי לא יוכל להסתירה עכ"ז לא תזכרו שם משא רק בלשון הזה תאמרו מה ענה לך ה' אם יהיה השאלה על המענה או מה דבר ה' אם יהיה על דבר מבלי שאלה קודמת: (לח) ואם וגו'. ואם אחר כל האזהרות תאמרו עוד לשון משא ה': לכן. בעבור זה כה אמר וגו': ואשלח. ר"ל ואף כי שלחתי אליכם אשר לא תאמרו לשון משא ה' ועכ"ז לא שמעתם: (לט) לכן הנני. בעבור זה הנני מוכן לשלם גמול ועל העון הזה בלבד אסיר אתכם בהסרה מלפני ואעזוב אתכם כאדם העוזב משא הכבידה עליו ר"ל העון הזה לבד כדאי הוא לזה העונש

If you say מַשָּׂא ה׳ in order to provoke Me.—[*Abarbanel*]

and I sent to you—Although I sent to you saying etc.—[*Mezudath David*]

39. **Therefore, here I am**—I am ready to visit retribution upon you.—[*Mezudath David*]

and I will exile—Heb. וְנָשִׁיתִי, *an expression of 'the sinew that was dislocated* (גִּיד הַנָּשֶׁה)*'* (Gen. 32:33), *and an expression of 'their might has failed* (נָשְׁתָה)*,' it jumps and moves from place to place.*—[*Rashi*]

Others render: And I will forget you.—[*Redak, Abarbanel*]

shall be to the man of His word although you pervert the words of the living God, the Lord of Hosts, our God. 37. So shall you say to the prophet, "What has the Lord replied to you?" Or "What has the Lord spoken?" 38. But if you say, "The burden of the Lord," therefore, so says the Lord, since you have said this thing, "the burden of the Lord," and I sent to you saying, "You shall not say, 'the burden of the Lord,'" 39. Therefore, here I am, and I will exile you,

for the prophecy shall be for the man of His word—*The unexplained expression the Holy One, blessed be He, said unexplained to the man of His counsel, who is not suspected of perverting it, but you ask it in order to pervert it, and you pervert the words of the Holy One, blessed be He, and that is what is stated above* (v. 30): *'those who steal My words from one another.' This too is a correct explanation.*—[*Rashi*]

Rabbi Joseph Kara follows *Rashi*'s second interpretation, the one he heard from his masters. He elaborates that since the inquirer has perverted the word *massa* from 'prophecy' to 'burden,' it will become a *burden* of retribution upon him.

Redak explains that the inquirer does not ask derisively. He merely uses the expression of מַשָּׂא, a legitimate expression for prophecy. The intention of the wicked, however, was 'the burden of the Lord.' He renders: But the *massa* of the Lord you shall no longer mention, for 'the prophecy' shall be to a man in his speech, but you pervert the words of the living God, the Lord of Hosts our God.

I.e., you pervert the meaning of the word in your heart from 'prophecy' to 'burden.'

Rabbi Joseph Kimchi explains: For the *massa* shall be the speech of a man. I.e. the speech that a man raises to his lips is called מַשָּׂא, from the root נשא, to *bear*. But you pervert it to mean 'a burden.'

Others interpret: **For the burden shall be to the man of his word.** I.e., the prophecy is a burden only to the prophet himself, who feels the prophecy burning within him and he cannot conceal it, but you pervert the words of . . . to call it a burden to the people.—[*Abarbanel, Mezudath David*]

the Lord of Hosts—For He is the Lord of the hosts of heaven and the hosts of the earth, and it is within His power to bring upon you all that He has spoken.—[*Redak*]

our God—He is our God but not your God, for you do not believe in Him.—[*Redak*]

37. **So shall you say to the prophet**—*when you come to ask My words of the prophet.*—[*Rashi*]

38. **But if you say**—If after all these warnings, you still say.—[*Mezudath David*]

וְנָטַשְׁתִּי אֶתְכֶם וְאֶת־הָעִיר אֲשֶׁר
נָתַתִּי לָכֶם וְלַאֲבוֹתֵיכֶם מֵעַל פָּנָי׃
מ וְנָתַתִּי עֲלֵיכֶם חֶרְפַּת עוֹלָם וּכְלִמּוּת
עוֹלָם אֲשֶׁר לֹא תִשָּׁכֵחַ׃ כד א הִרְאַנִי
יְהוָה וְהִנֵּה שְׁנֵי דּוּדָאֵי תְאֵנִים מוּעָדִים
לִפְנֵי הֵיכַל יְהוָה אַחֲרֵי הַגְלוֹת
נְבוּכַדְרֶאצַּר מֶלֶךְ־בָּבֶל אֶת־יְכָנְיָהוּ
בֶן־יְהוֹיָקִים מֶלֶךְ־יְהוּדָה וְאֶת־שָׂרֵי
יְהוּדָה וְאֶת־הֶחָרָשׁ וְאֶת־הַמַּסְגֵּר

ג"א יכניה

מְרַטֵּשׁ וְאַרְחֵיק יָתְכוֹן וְיָת קַרְתָּא דִיהָבִית לְכוֹן וְלַאֲבָהָתְכוֹן מְקַבֵּיל מֵימְרִי׃ מ וְאֶתֵּן עֲלֵיכוֹן חִסּוּדֵי עֲלַם וְהִתְחַפִּינוּן אִתְכַּנְעוּת עֲלַם דְלָא תִפְסוֹק׃ א אַחְזְיַנִי יְיָ וְהָא תְּרֵין סַלֵּי תְאֵינִין מַחְתִין מִקֳדָם הֵיכְלָא דַיְיָ בָּתַר דְאַגְלֵי נְבוּכַדְרֶצַּר מַלְכָּא דְבָבֶל יָת יְכָנְיָה בַּר יְהוֹיָקִים מַלְכָּא דְשִׁבְטָא דְבֵית יְהוּדָה וְיָת רַבְרְבֵי יְהוּדָה וְיָת אוּמָנַיָּא וְיָת תַּרְעַיָּא מִירוּשְׁלֵם

תולדות אהרן

שני דודאי תאנים . עירובין כא׳

רש"י

כד (א) דודאי. קדרות: מועדים. מוכנים: החרש והמסגר. ת"ח שגלו עם יכניה וככר פרשתי בספר (מלכים ב׳ כ"ד) החרש והמסגר (לימי־טרא"ה ליפירטי"ר בלע"ז). ל"א החרש והמסגר החרש לשון חרש

מהר"י קרא

כד (א) דודאי תנאים. סלי תאנים: מועדים. מזומנים כך אכיר את גלות יהודה לטובה:

רד"ק

אתכם נשא. מה שאמר בזה הענין בכל דבר ודבר הנני מורה על מהירות הפורענות עליהם כלומר הנני מוכן ומזומן להביא עליכם רעה. ונשיתי. ושכחתי וכבר כתבנו כי בבא המקור אחרון הוא לחזק הפעולה ר"ל כמו שאתם שוכחים דברי ואיתותי שעשיתי על ידי נביאי ועתה אתם מואסים נבואתי ומבזים אותה אני ג"כ אשכח אתכם אף על פי שקניתי אתכם וכרתי ברית אתכם כי אתם בטלתם הברית תחלה: ונטשתי אתכם. אעזוב אתכם ואת העיר שאסלק שכינתי ממנה ובאכרו מעל פני טעמו למלת אתכם ר"ל כי בעזבי אתכם תגלו מעל פני כמ"ש שלח מעל פני ויצאו וי"ת וארטיש יתכון מרטש וארחק יתכון וית קרתא דיהבית לכון ולאבהתכון מקביל מימרי: ויש לפרש ונשתי כמו ונתשתי בתי"ו והיא הנכון כי התי"ו והשי"ת ממוצא אחד הן ויבאו בענין אחד וכן טעה בטי"ת ותעה בתי"ו ענין אחד הוא וכן אם ינתשו מים זרים בתי"ו כמו ינטשו בטי"ת: (מ) ונתתי. וכלימות. שם בשורק הוי"ו ודגש המ"ם: (א) הראני ה׳. בחירק הה"א: והנה שני דודאי תאנים. אמר הראני במראה הנבואה שני דודאי תאנים ואל"ף דודאי תאנים נוספת האל"ף המשים לולאית וכן אביר הדוד אחד בלא אל"ף וענינו סלים וכת"י סלי: מועדים. מוכנים ומזומנים לאכול והיה

מנחת שי

נמסר בד"ה ב׳ י"ד: (לט) ולאבותיכם. לפי המסורת מלא וא"ו וכן הוא בספרים מדוייקים: (מ) וכלמות. י"ם שהמ"ם בוא"ו חולם אבן ברוב הספרים בשורק וכ׳ כתב רד"ק בפירוש ובשרשים: כד (א) הראני. בחירק הה"א: יכניהו. ס"א יכניה:

מצודת דוד

מדה כמדה על שאמרו לשון משא יעזוב אותם כמשא: ואת העיר. גם את העיר אשר וגו׳ אעזוב ואשליך מעל פני ותהיה מסורה ביד האומות: (מ) חרפת עולם. זמן מרובה תהיו בהחרפה גולים בין האומות: וכלימות עולם. זמן מרובה יהיה הכלימה שיהיה לכם בעת תלכו שבי לפני כי אשר לא תשכח הכלימה ההיא על כי תהיה מרובה וגדולה:

כד (א) הראני ה׳. במראה הנבואה: דודאי. כלים מלאים תאנים היו מזומנים לפני ההיכל: אחרי הגלות. חוזר לתחלה המקרא לומר שזה ראה אחר שהגלה כ"כ וגו׳: ואת החרש ואת המסגר. הם האומנים ושומרי השערים אשר סגרו אותם בפתח

מצודת ציון

כד (א) דודאי. שם כלי כענין קדרה וכן כפיו מדוד תעבורנה (תהלים פ"א): מועדים. מזומנים וכן אנה הנך מועדות

Moreover, the French does not match the Hebrew explanation. It rather matches *Jonathan*'s Targum of *craftsmen and sentries of the gates*. Another difficulty is that Rashi in Kings does not explain any more explicitly than he does here.

As mentioned above, *Jonathan* renders: the craftsmen and the sentries of the gates. He translates חָרָשׁ as *craftsmen*, as in Ex. 28:11, and מַסְגֵּר as *closing*, i.e. those who close the gates. The other explanation originates from *Gittin* 88a, *San.* 38a, and *Seder Olam* ch. 25. In *Gittin, Rashi* explains that these were such great scholars, that when they would leave a question unanswered, no one could volunteer any information to reopen the

and I will forsake you and the city that I gave you and your forefathers from before My presence. 40. And I will place upon you everlasting shame and everlasting embarrassment that shall not be forgotten.

24

1. The Lord showed me two pots of figs, prepared before the Temple of the Lord after Nebuchadrezzar, king of Babylon, had exiled Jeconiah son of Jehoiakim king of Judah and the princes of Judah and the craftsmen and the sentries of the gates

Since you forget My words and My signs that I have performed through My prophets, and now you reject My prophecy and condemn it, I will forget you as well. Although I made a covenant with you, you have already abrogated that covenant.—[*Redak*]

Abarbanel takes this as a distortion of מַשָּׂא Since you have perverted the meaning of מַשָּׂא, *prophecy*, I will pervert it to נְשִׁיתִי, *forgetting*, and forget you.

and I will forsake you—I will forsake you and the city, for I will remove My presence therefrom.—[*Redak*]

from before My presence—When I forsake You, you will be exiled from before My presence. *Jonathan* renders: And I will forsake you and I will drive you and the city that I gave to you and to your forefathers far from My presence. Accordingly, the word וְנָטַשְׁתִּי is rendered as וְנָתַשְׁתִּי; since the 'teth' and the 'tav' are linguals, they are sometimes interchangeable.—[*Redak*]

1. **showed me**—in a prophetic vision.—[*Redak, Mezudath David*]

pots—Heb. דּוּדָאֵי.—[*Rashi*] Most exegetes render it as 'baskets.'—[*Targum, Kara, Redak*]

prepared—Heb. מוּעָדִים.—[*Rashi, Kara, Mezudoth*] I.e., they were ready to eat.—[*Redak*]

after ... had exiled—I.e., this vision came to me after Nebuchadnezzar had exiled Jeconiah son of Jehoiakim etc.—[*Mezudath David*]

the craftsmen and the sentries of the gates—Heb. הֶחָרָשׁ וְהַמַּסְגֵּר, *Torah scholars who were exiled with Jeconiah, and I already explained in the Book of Kings* (II 24:14) הֶחָרָשׁ וְהַמַּסְגֵּר (*les maîtres, les portiers in French*). *the masters, the sentries of the gates. Another explanation:* הֶחָרָשׁ וְהַמַּסְגֵּר. הֶחָרָשׁ *is an expression of silence,* וְהַמַּסְגֵּר *is an expression of closing. That is to say, great sages in Torah,* to the extent *that when one of them would speak, everyone would remain silent.* מַסְגֵּר *means that* when *they would close* the discussion, *no one would reopen it.*—[*Rashi*] This passage of Rashi presents many difficulties, viz. that there is no apparent differences between the first interpretation and the second.

מִירוּשָׁלַ֔͏ִם וַיְבִאֵ֖ם בָּבֶֽל׃ ב הַדּ֣וּד אֶחָ֗ד
תְּאֵנִים֙ טֹב֣וֹת מְאֹ֔ד כִּתְאֵנֵ֖י הַבַּכֻּר֑וֹת
וְהַדּ֣וּד אֶחָ֗ד תְּאֵנִים֙ רָע֣וֹת מְאֹ֔ד אֲשֶׁ֥ר
לֹא־תֵאָכַ֖לְנָה מֵרֹֽעַ׃ ג וַיֹּ֨אמֶר יְהוָ֜ה אֵלַ֗י
מָֽה־אַתָּ֤ה רֹאֶה֙ יִרְמְיָ֔הוּ וָאֹמַ֖ר תְּאֵנִ֑ים
הַתְּאֵנִ֤ים הַטֹּבוֹת֙ טֹב֣וֹת מְאֹ֔ד וְהָֽרָעוֹת֙
רָע֣וֹת מְאֹ֔ד אֲשֶׁ֥ר לֹא־תֵאָכַ֖לְנָה מֵרֹֽעַ׃
ד וַיְהִ֥י דְבַר־יְהוָ֖ה אֵלַ֥י לֵאמֹֽר׃ ה כֹּֽה־
אָמַ֤ר יְהוָה֙ אֱלֹהֵ֣י יִשְׂרָאֵ֔ל כַּתְּאֵנִ֥ים
הַטֹּב֖וֹת הָאֵ֑לֶּה כֵּֽן־אַכִּ֞יר אֶת־גָּל֣וּת

תרגום

מִירוּשְׁלֵם וְאוֹבֵילִינוּן
לְבָבֶל: ב סַלָּא חֲדָא
תֵּינִין טָבָא לַחֲדָא כְּתֵינִין
בַּכִּירִין וְסַלָּא חַד תֵּינִין
בִּישִׁין לַחֲדָא (וּדְבִישִׁין
בִּישִׁין לַחֲדָא) דְּלָא
מִתְאַכְלִין מִבִּישׁוּ:
ג וַאֲמַר יְיָ לִי מָה אַתְּ חָזֵי
יִרְמְיָה וַאֲמָרִית תֵּינִין
תֵּינַיָּא טָבְתָא טָבָן לַחֲדָא
וּדְבִישִׁין בִּישָׁן לַחֲדָא
דְּלָא מִתְאַכְלִין מִבִּישׁוּ:
ד וַהֲוָה פִּתְגָם נְבוּאָה
מִקֳּדָם יְיָ עִמִּי לְמֵימַר:
ה כִּדְנַן אֲמַר יְיָ אֱלָהָא
דְיִשְׂרָאֵל כְּתֵינַיָּא טָבְתָא
הָאִלֵּין כֵּן אַשְׁהְמוֹדַע
יָת

רש"י

והמסגר ל' סגור כלומר חכמים גדולים בתורה שכשהיה אחד מהם מדבר הכל שותקים מסגר שהיו סוגרים ואין פותח: (ב) כתאני הבכרות. שבישלו כל צרכן בתחלת בכורי תאנים שהם חביבות על מוצאיהם בראשיתם: (ה) כן אכיר את גלות וגו'. הרי זה מקרא מסורס כן אכיר לטובה את גלות יהודה שהגליתי כבר יכניה וגלותו:

רד"ק

זה אחר הגלית נבוכדנאצר מלך בבל את יכניהי: ואת החרש ואת המסגר. יועצים וחכמים היו וי"ת ית אומניא וית תרעיא: (ב) הדוד אחד. כתאני הבכורות. הסמוכות לעצים כאילו אמר כתאני עצי התאנה המבכרות. בכורות תאר וזכר אותם תאנים

מצודת ציון

(יחזקאל כ"א): החרש. קבוצת האומנים כמו חרש עצים (ישעיה מ"ד): (ב) הבכרות. המבושלות כל צרכן וכן בכורי ענבים (במדבר י"ג): (ה) אכיר. מלשון הכרה:

מצודת דוד

וכן ת"י: (ב) תאנים. מלאה תאנים וגו': כתאני הבכורות. כתאנים המבושלין כל צרכן: מרוע. בעבור רעותן לא היה אפשר לאכלן: (ג) טובות מאד. המה טובות מאד: רעות מאד. המה רעות מאד: (ה) כתאנים הטובות האלה. שהמה חביבה ובני

אדם מתקרבים אליהן כן אכיר את גלות יהודה ר"ל עם כי נעשו זרים ממני כי הרחקתים מעל גבולי הנה עתה אכיר אותם ואתקרב

from Jerusalem and brought them to Babylon. 2. One pot [contained] very good figs like the first ripe figs, and the other pot [contained] very bad figs that could not be eaten because they were so bad. 3. And the Lord said to me: What do you see, Jeremiah? And I said, "Figs. The good figs are very good, and the bad ones are very bad, which cannot be eaten because they are so bad." 4. And the word of the Lord came to me, saying: 5. So said the Lord God of Israel: Like these good figs, so will I recognize the exile of

question. These scholars preserved Torah learning in Israel during the Babylonian exile.

Redak, too, interprets הֶחָרָשׁ וְהַמַּסְגֵּר as *advisers and sages.*

2. **like the first ripe figs**—*that have ripened completely in the beginning of the ripening of the figs, which are dear to all those who find them in their beginning.*—[*Rashi*]

Redak renders: like the figs of the ripening figtrees.

When ripe figs are not picked in time, but allowed to remain on the tree in the sun, they become wormy, as the Rabbis state in the Midrash. If they are picked in time, however, they are preserved. So was the exile of Jehoiachin plucked from the land of Israel in time, before they would become corrupted.—[*Malbim*]

3. **are very good**—Not merely better than the others, but very good because they were picked in time.—[*Malbim*]

are very bad—Not merely are they not as good as the other, but they are very bad because they were allowed to remain on the tree and were not picked in time.—[*Malbim*]

5. **Like these good figs**—that were picked in time.—[*Malbim*]

so will I recognize the exile of etc.—*This is an inverted verse: So will I recognize for good the exile of Judah which I have already exiled,* viz. *Jeconiah and his exile.*—[*Rashi*]

Malbim explains: So will I recognize the exile of Judah that were plucked in their time and have become very good, so good that My exiling them to the land of the Chaldeans was for good.

As mentioned above, *Rashi* explains: So will I recognize for good . . . *Malbim* renders: So will I recognize . . . that I sent forth . . . for good. 'For good' modifies 'have sent forth.' I have exiled them earlier for their own good.

יהודה אשר שלחתי מן־המקום הזה
ארץ כשדים לטובה: ו ושמתי עיני
עליהם לטובה והשבתים על־הארץ
הזאת ובניתים ולא אהרס ונטעתים
ולא אתוש: ז ונתתי להם לב לדעת
אתי כי אני יהוה והיו־לי לעם ואנכי
אהיה להם לאלהים כי־ישבו אלי
בכל־לבם: ח וכתאנים הרעות אשר
לא־תאכלנה מרע כי־כה ׀ אמר יהוה
כן אתן את־צדקיהו מלך־יהודה ואת־

תרגום

ית גלות יהודה דאגליתי
מן אתרא הדין לארע
כסדאי לטבתא: ו ואשוי
מימרי עליהון לטבא
ואתיבינון לארע הדא
ואבנינון ולא אפגר
ואקימינון ולא אטלטל:
ז ואתן להון לב למידע
דדחלתי ארי אנא יי
ויהון קדמי לעם ואנא
אהוי להון לאלה ארי
יתובון לפולחני בכל
לבהון: ח וכתיניא
בישתא דלא מתאכלא
מבישו. ארי כדנן אמר
יי כן אתן ית צדקיהו
מלך שבטא דבית
יהודה וית רברבוהי

רש"י

(ו) אתוש. לשון עקירה:

מהר"י קרא

(ו) והשבותים על הארץ הזאת. לירושלים לבנות בית שני: (ז) כי ישבו אלי בכל לבם. אלו דניאל וחביריו ועזרא שאתה מוצא בספרים שלהם שהתוודו על עונם:

רד"ק

כי הן נחמדות בעיני מוצאיהן לפי שהן בכורות וכן אמר כבכורה בתאנה בראשיתה ראיתי את אבותיכם: (ח) וכתאנים. כאילו אמר והנשברים יהיו תאנים הרעות ואחר כן פירש ואמר כה אמר ה': והיושבים בארץ מצרים. השארית שהיו יושבים אז

מצודת דוד

עליהם: לטובה. חוזר למעלה לומר כן אכיר לטובה: (ו) ושמתי עיני. אשגיח עליהם לטובה ולשמרם בגולה: והשבותים. בזמן בית השני: ובניתים ולא אהרס. ר"ל הואיל וכבר עבר עליהם הגלה לא יקוו עוד מאתה הריסה כ"א בנין בטובה לירושלים בבית השני לא כמו הנשארים בירושלים אשר יקוו אל הריסה הואיל ועדיין לא עבר עליהם הגלה ולא קבלו הגמול: ונטעתים וגו'. כפל הדבר במ"ש: (ז) ונתתי וגו'. אתן להם לב מבין לדעת אותי אשר אני ה': והיו לי לעם. להאמין בי ולקבל עול מוראי: ואנכי וגו'. להיות בעזרתם: (ח) וכתאנים הרעות. כאלו אמר והנשארים הם יהיו כתאנים הרעות אשר אין לאכלן בעבור רעתן הנבזים ומרוחקים

מצודת ציון

(ו) והשבותים. מלשון השבה: אהרס. מל' הריסה ונפילה: **אתוש.**

Judah, which I have sent forth from this place to the land of the Chaldeans, for good.
6. And I will place My eyes upon them for good, and I will return them to this land, and I will build them and not destroy, and I will plant them and not pluck them.
7. And I will give them a heart to know Me, for I am the Lord, and they shall be to Me for a people, and I will be to them for a God, for they shall return to Me with all their heart.
8. And like the bad figs that cannot be eaten because they are so bad, for so said the Lord: So will I make Zedekiah King of Judah and

6. **And I will place My eyes**—I will oversee them for good and guard them in their exile.—[*Mezudath David*]

Because of their exile, I will place My eyes upon them.—[*Malbim*]

and I will return them to this land—To Jerusalem, to build the second Temple.—[*Kara*]

This refers to the return to Zion in the days of Cyrus.—[*Malbim*]

and I will build them—as a kingdom.—[*Malbim*]

and I will plant them—as a settlement in the land.—[*Malbim*]

and not pluck them—Heb. אֶתּוֹשׁ, *an expression of uprooting.*—[*Rashi*]

This refers also to the release of Jehoiachin from prison and to the honor afforded him by the king of Babylon.—[*Abarbanel*]

7. **and they shall be to Me for a people**—to believe in Me and to accept the yoke of My fear.—[*Mezudath David*]

and I will be to them for a God—i.e to be at their assistance.—[*Mezudath David*]

for they shall return to Me with all their heart—These are Daniel and his colleagues and Ezra, as we find in their Books that they confessed their sins. See Daniel 9:4–20, Nehemiah 9:16–37.—[*Kara*]

For through the exile they shall return to Me with all their heart.—[*Malbim*]

8. **And like the bad figs**—And the

שָׂרָיו וְאֵת ׀ שְׁאֵרִית יְרוּשָׁלַ͏ִם הַנִּשְׁאָרִים
בָּאָרֶץ הַזֹּאת וְהַיֹּשְׁבִים בְּאֶרֶץ מִצְרָיִם׃
ט וּנְתַתִּים לְזַוָעָה לְרָעָה לְכֹל מַמְלְכוֹת
הָאָרֶץ לְחֶרְפָּה וּלְמָשָׁל לִשְׁנִינָה
וְלִקְלָלָה בְּכָל־הַמְּקֹמוֹת אֲשֶׁר־אַדִּיחֵם
שָׁם׃ י וְשִׁלַּחְתִּי בָם אֶת־הַחֶרֶב אֶת־
הָרָעָב וְאֶת־הַדָּבֶר עַד־תֻּמָּם
מֵעַל הָאֲדָמָה אֲשֶׁר־נָתַתִּי לָהֶם
וְלַאֲבוֹתֵיהֶם׃ כה א הַדָּבָר אֲשֶׁר־הָיָה

תרגום

וְיַת שְׁאָרָא דִירוּשְׁלֵם דְאִשְׁתְּאָרוּ בְּאַרְעָא הָדָא וּדְיָתְבִין בְּאַרְעָא דְמִצְרָיִם׃ ט וְאֶתְּנִינוּן לְזִיעַ וּלְבִישָׁא לְכָל מַלְכְּוָת אַרְעָא לְחִיסוּדִין וּלְמַתַל וּלְשׁוֹעִי וּלְלְוָטָא בְּכָל אַתְרַיָא דְאַגְלֵינוּן לְתַמָן׃ י וְאֶגָרֵי בְהוֹן יַת דְקַטְלִין בְּחַרְבָּא בְּכַפְנָא וּבְמוֹתָא עַד דִיסוּפוּן מֵעַל אַרְעָא דִיהָבִית לְהוֹן וְלַאֲבָהַתְהוֹן׃ א פִּתְגָם נְבוּאָה דַהֲוָה עִם יִרְמְיָה עַל

מהר"י קרא

לזועה קרי

כה (א) הדבר אשר היה אל ירמיהו אל כל עם יהודה וגו׳ עד היום הזה לא שמעתם אלי. וגם לא לקיתם שלא שילטתם כפי מעלליכם ומאחר שלא שבתם:

רש"י

(ט) לזועה לרעה לכל ממלכות הארץ. שישמעו הרעה הבאה עליהם ויזועו: לשנינה. שיננו וידברו הכל בפורענותם:

מנחת שי

(ט) לזעוה. לזועה קרי: לחרפה. בלא וא״ו: לשנינה בלא וא״ו: (י) את הרעב. בלא וא״ו על פי המסורת דרים מספטים וכ״כ רד״ק:

רד"ק

בארץ מצרים אותם שילכו עם יוחנן בן קרח: (ט) לזועה. כתיב וקרי לזעות והענין אחד כמו כבש וכשב: לחרפה. בלא וי״ו: לשנינה. בלא וי״ו: (י) את הרעב. בלא וי״ו: (א) הדבר. על ירמיהו. כמו אל: היא השנ. הראשונית לנבוכדנאצר. והנה

מצודת ציון

ענין עקירה כמו לנתוש ולנתוץ (לעיל א׳): (ט) לזועה. ענין רעד ורתת וכן והיה רק זועה (ישעיה כ״ח): לשנינה. ענין ספור ואמירה כמו ושננתם לבניך (דברים ו׳): (י) תומם. ענין כליון והשלמה כמו תם הכסף (בראשית מ״ז):

מצודת דוד

מבני אדם: כן אתן וגו׳. להיות שנוא ומרוחק: והיושבים בארץ מצרים. שהלכו עם יוחנן בן קרח למצרים ונתיישבו שמה אשר לא כמצות ה׳: (ט) ונתתים וגו׳. ר״ל אמסרם לכל ממלכות הארץ להיות לזועה ולרעה כי כולם יחרידום וירעו להם: לחרפה וגו׳. ר״ל בכל המקום אשר אדיח אותם שם יהיו לחרפה כי כולם יחרפו אותם: ולמשל. יכילו משל מהפורעניות הבאה עליהם: לשנינה. יתמידו לספר מהצרות הבאות עליהם: ולקללה. המקלל יתלה הקללה בהם לומר תהיה כהיהודים המקוללים: (י) עד תומם. עד יכלו מעל האדמה וגו׳:

his princes and the remnant of Jerusalem remaining in this
land, and those dwelling in the land of Egypt. 9. And I shall
make them for a horror [and] for evil for all the kingdoms of
the earth, for a disgrace and for a proverb, for a conversation
piece and for a curse in all the places where I will exile them.
10. And I will send forth the sword, the famine, and the pesti-
lence against them until they are consumed from upon the land
that I gave them and their forefathers.

25

1. The word that came

remaining ones shall be like the bad figs. Then he explained: So said the Lord etc.—[*Redak*]

and those dwelling in the land of Egypt—The remnant that was then dwelling in Egypt, viz. those who went with Johanan son of Kareah. See below 43:4–7.—[*Redak, Mezudath David*]

9. **for a horror [and] for evil for all the kingdoms of the earth**—*For they will hear the evil that came upon them and quake.*—[*Rashi*]

Since it was decreed that Nebuchadnezzar would pursue them, all the kingdoms among whom they were exiled would feel the evil coming upon them and quake. They would also be for a disgrace even in those places that Nebuchadnezzar would not reach.—[*Malbim*]

and for a conversation piece—*that everyone will repeat and discuss their retribution.*—[*Rashi*]

10. **And I will send forth the sword etc**—wherever they will be. Also, Zedekiah will die in misery in prison. God had decreed that all the kingdoms of the earth submit to Nebuchadnezzar. Therefore, Jeremiah served as an adviser to the Jews and to the other nations and exhorted them to obey this decree. Since Jeconiah and his princes and wise men heeded the prophecy and surrendered to him, God saw that they be spared. Since Zedekiah and his people did not heed the prophecy and did not surrender to Nebuchadnezzar, they were like the bad figs, for evil would befall them. Zedekiah would not be released from prison and no ruler would come from his seed. For this reason, the prophet mentioned those dwelling in Egypt along with Zedekiah and his people, since both groups acted contrary to God's command.—[*Abarbanel*]

עַל־יִרְמְיָהוּ עַל־כָּל־עַם יְהוּדָה בַּשָּׁנָה
הָרְבִעִית לִיהוֹיָקִים בֶּן־יֹאשִׁיָּהוּ מֶלֶךְ
יְהוּדָה הִיא הַשָּׁנָה הָרִאשֹׁנִית
לִנְבוּכַדְרֶאצַּר מֶלֶךְ בָּבֶל׃ ב אֲשֶׁר דִּבֶּר
יִרְמְיָהוּ הַנָּבִיא עַל־כָּל־עַם יְהוּדָה וְאֶל
כָּל־יֹשְׁבֵי יְרוּשָׁלִַם לֵאמֹר׃ ג מִן־שְׁלֹשׁ
עֶשְׂרֵה שָׁנָה לְיֹאשִׁיָּהוּ בֶן־אָמוֹן מֶלֶךְ
יְהוּדָה וְעַד ׀ הַיּוֹם הַזֶּה זֶה שָׁלֹשׁ
וְעֶשְׂרִים שָׁנָה הָיָה דְבַר־יְהוָה אֵלָי
וָאֲדַבֵּר אֲלֵיכֶם אַשְׁכֵּים וְדַבֵּר וְלֹא
שְׁמַעְתֶּם׃ ד וְשָׁלַח יְהוָה אֲלֵיכֶם אֶת־
כל

א׳ במקום ה׳

תרגום

על כל עמא דבית
יהודה בשתא רביעיתא
ליהויקים בר יאשיה
מלכא דשבטא דבית
יהודה היא שתא
קדמיתא לנבוכדרצר
מלכא דבבל׃ ב דאתנבי
ירמיה נביא על כל
עמא דבית יהודה ועל
כל יתבי ירושלם
למימר׃ ג מן תלת
עשרי שנין ליאשיה בר
אמון מלכא דשבטא דבית
יהודה ועד יומא הדין
דנן עשרין ותלת שנין
הוה פתגם נבואה מן
קדם יי עמי ומלילית
עמכון מקדם וממליל
ולא קבילתון׃ ד ושלח
יי לותכון ית כל עבדוהי

רש"י

כה (א) בשנה הרביעית. שנה שנתחתם גזר דינם שיגלו וישתו כוס החמה כמו שאמר בענין קח את כוס וגו' וקודם גזר דין אמר לנביא להוכיחם אולי ישובו ולא יתחתם גזר דינם: (ג) שלש ועשרים. יאשיהו מלך שלשים ואחת צא מהם י"ב שנה נשארו י"ט וארבע של בנו הרי שלש ועשרים: אשכים ודבר. לשון הווה הייתי משכים ומדבר תמיד:

רד"ק

כתב בתחלת ספר דניאל בשנת שלש למלכות יהויקים מלך יהודה בא נבוכדנצר מלך בבל ירושלם ויצר עליה אך נאמר כי בשנת שלש למלכות יהויקים בנו שהמליכו פרעה נכו מלך נבוכדנצר ובא לירושלם ויצר עליה ובשנת הרביעית ליהויקים בתחלת השנה נתן ה׳ בידו את יהויקים והיא שנה ראשונה לנבוכדנצר: (ב) על כל עם יהודה. כמו אל: ואל כל יושבי ירושלם. עם יהודה מן הערים האחרות שבאו לירושלים ודברי ירמיהו אליהם ואל יושבי ירושלם: (ג) זה שלש ועשרים שנה. יאשיהו מלך שלשים ואחת שנה ובי"ג שנה למלכו תחלת נבואת ירמיהו נמצא ירמיהו נתנבא בימי יאשיהו י"ט שנה ונבואה זו היתה בשנת הרביעית ליהויקים בנו הנה שלש ועשרים שנה: אשכים ודבר האל"ף במקום ה"א השכם כי

מנחת שי

כה (א) בשנה הרביעית. בספרים מדוייקים חסר יו"ד קדמאה וכן נראה מהמסורת דסוף יחזקאל: (ג) אשכים ודבר. האל"ף במקום ה"א

מצודת דוד

כה (א) על ירמיה. אל ירמיה: ליהויקים. למלכות יהויקים: (ב) על כל עם. אל כל עם: (ג) ליאשיהו. למלכות יאשיהו: זה שלש ועשרים שנה. י"ט שנה בימי יאשיהו כי מלך ל"א שנים וד׳ בימי יהויקים בנו הרי כ"ג: היה דבר ה׳ אלי. דבר בי הנבואה: ואדבר. ואני דברתי אליכם הנבואה והייתי משכי׳ ומדבר ר"ל אני הייתי זריז לומר הנבואה אבל אתם לא שמעתם: (ד) ושלח ה׳. ועוד שלח ה׳ שאר נביאים והיה משכים ומשלח בזריזות רב ואתם לא שמעתם: ולא וגו׳. כפל הדבר במלות שונות:

מצודת ציון

כה (ג) אשכים. מלשון השכמה והוא ענין זריזות:

twenty-three years after the commencement of his prophetic career. —[*Redak*]

arising early—*This is a present tense. I would arise early and speak constantly.*—[*Rashi*]

to Jeremiah concerning all the people of Judah in the fourth year of Jehoiakim son of Josiah, king of Judah—that is the first year of Nebuchadrezzar king of Babylon. 2. Which Jeremiah the prophet spoke to all the people of Judah and to all the inhabitants of Jerusalem, saying: 3. From the thirteenth year of Josiah son of Amon, king of Judah, until this day, these twenty-three years the word of the Lord has come to me, and I spoke to you, arising early and speaking, but you did not hearken. 4. And the Lord sent to you

Malbim explains that this verse refers to the exiles who wished to return to the land of Israel.

1. **in the fourth year**—*The year that their decree was sealed that they be exiled and that they drink the cup of wrath, as he says in this section:* '(v. 15) *Take the cup etc.,' and before the decree He commanded the prophet to reprove them, perhaps they would repent, and their decree would not be sealed.*—[*Rashi*]

that is the first year of Nebuchadnezzar—In the beginning of the Book of Daniel (1:1), we read, "In the third year of the reign of Jehoiakim, king of Judah, Nebuchadnezzar, king of Babylon, came upon Jerusalem and besieged it." It is possible that in the third year of Jehoiakim's reign, when he was crowned by Pharaoh-Neco, Nebuchadnezzar assumed the throne of Babylon, and marched on Jerusalem, besieging it. In the fourth year of Jehoiakim, still the third year of Nebuchadnezzar, God delivered Jehoiakim into his hand.—[*Redak*]

According to *Seder Olam,* ch. 25, Nebuchadnezzar besieged Jerusalem in the third year of Jehoiakim's revolt. We find that Nebuchadnezzar vanquished Jehoiakim in the fifth year of the latter's reign, which was the second year of the former's. Jehoiakim was faithful to Nebuchadnezzar for three years, making eight years from the beginning of his reign. He, then, rebelled against Nebuchadnezzar for three years. After the third year of his revolt, Nebuchadnezzar vanquished him again and carried him off to Babylon.

2. **to all the people of Judah**—The people of Judah came from other cities to Jerusalem, where Jeremiah addressed them together with the inhabitants of Jerusalem.—[*Redak*]

3. **twenty-three years**—*Josiah reigned thirty-one years* (II Kings 22:1). *Subtract twelve years from them* (Jer. 1:2). *This leaves nineteen, and four of his son amount to twenty-three.*—[*Rashi*] I.e., Jeremiah prophesied during the last nineteen years of Josiah's reign. Since this prophecy came to him in the fourth year of Jehoiakim, it was

כָּל־עֲבָדָיו הַנְּבִאִים הַשְׁכֵּם וְשָׁלֹחַ וְלֹא
שְׁמַעְתֶּם וְלֹא־הִטִּיתֶם אֶת־אָזְנְכֶם
לִשְׁמֹעַ׃ ה לֵאמֹר שׁוּבוּ־נָא אִישׁ
מִדַּרְכּוֹ הָרָעָה וּמֵרֹעַ מַעַלְלֵיכֶם וּשְׁבוּ
עַל־הָאֲדָמָה אֲשֶׁר נָתַן יְהוָה לָכֶם
וְלַאֲבוֹתֵיכֶם לְמִן־עוֹלָם וְעַד־עוֹלָם׃
ו וְאַל־תֵּלְכוּ אַחֲרֵי אֱלֹהִים אֲחֵרִים
לְעָבְדָם וּלְהִשְׁתַּחֲוֺת לָהֶם וְלֹא־תַכְעִיסוּ
אוֹתִי בְּמַעֲשֵׂה יְדֵיכֶם וְלֹא אָרַע לָכֶם׃
ז וְלֹא־שְׁמַעְתֶּם אֵלַי נְאֻם־יְהוָה לְמַעַן
הַכְעִסוּנִי בְּמַעֲשֵׂה יְדֵיכֶם לְרַע לָכֶם׃
ח לָכֵן כֹּה אָמַר יְהוָה צְבָאוֹת יַעַן אֲשֶׁר
לֹא־שְׁמַעְתֶּם אֶת־דְּבָרָי׃ ט הִנְנִי שֹׁלֵחַ

נביא מקדם ומשלח
ולא קבילתון ולא
ארכינתון ית אודנכון
לקבלא: ה למימר תובו
כען גבר מאורחיה
בישתא ומבישות
עובדיכון ותיבו על
ארעא דיהב יי לכון
ולאבהתכון למן עלמא
ועד עלמא: ו ולא
תהכון בתר טעות פלחי
כוכביא למפלחהן
ולמסגד להן ולא תרגזון
קדמי בעובדי ידיכון
ולא אבאיש לכון: ז ולא
קבילתון למימרי אמר
יי בדיל דלא לארגזא
קדמי בעובדי ידיכון
לאבאשא לכון: ח בכן
כדנן אמר יי צבאות
חלף דלא קבילתון ית
פתגמי: ט הא אנא
שלח

יתיר וא"ו

מהר"י קרא

(ח) לכן כה אמר ה' צבאות יען אשר לא שמעתם את דברי. (ט) הנני שולח ולקחתי את כל משפחות צפון. ואל נבוכדנצר.

מנחת שי

יצא מלא יו"ד על פי המסורת: (ה) שובו נא. בספרים מדוייקים הוא"ו שורק לא בשלש נקודות וכן דינו מכח המסורת שלא נמנה עם החסרים במסורת דקאי סיפרא סימן ל"ה: ולאבותיכם. בספרים מדוייקים מלא וא"ו וכן ראוי לפי המסורת: (ז) הכעסוני הכעסוני קרי:

רד"ק

אותיות אחו"י מתחלפות ונכתבה יו"ד המשך שלא כמנהג עם הצר"י ברוב: (ה) למן עולם ועד עולם. מזמן רב נתנה לאבתיכם ועד עולם יתננה לכם ולבניכם אם תרצו ולמ"ד למן עולם לא בא על ענין הדבר אלא לאמתת עצם הדבר ויספיק הענין זולתה וכמוהו למן היום אשר יצא מארץ מצרים למתי אעתיר לך והדומים להם: (ז) למען הכעיסוני. כתיב ר"ל

מצודת ציון

(ו) ארע. מלשון רעה: (ח) יען. בעבור:

מצודת דוד

(ה) לאמר. ר"ל הלא כל הנבואות היו לטובתכם לאמר שובו אתם כל איש מדרכו וגו' ובעבור זה תשבו על האדמה וגו': למן עולם. ר"ל מעת הנתינה עד עולם: (ו) במעשי ידיכם. בהעכו"ם העשויות במעשה ידיכם: ולא ארע לכם. לא אעשה עמכם רעה: (ז) ולא שמעתם. עם כי הדבר היה לטובתכם לא שמעתם וגו': למען הכעיסני. לא היה זה אלא למען הכעיסני וגו' וההכעסה תהיה באמת לרע לכם: (ט) הנני שולח. ר"ל אעיר לבות אומות שונות מפאת צפון: עבדי. ר"ל עושה שליחותי בדבר זה: סביב. היושבים

all His servants, the prophets, sending them early, but you did not hearken and you did not incline your ear[s] to listen.
5. Saying: Repent now, each man of his evil way and of the evil of your deeds, and dwell on the land that the Lord gave you and your forefathers from days of yore and forever. 6. And do not go after other gods to worship them and to prostrate yourselves to them, and you shall not provoke Me with the work of your hands, and I will not harm you. 7. But you did not hearken to Me, says the Lord, in order to provoke Me with the work of your hands for your harm. 8. Therefore, so said the Lord of Hosts: Since you have not hearkened to My words, 9. Behold, I send

4. **sending them early**—I.e. sending them early every morning, not all at once. Nevertheless, you did not hearken, and did not even incline your ears to listen.—[*Malbim*]

Although God sent them with great eagerness, sending them early every morning, you did not obey them.—[*Mezudath David*]

and you did not incline your ear[s]—This expression is synonymous with the previous.—[*Mezudath David*]

5. **Saying**—All these prophecies were for your benefit, exhorting you to repent so that you remain in your land.—[*Mezudath David*]

from days of yore and forever—It was given to your forefathers long ago, and it will remain their children's forever if they so desire.—[*Redak*]

You yourselves prevent My bestowing good upon you. He states this regarding murder, immorality, oppression, and theft that were among them.—[*Abarbanel*]

7. **in order to provoke Me**—Not for your benefit, but only to provoke Me.—[*Redak*]

with the work of your hands—I.e. with the idols you have made with your own hands.—[*Mezudath David*]

for your harm—Your provocation of Me will only bring harm upon you.—[*Mezudath David*]

9. **Behold I send**—This prophecy was said in the first year of Nebuchadnezzar, which, according to *Seder Olam* was the year he vanquished Jehoiakim.—[*Kara*] See *Megillah* 11b, that he vanquished Jehoiakim in his second year, also *Seder Olam* ch. 24.

וְלָקַחְתִּי אֶת־כָּל־מִשְׁפְּחוֹת צָפוֹן נְאֻם־
יְהוָה וְאֶל־נְבוּכַדְרֶאצַּר מֶלֶךְ־בָּבֶל
עַבְדִּי וַהֲבִאֹתִים עַל־הָאָרֶץ הַזֹּאת
וְעַל־יֹשְׁבֶיהָ וְעַל כָּל־הַגּוֹיִם הָאֵלֶּה
סָבִיב וְהַחֲרַמְתִּים וְשַׂמְתִּים לְשַׁמָּה
וְלִשְׁרֵקָה וּלְחָרְבוֹת עוֹלָם׃ י וְהַאֲבַדְתִּי
מֵהֶם קוֹל שָׂשׂוֹן וְקוֹל שִׂמְחָה קוֹל חָתָן
וְקוֹל כַּלָּה קוֹל רֵחַיִם וְאוֹר נֵר׃ יא וְהָיְתָה
כָּל־הָאָרֶץ הַזֹּאת לְחָרְבָּה לְשַׁמָּה
וְעָבְדוּ הַגּוֹיִם הָאֵלֶּה אֶת־מֶלֶךְ בָּבֶל
שִׁבְעִים שָׁנָה׃ יב וְהָיָה כִמְלֹאות

שְׁלַח נָאֲדַבַּר יָת כָּל
מַלְכְוָת צִפּוּנָא אֲמַר יְיָ
וְלִנְבוּכַדְנֶאצַר מַלְכָּא
דְבָבֶל עַבְדִי וְאַיְתֵינוּן
עַל אַרְעָא הָדָא וְעַל
יָתְבַהָא וְעַל כָּל עַמְמַיָא
הָאִלֵין סְחוֹר סְחוֹר
וְאֶגְמְרִינוּן וַאֲשַׁוִינוּן
לְצָדוּ וּלְאִשְׁתְּמָמוּ
וּלְחָרְבַת עָלָם: י וְאוֹבֵד
מִנְהוֹן קָל בִּיעַ וְקָל
חֶדְוָא קָל חַתְנִין וְקָל
כַּלָּן קָל סִיעַן דִמְשַׁבְּחִין
בְּנִיהוֹר בּוֹצִין: יא וּתְהֵי
כָּל אַרְעָא הָדָא לְחָרְבָּא
לְצָדוּ וְיִפְלְחוּן עַמְמַיָא
הָאִלֵין יָת מַלְכָּא דְבָבֶל
שַׁבְעִין שְׁנִין: יב וִיהֵי
כְּמִשְׁלַם שַׁבְעִין שְׁנִין
אסער

יתיר וא׳ו.

רש״י

(י) קול רחים. סימן הוא לסעודת ברית מילה על שם שטוחנין ושוחקין לה סממנין לרפואה: אור נר. סי׳ משתה

מהר״י קרא

ונביאה זו נאמרה בשנה הראשונה לנבוכדנצר ושנינו בסדר עולם שאותה שנה כיבש את יהויקים: (י) קול רחים. שמעצמך אתה למד כששאו ערים מאין יושב בטלו קול הטוחנות של

רד״ק

בעבור שהכעיסוני וקרי הכעיסני למען הכעים אותי עושים העכו״ם לא להנאה שיש להם בה: (ט) את כל משפחות צפון. ולמעלה בתחלת הספר אמר לכל משפחות ממלכות צפונה ושם פי׳ כי משפחות אומר על העם וממלכות אומר על ראשי הממלכות ולפי שאמר ונתנו איש כסאו זכר שם ממלכות: ואל נבוכדנצר מלך בבל עבדי. וטעם ואל אל שולח לא אל ולקחתי או יהיה ואל במקום ואת כמו אספרה אל חק ה׳ וירדפו אל מדין: ועל כל הגוים האלה. הסמוכים לא״י או האלה על הגוים שעתיד לזכר׳ בסמוך בפרשת כוס יין החמה: (י) קול רחים ואור. קול רחים שטוחנין תבלין לסעודת שמחה וכן מדליקין נרות רבות בבית המשתה וי״ת קל סיען דמשבחין בניהור בוצין: (יב) כמלאת שבעים שנה. כי נבוכדנצר מלך מ״ה שנה והיאך ידענו זה שהרי אויל מרודך נמ מלך בשנת ל״ז לגלות המלך יהויכין כמ״ש בספר מלכים בסופו ובסוף זה

מצודת דוד

סביבות א״י: והחרמתים. את כולם אחרים ואשימם לתמהון ולהיות שורקין עליהם ועד זמן רב יהיו חרבים: (י) והאבדתי וגו׳. ר״ל לא ישמע עוד קול ששון וגו׳: קול חתן. קול שמחת החתן: קול רחים. מגודל הרעה לא ימלאו תבואה לטחון ברחים: ואור הנר. מחסרון השמן ישבו באפלה: (יא) הגוים האלה. היושבים סביבות ארץ ישראל: (יב) כמלאות. כאשר יהיה נשלם שבעים שנה:

מצודת ציון

(ט) והחרמתים. ענין הרג ואבדון כמו כי החרם תחרימם (דברים כ׳): לשמה. ענין תמהון: לשרקה. ענין השמעת קול נקבין שפתים ונעשה על דבר השוב שנחרב: ולחרבות. מל׳ חורבן: (יב) כמלאות.

formance of circumcision, they were afraid to publicize the occasion and chose the mill as a symbol since it was used for grinding the ingredients for healing the wound. The light of a candle in the daytime or the light of many candles was the sign of a feast. *Rashi* does not explain the reason for concealing the feast. According to *Yerushalmi, Kethuboth* 1:5, this feast was a wedding, concealed from the rulers lest they assault the bride as was their wont. Accordingly, the connection to this verse is obscure. Why should Scripture choose a symbol used only in times of persecution to conceal these occasions? *Tosafoth* asserts that these signs were present at all times, even when circumcision was permitted. [In such times, however, the public was not notified by these signs, but by a public announcement. When public announcements

and I will take all the families of the north, says the Lord, and
to Nebuchadrezzar the king of Babylon, My servant, and I will
bring them upon this land and upon its inhabitants and upon
all these nations around, and I will destroy them and make
them for a desolation and for a hissing and for perpetual ruins.
10. And I will cause to cease from them a voice of mirth and a
voice of joy, the sound of a bridegroom and the sound of a
bride, the sound of a mill and the light of a candle. 11. And all
this land shall become waste [and] desolation, and these
nations shall serve the king of Babylon for seventy years.
12. And it shall be at the completion of

The intention is that I will inspire various nations from the north.—[*Mezudath David*]

all the families of the north—Compare 1:15, "all the families of the kingdoms of the north." The 'families' are the populace, and the 'kingdoms' are the heads of the kingdoms. That expression is used there in conjunction with the following passage, "and they will come and place, each one his throne etc."—[*Redak*] *Jonathan,* however, renders: all the kingdoms of the north.

and for Nebuchadrezzar—I.e., I will send for Nebuchadrezzar the king of Babylon. It may also be rendered: and Nebuchadrezzar the king of Babylon, meaning: and I will take Nebuchadrezzar the king of Babylon.—[*Redak*]

My servant—I.e. the one who will perform My errand in this matter.—[*Mezudath David*]

and upon all these nations—I.e. those who dwell near the Holy Land. It may also mean these nations mentioned below.—[*Redak*]

around—Those who dwell around the Holy Land.—[*Mezudath David*]

10. **And I will cause to cease**—I.e., there no longer shall be heard.—[*Mezudath David*]

the sound of a bridegroom—I.e. the sound of the rejoicing of a bridegroom.—[*Mezudath David*]

the sound of a mill—*That is an indication of a circumcision feast, since they would grind and crush ingredients for healing* the wound.—[*Rashi*]

the light of a candle—*An indication of a feast. So we learned in Sanhedrin* (32b).—[*Rashi*]

The Talmud does not state this explicitly on this verse. The passage reads: The sound of a mill in Burni announces: "The week of the male child! The week of the male child!" The light of a candle in B'ror Hayil announces: "A feast is there! A feast is there!" *Rashi* explains that when the government prohibited the per-

שִׁבְעִים שָׁנָה אֶפְקֹד עַל־מֶלֶךְ־בָּבֶל
וְעַל־הַגּוֹי הַהוּא נְאֻם יְהוָה אֶת־עֲוֺנָם
וְעַל־אֶרֶץ כַּשְׂדִּים וְשַׂמְתִּי אֹתוֹ
לְשִׁמְמוֹת עוֹלָם׃ יג וְהֵבֵאוֹתִי עַל־הָאָרֶץ
הַהִיא אֶת־כָּל־דְּבָרַי אֲשֶׁר־דִּבַּרְתִּי
עָלֶיהָ אֵת כָּל־הַכָּתוּב בַּסֵּפֶר הַזֶּה
אֲשֶׁר־נִבָּא יִרְמְיָהוּ עַל־כָּל־הַגּוֹיִם׃
יד כִּי עָבְדוּ בָם גַּם־הֵמָּה גּוֹיִם רַבִּים
וּמְלָכִים גְּדוֹלִים וְשִׁלַּמְתִּי לָהֶם כְּפָעֳלָם
וּכְמַעֲשֵׂה יְדֵיהֶם׃ טו כִּי כֹה אָמַר יְהוָה
אֱלֹהֵי יִשְׂרָאֵל אֵלַי קַח אֶת־כּוֹס הַיַּיִן

תרגום

אֲסָעַר עַל מַלְכָּא דְבָבֶל
וְעַל עַמָּא הַהוּא אֲמַר
יְיָ יָת חוֹבֵיהוֹן וְעַל אֲרַע
כַּסְדָּאֵי וַאֲשַׁוֵּי יָתַהּ
לְצָדוּת עָלַם׃ יג וְאַיְתֵי
עַל אַרְעָא הַהִיא
יָת כָּל פִּתְגָמַיָא
דְגָזְרִית עֲלַהּ יָת כָּל
דִכְתִיב בְּסִפְרָא הָדֵין
דְאִתְנַבֵּי יִרְמְיָה עַל כָּל
עַמְמַיָא׃ יד אֲרֵי פְלָחוּ
בְהוֹן אַף אִינוּן עַמְמִין
סַגִיאִין וּמַלְכִין רַבְרְבִין
וַאֲשַׁלֵּים לְהוֹן כַּאֲגוּרֵיהוֹן
וּכְעוֹבָדֵי יְדֵיהוֹן׃ טו אֲרֵי
כִדְנַן אֲמַר יְיָ אֱלָהָא
דְיִשְׂרָאֵל לִי קַבִּיל יָת
כָּסָא דַחֲמַר לְוָטָא הָדֵין

והבאתי קרי

מהר"י קרא

רחים ואף כשחרבו בתים מאין אדם בטל מתוכם אור הנר: (יג) והבאתי על הארץ ההיא את כל דברי אשר דברתי עליה. על ידי ישעיה. אם ימצא בספר מדוייק ואת בפסוק זה או נוכל להשיג זה פת׳ ואם הוא את אינו אלא מפרש הוא את שלמעלה הימנו. ואת כל הכתוב בספר הזה על ידי ירמיה *). כי ישעיה וירמיה ניבאו במפלת בבל יותר משאר כל הנביאים:

*) בנדפס כתוב ישעיה וירמיה.

רש"י

כך שנינו בסנהדרין: (יג) את כל הכתוב. על בבל: בספר הזה. בסופו: (יד) כי עבדו בם. כמו כי יעבדו בם בבני בבל: גם המה גוים רבים. מדי ופרס: (טו) כום היין החמה. נבואת הפורענות: והשקית אותו. הנבא להם שלא תשוב עוד בשום תשובה:

מנחת שי

(יג) לְשִׁמְמוֹת. כן כתיב: (יג) והבאותי. והבאתי קרי:

רד"ק

הספר ויהויכין גלה בשנת ה׳ לנבוכדנצר הרי מ"ה ואויל מרודך מלך כ"ג שנה והאיך ידענו זה שהרי מצאנו לבלשצר בנו מלך ג׳ שנים נשארו כ"ג בינתים והשלש לא שלמו לו לבלשצר כי בשנת השלישית נהרג הרי מ"ח וכ"ג הרי ס"ח ושתים לבלשצר הרי ע׳ לפיכך אמר כמלאת כי שלמים היו להם ע׳ שנה כי לא מת בלשצר עד שנת שלישית לו: לשממות עולם. שם מקובץ מן שממה והוא סמוך: (יג) את כל הכתוב בספר הזה. עם כל הכתוב. כלומר אביא על ארץ בבל את כל זה הדבר כמו שאביא על כל הגוים כל הכתוב בספר הזה אשר ניבא ירמיהו: (יד) כי עבדו בם גם המה. עבדו עבר במקום עתיד אמר יעבדו בכשדים גם המה כמו שעבדו הם בכל הגוים כן יעבדו בהם גוים רבים ומלכים גדולים והם מלכי מדי ופרס: (טו) כי כה אמר. קח. והשקית. הכל במראה הנבואה: היין החמה. חסר הנסמך ומשפטו היין יין החמה וכמוהו העם

מצודת ציון

ענין השלמה כמו ובמלאות ימי טהרה (ויקרא י"ב): אפקוד. ענין

מצודת דוד

אפקד. אזכיר עליהם עונם: ועל הגוי ההוא. זה בבל: (יג) בספר הזה. בסוף הספר: על כל הגוים. שהם יבאו ויחריבו את בבל עד היסוד בה: (יד) כי עבדו. עבר במקום עתיד ור"ל יעבדו בבבל: גם המה. ר"ל כמו שעבדה בבל באומות כן גם המה יעבדו בה ומוזר ומפרש גוים רבים וגו׳ הם יעבדו בבבל: להם. לבני בבל: (טו) את כום היין החמה. כמשיל חמת ה׳ ונזרת

prophecies of Isaiah, who dwelt at length on the downfall of Babylon. He hesitates, however, because he has not found any edition of Jeremiah reading: and all. *Jonathan*, too, renders: all.

14. **For . . . will enslave them**—Lit. have enslaved them. *Like 'For . . . shall enslave them,'* i.e. shall enslave *the people of Babylon.*—[*Rashi*]

As in many places, this is the prophetic past.

many nations . . . too—Viz. Media and Persia.—[*Rashi, Redak*]

Others state that all the nations mistreated by Babylon will enslave that nation and repay them for their mistreatment.—[*Abarbanel, Mezudath David, Malbim*]

and I will recompense them according to their deed—They will

seventy years, I will visit upon the king of Babylon and upon that nation, says the Lord, their iniquity, and upon the land of the Chaldeans, and I will make it for everlasting desolations.
13. And I will bring upon that land all My words that I have spoken about it, all that is written in this book, which Jeremiah prophesied concerning all the nations. 14. For many nations
and great kings will enslave them too, and I will recompense them according to their deed and according to the work of their hands. 15. For so said the Lord God of Israel to me: Take this
cup of the wine of

were impossible, these signs were used to inform the public of these celebrations.] *Ran* (*San.* ad loc.) explains that the Talmud indeed wishes to explain our verse and that these signs are not related to persecutions. See *Pethach Einaim.*

Redak explains that they would grind spices for festive occasions and light many candles. *Jonathan* renders: the sound of groups that praise with the light of candles.

When the cities became desolate, it goes without saying that the mills would no longer be heard and the light of the candles no longer seen.—[*Kara*]

12. **at the completion of seventy years**—For Nebuchadnezzar reigned forty-five years. This can be derived from the fact that his son Evil-Merodach assumed the throne in the thirty-seventh year of the exile of Jehoiachin, as is stated at the end of II Kings (25:27) and at the end of this Book (52:31), and Jehoiachin went into exile in the eighth year of Nebuchadnezzar (II Kings 24:12), thus equalling forty-five years. Evil-Merodach reigned twenty-three years, since Belshazzar his son reigned three years, leaving twenty-three years for Evil-Merodach. Belshazzar's third year was not complete, since he was slain in the third year. Hence, we have seventy years.—[*Redak*] See *Megillah* 11b.

all that is written—*concerning Babylon.*—[*Rashi*]

in this Book—*at its end.*—[*Rashi*]

Others render: with all that is written in this Book, which Jeremiah prophesied concerning all the nations. I will bring upon Babylon all that I have spoken about it, along with all that is written in this book concerning the doom of the other nations.—[*Redak*]

Malbim explains that Jeremiah's prophecies concerning the other nations, starting from ch. 46, include Babylon as well. Hence, in addition to the catastrophe destined to befall Babylon, the catastrophes destined for all other nations will also befall Babylon.

Kara renders: *and* all that is written in this Book etc. The beginning of the verse, 'all my word which I spoke concerning it,' refers to the

הַחֵמָה הַזֹּאת מִיָּדִי וְהִשְׁקִיתָה אֹתוֹ
אֶת־כָּל־הַגּוֹיִם אֲשֶׁר אָנֹכִי שֹׁלֵחַ אוֹתְךָ
אֲלֵיהֶם׃ טז וְשָׁתוּ וְהִתְגֹּעֲשׁוּ וְהִתְהֹלָלוּ
מִפְּנֵי הַחֶרֶב אֲשֶׁר אָנֹכִי שֹׁלֵחַ בֵּינֹתָם׃
יז וָאֶקַּח אֶת־הַכּוֹס מִיַּד יְהוָה וָאַשְׁקֶה
אֶת־כָּל־הַגּוֹיִם אֲשֶׁר־שְׁלָחַנִי יְהוָה
אֲלֵיהֶם׃ יח אֶת־יְרוּשָׁלַםִ וְאֶת־עָרֵי
יְהוּדָה וְאֶת־מְלָכֶיהָ אֶת־שָׂרֶיהָ לָתֵת
אֹתָם לְחָרְבָּה לְשַׁמָּה לִשְׁרֵקָה
וְלִקְלָלָה כַּיּוֹם הַזֶּה׃ יט אֶת־פַּרְעֹה מֶלֶךְ־
מִצְרַיִם וְאֶת־עֲבָדָיו וְאֶת־שָׂרָיו וְאֶת־

מִן קֳדָמַי וְתַשְׁקֵי יָתֵיהּ
יַת כָּל עַמְמַיָא דַאֲנָא
שָׁלַח יָתָךְ עֲלֵיהוֹן׃
טז וְיִשְׁתּוּן וְיִשְׁתַּגְשׁוּן
וְיִטְרְפוּן מִן קֳדָם דִקְטָלִין
בְּחַרְבָּא דַאֲנָא שָׁלַח
בֵּינֵיהוֹן׃ יז וְקַבֵּלִית יָת
כָּסָא מִן קֳדָם יְיָ וְאַשְׁקֵיתִי
יָת כָּל עַמְמַיָא דִשְׁלָחַנִי
יְיָ לְוָתְהוֹן׃ יח יָת
יְרוּשְׁלֶם וְיָת קִרְוַיָא
דְבֵית יְהוּדָה וְיָת
מַלְכָהָא וְיָת רַבְרְבָהָא
לְמִתַּן יָתְהוֹן לְחָרְבָּא
לְצָדוּ לְאִשְׁתְּמָמוּ
וּלְלוּטָא כְּיוֹמָא הָדֵין׃
יט יָת פַּרְעֹה מַלְכָּא
מִצְרַיִם וְיָת עַבְדוֹהִי וְיָת
רַבְרְבוֹהִי וְיָת כָּל עַמֵּיהּ׃
וית

רש"י

(טז) והתגעשו. ויתרגזון: והתהללו. לשון הוללות ישתטו: (יח) כיום הזה. כאשר הם היום. לאחר החרבן

רד"ק

המלחכה הספר הבקנה והדומים להם: (טז) ושתו והתגועשו. התפעל מורכב עם פעל שלא נזכר פועלו ועניינו ענין והגעש ותרעש הארץ: והתהללו. ענין הוללות והוא התפעל מורכב עם פעל הדומה לכרובע: (יז) ואקח, ואשקה, הכל במראה הנבואה: (יח) את ירושלם. היא שתתה תחלה כי כל אלה הגוים לקו על ידי נבוכדנצר ושנה ראשונה שמלך והיא השנה הרביעית ליהויקים בא על ירושלם: ואת מלכיה. יהויקים ויהויכין וצדקיהו: את שריה. בלא וי"ו: לשרקה.

מנחת שי

(טז) והתהללו. בספרים מדוייקים חסר וא"ו אחר הה"א: (יח) את שריה. י"ס ואת ונמצא בספרים בלא וא"ו וכ"כ רד"ק והוא חד מן פסוקים דכתיב בהון את ואת ואת את וסימן נמסר במלכים א' סימן ז': לשרקה. בלא וא"ו:

מצודת דוד

המסורעכיות ניין המבלבל את המוח: והשקיתה. ר"ל התנבא עליה': (טז) והתגועשו והתהוללו. ינועו בתנועה חזקה וישתטו מאימת החרב אשר אשלח ביניהם: (יז) ואקח וגו'. ר"ל קבלתי הנבואה ונבאתי להם: (יח) את ירושלים. חוזר למעלה שאמר והשקיתה וגו' אל ירושלים וגו': ואת מלכיה. עם כי לא היה אלא מלך אחד אמר מלכיה כי גם בני מלך נקראו בשם מלכים: כיום הזה. כי ירמיה כתב ספרו אחר החורבן לזה אמר כיום הזה בהמה חרבים:

מצודת ציון

זכרון: (טז) והתגועשו. ענין תנועה חזקה כמו ותגעש ותרעש הארץ (תהלים י"ח): והתהוללו. מלשון הוללות ושטות כמו והתהוללו

three exiles took place during the reigns of these three kings.

Abarbanel and *Mezudath David* assert that the king's sons are referred to here as kings.

as of this day—As they are today. Jeremiah wrote his Book after the destruction.—[*Rashi, Mezudath David*] The intention is that these words were added when the Book was completed and edited by the prophet, which was after the Temple was destroyed.

19. **Pharaoh the king of Egypt**—

fury from My hand, and you shall give it to all the nations to
whom I send you, to drink. 16. And they shall drink and reel to
and fro and be like madmen because of the sword that I am
sending among them. 17. And I took the cup from the hand of
the Lord, and I gave it to all the nations to whom the Lord had
sent me, to drink. 18. Jerusalem and the cities of Judah, and its
kings and its princes, to make them a waste, a desolation, a
hissing, and a curse, as of this day. 19. Pharaoh the king of
Egypt and his servants and his princes and all his people.

receive the very evil they dealt out to others.—[*Abarbanel, Malbim*]

15. **cup of the wine of fury**—*The prophecy of retribution.*—[*Rashi*]

and you shall give ... to drink it—*Prophesy to them that it will no longer be retracted for any repentance.*—[*Rashi*]

Rashi, apparently, interprets this verse figuratively. *Redak* explains that God showed Jeremiah the cup of wine in a prophetic vision and ordered him to take it and give it to the nations to drink.

Malbim explains that rebellions and chaos would transpire. This is symbolized by the wine, which intoxicates and confuses.

Mezudath David explains that the decree of retribution is compared to wine that confuses the mind.

Redak renders: this cup of wine, the wine of fury.

16. **and reel to and fro**—Heb. וְהִתְגֹּעֲשׁוּ *Jonathan renders: and they shall be confused.*—[*Rashi*] for variant readings, see *Ibn Nachmiash, Lexicon Chaldaicum, Aruch Completum.*

The intention is that nations will be locked in combat as will individuals.—[*Malbim*]

and be like madmen—Heb. וְהִתְהֹלָלוּ, *an expression of madness, they shall be mad.*—[*Rashi*]

17. **And I took, and I gave ... to drink**—All this was in the prophetic vision.—[*Redak*]

Mezudath David renders: And I received the prophecy and prophesied to them. *Abarbanel,* however, rejects the idea that Jeremiah went to all the nations with his prophecy. He prefers *Redak*'s interpretation that all this was a vision.

18. **Jerusalem**—She will be first, for all these nations suffered through Nebuchadnezzar, and the first year that he reigned—the fourth year of Jehoiakim—he marched on Jerusalem.—[*Redak*]

and its king—Jehoiakim, Jehoiachin, and Zedekiah.—[*Redak*] The

כָּל־עַמּוֹ׃ כ וְאֵת כָּל־הָעֶרֶב וְאֵת כָּל־
מַלְכֵי אֶרֶץ הָעוּץ וְאֵת כָּל־מַלְכֵי אֶרֶץ
פְּלִשְׁתִּים וְאֶת־אַשְׁקְלוֹן וְאֶת־עַזָּה
וְאֶת־עֶקְרוֹן וְאֵת שְׁאֵרִית אַשְׁדּוֹד׃
כא אֶת־אֱדוֹם וְאֶת מוֹאָב וְאֶת־בְּנֵי
עַמּוֹן׃ כב וְאֵת כָּל מַלְכֵי צֹר וְאֵת כָּל־
מַלְכֵי צִידוֹן וְאֵת מַלְכֵי הָאִי אֲשֶׁר
בְּעֵבֶר הַיָּם׃ כג אֶת־דְּדָן וְאֶת־תֵּימָא
וְאֶת־בּוּז וְאֵת כָּל־קְצוּצֵי פֵאָה׃ כד וְאֵת
כָּל־מַלְכֵי עֲרָב וְאֵת כָּל־מַלְכֵי הָעֶרֶב
הַשֹּׁכְנִים בַּמִּדְבָּר׃ כה וְאֵת ׀ כָּל־מַלְכֵי

תרגום

כ וְיָת כָּל מַלְכֵי סוּמְכְוָתָא
וְיָת כָּל מַלְכֵי אֲרַע עוּץ
וְיָת כָּל מַלְכֵי אֲרַע
פְּלִשְׁתָּאֵי וְיָת אַשְׁקְלוֹן
וְיָת עַזָּה וְיָת עֶקְרוֹן
וְיָת שְׁאָרָא דְאַשְׁדוֹד׃
כא יָת אֱדוֹם וְיָת מוֹאָב
וְיָת בְּנֵי עַמּוֹן׃ כב וְיָת
כָּל מַלְכֵי צוֹר וְיָת כָּל
מַלְכֵי צִידוֹן וְיָת כָּל מַלְכֵי
נִיסְּא דִי בְעִבְרָא דְיַמָּא׃
כג יָת דְדָן וְיָת תֵּימָא
וְיָת בּוּז כָּל מַקְפֵי פָאתָא׃
כד וְיָת כָּל מַלְכֵי עֲרָב
וְיָת כָּל מַלְכֵי עַרְבָאֵי
דְשָׁרָן בְּשְׁכוּנִין
בְּמַדְבְּרָא׃ כה וְיָת כָּל
מַלְכֵי

מהר"י קרא

(כ) ואת כל הערב. הם האומות שנתערבו בהן וי"ת כל סומכוותא: ואת שארית אשדוד. שנשארו כשהכם עוזיהו כשנלחם בהם דכתיב בדברי הימים ויצא ונלחם בפלשתים: מלכי האי. תרגום ניסא. והם איי הים: (כד) ואת כל מלכי ערב. הם ערבייא השוכנים ביישוב ואת כל מלכי הערב

רש"י

כתב ירמיה ספרו: (כ) ואת כל הערב. כל סומכוותא אשר ערוכת פרעה ומשענתו עליהם לעזרה: הערב. (גרנטיא"ה בלע"ז): (כב) ואת מלכי האי. כל אלו שמנה עד כאן שכיני א"י הם: (כג) קצוצי פאה. המוקצים בקצה אותה הרוח: (כד) מלכי ערב. ערביא: ואת כל מלכי הערב. סומכוותא של ערביים:

מנחת שי

(כב) ואת מלכי האי. מהלפין ואת כל מלכי האי וכן תרגם יונתן. ורד"ק כתב אין בו כל בספר מוגה: (כג) את דדן. תיבת פלוגתא רבתא ביני ספרי וספרייא בהאי תיבותא איכא מאן דכתב לה בוא"ו ואיכא מאן דכתב לה בלא וא"ו ולפום מאי דחזינן במסרה נוסחא בתרייתא עדיפא מדמסירא ד' את ריש פסוק בסיפרא וכולהו איתנהו בפסוקי דלעיל ודין חד מנהון:

רד"ק

בלא וי"ו: (כ) ואת כל הערב. עם מקובץ מעמים נתערבו יחד ות"י סומכוותא ל' ערבוביא: ואת כל מלכי ארץ פלשתים. שאר ארץ פלשתים לבד הערים הנזכרות וכ"כ בספר שמואל אחר שזכר הערים בענין טחורי הזהב אמר עוד מעיר מבצר ועד כפר הפרזי ולא זכר הנה גת כי לישראל היתה כי דוד לקחה מיד פלשתים כמ"ש בדברי הימים ויקח את גת ואת בנותיה מיד פלשתים והיא מתג האמה הנזכרת בספר שמואל: ואת שארית אשדוד. נראה כי כשלכדה נבוכדנצר כצאה נחרבת מקצתה על ידי מלך מצרים או זולתו: (כב) ואת מלכי האי. אין בו כל בספר מוגה: (כג) קצוצי פאה. השוכנים בקצה העולם בפאתו כי הפאה הוא קץ הדבר וי"ת מקפי פאתא: (כד) ואת כל מלכי ערב. הם הערביים יושבי אהלים כמ"ש לא יהל שם ערבי: ואת כל מלכי הערב השוכנים במדבר. לפי שזכר למעלה ואת כל הערב פירש הנה כי אלה הם אחרים שהם שוכנים במדבר: (כה) ואת כל מלכי זמרי. אפשר כי זמרי

מצודת ציון

הרכב (נחום ב'): בינותם. ביניהם: (כג) קצוצי. מלשון קלס: (כב) האי. קבוצת האיים אשר בשפת הים: (כג) קצוצי פאה. השוכנים בקצוות פאת העולם: (כד) מלכי ערב. שם אומה מה: מלכי הערב. הם הערביים:

מצודת דוד

(כ) כל הערב. עם המקובץ מעמים רבים כמו וגם ערב רב (שמות י"ב): ואת אשקלון וגו'. הם ערי פלשתים: שארית אשדוד. יתכן שנחרבה עד לא כא כ"כ ונשאר בה שארית:

today as Tema, found in the Arabian desert, approximately four hundred kilometers from the borders of Tiran.—[*Daath Mikra*]

and all those separated in that corner—Heb. קְצוּצֵי פֵאָה, *those separated at the end of that corner.*—[*Rashi*] *Jonathan* appears to explain it as 'those who have the corners of their hair polled.' This is the usual English translation. See Lev. 19:27, *Targum Onkelos*. *Malbim* takes it to mean those who are circumcised. See above 9:25.

24. **the kings of Arabia**—Heb. עֲרָב, *Arabia.*—[*Rashi*]

These are the Arabs who dwell in tents. See Isaiah 13:20.—[*Redak*]

20. And all the allies and all the kings of the land of Uz, and all
the kings of the land of the Philistines and Ashkelon and Gaza
and Ekron and the remnant of Ashdod. 21. And Edom and
Moab and the children of Ammon. 22. And all the kings of
Tyre and all the kings of Sidon and the kings of the isle that is
on the other side of the area. 23. Dedan and Tema and Buz and
all those separated in that corner. 24. And all the kings of
Arabia and all the kings of the allies who dwell in the desert.
25. And all the kings of

Immediately after the destruction of Jerusalem, Nebuchadnezzar destroyed Egypt.—[*Abarbanel*]

20. **And all the allies**—*All the supports* (סוּמְכָנְוָתָא) *which are Pharaoh's guarantee, and he leans upon them for aid.*—[*Rashi*]

Uz—A part of Edom. See Lam. 4:21.—[*Daath Mikra*]

and all the kings of the land of the Philistines—The rest of the land besides the cities mentioned further. See also I Sam. 6:17f., where other cities are mentioned after the five main cities.—[*Redak*]

and the remnant of Ashdod—It appears that Ashdod had been partly destroyed by Egypt or another nation before it was conquered by Nebuchadnezzar.—[*Redak*] *Malbim* asserts that Ashdod was conquered by Pharaoh, referring to ch. 48. It is, however, not found in that chapter nor in ch. 47, which deals with the downfall of the Philistines. Rabbi Joseph Kara takes this as an allusion to Uzziah's conquest of Ashdod, mentioned in II Chron. 26:6.

Gath, the metropolis of the Philistine kings, known as Metheg-ammah, an ox-goad, since it was the rod that governed all the Philistines, is not mentioned here. That city had long been taken by David. See II Sam. 8:2, I Chron. 18:1.—[*Redak, Ibn Nachmiash*]

22. **and the kings of the isle**—*All these that he counts* (שֶׁמּוֹנֶה) until here are neighbors of Eretz Israel.—[*Rashi*] *Ibn Nachmiash* explains *Rashi* to mean: *All these eight* (שְׁמֹנָה) *until here are neighbors of Eretz Israel.* He conjectures that Pharaoh the king of Egypt with his allies are counted as one. The land of Uz is counted as the second, the Philistines as the third, Edom as the fourth, Moab and Ammon, the descendants of Lot, as the fifth, Tyre as the sixth, Sidon as the seventh, and the kings of the isle as the eighth.

23. **Dedan**—Of the children of Keturah, mentioned in Gen. 25:3.

Tema—Of the sons of Ishmael, mentioned in Gen. 25:15. Both these nations lived in Arabia. Dedan was a nation of merchants whose center was in the north of the Arabian desert in Wadi-el-Kura and its environs. See Isaiah 21:13. Tema was located in a place still known

זִמְרִי וְאֵת כָּל־מַלְכֵי עֵילָם וְאֵת כָּל־
מַלְכֵי מָדָי: כו וְאֵת ׀ כָּל־מַלְכֵי הַצָּפוֹן
הַקְּרֹבִים וְהָרְחֹקִים אִישׁ אֶל־אָחִיו
וְאֵת כָּל־הַמַּמְלְכוֹת הָאָרֶץ אֲשֶׁר עַל־
פְּנֵי הָאֲדָמָה וּמֶלֶךְ שֵׁשַׁךְ יִשְׁתֶּה
אַחֲרֵיהֶם: כז וְאָמַרְתָּ אֲלֵיהֶם כֹּה־אָמַר
יְהוָה צְבָאוֹת אֱלֹהֵי יִשְׂרָאֵל שְׁתוּ
וְשִׁכְרוּ וּקְיוּ וְנִפְלוּ וְלֹא תָקוּמוּ מִפְּנֵי
הַחֶרֶב אֲשֶׁר אָנֹכִי שֹׁלֵחַ בֵּינֵיכֶם:
כח וְהָיָה כִּי יְמָאֲנוּ לָקַחַת־הַכּוֹס מִיָּדְךָ
לִשְׁתּוֹת וְאָמַרְתָּ אֲלֵיהֶם כֹּה אָמַר יְהוָה
צְבָאוֹת שָׁתוֹ תִּשְׁתּוּ: כט כִּי הִנֵּה בָעִיר

תרגום

מַלְכֵי זִמְרִי וְיַת כָּל מַלְכֵי
עֵילָם וְיַת כָּל מַלְכֵי מָדָי:
כו וְיַת כָּל מַלְכֵי צִפּוּנָא
דְקָרִיבִין וּדְרָחִיקִין גְבַר
לַאֲחוּהִי וְיַת כָּל מַלְכְוָת
עַמְמַיָא דְעַל אַפֵּי אַרְעָא
וּמַלְכָּא דְבָבֶל יִשְׁתֵּי
בָּתְרֵיהוֹן: כז וְתֵימַר
לְהוֹן כִּדְנַן אֲמַר יְיָ
צְבָאוֹת אֱלָהָא דְיִשְׂרָאֵל
שְׁתוּ וּרְוּוּ וְאִשְׁתַּגִישׁוּ
וּנְפָלוּ וְלָא תְקוּמוּן מִן
קֳדָם דְקַטְלִין בְּחַרְבָּא
דַאֲנָא שְׁלַח בֵּינֵיכוֹן:
כח וִיהֵי אֲרֵי יְסָרְבוּן
לְקַבָּלָא כַּסָא מִן יְדָךְ
לְמִשְׁתֵּי וְתֵימַר לְהוֹן
כִּדְנַן אֲמַר יְיָ צְבָאוֹת
מִשְׁתָּא תִשְׁתּוּן: כט אֲרֵי
הָא בְקַרְתָּא דְאִתְקְרֵי
שְׁמִי

רש"י

(כו) ששך. הוא בבל בא"ת ב"ש: (כז) וקיו. כאדם ששותה

מהר"י קרא

השוכנים במדבר: (כו) ששך. זו בבל באלפא ביתא דא"ת

רד"ק

הוא זמרן מבני קטורה: (כו) הממלכות הארץ. בא הסמיכות עם ה"א הידיעה שלא כמנהג ברוב וכן באו כמוהו הלשכות הקדש היתד הארג והדוכים להם מעמים: ומלך ששך. מלך בבל וכן ת"י וששך הוא בבל באלפא ביתא דא"ת ב"ש: (כז) וקיו. כן דרך השכור להקיא אבל השכור אחר שיקיא ישוב מעט לדעתו ויקום אבל להם אמר ונפלו ולא תקומו:

מנחת שי

(כז) וקיו. כ"כ ביו"ד וי"ס שכתוב וקוו וקרי וקיו ושבוש הוא:

מצודת דוד

(כו) איש אל אחיו. כוס החמה יתנו זה אחר זה כסמוך לו ר"ל כולם ילקו זה אחר זה: ומלך ששך. הוא בבל בא"ת ב"ש וכן נקרא בסוף הספר: ישתה אחריהם. ר"ל הוא ילקה אחר כולם בסוף: (כז) שתו ושכרו. שתו יין החמה והיו שכורים והקיאו והפלו לארץ ולא תקומו כדרך השותה יין הרבה ור"ל קבלו עליכם עול השעבוד וכלעד מפני חרב האויב: (כח) כי ימאנו לקחת הכוס בידך וגו'. ר"ל אם יתעלמו להנצל מן השעבוד: שתו תשתו. ר"ל בע"כ תהיו משועבדים:

מצודת ציון

פאת. ענין עבר וצד: (כו) איש אל אחיו. זה אחר זה כסמוך לו וכן ונפלתים איש אל אחיו (לעיל י"ג): (כז) וקיו. מלשון הקאה והוא החזרת המאכל מן הגוף דרך הפה: (כח) ימאנו. מל' מיאון:

the sword—*the strife of war.*—[*Rashi*]

28. **if they refuse**—I.e., if they endeavor to avoid subordination to Babylon.—[*Mezudath David*]

you shall surely drink—Perforce you will be subordinated to Babylon.—[*Mezudath David*]

drinks too much, who vomits.—[*Rashi*]

and fall and you shall not rise—Usually, after a drunken person vomits, he sobers up somewhat and stands up. But to the nations, the prophet says: Fall and you shall not rise.—[*Redak*]

Zimri, and all the kings of Elam and all the kings of Media.
26. And all the kings of the north, both near and far, one after
the other, and all the kingdoms of the earth that are upon the
face of the earth; and the king of Sheshach shall drink after
them. 27. And you shall say to them: So said the Lord God of
Israel: Drink, become drunk, and vomit, fall and you shall not
rise, because of the sword that I am sending among you.
28. And it shall be, if they refuse to take the cup from your
hand to drink, that you shall say to them: So said the Lord of
Hosts: You shall surely drink. 29. For behold, with the city

and all the kings of the allies—*The allies of the Arabs.*—[*Rashi*] See above v. 20. *Redak,* who explains this as 'a mingled people,' explains here that this mingled people is distinguished as those who dwell in the desert, unlike those mentioned above. *Abarbanel* points out that the aforementioned had no king, whereas these had kings.

25. **Zimri**—Perhaps Zimran, one of the sons of Keturah, mentioned in Gen. 25:2.—[*Redak*] See *Daath Mikra* for another theory.

one after the other—They will drink the cup of fury one after the other. I.e., one will suffer soon after the other.—[*Mezudath David*]

Sheshach—*That is 'Babylon' in* א״ת ב״ש.—[*Rashi, Kara, Redak, Mezudath David*] א״ת ב״ש is a code, substituting the last letter of the Alephbeth for the first one, and vice versa. Then the second from the end for the second from the beginning, and so on. Hence, the complete code is as follows: א״ת ב״ש ג״ר ד״ק ה״צ ו״פ ז״ע ח״ס ט״נ י״מ כ״ל. The result is that שֵׁשַׁךְ corresponds to בָּבֶל. *Jonathan,* too, explains in this manner. The reason for this substitution in this case is obscure. Azulai conjectures that שֵׁשַׁךְ equals 620.

300 = ש
300 = ש
20 = ך
620

כֶּתֶר, *crown,* too, equals 620, as follows:

20 = כ
400 = ת
200 = ר
620

Thus, we deduce that Nebuchadnezzar met his downfall because of his pride in assuming a crown not due him. See Isaiah 14:14.—[*Homath Anach*]

shall drink after them—He will suffer his downfall after all the other nations.—[*Mezudath David*]

27. **Drink, become drunk**—I.e., accept the yoke of slavery and the pain of the sword of the enemy.—[*Mezudath David*]

and vomit—*Like a person who*

אֲשֶׁר נִקְרָא־שְׁמִי עָלֶיהָ אָנֹכִי מֵחֵל
לְהָרַע וְאַתֶּם הִנָּקֵה תִנָּקוּ לֹא תִנָּקוּ כִּי
חֶרֶב אֲנִי קֹרֵא עַל־כָּל־יֹשְׁבֵי הָאָרֶץ
נְאֻם יְהוָה צְבָאוֹת׃ ל וְאַתָּה תִּנָּבֵא
אֲלֵיהֶם אֵת כָּל־הַדְּבָרִים הָאֵלֶּה
וְאָמַרְתָּ אֲלֵיהֶם יְהוָה מִמָּרוֹם יִשְׁאָג
וּמִמְּעוֹן קָדְשׁוֹ יִתֵּן קוֹלוֹ שָׁאֹג יִשְׁאַג
עַל־נָוֵהוּ הֵידָד כְּדֹרְכִים יַעֲנֶה אֶל כָּל־
יֹשְׁבֵי הָאָרֶץ׃ לא בָּא שָׁאוֹן עַד־קְצֵה
הָאָרֶץ כִּי רִיב לַיהוָה בַּגּוֹיִם נִשְׁפָּט
הוּא לְכָל־בָּשָׂר הָרְשָׁעִים נְתָנָם לַחֶרֶב

תרגום

שְׁמִי עֲלַהּ אֲנָא מְשַׁרֵי לְאַבְאָשָׁא וְאַתּוּן מִדְמַן דְמִזְכָּא תִּזְכּוּן לָא תִזְכּוּן אֲרֵי דְקַטְלִין בְּחַרְבָּא אֲנָא מְכַלֵי עַל כָּל יָתְבֵי אַרְעָא אֲמַר יְיָ צְבָאוֹת׃ ל וְאַתְּ תִּתְנַבֵּי לְהוֹן יַת כָּל פִּתְגָמַיָא הָאִלֵין וְתֵימַר לְהוֹן יְיָ מִמְרוֹמָא יְכַלֵי וּמִמְדוֹר קוּדְשֵׁיהּ יָרִים מֵימְרֵיהּ אַכְלָאָה יְכַלֵי דְיֵיתוּן בְּזוֹזִין עַל אֲרַע בֵּית שְׁכִנְתֵּי הָא כְּנַחְתֵּי מַעְצְרָא דְמְרִימִין קָלְהוֹן כֵּן יֵיתֵי זְוָעָא לְכָל יָתְבֵי אַרְעָא׃ לא מְטָא אִתְרְגוּשָׁא עַד סְיָפֵי אַרְעָא אֲרֵי דִינָא קֳדָם יְיָ בְּעַמְמַיָא מִתְפְּרַע הוּא לְכָל בִּשְׂרָא רַשִׁיעַיָא דִבְהוֹן מְסָרִינוּן לְקַטָלָא

ת״א ממרום ישאג. ברכות ג׳ (ברכות יג): הידד. ברכות נט:

קמץ בקדמא

מהר״י קרא

ב״ש: (ל) שאוג ישאג. ממקום נוהו שהוא יושב שם וגוזר גזירות על האומות כזה שדורך בגת שמשורר הידד כך יענה הידד של פורענות על יושבי הארץ: הידד. קול שאון:

רש״י

יותר מדאי שמקיא: החרב. התגר של המלחמה: (כט) מחל. מתחיל: (ל) על נוהו. מתאבל על חרבן ביתו: הידד. לשון הוי שצועקין עושי מלאכה כבדה בקול רם לזרז זה את זה להתחזק ודורכי גתות רגילין כה: יענה. כל לשון ענייה לצעקת קול רם היא: (לא) נשפט. מתווכח כדין:

רד״ק

וקיו. שרשו קאת ובאה היו״ד תמורת האל״ף: (ל) ממרום ישאג. על דרך משל כאילו ישאג וירים קולו ויבאו הגוים לקולו להחריב נוהו והוא בית המקדש: הידד כדרכים יענה. יצעק כמו הדורכים בגת שמרימין קול לחזק עצמם ואיש את אחיו במלאכה ודבר הקול הוא הידד ובלע״ז דואיד״ו: (לא) נשפט. כאילו נכנס במשפט עמהם שיענישם על רעתם ונתנם ביד

מצודת ציון

(כט) מחל. מלשון התחלה: (ל) ממרום. מהשמים הרמים: ישאג. ענין צעקה: וממעון. ענין מדור כמו השקיפה ממעון קדשך (דברים כ״ו): נוהו. מדורו כמו ואת נוהו השמו (תהלים ע״ט): הידד. המלה היא מיוחדת לקריאת דורכי היין לזרז עצמם וכן הידד השבתי (ישעיה ט״ז): כדורכים. הם הצועדים ופוסעים על הענבים להוציא היין: יענה. ענין הרמת קול וכן וענו הלוים וגו׳ קול רם (דברים כ״ז): (לא) שאון. ענין המייה: נשפט. ענין ויכוח: לכל

מצודת דוד

(כט) אשר נקרא שמי עליה. להיות נקראת עיר ה׳: אנכי מחל. אני מתחיל להביא הרעה ואתם תהיו נקיים מהרעה בתמיה הנה לא תנקו: (ל) ממרום ישאג. וכפל הדבר ואמר וממעון קדשו וגו׳ וחזר ומפרש שהוא ישאג על נוהו ור״ל סוף קרא גזירת חורבן על ירושלים: הידד. כדרך דורכי היין המרימים קול הידד לזרז זא״ז כן ירים קול אל כל יושבי הארץ לגזור עליהם חורבן שאון ואבדון: (לא) בא שאון. קול שאון המקום בא עד קצה הארץ ר״ל הגזירה היא על כולם: נשפט הוא. יתוכח עם כל בשר והויכוח יהיה אשר יתן את הרשעים להרג כי בזה מודיע להם הרשע והחטא לויכוח וכן כי באש ה׳ נשפט (ישעיה ס״ו):

upon them destruction and desolation.—[*Mezudath David*]

He shall call out—Heb. יַעֲנֶה. *Every expression of* עֲנִיָּה *is* an expression of *a cry with a loud voice.*—[*Rashi*] *Rashi* clarifies this matter lest we understand יַעֲנֶה as 'He shall answer.'

31. **A stirring has come**—A sound of stirring of the Almighty has come to the end of the earth; i.e. the decree is upon all of them.—[*Mezudath David*]

He contends—*He contends in judgment.*—[*Rashi*]

It is as though He enters litigation with them to punish them for their evil, and He will deliver them into the hand of the king of Babylon.—[*Redak*]

upon which My name is called, I commence to bring evil, and
shall you be cleared? You shall not be cleared, for I call a sword
upon all the inhabitants of the earth, says the Lord of Hosts.
30. And you prophesy to them all these words, and you shall
say to them: The Lord shall roar from above, and from His
Holy Habitation He shall give forth His voice; He shall roar
over His habitation; "Hedad!" He shall call out like those
who tread grapes, to all the inhabitants of the earth. 31. A stir-
ring has come until the end of the earth, for God has a contro-
versy with the nations; He contends with all flesh. The wicked
He has delivered to the sword, says the Lord.

29. **upon which My name is called**—to be called the city of the Lord.—[*Mezudath David*]

commence—Heb. מֵחֵל.—[*Rashi*]

shall you be cleared—If I bring evil first upon the city upon which My name is called, can you other nations expect to be cleared of evil?—[*Mezudath David*]

a sword—*Jonathan* paraphrases: those who slay with the sword.

Sometimes God brings retribution upon the nations of the world so that Israel should witness it and repent, lest the same retribution befall them. In that case, He commences with the nations of the world. In this case, however, He commences with Israel. This is surely not meant as a warning to the nations to repent. How, then, can you be cleared?—[*Malbim*]

30. **over His habitation**—*He mourns over the destruction of His house.*—[*Rashi* from *Ber.* 3a]

The Rabbis state there that the night is divided into three watches, when the various groups of angels recite God's praises in shifts. In each watch, the Holy One, blessed be He, sits and roars like a lion and says: Woe to the children for whose iniquities I have destroyed My house and burnt My temple and exiled them among the nations of the world.

Rashi explains that the mention of God roaring is repeated three times. This intimates that He roars, so to speak, in each of the three watches.

Redak explains this figuratively. It is as though God roars and raises His voice to call the nations to come and destroy His Temple. This follows *Targum Jonathan,* who paraphrases: He shouts that plunderers should come upon the land of the house of His presence.

"Hedad!"—*A cry of "Ha!" that those engaged in hard work cry out aloud to urge each other on to strengthen themselves, and those who tread the winepresses are accustomed to it.*—[*Rashi, Redak*]

So will God call out to the inhabitants of the world to decree

נאם-יהוה: לב כה אמר יהוה צבאות
הנה רעה יצאת מגוי אל-גוי וסער
גדול יעור מירכתי-ארץ: לג והיו חללי
יהוה ביום ההוא מקצה הארץ ועד-
קצה הארץ לא יספדו ולא יאספו ולא
יקברו לדמן על-פני האדמה יהיו:
לד הילילו הרעים וזעקו והתפלשו
אדירי הצאן כי-מלאו ימיכם לטבוח
ותפוצותיכם ונפלתם ככלי חמדה:

אמר יי: לב כדנן אמר
יי צבאות הא בישתא
נפקא מעם לעם ועממין
רברבין ייתון בגלי
מסיפי ארעא: לג ויהון
קטילי רמן קדם יי
ביומא ההוא מסיפי
ארעא ועד סיפי ארעא
לא יתספדון ולא
יתכנשון ולא יתקברון
לזיבל כבדר על אפי
ארעא יהון: לד אלילו
מלכיא וצוחו וחופו
רישיכון בקטמא תקיפי
עמא ארי שלימו יומיכון
לקטלא ותתבדרון
והפלון דהויתון רגיגין
כמני

הפ' בחולם ובחירק הת'

רש"י

(לב) מגוי אל גוי. שאני מסכסכן זה בזה: מירכתי. כתרגומו מסיפי: (לד) הילילו. לשון יללה: והתפלשו. התגלגלו בעפר (ווטרלייר בלע"ז): ותפוצותיכם. הרי זה מקרא קצר כלומר והפוצותיכם תקרבנה לבא: ככלי חמדה. כלומר אם תאמרו חשובים אנחנו הרבה יש כלי חמדה של

מהר"י קרא

(לד) הילילו הרועים. אלו מלכי יהודה ומלכי האומות: והתפלשו. ויפל"ו בלע"ז: ותפוצותיכם. הצאן שהייתם שומרים בהיותכם קיימים תהיינה נפוצות: ונפלתם ככלי חמדה. הוא ערקיי"א

רד"ק

מלך בבל: (לב) כה אמר ה'. אפשר שפרשה זו כענין שלפניה ויהיה פי' עזב ככפיר סכו על חרבן בית ראשון ע"י נבוכדנצר או תהיה עתידה והוא הנכון ויהיה פי' עזב ככפיר סכו על חרבן בית שני: (לד) הילילו הרועים. הרועים ואדירי הצאן הם מלכי הארץ: והתפלשו. התגללו בעפר או באפר: לטבוח. שיהיו טובחים איש את רעהו: ותפוצותיכם. זאת המלה באת שלא כמנהג כי הפ"א בחולם והתי"ו בחיר"ק והנכון הפ"א בשור"ק והת"ו בצר"י כי הוא מן תפוצה בשקל תבונה תמותה והקבוץ תפוצות בשקל תבונות תשובות ועם כנוי הנמצאים תפוצותיכם בשקל ותשובותיכם נשאר מעל ונאמר כי בא הפ"א בחולם לזוג התנועות כמו תהומות יכסיומו ובא התי"ו בחיר"ק כמו אם לא שריתך לטוב שראני שאריתך כמו שפירשנו: ונפלתם ככלי חמדה. אתם שהייתם ככלי חמדה בשלותכם עתה תפלו ותשברו וכת"י ותפלון דהויתון רגיגין

מנחת שי

(לד) כי מלאו ימיכם. מלא דכתיב ידיכם מפתבם: ותפוצותיכם. יש ספרים שהפ"א בשורק והתי"ו בצירי וברוב הספרים הפ"א בחולם והתי"ו בחירק וכן כתב רד"ק בפירוש ובמכלול דף קפ"ח ודף רנ"ה ובשרשים שזאת המלה באה כן בחולם ובשפטה בשורק ובאה גם כן בחירק שלא כמנהג ובשפטה בצירי וכ"כ

מצודת דוד

(לב) הנה רעה יוצאת. הרג והאבדון תלך מעם בכל אל כל עם ועם: וסער גדול. המיית מלחמה יתעורר מסוף הארץ והוא בבל: (לג) חללי ה'. הנהרגים בגזירת המקום: לא יספדו. על כי יהיו רבים לא יספיקו להספידם ולהכניסם במקום מיוחד או לקברם אבל יהיו מונחים ע"פ האדמה כמו הזבל: (לד) הילילו הרועים. למלכי יהודה ושריו יאמר הילילו וזעקו אתם מנהיגי העם ואתם אדירי הארץ ר"ל אתם הגבורים שבהם התפלשו בעפר דרך צער ואבלות כי מלאו ימיכם להביא מקלתכם לטביחה ובא זמן תפוצותיכם להיות מקלתכם נפוצים בגולה: ונפלתם ככלי חמדה. ר"ל לא תהיה נפילתכם ככלי

מצודת ציון

בשר. לכל אדם: (לב) וסער. רוח סערה: יעור. מל' התעוררות: מירכתי. מסוף וכן ולירכתי המשכן (שמות כ"ו): (לג) יאספו. ענין הכנסה כמו ואין איש מאסף אותם (שופטים י"ט): לדומן. ענין זבל: (לד) הילילו. מלשון יללה: והתפלשו. ענין התגלגול והתכסות בעפר כמו בעפר התפלשי (מיכה א'): אדירי. ענין חוזק: מלאו. נשלמו וכן וכמלאות ימי טהרה (ויקרא י"ב): ותפוצותיכם.

Rabbi Joseph Kara explains that the leaders would be slaughtered and the 'flocks' whom they guarded and protected during their lifetime would therefore be scattered.

like a precious vessel—*That is to say: If you say, "We are important," there are many precious glass vessels that fall, break, and are lost.*—[*Rashi*]

Redak explains: You, who were like a precious vessel during your prosperity, will now fall and be broken.

Others explain that the fall of a precious vessel is much greater than

32. So said the Lord of Hosts: Behold evil goes forth from
nation to nation, and a great storm shall be awakened from the
ends of the earth. 33. And those slain by the Lord shall be on
that day from the end of the earth to the end of the earth; they
shall not be lamented; neither gathered nor buried. They shall
be as dung on the face of the earth. 34. Howl, O you shepherds,
and cry out, and roll, you mighty of the sheep, for your days
have filled to slaughter, and your scatterings, and you shall fall
as a precious vessel.

32. **So said the Lord of Hosts**—*Redak* prefers the interpretation that this section is a prophecy of the destruction of the Second Temple by the Romans. *Abarbanel,* however, points out that the account of the storm being awakened from the ends of the earth resembles more closely Nebuchadnezzar's conquest of all the nations. Hence it is related to the preceding section.

from nation to nation—*whom I incite against one another.*—[*Rashi*]

and a great storm—I.e., stirring of war shall be awakened from the end of the earth. This refers to Babylon. —[*Mezudath David*]

from the ends—Heb. מִיַּרְכְּתֵי, *as the Targum* renders it: מִסְּיָפֵי, *from the ends of.*—[*Rashi*]

33. **those slain by the Lord**—I.e. those slain by the decree of the Omnipresent.—[*Mezudath David*]

they shall not be lamented—They will be so numerous that it will be impossible to lament them, to gather them to one place or to bury them. Instead, they will lie on the ground like dung.—[*Mezudath David*] *Abarbanel* notes that this prophecy was fulfilled only in Israel, not in the other nations.

34. **Howl**—Heb. הֵילִילוּ, *an expression of* יְלָלָה, *howling.*—[*Rashi*]

O you shepherds . . . you mighty of the sheep—Both these expressions refer to the kings of the world.—[*Redak*] *Abarbanel* identifies the shepherds as the kings of Judah, its princes, and the priests of God. The mighty of the sheep are the judges and the officers of the people. *Mezudath David* identifies the latter as the mighty men of the people.

and roll—I.e. *roll in the dust* (*se vautrer in French*).—[*Rashi*]

to slaughter—I.e to slaughter one another.—[*Redak*] *Redak* follows his interpretation of the verse that Scripture refers to the kings of the nations. *Abarbanel* and *Mezudath David* explain that the Jewish kings and leaders should wallow in the dust in sorrow and mourning for many of them would be slaughtered and many of them would be scattered in exile.

and your scatterings—*This is a short verse; i.e. to say: and your scatterings shall come near.*—[*Rashi*]

לה ואבד מנוס מן-הרעים ופליטה
מאדירי הצאן: לו קול צעקת הרעים
ויללת אדירי הצאן כי-שדד יהוה
את-מרעיתם: לז ונדמו נאות השלום
מפני חרון אף-יהוה: לח עזב ככפיר
סכו כי-היתה ארצם לשמה מפני חרון
היונה ומפני חרון אפו:

תרגום

כמני חמדתא: לה ויבד
בית ערוקי מן מלכיא
ושיזבא מתקיפי עמא:
לו קל צוחת מלכיא
ויללת תקיפי עמא ארי
אבז יי ית עמהון:
לז ויצדון מדורי שלמהון
מקדם תקוף רוגזא דיי:
לח גלא מלכא מכרכיה
ארי הות ארעהון לצדו
מן קדם חרב סנאה
דהיא כחמר מרויא ומן
קדם תקוף רוגזיה:

מהר"י קרא

בלע"ז: (לז) ונדמו נאות השלום. ת"י ויצדון מדורי שלמהון: (לח) עזב ככפיר סוכו. כל מלך ומלך יעזוב מלכותו ככפיר הזה שמניח מלונו כשהוא רעב: מפני חרב היונה. ת"י מן קדם חרב סנאה דהוא כחמר מרויא:

רש"י

זכוכית נופלים ונשברים ואובדים: (לז) ונדמו. לשון הורבה ל' הדימגו ונדמה שם (לעיל ח'): (לח) עזב ככפיר וגו'. גלה מלכא מכרכיה ככפיר העוזב את סוכו: היונה. משתכרת ביין כן תירגם יונתן. דבר אחר לשון אונאה:

מנחת שי

כהנהגם לוים תן פ"א פ' י"ד: (לו) ויללת. במק: ספרים הוא"ו בשוא וביו"ד בחירק ואי הוא לקריאה. ב"נ כמו שכתב רד"ק אבל לב"א שאנו סומכים עליו הוא"ו בחירק והיו"ד נחה. ועיין עוד מה שכתוב בשרשים שרש ילל:

רד"ק

כמני חמדתא: (לו) ויללת. בחיר"ק הוי"ו ונוח היו"ד לבן אשר ולבן נפתלי בשו"א הוי"ו וחיר"ק היו"ד: מרעיתם. צאן מרעיתם והם הגוים שהם מלכיהם ורועיהם: (לז) ונדמו. נכרתו כמו גם מדמן תדמי: נאות השלום. מקומות המרעה שהיו רועים בשלום והוא משל על עריהם ומדינתם: (לח) עזב ככפיר סכו. הראוי סכתו כי הנפרד סכה או יהיה הנפרד סך בפלס עז חום יאמר ממנו סכו בשקל עזו אמר כמו שהכפיר עוזב סכו מפני שאינו מוצא שם טרפו כן עזב האל יתברך בית המקדש מפני שלא מצא שם רצונו וכיון שעזבו והסתיר פניו ממנו נחרב: כי היתה ארצם לשמה. כי טרם חרבן הבית היתה ארצם לשמה ועם כל זה מוסר לא לקחו ולא יכול להתאפק עוד ועזבו: מפני חרון היונה. חרון חרב היונה ר"ל חרב האויב האונסת אותם מן ולא יונו נשיאי עוד את עמי: ומפני חרון אפו. והחרב באה מפני חרון אפו ויונתן פי' היונה מן יין שתרגם מן קדם חרב סנאה דהיא כחמר מרויא:

מצודת ציון

ענין סזור וכן כי נפן המס (ש"א י"ג): (לה) מנוס. ענין בריחה: ופליטה. שארית וכן לא יהיה לה פליטה (לקמן נ'): (לו) ויללת. מלשון יללה: שודד. ענין עושק וגזל: מרעיתם. מלשון מרעה: (לז) ונדמו. ענין כריתה וכליון כמו גם מדמן תדומי (לקמן מ"ח): נאות. מדור כמו בנאות דשא (תהלים כ"ג): (לח) ככפיר. כן יקרא ארי בחור: היונה. מלשון אונאה ועניינו קחה הסנן וכן הסיל היונה (צפניה ג'):

מצודת דוד

כזוי הטוטל בארץ שאין היזק בנפילתה אלא היזק רב וקלון מתמיד יהיה לכם בהנפילה הזה כבלי חמדה המוטל לארץ שההיזק רב כמה שנפחתת בנפילה: (לה) ואבד מנוס. לא יוכלו לברוח מיד האויב: ופליטה. אלא יאבד משמשת בשתים לומר שיאבד פליטה ושארית מן מאדירי הצאן המה הגבורים: (לו) קול צעקת. ר"ל הנה נשמע קול צעקת וגו': כי שודד ה'. ר"ל מה' באה השדידה בגזירה: מרעיתם. מקום שהרועים ירעו את הצאן והוא למשל על ירושלים: (לז) ונדמו. המדורות היושבות בשלום יהיו חרבים מפני חרון אף ה' שיחרב בהם: (לח) עזב ככפיר סכו. כל מדור יהיה נעזב מבעליו ולא יזכור בו כמו כפיר אריות שאינו זוכר בסוכתו אחר שעזבה: חרון היונה. חרון האויב המאנה ואונה אותם לקחת ההון וזה בא מפני חרון אף ה' שחרה בם ולא במקרה:

for their land has become waste—Before the destruction of the Temple, the land became waste. Yet they did not learn their lesson. Therefore, God could no longer resist abandoning them.

because of the wrath of the oppressing sword—Heb. הַיּוֹנָה, *drunk from wine. So did Jonathan translate. Another explanation: It is an expression of oppression* (אוֹנָאָה).—[*Rashi*] *Rashi*'s first explanation is unclear. Moreover, it does not match our edition of *Targum Jonathan* which coincides with that of *Redak*. Our edition reads: because of the sword of the enemy which is like intoxicating wine. The word הַיּוֹנָה is derived from יַיִן, *wine*.

According to the second explanation, we render: because of the wrath of the oppressing sword. Although 'sword' is absent from the text, it is understood. The intention is the sword of the enemy which oppresses and robs them.—[*Redak*]

and because of His furious wrath—I.e., the sword comes because of His furious wrath.—[*Redak*]

35. And flight shall fail the shepherds and deliverance the
mighty of the flock. 36. Hark! the cry of the shepherds and the
howling of the mighty of the flocks, for the Lord plunders their
pasture. 37. And the tranquil abodes shall be destroyed
because of the Lord's furious wrath. 38. He has left His hut like
a young lion, for their land has become waste, because of the
wrath of the oppressing sword, and because of His furious
wrath.

the fall of a cheap one, hence the comparison to the precious vessel.—[*Abarbanel, Mezudath David*]

35. **And flight shall fail the shepherds**—They will not be able to flee from the enemies.—[*Mezudath David*]

and deliverance the mighty—I.e., deliverance shall fail the mighty of the flocks. They will have no remnant.—[*Mezudath David*]

36. **Hark!! the cry of the shepherds**—This may also be rendered: Behold, the sound of the cry of the shepherds is heard.—[*Mezudath David*]

their pasture—I.e. the flocks of their pasture, the nations over which they rule.—[*Redak*] *Jonathan,* too, renders: their people.

As mentioned above, *Abarbanel* and *Mezudath David* explain this section as referring to the kings and officers of Judah. *Abarbanel* explains here that the prophet laments the fact that the shepherds and the mighty of the flocks do not cry out to God before the destruction, but will first cry out when calamity befalls them. *Mezudath David,* following this explanation, explains that they cry out and howl because the Lord plunders their pasture; i.e. because the Lord has decreed that Jerusalem, the place where the kings govern their people, be plundered and destroyed.

37. **And the tranquil abodes**—The pasturelands where they graze their flocks, i.e. their cities and provinces.—[*Redak*]

shall be destroyed—Heb. וְנָדַמּוּ, *an expression of destruction, an expression related to 'has silenced us* (הֲדִמָּנוּ),*' 'and there let us sit in silence* (וְנִדְּמָה).*'*—[*Rashi*] *Rashi,* apparently compares silence with destruction and desolation since a desolate place is always accompanied by silence.

Redak renders: shall be cut off.

38. **He has left his hut like a young lion**—*The king has gone in exile from his city like a young lion that leaves his hut.*—[*Rashi* after *Jonathan*]

Kara explains this to mean that every king will abandon his kingdom just as the lion leaves his den when he is hungry.

Redak explains that, just as the lion abandons his den when he does not find food there, so did the Lord abandon the Temple when His will was not executed there, and since He abandoned it and hid His countenance from it, it was destroyed.

APPENDIX

1:1

Many exegetes identify Hilkiah as the priest who discovered the *sefer torah* in the Temple during the reign of Josiah. His son Jeremiah commenced to prophesy in the thirteenth year of Josiah's reign. At that time, Josiah and the people had not yet returned to God. Their repentance took place in the eighteenth year, when the *sefer torah* was discovered.—[*Redak,* quoting his father, *Abarbanel, Alshich*] If this is the case, he was descended from a righteous man, who found the original *sefer Torah* written by Moses, rolled to the passage which reads: "The Lord will lead you and your king, whom you will appoint over yourselves, to a nation that neither you nor your ancestors have known . . . (Deut. 28:36). Hilkiah commenced to reprove the people by telling them of the impending exile. After him, his son Jeremiah continued to remind the people of the exile.—[*Abarbanel*] [This is astonishing since Jeremiah commenced to prophesy in the thirteenth year of Josiah, whereas Hilkiah found the scroll in the eighteenth year, five years after Jeremiah had commenced his prophecy.]

1:5

Abarbanel renders: Before I formed you in the womb, I gave you knowledge, and before you emerged from the womb, I sanctified you. I.e., before I formed your body, I endowed your soul with knowledge, and before you emerged frrom the womb, i.e. after your formation but before your birth, I sanctified your body with admirable traits.

1:10

to uproot and to crush—(*dépayser in French,* to uproot) *and over Israel to build and to plant if they heed. So did Jonathan paraphrase it.*—[*Rashi*]

This accounts for the two opposites, the many expressions of destruction and the building and planting. Rabbi Joseph Kara explains that the destruction is destined for the sinners and the building and planting for the repentant. *Redak* explains that each nation destined for misfortune would later be restored to its land after its exile, as we find further in the Book. The many expressions of destruction and the few expressions of building denote the prophet's numerous prophecies of doom and his few prophecies of consolation.

Ibn Nachmiash explains *the nations* as referring to the population and *the kingdoms* as referring to the kings, upon whom he prophesied evil and good.

2:3

Redak goes further by explaining that, despite Israel's sins, they are still considered holy. Although the Holy One, blessed be He, brings the enemy upon them, that enemy is punished because of them, since He remembers for them the lovingkindness of their youth, meaning the good deeds of the patriarchs, as we have seen in the case of Sennacherib, and so it was with Nebuchadnezzar, that because of Israel, Babylon was destroyed.

2:8

Jonathan renders: The teachers of the Torah did not teach to know My fear.—[*Redak*]

They studied the Torah without sincerity or for the sake of aggrandizement. This is accounted as though they did not know Me.—[*Abarbanel*]

and the rulers—Lit. the shepherds. This refers to *the kings.—[Rashi, Jonathan]* They lead the people as the shepherds lead the flocks.—[*Redak*]

and the prophets—They are the false prophets.—[*Redak*]

prophesied by Baal—*In the name of Baal.*—[*Rashi* from *Jonathan*]

and followed what does not avail—In this manner, all their deeds were acts of no avail.—[*Abarbanel*]

9. **Therefore, I will still contend**—*Before I bring misfortune upon you, I will still contend with you through My prophets although I have already contended with you many days.*—[*Rashi*]

Just as I have already contended with you in the above verses, when I said, "What wrong did your forefathers find in Me. . . ?" So will I continue to contend with you, reproving you for your own evil deeds, for you are as bad as they were. And so will your children's children be as bad as you. *Jonathan* renders: And with your children's children will I contend if they do as your deeds.—[*Redak*]

2:12

and storm—Heb. וְשַׂעֲרוּ, *an expression of* סַעַר, *a storm.*—[*Rashi, Redak*] The *sin* and the *sammech* are interchangeable.—[*Minchath Shai*]

become very desolate—*As though you are becoming desolate because of the Temple that is destined to be destroyed.*—[*Rashi*]

2:15

they have raised their voice—They have raised their voice and frightened him, only to prey upon him. As explained, the lions are the kings of the nations. The prophet depicts Israel as asking this question, why all this has befallen them, and the prophet replies in verse 17.—[*Redak*]

Another explanation is: Israel should have known that they were punished because of their sins, for 'Is Israel a slave? Is he a home-born slave? Why then has he become prey? . . .' It is only because of their sins, as further in the prophecy.—[*Kara*]

2:19

The kabbalists teach us that when a person infracts one of God's commandments by performing a forbidden act, the damage and the destruction are immediately impressed on high upon his heavenly root. And, corresponding to this,

he lends power to the forces of evil. From there, he draws upon himself a spirit of contamination which envelops him when he commits the sin, and after committing the sin, it returns to its place. Hence, he is actually in Gehinnom during his lifetime when he commits a sin, but he does not feel it until he dies, when he is caught in the trap he set for himself, viz. the forces of contamination and the destructive angels that were created by his deeds.—[*Nefesh Hachaim*, Gate 1, ch. 12] [This is Jeremiah's intention when he states: Your evil will chastise you. I.e., the evil you commit will, by itself, bring retribution upon you.]

2:23

See your way in the valley—*See what you have done opposite Beth Peor, and until now you adhere to that way like a swift she-camel clinging to her ways.—[Rashi* after *Jonathan*] See your way today. It is as it was in the plains of Moab when you worshipped Baal-peor.—[*Redak*]

young she-camel—Heb. בִּכְרָה, *a young female camel, that loves to wander. 'The young camels of Midian* (בִּכְרֵי)' (Isa. 60:6) *is translated* הוּגְנֵי, *and they are young camels, as we find in Sanhedrin* 52a: *There are many old camels laden with the skins of young camels* (הוּגְנֵי).—[*Rashi*]

Redak suggests further that the prophet castigates the people for the roads they made in the valleys leading up to the mountains where they worshipped the Baal.

clinging—*Adhering to the ways of her youth, an expression similar to: 'it would have clung* (מסריך סריך)' (*Chullin 51a*). *This may be associated with 'a shoe-thong'* (שְׂרוֹךְ נַעַל) (Gen. 14:23). *She binds the ways of her youth in her heart.*—[*Rashi*]

Redak, too, associates it with שְׂרוֹךְ נַעַל, explaining it in a different manner. Just as the shoe-thong is bound around the shoe many times, on one side one way and on one side the other way, so did you pervert your ways, once following one pagan deity and once following another. Thus, we render as *Jonathan*; perverting her ways. Scripture compares them to the female camel rather than to the male, since the female is more accustomed to run than the male.

2:24

accustomed to the desert—*Accustomed to be in the deserts, so she loves to wander.*—[*Rashi*]

The wild donkeys love to run in the flat desert lands.—[*Redak*]

that snuffs up the wind—*She opens her mouth and snuffs up the wind, and he always returns to his place.*—[*Rashi*]

her tendency like the sea creatures, who can hinder her?—*That trait of the sea creatures that she has, for also the sea creature snuffs up the wind, as it is said: 'They snuff up the wind like sea creatures'* (infra 14:6). *Who can hinder her from that trait? So it is with you—who can return you from your evil way?*—[*Rashi*]

Redak explains that the snuffing up the wind enables the wild donkey to run swiftly.

All who seek her will not weary—*For they will weary needlessly, for they will be unable to overtake her. What will her end be? In her month they will find her. There is one mouth in the year that she sleeps for the whole month, and then she is cap-*

tured. You, too—one month (*viz. Ab*) *was already prepared for you from the days of the spies, when your forefathers established it as a time of vain weeping; therein you will be captured.*

2:30

Your sword devoured—*your prophets, Zechariah and Isaiah.—[Rashi]*

Zechariah the son of Jehoiada was slain by the command of Joash, king of Judah, because he castigated the people for their idolatrous practices (II. Chron. 24:20ff.).

Isaiah was slain by Manasseh, as in *Yebamoth* 49b. See II Kings 21:16, Commentary Digest.

Redak quotes exegetes who explain this as a reference to Zechariah and Uriah. Uriah was a contemporary of Jeremiah who was slain by Jehoiakim. See 26:20–23. Accordingly, this prophecy was delivered at a much later time, not in the order it is written here.

Redak, however, disagrees with these exegetes. He then interprets *your prophets* to mean the false prophets who prophesied what the people wanted to hear, as in verse 26. He explains that the people were responsible for the death of the false prophets because they encouraged them to prophesy by listening to them. It was, therefore, as though they had slain them with the sword.

Abarbanel rejects *Redak*'s interpretation since it was their ears that 'slew the prophets,' not their sword. He approves of *Rashi*'s interpretation. *Daath Sofrim,* too, prefers *Rashi* since the context appears to support this explanation. Not only did your children not receive correction from the prophets, but you slew them with the sword when they castigated you for your sins and prophesied the doom of the kingdom. *Alschich,* too, explains this as regards the true prophets. He conjectures that, either they had killed many prophets much as they had killed Isaiah and Zechariah, or that through their sins, they were instrumental in the death of many prophets. The truth is, in any case, that the only prophets living at that time were Jeremiah and Zephaniah and Huldah the prophetess.

2:31

Most exegetes interpret this verse as referring to Israel's travels in the desert, viz. Rashi, Redak, Kara, Isaiah da Trani, and Ibn Nachmiash. *Abarbanel,* however, interprets it as a reference to the commandments of the Torah. God asks: Was I a desert to Israel or a land of thick darkness? Are My precepts an unbearable burden? Am I like a desert or a land of darkness, where one cannot find his necessaries? Did Israel not have all they needed when they followed Me through the desert? Why should you not have all you need when you observe My commandments?

Why have My people said, "We have been separated. . . "?—Heb. רַדְנוּ, *we have been separated from You. Like one who separates* (רוֹדָה) *bread from the oven. So is the midrash of Rabbi Tanhuma* (Bamidbar 2). *Menahem, however, explains* רַדְנוּ, *as an expression of descending* (יְרִידָה), *and also in other manners* (*Machbereth Menahem,* p. 162).—*[Rashi]* Accordingly, we render: we have gone down. *Jonathan* renders: we have wandered.

2:33

33. **How you adorn**—Heb. תֵּיטִבִי. *You adorn yourself to greet your adulterers. Comp. "And she adorned her head"* (I Kings 9:30) *concerning Jezebel in the section dealing with Jehu.*—[*Rashi*]

Others render: What have you to adorn your way to seek love?—Why do you try to improve your way to adopt the Baal worship in order to seek the love of the heathen nations?—[*Mezudath David*]

2:35

I contend with you—*I will come with you in judgment.*—[*Rashi*]

Others render: I will judge you.—[*Kara*]

2:37

Redak renders: Also from here shall you go out with your hands on your head. This alludes to the exile of Samaria. Just as the kingdom of Israel went out of Samaria amidst great sorrow, so will you leave Jerusalem with your hands on your head like a woman lamenting, as we find in the case of Tamar who behaved in this manner after being ravished by Amnon. *Jonathan* renders: And the shame of your sins on your head.—[*Redak*]

3:1

In many places, the Scriptures compare the Jewish people to a woman, and the Holy One, blessed be He, to her husband. That is to say that He took them as the nation of His inheritance. She is to Him as a wife and He is to her as a husband, and just as a woman who commits adultery is liable, so Israel, who followed foreign nations and clung to their beliefs, is referred to as having played the harlot. This allegory is found in many places in the Prophetic Books, where harlotry is symbolic of idolatry. We find this allegory especially in the Book of Ezekiel (ch. 23). God says: Since you went to the Baalim, how can you return to Me again? Even if you repent, you will be unable to return to Me until you go in exile from your land and stay in the land of your captivity until you forget your first sin, and idolatry no longer enters your mind. Then you will return to Me and I will return to you.—[*Redak*] It is apparent that *Redak* explains this as an interrogative form of the infinitive. And to return to Me, says the Lord. I.e., will you return to Me? Will you be able to return to Me? *Abarbanel*, too, explains the words in this manner. In his understanding of their meaning, however, he differs greatly. He interprets it to mean that Israel cannot return to God's worship and continue to worship idols simultaneously. It does not mean, however, that their repentance will not be accepted.

Jonathan renders: But you have erred and have joined many nations, yet return now to My worship, says the Lord.

Malbim explains that, according to the analogy of the divorced wife, God may still accept Israel's repentance. Since they did not accept idolatry as the heathen nations, each nation officially attached to its deity, but worshipped the pagan deities only occasionally, they are not analogous to the woman who married another husband. Moreover, they did not worship one particular deity, but many. They are, therefore,

analogous to a woman who played the harlot after her divorce, who may return to her former husband.

3:3

and the latter rain—Heb. מַלְקוֹשׁ, *the rain that falls in Nissan on the ears* (מְלִילוֹת) *and the straws* (קַשִּׁים). מַלְקוֹשׁ *is* (*tardif in O.F.*).—[*Rashi* from Ta'anith 6a].

3:5

I.e., instead of returning to Me, you spoke and have done evil things.—[*Redak*]

and you were able—*And you prevailed in rebelling with a victorious and irrefutable reply.*—[*Rashi* as emended by *Shem Ephraim*]

Jonathan renders: You increased. The intention is: You did as much evil as you were able.—[*Redak*] Another interpretation is: You were permitted. Your sins became to you as permissible acts, you became so accustomed to do them.—[*Sha'arei Teshuvah,* 1:5]

This explanation is according to the '*keri,*' the traditional reading דִּבַּרְתְּ. According to the '*kethib,*' the written text, דִּבַּרְתִּי, however, we interpret: I spoke to you to repent, but you did evil things and were able.—[*Redak*]

Others render verses 4 and 5 as relating to the time in Josiah's reign when the king repented and compelled the people to repent. In fact, many of the people still worshipped idols clandestinely. The prophet castigates them for their hypocrisy and states: Is it not recent, that you called me, "My Father; You are the Master of my youth." [And you said], "Will He bear a grudge forever? Will He keep it to eternity?" Behold, you spoke [that you wish to repent,] but you did evil things, and you were able.—[*Redak,* quoting his father, *Mezudath David*]]

3:6

and she played the harlot there—Heb. וַתִּזְנִי. I.e., she played the harlot *by worshipping idols.* וַתִּזְנִי *is the equivalent of* וַתִּזֶן, *the 'yod' being superfluous.*—[*Rashi, Redak*] Since this is the feminine form for the third person, the 'yod' does not belong in the verb. The 'yod' belongs only to the second person feminine.

3:7

And her treacherous sister Judah saw it—I.e. saw *all this.* The appellation '*treacherous' is harsher than 'backsliding.' Israel, since they were the first to sin, and they did not see any retribution from which to learn and to repent, are called 'backsliding.' Judah, who saw that these went in exile and did not receive correction, are called 'treacherous.'*—[*Rashi*]

The intention is that Judah saw what had befallen her sister kingdom and did not learn a lesson from her fate. Although this is not stated in the Scriptures, it is understood.—[*Redak*]

3:8

It is also possible that the prophet alludes to the fact that Judah returned to its land after seventy years of exile and remained there for four hundred twenty years. Although they had not yet been exiled, the prophet speaks of the future and comforts them that they, who will be in this exile, will return to their land since they were sold

only because of their sins, and by repenting, God will restore them to their land. He, therefore, says to the kingdom of Judah: "Where is your mother's bill of divorce that I sent her away?" You are close to return to Me as you have been before, for there is no bill of divorcement between us, and when you return, all the tribes will return, for David will reign over all Israel. Ezekiel, too, announced, "(37:19) Behold I take the stick of Joseph which is in the hand of Ephraim and the tribes of Israel, his companions, and I will place with them upon it the stick of Judah, and I will make them into My hand." Although He gave them a bill of divorcement, since the separation was intense and the exile very long, He shall return them with the tribe of Judah.—[*Redak*]

The Rabbis of the Midrash (*Lamentations Rabbah* 1:1) present this difficulty and reconcile it in the following manner: The Rabbis say: It is analogous to a king who became wroth with his queen. He wrote for her a bill of divorcement and then rose and seized it from her. Whenever she wished to remarry, he would say to her, "Where is your bill of divorcement?" If she would demand food, he would say, "But have I not divorced you?" Similarly, whenever Israel seeks to worship pagan deities, He says to them, "Where is your mother's bill of divorce?" Whenever they request that He perform miracles for them, the Holy One, blessed be He, says to them, "I have already divorced you." This is the intention of the words, "I sent her away, and I gave her her bill of divorcement."—[*Ibn Nachmiash*]

Redak, however, bases his interpretation on the second opinion of the Midrash, that Israel was 'like a widow,' meaning that she was widowed of the Ten Tribes but not of Judah and Benjamin.—[*Wertheimer*]

3:9

Others render: From the report of her harlotry. I.e., because they wished to conceal their idolatry, and it was discovered.—[*Ibn Nachmiash*]

and she committed adultery with the stones—Jonathan paraphrases: *And she strayed with the worshippers of stones and wood. And Jonathan renders:* מִקֹּל *as an expression of lightness, since her idols were light in her eyes.*—[*Rashi*]

3:12

to the north—*To the places where they were exiled there to Assyria.*—[*Rashi*]

Hence, *Rashi* understands this verse to mean that Jeremiah was to go to the north and to recite this prophecy to the Ten Tribes and to bring them back to the Holy Land. *Redak,* however, rejects the idea that Jeremiah was to go to the far northeast, to Halah, Habor, and the cities of Media. He explains הָלֹךְ to mean, come and speak, an expression of urging, not necessarily to go from one place to another. This is a common expression in Scriptures. He commands him to proclaim these words in Jerusalem before the elders of Judah and to pronounce these words as though speaking to the exiled tribes of Israel face to face. He is to announce to them that they are destined to return at the end of days.

My anger—Heb. פָּנַי, lit. My face.

My anger, so did Jonathan render it.—[*Rashi*] I.e., I will not let My anger rest upon you forever, but I will bring you back at the end of days.—[*Redak*]

for I am pious—Although you are liable to complete annihilation, I am pious with much lovingkindness, and I will bring you back.—[*Redak*]

I will not bear a grudge forever—but will bring you back when the exile of Judah is gathered.—[*Redak*] This appears to be the explanation of the verse according to *San.* 110b. See *Rashi* ad loc.

3:14

The Rabbis explain that if there will be one righteous man in a city, his merit will cause the whole city to be accounted meritorious, and if there will be two righteous men in an entire nation, they will cause the whole nation to be accounted meritorious, and in their merit, all of them will be redeemed from exile.—[*Redak, Kara* from *San.* 111a]

Jonathan renders: Return, children who exert themselves to repent, says the Lord; for I have chosen you and I will bring you near to Me as though you were left, one from a city and two from a family, and I will bring you to Zion.

The Talmud infers from this verse that, if one sins by neglecting to fulfill a positive precept, and he repents of his neglect, his sin is forgiven immediately.—[*Yalkut Shimoni* from *Yoma* 86a]

3:19

the beauty of the hosts of nations—Others render: the desire of hosts of nations.—[*Redak*] The Midrash (*Tanhuma, Mishpatim* 17) illustrates the status of Eretz Israel among the kings of the nations. In the Book of Joshua, we find that Israel vanquished thirty-one kings, kings of city-states. We find that Jericho had a king and Ai had a king, although one is less than three miles from the other. Yet each city had a king. We conclude, therefore, that these kings were foreign potentates, each one owning a small territory in Eretz Israel, for every king who did not own territory in Eretz Israel was not considered a king.

The Midrash also compares the Holy Land to a deer. Just as a deer, after being flayed, its hide does not contain its flesh, so does the Holy Land have so much produce that the land does not contain it. The Talmud (*Gittin* 57a) states that, whereas the Holy Land, when populated, is of ample size to accomodate its inhabitants, when desolate, it shrinks. In this respect, it resembles the deer, whose skin shrinks when it is flayed and stretches when it is living.

3:25

for they perverted their way—This is a parenthetic phrase. They are crying because they are lost.

they forgot the Lord their God—They do not recognize the shepherd's voice.

[22] **Return, backsliding children**—This is the voice heard on the high places. God calls to Israel to return to Him and He will cure their backslidings.

Here we are; we have come to You—Israel cries toward Him in the valley and replies to the voice on the heights, saying, "We are ready to

return to You, and we have already come to You for You are the Lord our God, but we do not recognize Your voice, and we do not know where to return.

[23] **Truly, to the falseness of the hills, the uproar of the mountains**—He points out that opposite the voice that emanates from between the mountains, the hills on the other side produce an echo, so that one standing in the valley does not recognize the true voice from the echo. Therefore, although a voice emanates from the mountains to show us the true way, from the hills there is heard the uproar of the mountains, the false voice answering it. This symbolizes the true prophets instructing us to return to You and the false prophets leading us to falsehood, viz. to worship idols, and we are unable to discern the true voice of God from the imaginary one.

but in the Lord our God is Israel's salvation—We cannot repent because we are at a loss to do so. The only salvation is in the hands of the Lord our God, Who can assist us from above to repent and be saved.

[24] **And the shameful thing consumed**—The idol worship has already destroyed all we have, leaving us in the depths of despair.

[25] **We will lie in our shame**—since we cannot lift our heads or do anything . . .

for we have sinned against the Lord our God since our youth—and we can no longer return to Him.—[*Malbim*]

4:2

Redak suggests that the intention is that in the future, the nations of the world will bless themselves and praise themselves with God, not with their idols. In that case, we render: bless themselves with Him and praise themselves with Him.

4:4

Jonathan renders: Return to God's worship and remove the wickedness of your heart.

lest My anger go forth—Lest My anger go forth like a burning fire and burn you up with no one there to quench it; i.e., there will be no one there to appease Me and cause My anger to subside, because of the evil of your deeds which have increased, and no one has the merit necessary to appease My anger.—[*Mezudath David*]

4:5

let it be heard—by an announcement.—[*Redak*]

and say, "Sound a shophar . . ."—*Warn the inhabitants of the land that they sound the shophar to flee..*—[*Rashi*]

This is to spread the word more than the telling and the announcing.—[*Redak*]

assemble—Heb. מַלְאוּ *An expression of gathering, and there are many in the Scriptures*: "(Isaiah 31:4) *Although a band of* (מְלֹא) *shepherds gather against him,*" Also "(infra 12:6) *They called after you a band* (מָלֵא)." Also "(Job 16:10) *Together they gather* (יִתְמַלָּאוּן) *against me.*"—[*Rashi*]

and let us come into the fortified cities—The prophet pictures them all gathering together in the fortified cities and raising a standard in the tower of Zion so that it should be seen from afar and they should be

able to flee to the fortified cities or to Jerusalem; although they all will be conquered, he exhorts them to flee for temporary refuge. Possibly, he is saying this to them according to what they think that they will be saved.—[*Redak*]

4:9

the heart of the king and the heart of the princes shall fail—It is usual for the king and the princes to encourage the people when they are under attack by the enemy. In this case, however, the king and the princes will panic when the city falls to the Chaldeans. The king mentioned is Zedekiah.—[*Redak*]

The Rabbis explain this as referring to the day the Chaldeans captured Zedekiah, slaughtered his sons before him, and blinded his eyes (below 52:10). They ask: How did Zedekiah stand there and see his sons being slaughtered before him and see others putting out his eyes? Should he not have dashed his head against the wall and died? Concerning that time it was said: And it shall be on that day, says the Lord, the heart of the king and the heart of the princes shall fail.—[*Ibn Nachmiash* from *Lam. Rabbah* 1:51] Accordingly, the failing of the 'heart' represents the loss of sense.

4:11

and not to cleanse—*And not to cleanse grain does it come. That is to say, not for good but for evil, to exile men (women), and children, and livestock.*—[*Rashi*]

Redak explains the verse similarly: At that time, i.e. when the enemy comes, it will be said of them, Behold the enemy has come upon them like a dry wind that passes over the high places, like the mountains and the hills, or like a wind that passes through the desert, for in these places the wind can pass without hindrance, for in settled regions the wind finds many hindrances: it cannot pass the houses, the walls, or the fences, but in the high places and in the desert, it finds no hindrances. Similarly, the enemy will come without hindrance. Now which way will he come? The way of the daughter of My people. From this wind, no satisfaction will be derived, like a wind with which the grain is winnowed and cleansed of the chaff. When a wind is not very strong, although it causes some damage, it is beneficial for some things, but this wind to which the enemy is likened, will come to Israel only to harm them, and they will not derive any benefit from it.

רוּחַ צַח may be rendered as a bright wind, denoting that the enemy will come with all that he wishes, with a huge army, with armored steeds and riders. It may also be rendered: a dry wind, one which will dry out the land and lay it waste.

4:14

how long will you harbor—I.e. how long will you persist with your iniquitous thoughts?—[*Redak*]

4:16

Jonathan renders: חָטוֹפִין כְּקָטוֹפִין, *plunderers like vintagers*. He explains נֹצְרִים as equivalent to בּוֹצְרִים, *vintagers*, grape pickers.—[*Redak*] *Abarbanel* objects to this assertion as well. Grammatically, there is no connection between a 'beth' and a

'nun.' He theorizes that this prophecy alludes to the destruction of the Second Temple by the Romans, who came from a distant land, much farther from the Holy Land than Babylon. The Romans were later called נוֹצְרִים. He perceived through prophecy that the Romans would later accept the Nazarene and be called *Notzerim*. *Ibn Nachmiash* suggests: *watchmen*, synonymous to שֹׁמְרֵי in the following verse. This is similar to Rashi's interpretation, although the word has a different meaning.

4:19

the alarm of war—The enemy will come and sound the shofar when they attack.—[*Mezudath David*]

The prophet is in great pain because of the impending doom to his people. Were the people really evil, the pain would not be so great. The truth was, however, that that generation was not as wicked as previous generations. There were times during Manasseh's reign that were much worse. The impending doom was because of the verdict issued during Manasseh's reign that had not been revoked. It was Jeremiah's mission to frighten the people and to inform them that the situation would become much worse until the land would be invaded and the Temple destroyed. He hoped to arouse the people, who outwardly obeyed Josiah's orders while sinning clandestinely. Even in the times of Jehoiakim and Zedekiah, most of the people performed many good deeds. To see with his prophetic eye what was destined to happen to these people caused him great pain.—[*Daath Soferim*]

4:28

This was Jeremiah's prophetic vision, that of the heavens darkening.—[*Abarbanel*]

I planned—Heb. זַמֹּתִי, *an expression of thought.*—[*Rashi*]

For what I spoke to the prophets as I had planned, I did not regret until now, and I will not turn back from it in the future.—[*Redak*]

Abarbanel explains this as the words of the prophet, declaring to the people that he constantly spoke of the impending doom and never turned back to predict peace as the false prophets had claimed. There was, therefore, no reason to believe that God had conveyed a message that was possible to interpret in that manner.

for that which I spoke—*I.e. this retribution, and I will fulfill it.*—[*Rashi*]

and I will not turn back—*And I will not repent to think good thoughts about them.*—[*Rashi*]

4:30

paint—Heb. בַפּוּךְ, *an expression of a blue paint.*—[*Rashi*]

He compares her to a harlot, who customarily wears pretty clothes and beautifies herself by painting her eyes, to attract lovers. So do the people of Israel try to conform to the heathens, to worship their gods, to wear their garments, in order to impress them with their beautiful garments and their beautiful chariots so that they should love them and say, "He is like me."—[*Redak*]

lovers—Heb. עֹגְבִים, *those who jest with the women with sides* (?) *of types of adultery. Comp. '(Ezekiel 23:20) She lusted* (וַתַּעְגְּבָה) *for concubinage with them.'*—[*Rashi*]

Redak and others explain it as 'lover.'

Kara explains that those nations whom Israel loved, viz. Egypt, Assyria, and the Chaldeans, whom Israel once wooed, will all turn against her.

they seek your life—*They seek to kill you.*—[*Rashi*]

Instead of loving you, as you had hoped, when you ceased to hope in Me and relied on them, they will seek to kill you and destroy you.—[*Redak*]

5:1

whether there is one who performs justice, who seeks faith—I.e., see whether there is a judge appointed to execute justice and to prevent the people from sinning. Indeed, there were righteous people, but there was none sitting on the bench in the streets of the city to execute justice and to seek faith, [i.e. to see that the people should be honest in their dealings.]

Redak, explains: a good man, great in deeds.

5:10

The first definition, 'upon its plains' apparently originates with Rabbi Joseph Kara who derives it from 'Sharon,' denoting flat land. Rashi rejects both this definition and that of Menahem because of their irrelevance with the roots of the vineyard. Redak, however, accepts Menahem's definition of 'walls.' He explains that the prophet is addressing the enemies and exhorting them to 'scale her walls and destroy . . . remove the points of her walls.' Others explain: Remove its branches, i.e. the spreading branches of the trees.—[*Redak*]

but make no complete end—I.e., make no complete end of the people. The wall, however, *was* completely destroyed by the Chaldeans.—[*Redak*]

5:13

Others explain that verse 13 refers to the true prophets of God. The wicked, who do not believe in the prophecy of the true prophets, say, "And the prophets shall become wind . . ." So shall be done to them. Jeremiah pronounces this curse on all those who speak in this manner.—[*Ibn Nachmiash*]

Abarbanel explains that the people curse the true prophets by saying, "So shall be done to them," i.e. the catastrophe that they prophesy for us.

6:1

Beth ha-kerem—*That is a place name.*—[*Rashi*]

Indeed, such a place is mentioned in Neh. 3:14 as the name of a province in the period of the return to Zion. This was the source of the stones used in the construction of the altar and the ramp leading up to the altar (*Middoth* 3:4). Some identify it with En-kerem, west of Jerusalem, and others with Ramat-Rachel, south of Jerusalem.—[*Daath Mikra*]

Others interpret this as the tower amidst the vineyards whence all the vineyards can be viewed. Over the house of the vineyard raise a beacon. This will warn the inhabitants of all the surrounding cities.—[*Redak, Mezudath David*] *Kara* interprets it as figurative of the people of Israel, known as 'the vineyard of the Lord of Hosts.' See Isa. 5:7.

raise a standard—*a standard to gather and fight for your lives.*—[*Rashi*]

from the north—That is Babylon, situated on the north of Judea.—[*Redak, Mezudath David*]

6:19

and they rejected My instruction—Heb. וְתוֹרָתִי וַיִּמְאֲסוּ בָהּ. *This follows the pattern of* '(Exodus 15:2) *The strength and destruction of God was my salvation* (וַיְהִי לִי לִישׁוּעָה),' *for he should have said:* וְתוֹרָתִי מָאֲסוּ בָהּ, *and it is the style of Scripture to speak in this manner.*—[*Rashi*]

'My words' denote the word of the prophets who admonished them to repent. To these words they did not wish to hearken. 'My instruction' denotes the Torah given to Moses, which they had entirely rejected, being unwilling to read it or to hear it read. We find that, when the Torah was found by Hilkiah the priest in Josiah's time, it appeared new to them for they had forgotten it.—[*Redak*]

Because they broke off the yoke of Torah and mitzvoth, they deserve the disaster that awaits them.—[*Abarbanel*]

6:23

and they will ride on horses—Not only will there be many foot soldiers, but there will also be horsemen, who are more dangerous than foot soldiers.—[*Redak*]

6:26

upon us—*So to speak, upon Me and upon you.*—[*Rashi* from *Gittin* 58a]

Rashi alludes to the Talmud's account of an incident that took place at the time of the destruction. There was a woman named Zofnath the daughter of Peniel, named so because all would gaze (צוֹפִים) upon her beauty. Her father was called Peniel because he was the High Priest who would enter the inner sanctum (לִפְנַי וְלִפְנִים). Her captor humbled her repeatedly during the whole night. On the morrow, he dressed her with seven chemises and took her out into the market to sell her. Along came a very ugly man and demanded to see her beauty. The captor retorted, "Empty-head, if you wish to buy her, buy, for there is none as beautiful as she in the world." "Nevertheless," he replied. He stripped her of her six chemises. When she came to the seventh, she rent it and wallowed in ashes. She said before Him, "O Lord of the world, if You have no pity on us, why have You no pity on the sanctity of Your great name?" It was concerning her that Jeremiah lamented: O daughter of My people, gird yourself with sackcloth and roll in ashes; . . . for suddenly the plunderer will come upon us. It does not say, 'upon you,' but 'upon us,' so to speak, upon Me and upon you.—[*Yalkut Shimoni* from *Gittin* 58a]

6:29

in vain—*In vain does the founder refine, for it is of no avail.*—[*Rashi*]

7:31

I did not desire this, and I did not command them to burn their sons and daughters before Me. If I commanded to sacrifice burnt offerings of cattle and sheep, I did not command them to burn their children. Yet, they burn them before

other gods, and they have no pity on them out of their love for paganism. *Jonathan* renders: Which I did not command in My Torah, neither did I have any desire for it. The Rabbis explained: **Which I did not ordain**—This refers to Jephthah [who sacrificed his daughter, as in Jud. 11:29–34], **and it did not enter My mind**—This refers to Mesha, king of Moab, as it is said (II Kings 3:27): And he took his first-born who would reign after him, and brought him up for a burnt-offering. Their view was that he offered him up to God.—[*Redak* from unknown *Midrash*] See *Yalkut, Ta'anith* 4a, *Aggadath Bereishith* 31:1. These midrashim are based on Jeremiah 19:5, not on our verse. See below.

8:2

they shall neither be gathered—as the custom is to gather the bones of the princes and to place them in elaborate coffins.—[*Malbim*]

8:7

await—Heb. שָׁמְרוּ.—[*Rashi*] *Redak* renders: keep. They keep the time of their coming in one place at one time, and at another time in another place according to the change of seasons. They keep their habits, not so My people.

and the turtledove and the crane and the swallow—*Jonathan* renders: וְשַׁפְנִינָא וְכוּרְכְיָא וּסְנוּנִיתָא. כּוּרְכְיָא *is* (*grue in French*), *a crane*.—[*Rashi*] סְנוּנִיתָא *is* (*hirondelle in French*), *a swallow*. —[*Rashi*]

Redak, too, cites Rav Hai Gaon, who renders it in this manner. He quotes others who interpret it as the magpie.

8:8

Redak's and *Kara*'s explanations are more in agreement with the traditional punctuation signs than *Rashi*'s. *Malbim* explains that the people of Jeremiah's generation believed that no one could receive God's Torah through tradition or prophecy. All concepts of right and wrong are inborn and perceived through a person's own intelligence. The prophet questions them: How do you say, "We are wise, and the Law of the Lord is with us. Verily, behold the pen has wrought falsely, the scribes falsehood"? How do you say that we are wise and that we have the Torah within us? Also, how do you say that the pen that wrote the Torah as received from God is false, and that the prophets who wrote their prophecies from God did falsely?

8:9

Malbim explains that since they rejected the word of the Lord, their wisdom is of no use. It is impossible to determine God's will through one's own intelligence. It can be determined only through prophecy and tradition.

8:10

for from the smallest to the greatest—This is already written above, as well as the two following verses. See 6:13–15.

from prophet—I.e. from false prophet.—[*Mezudath David*] *Jonathan* renders: from scribe.

and to priest—I.e. the priests of Baal.—[*Mezudath David*]

8:14

poisoned water—Heb. מֵירוֹשׁ, *Jona-*

than renders: *the cup of the curse, like the venom of serpents. The venom of the serpents is the poison that is in his teeth.*—[*Rashi*]

Redak explains this as poisonous water extracted from a certain grass. *Mezudath Zion* associates it with '(Deut. 29:17) gall (רֹאשׁ) and wormwood.' Scholars have not yet discovered its exact identity. See *Nature & Man in the Bible* by Yehuda Feliks, ch. 36.

Malbim continues with his interpretation, that the people now respond: Why do we sit still and not prepare for war? Gather and let us go to the fortified cities from where we can wage war against the enemy. The prophet replies: But there we will sit in silence and do nothing, for the Lord our God has silenced us, has likened us to mourners who sit and remain silent, and instead of the custom to give the mourners to drink a cup of consolation, He has given us to drink a cup of poisoned water, and this is because we have sinned against the Lord.

8:15

Malbim explains that the people say to the prophet: Is it not proper to hope for peace? Why, then, is there no good? The prophet replies: You should hope for healing of your spiritual ills by repenting your sins, but there is terror, for they cling yet to their wickedness.

8:16

the snorting of their horses—*The sneezing of his nostrils.*—[*Rashi*] The word נַחְרַת, *snorting*, is derived from נְחִירַיִם, *nostrils*.—[*Redak*]

the neighing of their stallions—*The neighing of joy of his horses, and we find elsewhere that horses are called* אַבִּירִים, '(Jud 5:22) *by reason of the prancings, the prancings of their mighty ones* (אַבִּירָיו),' *an expression of* '(Nahum 3:2) *a prancing horse.' And Jonathan renders: from the sound of the steps of their mighty ones.*—[*Rashi*]

Malbim explains that the people ask the prophet: Did not Jacob bless Dan with the blessing '(Gen. 49:17) Dan shall be a serpent on the road, an adder on the path, who bites the heels of the horse and its rider falls backwards'? Since the Danites were trained to battle with horsemen, how has the opposite now come true, that from Dan is heard the snorting of their horses, and yet no 'serpent' has bitten the heels of their horses, for at the neighing of their stallions the whole land quakes, and they have even penetrated into the land and eaten the land and its produce?

9:2

and they have grown strong in the land not for the sake of truth—Those who have power over others do not exercise that power for the sake of truth, in order to execute justice.—[*Redak, Mezudath David*]

9:9

they are withered—*An expression of aridness. Comp.* '(v. 11) *withered* (נִצְּתָה).'—[*Rashi*]

9:11

Kara explains as follows: Who is the man so wise that he can help others to understand this? If someone wonders about this, why God did this to this land, that all creatures wandered away, both the

fowl of the heavens and the cattle, and the dwellings of the wilderness are withered, without any one passing through, and they do not hear the lowing of the cattle, there is no wise man who can understand it and be able to explain it to those who ask him. It is a commonplace occurrence that a person is exiled from his place and that he takes his livestock with him, but here, what was the great anger that all the fowl and the cattle have left? Only the prophet to whom the mouth of the Lord has spoken, can declare it, and he will say, "Do you wish to know why the land is ruined so much that it is withered like a desert any one passing through?"

9:16

16. **Consider**—the impending catastrophe, and call the women mourners.—[*Redak*]

9:22

nor the strong man boast of his strength—for wisdom, strength, and riches will not stand up for a man to protect him from the Judge. But, if he comes to boast . . .—[*Kara*]

Redak explains this verse as regarding the impending siege and exile. If there are wise men, let them not boast of their wisdom, for it will not avail them, since they do not know the Lord and have not walked in His ways, so what wisdom have they? Likewise, if there are strong men among you, your strength will not avail you to save you from death or captivity. Likewise, if there are wealthy people, let them not boast of their riches, since it will not avail them to ransom them from death, for he and his riches will perish. He mentions these three characteristics since oftentimes the wise man can save himself through his devices and his stealth, and the strong man can save himself through his strength, and the rich man can ransom himself from the enemy. The prophet warns them that in this case, they will be unable to save themselves in any of these three ways. How then will they be able to save themselves? . . .

Jonathan paraphrases: So said the Lord: Let not Solomon son of David boast of his wisdom, and let not Samson son of Manoah, the strong man, boast of his strength, and let not Ahab son of Omri, the rich man, boast of his riches.

9:23

Rambam (*Guide to the Perplexed* 3:54) explains that kindness involves doing favors to people to whom one is not required to recompense or to bestow upon them more than they deserve. Righteousness is the bestowal upon a person what he deserves, and justice is the meting out recompense, either punishment or reward as it is deserved.—[*Redak*]

Rabbi Joseph Kara explains that God practices kindness with those who perform His commandments.

for in these I delight—I.e., in people who teach wisdom with the intention of learning, observing, and practicing, not like those people mentioned above, who boast that they are wise and have the Torah of the Lord with them, when, in reality, they have rejected God's word.—[*Kara*]

9:25

This refers to Kedar and the kingdoms of Hazor (infra 49:28f.) which

Nebuchadnezzar conquered. They are called 'cast off to the corners' since they are located at the far border of the desert.—[*Redak*]

From *Targum Jonathan,* it appears that he renders: those who have the corners of their hair polled. This was a custom of the pagans, and was prohibited by the Torah (Lev. 19:27). All these nations, although apparently practicing circumcision, still followed idolatrous customs.—[*Daath Mikra*]

for all the nations are uncircumcised—Now he explains 'circumcised' and 'for his uncircumcision.' All the nations are uncircumcised, and the house of Israel, although physically circumcised, have hearts closed up to God's teachings, and are, therefore, deserving of punishment. He does not state that the gentiles deserve punishment for not circumcising themselves, since they were not commanded to do so. He states only that Israel deserves punishment for their closed up hearts. They were commanded to circumcise themselves in order to be different from the nations in their actions as well as in their body, but since they are of uncircumcised hearts, the circumcision of the flesh did not avail them, and they are as though they had not been circumcised, for the circumcision of the flesh was given as a covenant to be a peculiar treasure, to serve God, as He states (Gen. 17:7): 'to be to you for a God and for your seed after you.' And a sign was sealed in their flesh in order that they remember constantly that they are different from the nations. Since they mingled with the nations and learned from their customs, it is as though they had broken the covenant and the sign, and that He is not their God, for they chose other gods in His stead. Therefore, the prophet continues after this with the exhortation not to learn from the way of the nations.—[*Redak*]

Although many of these nations were known to practice circumcision, as above, the Sages learn from this verse that gentiles, even if they are circumcised, are accounted as uncircumcised, and Jews, even if they are uncircumcised, are called 'circumcised.'—[*Ned.* 31b]

10:5

fear them not—*if you separate from them for they will not harm you.*—[*Rashi*]

10:8

Redak explains: But they are altogether brutish. I.e., even the wise of the nations are brutish and foolish. The instruction of vanities, which is wood. I.e., they instruct the people to worship the idols, which are vanity and wood, for it is plated with silver and gold, and it cannot move by itself. It is fashioned from the lowest of the creations, mineral, for the entire Creation is composed of animal, vegetable, and mineral.

10:9

Tarshish—*Jonathan* identifies Tarshish with Africa. See I Kings 10:22 Isa. 2:16, Commentary Digest. Some identify it as Carthage in North Africa, now known as Tunis, and others as Tartessus in Spain. See also Appendix of Isa. 1, 23:12, where it is identified as Tarsus on the coast of the Mediterranean. See Ibn Ezra, Jonah 1:3. *Daath Mikra* suggests also that it was in Italy, or on the Island of Sardinia.

Uphaz—According to *Jonathan,* this is Ophir. See I Kings 9:28, where the location of Ophir is discussed. Uphaz is mentioned only here and in Daniel 10:5.

10:13

and He brought up clouds—I.e., He caused it to rain after He brought up clouds.—[*Redak*]

Clouds are called נְשִׂאִים because they are lifted high above the earth or because they carry the water for rain.—[*Ibn Nachmiash*]

He made lightning for the rain—This is another wonder, that the rain does not extinguish the fire of the lightning.—[*Redak*]

10:17

Redak explains that the prophet is addressing Babylon after the Jews have been exiled there. He explains כִּנְעָתֵךְ as 'your conquest.' The prophet exhorts Babylon not to become haughty about her conquest of Judea because it was not accomplished through her merits. Do not order them to worship your idols because you rule over the nations, for now, God says to Babylon, "Gather in from the land your conquest." Cease your conquest of the nations for you will no longer conquer.—[*Redak*]

you who sit in the fortified cities—Heb. בַּמָּצוֹר. You who sit in a strong fortification and think that no nation will ever conquer you. This follows *Jonathan.* Others explain: You who are destined to sit in the siege. I.e., you Babylon, who will be besieged by Persia and Media.—[*Redak*]

10:23

Mezudath David explains this as the supplication that the Judeans will utter before God. We know that no man among the Judeans has the proper way to follow, and there is no man among us who goes and prepares his steps according to the proper way, but each one goes and does whatever he chances to do.

10:24

but with justice—*With chastisements.*

with justice—(*justice in French*).

but with justice—*Jonathan renders: but with mild judgment.*

not with Your wrath—*lest there be complete destruction.*—[*Rashi*]

Rashi's intention is apparently the same as *Mezudath David,* that the people beg the Lord to chastise them, but in a manner of one who chastises for the sake of instruction, of teaching to improve one's ways, not with wrath, as one who wreaks vengeance on another, lest He destroy them completely.

Kara explains that the prophet supplicates God not to turn the people into the hands of the nations since that is a chastisement of wrath, and the nations diminish them, as the Torah states: '(Lev. 26:38) And the land of your enemies shall consume you.'

10:25

families—This is synonymous with 'nations.' Cf. '(Zech. 14:18) And if the family of Egypt will not ascend.'—[*Redak*]

they have devoured—(*devorèrent in French*). *The same applies to 'and consumed him'* (וַאֲכָלֻהוּ).—[*Rashi*]

Although they are the rod of Your wrath upon Israel, they deserve punishment, since You were only a little displeased, and they helped for

evil. Therefore, pour out Your wrath upon them.—[*Redak*]

and have wasted his dwelling—As the Targum renders: And they have made their dwellings desolate. It is also possible that the reference is to the Temple and that the prophet deals with the future.—[*Redak*]

11:1

to say—I.e., to say to the men of Judah. The word was that they should say to them, "Hearken to the words of this covenant." The words of the covenant are those written in the Torah, in Deut. 28, 'And it shall be if you hearken to the voice of the Lord your God . . . And it shall be, if you do not hearken to the voice of the Lord your God . . . These are the words of the covenant that the Lord commanded Moses to make with the children of Israel, in addition to the covenant that He made with them in Horeb.' In Horeb, it is written: '(Ex. 24:7) And he took the book of the covenant and read it in the presence of the people, and they said, "All that the Lord spoke, we will do and we will hearken." And Moses took the blood and sprinkled on the people, and he said, "Behold the blood of the covenant that the Lord made with you concerning all these things." The words of the covenant are to obey God's commandments, and that He should be their God and they should be His people.—[*Redak*]

11:4

on the day—I.e. at the time I took them out of Egypt, on the fiftieth day after their departure.—[*Redak*]

out of the iron furnace—They were refined as silver and gold are refined in an iron furnace.—[*Redak, Mezudath David*]

11:16

fair with goodly fruit—With goodly fruit and with a goodly form. This alludes to the congregation of Israel. In the beginning, the Lord called your name 'a leafy olive tree, fair with goodly fruit.' When you obeyed His will, you were like a leafy olive tree, whose leaves do not wither; i.e., you were always prosperous, and you performed good and beautiful deeds, as an olive tree in its prime, 'with whose fatness they honor God and men.'—[*Redak*]

Now that you transgress My Torah, I will do to you what they do to a tree that no longer produces fruit, when its owners no longer benefit from it, that they break it and use the branches for firewood, so will I do to you.—[*Kara*]

12:4

Draw them out like sheep to the slaughter—Pay them in kind, for they wished to kill me as a lamb brought to the slaughter.

[4] **How long will the land mourn**—How long will the land be desolate because of the sins of the men of Anathoth? They said, "He does not know our end." When Jeremiah prophesied that they would have no remnant, they retorted that their future would not be during the lifetime of the prophet and that he did not know what was in store for them. The prophet feels that the destruction of the land will be due to the sins of the people of Anathoth and that the others are innocent. God's reply commences here with verse 5.

Redak explains these verses in a slightly different manner. As mentioned above, Jeremiah questions the prosperity and the tranquility of the wicked of Israel. He entreats God to draw them out like sheep to the slaughter and to prepare them for the day of slaughter. I.e., prepare them for the day of the destruction, that they should be unable to escape the sword. Then it will be known by the world that their wickedness caused their destruction. Now, however, there is confusion because of their prosperity.

[4] **How long will the land mourn**—I.e., how long will this be that they will be prepared for the day of slaughter, when the land will mourn, and the grass of all the field will dry out . . . because of the evil of its inhabitants, for as long as they have peace they say, "He will not see our end"? When the true prophets announce that God will bring misfortune upon them, they retort, "He will not see our end." This is the end of Jeremiah's question. God's reply commences with verse 5.

12:5

and in the peaceful land that you trust—*there they wearied you.*—[*Rashi*]

how will you do in the heights—*The princes of Judah. The pride of the Jordan is symbolic since it is a place of lions and tigers, and Jonathan taught us this in many places. And here he paraphrased: And how do you expect to do against the wild beasts that are on the height of the Jordan? 'And behold, as a lion ascends from the height of the Jordan,' Jonathan renders in two places* (infra 49:19, 50:44): *like a lion that ascends from the height of the Jordan.*—[*Rashi*]

The implication is that if the men of Anathoth attempted to kill Jeremiah, how much more will the princes of Judah attempt the same thing!

Since Jeremiah was still unaware of the wickedness of the men of Judah and Jerusalem, God says to him allegorically, "You have joined footmen like yourself and they wearied you, for you became weary trying to run along with them.

how will you compete—How can you attempt to run along with horse riders? If the people of Anathoth who are your kin did you so much harm that you fear them, how much more will you fear to join the people of Jerusalem and their princes! For then you will recognize that their wickedness far exceeds that of the people of Anathoth. Since their wickedness has come to such a state, it is necessary to bring Nebuchadnezzar to rule over them and destroy them.—[*Mezudath David*]

and in a peaceful land—Now He explains the parable. When you were in a peaceful land, in Anathoth, with your kinsmen, do you trust them that they will do you no harm? How then can you trust the height of the Jordan, the lions' lair; i.e., how will you contend with the men of Jerusalem and its princes?—[*Mezudath David*]

Redak explains that God does not answer the prophet. He reprimands him for his question. I see that you have run with mortals like yourself, and they have wearied you, for they have run faster than you, and you were unable to overtake them, and they wearied you in your running to overtake them.

Rabbi Joseph Kara, who explains the question as regarding the men of

Anathoth, explains that God replies: You are like a man who boasts that he can run with horses, and a footman comes along and wearies him with his running and runs ahead of him. Those who witness this, say to him, "You were boasting. Now you became weary from racing with a footman. How will you compete with the horses?"

and in the peaceful land which you trust, how will you do in the heights of the Jordan?—When I send you in the territory of Judah and Benjamin, you should trust them, yet you complain about the men of Anathoth that they seek to kill you, had I sent you to the height of the Jordan—i.e. Reuben and Gad who dwelt on the other side of the Jordan before they were exiled—you would surely complain about them.

and how can you compete with horses?—How can you compete with horses to race with them? The explanation of the parable is: You are among people like yourself, yet you do not know their thoughts, for they attempted to poison you, yet you did not know it and you did not realize it until I informed you. Now, how can you understand My thoughts and My secrets in guiding the world, why the wicked prosper and the righteous suffer in this world? Therefore, be silent and do not attempt to fathom My ways. He then includes Jeremiah's personal matters, as the others explain it, and He exhorts him to take courage and not to fear the princes of Jerusalem.

12:11

the wasted one mourns before Me—Heb. עָלַי, lit. on Me.—[*Rashi*]

The wasted one is the congregation of Israel, which has become waste. She mourns before Me about her wastelands, saying that I laid her waste.—[*Redak*]

for no one lays it to his heart—I.e., no one ponders over the matter, why the land was devastated, for no one takes to heart My words and My reproof, that I reprove you through My prophets. They did not take this to heart, neither did they hearken to it. *Jonathan* renders: They did not lay My fear to their heart.—[*Redak*]

12:13

and be ashamed of your increase—You should be ashamed of the thorns that your sowing produced. *Jonathan* renders: Do not be like those who sow wheat in an uncultivated field, and find nothing to gather in but thorns, and from their increase they have no benefit, and be ashamed of your deeds when the fierce anger of the Lord comes upon you.

12:14

who touch—I.e., who touch with the intention of harming. Cf. '(Gen. 26:11) Whoever touches this man.' Onkelos renders: whoever harms. Here too, *Jonathan* renders: who harm.—[*Redak*]

behold I uproot them—They too will be exiled just like My people. Therefore, let them not rejoice upon their exile.—[*Redak*]

I will uproot from their midst—I will take out those who were exiled among them when it comes time for Me to return the exile of My people.—[*Redak*]

13:7

7. **and I dug**—Apparently, he had covered it with earth.—[*Mezudath David*]

it was of no use for anything—*It was not fit for anything.*—[*Rashi*]

14:1

How Menahem explains the chapter according to this definition is not clear. Other exegetes explain the word as an expression of withholding or scarcity. *Redak* accounts for the plural form as referring to a scarcity of both produce and money. God informed the prophet prior to the coming of this drought.

Abarbanel understands the chapter as a story rather than a prophecy. He explains the general intention of the chapter as follows: This chapter comes to tell us that a year of drought came to the land of Judah, when there was neither bread nor meat and vegetables to eat. Neither was there water to drink. When the prophet prayed for the people, God replied that, because of the wickedness of the generation, his prayer would not be accepted, and that God would not repent of His anger. When the prophet complained that they were misled by the prophets, God replied that they were not prophets and that all their words were lies, and that he would, therefore, pour out His wrath on the false prophets and those who follow them, and He predicted the troubles that would befall them. Since Jeremiah complained of the hatred they harbored against him because of his prophecies, God promised him that He would spare him and that the enemy would pity him.

He explains the plural to denote the shortage of both food and drinking water. The verse is to be understood as: The following is the story of the matter about which the word of the Lord came to Jeremiah concerning the droughts. The reference is to God's reply to Jeremiah's prayers. The story is that of the droughts and the prayer, and the word of the Lord is the reply.

Kara places these droughts in the reign of Zedekiah.

14:7

for our backslidings have increased, we have sinned to You—True, it is fitting that You punish us because our backslidings have increased, for we have rebelled against You in many respects, by worshipping other gods, by stealing and robbing, and by following false prophets rather than true ones. Therefore, he says, "Our backslidings have increased." Nevertheless, do for the sake of Your name which is called upon us, for we are called the people of the Lord.—[*Redak*]

14:11

Malbim explains that sometimes evil befalls someone because God has hidden His face from him. In that case, prayer may help so that God should not hide His face. In other cases, God Himself metes out the punishment upon the guilty party. In that case, prayer is of no avail. Only intense remorse may help to repeal the decree. In this case, Jeremiah thought that the misfortune would befall them through God's hiding His face. He, therefore, prayed for them. God replies that he should not pray for good since He is meting out the punishment, and no prayer will avail.

14:16

and no one will bury them—There

will be so many corpses that they will be unable to bury them.—[*Mezudath David*]

This will be their punishment in addition to the torments and death.—[*Redak*]

their wives—The women were more prone to listen to the false prophets than the men.—[*Redak*]

their sons, and their daughters—This refers to minors, who are punished for the sins of the fathers, for this is God's sense of justice.—[*Redak*]

14:21

for Your name's sake—*that you are called merciful.*—[*Rashi*]

15:1

desire—Heb. נַפְשִׁי, lit. My soul.—[*Rashi, Redak*]

Why should you continue to pray to Me? Even if Moses and Samuel, who were greater than you, would stand before Me, I have no desire for this people. He mentions Moses and Samuel, who were Levites and prophets. Also, Samuel was the greatest prophet after Moses, as the Psalmist (99:6) states: 'Moses and Aaron among His priests and Samuel among those who call in His name.' We find also (I Sam. 3:19f.): 'And did not let any of his words fall to the ground. And all Israel from Dan to Beer Sheba knew that Samuel was established as a prophet to the Lord.'—[*Redak*]

send them away—This is addressed to the prophet. God says to him, "If you have the power to send them away, do so rather than pray for them."—[*Redak*]

Others explain: Tell them My message that I decreed that they be expelled from My land, and let them go forth.—[*Abarbanel, Mezudath David*]

15:4

son of Hezekiah—Scripture points out that Manasseh had a righteous father from whom to learn. Yet he was wicked and misled the people.—[*Daath Soferim*]

15:9

[7] **And I winnowed them with a sieve in the cities of the earth**—During Jehoiakim's reign, Daniel, his companions, and many of the princes of Judah were exiled.

I bereft, I destroyed My people—for they did not return from their ways.

[8] **His widows are to Me more numerous than the sand of the seas**—For since the day you rebelled against Me, your slain have increased, thereby increasing your widows.

I have brought—I have brought Jehoiakim and Jehoiachin and the craftsmen and the gate sentries.

I have cast upon her suddenly a city—The people of the city of the king of Babylon and with terrors.

9. **She who bore seven**—*Samaria and the nation of the Ten Tribes, from whom rose seven dynasties of wicked kings, has already been cut off and exiled.*—[*Rashi*]

and their remnant—*These are Judah and part of Benjamin, who remained in Israel. I shall deliver them to the sword. These are the seven dynasties: Jeroboam son of Nebat and his dynasty, Baasha and his dynasty, Omri and his dynasty, Jehu and his dynasty, Menahem and his dynasty, Pekah and his dynasty,*

Hoshea and his dynasty.—[*Rashi* from *Gittin* 88a]

The difficulty here is that Pekah and Hoshea did not have any dynasties since they were not succeeded by their sons. Pekah was assassinated by Hoshea, and Hoshea was the last king of Israel. Perhaps the intention is: Jeroboam son of Nebat and his tribunal etc. This would be closer to the quotation from the Talmud. Rashi, however, does not mention tribunals, but families. Also, the Talmud mentions Ahab instead of Omri. Rashi accounts for this by stating that Ahab outdid his father Omri in wickedness. Therefore, the tribunal is called on his name. On our verse, however, Rashi mentions Omri rather than Ahab. Apparently, he means to mention the first king of each dynasty. Hence, we are dealing with dynasties rather than with tribunals. Interestingly, Abarbanel states: Pekah and Hoshea, omitting the dynasties.

Other exegetes explain this passage as referring to Jerusalem or the people of Israel, who bore many children, seven being the symbol of many; i.e. had a large population, and they were all slain or exiled.—[*Redak, Kara*]

15:9

Jehoiachin is not counted although Scripture testifies: '(II Kings 24:9) And he did what was evil in the eyes of the Lord like all that his father had done.' In Rabbinic literature, however, we find that Jehoiachin repented of his sins while in Babylonian prison. His sins were therefore forgiven and he is accounted as a righteous man. See II Kings 25:30, Commentary Digest for all sources. Abarbanel, however, substitutes Jehoiachin for Jehoiakim. In light of these Midrashim, this presents a difficulty. Moreover, the verses quoted by the Midrash relate to Jehoiakim, rather than Jehoiachin.

and confounded—Heb. וְחָפֵרָה, *an expression of shame.*—[*Rashi*]

and their remnant—I.e. Zedekiah's generation.—[*Kara*] I.e., those who will not go into exile will be delivered to the sword of the enemy. It may also be interpreted as 'their descendants.'—[*Redak*]

15:10

they curse me—Heb. מְקַלְלְוַנִי. *I do not quarrel with them concerning matters of money that I claim from them, neither have they made any claim on me, yet all the people curse me.*—[*Rashi*]

The peculiar structure of this word leads *Redak* to conjecture that it is a combination of two roots: קלל, *curse,* and קלה, *to treat with contempt.*

15:18

You are to me—Heb. הָיוֹ תִהְיֶה.—[*Rashi*]

as a failing spring—*Like a man whose trust has been cut off from him, for you allow me to suffer at their hands.* אַכְזָב *is a spring that stops* (*faylayne in O.F.*), *failing.*—[*Rashi*]

water that is not faithful—*to rely upon it.*—[*Rashi*]

At the beginning of my prophecy, You promised me that I would be like a fortified city, a pillar of iron, and a wall of copper, yet the people humiliate me and strike me. Although God had stated: And they shall fight against you,' Jeremiah

expected this fight to be shortlived, but now, when he saw that his persecutions were unending, he complained to God.—[*Redak*]

16:2

Although there was a decree upon the men of Anathoth that they have no remnant, they, in fact, did have a remnant because they repented at the time of the conquest of the land. We find that when they returned from Babylonian exile, there were one hundred twenty-eight men of Anathoth (Ezra 2:27). [See Commentary Digest on 11:23]. Nevertheless, God commanded the prophet not to marry or beget children in Anathoth in accordance with the original decree, and He did not reveal their repentance to him, since God told him that the decree was so harsh that He commanded him not to marry in that place.—[*Redak*]

16:5

Redak quotes his father, who explains it as an expression of raising the voice, either in joy or in sorrow. He derives this from the Arabic cognate.

you bemoan—Heb. תָּנֻד, *you shall lament.*—[*Rashi*] See above 15:5.

for I have gathered in My peace etc—*When their father Abraham performed charity and justice, I gave his children lovingkindness and mercy,* as in Deut. 7:12: '*And the Lord your God shall keep for you* the covenant and the lovingkindness *etc.*' Also, '(Deut. 13:18) *And He shall give you mercy.' They turned 'justice into wormwood, and cast righteousness to the ground'* (*Amos 5:7*). *I, too, have returned and gathered in to Me My lovingkindness and My mercies.*—[*Rashi*]

I have gathered in—Heb. אָסַפְתִּי (*ôté in O.F.*), *taken off. Comp.* '(Gen. 30:23) *God has gathered* (אָסַף) *in my disgrace.*'—[*Rashi*]

The peace, the kindness, and the mercy that I was accustomed to bestowing upon this people, I have taken away from them and gathered it in to Me, and, since I gathered in My peace from them, you shall not seek their peace either in their mourning or in their joy.—[*Redak*]

16:15

The reference is to the precept of mentioning the departure from Egypt every day, as in Deut. 16:3. Rabbi Eleazar ben Azariah rules that this obligation obtains at night as well as by day but it will not obtain in Messianic times. The Rabbis, however, rule that the obligation obtains only by day, but the precept does extend to Messianic times (*Ber.* 12b).

16:18

Abarbanel explains that they profaned the land by failing to observe the laws of the release year and the jubilee year, in addition to their other abominations.

My heritage—My land, the land fit for Me to rest My Shechinah, the land hallowed over all lands.—[*Redak*]

16:21

I.e., before I redeem them, I will punish them this time and let them know My power and My might, for I will castigate them through the nations in order that they recognize My power and My might, and they know that I am the Lord. Then I will redeem them.—[*Kara*]

that My name is the Lord—*As its apparent meaning, a ruler and a sovereign to fulfill My decree.*—[*Rashi*]

The expression, 'My name is the Lord,' is synonymous with 'I am the Lord,' for He and His Name are one.—[*Redak*]

17:8

8. **And he shall be . . . by water**—which will never thirst.—[*Redak*]

and by a rivulet—I.e., even the roots that spread over a distance will be by rivulets of water.—[*Redak*]

and will not see—*The tree will not see when heat comes.*—[*Rashi*]

Even when there is heat in the world, it need not be concerned, since it is planted by water and the heat cannot dry it out, for even its leaves will be green. They will not fall off as the leaves of other trees in winter.—[*Redak*]

17:13

Rav Saadiah Gaon connects verses 11 and 12 as follows: He will be dishonored by the Throne of Glory i.e., he will be cast down by the Throne of Glory. *Jonathan* paraphrases: Retribution will be wrought upon him by Him Whose Shechinah is on the Throne of Glory, exalted from the beginning, opposite the place of our Sanctuary. Rabbi Samuel Ibn Tibon connects verse 12 with verse 10: I, the Lord, search the heart, test the kidneys . . . Just as God dwells in the heavens, the Throne of Glory, exalted from the beginning, so does He dwell in the place of our Sanctuary,' and He knows all that transpires on earth, everyone's thoughts and deeds.—[*Redak*]

Redak proceeds to explain verse 13 as a supplication: O Lord, source of the hopes of Israel, may all those who forsake You and have no trust in You be shamed with their trust in mortals as he mentioned before, 'and whose heart turns away from the Lord.'

and they who turn away from me—Heb. וְסוּרַי. Since I cleave to the Lord, those who turn away from me, in fact, turn away from the Lord and forsake Him. Those who turn away from my good ways forsake the Lord. It may also be rendered: And they who turn away.—[*Redak*]

shall be marked out on the earth—Since they have forsaken You, let them have no share in You, but let them be marked out on the earth like the beasts, of which nothing remains after death. So shall nothing remain of them since they forsook You.—[*Redak*]

for they have forsaken the source of living waters—This is payment in kind, since they forsook You, the source of living waters. Those who cleave to You will constantly receive Your bounty both in this world and in the next, but those who forsake You and put their trust in mortal man, who is a part of the earth, shall be written on the earth and not in the heavens.—[*Redak*]

17:23

23. **But they did not hearken**—I.e., *your forefathers* did not hearken *to what I commanded them.*—[*Rashi*]

and they hardened their napes—They did not turn their faces toward the prophets so as not to hearken to their reproof.—[*Mezudath David*]

17:26

and from the Negev—From those

living in the south.—[*Mezudath David*]

18:8

I will repent—*And I will think another thought*.—[*Rashi*]

18:14

the field—Heb. שָׂדָי, *like* שָׂדֶה, *a field*.—[*Rashi*]

cold—(*froids in French*).—[*Rashi*]

flowing—(*courants in French*).—[*Rashi*]

And we can also interpret it: 'Shall it be abandoned to be strange rejected water, the water that is cold running water?—[*Rashi*] (זָרִים—*According to the first interpretation, it is an expression of a stream* [זֶרֶם]. *According to the second interpretation, it is an expression of strangeness, i.e. rejected water.*) This appears both in the Lublin edition and in the Warsaw edition, but in parentheses. It does not appear to be correct, because *Rashi*'s first interpretation also defines זָרִים as 'strange,' not strange in the sense of being rejected, but strange in the sense of being unknown.

Redak explains that the prophet uses easily accessible water as his example. He first mentions the water that flows from the rock of the field, which is easily accessible to all, and then he mentions the strange cold water, i.e. the water that is piped into the city or near the city from a long distance. Would anyone neglect to drink these easily accessible waters? Yet I, Who am far from them according to My greatness, draw near to them to bring them benefit, but they have forgotten Me.

18:15

15. **For**—*so have My people done, that they have forgotten Me and burnt incense to vanity*.—[*Rashi*]

Lebanon—A mountain in Eretz Israel whose peak is white with snow. It is, therefore, called Lebanon from לָבָן, *white*.—[*Ibn Nachmiash*]

Rabbenu Tam (*Teshuvoth Dunash* p. 81) defines זָרִים as 'strange,' like *Rashi*'s first definition, and מַיִם קָרִים as 'spring water.'

18:18

18. **And they said, "Come etc.**—*Jeremiah was complaining about the men of Anathoth and saying that they say this*.—[*Rashi*]

I reprove them with Your words, and they say to each other, "Come let us devise plots against Jeremiah."—[*Redak*]

Come—An expression of urging, common in Scripture.—[*Redak*]

Torah . . . from the priest—*For it is incumbent upon the priests to teach the Torah, as it is stated:* '(Deut. 33:10) *They shall teach Your ordinances to Jacob*.'—[*Rashi*]

Come, let us strike him with the tongue—*Let us testify falsely against him*.—[*Rashi* from *Jonathan*]

Let us incite the princes against him and say that he prophesies only evil about this place.—[*Kara*]

Let us inform upon him.—[*Redak*]

The end of the verse explains the beginning, that their intention was to cause his death by testifying against him.—[*Kara*]

18:23

Redak renders: And do not erase their sin, making תֶּמְחִי a substitute for תִּמְחֶה, the active second person masculine future. For this, there are

examples in Scripture. See Deut. 32:18.

The intention is: Do not erase what they are doing to me.—[*Kara*]

and let them be made to stumble before You—Said Jeremiah before the Holy One, blessed be He, "Lord of the universe, even at the time they are performing charity, make them stumble with undeserving people, so that they should not receive reward for them."—[*Baba Kamma* 16b]

I.e., even when they walk before You to perform precepts, cause them to stumble.—[*Mezudath David*]

at the time of Your anger do it to them—At the time of Your anger wreak vengeance upon them so that they will be unable to contain it.—[*Mezudath David*]

Azulai (*Chomath Anach*) quotes Rabbi Isaac Luria (ARI zal) who associates this with the Talmudic maxim that in time of anger, God punishes for failure to perform a positive commandment (*Menahoth* 41a). Therefore, Jeremiah prayed that they be deprived of the precept of charity at just such a time. Azulai himself suggests that Jeremiah prayed that the Divine attribute of justice take preference to mercy. When God bestows mercy upon the world, He does not immediately punish the sinners with bodily harm, but with loss of their possessions. Jeremiah knew that the performance of charity changes the Divine attribute of justice to mercy. He, therefore, petitioned God to disqualify their charity and to punish them with justice, expressed as 'at the time of Your anger,' and then to 'do to them,' to inflict bodily harm upon them.

19:2

The reference is to the Dung Gate, mentioned in Neh. 2:13. From this gate, one goes out to the valley of the son of Hinnom. The Rabbis, however, identify this with the eastern gate of the Temple court. They enumerate seven names by which this gate was known: (1) The Sur Gate, from which all ritually unclean persons had to turn away (סורו); (2) the Yesod (foundation) Gate, for there they founded the halachah; (3) the Harsith Gate, which was directed opposite the rising sun (חֶרֶס); (4) the Ethun Gate, made for entrance and exit (from the root אתה, to come); (5) the Middle Gate, situated between two gates, the gate of the Temple proper and the gate of the Women's Court; (6) the New Gate, where the halachah was renewed; (7) the Upper Gate, situated above the Israelites' Court (see *Korban Ha-edah* ad loc.).—[*Redak* from *Yerushalmi Erubin* 5:1]

According to *Rashi*, this gate would be called the Potsherd Gate, whereas according to Yerushalmi, it would be called the Sun Gate. *Kara* conjectures that at this gate, earthenware vessels were manufactured. Hence, it would be called the Earthenware Gate. See above 18:2.

19:15

Malbim asserts that Jeremiah was not commanded by God to make this announcement. Consequently, he was vulnerable to Pashhur's attack. When he prophesied by the command of God, however, no one had the power to harm him.

20:2

Scripture describes Jeremiah with

his title of prophet to emphasize Pashhur's audacity to strike the prophet of God. We do not know whether he did so because he was confident that Jeremiah's prophecy would not be fulfilled or whether he felt that Jeremiah had spoken too harshly when announcing his prophecy, humiliating the people and the city of Jerusalem. Perhaps, too, it was just as the reaction of an elderly man seeing a youngster usurping a position unfitting for him.—[*Daath Soferim*]

and placed him in the prison—Heb. הַמַּהְפֶּכֶת, *the name of a place of a prison, and Jonathan rendered:* לְכִיפְתָא (*arvolud in O.F.*), *a vault.*—[*Rashi*] This is a room whose ceiling is just high enough to accomodate the prisoner's height.—[*Sanhedrin* 81b]

Rabbi Joseph Kimchi describes it as a pillory. *Daath Soferim* conjectures that it was customary to place someone who disturbed the Temple service into this prison, vault, or pillory. He was left there until his fate was decided. We do not know when this was instituted. It was not a standard form of punishment since it is not mentioned in the Torah as a punishment for any sin. It is again mentioned below (29:26), as a place 'for every man who is mad and makes himself a prophet.' I.e. for every man who makes himself a prophet and disturbs the order of the Temple. Pashhur saw Jeremiah as just such a person.

in the upper gate of Benjamin—This gate was in Benjamin's territory, for the Temple was partly in Judah's territory and partly in Benjamin's.—[*Redak*]

This gate was situated at the top of the mountain.—[*Mezudath David*]

20:10

a gathering—Heb. מָגוֹר, *an expression of gathering, and so did Jonathan render it.*—[*Rashi*]

Redak renders: terror. They frighten me all around, from all sides.

Some take this as an allusion to Pashhur, who was dubbed Magor Missaviv by the prophet. I heard the slander of many, also Magor Missaviv.—[*Abarbanel, Malbim*]

tell—*false testimony against him.*—[*Rashi*]

and let us tell about him—Heb. וְנַגִּידֶנּוּ, *and let us testify against him. And Menahem* (*Machbereth* p. 53) *explained* וְנַגִּידֶנּוּ *like* '(Deut. 14:1) *You shall not cut yourselves* (לֹא תִתְגֹּדְדוּ).' *He also joined* '(Job 17:5) *For the sake of flattering, he destroys* (יַגִּיד) *his friends.' This is an expression of destruction. Comp.* '(Dan. 4:11) *Cut down* (גֹּדּוּ) *the trees.' But Dunash* (*Teshuvoth* p. 54) *interpreted it as an actual expression of telling, and this is its interpretation: Tell false things about him and we will tell about him to the king.' And we have like* נַגִּידֶנּוּ, *we will tell about him, many words in the Scriptures that cannot be interpreted unless they are divided into two words or three. Comp.* '(Gen. 37:4) *And they could not speak with him* (דַּבְּרוֹ) *peacefully.' Also,* '(supra 10:20) *My children have left me* (יְצָאֻנִי),' lit. 'have gone away from me.'—[*Rashi*] *Dunash* attempts to illustrate that the suffix of a verb appearing to be a direct object may sometimes follow an intransitive verb representing a phrase, implying the preposition,

with, about, or *from.* Therefore, we may interpret נְגִידֶנּוּ as 'let us tell about him.' For the idea expressed in this verse, *Dunash* refers us to 18:18, where Jeremiah's enemies plot to strike him with their tongue.

everyone who was friendly with me—I.e. those I thought to be my friends.—[*Redak*]

await my destruction—Heb. צַלְעִי.—[*Rashi*]

Others render: **await my stumbling.** Perhaps I will stumble and they will be able to wreak vengeance upon me, as below. This expression is figurative.—[*Abarbanel, Mezudath David*]

20:14

Other exegetes explain the verse simply as: Cursed be the day in which I was born etc. Out of the bitterness of their soul, the righteous curse the day of their birth although no curse can effect a day that has already passed. Job, too, (3:3) states: "May the day in which I was born be lost, the night wherein it was said, 'A man-child has been brought forth.'" He continues the matter by saying, "The day in which my mother bore me shall not be blessed."—[*Redak*]

The Rabbis, however, wish to avoid repetition (*Abarbanel*). Also, they explain the verse in Job to mean, 'the night wherein she should have said, "Shall a man beget?"' The Midrash explains that Job cursed the night of his conception. He lamented the fact that his mother was not a menstruant when his father approached her and that she did not say, "Shall a man impregnate me now in my unclean state?" The Midrash draws an analogy between Job and Jeremiah, concluding that both of them cursed the day of their conception and the day of their birth. Yet, Job curses the night whereas Jeremiah curses the day. Would the righteous Hilkiah, the father of Jeremiah, perform the sex act in the daytime? They, therefore, conclude that he did so under compulsion, for he was fleeing from Manasseh, who was killing the prophets. The halachah is that, if a man is embarking on a journey, he must 'visit' his wife. Since he was unable to wait for nightfall, he performed his conjugal duty during the day before fleeing. —[*Maharzav*]

In our editions of *Gen. Rabbah,* as well as in *Yalkut Shimoni,* the reading is, 'when Jezebel killed the prophets.' *Maharzav* questions the possibility of this, since Jezebel lived at the time of Jehoshaphat, eleven generations before Zedekiah, when Jeremiah prophesied. He points out that, according to *Rashi,* the massacre took place during Manasseh's reign. This does not completely solve the problem, however, since Manasseh reined fifty-five years and he repented at the age of thirty-four, in the twenty-second year of his reign. Since the massacre must have taken place before he repented, we have at least thirty-three years left to his reign after the massacre, two years of Amon's reign, and thirteen years of Josiah's reign, when Jeremiah embarked on his prophetic career. Accordingly, at the time, he was forty-eight years old, yet he pleads, "I am a youth." See above (1:6) for various explanations.

Maharzav conjectures that, when Manasseh killed Isaiah, he also

killed other prophets. There is no other mention made of Manasseh's massacre of the prophets. See II Kings 12:16, Commentary Digest.

Malbim renders: Cursed is the day in which I was begotten—That was the day of the massacre of the prophets.

the day in which my mother bore me shall not be blessed—That was the ninth of Av, the day the Temple was to be destroyed. This is mentioned by *Abarbanel, Malbim,* and *Ibn Nachmiash* in the name of a Midrash. This Midrash is unknown to us.

The Rabbis (*Yalkut Shimoni* from *Pesikta Rabbathi* 27:3) depict Jeremiah's pitiful state with a touching episode of a high priest whose lot fell to officiate at the ceremony of a *sotah,* a suspected adultress. He uncovered her hair as is prescribed by the Torah. When he was ready to give her the cursing waters to drink, he looked at her face and recognized her as his own mother. He began to cry out and say, "Woe is me! My mother, whom I strove to honor, I must now disgrace!" So said Jeremiah, "Zion, upon whom I hoped to prophesy good things and consolations, I must prophesy words of retribution!"

20:16

And he heard an outcry in the morning—That was when he was arrested and brought to trial.

and a blast at noontime—That was the blast of the shophar announcing the verdict to execute him.

21:4

Although not matching it identically, *Rashi*'s interpretation resembles *Midrash Tehillim* 36:8: And some say that even in the generation of Hezekiah and in the generation of Zedekiah, they knew the Explicit Name, as it is stated: Behold I turn back the weapons of war that are in your hands—What were the weapons of war? This is the Explicit Name, for they would go out to war, and, although they did not wage war, the enemies would fall. But since the iniquities took their toll and the Temple was destroyed, they would fall into the hands of their enemies. [There is a dispute between] Rabbi Aivu and the Rabbis. Aivu said: The angels would peel the Name that was on them. And the Rabbis said that it would peel off by itself. And since the Temple was destroyed, they would go out to war. They began to say, "(Psalms 38:4) There is no perfection in my flesh because of Your fury." See Isaiah 29:10ff., Commentary Digest; also 43:28, Appendix.

Abarbanel interprets this to mean that they were able to bring down spiritual powers from heaven in order to defend themselves.

21:10

This appears to be more correct. According to Targum, why the necessity of 'for evil and not for good'? Possibly, God's anger could be for good, that they repent of their sins and the city would be saved. In this case, however, God says that the destruction has already been decreed, and His anger is to deliver the city 'into the hands of the king of Babylon, and he shall burn it with fire.'—[*Malbim*]

21:13

rock of the plain—*Mountain,*

entirely surrounded by plain.—[*Rashi*]

22:14

That wide house is ceiled with beams and boards of cedar.—[*Redak*]

and painted with vermilion—Heb. וּמָשׁוֹחַ בַּשָּׁשַׁר, *painted with dyes, so does Jonathan render.* בַּשָּׁשַׁר *is a color of a type used for painting. Rashi*'s intention appears to be that this is used for painting pictures and decorating the walls or the ceiling. *Another explanation*: וּמָשׁוֹחַ בַּשָּׁשַׁר *is like 'a cord used for measuring* (חוּט הַמִּשְׁחָה) (*[à] lignant en sinople in O.F.*) drawing green lines, delineate with a green color.—[*Rashi*]

Redak identifies it as a red color called *minium* in Latin, *color di miniare* in Italian, a red color. Hence, our translation, vermilion. He explains that וּמָשׁוֹחַ, literally anointing, means 'painted,' since painting is accomplished by drawing the hand over the article to be painted, as in anointing.

22:19

In II Kings 24:6, Scripture states: And Jehoiakim slept with his forefathers. *Rashi* comments: Not in his bed, for Nebuchadnezzar bound him with copper chains to take him to Babylon, and they were dragging him, and he died in their hands, as it is said, '(Jer 22:19) A donkey's burial shall he be buried, dragged and tossed past the gates of Jerusalem.' And in 11 Chron. 36:6, it is written that Nebuchadnezzar bound him to take him to Babylon.

This account resembles that of *Seder Olam*, ch. 25, which states that Jehoiakim died as soon as he was bound. Then they took him out and dragged him, in fulfillment of Jeremiah's prophecy.

Lev. Rabbah (19:6) relates that when Nebuchadnezzar came to destroy Jerusalem, he encamped in Riblah. The Great Sanhedrin came down to him. They asked him, "Has the time arrived for the Temple to be destroyed?" He replied, "No, but Jehoiakim has rebelled against me. Deliver him to me, and I will go." They went to them and told him, "Nebuchadnezzar wants you." After refuting his protests, they lowered him over the wall into the Chaldean camp. Some say that they lowered him alive, and some say that they lowered him dead. Some say that he died in their hands because of his frailty. Some say that Nebuchadnezzar judged him, executed him, and inserted his body into the carcass of a donkey, to fulfill the prophecy tht he would be buried "a donkey's burial." He was then dragged around all the cities of Judea. Still others say that Nebuchadnezzar dragged him around while he was still alive, then killed him and fed his flesh to the dogs, as donkey flesh is usually "buried."

22:20

and on Bashan give forth your voice—*On Bashan which will be destroyed. And Jonathan paraphrased: And in the gates of the Temple Mount. And I do not know how to explain how the expression 'Bashan' fits to the gates of the Temple Mount, unless it is because of the doors which they make from the terebinths of Bashan, and that is the name of a place, or the expression,*

'Bashan' denotes a place of a wide valley. So is the area of the Temple Mount an open area around the Temple.—[Rashi] Redak explains that the area on the Temple Mount surrounding the Temple was pasture-land for sacrificial animals. Hence, the analogy to Bashan.

and cry for Avarim—*And cry for Megizatha. They are place names.—[Rashi]* See Num. 33:48, where the name עִיֵּי הָעֲבָרִים appears. *Onkelos* renders: מְגִזַּת עֲבָרָאֵי *the crossing of the sides. Rashi* explains עִיֵּי as *wastelands.* These were the wastelands of Avarim. The reason for lamenting over the wastelands is obscure. Perhaps the intention is that he bewail the loss of Israel's borders, which once reached to the mountains of Avarim, which were at the border of Moab. See *Daath Mikra.*

Others explain that the prophet sarcastically exhorts them to call upon their friends, upon whom they relied for aid, namely Assyria and Egypt, instead of placing their trust in God. He exhorts them to ascend to the highest mountain peaks to shout to their allies to come and help them. He chooses Lebanon and Bashan as examples of lofty mountains from which the voice will carry over long distances. He exhorts them further to cry from עֲבָרִים, *from all sides.*

22:23

Redak explains this expression in two ways. The word מַה, *what,* can be used in expressing greatness or insignificance. In this case, it is used for both. 'What grace and beauty you had when the birthpangs came upon you!' This refers to the grace and glory the nation had before the invasion. It may also be interpreted: 'What grace did you have when the birthpangs came upon you?' What grace and beauty were left you when the enemy invaded and attacked you?

Jonathan renders: You who abide in the Temple among the kings, who raises her sons, what will you do when trouble and terror come upon you like the pangs to a woman in travail? The derivation of the words is obscure.

22:24

I will remove you—Heb. אֶתְּקֶנְךָּ. *Cf.* '(supra 12:3) *Draw them out* (הַתִּקֵם) *like sheep to the slaughter,*' '(Jos. 8:6) *Until we have drawn* (הַתִּיקֵנוּ) *them. And the 'nun' is superfluous. And, according to the Midrash Aggadah* (*Pesikta d'Rav Kahana,* p. 163a): *In the place to which he was removed* (נִתַּק), *there he was rectified* (נִתְקַן), *for he repented in Babylon, and the Holy One, blessed be He, applied for absolution of the oath He had sworn, "Inscribe this man childless," and Zerubbabel was born to him in Babylon, and it was said to him through the prophet,* '(Haggai 2:23) *On that day . . . I will take you, Zerubbabel, and I will make you as a signet,' directed toward what He said to his father, "Though . . . be a signet on My right arm, . . . I will remove him* (sic).'—*[Rashi]*

Although Zerubbabel was not actually Jeconiah's son, but the son of Pedaiah, who was the son of Shealtiel, who was the son of Jeconiah, as in I Chron. 3:17ff., he is considered his son, for until four generations, the descendants are considered as children since a per-

son may see these generations during his lifetime.—[*Ibn Nachmiash*]

Concerning Jeconiah's repentance, see II Kings 25:30, Commentary Digest.

23:1

the flocks of My pasture—Israel, to whom I am like a shepherd.—[*Mezudath David*]

you have scattered—Because of your sins, they have been scattered among the nations and driven into the lands of their enemies.—[*Mezudath David*]

23:4

nor shall they be dismayed—Unlike the days of the Second Temple, when the Holy Ark with the *cherubim*, prophecy, the Urim and the Thumim, and the fire that descended from heaven were no longer among them, in the days of the Messiah, they will have all these Divine gifts. Then, they will no longer be dismayed by their absence: for then all these sanctities will return to them as in days of yore.—[*Abarbanel*]

nor shall [any of them] be missing—Heb. וְלֹא יִפָּקֵדוּ, *and they shall not be missing. Cf.* '(Num. 31:49) *And no one of us was missing* (נִפְקַד).—[*Rashi, Redak*]

Unlike the days of the Second Commonwealth, when only a small part of the nation returned to the Holy Land, in the Messianic Era, no one will be missing. After the return from Babylonian exile, the Ten Tribes did not return, neither did the Judeans in exile in the western countries nor those in Ammon and Moab, as is related by Joseph ben Gurion. Moreover, of those exiled in Babylon, only a small number of the poor people returned.—[*Abarbanel*]

23:5

and prosper—Heb. וְהִשְׂכִּיל.—[*Rashi* according to *Targum Jonathan*] *Abarbanel* renders: and become wise. This parallels Isaiah's prophecy (11:2): 'And the spirit of the Lord shall rest upon him, a spirit of wisdom and understanding.'

and he shall perform judgment and righteousness in the land—This parallels Isaiah's prophecy of '(11:4) And he shall judge the poor justly, and he shall chastise with equity the humble of the earth.'—[*Abarbanel*]

23:10

because of oaths—*False oaths.*—[*Rashi*]

mourns—*I.e. is destroyed.*—[*Rashi*]

the dwellings of the wilderness—The place where animals are pastured.—[*Redak*]

their eagerness—Heb. מְרוּצָתָם, (*course in French*), *their course, their running. But Jonathan renders it as an expression of desire.*—[*Rashi*]

Most exegetes follow *Rashi*'s first interpretation, that מְרוּצָתָם is derived from רוץ, *to run*. Their running is only to do evil. They never run to perform a mitzvah or to do God's service, but only to evil.—[*Redak, Kara, Ibn Nachmiash*] *Jonathan*, however, derives the word מְרוּצָתָם from רצה, *to desire*. He paraphrases: And since they go with the will of their souls, evil shall come upon them.

23:19

19. **has gone forth**—This is the prophetic past.—[*Mezudath David*]

23:22

Redak explains: If they stood in My council, as they claim, and they are in possession of My prophecy, they should have taught the people My true words, not falsehoods, and brought them back from their evil way and from the evil of their deeds.—[*Redak*]

Kara explains: Let them now let My people hear My words and let them bring them back from their evil way etc.

With this, he refutes the claims of the false prophets who predict only peace and good, for it does not make sense that God should send prophets to support the wicked in their ways and not to exhort them to repent. —[*Malbim*]

23:31

Hence, according to *Rashi*, the root is לקח, *to teach*, as in the word לֶקַח, *teaching*. *Redak*, however, sees it as an inverted form of חָלָק, *smooth*. They speak with a smooth tongue and say, "He says." They would say to the people in God's name, "You shall have peace." Concerning this group, the Rabbis say, "They prophesy what they did not hear."

23:34

Abarbanel explains that when the wicked of his generation would see Jeremiah falling into a prophetic trance, they would ask derisively, "What is the burden of the Lord?" implying that prophecy was burdensome and painful to him. God ordered him to reply, "What is proper to do with a burden? If it is heavy, we cast it off. And I will forsake you, says the Lord."

you shall say to them, "What burden? And I will forsake you etc."—*They say to you* (sic), *"What is the burden?" You are the burden of the Holy One, blessed be He, and He says that He will forsake you and cast you off His arms from heaven to earth. So I heard.*—[*Rashi*] Perhaps the correct reading is: And you shall say to them.

When they ask you this question, retort to them with the same expression they use.—[*Kara*]

Redak explains: When they ask you "What is the prophecy of the Lord, you shall say to them what the prophecy is, viz. And I will forsake you, says the Lord.

and I will forsake—Heb. וְנָטַשְׁתִּי.—[*Rashi*]

23:36

For the burden shall be to the man of His word—*Although you pervert the massa into a pejorative, the prophecy* (מַשָּׂא) *of the word of the Lord shall be to the man of His word, and to the man of His counsel He reveals it, but you pervert it to an expression of a burden. This interpretation I did not hear, but it is the main interpretation. But this is how I heard it, namely that the burden shall be a burden of retribution for the one who says it, who asks, "What is the burden?" Another interpretation:* מַשָּׂא ה' *is an expression of prophecy, and the false prophet would ask the true prophet to tell him the word of the Holy One, blessed be He, in the language in which the expression came to him, and the expression did not explain the speech adequately. Therefore, the false prophet would pervert it to another meaning and would speak after the fashion of the true prophet in order that they should*

believe him. And so did Hananiah son of Azzur do. Therefore, he says, "Do not ask the prophecy of the Lord," the language of the expression, but "What did He speak?" or "What did He reply?" The explanation of the words you shall ask the true prophet to tell you what the Holy One, blessed be He, says, and to what His words are inclined.—[*Rashi*]

25:20

the allies—*Garantie in French.*—[*Rashi*] *Rashi* explains הָעֶרֶב as 'guarantee.' This is related to the word עָרֵב, *a guarantor,* עֵרָבוֹן, *security.* He interprets *Jonathan*'s סוּמְכְוָתָא, as being derived from סֶמֶךְ, *a support.*

Redak, however, derives it from ערב, *to mix.* He interprets it as a mingled people, similar to עֶרֶב רַב (Ex. 12:38). This interpretation is followed by *Ibn Nachmiash, Abarbanel, Kara, Mezudath David,* and *Malbim.* They interpret the Aramaic סוּמְכְוָתָא to mean 'a thick mixture,' hence a mingled people.

Malbim points out that no king is mentioned since they had no king. *Jonathan,* however, according to our edition, renders: kings. *Rashi,* apparently, did not have that reading. Perhaps *Malbim* follows *Rashi*'s reading in *Targum Jonathan.*

Daath Mikra interprets it as 'the west,' similar to מַעֲרָב.

BIBLIOGRAPHY

I. Background Material

1. Bible with commentaries ("Mikraoth Gedoloth"), commonly known as "Nach Lublin," including Rashi, Rabbi Joseph Kara, contemporary of Rashi, Redak (R. David Kimchi) and Minchath Shai.

2. Talmud Bavli or Babylonian Talmud. Corpus of Jewish law and ethics compiled by Ravina and Rav Ashi 500 C.E. All Talmudic quotations, unless otherwise specified, are from the Babylonian Talmud.

3. Talmud Yerushalmi or Palestinian Talmud. Earlier and smaller compilation of Jewish law and ethics, compiled by R. Johanan, first generation *Amora* in second century C.E.

4. Midrash Rabbah. Homiletic explanation of Pentateuch and Five Scrolls. Compiled by Rabbi Oshia Rabbah (the great), late Tannaite, or by Rabbah bar Nahmani, third generation *Amora*. Exodus Rabbah, Numbers Rabbah, and Esther Rabbah are believed to have been composed at a later date.

5. Midrash Tanhuma. A Midrash on Pentateuch, based on the teachings of R. Tanhuma bar Abba, Palestinian *Amora* of the fifth century C.E. An earlier Midrash Tanhuma was discovered by Solomon Buber. It is evident than this is the Tanhuma usually quoted by medieval scholars, e.g. Rashi, Yalkut Shimoni, and Abarbanel.

6. Pirke d'Rabbi Eliezer. Eighth century aggadic compilation, attributed to Rabbi Eliezer ben Hyrcanus, early Tannaite of first generation after destruction of second Temple. Also called Baraitha d'Rabbi Eliezer, or Haggadah d'Rabbi Eliezer. Commentary—Radal (R. David Luria) 1798–1855. Om Publishing Co., New York 1946

7. Yalkut Shimoni. Talmudic and Midrashic anthology on Bible, composed by R. Simon Ashkenazi, thirteenth century preacher of Frankfort on the Main. Earliest known edition is dated 1308, in Bodlian Library. Sources traced by Arthur B. Hyman, M.D. in "The Sources of the Yalkut Shimeoni," Mossad Harav Kook, Jerusalam 1965.

8. Pesikta d'Rav Kahana. Homiletic dissertations of special Torah readings and haftorah. Composed by Rav Kahana, early *Amora,* at time of compilation of Talmud Yerushalmi. Solomon Buber, latest edition Jerusalem 5723.

9. Pesikta Rabbathi. Later compilation similar to that of Rav Kahana. Composed 4605. Warsaw, 5673, Jerusalem—Bnei Brak 5729.

10. Midrash Tehillim, Or Shoher Tov. Homiletic explanation of Book of Psalms. Authorship not definitely established. New York 1947

11. Mechilta. Tannaitic work on Book of Exodus. Some ascribe its authorship to Rabbi Ishmael, some to Rabbi Akiva, and others to Rav, first generation *Amora*. Printed with Malbim below text of Exodus.

12. Sifrei. Tannaitic work on Numbers and Deuteronomy. Some attribute its authorship to Rav, first generation *Amora*. Printed with Malbim below text of Numbers and Deuteronomy.

13. Seder Olam. Early Tannaitic work, recording chronology of entire Biblical era. Composed by Rabbi Jose son of Halafta. Jerusalem 5715

II. Medieval Commentaries and Source Material

1. Don Isaac Abarbanel or Abravanel. Commentary on Jeremiah, by renowned scholar, onetime finance minister of Spain. 1437–1509

2. Adne Kesef, by Rabbi Joseph Ibn Kaspi, medieval exegete, London 1911

3. Rambam, Rabbenu Mosheh ben Maimon, also known as Maimonides. Leading medieval authority on halachah, philosophy, and medicine. After having fled Spain, his native land, he became court physician to the sultan of Egypt. His works include a commentary on the Mishnah, Sefer Hamitzvoth (a concise presentation of the 613 commandments, of the Torah, together with comments of Ramban), Mishneh Torah or Yad Hachazakah—Rambam's "opus magnum," containing a decision on all problems of Jewish, whether discussed in the Talmud, Midrash, or later Gaonic writings. 1134–1204, and a philosophic treatise, entitled, "Guide to the Perplexed." Relevant quotations appear in "Torath HaRambam, Neviim Uchtuvim," by Meir David ben Shem, Jerusalem, 1978.

4. Ibn Nachmiash, Joseph, fourteenth century Biblical exegete, commentary on Jeremiah, first edition, Frankfort a/M, 1912, recent Israeli ed., no date.

5. Rabbi Isaiah da Trani. Commentary on Early prophets, Isaiah, and Jeremiah, Wertheimer, Jerusalem 1959.

III. Modern Commentaries

1. R. Chaim Joseph David Azulai. Author of Homath Anach and other

commentaries on the Bible by a famous 18th century authority on all fields of Torah study.

2. R. Meir Leibush Malbim. Commentary on Biblical literature, which combines ancient tradition with keen insight into nuances of meanings in the Hebrew language, by a leading nineteenth century scholar. 1809–1879

3. Shem Ephraim on Tanach by the renowned authority, R. Ephraim Zalman Margolis of Brodi, emendations on Rashi text, Munkacz 5673, Eretz Israel 5732

4. R. Moshe Alschich, Mar'oth Hazov'oth. Biblical exegesis by renowned scholar in Safed Brooklyn, 1977

5. Mezudath David and Mezudath Zion, by Rabbi Yechiel Hillel Altschuller. Simple and concise 18th century Bible commentary.

6. Daath Mikra, contemporary scholarly and traditional commentary on Jeremiah, Mosad HaRav Kook, 1983.

7. Daath Soferim, by Rabbi Chaim Rabinowitz. Biblical exegesis by contemporary historian, exegete and educator, Jerusalem 1969.

IV. Other Sources

1. Machbereth Menachem. Lexicon by Menachem ben Saruk, early grammarian, Spain 920–980.

2. Teshuvoth Dunash. Dunash ben Labrat, opponent of Menachem ben Saruk. 920–990.

3. Sefer Hashorashim, Redak. Lexicon of Biblical roots. Berlin, 5607, New York, 5708

4. Sefer Hashorashim, R. Jona ibn Ganah, earlier lexicon of Biblical roots, Berlin (5656) 1896, Jerusalem 5726

5. Aruch, R. Nathan of Rome. Talmudic dictionary by early medieval scholar. Died 4866

6. Otzar Midrashim. Encyclopedia of all Midrashim. J.D. Eisenstein. New York, 1915, 1956

7. Methurgeman. Lexicon Chaldaicum. Aramaic lexicon, comprising all roots found in *Targumim* and in Bible. Composed by Eliia Levita, grammarian and lexicographer. 1541. No date on reprint.

8. Sepher Hagaluj, Rabbi Joseph Kimchi, father of Redak, grammarian and Biblical exegete, decisions of grammatical conflicts between Menachem and Dunash.

9. Aruch Completum, Dr. Alexander Kohut, critical edition of Aruch with elaboration and theories of word origins.

10. Barzilai, history of development of Hebrew language. Aaron Marcus, nineteenth century scholar and archeologist. Records of ancient inscriptions relevant to the period covered in Jeremiah.

11. Nefesh Hachaim, Popular Kabbalistic work, Chaim of Wolozhin, disciple of Elijah Gaon of Vilna, 1649–1721.